FORENSIC PSYCHOPHYSIOLOGY

USING THE

POLYGRAPH

Scientific Truth Verification - Lie Detection

FORENSIC PSYCHOPHYSIOLOGY USING THE POLYGRAPH

Scientific Truth Verification - Lie Detection

By

JAMES ALLAN MATTE, Ph.D.
Forensic Psychophysiologist

President
Matte Polygraph Service, Inc.
Williamsville, New York 14221-6915

Member, American Polygraph Association
Member, Florida Polygraph Association
Charter Member, Empire State Polygraph Society
Honorary Life Member, Pennsylvania Polygraph Association
Member, Society for Psychophysiological Research
Member, American Psychological Society

Former Special Agent, USAF office
of Special Investigations (OSI)
Retired U.S. Army CID Agent

J. A. M. Publications
Williamsville • New York • U.S.A.

Published and Distributed throughout the World by
J. A. M. Publications
43 Brookside Drive
Williamsville, New York 14221-6915
Tel: (716) 634-6645 - Fax: (716) 634-7204
E-Mail: JAMpublications@mattepolygraph.com
Website URL: http://www.mattepolygraph.com

ISBN 0-9655794-0-9

Library of Congress Catalog Card Number: 96-95246

Library of Congress Cataloging in Publication Data

Matte, James Allan
FORENSIC PSYCHOPHYSIOLOGY USING THE POLYGRAPH
Scientific Truth Verification - Lie Detection

Includes Bibliographical References and Index.
1. Lie Detectors and Detection.

Printed in the United States of America
by the Buffalo Printing Company
Williamsville, N. Y.

to my mother

Noella

FOREWORD

Having completed my basic polygraph training in 1948 under the direct tutelage of the late Leonarde Keeler, my field experience until 1959 primarily involved the use of the Relevant-Irrelevant polygraph technique. Although the late John E. Reid had advocated the use of the reviewed control question for years, until 1959 I was not motivated to fully understand the Reid Technique until confronted with the challenge of sharing instruction in a school teaching that technique. This was part of shared instruction with my about-to-be partner, Richard O. Arther, who, along with myself, was co-founder of the National Training Center of Lie Detection. As I became engrossed in this project I felt that a number of logical changes could be made building upon the Reid Technique. The result of these changes constituted the birth of the Backster Zone Comparison Technique. These changes primarily involved alteration of the Reid question sequencing, which has remained unchanged since first appearing in published form in 1947. The Zone Comparison Technique also embraced the first numerical system for the objective evaluation of polygraph charts.

From its outset, challenges were made demanding my "empirical data" to support such changes. My consistent response was "common sense" does not require empirical data. Privately though, I knew that the Zone Comparison Technique would have to withstand experimentation by those more prone to conduct laboratory studies.

Finally, more than thirty years after its inception, through the dedicated efforts of Dr. James Allan Matte, a comprehensive assessment has been compiled exploring and summarizing the extended research by others within and outside the polygraph profession. This includes a logical analysis of those original factors involving that which I initially considered as basic common sense changes in then existing techniques. I truly believe that this textbook laboriously compiled by Dr. Matte will be the enduring source within the polygraph profession for many years, and it is without reservation that I highly recommend this text to all individuals directly and indirectly involved in forensic psychophysiology using the polygraph.

Cleve Backster, Hon. Ph.D., Director
The Backster School of Lie Detection
San Diego, California

FOREWORD

Doctor James Allan Matte has once again asked me to write a Foreword to this, his new textbook. I had been so impressed with his first work, "The Art and Science of the Polygraph Technique," published in 1980, that I was moved to write the Foreword to that book, wherein I described my knowledge of James Allan Matte, Ph.D., and my work with him when I was in private practice almost 20 years ago.

Doctor James Allan Matte has continued his endeavors on behalf of his science. As can be seen from his curriculum vitae, he has been most active in various polygraph associations as well as societies involved in psychophysiological research and study. As Doctor Matte points out, the Federal Rules of Evidence, as recognized by Daubert v. Dow Pharmaceutical (1993), have changed the test for the admission of expert testimony and scientific evidence in the Federal Court. The author Matte makes a very convincing argument that the new standard opens the door for polygraph evidence to be considered by the jury along with any and all other evidence, direct, circumstantial and expert. His chapter on the legal aspects of the PV examination is most comprehensive and enlightening.

Students of this science, as well as lawyers who seek to understand it, would be well served by reading Doctor Matte's exhaustive treatise which is written with great clarity and based upon painstaking research.

Hon. Vincent E. Doyle
New York State Supreme Court
Administrative Judge
Eighth Judicial District
Buffalo, New York

FOREWORD

Twenty five years ago, I put on a hearing to admit polygraph evidence in a federal court criminal case on behalf of a client I was representing. Although coming close, I failed to convince the court to admit the evidence. See *United States v. DeBetham* (S.D. Cal. 1972) 348 F.Supp. 1377, aff'd 470 F.2d 1367 (9th Cir. 1972) (admission denied, but trial and appellate courts both noted the evidence for polygraph reliability). That experience stimulated a law career-long interest in the subject such that I have written① and lectured on the subject for lawyers and served as a polygraph-law instructor at the Backster School of Lie Detection for the last twenty years.

Almost a quarter century later, I am currently involved in another federal criminal case again attempting to admit evidence that my client (a new one) passed a polygraph test. This time, for two reasons, I may succeed. First, polygraph has made undeniable strides in proving itself a more reliable veracity test. The advent of computerization of the test has done much to guarantee standardization of the administration and scoring of the exam. Second, the long-standing rule of *Frye v. United States* (D. C. Cir. 1923) 293 F.1013, for admission of scientific evidence--"general acceptance in the field to which it belongs"-- has been supplanted in federal and other jurisdictions with a more inclusionary rule which permits trial courts additional discretion in the admission of the evidence. See *Daubert v. Merrell Dow Pharmaceuticals* (1993) 509 U.S. 579.

The result of these two phenomena is that polygraph evidence is finally penetrating what has been a fairly solid wall of court precedent excluding the polygraph evidence. Published opinions are emerging in criminal cases recognizing the advances in polygraph and cautiously fashioning orders for admission of the evidence. See *United States v. Piccinonna* (11th Cir. en banc 1989) 885 F.2d 1529 (admission on guilt or innocence); *United States v. Posada* (5th Cir. 1995) 57 F.3d 428 (admission at suppression pre-trial hearing); *United States v. Crumby* (D. Ar. 1995) 895 F.Supp. 1354 (D. Ariz. 1995) (admissible on guilt or innocence).

With this trend toward increasing admission of the evidence, there will come an increasing necessity for lawyers and judges to become familiar with polygraph law, history and science. Unfortunately, there has not been a publication available to comprehensively address all three topics.

Until now. Dr. James A. Matte's *Forensic Psychophysiology Using The Polygraph* is the best text on the subject I have seen. For too many years there has been a lack of a single resource for polygraphers, lawyers, judges and scientists to resort to learn

---

① E.g. "Polygraph 1984; Behind the Closed Door of Admissibility," 16 *Univ. West Los Angeles L. Rev.* 1 (1984; "Reliability of Polygraph Examination," 14 *Am Jur Proof of Facts* 1 (1977).

about polygraph issues. This book will solve that problem. It contains comprehensive discussions of the history, validation research, as well as test technique, application and interpretation. In future court hearings on polygraph, this will be a tremendous aid in demonstrating validity and overcoming the historic judicial reluctance to admit the evidence.

That reluctance stems from three judicial concerns: l) the lack of demonstrable polygraph standards in test technique, 2) proven validity, and 3) the impact on the administration of justice if polygraph were admitted. These are legitimate concerns. Previous foundation hearings tended to show wildly variant expert opinions on such fundamental matters as question formulation, test technique and interpretation. The result was lengthy court hearings simply to allow a judge to rule on admission. Courts do not have the time to resolve such scientific disputes in the middle of a trial.

This volume should go far in alleviating concerns over the first two issues. Polygraph has progressed to the point that standardization of test technique is accepted by competent examiners. Indeed, the current advances in computerization would be impossible were there not accepted technique standards. Also, peer-reviewed validity studies abound in the journals of psychophysiologists to show that properly conducted exams will show high degrees of validity. As to the impact on the justice system, with the first two concerns largely met, the courts are now carefully crafting tight rules for admission to insure that valuable court time is not wasted in a confusing battle of experts.

For the attorney or judge, the chapter on the legal aspects of the polygraph (or psychophysiological veracity test, as the author calls it), contains a review of the recent cases and also a discussion of the factors which should be considered in selecting an examiner. The latter is crucial to meet the three judicial concerns noted above. Simply put, proper examiner selection - one who is properly trained at an accredited polygraph school and who uses the proper test technique - is the key to any hope for judicial acceptance.

Dr. Matte's book is an invaluable resource and an enormous contribution to the field.

Charles M. Sevilla, Esquire
Cleary & Sevilla, Attorneys at Law
San Diego, California

SPECIAL ACKNOWLEDGMENT

This author is especially grateful to his friend and colleague Dr. Ronald M. Reuss, Ed.D., Professor Emeritus of Biology and instructor in anatomy and physiology, medical physiology, cardiovascular physiology and muscle physiology at the State University College at Buffalo, New York, who for the past fifteen years has assisted me in various polygraph research projects and acted as my mentor and faculty advisor which resulted in publication of my doctoral dissertation consisting of a validation study on the Polygraph Quadri-Track Zone Comparison Technique which has been incorporated into this book. Dr. Reuss has co-authored several published articles on polygraphy as reflected in the index of this book. Dr. Reuss' input and critical review of chapter 4 of this book dealing with physiology and its relationship to psychophysiological veracity examinations using the polygraph was invaluable. Dr. Reuss' expertise in related fields of knowledge including physics, math, electronics, statistics and education provided this author with the kind of guidance most authors pray for but few ever realize. In addition to his valuable contribution to chapter 4 of this book, Dr. Reuss applied his scientific no-nonsense approach in his critical review of related chapters which resulted in many improvements. Dr. Reuss' intimate knowledge of the psychophysiological veracity examination using the polygraph makes him an ideal expert witness in establishing the foundation for the admissibility of such examinations in a court of law. It is with the greatest respect and deepest gratitude that this author sincerely expresses this special acknowledgment of Dr. Ronald M. Reuss' contribution to this book.

James Allan Matte, Ph.D.
Forensic Psychophysiologist

ACKNOWLEDGMENTS

This author extends his sincere appreciation for the contributions made by the following persons:

Stan Abrams, Ph.D., Clinical and Forensic Psychophysiologist, Director of the School of Polygraph, Western Oregon State College for his critical review of material in chapter 9 and his helpful insight and advice concerning the use of forensic psychophysiology in the treatment and monitoring of convicted sex offenders on parole or probation discussed in Chapter 24 of this book.

Norman Ansley, President of Forensic Research, Inc., Severna Park, Maryland, and editor of Polygraph, Journal of the American Polygraph Association, whose vast knowledge of forensic psychophysiology is perhaps unequaled, for his guidance and assistance in the acquisition of information and materials for this book. This author is also grateful for his critical review of Chapter 2 regarding the history of forensic psychophysiology, and his invaluable contribution of historical information and photographs used in this book.

Thomas E. Armitage, Forensic Psychophysiologist, Buffalo Police Department, Buffalo, New York for his participation in polygraph research conducted by this author and Dr. Ronald M. Reuss, reported in Chapters 3, 5, and 22 and his appearance in Figures XXII-2 and XXII-3, Chapter 22 of this book.

Richard O. Arther, M.A., Director, National Training Center of Polygraph Science, New York, N. Y., for his critical review of this author's description of the Arther Technique depicted in Chapter 15 of this book.

Cleve Backster, Hon. Ph.D., Director, Backster School of Lie Detection, San Diego, California, for his guidance, encouragement and moral support in the writing of this book. This author is also grateful for his contribution of information and forms depicting the Backster Zone Comparison Technique used in chapters 11 and 12 of this book, and his critical review of those terms attributed to him in the Glossary. This author believes that history will recognize Cleve Backster as the twentieth century's greatest logician in this profession. His genius is an inspiration to all of us who seek improvement in forensic psychophysiology.

Gordon H. Barland, Ph.D., Chief, External Research, Department of Defense Polygraph Institute, for his contribution of historic information regarding forensic psychophysiology in Russia and China.

Steven K. Bartlett, Forensic Psychophysiologist, District Attorney's Office, Salt Lake City, Utah, and President of the American Polygraph Association, for his generous contribution of information regarding the Utah Zone Comparison Technique described in Chapter 11 of this book, and his unwavering support of this author's position on defense access to police psychophysiological veracity examinations set forth in Chapter 23.

Gayle Beck, Ph.D., Clinical Psychologist and Associate Professor, Department of Psychology, State University of New York at Buffalo for her assistance and supervision of David Direnfeld and Jillian Shipherd in their revision of Chapter 7 of this book and her critical review.

Robert A. Brisentine, Forensic Psychophysiologist, Brisentine & Associates, Bowie, Maryland, former Director, U. S. Army Crime Records Center and Chief Forensic Psychophysiologist for Army Law Enforcement, for the invaluable information he provided this author regarding polygraph research conducted at the Office of the Provost Marshal General, U. S. Army, and other information of historical significance reported in Chapter 2 of this book.

J. Alton Cantrell, Director, Loss Prevention, Harco Incorporated, Tuscaloosa, Alabama for his revision and editing of Chapter 20 of this book on the effects of drugs in psychophysiological veracity examinations.

Michael H. Capps, M.S., Director, Department of Defense Polygraph Institute, for his critical review of a thesis by this author, which formed the basis for Chapter 9 of this book, and his generous contribution of information regarding polygraph research conducted by the Department of Defense.

Adrian Coman, Lt. Colonel, Criminology Institute, Police Headquarters, Ministry of Interior, Bucharest, Romania, for his most generous contribution of information regarding the history of forensic psychophysiology using the polygraph in Romania.

Ronald E. Decker, Forensic Psychophysiologist, first Director of the Department of Defense Polygraph Institute, and former Director, U.S. Army Polygraph School, for his contribution of historical photographs of polygraph instruments, some of which were used in Chapter 2, and invaluable historical information also used in this book. Ronald E. Decker known amiably at the *Wizard* by his numerous polygraph students and seasoned graduates reflects his vast knowledge and versatility in polygraph instrumentation and technology that was used to design the polygraph curriculum for the Canadian Police College Polygraph Training School, and the Security Service of the Israeli government.

David Direnfeld, B.A. Honors and Jillian Shipherd, B.A., Doctoral students, Department of Psychology, State University of New York at Buffalo for their excellent revision of Chapter 7 of this book under the supervision of Dr. Gayle Beck, also acknowledged herein.

Christopher L. Fausett, Vice-President, Lafayette Instrument Company, Inc., for his contribution of information regarding its computerized polygraph systems and photographs of its instrumentation for publication in this book.

Nathan J. Gordon, Director, Academy for Scientific Investigative Training, Philadelphia, Pennsylvania, for his generous contribution of information regarding the Integrated Zone Comparison Technique described in Chapter 11 of this book.

Helen D. Haller, Ph.D., for her excellent editing and professional indexing of this book.

Charles C. Honts, Ph.D., Associate Professor of Psychology, Department of Psychology, Boise State University, Boise, Idaho, for his generous contribution of information regarding the Utah Zone Comparison Technique described in Chapters 11 and 15 of this book.

G. Jeffrey Johnson, Special Agent and senior forensic psychophysiologist, Department of Defense, for his generous contribution of information regarding polygraph research in computerized polygraph systems conducted for the Department of Defense.

Richard W. Keifer, forensic psychophysiologist, Federal Bureau of Investigation, and Director, American Polygraph Association, for his invaluable advice relating to polygraph techniques, and his effort in developing a criteria for technique acceptance by the American Polygraph Association as suggested by this author in Chapter 23 of this book.

John C. Kircher, Associate Professor of Educational Psychology, University of Utah, for sharing his research and knowledge of computerized polygraph systems with this author.

Robert G. Lundell and Susan A. Holmes, Polygraph Associates of Oregon, Medford, Oregon for their generous contribution of information and procedures pertaining to the administration of probationary psychophysiological veracity examinations in the treatment and maintenance/monitoring of convicted sex offenders on parole or probation which are set forth in Chapter 24 of this book. .

Lynn P. Marcy, M.A. Director, American Institute of Polygraph Technology and Forensic Psychophysiology, Dearborn, Michigan, for his generous contribution of information regarding the Marcy Technique described in Chapter 15 of this book.

Slavko Maric, Director, Centre for Criminal Forensics, Criminal Police Sector, Ministry of the Interior, Republic of Croatia, Zagreb, Croatia, for his most detailed report on the history and status of forensic psychophysiology using the polygraph in the Republic of Croatia.

Paul S. Meade, M.D., Director of the Niagara County Public Health Laboratory, Niagara Falls, New York, and Assistant Director of Laboratories, Mount St. Mary's Hospital, Lewiston, New York, for his critical review and analysis of Figure VI-1 Neurological Pathway From The Auditory System To the Sympathetic System, and Figure VI-6 Neurological Pathway For Respiratory Control, contained in Chapter 4 of this book. This author is also grateful to Dr. Meade for his contribution to the Addendum in aforesaid chapter and his coordinating the efforts of Dr. Ladislav Mrzljak, also acknowledged herein, who critically reviewed aforesaid figuges and also contributed to the Addendum.

Lavern A. Miller, Chairman and CEO, Stoelting Company, for his generous contribution of information and permission to portray polygraph instrumentation manufactured by his company.

Paul K. Minor, M.S., former Chief Forensic Psychophysiologist of the Federal Bureau of Investigation, and current President of American International Security Corporation, Fairfax, Virginia, for his generous contribution of information regarding the Modified Relevant-Irrelevant (MRI) technique described in Chapter 15 of this book.

Ladislav Mrzljak, M.D., Neurophysiologist and Senior Research Scientist at Yale University, New Haven, Connecticut, for his critical review and analysis of Figure IV-l Neurological Pathway From The Auditory System To The Sympathetic System, Figure VI-6 Neurological Pathway For Respiratory Control, and his invaluable contribution to the Addendum contained in Chapter 4 of this book.

John J. Nash, M.A., Professor of English, Erie Community College, Buffalo, New York for his occasional editorial assistance, along with his wife Diane M. Nash, M.A., M.S., English Teacher, who also posed as the polygraph subject in Chapter 6 of this book.

Dale E. Olsen, Ph.D., Program Manager, Applied Physics Laboratory, Johns Hopkins University, Laurel, Maryland for providing this author with the results of research conducted during the development of the computer algorithm used in computerized polygraph systems, and his critical review of Chapter 13 of this book.

Parn Kyou Park, Chief Polygraph Section, Ministry of National Defense, Seoul, Korea, for his generous contribution of historical information and current status of forensic psychophysiology using the polygraph in Korea.

Coen Pretorius, President, Polygraph Institute of South Africa, Halfway House, South Africa, for his contribution of historical information and current status of forensic psychophysiology using the polygraph in South Africa.

John R. Schwartz, Deputy Director, Department of Defense Polygraph Institute, Fort McClellan, Alabama, for his assistance in acquiring research data pertaining to forensic psychophysiology.

Charles J. Scibetta, Attorney at Law, Amherst, New York for his critical review of Chapter 23 regarding the legal aspects of psychophysiological veracity examinations, and his assistance in the development of a model Agreement and Stipulation form depicted in Appendix F. .

Akihiro Suzuki, National Research Institute of Police Science, Tokyo, Japan, for his generous contribution of information regarding techniques and research in forensic psychophysiology using the polygraph in Japan.

Donald A. Weinstein, Special Agent, Primary Instructor of Physiology and Anatomy for the Forensic Psychophysiologist, and Chair of the Curriculum Committee at the Department of Defense Polygraph Institute. This author is deeply appreciative of SA Weinstein's generous contribution of information regarding polygraph research conducted for DoDPI, and the unselfish sharing of his knowledge of forensic psychophysiology as contained in his June 1994 DoDPI Manual of Anatomy and Physiology for the Forensic Psychophysiologist. Special Agent Weinstein's critical review and in-depth discussions regarding polygraph chart interpretation rules were of immense value to this author.

Bruce White, President, Axciton Computerized Polygraphs, Inc., Houston, Texas for the invaluable information he provided this author regarding computerized polygraph systems, and photographs of its instrumentation for publication in this book.

Richard Widup, Special Agent, U.S. Army Criminal Investigation Division Command, for his generous contribution of research he conducted with Dr. Gordon H. Barland on the Stimulation Test, reported in Chapter 10 of this book.

Heidi Herbold-Wootten, Ph.D., Adjunct Professor, St. Leo College, Little Creek, Norfolk, Virginia, for her generous contribution of historical information regarding the early development of techniques and instrumentation in forensic psychophysiology in Europe.

James R. Wygant, Forensic Psychophysiologist and Editor of Polygraph News and Views, for his generous contribution of information relating to the probationary sex offender treatment and maintenance program in the state of Oregon, and his input in the practical use of computerized polygraph systems.

CONTENTS

Appendices

FORENSIC PSYCHOPHYSIOLOGY

USING THE

POLYGRAPH

Scientific Truth Verification - Lie Detection

Chapter l

INTRODUCTION

When my first book The Art and Science of the Polygraph Technique was published in 1980, I had great hopes that by the end of that decade, most of the polygraph techniques currently being taught at polygraph schools accredited by the American Polygraph Association would be validated by research studies (Chap.3), polygraph instruments would be computerized with validated algorithms exceeding ninety-eight percent in their accuracy to quantify, analyze and evaluate the physiological data (Chap.13) and the results of aforesaid polygraph examinations would have received judicial notice of acceptance in our courts. Only the latter has not been achieved.

However, the supersedence of the *Frye* standard by the *Federal Rules of Evidence* in *William Daubert v. Merrell Dow Pharmaceuticals, Inc.* in 1993 has paved the way for forensic psychophysiology to take its rightful place among those scientific procedures accepted by the courts (Chap.23).

The enormous amount of polygraph research conducted since 1980 which is discussed in Chapter 3 was spurred by the birth of the Department of Defense Polygraph Institute (DoDPI) in 1986 which assumed the U. S. Army Criminal Investigations Division Command's role and responsibility for the polygraph training of all military branches and federal agencies, including the Central Intelligence Agency (CIA). The DoDPI established a basic polygraph training program that is nationally accredited as a graduate level program, and a program of continuing education in advanced polygraph technique and instrumentation. The DoDPI initiated a research program within DoDPI to validate current federal test formats, and conducted basic research into current theories of lie-detection. Its mandate also included the exploration of the central and autonomic nervous system correlates of deception, improvement of current methodologies and development of advanced lie-detection methodologies, the examination of factors affecting polygraph accuracy, the study of the effectiveness of polygraph countermeasures and the development of counter-countermeasures, test and evaluation of current and new polygraph equipment and concepts, and the development of a curriculum and instructional research program. (DoDPI Report 1987)

Dr. William J. Yankee, Director of the Department of Defense Polygraph Institute (DoDPI) in his welcoming remarks at the 1990 Federal Interagency Polygraph Seminar at the FBI Academy, stated that "we must recognize that an examiner is more than a skilled operator, more than a cop. We must realize that a polygraph examination is one of the most complex psychophysiological examinations ever developed." In a published paper *A Case For Forensic Psychophysiology and Other Changes in Terminology* Dr. Yankee points out that for years the word psychophysiology and the term psychophysiological detection of deception (PDD) have been associated with detection of deception by scientists and others, and cites a 1935 proposal by the first National Crime Laboratory at Northwestern University School of Law for "...two psychophysiological laboratories for lie detection..." Dr. Yankee explains that psychophysiology is a science involving the presentation of stimuli to one or more of the human senses to determine the effects of those stimuli, when psychologically processed, on selected physiological activities (Coles, Donchin & Porges, 1986). Forensic psychophysiology is a science that deals with the relationship and application of psychophysiological detection of deception examinations to the legal system. The use of the modifier forensic in Forensic Psychophysiology, delineates and delimits the scope of the science of psychophysiology, as it applies to the legal system, to those systems, processes and applications that are an integral and functional part of the psychophysiological detection of deception. (Yankee 1994). Henceforth, the DoDPI replaced the term *polygraph examiner* and *polygraphist* with the new term *Forensic Psychophysiologist*, and further replaced the term *polygraph examination* or *test* with the new term *Psychophysiological Detection of Deception* (PDD) *Examination* or *Test*. These changes were made official and incorporated in all Department of Defense regulations. The distinction made by the Department of Defense between the term *examination* and *test* was previously articulated by this author as follows: "We can look upon the polygraph examination as a complex system encompassing the entire examination which includes all parts of the pre-test interview to include test question formulation, their review and presentation and assurance of intended interpretation, to the conduct of the polygraph test resulting in polygraph charts which are quantified for a determination. Therefore, the system (examination) includes all of the aforementioned interacting parts, anyone of which if omitted or altered effects the psychophysiological results of the polygraph test. The whole is the sum of its parts and the interactions of its parts."(Matte 1993)

We must recognize that several tests such as the Stimulation Test, the Quadri-Track Zone Comparison Test, the Silent Answer Test, the Guilty Knowledge Test can all be administered within one examination. We must also recognize that the polygraph is merely an instrument which records physiological data, hence is a recording device used to administer a Psychophysiological Detection of Deception Test. Therefore it is the physiological data recorded on the polygraph charts as it relates to the type of PDD test within the examination, which is analyzed and quantified for a determination of truth or deception.

This author believes that the aforesaid change in terminology by the DoDPI is a significant improvement in the description of the forensic psychophysiologist's role and duties. However, this author also believes that inasmuch as the Forensic Psychophysiologist's objective is to seek the truth, and the Forensic Psychophysiologist verifies the truth as well as detects deception, the term *Veracity* is a more positive and appropriate term than Detection of Deception therefore this author has adopted the title of *Psychophysiological Veracity Examination* in lieu of Psychophysiological Detection of Deception Examination in his practice and in this book.

In 1992, all polygraph schools accredited by the American Polygraph Association formed the *International Association of Forensic Psychophysiological Institutes* (IAFPI) which are listed in Appendix P.

While the use of psychophysiological veracity examinations using the polygraph in the private sector has significantly decreased as a result of the enactment of the Employee Polygraph Protection Act of 1988, their use and acceptance in the legal community has increased due to the courts' awareness of research studies (Chap. 3 & 23) published after the Office of Technology Assessment's (OTA) 1983 report, which repudiated many of the criticisms levied by OTA against forensic psychophysiology and legitimized its methodology as a sound, scientific procedure which should be admitted in court when proper safeguards are applied. In 1989, the United States Court of Appeals for the 11th , in U. S. v. Piccinonna, declared that "there is no question that in recent years polygraph testing has gained increasingly widespread acceptance as a useful and reliable scientific tool" "The science of polygraphy has progressed to a level of acceptance sufficient to allow the use of polygraph evidence in limited circumstances when the danger of unfair prejudice is minimized." (885 F.2d 1529 11th Cir. 1989).

With the recent demise of the long-standing Frye v. United States standard which held back the introduction of PV examination evidence, the United States Supreme Court decision in William Daubert v. Merrell Dow Pharmaceuticals, Inc., which was decided on 28 June 1993, now permits trial judges more discretion in what they accept as evidence. This Supreme Court decision will be important in future cases involving the admissibility of PV examination results in federal courts, and in state courts which adopted the Frye standard. Interestingly, in 1978, an "Experimental Investigation of the Relative Validity and Utility of the Polygraph Technique and Three Other Common Methods of Criminal Identification" namely Fingerprint Identification, Handwriting Analysis, and Eyewitness Identification conducted by Drs. J. Widacki and F. Horvath, revealed that the forensic psychophysiologist using the polygraph correctly resolved 95% of the cases, the handwriting expert 94% of the cases, the eyewitnesses 64% and the fingerprint expert 100% of the cases. However, when Inconclusives are included, the percentage of correctly resolved cases changes dramatically to 90% polygraph; 85% handwriting, 35% eyewitnesses; and 20% fingerprint. Thus, the aforesaid study supports Reid and Inbau's statement (Chap. 23) that the accuracy of the psychophysiological veracity (PV) examination is commensurate with and even superior to most of the presently approved forms of evidence. The scientific and legal status of forensic psychophysiology are fully discussed in Chapters 3 and 23 of this book, respectively.

After seventy years of employing PV examinations, the United States finds itself far from being alone in their use. At last count, fifty-seven countries administer PV examinations using the polygraph either by the government, in the private sector or both. Twenty of those countries have significant PV examination capability, and several manufacture their own polygraph instruments, including computerized polygraph systems. The Ministry of Internal Affairs in Russia is currently awaiting passage of a law that will allow its law enforcement agencies to administer PV examinations using the polygraph. Its passage is almost certain and the result will be the training of 5000 to 7000 forensic psychophysiologists. Two Russian companies are currently manufacturing computerized polygraph instruments, the Inex and the Avex polygraphs. The Inex is being marketed worldwide, but the Avex is restricted to Russian users. The Ministry of Internal Affairs opened a polygraph institute in Moscow in 1993 for the training of forensic psychophysiologists to provide the methodology necessary in the use of its technology. (Barland 1994). If all of the above events transpire, Russia will have more than twice as many forensic psychophysiologists as does the United States. Additionally, China developed and manufactured its own computerized polygraph instrument which it uses with methodology gained from American training facilities and experts. China plans on having at least one forensic psychophysiologist for each of their three thousand police districts. (Wang Bu, 1995). (Chap. 2). The United States is currently the leader in forensic psychophysiology and its experts are being sought for their knowledge throughout the world. However, unless the United States devotes more resources in the research and development of forensic psychophysiology and abandons anti-polygraph legislation in favor of non-biased regulatory statutes, there will be a dramatic shift in forensic psychophysiology dominance to Asiatic and European countries.

In the United States, a new application to psychophysiological veracity (PV) examinations has emerged. Following its remarkable success in the state of Oregon, eight states have adopted its supervision and treatment program of convicted sex offenders, which comprise a triad of therapist, probation/parole officer, and forensic psychophysiologist. The success of this program was reported in a recidivism study of 173 sex offenders conducted in 1991 by Charles F. Edson, Parole and Probation Officer and Sex Offender Specialist for the Medford Department of Correction, Oregon, during the period from 1982 to 1991 which revealed that 95% of individuals in the PV examination program were free of new sex crime conviction, 96% were free of new felony conviction, 89% were crime free in terms of any new criminal conviction, and 65% experienced no parole/probation revocations. The Jackson County Sex Offender Treatment Program (JCSOTP) developed by the Oregon Department of Corrections Community Programs Division reported its success in a study conducted of one hundred and seventy-three JSCOTP cases supervised between 1982 and 1990. The study covered all open cases and a random sample of closed cases. For over 60% of the cases, the offender had been on community supervision for more than three years. The study showed the following: No subsequent sex crime convictions 95%; No other new criminal convictions 89%; No other new felony convictions 96%; No parole/probation violations 65%; No parole/probation revocations to prison 87%. (Chap. 24). As the positive results of this program become known, more states are likely to adopt it due to its impact in the reduction of the prison population and the cost of housing these individuals, and the saving of supervisory time by busy probation officers which can be applied to other probationers whose reoffending was discovered by the PV examination, plus the deterrent effect on the majority of the others on probation, which amount to additional protection for society. Additionally, therapists involved in these programs have reported that the use of PV examinations has helped the treatment process because if a pedophile was reoffending, he or she would be reinforcing the very behavior they were attempting to eliminate. (Abrams 1992, Morris 1994, Grindstaff 1993)

This author's previous textbook published in 1980 presented a chart depicting the test structure of the different PV examination techniques in use at that time. It is quite apparent that the legal community, the public, and the news media in particular still do not comprehend that there are significant philosophical as well as psychological differences in the test construct of the various PV examination techniques, each with its own method of addressing the known and identified variables capable of affecting the validity and reliability of the physiological data recorded by the polygraph instrument on its polygraph charts. This book therefore endeavors to present a thorough explanation of these differences in chapters 9, 11, 15, 17 and 18 with supporting research validating each technique.

The aforesaid PV examination techniques fall into one of two categories: the *numerical approach* and the *clinical approach*.(Chap. 9). The distinction between the two approaches was dramatically realized by the Central Intelligence Agency (CIA) in 1994 when it was discovered that one of their own spymasters, Aldrich Ames, had been working as a double agent for the Soviet Union and his espionage activities went undetected in spite of his routine submission to three periodic PV examinations. Had the CIA employed the *numerical approach* of forensic psychophysiology on CIA spy Aldrich Ames, his treachery would have been detected and exposed in his very first PV examination inasmuch as the results of such a test are based solely on the quantified physiological data. The post-mortem investigation of the Aldrich Ames case revealed that in all three *clinical* PV examinations, Ames' polygraph charts contained specific and significant physiological responses to the relevant test questions, but the forensic psychophysiologist in each test allowed Ames' behavior and demeanor to influence the results, which is intrinsic to the *clinical approach*.

Lawyers, especially, must familiarize themselves with these different techniques in order to be effective in their examination and cross-examination of a forensic psychophysiologist in court as demonstrated in Chapter 23. Members of the news media who report the results of psychophysiological veracity examinations would better serve the public if they reported the distinct type of PV examination administered, whether the test conclusion was based on numerical scores (Chap. 11) or global evaluation (Chap. 15) and the qualifications of the forensic psychophysiologist, rather than painting all PV examinations and forensic psychophysiologists with the same brush.

The media's producers, directors, editors and reporters must all recognize the enormous impact their work has on the citizenry of this country, and the responsibility that goes with it. Crime statistics in the United States clearly show an epidemic in homicides, rapes, burglaries, robberies, larcenies and child abuse. Court dockets are overwhelmed and prisons are bursting at the seams from overpopulation. Perjury is rampant and juries are unable to detect it. Worse, judges as well as juries are hard-pressed to identify the wrongfully accused defendant, hence the potential for a wrongful conviction. The American Polygraph Association has been striving for three decades to improve the educational standards of its members, and the polygraph schools it accredits which, with some exceptions, currently require its applicants possess a minimum degree at the baccalaureate level, and provides eligibility for a Master's Degree in Forensic Psychophysiology to its graduates.(Chap. 23)

The results of improved education and training can be seen in a report (Ansley 1990) on the validity and reliability of all studies of real cases conducted from 1980 to 1990 which considered the outcome of 2,042 cases from ten studies which indicated a validity of 98% for deceptive cases and 97% for non-deceptive cases (Chap. 3). The methodology and technology of forensic psychophysiology has undergone significant improvements through research and development in the private and public sectors including the Department of Defense Polygraph Institute and the Applied Physics Laboratory at Johns Hopkins University which developed a mathematical algorithm for the computerized polygraph system demonstrating an accuracy exceeding 98 percent (Chap. 13). Society desperately needs this technology as a preventive measure to persuade our young generation that the truth will prevail in our courts which now have the capacity to uncover mendacity and punish the offenders (Chap. 23), and to distinguish habitual career criminals from those who can be safety placed on probation or parole through PV examination monitoring and treatment programs (Chap. 24), and last but not least, to identify the wrongfully accused defendant.(Chap. 23)

It is expected that this book will be read not only in the United States, but in most of the foreign countries that employ forensic psychophysiology. It is hoped that they will not repeat our mistakes but will benefit from our successes in the research and development of this complex technology and its application in our society as depicted in this book. This book is dedicated to all people who seek the truth through the art and science of forensic psychophysiology.

REFERENCES:

Abrams, S. (1992, July 26-31) Polygraphing the child abusers. Thesis presented at the 27th Annual Seminar/Workshop of the American Polygraph Association at Orlando, Florida.

Ansley, N. (1990). The validity and reliability of polygraph decisions in real cases. *Polygraph*, 19(3): 169-181.

Ansley, N. (1992). IAFPI met in Orlando. *APA Newsletter*, 25(4): 12.

Ansley, N. (1994). Notes and Comments, The Editor's Column. *APA Newsletter*, 27(2): 14-16.

Ansley, N. Editor (1989). Eleventh Circuit Admits Polygraph Evidence. *Polygraph*, 18(3): 125-143.

Ansley, N. Editor (1993). Supreme Court of the United States No. 92-102: William Daubert, et, ux, etc. et al., Petitioners v. Merrell Dow Pharmaceuticals, Inc., 113 S.Ct. 2786, 125 L.E.2d 469, 509 U.S.__. *Polygraph*, 22(3), 270-283.

Ansley, N. (1994). Ames did not pass polygraph tests as first reported. Aldrich Ames failed polygraph tests, results ignored. Notes and Comments, The Editor's Col umn. *APA Newsletter*, 27(2): 1-2, 14-16.

Ansley, N. Editor (1993). Computerized 'Lie Detector' Scoring. *APA Newsletter*, 26(4):9

Ansley, N. Editor (1995). Notes and Comment, The Editor's Column. *APA Newsletter*, 28(5),24.

Bailey, F. L., Zuckerman, R. E., Pierce, K. R. (1989). *The Emplovee Polygraph Protection Act: A Manual for Polygraph Examiners and Employers.* American Polygraph Association, Severna Park, Maryland.

Barland, G. H. (1994). Report of the International Liaison Committee. *APA Newsletter,* 27(4): 31-33.

Barland, G. H. (1995, Apr 17). Telephone conversation with J. A. Matte.

Brisentine, R. A. (1974). Polygraph research in the U. S. Army. *Polygraph,* 3(1): 66-80.

Department of Defense. (1984). *The Accuracy and Utility of Polygraph Testing.* DoD, Washington, D. C.

Department of Defense. (1987). Department of Defense Polygraph Program - Report to Congress for the Fiscal Year 1987. *Polygraph,* 17(2): 56-80.

For University of Pennsylvania Report. (1972). See Greenfield, Norman, S., and Stemback, Richard A. (Eds.): *Handbook of Psychophysiology.* New York, Holt, Rinchart and Winston, Inc.

Kubis, J. F. (1974). Comparison of voice analysis and polygraph as lie detection procedures. *Polygraph,* 3(1)1-47.

Lykken, D. T. (1981). *A Tremor in the blood: Uses and abuses of the lie detector.* New York: McGraw-Hill.

Matte, J. A. (1993). The Review, Presentation and Assurance of Intended Interpretation of Test Questions is Critical to the Outcome of Polygraph Tests. *Polygraph,* 22(4): 299-313.

Matte, J. A. (1980). *The Art and Science of the Polygraph Technique.* Charles C. Thomas - Publisher, Springfield, Illinois.

Matte, J. A., Reuss, R. M. (1995). *Psychophysiological Methodology in Numerically Evaluated Psychophysiological Veracity Examinations.* Thesis presented at the 30th Annual Seminar/Workshop of the American Polygraph Association on 16 Aug 95 at Las Vegas, Nevada.

McCauley, C., Forman, R. F. (1988). A review of the Office of Technology Assessment report on polygraph validity. *Basic and Applied Social Psychology.* 9(2): 73-84.

Morris, J. R. (1994, July 24-29). *Managing Monitoring/Testing Programs of Convicted Sex* Offenders. Thesis presented at the 29th Annual Seminar/Workshop of the American Polygraph Association at Nashville, Tennessee.

Office of Technology Assessment (OTA)(1983). *Scientific Validity of Polygraph Testing - A Research Review and Evaluation.*. Technical Memorandum for the Congressional Board of the 98th Congress of the United States, OTA-TM-H-15.

Public Law 100-347. (1988, June 27). Employee Polygraph Protection Act of 1988. 100th Congress. *Polygraph,* 17(4): 138-149.

Raloff, J. (1995, October 28). Assessing OTA's Legacy; examining what remains, now that OTA is gone. *Science News,* 148, 286-287.

Szucko, J. J., Kleinmuntz, B. (1981). Statistical Versus Clinical Lie Detection.. *American Psychologist.* 26:488-496.

U. S. Department of Labor. (1988). Application of the Employee Polygraph Protection Act of 1988; Final Rule. *Polygraph,* 17(4):149-194.

Widacki, J., Horvath, F. (1978). An experimental investigation of the relative validity and utility of the polygraph technique and three other common methods of criminal identification. *Polygraph*, 7(3), 215-222.

Yankee, W. J. (1995, Jan 9). Letter from Department of Defense Polygraph Institute regarding the *Computerized Voice Stress Analyzer (CVSA),* to Dr. James A. Matte.

Yankee, W. J. (1990). Welcoming Remarks of Dr. William J. Yankee at the 1990 Federal Interagency Polygraph Seminar FBI Academy, Quantico, Virginia. *Polygraph*, 9(3): 182-188.

Yankee, W. J. (1994). A Case for Forensic Psychophysiology and Other Changes in Terminology. *Polygraph*, 23(3): 188-195.

Chapter 2

HISTORY

Since the beginning of time man has sought to verify the truth and detect deception by various means including torture and trial by ordeal, which still persist in many civilized as well as underdeveloped countries. But in 1730, a year before he died, Daniel Defoe wrote an essay entitled "An Effectual Scheme for the Immediate Preventing of Street Robberies and Suppressing all Other Disorders of the Night" wherein he suggested "taking the pulse" as a practical and more humane method of identifying a criminal. Defoe wrote:

> Guilt carries fear always about with it; there is a tremor in the blood of a thief, that, if attended to, would effectually discover him; and if charged as a suspicious fellow, on that suspicion only I would always feel his pulse, and I would recommend it to practice. The innocent man which knows himself clear and has no surprise upon him; when they cry "stop thief" he does not start; or strive to get out of the way; much less does he tremble and shake, change countenance or look pale, and less still does he run for it and endeavor to escape.
>
> It is true some are so harden'd in crime that they will boldly hold their faces to it, carry it off with an air of contempt, and outface even a pursuer; but take hold of his wrist and feel his pulse, there you shall find his guilt; confess he is the man, in spite of a bold countenance or a false tongue: This they cannot conceal; 'tis in vain to counterfeit there; a conscious heart will discover itself by faltering pulse; the greatest stock of brass in the face cannot hide it, or the most firm resolution of a harden'd offender conceal and cover it. The experiment perhaps has not been try'd, and some may think it is not a fair way, even with a thief, because 'tis making the man an evidenced against himself: As for that, I shall not enter into the enquiry farther than this: if it is agreeable to Justice to apprehend a man upon suspicion, if the particulars are probably and well grounded; it cannot then be unlawful by any strategem that is not injurious in itself, to seek out collateral grounds of suspicion, and see how one thing concurs with another.
>
> It may be true, that this discovery by the pulsation of the blood cannot be brought to a certainty, and therefore it is not to be brought into evidence; but I insist if it be duly and skillfully observed, it may be brought to be allowed for a just addition to other circumstances, especially if concurring with other grounds of suspicion.

(Scott-Kilvert 1965; Ansley 1989).

But Daniel Defoe was hardly the first person to suggest the use of the pulse to detect deception. In the book *Gesta Romanorum* (1906) it is related that during the Middle Ages, a nobleman suspected his wife of infidelity and informed one of his advisers of his suspicions. A test of the wife's faithfulness was arranged at a dinner where the adviser sat next to the nobleman's wife and casually laid his hand upon her wrist while conversing with her. During the conversation he mentioned the name of the man suspected by the nobleman, whereupon the wife's pulse immediately quickened, but when he later mentioned the name of her husband he perceived no similar response. It is reported that a confession was later elicited. (Trovillo 1939).

While Defoe's essay called upon criminologists to employ medical science in the fight against crime, it was not until the nineteenth century, that science came to the aid of the truth seeker through the research of Italian physiologist Angelo Mosso.

Encouraged by Cesare Lombroso, his tutor and contemporary, Mosso pursued his studies of emotion and fear and its influence on the heart and respiration with an instrument for measuring blood pressure and pulse change called a "plethysmograph" invented by Francis Franke, which revealed periodic undulations in blood pressure caused by the respiration cycle. Mosso's studies of the circulation of blood in the brain contributed immensely to the study of the influences of fear.(Trovillo 1939). It was Mosso (1878) who first reported experiments in which he observed that the breathing pattern changed under certain stimuli. (Herbold-Wootten 1982)

In his writings, Mosso described one particular observation of a female patient whose brain was partially exposed through an opening in the skull as a result of a disease, as an example of the disrupting nature of fear, especially for one's own security. As the patient sat quietly in an armchair seemingly absent-minded while her cerebral pulse was being recorded, the pulsations suddenly rose higher and the brain increased in size. In the absence of any external cause, the patient was queried regarding her thoughts immediately prior to this physiological occurrence, which revealed that the patient had caught sight of a skull resting between books in a bookcase facing her, which had frightened her by reminding her of her malady. (Trovillo 1939)

Mosso also observed that variations in blood pressure and the circulation of blood in the brain during fear are far greater than those resulting from the effect of mere noises and sounds. In an attempt to further measure the influence of fear, Mosso devised a "scientific cradle," which was designed to measure the flow of blood while a person lay on his back in a prone position, as it became concentrated first in one part of the body and then in another.

The "cradle" consisted of a large, heavy table at the center of which was a delicate knife-edge fulcrum. A heavy wooden plank rested securely and evenly on the fulcrum. To prevent constant swaying of the balance with each small oscillation of respiration, a heavy metal counterpoise, which could be adjusted up or down, was fastened vertically in the middle of the plank, underneath it, and secured with two metal bars at each end of the plank. When the subject experienced emotion. the blood would rush to the head and throw the cradle out of balance, which in turn would be recorded on a revolving smoked drum.

A rubber cuff was also wrapped around the subject's foot and connected by a tube to a tambour recording pulse fluctuations.(Trovillo 1939)

Mosso concluded from these experiments that he could identify a subject who is afraid as opposed to one who is tranquil from their pulsation records. Mosso's contribution to the science of forensic psychophysiology is especially meaningful since fear of detection is a primary element in the detection of deception as pertains to forensic psychophysiology, as will be seen and explained in later chapters.

Mosso's tutor, Cesare Lombroso, M. D. (an Italian criminologist), unlike his contemporaries and predecessors who limited their experiments to the laboratory, applied the blood pressure-pulse tests to actual criminal suspects on several occasions while assisting the police in the identification of criminals. In 1895, Lombroso published the second edition of *L'Homme Criminel* in which he relates his use of a plethysmograph and a sphygmograph during the interrogation of criminal suspects.(Trovillo 1939)

Of particular interest is Lombroso's modification of the plethysmograph resulting in the hydrosphygmograph. The suspect's fist would be placed in a water-filled tank. The immersed fist was sealed across the top of the tank by a rubber membrane. Pulsations of blood in the fist were transferred to the water and the changes in water level were carried over into an air-filled tube, which in turn recorded the pulsations on the revolving smoked drum. (Trovillo 1939)

Lombroso in one particular instance, using the hydrosphygmograph, correctly concluded that a suspect was innocent of a 20,000 francs railroad robbery but was guilty of stealing certain passports and documents. During the examination, the suspect showed no change in the sphygmographic lines to questions pertaining to the railroad robbery, but a fall of 14 mmHg reflecting a drop in blood pressure occurred when the theft of the documents was mentioned. Lombroso concluded from the absence of a response to the railroad questions versus the presence of a response to the documents questions that the suspect was truthful to the former and deceptive to the latter issue, documenting one of the earliest usage of a comparative control question. Lombroso's conclusions were later verified. (Trovillo 1939; Lombroso 1911).

The United States military in the nineteenth century was not without ideas about novel methods of procuring information from unwilling subjects. Dr. Charles E. Cady, a military surgeon, recommend the use of chloroform for solving Lincoln's assassination including identification of its conspirators. Based on his three years of experience as a surgeon in the army where he had observed Rebel officers divulge important information while they were partially under the influence of chloroform which they had positively refused to communicate in their normal state, Dr. Cady suggested that men skilled in the administration of chloroform, administer pure unadulterated chloroform to the patient who had been placed flat on his back with his head slightly elevated in a well ventilated room to insure perfect admixture of air with the vapor of the anesthetic, and while the patient is in a semiconscious condition, he is questioned bluntly and pointedly. (Eisenschiml 1940).

In 1879, a much acclaimed psychological test was developed by F. Galton, whereby the patient is presented with a group of words sufficiently separated in time to allow the patient to utter his first thought generated by each word. For that reason it was called the word-association test. The application of this test to determine criminal guilt required the insertion of several neutral questions that were irrelevant to the crime into the word association test interspersed with words relevant to the crime situation. The premise of this test is that a guilty examinee when confronted with a relevant word, will suffer from an inner conflict in his attempt to utter an associated word lacking in culpability, which may be manifested by a delay in reaction time, a more rapid reaction time, repetition of relevant or stimulus words, stereotyped or identical responses to several different words, blocking of response, informative nature of the response, or uncoordinated physical movements. Galton, commenting on the effectiveness of his test, stated "They lay bare the foundations of a man's thoughts with curious distinctness and exhibit his mental anatomy with more vividness and truth than he would probably care to publish to the world." (Trovillo 1939)

In 1879, Wilhelm Wundt founded the first psychological Laboratory in Leipzig, Germany and he immediately attracted students from all over the world. Most first generation psychologists studied under Wundt or at least visited him, i.e. G. S. Hall, James McKeen Cattell, G. M. Stratton, C. H. Judd, Titschener; the last four received their doctorates from Leipzig University. In the summer of 1880 Trautscholdt conducted a study with the association method in which Wundt and Hall both served as subjects. Wundt modified Galton's association method to an almost standardized form, a process which took several years. (Lowenstein, 1920, 1922; Herbold-Wootten 1995)

The earliest application of the psychogalvanometer to forensic problems was made by Sticker in 1897. Sticker believed that the origin of the galvanic skin phenomenon is under the influence of exciting mental impressions and that the will has no effect upon it. Sticker based his conclusions on experiments conducted by several predecessors such as Adamkiewicz who in 1878 was the first to offer experimental proof that the secretion of sweat is closely linked to psychological processes. (Trovillo 1939).

In 1904, Max Wertheimer, a German scientist at the Physiological Institute of the University of Prague, published a paper together with Julius Klein entitled "Psychologische Tatbestandsdiagnostik" with subtitle "Ideas about experimental methods for the purpose of revealing the involvement of a person in a criminal act (Tatbestand)". The article began with a question: "Isn't it possible to diagnose in a perpetrator the concealed knowledge of his criminal action independent of his statements?" In his 1906 dissertation, Wertheimer stated: "Isn't it possible to find experimental methods that allow us to discriminate between persons that know about a crime and those that do not?" In the first paper, Wertheimer and Klein presented a complete program designed to solve the problem of detection of traces of special, unusual or extraordinary experiences in the consciousness of the examinee which they called "complexes." They suggested the use of the word association method and the employment of the physiological recording devices available during that period to detect those "complexes" such as the plethysmograph, which was known through the writings of Muller and Mosso, the pneumograph, the hydrosphygmograph, known through the work of Lombroso, the psychograph, which was a device that recorded involuntary trembling of the finger used by Bekhterev and later by Luria. Wertheimer and Klein's program further suggested the creation of altered states of consciousness through the use of narcotics and hypnosis to detect these complexes. (Herbold-Wootten 1982)

In 1908, Hugo Munsterberg, a Harvard psychology professor and former student of Wilhelm Wundt, introduced the forensic application of the word association technique in detecting deception in the United States and further suggested possibilities in detecting deception through the recording of physiological changes.(Trovillo 1939; Herbold-Wootten 1982). Following Max Wertheimer and Julius Klein's paper on what is currently known as the Guilty Knowledge Technique, Munsterberg wrote about the problem of testing the nervous innocent person and said the "real use of the experimental emotion method is therefore so far probably confined to those cases in which it is to be found out whether a suspected person knows anything about a certain place or man or thing. Thus if a new name, for instance, is brought in, the method is reliable; the innocent, who never heard the name before, will not be more excited if he hears that one among a dozen others; the criminal, who knows the name as that of a witness of the crime, will show the emotional symptoms."(Munsterberg 1907)

While Munsterberg was promoting Galton's word association technique in detecting deception, Arthur MacDonald (an acquaintance of Lombroso) appeared before a Congressional hearing proposing a federal laboratory to study criminals and suggested the use of an apparatus containing all of the elements of a modern polygraph (pneumograph, galvanometer, and cardiosphygmograph). (Trovillo 1939).

Before the turn of the twentieth century, Verdin of Paris (a manufacturer of physiological apparatus) was producing ink-recording polygraphs with pneumatic tambours. However, despite the availability of ink-recording kymographs, smoked drum apparatus still remained popular because of the reuse of the paper, and the lack of problems with ink feed in the pens, i.e. jamming and skipping.

S. Veraguth (1907) was one of the first scientists to use the word-association test with the galvanometer, although H. Munsterberg was concurrently referring its application to criminal cases (1908). In 1907, Veraguth described his observations of the galvanic phenomena and emotions, noting that emotional complexes, unveiled in word-association experiments, made an *ascending* galvanometer curve, in contrast with the *rest curve* of non-crucial stimuli, and that these personally significant stimuli produced larger fluctuations of the galvanometer than indifferent stimuli. Veraguth also noted that the first indifferent stimulus words caused larger responses than succeeding indifferent stimuli. He is believed to be the first to use the term "psychogalvanic reflex" which was later repudiated by Ruckmick (1936) in that the reaction is not a reflex; its psychological nature not being completely understood, thus he proposed the term "electrodermal response." Veraguth however believed that the electrical phenomena noticed by Fere , Tarchanoff, and Muller, for both the endosomatic and exosomatic currents, were attributable not to vascular changes in the skin but to activity of the sweat glands. He ascribed the mental counterpart of these changes to a feeling of reality or compulsion, or an emotional situation, or both. Jung and Peterson of Zurich subsequently used the phenomenon for detection of emotional complexes. (Trovillo 1939)

In the early twentieth century several hundred papers dealing with the "psychogalvanic reflex" were published, but very little research was conducted in its relation to deception.

In 1919, Binswanger noted that "The analysis in many (of Veraguth's) cases discloses undoubted relationships of an 'old' complex to the present; in the same way an apparently 'actual' complex which momentarily seems very much to occupy the subject, may derive its essential effect from events of long ago." Trovillo (1939) points out that "Modern police interrogations which depend upon the electrodermal or psychogalvanic responses of a criminal suspect may find this very situation embarrassing. A suspect may give a large response, for example, not because he is guilty or robbing the place in question, but because he has robbed other and similar places. The operator is not always able to identify the basis for the reaction until after prolonged questioning about related or associated experiences." (Jung 1919; Trovillo 1939). Binswanger appears to be the first person to consider the "*outside issue*" in his study of many of Veraguth's cases.

Vittorio Benussi was born on 17 January 1878 in Trieste, Italy. He studied philosophy in Graz, Austria where in 1900 he received a doctoral degree in philosophy inasmuch as psychology was not yet an independent field of science. During the period 1902 to 1914 Benussi was Privatdozent of Philosophy in Graz and conducted extensive experimental research in the field of perception of forms, optical illusions, visual and tactile perception of movement, spaced perception, weight perception and perception of time, and while in Graz Benussi also acquired experience in hypnotic induction techniques. After years of working in a well-equipped laboratory in Graz and subsequently from 1914 to 1919 at the University of Vienna, Benussi accepted a position at the University of Padua, Italy which had no laboratory, in fact the entire available equipment consisted of a box of chalk. Due to these limited research facilities, he focused his research efforts to hypnosis which Benussi used as a tool to investigate perception, that is when he discovered that it was possible to discriminate sleep, wakefulness and the state of hypnosis by certain breathing patterns which he used as a criterion of the hypnotic state which he had created in his subjects. But Benussi had conducted experiments about the respiratory symptoms of lying while in Graz, Austria, which was secondary to his interest in psychology and hypnosis, and it is there that he discovered a methodology for calculating the quotient of the inhalation to exhalation time as a means of determining truth from deception. (Herbold-Wootten 1989, 1995).

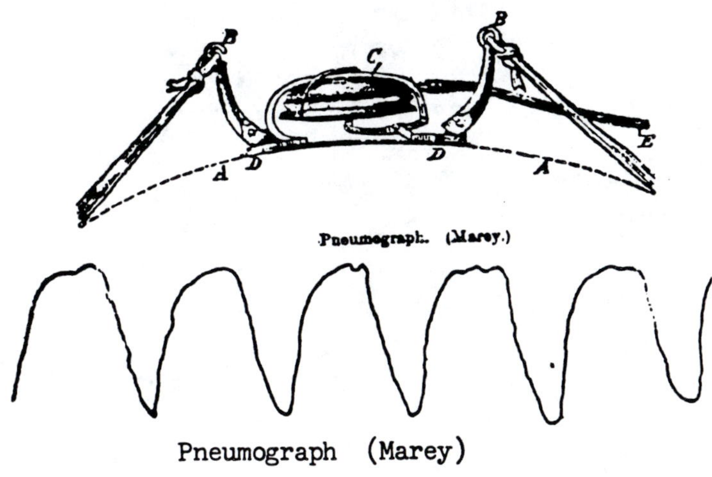

Figure II-1. From Norman Ansley. Courtesy of the American Polygraph Association.

In March 1913, Vittorio Benussi presented a paper before the second meeting of the Italian Society for Psychology in Rome, on the subject of his experiments regarding respiratory symptoms of lying. Benussi described how he recorded a subject's breathing patterns using a Marey pneumograph (Fig.II-l), which recorded on a moving chart consisting of long blackened strips 2.10 meters long with the use of bamboo pens 12 centimeters in length a subject's inspiration reflected by a proportionate upward movement of the pen and expiration reflected by a proportionate downward movement of the pen. Benussi detected deception by changes in the inspiration-expiration ratio, using sophisticated statistical methods to analyze his data. Benussi was possibly the first to employ more than one physiological measure in detection of deception by recording heart rate and a blood pressure curve (Fig.II-2) in addition to respiration. (Marey was a manufacturer of physiological apparatus for many years and a competitor of Verdin of Paris.) (Benussi 1914, translated and reprinted 1975)

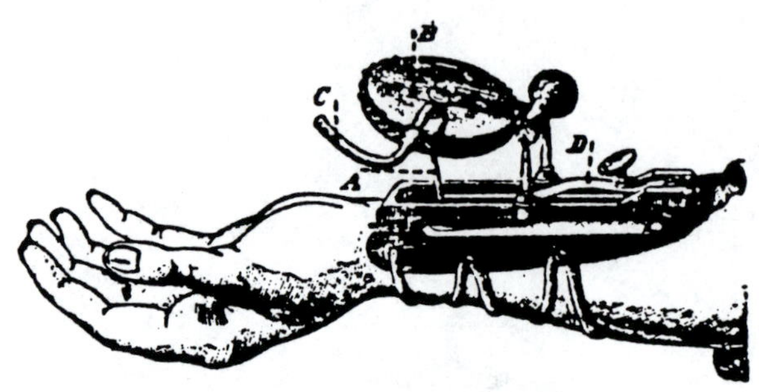

Marey's Sphygmograph

Figure II-2. From Norman Ansley. Courtesy of the American Polygraph Association

Benussi's comprehensive experiments revealed that his respiratory diagnosis failed in only one case of truth and one case of lie, and that these two cases could easily be explained on the basis of the experimental circumstances. Benussi's experiments considered countermeasures which revealed that even practiced controlled breathing did not prevent a correct diagnosis. Vittorio Benussi also experimented with the accuracy of behavioral observation versus respiratory recordings and found that behavioral observations did not fare better than chance while respiration recordings were nearly 100% accurate. Benussi stated "while on the average the personal observations yield practically no useful diagnosis at all the respiratory quotients in practically every single case disclose whether the statement of the EP (Experimental Person) was false or true. A comparison of the values shows the extent to which the diagnostic aids exceed the ability of the observers - which are by no means unskilled. An expert diagnosis has entirely the character of the accidentally correct hit when it is correct and of the accidentally incorrect hit in the other case (as mentioned above, the evaluation percentages fluctuate around 50%), while the respiration diagnosis is correct with a frequency of nearly 100%." Benussi questioned whether "the respiratory symptoms in the case of lie and sincerity show characteristic differences" and determined that "two forms of interpretation must be conceded. The respiratory changes can result from (a) differences in the intellectual or (b) the emotional states, which differ in the case of lying and sincerity." Benussi observed that "it cannot be the intellectual processes specific for the lie that give rise to the observed respiratory changes. In the pretended lie these processes remain qualitatively untouched and the respiratory symptoms of the lie do not appear." Benussi concluded that the respiratory symptoms of lying are caused by the *emotion of lying* rather than *intellectual*

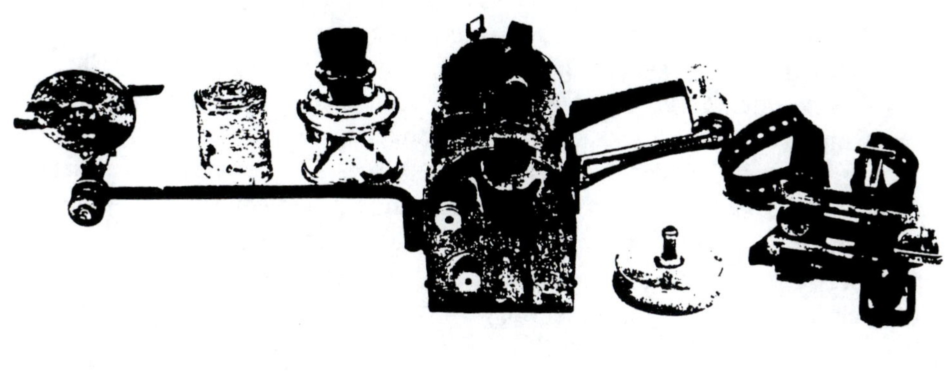

MACKENZIE'S CLINICAL POLYGRAPH, C. 1910

Figure II-3. From Norman Ansley. Courtesy of the American Polygraph Association. Photo by W. D. Haman, Assistant Curator, Oxford Museum of History and Science.

conflict.(Benussi 1914; Ansley 1988). Benussi used students as subjects in his experiments, and in order to enhance the effects of deception he introduced "observers" in the experimental situation. As it was not custom in those days to describe experimental procedures in exact details as we would do today, it is impossible to determine whether the experimental situation was indeed identical for all subjects. It is unexplained why H. Burt could not replicate Benussi's findings.(Herbold-Wootten 1995).

James Mackenzie, an English clinician and cardiologist described his 'clinical polygraph' in 1892 as an 'ink polygraph' with an accurate clockwork which drives a paper ribbon with time markers at one-fifth of a second. The instrument is encased in a nickel-plated housing from which an arm projects for two registering tambours connected by means of rubber tubing to the receiving apparatus composed of simple aluminum cups for the heart beat (cardiogram) and venous pulse, and the pelotte (metal cup with a perforated nipple at its center), fixed to the arm by straps for the arterial pulse.(Fig. II-3). The first such instrument was manufactured for Mackenzie by Krohne and Seseman of London, and later by several companies including Down Brothers of London and the Cambridge Scientific Instrument Company. In 1908, Mackenzie authored an article describing his 'Ink Polygraph' published in the British Medical Journal. (Mackenzie 1908; Reid, Inbau 1977; Ansley 1992).

In 1915, Dr. William M. Marston (an American scientist) after years of research devised the systolic blood pressure deception test, which consisted of intermittent recordings of a suspect's systolic blood pressure during questioning, using a standard medical blood pressure cuff and stethoscope, requiring repeated inflation of the pressure cuff to obtain readings at intervals during the examination. Hence, it was also called the "discontinuous" technique. (Ferguson 1973) Marston conducted a research project for the Psychological Committee of the National Research Council in 1917 involving twenty tests of criminal defendants referred by a court or probation office for a medical or psychiatric evaluation. The guilt or innocence of these 16 women and 4 men was established by physical and medical evidence, testimony, and judicial disposition. Each subject was administered the discontinuous systolic blood pressure test which revealed that the examiner's conclusions were in agreement with the evidence in all 20 cases. In 8 cases the examiner found the subject truthful and in 12 cases he found some or all of the testimony was deceptive. In 5 of the deceptive cases the examiner identified specific issues about which they were truthful and other specific issues about which they were deceptive. Dr. Marston describing his methodology "Other tests of the nature of which the subject is ignorant, as well as periods of rest and series of questions upon irrelevant and indifferent subjects are also interjected into the examination of the subject," indicates one of earliest applications of the Relevant/Irrelevant technique. (Marston 1921; Ansley 1990). Norman Ansley, Editor in Chief of the American Polygraph Association advised this author that many years ago he had conversations with Mrs. Elizabeth Marston and her close friend and colleague Olive Richard, both of whom had worked with Dr. Marston as forensic psychophysiologists in the 1920s and 1930s.(Fig. II-4). Both related to Ansley that, depending on the type of case, they would sometimes insert a "hot question" into the test, whose description corresponds to the non-exclusive control question subsequently published by Reid & Inbau in 1966. When asked by Ansley the reason for Dr. Marston's failure to publish his development and usage of his "hot question" they replied that Dr. Marston did not want examinees to read and learn about it. (Ansley 1995). Dr. Marston who had studied under Munsterberg developed a technique for use in practical cases with the assistance of his wife Elizabeth Holloway Marston and Olive Richard. Marston was apparently acquainted with the principle of a Guilty Knowledge Test in describing an "elimination test." Marston said that in this examination "another series of critical questions may be asked, and another polygraphic record run. These questions are designed to reveal the testee's knowledge of other suspects connected with the case. For example, if the testee is known to be a member of a certain gang, and the examiner wishes to identify other members of the same mob, a series of this sort is asked: 'Was Jones with you on the night of the murder?', 'Was Smith with you?', 'Was Doe with you?', and so on. The testee in such cases usually answers 'no' to all of the identification questions, but his uncontrollable b.p. responses reveal which individuals were present in the murder gang. Other types of questions may be arranged similarly in groups, and further b.p. records may be taken as desired." (Marston, 1938; Ansley 1992)

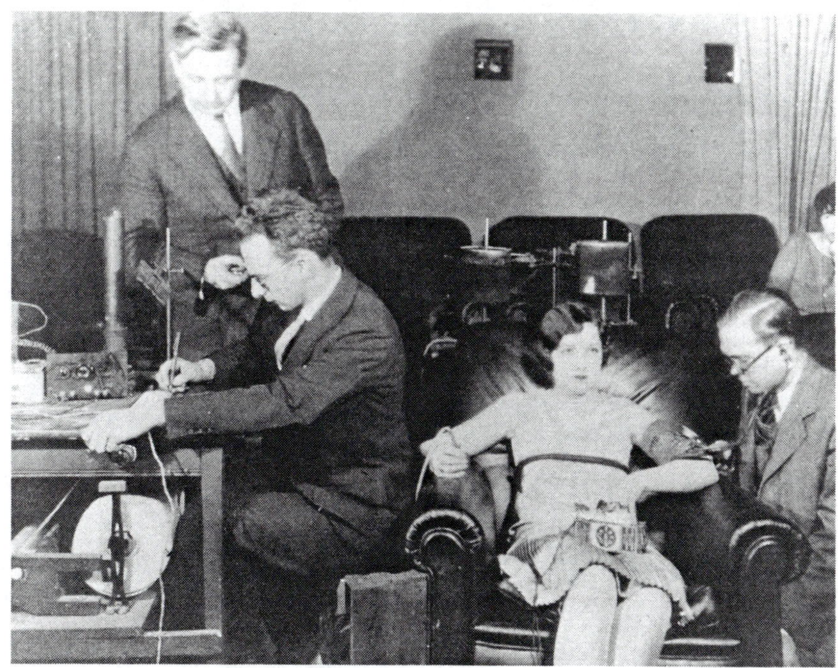

A Laboratory Set-Up of Lie Detector Apparatus - Used by Dr. Marston at Columbia University. Blood pressure, discontinuous method, is taken by Tycos. Psycho-galvanometer is connected to subject's fingers. Grip and respiration make record on smoked drum. Above photograph depicts Bill Marston standing and Olive Richard is in the back watching the smoked drum recording which is directly behind the model who is posing as the subject. A chronoscope is in her lap, her right hand holds the device for recording muscle tension. The electrodes are on her left hand and the student on the left is recording the galvanometer fluctuations. The student on the right is monitoring blood pressure.

Figure II-4. From Marston, William Moulton (1938). The Lie Detector Test. New York: Richard R. Smith, Reprinted by the American Polygraph Association, 1989.

During World War I, a committee of psychologists formed by the National Research Council for the purpose of evaluating the known deception tests for possible use in counterintelligence investigations determined after a number of experiments that the systolic blood pressure deception test was superior to other deception tests and enjoyed a 97 percent reliability. As a result, Marston was recommended for appointment as Special Assistant to the Secretary of War with authority to employ his technique in counterintelligence investigations. It is said that the first use of the polygraph in an espionage case was conducted by Dr. Marston in 1917-1918 (Ansley 1995). Marston did not however receive aforementioned appointment, but his work did arouse the interest of a young psychologist named John Larson (employed by the Berkeley California Police Department). The blood pressure test excited his curiosity and in 1921 Larson developed an instrument that continually and simultaneously measured respiration and cardiovascular changes on a Jacquet polygraph which apparently also included an event marker (Larson 1932; Barland 1988). This polygraphic apparatus, which Larson assembled in portable form, was used extensively in criminal cases with much success.(Fig. II-5).

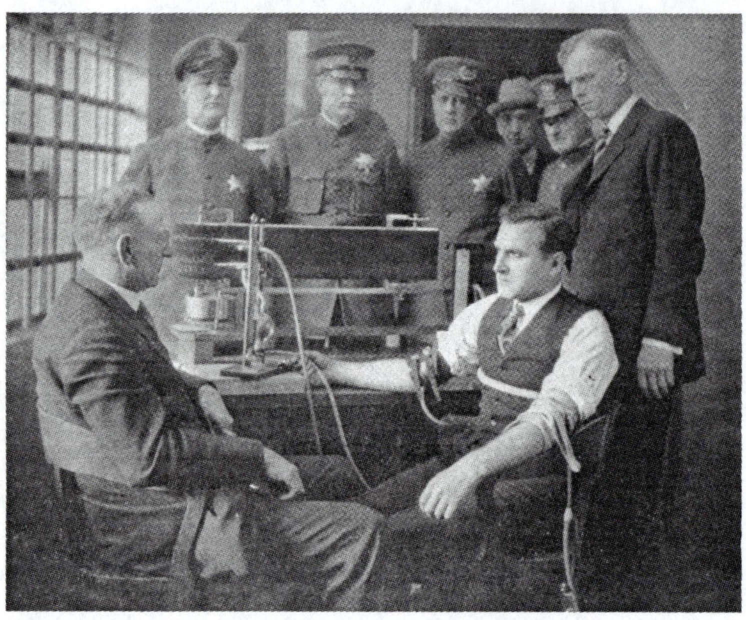

John Larson's Portable Polygraph

Figure II-5. From D. C. Lee: Instrumental Detection of Deception. Springfield, Illinois. Charles C. Thomas, 1953.

In one particular case at the Berkeley Police Department, Larson used a cardio-pneumo-psychogram which recorded pulse rate, vascular volume and respiration on a smoked-drum kymograph on a group of 38 college girls residing in the same house, to determine which one was a shoplifter. One of the girls produced deceptive records and was tested again several days later which again produced deceptive results. Confronted with the results of her test, she confessed to having sold over $500.00 worth of stolen books, articles and clothing from stores. (Larson 1923; Ansley 1990).

In another case reported by Ansley (1990), John Larson wrote in 1932 of a case wherein ninety college girls who lived in a college boarding house had been victimized by a series of larcenies including silk underwear, registered letters and a diamond ring, which police investigators had been unable to solve. All of the girls were tested with their consent, using a cardio-pneumo-psychogram (CPP)which recorded pulse rate, vascular volume and respiration on a smoked-drum kymograph. All of the tests were conducted as nearly alike as possible. The CPP recordings showed a marked uniformity for all the girls with one exception. The exceptional record showed very marked effects in the respiratory rate and the blood pressure. In one instance there seemed to be an involuntary holding of the breath and a marked drop in the height of the beats, following which there was a marked increase in rate, pressure and amplitude. The test was not completed because the subject "blew up." At the point at which the subject forced discontinuance of the test, the pressure rate, and force were steadily increasing. This same subject confessed to the thefts a few days later and paid for the stolen property. (Larson 1932; Ansley 1990).

In 1920, Otto Lowenstein, a psychiatrist in Bonn, Germany introduced an apparatus that could record simultaneously the movement of each foot, each hand, the head in all three dimensions; it had two pneumographs. The subject was placed in a huge chair with his feet hanging free in the air, the head attached to a kind of helmet. The instrument recorded ten tracings. Lowenstein used this apparatus experimentally, and also in actual cases to detect whether or not inmates in his hospital were suffering from true or false amnesia. The instrument was huge, impractical and difficult to maintain in working order, but is considered a true polygraph. (Herbold-Wootten 1982).

During the 1920's, several Japanese psychologists became keenly interested in the electrodermal activity (EDA) as an indicator of emotions. Akamatsu, Uchida and Togawa (1933) suggested the use of EDA for the detection of deception because the skin conductance level was found to decrease during emotional changes. The first report of psychophysiological detection of deception in Japan was by Akamatsu, et al., (1937), when they reported the successful use of skin conductance level. In 1938 and 1939 they reported additional experiments using skin conductance level for the detection of deception. Togawa later applied this method for testing a spy, in Japan's first practical application of psychophysiological detection of deception. (Fukumoto 1982)

The original lie detection apparatus used in Japan in the 1930's was a galvanometer which measured skin conductance level changes. During the Second World War the Yokokawa Denki Company introduced a psychogalvanometer on the Japanese market which was subsequently adopted in 1947 as a lie detector by the Metropolitan Police. Before long, most police departments in Japan were using the Denki psychogalvanometer, but operation of the apparatus was deemed too complicated, therefore it was replaced with the purchase of the Keeler model 302 polygraph in 1953. The Keeler instrument was subsequently used as a pattern for two Japanese polygraph instruments in 1955; the YKK Polygraph manufactured by the Yamakoshi Seisakusho Company, and the TKK Polygraph manufactured by the Takei Kikikogyo Company, both of which were gradually adopted at all prefectural police headquarters. (Fukumoto 1982)

Because the Japanese laws give the police greater control over the crime scene than in the United States, the Japanese police are able to protect critical investigative information from the media and suspects. This enables the Japanese forensic psychophysiologists (FPs) to utilize Guilty Knowledge tests in a significantly greater percentage of cases, hence less reliance on control question techniques. Akihiro Suzuki, a leading polygraph researcher at the National Research Institute of Police Science, Tokyo, Japan advised this author in 1989 that the control question type of questioning method was controversial among Japanese FPs because the use of control or fictitious questions is beyond an examinee's agreement, and there is some question in their minds about the effectiveness of the control and the fictitious questions when the examinee understands the purpose of those questions.(Suzuki 1977, 1989). Since the Second World War the use of the polygraph in Japan has greatly expanded to the extent that they currently have more than one hundred practicing forensic psychophysiologists, and its results have frequently been admitted as evidence in Japanese Courts. (Fukumoto 1982; Barland 1995).

In the mid 1920's, A. R. Luria, a 24-years old psychologist at the Moscow Institute of Psychology conducted experiments with Alexei N. Leontiev, using a theory developed by the Institute's Director S. Kornalov that there was a finite amount of energy available for a task, and that mental effort and physical effort competed for the use of energy. Therefore, increased mental effort would interrupt or distort motor activity. Using Jung's work on word-association, the subjects were directed to engage in a motor project response simultaneously with each verbal associative response (Jung, 1905, 1910). This research project lasted several years and its results appeared to support Kornalov's theory. Luria then used aforesaid procedure on actual or suspected criminals. Luria hypothesized that he could use the known details of the crime as the critical stimuli in the combined motor test, which would reveal the guilty subject. Several years of study resulted in the collection of data on more than fifty subjects, most suspected of murder, which revealed that "strong emotions prevent a subject from forming stable automatic motor and speech responses... It appeared as if subjects influenced by strong emotions adapted to each situation in a unique way and did not settle into a stable reaction pattern."Luria said the work was of "practical value to criminologists, providing them with an early model of the lie detector." (Luria 1932,1979; Ansley 1992).

In 1925, Leonarde Keeler (a Stanford University psychology major who had gained firsthand experience in polygraph interrogations from Larson at the Berkeley Police Department) developed an improvement of Larson's apparatus. Keeler's instrument, like Larson's, recorded relative changes in blood pressure, pulse rate, and respiration patterns. However, Keeler developed a metal bellows, also known as a tambour, which was connected by mechanical actuating devices to small fountain pens. Volume changes within a blood pressure arm cuff and an accordion type tube also known as a pneumograph tube circling the chest or stomach of the subject (depending on whether the subject was a chest or stomach breather) were transferred in heavy walled rubber tubes to the aforementioned tambours. Keeler further designed a kymograph that pulled, at a constant speed, chart paper under the recording pens from a roll of chart paper located inside the instrument.

Leonarde Keeler is also credited with the development of the relevant/irrelevant (question) technique which he described in an article which he presented as "Deception tests and the lie detector" at the International Association for Identification in 1930,

(Stevens 1994; Keeler 1930; Ansley, Pumphrey 1994), although prior usage of a relevant/irrelevant question technique by Dr. William Marston has been documented. Keeler is also credited with the development of Peak of Tension tests which he categorized as the Name Test, the Amounts Test, the Object Test, the Map Test, the Age Test, and the Type of Crime Test, which would currently be identified as Guilty Knowledge and Concealment tests (Stevens 1994; Keeler 1936, 1938). Keeler is further credited with the introduction of the Card Test designed to ascertain the examinee's capability of response, currently known as the stimulation or concealed knowledge test. (Keeler 1936, 1938). It should be noted that Keeler collaborated with John A. Larson in Larson's classic 1932 work *Lying and its Detection*, wherein Larson described a 1928 case wherein a "Maps" test (Searching or Probing Peak of Tension test) was used to located a victim's body.(Ansley 1992). Keeler's 1938 book *The Detection of Deception* may be the first time that the test format now known as the Known-Solution Peak of Tension Test or Guilty Knowledge test was described specifically as a "peak of tension test." Keeler gave a case example and specific instructions for making up the list. (Ansley 1992).

In 1938 Keeler included a third physiological measuring component in his instrument, namely the Psychogalvanometer (PGR) also known as the galvanic skin reflex (GSR), developed by the Italian physiologist Galvani in 1791. The PGR reflected emotional changes by measuring changes in a person's skin resistance to electricity. This was accomplished by transmitting a constant minute electrical current through the skin of a selected fingertip.(Fig. II-6). That same year (1938), Leonarde Keeler was awarded a Legum Doctoris by Lawrence College (now Lawrence University) of Appleton, Wisconsin. On 3 January 1940, Leonarde Keeler incorporated as Keeler, Inc. (Ansley, (Harrelson) 1995).

Prior to Keeler's implementation of the psychogalvanometer in his instrument for the detection of deception, few attempts were made to utilize the PGR due to a lack of understanding regarding the causative factors for the resulting responses. The PGR has been the least understood physiological phenomenon of the three parameters.

It must be noted that Father Walter G. Summers, Department of Psychology, Fordham University (who developed the "pathometer," which measured apparent changes in skin resistance to electricity) conducted more than 6,000 laboratory experiments and further conducted about 50 actual cases involving the question of guilt or innocence of criminal suspects, obtaining an accuracy of between 98 and 100 percent. His technique was interesting in that it consisted of three tests for comparison in the amounts of deflection of the recording pen in relevant and irrelevant questions. A gradual decrease in pen deflection would indicate innocence; repeated responses to relevant questions of equal or greater magnitude than preceding tests would indicate guilt. (Trovillo 1939; Summers 1936).Father Summers also used control questions which he called "*emotional standards*" carefully selected from the suspect's life in an attempt to evoke "intense psychogalvanic reactions to surprise, anger, shame or anxiety..." such as 'Are you living with your wife' or 'Were you ever arrested.' Examinees who showed consistently greater reactions to the relevant questions than to the *emotional standard* questions contained in the same test

The Keeler Polygraph - Model 302C
Manufactured by Associated Research

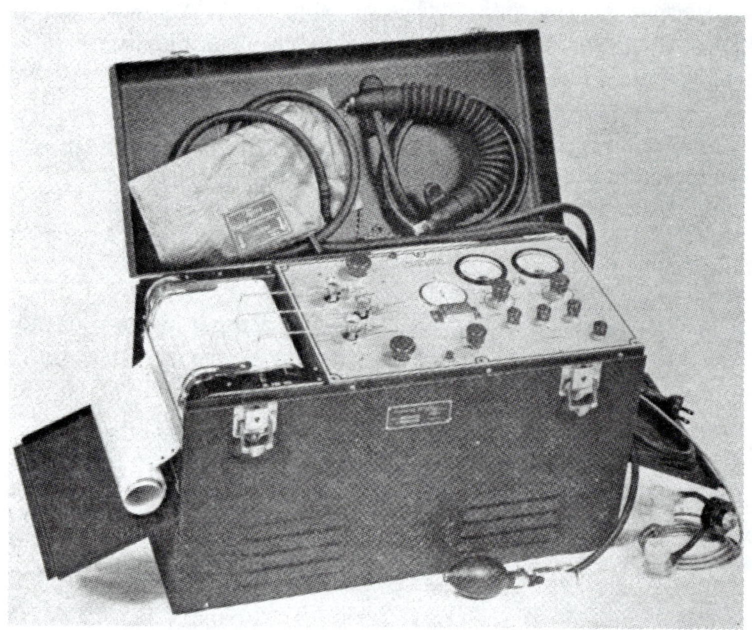

The above model succeeded Keeler's original 1925 model. It is housed in a steel case with wrinkle finish and chromium trim. The cover is attached to case with slip hinges permitting cover to be removed when instrument in use. The chart drive unit is powered by a synchronous motor at speeds of either six or twelve inches per minute, with two switches to regulate speed. There are four recording pens. The lower pen and its associated controls comprise the pulse-blood pressure unit. The longer pen records electrodermal variations. Above the electrodermal pen is the pen for recording respiration changes. At the top of the panel is the stimulus marker pen actuated by means of a flexible cable attached at the lower left of the panel. At the center of the panel is a standard sphygmomanometer, used as a guide to proper inflation of the blood pressure cuff.

Figure II-6. From C. D. Lee: Instrumental Detection of Deception, Springfield, Illinois. Charles C. Thomas, 1953.

were diagnosed as deceptive whereas examinees whose reactions to the *emotional standard* questions were consistently greater than the relevant questions were diagnosed as truthful to the relevant issue.(Summers 1939).

The Darrow Behavior Research Photopolygraph

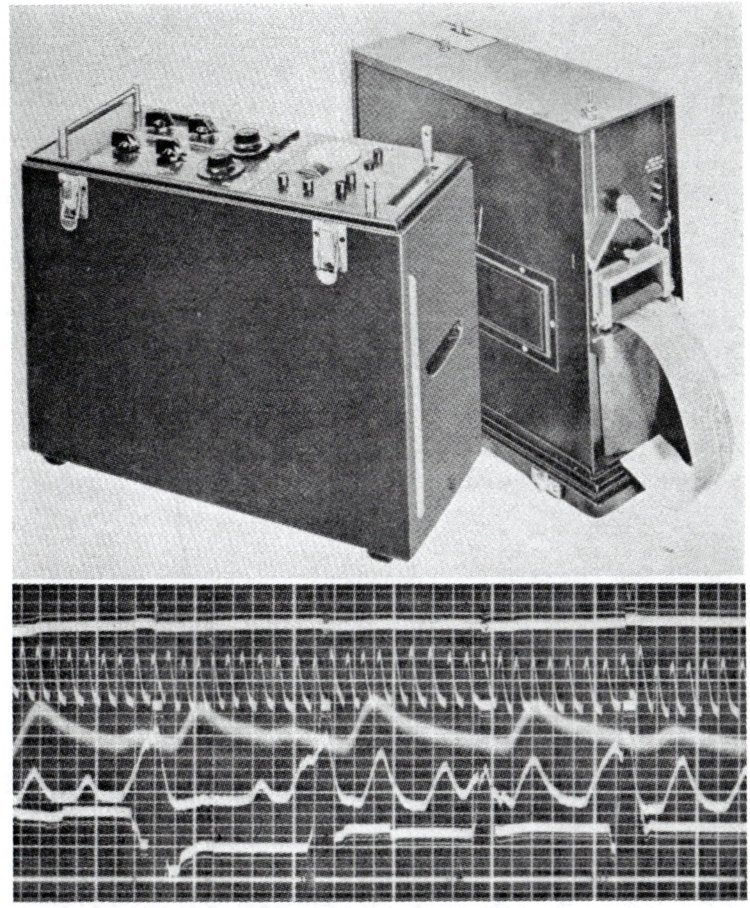

The Darrow Behavior Research Photopolygraph, distributed by the C. H. Stoelting Company. The recordings are made on a photographic film. The unit on the left contains the recording device, the one on the right, the complete developing mechanism. A short section of developed film is also shown. Reading from top to bottom, the recordings are: Voice or reaction key, tremorgraph, pulse-blood pressure, electrodermal response, respiration, tremorgraph (after Luria), voice or reaction key.

Figure II-7. From C. D. Lee: Instrumental Detection of Deception, Springfield, Illinois. Charles C. Thomas, 1953.

In 1930, Wilson (of the Scientific Detection Laboratory of Northwestern University School of Law) constructed a nonrecording psychogalvanometer. In 1931, Wilson and Keeler used it in several investigations. Subsequent studies conducted by the Chicago Police Scientific Crime Detection Laboratory revealed that electrodermal responses recorded simultaneously with cardiac and respiratory indices of deception in experimental cases provided a GSR accuracy of about 95 percent. (Trovillo 1939).

In the early 1930's C. W. Darrow developed the Darrow Behavior Research Photopolygraph which was built by C. H. Stoelting Company, Chicago, Illinois. (Fig. II-7). It recorded respiration, galvanic skin response, two tremorgraph recordings, one for each hand, and a verbal stimulus, response record. The two tremorgraph tambours could be used instead for a stabilometer, abdominal respiration, gastrointestinal balloon, plethysmograph, and carotid or radial pulse records. The photographic shadographic method avoided the problems of inked pens. However the price of Darrow's instrument was $999.00 versus Keeler's instrument which at that time sold for $450.00. It was reportedly in use by the U. S. Bureau of Prisons at two of their sites, namely at the Lewisburg Penitentiary and the Narcotic Farm in Kentucky. One of Darrow's instruments was also shipped to Poland. (Coffey 1936, Wideman 1935, Ansley & Furgerson 1987). The FBI considered using it in 1935, however after much investigation of existing polygraph instruments, the FBI purchased a polygraph instrument patented by Leonarde Keeler and manufactured by the Western Electro Mechanical Company at Oakland, California.(Ansley & Furgeson 1987)

Keeler, armed with a polygraph instrument consisting of three components, namely the pneumograph, the psychogalvanometer, and the cardiosphygmograph, which simultaneously recorded on a moving chart a person's breathing pattern; galvanic skin response; and heart beat, pulse rate, and strengths plus changes in mean blood pressure, applied his relevant/irrelevant questioning technique on suspects in actual criminal investigations with great success. This test-question technique consisted of relevant or crime questions designed to elicit a reaction from the guilty subject. These relevant questions were interspersed with irrelevant questions of a neutral nature, i.e. "Were you born in the U.S.?" or "Are you now wearing a white shirt?" the irrelevant questions were designed to establish a normal tracing pattern or average tracing segment and allow any reaction on a relevant question to dissipate itself before asking another relevant question. It was assumed that the guilty person would show deception to the relevant question(s) and the innocent would not. In spite of the technique's shortcomings, it formed the basis for the development of more sophisticated techniques.

Keeler added a personally embarrassing question (PEQ) to his relevant/irrelevant technique, which was designed to elicit a reaction only from the innocent subject, reasoning that the guilty would be still more concerned with the relevant or crime question. However, it was found that an unacceptable percentage of both the innocent and the guilty reacted to that question. Keeler also included an unreviewed control question (surprise question), which served the same purpose as the PEQ. Although the PEQ apparently ceased being taught at the Keeler Institute in 1951, the surprise control question is still part of some relevant/irrelevant techniques in use today. However, the relevant/irrelevant technique has adapted to evolutionary change with the incorporation of relevant connected questions referred to as *situational controls*. These control questions are carefully designed to pertain to the situational setting of the examinee's involvement in the crime to be resolved. These questions allow the truthful examinee to react to the reasons he/she is tied to or associated to the issue in question. (Minor, Abrams 1989). Interestingly, the first polygraph examiners were either self-taught or underwent tutorial training by the practitioners. By 1942, Keeler was teaching a two-week course for police and military examiners, then expanded it to a six-week, formal course of instruction in 1948. (DOD 1984; Barland 1988).

On 4 March 1935, E. P. Coffey, Head of the new crime laboratory at the FBI wrote a lengthily memo to Clyde Tolson, Deputy Director of the FBI, reporting on the training he had received from Leonarde Keeler in Chicago during the period from 25 February 1935 to 3 March 1935. Coffey observed and conducted cases with Keeler and reported on the test methods used to solve a number of cases some of which involved banks. Coffey described the "amounts test" which would currently be known as a searching or probing peak of tension test within the Guilty Knowledge family of tests, which was used when a prior test indicated some guilt. "The subject is asked whether his thefts from the bank exceed any of a series of amounts which are called off to him which generally range from a nominal sum to $20,000.00. Invariably the charts would indicate relief in emotion as the amounts passed into larger sums and according to Keeler the amount of the theft on the mind of the subject is accurately indicated on the charts." Later confessions seemed to confirm that statement. Special Agent Coffey was the first FBI polygraphist (FP) and probably the first examiner in the Federal Government. He established the first Federal polygraph research program. (Ansley & Furgerson, 1987; Ansley 1992). The first FBI use of the polygraph in espionage was in 1938. Leon G. Turrou, an FBI agent was fired by FBI Director J. Edgar Hoover for botching the case and letting too many German agents escape. Turrou subsequently wrote a book *Nazi Spies in America* in which he never mentions Hoover. (Ansley, 1995).

There was also a brief description of a Guilty Knowledge Test by Thomas Hayes Jaycox, Polygraph Examiner for the Wichita Police Department, writing in *The Scientific American* in 1937, of conducting a "name test" which he described as a group of names of men who might have committed the crime to a suspect who gave little or no apparent response except to one name at which his blood pressure and respiration became abnormal. The suspect confessed. (Jaycox 1937)

The first legitimate laboratory study involving a Peak-of-Tension test resembling the current format was probably conducted by Christian A. Ruckmick (1938). Using an electrodermal meter with a 30,000 ohm range, considered quite limited by current instruments which have a range of one million ohms, Ruckmick tested 89 students. In his first experiment, Ruckmick attempted to detect with meter deflection the number the examinee chose from a pile of cards with little success. Ruckmick then changed his experiment by using only ten cards with three letter words such as "nor" "and" etc.There were buffer words at the beginning and end of the list which were not written on cards. The question prefix was "is it...?" and the answer was "no" to all words. The detection rate was 78%. The number of judges was not listed but the removal of an undergraduate student's work raised the detection rate to 83%. The experimenter had an additional phase in which a half a dozen students who "got excited" about the wrong word were generally successful in "throwing the examiner off." That was the first and one of the few POT projects that mentions application of a countermeasure. (Ruckmick 1938)

The 8 October 1938 edition of the Saturday Evening Post depicted what may be the first time that a *Lie Detector* instrument has been used to validate a commercial product. The sub-heading reads "World-Famous Psychologist Proves Vital Importance of Using a Gillette Blade in Your Gillette Razor!" The ad continues "Strapped to Lie Detectors, the same scientific instruments used by G-men and police officers throughout the country, hundreds of men take part in an astonishing series of tests that blast false claims and reveal the naked truth about razor blades. These men, shaving under the

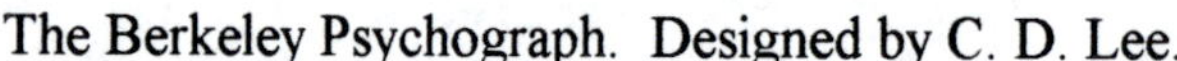

The Berkeley Psychograph. Designed by C. D. Lee.

The middle pen was a stimulus marker, upper pneumo, lower cardio.

Figure II-8. From C. D. Lee: Instrumental Detecton of Decepton, Springfield, Illinois. Charles C. Thomas, 1953.

piercing eye of Dr. William Moulton Marston, eminent psychologist and originator of the famous Lie Detector test, come from all walks of life, represent all types of beards and every kind of shaving problem. Knowing that the Lie Detector tells all... reveals the innermost thoughts and sensations...these men shave one side of the face with a Gillette Blade, the other side with substitute brands." The article shows a graph containing a linear blood pressure tracing, and a photograph of Dr. Marston analyzing a graph strip exiting a lie detector instrument while a male subject is shaving. (Marston 1938).

In 1938, Captain Clarence D. Lee of the Berkeley Police Department designed the Berkeley Psychograph (Fig. II-8) consisting of a chart drive or recording unit, a pneumograph or respiration unit, a cardiograph or pulse-blood pressure unit, and a stimulus signal unit. All of these units were functionally similar to those in the Keeler polygraph. However, mechanically, the principal difference between the two systems was in the pulse-blood pressure unit. In place of the Erlanger capsule with its rubber bulb, a mechanically simple chamber of cast aluminum was substituted in which there were two diaphragms of special heavy, elastic and resilient membrane, so placed that the air mass in the low pressure area was always small, which in turn meant that practically all of the original force of the pulse was delivered to the oscillating pen shaft. Lee also substituted a mechanically simple tambour of cast aluminum in place of the Marey tambour of the early Larson instrument, and of the metal bellows in the Keeler model. In his book "The Instrumental Detection of Deception" Clarence D. Lee relates a technique for differentiating between a guilty subject and one who is innocent but nervous and apprehensive by the introduction into the question series of one relating to a fictitious or non-existent crime of equal significance to the one under investigation, thus the first published use of the guilt complex control question. Lee also described his use of guilty knowledge and concealment tests which he called the "*association method*" and the "*clue-seeking method*" respectively. On 26 August 1937, Lee wrote to John Edgar Hoover, Director of the FBI, in reply to a letter of inquiry from Hoover. In explaining the various techniques, Lee gave examples of tests that have the elements of the Guilty Knowledge Technique including the Known Solution and the Searching Peak of Tension tests. Lee commented that "If our stimuli here is properly balanced, the consciousness of an innocent suspect should react about equally to all the suggestions, but if guilty there should be pronounced reactions at certain points which would indicate real facts of the case."(Ansley & Furgerson, 1987; Ansley 1992). Lee also used a "Control Test" when an examinee has shown no response whatsoever on any of his polygrams, to determine the examinee's capability of response. This control test now known as a Stimulation Test or Concealed Knowledge Test, consisted of having the examinee select a numbered card from several cards whose number is known only to the examinee, who is then instructed to answer in the negative to all card numbers including the card number he selected, hence lying to one of them, which should elicit a response on the polygram. If the examinee showed no response, the results of his previous test regarding the crime would be declared inconclusive rather than truthful due to his demonstrated inability to produce a response. Lee acknowledged that some FP's used the aforesaid control test before or after the relevant issue test as a "yardstick of sorts for evaluating the reactions which may follow the crucial questions in the formal question series." Lee further acknowledged John E. Reid's suggestion published in the Journal of Criminal Law and Criminology in 1947, of incorporating in the formal test question series what he termed "comparative response" questions, which Reid claimed afforded a far better criterion of subject's responsiveness than the number or card control tests run separately. In describing his "control question" Lee reported Reid as stating that reaction to such control questions served two useful purposes: (1) Definitely to establish that testee is normally responsive, and (2) to serve as a yardstick for evaluating his reactions to the relevant questions. Regarding the latter purpose, supposing the reaction is greater to the control question than to the major crucial question ("Did you kill X?" or "Did you rob the bank?"), the presumption is that he is innocent of the present offense. (Lee 1953).

In 1942, Edward W. Geldreich conducted a study of the effect of fear on detection. Using his previous 1941 study with a detection rate of 74% as a control group, Geldreich gave his experimental subjects the same instructions and test as those in the control group except that each subject was told they would be given an electric shock if the galvanometer revealed their card selection. Prior to the test, each subject was given an electric shock so severe that it made them jump. However, no shocks were given during the tests, but that was not what the subjects believed. The detection rate for the experimental group was 43 of 50, or 86% correct. The average electrodermal response for the irrelevant responses in the control was 3.6mm, while the aroused experimental group averaged 4.4 mm. The average response to lying by those in the control group was 13.9 mm, while the shocked experimental group averaged 16.8 mm. Many of the laboratory research projects that followed Geldreich's lab study lacked the useful data he included. (Geldreich 1941).

In 1942, Fred E. Inbau, professor of law at Northwestern University and former director of the Chicago Police Scientific Crime Detection Laboratory, wrote a book *Lie Detection and Criminal Interrogation*, wherein Inbau referred to the "peak of tension test" in describing the methodology for the administration of a guilty knowledge test where the subject has not been informed of the essential details of the case such as the object stolen, the amount of money missing, or the implement used in the commission of the crime. Inbau's instructions appeared in the second (1948) and third (1953) editions of the book, the third edition being co-authored by John E. Reid. Interestingly, Inbau had worked with Leonarde Keeler utilizing Keeler's relevant-irrelevant (R-I) technique in numerous criminal cases.(Ansley 1992)

In the early 1940's, China imported United States polygraph technology and as early as 1943 in the Chongqing Sino-American Cooperative Institute, the U.S. Intelligence Department had trained Chinese polygraph examiners for the military, and began a polygraph curriculum at the Central Officers School. After the mainland was liberated, the equipment and personnel all went to Taiwan. By 1950 however, polygraph technology in China met with total rejection mainly due to the influence of the Soviet Union who considered polygraphy a "bogus science" "a false witness tool of the imperialists" which was echoed accordingly by the Chinese. In the 1950's a famous Chinese movie which totally repudiated polygraph technology had widespread influence throughout China right through the 1980's when various Chinese scientists wrote papers criticizing polygraphy citing the aforesaid movie as the basis for their argument in spite of the fact that no one connected with the movie, including the playwright-director, had read any scientific books on polygraph technology or seen any polygraph instrument. After Sino-Soviet relations deteriorated, the polygraph issue in China once again was resurected and certain Chinese governmental agencies broke through the United States technology blockade and imported a multiple-line physiological recorder for use as a lie-detector. After review and approval, Central Leadership Comrades entrusted the Chinese Academy of Sciences Psychological Research Institute to perform research on its scientific nature. Unfortunately, the research was discontinued due to the commencement of the Great Cultural Revolution in China (Wang Bu, 1995)

In 1980, the Chinese Central Department Chief Liu Wen of the International General Bureau led a technological study group to study polygraph technology in Japan, and concluded that "Lie detectors have a scientific basis. Attitudes of total rejection held in the past were wrong." In 1981, the Chinese Public Security Bureau imported a U. S. made MARK-1 model voice analyzer and conducted internal tests of its accuracy with good results. In 1987, Huadong Teachers University Psychology Department lecturer Yue Jinghong used biomedical measuring equipment to assist such units as the Shanghai City Public Security Bureau on a group of cases with very good results. Jinghong also devised a multiple-line physiological measuring set in the laboratory. The achievements of these initial studies on polygraph technology drew the attention of individuals from the Chinese Peoples Politics and Law College and Chinese Peoples Public Security College who began organizing a course of lectures, published thesis and revised teaching material that accurately evaluated polygraph technology. In the summer of 1990, United States polygraph experts were invited to lecture in China and the Chinese registration to attend these lectures exceeded the original estimate by sixty percent, attesting to the renewed popularization of polygraph technology. (Wang Bu, 1995)

In 1990, Yang Chen, Senior Engineer at the Chinese Ministry of Public Security Science and Technology Department made arrangements with the Director of the Michigan State Police Polygraph Department to give lectures in China with a request for the Chinese to prepare substitute polygraph equipment due to the difficulty in taking a polygraph instrument out of the United States. Thus, through research, the Chinese found an LZ-1 model psychological measuring device manufactured by the Chinese Academy of Sciences Automation Institute, which was originally designed to measure and regulate the psychological state of a mobile person and measured two physiological parameters: blood pressure and electrodermal response. Several simulated tests were conducted which appeared to satisfy basic polygraph requirements. However, two weeks before the scheduled lectures, the Chinese scientists received a teletype message from the American lecturer advising that "My superiors have informed me that exchanging this technology with Communist China is a future matter and not a current one." (Wang Bu, 1995)

This abrupt break in the Chinese-American contract encouraged the Chinese to pursue a route of self-reliance which gained the support of the Ministry of Public Security and the Ministry of Public Security Science & Technology Department which brought the manufacture of a polygraph instrument on line with the Ministry's scientific research plan which resulted in the manufacture of the PG-1 model psychological measuring device in May 1991. The PG-l is a computerized polygraph system which uses an analog/digital converter to convert the collected data from an analog signal into a digital signal. The converter is connected to a computer by an input board. The monitor screen displays the charts in real time and after the test is completed the charts are printed out on a printer. The sensors that collect pulse waves and breathing waves use new press down/pull up sensors that are small and highly sensitive. The direct collection of electrical pulse signals simplifies subsequent circuit design. The Chinese model has a simplified faceplate which compresses the multitude of control knobs normally found in other models, to only four knobs. In September 1991, the Director of the Michigan State Police Polygraph Department finally arrived in China to give lectures and upon seeing China's indigenously made polygraph instrument, praised it as perhaps the best polygraph instrument he had ever seen. (Wang Bu 1995)

China's development of a computerized polygraph instrument enabled them to launch a substantive polygraph research program. After experimenting with several different polygraph techniques, the Chinese adopted the Guilty Knowledge Test as their primary polygraph method. (Wang Bu, 1995). China currently has about 50 active forensic psychologists and plans on having one forensic psychophysiologist for each of the 3000 police districts in China. (Barland 1996).

It should be noted that in 1948, Henry V. Baesen, Chia-Mou Chung, and Chen-Ya Yang conducted polygraph studies in the United States at Washington State College and published *A Lie Detector Experiment* in which they reported on a peak of tension test which appeared to have been mixed in with another test format, both relating to a mock crime. The objective was to separate perpetrators from witnesses. Their format of relevant questions included: Set 1 - (4) Does (amount stolen) have particular significance to you? (8) Did (name of accomplice) steal the money? (10) Did you steal the money? which was followed by Set 2 - (3) Did you steal the money? (9) Does (amount stolen) have particular significance to you? (12) Did you watch (name of accomplice) steal the money? (16) Did (name of accomplice) watch you steal the money? The authors referred to the above list of questions as a Peak of Tension test, and stated the following "The peak of tension on the stolen sum was brought about by arranging the questions in consecutive order beginning with two amounts not stolen and then the third question as the critical sum followed by the last sum known not to be critical. With the exception of the peak of tension series of questions, the relevant questions were adequately separated by irrelevant and control questions." The instrument recorded cardio and respiratory functions. It is not clear from the description as to whether the amounts were consecutive or spread out among the irrelevant, other relevant, and control questions. It does appear that both test methods appeared together on one chart. They were correct in 86% of their trials which is remarkable considering the mixed format. (Ansley 1992)

By 1951, at the Keeler Institute, the Peak of Tension Test with the use of one item per list was being taught as being more accurate than the 'relevant/irrelevant' or 'general question' test. A Peak of Tension 'Type A' was one where the forensic psychophysiologist (FP) knew the key item, and 'Type B' was a Searching Peak where the key item was unknown to the FP. The list of test questions was always shown to the subject before the test to build upon the anticipation and to accentuate relief afterwards. FP's were taught to place the critical item in the center of the list, and to use a logical progression when appropriate as in the case of room numbers or amounts of money. Illogical items were to be avoided. The Deception criterion was a rise and drop in blood pressure, which was deemed ideal; or an irregular cardio pattern before the key and a regular, straight or down pattern afterwards. There could also be a single rise and fall of the blood pressure in response to the key item, and irregular thereafter. In the pneumograph the pattern could be irregular to the key item, regular thereafter, or the reverse. There could also be a specific reaction to the key item, between regular patterns. While the cardio pattern was considered the most reliable, the galvanometer was considered the least reliable, which would probably rise at each item, a large rise at the key item, then level off or drift after the key item. However in a Searching or Probing Peak of Tension test where the key item is unknown to the FP, the galvanometer was considered much more useful, and respiration second, although a cardio reaction could be expected. Further, Colonel Ralph W. Pierce, US Army (retired) in a 1950 article on "The Peak of Tension Test" wrote that "the psychogalvanic reflex, or electrodermal response, is also very important in peak of tension tests. In fact, in some cases where little, if any, change is found in either the blood pressure-pulse or respiration recordings, it becomes the most important indication of deception."(Ansley 1992)

In 1944, the German press reported that two French psychiatrists, Dr. Bernard and Professor Gelma had built a device to measure emotions and brain waves under experimental conditions. They had constructed a 'psychoelectrometer' which they attached to the scalp of the subject being questioned about matters requiring an immediate response which in turn caused a pen deflection. "As soon as the relevant thought flashes through the mind, an electric wave of very low frequency is allegedly elicited and the needle of the thought-registration device deflects. If the answer contains a discrepancy or perhaps an open falsehood, there is a deflection of 10 to 15 divisions from zero." Professor Gelma also allegedly "determined the degree to which an adolescent liked a girl. In one case he made a murderer confess; cross examination proved him guilty, although he denied the crime." The press further stated "For the forensic psychologist a significant advance would be achieved with this technical novelty." (Von Heindl 1944, Barland 1979)

However, Von Heindl claimed to have conducted the same experiments and pursued the same idea in Munich, Germany in 1909 when he was in the physics laboratory of Professor Wilhelm K. Roentgen, a German physicist who received the first Nobel prize for his work with cathode (x) rays and the penetrating power of radiation at the University of Wurzburg in Bavaria in 1895. Roentgen lent Von Heindl an old electroscope which was probably a galvanometer, a common instrument in physics and psychology laboratories at that time, to enable Von Heindl to conduct experiments on the measurement of electrical currents during criminal interrogations. Von Heindl had a master harnessmaker in Munich make two leather belts which contained copper wires designed to be strapped on the wrists of the subject of interrogation. These wires were then connected to the electroscope and to a Leclanche element which was a battery consisting of a carbon cathode covered with manganese dioxide and a zinc anode dipped into an ammonium chloride solution with the manganese dioxide retained in a porous pot (currently known as a dry cell). Von Heindl's device "indicated the innermost excitement of the suspect by a swinging of the pointer of the electroscope a few divisions of the scale at every insidious question, and particularly at every dishonest answer." (Von Heindl 1944; Barland 1979)

In 1947, John E. Reid (attorney at law, former staff member of the Chicago Police Scientific Crime Detection Laboratory, polygraphist, and director of John E. Reid and Associates) published and was credited with the development of the reviewed control question consisting of a probable lie incorporated into the relevant-irrelevant test, although Dr. William Marston and Father Walter Summers both had used such a control question in their test format. Indeed, Father Summers described his use of an "emotional standard" in his 1939 article "Science Can Get The Confession" and by 1952 the New York State Police was employing Father Summers' "emotional standard" as a control question for comparison with the relevant questions in their test format. (Kirwan 1952). Nevertheless, publication of what became known as the Reid Control Question Technique represented a major breakthrough in polygraph technique. Reid also introduced the guilt-complex test, (previously described and used by Lee 1943), administered to the overly responsive subject. Reid developed a means of recording arm and leg movement in addition to the recording of breathing, GSR, and cardio. In 1966, Reid, in collaboration with Professor Fred E. Inbau (of Northwestern University), wrote a comprehensive textbook regarding modern polygraph instrumentation and techniques entitled *Truth and Deception.*

Norman Ansley began his long and distinguished career in the U. S. Army National Guard in 1947 followed by duty in the U. S. Army Reserve. In 1949, Ansley attended the U. S. Army C.I.D. Criminal Investigations School and graduated as a C.I.D. Special Agent. In 1951, as a civilian, he graduated from the Keeler Polygraph Institute which marked the beginning of a career unequaled in authorship of publications related to forensic psychophysiology. Indeed, Ansley authored or co-authored one hundred and four published articles related to forensic psychophysiology and twelve books including three editions of *Truth and Science* and three volumes of *Polygraph and the Law*. Ansley's vast in-depth knowledge of polygraphy has invited consultation from the Office of Naval Research; the Commission on Protecting and Reducing Government Secrecy, Washington, D. C.; The President's Foreign Intelligence Advisory Board; the Committee on Governmental Affairs, U. S. Senate on National Security Decision Directive 84; the U. S. Senate Select Committee on Intelligence; the Committee on the Armed Forces, U. S. Senate on "Polygraphs for Counterintelligence Purposes in the Department of Defense"; the Committee on Armed Services, U. S. House of Representatives "Relating to the

Administration of Polygraph Examinations and Prepublication Review"; and the President's Intelligence Oversight Board. Norman Ansley served as Chief of the polygraph program for the National Security Agency, U. S. Department of Defense, and later as Chief of Polygraph and Personnel Security Research at the National Security Agency. In 1972, Norman Ansley became the Editor in Chief of the American Polygraph Association (APA). Ansley's contribution to the field of forensic psychophysiology can best be described by his receipt of almost all of the prestigious awards that the American Polygraph Association could bestow upon him. The American Polygraph Association's Journal *Polygraph*, and its APA *Newsletter* have been the lifeblood of the organization with its continuous high quality publications which have served well in the defense of forensic psychophysiology against its numerous challenges in the legal and political arenas. An examination by historians of the literature on forensic psychophysiology in the 20th century will most certainly single out Norman Ansley as the most prolific author on the subject in this century.

In about 1951, Associated Research introduced a two-pen polygraph instrument, model 305, which recorded cardiovascular and respiratory data on a chart driven by a spring-wound kymograph made by Esterline Angus. The two pens had central inking. There were also centering and resonance knobs for the cardio and pneumo channels plus vents. The resonance knob squeezed the tube under the panel and reduced the size of the pattern with reported effectiveness. The tube connections for the pneumograph and cardiograph were on top of the instrument. The crank handle inserts at the kymograph end. The whole instrument was contained in a samsonite case which had a large storage area. The clockwork drive was especially useful on occasions when the forensic psychophysiologist conducted tests where AC current was not available, such as on overseas assignments.(Ansley 1995)

According to notes made in 1952 by Norman Ansley, Editor in Chief of the American Polygraph Association, Russell Chatham, Inc. had the contract for conducting PV examinations on employees of the contractor (probably Union Carbide) who performed classified work at the Atomic Energy Facility at Oak Ridge, Tennessee. The notes list the forensic psychophysiologists at that time by Chatham, Inc., as Russell Chatham, Rex Ames Ramsey, Havey F. Payne, J. Arnold Cohen, George F. Haney, and Paul V. Trovillo. Chatham identified Trovillo as Director of Research of his organization. In addition, Chatham also had a contract to provide two forensic psychophysiologists (Ramsey and Cohen) for three months to the Armed Forces Security Agency in June, July, and August 1951. Chatham also had a contract in the early 1950's to provide polygraph screening for the Johns Hopkins Applied Physics Laboratory in Maryland. (Ansley 1995).

The original contract at Oak Ridge was handled by Leonarde Keeler. When Chatham was awarded the contract, he had Associated Research build polygraph instruments for him with his name on them. They were two pen units, a cardiosphygmograph and a pneumograph with an Esterline Angus two-speed sprocket drive kymograph. At least 25 and possibly 50 of these were manufactured, and because it was more than the company needed, Chatham was reported to have given some away to colleges and friends, including Louisiana State, Alabama at Tuscaloosa, and Barnard College of Columbia. Norman Ansley reported having an AR Model 304 in his possession. (Ansley 1995).

In 1952, D. G. Ellson at Indiana University conducted several lie detection studies for the United States Navy. In one of his experiments, Ellison used 23 students, 11 in one group and 12 in a second group. The experimental method consisted of providing each student with a sheet of paper and instructed to circle any one of the six months listed from a list of the first six months of the year. The questions by the experimenter were "Is it January?" "Is it March?" and so forth. Each question was answered in the negative producing five truthful answers and one lie in each series. The question interval was 20 seconds. A B&W meter was used to record the subjects' electrodermal responses. After the first test was conducted, the subjects of group one were told the month the experimenter believed was correct, based on the mean meter deflection, and the subjects of group two were told a month that was probably wrong, as it was the month with the least deflection. The subjects of both groups were then tested again on which month they circled on a list of the last six months of the year. For group one, the detection rate on the first test was 9 of 11 (82%) and was 3 of 11 (27%) on the second run, after being correctly informed of the first test results. The two failures on the first run were also failures on the second run, and the three successes on the second run were also successes on the first run. For group two, who were misinformed of the first test results, the initial detection rate was 9 of 12 (75%), and was 10 of 12 (83%) on the second run. Eight of the nine correct decisions on the first run were persons who were among the ten of 12 correct decisions on the second run. One of the failures on the first run was among the two failures on the second run. The novel aspect of this project was informing one group correctly of their decision in the first series and misinforming a matching group, and assuming the difference in results was related to the differing instructions. The results, however, defy conventional wisdom, as one would expect the misinformed to be detected at a lower rate or at the same rate. (Ansley 1992). In fact, Leonard Saxe (1986), a polygraph critic, has insisted that belief in the validity of testing was necessary for it to work. However, research conducted by William Yankee and Douglas Grimsley (1986) using a Zone Comparison format and a mock crime, found a trend in which accurate feedback was 94% accurate, inaccurate was 86%, and 79% for no feedback. However the differences did not reach statistical significance ($p > .05$). Gordon H. Barland and David Raskin (1972) used a peak of tension stimulus test with a Backster Zone Comparison technique in which one group was shown a polygraph chart which correctly indicated the card picked (Stimulation test), another group was shown a polygraph chart which depicted an incorrect selection, and a third group did not receive a stimulus test. The manipulation of these stimulus test results did not produce any significant effect on the detection of guilt or innocence for the mock crime. Raul Diaz (1985) found that of those told they were detected after the first card test, the subsequent detection was 27 of 40 (68%) while those who were told they were not detected by the card test were subsequently detected in 28 of 40 (70%) tests. Ellson was the first to explore the effect of positive feedback and false feedback on subsequent tests.(Ansley 1992)

D. G. Ellson (1952) appears to also be the first to research the effect of answering test questions in the Negative, in the Positive, and with no answer (mute) to determine their effect on the test results. Using a galvanometer, Ellson tested eight students to determine the month of their birth. Each test list contained four months of the year, and each series was tested twice with the four months asked twice, each time in a different sequence. The eight students were tested three times in this manner, once with instructions to say "no," once with instructions to say "yes," and once with instructions to remain mute. The sequence of these conditions was varied so as to offset the serial effect. Detection for the "no" tests was four of eight, two of eight for "yes" answers, and one of eight from the mute tests. (Ansley 1992).

In a 1955 review of the accuracy and status of lie detection, Benjamin Burack referred to the Peak of Tension Test as the "disguised questions test" and suggested a variation in which no answer is given, and another variation in which only key words in each question were asked such as "pearl necklace?" "diamond ring?" (Burack 1955).

Cleve Backster, born Grover Cleveland Backster, Jr., on 27 February 1924 at Lafayette, New Jersey, received an appointment on 12 April 1948 as Plans Officer at the newly formed Central Intelligence Agency (CIA) whose near total operation was headquartered at 2430 E. Street, N. W. in Washington, D. C., as a result of his pioneering work in hypno-interrogation, narco-interrogation (with medical assistance) and impressive credentials as an interrogation instructor at the U. S. Army Counterintelligence Corps (CIC) at Fort Holabird, Maryland, which attracted the attention of the newly formed CIA., While serving in the U. S. Army CIC, Cleve Backster's innovative and avant guarde approach to interrogation with the use of hypnosis and medically supervised narcosis was met by his superiors with much skepticism and paltry support. Frustrated by the lack of concern for the potential usefulness of the technique to CIC and the danger of its use by inimical foreign intelligence agencies, Backster decided to "risk all" to bring this point home, by hypnotizing the secretary of CIC Chief of Counterintelligence Corps Brigadier General George V. Keyser into opening and removing from the General's office safe a classified document and giving it to Backster who imposed post-hypnotic amnesia of the event. The following day, Backster brought the classified document to General Keyser at his office, offering the General the choice of either court-martialing him for the unauthorized removal of the classified document or furnishing him with the much needed support required to energize the program. General Keyser chose the latter. On 9 August 1948, a few months following his appointment as Chief of a security section at the CIA that later included use of the polygraph, Backster received his polygraph completion certificate from Leonarde Keeler, after frequent trips to the Keeler Polygraph Institute in Chicago, Illinois constituting an equivalency of six weeks of training. The polygraph technique in use at the CIA during that early period was Keeler's relevant-irrelevant technique, although John Reid at that time was promoting the use of his reviewed non-exclusive control question technique.(Backster 1995)

In 1948, Cleve Backster joined a group of polygraph examiners which included Paul Trovillo, Vern Lyon, Arthur Eggert, George Haney, John Reid and Leonarde Keeler, who had been meeting to exchange ideas regarding the desirability of forming a society of polygraph examiners. Although it is recorded that this society officially incorporated on 30 Dec 47 at Bismark, North Dakota, it was at Backster's suggestion in mid-1948 that the official title of the organization was named the International Society for Detection of Deception to embrace polygraph activity outside of the United States. Membership cards were issued to its members commencing in 1948. (Backster 1995)

In 1948, India began the use of polygraph examinations after an Inspector of the CID in Bangalore completed a six-week course at a polygraph school in the United States. It is said that the polygraph was used in narrowing down the field of suspects in the Mahatma Ghandi assassination plot. After some research and a few cases, use of the polygraph ceased until 1974. However from 1974 to 1987, the Central Forensic Laboratory conducted over 3,000 polygraph examinations. In India there have been a few cases where the results of polygraph tests have been accepted by the courts, but generally, the results of polygraph tests conducted by police officers are not accepted by the courts, but the courts are more receptive to the results of polygraph tests conducted by non-police examiners for the defense. (Kiang 1996)

In 1950, shortly after Leonarde Keeler's untimely death, Backster was offered the job of Director of the Keeler Polygraph Institute by its major stockholder Jack Harrison, and Backster accepted the position. Backster learned that Keeler's chief polygraph examiner Colonel Ralph Pierce who had been working out of town when Keeler died, was fired by Harrison upon his return. Backster resigned his position as Director in 1951 and moved to Washington, D.C. where he established Lie Detection, Inc., and Security Screening Specialist, Inc., which handled classified work for different government agencies. (Backster 1995)

In 1951, Colonel Ralph Pierce who had been fired by Jack Harrison (Keeler Institute), was instrumental in the establishment of the U. S. Army Provost Marshal Polygraph School at Fort Gordon, Georgia, a branch of the United States Army Military Police School (USAMPS), which provided a polygraph training program with a curriculum oriented to criminal investigations.(Backster 1995). Fred Olsen was appointed as the first Director of the U. S. Army Provost Marshal Polygraph School. Keeler's relevant-irrelevant technique and the Reid technique were adopted by the U.S. Army Provost Marshal Polygraph School. (Decker 1995)

In 1952, the U. S.Army C.I.D. adopted the Deceptograph manufactured by C. H. Stoelting Co., Chicago, Illinois which was given the U.S. Army nomenclature of Lie Detecting Set AN/USS-2A. (Fig. II-9).

The C. H. Stoelting three-channel polygraph instrument was initially mounted in an upright, wooden box which was not easily portable. Sometime in the mid or late 1950's, Cleve Backster disassembled and remounted the Stoelting instrument into a Samsonite luggage case which was the first suitcase style polygraph, and several hundred were subsequently sold by Stoelting. (Backster 1995)

In 1959, Cleve Backster formed an equal partnership with Richard O. Arther, former chief associate of John E. Reid, and established the National Training Center of Lie Detection in New York City, New York. (Fig. II-10). The partnership lasted only three years. But in 1960, Backster developed the *Backster Zone Comparison Technique*. Backster devised a standardized technique incorporating relevant-irrelevant questions, including his development and introduction of a *sacrifice relevant question*, two *earlier-in-life control questions* which excluded the time period in which the crime or incident occurred with the use of time bars, hence called *exclusive earlier-in-life control questions*, and *symptomatic questions* first introduced by Backster to identify any *outside issue factor* that might interfere with the test. Backster adopted the dormant *psychological set* theory and conceived the *anticlimax dampening concept*, which form the basis of his Zone

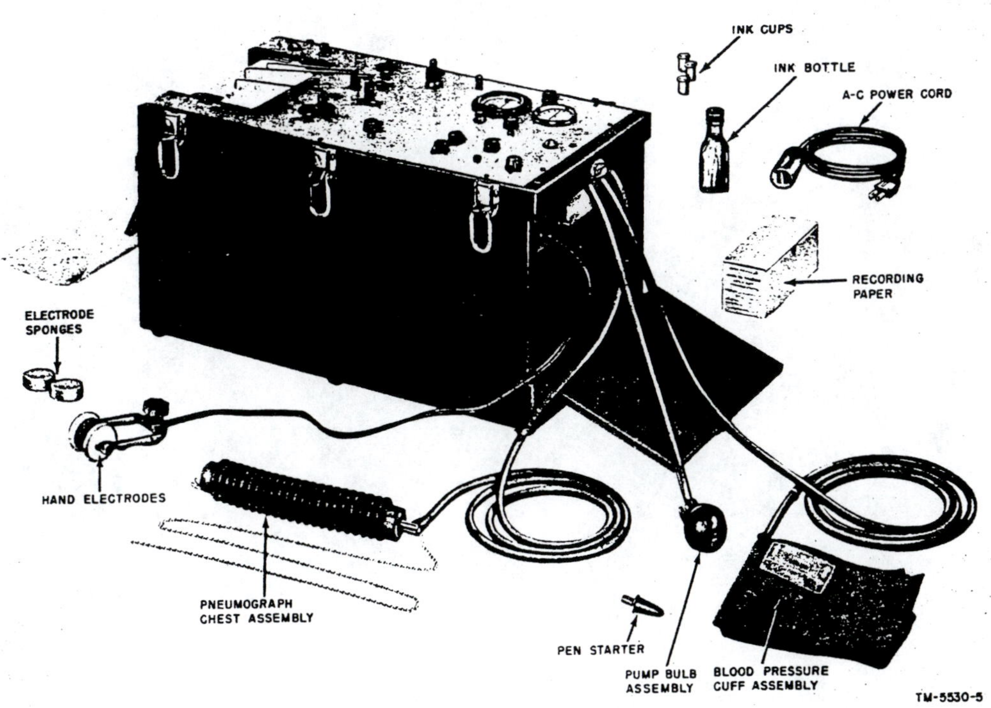

Figure II-9. Deceptograph manufactured by C. H. Stoelting Co.
U. S. Army nomenclature AN/USS-2A (1952).

Comparison technique (Chapter 11). Backster also introduced a *quantification system* of chart analysis, which permits the forensic psychophysiologist to score numerically each relevant and neighboring control question tracing according to standard rules and penalties for rule violations. This standardized quantification system, which permits completely objective chart analysis by any forensic psychophysiologist trained in the Backster

Figure II-10. First National Training Center of Lie Detection Class (PE-1). New York City, N.Y. 6 April 1959 to 15 May 1959. Sitting from left to right: Richard O. Arther, Chief Instructor; Margaret (Gale) D. Neff; student; Cleve Backster, Director; Standing from left to right: Joseph Heger, Jr., student; C. A. (Ken) Schorr, student; Johnny G. Lough, student; Marvin A. Marcus, student; Robert D. Weir, student.

technique regardless of distance, is considered a major contribution to forensic psychophysiology because of its scientific, objective approach to chart evaluation and analysis. However, Arther espoused the Reid technique which placed heavy emphasis on behavioral factors in the assessment of an examinee's truthfulness in addition to the physiological data recorded on the polygraph charts, hence a *global* or *clinical approach* in contrast to Backster's *numerical approach* which vigorously excluded all non-polygraphic data from the decision making process. (Backster 1995). That same year, Backster developed a four-page *Uniform Chart Markings* which was published by C. H. Stoelting Co (1960). These standardized chart markings to be made by the forensic psychophysiologist conducting a PV examination, enable the reconstruction of the test conditions for subsequent independent review and analysis. (Stoelting 1960).(See Chap. 11).

In 1961, Backster's Zone Comparison technique and quantification system which then included the S-K-Y test questions at the tail end of the test, was adopted by the U. S. Army C.I.D. Polygraph School at Fort Gordon, Georgia. The Backster Zone Comparison Technique became the only authorized technique for specific issue examinations in the U. S. Army. (Decker 1995). In November 1961 Backster removed the S-K-Y test questions from his Zone Comparison Test and made it a separate S-K-Y test, but the C.I.D. Polygraph School did not follow Backster's lead and retained the S-K-Y. test questions in their U.S. Army Zone Comparison Test Format. The U. S. Army C.I.D. applied their Zone Comparison technique to their worldwide quality control and case review, permitting objective critique of psychophysiological veracity examinations conducted as far away as Asia and Europe. (Capps 1994; Brisentine 1974; Backster 1995)

During that period, Backster and Arther's philosophical and methodological differences in their approach to lie detection became increasingly divergent until one day in 1962, Backster who was the school director, fired Arther, his equal partner. Arther sued Backster and won retention of the National Training Center of Lie Detection. Backster then established the Backster School of Lie Detection in the same building and on the same floor as the National Training Center of Lie Detection in New York City, to the consternation of Arther whose students would meet the Backster students in the hallway when the coffee and doughnut cart came around each morning. (Backster 1995)

Arther developed his own test format which has no similarity to Backster's Zone Comparison Technique. The Arther technique as it became known by his graduates uses the clinical approach. (See Chapter 15 for details).

Backster continued his research and development adding the *Examination Reliability Ratings* to determine numerically the Adequacy of Target Information, Distinctness of Issue, and Target Intensity for each separate issue to be tested, to insure that only those issues which contain sufficient combined case information, distinctness and intensity are scheduled for examination in the preferred order of those issues with the greatest scores. The net effect was to reduce inconclusives. Backster also developed the S-K-Y test which incorporated questions regarding suspicion, knowledge and a direct involvement question, using the suspicion question as a control question, which Backster later (1978) changed to include two exclusive control questions. Backster had hypothesized that the Zone Comparison test should cover only one single issue to optimize the subject's psychological set; other issues to be covered in separate single-issue Zone Comparison tests, or the S-K-Y test.

In 1959, Ivan Babic, Head of the forensic Laboratory in Zagreb, Croatia, conducted the first polygraph experimental tests using a Keeler polygraph instrument purchased in the United States. At that time, psychophysiological veracity (PV) examinations using the polygraph were conducted secretly because the orthodox socialist doctrine had a negative or at least ambivalent attitude towards police usage of the polygraph, as was the case in the USSR. It was well known that the PV examination was an efficient means of combating crime from the experience of the American police, but ideologically it was a "capitalistic inquisitorial means of getting admission of guilt." Hence, only a small number of police executives and chiefs knew about these experiments. At that time, the results of these experiments on the criminal population were not being published in internal police publications nor in the press. Apart from aforesaid reasons, there was a certain aversion of police chiefs towards writing about PV examinations, to prevent criminals from learning their methodology, and further that judicial bodies would not raise questions about their legal justifiability. However this secretive situation did not last long, when the experimental phase ended with the commencement of the operative phase in the usage of PV examinations using the polygraph in combating crime. The first significant case solved by using the polygraph was in November 1959. The forensic psychophysiologist D. Papes used the Peak-of-Tension (POT) technique with spectacular results, which inspired the interest of the entire police community to use the polygraph throughout the Republic of Croatia and Yugoslavia. During that period, neither expert literature on the polygraph nor polygraph schools were available, and for ideological and security reasons forensic psychophysiologists were not allowed to specialize abroad. However a significant step forward was made when, for police purposes, several American publications on polygraph such as C. D. Lee's *Instrumental Lie Detection* (1953), Inbau-Reid's *Lie Detection and Criminal Interrogation* (1953), Inbau-Reid's *Truth and Deception* (1966 & 1977), were translated into Croatian. During the period 1959 to 1967, PV examinations using the polygraph were only conducted by the Zagreb police. Other police administrations had neither polygraph instruments nor forensic psychophysiologists (FP) to operate them. Therefore FPs from Zagreb had to cover all of Croatia and the Federation of former Yugoslavia when serious crimes demanded their expertise. The development of forensic psychophysiology in Croatia experienced a breakthrough in 1967 when a student of psychology and criminal inspector named Zvonimir Roso, who had established a positive reputation in the administration of PV examinations using the polygraph in several serious crimes, had the results of a Peak-of-Tension (POT) admitted into evidence in the Croatian Supreme Court, which represented the first case that a Supreme Court of a European country had accepted polygraph results as evidence. However, legal regulations were later changed to exclude polygraph test results as evidence in Croatian legal proceedings. On the positive side though, forensic psychophysiology was afforded a full-time occupation with police investigators, hence it became a profession. Roso introduced standards of practice modeled after those of the American Polygraph Association. The polygraph laboratory was equipped with new instruments, and professional literature was being read regularly. The education of policemen on the possibilities of forensic psychophysiology in their investigative work was promoted, and the Zagreb Polygraph School was established. Roso wrote some thirty professional works and studies on the use of polygraphy in police investigations and two books: *Polygraph in Criminalistics* (1987) and *Police Investigation (Policijsko ispitivanje*, 1988, 1995). During the period 1967-1979 Zvonimir Roso trained all the forensic psychophysiologists in Croatia and Yugoslavia, which made possible the establishment of polygraph laboratories in all of the important police centers. Roso retired in 1990, to pursue theoretical work in criminology and forensic psychophysiology. During the period 1960 to 1994, five polygraph laboratories were established in the Republic of Croatia, with locations at Zagrebacka, Primorsko-Goranska, Splitsko-Dalmatinska, Osjecko-Baranjska and Istarska. These laboratories are staffed by eight forensic psychophysiologists with varied backgrounds as psychologist, investigator or lawyer who have conducted a combined total of 33,393 PV examinations as of 1 January 1995. In 1994 alone, an average of 251 persons per forensic psychophysiologist were tested. Since then, two new polygraph laboratories have been established: one at Police Administration Varazkinska employing a conventional electronic polygraph instrument, and one at Police Administration Dubrovancko Neretvanska employing an American computerized polygraph system. (Maric 1995)

In 1961, an article entitled "Integrated Control-Question Technique" authored by J. Arnold Cohen appeared in *Police*. The article described the use of a novel *known-Lie* in a control question test. The examinee is first administered a *card test* using several cards of different suits from a deck of playing cards. Then the card number that the examinee lied to in the Card Test is inserted into the Integrated Control Question Test as a control question, along with several of the other card numbers the examinee did not select or lie to, which act as irrelevant questions, interspersed with the relevant questions and a guilt complex question. (Cohen 1961; Ansley 1995)

In 1962, Dr. Joseph F. Kubis, Fordham University, New York, N.Y. completed *Studies in Lie Detection, Computer Feasibility Considerations*, for the Rome Air Development Center, Air Force Systems Command, US Air Force. Kubis' experiments involved a Simulated Theft, Denial-of-Actual-Crime, Denial-of-Classified-Information, and Countermeasure Techniques. Cardiovascular (Plethysmograph), respiratory (one channel) and psychogalvanic response systems were monitored, recorded, and evaluated for lie detection capabilities. Questionnaire, Peak-of-Tension, and Association techniques were employed. In spite of the fact that the five examiners, all psychologists, were not graduates of a polygraph school and had no field experience, but were trained for a period of three months by an experienced lie detector expert, significant results were obtained in the Simulated Theft Experiment. Kubis' examiners were trained to use a crude numerical scoring system wherein the numbers 3, 2, 1 and 0 were assigned to the "very significant", "Significant", "Doubtfully Significant", and "Non-Significant" categories of responses, respectively, without specific, standardized physiological interpretation rules, in what can best be described as a multiple-issue General Question Test structure. Using this ordinal scale, the lie detection examiners were able to differentiate with significant accuracy among the Thief, the Lookout, and the Innocent Suspect. Independent raters, who based their decisions only on the physiological recordings, were able to attain the same degree of accuracy as the examiners. Of the three physiological systems employed, the psychogalvanic response was evaluated with greatest objectivity and was found to yield the most valid results. In the Denial-of-Actual-Crime and in the Denial-of-Classified-Information experiments, success in detecting lies was limited, most likely due to the use of fictitious crime control questions and a poor test model. The countermeasure techniques experiment indicated that individuals with a moderate amount of training can contaminate the physiological records with irrelevant responses which enabled them to confuse the lie detector examiner and thus elude detection. Dr. Kubis opined that despite the aforesaid positive findings, limitations in objectivity, uncontrolled invalidating influences and non-standardized instrumentation in the polygraph field warrant further definitive research before the computer can be considered as an integral component of the lie detection decision. However, Dr. Kubis felt that there was a critical need for the objectification of the measurements of various aspects of the physiological patterns used in lie detection interpretation, and computer type programs could be of great service in the solution of this problem. (Kubis 1962). Ironically, in the same city of New York at that same period of time, Cleve Backster had been teaching his standardized Zone Comparison Technique with its sophisticated numerical scoring system since 1960. We can only wonder how much sooner the computerized polygraph system would have emerged had Kubis and Backster collaborated on the aforementioned study.

In 1963, Cleve Backster introduced his first *Standardized Polygraph Notepack* booklet which included Subject and Examination Data, Case Information, Target Selection Guide, Pre-Test Interview Data, Subject's Version, "You" Phase (Specific-Issue) Question Formulation, Tri-Zone Reaction Combinations Scanning, Spot Analysis and Score Tally, the S-K-Y Phase Series, the Known-Solution Peak of Tension Test, the Probing Peak of Tension Test, and the Exploratory Series. Backster's Known Solution and Probing Peak of Tension tests each contained a Preparatory Question and a Question Prefix. They can be classified as Guilty Knowledge tests. Backster incorporated changes in his Standardized Polygraph Notepack with new editions published in 1969 and 1979. Backster's 1969 Notepack completed with examples of its use was also published in full in Bailey and Rothblatt's book *Investigation and Preparation of Criminal Cases, Federal and State* in 1970.

In 1966, Backster commenced his extensive research related to observed electrical responses in plant life and at a cellular level in other living organisms. His research into what has been called the "Backster Effect" has attracted world-wide attention and continuing invitations to lecture before academic and scientific groups on the progress of his ongoing research.(Stone 1989). Backster also served as Chairman of the Research and Instrument Committee of the Academy for Scientific Interrogation from 1958 through 1965, and during the period 1978 through 1986 Backster served simultaneously as chairman of the Research and Instrumentation Committee of the American Polygraph association and Chairman of the Research and Development Committee of the American Association of Police Polygraphists. Since 1987 Backster has confined his conventional polygraph activity to instructing at the Backster School of Lie Detection and polygraph quality control consultant services. (Backster 1995)

Richard O. Arther, as director of the National Training Center of Lie Detection distinguished himself as the first FP to record simultaneously on a regular basis chest and abdominal breathing patterns and discovered that approximately one out of three times the two differed. Arther was also the first forensic psychophysiologist to record simultaneously two galvanic skin responses. The expert has two choices, the "self-centering" (or automatic) mode and the "floating" (or manual) mode. By recording both modes from 1958 to 1965, it was Arther's opinion that the automatic or "self-centering" mode was superior, (Arther 1971, 1986) but subsequent research (Raskin, et al 1978) found opposite results.

In 1965, Arther introduced the Arther II polygraph manufactured by the Stoelting Company which contained a stimulus marker that recorded the beginning and ending of a question and the moment the examinee gave his answer. In 1966 Arther founded the

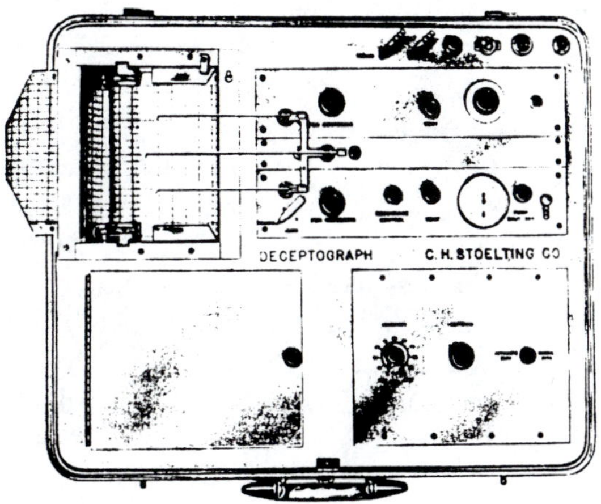

Figure II-11. Deceptograph Model Cat. No. 22500 manufactured by Stoelting Co. Vacuum Tubes Amplifier.

Journal of Polygraph Science, the oldest of the polygraph publications. The stimulus marker was not new in polygraph instruments. The stimulus marker was an optional feature in all Berkeley Psychographs, Keeler (western Electro-Mechanical), Keeler (Associated Research) models. All of the stimulus markers were hand operated and were not "exact." Norman Ansley reported that the only "exact" stimulus marker he ever used was a Stoelting model that had the stimulus marker operated by a microphone and amplifier that moved the stimulus marker. The National Security Agency had a field model which in addition to a stimulus marker, also had two pneumos, a GSR, a cardio and a plethysmograph, all in an aluminum chassis. (Ansley 1996).

In about 1955, the Stoelting Company in Chicago, Illinois which had been producing polygraph instruments since 1935, introduced the Deceptograph model Cat. No. 22500 (Fig. II-11). This model contained vacuum tubes in its amplifier which required significant warm-up time before use (30 minutes) (Decker 1996). It contained three recording channels: cardio, pneumo and GSR. The A. C. operated unit was packaged in an aluminum halliburton case with sectionalized components and a built-in microphone cartridge. The 22500 model was advertised as the most widely used polygraph instrument in the world.

In 1966, the Stoelting Company introduced the Emotional Stress Monitor, catalogue number 22600 (Fig. II-12) which was a three-pen polygraph instrument. The most important change in this instrument was the replacement of the vacuum tubes with transistors which reduced the weight and size of the instrument, and eliminated the need for the thirty minutes warm-up previously required in instruments which used vacuum tubes. The top channel was a mechanical recording channel for recording respiration which did not have any means of controlling tracing size, except perhaps by adjustment of the pneumograph tube. The next recording channel was the GSR which was a 250,000 ohm amplifier, balancing a twenty three micro amp current to the subject to record changes in galvanic skin response. The bottom channel was used to record heart rate and changes in relative blood pressure. Due to the mechanical nature of the recording, optimum tracings were not always obtainable. (Cross 1986). A couple of years later, the Stoelting Company introduced a four-pen Emotional Stress Monitor consisting of a double pneumograph which recorded simultaneously the thoracic and abdominal breathing patterns, in addition to the GSR and the cardiograph. In addition this new instrument provided a kymograph which recorded on an eight inch rather than the previous six inch chart to accommodate the fourth channel. This was considered a major improvement in instrumentation by professional polygraphists.

In 1967, Ronald E. Decker was appointed Director, U. S. Army Polygraph School. That same year, Decker visited John E. Reid at his office in Chicago, Illinois and asked Reid if he would approve four changes that the U.S. Army Polygraph School wanted to make to his Reid Technique, to wit: (1) Use a single issue only, inasmuch as Reid in his (1966) book gave an example of a test in which the examinee is asked if he

EMOTIONAL STRESS MONITOR

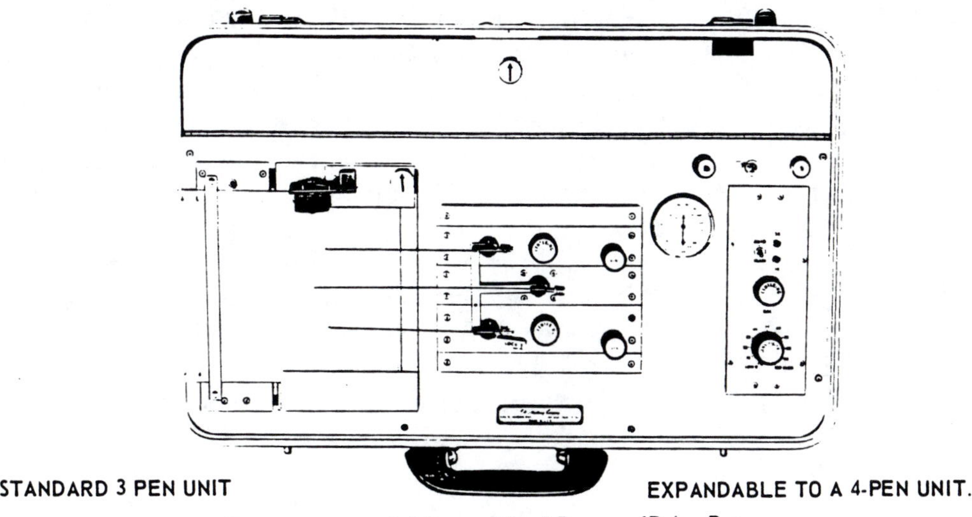

Figure II-12. Stoelting's Cat. No. 22600. Transistorized Amplifier.

stole the man's watch and also if he shot the man. (2) use isolated Backster control questions. (3) use Backster's Spot Analysis, and (4) use a numerical scoring system. According to Decker, Reid became visibly upset over the suggested changes to his technique and told Decker that he could call it anything he wanted, but not to call it the Reid Technique and not even associate Reid's name to it. Decker than replied that if Reid had no objections he would call it the Modified General Question Test or MGQT which henceforth was added to the polygraph techniques taught at the U. S. Army Polygraph School. (Decker 1995)

In 1968, Dr. William J. Yankee, Dean of Academic Affairs, Delta College, University Center, Michigan presented A Report on the Computerization of Polygraphic Recordings to the Keeler Polygraph Institute Alumni Association's fifth annual seminar in Chicago, Illinois. Dr. Yankee explained the basics of scientific research and a method of quantifying those variables affecting the polygraphic recordings as a means of computerizing the polygraph system.

In 1970, Richard O. Arther introduced a novel concept into the Known-Solution Peak-of-Tension Test, namely the "False Key." Arther reasoned that the truthful examinee does not know which is the key, but the deceptive examinee will recognize the key. However, Arther observed a danger in that the truthful examinee may have learned the key but does not want to admit it perhaps because he/she got the information improperly, such as reading the case file when the investigators were out of the room; or the information was given to him/her by the perpetrator. Another danger is that the key is relevant to the truthful examinee for other reasons, such as involvement in another crime or incident in which that particular key was relevant. Arther related a case in which a prior Control Question test indicated truthfulness, and in the seven-item peak of tension test the examinee always reacted to the same irrelevant item, even though the sequence of the items was changed around for each of the three charts. The item was a rather obvious one for an innocent examinee. However, there was no more reaction to the key item than there was to the remaining irrelevants. The examinee's innocence was later verified. Following that 1960 case, Arther reported another case in which a suspect in a robbery of a woman who had just shopped at a grocery store did not respond to the key item at number four position, a hat box, but to the more logical paper bag at number two, which was irrelevant. Since then, Arther has always used a false key at number two position in each Known-Solution Peak-of-Tension test. Whenever possible, the False Key is an item that is the most obvious item. If the obvious item is the Key, then it is necessary to subtly overemphasize an irrelevant at number two position so that the truthful examinee will guess that is probably the key item. The subtle emphasis is done by saying a little more about the item, the use of a gesture, or possibly by reading the item in a louder voice. Otherwise, Arther's peak of tension tests followed a fixed pattern, seven items if possible with the key at position number four in Known-Solution Peak-of-Tension tests, and seven items if possible in Searching (Probing) Peak-of-Tension tests, with number seven being a question about something else not mentioned. (Arther 1970; Ansley 1992)

In contrast to previous employers of the Known-Solution Peak-of-Tension test, John E. Reid and Fred E. Inbau in their 1977 textbook *Truth and Deception* (2d Edition of their 1966 textbook), differ in their administration of this guilty knowledge test by recommending that the examinee not be told the order of the question or articles before the first Peak-of-Tension test, and not even told what the various named articles will be. The object was to "achieve an element of surprise on the first peak of tension test, but only on this first test. Thereafter, on the subsequent peak of tension tests (of which there should be three in all), the original order of the questions should be maintained and the subject so advised prior to each test." The second peak of tension test should be given shortly after the first one and the examinee told that the questions would be the same, and asked in the same order. After the second test the Reid and Inbau instructions called for the FP to leave the room for a few minutes, and to tell the examinee that when the third test is administered, their blood pressure may rise at the exact time the question is asked that includes the item which only the guilty person knows. The FP adds a comment to the examinee that if he/she is not telling the truth, the next test will reveal his culpability by his reaction to the correct item. The FP leaves the examination room to allow the examinee some time to review in his/her own mind the prior test. Reid and Inbau were very specific in their directions for the conduct of such tests and included thirty-two charts from their case files to illustrate the manner in which such charts are analyzed which included Known Solution and Searching Peak of Tension tests. (Reid & Inbau 1977; Ansley 1992).

Dr. David Thoreson Lykken, professor of psychology and psychiatry at the University of Minnesota Medical School, conducted several research studies regarding the Guilty Knowledge test and in one experiment (Lykken 1960) employed a number of medical students, several staff psychologists and psychiatrists, and a number of female members of the secretarial staff. They were informed on the nature of the Galvanic Skin Response (GSR), the lie detector in general, and the principle of the guilty knowledge method in particular. After being attached to the GSR electrodes, each subject was allowed to sit before the recording instrument and practice producing voluntary GSRs by various methods. Each subject was told what the format of the questioning would be, was cautioned against attempting to defeat the test merely by inhibiting responses, and was correctly advised that the best way to confuse the scoring system would be to produce GSRs of various amplitudes to the innocent alternatives in as random a pattern as possible. A prize of $10.00 was offered to any subject who could manage to defeat the objective scoring system used to evaluate the GSR tracing. In spite of aforesaid training in countermeasures, all of the subjects of the experiment were correctly matched with their own sets of questionnaire responses with no ambiguities and by a completely objective a priori scoring system resulting in 100% correct identification. Dr. Lykken opined that the aforesaid experiment testified as conclusively as such laboratory studies can, that the guilty knowledge method can yield extremely high validities, even with sophisticated defensive subjects, under conditions appropriate to its use, when enough guilty knowledge is available to the FP to enable him/her to construct an adequate interrogation list. (Lykken 1960)

However, analog research conducted by C. B. Honts, M. K. Devitt, M. Winbush, and J. C. Kircher (1996) regarding the effects of mental and physical countermeasures on the accuracy of the Concealed Knowledge Test (CKT), also known as the Guilty Knowledge Test (GKT) revealed that when the polygraph charts were evaluated and scored by Human Evaluation, the Innocent were correctly identified in 100% of the cases, the Guilty 70%, but when physical countermeasures were applied, correct decisions dropped to 10% and mental countermeasures dropped them to 50%. But when the Kircher and Raskin (1988) Discriminant Analysis Algorithm was used, it correctly classified 80% of the innocent, 80% of the guilty control, 40% of the physical countermeasure, and 80% of the mental countermeasure subjects. However, it should be noted that in this experiment, Honts, Devitt, Winbush and Kircher used a Lafayette Model 761-65GA field polygraph instrument but only recorded thoracic and abdominal breathing patterns, plus galvanic skin response. No cardiovascular recording was used. Many experts including this author believe that the cardio cuff pressure has a psychophysiological effect on the breathing patterns, and the cardiograph channel provides an excellent means of detecting some countermeasures. Many practicing forensic psychophysiologists including this author use the Closed-Eyes and Shoeless Feet techniques as anti-countermeasures. Additionally, Honts, Devitt, Winbush and Kircher make no mention of the availability of movement/motion detection devices attached to polygraph examination chairs (Stoelting, Lafayette, Axciton) which research has shown were able to identify 92% and 85% of countermeasure movements by Abrams & Davidson 1988, and Stephenson & Barry 1988, respectively. Thus this *analog* study did not replicate the psychophysiological dynamics and instrumentation as found in a *field* situation.

Dr. Lykken popularized the Guilty Knowledge Test among scientists as the only sound test for the detection of deception and stated "I developed what I called the Guilty Knowledge Test as a young psychology professor who routinely used multiple-choice test questions both in the classroom and in constructing research instruments, personality questionnaires and the like. It was natural to think of using this same format to determine whether a subject possessed guilty knowledge, i.e., whether he could identify the correct alternative to several equally plausible alternative answers to questions about the crime. Since a guilty suspect would be unlikely to answer such questions truthfully, it was natural to think of letting his involuntary, autonomic nervous system answer for him." (Lykken 1992). However, in 1960 Lykken wrote "The guilty knowledge technique, of course, is not new. Every psychology student has seen it demonstrated using the GSR and 'a number between one and five.' In one form or another it also appears repeatedly in the lie detection literature. Thus, the 'peak of tension' test as described by Keeler (1933) originally involved presenting to the suspect a list of related items of which one was a 'significant' item and looking to the response record for signs of increased physiological 'tension' up to the significant item, decreasing thereafter. When only the guilty suspect knows which is the significant item, this is a crude form of the guilty knowledge test and is, potentially, an objective and accurate method of guilt detection." Dr. Lykken's definition of the Guilty Knowledge Test is similar to Ben-Shakhar's. Lykken writes "I consider a GKT to be any procedure that uses some involuntary physiological response to indicate whether the subject identifies the 'correct' or crime-related alternative as distinctive or different from a set of control alternatives that are not in fact crime-related but chosen to seem equally plausible to an innocent suspect. And the crucial thing about the procedure is that, in contrast with the CQT, the incorrect alternatives provide genuine controls in the scientific sense of that term. That is, the subject's mean response to the incorrect alternatives provide an estimate of how this person ought to react to the correct alternative if he is innocent and does not recognize the correct alternative as being crime-related." (Lykken 1992) This definition can also include all of the present Peak of Tension and Stimulation formats. (Ansley 1992)

Richard O. Arther (1970) appears to be the first FP to use what is known as the *Mode of Answer* methodology in which an examinee repeats a word from the question before answering "no." Arther used this method, taught it and wrote about it as a method to improve Peak of Tension tests. In the Arther version the subject answers with the essential word from each peak of tension test question before saying "no" i.e. "Do you know if the gun used in the robbery was a Colt revolver?" Answer, "Colt, no." (Ansley 1992)

In 1985, Douglas L. Grimsley and William J. Yankee completed a research project for the Department of Defense in which the examinee answered with the last word in the question, then said "no." The research, performed jointly by the University of North Carolina at Charlotte and the A. Madley Corporation, involved mock screening examinations with the relevant/irrelevant technique. Use of the Mode of Answer increased the accuracy. Accordingly, the A. Madley polygraph school began to teach the method to students, and there are probably a number of FP's who are using the method in the field. (Ansley 1992)

In 1987, W. Michael Floyd published a study in which the mode of answer was used in real cases, and the results compared to cases when it wasn't used. Floyd's variation used the verb in the question as opposed to a descriptive word or the last word in the question. There was no discernible difference in inconclusive rates, admission rates, time of administration, or confusion by examinees. Accuracy, in the field, could not be measured. (Ansley 1992)

In the laboratory, Kristen D. Balloun and David S. Holmes (1979) conducted research involving students cheating and used a guilty knowledge test in which the last word of the question became the answer, but the subject did not say "no." The last word was also the descriptive or essential word, i.e. "Was it tobacco?" Answer, "Tobacco." Balloun and Holmes tested their subjects twice, using heart rate, finger pulse volume, and skin resistance. They were correct in 11 of 18 cheaters (61%) and 14 of 16 truthful (87%) on the first test. Detection of cheaters fell significantly on the second test to 3 of 18 (17%), while truthful was 15 of 16 (94%). (Ansley 1992).

Although Reid & Inbau (1977) report their usage and instruction in the use of a Silent Answer test (SAT) in conjunction with the Reid Control Question Test in which verbal answers have been given in earlier charts, Akihiro Suzuki and J. Yatsuda (1965) reported a case study of a Silent Answer Test on a murder suspect in a PV examination. Reid used the SAT when the first few polygraph charts did not clearly reveal the examinee's status as truthful or deceptive. It was further used when the effort of the subject to answer caused some distortions in the tracings. It was also used when the examinee was engaging in countermeasures involving respiratory distortions. (Ansley 1992)

Reid and Inbau (1977) also include a "Yes Test" as part of the Reid Technique. It is used primarily "where the subject has tried to evade detection by distortion of the tracings" on the stimulation chart or the relevant charts. The subject is instructed to say "yes" to all test questions, including the relevant questions. The Reid experience has been that subjects who lied while answering relevant questions often tried to distort their responses to the yes answered questions to make their responses look like lies. Control questions are often deleted from the format when a "Yes Test" chart is administered. Reactions to the "yes" answers are often genuine because the "yes" answer is disturbing. Although Christopher Horneman and J. G. O'Gorman (1985) found "yes" answers in Guilty Knowledge Tests produced detection rates only at chance level, other researchers have found that "yes" answers produced detection rates above chance (Dufek, Widacki & Valkova, 1975; Elaad & Ben-Shakhar, 1989); and Gudjonsson, 1977). Answering "yes" to the critical item and "no" to the other items also produced detection rates above chance (ohkawa, 1963). However, when there was a comparison of detection rates for "yes" answers with "no" answers, the "no" answers provided higher rates of accuracy (Elaad & Ben-Shakhar, 1989; Ellson, 1952; Furedy, David & Gurevich, 1988; Gustafson & Orne, 1965; Horneman & O'Gorman, 1985; Janisse & Bradley, 1980; Ohkawa, 1963). Only one study found a higher detection rate for the "yes" answers than the "no" answers (Kugelmass, Lieblich & Bergman, 1967) but the difference was not significant. (Ansley 1992).

In 1959, H. Victor Cohen of the Government of Israel and an Israeli police officer attended the Reid College of Detection of Deception at Chicago, Illinois, after reading the book *Lie Detection* by Inbau and Reid. This marked the beginning of the use of the polygraph in psychophysiological veracity examinations in Israel, which currently has more than sixty forensic psychophysiologists, half of which are in private practice. (Cohen 1976). They rely heavily upon the control question test in criminal investigations. (Barland 1988).

Korea which is now a major user of the polygraph in forensic psychophysiology had its first forensic psychophysiologists (FP) trained by U. S. Army FPs stationed in Korea in the 1950s, but unlike the Japanese, some Korean FPs were subsequently trained outside their country, primarily in America and Japan. Consequently, both the control question and peak of tension tests are used in criminal investigations. (Barland 1988). In fact, in 1960, a Korean Military Police Captain Soung-Han Je received polygraph training at the U. S. Army Military Police Polygraph School in the United States, and he was followed by MP Captain Sun-Do Kwang in 1961. In 1979, twelve investigators from the Prosecutor's Office and the Police received polygraph training from the U. S. Army C.I.D. forensic psychophysiologist (FP) stationed at the 8th US Army, Seoul, Korea. Subsequently, several Korean investigators of the Prosecutor's Office attended the Backster School of Lie Detection, San Diego, California and the Reid College in the Detection of Deception, Chicago, Illinois. Currently there are about 123 forensic psychophysiologists in Korea but only 70 FPs are members of the Korea Polygraph Association (KPA), the rest of them are no longer practicing polygraphy. In Korea, the polygraph is used only by military and law enforcement agencies; the private sector is excluded. At the present time most polygraph instruments in use in Korea are Stoelting conventional polygraph instruments. In 1994, the Ministry of National Defense, Scientific Investigations Laboratory (MNDSIL) in Korea purchased its first and only computerized polygraph system, a Stoelting CPS. (Parn Kyou Park 1996).

In 1964, Akihiro Suzuki, Polygraph Training Instructor and Researcher at the National Institute of Police Science in Japan and Yoshio Hikita, a Forensic Psychophysiologist and Vice Director of the Crime Detection Laboratory at the Nara Prefectural Police Headquarters, Japan reported their experiments in the analysis of responses recorded by the pneumograph, cardiograph and galvanometer on polygraph

Cardio Activity Monitor With Water Chamber

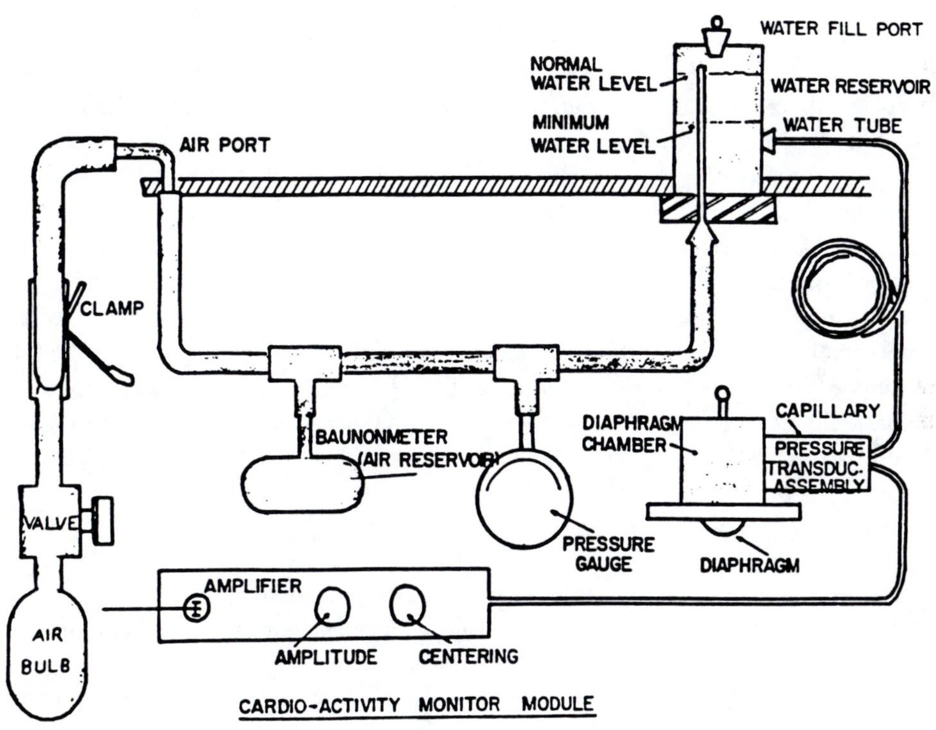

Figure II-13. From R. E. Decker, A. E. Stein and N. Ansley: A Cardio Activity Monitor. Polygraph, 1(3), Sep 72.

charts and their diminution indicative of the subject's habituation using Cleve Backster's "Total Chart Minutes Concept" model.(Backster 1963). Backster had recognized the individual differences of examinees in the index reliability, or performance, which are caused by differences of habituation in each index, and stated that forensic psychophysiologists can eliminate individual differences in index reliability and achieve standardization by taking this difference in adaptability into consideration, thus achieving a higher rate of accuracy. (Suzuki, Hikita 1981). Their experiment "showed the degree of validity in a descending order from respiratory, GSR to pulse rate test. However, it is still too early to make any conclusion from this because of the contradictory results obtained by others. The differences are due to the analysis methods and individual examiners characteristics affecting the results." (Suzuki, Hikita 1964, 1981) The psychodynamics of analog studies and mock crime paradigm are quite different than real-life cases which no doubt elicit emotions not present in the former. (Matte 1989)

In 1969, Biometrics Inc. of Waltham, Massachusetts, under research contract by the U.S. Air Force, developed a cardio activity monitor (CAM) designed to obtain from the wrist or thumb the same recording and chart pattern obtained with the conventional sphygmograph using the cardio medical cuff normally placed against the brachial artery at the inside upper arm. (Fig. II-13). The sensor assembly consisted of a water-filled chamber with a very thin rubber diaphragm placed over the radial artery at the wrist. The diaphragm was hydraulically inflated, partially compressing the artery. The artery pulsations were transmitted through the wall of the diaphragm into the hydraulic chamber of the sensing module where it is connected by a pressure transducer. The flow of blood is relatively unobstructed due to the smallness of the diaphragm area, which compresses only tissue immediately overlying the radial artery. Furthermore, the radial pulse can be partially occluded for long periods of time without discomfort because the ulnar artery distributes blood to the same general area through parallel channels.(Decker, Stein, Ansley 1972).

The early structure of the CAM presented several problems that were resolved after the Stoelting Company conducted a three-year transducer development program resulting in a low cost design that is nearly indestructible. The "dry" CAM, introduced by the Stoelting Company in 1975, is a finger or wrist attachment that contains a pressure sensitive metal diaphragm. Two tiny silicone strain gauges are bonded to the inside surface of the metal diaphragm. When the metal disc flexes with pressure changes the strain gauges convert this to an electrical signal. (Fig. IV-5, IV-6, IV-7, IV-8, IV-9)

In 1973, the electronic trend in polygraph instrumentation began with the introduction of the electronic cardio by the Lafayette Instrument Co. With its adjustable and greater sensitivity, the electronic cardio covered a wider range of subjects and allowed the FP to record at significantly lower cuff pressure with sufficient tracing amplitude for adequate interpretation. That same year, the Lafayette Instrument Company added "selective enhancement" to the electronic cardio circuit which allowed the FP to further amplify the dicrotic notch area of the cardio tracing for better viewing of the position changes. This added enhancement or amplification to the base line response allowed the FP to lower the overall amplification and still be able to see the base line changes. (Decker, Pochay 1985).

In 1974, the Stoelting Company departed from the purely mechanical polygraph instrument to the electronic instrument permitting electronic enhancement of each and all tracings commencing with the Polyscribe series, the first solid state all electronic polygraph instrument with multi-function amplifiers on each of the four channels, activated by a mode switch on the channels' top panel. The Polyscribe series was discontinued in 1979 with the introduction of the Ultra-Scribe series (Fig. IV-3), which can simultaneously record a person's heart beat, pulse rate and strength, and changes in mean blood pressure using both the conventional cardio cuff on the arm and the CAM on the wrist or thumb of the other arm in two separate channels, enabling comparison of the two modes of recording. This electronic enhancement enables the forensic psychophysiologist to adjust the amplitude of both breathing channels and the cardiograph channel to ideal tracings on the polygraph chart. The GSR channel's amplifier was increased to one million ohm, to assure ample capability for the most difficult subjects. (Miller 1995).

In 1979, the Stoelting Company introduced the Cardio Tach, a self powered device with a meter for visual read out to detect changes in heart rate, which could be connected to the multi-function amplifier in the Ultra-Scribe polygraph instrument for a graphic display on the polygraph chart. (Decker, Pochay 1985).

The Lafayette Instrument Company, in Lafayette, Indiana, a competitor of the Stoelting Company in the manufacture of polygraph instruments who had also marketed three and four-pen mechanical polygraph instruments, also introduced its electronic polygraph instruments, some of which were partly mechanical and electronic and some all electronic with minor variations from Stoelting's instruments, shortly thereafter. Both manufacturers' polygraph instruments recorded the same physiological parameters. But in 1984, the Lafayette Instrument Company added to its electronic polygraph instruments the Auto Base Response circuit, designed to increase the amount of base line amplification at a constant rate, as the overall amplification is decreased, which provided greater resolution of the base line changes at lower sensitivity settings. That same year, Lafayette also introduced the "Factfinder" polygraph instrument with a 10 inch chart drive, available with three, four and five channels. (Decker, Pochay 1985).

Polygraph manufacturing companies such as Stoelting, Lafayette and Axciton have responded to claims made by polygraph critics (Lykken 1978) that countermeasures in the form of physical movement during the polygraph examination can successfully defeat the polygraph, by manufacturing and marketing a "movement sensing chair." But the first movement chair was designed by John E. Reid, noted forensic psychophysiologist in 1946 as a result of research which reflected that blood pressure changes could be artificially induced by muscular contraction and relaxation. Even the medical profession failed to recognize the possibility that the mere exertion of unobserved muscular

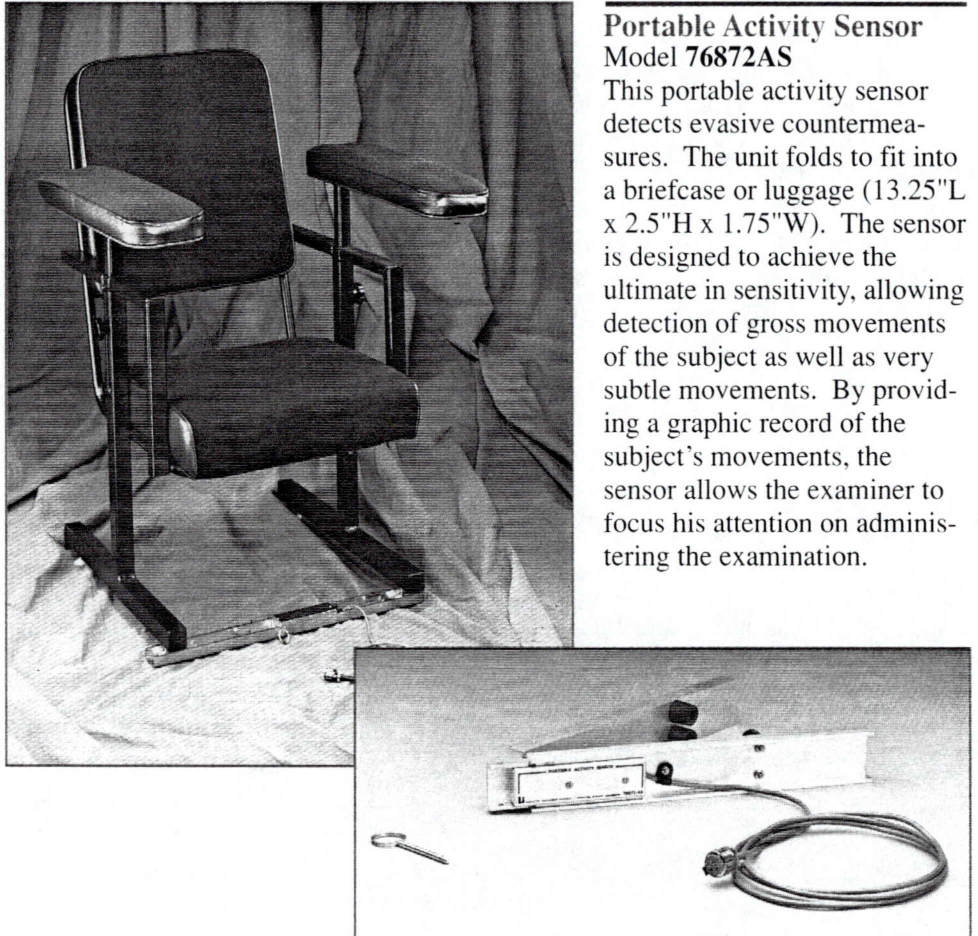

Figure II-14. Lafayette Portable Activity Sensor. A foldable (silvery) sensor bar inserted underneath the two front legs of the polygraph examination chair as illustrated in above photo. This sensor works with any electronic multiple function amplifier.

pressure could produce a similar effect. Reid's original model consisted of metal bellows in the arms and seat bottom of the chair which pneumatically activated recording pens on the polygraph chart. This instrument was so effective in identifying physical movements that it prompted attorney F. Lee Bailey to offer a reward of $10,000.00 to anyone who could beat the polygraph. Dr. Lykken admitted in his book (1981) that Mr. Bailey's money is quite safe if the test is administered by a competent forensic psychophysiologist utilizing a movement sensing chair. Dr. Lykken explains however that a forensic psychophysiologist of Reid's experience would be looking for the slightest movement which would be interpreted as a deliberate countermeasure. Dr. Lykken raises the question of tongue biting as one covert self-stimulation which Reid's special chair cannot detect. Dr. Lykken admits that "there is no doubt that it would be hard to beat a lie test when the examiner expects you to try and knows how you mean to do it." (Lykken 1981). Over the years, the motion chair has been refined from a bulky, mechanical pneumatic device to the current electrically enhanced strain-gauge transducer type of device. (Fig. II-14 & II-15)

Research conducted by Mike Stephenson and Glenn Barry at the Canadian Police College Polygraph School (Stephenson, et al 1988) involving twelve subjects who used thirty-six physical countermeasures such as pushing left/right foot onto the floor, contraction of anal sphincter, curling toes, right/left thigh contraction, left/right forearm push, pressing on GSR plates, right/left heel press, right/left palm press, left/right elbow pushed down, resulted in a percentage detection rate for the forensic psychophysiologist (FP) using the movement chair of 85 percent. Without the benefit of the movement chair the FP obtained a detection rate of only 9 percent. An observer placed directly in front of the subject obtained a detection rate of 36 percent. It must be noted that the subjects of Stephenson-Barry's research were FP trainees who completed ten weeks of a twelve-week polygraph examiners course well versed on physical countermeasures in a non-test situation. The results indicate that the motion chair is a very useful piece of equipment for the forensic psychophysiologist in a time when various ways to defeat the polygraph are broadly published. However Stephenson and Barry specifically directed subjects to move parts of their bodies and observed whether these movements could be detected, and whether or not they could be evaluated on the charts as countermeasures, with and without the Lafayette Activity Sensor.

Dr. Stanley Abrams and Lt. Michael Davidson (Abrams, Davidson (1988) conducted a study to evaluate the impact of movement as a countermeasure upon polygraph testing and to ascertain further if the activity sensor is an effective counter to these attempts to distort the findings. In this study, additional movements were incorporated in the form of tongue biting, stepping on a tack, tensing of the jaw, and tightening of the buttocks. The results of this study revealed that in every movement made by the subjects, a change resulted in the tracings in at least one of the three measures being employed. In 36 percent of the cases, the tracings demonstrated distortion caused by the movements which were readily interpreted as movements. This was particularly the case when the movement was on the upper portion of the body and

Figure II-15. Axciton Portable Movement Sensor. This sensor attaches to the rear leg of the polygraph examination chair. It connects and is designed to be used with the Axciton Computerized Polygraph System.

on the same side as the blood pressure cuff. Despite concentrating on that part of the body to be moved, only 12 percent of the movements were actually observed. In 5 percent of the movements that were seen, no changes in the tracings occurred that would indicate that a movement had been made. Combining both the behavioral reactions not seen in the tracings and those indications of movement present in the tracings, a total of 44 percent of the countermeasures were detected. The activity sensor, however, was able to detect 92 percent of these movements. This included both the tongue biting and stepping down on a tack. As Dr. Abrams points out in his discussion of the study, it would take a sophisticated subject to create responses to the right questions (Control Questions) and he/she would still face the problem of suppressing an arousal at the relevant questions. Inasmuch as this study involved a mock paradigm where the "fear of Detection" is not present, the question arises regarding a real-life situation where the relevant questions offer a real threat to the subject, as to whether that real threat would still elicit a greater arousal from the Guilty subject than the Control questions to which the subject is applying a physical countermeasure. It appears from the higher rates of accuracy reported in the research for deceptive subjects, that the majority of individuals are not employing countermeasures of this nature (Patrick and Iacono, 1987; OTA 1983).It may be that the reactions to the relevant questions in real-life testing exceed the reactions of the controls even though purposeful movements are made. This author reported in 1991 a confirmed deceptive case wherein the subject had successfully caused an inconclusive result in a PV examination administered by the police which employed the Clinical Approach, by controlling his breathing and using a tack inside his boot to cause pain to all test questions except the relevant ones. However when this same examinee was retested privately by this author at the request of his attorney, employing the Quadri-Track Zone Comparison Technique, those same countermeasures failed inasmuch as his numerical scores far exceeded the scores necessary to render a conclusion of deception, which was confirmed by his post-test confession.(Matte 1991). Apparently, differences in methodology and test structure do have an influence on the effectiveness or non-effectiveness of countermeasures. It is also quite apparent from aforementioned research that when either pain, muscular tension or movements are used, the activity sensor is highly effective in detecting these countermeasures. However its use was not popular inasmuch as the manufacturers of activity sensors required FP's to sacrifice one of the channels on their polygraph instruments for the recording of subject movement, which was not practical as most mechanical and electronic polygraph instruments only have four channels, the minimum required for an adequate polygraph test. The alternative is to add a channel to existing ones which is easily accomplished since current four and five pen polygraph instruments are designed to accept an additional channel. With the advent of the Computerized Polygraph System, the addition of a movement sensor, as well as other newly developed sensors, can be easily made without affecting the quality and/or integrity of the other existing sensors, although the number of physiological tracings displayed on the computer monitor or the computer chart printout is limited in the same manner as conventional polygraph instruments with their printed charts. (See Chap. 21)

In 1969, Richard I. Golden presented a paper at the Annual Seminar of the American Polygraph Association at Houston, Texas, regarding his experiments using existing control question techniques but requiring the subject to answer each test question twice, the first time truthfully and the second time with a lie, for the purpose of acquiring additional psychophysiological data from the examinee by comparing his subjective truthful answer with a known *directed* lie to the same question. Golden gave full credit for the invention of aforementioned "Yes-No Technique" to Morton Sinks, a forensic psychophysiologist in Cleveland, Ohio, who first thought of the technique in 1965.

In 1973, Silvestro F. Reali, who was President of Polygraph Personnel Research School for Lie Detection, introduced the Reali positive control technique, which also requires the examinee to answer each test question twice as in Golden's technique. However, Reali's technique requires the examinee to answer each test question with a *directed* lie the first time, and truthfully the second time. The examinee is not instructed to specifically give a "yes" or "no" answer to either question. Reali's positive control technique does not incorporate existing comparison techniques and contains no earlier-in-life control question. The test is comprised of irrelevant questions, semirelevant questions, relevant questions, verified disclosure questions, a question regarding previous polygraph tests, and a medical question. Each question in the test, regardless of type, is formulated to have its own control by eliciting a deliberate lie to each question from the examinee, which theoretically should elicit the greater response from the innocent examinee while the guilty examinee should reflect his greatest response to the identical question to which he denies culpability. (Reali 1978) It should be noted that the title Positive Control Question Technique was initially developed at the U. S. Army Polygraph School, Fort Gordon, Georgia. (Ansley 1996)

Implementation of Golden's yes-no technique and Reali's positive control technique obviously doubles the amount of time the examiners arm is under pressure from the cardio *cuff* normally maintained from 70 mm to 90 mm. This presents a problem for those polygraphists still using mechanical polygraph instruments that lack an electrically enhanced cardiograph permitting substantially lower cuff pressure or the Cardio Activity Monitor that requires no significant pressure. However, reduction of cuff pressure below 70 mm invites problems in the cardiograph tracings in that lower pressure requires increased sensitivity to obtain adequate amplitude which in turn can cause unmanageable, erratic pattern movement, depending of course on the examinee's physiology. Furthermore, a high pressure cuff theoretically shows the most dramatic change in amplitude during a reaction because the *percent* change in the mismatch between mean arterial blood pressure (MABP) and mean cuff air pressure (MCAP) during a reaction is very significant, whereas a low cuff pressure shows little change in amplitude during a reaction because the *percent* change in the mismatch during a reaction is relatively small. (Barland 1984). (Full discussion in Chap. 4).

In 1987, an analog study on the "Validity of the Positive Control Physiological Detection of Deception Technique" was conducted by Lawrence N. Driscoll, an instructor at Indiana University of Pennsylvania and a self-employed forensic psychophysiologist, Charles R. Honts, Ph.D., a research associate in the Department of Psychology at the University of Utah, and David Jones, J.D., Ph.D., a professor of administration of justice at the University of Pittsburgh. The results of this experiment "indicate the positive control test to be an inferior detection of deception technique as compared to the control question test. This finding is indicated by the dramatically increased percentage of inconclusive outcomes for the positive control (45 percent) as compared to the control question test (10 percent), and in an increased false negative rate for the positive control test (22 percent) as compared to the control question test (0 percent).... the positive control test was not demonstrated to be a valid discriminator of truthtellers and deceivers." (Driscoll, Honts, Jones 1987).

Millard E. Addison, Special Assistant for Scientific Investigations at the Department of the Navy Naval Investigative Service communicated to this author on 11 May 1982 the results of a study he conducted on Si Reali's Lie/Truth (Positive Control) technique by having his ten forensic psychophysiologists use it on various types of criminal and counterintelligence cases after an MGQT, Zone Comparison Test or Relevant-Irrelevant test to see if the two tracked. They "found the two tracked on approximately 95 percent of the NDI (No Deception Indicated) calls, were inconclusive in 4 percent, and DI in less than 1 percent; however, on DI (Deception Indicated) calls, we found only a 60 percent tracking ratio with 40 percent NDI or inconclusive." (Addison 1982).

In 1986, a study based on the doctoral dissertation of Robert F. Forman entitled "Validity of the Positive Control Polygraph Test Using the Field Practice Model" tested thirty-eight subjects and obtained an average accuracy of 73% for the examiner and 78% for a "blind" judge of the polygraph record. (Forman, McCauley 1987)

In about 1980, the collective work of Dr. David C. Raskin and Dr. John C. Kircher from the University of Utah, aroused the interests of many field forensic psychophysiologists some of whom adopted the control test format used by aforesaid researchers in their studies. One of them was the Arizona School of Polygraph Science which began teaching one version of the control question test that the aforesaid researchers had used in some of their research and labeled it as the Utah Zone Comparison Technique (UZCT) (Honts 1996). Dr. Charles R. Honts who later joined the Raskin, Kircher team, stated to this author (1996) that they never promoted any particular questions sequence. Their "collective view was that a control question test was a control question test." Dr. Honts saw no scientific reason to prefer one order of control, relevant, and neutral questions over another, hence saw no reason to promote any one formulation. However the most common format in their published research was a three relevant question test with three Backster type (exclusive) control questions. The format also included a sacrifice-relevant question but no symptomatic questions. Control/relevant pairs were separated by a neutral question, and the neutral and control questions were rotated after each chart. The ordinal position of the relevant questions was not changed. Furthermore, the relevant question was compared to the control to the left, unless the control zone was considered to be a distortion zone. If a control question was not scorable, the relevant was compared to the control nearest in time that was acceptable for scoring. Backster's 7-position scale was used but unlike Backster, a fixed numerical threshold of +/-6 was used. (Honts 1996).

During the period 1983-1987, David C. Raskin introduced a *directed lie control question* (DLCQ) into his Utah Zone Comparison Technique as a replacement for one or more of the traditional earlier-in-life control questions. In about 1993, Dr. Raskin replaced all of the traditional earlier-in-life control questions with directed-lie control questions. (Bartlett 1995; Abrams 1996). Dr. Honts followed suit with the adoption of all exclusive directed lie controls. However Honts has no objection to the use of non-exclusive directed lies (Honts 1996). This approach simplifies the construction of the control question and assures that the examinee's answer is in fact a lie, purportedly reducing the likelihood of false positives.

Earlier use of the directed-lie control question was reported by L. S. Fuse in 1982, wherein he indicated that the DLCQ had evolved over the previous sixteen years and was found to be most effective in multiple issue tests. However Fuse cautioned that there had to be the right amount of emphasis on the DLCQ *because too much would dampen the response to the relevant question*, and *too little could cause a false positive reaction*. In his 1989 Doctoral dissertation for the Department of Psychology at the University of Utah, S. W. Horowitz conducted a study of *The Role of Control Questions in Physiological Detection of Deception* wherein he used a mock crime paradigm with sixty truthful and sixty deceptive subjects. He compared the effectiveness of the control question technique (CQT), the relevant-irrelevant (R&I) technique, and two *directed lie* control question (DLCQ) procedures in which one used lying to neutral questions and the other lying to personal issues. Comparing the various procedures among the truthful subjects, 87% accuracy was obtained on the "personal lie" approach in contrast to 67% when the "neutral lie" was used. Employing the usual control question technique, 80% accuracy was reported while only 20% was found on a R&I procedure. For the deceptive subjects, the "personal lie" approach again was found to be more effective than the "neutral lie" with accuracy at 75% and 53% respectively. For the group in which the usual control question procedure was used, 53% accuracy was obtained while 100% accuracy was reported for the R&I approach. (Abrams 1991)

In 1981, Dr. Gordon H. Barland reported his results of *A Validity and Reliability Study of Counterintelligence Screening Tests*, wherein he used fifty-six U. S. Army employees in a mock screening situation to determine the accuracy of PV examinations with the Counterintelligence Screening Test (CIST) using *directed-lie control questions*. This CIST is derived from the federal version of the Zone Comparison Test. The test contains 13 questions: five different models of field polygraph instruments were used which recorded respiration, skin resistance and relative blood pressure. Three methods were used to evaluate the polygraph charts. (1) The Zone method where each relevant question was evaluated against the larger control question in its zone for each channel and scored from +3 to -3. (2) The Greatest Control method which used the same procedure as the Zone method except that the five relevant questions were evaluated against the one control question on the chart with the largest overall reaction. (3) The Relevant-Irrelevant method wherein there was no numerical scoring and each relevant question was evaluated in terms of size and consistency of response without reference to the control questions. (Barland 1981).

In the aforementioned study, the first method (Zone) correctly identified 81% of the Deceptive subjects and 76% of the Non-Deceptive (Truthful) when inconclusives are omitted. The second method (Greatest Control) correctly identified 68% of the Deceptive and 83% of the Non-Deceptive (Truthful) when inconclusives are omitted. The third method (R-I) correctly identified 86% of the Deceptive and 76% of the Non-Deceptive (Truthful) when inconclusives are omitted. However, in evaluating the aforementioned results, it should be noted that in the initial analysis, if the subject was in fact *deceptive to any relevant question*, and he reacted deceptively to any of the questions, it was considered a *hit* even though the forensic psychophysiologist (FP) may have *misidentified* which relevant question the subject was deceptive to. Thus when the *specifically correct* rather than *gross* identification is factored into the equation, the first method (Zone), excluding inconclusives, reveals only a 63% correct identification of the deceptive questions, hence was unable to identify the programmed deceptive questions *significantly better than chance*. The second method (Greater Control) reveals only a 54% correct identification of the deceptive questions, thus was *totally unable to identify* the programmed deceptive questions *any better than chance*. The third method (R-I) reveals a 69% correct identification of the deceptive questions, which *appears* to be superior to the other two methods in the identification of the deceptive questions. (Barland 1981). However it should be further noted that while the FPs in the third method (R-I) were instructed to disregard the control (directed-lie) questions when evaluating the relevant questions, they certainly could not omit the psychophysiological effect of the control questions on the examinees, and its influence on the neighboring relevant questions which were evaluated as if a Relevant/Irrelevant test had been conducted. This research demonstrated that the Greatest control method was unable to detect either the deceptive subjects or the deceptive questions at greater than chance levels. It further demonstrated that the *Directed-Lie* control question identified the truthful significantly better than chance but *failed to identify the deceptive subjects or the deceptive questions at better than chance levels*.

In 1988, C. R. Honts and D. C. Raskin conducted A Field Study of the Validity of the Directed Lie Control Question, assessing twenty-five confirmed criminal tests in which the directed lie control question (DLQC) procedures were used. Confirmation (ground truth) was acquired through admissions, physical evidence that conclusively exonerated the examinee, or if the accusations were retracted. Regarding the latter, the alleged victim recanted, denying that the accusation was real. One DLCQ and two control questions were compared with three relevant questions on each administration of these tests. Using this approach, the researchers reported that of the 25 cases, one was inconclusive, one error occurred on a deceptive subject, and the remainder were accurate. When blind scoring was employed, 90% accuracy was obtained when control questions alone were used, with both errors being false positives. Using both controls and one DLCQ, an accuracy of 95.6% was obtained, with the one error being a false negative. Dr. Stan Abrams (1991) expressed his concern about the criteria used to establish ground truth in eleven (11) of the twenty-five (25) subjects used in aforesaid Honts-Raskin study, inasmuch as those eleven subjects were suspects in child sexual abuse cases and one of the criteria used for verification was retraction of an accusation. Dr. Abrams, a Clinical Psychologist and Forensic Psychophysiologist, stated that it is not at all unusual for a child victim of sexual abuse to retract his or her accusation, but that does not necessarily mean that the abuse did not occur, and quoted Toth & Whalen (1987) "Whatever a child says about sexual abuse, she is likely to reverse it. Beneath the anger of impulsive disclosure remains the ambivalence of guilt and the martyred obligation to preserve the family. In this chaotic aftermath of disclosure, the child discovers that the bedrock fears and threats underlying the secrecy are true. Her father abandons her and calls her a liar. Her mother does not believe her and decompensates into hysteria or rage." (Abrams 1991)

In 1991, Dr. Stan Abrams studied the *directed lie* control question approach in ten verified cases consisting of six confirmed deceptive subjects and four confirmed truthful subjects. In all ten cases, verification was determined by confessions. The instructions given to the subjects were taken verbatim from an audio-taped examination conducted by Dr. Raskin. Not only was the wording exactly the same, but a very strong effort was made to maintain the same inflection. All of the polygraph charts were numerically scored using the traditional seven-position scale (+3 0 -3). The results revealed that all four truthful subjects' scores increased from an average score of +2.75 to +5.25. However, five of the six deceptive subjects' scores increased from an average score of -1.6 (deception) to an average score of +3.6 (truthful), and the sixth deceptive subject's score increased from Zero (inconclusive) to +4 (truthful). Thus, five of the six subjects produced minus (deception) scores and one produced a score of zero (inconclusive) when the relevant questions were compared to the normally used control questions, but when compared to the DLCQ, all six confirmed deceptive subjects produced plus (truthful) scores, hence false negatives for all six confirmed deceptive subjects. Apparently, the same factors that caused the unacceptable number of false negatives when using the DLCQ in studies conducted by Driscoll, et al. (1987), and Addison (1982) were operative in Abrams' study. (For further discussion of DLCQ see Utah Zone Comparison, Chap. 11)

Canada was slow in its adoption of the polygraph in forensic psychophysiology, primarily due to British influence on its investigative and judicial processes. Initially, Canadian FPs received their training in American schools until the Canadian Police College established a polygraph training course in 1978, which was patterned after the United States Department of Defense Polygraph Institute. The Zone Comparison format is the technique of preference and the polygraph is used primarily for criminal investigations, seldom for screening, be it by government or industry. (Barland 1988; M. T. Bradley, M. E. Cullen, S. B. Carle 1996).

South Africa first experienced the use of a polygraph instrument to detect lies in 1978 when Brenda Selkon, a clinical psychologist and 1977 graduate of the Reid College, conducted PV examinations using a Stoelting instrument for Fidelity Guards, a company in the Rennies Group, with an office in Hillbrow, Johannesburg. Shortly thereafter, Gerry Higgins, presumably trained in the United States, worked as an FP with Lodge Security in South Africa, and operated from a professional office in Parktown, Johannesburg. In 1985, Coen Pretorius and Henk Van Rooyen of the National Intelligence Service (NIS) of South Africa were obliged to receive their polygraph training at the Polygraph Institute of Israel due to United States sanctions against South Africa. A number of professors from the University of Pretoria Medical School also attended the Polygraph Institute of Israel inasmuch as the course included pharmaceutical/medical issues of interest to the attending clinical psychologists and psychiatrist. In 1987, a meeting was arranged by the Johannesburg Chamber of Commerce regarding "lie detection." The FPs disagreed about almost everything and the meeting was described by one of the attendees (Pretorius) as a *disaster*. Serious mistakes made by some of the earlier FPs in South Africa changed the perceptions of potential clients and users for the worst. But some members of the South Africa Army and the National Intelligence Service were nevertheless sent to polygraph school. Following the death of Gerry Higgins, Lodge Security hired Alan Shaw and Kevin Condon to conduct PV examinations using two Lafayette, four-pen instruments. Alan Shaw subsequently received training at the Backster School of Lie Detection. Apparently South Africa experienced the same abuses reported at congressional hearing in the United States in the 1970's, in that many of the FPs' focus was only on acquiring confessions to the detriment of the innocent, and perceptive trained other people to conduct only pre-employment screenings as they were not completely competent. However with the establishment of the Polygraph Association of South Africa (PASA) consisting of ten members (total of 13 active FPs in SA, half employed by Govt.), standards of practice similar to that of the American Polygraph Association have been adopted. In the late 1980's a young electronics engineer (NFI) developed a computerized polygraph instrument. It is believed that the project fell through when it was almost ready to be used because the FPs wanted immediate online printing of the chart; the printer was too loud and the printing not continuous; the tracings were shown only in bursts, and its full development too costly. Coen Pretorius investigated the possibility of having a 4-pen polygraph instrument built in South Africa similar to the Lafayette Ambassador instrument, but the cost of such a project was exorbitant hence not viable. Pretorius then learned that United States sanctions applied only to the Government sector, thus he was able to procure a Lafayette Ambassador polygraph instrument. In September 1995, a PV examination conducted by Coen Pretorius was admitted into evidence by the magistrate in Pretoria North Criminal Court. In September 1995, PV examination results were also used to strengthen the case of the police in the bail application of a person charged with arson in Cape Town. Results of PV examinations in South Africa have been recently used by companies in disciplinary hearings internally, and also in the Industrial Court. The present state of forensic psychophysiology in South Africa is undergoing the same growing pains felt in the United States in the 1980's. The Polygraph Association of South Africa is seeking a national licensing law to regulate the training and use of the polygraph in PV examinations. At the present time, the PASA is discouraging the training of FP in South Africa, opting instead for training at APA accredited polygraph schools. The techniques in use by FPs in South Africa are the Backster and Reid techniques for specific issues and the Relevant/Irrelevant technique for pre-employment screenings. (Pretorius 1995).

In 1974, the Criminalistic Institute of Romania began their evaluation of new forensic methods in their fight against crime, such as anthropological examination, the examination of the stress in the voice, the examination of the voice and of speech. During that same period the Institute reviewed information referring to the existence of the polygraph technique in the United States and its success in law enforcement, which generated a desire for its use by the Romanian police. (Coman 1995)

In 1975, Tudorel Butoi, a Romanian psychologist graduate of the Faculty of Psychology who had just completed his three years of probation in medical psychology was hired by the Romanian police and assigned the rank of lieutenant at the Criminalistic Institute following six months training as a policeman. Butoi's first step was to study all available material on forensic psychophysiology (polygraph) including the works of the early pioneers such as Cesare Lombroso, William Marston, Vittorio Benussi, Hugo Munsterberg, John A. Larson, Robert Gisele, Leonarde Keeler, and the works written by John Reid and Fred Inbau upon which is based the polygraph methodology used in Romania. The works of American forensic psychophysiologists comprised the major contribution and are the current principal guide in polygraph research in Romania. The results of the study have been promoted with the total support of the Chief of the Criminalistic Institute headed by Colonel Ion Anghelescu, criminology expert with a doctorate in law, who subsequently died in the rank of General-Major in 1985. Lieutenant Tudorel Butoi was placed in charge with "full truth and responsibility of pioneerdom" in polygraph technique in Romania. In this direction, he applied to the United States for the purchase of polygraph instruments which was rejected by the United States because of the embargo against communist countries at that time. Therefore, Romania purchased four polygraph instrument from Japan. With the American test models as a guide, they learned the principles in the use of the instruments and tested the polygraph methods. Due to the distrust by the majority of Romanian policemen concerning the accuracy of the polygraph, Lieutenant Butoi was forbidden to work on current, actual cases but was relegated to employing the polygraph in ancient cases (2 to 10 years old) which had remained unsolved. This distrust created a most pleasant situation due to the spectacular results of the polygraph in cases with a minimum of solutions. The ensuing success in the use of the polygraph in several major cases with a high level of difficulty and seriousness resulted in a request for assistance in the establishment of a preparatory program in the field of simulated behavior detection at the laboratories of Rijeka, Split, Zagreb and Belgrade in Yugoslavia in 1977. This was not only useful as an operational transfer, but especially as a modality of organization on territorial laboratories in the Federal Yugoslavian Police. (Coman 1995)

Lieutenant Butoi recruited three experimental psychologists, namely Major Bus Ioan from the district laboratory in Cluj, Major Balan Vasile from the district laboratory in Iasi, and Major Voiculescu Toma from the district laboratory in Timisoara. Their training lasted about one year and was accomplished by Tudorel Butoi, assisted by specialists in judicial psychology and criminology. A committee including criminology experts lead by judicial psychology specialist Tiberiu Bogdan and General-Major Ion Anghelescu, certified Ioan, Vasile and Voiculescu as experts. During their training, the polygraph laboratories were arranged following the American model in the towns where they were to be assigned to conduct their work. (Coman 1995)

In 1978, the Faculties of Psychology and The National Institute of Psychology were canceled because of the political system in Romania which in turn severely limited the psychological activity in every field including forensic psychophysiology. They were re-established in 1990. Nevertheless, in 1980, the Criminology Institute of Romania acquired two American polygraph instruments (Lafayette) for use in the Central Laboratory and Police Headquarters Laboratory. About 600 to 800 subjects were examined annually in the polygraph laboratories with a combined accuracy of approximately 92%. This success prompted previously reluctant policemen to solicit the use of the polygraph technique, especially in cases in which classical methods didn't produce any results. Beginning in 1978, Tudorel Butoi conducted his first polygraph tests at the request of prosecuting attorneys and courts and no errors were noted. (Coman 1995)

At the present time, the first stage in the development of a national polygraph training school in Romania has been completed through the efforts of Tudorel Butoi, Chief of the Polygraph Laboratory at the Police Department of Bucharest, and Major Adrian Coman, criminology expert and bachelor in law who replaced Butoi at the Criminalistic Institute of the Police Headquarters. Standards of practice and legal protections for the rights and liberties of Romanian citizens in the administration of psychophysiological veracity (PV) examinations have been established. Furthermore, forensic psychophysiologists' expertise are checked by annual examinations at the central laboratory, and professional meetings have been organized in order to analyze and exchange experiences and promote any idea which may improve their methodology. There are also conferences at the Jurists Association and presentations at police schools and the Faculty of Psychology and Law. The courts more frequently stop trials and apply to the polygraph test by admitting the technical-scientific report as a separate proof. Furthermore, with the consent of the State Department, polygraph usage has extended to cases concerning the corruption of policemen, in which the classical methods of investigation did not work. Currently the Institute has acquired eight computerized polygraph systems from American Companies (Stoelting and Lafayette). (Coman 1995)

During the period 1984 to 1995, the number of polygraph laboratories in Romania has increased from six to eighteen, and there is a plan to have all forty-one districts with their own polygraph laboratories. One of the major problems in the recruitment of candidates for polygraph training was the lack of psychology graduates inasmuch as the Faculties of Psychology had been canceled for twelve years. This problem now appears to have been remedied and the State Department has agreed to recognize forensic psychology as a separate, distinct field with new terminology to describe the laboratories as *Laboratory of Simulated Behaviour Detection* and the experts have been named *Specialist-Psychologist Officers*. Also in development is the Romanian Judicial Biodetection School with the assistance of Tudorel Butoi and Voicu Zdrenghea. Beginning in 1990, some fundamental works in the field of biodetection were published such as *Psychological Investigation Concerning Simulated Behaviour* (1991), *Judicial Biodetection* (1992), and a book by professor Nicolae Mitrofan entitled *Judicial Psychology* dedicated to judicial biodetection, which became the course of lectures in the police schools, Faculties of Psychology and Law, and a work accessible to the public, psychologists and jurists. In 1993 specialization courses in judicial biodetection were organized, with the support of forensic psychophysiologists, at the unions of jurists and at the Bar. In 1994, Romanian forensic psychophysiologists had meetings with experts from the American Polygraph Association and the Department of Defense Polygraph Institute (USA) to further their knowledge about forensic psychophysiology. This has resulted in a well-received invitation by the APA for affiliation of Romanian forensic psychophysiologists with the APA. Romania is interested in founding a department for scientific research in forensic psychophysiology and a national association of psychologists experts in polygraph testing. (Coman 1995).

Turkey is an example of the speed with which a country can acquire a major polygraph capability. As recently as 1984 there was not a single forensic psychophysiologist (FP) known to be in Turkey. As of 1988 there were more than sixty FPs all trained in American schools and using the latest polygraph equipment and techniques. They have established quality control procedures modeled after that used by the United States Department of Defense. (Gale, Barland 1988). Turkey now trains its own forensic psychophysiologists. (Ansley 1996).

In 1980, Paul K. Minor, Chief Polygraph Examiner of the Federal Bureau of Investigation (FBI) modified the Relevant/Irrelevant (R-I) technique to include control questions of *measured relevance* to the target issue but not designed to cause an arousal. Instead, they serve as a vehicle to introduce the examinee to the issue in a logical interrogatory form and allow possible guilt feelings, anger, frustration, and so forth to be vented in areas other than at the direct relevant questions. These *relevant connected* questions referred to as *Situational Controls* provide a means for the truthful examinee to respond to the reasons he/she is tied to or associated to the target issue. These Situational Control questions provide a baseline of comparison that includes the excitement level of the target issue itself. This latest modifification of the R-I technique is known as the Modified Relevant-Irrelevant (MRI) Technique. (Minor, 1995). (For further details see Chapter 15).

The Department of Defense Polygraph Institute (DoDPI) subsequently modified Keeler's Relevant-Irrelevant technique which they referred to as the General Question Test (GQT). DoDPI uses formalized (disguised) control questions such as "Do you intend to lie to any of the questions on this test?" or "Have you lied to me in any way since we have been talking today?" The sequence of the relevant questions, interspersed with irrelevant questions, "walk" the examinee through the crime. (DoDPI 1995) (Chapter 15 for details).

On 11 March 1983, the President of the United States Ronald Reagan issued National Security Decision Directive 84 (NSDD-84) which authorized Federal executive agencies and departments to administer psychophysiological veracity (PV) examinations using the polygraph to their employees pursuant to investigations of unauthorized disclosure of classified information. This presidential directive which affected more than 2.5 million government employees and 1.5 million employees at companies doing business with the United States government resulted in a quick response by the Committee of Government Operations, U. S. House of Representatives which formally requested the Office of Technology Assessment (OTA) of the U. S. Congress to conduct a study on the validity of polygraph tests. This study which OTA admittedly should have taken between twelve to eighteen months to complete (Gibbons 1983) was published in November 1983, after only one meeting with the project's advisory panel, and only eight months after the issuance of president Reagan's directive. OTA's 132-page technical memorandum entitled *Scientific Validity of Polygraph Testing: A Research Review and Evaluation* has been regarded by many entities as the definitive, authoritative evaluation of psychophysiological veracity examinations using the polygraph, and now twelve years after publication, its results and conclusions are still quoted in the public and private sectors, the courts, and the news media whenever an apparent scientific source is needed to support an assertion that polygraph tests are unreliable. Regardless of the fact that the OTA study suffers many serious flaws, is now outdated by more recent, thorough analog and field research studies on PV examinations using the polygraph, and fails to consider advanced polygraph techniques which have incorporated additional safeguards (Chapters 10, 12, 14, 15, 16, 17), it continues to overshadow a comprehensive 143-page study on *The Accuracy and Utility of Polygraph Testing* published by the Department of Defense in 1984 which reflected the accuracy of control question tests in criminal investigations which ranged from 80 to 95 percent (DOD 1984), and a study conducted by Norman Ansley (1990) on The Validity and Reliability of Polygraph Decisions in Real Cases which reviewed ten studies which considered the outcome of 2,042 cases, from 1980 to 1990 with the result indicating a validity of 98 percent for deceptive cases and 97 percent for non-deceptive cases. These studies were from police and private cases using a variety of polygraph techniques, conducted in the United States, Canada, Israel, Japan and Poland. (Ansley 1990).

In February 1984, shortly after publication of the OTA study, President Reagan's National Security Decision Directive 84 was rescinded. OTA was subsequently abolished by Congress in September 1995. (Ansley 1995)

In about 1984, Nathan J. Gordon, Director of the Academy for Scientific Training in Philadelphia, Pennsylvania, while teaching a polygraph class, decided to compare the *automatic* versus the *manual* galvanic skin response (GSR) by attaching two instruments to a student. Two other students ran the instruments and marked the charts. One instrument was in the automatic mode and the other in the manual mode. After the test, Gordon instructed each student to mark their GSR's whose tracings appeared different. Gordon then instructed them to set up a *hierarchy* of GSR reactions on each of their charts, from the greatest reaction to the smallest reaction. Gordon found that although the tracings appeared to be different, the hierarchy each student established was identical. This hierarchy approach to a single parameter again crossed Gordon's mind while teaching the various methods of traditional numerical scoring systems (Backster/US Army/Utah) which employed a seven-position scale of comparing each relevant to a selected control question. Gordon discussed the objectivity of his newfound method with Philip M. Cochetti, an instructor at Gordon's polygraph school, and they subsequently named it the "Horizontal Scoring System" inasmuch as they were scoring a single parameter horizontally against itself. That same year, Gordon and Cochetti together submitted a thesis introducing the *Horizontal Scoring System* to the American Polygraph

Association for publication in *Polygraph*. (Gordon, N. J. & Cochetti, P. M. 1987). By 1985, Gordon and Cochetti were already using it in comparison to the Utah method of numerical analysis with apparent comparable success. The Horizontal Scoring System also known as the Rank Order Scoring System forms the basic structure of the algorithm of several computerized polygraph systems. (Gordon 1995). It should be noted that Dr. David T. Lykken developed a method of scoring his Guilty Knowledge Test by ranking the responses for each item and then averaging the ranks of the relevant alternatives for an *average rank score*. (Lykken 1981)

In 1987, Nathan J. Gordon, William M. Waid, and Philip M. Cochetti modified the Backster Zone Comparison Technique to include two Backster Exclusive Control questions and one Reid Non-Exclusive control question for comparison with three relevant questions which, at the option of the FP, may be interspersed with Irrelevant questions. A Symptomatic question, a Sacrifice Relevant question, and a Countermeasure question are also included in this format which they named the *Integrated Zone Comparison Technique* (IZCT). The physiological data from the polygraph charts is evaluated with the *Horizontal Scoring System* developed by Gordon and Cochetti in 1984. Uniquely, the first test (chart) is administered as a *Silent Answer Test* (SAT) which is scored and included in the overall evaluation. A Stimulation Test is administered after the first test (chart). (Gordon 1995). (For details see Chapter 11)

In the early 1970's, a device for the detection of emotional stress in the voice was developed by Dektor CI/S Inc. This device called a Psychological Stress Evaluator (PSE), was being used extensively in both the public and private sector of the United States. According to its manufacturer, the PSE detects inaudible and involuntary frequency modulations (FM) in the 8-12 Hz region. These frequency modulations, whose strength and pattern are inversely related to the degree of stress in a speaker, are believed to be a result of physiological tremor or microtremor (Lippold 1971) that accompanies voluntary contraction of the striated muscles involved in vocalization. During nonstressful periods the modulations are under control of the central nervous system. As stress is imposed the autonomic nervous system gains dominance, resulting in a suppression of FM. This suppression, indicative of emotional stress, is displayed by the PSE as a characteristic blocked or rectangular wave form. The PSE processes voice frequencies, preserved on a normal tape recording, using electronic filtering and frequency discrimination techniques. The stress-related FM patterns, displayed on a moving strip of heat sensitive paper, can be processed in four different modes of display for either gross or more detailed analysis. Because the recovery of the FM indicator spontaneously occurs with the removal of the stressing stimulus, stress in either narrative or monosyllabic speech can be evaluated. (Horvath 1979). On 5 June 1974, the Deputy Assistant Secretary of Defense submitted a report on the psychological stress evaluator (PSE) to the Foreign Operations and Government Information Subcommittee of the Committee on Government Operations, U. S. House of Representatives. This report reflected that the Department of the Army contracted a test and evaluation project from Fordham University (Kubis 1974), which found that "the PSE produced valid results in less than one-third of the tests administered and its reliability was less than pure chance." The report further reflected that the Air

Force Office of Special Investigations (OSI) conducted validation testing and concluded that "the PSE was not useful." The National Security Agency also conducted studies on the PSE and found it to be "insufficiently reliable." (Cooke 1974). In addition, Dr. Malcolm Brenner, University of Oregon, and Dr. Harvie H. Branscomb, Massachusetts Institute of Technology presented a paper at hearings on senate Bill 1845, United States Senate, Subcommittee on the Constitution, Committee on Judiciary, on 19 September 1978, regarding the Psychological Stress Evaluator - Technical Limitations Affecting Lie Detection, which concluded that "Based on our research experience with this device, we believe that the PSE measure is not of sufficient technical quality to be used in lie detection and our testimony documents five technical shortcomings which affect the present instrument."(Brenner, Branscomb 1979). Dr. Frank Horvath, Michigan University conducted an analog study of the PSE which is asserted to be a voice-mediated lie detector, and the galvanic skin response (GSR) of a standard field polygraph instrument. "Evaluations of response data was subjectively carried out by two trained evaluators; their interrater agreement was .38 for PSE analysis and .92 for GSR evaluation." "These findings were consistent with previous research and do not indicate that the PSE is effective in detecting deception." (Horvath 1979)

A field research study entitled "Possibility of Detecting Deception by Voice Analysis" conducted by Akihiro Suzuki and Shoichi Watanabe, Research Psychologists for the National Institute of Police Science, Tokyo, Japan, and Utaka Taheno, Tsuneo Kosugi and Takumi Kasuya, Police Psychologists for the Criminal Investigation Laboratory, Metropolitan Police Department, Tokyo, Japan, was published from Reports of the National Institute of Police Science in 1973. This study measured and recorded voice pitch, intensity and duration with apparatus used for the analysis of voice from tape recordings. Analysis was made of seventy-five answers to relevant crime questions from polygraph tests in real criminal cases in which the answers were verified as deceptive by subsequent confession or by medical jurisprudence. The results indicated that "Each of the three methods were measured against chance, and none exceeded chance." "The authors concluded that these voice measures were not reliable or useful." (Suzuki, Watanabe, Taheno, Kosugi, Kasuya 1979)

In 1979, a validity study of the Psychological Stress Evaluator (PSE) manufactured by Dektor Counterintelligence & Security, Inc., Springfield, Virginia, was conducted by Brian E. Lynch and Donald R. Henry of the Royal Ottawa Hospital, Ottawa, Ontario, Canada and published in the Canadian Journal of Behavioural Science. The PSE was assessed for its ability to display and detect arousal in the spoken word. Forty-three university students were asked to read aloud ten words composed of random proportions of taboo and neutral words. PSE recordings of these words were than given to two trained and ten untrained analysts for identification of stress patterns. Results indicated that "although the students rated the taboo words significantly more arousing than the neutral, the accuracy of identification of such words was no greater than chance for all analysts, regardless of training." (Lynch, Henry 1979, 1980)

In 1980, a field study comparing the Psychological Stress Evaluator (PSE) to Polygraph in evaluating Truth or Deception in criminal cases was conducted by Robert Peters, Forensic Psychophysiologist with the Wisconsin Department of Justice. The results of this study indicated that the PSE agreed with the polygraph in only 44% of the cases.

In 1982, Dr. Frank Horvath, Associate Professor, School of Criminal Justice, Michigan State University, published a study "Detecting Deception: The Promise and the Reality of Voice Stress Analysis" and reported that "A review of the evidence now accumulated about these devices shows that the evidence for the existence of a microtremor in the voice is problematic and that the capability of these devices in detecting stress is equally questionable. Without exception, however, the scientific evidence reported to date shows that voice stress analyzers are not effective in detecting deception; none of these devices has yet been shown to yield detection rates above chance levels in controlled situations."(Horvath 1982)

In 1994, this author became aware of a Computer Voice Stress Analyzer (CVSA) developed and marketed by Charles Humble, Ph.D., National Institute of Truth Verification (NITV) at West Palm Beach, Florida. On 26 April 1995, this author contacted Dr. Humble by letter informing him about the writing of this textbook and the need for information regarding the difference between the CVSA and its predecessor the Psychological Stress Evaluator (PSE) and the existence of any validation studies conducted on the CVSA. Dr. Humble, in a letter of reply dated 2 May 1995, refused to provide this author with any of the requested information about the CVSA, stating that it was the policy of NITV to provide only law enforcement agencies with information concerning the CVSA, and that there were no exceptions to this policy.

In a project funded by the Department of Defense Polygraph Institute as DoDPI94-P-0027, Dr. Victor L. Cestaro (1996a) conducted a study to test the underlying electronic theory of operation of the Computer Voice Stress Analyzer (CVSA). During this experiment the CVSA input/output was evaluated using simulation signals from laboratory test generators. The laboratory simulations established that the CVSA performs electrically according to the manufacturer's theory of operation. In that same project, an analog study was conducted to evaluate the decision accuracy and agreement rates obtained using the traditional polygraph instrument and the CVSA. Forty-two subjects (22 males, 20 females) took psychophysiological veracity (PV) examinations administered with the polygraph and CVSA instruments using Known-Solution Peak of Tension (POT) tests wherein the selected number is posted in full view of both the examiner and the examinee prior to the actual use of the instruments. Half of the subjects were tested with the polygraph instrument, then the CVSA instrument. The remaining half were tested using the instruments in the opposite order. The Peak of Tension tests employing the polygraph and the CVSA instruments were blind-evaluated by four independent examiners for each instrument. The frequencies of accurate determinations made using each instrument were compared using proportionality tests. The CVSA instrument and associated processes were significantly less accurate than the polygraph instrument and PV examination processes tested in similar circumstances (38.7% vs. 62.5%, with chance =25%. Interrater reliability, assessed using a multiple rater Kappa test, showed that agreement among all blind evaluators within each instrument category was significantly better than chance (p<.05). These data indicate there may be a systematic and predictable relationship between voice patterns and stress related to deception, and that the differences observed in accuracy rates between the two instruments are attributable to instrument/procedure sensitivity rather than examiner data evaluation skills. Thus the accuracy of examiner decisions concerning subject veracity obtained using the polygraph instrument and procedures was significantly greater than both chance and that obtained using the CVSA instrument. Furthermore, the accuracy of examiner decisions concerning subject veracity obtained using the CVSA instrument and procedures was not significantly greater than chance. While the study design was sufficiently powerful to detect such differences had they existed, subject did not experience jeopardy during

---

Cat. No. 83490 Matté Polygraph Chart Template

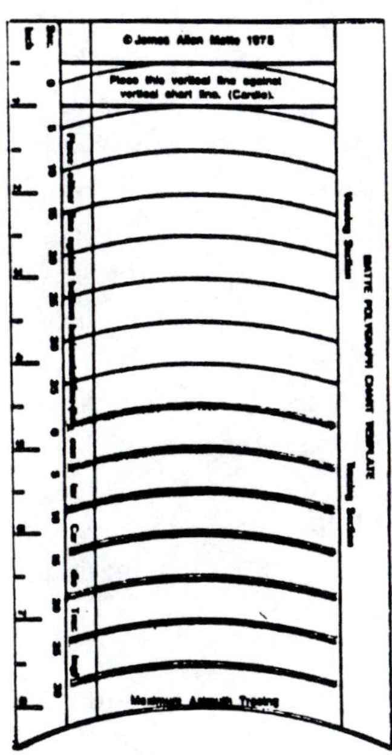

- **Facilitates Chart Interpretation**
- **Provides Accurate Visual Pulse Rate Calculation**
- **Allows Arcs to be drawn on the Charts for Subsequent Evaluation**

The Matte' Polygraph Chart Template provides the polygraphist with an accurate visual means of calculating pulse rate changes by viewing the cardio tracing through measured arc lines. This eliminates the inaccuracies inherent when viewing curvilinear tracing drawn on rectilinear chart paper. Both viewing and tracing sections are combined into one convenient template for immediate or subsequent chart evaluation.

The Template is easy to use. Simply align the template with the cardio tracing and view the pulses between the template's arc lines which repeat every 0.5 inches (5 seconds). Count the pulses between two consecutive arc lines and multiply by 12 to compute the pulse rate in beats-per-minute. Also the template can be used to draw accurate arcs on the chart. These lines can then be used for subsequent chart analysis or analysis by a group of examiners.

The Template can be used with any cardio tracing made with the standard 5 inch long recording pen which includes all polygraph models ever produced by Stoelting.
Cat. No. 83490 .... $7.50

Figure II-16. Matte Polygraph Chart Template. A clear plastic chart overlay.

testing, as they would in the field in real-life situations. The lack of jeopardy may have contributed to the acquired relatively low accuracy rates for both instruments. However, interrater agreement for the CVSA and polygraph instruments and procedures were both relatively high and significantly better than chance, suggesting that the observed difference in accuracy rates are attributable to instrument/procedure sensitivity, or the lack thereof, rather than examiner test data evaluation skills. (Cestaro 1996b)

On 11 September 1996, the Department of Defense Polygraph Institute (DoDPI) issued a Position Statement on *voice stress analysis* including the CVSA which stated "To date, we have found no credible evidence in information furnished by the manufacturers, the scientific literature, or in our own research, that voice stress analysis is an effective investigative tool for determining deception." (Capps, 1996)

During the period of 1974 and 1975 the author (Matte) conducted research to determine whether the belief held by many forensic psychophysiologists and certain authorities in the field of forensic psychophysiology, that the heart rate only decreases during reaction time when an examinee attempts deception, had any validity. This author devised a more accurate means of time-framing the reaction segment for pulse count, which resulted in the development and manufacture of the first polygraph chart template (Fig. II-16), subsequently marketed by the Stoelting Company in 1982 as the Matte Polygraph Chart Template, Cat. No. 83490. This template facilitates chart interpretation, provides accurate visual pulse rate calculation and allows arcs to be drawn on the charts for subsequent evaluation. The author (Matte) was able to illustrate that the heart rate in some individuals does increase during reaction time, while others will decrease, but a majority will experience no change. This discovery revealed that in the analysis of the cardiograph tracing, deception could not be ruled out in the absence of the traditional heart rate decrease at reaction time. The author, with the assistance of Dr. Joseph A. Zizzi, M. D. (president of the medical-dental staff and cardiologist at the E.J. Meyer Memorial Hospital, buffalo New York) was able to provide the physiological explanation for each phenomenon, which was grouped as alpha. beta, or alpha-beta adrenergic responder, respectively. As a result of these findings, a proposed classification system for polygraph subjects was formulated employing both the cardiograph and the pneumograph tracings as the basis. (Matte 1980)

In 1982, Dr. Gordon H. Barland developed a plastic chart overlay to facilitate the analysis of the pneumograph, GSR and cardio tracings on polygraph charts (Fig II-17), which was marketed by the Stoelting Company simultaneously with the Matte Polygraph Chart Template.

In 1973, Kazunoba Yamaoka, M.D., Chief of the Psychology Section, and Akihiro Suzuki, Senior Researcher of the same section at the First Forensic Science Division, National Institute of Police Science, Japan, reported their studies on skin-blood flow as an index of lie detection. The skin-blood flow changes were measured by placing warm metal and comparison metal electrodes on the skin surface. An electric current (6V) to the warming plate produced a temperature difference of 1.5-2.5 degrees centigrade between the two metal plates. The changes in temperature difference caused by the localized increase-decrease of the blood flow were measured and recorded (Hagiwara, et al., 1968). The experiment using the aforesaid thermoelectric effect was conducted to study the effectiveness of the skin-blood flow changes as an index of lie detection test based on the technique developed by Chiba University. Five playing cards were used with thirteen subjects, each requested to select a card and lie about its selection on the test which was conducted twice for each subject. Simultaneous to the recording of skin-blood flow was also recorded the subjects' skin potential response (SPR) and skin resistance response (SRR) for comparison. The results revealed a detection rate by the skin-blood flow was inferior to SPR and was neither superior nor inferior to SRR. (Yamaoka, Suzuki 1973, 1980)

Cat. No. 83500 Barland Chart Overlay

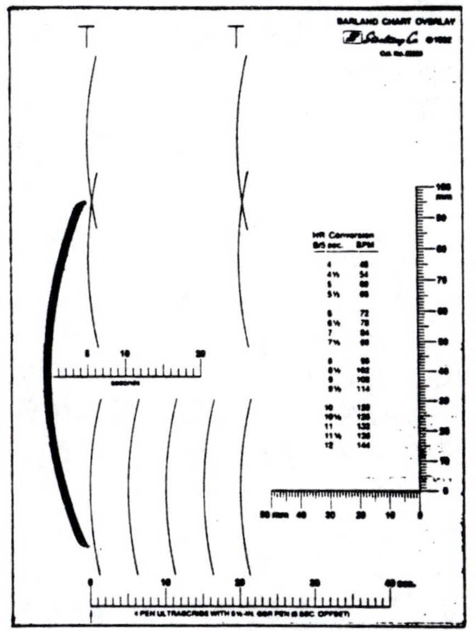

- **Permits Accurate Visual Pulse Rate Calculation**
- **Measures both GSR Latency and Reaction Size**
- **Permits Accurate Pen Position Determination of each Pen at any given Moment in Time**
- **Allows Rapid Measurement of Chart Minutes**

The Model 83500 Barland Chart Overlay is an inexpensive aid for more rapid and accurate chart analysis. The various arcs, scales, and charts facilitate analysis of the entire polygraph chart, i.e., two pneumos, GSR, and cardio.

Primary pen arcs are provided for: thoracic respiration, abdominal respiration, GSR, and cardio. The GSR arc is die cut into the overlay, rather than printed, to provide an unobstructed field of view and to prevent interference with the other arcs. The primary pen arcs show the possible positions of the polygraph pens at any given moment, such as the beginning of a question.

The auxiliary pen arcs (cardio) permit rapid pulse rate determination when used with the heart-rate conversion table. Simply count the pulses between two cardio arcs and look up the conversion on the table to obtain the rate in beats-per-minute.

The two horizontal scales can be used to measure GSR latency. The width of the overlay is precisely 6 inches and can be used to gauge total chart time (1 minute per chart) width). The vertical scale can be used to quickly and accurately measure the amplitude of GSR and cardio reactions. Even event marks are provided to indicate the location of this optional recording pen.

The Chart Overlay is designed to be used with any Stoelting four pen UltraScribe Polygraph (with or without stimulus marker), and the Arther VI polygraph.
Cat. No. 83500 .... $7.50

Figure II-17. Barland Chart Overlay made of clear plastic.

During the period from 1961 to 1966, several government hearings were held on polygraph in the government and in industry. In 1974, hearings were again held by the government, this time by the Subcommittee of the Committee on Government Operations, House of Representatives, chaired by the Honorable William S. Morrhead to investigate *The Use of Polygraphs and Similar Devices by Federal Agencies.* After the testimony from forensic psychophysiologists, scientists, representatives from the federal government, labor and civil liberties unions were heard, the committee members were changed with Bella Abzug as the new chairperson. None of the original committee members who were present at the hearings were involved in the preparation of the final report. Immediately following the Table of Contents of the 790-page report of the SubCommittee of the Committee on Government Operations, House of Representatives, is the testimony of Robert E. Smith of the American Civil Liberties Union Foundation, followed by a 75-page American Civil Liberties Union Report. Transcripts of the hearing sessions provide ample evidence of the biasness in the attitude and treatment of those interviewed by the committee. The committee recommended that all government agencies discontinue the use of polygraph testing. Fortunately, the committee's recommendation was not adopted. But that was not to be the end.

In 1977, hearings were held by the Subcommittee on the Constitution of the Committee on the Judiciary, United States Senate, chaired by the Honorable Birch Bayh, U. S. Senator from the State of Indiana who introduced a bill (S1845) in the senate of the United States "To protect the rights of individuals guaranteed by the Constitution of the United States and to prevent unwarranted invasion of their privacy by prohibiting the use of polygraph type equipment for certain purposes." That bill was defeated but it was not to be the last.

In 1974, this author (Matte) developed "A Technique for Polygraphing the Deaf" as a result of having a client who had an entire department at a gold refining plant manned by deaf persons. Usually the company or agency requesting the PV examination(s) has a person on their staff knowledgeable in the deaf person sign language, especially if there are several deaf persons employed there, to provide essential communication between deaf employees and non-deaf employees. The temptation of the FP to use such a person as an interpreter in the conduct of PV examinations is certainly hard to resist, but great caution must be exercised inasmuch the loyalty of the interpreter may be with the subject, not the company and FP; the interpreter who is also a co-worker of the subject may be an accomplice; the interpreter may yield to an offer of a bribe by the subject with whom he/she is acquainted; the interpreter may yield to blackmail by the subject (co-worker) knowledgeable about the interpreter's own illegal activities at the company; the interpreter may inadvertently make an error in communicating the test question(s) as a result of ineptitude or own misinterpretation. Furthermore, the interpreter so inclined may sabotage the PV examination by not actually conveying the relevant questions; rewording the relevant question(s) (in sign language) so that the examinee's answer(s) will not be a lie to the examinee; by substituting an irrelevant or neutral question for the relevant question(s). The FP not knowledgeable in the sign language for deaf persons would be unable to detect any of the above means of sabotage. The system developed by this author which is fully explained in Chapter 22, involves the use of an assistant who presents each test question typed on separate 3x5 cards to the examinee who is seated in the PV examination chair with both a cardio activity monitor and electrodermal electrodes fastened to one hand while the other hand is free to move the index finger only, onto one of six choices presented on a 3x5 card taped to the surface of the arm rest at the examinee's fingertips. The choices are a plus or minus sign in the color of green, red, and yellow (also written for color blind people). Somewhere inserted into each test question is written the color code, which compels the examinee to read the question in order to choose the right color in which to answer the test question with a plus or minus indicating yes or no to the posed question. It should be noted that the normal procedure of not reviewing the test questions in the same order they are asked on the test, some eliciting an affirmative and some a negative answer, further provides the FP with a means of determining whether the subject read the question by verifying a correct answer was given. This author found that the aforementioned technique removes the possibility of subject countermeasure or interpreter sabotage, and identifies the presence of communication problems at the most critical stage of the PV examination. (Matte 1980)

In 1975, the author (Matte) conducted research to provide forensic psychophysiologists with a means of verifying the effectiveness of control questions, i.e. the probable lie or known-lie question (considered the most critical portion of the test structure) immediately prior to each examination. This research resulted in a polygraph control question validation procedure known as the CQV test which is covered in detail in Chapter 14. The procedure also provides researchers with the methodology to conduct experiments to validate PV examinations using a hybrid model which avoids the non-threatening nature of analog studies while benefiting from its absolute ground truth, yet enjoy the intense emotionality present in field studies, inasmuch as the examinees are criminal suspects, tested about a fictitious crime related to the actual crime for which they reported for the PV examination. Hence, each examination indicative of deception which is verified by a confession, automatically provides the researcher with *confirmed truthful* charts and *confirmed deceptive* charts from a real-life field setting. (Matte 1976)

On 30 August 1976, a research project (funded by a grant from the University of Utah Research Committee; the Biomedical Sciences and Research Support Branch of the National Institute of Health; and the National Institute of Law Enforcement and Criminal Justice, U.S. Department of Justice) was launched under the direction of David C. Raskin, Ph.D. (professor of psychology at the University of Utah, Salt Lake City, Utah), John A. Podlesny, Ph.D. (adjunct professor at the University of Utah), and Gordon H. Barland, Ph.D.) (polygraphist in private practice). The results of this project indicated that polygraph examinations utilizing control-question or guilty-knowledge tests are highly accurate (90% accuracy), but the relevant-irrelevant test possesses many weaknesses and, therefore, should not be used as a substitute for control-question tests. This research also concluded that numerical scoring of polygraph charts produces higher rates of accuracy and reliability of chart interpretation than other methods of chart interpretation. It supported the continued use of breathing pattern, skin conductance (galvanic skin response), and cardiovascular measures (blood pressure) as physiological indices. highlighting the clear superiority both in laboratory experiments and in field situations of the galvanic skin response. Additionally, the research indicated that a properly designed photoelectric plethysmograph would make a useful addition to polygraph instruments. Results of this research also revealed that the electronic, low-pressure cardiograph offered superior performance by reducing subject discomfort and allowing a slower rate of question presentation (20 to 25 seconds between questions) than the mechanical cardiograph, which is a high-pressure system.

However, several scientists in forensic psychophysiology including Cleve Backster and this author believe that the best cardio tracings are obtained at cuff pressures of at least 70 mmHg which in addition to the physiological explanation given above and in Chapter 4, also produce more productive and accurate pneumograph tracings because the cuff pressure elicits the examinee's greater attention. (Backster 1995)

A significant discovery of Raskin, et al's research was the demonstration that longer lasting responses in the galvanic skin response parameter are associated with reactions. It clearly indicates that additional weight may be given to galvanic skin responses, which show a slower recovery towards baseline level. It therefore concluded and recommended that the automatic mode of recording the galvanic skin response be eliminated and only the manual or free-floating mode be used, inasmuch as the automatic mode almost immediately and automatically brings the galvanic skin response pen back to normal baseline, having the effect of eliminating information concerning recovery time. This new data is in direct conflict with earlier research on the galvanic skin response by Richard O. Arther, who recommended that only the automatic mode be used.

In this research the common belief that psychopaths could "beat" the polygraph was dispelled and investigation into the relationship between the variety of personality, biographical and circumstantial factors, and its effect on polygraph results revealed that in the absence of very low intelligence or an incapacitating psychological or physical illness, polygraph examinations are effective with a wide variety of persons with respect to the broad range of crimes typically investigated.

The University of Utah research project disclosed that decisions based on the observation of gestures, verbal behavior, and mannerisms produced more than 50 percent incorrect designations of innocent subjects as deceptive. This is especially meaningful in view of the fact that at least one polygraph school and many polygraphists in the field place great emphasis on behavioral observations to support their chart analysis. These findings clearly indicate that FP's should restrict their basis for decisions to the physiological recordings on the polygraph charts.(For full discussion see Chapter 9).

In 1976, Takeshi Wakamatsu of the Criminology Laboratory, Fukuoka Prefectural Headquarters, Fukuoka City, Japan reported his study on the "Effects of Motivating the Suspect to Deceive the Polygraph Test," using sixty subjects divided into three groups who were tested under a mock crime paradigm, employing an instrument that recorded only the galvanic skin response and heart rate. The first group of subjects received 1000 yen if they could defeat the test, but were punished if they failed. The second group was merely encouraged to deceive the FP, the third group was not given any motivation to deceive. The two groups who were motivated showed significantly greater GSR responses and more instances of increased heart rate during the test than the unmotivated group.(Wakamutsu 1976. 1987). While aforesaid analog research shows increased responsitivity from subjects motivated to deceive, it also reveals an expectation that field studies of real-life cases should produce greater responsitivity from its subjects than those from analog studies using mock crime paradigms.

In 1977, the author (Matte) developed the Polygraph Quadri-Zone Comparison Technique, renamed *Quadri-Track Zone Comparison Technique* in January 1995, which is a modification of Backster's Tri-Zone Comparison Technique, in that it provides a fourth Track or Spot for quantification designed to recoup response energy lost by the other tracks/spots as a result of "*inside issue*" factors which this author identified as "*Fear of Error*" by the Innocent, and "*Hope of Error*" by the Guilty, thus labeled the *Inside Track*, identified in Chapters 9 and 11. Interestingly, Backster in his 1974 testimony at the Hearings before a Subcommittee of the Committee on Government Operations House of Representatives also recognized that there are varieties of fear, stating 'It is extremely important that this problem be overcome by the use of a carefully structured procedure that is designed to allow the examiner to isolate not only "fear" as the emotion involved, but also to distinguish "fear of the detection of deception" from the other varieties of "fear."'(Govt. Hearings 1974). The author further developed a qualitative modification of the conversion table currently used in the numerical scoring system of chart analysis as developed by Cleve Backster on the basis of scientific principle supported by a 1989 validation study (Matte, Reuss 1989).

That same year (1977), this author (Matte) also developed the Suspicion-Knowledge-Guilt (SKG) test to provide the forensic psychophysiologist with a single test capable of identifying the examinee(s) who has major involvement, some direct involvement, or guilty knowledge, yet containing similar controls to that found in the Quadri-Track Zone Comparison Technique. (See Chapter 17). At that time Backster's S-K-Y (Suspicion-Knowledge-You) test did not contain any ealier-in-life control questions. That changed in 1979 with the publication of Backster's (1979) edition of his Standardized Polygraph Notepack and Technique Guide wherein he introduced two earlier-in-life control questions into his S-K-Y test. (Backster, 1996)

In 1986 the Department of Defense Polygraph Institute was established under Department of Defense Directive 5210.78. The foundation for this Institute was inherited from the Polygraph Branch of the U. S. Army Military Police School (USAMPS). The Army Provost Marshal General's School and USAMPS provided a polygraph training program from 1951 to 1986. As a result of this inheritance, the Secretary of the Army was designated the Executive Agent for DoDPI. In September 1991, DoD Directive 5210.78 was revised and the Secretary of the Army executive agency responsibility was eliminated. This change placed authority, direction and control for DoDPI under the Assistant Secretary of Defense for Command, Control, Communications and Intelligence. (DoDPI 1995). Ronald E. Decker who had been Acting Director of DoDPI during the previous year, became the Deputy Director of DoDPI with the appointment of Dr. William J. Yankee as the first Director of the Department of Defense Polygraph Institute. The second and current director of DoDPI is Michael H. Capps. (Decker 1995)

During the period 1986 to 1988, Dr. David C. Raskin and Dr. John C. Kircher developed the first commercial, U. S. made computerized polygraph system (CPS) (Fig. II-18) which was introduced into the market place by the Stoelting Company in 1991.(Miller 1995). Its algorithms developed by Scientific Assessment Technologies were based on thirteen years of research conducted at the University of Utah by Drs Raskin and Kircher. The models were field tested on a grant from the National Institute of Justice, U. S. Department of Justice, using data collected from PV examinations conducted during criminal investigations by an agency of the U. S. Department of the Treasury. The CPS used an A/D Converter System software. Its algorithm analyzes the physiological changes and reports the probability that a subject was truthful or deceptive. The results are based on the traditional physiological parameters: respiration, galvanic skin response/conductance and cardio. In addition, the six-channel CPS displays and records finger pulse (plethysmograph) and countermeasure activity (movement sensor).(Stoelting

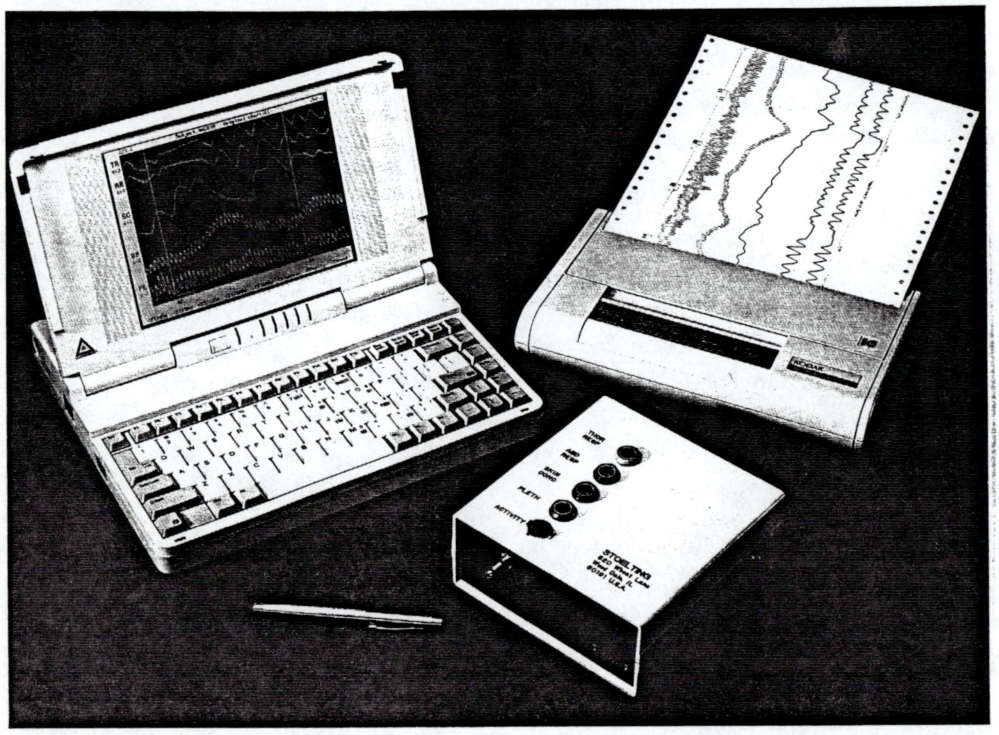

Figure II-18. Stoelting Computerized Polygraph System. Includes 2 respiratory sensors, 1 galvanic skin conductance sensor, 1 cardio cuff, 1 plethysmograph, 1 countermeasure activity monitor.

1995). This CPS was not without its critics who faulted the system for its limited criteria for deception and its combining all control questions into a "super" control question for comparison to the relevant questions. This CPS could be used with any standard control question technique, i.e. Backster, Matte, DoDPI Zone Comparison, MGQT, Reid, Arther, Marcy.

In 1988, Bruce White, a seismic wave theory researcher with a physics background specializing in signal processing and data acquisition system design, developed and introduced the Axciton Computerized Polygraph System with its own A/D converter system and custom hardware/software which was very flexible, user friendly, but at that time had an inadequate algorithm. (Schwartz 1994, White 1995)

In 1988, the Employee Polygraph Protection Act (EPPA), was enacted in the United States (Public Law 100-347 1988, June 27; Federal Register 1991, March 4). No doubt the Office of Technology Assessment (OTA) study played a major role in the near total abolishment of pre-employment and employee screenings using the polygraph in the private sector, with few exceptions. At the same time, employers retained the use of the polygraph to resolved specific losses or injuries but with severe limitations and restrictions which are fully discussed in Chapter 25. The OTA Study is a prime example of what can happen when a Congressional Board of politicians govern a scientific group such as the OTA which owes its existence to that Board. The tragedy of its effects on society is that most of the research and development of polygraph techniques and instrumentation for the advancement of truth verification and lie detection were conducted in the private sector which suffered immense losses of personnel, some of whom would otherwise have been engaged in polygraph research and development. Society is willing to spend billions of dollars in the construction of more prisons, the training and hiring of more guards and more police officers, but nay a penny for the advancement of truth verification which could revolutionize the criminal justice system by requiring its citizenry to tell the truth when under oath or have the lie detected. But societies outside of the United States have picked up the baton in the technological race of truth verification, with fifty-seven countries having some polygraph capability of which eighteen have significant capability in psychophysiological veracity examinations using the polygraph including computerized polygraph systems.

In 1989, this author (Matte) with the assistance of his mentor and faculty advisor Dr. Ronald M. Reuss, completed a three-year field validation study on the Quadri-Zone Comparison Technique, subsequently renamed the Quadri-Track Zone Comparison Technique, using 122 confirmed real-life cases from two separate entities, the files of a Metropolitan Police Department and a Private Polygraph firm. The Quadri-Track's unique Inside Track accurately identified and remedied a major cause (Fear/Hope of Error) of false positives/negatives and inconclusives in specific single-issue tests. The Quadri-Track Zone Comparison Technique correctly identified 91% of the Innocent as Truthful and 9% as Inconclusive, with no errors. It further correctly identified 97% of the Guilty as Deceptive and 3% as inconclusive, with no errors. Inconclusives excluded, the Quadri-Track Zone Comparison Technique was 100% accurate in the identification of the

Innocent and the Guilty. Inconclusives included, the utility rate was 94%. This field study further examined Dr. Martin Orne's *Friendly Polygraphist Concept* that PV examinations conducted for defense attorneys should experience a high rate of false negatives due to a purported lack of fear of detection by the client polygraphed. The data from the scores of verified real-life cases from a police department and a private polygraph firm, both using the Quadri-Track Zone Comparison Technique revealed that from the total number of cases examined in this study (122), 39 were conducted for defense attorneys under attorney-client privilege, and 34 of those were scored deceptive, and subsequently confirmed. Furthermore, defense attorney cases showed a mean chart score of -9.38 compared with police cases which showed a mean chart score of -9.10, which suggest similar states of autonomic arousal. Another group, commercial cases which were not tested under privilege, showed a mean chart score of -9.90, thus there was no statistical difference in the scores obtained from police versus private PV examinations. This field study also examined the relative effectiveness of physiological data in field PV examinations which revealed the most productive of the physiological channels was the pneumograph (43%), followed by the cardio (32%) and the electrodermal (24%). A further breakdown of productivity and accuracy of each channel by gender, guilt and innocence and other combinations of truth and deception were also examined and are reported in Chapter 3. A Predictive Table for estimating error rates was developed from the data of this study for use by FP's and attorneys.(See Chap. 11) (Matte-Reuss 1989, 1990)

In 1989, The Johns Hopkins University's Applied Physics Laboratory (APL) under a series of contracts with Department of Defense agencies, under the direction of Dr. Dale E. Olsen, Project Manager who was assisted by John C. Harris, commenced the

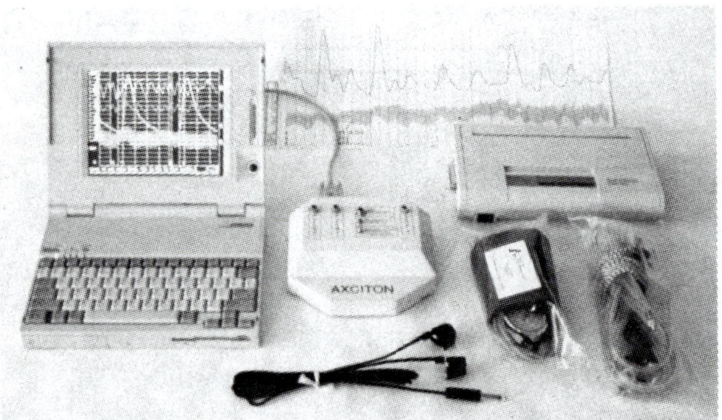

Figure II-19. Axciton Computerized Polygraph System. Includes 2 respiratory sensors, 1 galvanic skin conductance sensor, and 1 cardio cuff. An additional channel can be added for auxiliary sensors such as the plethysmograph, or an activity monitor.

development of a Polygraph Automated Scoring System (Polyscore). At that time, the only computerized data collection system were the CODAS system, the Computerized Polygraph System (CPS), and the Axciton System. The CODAS system, a general-purpose data collection system was not as suitable for standard polygraph tests as the other systems. The CODAS system allowed automatic spectral analysis of the data. These early computerized polygraph systems stored only twenty-five seconds of data for each question and did not store pulse information. However this system included the first true automated scoring system. (Kircher,1983; Kircher & Raskin, 1988, Olsen & Harris 1995).

The Axciton Computerized Polygraph, Inc., located at Houston, Texas was selected by APL at the Johns Hopkins University for data collection because it was the only computerized data collection system available at the time which met all of their requirements (Fig. II-19). It contained a system for the rank order scoring of the responses, but the scoring system did not produce a probability of deception. Axciton systems were purchased and placed with two federal, two state, and two county law-enforcement agencies and one city agency located in the eastern United States. These agencies were selected because their forensic psychophysiologists had been trained at the Department of Defense Polygraph Institute in the use of the Zone Comparison technique. The sample of cases represented a reasonable mix of law enforcement cases including

Figure II-20. Lafayette LX2000-305 Computerized Polygraph System. This system consists of 2 respiratory sensors, 1 galvanic skin conductance, 1 cardio cuff, and an auxiliary channel for use of a plethysmograph or movement/activity sensor.

murder, larceny, witness statement verification, forgery, arson, assault, bribery, child molestation, incest, patient abuse, kidnapping and drug violations. The algorithm was developed specifically for the Zone Comparison technique test question sequence which included a sacrifice/preparatory relevant question, two symptomatic questions, three earlier-in-life control questions and three relevant questions. By 31 March 1991, APL had received data from 857 cases, but not all of these cases were used because in 37% of the cases, two or more FP's called the charts inconclusive. PolyScore version 2.3 was developed with 539 usable cases and of these 270 were nondeceptive cases and 269 were deceptive cases, and the number of polygraph charts averaged three charts per subject. Version 3.0 used a confirmed sample of 218 cases with an accuracy of over 98%. In 1993, the Lafayette Instrument Company implemented APL's PolyScore in its new computerized data collection system (Fig. II-20) after APL analyzed its signals and developed data transformation software to account for differences between the two collection systems. APL continues its work to improve its algorithm for the Zone Comparison and other question sequences.(Olsen & Harris 1995).

In 1993, the Ministry of Internal Affairs of Russia opened a polygraph institute in Moscow for the training of forensic psychophysiologists to provide the methodology necessary in the use of its technology recently developed by two soviet companies in the manufacturing of the Inex and the Avex computerized polygraph systems. (Barland 1994)

In early 1995, forensic psychophysiology using the polygraph was first introduced in Malaysia with the purchase of a Lafayette LX2000W computerized polygraph system by the Royal Malaysian Police (RMP), to be used in the Criminal Investigation Department (CID) for specific testing of criminal cases in the National Police Force. In April 1995, an officer was sent for basic training in forensic psychophysiology at the Maryland Institute of Criminal Justice, with the possibility of more officers receiving similar training. (Kiang 1996).

In August 1995, this author, assisted by Dr. Ronald M. Reuss, presented a thesis at the 30th Annual Seminar/Workshop of the American Polygraph Association, Las Vegas, Nevada. This thesis identified forty-five variables separated into four psychophysiological categories (See Chap. 9), which have the capability to adversely affect the physiological responses to the critical questions recorded on the polygraph charts which are used to arrive at a determination of truth or deception. It demonstrates how those relevant variables can be effectively controlled and/or factored into the examination process with the utilization of the Zone Comparison Test such as the Matte Quadri-Track Zone Comparison Technique or the Backster Tri-Zone Comparison Technique which employ a numerical scoring system of chart analysis, hence is called the Numerical Approach, and further demonstrates the validity and reliability of results based solely upon the numerical scores acquired from the physiological data recorded on the polygraph charts. This thesis argues against the use of the Clinical Approach which augments its visual inspection or quantification of the polygraph charts with an evaluation of the examinee's verbal and non-verbal behavior and other auxiliary information to reach a conclusion of truth or deception, which is also known as Global Evaluation. A strong case is made for unification of the methodology used by forensic psychophysiologists under the model of the Numerical Approach which excludes all non-polygraphic data from its decision making process, hence superior in objectivity.

With the recent advent of computerized polygraph systems, both in the United States and abroad, data collection will broaden and be more readily and objectively analyzed. Conventional polygraph instruments with their limited number of channels due to the recording of pen on paper graph, are being replaced by computerized polygraph systems which fulfill the critical need for objectivity and allow the exploration and use of many more sensors which must be analyzed by computers. Various computer algorithms are being developed for the Modified General Question Test (MGQT), Test for Espionage and Sabotage (TES-CI), Test Format for Criminal Testing (TES-C), Relevant/Irrelevant (Screening) (R/I), Event Related Controls (ERC), and Countermeasures (CM). However, it must be remembered that the validity of the physiological data from which the computer derives its statistical conclusions is entirely dependent on the methodology used by the forensic psychophysiologist in the psychological preparation of the examinee, the scientific formulation of the various types of test questions within a validated test format, administered in an objective, unbiased manner, which should be verified by video recording.

The present state of computerized polygraph systems has not yet displaced the conventional electronic polygraph instrument because not all of the traditional, verified criteria for deception have been factored into current computer algorithms, although the computerized algorithm does use criteria not available to the field FP, including the statistical probability feature of PolyScore (See Chap. 15). However, since traditional analysis and numerical scoring of the physiological data is permitted from the recorded display on computerized polygraph systems, the need for conventional polygraph systems will soon expire. Truly, forensic psychophysiology has embraced the technology of the twenty-first century with endless possibilities. Law enforcement agencies are reaping its benefits. The courts cannot be far behind.

There are no doubt many persons not mentioned in this chapter whose scientific research nevertheless made it possible for forensic psychophysiology to attain its present status within the scientific community as a valid means of determining truth and deception. No one person invented a so-called lie-detector. As evidenced by this chapter, scientific truth verification and lie-detection involves a marriage of physiology and psychology dating back several centuries, encompassing the work of many pioneers whose zeal and vision is to be admired and respected, for they formed the evolutionary chain of discoveries and developments responsible for the present status of forensic psychophysiology.

REFERENCES

Abrams, S. (1996, January 25). Telephone conversation with J. A. Matte.

Abrams, S., Davidson, M. (1988). Countermeasures in polygraph testing. *Polygraph*, 17(1), 16-20.

Addison, M. E. (1982, May 9, 11). Letters from Dept. of the Navy's Special Assistant for Scientific Investigations to J. A. Matte.

Ansley, N. (1988). Historical Note: Vittorio Benussi and research. *Polygraph*, 17(3), 121-122.

Ansley, N. (1992). The History and Accuracy of Guilty Knowledge and Peak of Tension Tests. *Polygraph*, 21(3): 174-247.

Ansley, N. (1990). Historical Notes: Abstracts of Early Research. *Polygraph*, 19(3), 227-228.

Ansley, N. (1990). The validity and reliability of polygraph decisions in real cases. *Polygraph*, 19(3), 169-181.

Ansley, N. (1995, May 15). Historical Note dated 21 Dec 87 relating to telephone conversation between Norman Ansley and Mary A. Harrelson of Keeler, Inc., on 16 Dec 87, forwarded to J. A. Matte.

Ansley, N. (1995, May 15). Historical Note dated 23 Jun 87 relating notes Ansley made in 1952 re: Russell Chatham, Inc. Oak Ridge, TN, forwarded to J. A. Matte.

Ansley, N. (1989). Feel the Pulse: Defoe's 1730 Proposal. *Polygraph*, 18(2): 122.

Ansley, N. (1992). Historical Note: Mackenzie's early polygraph instrument. *Polygraph*, 21(4): 349-351.

Ansley, N. (1995, May 10, 28). Telephone conversation with J. A. Matte.

Ansley, N. (1995, November 20). Handwritten memo on copy of title page of Leon G.Turrou's *Nazi Spies in America*, published by Random House, New York, to J. A. Matte.

Ansley, N. (1995, December 4). Handwritten note regarding Associated Research model 305 polygraph instrument, to J. A. Matte.

Ansley, N. (1992). Historical Note: A. R. Luria: Motor reactions and lie detection in the 1920s. *Polygraph*, 21(1). 80-81.

Ansley, N. (1990). *Polygraph and the Law* (three volumes). Severna Park, MD: JKP Publishing.

Ansley, N. (1995, Nov-Dec.) Notes and Comments - The Editor's Column. *Newsletter*, American Polygraph Association, 28(6), 18-20.

Ansley, N., Horvath, F., Barland, G. H. (1992). *Truth and Science* (3rd ed., rev.). Severna Park, MD: American Polygraph Association.

Ansley, N., Pumphrey, J. K. (Comp.) (1994). Special Issue: Leonarde Keeler. *Polygraph*, 23(2), 118-188.

Ansley, N., Ferguson, R. M. (1987). Pioneers in the Polygraph: The federal Bureau of Investigation in the 1930's. *Polygraph*, 16(1): 33-52.

Arther, R. O. (1970). Peak of tension: Question formulation. *Journal of Polygraph Studies*, 4(5), 1-4

Arther, R. O. (1971). The GSR unit. *Journal of Polygraph Studies*, 5(6), 1-4

Arther, R. O. (1986). Updating Arther's infamous golden rules. *The Journal of Polygraph Science*. 20(6), 1-4.

Backster, C. (1963/1979). Standardized Polygraph Notepack and Technique Guide: Backster Zone Comparison Technique. *Backster School of Lie Detection*, New York, N. Y.

Backster, C. (1963). Total Chart Minutes Concept. *Law and Order*, 11(10), 77-79.

Backster, C. (1974). Anticlimax Dampening Concept. *Polygraph*, 3(1), 48-50.

Backster C. (1969). Technique fundamentals of the Tri-Zone Polygraph Test. New York: *Backster Research Foundation.*

Backster, C. (1995, May 20). Facsimile with J. A. Matte

Backster, C. (1995, May 22). Telephone conversation with J. A. Matte.

Backster, C. (1995, October 22). Telephone conversation with J. A. Matte.

Backster, C. (1996, March 13). Telephone conversation with J. A. Matte.

Baesen, H. V., Chung, C-M., Yang, C-Y. (1948). A lie detection experiment. *Journal of Criminal Law and Criminology*. 39: 532-537.

Bailey, F. L., Rothblatt, H. B. (1970). *Investigation and Preparation of Criminal Cases, Federal and State*. Rochester, N.Y. The Lawyers Co-operative Publishing Co.

Balloun, K. D., Holmes, D. S. (1979). Effects of repeated examinations on the ability to detect guilt with a real polygraphic examination: A laboratory experience with real crime. *Journal of Applied Psychology*, 64(34), 316-322.

Barland, G. H. (1995, May 17). Telephone conversation with J. A. Matte.

Barland, G. H., Raskin, D. C. (1972). An experimental study of field techniques in "lie detection." *Polygraph*, 1(1), 22-26.

Barland, G. H. (1981, May). *A validity and reliability study of counterintelligence screening tests*. Unpublished manuscript, Security Support Battalion, 902nd Military Intelligence Group, Ft. George G. Meade, MD.

Barland, G. H. (1984, June 1-2). *The Cardio Channel: A Primer*. Paper presented at the Florida Polygraph Association Seminar.

Barland, G. H. (1988). The polygraph test in the USA and elsewhere, in A. Gale (Ed). *The Polygraph Test: Lies, Truth and Science*. London: Sage Publications. 73-95.

Barland, G. H. (1995, Dec 26). Telephone conversation with J. A. Matte.

Barland, G. H. (1994). Report of the International Liaison Committee. *APA Newsletter*, 27(4): 31-33.

Barland, G. H. (1996, March 12). Telephone conversation with J. A. Matte.

Bartlett, S. K. (1995, December 20). Letter of reply regarding the Utah Zone Comparison Technique, to J. A. Matte.

Benussi, V. (1914). Die Atmung symtome der luge. Archiv Fuer Die Gesampte Psychologie. 31 244-273 (Tr. and reprinted, 1975). The respiratory symptoms of lying. Polygraph, 4(1), 52-76.

Bradley, M. T., Cullen, M. E., Carle, S. B. (1996). Control question tests by police and polygaph operators on a mock crime and real events. *Polygaph*, 25(1)1-___(in press).

Brenner, M., Branscomb, H. H. (1978). Testimony at hearings before the Sub-Committee *on the Constitution of the Committee on the Judiciary, United States Senate, Ninety-Fifth Congress*, first and second sessions on S.1845.449-460.

Brenner, M., Branscomb, H. H. (1979). The psychological stress evaluator; technical limitations affecting lie detection. *Polygraph*, 8(2), 127-132.

Brisentine, R. A. (1974). Polygraph Research in the U. S. Army. *Polygraph*, 3(1), 66-80.

Burack, B. (1955). A critical analysis of the theory, method, and limitations of the 'lie detector.' *Journal of Criminal Law, Criminology and Police Science*, 46, 414-426.

Bu, Wang (1995. June 20). The 90's will be a decade when polygraph technology will start to soar in China. Unpublished paper in Chinese sent to Dr. Gordon H. Barland, Research Division, Department of Defense Polygraph Institute. Translated in English (9 pages) on 12 February 1995)

Capps, M. H. (1994, Sep 12, 16). Telephone conversation with J. A. Matte.

Capps, M. H. (1996, September 11). *Voice Stress Analysis Position Statement*. Department of Defense Polygraph Institute, Fort McClellan, AL.

Cestaro, V. L. (1996a). A test of the computer voice stress analyzer (CVSA) theory of operation. *Polygraph*, 25(2), 101-116.

Cestaro, V. L. (1996b). A comparison between decision accuracy rates obtained using the polygraph instrument and the computer voice stress analyzer (CVSA) in the absence of jeopardy. *Polygraph*, 25(2), 117-127.

Coffey, E. P. (1936, April 10). Memorandum for Mr. Edwards "Re: Visit to C. H. Stoelting Company.

Cohen, V. H. (1976). The polygraph and research in Israel. *Polygraph*, 5(3), 235-243.

Cohen, J. A. (1961, Sep-Oct). Integrated Control-Question Technique. *Police*: 56-58.

Coman, A. (1995, November 24). 10-page letter to J. A. Matte.

Cooke, D. O. (1974). *Prepared statement by the Deputy Assistant Secretary, Office of the Comptroller, Department of Defense, to the Chairman, House of Representatives, Foreign Operations and Government Information Subcommittee of the Committee on Government Operations*, Wash. D.C., Ninety-Third Congress, Second Session, 423-429.

Cross, A. J. (1986, Oct. 28). Letter from the Stoelting Company to J. A. Matte.

Decker, R.E., Stein, A.E., and Ansley, N. (1972). A cardio activity monitor. *Polygraph*. 1{3):108-124.

Decker, R. E., Pochay, M. (1985). Polygraph History. Unpublished manuscript.

Decker, R. E. (1995, November 21). Telephone conversation with J. A. Matte.

Decker, R. E. (1996, February 23). Telephone conversation with J. A. Matte.

Department of Defense (1984). *The Accuracy and Utility of Polygraph Testing*. An analysis of the scientific literature on the accuracy of the polygraph. DOD Publication.

Department of Defense Polygraph Institute (1995). History and schedule of courses April - September 1995. DoDPI, Fort McClellan, AL.

Diaz, R. (1985). *The effects of pre-experimental expectancy, opinion, and demonstration of accuracy on the physiological detection of information.* Doctoral dissertation, Bowling Green State University.

Department of Defense (1995). General Question Technique (GQT). Department of Defense Polygraph Institute. 42 page outline.

Driscoll, L. N., Honts, C. R., Jones D. (1987). The validity of the positive control physiological detection of deception technique. *Polygraph*, 16(3), 218-225.

Dufek, M., Widacki, J., Valkova, V. (1975). Experimental studies of the use of the polygraph for a house search. *Archiv Med. Sad. I Krym.*, 25(2), 163-166.

Eisenschiml, O. (1940). *In the Shadow of Lincoln's Death*. Wilfred Funk, Inc., New York, NY.

Elaad, E., Ben-Shakhar, G. (1989). Effects of motivation and verbal response type on psychophysiological detection of deception. *Psychophysiology*, 26(4), 422-451

Ellson, D. G. (1952). *A report on research on detection of deception*; Office of Naval Research Contract No. N6-ONR-18011. Lafayette, IN: Indiana University.

Federal Register (1991, March 4). Application of the Employee Polygraph Protection Act of 1988; Final Rule. Part II Department of Labor, Employment Standards Administration, Wage and Hour Division. 29 CFR Part 801.

Ferguson. R.J. and Miller. A.L.; *The Polygraph in Court.* Springfield, Thomas, 1973.

Floyd, W. M. (1987). Comparison of standard 'yes/no' response and 'keyword' response in a counterintelligence-suitability polygraph examination. *Polygraph*, 16(2), 97-105.

Forman, R. F., McCauley, C. (1987). Validity of the positive control polygraph test using the field practice model. *Polygraph*, 16(2), 145-160.

Fukumoto, J. (1982). Psychophysiological detection of deception in Japan: The past and the present. *Polygraph*, 11(3), 234-239.

Furedy, J. J., Davis, C., Gurevich, M. (1988). Differentiation of deception as a psychophysiological process: A psychophysiological approach. *Psychophysiology*, 25(6), 683-688.

Fuse, L. S. (1982). Directed lie control testing (DLCQ) technique. Unpublished manuscript.

Geldreich, E. W. (1941). Studies of the galvanic skin response as a deception indicator. *Transactions of the Kansas Academy of Science*, 44, 346-351.

Geldreich, E. W. (1942). Further studies of the use of the galvanic skin response as a deception indicator. *Transactions of the Kansas Academy of Science* 45, 279-284.

Gibbons, J. F. (1983, Nov. 1). Letter of Reply to Dr. Frank Horvath's letter of 24 Oct 83.

Gordon, N. (1995, May 17). Letter of reply to J. A. Matte's letter of 26 Apr 95.

Gordon, N. J. & Cochetti, P. M. (1987). The horizontal scoring system. Polygraph, 16(2), 116-125.

Government Hearings (1974). *The Use of Polygraphs and Similar Devices by Federal Agencies*. Hearings before a Subcommittee of the Committee on Government Operations House of Representatives, Ninety-Third Congress, Second Session. Wash. D. C.

Gudjonsson, G. H. (1977). *The efficacy of the galvanic skin response in experimental lie detection: Some personality variables*. Unpublished Master of Science Thesis, University of Surrey.

Gustafson, L. A., Orne, M. T. (1965). The effects of verbal response on the laboratory detection of deception. *Psychophysiology*, 2(1), 10-13.

Hagiwara, Y., Hakuno, N.(1968). Measurement of blood flow by means of thermoelectro effect (3): Psychophysiological study on emotion. *Medical Journal of Chiba University*, 44, 250-255. (Text in Japanese).

Heindl, V. (1944). Archiv fur Kriminologie 114, 100-101. (Translated by Barland, G. H. and published, June 1979). A device for reavealing lies during questioning. *Polygraph*, 8(2), 173-175.

Herbold-Wooten, H. (1982). The German tatbestandsdiagnostik; A historical review of the beginnings of scientific lie detection in Germany. *Polygraph*, 11(3). 246-257.

Herbold-Wootten, H. (1995, May 19). Fax reply to J. A. Matte.

Herbold-Wootten, H. (1989). More About Vittorio Benussi. *Polygraph*, 18(1). 42-45.

Honts, C. R. (1996, February 9). Letter of reply to letter of inquiry from J. A. Matte dated 13 January 1996.

Honts, C. R., Raskin, D. C. (1988). A field study of the validity of the directed lie control question. *Journal of Police Science and Administration*, 16: 56-61.

Honts, C. R., Devitt, M. K., Winbush, M., Kircher, J. C. (1996). Mental and physical countermeasures reduce the accuracy of the concealed knowledge test. *Psychophysiology*, 33(1), 84-92.

Horneman, C., O'Gorman, J. G. (1985). Detectability in the card test as a function of the subject's verbal response. *Psychophysiology*, 22(3), 330-333. Reprinted in *Polygraph*, 15(4), 264-271.

Horowitz, S. W. (1989, March). The role of control questions in physiological detection of deception. Doctoral dissertation, Department of Psychology, University of Utah.

Horvath, F. (1979). An experimental comparison of the psychological stress evaluator and the galvanic skin response in detection of deception. *Polygraph*, 8(2), 133-143.

Horvath, F. (1982). Detecting deception: The promise and the reality of Voice Stress Analysis. *Polygraph*, 11(4), 304-318.

Inbau, F. E. (1942). *Lie Detection and Criminal Interrogation*. Baltimore: Williams & Wilkins.

Inbau, F. E. (1948). *Lie Detection and Criminal Interrogation*, 2nd ed. Baltimore: Williams & Wilkins.

Inbau, F. E., Reid, J. E. *Lie Detection and Criminal Interrogation*, 3rd ed. Baltimore: Williams & Wilkins.

Janisse, M. P., Bradley, M. T. (1980). Deception information and the pupillary response. *Perceptual and Motor Skills*, 20, 748-750.

Jaycox, T. H. (1937, June). Lie detection useful only in expert hands. *Scientific American*.

Jung, C. G. (1910). The association method. *American Journal of Psychology*, 21, 219-240

Jung, C. G. (1905). Die psychologische diagnose des tatbestandes. *Schweizerische Zeitschrift fur Strafrecht.* 18, 368-408.

Jung, C. G. (1919). *Studies in Word Association*. New York: Moffat, Yard & Company.

Keeler, L. (1930). Deception tests and the lie detector. *International Association for Identification Proceedings*, 16, 186-193.

Keeler, L. (1933). Scientific methods of crime detection with polygraph. *Kansas Bar Association Journal.* 12, 22-31.

Keeler, L. (1936). Some modern trends in the detection of crime. Part I. *The Claim Investigator*, 6(8), 57-58, 62. Part II. *The Claim Investigator*, 6(9), 65.

Keeler, L. (1938). The detection of deception. In L. Keeler, C.W. Muelberger, L.M. Wilson, F.E. Inbau, K.Keeler, & M. E. O'Neill. *Outline of Scientific Criminal Investigation*. Chicago: Scientific Crime Detection Laboratory, Northwestern University School of Law. Ann Arbor, Michigan: Edwards Brothers, Inc. Reprinted in *Polygraph* (1976) 5(4), 293-302.

Kiang, L. E. (1996). Polygraph testing procedure in Malaysia. *Polygraph*, 25(1), 59-72.

Kircher, J. C. (1983). *Computerized decision-making and patterns of activation in the detection of deception.* A dissertation submitted to the faculty of the University of Utah in partial fulfillment of the requirements for the degree of Doctor of Philosophy.

Kircher, J. C., Raskin, D. C. (1988). Human versus computerized evaluations of polygraph data in a laboratory setting. *Journal of Applied Psychology*. 73, 291-302.

Kirwan, W. E. (1952, October 16). Letter to Norman Ansley, Executive Secretary, Board of Polygraph Examiners, Wash. D.C.

Kubis, J. F. (1962). *Studies In Lie Detection: Computer Feasibility Considerations*. Fordham University, New York, N. Y. RADC-TR-62-205. Project No. 5534, AF

30(602)-2270, prepared for Rome Air Development Center, Air Force Systems Command, USAF, Griffiss AFB, New York.

Kubis, J. F. (1974). Comparison of voice analysis and polygraph as lie detection procedures. *Polygraph*, 3(1), 1-47.

Kugelmass, S.,Lieblich, I., Bergman, Z. (1967). The role of 'lying' in psychophysiological detection. *Psychophysiology*, 3(3), 312-325.

Larson, J. A. (1932). *Lying and its Detection*. Chicago: University of Chicago Press. (Reprinted by Patterson Smith, 1969).

Larson, J. A. (1923). The cardio-pneumo-psychogram in deception. *Journal of Experimental Psychology*, 6(6), 420-454.

Lee, C. D. (1953). *The Instrumental Detection of Deception - The Lie Test*. Police Science Series, Charles C. Thomas - Publisher, Springfield, IL.

Lippold, O. (1971). Physiological tremor. *Scientific American*, 224, 65-73.

Lombroso, C. (1911). *Crime: Its Causes and Remedies*. Little, Brown & Company, Boston, MA.

Lowenstein, O. (1920). Uber den Nachweis psychischer Vorgange und die Suggestibilitat fur Gefuhlszustande im Stupor. *Zeitschrift fur die gesamte Neurologie uond Psychiatrie*, 61, 304-350.

Lowenstein, O. (1921). Uber die Bedeutung der unbewubten Audsttucksbewegungen. *Die Naturwissenschagten*, 403-.

Lowenstein, O. (1922). Uber subjektive Tatbestandmassigkeit und Zurechnunnngsnfahigkeit nebst kritischen Bemerkungen zur psychologischen Tatbestands-diagnostik. *Archiv fur Psychiatrie*, 65, 411-458.

Luria, A. R. (1932). *The nature of human conflicts: Or emotion, conflict and will.* New York: Liveright.

Luria, A. R. (1979). *The making of the mind: A personal account of Soviet psychology*. Cambridge, Harvard University Press.

Lykken, David T. (1959). The GSR in the detection of guilt. Journal of Applied Psychology, 43(6), 383-388. Reprinted in Polygraph, 7(2), 123-128.

Lykken, David T. (1960). The validity of the guilty knowledge technique: The effect of faking. Journal of Applied Psychology, 44(4), 258-262. Reprinted in Polygraph, 7(1), 42-48.

Lykken, D. T. (1978). Testimony. Hearings Before the Subcommittee on the Constitution, U. S. Senate on S1845. Polygraph Control and Civil Liberties Protection Act. U. S. Government Printing Office, pp. 8-33.

Lykken, D. T. (1981). *A Tremor in the Blood: Uses and Abuses of the Lie Detector*. New York: McGraw-Hill.

Lykken, David T. (1992, Jan 8). Letter to Norman Ansley, Editor in Chief of APA Publications.

Lynch, B. E., Henry, D. R. (1979). A validity study of the Psychological Stress Evaluator. *Canadian Journal of Behavioural Science*, 11, 89-94.

Lynch, B. E., Henry, D. R. (1980). A validity study of the Psychological Stress Evaluator. *Polygraph*, 9(1), 49-54.

MacKenzie, J. (1908). The ink polygraph. *British Medical Journal*, 1, 1411.

Maric, S. (1995, April 9). *History of Polygraph in Croatia*; with cover letter from Ministry of the Interior, Criminal Police Sector, Centre for Criminal Forensics, to James Allan Matte, Ph.D., President, Matte Polygraph Service, Inc., Williamsville, N. Y. 12 pages.

Marston, W. M. (1938, October 8). "New Facts About Shaving Revealed by Lie Detector!" *The Saturday Evening Post*.

Matte, J. A. (1976). A polygraph control question validation procedure. *Polygraph*, 5(2), 170-177.

Matte, J. A. (1980). *The Art and Science of the Polygraph Technique*. Springfield, Illinois: Charles C. Thomas.

Matte, J. A. (1980). A technique for polygraphing the deaf. *Polygraph*, 9(3), 148-153.

Matte, J. A. (1991). A countermeasure that failed. *APA Newsletter*, 24(4), 14-15.

Matte, J. A., Reuss, R. M. (1989). Validation study on the Quadri-Zone Comparison Technique. *Research Abstract*, LD 01452, Vol 1502, 1989, University Microfilm International.

Matte, J. A., Reuss, R. M. (1989). A field validation study of the Quadri-Zone Comparison Technique. *Polygraph*, 18(4), 187-202.

Matte, J. A., Reuss, R. M. (1990). A field study of the 'Friendly Polygraphist' concept. *Polygraph*, 19(1), 1-9.

Miller, L. A. (1995, July 14). Letter from Chairman and CEO of Stoelting Company to J. A. Matte.

Minor, P. K. (1989). The Relevant-Irrelevant Technique. Chap 10. *The Complete Polygraph Handbook*, Abrams, S. 1989, Lexinton Books, Lexington, MA.

Minor, P. K. (1995, December 14). Telephone Conversation with J. A. Matte.

Minor, P. K. (1995, December 14). Facsimile regarding the Relevant-Irrelevant Technique. 10 Pages. to J. A. Matte.

Munsterberg, H. (1907). On The Witness Stand. S. S. McClure Company, Republished by Bobbs-Merril in 1908 and Doubleday, Page & company in 1912/

Munsterberg, H. (1908). *On the Witness Stand. Essays on Psychology and Crime*. New York: Doubleday & Co.

Munsterberg, H. (1933). *On the Witness Stand.* (2d Ed.) New York: Doubleday & Co. 118-133.

Office of Technology Assessment (OTA) (1983). *Scientific Validity of Polygraph Testing - A Research Review and Evaluation*. Technical Memorandum for the Congressional Board of the 98th Congress of the United States, OTA-TM-H-15.

Office of Technology Assessment (OTA) (1972). *What OTA is; What OTA does; How OTA works.* Booklet, Congress of the United States, OTA, Wash. D.C.

Ohkawa, H. (1963). Comparison of physiological response of 'yes,' 'no,' and 'mute' conditions in peak of tension tests. *Reports of the National Institute of Police Science*, 21, 1-4.

Olsen, D. E., Harris, J. C., Capps, M. H., Johnson, G. J., Ansley, N. (1995). *Computerized Polygraph Scoring System*. Final draft provided by Dr. Olsen of The Johns Hopkins University, Applied Physics Laboratory to J. A. Matte in May 1995.

Park, P. K. (1996, March 2). Letter regarding history of polygraph in Korea to J. A. Matte.

Patrick, C. J., Iacono, W. G. (1987). Validity and reliability of the control question polygraph test: A scientific investigation. *Psychophysiology*, 24, 604-605 (abstract).

Peters, R. (1980). Comparison of Psychological Stress Evaluator to Polygraph in evaluating truth or deception in criminal cases: A pilot study. *Polygraph*, 9(2), 109-113.

Peterson, F. (1907). The Galvanometer as a Measurer of Emotions. *British Medical Journal* 2:804-806.

Peterson, F., Jung, C. G. (1907). Psychophysical Investigations with the Galvanometer and Pneumograph in Normal and Insane Individuals. *Brain* 30:153-218.

Pretorius, C. (1995, November 1). Facsimile from The Polygraph Institute of South Africa, 4 pages, in reply to Letter dated 27 June 1995 and Facsimile dated 1 November 1995 from J. A. Matte.

Pretorius, C. (1995, November 4). Facsimile from The Polygraph Institute of South Africa, 4 pages, to J. A. Matte.

Public Law 100-347. (1988, June 27). Employee Polygraph Protection Act of 1988. U. S. Government Printing Office: 1988 292-109/94912.

Raskin, D. C., Barland, G. H., Podlesny, J. A. (1976, Aug 30). *Validity and reliability of detection of deception*. Final Report, contract 75-NI-990001, National Institute of Law Enforcement and Criminal Justice, Law Enforcement Assistance Administration, U. S. Department of Justice and Department of Psychology, University of Utah, Salt Lake City, Utah.

Raskin, D. C., Barland, G. H., Podlesny, J. A. (1978). *Validity and Reliability of Detection of Deception*. National Institute of Law Enforcement and Criminal Justice, Law Enforcement Assistance Administration, U. S. Department of Justice.

Reid, J. E. (May 1946-April 1947). A revised questioning technique in lie detection tests. *Journal of Criminal Law and Criminology*. 37(6), 542-547.

Reid, J. E., Inbau, F. E. (1966). *Truth and Deception: The Polygraph ("Lie Detector") Technique*. Baltimore: Williams & Wilkins.

Reid, J. E., Inbau, F. E. (1977). *Truth and Deception: The Polygraph ("Lie Detector") Technique*, 2d ed. Baltimore: Williams & Wilkins.

Ruckmick, C. A. (1936). *The Psychology of Feeling and Emotion*. New York: McGraw-Hill. 345-373.

Ruckmick, C. A. (1938). The truth about the lie detector. *Journal of Applied Psychology*, 22(1), 164-167.

Saxe, L., Schmitz, M. & Zaichkowsky, L. (1986). *Polygraph examinations as placebos: A test of the fallibility of lie detection*. Unpublished manuscript.

Schwartz, J. R. (1994). Preparing today for our profession tomorrow: Computerized Polygraph History. Written presentation at the American Polygraph Association's 29th Annual seminar and workshop, Nashville, TN.

Scott-Kilvert, I. General Editor (1965). *British Writers, Daniel DeFoe to the Gothic Novel.* Vol III, Charles Scribner's Sons, N.Y.

Stevens, V. (1994). Biography of Leonarde Keeler. *Polygraph*, 23(2), 118-126.

Stevenson, M., Barry, G. (1988). Use of a motion chair in the detection of physical countermeasures. *Polygraph*, 17(1), 21-27

Stoelting (1995). CPS - Computerized Polygraph System. Advertising brochure, Stoelting Company, Wood Dale, Illinois.

Stone, R. B. (1989). *The Secret Life of Your Cells*. Whitford Press, A division of Schiffer Publishing, Ltd, Atglen, PA.

Summers, W. G. (1936) A recording psychogalvanometer. Bulletin of the *American Association of Jesuit Scientists*, 14(2): 50-56. Reprinted with permission of Loyola College in *Polygraph*, 13(4): 340-346. December 1984.

Summers, W. G. (1937). A new psychogalvanometric technique in criminal investigation. *Psychological Bulletin*, 34, 551-552.

Summers, W. G. (1939). Science can get the confession. *Fordham Law Review*. 8: 334-354.

Suzuki, A., Watanabe, S., Taheno, Y. Kosugi, T., Kasuya, T. (1979). Possibility of detection deception by voice analysis. *Polygraph*, 8(4), 318-324.

Suzuki, A., Hikita, Y. (1964). An analysis of responses on polygraph: A diminution of responses. *Reports of the National Institute of Police Science*. 17, 290-295. (Text in Japanese)

Suzuki, A., Hikita, Y. (1981). An analysis of responses on polygraph: A diminution of responses. *Polygraph*, 10(1), 1-7 (Text in English).

Suzuki, A., Yatsuda, J. (1965). Case study of silent answer of murder suspect in polygraph test. Research Materials No. 35, *Polygraph Reports*, pp. 17-29, National Institute of Police Science.

Suzuki, A. (1977). A survey of factors affecting the polygraph examination in Japan. *Polygraph*, 6(3), 218-233.

Suzuki, A. (1989, Aug 22). Letter to J. A. Matte.

Tatbestandsdiagnostik. *Archiv fur Psychiatrie*, 65, 411-458.

Toth, P. A., Whalen, M. P. (Eds.) (1987). *Investigation and Prosecution of Child Abuse.* National Center for the Prosecution of Child Abuse, 1033 N. Fairfax Street, Suite 200, Alexandria, VA.

Trovillo. Paul Y.: A history of lie detection. *Journal of Criminal Law, Criminology and Police Science,29:*848-881. March-April 1939 30:104-119, & May-Jun 1939. Reprinted in *Polygraph* (1972) 1(2), 46-74, and 1(3), 151-160.

Veraguth. S. (1907). *Das Psychogalvanische Reflexphanomen*, I. Bericht, Monatsschrift Fur Psych. und Neurol, Bd. XXI, Heft 5. See also his *Der Psychophysische Galvanische Reflex*. Bericht uber den, II. Kongress fur Experimentelle Psychologie. 219-224.

Wakamatsu, T. (1976). Effects of motivating the suspect to deceive the polygraph test. *Reports of the National Research Institute of Police Science*, 29 (2).(Text in Japanese). (Tr. and reprinted, 1987). *Polygraph*, 16(2), 129-144.

White, B. (1995, Oct 13). Telephone conversation with J. A. Matte.

Wideman, W. (1935, July 18). Letter to the Department of Justice, from the C. H. Stoelting Company, Chicago, Illinois.

Yankee, W. J. (1968). *A report on the computerization of polygraphic recordings*. Presented to Keeler Polygraph Institute Alumni Association, Fifth Annual Seminar, Chicago, Illinois.

Yamaoka, K., Suzuki, A. (1973). Studies on skin-blood flow as an index of lie detection. *Reports of the National Institute of Police Science*, 26, 206-209. (Tr. and reprinted, 1980). *Polygraph*, 9(4), 232-237.

Yankee, W. J. & Grimsley, D. L. (1986). The effect of a prior polygraph test on a subsequent polygraph test. *Psychophysiology*, 24(5), 621-622 (abstract).

Chapter 3

Research and Scientific Status of PV Examinations

Since the publication of this author's previous textbook *The Art and Science of the Polygraph Technique* in 1980, more research has been conducted on psychophysiological veracity (PV) examinations using the polygraph than in the previous sixty years. Some of the unparalleled advances in PV examination processes and procedures have emanated from the enactment of the Defense Authorization Act of 1986 which directed the Secretary of Defense to conduct research on PV examinations, and by DoD Directive 5210.78 which established the Department of Defense Polygraph Institute (DoDPI) as a higher education and research facility. While not all published research relating to PV examinations during the past fifteen years was conducted by DoDPI, its role as a leading research entity certainly gave impetus to other research facilities and individuals, either through government grants, technical assistance, or its mere presence in the field of forensic psychophysiology, to engage in research regarding PV examination test formats, physiological data collection processes, physiological data analysis, diagnostic procedures and the recognition and identification of countermeasures.

The major emphasis since 1986 appears to be in the development of the computerized polygraph systems, although it has been in the developmental stages since J. F. Kubis, Fordham University completed his "Studies in Lie Detection, Computer Feasibility Considerations" in 1962 for the Rome Air Development Center, Air Force Systems Command, US Air Force, followed by Dr. W. Yankee (1968), N. R. Burch (1969), F. J. McGuigan and G. U. Pavek (1972), J. A. Podlesny (1976), E. James (1982), H. W. Timm (1989), J. Honts (1986), D. Raskin, J. Kircher, J. Honts, and Horowitz (1988), all of whom used various methods to collect, quantify and evaluate physiological data collected with laboratory or traditional polygraph instruments. It was during that 1986-1988 period that John C. Kircher and David C. Raskin produced the first computer assisted polygraph system (CAPS), and developed the first algorithm to be used for diagnostic purposes (Yankee 1995).

We currently have three American computerized polygraph systems manufactured by Stoelting, Axciton, and Lafayette. The Stoelting Computerized Polygraph System (CPS) IBM compatible, with an algorithm developed by Scientific Assessment Technologies based on thirteen years of research conducted at the University of Utah by Drs Raskin and Kircher; the Axciton Computerized Polygraph System, also IBM compatible, initially developed by Bruce White in 1988 which was subsequently selected by the Johns Hopkins University Applied Physics Laboratory for data collection and use of the newly developed algorithm for the Zone Comparison Technique and later versions of the APL algorithm. The third computerized polygraph system manufactured in the United States was the Lafayette LX-2000-101/105 (1993) which also uses the APL algorithm. The Lafayette LX-2000-101 initially used the Macintosh computer, but was later modified for compatibility with both IBM and Macintosh computers. The aforesaid algorithms have produced impressive results when compared to traditional scoring of verified polygraph charts, but at this stage of development, the difference between the accuracy rates for FPs using traditional scoring and the aforesaid algorithms is not statistically significant.(Kircher, Raskin 1988; Raskin, Kircher, Honts, Horowitz 1988; Honts 1992). Hence most FPs use the algorithm as a quality control to confirm their manual traditional scoring. There is no question however that in the near future, advanced computerized polygraph systems with more sophisticated algorithms will surpass human analysis and traditional numerical evaluation of the physiological data on polygraph charts.

While the computerized polygraph systems play a significant role in the decision making process of truth or deception, the excitement generated by this new polygraph technology appears to have eclipsed the value and essentiality of a validated psychological test structure administered with a validated methodology. It must be recognized that an invalid test structure or methodology will produce invalid physiological data on the polygraph charts which the most sophisticated computerized polygraph system cannot correct. We only need to look at the numerous variables listed in Chapter 9 to understand the major role that the forensic psychophysiologist plays in the preparation and administration of the psychophysiological veracity examination. While validity and reliability of the method by which the physiological data produced from the administration of the psychologically structured test (PST) is analyzed and evaluated (APL, CPS) are essential, the validity and reliability of the PST and the methodology used to administer it are not only essential but critical in establishing overall PV examination validity and reliability.

Although there are numerous variables which may affect its accuracy, existing research has shown that the PV examination works significantly better than chance in a wide range of testing situations, including criminal investigations, intelligence matters, security screenings, and even in mock crimes in a laboratory environment. In fact, it is difficult to find experiments in which PV examinations using the polygraph did not perform better than chance. The PV examination apparently works well with many cultures because many of the research studies were conducted in foreign countries such as Israel, Poland, Japan, and India. It is recognized that imperfections can be found in any study, either from its design, its execution, or in the selection, analysis, and reporting of its data. Sometimes the flaws are serious enough to disqualify the study from serious consideration. Unfortunately, many studies which failed to duplicate actual field situations by using untrained and/or inexperienced forensic psychophysiologists (FP) with instruments which recorded fewer channels or sensors than the customary four-channel polygraph instruments used by professional FP's, have found their way into the literature used to assess the validity and reliability of PV examinations. Furthermore, in many cases the study failed to duplicate either the psychological structure of the test format being evaluated, the methodology normally used in the administration of the test being evaluated, or in analog studies the emotional elements normally found in real-life cases. Some researchers have misclassified studies which investigated the ability of FP's working in the blind to correctly classify subjects as truthful or deceptive using verified cases as *validity* studies, when in fact these studies are evidence of reliability only. It is therefore imperative that the reader understand the difference and definition of validity versus reliability.

VALIDITY: It is described in Webster's dictionary as "the state, quality, or fact of being valid; (legal) soundness." An index of validity shows the degree to which a test measures what it purports to measure, when compared with accepted criteria, hence the validity of a psychophysiological veracity (PV) examination using the polygraph depends on whether it can accurately determine truth and deception. Selection of satisfactory validation criteria and demonstration of a reasonable degree of validity are fundamental in psychological testing. The first necessary condition of a valid test is that it have an adequate degree of reliability. *Reliability* is that which can be relied on; dependable; hence the reliability of a PV examination depends on whether the same set of data will consistently produce the same results. This consistency, known as reliability, is usually the degree to which a test yields repeatable results. Therefore, to assess the validity of any type of PV examination, it is necessary to obtain a *criterion measure* against which to compare the test results. The *criterion* is easily obtained in a laboratory experiment (analog study) where the experimenter can decide in advance which examinees will lie and which will tell the truth on the test. In field studies where actual suspects of criminal investigations are administered PV examinations, it is usually much harder to obtain dependable *criterion measures* and the experimenter may have to make do with a criterion that has less certainty.

Face Validity: Whenever an author bases his/her test upon his/her own logical analysis of what is to be evaluated or measured, without subjecting the device to comparison with external standards, he/she is using "face validity" as his/her criterion. (Freeman 1950). Face validity can also refer to a consensus of opinion, usually by a panel, regarding the logic of a theory, usually presented for further study or validation. Earlier PV examinations were structured on the basis of face validity, supported by empirical data.

Construct Validity: Refers to whether a test adequately measures the underlying trait it is designed to assess. A PV examination is designed to verify the truth and detect deception. It is therefore important to clearly define the constructs of truth and deception, and distinguish them from other concepts such as shame or guilt. To measure construct validity, it is necessary to both describe the construct and show its relation to a conceptual framework. Construct validation thus requires that a test be based on some theory or conceptual model. The process of assessing construct validity is typically done by logical analysis and the testing of hypothesized relationships among variables. Since different types of PV examinations have different theoretical bases, there are multiple forms of construct validity. Construct validity is established by various means but is primarily based on theoretical predictions of how items should interrelate or how other tests should intercorrelate (concurrent validity), and actual evidence, i.e. scores from similar tests examined. If no such predictions are possible, it is impossible to establish construct validity. (OTA 1983) Construct Validity for PV examinations is sub-categorized as follows:

> *Psychological Structure*: The psychological components that make up the test structure must initially be in conformance with acceptable scientific principles, have face validity, and be in harmony with the theory's objectives. Then the psychological test structure must be tested for Construct

Validity. Each of its components can be validated separately or in concert with each other, i.e. Symptomatic questions (Capps, Knill, Evans 1993), Exclusive control questions (Raskin, Barland, Podlesny 1978), Fear/Hope of Error questions (Matte, Reuss 1989, 1990). A test structure may have face validity, meet acceptable scientific principles, and be in harmony with the theory's objectives yet fail the test for Construct Validity. The Positive Control Technique held great promise but studies (Driscoll, Hontz, Jones 1987; Adison 1982; Forman, McCauley 1987) showed the technique produced an unacceptable percentage (35% - 45%) of false negatives and inconclusives.

Methodology: The methodology used to administer the psychologically structured test (PST) must consider and address all of the known variables that may affect the physiological data produced from the administration of the PST (Chap. 9). Methodologies do vary. For instance, most methodologies review the test questions with the examinee prior to the administration of the PV test, but some do not. Most methodologies employ a non-accusatory, non-threatening approach during the pre-test interview, but violations do occur. Most methodologies review the control questions last, after the relevant questions; others do not. Some methodologies use behavior-provoking questions during the pre-test interview, while other methodologies prohibit their use. Some methodologies use a Stimulation test as the first test, before the administration of the test regarding the relevant issue, while other methodologies use a Stimulation test after the conduct of the first test chart regarding the relevant issue. Other methodologies use no Stimulation test. Each of these methodologies must be validated within the PST for which it was designed. Departure from a validated methodology risks invalidation of that PV examination.

Data Analysis: The method by which the physiological data produced from the administration of the PST is analyzed and evaluated for a conclusion (Truth or Deception) must be validated. The mechanics of administering the test should be objective, and the test items should be amenable to objective and relatively simple scoring. Objectivity of administering and scoring provides a basis for uniformity of interpretation of results. The numerical scoring system (Backster, Matte, DoDPI) or the mathematical algorithm (APL, CPS) must be based on validated physiological criteria for deception, i.e. pneumograph, galvanic skin response/conductance, cardiograph. (Raskin, Barland, Podlesny 1978; Matte, Reuss 1989, 1992; Olsen, Harris, Capps, Ansley, Johnson 1995; Kircher 1983; Kircher, Raskin 1988).

Criterion Validity: Theoretically, construct validity is most important, but practically, criterion validity is the central component of a validity study. In PV examinations, this aspect of validity refers to the relationship between test outcomes and a criterion of ground truth. In this respect, criterion validity is what is meant by test accuracy. In the absence of construct validity evidence, however, it is difficult to determine to what extent criterion validity data can be generalized. In certain situations, it is not clear which aspects of a test are responsible for accuracy, and what factors cause a test to be inaccurate. (OTA 1983)

<u>*Internal Validity:*</u> Refers to the degree to which a study has control over extraneous variables which may be related to the study outcome. In the case of a study of PV examinations, internal validity is usually enhanced by the presence of control groups. Typically, such conditions of an experiment permit analysis of variables such as different question formats. In most field studies, internal validity is difficult to establish because the investigation cannot control or, in many cases, have definitive knowledge about whether a subject is guilty or innocent. (OTA 1983)

<u>*External Validity:*</u> Refers to the nature of the subjects and settings tested. The broader the population examined and the type of setting investigated, the wider that study's results can be generalized. In a parallel way, the more similar the research situation to the "real life" situation, the greater a study's external validity. Evidence about external validity is developed both from investigations that test a broad range of subjects and situations and from investigations that identify subject and setting interactions with PV examination outcomes. The broader the population examined and the type of setting or the more similar it is to the situation for which one wants to use a test or a theoretical construct, the greater a study's external validity. (OTA 1983)

<u>*RELIABILITY:*</u> The assessment of the validity of any psychophysiological veracity test is based on the assumption that the test consistently measures the same properties. This consistency, known as reliability, is usually the degree to which a test yields repeatable results, i.e. the extent to which the same examinee retested is scored similarly. Reliability also refers to consistency across forensic psychophysiologists/scorers. A reliable PV examination should yield equivalent results/scores when examinees are retested by the same forensic psychophysiologist (FP) or other FPs. As an example, if a forensic psychophysiologist concluded from the analysis of a set of polygraph charts that an examinee was deceptive, any other forensic psychophysiologist trained in that technique should be able to review the same charts and conclude that deception was indicated. This illustrates interrater reliability. Obviously, such reliability will be affected by the amount and type of training and experience of the forensic psychophysiologist. (OTA 1983)

<u>*Internal Reliability*</u>: In PV examinations, internal reliability is established by repetition of a test segment. In single-issue zone comparison tests such as Backster's Tri-Zone Comparison test or the Matte Quadri-Track Zone Comparison Test, the single relevant issue is addressed with two relevant questions, differently worded, but asking the same question. Hence the three parameter scores from each relevant versus control question can be combined for a total score inasmuch as both relevant questions deal with the same issue. Thus the scores from both relevant/control questions must be in consonance to attain

the minimum score required for a definite conclusion. Such test construct provides opportunity for demonstration of consistency, hence internal reliability.

External Reliability: In PV examinations, external reliability is established by repetition of the test itself, hence two or more polygraph test charts are required to be administered before a conclusion of truth or deception can be rendered. (American Polygraph Association standards).

Three types of studies have been used to validate PV examinations: the analog study, the field study, and the hybrid study (mixed origin). An analog study employs a mock crime paradigm, whereas a field study involves the testing of real-life suspects of criminal offenses. The rarely used hybrid study attempts to avoid the apparent weaknesses of both analog and field studies by combining the best features of each. The researcher arranges matters so that a real crime can occur. Ground truth is known as in an analog study, and similar to a field study, there is a lot at stake for both the truthful and deceptive subjects. Researchers, most of whom are academicians, prefer analog studies because they are easier to conduct, provide absolute ground truth, and the researcher has complete control over the experiment. Whereas field studies demand the employment of a professional forensic psychophysiologist (FP) in an environment appropriate for the testing of criminal suspects, where ground truth is difficult to acquire. That is probably the reason that twice as many analog studies as field studies have been conducted on PV examinations. Hybrid studies are difficult to construct, require opportune circumstances and discretionary control of the facts by the experimenter.

We must be careful in the evaluation of the results of validation studies involving mock paradigms (analog), inasmuch as the psychodynamics are quite different than those found in real-life cases (Abrams 1972). Analog studies in general, fail to duplicate the three major emotions normally responsible for the autonomic arousal(s) found in field studies involving real-life suspects, i.e. fear of detection by the guilty examinee, fear of error by the innocent examinee, and anger by the innocent examinee. Most analog studies have used small amounts of money, generally between $2.00 to $20.00, as a reward for defeating the test - hardly comparable to the loss of liberty or life as found in field studies. Furthermore, truthful examinees in analog studies cannot be expected to be fearful that an error will be made on their examination. However that is precisely the emotion that can prevail in a real-life case where a truthful examinee is erroneously found deceptive, which is called a *false positive*. In analog studies reported by Gordon H. Barland (1985), he showed the mean strength of scores for three charts to be plus 6.9 for the truthful and minus 8.3 for the deceptive. In a field study by Matte and Reuss (1989) they showed a mean strength of scores for three charts of plus 18 for the truthful and minus 27 for the deceptive. The emotion of *anger* which may be provoked by an incompetent and/or biased FP is absent in analog studies. A complete list of the variables which are capable of adversely affecting the physiological responses to the critical questions recorded on the polygraph charts which are used to arrive at a determination of truth or deception can be found in Chapter 9. A double cross-validation procedure was conducted by Raskin, et al (1988) to determine the accuracy of computer classifications of criminal suspects based on a discriminant function derived from laboratory data and the accuracy of computer classifications based on a discriminant function developed on criminal suspects which revealed that the laboratory model produced an increase in false positive errors when applied to field suspects and the field model showed an increase in false negative errors when applied to laboratory subjects. Furthermore, a comparison of the means of the computer-generated indices of differential reactivity to control and relevant questions by laboratory subjects and criminal suspects revealed that the differential reactivity indices for laboratory subjects were symmetrical around zero, but the means for the field suspects were shifted in the negative direction. The authors stated "These results reinforce an interpretation that compared to deceptive laboratory subjects, deceptive field suspects show stronger differential reactions to relevant questions than to control questions; and compared to truthful laboratory subjects, truthful field suspects showed much weaker differential reactions to control than to relevant questions." (Raskin, et al 1988)

Norman Ansley (1995) reported on data acquired from unpublished manuscripts in the Department of Defense regarding a comparison of anticipatory heart rate during the beginning of the first chart between 116 examinees involved in a laboratory research conducted by a federal agency in 1987, and 120 examinees involved in real federal cases conducted by that same federal agency in 1988 using the same FPs, same test questions, and similar population.. The average anticipatory heart rate of the laboratory examinees was 73.7 beats per minute, while the field average was 87.3 beats per minute. (Barland, Honts & Barger 1989). Ansley stated that "simulating field conditions is not always necessary or even useful in some types of developmental research, but when researchers want to know about field accuracy or utility, or want to apply their findings to field use, then they need to strive to match field condition as closely as possible with representative subject populations, standard test formats and the accompanying analytic technique, imaginative scenarios, and a setting that creates arousal approximating that in field psychophysiological detection of deception." (Ansley 1995)

Analog studies have been used to validate all types of psychophysiological veracity (PV) examinations including Zone Comparison Tests (ZCT), Mixed General Question Tests (MGQT), Relevant/Irrelevant Tests (R/I) also known as General Question Tests (GQT), and Guilty Knowledge Tests (GKT). This author believes that analog studies are better suited for the validation of Guilty Knowledge Tests (Balloun, Holmes 1979; Davidson 1968; Lykken 1959, 1960; Ohnishi, Tada, Tanaka 1965; Suzuki, Watanabe, Ohnishi, Matsuno, Arasuna 1973; Stern, Breen, Watanabe, Perry 1981) because they are not classified as lie tests inasmuch as the relevant question is not known to the innocent examinee hence not a factor that should elicit a false response to the relevant question due to *Fear of Error* or *Anger* by the innocent examinee. *Recognition* of the incriminating item is the essential element which causes autonomic arousal in Guilty Knowledge Tests. However it should be remembered that the psychodynamics in analog studies are quite different from those found in field studies, the latter containing a heightened, true *fear of detection*. Analog studies have been useful to determine the *effects of various drugs* (Gatchel, Smith & Kaplan 1983; Waid, E.C. Orne, Cook, M.T. Orne 1981), *subject characteristics* (Raskin and Hare 1978; Hammond 1980), *countermeasures* (Honts 1982; Abrams, Davidson 1988; Stevenson, M., Barry, G. 1988), *hypnosis* (Bitterman, Marcuse 1945; Cumley, Berry 1959; Berry 1960; Germann 1961; McInerney 1956; Coe, Yashinski 1985; Weinstein, Abrams, Gibbons 1970) *biofeedback* (Stern, Breen, Watanabe, Perry 1981; Corcoran, Lewis, Garver 1978; Corcoran, Wilson 1979). However, in spite of analog studies' aforesaid shortcomings, they have shown remarkable results attesting to the validity of various types of PV examinations. (Barland & Raskin 1975; Rovner, Raskin, Kircher 1978; Raskin & Hare 1978; Podlesny & Raskin 1978; Correa. E. J., Adams, H. E. 1981).

Some analog studies used only one parameter such as the galvanic skin response or conductance in their experiment. Other analog studies used FP (forensic psychophysiologist) trainees and allowed them to base their decision as to truth or deception on only one polygraph chart (Kleinmutz, Szuko 1982), which may account for its reported mediocre accuracy, whereas in the field, FP's are required by American Polygraph Association standards which have been adopted in many state statutes governing the use of the polygraph, to base their decision on a minimum of two or more polygraph charts employing a polygraph instrument that records at a minimum an examinee's respiration, electrodermal response and cardiovascular acvitity. There is no doubt that the level of FP experience and the type of test and methodology affect the accuracy of decisions. PV examinations are most accurate when only one issue is to be resolved. When more than one issue must be included in the test, such as in intelligence applications and in pre-employment screenings, the accuracy is expected to decrease due to an increased burden on the examinee's selective attention process and the effect of anti-climax dampening (Chap. 9), the lack of certain control questions unique to single-issue test structures, the lack of internal reliability offered by lateral scoring in single-issue tests (Backster, Matte, DoDPI Zone Comparison Techniques), and the inability to use the computer algorithm designed for single-issue Zone Comparison Test developed by Johns Hopkins University's Applied Physics Laboratory, which has been shown to be superior to the algorithm developed by APL for multiple-issue tests (MGQT). (Olsen, Harris, Capps, Ansley, 1995).

It becomes increasingly clear that PV examinations embrace a number of varied techniques, each with its own methodology of implementation. Some techniques use a global evaluation, incorporating case information, examinee verbal/non-verbal behavior in addition to the physiological data on the polygraph charts to reach a conclusion of truth or deception, which is referred to as the Clinical Approach, while others use the Numerical Approach which vigorously excludes all non-polygraphic data from their decision making process. Both have been shown to attain high accuracy rates, (Ansley 1990) but validation of one type of technique does not validate another, unless they are closely related in structure and methodology. Hence one cannot use a validity study on the Reid technique (Clinical) which employs two *non-exclusive* control questions for comparison against four relevant questions dealing with varied aspects of a crime, to support or criticize the validity of the Backster technique (Numerical) which employs two *exclusive* control questions for comparison against two relevant questions dealing with the same issue, not to mention other differences in test structure and methodology of application and evaluation. Indeed, Dr. David T. Lykken, a proponent of the Guilty Knowledge Test but a severe critic of the "lie test" stated that we needed to distinguish between the Clinical Approach (Keeler,

Reid, Arther schools) from the Numerical Approach (Backster, Matte, DoDPI) in that "Both are psychological procedures aimed at arriving at a judgment about the subject's psychological state. The Backster (Numerical Approach) is arguably a psychological test, but the Keeler-Reid-Arther procedure is clearly not a test at all, although it is commonly referred to in this way...these (Keeler-Reid-Arther) all can be described as clinical assessments rather than as tests." (Lykken 1981). Yet many scientists, academicians, politicians, lawyers and judges have assumed or found it convenient to paint all PV examinations with the same brush. Thus, many court judges routinely deny admissibility of validated PV examinations on the basis of a prior precedent setting case derived from testimony given perhaps three decades ago on a PV examination which employed a different technique and methodology.

Since 1980, this author has been arguing the need for *field* validation studies as the best means of determining whether a PV examination's psychological test structure and methodology have the capability of addressing all of the known variables which may affect the physiological data recorded on polygraph charts and provide an accurate, reliable conclusion. But the question of establishing ground truth is always raised as the main obstacle for its implementation. In field studies of PV examinations, the FP's decisions are compared against some post hoc determination of whether examinees/suspects are truthful or deceptive, hence *ground truth*. These post hoc determinations may consist of confessions by the presumably guilty person, decisions by a panel of attorneys or judges assembled specifically for a particular study who base their decisions on investigative files excluding references to polygraph decisions (i.e. Bersh 1969), judicial outcomes (dismissals, acquittals, convictions), and other criteria. The fact that determinations of guilt or innocence are made post hoc makes drawing conclusions from field studies difficult but not impossible. Some FP's are especially gifted as interrogators, thus acquire a high rate of confessions from deceptive subjects. Critics argue that a confession is not an absolute confirmation of the test results because the criminal justice system has often discovered a wrongful conviction based on a false, coerced confession from an innocent defendant. However, it should be recognized that a valid PV examination must necessarily be conducted in a non-accusatory, non-threatening, low-key manner, hence very unlikely to produce a false confession. Furthermore, a post-test interrogation is not conducted unless the PV examination results reveal deception to the target issue. Therefore PV examination results which are confirmed by a confession should have a high degree of credibility, and contrary to what some researchers have stated (Bersh 1969), can also serve to confirm the truthful test results of other suspects *in that same case*. Iacono (1987) argued that studies that select PV examinations for analysis using a criterion of ground truth based on confessions, overestimate accuracy because they do not include the polygraph charts of innocent suspects who failed the test and did not confess and guilty suspects who were identified as truthful hence were not interrogated or failed to confess. He also argued that guilty suspects selected for studies that used confessions as the criterion were only those who produced charts which contained strong enough autonomic arousals to indicate guilt resulting in a confession. However this argument implicitly recognizes the accuracy of PV examination charts that are strongly indicative of deception, but also implies that the test results of suspects identified as deceptive and did not confess are weaker than those who failed the test and did confess. Therefore Raskin, et al. used a method of selecting cases which prevented the problem of not selecting truthful suspects identified as deceptive (false positives) by acquiring confirmed truthful suspects from multiple-suspect cases. The truthfulness of aforesaid suspects was established by corroborated confessions of other suspects, and all truthful suspects who might have failed the tests were included in the sample and would have contributed to the observed error rate. The large majority of confirmed deceptive suspects were also obtained from multiple-suspect cases in which there was usually more than one deceptive suspect who could, and often did, confess and incriminate one or more of the other suspects who were tested. Therefore the potential problems of false positives and negatives proposed by Iacono were reduced or eliminated by the methodology of Raskin, et al study, which also investigated Iacono's proposition that suspects who were identified as deceptive and confessed produced stronger physiological reactions on their deceptive charts than those who failed the tests and did not confess. A comparison and analysis of the physiological reactions on the polygraph charts of the deceptive suspects who confesses versus deceptive suspects who did not confess revealed that there was an approximate 20% difference in magnitude of negative scores assigned to confirmed and unconfirmed deceptive results. However, the mean scores for unconfirmed deceptive results were 63% higher than the minimum score required for conclusive deceptive decision. These results indicate that the success or failure in eliciting a confession was unrelated to the strength of the physiological reactions to the relevant questions, hence provide little support for Iacono's argument concerning the lack of validity of confession-based field polygraph studies. (Raskin, et al. 1988).

Another means of establishing ground truth is with the use of court records when the subject of a PV examination found deceptive is subsequently convicted of that offense. A plea of guilty would be more confirmatory than a conviction over a plea of not guilty. It is recognized that on rare occasions individuals are sometimes wrongfully convicted, but the statistics do not warrant the exclusion of convictions to establish ground truth. Another means of confirmation can be the results of a thorough investigation which produced sufficient evidence for a conviction but the case never went to trial due to various reasons such as the victim or complainant dropped the charges, withdrew from the case, or settled out of court. Oftentimes we get a combination of confirmatory evidence such as a confession and conviction.

It is a well-known fact that PV examinations conducted for defense attorneys under the protective umbrella of privileged communication result in an exceptionally high rate of confessions from deceptive subjects because their confessions cannot be used against them in court. In some instances the deceptive subject will not confess to the FP but will verbalize a confession to his/her attorney who will then confirm the test results inasmuch as the privilege extends to the FP who acted as the attorney's agent. Indeed, this author conducted a field study published in 1990 (Matte, Reuss 1990) which involved 39 defense attorney cases under attorney-client privilege, and 34 of those were numerically scored deceptive and subsequently confirmed by confession. There is no reason to believe that PV examinations conducted under those protective conditions have any less credibility than PV examinations conducted by the police or commercial cases where no privilege exists. The aforementioned study examined the numerical scores from the aforementioned defense attorney cases and compared them with confirmed PV examinations conducted by a Metropolitan Police department, and confirmed commercial PV examinations without the privilege and found that the defense attorney cases showed a mean chart score of -9.38 compared with police cases which showed a mean chart score of -9.10, which suggests similar states of autonomic arousal. The commercial cases which were not tested under privilege, showed a mean chart score of -9.90. Because these guilty cases have similar scores, the idea that defense subjects lack the fear of arousal found in other populations is clearly without merit. (Matte, Reuss 1990)

Another method of establishing ground truth is with the use of panel judgments. A Validation Study of Polygraph Examiner Judgments was conducted by Philip J. Bersh, Temple University (1969) under the sponsorship of the Department of Defense Research and Engineering Joint Working Group on Lie Detection. The data collection was carried out by Robert A. Brisentine, Office of the Provost Marshal General, U. S. Army, also a member of the Working Group. This study consisted of an independent comparison of polygraph results with the investigative file, by comparing polygraph results in criminal cases against judgments of guilt or innocence made by a panel of lawyers having access to the complete investigative file from which all reference to the polygraph examination were removed. Cases were selected at random from the period 1963 to 1966, and of an initial 323 case files, a final number of 157 cases that were complete enough to permit a lawyer to judge guilt or innocence were selected. Cases were selected so that there were similar number of deception and no deception examiner judgments and a mix of Zone Comparison tests and Relevant-Irrelevant tests referred to as General Question Tests* (Brisentine 1995). Seventy-two of the aforementioned cases had been interpreted by the forensic psychophysiologists (FPs) as deceptive and eighty-five as truthful. The attorneys had been instructed to disregard all legal technicalities and to judge each case solely on the evidence in the file. The results revealed that the FPs and the panel of lawyers agreed on 92 percent of all cases when the panel was unanimous in its findings. A breakdown of the statistics reflects deception indicated 90 percent agreement, no deception indicated 94 percent

---

*The Bersh study contains a footnote #3 which states "The GQT type of examination begins with a control question but thereafter presents control and relevant questions in random order. In the ZOC type of examination, each relevant question is interpolated between a pair of control questions. The polygraph response to a relevant question is compared only with its surrounding control questions. In the case of the GQT type examination, the polygraph response to a relevant question is compared with the level of response to control questions in general." This statement by Bersh is in error and is misleading because the GQT (General Question Test) in that study began with a sacrifice relevant question, and thereafter only relevant and irrelevant questions were used, hence there were no control questions in the GQT because it was in fact a Relevant/Irrelevant test. (Brisentine 1995). The term control question in PV examinations is usually reserved for questions that are designed to elicit a lie from the examinee, whereas an irrelevant question is a neutral question, designed to lack any stimulating qualities for both the innocent and guilty examinee.

agreement. Of the 157 total cases, 89 were Zone Comparison tests divided into 37 deception indicated and 52 no deception indicated. These Zone Comparison tests had been administered by U. S. Army CID and MI agent forensic Psychophysiologists (FP) and U.S. Air Force OSI agent FPs. The General Question tests had been administered by U. S. Navy ONI agent FPs. All of the Zone Comparison tests were numerically scored and the decisions as to truth or deception were based solely on the test scores. Further, a group of 10 CID and MI agent FPs and 10 OSI Agent FPs independently scored the charts of all Zone Comparison tests without the benefit of the file. The percentages of agreement between FPs and the JAG panel were 92.6% for (GQT) General Question cases, and 92.1% for (ZCT) Zone Comparison cases. A review of the data in Table 3 of Bersh's study necessitated a correction to the reported calculation of 91.0% agreement for Zone Comparison cases. Aforesaid table reflects that the FP correctly identified 34 of the 38 cases found Guilty by the JAG Panel, and the FP correctly identified 48 of the 51 cases found Not Guilty by the JAG Panel. Therefore the FP and the JAG Panel agreed on 82 of the 89 cases for a 92.1% agreement. When Bersh released his report, Robert A. Brisentine, Jr., who carried out the data collection and was also a member of the Department of Defense Polygraph Research Committee working group, objected to Bersh's statement that "the study did not permit isolation of the role played by the polygraph record itself, the examiner's judgment was considered the end product of his complete interrogation of a suspect." inasmuch as it did not correctly reflect the decision making process of the Zone Comparison tests (ZCT) which comprised half of the cases in the study. However Bersh who at that time was convinced that global evaluation was the primary method of evaluating polygraph tests, declined to change his report for what he believed was a minor point. (Brisentine 1995). This is unfortunate because the data in this study shows that there is no statistical difference in the accuracy of test decisions (GQT) using global evaluation (Clinical Approach) versus the Numerical Approach (ZCT) where the decisions are based solely on the physiological data recorded on the polygraph charts, the latter providing better construct and internal validity hence superior reliability.

Correlations between total numerical scores assigned by comparably trained numerical scorers usually exceed 93% (Raskin, 1982). Kircher and Raskin (1983) performed lens model analysis of the decision policies of five forensic psychophysiologists who performed numerical evaluations of polygraph charts and found only minor differences among them. Others have reported substantial differences among forensic psychophysiologists who used global methods (Clinical Approach) (Forman & McCauley, 1986). Those laboratory data are consistent with the results of a field study reported by Raskin (1976). Dr. Raskin found that field forensic psychophysiologists who used numerical methods of evaluation were significantly more accurate in their decisions then were global evaluators (98.9% vs 88.5%). (Kircher & Raskin 1988)

Several studies have been rightfully criticized for not having separate base rates for the guilty and the innocent.(Lykken 1981). Conclusions about the validity of PV examinations may depend on whether the researcher attends to the average accuracy rate or to the accuracy for guilty and innocent subjects separately. The conclusions of all decision statistics contribute to the ability to make an accurate assessment of PV examination validity. If the base rate is l guilty and 99 innocent and the FP concludes that all 100 examinees are truthful, the researcher who fails to separate the statistics and combines the statistics for an overall percentage of accuracy could thus report a 99 percent accuracy. However a more appropriate and accurate report would be to calculate the guilty as 0 percent accuracy and the innocent as 100 percent accuracy, which percentages are added and divided by two for a total accuracy of 50 percent - no better than chance. However a sample size of one (guilty) is an invalid statistic to be used in statistical calculations. It is therefore imperative that researchers attempt to acquire as near equal samples of guilty and innocent subjects when attempting to evaluate validity and reliability of PV examinations, and use the latter statistical procedure. An example is the Matte-Reuss Validation Study of the Quadri-Zone Comparison Technique (1989) wherein 122 confirmed real-life cases from a Metropolitan Police Department and Private Polygraph firm were used which consisted of 62 deceptive cases and 53 no deception cases and 7 inconclusive cases of which 5 were solved as innocent and 2 as guilty. The Innocent and the Guilty were reported separately. The Quadri-Zone Comparison Technique correctly identified 91 % of the Innocent as Truthful and 9% as Inconclusive, with no errors. It further correctly identified 97% of the Guilty as Deceptive and 3% as Inconclusive, with no errors. Inconclusives excluded, the Quadri-Zone Comparison Technique was 100% accurate in the identification of the Innocent and the Guilty. Inconclusives included, the utility rate was 94%. (See Chap. 11 for details)

Another significant study entitled *Validity and Reliability of Detection of Deception* conducted by Drs. David C. Raskin, Gordon H. Barland, and John A. Podlesny at the University of Utah, for the National Institute of Law Enforcement and Criminal Justice, Law Enforcement Assistance Administration, U. S. Department of Justice which was published in 1978, involved six different field studies of criminal suspects and two analog studies with a mock-crime paradigm. The two Laboratory experiments used the Numerical Approach with an evenly divided base rate of guilty and innocent subjects. Experiment I realized 95% correct decisions excluding 8% inconclusives, and Experiment II realized 89% correct decisions excluding 10% inconclusives. In the field studies the accuracy of PV examinations with criminal suspects was evaluated using the decisions based on the numerical scores obtained from the independent chart interpretations. The same standard plus or minus 5 score boundaries as used in the analog studies were used for the inconclusive region. Those decisions were compared to the combined judgments of a panel and also to the judicial outcomes. When both the panel and the polygraph scores yielded a decision, the PV examination outcome agreed with the majority panel in 86% of the cases. More than half of the suspects found truthful with the polygraph produced inconclusive outcomes from the panel, and six of the seven disagreements were false positives (deceptive polygraph results on subjects considered innocent by the panel). PV examination results were also compared to the judicial outcomes which were considered conclusive and were not influenced by the polygraph results. There was 88% agreement between the polygraph decisions and the judicial outcomes. All of the disagreements (4) occurred on suspects who produced deceptive polygraph charts and who were acquitted in court. (Raskin, Barland, Podlesny 1978)

In aforementioned *Utah study*, two types of data were obtained to assess the effectiveness of examinations performed on persons diagnosed psychopathic (sociopathic). Among the 24 subjects who had been diagnosed as psychopaths, decisions were 96% correct. The single error was a false positive, and not a single guilty psychopath was able to produce a truthful polygraph outcome. In fact, the PV examinations were slightly more effective with the psychopaths than with the nonpsychopaths, but the difference was not statistically significant. The subjects from the study of criminal suspects were also compared on a number of biographical and personality variables. Those comparisons were made for sex, education, number of previous arrests, religiousness, previous polygraph tests, age, and the MMPI scores for the lie scale, K-scale, hypochondriasis scale, and depression scale. There were no indications that any of those variables were related to the polygraph results. This study also examined the strength of polygraph reactions exhibited by deceptive suspects and compared them for different crime categories using the total scores for the first three polygraph charts for suspects accused of sex crimes, drug crimes, crimes of violence, and crimes of financial gain. There were no discernible differences among the groups. A similar analysis was performed to compare the categories of sex crimes, drug crimes, and crimes involving confrontation between criminal and victim, and crimes without confrontation between the criminal and victim. Again, there were no discernible differences among polygraph scores for deceptive suspects divided into those categories. Thus there was no evidence that the type of crime affected the strength of polygraph reactions among suspects found deceptive on the polygraph test. (Raskin, Barland, Podlesny 1978)

The Utah Study also examined the effectiveness and value of behavior symptoms in PV examinations. The predictions based upon the observation of behavior during the pretest phase of the PV examinations of criminal suspects were compared to the judgments of guilt or innocence made by a majority of the panel. The initial predictions agreed with the panel in 56% of the cases and the later predictions agreed with the panel in 69% of the cases. Neither of those results was significantly above chance, indicating that systematic observation of behavior during the pretest phase of the PV examination was of no value in determining truth or deception. (Raskin, Barland, Podlesny 1978)

The Utah Study's investigation of the reliability of chart interpretation is of special importance to proponents of the Numerical Approach, for their exclusive reliance on the physiological data recorded on the polygraph charts has been challenged by proponents of the Clinical Approach (Arther 1979, Jayne 1993). This project included four different assessments of the reliability of chart interpretation. The first involved 40 sets of polygraph charts obtained with the control question technique which were scored numerically by the original forensic psychophysiologist (FP) (Dr. Barland) and were independently scored by Dr. Raskin. Both FP's made a definite decision on 36 of the 40 subjects, and they were in agreement on l00% of them. The second involved the outcomes based on numerical scores by the original FP (Dr. Barland) and those based on blind evaluation of the charts by Dr. Raskin. Both FP's obtained the same categorization in 86 of the l02 cases (84.3%) when inconclusives were included. On cases in which both FP's made a decision, they were in agreement 100% of the time. The correlation between the numerical scores assigned by the two FP's was very high, r = .91. The third assessment involved an examination of the extent of agreement between polygraph decisions by law enforcement and private FP's and those based on independent numerical evaluation by Drs. Raskin and Barland. One private polygraph firm whose polygraph charts were included in this assessment utilized the relevant/irrelevant technique which did not permit numerical scoring of its polygraph charts. The rate of agreement for law enforcement was 92% compared to private polygraph firms 79%. The fourth assessment involved 400 judgments made by 25 FP's on the set of 16 PV examinations which resulted in 79% correct decisions, 8% errors, and 13% inconclusives. Excluding inconclusives, 90% of the decisions were correct. Accuracy ranged from 53% correct decisions for one FP to 100% correct decisions for nine FP's. The proportion of the errors that were false positives (60.6%) was more than twice as high as would be expected by chance. There was no significant difference in accuracy of decisions for examiners with at least one year of experience (92%) as compared to those with less than one year of experience (89%). However the seven examiners who employed numerical scoring of the charts were significantly more accurate in their decisions (99%) than the 18 examiners who did not use numerical scoring (88)%). Furthermore, even among examiners who had received formal training in numerical scoring, the seven examiners who explicitly employed numerical evaluation achieved significantly higher accuracy of decisions (99%) than the six examiners who knew how to numerically score charts but did not explicitly employ the technique (88%). (Raskin, Barland, Podlesny 1978)

The Utah Study also conducted a quantitative analysis of physiological responses involving respiration amplitude, respiration cycle time, skin conductance response amplitude, skin conductance response rise time, skin conductance response recovery, skin potential responses, cardio responses, finger blood volume, finger pulse amplitude, heart rate changes, and cardio activity monitor, and established an *analysis validity* of the physiological criteria for deception in aforementioned instrument channels.

The Utah Study also evaluated the psycho-structural validity of the Reid *non-exclusive* control questions as used in the Clinical Approach, versus the Backster *exclusive* control questions as used in the Numerical Approach. The rate of accuracy of decisions using control question tests with Backster *exclusive* control questions was 94%, and 83% with Reid *non-exclusive* control questions. The accuracy of guilty-knowledge tests (GKT) was also evaluated for comparison with control question tests which revealed that the GKT was 90% accurate. It should also be noted that in the comparison of Backster *exclusive* control questions and the Reid *non-exclusive* control questions, the tests using exclusive control questions which employed a time bar to exclude the period of the crime from the period encompassed by the control question, produced significant identification of innocent subjects (mean score = +13.6) and guilty subjects (mean score = -11.7), but the results with Reid *non-exclusive* control questions which included the period of the crime encompassed by the control question, were significant for innocent subjects (mean score = +14.2) but not guilty subjects (mean score = -6.3). A quantitative analysis of physiological responses also produced some results which indicated a superiority for test utilizing *exclusive* control questions. Measures of skin conductance response recovery times and amplitude of negative skin potential responses showed stronger reactions to relevant questions by guilty subjects and to control questions by innocent subjects only with *exclusive* control questions. The test which used *non-exclusive* control questions showed no discrimination for either of those measures. The study concluded that control questions which are separated from the relevant issue by age or time of occurrence have some advantages over control questions which do not have those exclusionary characteristics. (Raskin, Barland, Podlesny 1978)

It should be noted that in aforesaid Utah study, the test structure used to compare the effectiveness of the *exclusive* versus the *non-exclusive* control questions was with the exclusive control question format of an equal number of relevant and control questions not exceeding three of each. Dr. Frank Horvath (1991) used the *non-exclusive* control question format to test both types of control questions, wherein only two control questions were compared against five relevant questions on the same test. This major distinction between the two test formats was overlooked by both Raskin, et al and Horvath. Both studies failed to test the control questions with both formats. A factor which reduced the strength and effectiveness of the two exclusive control questions in Horvath's experiment was the use of the same age category for both exclusive control questions, not a recommended practice (Matte 1993). As expected, the two exclusive control questions normally compared against an equal number of relevant questions, were overwhelmed in Horvath's experiment by the five relevant questions on the same test. But had Horvath also tested the exclusive and non-exclusive control questions using the exclusive control question format of two relevant questions compared against two controls or an equal number of each, he would predictively have found a significant number of false negatives in that the non-exclusive control questions would have been too powerful for the two neighboring relevant questions. The Raskin and Horvath studies have shown that the Exclusive and Non-Exclusive control questions are most effective when used in the format in which they were initially designed to be used. The failure to duplicate in toto the PV examination's test structure and methodology when attempting to validate its components will expectedly produce distorted and misleading results.

Horvath's (1994) analog study regarding the value and effectiveness of the sacrifice relevant question is another example of what can happen when a researcher fails to duplicate in toto the PV examination's methodology and test structure component(s) he is testing. Horvath failed to use a Zone Comparison format consistent with the Backster Zone Comparison Technique or the Matte Quadri-Track Zone Comparison Technique, both of which use only two relevant questions plus a Sacrifice/Preparatory question that is designed to function as an orienting relevant question *which should not exceed the precise scope of its related two strong relevant questions*. In his study Horvath uses exclusive control questions that possess the same time frame within the test structure versus Backster and Matte formats which use a *different* time frame for each control question within each test for each examinee. Furthermore, Horvath rotates the position of the control questions whereas Backster and Matte rotate the position of the relevant questions. It should be noted that in the Backster and Matte techniques, the Sacrifice Relevant question is presented to the examinee as a Preparatory question to enhance the focus of the deceptive as later verified examinee's psychological set onto the two strong relevant questions included in the same test, a procedure not used in the Horvath study. In order to effectively determine the validity and productivity of the Sacrifice Relevant question, it must be compared against the two relevant questions affected by it on the same test chart. However, Horvath's analog study did not make that comparison. Instead, Horvath compared the magnitude of the Sacrifice Relevant question in the Zone Comparison format to various relevant questions in the MGQT format (Mixed General Question Test). Even though the study design was faulty, there was no adverse impact showing on the results of the Zone Comparison test by the use of a Sacrifice Relevant question. The fact that Horvath's research is an analog study using mock paradigms which lack the essential emotions present in field cases also leaves doubt as to the credibility of any conclusions based on his results. It is therefore imperative that forensic psychophysiologists thoroughly review and analyze a research study before formulating an opinion regarding the validity and reliability of the test component evaluated by that study.

The Utah study also examined Dr. Martin Orne's Friendly Polygrapher hypothesis which holds that defense attorney clients who are guilty are less likely to be detected in PV examinations due to their lack of fear of detection as a result of the protection afforded them under the umbrella of privilege communication. Dr. Orne (1975) hypothesized that their autonomic arousal to the relevant questions should be significantly diminished compared to guilty criminal subjects of PV examinations by the police where no privilege exists. The first sample showed that defense cases produced 78% truthful, 20% deceptive, and 2% inconclusive outcomes. The law enforcement cases produced 76% truthful, 20% deceptive, and 5% inconclusive outcomes. Contrary to the "friendly polygrapher" hypothesis, there was no difference in frequency of truthful outcomes for defense and law enforcement examinations conducted by the same examiner. The second sample produced mean numerical scores of -4.7 for defense cases and -2.0 for law enforcement/employer cases. Although the difference between those means was not significant, it was in the opposite direction from that predicted by the "friendly polygrapher" hypothesis. The third sample produced mean numerical scores of -10.4 for defense cases and -0.7 for law enforcement cases. The difference between those means was statistically significant and in the opposite direction from that predicted by the "friendly polygrapher" hypothesis. Thus, the three samples of data obtained to test the predictions from the "friendly polygrapher" hypothesis not only failed to produce any evidence to support that hypothesis, but some of the results indicated effects which were totally contrary to Orne's speculations. (Raskin, Barland, Podlesny 1978). Raskin, et al study supports a subsequent study on the "Friendly Polygraphist" concept conducted by Matte, Reuss (1989) which was reported earlier in this chapter.

A remarkable hybrid study was conducted by Netzer Daie, a member of the Scientific Interrogation Unit of the Israeli Police in Jerusalem, with colleagues Avital Ginton, Eitan Elaad, and Bershon Ben-Shakhar in 1982. Twenty-one male Israeli policemen were administered a series of pencil-and-paper tests presented as part of a police course. Beneath the answer sheet for one of the tests was a hidden chemical page that recorded what was written on the answer sheet. The chemical page was removed, the answer sheet returned and subjects scored their own tests. Seven subjects actually changed their answers during the scoring. Several days later, subjects were informed that cheating was suspected and were offered an opportunity to take a polygraph test. They were told that their career would depend on the test results. Fifteen subjects, thirteen innocent and two guilty, were actually tested with control-question procedures administered at police laboratories by professional FP's. Electrodermal activity, cardiovascular activity, and respiration were recorded. There were three participants in each case, an FP, an observer in an adjacent room, and a blind chart evaluator. Thus, each participant had different information by which to make a decision of truth or deception. The FP made his decision based on the polygraph charts and subject behavior, the observer made his decision based only on subject behavior, and the chart analyst used only the polygraph charts. In addition to their overall impressions, the FP and the blind chart evaluator also scored the tests using field scoring techniques. Each relevant-control pair was scored from +3 to -3 and summed across physiological response systems, questions, and charts. Total scores from +5 to -5 were called inconclusive. Additionally, eight other FP's analyzed the charts using both general chart scrutiny, and the numerical scoring method.

The results of aforementioned hybrid study revealed that the original FP, using only his clinical judgment, correctly classified 100% of the guilty subjects and 85% of the innocent subjects; there were no inconclusive decisions. Numerical field scoring increased the number of inconclusives; one guilty subject and six innocent subjects were classified inconclusive. Omitting inconclusives, the original FP correctly classified 100% of the guilty subjects and 86% of the innocent subjects using numerical field scoring techniques. The blind evaluator correctly classified 50% of the guilty subjects (none of the guilty were classified inconclusive) and 70% of the innocent subjects using only general chart scrutiny (omitting inconclusives). Numerical field scoring increased the number of inconclusive decisions and improved the accuracy (omitting inconclusives) of the blind evaluator: 100% of the guilty subjects and 83% of the innocent subjects were correctly classified. The eight additional FP's correctly classified 94% of the guilty subjects with chart scrutiny and 100% (omitting inconclusives) of the guilty subjects with numerical analysis. Omitting inconclusives, their decisions from general chart scrutiny correctly classified 82% of the innocent subjects and their decisions from numerical analysis correctly classified 83% of the innocent subjects. The observer (behavior only) identified both guilty subjects as innocent, and 2 of the 13 innocent as guilty. (Ginton, et al. 1982)

The most difficult task of researchers in field PV examinations is the establishment of ground truth for the *innocent* cases. After attending one of my lectures in August 1995, Dr. Dale E. Olsen, Program Manager at The Johns Hopkins University Applied Physics Laboratory recently suggested to this author that this problem could be resolved with the use of a hybrid study using the *Matte Control Question Validation Procedure* (Matte 1976) originally designed to verify the effectiveness of the control questions prior to their use in the actual crime test. The procedure is as follows. The criminal suspect reports for a PV examination for a specific issue to be resolved and is told during the pretest interview of another crime (Fictitious) associated with the offense in question which has been reported and also needs to be resolved. It is imperative that the fictitious crime be in the same category as the actual crime in order for the control questions to be appropriate and useful. Thus the suspect is administered a minimum of two separate polygraph tests (charts) regarding the fictitious crime which is very real to the suspect. The numerically scored polygraph charts should produce truthful results affirming the effectiveness of the control questions. Furthermore, verified truthful charts are available for comparison with the polygraph charts produced by the second PV examination regarding the real issue which could produce deceptive charts, possibly confirmed by a confession, in which case the FP has confirmed truthful and deceptive charts from the same subject. This author has found that when a guilty subject is confronted with the truthful chart scores for comparison with the deceptive chart scores, denial of his/her guilt becomes extremely difficult, and confirmation of the results by confession is usually the result.

Since 1980 when this author's previous textbook was published, Norman Ansley, Editor in Chief of the American Polygraph Association, authored two major reports on the validity and reliability of psychophysiological veracity examinations. The first, published in 1983, entitled a *Compendium on Polygraph Validity*, reports on the validity of field (criminal) cases totaling 1,964 examinees tested, and analog (laboratory) studies totaling 1,113 examinees tested. The second report was published in 1990 entitled *The Validity and Reliability of Polygraph Decisions in Real Cases.* This report presented all studies of real (field) cases conducted between 1980 and 1990. Due to the succinctness of aforesaid reports and their excellent tables, they are both described, with permission of the author and the American Polygraph Association, in near toto below.*

A Compendium on Polygraph Validity: Norman Ansley (1983)

<u>Summary</u>

When research is conducted using real polygraph cases in which independent means are employed to check truth or deception, the average validity is 96 percent, with a range of 86.3 to 100 percent. These statistical results, based on the follow-up of nearly two thousand real cases, do not include those examinations in which the results were reported as inconclusive. It is the use of the inconclusive range that gives the field examiner the opportunity to be fair and safe, and say "I don't know."

Inspector William Y. Doran (1981), Deputy Assistant Director, Laboratory Division, Federal Bureau of Investigation has spoken of the importance of this inconclusive range. He said, "the inconclusive range serves a purpose - it is the safety zone and should be protected to avoid unnecessary errors. No examiner should render a judgment if he/she is not completely comfortable with his/her findings."

*Ansley, Norman (1983). A Compendium on Polygraph Validity. *Polygraph*, <u>12</u>(2), 53-61. Ansley, Norman (1990). The Validity and Reliability of Polygraph Decisions in Real Cases. *Polygraph*, <u>19</u>(3), 169-181.

When research is conducted in a laboratory setting where truth and deception is known (except to the examiner), the validity of polygraph techniques average 93.6 percent, with a range of 69.0 percent to 100 percent. Not all of the laboratory projects cited in this compendium were conducted to determine validity. Some were projects to evaluate variations in techniques, methods of analysis, specific and often single physiological recordings, and specific types of subject populations. For example, the third study by Heckel was of delusional psychotics which showed low validity, 69%; while the studies of psychopaths resulted in a surprise, with an average detection rate in excess of 90%. That polygraph techniques are cross-cultural is evident from the similarity of the results of studies made in Poland, Israel, Iceland, Japan, Canada and the United States.

Among the major techniques, there is little difference in their accuracy. The validity of control question formats average 95.2 percent, relevant-irrelevant formats average 96.8 percent, peak of tension formats average 91.2 percent, guilty-knowledge formats average 94.4 percent, and screening examinations average 96.7 percent. Since field examiners often use combinations of these techniques, no average can describe the accuracy of examinations in individual cases. The research also shows that polygraph techniques are slightly better at verifying truthfulness than detecting deception.

On the following pages are a table for quick comparisons of the results of the studies, and two sections of material describing each of the research projects with the source of the material. The first section describes follow-up studies on real cases, while the second section describes the results obtained from laboratory studies.

VALIDITY

Criminal Cases			**Laboratory Cases**		
Researcher Tested	Validity	No Tested	Researcher	Validity	No
Ben Ishai 1	94.0%	100	Benussi	97.5%	80
Ben Ishai 2	100.9%	10	Blum	96.2%	106
Bersh	92.4%	157	Correa	92.0%	40
Bitterman	100.0%	81	Davidson	97.9%	48
Edwards	98.3%	959	Dufek 1	83.3%	30
Elaad	96.6%	184	Dufek 2	90.0%	20
Lyon	100.0%	40	Dufek 3	100.0%	10
Peters	90.2%	172	Dufek 4	85.0%	20
Raskin 1	86.3%	92	Gudjonsson 1	91.7%	12
Raskin 2	88.2%	41	Gudjonsson 2	83.3%	12
Summers	100.0%	90	Gudjonsson 3	94.4%	12
Widacki	91.6	38	Gudjonsson 4	72.3%	12
		1,964	Hammond	96.8%	62
			Heckel 1	100.0%	5

Criminal Cases

The average validity for 1,964 persons tested was 96.3%.

Laboratory Cases

Heckel 2	87.5%	5
Heckel 3	69%	5
Kircher	95.6%	100
Krenbergerova	96.7%	10
Lieblich	97.0%	58
Lykken 1	93.9%	49
Lykken 2	100.0%	20
McNitt	100.0%	59
Ohkawa	90.2%	40
Ohnishi	92.0%	50
Podlesny 1	89.0%	60
Podlesny 2	90.0%	60
Raskin	87.5%	48
Widacki	95.0%	80
		1,113

The average validity for 1,113 persons tested was 93.6%.

VALIDITY OF CRIMINAL (FIELD) CASES

Research	Cases	Percent

Akiva Ben-Ishai. "Some Remarks on Polygraph Research." Paper presented at the Ninth Annual Meeting of the American Academy of Polygraph Examiners, Chicago, 1962.

		Cases	Percent
#1	Independent judgments of case file compared to polygraph results:	100	94.0%
#2	Blind review of charts from confirmed cases:	10	100.0%

Philip J. Bersh. "A Validation Study of Polygraph Examiner Judgments." *Journal of Applied Psychology* 53 (1959): 399-403.

	Cases	Percent
Independent judgment of case files compared to polygraph results:	157	92.4%

M. E. Bitterman and F. L. Marcuse. "Cardiovascular Responses of Innocent Persons to Criminal Interrogation." *American Journal of Psychology* 60 (1947): 407-412.

	Cases	Percent
Test results compared to investigative outcome:	81	100.0%

Research	Cases	Percent
Robert H. Edwards. "A Survey: Reliability of Polygraph Examinations Conducted by Virginia Polygraph Examiners." Bureau of Forensic Science, Department of General Services, Commonwealth of Virginia, July 31, 1981. Reprinted in *Polygraph,* 10 (4) (1981: 229-272.		
Test results compared to investigative or judicial outcome of the cases:	959	98.3%
Eitan Elaad and Esther Schahar. "Polygraph Field Validity." In I. Nachshon (Ed.) "Scientific Interrogation in Criminal Investigation." Selected papers presented at the First National Conference on Scientific Interrogation in Criminal Investigation, Bar-Ilan University, Ramat-Gan, Israel, November 3-4, 1976.		
Test results compared to investigative or judicial outcome of the cases:	184	96.6%
Verne W. Lyon, "Deception Tests with Juvenile Delinquents." *Journal of Genetic Psychology* 48(3) (1936): 494-497.		
Test results compared to investigative or judicial outcome of the cases:	40	100.0%
Robert B. Peters. "A Survey Polygraph Evidence in Criminal Trials." *The of American Bar Association Journal* 68 (February 1982); 162-175.		
Test results compared to the outcome of the trials, pleas, or disposition of charges:	172	90.2%
David C. Raskin, Gordon H. Barland and John A. Podlesny. *Validity and Reliability of Detection of Deception*. Washington, D. C.: National Institute of Law Enforcement and Criminal Justice, U. S. Department of Justice, 1978, pp. 4, 8, 10.		
#1 Results from blind analysis of the polygraph charts compared to the independent judgments of the case files:	92	86.3%
#2 Results from blind analysis of the polygraph charts compared to the judicial outcome of the cases:	41	88.2%

Research	Cases	Percent
Walter B. Summers. "The Electric Pathometer." *Proceedings of the International Association of Chiefs of Police*. Washington, D. C.: IACP, 1938, pp. 142-143.		
Test result compared to judicial outcome of cases:	90	100.0%
Jan Widacki. *Analiza Przestanek Diagnozowania w Badanich Poligraficznych*. (The Analysis of Diagnostic Premises in Polygraph Examination.) Uniwersytetu Slaskiego, Kakktowice, Poland, 1982.		
Results from the blind analysis of the polygraph charts compared to the judicial outcome:	38	91.6%

VALIDITY OF LABORATORY (ANALOG) CASES

Research	Experiments	Percent
Vittorio Benussi. "Die atmungssymptome der Luge." *Archiv fur die Gestamte Psychologie*. ("The Respiratory Systems of Lying.") Tr. and reprinted in *Polygraph* 4(l) (March 1975: 52-76.		
Measured inspiration/expiration ratios before and after lying.	80	97.5%
Richard H. Blum and William Osterloh. "The Polygraph Examination as a Means for Detecting Truth and Falsehood in Stories Presented by Police Informants." *Journal of Criminal Law, Criminology and Police Science* 59 (1968): 133-137.		
With a polygraph had to determine which informants were telling the whole truth, telling partly true stories, or telling totally false stories. There were 106 issues to be decided, told by 20 subjects.	106	96.2%
Eilleen J. Correa and Henry E. Adams. "The Validity of the Preemployment Polygraph Examination and the Effects of Motivation." *Polygraph* 10 (3) (September 1981): 143-155.		
Determine from 40 subjects who was truthful on their application forms, and among the untruthful, what items		

Research	Experiments	Percent
on the form were not truthful.	40	92.0%
P. O. Davidson. "Validity of the Guilty-Knowledge Technique: The Effects of Motivation." *Journal of Applied Psychology* 52 (1) (1968): 62-65.		
Simulated crime in which the motivation varied, one group getting .10 cents to a $1.00, the other $25 to $50, if they committed the crime and escaped detection by the polygraph test. Missed one low motivation S.	48	97.9%
Miroslav Dufek. "A Contribution on the Problem of Polygraph Examinations." *Czechoslovak Criminalistics* (February 1969). Tr. from Czech.		
#1 Thirty subjects wrote a number from two to ten. Searching peak of tension test to pick the number. Change was 11.0%. (Five inconclusive, no errors.)	30	83.3%
#2 20 subjects who examined one of six items. Searching peak of tension test to pick the item. Chance was 16.7%. (Two inconclusive, no errors.)	20	90.0%
#3 Ten subjects picked a first name with personal meaning, placed with nine neutral. Searching peak. Chance was 11.1%.	10	100.0%
#4 Experiment like #2, but subjects knew the exact order of the items prior to the peak of tension test. Chance was 16.7%. (Three inconclusive, no errors.)	20	85.0%
G. H. Gudjonsson. "The Efficacy of the Galvanic Skin Response in Experimental Lie Detection. Some Personality Variables." Master of Science Thesis, Department of Psychology, University of Surrey, England.		
#1 12 uniformed Icelandic policemen took three peak of tension tests. One on their month of birth (91.7%), one on a number (100.%), and one on a word (83.3%). Chance was 14.3%.	36	91.7%
#2 12 Icelandic detectives took three peak of tension tests. One on their month of birth (83.3%), one on a number (83.3%), and one on a word (83.3%). Change was 14.3%.	36	83.3%

Research		Experiments	Percent
#3	12 Icelandic clergymen took three peak of tension tests. One on their month of birth (100%), one on a number (100%), and one on a word (83.3%). Chance was 14.3%.	36	94.4%
#4	12 Icelandic criminals took three peak of tension tests. One on their month of birth (75%), one on a number (83.3%), and one on a word (58.3%). Chance was 14.3%.	36	72.2%

David L. Hammond. "The Responding of Normals, Alcoholics and Psychopaths in a Laboratory Lie Detection Experiment." Doctoral Dissertation, California School of Professional Psychology, 1980.

	Subjects were 21 normals, 20 alcoholics, 21 psychopaths, all tested by students in a polygraph course about a mock crime. Control question technique. Charts read blind by expert examiner.	62	96.8%

R. V. Heckel, J. R. Brokaw, H. C. Salzberg, and S. L. Wiggins. "Polygraphic Variations in Reactivity Between Delusional, Nondelusional, and Control Groups in a Crime Situation." *Journal of Criminal Law, Criminology and Police Science* 53(3) (1962): 380-383.

#1	Subjects were 5 normal males who took polygraph test in regard to what they thought was a real theft. Charts were read blind by four examiners. All S's were innocent. Chart analysis indicated:	5	100.0%
#2	Subjects were 5 nondelusional psychiatric patients. Procedure as in #l.	5	87.5%
#3	Subjects were 5 delusional psychotic psychiatric patients. Procedures as in #l.	5	69.0%

John C. Kircher and David C. Raskin. "Cross-Validation of a Computerized Diagnostic Procedure for Detection of Deception." Paper presented at the meeting of the Society for Psychophysiological Research, October 1982, Minneapolis, Minnesota.

#1	100 subjects of which half committed a mock crime, half innocent. Computer analysis of the polygraph charts.	100	91.3%
#2	Same as above but charts scored blind by expert examiner.	100	95.6%

Research	Experiments	Percent
Jana Krenbergerova. "Experimental Experiences With the Use of the Polygraph." Socialist Legality (May-June 1969). Tr. from Czech.		
Ten men hid weapons in various buildings. Searching peak of tension tests were given to locate (1) the building, (2) the floor, and (3) the room. Each list had 18 items. Chance was 5.6%. There were 30 tests given.	30	96.7%
Israel Lieblich, Gideon Naftali, Joseph Shmueli and Sol Kugelmas. "Efficacy of GSR Detection of Information With Repeated Presentation of Series of Stimuli in Two Motivational States." *Journal of Applied Psychology*, 59 (1) (1974): 113-115.		
There were 58 subjects, half in low and half in high motivational states. Searching peak of tension for their first name among five names (chance 20%) produced 60% results for low and high at end of first test. Ten tests conducted on each subject, scored cumulatively produced the results below. 20 of 28 high motivational subjects admitted after the test they tried countermeasures.		
#1 Low motivational group	29	96.0%
#2 High motivational group	29	98.0%
David T. Lykken. "The GSR in the Detection of Guilt." *Journal of Applied Psychology*, 43 (6) (1959): 385-388.		
49 subjects in 4 groups. 13 enacted 2 "crimes," a "murder" and a "theft." 12 enacted only the "murder" and 12 enacted only the "theft." There were 12 innocent. Chance was 25%.	49	93.9%
David T. Lykken. "The Validity of the Guilty Knowledge Technique: The effects of Faking." *Journal of Applied Psychology*, 44 (4) (1960): 258-262.		
20 subjects were taught to give false GSR responses, and to do so during the tests. Also, offered a $10.00 prize to beat the test, a searching peak of tension on personal information.	20	100.0%

Research	Experiments	Percent
Reginald D. MacNitt. "In Defense of the Electrodermal Response and Cardiac Amplitude as Measures of Deception." *Journal of Criminal Law, Criminology and Police Science* <u>33</u> (1942): 266-275.		
Subjects were employees, some who had stolen merchandise (confessed) who were told to lie during the tests and some employees considered honest. Relevant-irrelevant screening tests conducted on the 59 subjects by examiner blind to situation.	59	100.0%
Hisatsugi Ohkawa. "Comparison of Physiological Response of 'Yes,' 'No,' and 'Mute' Conditions in Peak of Tension Test." *Reports of the National Institute of Police Science* (1963): 1-4. Tr. from Japanese.		
A mock theft involving 40 subjects, who stole one of eight items. Searching peak of tension. Chance was 12.5%. (Mute results 87.5%, honest answer, 75.0%).	40	90.2%
Kazuo Ohmishi, Katsunori Matsuno, Masana Arasuna and Akhiro Suzuki. "The Objective Analysis of Physiological Indices in the Field Detection of Deception." *Reports of the National Institute of Police Science* <u>29</u> (3) (August 1976): 181-188. Tr. from Japanese, Abstract in English.		
Searching peak of tension to pick the correct number from six numbers. Subjects were 50 suspects in criminal cases. Chance was 16.7%.	50	92.0%
John A. Podlesny, David C. Raskin and Gordon H. Barland. "Effectiveness of Techniques and Physiological Measures in the Detection of Deception." Report No. 76.5, Contract 75-NI-99-0001, National Institute of Law Enforcement and Criminal Justice; Department of Psychology, University of Utah, Salt Lake City, Utah. August 20, 1976.		
#1 Control question technique used to detect participation in a mock theft experiment, in which 30 were guilty, 30 were innocent.	60	89.0%
#2 As above, but a guilty knowledge technique was used.	60	90.0%

Research	Experiments	Percent
David C. Raskin and Robert D. Hare. "Psychopathy and Detection of Deception in a Prison Population." *Psychophysiology* 15 (2) (1978): 126-136.		
48 prison inmates of which half were diagnosed psychopaths were tested in a mock crime with a control question technique. (There was no difference in detectability of psychopaths from non-psychopaths.)	48	87.5%
Jan Widacki and Frank Horvath. "An Experimental Investigation of the Relative Validity and Utility of the Polygraph Technique and Three Other Common Methods of Criminal Identification." *Journal of Forensic Sciences* 23 (3) (July 1978): 596-601.		
80 students participated in an experiment in which 20 of them were guilty of participating in the delivery of an envelope to a specific location	80	95.0%

* * * * * *

The Validity and Reliability of Polygraph Decisions in Real Cases: Norman Ansley (1990)

Abstract

A report on validity from all studies of real cases, conducted since 1980 is presented. Examiner decisions in these studies were compared to other results such as confessions, evidence, and judicial disposition. The ten studies reviewed considered the outcome of 2,042 cases, and the results, assuming that every disagreement was a polygraph error, indicate a validity of 98%. For deceptive cases, the validity was also 98%, and for non-deceptive cases, 97%. The studies were from police and private cases, using a variety of polygraph techniques, conducted in the United States, Canada, Israel, Japan and Poland.

A report on all the studies of the reliability of blind chart analyses from real cases conducted since 1980 is also presented. Blind analysis of polygraph charts is not a complete measure of reliability, despite frequent misrepresentations. It is, however, related to reliability and validity. True reliability studies involve retesting, and there are no such studies involving real cases. The eleven studies of blind chart analyses included 922 cases, of which 828 were correctly decided, being 90%. The confirmed deceptive cases were correctly decided at 94%, the non-deceptive at 89%. The charts were from police and private cases, with numerical and global evaluation and a variety of polygraph techniques.

Four of the studies involved analyses of the examiners' decisions and the decisions of blind evaluators. Based on 320 police and private cases, examiners were correct in 313, being 98%, blind evaluators in 227 for 95%. Examiners and evaluators were both at 98% accuracy with deceptive cases, but differed considerably in truthful cases. Examiners were correct in 97% of the non-deceptive cases while blind evaluators were correct in 89%.

These studies, which represent all that are available in the last decade, suggest that polygraph testing is highly accurate but an imperfect technique for detecting deception and verifying truth.

The following analyses are based on the results of research studies involving field polygraph tests. Ground truth was established in these studies by either confession of the subject or of another person in the same case, or was based on court decisions. Sometimes the follow-up was based on both, and may have also evaluated physical evidence. There are two weaknesses in this form of ground truth. One is that court decisions and physical evidence are themselves unreliable. Confessions are probably a good measure, when you have them, as false confessions are rare. However, some critics have suggested that the personality of those who confess is somehow different from those who don't, and that our accuracy in detecting deception in the confession group is not representative of the accuracy of detecting deception in the non-confession group. Also, when police examiners err by calling a deceptive person truthful, a false negative, the error is not often discovered because the subject is not interrogated, and the test result affects the subsequent investigation. These and other problems inherent in validity and reliability studies involving real cases create data that must be used with a caution somewhat different from the limitations imposed on the use of laboratory results. The combination of field and laboratory research results probably creates the best approximation of validity. The laboratory studies are most valuable when the control subjects are evaluated and the tests simulate field conditions with standard instruments, standard test formats, and trained examiners.

In this paper, the studies and tables are limited to studies published in the last ten years. They are of two types. In one, the testing examiners' numerical scores or his decision is compared with the ground truth derived from confession, judicial outcome, evidence, or a combination. These are studies of validity. The second group represents an estimate of reliability. In most of the reliability studies the evaluator sees only the sets of charts, and does not see the question lists, information about the subject, or case facts. Because of this restriction, the research only tells us the value of what is on the charts, with the evaluator not knowing the other information that was available to the examiner. It is not a full measure of total examination reliability. There is research that suggests that evaluators are more accurate in their decisions from the charts when they also have information about the case and subject (Holmes, 1958; Wicklander & Hunter, 1975). A different test of reliability might be to give the evaluators the case materials, a briefing on the case by the investigators, a video of the pretest and test, and the charts. That has not been done. Another approach to a field test measure of validity is to test after the fact, persons whose cases have been adjudicated or are confirmed by confession, evidence, and court adjudication. Marston came close to that in 1921 when he conducted twenty cases referred by the court or probation office and selected by a physician who believed their guilt or innocence was already well established by physical or medical evidence, testimony, or by judicial disposition. Two studies have assessed validity by comparing the decision of polygraph examiners who conducted criminal cases with the decisions of a panel of attorneys, assuming the attorneys were unfailingly correct when they all agreed after reading the evidence (Bersh, 1969; Barland & Raskin, 1976). That research would have been better if some confirmed cases were given to the panel mixed in with the other cases to determine how accurate they were at making decisions.

Because there are numerous studies of validity or reliability involving real cases, it seemed appropriate to confine this review to studies published in the past ten years because they are more apt to represent what is happening in the field now.

Not all of the results are about control question tests. In regard to the largest study, the Edwards study, we do not know what kind of tests were given by the various police agencies in Virginia, some were probably Relevant-Irrelevant Technique (RI) and others were Control Question Tests (CQT), and perhaps a few were Peak of Tension tests (POT) alone or as supplements. Edwards also differs from the other studies in that the methods of follow-up are unknown, and it appears to be more of a survey than the other studies. Yamamura, reporting on a Japanese riot in which 95 were polygraphed, was able to use all POT tests. Like Edwards, his research needs special consideration. The other studies involve CQT test formats. Inconclusive decisions have been excluded from these tables.

Of the CQTs (excluding Edwards and Yamamura), examiners were correct in 301 of 316 NDI (No Deception Indicated) calls for 95%. They were correct in 629 of 634 DI (Deception Indicated) calls, for 99%. Unlike the peak of tension tests, control question tests were more accurate with guilty subjects. If you include Edwards' study there is minimal difference in the total results.The total NDI decisions were correct in 657 of 679 cases, for 96%, and correct in 1,216 of 1,230 DI cases, for 99%. The overall accuracy for all cases (except POT) was 1,873 correct out of 1,909 cases, for 98%. When you include Yamamura and Edwards, the data is similar: 718 of 744 NDI decisions were correct for 97%; 1,240 of 1,260 DI decisions were correct for 98%; and total figures were 1,993 decisions in 2,042 tests were correct for 98%.

The only research on field use of the peak of tension tests in the past ten years is by Yamamura. The accuracy for the 95 subjects averaged 89%, and was more accurate with the nondeceptive than with the deceptive. When they polygraphed the guilty subjects to learn which of five riot acts they had committed, they were only 79% accurate, but chance was also lower, at 20%. Also, many subjects were guilty of more than one act. Verifying the acts was also more difficult, but they did verify 179 of 226 DI decisions.

TABLE 1

Results

Table 1
Validity of Examiners' Decisions
(inconclusives excluded)

Authors/Date	NDI #	NDI # Correct	NDI %	DI #	DI # Correct	DI %	Total #	Total # Correct	Total %	Technique
Arellano (1990)	18	18	100%	22	22	100%	40	40	100%	Backster Zone
Edwards (1981)	363	356	98%	596	587	98%	959	943	98%	variety
Elaad & Schahar (1985)	100	95	95%	74	73	99%	174	168	97%	Reid CQT & Backster Zone
Matte & Reuss (1989)	54	54	100%	60	60	100%	114	114	100%	Quadri-zone
Murray (1989)	21	18	86%	150	150	100%	171	168	98%	Arther CQT
Patrick & Iacono (1987)	30	27	90%	51	51	100%	81	78	96%	CQT
Putnam (1983)	65	62	95%	220	219	99%	285	281	99%	Backster Zone & MGQT
Raskin et al (1988)	28	27	96%	57	54	95%	85	81	95%	CQT
Widacki (1982) *	--	--	--	--	--	--	38	35	92%	Backster Zone
Yamamura & Miyake (1980)	65	61	94%	30	24	80%	95	85	89%	POT
TOTALS	744	718	97%	1260	1240	98%	2042	1993	98%	
TOTALS (less Edwards and Yamamura & Miyake)	316	301	95%	634	629	99%	988	965	98%	

* Only the totals reported.

Norman Ansley, Polygraph, 19(3), 1990

Reliability of Blind Chart Analysis

Blind analysis of charts, where the evaluator knows no facts of the case is only a measure of reliability. This approach is often misrepresented as a measure of validity, but it is not so for several reasons. First, we assume in these studies that the blind evaluators are as competent as the examiner, are as experienced as the examiner, and are trained and experienced in the technique used by the examiner. The last point is vital. When there is a gathering of examiners where they have been trained at different schools in different test methods, and employ different scoring methods, the examiners will have difficulty scoring each other's charts (Weaver 1980, Koll 1979). Many studies do not cite the qualifications, training, and experience of the evaluators. It is not always safe to assume in these studies that the evaluators had experience with the technique, or had adequate training in the appropriate scoring method for the technique. Another variable is the quality of the polygraph charts and the details of marking. The evaluator may have made assumptions about some markings, or the lack of markings, assumptions that were not correct.

Excluded from this study are those research projects in which the reviewers saw only one chart of a set, or chart segments (Kirby, 1981; Kleinmuntz & Szucko, 1985; Rafky & Sussman, 1985; and Yankee, Powell & Newland, 1985). That all of these studies showed decisions above chance is interesting and instructive, but no one of those studies represent a measure of the reliability of blind chart interpretation. Also deleted is the study by Edel and Moore (1984) because it is only a study of interrater reliability at judging reactions, not truth and deception. Included in the tables are three studies that do not separate data by DI and NDI status (Honts & Driscoll, 1988; Jayne, 1990; Widacki, 1982), but do have total figures.

Results

When we total the CQT studies in Table 2, the evaluation of confirmed NDI charts was correct in 193 of 218 cases, for 89%; the DI chart decisions were correct in 279 of 297, for 94%; and the total decisions were correct in 828 of 922, for 90%. Three studies give only totals, no data of NDI and DI decisions. One study, Elaad (1985), was included twice, as he used numerical scoring in one, global in the other. Global was superior.

The blind numerical analysis of charts was less accurate than the decisions by the initial examiners. The difference in examiner decisions compared to the blind evaluators for standard field CQTs are: for NDI, Examiners 95%, Blind Evaluators 89%; for DI, Examiners 99%, Blind Evaluators 94%; and overall, Examiners 98%, Blind Evaluators 90%.

Table 3 displays the results of four novel scoring methods applied to the analysis of confirmed polygraph charts from real cases. Two involve computer assisted scoring methods, methods that are quite different. In the work by Jayne, his numerical analysis of the charts was correct in 92 of 100 cases, for 92% while his computer analysis was correct in 90 of 100 cases for 90%. Franz, however, was more accurate with his computer analysis, correctly deciding 89 of 100 examinations for 89%, while his numerical scoring correctly called 83 of 99 cases (one inconclusive) for 84%. In the Honts & Raskin research they added a directed lie control question to 23 cases. When they scored the charts without the directed lie they were correct in 19 of 21 decisions (two inconclusives), for 90%; while they were correct in 22 of 23 decisions when they included the directed lie, for 96%. Matte and Reuss decided to score their Quadri-Zone charts with the Backster scoring system applied to all but the fourth zone (third spot), which provides additional control data. Because they were correct in the analysis of all tests in the original cases, the application of Backster's method could not improve the record. In fact, there were more inconclusive results, and the accuracy was 93 of 97 decisions, for 96%. While this may tell us how important the fourth zone is to the success of the Quadri-Zone test, it is not an indication of the accuracy of the Backster Zone Comparison Test.

When we compared those few studies that included the original examiners' accuracy and the blind evaluators' accuracy we had the results shown in Table 4.

All four of these studies were CQTs and all were numerically scored. The examiners were correct in NDI charts in 126 of 130, for 97%, and the blind evaluators were correct on 102 of 114 for 89%. The differences disappeared with DI charts where examiners were correct on 187 of 190 charts and the blind evaluators were correct 175 of 179, both at 98%. The total examiners' decisions were correct in 313 of 320 cases, for 98%, and the total blind evaluators' decisions were correct in 277 of 293 cases, for 95%. The blind evaluators were not better than the original examiners in any phase of these four studies, but they were similar in their accuracy at judging deceptive charts. The blind evaluators were considerably less accurate in judging truthful charts. When the results are from separate studies, the trend remains, but the accuracy with DI charts is not alike. See Tables 2 and 3.

Table 2
Reliability of Blind Chart Analysis
(inconclusives excluded)

Authors/Date	NDI #	NDI # Correct	NDI %	DI #	DI # Correct	DI %	Total #	Total # Correct	Total %	Technique
Arellano (1990)	18	18	100%	22	22	100%	40	40	100%	Backster Zone (numerical scoring)
Elaad (1985)	30	23	77%	30	23	77%	60	46	77%	CQT (numerical scoring)
Elaad (1985)	30	27	90%	30	23	77%	60	50	83%	CQT (global scoring)
Franz (1989)	34	33	97%	47	47	100%	81	80	99%	Reid CQT (numerical scoring)
Honts & Driscoll (1988) *	--	--	--	--	--	--	52	46	88%	CQT (numerical scoring)
Honts & Raskin (1988)	10	8	80%	11	11	100%	21	19	90%	Utah zone, less one control (DL) (numerical scoring)
Jayne (1990) *	--	--	--	--	--	--	100	92	92%	Reid CQT (numerical scoring)
Matte & Reuss (1989)	54	54	100%	60	60	100%	114	114	100%	Quadri-zone (numerical scoring)
Patrick & Iacono (1987)	20	11	55%	49	48	98%	69	59	86%	Canadian CQT (numerical scoring)
Raskin et al (1988)	22	19	86%	48	45	94%	70	64	91%	CQT (numerical scoring)
Ryan (1989) *	--	--	--	--	--	--	255	218	85%	Reid CQT (numerical scoring)
TOTALS	218	193	89%	297	279	94%	920	828	90%	

* Only the totals reported.

Norman Ansley, Polygraph, 19(3), 1990

Table 2

Table 3
Reliability of Blind Chart Analysis, Novel Scoring Methods
(inconclusives excluded)

Authors/Date	NDI #	NDI # Correct	NDI %	DI #	DI # Correct	DI %	Total #	Total # Correct	Total %	Novel Technique
Franz (1989)	50	43	86%	50	46	92%	100	89	89%	Computer analysis of CQT charts
Honts & Raskin (1988)	11	11	100%	12	11	92%	23	22	96%	Directed Lie Control scored with CQT charts
Jayne (1990) *	--	--	--	--	--	--	100	90	90%	Computer analysis of Reid CQT charts
Matte & Reuss (1989)	38	35	92%	59	58	98%	97	93	96%	Backster numerical applied to Quadri-zone charts, fourth zone deleted

* Only the totals reported.

Norman Ansley, Polygraph, 19(3), 1990

Table 3

Table 4
Validity of Examiner and Blind Scorers
(inconclusives excluded)

Authors/Date	NDI #	# Correct	%	DI #	# Correct	%	Total #	# Correct	%	Scorer
Arellano (1990)	18	18	100%	22	22	100%	40	40	100%	Examiner
	18	18	100%	22	22	100%	40	40	100%	Blind Evaluator
Matte & Reuss (1989)	54	54	100%	60	60	100%	114	114	100%	Examiner
	54	54	100%	60	60	100%	114	114	100%	Blind Evaluator
Patrick & Iacono (1987)	30	27	90%	51	51	100%	81	78	96%	Examiner
	20	11	55%	49	48	98%	69	59	86%	Blind Evaluator
Raskin et al (1988)	28	27	96%	57	54	95%	85	81	95%	Examiner
	22	19	86%	48	45	94%	70	64	91%	Blind Evaluator
TOTALS	130	126	97%	190	187	98%	320	313	98%	Examiner
	114	102	89%	179	175	98%	293	277	95%	Blind Evaluator

Norman Ansley, Polygraph, 19(3), 1990

Table 4

Table 5
Test Formats and Subject Populations

Authors/Date	Test Format	#/Subjects	Population Tested
Arellano (1990)	Backster Zone	40	Hispanic. Illegal aliens in U.S. suspected of theft by employer. Tested in Spanish.
Edwards (1981).	variety	959	Criminal suspects in Virginia.
Elaad & Schahar (1984)	Backster Zone	174	Criminal suspects in Israel.
Elaad et al (1988)	Guilty Knowledge Test (after Reid CQT)	40	Criminal suspects in Israel. All but one GKT test followed a Reid CQT.
Franz (1989)	CQT (not described)	100	Criminal suspects in U.S.
Honts & Driscoll (1988)	CQT (not described)	52	Criminal suspects in U.S. (federal cases). ROSS (novel) scoring used.
Honts & Raskin (1988)	Directed lie incorporated	21	Criminal suspects in U.S. (private cases).
Matte & Reuss (1989)	Quadri-Zone	114	Criminal suspects in Buffalo, NY (police and private cases).
Murray (1989)	Arther CQT	171	Police screening and criminal cases in Colorado.
Patrick & Iacono (1987)	Canadian CQT	81	Criminal suspects in British Columbia.
Putnam (1983)	Modified General Question Test & Backster Zone	285	Criminal suspects in Reno, Nevada.
Raskin et al (1988)	CQT (not described)	85	Criminal suspects in U.S. (federal cases).
Ryan (1989)	Reid CQT	255	Criminal suspects in Chicago, IL.
Widacki (1982)	Backster Zone	38	Criminal suspects in Poland.
Yamamura & Miyake (1980)	Peak of Tension	95	Criminal suspects in riot case in Japan.

Norman Ansley, Polygraph, 19(3), 1990

Table 5

Discussion

Based on these studies involving real cases and excluding inconclusive decisions, it appears that field examiners are about 98% accurate in their overall decisions. When they employ control question tests they are more accurate with deceptive (DI) subjects at 99% than they are with truthful (NDI) subjects at 95%.

The blind reliability studies of control question tests also showed the same trend for accuracy comparing results from deceptive subjects with results from truthful subjects. Blind evaluators were correct in 93% of the DI charts and 83% of the NDI charts.

In the one field study of peak of tension tests, the examiners' truthful decisions, at 94%, were more accurate than their deceptive decisions, at 80%. In the one study of blind analysis of GKT charts, the truthful decisions, at 90%, were more accurate than the deceptive decisions, at 65%. Suggesting that these studies show a trend is questionable because one study is from Japan, the other is from Israel. The techniques are somewhat related, but not alike, and in the Elaad study, the GKT charts were run after Reid CQT charts. Also, in Elaad, the results were from blind evaluators while in Yamamura & Miyake the results are based on the examiners' decisions.

There is a recent tendency to treat the class of control question tests (CQTs) as a generic test, something specific, rather than a category of tests with important differences among the members. While I have grouped CQTs in this study there are several different CQT formats, with one appearing in four studies: Arther CQT (Murray 1989), Backster Zone (Arellano, 1990; Elaad & Schahar, 1987; Putnam, 1983; Widacki, 1982), Canadian CQT (Patrick & Iacono, 1987), Directed Lie Control Questions Test (Honts & Raskin, 1988), Matte Quadri-Zone (Matte & Reuss, 1989), Modified General Question Test (Putnam, 1983), and Reid CQTs (Elaad et al., 1988; Jayne, 1990; Ryan, 1989). See Table 5. There is no evidence to show that differences in pretest and format are important in determining validity of CQTs. It is logical to think they probably do make some difference but it may be a difficult task to separate pretest and format from other variables in field research. For example, the studies here include significant population differences in terms of culture. There is probably a diverse population represented among the subjects tested in Israel. Arellano tested Hispanics who were in the United States illegally, and tested only in the Spanish language. Yamanura & Miyake tested the riot suspects in Japanese. However, the Canadian and American subjects may have much in common. Variations in technique and populations must be recognized as a limiting factor in generalizing from these studies.

* * * * * *

There are only three known research studies dealing with test-retest reliability involving the same examinee. (Yankee & Grimsley 1987; Grimsley & Yankee 1986; Balloun & Holmes 1979). Most PV examination reliability studies have used inter-rater agreement as the measure of consistency. However we should not overlook the fact that conclusions as to truth or deception when conducted in accordance with the standards of the American Polygraph Association, are based on a minimum of two separate polygraph charts containing the same test questions administered to the same examinee, and the median number of charts usually numbers three and can go as high as five. The relatively high numerical threshold which increases with each chart administered as required by the Backster Tri-Zone and Matte Quadri-Track Zone Comparison techniques before a definite conclusion can be rendered, cannot be attained without consistency of all charts' scores.

Both of aforesaid studies by Yankee and Grimsley used college students in mock paradigms, hence are classified as *analog* studies. The former, entitled *The Effect of a Prior Polygraph Test on a Subsequent Polygraph Test*, employed an analog control question specific issue methodology to determine among other things (1) the overall accuracy of FP decisions for the first PV examination and the subsequent retest of the same examinee, and (2) the accuracy of FP decisions after one group of examinees has been given *accurate feedback* regarding the results of their first PV examination; a second group has been given *inaccurate feedback*; and a third group has been given *no feedback*. The results of aforesaid study revealed that the overall accuracy of FP decisions, excluding inconclusives was 93% for the first test and 86% for the second test on the same subjects. In experiment (2) above, the accuracy (excluding inconclusives) for *accurate feedback* (AF) for the second test was 94% (from 100% in first test); *inaccurate feedback* (IF) was 86% (from 95% in first test); and *no feedback* (NF) 79% (from 90% in first test). Furthermore, *inaccurate feedback* caused an increase in *Inconclusives* from 17 % in first test to 42% in second test. The number of correct decisions declined for all groups on the second test, but was more pronounced for the *inaccurate feedback* (IF) group, where the values almost reached statistical significance at .05.(AF 83% to 63%; IF 79% to 50%; NF 75% to 63%).Thus it appears that giving inaccurate feedback to examinees does reduce correct decisions and increases inconclusives. Caution must be exercised in the evaluation of aforesaid results inasmuch at it is based on an analog study whose psychodynamics are considerably different than field studies dealing with real-life fears.

In a real-life situation, it is expected that an innocent (as later verified) examinee who is advised that his/her PV examination results show deception regarding the target issue, will become quite upset and lose faith in the examination procedure. Hence such an examinee should experience a pronounced "fear of error" in any subsequent test, which has been shown (Matte 1980; Matte-Reuss 1989) to impact on the innocent examinee's selective attention process (psychological set) involving control versus relevant questions, wherein the innocent examinee's plus (truthful) scores are diminished below the threshold thus causing an inconclusive result (52% in Matte-Reuss study), and in some cases the scores fall below zero for negative (minus) scores causing a false positive result (5% in Matte-Reuss study). (See Chapters 9 and 14 for details). Furthermore, in a real-life situation, such erroneous feedback can also arouse anger from an innocent examinee (also discussed in Chapter 9) which can cause a false positive or inconclusive result.(Hunter 1974). These aforementioned *emotions* were certainly not duplicated in the aforesaid Yankee-Grimsley laboratory experiment, yet that is the *essence* of the study's purpose. The fact that a mock paradigm devoid of aforesaid emotions reflected a decrease in accuracy of 8% by inaccurate feedback versus accurate feedback and increased the inconclusives from 17% to 42% should underscore the potential for a significantly greater decrease in accuracy when such emotions are present in real-life situations. Thus a field study would be a more appropriate method of evaluating such a hypothesis.

The second reliability study conducted by Grimsley and Yankee (1986) is entitled *The Effect of Multiple Retests on Examiner Decisions in Applicant Screening Polygraph Examinations*. This study also employed college students in mock paradigms, hence is classified as an analog study. This methodology employed the relevant-irrelevant technique, normally used in screening type of examinations. Three tests were administered to each examinee by a different forensic psychophysiologist (FP), using the relevant-irrelevant test format. After each test, all examinees were told that they had failed the test.

Overall diagnostic accuracy was 78% for test 1, 73% for test 2, and 77% for test 3, hence no statistical difference between tests 1, 2, and 3. For the guilty, inconclusives excluded, the accuracy was 72%, 63%, and 64% for tests l, 2, and 3 respectively. For the Innocent the accuracy was 81%, 80%, and 83% for tests l, 2, and 3 respectively. An examination of the data reveals that repeated PV examination testing of the same examinees increases the likelihood that nondeceptive subjects will eventually be called nondeceptive (reduces the false positive decisions) and that they will pass the test. The accuracy of the decisions for nondeceptive subjects increases from 81% to 96% excluding inconclusives. The false negative rate (calling a deceptive subject truthful) decreases with repeated testing, from 73% to 90%. Because this is an analog study, caution must be exercised in the evaluation of aforesaid results. Furthermore, all of the examinees in this experiment were told that they were deceptive regardless of the results for analytical purposes, but not an ethical or realistic practice in field testing. As related in the first analog study conducted by Yankee & Grimsley (1986) involving specific-issue control question testing, the psychodynamics in analog studies are significantly different than field studies.

The third reliability study was conducted by Kristen D. Balloun and David S. Holmes (1979) involving a laboratory experiment with a real crime (cheating on an examination), hence a hybrid study. In this study, a guilty knowledge test was employed, using a galvanometer (GSR) and a plethysmograph. Eighteen males with high psychopathic deviate scores on the Minnesota Multiphasic Personality Inventory (MMPI) were compared with sixteen males with low psychopathic deviate scores, regarding their detectability in a guilty knowledge test using aforementioned instruments. The results indicated that only the GSR was effective in detecting guilt and there was a decline in accuracy from 75% correct overall on test 1 to 56% correct on test 2. The decline in accuracy for the second test was particularly striking for the deceptive subjects (cheaters) where the number of correct calls declined from 61% to 17%, but there was a slight increase in the number of correct decisions for the truthful subjects (non-cheaters), from 88% in test 1 to 94% in test 2. There was no difference in the detection rates for subjects with high or low psychopathic deviate scores. It should be noted that this study did not employ a pneumograph to record thoracic and abdominal breathing patterns, nor a blood pressure cuff to record cardiovascular responses, normally used in field polygraph instruments. While aforementioned study reflects a significant decrease in accuracy between test 1 and test 2 for the detection of the guilty, there was no statistical difference in the accuracy of identification of the innocent between test 1 and test 2. There is some question regarding the distinctness of issue and recall motivation of the deceptive subjects in the guilty knowledge test used in this study. Finally, the results of this study only apply to the guilty knowledge test.

In 1988, a final report to the National Institute of Justice entitled *A Study of the Validity of Polygraph Examinations in Criminal Investigation* by D. C. Raskin, J. C. Kircher, C. R. Honts, S. W. Horowitz, evaluated the accuracy of polygraph decisions using confirmed criminal cases which revealed that the Secret Service FPs, using the Numerical Approach, were significantly more accurate in their identification of truthful and deceptive subjects in the analysis of single-issue tests (96% and 95% respectively) where the suspects were either truthful to all confirmed relevant questions or deceptive to all confirmed relevant questions, than they were in multiple-issue tests (91% and 85% respectively) where the suspects were confirmed as deceptive to at least one relevant question and also truthful to at least one relevant question in the same test. Furthermore, the accuracy of blind interpreters on single-issue tests where all answers to the relevant questions are either truthful or deceptive was 85% on truthful and 94% on deceptive subjects. However in multiple-issue tests the blind interpreters' accuracy dropped to 63% on truthful answers and 84% on deceptive answers. The authors opined from these results that "control question polygraph tests perform best when the relevant questions deal with issues that elicit either all truthful or all deceptive answers from the subject... A related problem is raised by the finding of higher false positive rates for questions answered truthfully by suspects who were also deceptive to at least one relevant question in the same test. It appears that answering deceptively to at least one relevant question in the test tends to weaken the reactions to the control questions, thereby making it difficult for them to produce reactions that are larger than those to relevant questions that answered truthfully."(Raskin, et al 1988)

The aforementioned study also made comparisons in the ability of human interpreters to make correct diagnosis of truth or deception on the basis of the physiological data contained in polygraph charts versus the computer and its algorithm. The study revealed that, using a lens model, on the average, the blind evaluators were able to predict 18% of the criterion variance that was not predicted by the four computer-generated variables. This finding suggests that significantly more diagnostic information was available in the physiological recordings than was represented in the four parameters quantified by the computer. The authors felt that "some of the variance may be attributed to the human interpreter's ability to make reasonable approximations of the amplitudes of physiological reactions even when the recording pens exceeded the limit of travel because the examiner had set the amplifier sensitivity too high, a common occurrence in the polygraph charts used in the present study. The computer merely quantified the amplitude of the response as it appeared on the chart, and no attempt was made to estimate the true amplitude of the response when the limit of pen travel was exceeded." Interestingly, all of the original FPs and one of the blind interpreters outperformed the computer model. However the computer model used in aforementioned study did not have the sophistication of current computer systems and algorithms such as APL's PolyScore used by Axciton and Lafayette. The results obtained with the computer models in this study derived from the data on criminal suspects demonstrated higher accuracy than the majority of blind numerical interpretation. This indicates that computer evaluations are a realistic means of providing an objective, rapid and readily available form of quality control for field examiners.(Raskin, et al 1988)

In 1988 a study entitled "Human Versus Computerized Evaluations of Polygraph Data in a Laboratory Setting" by J. C. Kircher and D. C. Raskin, evaluated computer algorithms that process physiological reactions to PV examination test questions and assess the probability that the questions were answered truthfully against data obtained in two mock crime experiments. The subjects of the experiments were equally divided into guilty and innocent groups. A standardization sample data from 100 subjects was used to develop a discriminant function of electrodermal, cardiovascular, and respiration measures. The distributions of discriminant scores were used to derive Bayesian assessments of the probability of truthfulness. Data validation sample from 48 subjects in another experiment were used to cross validate the computer model. Dichotomous computer classifications of subjects in the standardization sample were 93% correct. Blind numerical evaluations of the same data by an expert interpreter were 89% correct. On cross-validation, computer outcomes were 94% correct, and numerical evaluations were 92% correct. There were no significant differences between computer and human evaluations. It should be noted that the accuracies achieved by the numerical evaluators replicated findings obtained with numerical evaluations in previous mock crime experiments (Bradley, Ainsworth 1984; Dawson 1980; Ginton, Daie, Elaad, Ben-Shakhar 1982; Podlesny, Raskin 1978; Raskin, Hare 1978). However, such results must be viewed with caution as they represent *estimates* of the validity of the numerical methods utilized in real cases in the field. The correlations between the physiological measures and the guilt or innocence criterion and the corresponding correlations for the numerical scores assigned by the polygraph interpreter were more informative than the detection rates. Those correlations revealed that computer and numerical methods extracted similar amounts of diagnostic information from cardiovascular responses to test questions, whereas computer assessments of respiration suppression were somewhat less diagnostic than those of the numerical evaluator on cross-validation. Three of the five computer-generated measures selected for the discriminant function were obtained from skin conductance which accounted for more than 70% of the predictable linear variance in the criterion. In one experiment skin conductance amplitude correlated .77 with the criterion and .82 in another experiment, making it the most heavily weighted variable in the discriminant function. These findings and those from other experiments suggest that the skin conductance response (in analog studies) is the most useful measure for discriminating between truthful and deceptive subjects (Barland, Raskin 1975; Bradley, Ainsworth 1984; Bradley, Janisse 1981; Dawson 1980; Kubis 1973; Podlesny, Raskin 1978; Raskin, Hare 1978). However field studies have shown contrary results where respiration was found to be the most productive and accurate, with the electrodermal response finishing last ((Jayne 1990; Slowik, Buckley 1975; Matte, Reuss 1989, 1992).

In aforementioned study by Matte and Reuss (1989), the physiological data and ensuing numerical scores from 311 polygraph charts from l22 confirmed field cases acquired from a metropolitan police department and a private polygraph firm employing the same polygraph technique (Matte Quadri-Track Zone Comparison), were analyzed to determine the effectiveness of each of the four recorded channels, namely the upper (thoracic) and lower (abdominal) respiration, electrodermal (GSR), and cardiovascular activity. Of the original tests, 62 were called "deception indicated" (DI) and 53 "no deception indicated" (NDI). Subsequently these decisions were verified as correct. In addition, there were seven inconclusive decisions, of which five proved to be innocent and two guilty. The instruments were electronically enhanced four-channel Stoelting polygraph units. The productivity of each channel was determined on the basis of the sum of the *verified* scores attained in each tracing, thus the tracing which accumulated the highest score *consistent with ground truth* was deemed the most productive, followed by the next highest score consistent with ground truth and so forth. Hence productivity is also indicative of accuracy.

The results of aforementioned Matte-Reuss study revealed that the most productive of the physiological channels was the pneumo tracing at 43%, followed by the cardio at 32%, and the electrodermal at 24%. Among men, the most productive channel for the innocent cases was the pneumo at 67%, the cardio at 22%, and the electrodermal at 11%. For guilty men the most productive was the cardio at 46%, the pneumo at 37%, and the electrodermal at 15%. Among innocent women the most productive was the electrodermal at 43%, the pneumo at 38%, and the cardio at 18%. For guilty women the most productive channel was the pneumo at 44%, the cardio at 39%, and the electrodermal at 17%. There were also major sex differences in the pneumo tracings. The upper (thoracic) is more significant in 33% of the females, but not in the males. The lower (abdominal) is significant in 75% of the males, but in only 26% of the females. This difference was found to be significant ($p = <.0000011$). There is a major difference in the breathing response of males and females. For the females 74% produce an Upper breathing response, or produce an equal Upper and Lower response. Only 26% of the females show a lower dominance in breathing response. For the males 100% favor a Lower response or an equal Upper and Lower breathing response. In this study no males showed an Upper dominance in breathing response. This indicates that males show a definite tendency to show stronger Lower (abdominal) breathing responses. The study fails to reject the hypothesis that there is a significant difference for females ($p = <.339$). This indicates that there is a stronger probability of an equal chance of Upper, Lower, or Equal dominance in the pneumo tracing for females. (Matte, Reuss 1989, 1992)

In comparing the results of aforementioned field research study with previous research on the effectiveness of the Pneumo, GSR and Cardio polygraph components, it becomes apparent that the ineffectiveness of the pneumograph in some studies (Barland 1986, Thackray 1968, Cutrow 1972) was most likely due to the positioning of the *single* pneumograph component on the least productive breathing area. In some *mock crime* studies the GSR is the most effective overall parameter (Raskin et al. 1978; Thackray et al, 1968; Cutrow et al. 1972), but in many *field* studies the pneumograph is the most effective overall parameter (Jayne 1990; Slowik & Buckley 1975; Matte & Reuss 1992; Suzuki 1975; Buckley & Senese 1991; Elaad & Kleiner 1990; Elaad 1985) and the GSR is often the least effective parameter (Jayne 1990, Orlansky 1964; Matte & Reuss 1989,

1992). However Barland and Raskin (1974 used field cases of confirmed deceptive subjects only; no truthful subjects were used in this research; and they found the electrodermal to be the most accurate, followed by the pneumo and the cardio. Franz (1989) used a computer analysis of 100 confirmed field cases and found the electrodermal to be the most accurate, followed by respiration and cardio. In Ryan's (1989) study the GSR was most effective in identifying the Guilty, but respiration was the most effective in identifying the Innocent. When Inconclusives are omitted from Ryan's data, the respiration parameter was found to be significantly more useful than the GSR and Cardio for both the truthful and deceptive subjects. Interestingly, in the study by Elaad and Kleiner (1990) it was reported that the experienced forensic psychophysiologists had significantly better detection rates with the respiration, but there was no significant difference between the groups in scoring electrodermal or cardio patterns.

This author believes that the difference in psychodynamics between subjects in mock paradigms (laboratory studies) and field studies (real-life cases) explains the significant differences seen in the reported research for these different types of studies. The key factors for the psychodynamic differences are felt to be the *Fear of Detection* by the Guilty and the *Fear of Error* by the Innocent. Even if laboratory models were unsuitable for field application, the use of automated methods for collecting and storing physiological data in field settings would greatly facilitate development of statistical models that may be of value in field settings. The accumulation of physiological data from large numbers of verified criminal cases would make it possible to develop and test computer models utilizing data acquired from actual criminal cases.

Such data accumulation was subsequently conducted for the Department of Defense by the Applied Physics Laboratory at the Johns Hopkins University in the development of a mathematical algorithm to score PV examination Zone Comparison tests from field test data collected on Axciton computerized polygraph systems. The Polygraph Automated Scoring System (PASS) version 2.1 software was in service for a very brief period and was replaced by PolyScore, version 2.3. PolyScore 2.3 software used a sophisticated mathematical algorithm to analyze the data, then displayed a probability to indicate deception, no deception, or inconclusive. The data base for version 2.3 was established by using 539 PV examinations in field criminal cases. Of the 539 PV examinations, 162 were confirmed. The remaining 377 cases were included in the data base if the decisions made by the field FPs were agreed upon by two different examiners or if verified by independent means. Of the 162 confirmed cases, 142 were correctly identified and 20 were called inconclusive by the original FPs. The algorithm diagnosed 150 of the 162 correctly, identified 11 as inconclusive, and produced one error. Thus, the algorithm reduced the inconclusives by nine and increased the number of correct identifications from 142 to 150. (Yankee 1995).

The current version of the APL software, PolyScore 3.0, was developed with 624 usable cases. Of these, there were 301 nondeceptive cases and 323 deceptive cases. The number of charts for each subject averaged three charts and typically there were nine relevant responses for each subject. There were 7 basic processing steps in the development of the algorithm: the conditioning of the data, standardization of the data, development of data features, standardization of features, evaluation of the features, development of the decision rule, and evaluation of the algorithm. Inasmuch as the subject status was determined by examiner (FP) decision for many of the cases in the data set, the results set forth demonstrate that the algorithm is consistent with experienced FP decisions. However the computerized evaluation system is fundamentally different than those used by FPs. The two methods of chart evaluation use different scoring criteria and weight the channels differently. This was evidenced by eight cases scored as inconclusive by the original FP and later confirmed as 6 deceptive and 2 truthful. These eight examinations were dropped from the database and the model was refitted using the same features to render this evaluation independent of the training data. A clear decision was made in seven of the eight cases by the algorithm and all of these decisions were correct. The results were inconclusive for one case. These results appear to confirm that the algorithm does not mimic traditional chart interpretation. Furthermore, this conclusion can be reached without the empirical support, inasmuch as the manner in which the algorithm processes the data is fundamentally different than traditional methods. It is also apparent that the algorithm could be effective in reducing inconclusive decisions. (Olsen, Harris, Capps, Johnson, Ansley 1995) The mathematical algorithm used in the Applied Physics Laboratory software called PolyScore employed in computerized polygraph systems devotes an average 54 percent of its criteria for deception to Electrodermal activity, 24 percent to Blood Volume, 8 percent to Pulse Rate, and only 14 percent to Respiration (Johnson 1994; Olsen 1995).

Judging from aforementioned studies, the difference between the accuracy rates for FPs using traditional scoring systems and the computer algorithms is not statistically significant, hence most field FPs are using the algorithm results as a second opinion for quality control. Computer algorithms will continue to be used in that manner until more sophisticated systems, capitalizing on broader data bases, including a broader range of test formats, are developed that will significantly surpass human evaluation capabilities. When new methods of collecting physiological data, not amenable to human interpretation, are developed, computer algorithms will be the only method capable of making a diagnosis. However, caution must always be exercised in the weight attributed to the analysis of the physiological data, whether evaluated by a traditional scoring system or computer algorithm, inasmuch as it is the end product of a psychologically structured and administered examination with its own specific construct and criterion validity.

REFERENCES:

Abrams, S., Davidson, M. (1988). Countermeasures in polygraph testing. *Polygraph*, 17(l): 16-20.

Addison, M. E. (1982, May 9, 11). Letters from the Department of the Navy's Special Assistant for Scientific Investigations to J. A. Matte.

Ansley, N. (1983). A compendium on polygraph validity. *Polygraph*, *12*(2): 53-61.

Ansley, N. (1990). The validity and reliability of polygraph decisions in real cases. *Polygraph,* 19(3): 169-181.

Ansley, N. (1995). Simulations and polygraph research. *Polygraph,* 24(4), 275-290.

Arellano, L. R. (1990). The polygraph examination of Spanish speaking subjects. *Polygraph,* 19(2), 155-156. (abstract)

Arther, R. O. (1979). Observing Gestures, Part I. *The Journal of Polygraph Science*. Vol. XIV, Nr. 2, Sep-Oct 1979.

Balloun, K. D., Holmes, D. S. (1979). Effects of repeated examinations on the ability to detect guilt with a polygraphic examination: A laboratory experience with a real crime. *Journal of Applied Psychology,* 64(3): 316-322.

Barland, G. H. (1975). *Detection of Deception in Criminal Suspects*: A Field Validation Study. Unpublished dissertation. University of Utah.

Barland, G. H., Raskin, D. C. (1975). An evaluation of field techniques in detection of deception. *Psychophysiology,* 12, 321-330.

Barland, G. H., Raskin, D. C. (1976). *Validity and reliability of polygraph examinations of criminal suspects*. Report No. 76-1, Contract No. 75-NI-99-001 for the National Institute of Law Enforcement and Criminal Justice.

Barland, G. H. (1985). A method for estimating the accuracy of individual control question tests; *Anti-Terrorism; Forensic Science; Psychology in Police Investigation*. Proceedings of IDENTI-!85. The International Congress on Techniques for Criminal Identification, Jerusalem, Israel: Heiliger and Company Limited, 142-147.

Barland, G. H., Honts, C. R., Barger, S. O. (1989). *Studies of the accuracy of security screening polygraph examinations*. Ft. McClellan, AL: Department of Defense Polygraph Institute.

Berry, R. L. (1960). A study of the effect of hypnotically induced amnesia upon the accuracy of the lie detector test results. Lie Detector Committee, The Provost Marshal General's School, Fort Gordon, Georgia.

Bersh, P. J. (1969). A validation study of polygraph examiner judgments. *Journal of Applied Psychology,* 55(5): 399-403.

Bitterman, M. E., Marcuse, F. L. (1945). Autonomic response in post-hypnotic amnesia. *Journal of experimental psychology* 35, 248-252.

Bradley, M. T., Janisse, M. P. (1981). Accuracy demonstrations, threat, and the detection of eception: Cardiovascular, electrodermal, and pupillary measures. *Psychophysiology*, 18(3): 307-315.

Bradley, M. T., Ainsworth, D. (1984). Alcohol and the psychophysiological detection of deception. *Psychophysiology*, 21, 63-71.

Brisentine, R. A. (1995, Oct 19). Telephone conversation with J. A. Matte.

Brisentine, R. A. (1995, Nov 13). Telephone conversation with J. A. Matte.

Burch, N. R. (1969, October). *Online classification of polygraph responses*. Final Report, Department of the Navy, Office of Naval Research, Washington, D. C., Contract N014- 67-C-0493.

Capps, M. H., Knill, B. L., Evans, R. K. (1993). Effectiveness of the Symptomatic Questions. *Polygraph*, 22(4), 285-298.

Capps, M. H. (1991). Accuracy of individual parameters in field polygraph studies. *Polygraph*, 20(2), 65-70.

Capps, M. H., Ansley, N. (1992). Anomalies: The contributions of the cardio, pneumo, and electrodermal measures towards a valid conclusion. *Polygraph*, 21(4), 321-340.

Coe, W. C., Yashinski, E. (1985). Volitional experiences associated with breaching post hypnotic amnesia. *Journal of Personality and Social Psychology*, 48(3), 716-722.

Corcoran, J. F. T., Lewis, M. D., Garver, R. B. (1978). Biofeedback conditioned galvanic skin response and hypnotic suppression of arousal: A pilot study of their reaction to deception. *Journal of Forensic Science*. 23:155-162.

Corcoran, J. F. T., Wilson, D. H. (1979). Biofeedback conditioned responses and the polygraph: A case report. *Polygraph*, 8(2), 120-126.

Correa, E I., Adams, H. E. (1981). The validity of the Pre-employment polygraph examination and the effects of motivation. *Polygraph* 10, 143-156.

Cumley, W. E. (1959). Hypnosis and the polygraph. *Police* 4(2), 39-40.

Cutrow, R., Parks, A., Lucas, N., Thomas, K. (1972). The objective use of multiple physiological indices in the detection of deception. *Psychophysiology*, 9, 578-589.

Davidson, P. O. (1968). Validity of the guilty - knowledge technique: The effects of motivation. *Journal of Applied Psychology*, 52(1): 62-65.

Dawson, M. E. (1980). Physiological detection of deception: Measurement of responses to questions and answers during countermeasure maneuvers. *Psychophysiology*, 17, 8-17.

Driscoll, L. N., Honts, C. R., Jones, D. (1987). The validity of the positive control physiological detection of deception technique. *Polygraph*, 16(3), 218-225.

Edwards, R. H. (1981). A survey: Reliability of polygraph examinations conducted by Virginia polygraph examiners. *Polygraph*, 10(4), 229-272.

Elaad, E. (1985). *Validity of the control question test in criminal cases*. Unpublished manuscript. Scientific Interrogation Unit, Criminal Investigation Division, Israel National Police Headquarters, Jerusalem, Israel.

Elaad, E., Ginton, A., Jungman, N. (1988). *Respiration line length and GSR amplitude as detection measures in criminal guilty knowledge tests*. Unpublished manuscript. Division of Criminal Investigation, Israel National Police Headquarters, Jerusalem, Israel.

Elaad, E., Schahar, E. (1985). Polygraph field validity. *Polygraph*, 14(3), 217-223.

Forman, R. F., McCauley, C. (1987). Validity of the positive control polygraph test using the field practice model. *Polygraph*, 16(2), 145-160.

Franz, M. L. (1989). *Technical report: Relative contributions of physiological recordings to detect deception*. DoD contract MDA 904-88-M-6612, Argenbright Polygraph, Inc., Atlanta, GA.

Freeman, F. S. (1950). *Theory and practice of psychological testing*. New York: Henry Holt and Company.

Gatchel, R. J., Smith, J. E. Kaplan, N. M. (1983). The effect of propranolol on polygraphic detection of deception. Unpublished manuscript, University of Texas Health Sciences Center.

Germann, A. C. (1961). Hypnosis as related to the scientific detection of deception by polygraph examination: A pilot Study. *International Journal of Clinical and Experimental Hypnosis*. 9, 309-311.

Ginton, A., Daie, N., Elaad, E., Ben-Shakhar, G. (1982). A method for evaluating the use of the polygraph in a real-life situation. *Journal of Applied Psychology*, 67(2): 131-137

Hammond, D. L. (1980). The responding of Normals, Alcoholics, and Psychopaths in a laboratory lie-detection experiment. Unpublished Doctoral dissertation, California School of Professional Psychology.

Holmes, W. D. (1958). Degree of objectivity in chart interpretation. In V.A. Leonard (Ed.), *Academy lectures on lie detection* (Vol. 2, pp. 62-70). Springfield, IL: Charles C. Thomas. Abstract in Polygraph, 19(2), 156-157.

Honts, C. R. (1982). The effects of simple physical countermeasures on the physiological detection of deception. Unpublished Master's Thesis, Virginia Polytechnic Insti- tute and State University, Blacksburg, Virginia. Presented at the Society for Psycho-physiological Research, Minneapolis, Minnesota, October 1982, with R. L. Hodes.

Honts, C. R. (1986). Countermeasures and the physiological detection of deception: A psychophysiological analysis. Unpublished doctoral dissertation, University of Utah. 1986.

Honts, C. R. (1992). Bootstrap decision making for polygraph examinations. University of North Dakota, Grand Forks, ND, Grant #N000140-92-J-1794, Final Report, August 24, 1992. (Processed by PERSEREC and funded by DoDPI).

Honts, C. R., Driscoll, L. N. (1988). A field validity study of the Rank Order Scoring System (ROSS) in multiple issue control question tests. *Polygraph*, 17(1), 1-15.

Honts, C. R., Raskin, D. C. (1988). A field study of the validity of the directed lie control question. *Journal of Police Science and Administration*, 16(1), 56-61.

Horvath, F. (1991). The utility of control questions and the effects of two control questions tests on field polygraph techniques. *Polygraph*, 20(1), 7-25.

Horvath, F. (1994). The value and effectiveness of the sacrifice relevant question: an empirical assessment. *Polygraph*, 23(4), 261-279.

Hunter, F. L. (1974). Anger and the Polygraph Technique. *Polygraph*, 8(4), 381-395.

Iacono, W. G. (1987). Can we determine the accuracy of polygraph tests? In P. K. Ackles, J. R. Jennings, M.G.H. Coles (Eds.), *Advances in Psychophysiology*, (Vol._ 4). Greenwich, CT: JAI Press.

James, E. (1982). Produced and distributed a program for the VIG 20 Commodore com puter and later for the Commodore 64, to provide "...computer assisted chart evaluation."

Jayne, B. C. (1990). Contributions of physiological recordings in the polygraph technique. Polygraph, 19(2), 105-117.

Jayne, B. C. (1993). The use of alternative opinions in the polygraph technique. *Polygraph*, 22(4), 299-312.

Johnson, G. J. (1994). Information facsimile regarding APL Zone Scoring Results, Zone features, Algorithm Data, Scoring Weights and Response Intervals. U. S. Government Department of Defense, Office of Security Facsimile, 12 Oct 94 to Dr. James A. Matte.

Kirby, S. L. (1981). The comparison of two stimulation tests and their effect on the polygraph technique. *Polygraph*, 10(2), 63-76.

Kircher, J. C. (1983). *Computerized decision-making and patterns of activation in the detection of deception*. A dissertation submitted to the faculty of the University of Utah in partial fulfillment of the requirements for the degree of Doctor of Philosophy.

Kircher, J., Raskin, D. C. (1988). Humans vs. computerized evaluations of polygraph data in a laboratory setting. *Journal of Applied Psychology*, 73(2), 291-302.

Kircher, J. C., Raskin, D. C. (1989). *Computer-assisted polygraph systems, version 6.00 and 6.01 user's manual*, Scientific Assessments Technologies, Inc., 1865 Herbert Avenue, Salt Lake City, UT.

Kleinmuntz, B., Szucko, J. J. (1982). On the fallibility of lie detection. *Law and Society Review*, 17: 84-104.

Kleinmuntz, B., Szucko, J. J. (1984). A field study of the fallibility of polygraph lie detectors. *Nature*, 308(5958), 449-450.

Koll, M. (1979). Analysis of zone charts by various pairings of control and relevant questions. *Polygraph*, 8(2), 145-160.

Kubis, J. F. (1962). *Studies in lie detection: Computer feasibility considerations*. Fordham University, New York, N. Y. RADC-TR-62205. Project No. 5534, AF30(602)-2270, prepared for Rome Air Development Center, Air Force Systems Command, USAF, Griffiss AFB, New York.

Kubis, J. F. (1973). Analysis of polygraphic data (Pt. 2). *Polygraph*, 2, 89-107.

Lykken, D. T. (1959). The GSR in the detection of guilt. *Journal of Applied Psychology*, 43(6), 383-388. Reprinted in Polygraph, 7(2), 123-128.

Lykken, D. T. (1960). The validity of the guilty knowledge technique: The effect of faking. *Journal of Applied Psychology*, 44(4), 258-262. Reprinted in *Polygraph*, 7(1), 42-48.

Lykken, D. T. (1981). *A Tremor in the Blood: Uses and Abuses of the Lie Detector*. New York: McGraw-Hill.

Matte, J. A. (1976). A polygraph control question validation procedure. *Polygraph*, 5(2), 170- 177.

Matte, J. A. (1978). Polygraph Quadri-Zone Comparison Technique. *Polygraph*, 7(4), 266-280.

Matte, J. A. (1979). Privileged communication between attorney-client-polygraphist. *New York State Bar Journal*. 51(6), 466-469, 500-504.

Matte, J. A., Reuss, R. M. (1989). A field validation study of the Quadri-Zone Comparison Technique. *Polygraph*, 18(4), 187-202.

Matte, J. A., Reuss, R. M. (1989). Validation Study on the Quadri-Zone Comparison Technique. *Research Abstract*, LD 01452, Vol. 1502, 1989, University Microfilm International.

Matte, J. A., Reuss, R. M. (1990). A field study of the 'Friendly Polygraphist' concept. *Polygraph*, 19(l), 1-9.

Matte, J. A., Reuss, R. M. (1992). A study of the relative effectiveness of physiological data in field polygraph examinations. *Polygraph*, 21(1), 1-22.

Matte, J. A. (1993). Defense access to police polygraph tests. *New York State Bar Journal*. 65(5), 36-41.

Matte, J. A., (1993). The review, presentation and assurance of intended interpretation of test questions is critical to the outcome of polygraph tests. *Polygraph*, 22(4), 299-312.

McGuigan, F. J., Pavek, G. U. (1972). On the psychophysiological identification of covert, non-oral language processes. *Journal of Experimental Psychology*, 92(2), 237- 245.

Mclnerney, C. A. (1956, August 30). Hypnosis and the lie detector. Paper presented at the annual seminar of the Academy for Scientific Interrogation.

Murray, K. E. (1989). Movement recording chairs: A necessity? *Polygraph*, 18(1), 15-23.

Office of Technology Assessment (OTA). (1983). *Scientific Validity of Polygraph Testing - A Research Review and Evaluation.* Technical Memorandum for the Congressional Board of the 98th Congress of the United States, OTA-TM-H-15.

Olsen, D. E. (1995, August 16). Personal conversation with J. A. Matte. American Polygraph Association, 30th Annual Seminar/Workshop, Las Vegas, Nevada.

Olsen, D. E., Harris, J. C., Capps, M. H., Ansley, N., Johnson, G. J. (1995, October 20). Computerized polygraph scoring system. *Final draft*, awaiting publication.

Olsen, D. E. (1995. Mar 8). Telephone Conversation with J. A. Matte.

Olsen, D. E. (1995, Apr 28). Telephone Conversation with J. A. Matte.

Ohnishi, K., Tada, T., Tanaka, S. (1965). Response patterns in POT. *Research Material* No. 35, NRIPS, 29-37. (In Japanese).

Orne,M. T. (1975). Implications of laboratory research for the detection of deception. In N. Ansley (ed.) *Legal Admissibility of the Polygraph.* Springfield, Illinois: Charles C. Thomas, 114-116.

Patrick, C. J., Iacono, W. G. (1987). Validity and reliability of the control question polygraph test: A scientific investigation. *Psychophysiology*, 24, 604-605. [abstract]

Podlesny, J. A. (1976). Effectiveness of techniques and physiological measures in the detection of deception. *Dissertation*, University of Utah.

Podlesny, J. A., Raskin, D. C. (1978). Effectiveness of techniques and physiological measures in the detection of deception. *Psychophysiology*, 15, 344-359.

Putnam, R. L. (1953). *Field accuracy of polygraph in the law enforcement environment.* Unpublished manuscript. American Polygraph Association archives.
Rafky, D. M., Sussman, R. C. (1985).Polygraphic reliability and validity: Individual components and stress of issue in criminal tests. *Journal of Police Science and Administration*, 13(4), 283-292.

Raskin, D. C., Hare, R. D. (1978). Psychopathy and detection of deception in a prison population. *Psychophysiology*, 15; 126-136.

Raskin, D. C., Barland, G. H., Podlesny, J. A. (1978). *Validity and reliability of detection of deception.* Washington, D. C.: National Institute of Law Enforcement and Criminal Justice.

Raskin, D. C., Kircher, J., Honts, C. Horowitz, S. (1988). A study of the validity of polygraph examinations in Criminal investigations, *Final Report to the National Insti-*

tute of Jutice, Grant No. 85-IJ,CX-0040, Dept. of Psychology, University of Utah, Salt Lake City, UT.

Raskin, D. C., Kircher, J. C., Honts, C. R., Horowitz, S. W. (1988).Validity of control question polygraph tests in criminal investigation. *Psychophysiology*, 25(4), 464. [abstract]

Rovner, L. I., Raskin, D. C., Kircher, J. C. (1978). Effects of information and practice on detection of deception. Presented at the Society for Psychophysiological Research, Madison.

Ryan, R. (1989). *The accuracy of respiration, GSR, and cardiovascular polygraph re sponses utilizing numerical evaluation*. Unpublished master's thesis, Reid College.

Slowik, S., Buckley, J. (1975). Relative accuracy of polygraph examiner diagnosis of respiration, blood pressure, and GSR recordings. *Journal of Police Science and Administration*, 3(3), 305-310.

Stevenson, M., Barry, G. (1988). Use of a motion chair in the detection of physical countermeasures. *Polygraph*, 17 (l), 21-27.

Stern, R. M., Breen, J. P., Watanabe, T., Perry, B. S. (1981). Effect of Feedback of physiological information on responses to innocent associations and guilty knowledge. *Journal of Applied Psychology*, 66(6), 677-681.

Suzuki, A., Watanabe, S., Ohnishi, K., Matsuno, K., Arasuna, M. (1973). Polygraph examiners' judgments in chart interpretation: Reliability of judgment. *Reports of NRIPS*, 26, 34-39. (In Japanese.)

Szuko, J., Kleinmutz, B. (1981). Statistical versus clinical lie detection. *Polygraph*, 10(2), 92-105.

Thackray, R., Orne, M. (1968). A comparison of physiological indices in detection of deception. *Psychophysiology*, 4, 329-339.

Timm, H. W. (1989). Methodological considerations affecting the utility of incorporating innocent subjects into the design of guilty knowledge polygraph experiments. *Polygraph*, 18(3), 143-157.

Waid, W. M., Orne, E. C., Cook, M. R., Orne, M. T. (1981). Meprobamate reduces accuracy of physiological detection of deception. *Science*, 212, 71-73

Weaver, R. S. (1980). The numerical evaluation of polygraph charts: Evolution and comparison of three major systems. *Polygraph*, 9(2), 94-109.

Weinstein, E., Abrams, S., Gibbons, D. (1970). The validity of the polygraph with hyp notically induced repression and guilt. *American Journal of Psychiatry*, 126, 1159-1162.

Wicklander, D. E., Hunter, F. L. (1975). The influence of auxiliary sources of information in polygraph diagnosis. *Journal of Police Science and Administration*, 3(4), 405-409.

Widacki, J. (1982). *Analiza przestanek diagnozowania w. badanich poligraficznych* (The analysis of diagnostic premises in polygraph examinations). Uniwersytetu Slaskeigo, Katowice. [text in polish]

Yamamura, T., Miyake, Y. (1980). Psychological evaluation of detection of deception in a riot case involving arson and murder. *Polygraph*, 9(3), 170-181.

Yankee, W. J. (1968). *A report on the computerization of polygraph records*. Paper presented to the fifth annual seminar of the Keeler Polygraph Institute Alumni Asso ciation, Chicago, IL.

Yankee, W. J. (1995). The current status of research in forensic psychophysiology and its application in the psychophysiological detection of deception. *Polygraph*, 24(3), 137-150.

Yankee, W. J., Powell, III., James M., Newland, R. (1985). An investigation of the accuracy and consistency of polygraph chart interpretation by inexperienced and experienced examiners. *Polygraph*, 14(2), 108-117.

Chapter 4

PHYSIOLOGY

THE MODERN POLYGRAPH INSTRUMENT AND THE AUTONOMIC NERVOUS SYSTEM

Humans in their earliest development were endowed with an emergency system of nerves that reflexly and automatically prepared their body to meet situations that threatened their well-being. Their health and survival depends on the maintenance of a stable fluid and chemical balance in all the vital organs of their body despite sometimes drastic changes in the environment about them; this is referred to as homeostasis. The precision of the physiological mechanics in the maintenance of this stability is incredible. In the center of the brain is located a regulating mechanism, the hypothalamus, that corrects the slightest deviation from a particular standard within very fine limits. Sleep, oxygenation of the blood, body temperature, levels of potassium, sodium, calcium, magnesium and all the essential chemical substances that maintain the activity of cell membranes are finely adjusted. Medical authorities discovered that the autonomic nervous system (Table 1) is responsible for the regulation of all of these complex systems, and that its central control is in the hypothalamus, a series of groups of nerve cells of the brain that control the entire endocrine-hormonal system. All of our involuntary reflexes - those that we cannot consciously control such as our heart beat, pulse rate, increases and decreases in blood pressure, and the expansion and constriction of arteries - are governed by the autonomic nervous system. We do not have to think about inspiration and expiration in order to breathe; our heart functions without deliberation; our sweat glands are not consciously regulated, nor is the flow of blood in our vascular system. When one of our senses detects a threat to our well-being, it sends a signal to the autonomic nervous system, which activates its sympathetic division regardless whether the threat is physical or psychological.

Inside the medulla is a region of gray matter containing a network of interlacing nerve fibers called the *reticular formation*. The reticular formation extends throughout the brain stem and up into the diencephalon. In addition to receiving nerve impulses from the cerebellum, from the basal ganglia, and from various other nuclei in the brain, the *reticular formation* also receives input from all the sensory tracts as they ascend through the medulla. Selected impulses that pass through the reticular formation are relayed to the cerebral cortex and activate it. Because it exerts this control over the cerebral cortex, the reticular formation is considered to be an *activating* or *arousal system* that is essential in maintaining wakefulness, and alertness. For this reason, it is also referred to as the *reticular activating system* (RAS). Located in the reticular formation of the medulla are the *medullary centers*, which are groups of neurons involved in the control of a variety of vital functions, such as heart rate, respiration, dilation and constriction of blood vessels, coughing, and swallowing.

TABLE 1*

AUTONOMIC EFFECTS ON VARIOUS ORGANS OF THE BODY

Organ	Effect of Sympathetic Stimulation	Effect of Parasympathetic Stimulation
Eye		
Pupil	Dilated	Constricted
Ciliary muscle	Slight relaxation (far vision)	Constricted (near vision)
Glands	Vasoconstriction and slight secretion	Stimulation of copious secretion containing many enzymes for enzyme-secreting glands)
Nasal		
Lacrimal		
Parotid		
Submandibular		
Gastric		
Pancreatic		
Sweat glands	Copious sweating (cholinergic)	Sweating on palms of hands
Apocrine glands	Thick, odoriferous secretion	None
Blood vessels	Most often constricted	Most often little or no effect.
Heart		
Muscle	Increased rate Increased force of contraction	Slowed rate Decreased force of contraction (especially of atria)
Coronaries	Dilated (B2); constricted (a)	Dilated
Lungs		
Bronchi	Dilated	Constricted
Blood vessels	Mildly constricted	? dilated
Gut		
Lumen	Decreased peristalsis and tone	Increased peristalsis and tone
sphincter	Increased tone (most times)	Relaxed (most times)
Liver	Glucose released	Slight glycogen synthesis
Gallbladder and bile ducts	Relaxed	Contracted
Kidney	Decreased output and renin secretion	None
Bladder		
Detrusor	Relaxed (slight)	Contracted
Trigone	Contracted	Relaxed
Penis	Ejaculation	Erection
Systemic arterioles		
Abdominal viscera	Constricted	None
Muscle	Constricted (adrenergic a) Dilated (adrenergic B2) Dilated (cholinergic)	None
Skin	Constricted	None
Blood		
Coagulation	Increased	None
Glucose	Increased	None
Lipids	Increased	None
Basal metabolism	Increased up to 100%	None
Adrenal medullary secretion	Increased	None
Mental activity	Increased	None
Piloerector muscles	Contracted	None
Skeletal muscle	Increased glycogenolysis Increased strength	None
Fat cells	Lipolysis	None

* From A. C. Guyton & J. E. Hall: Textbook of Medical Physiology, 9th Edition. Philadelphia, W.B. Saunders Company, 1996.

That part of the sensory information received by the *Reticular Activating System* (RAS) is sorted out by the thalamus before nerve impulses are sent to the cerebrum. The *thalamus* is a central relay station for sensory impulses traveling upward from other parts of the spinal cord and the brain to the cerebrum. The separate sensory pathways have terminations in the thalamus, and then each separate pathway leads to the appropriate region of the cerebrum. It is therefore the last portion of the brain for sensory input before the cerebrum. The thalamus has connections to various parts of the brain by way of nerve fibers that radiate from the upper part of the RAS which extends from the *medulla* to the *thalamus*. The thalamic portion of the RAS sorts out stimuli received from sense organs including the eyes and *ears*, passing on only those that require immediate attention. The *thalamus* is the gatekeeper to the *cerebrum* because it alerts the *cerebrum* to only certain sensory input. The *midbrain* and the *pons* contain tracts that connect the *cerebrum* with other parts of the brain. In addition, the *pons* functions with the *medulla* to regulate *breathing rate*, and the midbrain has reflex centers concerned with head movements in response to visual and *auditory* stimuli. The hypothalamus is concerned with homeostasis or the constancy of the internal environment, and contains centers for hunger, sleep, thirst, body temperature, water balance, and blood pressure. The hypothalamus controls the pituitary gland and thereby serves as a link between the nervous and endocrine systems.

In psychophysiological veracity (PV) examinations, the ear of the subject is the receptor which receives the potentially threatening question or stimulus from the forensic psychophysiologist (FP). The stimulus is transmitted from the ear via sensory neurons of the auditory nerve which has direct connections to the temporal lobe of the cerebrum. There are also collateral branches of the neurons to the reticular activating system (RAS). The branches to the RAS can influence the state of arousal of the cerebrum depending upon the threatening nature of the stimulus. From the temporal region of the cerebrum, there are connections to the frontal lobe which is the center for judgment and reasoning, where the question is perceived and a judgment is made regarding, among other things, the threatening nature of the question. When a question is perceived as threatening, impulses are sent from the frontal lobe through the hypothalamus to the sympathetic system, triggering a sympathetic response. Therefore the sympathetic centers in the lower brain stem act as relay stations for control activities initiated at higher levels of the brain.

The spinal reflex is different and should not be confused with the reflex mechanisms regulated in the medulla which involves the maintenance of homeostasis. In the spinal cord there is a small, irregularly shaped internal section that consists of gray matter (nerve cell bodies) and a larger area surrounding this consisting of white matter, or nerve fibers. There are essentially three categories of spinal cord structures. These categories include *afferent* (sensory) nerves which conduct impulses upward to the brain, *efferent* (motor) nerves which conduct impulses from the brain and on to the nerves which supply the muscles and glands. A third category are *interneurons*, which are found between afferent and efferent nerves and serve as a processor. The spinal reflex involves the integration of messages not involving the brain, or reflex activities. Interneurons are sometimes referred to as creating a *shortcut* in nerve impulse transmission because cognitive processing

NEUROLOGICAL PATHWAY FROM THE AUDITORY SYSTEM

To The

SYMPATHETIC SYSTEM

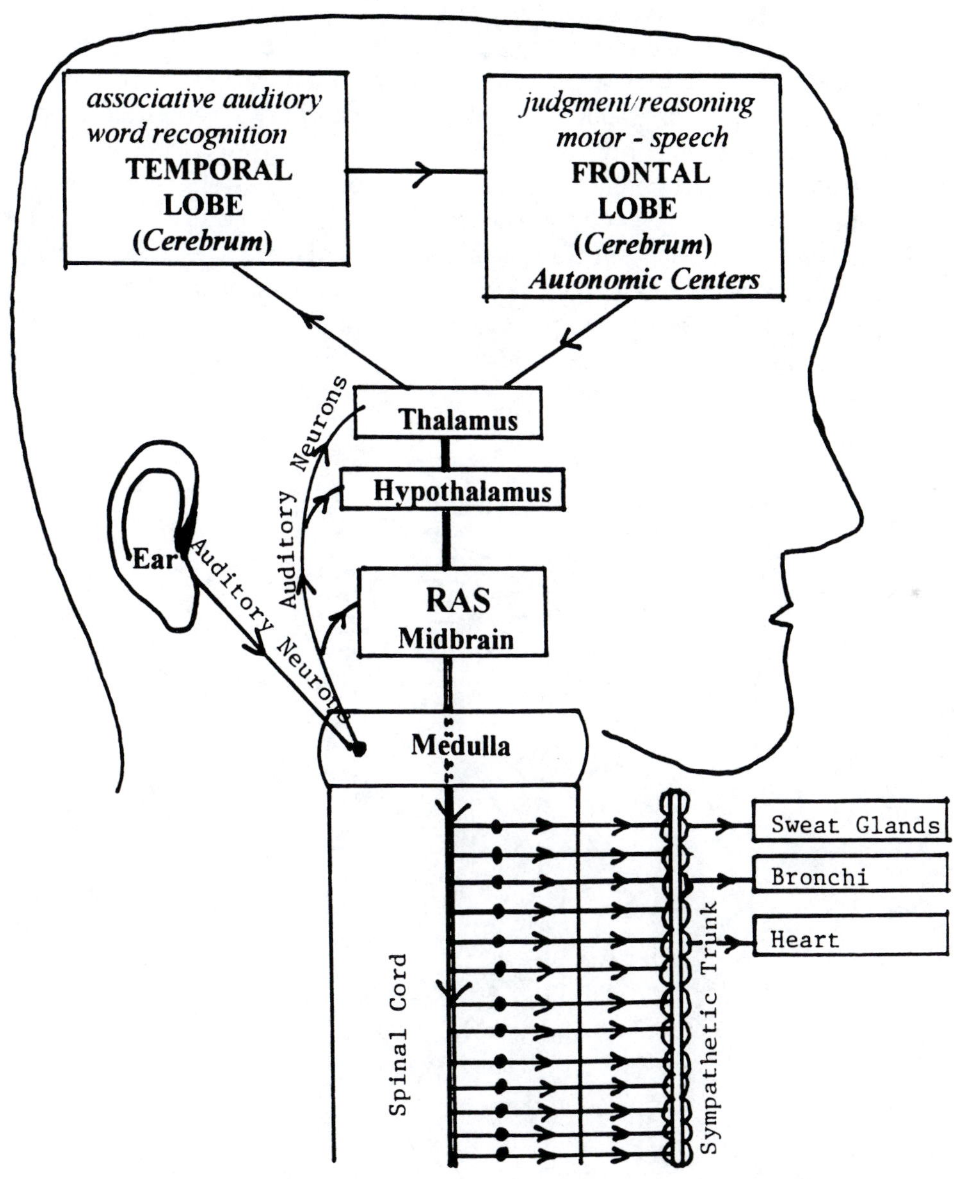

Figure IV-1. Above illustration developed and drawn by J. A. Matte & R. M. Reuss 1996.

from the brain is not required to obtain the immediate motor response from a stimulus. An example of this process can be seen if a person places his/her hand on a hot stove burner. He/she will immediately remove his/her hand because of a direct spinal reflex not requiring brain processing. The message is eventually transmitted to the brain arousing conscious awareness.

When the sympathetic system is activated, it immediately prepares the body for "fight or flight" by causing the adrenal medulla glands* to secrete hormones known as epinephrine and norepinephrine, so that among other functions, the blood will be distributed to those areas of the body where it is most needed to meet the emergency, such as the brain and the larger muscle groups. The chemical norepinephrine causes the arterioles in certain parts of the body to constrict, thereby preventing blood from entering those areas where it is not immediately needed. Certain portions of the body affected by the sympathetic system can be felt or seen by the individual affected. For instance, an athlete may feel "butterflies" in his stomach just before an athletic event. This is a result of the sympathetic system causing the secretion of norepinephrine, a hormone, to constrict arterioles leading to the stomach thereby significantly reducing the amount of blood normally routed to the stomach, producing that nauseated feeling of "butterflies." Constriction of arterioles

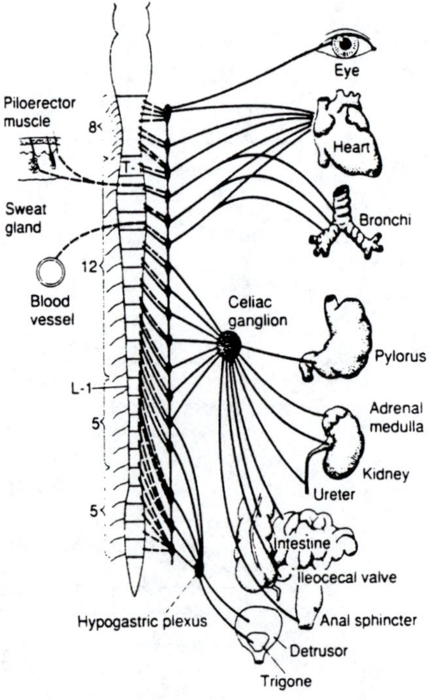

Figure IV-2. Sympathetic nervous system. Dashed lines represent postganglionic fibers in the gray rami leading back into the spinal nerves for distribution to blood vessels, sweat glands, and pilorector muscles. From A. C. Guyton and J. E. Hall. Textbook of Medical Physiology, 9th Edition, Philadelphia: W. B. Saunders Company, 1996.

in other parts of the body also takes place when the sympathetic system activates the secretion of norepinephrine, which in time affects the skin capillaries in the same manner, producing pallor in the face often found in people experiencing severe fright, as well as coldness or clamminess of the hands and fingers due to the reduction in the volume of blood in those extremities, as a mechanism to reduce bleeding from wounds.

Other obvious effects take place when the sympathetic system is activated. The heart pumps blood harder and faster, increasing blood pressure, pulse rate, and strength, thus furnishing more oxygenated blood to those areas of the body where it is vitally needed to meet the emergency, such as the brain when increased mental activity is demanded. The salivary glands in the mouth secrete a different, thicker saliva that has less volume, thereby causing a "dry mouth," which was a well-known phenomenon to early civilizations. The sympathetic system also affects covert symptoms such as a tensing of the involuntary muscles that in addition to causing a constriction of the cardiovascular system, causes a tightening of the involuntary muscles in the stomach thereby inhibiting the diaphragm-intercostal muscular complex, which causes a less than average enlargement of the chest cavity. Peculiarly enough, for those few seconds there is less than average air intake at a time when the brain, which consumes more than 75 percent of the total oxygen intake of the body, needs more than an average amount of oxygen because of the increased mental activity. Therefore, stimulation of the respiratory muscles by the brain will also cause some breathing changes.

The sympathetic preganglionic neurons are cholinergic and release acetylcholine. The sweat glands are stimulated to release perspiration by this mechanism. Thus the sympathetic system affects nervous impulses in a fraction of a second simultaneously stimulating sweat glands, organs with adrenergic receptors and release of norepinephrine from the adrenal medulla. Norepinephrine is transported by arterial blood flow making complete circulation of the body in about one minute, and also norepinephrine from sympathetic nerves, constrict arterioles that force blood away from the skin surfaces in the outer extremities of the body towards the larger muscle groups.

The sympathetic system also causes the iris of the eyes to dilate permitting more light to enter the eye, thereby increasing our vision and awareness of our surroundings. It also affects other organs of the body of less significance to the forensic psychophysiologist, such as contraction of the anal and urinary sphincters, relaxation of the bladder, and inhibition of the contractions of the small intestine wall.

Within the autonomic nervous system is another subdivision called the parasympathetic, which is functionally antagonistic to the sympathetic system. Its role is to maintain

---

*The SNS usually activates the target organs directly, usually by releasing norepinephrine at the myoneural junction between the second (postganglionic) neuron and the target organ (exception: sweat glands are activated by acetylcholine). One of the target organs is the pair of adrenal glands; their release of norepinephrine and epinephrine serves as a booster, coming several seconds after the other organs were directly innervated.

the homeostasis of the body necessary for normal functioning. Therefore, it follows that whenever the sympathetic activates, the parasympathetic follows to reestablish the chemical balance of the body. Without the parasympathetic system, the pressure in the circulatory system could build up so high as to cause an artery to rupture. Instead, the parasympathetic inhibits the heart and dilates the coronary arteries. It accelerates activity of the stomach and the small intestine, stimulates the salivary glands, relaxes the anal and urinary sphincters, and contracts the bladder.

The sympathetic and parasympathetic subdivisions of the autonomic nervous system are therefore responsible for maintaining the homeostasis or stability of the body's internal organs. Their function is unlearned and unconscious and forms the basis of all emotional and instinctual behavior. Claude Bernard (a French physiologist) once remarked that nature thought it prudent to place these functions outside the control of the ignorant will.

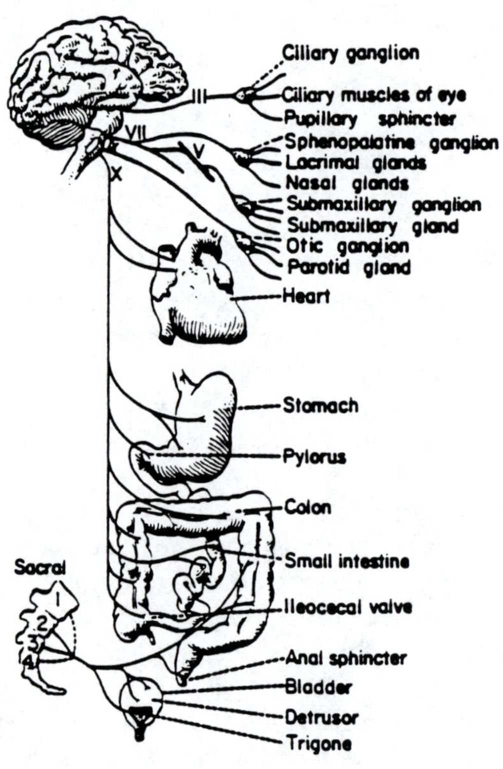

Figure IV-3. Parasympathetic Nervous System. From A. C. Guyton & J. E. Hall. Textbook of Medical Physiology. 9th Edition. Philadelphia: W. B. Saunders Company, 1996.

All of the above physiological activity can be measured and recorded. As a practical matter, however, the forensic psychophysiologist (FP) measures and records breathing patterns, heart beat, pulse rate and strength, changes in mean blood pressure, and electrodermal responses in order to obtain physiological evidence of hypothalamic activity including the sympathetic and the parasympathetic subdivisions of the autonomic nervous system during the psychophysiological veracity (PV) examination in response to particular questions(s) on the test.

Both the sympathetic nervous system and parasympathetic nervous system are continually active; under stress the sympathetic nervous system becomes more active than before, the parasympathetic nervous system less so (the balance of autonomic activity shifts in the sympathetic nervous system direction); vice versa when the stress is over.

Obviously the structure of the PV examination must be such that it isolates fear of detection and eliminates artifacts that might interfere with the test. This is fully discussed in Chapter 9.

The modern electronic polygraph instrument and the computerized polygraph system both use four basic components to record the examinee's physiology as demonstrated with a fully electronic polygraph instrument in Figure IV-4, and a computerized polygraph system in Figures II-18, II-19, and II-20.

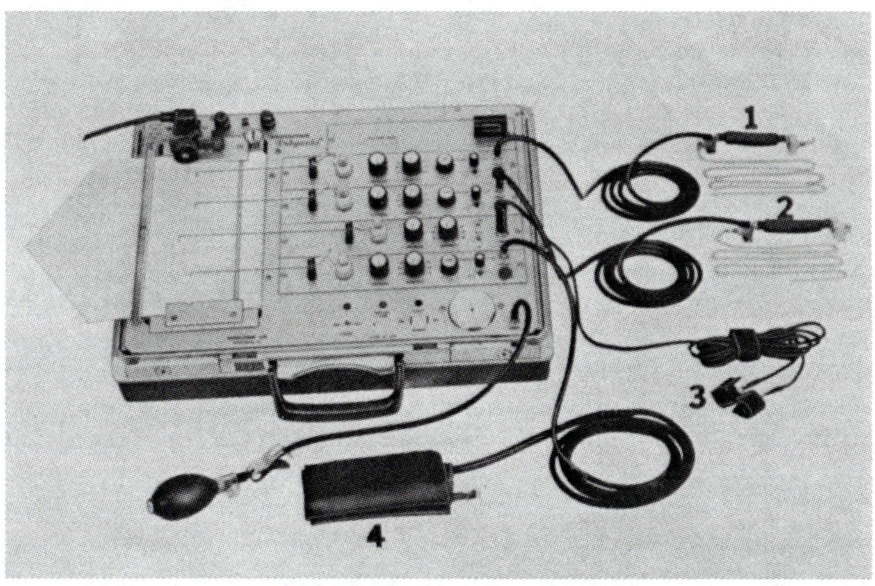

Figure IV-4. Stoelting Ultra-Scribe, fully electronic, four-channel polygraph instrument.

The top two pens record the thoracic and abdominal breathing patterns of respiration. This is accomplished through the use of a pneumograph consisting of two hollow corrugated tubes (components 1 and 2 in Fig IV-4) about seven inches in length, each attached to a unit by a rubber hose no longer than six feet and no larger than one-quarter inch in diameter. This breathing or pneumo unit is a low-pressure unit. A pneumo unit allows the FP to close off the air and lock the vent during the examination and release it upon completion of the test. The inhalation/exhalation of the subject causes the tubes to expand and contract, thereby reflecting the change through bellows to the pen onto the chart. When the pneumograph tube is extended with the vent closed, there is greater volume within the tube. Consequently, when there is greater volume the pressure within the tube is decreased. When the tube contracts, the volume is decreased and the internal pressure is increased. An inhalation causes the pen to go up (clockwise); exhalation causes it to go down (counterclockwise). A pen centering knob allows the FP to adjust the position of each pen to mechanical center so that tracings will not overlap each other and the pens will not collide with each other.

A shallow breather for example will create a pneumo tracing of narrow amplitude; a deep breather, large amplitude.

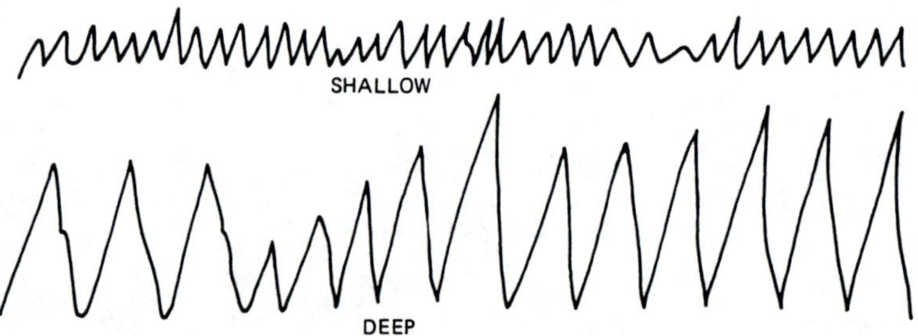

Figure IV-5. Shallow and Deep Breathing Patterns.

Amplitude is caused by the difference in pressure from inhalation/exhalation. The tighter the tube, the more amplitude. One inch expansion is the recommended maximum. Due to the accordion construction of the pneumo tube, which is fastened to a beaded chain (some have Velcro®), the pneumo tube can be attached to the chest or abdomen area of the body with the hands of the FP seldom touching the subject.

The mechanics of inspiration or inhalation referred to above is the taking in of outside air, bringing with it the oxygen that the body needs, and expiration or exhalation is the removal of air carrying those waste products that the body has filtered. Additionally, external respiration is the movement of oxygen (O_2) from the alveoli to the capillaries of the lungs and inversely, the removal of waste products, such as carbon dioxide (CO_2) and water (H_2O) from the capillaries of the lungs to the alveoli. Internal respiration is the exchange of oxygen (O_2) from the capillaries to the adjoining cells. Thus the delivery of oxygen to the lungs is called breathing or pulmonary ventilation, hence respiration is possible *because* of ventilation. Deep within the chest cavity, the trachea, which is a long tube-like structure comprised mostly of cartilage and some smooth muscle, divides into two bronchi which enter the lungs, one on the right and one on the left, at an area called the hilus. External respiration takes place in the lungs which are situated side by side in the thoracic cavity of the body. As the bronchi divide and enter the lungs, they subdivide a number of times, resembling the branches of a tree, sometimes referred to as the bronchial tree. The bronchial tree is comprised of a number of progressively smaller tubes which include the primary and secondary bronchus and bronchioles. The bronchiole walls have smooth muscle and are controlled by both the sympathetic and parasympathetic subdivisions of the autonomic nervous system. The bronchioles are innervated by parasympathetic nerve fibers from the vagus nerves and constrict when stimulated by acetylcholine from these nerves. Sympathetic stimulation by sympathetic nerves causes release of norepinephrine (noradrenaline) which relaxes the bronchioles. The smallest of bronchioles are the terminal bronchioles, the ends of which contain clusters of air sacs called alveoli. Each alveolus is of single-cell construction and has very thin walls surrounded by a network of capillaries also of single cell construction which permits the exchange of gases, the delivery of oxygen and the removal of carbon dioxide. Thus the cardiovascular system works in concert with the respiratory system in delivering oxygen to the cells. Therefore within the pulmonary circuit, oxygen deprived blood passes through the right side of the heart and into the pulmonary artery where it continues its travel through progressively smaller branches i.e. arterioles, metarterioles after entering the lungs and ultimately through the capillaries which surround each alveolus. As the blood vessels diverge in the capillary network, the gaseous exchanges take place with the alveoli, and oxygen rich blood is carried back to the heart via the pulmonary veins and the waste products of respiration are deposited for the purpose of removal from the body through the act of exhaling.(Weinstein 1994; Matte-Reuss 1995)

The act of breathing involves volume and pressure. Volume is the amount of space within the chest cavity. Pressure involves the amount of atmospheric (outside) pressure exerted against the chest versus the amount of pressure inside the chest. During inhalation there is a volume increase, and an internal pressure decrease which will ultimately cause air to fill the lungs to equalize against the forces of atmospheric pressure exerted against the outside of the chest cavity. During inhalation, the diaphragm flattens out and the chest cavity becomes longer thus increasing volume. The external intercostals cause the rib cage to lift up and extend outward, further increasing the width of the chest cavity hence increasing volume. Therefore as described above, when there is an increase in volume, there is a decrease in pressure and air fills the lungs. Conversely, during exhalation when there is a volume decrease, there will be an increase of pressure within the chest cavity. The diaphragm relaxes and the elasticity of the lung tissue allows the lungs to collapse and the diaphragm to rise. During forced exhalation, the abdominal muscles contract forcing extra air out of the lungs. The internal intercostals cause the rib cage to collapse forcing out more air. By using two separate pneumographs, the FP can monitor thoracic (intercostal) and abdominal (diaphragm) breathing patterns. (Weinstein 1994; Matte-Reuss 1995)

While the pneumograph tracings of the thoracic and abdominal area appear to be quite similar, they are affected through two completely different sources. The initial process of inspiration or intake of outside air commences with the activation of the phrenic nerve which cause the muscle cells in the diaphragm to contract. Because the diaphragm is located under the lungs, separating the thoracic and abdominal cavities, when the diaphragm contracts, the size of the thoracic cavity, specifically that part of the thoracic cavity beneath the ribs, increases. Simultaneously the intercostal nerves activate causing the external intercostal muscles located on the outside edge of the rib cage to contract raising the ribs thus increasing the size of the thoracic cavity further. The lungs then inflate because volume has increased and pressure has decreased. Inspiration at this point is *active*. Normal expiration which is *passive* involves the relaxation of the diaphragm and the external intercostal muscles. When the expiration of more air than normal is required, i.e. *forced* or *active expiration*, it is facilitated by the internal intercostal muscles, attached to and located on the interior edge of the rib cage. The contraction of these internal intercostal muscles, brought about by impulses carried on the intercostal nerve, causes the rib cage to be pulled down and in, thereby decreasing the size of the chest cavity, and volume is reduced. Forced expiration can also be increased through the contraction of the abdominal muscles which pushes organs such as the intestines and stomach up, forcing the diaphragm up even further into the chest cavity and pushing additional air out of the lungs. Forced expiration is said to be *active* while normal expiration is said to be *passive* because of the elasticity of the tissues which gives the force for expiration. The smooth muscles contained in the trachea and the bronchi and bronchioles are structures of the bronchial tree, thus receive their innervation from both the *sympathetic* and the *parasympathetic* nervous systems. The sympathetic nervous system opens these tube-like structures and the parasympathetic nervous system closes them. Conscious control of breathing uses the *somatic nervous system*, which provides innervation by way of the *phrenic nerve*, which stimulates the diaphragm, and the intercostal nerves for the intercostal muscles.(Weinstein 1994; Matte-Reuss 1995)

Breathing originates and is controlled by the *medullary rhythmicity center*, also known as the *respiratory center*, which is located in the medulla. This center consists of two divisions, the *inspiratory center* and the *expiratory center*. Normal breathing is considered to be automatic because it is controlled by the inspiratory center which is self-stimulating. As this stimulation occurs, an impulse is sent from the inspiratory center to the somatic nerves (phrenic and intercostal). Impulses from these nerves will then cause the diaphragm and the external intercostal muscles to contract. Furthermore, when the inspiratory center is firing, it sends a signal which inhibits the activation of the expiratory center. But within a few seconds the inspiratory center fatigues and stops firing; the signal to the somatic nerves stops, the muscles stop contracting and the inhibition to the expiratory center is stopped. While normal expiration is passive, the expiratory center is involved only in forced expiration. Because it is no longer inhibited, should there be a need for forced expiration, the expiratory center can cause this action to occur. Thus *normal*

NEUROLOGICAL PATHWAY FOR RESPIRATORY CONTROL

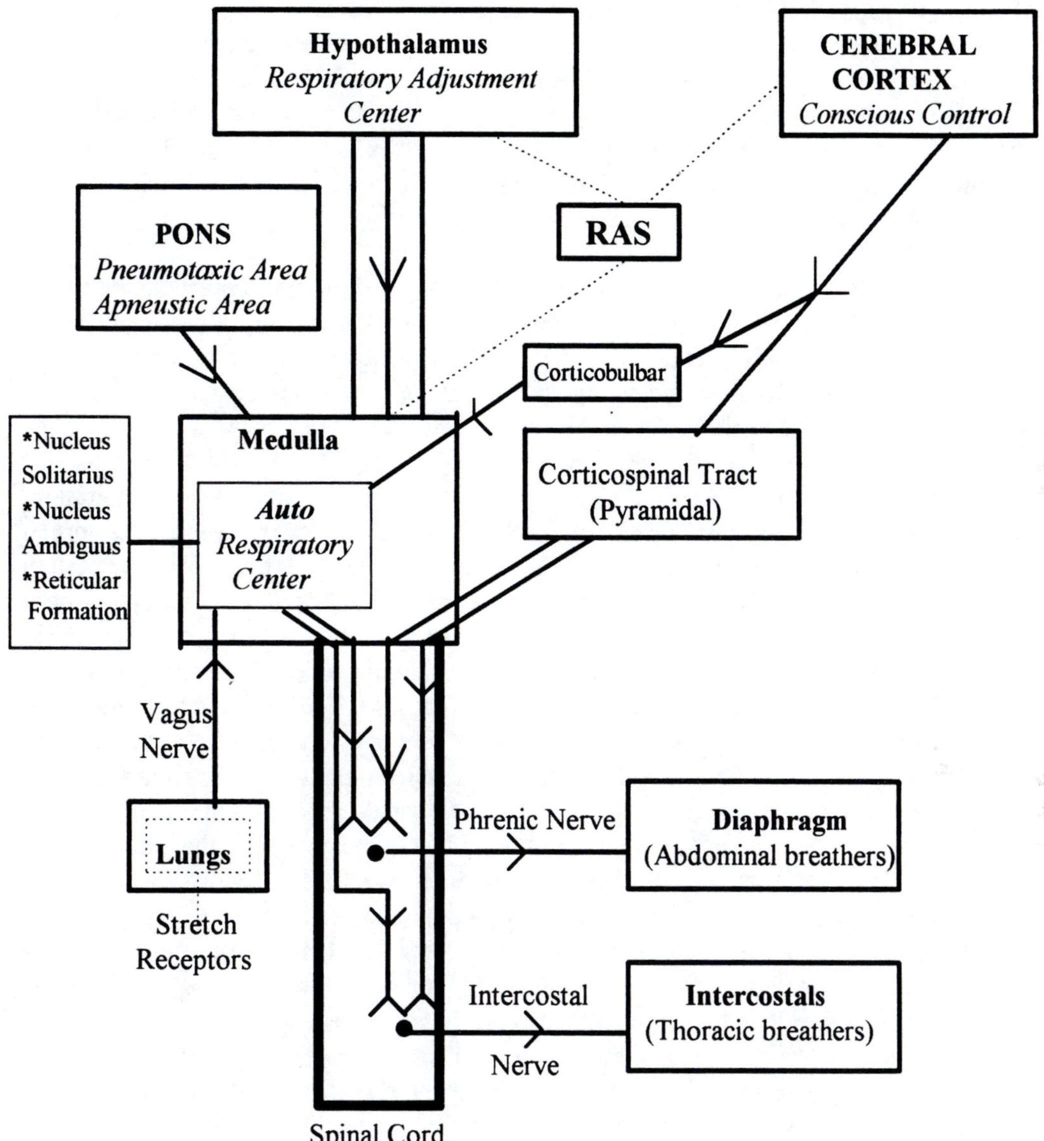

In the above illustration, the two black dots represent the cell bodies of neurons that form the phrenic and intercostal nerves. The connecting arrow heads represent the axon endings at the synapse.

*These three nuclei make-up the Auto Respiratory Center. See Addendum on page 186 for full discussion.

Figure IV-6. Above illustration developed and drawn by J. A. Matte & R. M. Reuss, 1996.

breathing is not affected by the autonomic nervous system. If this were the extent of the process of ventilation, the pneumograph tracing would only reflect consistent, regular inhalation and exhalation cycles. However, other areas of concern are the apneustic and pneumotaxic areas which are located within the pons. These areas affect the depth and length of time of inspiration which are deception criteria in PV examinations. The apneustic area affects the inspiratory center, keeping it from fatiguing and prolonging inspiration. The pneumotaxic center affects the apneustic center and the inspiratory center by inhibiting the firing of those centers. Thus the apneustic center increases inspiration and the pneumotaxic center decreases inspiration.(Weinstein 1994)

Therefore, as described in Figure IV-6, the auto-respiratory center located in the medulla maintains normal breathing function, but it is the respiratory adjustment center located in the hypothalamus acting in concert with the reticular activating system (RAS) which affects the diaphragm via the phrenic nerve and the intercostal muscles via the intercostal nerve both of which emanate from the spinal cord.

It must be recognized that there are reflex mechanisms which affect respiration. One is known as the Hering-Breuer inflation reflex which does not operate during normal breathing. The Hering-Breuer reflex stops inspiration if the lungs are stretching too much and causes expiration to begin. The Hering-Breuer reflex probably is not activated until the tidal volume increases to greater than about 1.5 liters. This reflex appears to be mainly a protective mechanism for preventing excess lung inflation rather than an important ingredient in the normal control of ventilation. (Guyton & Hall, 1996). The stretching of the lung is monitored by its nerve fibers which prevent overinflation. Another reflex mechanism of the respiratory system is the chemoreceptors which monitor chemicals in the circulatory system such as oxygen (O_2), hydrogen ions (H^+) and carbon dioxide (CO_2). These chemoreceptors are located in aortic and carotid bodies in the aorta and the carotid arteries, respectively. In order to sustain life, oxygen is taken into the body and waste products, such as carbon dioxide, are expelled. When carbon dioxide is being transported in the circulatory system, one of the by-products are hydrogen ions (H^+). If there are too many hydrogen ions, there is a significant amount of carbon dioxide in the bloodstream. If there is too much carbon dioxide in the blood, the inspiratory centers are activated to remove the excess carbon dioxide inasmuch as high levels of carbon dioxide are more dangerous than low levels of oxygen. A third reflex which can affect the respiratory pattern of concern to the forensic psychophysiologist involves the voluntary contraction of the anal sphincter muscle. When the anal sphincter is contracted, respiratory amplitudes will most likely increase. While not always the case, this reflex is usually the result of a countermeasure by a deceptive examinee. (Weinstein 1994)

With the use of electronic polygraph instruments, we change mechanical energy, in the form of pressure changes, as the volume in the pneumograph tubes increases or decreases, to electrical energy, and then, through the use of the pen motor, revert to mechanical energy to produce the tracings. The precise manner in which this *transducing* occurs involves the introduction of mechanical energy (pressure, volume, etc.) against a tambour in the *transducer*. This action stretches the tambour, across which are stretched thin wires or strain gauges. As the strain gauge stretches, electrical resistance, present in the circuit, is changed. The signal (converted to electrical energy) then passes through the various circuitry of the recording instrument. The pen motor of the component is then capable of once again changing the signal into mechanical energy to produce the tracing. The *coupler* adapts the circuitry of the recording instrument to accept the transduced signal. The *preamplifier* then provides the initial boost and a degree of filtering to the signal, which is then routed to the *power amplifier* to further increase power sufficiently to enable the pen motor to function. (Weinstein 1994)

The traditional field polygraph instruments are powered by *alternating current* (AC) which is comprised of a 60 cycle frequency that *fluctuates* (goes in both directions) which is subsequently changed from alternating current to *direct current* (DC), a *constant*, rectified current that travels in only one direction. Hence the recording components contained in aforementioned field polygraph instruments are powered by direct current, thus are designed to use only direct current to produce an output signal. An output signal produced by the responses of a subject comprises any number of frequencies, each of which contain a number of cycles over a period of time. These frequencies can be high (fast), or low (slow). These frequencies may sometimes have to be modified in order to acquire an interpretable and scorable tracing. This is accomplished through the use of *filters*. Low pass filters allow lower (slower) frequencies to pass while filtering out higher (faster) frequencies. *High pass filters* allow the passage of higher frequencies while blocking those of lower frequencies. A *notch filter* blocks the passage of a specified frequency, allowing all others to pass, while a *band pass filter* specifies a particular range of frequencies to pass and blocks all others. (Weinstein 1994; Reuss 1996)

An example of the filtering process is found in all field polygraph instruments which have an Auto/Manual switch on the GSR or GSG component. This filter is a high pass filter, which filters out low (slow) frequency signals when the switch is in the Auto position or mode. When the switch is in the Manual position, the output signal is essentially unfiltered. Thus when in the Auto position, the resulting signal will produce a tracing that rises quickly but with less amplitude than in the Manual mode, and an immediate return to baseline without recording the duration of the response as found in the Manual mode. Since a response can be comprised of a number of high and low frequency signals, the low (slow) wave activity which makes up the tracing baseline is filtered out when the switch is in the Auto mode. Furthermore, the filtering of frequency signals could reduce or attenuate one response differently than another within the same examinee even though they may appear to be of the same magnitude, hence referred to as a *differentially attenuated* signal. (Weinstein 1994)

It is recognized that on occasion, filtering a signal becomes necessary in order to acquire a stable recording and an interpretable tracing. When this is required, it should be accomplished to the minimum extent possible. Otherwise, it should be avoided to preclude the loss of valuable data and criticism that naturally occurring physiology was somehow modified. Research (Raskin, et al (1978) showed that electrodermal *recovery time* as well as *response rise time* is useful data in the evaluation and scoring of physiological responses, which would be lost in the Automatic mode of GSR/GSG, hence should be avoided whenever possible.

The longest pen in the polygraph, the third pen from the top in Figure IV-4, is called the galvanic skin response (GSR) or galvanic skin conductance (GSG) pen. While the other pens are all five inches long the GSR/GSG pen is seven inches long (Stoelting) but its base or pen cradle is located only 1.5 inch further onto the chart than its neighboring pens. The GSR/GSG pen also sits higher into its cradle so that it may ride over the other pens without colliding into them. This was found to be necessary inasmuch as the GSR/GSG tracing consists of clockwise and counterclockwise excursions of the pen often traversing into the pneumo tracing or the cardio tracing area. The extra length of the GSR/GSG pen to the other pens means that it records five seconds earlier than the pneumo and cardio pens on the polygraph chart. Conventional Lafayette instruments record their GSR/GSG eight seconds earlier than their neighboring pneumo and cardio pens.

The galvanometer components sense small changes in skin resistance to electricity. A simple Wheatstone bridge or voltage regulator circuit uses the finger electrodes (Component 3), which are placed against the last joint on two fingers of the same hand and compensating resistances in one arm, and is so arranged that the subject's general resistance level, across the electrode plate, can be electrically balanced against the other bridge arms. The subject's emotional response to stimuli introduced by the FP will trigger small changes in the subject's general resistance level, causing a positive or negative imbalance. This imbalance is picked up by the chopper converter, fed as a rectilinear wave into the first and second voltage amplifier stages, and transmitted to the power and phase detector stage, which receives the greatly magnified signal and translates it as an output signal according to polarity and magnitude. The recording galvanometer receives the signal, causing the pen to swing from the zero reference base line, depending on polarity and magnitude of the signal. The intensity of the subject's response to stimulus, as transmitted by the electrodes from general resistance level, can normally be measured by the arc of the GSR/GSG pen swing from the zero reference base line of the chart.

An understanding of the electrodermal system is essential for the proper evaluation of the data recorded by the galvanometers in polygraph instruments. The changes in electrodermal tonic level are caused by increases in sweat gland activity which are located within the skin, the largest organ of the human body whose role is vital to the maintenance of homeostasis. Although the function of the skin is to prevent harmful substances from entering the body while providing exteroreceptors as an alert and discriminatory system, the *sweat glands* provide the human body with a mechanism for thermoregulation or the maintenance of a constant body temperature, and a *primeval conditioning of the skin in certain areas of the body in preparation for fight or flight*. This latter function is of special importance to the forensic psychophysiologist (FP).

The anatomy of the skin includes three layers, namely the *epidermis* or outer layer, the *dermis* located beneath the epidermis, and the *sub-dermis* or *subcutaneous* layer where the sweat glands originate. The *corneum* which is the outermost layer of the epidermis consisting mostly of dead, dry skin cells offers a high resistance to any electrical charge. The dermis on the other hand is well supplied with nerves and blood vessels, while the subdermis below it serves as the seat of the two types of sweat glands. The *apocrine* sweat gland is generally found in the armpits and genital areas, hence not a practical area for the recording of electrodermal activity. However, the *eccrine* sweat gland has wide-spread distribution over the entire body with particular concentration on the *palmar* surfaces of the hands, and the *plantar* surfaces or the soles of the feet.

The *eccrine* sweat gland originates in a coiled form in the subdermis layer of the skin. It comprises the *secretory* portion of the sweat gland responsible for the *diffusion* or movement of sweat from the subdermis into the dermis, and the *excretory* portion of the eccrine sweat gland also known as the sweat gland duct, whose structure has straightened while traversing through the blood and nerve filled dermis to the epidermis where the duct coils again through the corneum until it reaches the sweat pore at the surface of the skin where the sweat emerges from the body. The coiled structure of the sweat gland in the epidermis permits increased *diffusion* of the sweat to the surrounding cells, especially when the corneum is dry. Since the post ganglionic neurotransmitter associated with the sweat gland is acetylcholine and the receptor involved is classified as muscarinic, the sweat gland is innervated by the sympathetic nervous system only, with no parasympathetic fibers. Therefore, the return of an electrodermal response to tonic level is dependent upon *passive reabsorption* of the sweat or *corneal hydration*, and *active reabsorption*.

The sweat gland is normally empty during its *homeostatic condition*, hence in a PV examination, the GSR/GSG recording pen is recording the *tonic level* or average moisture level of the skin surface, and as long as the skin remains moist, the pen will remain (float) at mechanical center, unless the skin is or becomes dry in which case the pen will move to the lower mechanical limit. This latter condition is the result of a high degree of resistance and essentially a lack of sweat in the sweat gland duct. The sweat gland begins to secrete sweat when it receives a signal from the sympathetic nervous system. As the sweat rises in the duct, there is a biologically adaptive mechanism known as *passive reabsorption* which prevents the skin from becoming overly moist. There is also another mechanism known as *active reabsorption* which is designed to remove the sweat from the duct and return it to its homeostatic state. The upward movement or excursion of the GSR/GSG pen reflects the filling of the sweat gland ducts as the sweat moves toward the surface of the skin. The examination environment can have an impact on the functioning of the GSR/GSG component. A high degree of humidity may increase skin moisture versus no humidity, which will impact on the examinee's tonic level. Changes in tonic level are likely to appear as the sweat rises in the sweat gland duct, however corneal hydration is the main mechanism affecting tonic level. A change in the amplitude of the electrodermal recording is in all probability the product of a change in the level of the sweat in the sweat gland duct, and more specifically, that portion of the duct contained in the corneal layer of the skin. When the duct is filled with sweat, there cannot be any further phasic activity. It is therefore important that the sweat glands being recorded are allowed to return to their pre-stimulus tonic level by themselves through passive and active reabsorption, before attempting mechanical recentering of the pen. As previously mentioned, the *duration* of the recording is dependent upon the duration of the sweat glands continuing to produce sweat which is keeping the ducts filled. Thus the *amplitude* of the electrodermal recording is the result of sweat rising in the sweat gland duct, and duration of the recording reflects a continuance of sweat production which keeps the duct filled. The *tonic level* represents the level of moisture on the surface of the skin, and *latency* which is the period of time between stimulus onset and response onset, is the degree to which the corneum is already hydrated when the stimulus is applied. Hence in a humid environment, latencies will be shorter and amplitudes will be higher because the already hydrated skin will facilitate the rise of the sweat through the duct and retard passive reabsorption. Conversely, in a dry environment, amplitudes will be smaller and latencies longer. (Weinstein 1994).

As indicated above, some instruments measure and record galvanic skin *resistance* while others measure and record galvanic skin *conductance*. Resistance is an exosomatic measure of how much difficulty electrical current has in passing through the skin. Conductance, which is also an exosomatic measure, reflects how easily current passes through the skin. In research it is considered important to determine absolute values and absolute levels. Researchers are infinitely more concerned with evaluating data collected between subjects rather than single subject methodology which is of more importance to the forensic psychophysiologist. Conductance measures facilitate such absolutes and comparisons and therefore conductance is the preferred measure of the researchers. (Weinstein 1994) However research has shown no considerable differences in the magnitude of GSR versus GSG responses. Conductance measures have been shown to be more stable, thus requiring less recentering by the FP. Furthermore, conductance measures are less affected by some of the problems associated with resistance measures, such as plunging baselines. Nevertheless, research has not shown any difference in accuracy between the GSR and the GSG.

One American manufacturer of a computerized polygraph system uses electrodes composed of a combination of superior metals which are referred to as *silver-silver chloride* or AgAgC1, while the other two American manufacturers of computerized polygraph systems use electrodes constructed of metal, typically brass, which have been plated with nickel; all are used to measure galvanic skin conductance. It is believed by some researchers that the latter enhance the likelihood of a variety of electrical interference problems such as polarization and bias potential. Electrodes can become polarized when certain electrical properties gather or build up on the electrodes, essentially acquiring an electrical charge of their own. This polarization can cause a departure from the skin's tonic level (baseline or resting level), typically a constant rise of a tracing requiring intermittent recentering before the application of a critical stimulus. This creates a dilemma for the FP in differentiating between a legitimate pen rise resulting from a *phasic response* (specific stimulus) and the effect of *polarized electrodes*. (Weinstein 1994) However, research set forth below (Yankee & Grimsley 1986, 1987) disputes some of those findings.

Another electrical interference problem known as *bias potential* can also occur which is caused by the buildup of aforementioned electrical properties between the two electrodes which are normally fastened on two fingers of the same hand. Weinstein described it as "being similar to having a battery placed into an existing electrical circuit, whereby an independent electrical potential is being generated. Here too, the question is raised as to what is being measured, the response of the subject, or the electrical potential being generated by the electrodes themselves. It should be noted that all electrodes, regardless of composition, are susceptible to problems such as polarization or bias potential." One method of minimizing polarization and bias potential is to periodically remove the wires attached to the electrodes and exchange them between the electrodes, thus reversing the direction of the electrical charge passing through the electrodes. But *silver-silver chloride* electrodes are designed for use only with *skin conductance units*, not skin resistance units. Silver-silver chloride electrodes require *more maintenance and care* of application than nickel-plated brass electrodes used with skin resistance units. Silver-silver chloride electrodes *require some type of medium* such as an electrode gel to insure contact between the electrode and the skin. Furthermore, the electrodes themselves must be regularly cleaned and may occasionally need re-chloriding to their original state to maintain optimum efficiency. It should be noted that polarization and bias potential are essentially the same thing, but occur at different places. (Weinstein 1994). Interestingly, stainless steel electrodes used in Stoelting's conventional polygraph instruments are more resistant to corrosion and easier to maintain than nickel-plated brass electrodes and silver-silver chloride electrodes, yet Lafayette and Axciton computerized polygraph instruments both employ nickel-plated brass electrodes in their GSG component.

It should be noted that Yankee and Grimsley (1987) used the galvanic skin response (GSR) measure with both silver/silver chloride (SSC) electrodes and stainless steel field (SSF) electrodes using a potassium chloride and agar mixture as the conducting medium, in an analog study, which revealed that in the first test the differences between the two measures were generally slight (SSC 48 correct, 6 incorrect) (SSF 49 correct, 7 incorrect). However in the second test, the stainless steel field electrodes were significantly more accurate than the silver/silver chloride electrodes (SSF 43 correct, 7 incorrect) versus (SSC 37 correct, 8 incorrect).

In another study by Grimsley and Yankee (1986), two GSR (Galvanic Skin Response) channels were used employing stainless steel field (SSF) electrodes and silver/silver chloride (SSC) electrodes with a potassium chloride and agar mixture as the conducting medium which revealed that in test 1 the SSF had 45 correct decisions, 7 false positives, 9 false negatives and 19 inconclusives, versus the SSC with 41 correct decisions, 7 false positives, 9 false negatives and 23 inconclusives. In test 2 the SSF had 39 correct decisions, 13 false positives, 15 false negatives and 13 inconclusives, versus the SSC which had 38 correct decisions, 14 false positives, 12 false negatives and 16 inconclusives. In test 3 the SSF had 35 correct decisions, 6 false positives, 9 false negatives and 30 inconclusives, versus the SSC which had 37 correct decisions, 8 false positives, 7 false negatives and 28 inconclusives.

It is apparent from the above two studies conducted by Yankee and Grimsley that the only significance in accuracy between the field stainless steel electrodes and the silver/silver chloride electrodes occurred in test 2 of aforementioned 1987 study where the stainless steel field electrodes yielded a greater number of correct decisions (43 versus 37) with fewer incorrect decisions (7 versus 8) than the silver/silver chloride electrodes. However, Weinstein (1994) warns that the silver/silver chloride electrodes were designed to specifically complement skin conductance units, not skin resistance units as employed in above studies.

The proper placement of the electrodes, whether silver-silver chloride or field electrodes using nickel-plated brass or stainless steel, is critical to the recording of electrodermal activity. The finger tips of the examinee's non-dominant hand usually offer the greatest density of eccrine sweat glands with the least amount of resistance, such as from calluses or scars, the former increasing resistance, the latter offering the electrical current a path of least resistance, thus avoiding neighboring sweat glands. Stability of the electrodes on the examinee's fingers can be improved with the use of a professional polygraph chair which has wide, elongated arms to fully support the arm, hand, fingers and electrodes without bending the wrist. The electrodes should not be fastened tightly as this may cause a pulsing action of the blood flowing through the fingers onto the polygraph chart tracing. Fastening of the electrodes too loosely can cause intermittent contact between the electrodes and the skin resulting in a plunging tracing. The momentary separation of the electrode from the skin breaking the continuity of the electrical circuit may be the result of a contraction of the forearm muscles that control the fingers as a deliberate countermeasure attempt, or may be the result of a phasic response. This author has found that the stainless steel or nickel-plated brass electrodes should be wiped clean after the conduct of each chart, and that no gel or other medium should be used on the examinee's fingers; rather when necessary, the examinee's fingers may be washed with soap and water, then thoroughly rinsed and wiped dry. On the other hand, the silver-silver chloride electrodes often require the use of an electrolyte to hydrate the corneum, improve contact between the electrode and the skin, and reduce resistance. Care must be exercised when hydrating the corneum not to use a preparation with too much saline content as it may impact on the continuity of responses throughout the PV examination as it is absorbed into the skin. Weinstein suggests a better alternative by mixing a neutral base and physiological saline, or else the use of KY™ jelly, which can be purchased at any drug or department store. Since electrical current flows more easily through a fluid than through the skin or air, hydrating the corneum will reduce electrical resistance and improve the surface contact area.

A rule of thumb when adjusting the sensitivity of the GSR or GSG channel at the commencement of a PV examination is to obtain a tracing that *floats* at mechanical center; that is, the tracing moves in a small-wave like action while maintaining its course at mechanical center, yet capable of significant clockwise excursion when a specific stimulus is applied, with the *least amount of component sensitivity*. The administration of an Acquaintance Chart followed by a Stimulation Test prior to the conduct of the relevant test charts offers the FP opportunities to make the necessary GSR/GSG sensitivity adjustments. Too much sensitivity is often the cause of continuing recording pen plunges.

Forensic psychophysiologists should be aware of pharmacological preparations that have antimuscarinic properties inasmuch as the receptor for the sweat gland is muscarinic. The electrodermal recording might lack responsiveness and in some cases be totally devoid of responsiveness due to the examinee's ingestion of a drug or medication which has anti-muscarinic properties such as antipsychotic and antidepressant medications. Over the counter medications such as antihistamines, cold and allergy type medications and medications intended for relieving menstrual discomfort also have anti-muscarinic properties. Other preparations which have antihistamine properties designed to relieve or prevent motion sickness, sleeping aids, and asthma medications, all tend to block the reception of the neurotransmitter and are classified as antagonists. (Weinstein 1994) (See Chapter 20 on Drugs).

The fourth or bottom pen records the action of the cardiosphygmograph. This cardio unit is a mechanically operated unit. It is a high pressure system. This system records changes in mean blood pressure, rate, and strength of pulse beat by means of a medical blood pressure cuff containing a rubber bladder that is wrapped around the upper arm, in a manner that places the bladder against the brachial artery. The bladder is connected to a rubber hose, past a pressure indicating gauge (aneroid sphygmomanometer), to a very sensitive bellows and its connected lever system that powers the pen. The FP inflates the bladder with a hand pump to a constant air pressure that will provide a tracing amplitude of 0.75 to 1 inch with the dicrotic notch situated about the middle of the diastolic limb of the tracing. This normally requires cuff pressure of 70 to 85 mm Hg. The pumped air is locked in the system by use of a vent.

A wrist or infant cuff is also available for placement over the wrist, but it is not as effective as the arm cuff because there are less volume changes at the wrist due to a lack of muscle, much bone and smaller blood vessels.

A person's heart is about the size of his fist and weighs about eight ounces. It is a highly efficient pump that moves blood through the body. The heart is a muscle that contracts and relaxes about seventy to ninety times per minute in most adults. Each contraction and relaxation of the heart muscle is a heartbeat that pumps about two ounces of blood resulting in about 13,000 quarts of blood being pumped each day. Adjustment of the rate of contraction of cardiac muscle is exercised by the vagus nerve, which retards, and the sympathetic nervous system, which accelerates. These act on a lump of special tissue in the wall of the right atrium called the sinu-atrial or S.A. node, to regulate the rate and strength of heartbeats. From it, an impulse spreads over the atria resulting in a contraction of the atria. This signal also reaches the AV node between the right atrium and right ventricle which sends a signal that spreads over the ventricles. The AV node is also regulated by the sympathetic and parasympathetic systems In spite of this heavy workload, the heart is actually at rest two-thirds of the time. The heart is divided into four chambers. The upper two chambers are called atria; the lower two are called ventricles. Each atrium is connected to the ventricle below it by a valve that allows blood to flow from the atrium to the ventricle, but not in the opposite direction.

When the heart beats, it is like a fist closing. As it closes, the blood inside is forced out from two different ventricles. The right ventricle sends venous blood to the lungs to leave carbon dioxide and pick up oxygen. The left ventricle pumps oxygenated blood received from the lungs to all parts of the body. When the heart relaxes, into the right ventricle enters the blood that the veins are returning from the rest of the body and into the left ventricle flows the oxygenated blood returning from the lungs. The complete cycle takes about one seventieth of a minute. When the heart beats it is called a systole, and when it relaxes it is called a diastole. Naturally, systolic pressure is the highest and diastolic pressure is the lowest.

While the heart relaxes, a phenomenon of importance to forensic psychophysiologists (FPs) is the collision of the fresh blood entering the aorta (main artery) with the blood already in the artery. This not only causes the blood already in the artery to be pushed forward, but it also causes some of the newer blood to bounce back towards the heart. This blood does not re-enter the heart because the *semi-lunar valve* (one-way valve) is forced closed by the returning blood. This causes a pressure wave which is seen as a dicrotic notch, usually located halfway down the diastolic limb of a polygraph cardio tracing.

Therefore, during the systolic phase when the heart pumps blood out, it causes an increase in pressure against the arteriole walls, including the brachial artery against which is tightly wrapped a bladder filled with air (the cardio cuff). This increased pressure in turn displaces a proportionate amount of air in the bladder, which is transmitted to a mechanism that moves the pen in an upward or clockwise motion on the polygraph chart. At that point we have recorded the systolic portion of the heart beat. When the heart starts to relax, the pen begins its descent, but then stops abruptly as a result of the returning blood bouncing against the semi-lunar valve, causing a dicrotic notch. As pressure descends in the arteries, the pen continues its descent to its normal base line, completing the diastole limb and the heart beat cycle on the chart.

Regulation of heart rate through the nervous system is accomplished by the autonomic nervous system. Nerve fibers of the sympathetic nervous system are provided to the SA node, AV node, the atria and to the ventricles. Nerve fibers of the parasympathetic nervous system are provided primarily to the SA node and AV node. Generally, when sympathetic nervous system fibers fire, the neurotransmitter norepinephrine is released and heart rate is increased. When parasympathetic nervous system fibers are activated, acetylcholine is released and heart rate is slowed. A person's "normal" heart rate is referred to as his *vagal tone*. It should be noted that withdrawal of parasympathetic activation can also produce a heart rate increase. Chemical regulation refers to the circulation, through the blood, of hormones such as adrenaline (epinephrine). Specifically, when such circulating hormones reach the sinoatrial node in the right atrium, a very definite heart rate increase will be initiated. Therefore, *intrinsic regulation* is responsible for steady heart rate, and the nervous system can produce either an increase or a decrease in heart rate, whereas hormonal influence is limited to heart rate increases only. To some extent, it would also be necessary to include the fact that regulation can be affected through the central nervous system (CNS) as well, acting through the sympathetic and parasympathetic nerves. In the brain, specifically within the pons and medulla, there are certain reflex mechanisms and cardiovascular regulatory centers. (Weinstein 1994; Matte-Reuss 1995)

TABLE 2*

ADRENERGIC RECEPTORS AND FUNCTION

Alpha Receptor	Beta Receptor
Vasoconstriction	Vasodilation (B_2)
Iris dilatation	Cardioacceleration (B_1)
Intestinal relaxation	Increased myocardial strength (B_1)
Intestinal sphincter contraction	Intestinal relaxation (B_2)
Pilomotor contraction	Uterus relaxation (B_2)
Bladder sphincter contraction	Bronchodilation (B_2)
	Calorigenesis (B_2)
	Glycogenolysis (B_2)
	Lipolysis (B_1)
	Bladder wall relaxation (B_2)

*From A. C. Guyton & J. E. Hall: Textbook of Medical Physiology, 9th Edition, Philadelphia, W. B. Saunders Company, 1996.

There are very specific events which occur during the entire cardiac cycle. These events include the *depolarization* of the atria, or a negative change in the electrical potential of that structure, depolarization of the ventricles, followed by atrial and ventricular *repolarization*, or return to their previous state. The cardiac cycle is divided into two segments. *Systole*, which is that period of time when the heart is contracting, or more specifically when the ventricles are contracting and *diastole* is when the atria and ventricles are in a state of relaxation. Sometimes, systole is called the time of excitation and diastole as the resting period. Upon the completion of systole, pressure will be greater in the arteries than it will be in the ventricles. Therefore, the aortic and pulmonary semi-lunar valves will be forced to close. Both the bicuspid and tricuspid valves (those valves between the atria and ventricles) are also closed. The functioning of the heart valves is dependent upon pressure and when pressure gradients are higher in one chamber than they are in another, the appropriate valves will be forced to close. As blood flows from the vena cava and the pulmonary veins, it passes through the atria and into the ventricles, and the ventricles begin to fill. This ventricular filling is deemed passive because the heart is in diastole. The atria then begin to fill. When the ventricles are nearly full (70%), the SA node fires and additional blood is forced into the ventricles from the atria. As this event occurs, the atria are depolarizing (P wave). Then begins the depolarization of the ventricles (QRS wave), stimulating contraction of the ventricles. Now there is more pressure in the ventricles than there is in the atria and this pressure change causes the AV valves (bicuspid and tricuspid) to close. As the AV valves close during this particular segment of time, the first heart sound, sometimes called "lubb" sound, can be heard. When the building pressure is greater in the ventricles than it is in the arteries, both the aortic and pulmonary artery valves (semi-lunar) will open, the ventricles strongly contract (mid R-S wave) and the blood in the ventricles is said to be ejected out of the heart and into the appropriate artery. When the ventricles are empty, a pressure change between the ventricles and the arteries occurs thereby causing the semi-lunar valve to close. The closing of these valves generates the second heart sound, or what is sometimes called the "dupp" sound. The heart sounds are caused by the turbulence of the blood created by the valve closing. When these valves close, some of the blood in the arteries, which was recently ejected from the ventricles, *bounces* against the closed valves. This is evidenced by the appearance of the dicrotic notch on the cardiograph tracing. (Weinstein 1994; Matte-Reuss 1995)

Blood pressure is the force that the blood exerts against the interior surface of the blood vessels. Among the components that affect blood pressure is the amount of blood ejected from the heart on one cycle, or *stroke volume* (SV); the amount of blood in the ventricles just prior to contraction, or *preload* (PL); the amount of pressure in the arteries which keeps the aortic valve closed, or *afterload* (AL); the amount of blood ejected per minute, or *cardiac output* (CO); the forcefulness of the contractions of the heart, or *contractile force* (CF). Other conditions, such as *constriction within the blood vessels*, as might be caused by plaque or cholesterol, *total blood volume* throughout the body, thickness, or *viscosity* of the blood and *elasticity* of the blood vessels, all have an impact on blood pressure. However what is being recorded by forensic psychophysiologists (FP) with the use of an inflated bladder encased in a cloth sleeve is not blood pressure, but blood volume. Also of interest to the FP are changes in heart rate and baseline changes. In fact what is measured by the cuff is a pulse rate due to a pressure wave in the blood generated by the heart contractions. Heart rate is a reflection of how fast the heart is beating. Baseline changes are manifested by increases and decreases of blood volume at the site where it is being recorded, either the brachial, ulnar or radial arteries. Although, at the present time our instrumentation does not measure blood pressure precisely, the amplitude of the cardiograph tracing provides the FP with a representation of what we know as *mean arterial blood pressure* (MABP), or an average of the pressure in the artery we are monitoring. When the blood pressure cuff is inflated, the FP is attempting to equal that pressure externally so that he/she can monitor any changes. When the cuff pressure (MCAP) is equal to the mean arterial pressure (MABP), the result will be a greater, or optimal amplitude of the cardiograph tracing. When physiological changes occur to the MABP, in the form of increased or decreased volume being recorded by the cuff, the result will be a constriction of the tracing. As the MABP approaches the cuff pressure, the tracing will increase in size until such time as it is once again equal to the MABP. Thus, changes in *baseline* in PV examinations reflect a change in blood volume, *amplitude* is affected by blood pressure, and *heart rate* represents how fast the heart is beating.(Weinstein 1994; Matte-Reuss 1995) It should be noted that a high pressure cuff theoretically shows the most dramatic change in amplitude during an autonomic response because the *percent* change in the mismatch between mean arterial blood pressure (MABP) and mean cuff air pressure (MCAP) during a response is very significant whereas a low cuff pressure shows little change in amplitude during a response because the *percent* change in the mismatch during a response is relatively small.

As a further explanation, the pulse amplitude measures changes in the pressure in the brachial artery. With each heart beat the arterial pressure changes from about 80 to 120 mm Hg. The increase in arterial pressure distends the artery which presses against the cuff, increasing the cuff air pressure. (Barland 1984). The amplitude recorded on the chart is a function of the relationship between the mean arterial blood pressure (MABP) in the brachial artery (usually about 100 mm Hg) and the mean cuff air pressure (MCAP) (Geddes & Newberg, 1977).

Barland (1984) provides the following explanation:

a. The maximum amplitude (both with mechanical, high pressure cardios and electronic, low pressure cardios when the electrical amplification remains constant) is obtained when the MCAP exactly equals the MABP.

b. Whenever a mismatch in either direction occurs (the MCAP is either higher or lower than the MABP) the amplitude decreases. The greater the mismatch, the smaller the amplitude.

c. If the MCAP is lower than the MABP, and the MABP increases, such as when the subject lies, the cardio amplitude gets smaller, because arterial blood pressure is going away from the cuff air pressure.

d. If the MCAP is higher than the MABP, and the MABP increases, such as when the subject lies, the cardio amplitude would actually get larger, because the arterial blood pressure is approaching the cuff air pressure.

Examples:

a. High pressure cuff:

Time:	MABP (mmHg)	MCAP (mmHg)	Difference (mmHg)
Before reaction	100	90	10
During reaction	120	90	30
			% change = 200%

b. Low pressure cuff:

Time:	MABP (mmHg)	MCAP (mmHg)	Difference (mmHg)
Before reaction	100	60	40
During reaction	120	60	60
			% change = 50%

In each case the subject's blood pressure increased 20 mmHg, but the percent change in the mismatch is small when the mismatch is large to begin with. Barland hypothesized that we should expect that the high pressure cuff would show much more dramatic amplitude changes during a reaction than would a low pressure cuff. Thus it would be a function of the change in cuff pressure, not the change from a mechanical to an electronic system. (Barland 1984)

The chart recording unit in mechanical and electronic polygraph instruments is called a kymograph. It has a synchronized motor that drives the chart at the rate of six inches per minute and its speed constant is vital because the vertical lines, which are spaced either at one-half or one inch intervals, represent five or ten second intervals on the chart. This provides the FP with a means of determining pulse rate, breathing rate, and question spacing. Since the GSR/GSG pen extends half an inch further onto the chart than the other pens (Stoelting) or seven eighths of an inch (Lafayette), its pen tip, when at mechanical center, records five seconds earlier (Stoelting) or eight seconds earlier (Lafayette) than its neighboring pens (Decker 1995). The FP must take this factor into consideration when analyzing the charts recorded by conventional polygraph instruments. Furthermore, PV examination reports should include the type of polygraph instrument used so that the correct GSR/GSG pen length will be known to outside forensic psychophysiologists hired to analyze the chart data. (See Chapter 12)

In the late 1970's, polygraph manufacturers produced a new generation of instruments which are fully electronic. Each of the aforementioned channels contains a transducer that permits a variety of pneumatic signals to be processed directly. There are no moving parts, no jewels, no bearings, no levers, no friction, only a metal diaphragm that flexes a few thousandths of an inch with changes in pressure. These transducers were specifically designed and built for application to polygraph instruments. Each channel contains an electronic amplifier. These transducers and amplifiers have the capability of handling input signals of one-thousand and more Hertz, although frequencies of such magnitude are not required by present day polygraph techniques. In addition, each channel contains a self-test button so that FP's can verify that each channel is functioning normally.

The significance of each channel containing a transducer and amplifier is that it permits the FP to amplify or reduce electronically a tracing to an ideal amplitude. For instance, exceptionally shallow or deep breathers no longer present a problem because the amplitude of the pneumograph tracings can be adjusted electronically, a feature not available on conventional mechanical instruments.

An added feature to this electronic polygraph instrument is the cardio activity monitor (CAM) transducer, which can continuously monitor blood pressure variations and heart rate with the simple placement of the transducer on the finger, thumb, or wrist using the artery feeler. The transducer can be quickly and simply attached using a Velcro fastening band. Minimal fastening pressure eliminates discomfort and allows continuous monitoring. Since the radial artery is deeply imbedded in some individuals, a semi-elastic artery

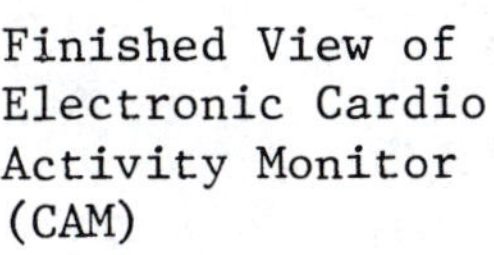

Figure IV-7

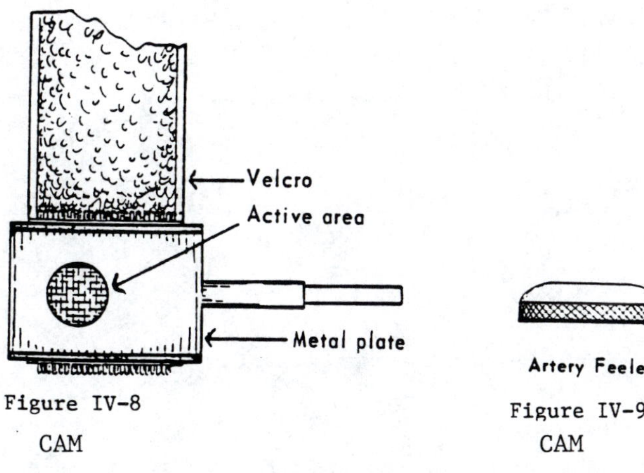

Figure IV-8
CAM

Figure IV-9
CAM

feeler is placed over the active area of the transducer. The transducer uses silicon strain gauges in its construction, is extremely sensitive but very rugged, and will withstand severe usage without damage.

Cardio Activity Monitor Wrapped Over Radial Artery of Wrist

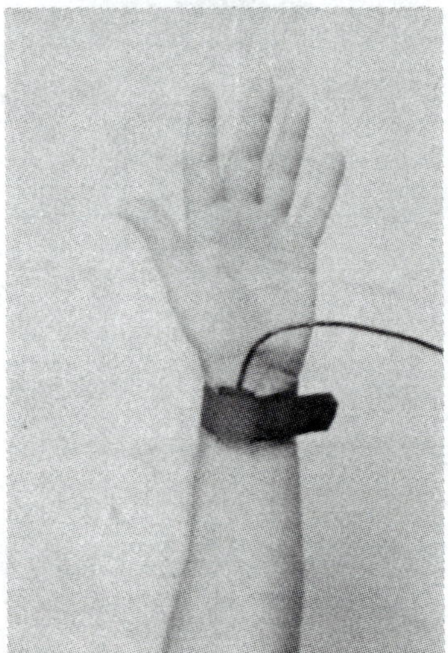

Figure IV-10

View of Thumb with 4 Positions of CAM Placement

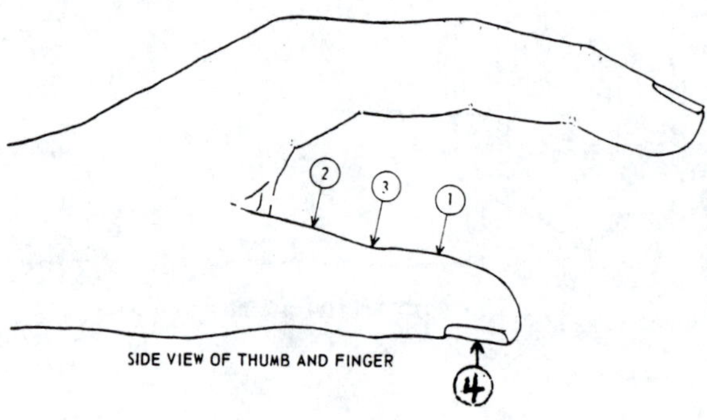

Figure IV-11

Figure IV-7 shows a picture of the CAM ready for use. Figure IV-8 is a diagram of the CAM minus the artery feeler exposing the metal disk, which is the active area of the transducer. Figure IV-9 is the artery feeler, which is bonded over the active area. Figure IV-10 shows the CAM placed tightly over the radial artery at the wrist with the palm facing upward during the test. Of course, the forearm, wrist and hand are resting on the wide, elongated arm rest (with the palm facing upward). This position is preferred because it records arterial pulse volume and rate which produces excellent tracing amplitude at low sensitivity with a steady pattern, and Figure IV-11 shows alternate locations for the CAM in order of preference. At location number 4, the artery feeler is placed directly over the thumb nail, recording capillary volume changes.

Interestingly, Grimsley and Yankee (1986) found that the Cardio Activity Monitor (CAM) was superior in accuracy when used alone compared to the cardiograph on all three multiple-issue tests conducted in their analog study. The percent correct calls (excluding inconclusives) for the CAM and the cardio were 72% to 68% for test 1, 64% to 42% for test 2, and 70% to 69% for test 3 respectively. William A. Davidson (1979) conducted a validity study on the CAM using polygraph charts from real cases which were reviewed blind by a panel of seven field FPs. No attempt was made in Davidson's study to compare the difference in decisions of FPs when reviewing Zone Comparison Tests (ZCT) versus Modified General Question Test (MGQT) due to the unequal samples selected. However the results showed that decisions based on the CAM alone were 88%, decisions with the pneumo, GSR and cardio combined were 86%, and with all components including the CAM were 89%. But Davidson cautions that in his instant study, the pressure of the cardio cuff was not absent, hence it could not be determined what effect the absence of cuff pressure would have had on the other components and the CAM.

While the CAM is more useful than the cardio in multiple issue screening type of examinations which can be quite lengthy, due to the lack of cuff pressure enhancing subject comfort, this author is convinced from his extensive experience with both components in the field that if a choice between the two is required, the *cardio cuff* should take precedence over the CAM in specific issue type examinations which generally do not exceed a total of four minutes of chart time per chart, as it produces a more *stable* yet *reactive* tracing from closer proximity to the heart, and the bicepts/tricepts area offers significantly greater arterial blood volume than at the wrist or thumb area. Whereas proper placement of the CAM's artery feeler directly over the radial artery, which is critical for an adequate recording, can sometimes be quite difficult, and its position can be easily displaced or disturbed by the slightest flexing of the muscles of the forearm or movement of the hand. Furthermore, the cardio cuff pressure elicits the examinee's attention away from the somewhat restrictive pneumograph tubes monitoring the examinee's breathing patterns.

Conventional blood pressure recording through the arm cuff over the brachial artery can also be recorded electronically as well as pneumatically with as little as 35mm of cuff pressure, due to the transducer amplifier, which means no more discomfort for the examinee. However, recording at such low pressure is not recommended unless absolutely necessary, i.e. medical condition, and for the reasons described by Barland above.

The advent of computerized polygraph systems somehow popularized the use of the plethysmograph, most likely due to the omission of the Cardio Activity Monitor (CAM) which was readily available with conventional electronic polygraph instruments and widely used in screening type of PV examinations due to a lack of cuff pressure hence increased comfort level. However, plethysmography, a Greek word meaning fullness, which is concerned with recording the volume of a body segment (Geddes 1974) can be sub-categorized as follows: *Volumetric,* which is what Cesare Lombroso used; *Occlusion,* which is the conventional cardiosphygmograph with cuff; and *Photoelectric,* currently being offered as a supplementary component in computerized and analog polygraph systems. (Barland 1984)

Initially, the Stoelting Company in the early 1970's introduced a photoelectric plethysmograph which used *transillumination* (light transmission) to measure blood changes in deep tissues. Stoelting reversed the leads to duplicate the cardio tracing with the dicrotic notch on the ascending limb. However, the type of pick-up used in this early model caused movement artifacts necessitating the repositioning of the unit after nearly every chart. A subsequent photoelectric plethysmograph was introduced which used a *back scatter* (light reflection) to measure vascular changes in the skin.(Fig. IV-12) (Barland 1984; Geddes 1974). This unit now used in American-made instruments attaches to a finger with a "clothes pin" clamp which permits easy placement/removal and no movement artifacts. (Barland 1984). It should be noted that the Japanese in 1973 (Yamaoka & Suzuki) used another type of plethysmograph in a research experiment called a Shin-ei's Shincorder which measured the skin-blood flow by *thermoelectric* effect with the use of a skin-blood flow element for measuring temperature which was taped to the subject's left thumb. In this Japanese analog study the aforesaid plethysmograph was compared with the accuracy of detection rate with skin potential response and skin resistance response which revealed that the *thermoelectric* plethysmograph was inferior to the skin potential response but was equal in accuracy to skin resistance response.(Yamaoka & Suzuki, 1980)

While heart rate can be calculated from the systole/diastole limbs of the cardio tracing acquired with the cardio cuff, the cardio activity monitor or the plethysmograph, another device is also available from American and Japanese manufacturers of polygraph instruments, namely the Heart Rate Monitor or cardiotachometer. An analog study conducted by Watanabe and Suzuki in 1972 with the use of a cardiotachometer revealed that a heart rate change, initially a brief decrease in rate for about 4 beats followed by an erratic increase for about 15 beats can be expected as a response to stimuli. (Watanabe & Suuzuki, 1977). It should be noted that in 1975, Ed Glassford and Jan Nyboer conducted studies on the action of the vasomotor system in the extremities which indicated that plethysmographic studies of the fingers indicate that there is sufficient vasoconstriction in the hand and arm to alter the oscillogram of the entire upper extremity when the subject is emotionally stressed, hence emotional stimuli will alter the blood pressure and flow in the fingers and arm. (Glassford & Nyboer, 1975)

The 1990's have seen the introduction of the computerized polygraph systems by Stoelting, Axciton, and Lafayette. All of them record and display on a monitor screen the thoracic and abdominal breathing patterns, the GSG, and cardiovascular tracings. However, unlike conventional polygraph systems, the GSG pen is vertically aligned with all of the other imaginary pens which display and record the physiological data for subsequent printing. Thus the FP does not have to contend with a GSG pen that extends half an inch or seven eighths of an inch further onto the chart than the other pens, hence recording five or eight seconds earlier than the other pens. It should be noted that Axciton's GSG default is in Auto mode. (White 1996). Lafayette's GSG default is in Manual mode. (Fauset 1996). The APL algorithm basically can compute the detrended manual from the auto and the auto from the manual. (Olsen 1996).

Two Types of Plethysmograph

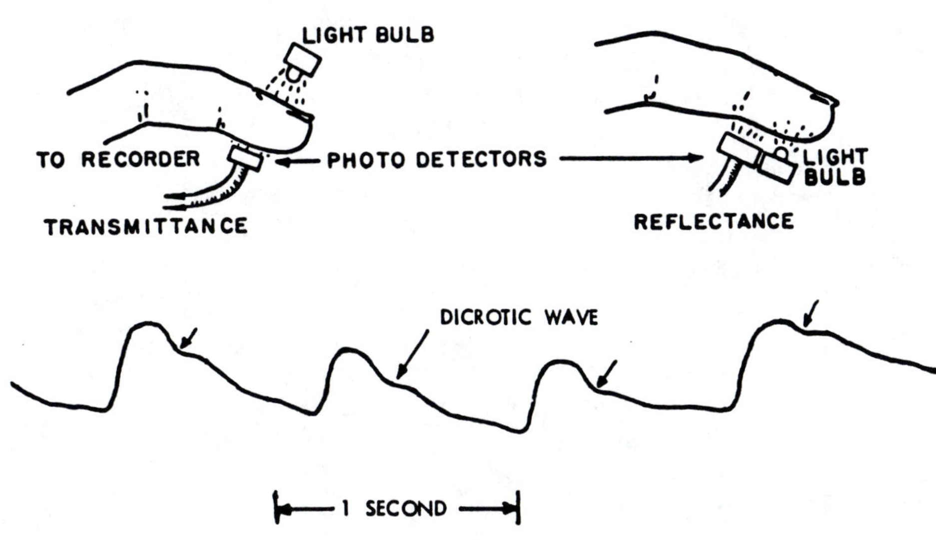

Figure IV-12. The two types of photoplethysmograph and a typical record. In one type the amount of transmitted light is measured and in the other, the amount of back-scattered reflected light is measured. From L. A. Geddes: What Does The Photoplethysmograph Indicate? *Polygraph*, 3(2), June 1974.

Somewhat troubling to this author is the current lack of a channel for the use of the Cardio Activity Monitor (CAM) in all of the American-made computerized polygraph systems. In lieu of the CAM, the Stoelting, Axciton and Lafayette companies have made available a plethysmograph which records pulse and blood volume changes at the fingertip through the use of a photoelectric cell. Unlike the plethysmograph, the CAM can be placed over the radial artery of the examinee's wrist, thus acting as an electronic mini cardio cuff, yet the CAM can also be placed at different areas of the examinee's thumb thus recording pulse and blood volume changes not unlike the plethysmograph but through pressure rather than skin color changes.

It should also be noted that at this time, both the thoracic and abdominal breathing patterns are displayed on the monitor screen and recorded for subsequent printing, but only the thoracic breathing pattern is evaluated and scored by the current algorithms. In view of the results of *field* research conducted by this author and others (Chap. 3) which testifies to the superior effectiveness of the abdominal pneumograph component in male examinees and the fact that some examinees are definitely either thoracic or abdominal breathers, plus the variable effectiveness of the pneumograph components described in Chapter 3 (Matte-Reuss 1992), it would appear advantageous for the computerized polygraph systems to evaluate both thoracic and abdominal breathing patterns and select and score the most productive pattern for each examinee tested. Research (Slowik, et al 1973) showed that overall, there was a significant difference in the SUMAM between the thoracic and abdominal breathing patterns, in that the sum of the lowest and highest amplitudes for the abdominal recording was consistently larger than the sum for the thoracic recording, which may simply indicate a difference in scale, but could be critical in examinees who produce poor physiological recordings. From the aforementioned information regarding the differences between the current electronic polygraph instruments and the computerized polygraph systems, it is quite understandable that a great number of experienced forensic psychophysiologists using the former instruments are at this time reluctant to convert to the latter computerized instruments which they feel do not yet provide overall superiority over the former, and indeed lack some of the former's versatility. There is no question that in the near future, computerized polygraph systems will incorporate all of the desirable features of the conventional electronic polygraph instruments, plus additional ones, all evaluated by the most sophisticated mathematical algorithms that scientists can produce which will most certainly exceed human evaluation.

ADDENDUM

As illustrated in Figure IV-6, the Auto Respiratory Center located in the Medulla, is comprised of the Nucleus Solitarius, the Nucleus Ambiguus, and the Reticular Formation. Although it is common to speak of a rostrally located inspiratory part and a caudally located expiratory part of the respiratory center, inspiratory and expiratory neurons to a large extent are intermingled in the respiratory center. In quiet breathing, only the inspiratory movement is active. The inspiratory center, which is driven by impulses from both central and peripheral chemoreceptors and various reflexes, sends impulses through reticulospinal pathways to the motor neurons that inervate the inspiratory muscles. When the inspiratory activity has reached a critical threshold, the inpiratory center is inhibited which allows for passive expiration. The "switching off" of the inspiratory center is controlled by a neural mechanism that obtains input from several sources, including impulses through the vagus nerve from stretch receptors in the lungs (Hering-Breuer reflex), and impulses from the chest wall.

The changes in respiration that are seen in different conditions are brought about by impulses generated by chemoreceptors in the large arteries of the heart and mechanoreceptors of the lungs. There is also a mechanism for direct chemical stimulation of the respiratory center, which responds especially to an increase in the carbon dioxide content of the blood and the pH of the extracellular fluid. (Heimer, 1989).

The mechanism for the variation seen in respiration in males versus females (Matte, Reuss, 1989 and 1992) with males showing a predominately abdominal response (phrenic nerve) and females a predominately thoracic (intercostal nerve) or equal thoracic/abdominal response (phrenic/ intercostal) can be explained by variations in the size and location of the inspiratory and expiratory loci in the nucleus solitarius, nucleus ambiguus and reticular formation forming as a whole the respiratory center in the medulla. (Fig. IV-6). (Meade 1996)

Research dating back to 1982 by DeLacoste-Utamsing on the human corpus callosum and up to recent research by Swaab, et al, have shown considerable variation in the gross and microanatomy of the brain and brainstem. Swaab's most recent studies in the sexual dimorphism in the hypothalamic nuclei are the most interesting. In these large studies on human material, males and females of all age ranges showed variable differences in the size and shapes of the suprachiasmatic nuclei (SCN) and paraventricular nuclei (PVN) in the human hypothalamus and the sexually dimorphic nucleus of the preoptic area (SDN-POA). (Hofman, Schaab, 1988, 1989)

It can be reasonably extrapolated from these studies that the nuclei in other areas of the brain and brainstem can be expected to display similar sexual dimorphism. This would explain the variation in the mechanism of breathing responses seen in males versus females as outlined above. Variations in the size, shape and even position of the nucleus solitarius, nucleus ambiguus and reticular formation in the medulla would alter the connections to the various efferent and afferent neural pathways controlling inspiration and expiration. The positional and size differences would also affect the feedback responses to the incoming stimuli from the stretch receptors located in the lungs (bronchi and vasculature) and in the intercostal muscles in the chest wall triggering expiration as well as the afferent pathways controling inspiration. The positional differences and connections between the neurons in foci within the nuclei making up the respiratory center would explain the variations in the end organ affected in respiration. This would explain the differences between the female and male respiratory response. The neuclei and their neurons, the connecting afferent and efferent nerve fibers and the respective end organ interfaces would all show a difference based on the sex of the subject studied - a sexually dimorphic response.

Thus there are variations in the phrenic nerve and/or intercostal nerve connections to and from the respiratory center nuclei and their respective end organs, the diaphragm (abdominal breathers) and the intercostal muscles (thoracic breathers). In the abdominal breathers the connection between the phrenic nerve and the nuclei of the respiratory center would predominate while in the thoracic breathers the connection of the intercostal nerve would predominate. This variation would be affected by the sexual dimorphism (differences between the sexes) of the brainstem respiratory center nuclei controlling each of the pathways, phrenic nerve vs. intercostal nerve vs. combinations of the two nerve pathways.

Therefore in males, the size and resultant neuronal density as well as the position of the nuclei within the respiratory center is shifted toward the region connecting with the phrenic nerve. In females these variables result in a shift in the nuclei either to the region connecting to the intercostal nerve or result in an overlaping of regions resulting in connections with both the intercostal and phrenic nerves. (Meade, Mrzljak, 1996)

REFERENCES:

Barland, G. H. (1984, June 1-2). The Cardio Channel: A Primer. Paper presented at the Florida Polygraph Association Seminar. 15 pages.

Davidson, W. A. (1979). Validity and Reliability of the Cardio Activity Monitor. *Polygraph*, 8(2), 104-111.

Decker, R. E. (1995, November 25). Telephone conversation with J. A. Matte.

DeLacoste-Utamsing, C., Holloway, R. L. (1982). Sexual dimosphism in the human corpus callosum. *Science*, 216(4553), l43l-2.

Geddes, L. A., Newberg, D. C. (1977). Cuff pressure oscillations in the measurement of relative blood pressure. *Psychophysiology*, 14, 198-202. Reprinted in *Polygraph*, 1977, 6, 113- 122.

Glassford, E., Nyboer, J. (1975). Emotional stress and oscillometric variations of the pulse curve. *Polygraph*, 4(2), 108-117.

Grimsley, D. L., Yankee, W. J. (1986). The effect of multiple retests on examiner decisions in applicant screening polygraph examinations. NSA contract MDA 904-85-C-A962, 1986. A. Madley Corporation, Charlotte, N.C.

Guyton, A. C., Hall, J. E. (1996). *Textbook of Medical Physiology*. (9th Ed.). Philadelphia: W. B. Saunders Company.

Heimer, L. (1989). *The Human Brain and Spinal Cord*. Berlin, Germany: Springer-Verlag.

Hofman, M. A., Fliers, E., Goudsmit, E., Swaab, D. F.(1988). Morphometric analysis of the suprachiasmatic and paraventricular nuclei in the human brain: sex differences and age-dependent changes. *Journal of Anatomy*, 160: 127-43.

Hofman, M. A., Swaab, D. F. (1989). The sexually dimorphic nucleus of the preoptic area in the human brain: a comparative morphometric study. *Journal of Anatomy*, 164: 55-72.

Lafayette Instrument Co. (1995-1996) Catalog of computerized and conventional analog polygraph instruments. 34 pages.

Mader, S. S. (1992). *Human Biology*. (3rd Ed.). Dubuque, Iowa: William C. Brown - Publishers.

Matte, J. A. (1980). *The Art and Science of the Polygraph Technique*. Springfield, Illinois: Charles C. Thomas - Publisher.

Matte, J. A., Reuss, R. M. (1989). A field validation study of the Quadri-Zone Comparison Technique. *Polygraph*, 18(4), 187-202.

Matte, J. A., Reuss, R. M. (1989). Validation study on the Quadri-Zone Comparison Technique. *Research Abstract*, LD 01452, Vol. 1502, 1989, University Microfilm International.

Matte, J. A., Reuss, R. M. (1995, September 20). Critique of Department of Defense Manual *Anatomy and Physiology for the Forensic Psychophysiologist* authored by Special Agent Donald A. Weinstein, US Air Force Office of Investigations. 1-10.

Matte, J. A., Reuss, R. M. (1992). A study of the relative effectiveness of physiological data in field polygraph examinations. *Polygraph*, 21(1), 1-22.

Meade, P. S., Mrzljak, L. (1996, November). Conferences between Dr. Mrzljak, Dr. Meade and Dr. J. A. Matte regarding differences in respiratory pathways of males versus females.

Raskin, D. C., Barland, G. H. Podlesny, J. A. (1978). Validity and Reliability of Detection of Deception. Washington, D. C.: National Institute of Law Enforcement and Criminal Justice. Also published in *Polygraph*, (March 1977) 6(1), 1-40.

Rathus, S. A. (1994). *Essentials of Psychology*. (4th Ed.). Orlando, Florida: Harcourt Brace & Company.

Slowik, S. M., Buckley, J. P., Kroeker, L., Ash, P. (1973). Abdominal and thoracic pneumograph recordings. *Polygraph*, 2(1), 12-27.

Spence, A. P. (1990). *Basic Human Anatomy*. (3rd Ed.). Redwood City, California: The Benjamin/Cummings Publishing Company.

Watanabe, S., Suzuki, A. (1977). The heart rate response as an index of the lie-detecting test. *Polygraph*, 6(2), 103-112. Originally published in *Reports of the National Institute of Police Science*, (Japan), 25 (1972): 51-56.

Weinstein, D. A. (1984, June). *Anatomy and Physiology for the Forensic Psychophysiologist* (Revised). Department of Defense Polygraph Institute.

White, B. (1995, November 27). Telephone conversation with J. A. Matte

Yamaoka, K., Suzuki, A. (1980). Studies on Skin-Blood Flow as an Index of Lie Detection. *Polygraph*, 9(4), 232-237. Originally published in *Reports of the National Institute of Police Science*, (Japan), 26, (1973), 206-209.

Yankee, W. J., Grimsley, D. L. (1987). The effect of a prior polygraph test on a subsequent polygraph test. NSA contract MDA 904-84-C-4249. University of North Carolina at Charlotte, N. C.

Chapter 5

Evolution of the Psychophysiological Veracity Examination

Humans are the slaves of their emotions and no one knows this better than a forensic psychophysiologist. The effectiveness of the forensic psychophysiologist (FP) lies in his/her knowledge of the causes and effects of emotions (see Chap. 9) and his/her ability to structure a test that will contain certain emotions while allowing others to release onto carefully prepared stimuli scientifically arranged to elicit responses that will distinguish truth from deception.

Emotions consist of intensified feelings regarding a situation, which are caused by an interaction between the mind and the body resulting in physiological changes within the body to cope with the situation. The pattern and the degree of physiological changes vary according to the intensity of the feelings and the type of situation. When these feelings are mild, the physiological changes are correspondingly slight. In mild fear, the changes include increases in digestive functions, changes in pulse rate, increase in blood pressure and rate of breathing. In order to better cope with the situation causing the fear, the body accelerates its activity correspondingly to provide the individual with additional energy. (Little, et al 1955)

When these feeling are strong, however, the accompanying physiological changes are extensive. Under strong fear, these changes have the effect of preparing the body for a fight or flight. The adrenal glands begin releasing adrenaline into the bloodstream stimulating the heart into greater activity, thereby increasing circulation. The circulatory system begins to redistribute the blood supply, taking it away from the stomach and the intestines where it is not needed at the moment, and sending it to the large muscle groups such as the arms and legs where it is more needed. The liver begins pumping glycogen into the bloodstream providing a quick source of extra energy. Breathing rate increases, and the spleen begins dispatching large numbers of additional red corpuscles into the bloodstream, thus enabling the lungs to extract more oxygen from the air. In the meantime, the pupils of the eyes dilate a little admitting more light. The hair bristles, bloodclotting hormones appear in the blood providing some protection against bleeding to death in the event of a wound. The body is in a state of full emergency. The individual is prepared to either run or fight. Emotions are an indispensable part of the body's adjustive machinery. Strong emotions, especially fear, usually hamper sound thinking in any situation where objectivity is required, for they intensify self-defensive behavior. Strong emotions prevent sound thinking in at least three ways. In the first place, whenever we interpret a situation as critical, we tend to become so concerned with the threat that we are unable to concentrate on the problem. Second, the redistribution of the blood supply occurring with strong fear tends to decrease the supply to the higher brain centers and to leave them undernourished so that they cease to function effectively. Third, emotions tend to reduce the control of behavior by thought. Under strong emotional tension we have an urge to do something immediately even if it is wrong rather than wait until we can consider the situation in the light of accumulated experience. Such behavior can be explained by the hypothesis that our behavior in the face of a threat is determined by the hindbrain, sometimes referred to as the old brain because it is the first part of the brain which develops in the embryo. The hindbrain or old brain which consists of the cerebellum, medulla, pons, and the reticular activating system, is responsible for our survival, or autonomic functions including heart rate and respiration. Overlying this is a larger area, the so-called "new brain," known as the cerebrum, which supposedly developed later in the evolution of humans. The old brain operating below conscious level is the source of impulsive behavior. When we encounter a situation that threatens safety of the self, the natural impulse, originating in the old brain, is to do violence to the threatening object or to flee from it. Under the influence of emotion our thinking is likely to be dominated by primitive brain centers, and to be primitive in quality at the very time when the highest grade of objective thinking is needed. The emergency situations we must face in this highly complex society are usually threats to self rather than to physical safety. It makes no difference, therefore, to the body whether a threat is physical or psychological; as long as the situation is interpreted as a serious threat, the body puts into effect its inherited pattern of adjustment by preparing for physical rather than mental action. The net effect of these physiological changes is to make high-level thinking more difficult, if not impossible, at the very time when clear thinking is needed most. (Little, et al 1955).

The system that prepares the body's defenses to meet these emergencies is none other than the sympathetic subdivision of the autonomic nervous system (a motor system) as discussed in the previous chapter.

In a psychophysiological veracity (PV) examination, it is fear, fear of detection, fear of the consequences if the individual is detected, that causes the sympathetic system to activate in order to prepare the body to meet the emergency. Therefore, a sense of guilt is not an essential element to activate the sympathetic system.

The act of lying does not necessarily activate the sympathetic system, but rather the reason for the act. Without fear of detection, the degree of significance of the act of lying to the examinee depends on the examinee's background as to the type and strength of inhibitions he/she acquired during his/her formative and later years. The examinee who suffers inhibitions caused by such factors as religious beliefs that lying for any reason is a sin, and conservative or disciplinarian upbringing equating lying with dishonor, etc. will show a response, even a strong response, to a lie which has no immediate threat to his/her well-being (immediate because such an examinee will consider any lie a threat to his/her moral well-being no matter how trivial); the lie will cause an inner conflict, even if he/she is asked to lie about a card he/she selected from a deck of cards for the purpose of determining which card he/she picked by use of the polygraph. (See Chapter 9 for further details)

However, if fear of detection is absent from an examinee who suffers no inhibitions, can we expect this individual to show a response in a PV examination? While such an individual has learned that he/she can lie quite successfully and may even find it a rewarding experience, such a person will also be considerably embarrassed at being caught lying. Conflict and anxiety to some degree is inevitable, and a response in a polygraph examination while milder perhaps can still be expected.

For this reason, experiments conducted in the laboratory for the purpose of validating the effectiveness and reliability of the PV examination, although successful, did not reflect the high degree of response, level of accuracy and effectiveness experienced by forensic psychophysiologists in the field, because it is most difficult if not impossible to simulate fear of detection in a laboratory situation as compared to an actual live situation where an examinee's well-being is truly being threatened by some form of punishment if the discovery of his/her lie becomes known.

Interestingly, Raskin, Barland and Podlesny (1978) conducted a study to assess the effectiveness of PV examinations performed on persons diagnosed psychopathic (sociopathic). Among the 24 subjects who had been diagnosed as psychopaths, decisions were 96% correct. The single error was a false positive, and not a single guilty psychopath was able to produce a truthful polygraph outcome. In fact, the PV examinations were slightly more effective with the psychopaths than with the nonpsychopaths, but the difference was not statistically significant.

Recognizing that the underlying basis of the PV examination technique is the emotion of fear, which is the most depressing of all emotions, we must also recognize that the emotion of anger, which is the most exciting emotion, also induces sympathetic excitation and adrenaline secretion. However, psychologically speaking, anger is different from fear. Unlike fear that conveys that something is so overwhelming that it is difficult to escape, anger conveys that something harmful can be overcome. Anger conveys a tendency to fight instead of an urge to escape. There is a sensation of tension and fullness in anger instead of the sensation of weakness and tremor experienced in fear. We must acknowledge that anger can turn to fear and sometimes fear can turn to anger. When escape becomes impossible and a threat is upon us, we may decide to fight and may even win. (Hunter 1974).

Published data and neurological evidence suggests that fear and anger both cause a strong arousal of the sympathetic subdivision of the autonomic nervous system. (Rathus 1994). It therefore became apparent to forensic psychophysiologist (FP) that adequate safeguards needed to be adopted to preclude the element or state of anger from entering and interfering with the PV examination. It became evident that the best safeguard against anger was to search for its existence prior to and during the PV examination. Hence pretest information was obtained to determine the subject's attitude towards the examination whenever possible. The best source of information about a subject's behavior is usually the subject himself/herself. The FP, for instance, may ask the subject how he/she feels about taking the PV examination. This should provide an outlet for the subject to vent his/her anger and release his/her anxieties, and it can also provide the FP with an answer from the examinee that will alert the FP about an angry emotional state on the part of the subject. For this reason, rules have been adopted by FPs who recognize the need to address this variable (see Chapter 9) which dictate that no accusatory approach should ever be used in a pretest interview nor during or between the conduct of the PV tests. No approach that could raise anger on the part of the examinee is to be used during the pretest interview. Interview techniques that convey to the examinee that the FP does not believe in the examinee's innocence are considered taboo in a pretest interview. This includes the use of behavior-provoking questions whose purpose is not unknown to the academic community nor unperceivable by the astute examinee. A completely unbiased and objective approach using a friendly but professional manner during the pretest interview as well as in the conduct of the PV examination was adopted in most PV examination techniques.

By evaluating the behavior of the examinee and following established procedures and safeguards, problems in rare instances where anger can be misinterpreted for fear can be easily overcome.

In early PV examination techniques, the only stimulus responsible for activation of the sympathetic subdivision of the autonomic nervous system was the crime question which was interspersed with irrelevant (neutral) questions. Through time, various types of control questions, some designed to determine whether the examinee was capable of response, while others were designed to be used for comparison with the relevant questions, appeared in various test formats. In this chapter we will examine the evolution of the psychological test structure of the PV examination which excludes the Guilty Knowledge Test and the Concealed Knowledge Test because the GKT and the CKT are not classified as *lie tests* (Lykken 1981) inasmuch as the relevant question is not known to the innocent examinee hence is not a factor that should elicit a false response to the relevant question due to *fear of error* or *anger* by the innocent examinee. Recognition of the incriminating item is the essential element which causes autonomic arousal in Guilty Knowledge Tests. The GKT and the CKT are fully discussed in chapter 18.

The first psychophysiological veracity (PV) examination technique to be used in a field situation involved the simplest test structure, namely the relevant-irrelevant technique. This technique included a series of relevant questions dealing with the issue or crime for which the examinee was being tested, interspersed with irrelevant or neutral questions designed to lack any stimulating qualities for both the innocent and guilty examinee. (Lombroso 1911, Marston 1921, Larson 1923, Keeler 1930). It was Leonarde Keeler who formally described it in an article (1930) by which the relevant-irrelevant technique became known as the Keeler technique.

Keeler added a *personally embarrassing question* (PEQ) and later an *unreviewed control question* to his relevant-irrelevant technique to determine the examinee's capability of response during the examination. Keeler eventually discarded the PEQ but retained the latter for optional use.

Keeler (1936) also introduced a *card test* also designed to determine the examinee's capability of response, which was later recognized and used as a *stimulation test*. The procedure required the examinee to select one card from several cards and memorize the number on the selected card without divulging it to the FP, who then instructed the examinee to give a negative answer to all of the test questions, including the card number that he had selected, thus lying to that particular question, which the FP was expected to distinguish from the other card numbers by the physiological arousal produced by the relevant card number.

While Keeler's relevant-irrelevant technique was the primary technique in use in the 1930s and 1940s, Father Walter G. Summers modified the technique to incorporate "emotional standards" which were control questions, carefully selected from the suspect's life in an attempt to evoke intense electrodermal reactions to emotions such as surprise, anger, shame or anxiety, i.e. Are you living with your wife? or Were you ever arrested? Examinees who showed consistently greater reactions to the relevant questions than to the *emotional standard* questions contained in the same test were diagnosed as deceptive whereas examinees whose reactions to the *emotional standard* questions were consistently greater than the relevant questions were diagnosed as truthful to the relevant issue. (Summers 1939). This was an important step in the evolutionary process of the psychological structure of the PV examination.

In 1947, John E. Reid published his *comparative response questions* which served two useful purposes: (1) to establish that the examinee is capable of response, and (2) to serve as a yardstick for evaluating the examinee's reactions to the relevant questions. Hence if the reactions to the control questions are greater than the relevant questions, the examinee is declared truthful to the relevant questions (issue); but if the examinee's reactions to the relevant questions are greater than the control questions, then the examinee is declared deceptive to the relevant questions (issue). (Lee 1953).

Reid inserted two reviewed control questions for comparison with usually four relevant questions dealing with the same crime (but not the same issue as later discussed). For instance, the crime questions may include direct involvement, indirect involvement, and guilty knowledge. Reid recommended the use of reviewed control questions that were in the same crime or offense category as the crime or matter for which the examinee is being tested. Reid's reviewed control questions were all-encompassing in that they included the period in which the crime was committed, i.e. "Did you ever steal anything in your life?" (Reid 1977). Furthermore, Reid's control questions were reviewed word for word with the examinee before the administration of the test, hence they were subsequently referred to as *reviewed control questions*. In fact, all of the test questions were reviewed with the examinee, to avoid the element of surprise which Reid recognized as an undesirable variable. Reid stated that "the examiner will seek to develop a *control question* - a question about an act of wrongdoing *of the same general nature as the main incident under investigation*, and one to which the subject, in all probability, will lie or to which his answer will be of dubious validity in his own mind." (Reid & Inbau 1966).

The following hypothetical case shows the Reid Control Test structure.(Reid & Inbau 1966).

(Irrelevant) 1. Do they call you Scottie? (known truth)
(Irrelevant) 2. Are you over 21 years of age? (or reference is made to some other age unquestionably but reasonably, and not ridiculously, below that of the subject.)
(Relevant) 3. Did you steal John Doe's watch last Friday night?
(Irrelevant) 4. Are you in Buffalo now? (known truth)
(Relevant) 5. Did you shoot John Doe last Friday night?
(Control) 6. Besides what you told about, did you ever steal anything else?
(Irrelevant) 7. Did you ever go to school? (known truth)
(Relevant) 8. Were those your footprints near John Doe's body? (Evidence connecting)
(Relevant) 9. Do you know who shot John Doe? (Guilty knowledge)
(Control) 10. Did you ever steal anything from a place where you worked?

Reid also included into his test structure a guilt complex control question which had been reported earlier by Clarence D. Lee (1953) which is used primarily for overly responsive examinees. This test is in two parts. The first part consists of administering a reviewed control question test using fictitious crime questions similar in nature to the actual crime the examinee is suspected of committing. The second part consists of administering a second reviewed control question test using both the fictitious crime questions juxtapositioned with the actual crime questions for comparison. If the fictitious crime questions produce consistently greater responses than the actual crime questions, the examinee is deemed truthful regarding the real issue for which he/she is being tested. Deception is indicated when the opposite occurs, (Lee 1953, Reid & Inbau 1966). Like Keeler, Reid relied equally on the observation of the examinee's verbal and non-verbal behavior plus the case facts and other auxiliary information in addition to the polygraph chart data in arriving at a decision of truth or deception, hence Reid employed a *global evaluation*, which this author identifies in this book as the Clinical Approach.

D. G. Ellson (1952) appears to be the first to research the effect of answering test questions in the Negative, in the Positive, and with no answer (mute) to determine their effect on the test results. Ellson's research revealed that the detection for the "no" tests was four of eight subjects, two of eight subjects for "yes" answers, and one of eight subjects for the mute tests. (Ansley 1992).

In 1961, an article entitled "Integrated Control-Question Technique" authored by J. Arnold Cohen appeared in *Police*. The article described the use of a novel ***known-lie*** in a control question test. The examinee is first administered a *card test* using several cards of different suits from a deck of playing cards. Then the card number that the examinee lied to in the Card Test is inserted into the Integrated Control-Question Test as a control question, along with several of the other card numbers the examinee did not select or lie to, which act as irrelevant card questions, interspersed with the relevant questions and a guilt complex question. Thus a typical test format would be structured as follows: 1. Irrelevant question. 2. Irrelevant question. 3. Relevant question. 4. Irrelevant Card question. 5. Relevant question. 6. *Card Control* question. 7. Irrelevant Card question. 8. Guilt Complex question. 9. Relevant question. 10. Irrelevant Card question. 11. Relevant question. 12. Irrelevant Card question. 13. Relevant question. 14. Irrelevant Card question. It should be noted that the examinee is not told the results of the card test, thus during the Integrated Control-Question Test the examinee is not sure whether the FP knows which card the examinee selected. (Cohen 1961; Ansley 1995)

Reid's *reviewed control question technique* was adopted and modified by several leading polygraph practitioners in the 1950s, most notably Richard O. Arther and Lynn Marcy (See Chapter 15), both of whom established their own polygraph schools.

In 1960, Cleve Backster, former Director of the Keeler Polygraph Institute, developed the *Backster Zone Comparison Technique*. Backster's technique was a significant departure from the Keeler and Reid techniques for several reasons. Backster introduced *reviewed probable-lie control questions* that used *time bars* to *exclude* the period in which the crime generating the test was committed. Hence Backster's control questions were named *exclusive* control questions versus Reid's control questions which were labeled *non-exclusive* control questions. By design, the time bars created a control question *structurally less intense* than the relevant (crime) question against which it is to be compared. Manipulation of the time bar could weaken or strengthen the control question when needed. Backster also limited the number of relevant questions to equal the number of control questions, thus two control questions versus two relevant questions. Backster further restricted the relevant questions to the same identical issue so that if the examinee is lying to one relevant question, he/she must also be lying to the other relevant question on the same test, hence optimizing the intensity and distinctness of the examinee's psychological set, thus avoiding competing variables. It was therefore called a single-issue test. Backster adopted the then dormant *psychological set theory* to explain that an examinee's focus of attention will be on the greatest threat to his/her well-being dampening out lesser threats also present on the same test which he labeled the *anti-climax dampening* concept. Thus by restricting the test to a single issue, and clearly separating, with the use of time bars, the earlier-in-life control questions from an equal number of relevant questions, the examinee's *selective attention process* as to which questions are most threatening to him/her is facilitated.

Backster also introduced a *sacrifice relevant question* which acts as a safeguard in that it allows for dissipation of excessive general nervous tension or undue anxiety prior to the asking of the primary relevant questions. It is structured as an orienting relevant question but serves as both a sacrifice relevant question which may elicit an emotionally induced sympathetic response , and as a preparatory question for the introduction of the two strong relevant questions, hence is a dual-purpose question. Backster further developed and introduced two *symptomatic questions* into his test structure to determine if an outside issue was bothering the examinee and interfering with the examinee's *psychological set*. Backster's test commenced with the use of an irrelevant (neutral) question. His test structure was designed to eliminate or identify variables that might interfere with the examinee's selective attention process and enhance the distinctness and intensity of the examinee's *psychological set* towards either the *relevant questions* which should dampen out the guilty examinee's concern over the exclusive control questions inasmuch as they are *structurally less intense*, or towards the *exclusive control questions* which are the only questions the innocent examinee is lying to. Backster categorized his test structure into three zones; the *red zone* for the relevant questions, the *green zone* for the exclusive control questions, and the *black zone* for the symptomatic questions, thus the *Tri-Zone Comparison Technique*. Backster also developed and applied a numerical scoring system using a seven-position scale to objectively evaluate the physiological data produced by the relevant and control questions being intercompared. Backster's test structure of comparing each relevant question dealing with the same issue against a neighboring control question permitted horizontal as well as vertical scoring of the three parameters (pneumograph, GSR, cardio), thus establishing an internal reliability method inasmuch as the same questions worded differently are asked twice, doubling the number of spots scored for a determination. Backster also established external reliability by requiring the conduct of two or more polygraph charts on the same test. As a safeguard against error, Backster established a *numerical threshold* which required that a minimum score be attained before a conclusion of truth or deception could be rendered, which increased in value with each test chart administered, thus a PV examination which failed to meet the minimum required scores was deemed *inconclusive*. Backster's Zone Comparison technique was designed to eliminate or isolate all of the known variables from the examination process and through an objective chart data analysis, render a valid and reliable opinion of truth or deception based solely on the numerical scores acquired from the analysis of the physiological data recorded on the examinee's polygraph charts, excluding all non-polygraphic data from the decision making process. Thus Backster's Tri-Zone Comparison Technique employs the *Numerical Approach*.

Backster initially included in his Zone Comparison Technique three additional questions labeled S-K-Y for Suspicion, Knowledge, You (Did You), which he had inserted at the end of his test structure. But Backster subsequently removed the S-K-Y questions from his Tri-Zone Comparison Technique and incorporated those three questions into a separate S-K-Y test.

In 1961, Backster's Zone Comparison technique and quantification system which then included the S-K-Y test questions at the tail end of the test, was adopted by the U. S. army C.I.D. Polygraph School at Fort Gordon, Georgia. In November 1961, Backster removed the S-K-Y test questions from his Zone Comparison Test and made it a separate S-K-Y test, but the C.I.D. Polygraph School did not follow Backster's lead and retained the S.K.Y. test questions in their U. S. Army Zone Comparison Test Format.

In 1963, Backster introduced his first *Standardized Polygraph Notepack* booklet which included among other things the Tri-Zone Reaction Combinations, Scanning, and Spot Analysis which provided the FP eight (8) separate reaction combinations with remedial action where necessary to use in the spot analysis of his/her charts, thus greatly aiding the forensic psychophysiologist (FP) in evaluating whether the questions within the zone comparison were functioning as designed or required remedial action prior to the administration of next test chart.

An example of the Backster Zone Comparison Technique Test Structure from the 1963 Edition of Backster's Standardized Polygraph Notepack and Technique Guide is depicted in Figure V-1.

Figure V-2 from the 1963 Edition of Backster's Standardized Polygraph Notepack depicts Backster's Tri-Zone Reaction Combinations; Spot Analysis Tally for Relevant Questions Number 33 and 35 which depicts the 7-position scale; and the Scoring Sheet used to enter the scores acquired from the comparison of the control questions (46 and 47) to the relevant questions (33 and 35); and the Conversion Table at the bottom of the table which indicates the test conclusion based on the final tally of all the scores.

The scientific formulation and proper introduction of aforementioned control questions (Reid and Backster) required formal training, intuitive skill and experience of application to attain the desired results. Furthermore, the nature of aforesaid control questions limited their use to test formats which contained no more than five relevant questions. Therefore, it was not surprising to find forensic psychophysiologists practicing in the private sector who were experimenting with novel techniques that hopefully would provide a simpler test format and procedure that could be used in multiple-issue tests such as pre-employment and employee screenings as well as single-issue tests. Thus, following a paper presented by Richard I. Golden at the American Polygraph Association seminar in 1969 regarding experiments with a "Yes-No" technique originally developed by Morton Sinks in 1965, which required the subject to answer each test question with an affirmative and a negative answer, Silvestro F. Reali in 1973 introduced the Positive Control technique which also required the examinee to answer each test question twice as in Golden's technique. However, Reali's technique did not incorporate existing comparison techniques and his technique contained no earlier-in-life control questions. Furthermore, Reali's technique required the examinee to answer each test question with a *lie* the first time, and truthfully the second time, but the examinee was not instructed to specifically give a "yes" or "no" answer to either question. The test comprised irrelevant questions, semi-relevant questions, relevant questions, verified disclosure questions, a question regarding previous polygraph tests, and a medical question. Each question in the test, regardless of type, was formulated to have its own control by eliciting a deliberate lie to each question from the examinee, which theoretically should elicit the greater response from the innocent examinee while the guilty examinee should reflect his greatest response to the identical question to which he/she denies culpability. In effect, the examinee's first answer to a test question is a "*directed lie*."

Unfortunately, subsequent research (Driscoll, Honts, Jones, 1987; Addison 1982; revealed that the Positive Control Technique produced an unacceptably high percentage (40% to 45%) of false negative and inconclusive results. A validity study of the Positive Control Polygraph Test by Forman and McCauley in 1986 using a field practice model revealed an average accuracy of 73% for the examiner and 78% for a blind judge of the-polygraph record. (Forman, McCauley 1987). As a result of its dismal performance, the aforesaid technique lost most of its credibility.

Backster Tri-Zone Comparison Test Structure in 1963

HE-... "YOU" PHASE TARGET "A" continued — USED ON CHART NO: 1 | 2 | 3 | 4 | 5

Symbol	No.	Question		
y	14 (J)	WERE YOU BORN IN THE UNITED STATES?	13 (J) (Last Name)	13 (K) (First Name
y|r	39	RE: WHETHER (OR NOT) YOU (YOURSELF)	DO YOU INTEND TO ANSWER TRUTHFULLY EACH QUESTION ABOUT THAT?	
●	25	ARE YOU COMPLETELY CONVINCED THAT I WILL NOT ASK YOU A QUESTION DURING THIS CHART THAT HAS NOT ALREADY BEEN REVIEWED?		
g	46	BETWEEN THE AGES OF ( ) AND ( ) -- DO YOU REMEMBER:		
r	33			
g	47	DURING THE FIRST ( ) YEARS OF YOUR LIFE -- DO YOU REMEMBER:		
r	35			
●	26	IS THERE SOMETHING ELSE YOU ARE AFRAID I WILL ASK YOU A QUESTION ABOUT -- EVEN THOUGH I TOLD YOU I WOULD NOT?		
y|r	44 (J)	REGARDING MEDICATION -- ARE YOU HOLDING BACK INFORMATION ABOUT ANY PILLS OR MEDICINE YOU HAVE TAKEN DURING THE LAST 8 HOURS?		
y|r	44 (K)	REGARDING OTHER LIE DETECTOR TESTS - ARE YOU HOLDING BACK INFORMATION ABOUT ANY OTHER TIME YOU HAVE TAKEN A LIE DETECTOR TEST?		

Figure V-1. From Backster's 1963 Edition Standardized Polygraph Notepack and Tech nique Guide.

Test Questions 14J, 13J, and 13K are Irrelevant (Neutral) Questions.
Test Question 39 is a Sacrifice/Preparatory Relevant Question.
Test Questions 25 and 26 are Symptomatic Questions.
Test Questions 46 and 47 are Non-Current Exclusive Control Questions.
Test Questions 33 and 35 are Relevant Questions.
Test Questions 44J and 44K are not used for a determination or conclusion, and were later removed by Backster from the test structure.

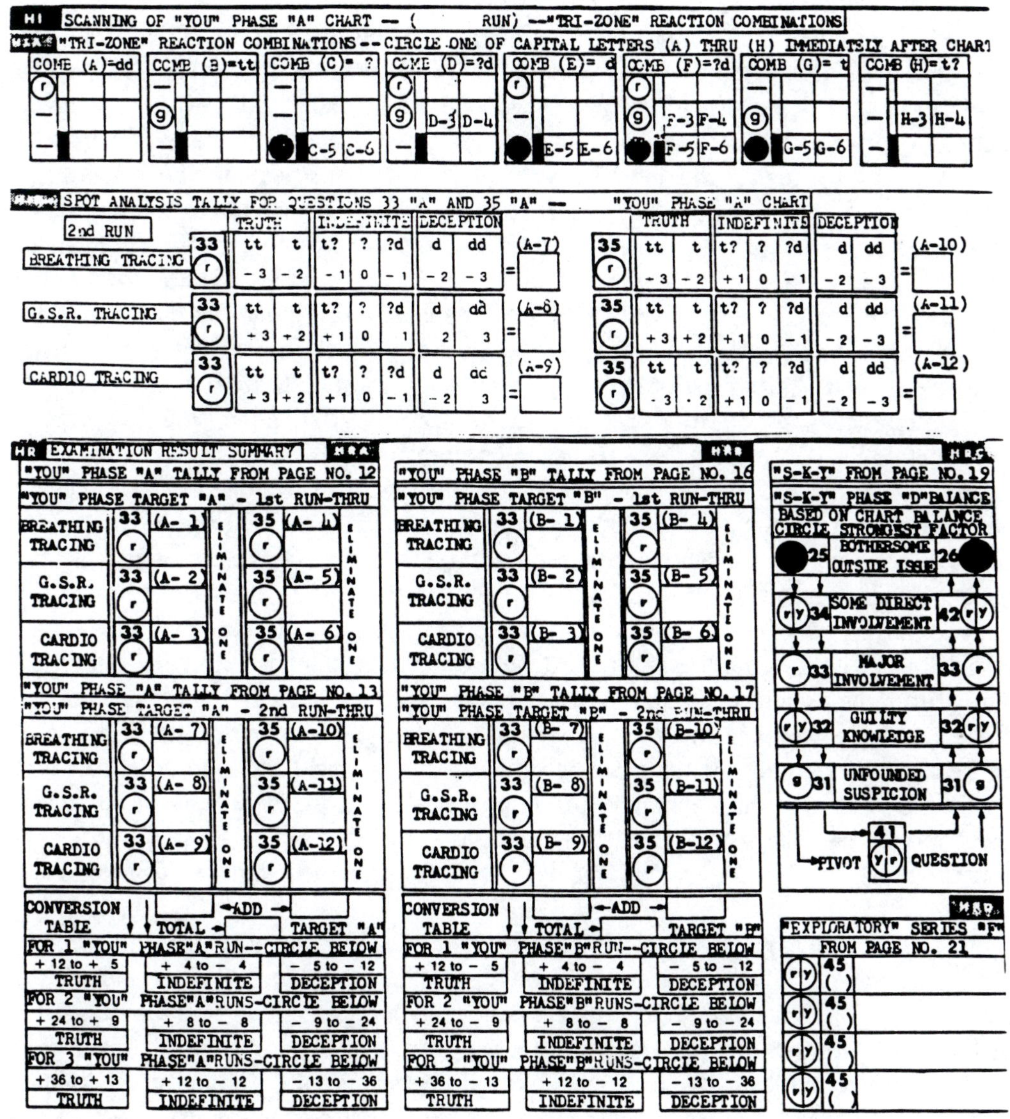

H1 SCANNING OF "YOU" PHASE "A" CHART — (RUN) —"TRI-ZONE" REACTION COMBINATIONS

"TRI-ZONE" REACTION COMBINATIONS — CIRCLE ONE OF CAPITAL LETTERS (A) THRU (H) IMMEDIATELY AFTER CHART

COMB (A)=dd	COMB (B)=tt	COMB (C)= ?	COMB (D)=?d	COMB (E)= d	COMB (F)=?d	COMB (G)= t	COMB (H)=t?
r	—	—	r	r	r	—	—
—	g	—	g D-3 D-4	—	g F-3 F-4	g	— H-3 H-4
—	—	C-5 C-6	—	E-5 E-6	F-5 F-6	G-5 G-6	—

SPOT ANALYSIS TALLY FOR QUESTIONS 33 "A" AND 35 "A" — "YOU" PHASE "A" CHART

2nd RUN

		TRUTH tt	TRUTH t	INDEFINITE t?	INDEFINITE ?	INDEFINITE ?d	DECEPTION d	DECEPTION dd	
BREATHING TRACING	33 r	-3	-2	-1	0	-1	-2	-3	(A-7) =
G.S.R. TRACING	33 r	+3	+2	+1	0	1	2	3	(A-8) =
CARDIO TRACING	33 r	+3	+2	+1	0	-1	-2	3	(A-9) =

		TRUTH tt	TRUTH t	INDEFINITE t?	INDEFINITE ?	INDEFINITE ?d	DECEPTION d	DECEPTION dd	
BREATHING TRACING	35 r	-3	-2	+1	0	-1	-2	-3	(A-10) =
G.S.R. TRACING	35 r	+3	+2	+1	0	-1	-2	-3	(A-11) =
CARDIO TRACING	35 r	-3	-2	+1	0	-1	-2	-3	(A-12) =

HR EXAMINATION RESULT SUMMARY

HRA "YOU" PHASE "A" TALLY FROM PAGE NO. 12

"YOU" PHASE TARGET "A" - 1st RUN-THRU

BREATHING TRACING	33 r (A- 1)	35 r (A- 4)	ELIMINATE ONE
G.S.R. TRACING	33 r (A- 2)	35 r (A- 5)	
CARDIO TRACING	33 r (A- 3)	35 r (A- 6)	

"YOU" PHASE "A" TALLY FROM PAGE NO. 13

"YOU" PHASE TARGET "A" - 2nd RUN-THRU

BREATHING TRACING	33 r (A- 7)	35 r (A-10)	ELIMINATE ONE
G.S.R. TRACING	33 r (A- 8)	35 r (A-11)	
CARDIO TRACING	33 r (A- 9)	35 r (A-12)	

CONVERSION TABLE — TOTAL ← —ADD→ — TARGET "A"

FOR 1 "YOU" PHASE "A" RUN—CIRCLE BELOW

+ 12 to + 5	+ 4 to − 4	− 5 to − 12
TRUTH	INDEFINITE	DECEPTION

FOR 2 "YOU" PHASE "A" RUNS-CIRCLE BELOW

+ 24 to + 9	+ 8 to − 8	− 9 to − 24
TRUTH	INDEFINITE	DECEPTION

FOR 3 "YOU" PHASE "A" RUNS-CIRCLE BELOW

+ 36 to + 13	+ 12 to − 12	− 13 to − 36
TRUTH	INDEFINITE	DECEPTION

HRB "YOU" PHASE "B" TALLY FROM PAGE NO. 16

"YOU" PHASE TARGET "B" - 1st RUN-THRU

BREATHING TRACING	33 r (B- 1)	35 r (B- 4)	ELIMINATE ONE
G.S.R. TRACING	33 r (B- 2)	35 r (B- 5)	
CARDIO TRACING	33 r (B- 3)	35 r (B- 6)	

"YOU" PHASE "B" TALLY FROM PAGE NO. 17

"YOU" PHASE TARGET "B" - 2nd RUN-THRU

BREATHING TRACING	33 r (B- 7)	35 r (B-10)	ELIMINATE ONE
G.S.R. TRACING	33 r (B- 8)	35 r (B-11)	
CARDIO TRACING	33 r (B- 9)	35 r (B-12)	

CONVERSION TABLE — TOTAL ← —ADD→ — TARGET "B"

FOR 1 "YOU" PHASE "B" RUN—CIRCLE BELOW

+ 12 to − 5	+ 4 to − 4	− 5 to − 12
TRUTH	INDEFINITE	DECEPTION

FOR 2 "YOU" PHASE "B" RUNS-CIRCLE BELOW

+ 24 to − 9	+ 8 to − 8	− 9 to − 24
TRUTH	INDEFINITE	DECEPTION

FOR 3 "YOU" PHASE "B" RUNS-CIRCLE BELOW

+ 36 to − 13	+ 12 to − 12	− 13 to − 36
TRUTH	INDEFINITE	DECEPTION

HRC "S-K-Y" FROM PAGE NO. 19

"S-K-Y" PHASE "D" BALANCE BASED ON CHART BALANCE CIRCLE STRONGEST FACTOR

25 BOTHERSOME OUTSIDE ISSUE 26

r y 34 SOME DIRECT INVOLVEMENT 42 r y

r 33 MAJOR INVOLVEMENT 33 r

r y 32 GUILTY KNOWLEDGE 32 r y

g 31 UNFOUNDED SUSPICION 31 g

41 → PIVOT y r QUESTION

HRD "EXPLORATORY" SERIES "F" FROM PAGE NO. 21

r y 45 ( )

r y 45 ( )

r y 45 ( )

r y 45 ( )

Backster Scanning, Spot Analysis, Quantification-Conclusion Table

Figure V-2. From Backster's 1963 Edition Standardized Polygraph Notepack and Technique Guide.

The original format of the Relevant-Irrelevant (R-I) technique originally consisted of relevant questions interspersed with irrelevant (neutral) questions, which was subsequently modified to include a surprise question as a type of control question. In 1980, Paul K. Minor, Chief Polygraph Examiner of the F.B.I. modified the R-I technique to include control questions of *measured relevance* to the target issue but not designed to cause an arousal. Instead, they serve as a vehicle to introduce the examinee to the issue in a logical interrogatory form and allow possible guilt feelings, anger, frustration, and so forth to be vented in areas other than at the direct relevant questions. These *relevant connected* questions provide a means for the truthful examinee to respond to the reasons he/she is tied to or associated to the target issue. These *relevant connected* questions provide a baseline of comparison that includes the excitement level of the target issue itself. The R-I technique is now also referred to as the General Question Technique (GQT), and the Modified Relevant-Irrelevant (MRI) technique as well as the Keeler technique. (Minor-Abrams, 1989) Unlike the other PV examination techniques (Reid, Backster, Marcy, Matte, DoDPI) which require that all test questions be reviewed word for word with the examinee prior to the conduct of the PV test, the MRI technique requires only that the irrelevant questions be specifically reviewed. The remaining test questions which should identify the relevant issue, determine the examinee's relationship to the offense or event, explore the examinee's suspicions and knowledge regarding the event, and determine indirect and direct involvement, are not specifically reviewed word for word with the examinee prior to the conduct of the PV test, but each of aforesaid issues is thoroughly discussed with the examinee and a clear, unequivocal answer regarding questions dealing with aforesaid issues are acquired from the examinee, so that the examinee will be familiar with the contents of the test questions which should then not be viewed as surprise questions on the test. However, because the laws in several states require the review of all test questions verbatim with the examinee prior to the administration of the PV test, the review of all test questions is optional and has been deemed by authorities in the MRI technique not to have any adverse effect on the PV examination. (Minor, 1995) (For further details see Chapter 15).

Forensic Psychophysiologist Richard I. Golden hypothesized that visual stimulation adversely affects a polygraph test; therefore, by testing the person with his/her eyes closed the stimulus would be removed. He further hypothesized that if the examinee is tested with his/her eyes closed he/she will be less aware of the cardio cuff pressure on his/her arm due to the fact that he/she cannot see the gradual discoloration of his/her arm and/or hand. He also hypothesized that inasmuch as a visual distraction can assist an examinee attempting to disassociate, a lack of visual distraction by the closing of the eyes would disarm disassociation attempts.(Golden 1966)

In Golden's experiments, over 2000 persons were tested with their eyes closed and over 2000 persons were tested with their eyes open. The findings of his research reflected that persons tested with their eyes closed generally showed greater reaction to the known-lie control questions when truthful to the crime questions and also showed greater reaction to the relevant or crime questions when deceptive to the relevant question. His findings also revealed a higher correlation among the three polygraph tracings of those persons tested with their eyes closed. They also revealed that the galvanic skin responses were more dependable, and did not manifest the "fatigue" or continued dropping of "GSR" baseline as seen with examinees whose eyes were open during the test. Golden discovered that the phenomenon of blind people hearing better than those with sight manifested itself during his research when examinees tested with their eyes closed during the first chart but with their eyes open during the second chart claimed that the questions had been asked in a louder voice while their eyes were closed. A replay of the tape recorder failed to disclose any difference in the volume of the voice. The fact that all of the examinees in the control group tested with eyes open for the first chart then closed for the second chart reported that the questions had more meaning to them when their eyes were closed and two-thirds of the same group reported that they could only concentrate on the test questions when their eyes were closed, because their minds wandered when their eyes were open, clearly indicates that when their eyes were closed they listened much more carefully to the test questions. Golden concluded that the closed-eyes polygraph technique enhances the reliability and validity of polygraph reactions and significantly increases consistency among the three polygraph tracings resulting in overall increase in accuracy and fewer inconclusive opinions. (Golden 1966). This author concurs with Golden's conclusions but cautions that some examinees become lethargic and even sleepy when their eyes are closed, while others become tired after several tests are conducted, in which case the FP should revert to the Open-Eyes technique for the remainder of the examination.

In 1975, this author developed the Control Question Validation (CQV) test as a means of verifying the effectiveness of the reviewed exclusive or non-exclusive control questions which are considered the most critical portion of the test structure, immediately prior to the administration of each PV examination. (see Chapter 14 for details). The CQV test incorporated a fictitious crime made very real to the examinee, of the same nature and category as the crime or matter for which the examinee is tested. A minimum of two tests (charts) would be administered to allow for adjustments or remedial action after the first test chart. The examinee should expectedly show consistently greater response to the control questions than to their neighboring relevant (fictitious) questions. A field research (Matte 1980) which employed both the Backster technique with exclusive control questions administered by this author, and the Arther technique with non-exclusive control questions administered by two Arther graduates, consisted of a total of ten cases divided equally between Backster and Arther type cases. Of the ten cases, two of the Arther cases involving non-exclusive control questions required that the control questions be changed as a result of no response to the control questions but a mild response to the relevant (fictitious) question in one of the Arther cases, and one Backster case involving an exclusive control question required that the control questions be changed as a result of no response to either the control or relevant questions. The aforesaid research further revealed that in two of the Backster cases, the control questions produced adequate responses to the control questions but also produced mild responses to the relevant (fictitious) questions, requiring re-emphasis of the control questions prior to the conduct of the second CQV test which effectively remedied the problem, producing significant responses to the control questions with an absence of response to the relevant (crime) questions. Subsequent to the aforesaid research, this author conducted a PV examination in a criminal case wherein the CQV test was used. The examinee in this particular case produced significant and consistent responses to the relevant (fictitious) questions in the CQV test. In fact, this author showed the charts to an FP with 20 years of experience who upon reviewing the two CQV charts asked this author if a confession had been obtained from the examinee, after which he was informed that it was a fictitious crime (CQV) test. His exclamation after recovering from his surprise was "Boy, do we have to work on our controls."

At that time, this author had been associated for more than three years with Arther School graduates who had been trained to use a stimulation (card) test immediately after the conduct of the first chart. Hence this author adopted their stimulation procedure which consisted of presenting the examinee with six cards, each containing a different number. The examinee is instructed to select one card and not show the card number to the FP, but memorize the number. The examinee is then given all the cards for safekeeping and is instructed to answer in the negative to all of the test questions including the card number that he/she selected on the test. The examinee is informed that the purpose of the test is to determine his/her suitability for the test and provide the FP with a physiological recording of a known lie from the examinee.

During the administration of aforementioned Stimulation tests, this author observed a dramatic change in the *psychological set* of many innocent (as later verified) examinees who had produced from mild to strong responses to the relevant questions in their first test (chart) but after the conduct of the Stimulation test, produced significant responses to the control questions with an absence of response to the relevant questions on the test that followed the Stimulation Test. This reflected a dramatic shift of their *psychological set* from the relevant questions on the first test to the control questions on the test which followed the Stimulation test. Conversely, it was also observed that guilty (as later verified) examinees who produced either mild or no response to the relevant questions during the first test (chart) subsequently produced strong responses to the relevant questions in the test that followed the Stimulation test. This author concluded that the reason for the shift in the Innocent subjects' psychological set from the relevant questions to the control questions was the positive influence of the results of the Stimulation test which reassured the Innocent examinee of the accuracy of the PV test, thus allaying any *fears that an error* might be made regarding their involvement in the crime for which they were being examined. Conversely, the results of the Stimulation test convinced the Guilty examinee that the test is accurate, thus increasing his/her *fear of detection* regarding his/her deception to the relevant questions. Feedback in post-test interviews verified this author's conclusions regarding the reason for aforesaid shifts in the psychological set of examinees administered a stimulation test after the first PV test.

Proponents of the Clinical Approach (Reid, Marcy, Arther) use *global evaluation* which includes any auxiliary information that will assist the FP in his/her evaluation, thus find such aforesaid shifts in an examinee's psychological set of value in their overall evaluation. Proponents of the Numerical Approach do not evaluate the reason for the aforesaid shift in the examinee's psychological set nor do they include it in their evaluation. However, the results of aforesaid shifts are manifested in the physiological data recorded on the polygraph charts which are numerically scored for a determination of truth or deception. It should be noted that in 1989, this author discontinued the administration of the Stimulation test as the second chart, that is, after the conduct of the first relevant test chart. Instead, this author administers the Stimulation test as the first chart, before any of the relevant test charts, so that all relevant tests will be equally influenced, and its order of administration will appear logical to the examinee, thus not raise any undesirable variable. Furthermore, research conducted by this author (Matte, Reuss 1989) revealed that the administration of the Stimulation test after the first relevant test chart has been conducted has the potential of raising *suspicion* on the part of some Innocent (as later verified) examinees that perhaps they did not do well on their first chart, thus arousing a *"fear of error"* regarding the target issue, which has been known to cause an arousal on the relevant questions resulting in an Inconclusive or False Positive finding.(Matte-Reuss 1989).

It became evident from this author's observations in the use of the Control Question Validation Test and the Stimulation Test as described above, that truthful (Innocent) examinees can and sometimes do produce from mild to strong physiological reactions to the relevant (crime) questions even though they are being truthful. It also became evident to this author that the primary reason for aforesaid phenomena is the truthful examinee's *fear that an error* will be made on his/her test regarding the target issue. This author also observed that in some instances, deceptive as later verified examinees upon realizing the futility of further deception, especially after the administration of a stimulation test, became placid and adopted a defeated attitude, hence became less responsive to the relevant questions while awaiting the eventual discovery of their deception. Indeed Stephen L. Kirby (1981) noted in his field study that the accuracy of the charts following the stimulation test (administered as the second chart) for the truthful examinees increased an average of 4.3 percent, while deceptive subjects decreased 15.8 percent. Kirby opined that this data falls in line with the theory (Reid & Inbau 1977) that some deceptive subjects who feel that the polygraph has detected their lie, give up, become less emotional, and therefore less responsive on each subsequent test. However, the introduction of a *Hope of Error* question (Matte 1978) into the test appeared to remotivate those deceptive subjects thus rechanneling their *fear* of detection into *hope* that an error would be made on the test regarding the target issue.

In 1977, this author developed the Quadri-Zone comparison Technique which this author subsequently (1995) renamed the *Quadri-Track Zone Comparison Technique* to be in consonance with Backster's definition of the term *Zone* which is: a twenty to thirty-five seconds block of polygraph chart time initiated by a question having a unique psychological focusing appeal to a predictable group of examinees. (Ansley 1990). Thus the *Exclusive Control Questions* which are designed to elicit a response from the Truthful (Innocent) examinee, comprise the *Green Zone*; the *Relevant Questions* (excluding the Sacrifice/Preparatory question) which are designed to elicit a response from the Deceptive (Guilty) examinee, comprise the *Red Zone*; and the *Symptomatic Questions* designed to elicit a response from the examinee who fears that an unreviewed question dealing with an outside issue will be asked on the test, comprise the *Black Zone*. Hence the *Black Zone* questions are designed to identify and eliminate the Outside Issue variable, and the *Red Zone* questions are individually compared with the *Green Zone* questions to determine which Zone (Red or Green) represented the greatest threat to the well-being of the examinee thus eliciting the greatest psychophysiological arousal indicative of truth or deception to the target issue.

The Quadri-Track Zone Comparison Technique test structure depicted below is the current version which has not changed in structure since its previous publication in 1980, except that the last question, number 44J regarding drugs was removed and its use discontinued in about 1982. Originally, question pairs 25-26, 46-33, 47-35, 23-24, were labeled Zones l, 2, 3, and 4 respectively. In January 1995, the aforementioned question pairs were renamed "Tracks" and specifically identified as follows: 25-26 Outside Track; 46-33 Primary Track; 47-35 Secondary Track; 23-24 Inside Track. The Primary, Secondary and Inside tracks which are numerically scored for a determination of truth or deception are each referred to as a Spot, in consonance with the Backster Tri-Zone Comparison system. The numerical threshold (cut-off) used in the decision making process was slightly modified in 1989 as a result of the Matte-Reuss validation study in 1989, wherein the plus (truthful) score required to reach a decision was reduced from plus 4 per chart to plus 3 per chart.

Irrelevant (Neutral)	14J	Were you born in the United States?
Preparatory/Sacrifice Relevant Question	39	Regarding whether or not you stole that $1000.00 discovered missing from the safe at ABC Markets on 12 January 1977: Do you intend to answer truthfully each question about that?
Symptomatic	25	Are you completely convinced that I will not ask you an unreviewed question during this chart?
Non-Current Exclusive Control	46	Between the ages of 18 and 23 - do you remember ever stealing anything?
Relevant	33	Did you steal that missing $1000.00 from ABC Markets?
Non-Current Exclusive Control	47	During the first 18 years of your life - do you remember ever stealing something from someone who trusted you?
Relevant	35	Regarding that $1000.00 discovered missing from the safe at the ABC Markets on 12 January 1977, did you steal that money?
Inside Issue Control	23	Are you afraid an error will be made on this test - regarding the target issue? (the theft of that $1000.00)
Inside Issue Relevant	24	Are you hopeful an error will be made on this test - regarding the target issue? (the theft of that $1000.00)
Symptomatic	26	Is there something else you are afraid I will ask you a question about, even though I told you I would not?

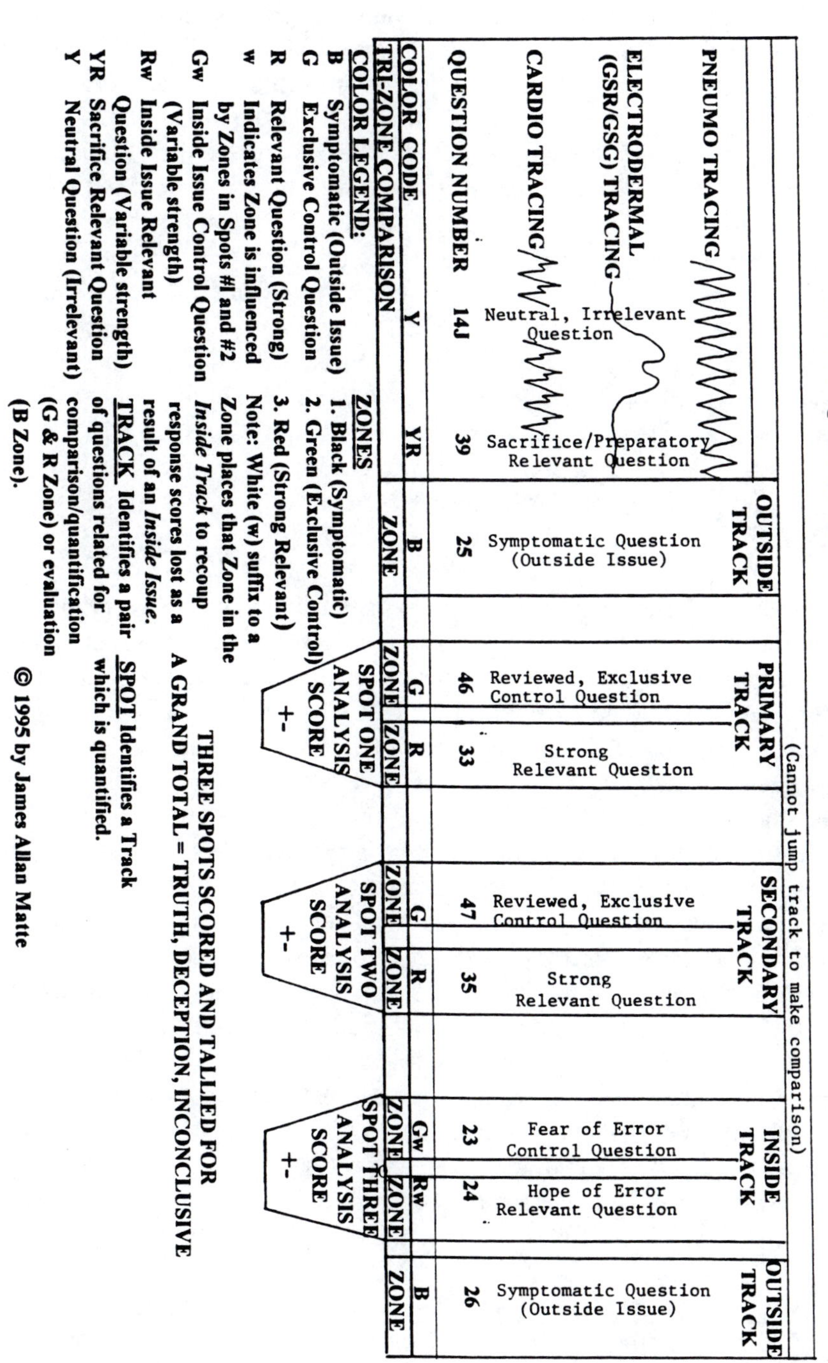

Figure V-3. Matte Quadri-Track Zone Comparison Test Structure.

Control question #23 is compared against Relevant Question 24 in the same manner that the other two pairs of control/relevant question pairs (46-33 and 47-35) are evaluated and scored. During the pretest interview and the review of the test questions, the examinee is motivated to furnish a *negative* answer to control question #23, and of course, all examinees furnish a negative answer to relevant question #24. The validated theory (Matte-Reuss 1989) holds that the innocent as later verified examinee who genuinely has a *fear of error* regarding the target issue will show a response to control question #23 and not to its neighboring relevant question #24. This quantified response should offset any negative scores produced by the innocent examinee's response to the relevant question(s) as a result of aforesaid fear of error. The Quadri-Track Zone Comparison Technique uses an increasing threshold (cut off) *averaging* a minimum score of plus 3 per chart for a truthful conclusion, and a minimum score of minus 5 per chart for a deceptive conclusion. Lower scores are called Inconclusive. In those *rare* instances when the examinee insists on furnishing an affirmative answer to control question #23, the examinee's affirmative answer is accepted and has been found by this author to still be an effective control question. (For full discussion and illustration of 23-Reaction Combo Guide see Chapter 11).

In about 1980, the control test format used by Dr. David C. Raskin and Dr. John C. Kircher in their research studies was adopted by several forensic psychophysiologists and the Arizona School of Polygraph Science which began teaching one version of the control test used in aforesaid researchers' studies which the school named the Utah Zone Comparison Technique (UZCT). The Raskin and Kircher team was later joined by Dr. Charles R. Honts. According to Honts, they never promoted any particular questions sequence inasmuch as their collective view was that a control question test was a control question test. They saw no scientific reason to prefer one order of control, relevant, and neutral questions over another, hence no reason to promote any one formulation. However the most common format in their published research was a three relevant question test with three Exclusive control questions. The format also included a sacrifice-relevant question but no symptomatic questions. Control/relevant pairs were separated by a neutral question, and the neutral and control questions were rotated after each chart. The ordinal position of the relevant questions was not changed. Furthermore, the relevant question was compared to the control preceding it, unless the control zone was considered to be a distortion zone. If a control question was not scorable, the relevant was compared to the control nearest in time that was acceptable for scoring. A 7-position scale was used but unlike Backster, a fixed numerical threshold of +/-6 was used, with lower scores meriting an inconclusive. (Honts 1996).* (Bartlett 1995; Barland 1995; Abrams 1995; Honts 1996).

In 1981, Dr. Gordon H. Barland reported his results of *A Validity and Reliability Study of Counterintelligence Screening Tests*, wherein he used fifty-six U. S. Army employees in a mock screening situation to determine the accuracy of PV examinations with the Counterintelligence Screening Test (CIST) using *directed lie questions*. This CIST is derived from the federal version of the Zone Comparison Test. The test contains 13 questions: five relevant, four directed lies, and two symptomatic. Five different models of field polygraph instruments were used which recorded respiration, skin resistance and relative blood pressure. Three methods were used to evaluate the polygraph charts. (1) The Zone method where each relevant question was evaluated against the larger control question in its zone for each channel and scored from +3 to -3. (2) The Greatest Control method which used the same procedure as the Zone method except that the five relevant questions were evaluated against the one control question on the chart with the largest overall reaction. (3) The Relevant-Irrelevant method wherein there was no numerical scoring and each relevant question was evaluated in terms of size and consistency of response without reference to the control questions.(Barland 1981)

In the aforementioned study, the first method (Zone) correctly identified 81% of the Deceptive subjects and 76% of the Non-Deceptive (Truthful) when inconclusives are omitted. The second method (Greatest Control) correctly identified 68% of the Deceptive and 83% of the Non-Deceptive (Truthful) when inconclusives are omitted. The third method (R-I) correctly identified 86% of the Deceptive and 76% of the Non-Deceptive (Truthful) when inconclusives are omitted. However, in evaluating the aforementioned results, it should be noted that in the initial analysis, if the subject was in fact *deceptive to any relevant question*, and he reacted deceptively to any of the questions, it was considered a *hit* even though the forensic psychophysiologist (FP) may have *misidentified* which relevant question the subject was deceptive to. Thus when the *correct* rather than *gross* identification is factored into the equation, the first method (Zone), excluding inconclusives, reveals only a 63% correct identification of the deceptive questions, hence was unable to identify the programmed deceptive questions *much better than chance*. The second method (Greater Control) reveals only a 54% correct identification of the deceptive questions, thus was *totally unable to identify* the programmed deceptive questions *any better than chance.* The third method (R-I) reveals a 69% correct identification of the deceptive questions, which *appears* to be superior to the other two methods in the identification of the deceptive questions.(Barland 1981). However it should further be noted that while the FPs in the third method (R-I) were instructed to disregard the control (directed-lie) questions when evaluating the relevant questions, they certainly could not omit the psychophysiological effect of the control questions on the examinees, and their influence on the neighboring relevant questions which were evaluated as if a Relevant-Irrelevant test had been conducted. This research demonstrated that the Greatest Control method was unable to detect either the deceptive subjects or the deceptive questions at greater than chance

---

* The Utah Zone Comparison Technique test structure depicted herein is based on information provided by Steven K. Bartlett, President (1995-1996) of the American Polygraph Association and a user of the Utah ZCT, Dr. Gordon H. Barland, a former colleague of Dr. Raskin at the University of Utah, Dr. Stan Abrams, Director of the Western Oregon State College School of Polygraph, and Dr. Charles R. Honts, Associate Professor of Psychology, Boise State University. A letter of inquiry dated 15 May 1995 regarding the Utah ZCT from this author to Dr. David C. Raskin who on 15 June 1995 retired to Alaska, has gone unanswered. It is recognized that the Utah ZCT has been modified by various users of the technique.

levels. It further demonstrated that the *Directed-Lie* control question identified the truthful significantly better than chance but *failed to identify the deceptive subjects or the deceptive questions at better than chance levels.*

During the period 1983-1987, David C. Raskin introduced a directed lie control question (DLCQ) into the (Utah) Zone Comparison Technique as a replacement for one of the traditional earlier-in-life exclusive control questions. In about 1993, Raskin replaced all of the traditional earlier-in-life control questions with directed-lie control questions.(Raskin 1995; Bartlett 1995). Dr. Honts subsequently replaced all of the exclusive non-directed lie control questions with exclusive directed lie control questions, and has no objections to the use of non-exclusive directed lies. (Honts 1996). This approach simplifies the construction of the control question and assures that the examinee's answer is in fact a lie, purportedly reducing the likelihood of false positives.

Earlier use of the directed-lie control question was reported by L. S. Fuse in 1982, wherein he indicated that the DLCQ had evolved over the previous sixteen years and was found to be most effective in multiple-issue tests. However Fuse cautioned that there had to be the right amount of emphasis on the DLCQ because too much would dampen the response to the relevant question, and too little could cause a false positive reaction. In his 1989 Doctoral dissertation for the Department of Psychology at the University of Utah, S. W. Horowitz conducted a study of The Role of Control Questions in Physiological Detection of Deception wherein he used a mock crime paradigm with sixty truthful and sixty deceptive subjects. He compared the effectiveness of the control question technique (CQT), the relevant-irrelevant (R&I) technique, and two directed-lie control question (DLCQ) procedures in which one used lying to neutral questions and the other lying to personal issues. Comparing the various procedures among the truthful subjects, 87% accuracy was obtained on the personal lie approach in contrast to 67% when the neutral lie was used. Employing the usual control question technique, 80% accuracy was reported while only 20% was found on the R&I procedure. For the deceptive subjects, the personal lie approach again was found to be more effective than the neutral lie with accuracy at 75% and 53% respectively. For the group in which the usual control question procedure was used, 53% accuracy was obtained while 100% accuracy was reported for the R&I approach. (Abrams 1991).

In 1987, Nathan J. Gordon, William M. Waid, and Philip M. Cochetti modified the Backster Zone Comparison Technique to include two Backster Exclusive Control questions and one Reid Non-Exclusive Control question for comparison with three relevant questions which may be interspersed at the option of the FP with Irrelevant questions. A Symptomatic question, a sacrifice relevant question, and a countermeasure question are also included in this format which they named the *Integrated Zone Comparison Technique*. The Horizontal Scoring System developed by Gordon and Cochetti in 1984 is used to evaluate the physiological data recorded on the polygraph charts.(Gordon 1995). (For details see Chapter 11)

In 1988, C. R. Honts and D. C. Raskin conducted A Field Study of the Validity of the Directed Lie Control Question, wherein they reported on twenty-five confirmed criminal tests in which the directed lie control question (DLQC) procedures were used. Confirmation (ground truth) was acquired through admissions, physical evidence that conclusively exonerated the examinee, or if the accusations were retracted. Regarding the latter, the alleged victim recanted, denying that the accusation was real. One DLCQ and two control questions were compared with three relevant questions on each administration of these tests. Using this approach, the researchers reported that of the 25 cases, one was inconclusive, one error occurred on a deceptive subject, and the remainder were accurate. When blind scoring was employed, 90% accuracy was obtained when control questions alone were used, with both errors being false positives. Using both controls and one DLCQ, an accuracy of 95.6% was obtained, with the one error being a false negative. Dr. Stan Abrams (1991) expressed his concern about the criteria used to establish ground truth in eleven (11) of the twenty-five (25) subjects used in aforesaid Honts-Raskin study, inasmuch as those eleven subjects were suspects in child sexual abuse cases and one of the criteria used for verification was retraction of an accusation. Dr. Abrams, a Clinical Psychologist and Forensic Psychophysiologist stated that is not at all unusual for a child victim of sexual abuse to retract his or her accusation, but that does not necessarily mean that the abuse did not occur, and quoted Toth & Whalen (1987) "Whatever a child says about sexual abuse, she is likely to reverse it. Beneath the anger of impulsive disclosure remains the ambivalence of guilt and the martyred obligation to preserve the family. In this chaotic aftermath of disclosure, the child discovers that the bedrock fears and threats underlying the secrecy are true. Her father abandons her and calls her a liar. Her mother does not believe her and decompensates into hysteria or rage." (Abrams 1991).

In 1991, Dr. Stan Abrams studied the directed-lie control question approach in ten verified cases consisting of six confirmed deceptive subjects and four confirmed truthful subjects. In all ten cases, verification was determined by confessions. The instructions given to the subjects were taken verbatim from an audio-taped examination conducted by Dr. Raskin. Not only was the wording exactly the same, but a very strong effort was made to maintain the same inflection. All of the polygraph charts were numerically scored using the traditional seven-position scale (+3 0 -3). The results revealed that all four truthful subjects' scores increased from an average score of +2.75 to +5.25. However, five of the six deceptive subjects' scores increased from an average score of -1.6 (deception) to an average score of +3.6 (truthful), and the sixth deceptive subject's score increased from Zero (inconclusive) to +4 (truthful). Thus, five of the six confirmed deceptive subjects produced minus (deception) scores and one produced a score of zero (inconclusive) when the relevant questions were compared to the normally used control questions, but when compared to the DLCQ, all six confirmed deceptive subjects produced plus (truthful) scores, hence false negatives for all six confirmed deceptive subjects. Apparently, the same factors that caused the unacceptable number of false negatives when using the DLCQ in studies conducted by Driscoll, et al. (1987), and Addison (1982) were operative in Abrams study. (For further discussion of DLCQ see Utah Zone Comparison, Chap. 11).

In order to understand the reason for the inordinate percentage of false negatives produced by the Directed-Lie control question, we must first take a look at the psychological structure of the Zone Comparison test originally developed by Cleve Backster. Backster originated the *earlier-in-life* control question which separates the time frame of the control question from the time frame of the relevant question by usually two or more years with the use of a time bar, thus the control questions do not offer an immediate threat, hence are *structurally weaker or less intense* than the relevant question. This purposeful imbalance between the control and relevant question optimizes the function of Backster's anticlimax dampening concept, in that the guilty-as-later verified examinee who is lying to both the control and the relevant question, will show a greater physiological arousal to the relevant question which offers an immediate threat to his/her well-being, dampening out the lesser threat offered by the control question. Conversely, the innocent-as-later-verified examinee who is not deceptive to the relevant question but is lying to the control question will show a physiological arousal to the control question because it is the only question which offers a threat to the truthful examinee's well-being. The *Fear of Error* question used in the Quadri-Track ZCT and Backster ZCT (optional) is designed to remedy those infrequent responses to the relevant questions due to an innocent examinee's *fear* that an *error* will be made on his/her test regarding the target issue. Unfortunately, many forensic psychophysiologists mistakenly believe that the control and relevant questions must be of equal strength and intensity in order to reduce their inconclusive rate and avoid false positives. To that end, they have substituted Backster's time bar with a prefix such as "Not connected with this (offense/matter)" to prevent the control question from embracing the target issue thus retaining its classification as an *exclusive* control question, yet this type of *exclusive* control question does embrace the same time frame as the relevant question, thus making it potentially equal and in some cases greater in strength and intensity. This author thus classifies such a question as a *Current-Exclusive* Control question versus Backster's *earlier-in-life* control question which is a *Non-Current-Exclusive* Control question. It is recognized that in some cases, use of the Current *Exclusive* control question is unavoidable, such as in cases involving young children where use of a time bar is difficult or impractical. Because the *Non-Current Exclusive* Control question is structurally weaker than the relevant question, it must be at least equal in number to the relevant questions against which it is being compared within the same test, whereas the *Non-Exclusive* Control question which embraces the time period of the offense as used in the Reid and Arther technique is usually compared with twice as many relevant questions due to its greater strength potential.

Therefore, within the various control question techniques, we now have the *Non-Current Exclusive* control question which employs a time bar to totally exclude the crime period, the *Current Exclusive* control question which uses a prefix to exclude only the crime, the *Non-Exclusive* control question which includes the crime and time period, and the *Directed-Lie* Control question which may employ any of the aforesaid control questions with a directed lie.

The *Current Exclusive* control question suffers the same weakness as the *Non-Exclusive* control question in that both embrace a current time frame which may include the commission of one or more recent crimes similar to the one for which the examinee is being polygraphed, thus rendering the Current Exclusive control question of potentially equal strength to the relevant question against which it is being compared. Nevertheless, proponents of the Clinical Approach who employ the *Non-Exclusive* control question reason that the inclusion of the crime period broadens the scope of the control question thereby increasing the likelihood of it being a lie by the truthful (Innocent) examinee and further increases the examinee's concern about the accuracy of his/her answer to the control question. The flaw in this reasoning is that since control questions are necessarily formulated to be in the same category of offense as the relevant questions, the guilty examinee may well interpret the Non-Exclusive control question as a Relevant question because its scope does contain the crime for which he/she is being tested. Furthermore, the Non-Exclusive control question does not contain a time buffer between the time of the crime and the time covered by the control question(s) as found in the Exclusive control questions, therefore the Non-Exclusive control questions may not only contain the crime for which the deceptive (guilty) examinee is being tested, but also other similar crimes he/she may have recently committed, rendering the Non-Exclusive control question a significantly stronger threat to the deceptive (guilty) examinee than the relevant question against which it is being compared for a determination, thus a formula for false negatives.

It is against this background that we now examine the Directed-Lie control question (DLCQ). The DLCQ represents an immediate threat to the examinee, especially the guilty, because it is usually perceived by the examinee as a measure of his/her physiological lie pattern against which the relevant questions will be compared, thus the DLCQ becomes equally if not more important than the relevant questions to both the guilty and innocent examinee. An example of the threatening power of the DLCQ to the guilty examinee was observed by this author who attempted to administer a Stimulation test to a guilty-as-later-verified examinee who had been directed to lie to the card number he had selected. On three consecutive Stimulation tests the examinee answered the question containing his selected card number with an affirmative (truthful) answer, contrary to instructions directing him to lie to that question. His refusal to lie was an obvious attempt to withhold his physiological "fingerprint" of a lie that he erroneously believed would be used for comparison with his physiological response(s) to the relevant questions. It was only after this author informed him that the PV examination would be terminated and the District Attorney would be informed of his non-cooperation that the examinee followed instructions resulting in a successful Stimulation test, which produced the greatest overall physiological response in all of the charts conducted on that deceptive examinee.

It is therefore not surprising to this author that the results of studies conducted by Driscoll, Honts, Jones 1987; Addison 1982; Barland 1981; and Abrams 1991, on the Directed-Lie control question revealed an extraordinary percentage of false negatives. Another concern about the Directed Lie Control Question (DLCQ) is that it is an invitation for the guilty (as later verified) examinee to distort the recording of his physiology on the DLCQ.

Also of concern to this author is the insertion of irrelevant questions between *tracks* containing Green (control) and Red (relevant) Zone questions as found in some of the modified Zone Comparison techniques (Utah ZCT, Integrated ZCT). Such an addition interrupts the *flow* of the examinee's *psychological set*, self-programmed to be absorbed by either the Red or Green Zone questions, which in turn are expected to produce physiological responses capable of *dampening* out potential arousals from their neighboring zone questions. For optimum performance, the *selective attention* process must be unhampered by irrelevant matter, and afforded clear, distinct and uninterrupted pathways to the appropriate zone questions which should be permitted to dampen the neighboring zone questions against which they are being compared.

While the quantified, single-issue PV examination originally developed by Cleve Backster has been validated in several studies as producing highly accurate and reliable results, multiple-issue tests such as Backster's Zone Comparison Exploratory test, Matte's Quinque-Track Zone Comparison test, the DoDPI General Question test, the Utah Zone Comparison test, and the US Air Force Modified General Question test, all of which have a quantified decision making process, are considered a degradation of the single-issue test because they do not offer the examinee's psychological set the singular, narrow scope of the former, which permits horizontal tallying of the vertical scores incorporating a repetition of the target issue questions, thus establishing internal reliability. Control Question techniques which include a Guilty Knowledge question or an Evidence Connecting question which may elicit a lie from an examinee who can potentially be truthful to the other relevant questions on the same test, are classified as multiple-issue tests. As an example, an examinee may have guilty knowledge of the identify of the offender but not himself/herself be guilty of committing the offense. Furthermore, an innocent examinee may respond to the Knowledge question due to his/her strong suspicion about someone. This potential problem is adequately addressed in separate tests such as the Backster S-K-Y test or the Matte S-K-G test which contains questions for both Knowledge and Suspicion.

To qualify as a single-issue test, all of the relevant questions must relate to a singular, specific issue, thus the examinee who is truthful to one of the relevant questions must also be truthful to the other relevant question(s) on the same test; and conversely, the deceptive examinee who is lying to one relevant question must also be deceptive to the other relevant question(s) on the same test. This permits the tallying of the numerical scores from all of the relevant questions into a single, total score to reach a conclusion of truth or deception regarding that single issue.

The presence of multiple issues in a PV examination invites competition between relevant questions for the guilty as later verified examinee's psychological set, with the relevant question having the most serious consequences potentially dampening out other relevant question(s) to which the examinee has been deceptive, thus producing misleading lack of responses to those relevant questions. However, multiple-issue tests have been especially popular in the private sector because of their utility as a time/cost saving device in resolving several issues with one test. There is a positive side to the multiple-issue test when used properly. This type of test can be useful in eliminating suspects who show no responses to any of the relevant questions yet respond adequately to the neighboring control questions. It can also be useful for an examinee showing reaction to all of the relevant questions. In the event that an examinee does show consistent, unresolved responses to one or two relevant question, but not to all relevant questions on the test, single-issue tests can then be administered to resolve each unresolved relevant issue. (Full discussion in Chapters 11 & 17)

It should be noted that the Reid Technique, the Arther technique, the Marcy technique, the Modified Relevant-Irrelevant technique, and the DoDPI General Question test, are structured to contain more than one issue dealing with the same case, thus can be classified as multiple-issue tests. A process of Global Evaluation is utilized in these techniques which employ factual analysis (except Arther), behavior analysis and chart analysis. (Full discussion in Chapter 15)

The evolutionary process of psychophysiological veracity examination techniques has taken the forensic psychophysiologist on a journey filled with trials and errors which eventually produced highly accurate psychological techniques with the use of the polygraph instrument, which have been separated into two major camps; the Clinical Approach and the Numerical Approach. Both approaches to forensic psychophysiology have demonstrated a high degree of accuracy, but the latter's objectivity is not contaminated with auxiliary information, and has demonstrated superior construct and criterion validity plus greater internal and external reliability. Furthermore, the psychological test structure of the Numerical Approach is in complete harmony with the computerized polygraph systems for which it was originally designed.

REFERENCES

Abrams, S. (1995, December 29). Telephone conversation with J. A. Matte.

Abrams, S. (1989). *The Complete Polygraph Handbook*. Lexington, Massachusetts: Lexington Books.

Abrams. S. (1991). The directed lie control question. *Polygraph*, 20(1), 26-31.

Addison, M. E. (1982, May 9, 11). Letters from Dept. of the Navy's Special Assistant for Scientific Investigations to J. A. Matte.

Ansley, N. (1990). Technical Note: Zone Comparison is the Proper Name. *Polygraph*, 19(2), 161-163.

Ansley, N. (1992). The history and accuracy of guilty knowledge and peak of tension tests. *Polygraph*, 21(3), 174-247.

Ansley, N. (1995, May 10). Telephone conversation with J. A. Matte

Ansley, N. (1995, Nov-Dec). Telephone conversations with J. A. Matte.

Arnold, M. (1950). *An excitatory theory of emotion*. In Reymert, M. I. (Ed.): *Feelings and Emotions*. New York: McGraw-Hill.

Backster, C. (1969). Technique Fundamentals of Tri-Zone Polygraph Test. New York: *Backster Research Foundation*.

Backster, C. (1963/1979). Standardized Polygraph Notepack and Technique Guide: Backster Zone Comparison Technique. *Backster School of Lie Detection*, New York, N. Y.

Backster, C. (1974). Anticlimax Dampening Concept. *Polygraph*, 3(1), 48-50.

Backster, C. (1994). 37th Annual Polygraph Examiner Work Conference Handout Note book. San Diego, CA 5-9 December 1994.

Backster, C. (1962 May-June). Methods of strengthening our polygraph technique. *Police*, 6(5), 61-68.

Backster, C. (1963). New standards in polygraph chart interpretation - Do the charts speak for themselves? *Law and Order*, 11(6), 67-68.

Backster, C. (1963). Polygraph Professionalization through technique standardization. *Law and Order*, 11(4), 63-64.

Backster, C. (1964). Polygraph spot analysis versus non-localized analysis. *Law and Order*, 12(2), 31-32.

Backster, C. (1996, March 11). Telephone conversation with J. A. Matte.

Barland, G. H. (1995, December 27). Telephone conversation with J. A. Matte.

Barland, G. H. (1981, May 12). *A validity and reliability study of counterintelligence screening tests*. Unpublished manuscript, Security Support Battalion, 902nd Military Intelligence Group, Ft. George G. Meade, MD

Bartlett, S. K. (1995, December 28). Telephone conversation with J. A. Matte.

Bartlett, S. K. (1995, December 20). Letter of reply regarding the Utah Zone Comparison Technique to J. A. Matte.

Cohen, J. A. (1961, Sep-Oct). Integrated Control Question Technique. *Police*: P. 56-58.

Driscoll, L. N., Honts, C. R., Jones D. (1987). The validity of the positive control physiological detection of deception technique. *Polygraph*, 16(3), 218-225.

Ellson, D. G. (1952). *A report on research on detection of deception*. Office of Naval Research Contract No. N6-ONR-18011. Lafayette, IN: Indiana University.

Forman, R. F., McCauley, C. (1987). Validity of the positive control polygraph test using the field practice model. *Polygraph*, 16(2), 145-160.

Golden, R. I., (1966 Sep-Oct). The closed-eyes polygraph technique. *Journal of Polygraph Studies*, I(2), 1-4.

Golden, R. I. (1969, August). The 'Yes-No' Technique. Paper presented at the American Polygraph Association Seminar in Houston, Texas.

Gordon, N. (1995, December 14). Telephone conversation with J. A. Matte.

Honts, C. R., Raskin, D. C. (1988). A field study of the validity of the directed lie control question. *Journal of Police Science and Administration*, 16: 56-61.

Hunter, F. L. (1974). Anger and the polygraph technique. *Polygraph*, 8(4), 381-395.

Keeler, L. (1930). Deception tests and the lie detector. *International Association for Identification Proceedings*, 16: 186-193.

Keeler, L. (1936). Some modern trends in the detection of crime, Part I. *The Claim Investigator*, 6(8) (September 1936): 57, 62; Part II, *The Claim Investigator* 6(9) (October 1936): 65.

Kirby, S. L. (1981). The comparison of two stimulation tests and their effect on the polygraph technique. *Polygraph*, 10(2), 63-76.

Larson, J. A. (1923). The cardio-pneumo-psychogram in deception. *Journal of Experimental Psychology*, 6(6), 420-454.

Lee, C. D. (1953). *The Instrumental Detection of Deception - The Lie Test*. Police Science Series. Springfield, IL: Charles C. Thomas, Publisher.

Little, W. W., Wilson, W. H., Moore, W. E. (1955). Applied Logic. Boston, Mass: Houghton Mifflin.

Lombroso, C. (1911). *Crime: Its Causes and Remedies*. Boston, Mass: Little, Brown & Company.

Lykken, D. T. (1981). *A Tremor in the Blood: Uses and Abuses of the Lie Detector*. New York: McGraw-Hill Book Company.

Marcy, L. P. (1995, January 30). Letter regarding the structure and methodology of the Marcy Polygraph Technique, to J. A. Matte.

Marston, W. M. (1921). Psychological possibilities in deception tests. *Journal of Criminal Law and Criminology*, 11: 551-570.

Matte, J. A. (1976). A polygraph control question validation procedure. *Polygraph*, 5(2), 170-177.

Matte, J. A. (1978). Polygraph Quadri-Zone Comparison Technique. *Polygraph*, 7(4), 266-280.

Matte, J. A. (1980). A technique for polygraphing the deaf. *Polygraph*, 9(3), 148-153.

Matte, J. A. (1980). *The Art and Science of the Polygraph Technique*. Springfield, Illinois: Charles C. Thomas - Publisher.

Matte, J. A. (1981). Polygraph Quadri-Zone Reaction Combination Guide. *Polygraph*, 10(3), 186-193.

Matte, J. A. (1993). The review, presentation and assurance of intended interpretation of test questions is critical to the outcome of polygraph tests. *Polygraph*, 22(4), 299-312.

Matte, J. A., Reuss, R. M. (1989). A field validation study of the Quadri-Zone Comparison Technique. *Polygraph*, 18(4), 187-202.

Matte, J. A., Reuss, R. M. (1989). Validation study on the Quadri-Zone Comparison Technique. *Research Abstract*, LD 01452, Vol. 1502, University Microfilm International.

Matte, J. A., Reuss, R. M. (1993). Predictive tables for estimating accuracy and error rates in single-issue control question tests. *The Truthseekers*, 5(3), 1-9.

Matte, J. A., Reuss, R. M. (1995, August 16). Methodology in numerically evaluated psychophysiological veracity examinations. Thesis presented at the 30th Annual Seminar/Workshop of the American Polygraph Association, Las Vegas, Nevada. 53 pages.

Minor, P. K. (1989). The Relevant-Irrelevant Technique. Chap. 10. *The Complete Polygraph Handbook*, Stan Abrams. Lexington, Mass: D. C. Heath and Company.

Minor, P. K. (1995, January 10). Telephone Conversation with J. A. Matte.

Minor, P. K. (1995, December 14). Telephone Conversation with J. A. Matte.

Raskin, D. C., Barland, G. H., Podlesny, J. A. (1978). Validity and reliability of detection of deception. Washington, D. C.: *National Institute of Law Enforcement and Criminal Justice.*

Raskin,D. C. (1995, May). Telephone conversation with J. A. Matte.

Rathus, S. A. (1994). *Essentials of Psychology*. Fourth Edition, Harcourt Brace College Publishers, Fort Worth, TX.

Reali, S. F. (1978). Reali's Positive Control Technique. *Polygraph*, 7(4), 281-285.

Reid, J. E., Inbau, F. E. (1966). *Truth and Deception*. Baltimore, MD: The Williams & Wilkins Company.

Reid, J. E., Inbau, F. E. (1977). *Truth and Deception: The Polygraph ("Lie Detector") Technique*, 2d ed. Baltimore: Williams & Wilkins.

Summers, W. G. (1939). Science can get the confession. *Fordham Law Review*. 8: 334-354.

Toth, P. A., Whalen, M. P. (Eds.) (1987). *Investigation and Prosecution of Child Abuse*. National Center for the Prosecution of Child Abuse, 1033, N. Fairfax Street, Suite 200, Alexandria, VA.

Chapter 6

THE REQUIRED SETTING FOR A PSYCHOPHYSIOLOGICAL VERACITY EXAMINATION: A CONTROLLED ENVIRONMENT

No one would seriously consider undergoing major surgery in a place other than an operation room designed to minimize the danger of infection and other elements that may impair the successful completion of the operation. A psychophysiological veracity (PV) examination also requires a special environment, free of artifact that might interfere with the examination. Yet no one seems to question the validity of PV examinations administered in facilities that are loaded with artifacts such as lack of privacy, noise, audible external voices, distracting decor, excessive room temperature, poor lighting, lack of proper table and subject examination chair, and general lack of professional atmosphere. Some forensic psychophysiologists (FP) for both law enforcement and private industry are often required to travel to distant places to conduct PV examinations at facilities such as hotel and motel rooms that fail to meet the required standards set forth in this chapter. Forensic psychophysiologists for the prosecution and the defense both have occasion to conduct PV examinations in jails and prisons which often ignore the requests of the forensic psychophysiologists for adequate facilities and compel them to conduct PV examinations in cells or rooms offering the worst kind of conditions imaginable, with a *take it or leave it attitude,* that totally disregards the right of the inmate to a valid and reliable PV examination which can only be conducted in a controlled environment, free of artifact.

Ideally, a polygraph suite should consist of a waiting room, an examination room, and a chart interpretation room. Charts should never be interpreted in front of the subject. The decor of the reception room should convey an air of professionalism with a calming effect, rather than an officious or police atmosphere. The examination room should not be smaller than eight by eight feet nor larger than ten by fifteen feet and, preferably, should be ten by ten feet. Too large an area loses the aura of confidentiality. The floor should be carpeted to absorb sound. The walls should be soundproof and covered with a paint of a warm light color. The lighting must be adequate but free of glare. The examination room must be soundproof from both internal and external noises. A likely source of external noise is from the hallway outside the examination room. Therefore, the door to the examination room should be solid and make full contact with the floor and the door jamb. It is also advisable whenever possible to have a second solid door separating the reception room from the examination room as a further barrier to external noise.

There should be three chairs in the examination room: the forensic psychophysiologist's chair, consisting of an office swivel armchair located behind the desk holding the polygraph instrument; a regular armless chair where the subject initially sits during the pretest interview, located alongside the desk; and the examination chair, which should have a straight back for better breathing patterns and adjustable arms to that the subject's arms will be maintained away from his or her rib cage to avoid the interference of subject's breathing with the cardio tracing. The examination chair should be located on the opposite side of the desk from the FP and facing in the opposite direction that the polygraph chart moves out of the instrument. The examination chair should be situated so that the subject's left arm will be farthest from the instrument desk. This will provide the FP with the necessary room required to attach the pneumograph tubes that

Diane Nash portraying the examinee with the author in pre-test interview setting. (circa 1979)

Figure VI-1

link to the subject's left side, and further place the cardio cuff on subject's left arm, which requires a certain amount of leverage to apply properly.

The wall facing the examinee when seated in the examination chair should be free of any fixture that may distract the subject or act as an aid at dissociation when for some reason the subject is tested with his or her eyes open. The windows may be covered with rehearsal room quality drapes that will significantly reduce internal sound.

In addition to the three rooms mentioned above, it is a good idea to have a bathroom nearby or adjoining the examination room so that the subject may wash his or her hands prior to the test to remove any grease or other substance that might impair sweat gland function at the fingertips. This is a good anti-countermeasure practice that should be implemented before any PV test. The bathroom also provides a ready place for the subject to urinate without a lengthy interruption and further provides the FP a means of acquiring a urine specimen from the subject for transmittal to the laboratory to test for the presence of drugs immediately upon completion of the PV tests.

Diane Nash portraying the examinee with the author in the actual testing phase of the examination. (circa 1979)

Figure VI-2

The chart interpretation room provides privacy for the forensic psychophysiologist (FP) in the analysis of the physiological data contained on the polygraph charts during the progress of the examination and affords him or her the opportunity of private consultation with another FP and/or the investigator in the case.

Interpretation of the physiological data on the collected polygraph charts in the presence of the subject should be avoided since examinees have been led to believe that the "machine" readily provides the answer of truth or deception. Careful study of the physiological data as is necessary by the FP may convey to the subject that the FP is not sure of his or her findings, creating doubt in the competency and expertise of the FP. This could cause undue anxiety in the innocent examinee and strengthen the guilty's resistance to post-test interrogation.

The examination room temperature should be controlled so it will not fall below 70°F or rise above 80°F, and its system must be quiet. The galvanometer will become progressively less effective outside of that temperature range.

The examination room should have an audio monitoring system at the very least and preferably the added feature of closed circuit television or a two-way mirror. Examinations of female subjects, psychiatric patients, etc., may require monitoring for the protection of the FP and the patient. Examinations whose results may end up in court should be recorded to show that all procedures were followed in accordance with scientifically valid standards, or that a confession was obtained without violation of the examinee's constitutional rights.

The examination room should be equipped with a three-prong electrical outlet that is grounded so that the instrument and its most affected component, the galvanometer, will operate at maximum efficiency. When using a computerized polygraph system, it is advisable to use a surge protector.

In essence, the polygraph examination room is designed to provide complete privacy in a professional surrounding that will convey confidence in the expertise of the forensic psychophysiologist. It further provides an environment that is free of external and internal noises that may interfere or interrupt the examination and is free of visual or audio elements that may be distracting or useful in attempting countermeasures by the examinee. The proper setting and examination procedures should include anti-countermeasures that prevent and/or deter the guilty (as later verified) examinee from employing countermeasures. In that regard it is advisable to have the examinee remove his or her shoes immediately prior to the actual testing phase when charts are collected, for observation of any feet or toe movement against instructions by the FP. This or any other movement by the examinee would of course be detected by examination chairs equipped with activity or movement sensors. (Chapter 21).

So far we have identified and provided controls for auditory variables. However, how do we control visual distractions such as the movement of the polygraph pens and the movement of the FP's hand when making instrument adjustments and writing on the polygraph chart during the administration of the polygraph tests? A normal person's vision is capable of perceiving objects on either side while looking straight ahead. Therefore, it is conceivable that an examinee while sitting in the examination chair parallel to the polygraph desk and facing away from the instrument may still be able to see the instrument and the FP. To position the examinee so that his or her back is facing the instrument and the FP is undesirable because it would prevent the FP from observing facial and other body movement on the part of the examinee which may cause distortion on the chart.

Forensic psychophysiologist Richard I. Golden hypothesized that visual stimulation adversely affects a polygraph test; therefore, by testing the person with his or her eyes closed the stimulus would be removed (Golden, 1966). He further hypothesized that if the examinee is tested with his or her eyes closed, he or she will be less aware of the cardio cuff pressure on his or her arm due to the fact that he or she cannot see the gradual discoloration of his or her arm and/or hand. Golden also hypothesized that inasmuch as a visual distraction can assist an examinee attempting to disassociate, a lack of visual distraction by the closing of the eyes would disarm disassociation attempts.

In Golden's experiments, over 2000 persons were tested with their eyes closed and over 2000 persons were tested with their eyes open. The findings of his research reflected that persons tested with their eyes closed generally showed greater reaction to the known-lie control questions when truthful to the crime questions and also showed greater reaction to the relevant or crime questions when deceptive to the relevant question than those persons tested with their eyes open. His findings also revealed a higher correlation among the three polygraph tracings of those persons tested with their eyes closed. They also revealed that the galvanic skin responses were more dependable and did not manifest the "fatigue" or continued dropping of GSR baseline as seen with examinees whose eyes were open during the test. Golden discovered that the phenomenon of blind people hearing better than those with sight manifested itself during his research when examinees tested with their eyes closed during the first chart but with their eyes open during the second chart claimed that the questions had been asked in a louder voice while their eyes were closed. A replay of the tape recorder failed to disclose any difference in the volume of the voice. The fact that all of the examinees in the control group tested with eyes open for the first chart then closed for the second chart reported that the questions had more meaning to them when their eyes were closed and two-thirds of the same group reported that they could only concentrate on the test questions when their eyes were closed, because their minds wandered when their eyes were open, clearly indicates that when their eyes were closed they listened much more carefully to the test questions. It therefore appears that the closed-eyes technique enhances the reliability and validity of polygraph reactions and significantly increases consistency among the three physiological tracings resulting in overall increased accuracy and fewer inconclusive opinions.

This author has used the closed-eyes technique for many years and concurs with Golden's conclusions, but cautions that some examinees become lethargic and even sleepy when their eyes are closed, while others become tired after several tests are conducted, in which case the forensic psychophysiologist should revert to the open-eyes technique where the examinee is instructed to look straight ahead during the testing phase, for the remainder of the psychophysiological veracity examination. The suggestion (Wygant 1996) that users of computerized polygraph systems position themselves toward the front of the examinee for a more direct view of him/her inasmuch the polygraph chart is on the monitor screen not within view of the examinee, fails to consider the distracting effect the forensic psychophysiologist's activities will have on the examinee facing him/her during the test, and the impeding variables it could add to the testing phase of the examination.

REFERENCES

Golden, R. I. (1966). The closed-eyes polygraph technique. *Journal of Polygraph Studies*, 1(2).

Wygant, J. R. (1999, September). Equipment tips. *Polygraph News and Views*. Portland, OR. 4(5). 1-4.

Chapter 7

IDENTIFICATION OF PROBLEM AREAS THROUGH BASIC PRINCIPLES OF PSYCHOLOGY

There are times when a Forensic Psychophysiologist (FP) will be requested to administer a psychophysiological veracity (PV) examination using the polygraph on an individual known to be suffering from a mental disorder. By knowing ahead of time the symptoms associated with a particular type of psychological diagnosis and the quality of polygraph charts that may be produced by such individuals, the FP can make an intelligent decision regarding the feasibility of testing this individual and the type of precautionary measures that must be taken if the test is to be administered. Additionally, the FP who is well versed in the mental disorders is in a better position to identify possible problems with examinees who have an undiagnosed disorder. The FP then is better equipped to produce an accurate PV examination when assessing such individuals. This chapter is not designed as a course in abnormal psychology, but to provide the FP with some basic information that may assist in identifying possible mental disorders in examinees. This is merely an overview of the topic, designed to guide the FP in acquiring further knowledge regarding this important but complex area of psychology. While American Polygraph Association accredited polygraph schools currently require that their students possess a bachelor's degree (with some exceptions) which preferably includes some course work in psychology, graduates who subsequently acquire certification from either national or state associations are required to attend continuing education courses which include psychology in order to retain their certification. It is expected that these courses will cover this important issue in much greater detail.

Some examinees who possess a psychological diagnosis will produce good polygraph charts while others will produce poor ones. A poor chart may yield inconclusive results due to excessive distortion and lack of tracing purity. Some knowledge of the emotional health of the examinee will help the FP understand the etiology of the polygraph chart. There will be some occasions where the FP will suspect from the physiological data on the polygraph charts that the examinee is experiencing psychological difficulties. A psychological evaluation of such an examinee should be recommended. If the examinee has been clearly diagnosed as suffering from a mental disorder, the FP should determine if it is best to request permission to administer the test at a later date since an inconclusive chart can result based on the state of the examinee at that time. In order to obtain a definitive polygraph chart, the examinee's symptoms must be alleviated to some extent. Pointing this out to the appropriate psychiatric staff should result in determining when the examinee is ready to be re-examined. By being forewarned as to the quality of charts for individuals with each type of mental disorder, the FP will not spend unnecessary time and effort exhausting the examinee and him/herself in an attempt to acquire satisfactory charts from an individual whose mental condition disqualifies him/her as a testable examinee. Therefore it is imperative that the FP distinguish between results of a PV examination due to psychopathological disorders and examinees who are clearly responding to the questions put forth. Though at times this distinction may not be well defined, the following explanations will provide information to assist in this decision.

Abnormal Behavior

Over the course of a lifetime, everyone has worries and fears as well as moments of feeling sad or blue. These are normal emotional and behavioral responses to life's stresses and in fact, if an individual did not respond in this way, he or she would be considered abnormal (due to a lack of affect). What distinguishes normal from abnormal responding is the degree to which one becomes distressed or disabled or is at risk for suffering pain, disability, death or loss of freedom due to behavioral/emotional responses. For example, many individuals do not like to give formal talks or speeches, thus evoking concerns over doing a bad job, becoming jittery or nervous. These concerns are not unusual and in most cases add a degree of preparedness and thus can be considered useful anxiety for the individual. However, should the degree of concern or anxiety result in avoidance of giving formal presentations or deliberately limiting career opportunities, a person could be considered psychopathological.

The example above provides a description of one anxiety disorder that will be explained in more detail later in this chapter. Other types of disorders will also be reviewed, including mood disorders, somatoform disorders, psychoses, and dissociative disorders. Each of these categories of disorders contains specific diagnoses, some of which are more common than others. Though it is unlikely that the FP will come in contact with an individual who has a psychotic disorder, it is important to be familiar with the clinical presentation of this disorder as well as other more common mental disorders. Each disorder will present with symptoms, both physical and cognitive, that will impact the reliability and validity of the PV examination. In certain disorders (e.g., anxiety) the central feature is the physiological responding of the individual that will have its greatest impact on the PV examination. In other cases (e.g., dissociative and psychotic disorders), the central feature is cognitive responding that will influence the PV examination. Yet other disorders (e.g., mood disorders, somatoform disorders) will effect the PV examination both physiologically and cognitively. Thus it behooves the FP to recognize the various symptoms in order to identify problem areas that may affect the pretest interview and the physiological data recorded on the polygraph charts.

Anxiety Disorders

A certain amount of anxiety is normal and adaptive in human beings. Anxiety has served an important role in the evolution of our species. However, anxiety exists on a continuum which ranges from normal to abnormal. In the following discussion, we will detail some of the elements of maladaptive anxiety, termed anxiety disorders. The anxiety disorders are among the most prevalent psychological diagnoses. Anxiety is defined as an intense state of fear or apprehension, typically concerning future events and their perceived consequences. In anxiety disorders, this fearful state is not easily attributable to an immediate threat in the environment, but is more likely to be a mis-firing of the fight or flight system (Cannon, 1929). There are several types of anxiety disorders, each having its own unique set of symptoms, yet certain common characteristics are present in all the anxiety disorders.

There are seven common anxiety disorders: (1) Panic Disorder with and without Agoraphobia; (2) Agoraphobia; (3) Specific Phobia; (4) Social Phobia; (5) Obsessive-Compulsive Disorder; (6) Posttraumatic Stress Disorder; (7) Generalized Anxiety Disorder. It can be expected that individuals who are undergoing PV testing will be somewhat nervous. This is a normal response. However, the key for the FP is in recognizing maladaptive anxiety and its impact on the polygraph chart. Moreover, the FP should consider the impact of the conditions under which the examinee is being tested and potential exacerbation of symptoms in individuals with anxiety disorders.

Panic Disorder: Panic disorder is characterized by recurrent and unexpected panic attacks. In addition to panic attacks, individuals usually fear the consequences of such attacks and/or fear suffering future attacks. These fears can cause individuals to change their behavior, for example refrain from exercising, reduce caffeine consumption or carry emergency phone numbers when leaving the house. The fears and behavioral changes can persist even when a significant amount of time has elapsed since the last panic attack. Panic attacks consist of an intense rush of anxiety, fear or feeling of impending doom. Symptoms which are commonly experienced during an attack include: accelerated or pounding heart, shortness of breath or smothering sensations, feeling dizzy or faint, depersonalization or derealization and fear of dying. Panic attacks can occur at any time and thus may come "out of the blue." In addition, panic attacks can be triggered while in various states of relaxation. The attacks can also occur with any of the anxiety disorders (e.g., specific phobia, obsessive-compulsive disorder, social phobia, etc.) as discussed below. Individuals with panic disorder can experience heightened physiological arousal between panic attacks that varies in intensity based on the severity of the panic. As a result, individuals with panic disorder will produce a poor to very good polygraph chart based on the intensity and severity of their attacks and chronic arousal (Zimbardo et al., 1975; APA, DSM-IV, 1994; Neale, Davison & Haaga, 1996).

Agoraphobia: Individuals who fear not being able to escape a situation or get help if they experience a panic attack may begin to fear and/or avoid situations. An individual who suffers from agoraphobia may experience an increase in anxiety and physiological arousal in anticipation of entering a feared situation, such as a small room with the door closed, though this is not always the case. Thus, if the individual thinks escape would be difficult during the PV examination in the event of a panic attack, this will probably cause a poor quality polygraph chart.

Specific Phobia: Individuals who have a specific phobia are fearful of particular situations or objects. These individuals have developed a fear of an object or situation to the extent that when confronted by it, they are overwhelmed with disabling anxiety. There are four common sub-types of phobias which include (a) Animal Phobia (e.g. snakes, dogs) (b) Natural Environment Phobia (e.g. storms, heights) (c) Blood-Injection-Injury Phobia (e.g. blood, needles) and (d) Situational Phobia (e.g. flying, elevators, or bridges). Each of these sub-types shares the common feature of unrealistic or excessive fearful responses to the object or situation. For example, when the individual is confronted with the situation or object he/she will have an anxious response which may include a panic attack (as described earlier). It is possible in the case of claustrophobic examinees that features of polygraph examination will evoke an anxious response. These individuals may become fearful due to the sensation of being trapped by the physiological monitoring devices. Thus, the perception of confinement inherent in the electrode configuration will reduce the quality of the resulting polygraph chart. Provided that the feared object is not present while the polygraph examination is being conducted, individuals with specific phobias should produce good to very good charts.

Social Phobia: Social Phobia is the fear of being evaluated negatively in social situations and/or a fear of embarrassing or humiliating oneself in public. The fear may be of specific situations, such as giving formal speeches or may be a general fear of social situations. The individual with social phobia may be concerned about displaying signs of autonomic arousal, such as sweating, blushing or trembling. As the concern intensifies, the individual becomes more sensitive to bodily changes, which in turn increases anxiety and autonomic responding, usually resulting in an increase in the demonstrated signs of autonomic arousal. Individuals can respond to the feared situation in the form of a panic attack (as described earlier). Due to the nature of the PV examination (e.g., scrutinizing questions), it is likely that the individual may produce a poor polygraph chart.

Obsessive-Compulsive Disorder: Obsessive-compulsive disorder is characterized by persistent, unwanted and distressing thoughts, images or impulses (obsessions) that cause marked anxiety and/or distress. Compulsions are behaviors or acts (including mental acts) which one feels driven to perform and are repetitive in nature. The purpose of compulsions is to reduce anxiety caused by the obsessions. Though the individual realizes that these thoughts are a product of his/her own mind (thus distinguishing them from a psychotic delusion), the thought or image is not characteristic of the individual (ego-dystonic). Examples of obsessions include thoughts of harming oneself and/or others, fears of contaminating oneself and thoughts/images of symmetry or exactness. Compulsive behaviors are sometimes seen as excessive or unreasonable but usually have a rational basis, such as excessive and/or repetitive washing to rid oneself of dirt or germs or constant checking of the stove to prevent the possibility of a fire. An individual with contamination obsessions may fear contracting germs from the polygraph equipment and thus may become anxious, physiologically aroused and have difficulty concentrating until he/she can perform a neutralizing compulsion. Thus, individuals with obsessive-compulsive disorder may produce a poor to good polygraph chart depending upon the severity and content of their obsessions and compulsions.

Posttraumatic Stress Disorder: Posttraumatic Stress Disorder (PTSD) can result if an examinee has experienced a traumatic event such as combat, natural disaster, assault, or motor vehicle accident. It is important to recognize that although not everyone who experiences a trauma will develop the disorder, most individuals will experience some of the symptoms of PTSD for a brief period of time. For trauma survivors, the onset of these symptoms can be immediate (Acute Stress Disorder) or may not begin until months or even years after the event (Delayed Onset). Typical symptoms include re-experiencing phenomena such as flashbacks, painful intrusive recollections, feeling as though the event is happening all over again, and nightmares. The PTSD sufferer often will have heightened autonomic arousal, exaggerated startle response, hypervigilance, and have feelings of irritability with outbursts of anger. Therefore, it is not surprising that they will often have difficulty with sleep and a decreased ability to concentrate. Understandably, individuals with PTSD will often attempt to avoid thoughts and feelings surrounding the trauma as well as things that remind them of the event. They may demonstrate a restricted range of affect, be unable to recall an important aspect of the traumatic event, feel detached from people and be disinterested in usual activities. These individuals may find it difficult to concentrate on the examiner's questions and will be particularly distracted if characteristics of the FP or the setting remind the examinee of the trauma in some way. In these cases, the examinee will probably produce a very poor chart.

Generalized Anxiety Disorder: Individuals with Generalized Anxiety Disorder (GAD) are often described as worriers due to their chronic and continuous feelings of apprehension and anxiety about matters when there is little or no basis for the excessive concern. They are preoccupied with the focus of this concern, which keeps them in a chronic state of worry. The prolonged anxiety and apprehension is not associated with particular objects or feared situations but represents a more pervasive mindset. Recurrent themes of worry are specific to the individual and vary greatly, but can include such things as excessive concern about family members, financial matters, minor matters such as repairs to the car or house, being late for appointments, etc. The continued state of heightened anxiety in individuals with GAD results in chronic arousal of the autonomic nervous system. These individuals cannot stop worries from coming into their minds and subsequently experience difficulty concentrating, difficulty sleeping, and are easily fatigued. Other symptoms include muscle tension, irritability, apprehension about the future, and hypervigilance. Individuals who have this diagnosis will demonstrate decreased variability in autonomic responses and higher resting rates on measures such as muscle tension (Hoehn-Saric, & McLeod, 1988; Hoehn-Saric, McLeod, & Zimmerli, 1989). This chronic state of anxiety can occasionally become acute with relatively minor environmental stress (e.g. being late for an appointment). The FP must be cautious when interpreting such profiles due to this chronic arousal which cannot be directly attributed to the FP's questioning but rather is a reflection of general nervous tension (Toth 1972).

Mood Disorders

Everyone has days when they feel down or sad or do not feel interested in activities they normally enjoy. Conversely, we all have days when we feel exceptionally good, and sometimes we feel both emotions within the same day. Feeling down and feeling good are descriptors of each end on a continuum of mood states. In most individuals, moods tend to be somewhere near the center of the continuum with minor fluctuations to either side. However, when a person's mood is at one end of the continuum for an extended period of time, a mood disorder may develop. In addition, mood disorders occur when a mood shifts from one extreme to another. Mood disorders are accompanied by somatic (physical) and cognitive symptoms. Experiencing either end of the continuum for prolonged periods or cycling back and forth can lead to tremendous dissatisfaction with life and possibly result in suicide. The following section outlines some of the more common mood disorders, including 1) Major Depression; 2) Dysthymia; 3) Mania; 4) Bipolar I and II; and 5) Cyclothymia and accompanying somatic and cognitive symptoms.

Major Depressive Episode: A major depressive disorder consists of depressed feelings or a lost of interest and/or pleasure in usual activities. Though everyone experiences days when they feel down and don't have much interest in activities, continuously feeling down or having a lack of interest for at least two weeks (for the majority of each day) constitutes a major depressive episode. In addition to feeling down and having little interest in activities, an individual also experiences some of the following symptoms; significant weight loss when not trying to lose weight, difficulty sleeping or sleeping too much, psychomotor agitation or retardation that is observed by others, fatigue or loss of energy, feelings of worthlessness or guilt, difficulty concentrating and recurrent thoughts of death, suicide or a suicide attempt. Individuals who are depressed may also report feeling anxious and experience difficulty relaxing. Due to diminished concentration and increased fatigue, it is likely that the depressed individual will produce a poor to moderate polygraph chart.

Dysthymia: Dysthymia is similar to major depression except it is of a lesser severity and intensity, though of a longer duration. Individuals will report feeling down for the majority of the past two years or longer and may feel that this state is normal for them. In addition to feeling down, some of the following symptoms are usually present: poor appetite or overeating, low energy or fatigue, difficulty sleeping or sleeping too much, low self-esteem, poor concentration or difficulty making decisions, and feelings of hopelessness. Individuals with dysthymia do not necessarily experience daily somatic and cognitive symptoms as in major depressive disorder and thus will provide from moderate to good polygraph charts.

Mania: Individuals with mania experience a drastic increase in energy, decreased need for sleep, and an inflated self-esteem. This increased energy becomes problematic because it is associated with rapid speech, racing thoughts, and being easily distracted. This abundance of energy can result in restless agitation, an increase in goal-directed behavior, and over-involvement in pleasurable activities which are likely to have negative consequences (e.g. uncontrolled shopping sprees, sexual indiscretions). People who are in a manic episode are easily recognizable and may at first give a fun-loving impression. However, fairly rapidly a FP will recognize the symptom picture as the serious disorder that it represents. Any individual who is in a manic state will most likely produce an erratic polygraph chart, thus should, whenever possible, not be examined until the manic episode is in remission.

Bipolar I and II: People with these disorders are frequently referred to in layman's terms as being manic-depressive. Manic depression is characterized by alternations between the two disorders (mania and depression) with small periods of normal mood between the remission of one disorder and the onset of the next. When the predominant symptoms are characterized by manic episodes with one or more major depressive episodes, the person is diagnosed with Bipolar I disorder. In contrast, if the person suffers predominantly from a recurrence of major depressive episodes with at least one manic period, they are diagnosed with Bipolar II disorder. The person with Bipolar disorder (I or II) will produce one of two polygraph charts. If he/she is in a manic state at the time of the test, the chart will reflect agitation with a general nervous tension. However, if he/she is in a depressive state at the time of the test, the chart may be unresponsive depending upon the degree of depression.

Cyclothymia: Cyclothymia is similar to bipolar disorder except it is of lesser severity and intensity, yet is present for longer periods of time. For two years of more, these individuals will fluctuate between mild to moderate levels of depressive and manic symptoms. This persistent mood fluctuation may result in the person being categorized as temperamental, moody, unpredictable, or unreliable. Since they often experience drastic mood changes including significant down periods, they are likely to be cynical people. An individual with cyclothymia will produce poor to good polygraph charts depending on the severity of his or her current symptoms.

Somatoform Disorders

When an individual complains of physical symptoms which cannot be explained by a medical condition, it is possible that they are suffering from a somatoform disorder. Most healthy individuals adapt to the presence of ordinary aches and pains or long bouts of discomfort. In contrast, individuals with somatoform disorders are overly alert to the presence of bodily symptoms such as aches, pains and minor defects and interpret them as signs of physical illness or disease. They frequently seek assistance from general practitioners and specialists in the medical field rather than mental health professionals. These disorders are not to be confused with factitious disorders or malingering where the physical symptoms are under voluntary control of the individual. People with somatoform disorders do not intentionally produce symptoms.

The five common somatoform disorders include: 1) Somatization Disorder; 2) Conversion Disorder; 3) Pain Disorder; 4) Hypochondriasis; and 5) Body Dysmorphic Disorder. It is not entirely clear what impact these disorders would have on a polygraph chart since the individuals themselves are often unaware that their difficulties have a psychological basis. However, it can be said that depending upon the intensity of the symptoms experienced, the polygraph charts will range from poor to very good.

Somatization Disorder: Somatization Disorder, also known as Briquet's syndrome, is marked by dramatic and frequent complaints of physical symptoms that cannot be explained by any known medical condition. Individuals with this disorder believe that their symptoms are serious despite the fact that no physical illness has been diagnosed. Typical symptoms include pain in various areas of the body (e.g., arms, legs, or head), gastrointestinal difficulties (e.g., nausea, sour stomach, or vomiting), problems with sexual performance (e.g., erectile dysfunction or menstrual irregularities), and unusual neurological complaints (e.g., double vision, loss of balance, or paralysis). People with this disorder may also suffer from anxiety or depression, abuse medications and may appear frustrated at the inability of medical practitioners to diagnose the source of their difficulties. This individual will produce from poor to very good polygraph charts depending upon the severity of the disorder and associated features such as anxiety, depression and abuse of medications (Toth 1972).

***Conversion Disorder*:** Conversion disorder is marked by the development of illness-related symptoms or the loss of motor functions or bodily sensations which are not explainable by current medical knowledge. These types of impairments can occur in one of the five senses (e.g., hallucinations, paralysis, or deafness), as a motor deficit (e.g., paralysis, poor coordination, or loss of balance) or as seizures or convulsions. The impairment typically has a sudden onset during a stressful period in the person's life. These individuals can be quite dramatic when describing their symptoms (like the somatization patient), but they are more likely to show relatively little concern about the nature or implications of the symptom. An example of this phenomenon includes a case of "glove paralysis." This is described as an absence of subjective feeling in the hand, despite the lack of medical explanation. Most people would be quite distressed by the presence of any type of paralysis, yet the individual with conversion disorder is likely to show relatively little concern. This individual will produce poor polygraph charts and inconclusive results if the symptoms interfere with his or her ability to concentrate or respond appropriately to the examiner's questions.

Pain Disorder: Individuals who have pain disorder become self-absorbed with the experience of pain. Typically, the pain has a sudden onset during a time of psychological stress in the individual's life. Pain is a subjective experience which is influenced by biological, psychological and social factors. However, in these individuals, the intensity and/or duration of the pain is greater than one would expect based on the type of injury, or there is no identifiable organic cause for the pain, despite medical assessment. If the examinee is experiencing an intense bout of pain, the PV examination should be postponed until the symptoms (pain) is no longer present, inasmuch as the *pain* can produce an autonomic arousal undistinguishable from *fear* of detection. (See Chapter 9).

Hypochondriasis: Individuals with hypochondriasis are preoccupied with the idea that they may have a serious illness. They become quite skilled at keeping records of changes in their bodies, while fearing a dreaded illness. Thus, they are likely to misinterpret normal bodily changes as signs or symptoms of a feared disease. These individuals are likely to be interested in any test which measures their physiological responding. These individuals will produce from poor to very good polygraph charts depending on the severity of their affliction.

***Body Dysmorphic Disorder*:** People with body dysmorphic disorder are concerned with imagined or exaggerated flaws in their appearance. Slight flaws such as thinning hair, acne, wrinkles, scars, or excessive facial hair become blown out of proportion. In addition, people may become overly concerned with the shape or size of other body parts such as their nose, eyes, mouth, teeth, or head. Usually these individuals experience a great deal of distress over their supposed deformity and often limit their social and/or occupational goals. It is likely that these individuals will seem distressed or nervous upon meeting the FP and will be overly concerned about the FP noticing or commenting on the defect. In a properly conducted PV examination comprising a low-key, non-accusatory pretest interview, polygraph charts of average quality may be expected.

Psychotic Disorders

Disorders which have symptoms typically involving alterations of perceptions, thoughts or consciousness (hallucinations and delusions) as their defining features are known as psychotic disorders. An individual who believes in his or her incorrect inferences about reality has a psychotic disorder. In addition to hallucinations and delusions, psychotic disorders can include disorganized speech, lack of drive (goal directed behavior) and flat or blunt affect (absence of emotional responding). Though individuals may exhibit psychotic symptoms as part of a separate disorder (e.g., major depression), the disorder is not considered psychotic unless the psychotic symptoms are the defining or central feature of the disorder.

Two common psychotic disorders that will be discussed in detail are schizophrenia and delusional disorder. Schizophrenia is classified into subtypes based on the most recent clinical evaluation. The following are some of the common subtypes that an FP may encounter: 1) Catatonic; 2) Disorganized; 3) Paranoid; and 4) Residual. Delusional disorder is classified into one of the following subtypes which correspond to the predominant theme of the delusion: 1) Erotomanic; 2) Grandiose; 3) Jealous; 4) Persecutory; and 5) Somatic.

Schizophrenia: Schizophrenia is the most devastating of all psychotic disorders in terms of its effect on an individual's life. Approximately half of those diagnosed with schizophrenia will become severely and permanently disabled, join the lowest socioeconomic class and depend on financial aid. In addition to the socioeconomic effects, the psychological effect on those with schizophrenia is very high. The rate of attempted suicides is one in four and successful suicides are one in ten. Many of those with schizophrenia hear voices that are not there (including voices which may criticize the individual or command him/her to do things), speak nonsense languages, laugh at inappropriate times, have difficulty separating themselves from their environment and generally lose touch with reality.

In studies comparing schizophrenics with normals (Colville, et al., 1960; Zimbardo, et al., 1975) the following obtained results are of particular interest to the FP:

1) Schizophrenics demonstrated a decrease in physiological responding to a variety of stimuli.

2) Schizophrenics manifested reduced response to thyroid medication, autonomic stress and various other types of stimuli that would normally produce physiological changes.

3) The homeostasis of the schizophrenic (that is, his/her capacity to maintain a constant level of physiological function) was impaired.

The above symptoms suggest a failure of the body to respond to external stimulation, which corresponds to his/her failure to respond emotionally. A PV examination should not be performed on an individual in the active phase of a schizophrenic episode. Additionally, medications used to treat schizophrenia can produce side effects such as tardive dyskinesia (involuntary movements of the mouth, lips, tongue, legs or body) and decreased autonomic response which will probably result in poor and/or invalid polygraph charts.

Schizophrenia is classified into various subtypes depending upon the clinical impression at the most recent evaluation. The most common subtypes include the catatonic, disorganized, paranoid and residual.

The <u>catatonic subtype</u> is characterized by psychomotor disturbances which may be evidenced by remaining immobile or excessive mobility, unusual movements and meaningless repetition of others' words. In the immobile state, for example, the individual will remain motionless, adopting a particular posture anywhere from hours to several days. This state could suddenly transform into a state of excessive mobility, also lasting from hours to days. This individual will produce unresponsive polygraph charts similar to those seen in patients in a state of depression. This type of individual will find it difficult to focus his/her attention on the examination. It is doubtful whether an adequate polygraph pretest interview could be conducted on such an individual, without which a valid PV examination cannot be administered.

The <u>disorganized subtype</u> is characterized by disorganized speech, behavior and flat or inappropriate affect. This may include incoherence in expression, giggling or disregard for social conventions. This type of individual will produce a sloppy polygraph chart which may reflect general nervous tension.

The paranoid subtype is characterized by delusions or hallucinations of extreme suspiciousness, yet intellectual functioning may be unaffected. Associated features may include anxiety, aloofness, anger and argumentativeness. This individual may produce from poor to medium quality charts, depending on the matter for which he or she is being administered a PV examination. If it concerns a matter that he/she actually witnessed, a good chart may be produced. However, if it concerns an incident that is associated with the theme of the delusion, the individual may indicate false responses because he/she believes the answers to be truthful and is unaware that he/she is lying.

The residual subtype is applied when at least one previous episode of schizophrenia has occurred, but the present picture is characterized without prominent positive psychotic symptoms such as hallucinations or delusions. Instead, the disturbance is supported by the presence of negative symptoms such as flat affect, lack of speech or lack of drive. However, if positive symptoms are present, they are not prominent and accompanied by strong affect. This subtype is the most common and occurs during a transition between a full blown episode and complete remission or can be present in this state for years without acute exacerbations. This individual will produce polygraph charts similar to those seen in patients with depression.

Delusional Disorder: Delusional disorder is associated with non-bizarre delusions that are not similar to those of schizophrenia. That is, a non-bizarre delusion involves situations that can conceivably occur in real life (such as being loved by someone far away, being followed or having a disease). The delusion(s) must persist for at least one month. An individual with delusional disorder usually is not markedly impaired in intellectual and occupational functioning, whereas social and marital functioning are more likely to be effected. The delusional disorder may be sub-typed based on the theme of the predominant delusion. The most common delusional subtypes include the erotomanic, grandiose, jealous, persecutory, and somatic. Generally, individuals with delusional disorder can produce poor to good polygraph charts depending upon the theme of the delusion and the relationship of the PV examination questions to the delusion. If questions relate to the veridicality of the delusions, the individual may respond in a manner that confirms the delusion, thus responding falsely though unknowingly. However, questions that are irrelevant to the delusional theme can be answered without bias due to the delusion.

The erotomanic subtype is characterized by a belief that one has some great talent, insight or important discovery. Additionally, though not as common, are the beliefs of having special relationships with prominent individuals or being a prominent person.

The grandiose subtype is characterized by a belief that one has great powers or abilities, knowledge or worth. Individuals may also believe that they are the relatives of famous people or those in high power.

The jealous subtype is characterized by a belief that the individual's spouse or lover is unfaithful. There is no basis for this belief other than erroneous inferences from inconclusive "evidence" (e.g., disarranged clothing or spots on the sheets). The "evidence" is used to confront the spouse or lover and attempts are made to stop the believed infidelity.

The persecutory subtype is applied when the theme of the delusion concerns the belief that one is being conspired against, cheated, spied on, followed, poisoned or drugged, maliciously maligned, harassed or obstructed from obtaining goals. The belief may be based on small slights which become exaggerated. Legal action may be pursued in order to bring justice against the believed perpetrator(s). Individuals with a persecutory subtype are often resentful and angry and may be prone to violence against the believed perpetrator(s).

The somatic subtype involves delusions of bodily functions or sensations. These may consist of beliefs that one is emitting a foul odor from various body parts, that one is infected with insects on or in the skin or that body parts are definitely misshapen or not functioning (contrary to all evidence).

Dissociative Disorders

Most people function in their day-to-day lives by relying on an integrated mental system which can answer such questions as Who am I? Where am I? What am I doing? at any given moment. The person with a dissociative disorder can no longer answer these basic questions because they can no longer tap information about their identity, memories, or consciousness. In effect, the person has become dissociated from a specific point of reality. These disorders can have a gradual onset but are more likely to begin quite suddenly after a particularly devastating incident. The symptoms can last for a few minutes, hours, days or the person could experience these difficulties for the rest of his/her life.

Although these disorders are typically brought on by environmental stress, the dissociative disorders are quite different from other reactions to stressful situations. For example, with Posttraumatic Stress Disorder (PTSD), which is described earlier in this chapter, individuals have repeated painful recollections of the event and they have difficulty getting rid of thoughts about the event. In contrast, with the Dissociate Disorders, the alteration of the person's identity, memory, or consciousness is designed to blot out painful experiences.

Dissociation is not necessarily a pathological trait; it exists on a continuum from normal to abnormal. In fact, almost everyone uses dissociation in their everyday lives. Any time we are working on more than one task at a time, we need to temporarily suspend the connection between ideas and emotions. For example, when a person is driving and simultaneously tuning in a radio station, they are using dissociation to divide their attention. A skilled actor is also likely to engage in dissociation as he struggles to portray the emotions of a character and not lose his own identity and emotions in the process.

On the abnormal end of the continuum, the intensity and/or duration of the dissociation becomes maladaptive. Dissociative disorders include: (1) Depersonalization (2) Dissociative Amnesia (3) Dissociative Fugue (4) Dissociative Identity Disorder. Each of these disorders represents an inability to recall information such as identity or specific memories and they involve major changes in social functioning. If the matter or event for which the examinee is being evaluated is what triggered the dissociative disorder, his/her polygraph charts may indicate no specific responses when in fact his or her answers may not be the truth, because he or she is unaware that he or she is responding untruthfully. Obviously, interpretation of such a case by the FP will be particularly difficult but fortunately, cases of this nature are rare. An example of PV examination procedures adopted in a suspected case of Dissociative Identity Disorder is set forth in the Addendum to this chapter.

Depersonalization: Depersonalization is a change in an individual's perception of themselves. People who are experiencing depersonalization might say things like "I feel like I'm in a dream." because their connection to reality feels as though it is temporarily lost or altered in some way. They may feel as though they are not in complete control over their own actions, speech, thoughts, etc. and may fear that they are going crazy. Depersonalization can occur suddenly in recurrent episodes or may be a more chronic state. An individual who is experiencing depersonalization will often be able to convey that they are not feeling grounded in reality and may appear drugged. If the examinee is experiencing an episode of depersonalization, testing should be deferred until the symptoms are alleviated.

Dissociative Amnesia: When an individual has dissociative amnesia, he/she experiences a loss of memory about specific events, people, places or objects while memory for all other information remains intact. These symptoms are not the same as ordinary absent-mindedness. Individuals with dissociative amnesia may appear as though they had never encountered the object, event or person they have forgotten. Amnesia is the most common dissociative disorder and usually occurs following an accident. Amnesia can be described in several ways: In Localized amnesia, a person forgets a specific time period, typically the first few hours after an accident; Selective amnesia occurs when the person can remember some but not all of the details from a given time period; Generalized amnesia occurs when the person has no memory of their life up to the current time and occurs very rarely; Continuous amnesia occurs when a series of events leading up to and including the person's current situation are forgotten; and Systematized amnesia occurs when only memories belonging to a certain category, such as memories of a specific person, are forgotten. Polygraph charts for these individuals will be very poor when questioning is about events, people or time points for which the examinee has no memory. Therefore, the quality of polygraph charts in general for people with amnesiac disorders will range from very poor to good.

Dissociative Fugue: Dissociative fugue is characterized by an abrupt and unexpected departure from home or place of work. This is compounded by an inability to recall all or parts of one's past, in addition to being confused about one's identity or the assumption about a new identity. When a return to the pre-fugue state occurs, an inability to recall events during the fugue state may be apparent. Typically, the onset of a dissociative fugue is related to a stressful, traumatic or overwhelming life event. An individual in a current state of dissociative fugue should not undergo a PV until he/she returns to a pre-fugue state. At this time, a poor to good polygraph chart can be produced depending upon the presence of associated features such as stress, amnesia or posttraumatic stress disorder.

Dissociative Identity Disorder: Dissociative Identity Disorder is often referred to as Multiple Personality Disorder. This disorder is extremely rare and is one of the most dramatic of all the dissociative disorders (Coville, et al 1960). With this disorder, the individual assumes alternate personalities, each with its own set of traits and memories. The transition from one personality to another may or may not be consciously experienced and the degree and completeness of the personality differences will vary. Sometimes the separate personalities are completely unaware of the actions of the alternate personalities while other times there is one personality that is aware of the actions of the alternate personalities. The striking behavioral differences and unique personality styles have brought a great deal of attention to this disorder. The media's depiction of stories such as Dr. Jekyll and Mr. Hyde, Sybil, and The Many Faces of Eve reflects the inherent interest this disorder holds. One possible theory about the development of this disorder is that it is the mind's method of adapting to traumatic childhood experiences. If an examinee has this disorder, PV examinations for that person must be conducted when they refer to themselves in the same way as the time period that the examination is about. For example, if Mary has dissociative identity disorder and had switched to an alternate personality named Beth while making airline reservations, Mary may not have any memory of the reservation and if questioned, could respond by stating that she had never made airline reservations. This profile will appear reliable because the examinee is not aware that she has not given a truthful response. Therefore, interpretation of a PV examination must be made carefully; the profiles will range from very poor to good. A more accurate profile will be produced in an individual who is aware of the actions of the alternate personalities. (See Addendum)

Summary

Whenever an examinee displays behavior that suggests that he or she may be suffering from an acute mental disorder, the FP should postpone the examination until a determination has been made regarding the examinee's state of mental health. When the FP knows in advance that an examinee is suffering from a mental disorder, but the PV examination is still required for one reason or another, the FP should obtain written permission from the examinee's psychiatrist and insist on having the psychiatrist monitor the entire examination through audio and, if available, visual systems, to enable the psychiatrist to stop the examination if and when he or she feels that his or her patient is unable to continue. The psychiatrist can be of invaluable assistance to the FP who should consult him or her at intervals during the examination when legitimate reasons for leaving the polygraph examination room are available to the FP.

The FP must also be alert to the examinee who may feign mental illness in order to be excluded from taking a PV examination. In this area, there may be a need for the use of the polygraph technique in determining whether a patient being considered for release into the community by the court or other authority has in fact recovered his or her mental health; whether a defendant/patient scheduled for trial is in fact competent to stand trial or is feigning mental illness; and whether a person being considered for release on parole is in fact rehabilitated. The FP working in conjunction with a psychiatrist or clinical psychologist can verify the truthfulness of certain key statements and other information furnished by the defendant-patient that form the nucleus of tests administered by the psychiatrist or psychologist from which an expert opinion regarding the patient's state of mental health is predicated.

ADDENDUM

Inasmuch as the individual with dissociative identity disorder will give the FP his or her biggest problem, the following procedure based on an actual case conducted by the author is set forth below:

A psychiatrist contacted the author and advised that upon his recommendation, a defense attorney would be requesting that their client/patient be administered a PV examination to determine whether his patient had in fact made obscene telephone calls to a woman as alleged. The defendant had been administered a truth serum test (sodium pentothal) by the psychiatrist who as a result of the test opined that the defendant had not made the obscene telephone calls as alleged. These results were in direct conflict with evidence furnished by the telephone company that two telephone calls had in fact been made from the defendant's house to the complainant on specified dates which the defendant denied. The polygraph results, if favorable to the defendant, were to be used to buttress the truth serum test.

Upon acceptance of this PV examination, the following were considered:

1) If the subject did in fact commit the offenses and therefore "beat" the truth serum test and the psychiatrist, his "fear of detection" by the polygraph would be greatly diminished. This "fear of detection" would be further reduced by his knowledge that the test results are protected from disclosure to anyone but his attorney and psychiatrist without his consent. Fear of detection is one of the primary elements that activates the sympathetic subdivision of the autonomic nervous system, causing what is commonly known as a reaction to a given question in a PV examination.

2) If the subject did in fact commit the offenses, the defeat of the truth serum test may be the result of a dissociative identity disorder. Dissociation, as mentioned earlier in this chapter, is a mechanism in which a group of mental processes are separated or isolated from consciousness and operate independently or automatically. This can result, in the case of dissociative identity disorder, in the splitting of certain mental content from the main personality or a loss of normal thought-affect relationships. Accepting the possibility of two personalities

existing in the subject's subconscious mind, each surfacing into the subject's conscious mind without the knowledge of the other, offered the plausible explanation that when the subject underwent the truth serum test, the "innocent" personality was in control of the subject's conscious mind.

3) If the subject suffers from a dissociative identity disorder and the innocent personality is in control of the subject's conscious mind during the PV examination, truthful charts can be expected from the subject.

4) If the PV examination produced truthful charts in the first series of tests, an attempt must be made to cause the "guilty" personality to surface into the conscious mind immediately after the first series of tests, whereupon the same tests are administered a second time to observe the appearance of deceptive results.

5) If deceptive results are obtained after the first series of tests, then the dissociative identity disorder theory can no longer be considered and the interrogation of the subject must follow in an attempt to obtain a confession.

6) The subject's psychiatrist must be apprised of the entire examination procedure for his comments and approval, and requested to monitor the entire examination.

A conference was held between the subject's attorney, his psychiatrist, and the author at which time the attorney produced a copy of a cassette tape containing the voice of an unidentified male uttering obscene remarks to the complainant. The attorney felt that the voice could be that of his client, but the psychiatrist felt that it was not subject's voice. The existence of this cassette tape was not known to the psychiatrist at the time he administered the truth serum test, and it was decided that its existence would be kept from the subject until after the first series of tests as planned.

It was agreed that two tests covering two separate targets would be conducted, each test consisting of a minimum of two charts for consistency of response. As is standard practice, a non-accusatory, low-key approach conveying complete objectivity in the pretest interview would serve to retain the "innocent" personality in the subject's conscious mind, if in fact this personality was in control. However, a detailed explanation of the functions of the autonomic nervous system and its recording by the polygraph instrument would serve to generate some fear of detection in the guilty subject. Utilization of a stimulation test after the first chart of test A would increase fear of detection regarding the relevant or probable-lie control questions, thereby stimulating the guilty subject and reassuring the innocent subject as the case may be.

It was further agreed that if the results of target A and B reflected truthful charts, the subject would then be given a *Playboy* magazine containing stimulating photographs for subject to read with instructions to select his preferred photograph, as a means of inviting the "guilty" personality into the subject's conscious mind. The subject would then be allowed to hear the tape recording previously mentioned and questioned as to whether he recognized the voice, as a further invitation to the "guilty" personality. No accusatory approach was to be used, merely an inquiry in order to retain an objective atmosphere. Tests A and B would then be readministered.

Pretest Evaluation: In the event that the first series of tests reflected truthful results but the second series of tests reflected deceptive results, hopefully supported by a confession from the subject, the PV examination could then be used by the psychiatrist to prove a diagnosis of dissociative identity disorder, which would prove invaluable in the treatment of his patient and invaluable to the attorney in the defense of his client.

The entire PV examination was monitored by the subject's psychiatrist. A Stoelting "PolyScribe" fully electronic polygraph instrument was used which recorded on a moving chart, thoracic and abdominal breathing patterns, electrodermal response (GSR), and cardiovascular activity. The subject made no admissions during the pretest interview. The author was unable to identify the subject during the pretest interview with the voice heard on the aforementioned cassette tape.

The subject was administered a stimulation test after the first chart of test A. At the conclusion of test B, all charts were scored numerically using a seven-position scale quantification system. The breathing tracing was the least productive tracing in spite of the fact that ideal amplitude was present, yet the overall results showed consistent responses to all of the relevant questions resulting in a final conclusion that the subject was attempting deception when he answered the relevant crime questions. This eliminated the dissociative identity disorder theory. The subject confessed to his crime within ten minutes after confrontation with the results of the PV examination, precluding the necessity of using the cassette tape.

REFERENCES

American Psychiatric Association. (1994). *Diagnostic and statistical manual of mental disorders* (4th ed.). Washington, DC: Author.

Cannon, W.B. (1929). *Bodily Changes in Pain, Hunger, Fear and Rage* (2nd ed.). New York: Appleton-Century-Crofts.

Coville, W. J., Costello, T. W., & Rouke, F. L. (1960). *Abnormal Psychology*, Scranton, PA: Barnes & Noble.

Hoehn-Saric, R., & McLeod, D. R. (1988). The peripheral sympathetic nervous system: Its role in normal and pathological anxiety. *Psychiatric Clinic of North America, 11,* 375-386.

Hoehn-Saric, R., McLeod, D. R., & Zimmerli, W. D. (1989). Somatic manifestations in women with generalized anxiety disorder: Psychophysiological responses to psychological stress. *Archives of General Psychiatry, 46,* 1113-1119.

Neale, J. M., Davison, G. C., & Haaga, D. A. F. (1996) *Exploring abnormal psychology*. New York: John Wiley & Sons.

Toth, M. (1972). *Basic Principles of Psychology*. New York: Backster School of Lie-Detection.

Zimbardo, P. G., & Ruch, F. L. (1975). *Psychology and Life*, 9th ed. Glenview, Il: Scott, Foresman & Company.

Chapter 8

FORMULATION, REVIEW, PRESENTATION AND ASSURANCE OF INTENDED INTERPRETATION OF TEST QUESTIONS CRITICAL TO EXAMINATION RESULTS

Background

The formulation of test questions is of such importance that most polygraph schools devote a distinct block of study and training designed to enable the student forensic psychophysiologist to formulate test questions that are clearly understood by the examinee, identify the issue succinctly, meet the requirements imposed by the technique used, and conform to the legal or investigative objectives necessitating the test. But the manner in which these test questions are reviewed and presented to the examinee is of equal importance to their formulation, and the intended objective interpretation must be assured to obtain consistent, accurate results.

The forensic psychophysiologist must deal with examinees of various ages, and cultural and educational backgrounds. While it is true that the age of computerization has entered the realm of polygraph chart interpretation and quantification, the methodology required to acquire those charts from the examinee will always require the expertise of a forensic psychophysiologist whose role has become more complex as we examine the psychological factors that make up the test.

Clarence D. Lee, Captain of Detectives at the Berkeley Police Department in his book *The Instrumental Detection of Deception* published in 1953 stated in regard to the formulation of relevant questions,

> On the mental side all effort must be avoided except that involved in the deception syndrome. In a number of experiments with students, it was found that even doing very simple mental problems in arithmetic caused a rise in blood pressure, the magnitude of which rise was probably proportional to the effort, indicating that those skilled in mathematics would react less than those unskilled. Also in an actual case when the suspect was asked if he was at a certain place at a date long past, his effort to remember the date resulted in increased blood pressure despite the fact that he answered truthfully.

The message here is that relevant test questions must be succinct, as short as possible, void of rationalization potential, and thoroughly reviewed with the examinee and thus not elicit any mental exercise from the examinee. "All effort must be avoided except that involved in the deception syndrome."

By the same token, non-current (earlier-in-life) exclusive control questions, current exclusive control questions, and non-exclusive control questions are all designed to elicit mental exercise which may account for physiological responses to control questions by innocent examinees whose truthful responses were to the best of their memory which remained in a search mode during the test.

We can look upon the psychophysiological veracity (PV) examination as a complex system encompassing the entire examination which includes all parts of the pre-test interview to include test question formulation, their review and presentation and assurance of intended interpretation, to the conduct of the psychophysiological veracity test resulting in polygraph charts containing physiological data which are quantified for a determination. Therefore, the system includes all of the aforementioned interacting parts, anyone of which if omitted or altered affects the psychophysiological results of the PV examination. The whole is the sum of its parts and the interactions of its parts.

The Pretest Interview

The failure of many forensic psychophysiologists (FP) to recognize the inherent relationship between question formulation and assurance of intended interpretation through proper review, presentation, and feed back is also shared by some researchers whose studies attempted to verify the effectiveness of some of the psychological components of the PV test directly affected by this relationship.

In my twenty-four years as a practicing forensic psychophysiologist, this author had occasion to observe forensic psychophysiologists trained at various polygraph schools in the conduct of PV examinations through closed-circuit television. During the pre-EPPA (Employee Polygraph Protection Act) era it was not unusual to have several forensic psychophysiologists working on the same case involving several subjects in a search to identify a single perpetrator. These cases gave this author opportunities to monitor and review the work of other forensic psychophysiologists, which revealed significant dissimilarities in the methodology of their pre-test interview, although all were testing subjects on the same case, using the same test questions. It became apparent that those forensic psychophysiologists who had developed a standardized method of test question review and presentation which informed and elicited information from the examinee that assured the forensic psychophysiologist of its intended interpretation and the examinee of the objectivity and the accuracy of the test, produced consistently better charts and more accurate results than those forensic psychophysiologists who treated the examinees as inanimate objects.

A disquieting number of forensic psychophysiologists merely reviewed the control questions with the examinee without any preamble, and with the assumption that all test questions were understood by the examinee in the manner intended. In fact, some forensic psychophysiologists played down the importance of the control questions by skimming through them quickly and lightly, giving the impression that they feared the examinee might otherwise bare his soul. An equally grave error was to assume that the examinee understood and interpreted the test questions as intended on the sole basis of a correct answer without feedback verification. In some instances, little or no importance was given to the manner of delivery of the test questions during the actual examination, which included variations within the test from monotone statement-like questions to animated inquisitorial questions, which in my view, could seriously affect the psychological set of the examinee.

The effectiveness of each psychological component of the PV examination in the form of test questions is therefore dependent upon the proper delivery of test questions, clearly understood, and interpreted by the examinee as designed and formulated.

Before we examine the aforementioned factors by implementing a mock review/presentation of test questions in a control question format, i.e., the Quadri-Track Zone Comparison Technique, I would like to briefly discuss certain aspects of the pretest interview which affect the review and presentation of the test questions.

The pre-test interview in the Quadri-Track Zone Comparison Technique as in other control question techniques is non-accusatory in nature. No accusatory or interrogative approach by the forensic psychophysiologist is used during any portion of the pre-test interview of the PV examination or between administration of the polygraph charts. No accusatory or interrogative approach is used until all PV tests (polygraph charts) have been conducted and a determination of deception has been concluded from the final tally of the chart scores. In the final analysis, truth or deception is determined by the examinee's consistent physiological responses on the polygraph charts either to the control questions if truthful or to the relevant (crime) questions if deceptive. The examinee's psychological set is self-directed to those test questions that he or she finds most threatening, either the control questions or the relevant questions. The forensic psychophysiologist must not introduce any factors that will increase the threat of the relevant questions or the truthful examinee's fear of them. This is especially important because the non-current, earlier-in-life, exclusive control questions are structurally less intense than the relevant questions. The pre-test interview is used to gather background data and the examinee's version of the event, refinement of the formulation of the test questions, and preparation of the examinee psychologically for the administration of the PV test, including the dissolution of any anger and the promotion of confidence in its impartiality and reliability. Furthermore, the actual PV test should be conducted without emphasis on a particular question. In fact, all test questions should be asked in a statement-like manner where the tone remains the same or drops at the end of the question, not rise in a questioning manner which might be interpreted as disbelief. This is consistent with the theme portrayed during the pretest interview. I advise all examinees at the beginning of the pretest interview that I assume that each examinee is innocent of the crime for which he or she is being polygraphed, until and unless the total scores from their polygraph charts indicate deception. As further corroboration, I sometimes relate to the examinee a true case of another examinee who was identified by two victims and a witness, nevertheless produced truthful polygraph charts which were confirmed with blind scoring by another forensic psychophysiologist, resulting in dismissal of the charges. The scoring of the polygraph charts is briefly explained to the examinee and the examinee is shown the scoring sheet containing the Conclusion Table as further evidence of the objectivity of the examination. The examinee is advised that after the polygraph charts in all issues to be tested have been administered, then they are taken into the next room for quantification at which time a determination is made as to truth or deception regarding each issue tested. Therefore, the examinee should not ask the forensic psychophysiologist about the results of his charts until they have all been conducted and scored. It is further explained to the examinee that the forensic psychophysiologist's concern during the administration of the PV test(s) is to obtain clear, readable charts, where the examinee followed all instructions and refrained from movement during the test and answered all of the test questions after they were asked in their entirety. His answers were expected to be consistent with his answers during the pretest review. (Familiarity with the test questions will sometimes prompt the examinee to give his answer while the question is still being asked.) The intended effect of withholding the chart results until all charts have been administered is to preserve the examinee's anxiety level towards the relevant questions if guilty, or toward the control questions if innocent, throughout each chart until all test charts have been conducted. Furthermore, the announcement of chart results before all charts have been administered could alter the examinee's psychological set on subsequent charts. To inhibit any attempt at countermeasures the examinee is advised that Innocent examinees want the instrument to produce accurate results therefore will cooperate fully and follow all instructions to the letter. Conversely, the guilty examinee does not want the instrument to produce accurate chart results therefore will attempt to prevent exposure of his/her guilt by not adhering to instructions such as subtle movements during the test. The examinee is also told of the sensitivity of the polygraph instrument which permits the forensic psychophysiologist to notice a mere swallow on the polygraph chart. Furthermore, only a guilty examinee would deliberately violate instructions, and that is as obvious as waving a red flag. This explanation also sets the stage for a better understanding by the examinee of the role of the "Fear of Error" question, versus the "Hope of Error" question, incorporated into the test structure, which is discussed later in this chapter.

The aforementioned pretest procedure precludes any attempt to obtain a confession until all PV test (polygraph) charts have been conducted and a determination of deception has been derived from the quantified chart scores. This requires self-discipline, especially when confronted with verbal and non-verbal behaviors normally associated with non-truthtelling styles. But to yield to the temptation can destroy the examinee's trust in the forensic psychophysiologist's impartiality and faith in his objectivity which in this author's view can cause a serious shift in the Innocent examinee's psychological set (from the control questions to the relevant questions), which may be proportional to the intensity of the interrogation and the sensitivity of the examinee. A serious challenge to the validity of the ensuing polygraph charts could be made in such a circumstance.

The likelihood that such a non-accusatory pretest interview would increase the potential for false negatives is not supported by research (Matte & Reuss, 1989) wherein thirty-nine (39) confirmed cases were conducted for defense attorneys under attorney-client privilege and thirty-four (34) of those were scored deceptive, three (3) were found truthful, and two (2) were inconclusive. It should be remembered that a guilty examinee is far more likely to yield a confession after being confronted with his polygraph scores, especially from a forensic psychophysiologist who maintained his impartiality and objectivity. Another factor which enhances the credibility of the forensic psychophysiologist is his bridge building rapport with the examinee. On the other hand, a premature interrogation could burn that bridge.

Quadri-Track Zone Comparison Methodology

We will now examine the methodology used in this formulation, review, presentation and assurance of intended interpretation of test questions in a single-issue test format, the Quadri-Track Zone Comparison Technique.

Type	No.	Question
Y	14J	Were you born in the United States?
YR	39	Regarding whether or not you stole that $5,000.00 deposit discovered missing from the safe at ABC Market, 999 Sunset Avenue, Buffalo, New York on 4 July 1993: Do you intend to answer truthfully each question about that?
B	25	Are you completely convinced that I will not ask you an unreviewed question during this chart?
G	46	Between the ages of (18) and (24) - Do you remember ever stealing anything?
R	33	Did you steal that missing $5,000.00?
G	47	During the first (18) years of your life - Do you remember ever stealing anything from someone who trusted you?
R	35	Regarding the $5,000.00 deposit discovered missing from ABC Market on 4 July 1993, did you steal that money?
Gw	23	Are you afraid an error will be made on this test regarding the target issue?
Rw	24*	Are you hoping an error will be made on this test regarding the target issue?
B	26	Is there something else you are afraid I will ask you a question about, even though I told you I would not?

*Note: In the past, this author used the word "hopeful" at question number 24 because it was grammatically correct, but have substituted the word "hoping" because it is more easily understood and appears to be more effective.

The above format reflects the order in which the test questions are asked during the psychophysiological veracity test. After the first chart, relevant questions number 33 and 35 are switched in their position in each subsequent chart, to allow each relevant question to be compared against each control question. The order in which the test questions are reviewed with the examinee are as follows: 39, 33, 35, 46, 47, 23, 24, 14J, 25, 26.

Legend - Question Types

YR	(Yellow Red)	Preparatory/Sacrifice Relevant Question
R	(Red)	Relevant Question (strong)
Rw	(Red white)	Inside-Issue Relevant Question (variable strength)
G	(Green)	Non-Current Exclusive Control Question
Gw	(Green white)	Inside-Issue Control Question (variable strength)
Y	(Yellow)	Neutral (irrelevant) question
B	(Black)	Symptomatic (Outside Issue) question

TEST QUESTION FORMULATION AND REVIEW

The formulation of test questions starts with the review of the case information during which time the FP makes note of all the facts which support and/or contradict the allegations from which the FP will set forth the target issues to be tested, usually in order of their combined *adequacy of case information*, *case intensity* and *distinctness of issue*. The aforesaid Adequacy, Intensity and Distinctness are rated on a scale from 1 (inadequate) to 5 (adequate). When the combined rating totals less than 9, abortion of the test should be considered. (See Chapter 11 for details). Each issue is then treated as a separate single-issue test. The relevant test questions are formulated first. Then the control questions are developed and formulated on the basis of the case information and the subject's background information, with alternative control questions to be used at test time in the event that the initial control questions are deemed unsuitable or inappropriate. Many FP's such as this author maintain a book or computer file of control questions categorized by type of offense or matter with the various types of applications.

The relevant question should be formulated so that it gets to the heart of the issue. It should be a direct question having an intense and specific relationship to the crime or issue. Its purpose is to elicit a reaction from a deceptive person. In the formulation of the relevant question, the FP should not rely too strongly on the accuracy of such items of information as time, date, location, amount, or method in the wording of this question. The vocabulary and terms used to formulate the relevant question should take into consideration the mental ability and schooling of the person being tested. The relevant question should not contain too much restrictive phrase information for the circumstances involved, thus making it unnecessarily long. Caution should be exercised in the formulation of relevant questions not to mistakenly include two distinctly different issues in the same relevant question, where the subject might be answering one part truthfully, but attempting deception in regard to the other part. The FP in the formulation of the relevant question should ask himself/herself, can the subject be attempting deception to this relevant question but not be guilty of the offense and can the subject be answering this relevant question truthfully but still be guilty of the offense? If the answer is yes to either of these two questions, then remedial action is obviously necessary. The FP should also ask himself/herself if the relevant question tends to be too weak, risking a lack of reaction to it because of "anti-climax dampening" by one or more stronger relevant questions he/she is using in the test. Legal terminology in the formulation of relevant questions should be avoided. For instance, in rape cases the term "sexual intercourse against your will" should be used rather than "rape." In homicide cases, words representing the actual act should be used rather than terms such as murder. Example, "Did you yourself shoot your wife?" rather than "Did you murder your wife?" "Did you shoot John Doe?" rather than "Did you kill John Doe?" In this manner, the FP brings the guilty (as later verified) subject back to the scene of the crime. Second, the guilty (as later verified) subject will not be given an opportunity to rationalize his/her act. In cases where the subject claims he or she was intoxicated at the time he or she allegedly committed the offense and thus *cannot remember* perpetrating the crime, the word "knowingly" should be added to the relevant question, e. g. "Did you *knowingly* set fire to that 1973 Ford Torino?" or "Did you *knowingly* break into the house of Susie Flowers?" The relevant questions are the first questions that are reviewed with the examinee during the pretest interview.

During the review of the relevant questions, a "sacrifice" relevant question is also reviewed with the examinee. It is sometimes called an "ice-breaker" question because it is the first relevant question asked during the actual test. Often the innocent as well as the guilty (as later verified) subjects will react to the first relevant question asked on the test. For this reason a sacrifice relevant question, which should not exceed the precise scope of its related relevant questions contained in the same test, is used at the beginning of the test to absorb anxieties of both innocent and guilty (as later verified) examinees.

The Sacrifice/Preparatory Relevant Question

Test question # 39 is the first test question that is reviewed with the examinee. It is structured as an orienting relevant question which may elicit an emotionally induced sympathetic response inasmuch as it serves as both a Sacrifice Relevant Question and also as a Preparatory Question for the introduction of the two strong relevant questions (33 and 35), hence is a dual-purpose question. The manner in which this weak relevant question is introduced as a Preparatory Question for the two strong relevant questions assures its function as a Sacrifice Relevant Question. (Full discussion of its psychological structure in Chapter 9)

The forensic psychophysiologist (FP) first reads question # 39 to the examinee in its entirety, than awaits the response. After acquiring an affirmative answer from the examinee the FP then states: "I have identified the issue for which you are being tested and I'm asking you if you intend to answer truthfully each question about that, isn't that correct?" to which the FP should obtain an affirmative answer. Then the FP states to the examinee: "The next test question is short and to the point" then the FP reads relevant question #33, to which the FP should obtain a negative answer. The FP then states to the examinee, "The next test question is the same question, it is just worded differently and is a bit longer." Then the FP reads relevant question #35, to which the FP should obtain a negative answer.

Inasmuch as question #39 is a Sacrifice Relevant question, the FP can afford to make it long without fearing its consequences because it is not considered or scored for a determination. The FP therefore uses this question to fully identify the matter being tested. Because this question serves as a Preparatory question for the introduction of the two strong relevant questions (33 & 35), the next and first strong relevant question can be very short without fear of misinterpretation or rationalization. This eliminates *mental exercise* as a possible cause for a physiological response to that test question. Thus one of the variables mentioned in Chapter 9 is addressed.

Relevant Question Review

We have partially explained the review of the two relevant questions (33 and 35) during the explanation of aforementioned Sacrifice/Exploratory relevant question. We have shown that relevant question # 33 should be formulated to be short and to the point in order to avoid the "mental exercise" variable. Since relevant question # 33 is reviewed immediately after Preparatory/Sacrifice Relevant question # 39, the former is directly related to the latter and its brevity can thus be defended.

Now we turn our attention to relevant question # 35. This test question is the second strong relevant test question. It is designed to identify the issue sufficiently to avoid the potential for examinee rationalization but not necessarily as long as question # 39. It should be noted that the question, "did you steal that money?" is located at the end of question #35 for effect.

In reviewing relevant question # 35, it is explained to the examinee that the amount of money reported missing from the safe may be slightly different than the amount actually stolen, therefore the amount quoted is merely to identify that theft of that deposit of money discovered missing from ABC Market on that particular day. If the examinee did in fact steal that deposit of money, regardless of the amount, they will respond on the test. This explanation is designed to avoid rationalization on the part of the examinee, as well as obtaining feedback of his or her understanding and interpretation of the test question.

Rationalization

The issue of rationalization must not be underestimated. Generally, relevant test questions should be the easiest to understand and interpreted inasmuch as they deal directly with the issue(s) for which the examinee is being polygraphed, which have been thoroughly discussed during the pre-test interview. However, guilty examinees (as later verified) must not be given an opportunity to answer the relevant test question truthfully yet be guilty of the offense, because of a technically or grammatically incorrect question.

An example of effective rationalization occurred in 1969 while this author was assigned as a U. S. Army C. I. D. Agent at Fort Dix, New Jersey. Someone threw a grenade into the parking lot of the Philadelphia Police Department causing damage to police vehicles. Several forensic psychophysiologists from the Philadelphia Police Department were authorized and conducted PV examinations at the Fort Dix C.I.D. Offices on Army enlisted personnel assigned to the ordnance section. After conducting PV examinations on a number of soldiers without identifying the perpetrator, one soldier produced responses to the Knowledge question and subsequently identified the perpetrator whom it was learned had already been tested but had failed to show responses to the relevant questions. That suspect was reinterviewed which resulted in a confession. It was then learned that the *civilian* forensic psychophysiologists, unfamiliar with U.S. Army ordnance, had used the wrong grenade classification in the wording of his relevant questions, which enabled the suspect to answer the relevant questions truthfully, although guilty of the crime. The forensic psychophysiologist would have been better off if he had simply used the word "grenade" without adding its numerical classification.

Sacrifice Relevant Question Effect

As testimony to the effectiveness of the Sacrifice Relevant Question #39 in its described role, I offer this incident which occurred at this author's polygraph office in 1991. An adult male was administered a PV examination by a law enforcement agency regarding the commission of a crime, but the results were inconclusive. Before submitting to a test by the police, his new attorney decided to have his client tested privately and brought him to this author. I administered the Quadri-Track Zone Comparison Technique consisting of a Stimulation Test followed by four separate charts dealing with the same issue. Each chart was scored as follows: Chart 1 was -10, Chart 2 was -2, Chart 3 was -13, Chart 4 was -8 for a total score of -33. For the Quadri-Track Zone Comparison System, a minimum score of -20 for 4 charts is required before a definite conclusion of Deception can be rendered. A minimum score of +12 for 4 charts is required before a definite Truthful conclusion can be rendered. The suspect was confronted with the results of his PV examination and after some interrogation the suspect confessed to the crime. During his explanation of the details surrounding the commission of the crime, the suspect, still sitting in the polygraph chair, reached down and unlaced his right boot, took off the boot and removed the insole. From the tip of the insole the suspect calmly removed a thumbtack from the toe area and placed it on the polygraph desk. The tack would most likely have escaped detection because it was in the insole which required pressure for the tip to surface. The suspect stated that he had read a booklet that told how to beat the polygraph, primarily by controlling his breathing and placing a tack in his shoe. This author asked the suspect on which questions did he press his toe on the tack and the suspect replied, "To all of the test questions except the two relevant questions." However, he did not use that countermeasure on the stimulation test. Using these countermeasures, he had successfully caused an Inconclusive result in his first PV examination administered by the police, but in spite of his success and practice, his countermeasures failed to defeat the Quadri-Track Zone Comparison Technique. The suspect apparently only considered the two strong relevant questions (#33 & #35) as worthy of consideration. This is most likely because of the manner in which the Sacrifice relevant question is presented to the examinee as a Preparatory question to the two strong relevant questions.

We have so far reviewed the Preparatory/Sacrifice Relevant question (39), and the two Strong Relevant questions (33, 35) with the examinee.

Control Question Formulation and Review

As discussed in Chapter 5, there are various types of comparative control questions, depending upon which polygraph technique is being utilized. There is the Non-Current (earlier-in-life) Exclusive control question used in the Matte Quadri-Track ZCT, the Backster ZCT, the DoDPI ZCT; the Current Exclusive control question used in the Integrated ZCT, the Utah ZCT, the Marcy technique; the Non-Exclusive control question used in the Reid and Arther technique; and the Directed Lie control question used by some employers of the Utah ZCT. The one common denominator that all of these control questions have is that they are normally formulated to be in the same category of offense or matter as the relevant issue questions against which they are being compared for a determination of truth or deception. While their presentation to the examinee differs with each technique, their purpose is identical. In this discussion, we are using the Quadri-Track Zone Comparison Technique, thus the Non-Current Exclusive control question is used. We now continue with the review of the Control Questions.

Even though the FP has formulated control questions on the basis of the case information and background data furnished to him/her prior to the scheduled PV examination, these control questions are tentative and subject to amelioration or change depending upon the information that is furnished by the examinee during the pre-test interview. During the pre-test interview the FP "draws out" the subject in areas fruitful for the development of controls, but the FP must exercise caution in not arousing a bothersome outside issue. The FP listens attentively for statements made by the examinee about himself/herself that the FP believes are not completely truthful on the basis of prior factual information, contradictions with other statements, and/or verbal and non-verbal behavior during the utterance of the statement. Such information can be most useful in formulating new and potentially more effective control questions.

Following the review of the Relevant test questions, the next series of test questions which are reviewed with the examinee are the Non-Current (earlier-in-life) Exclusive control questions numbered 46 and 47. The term Exclusive is used to identify control questions that exclude the period in which the crime was committed through the use of a time bar. They are reviewed with the examinee in the following manner:

> The next two questions are very important because some people are very sensitive about being asked questions that deal with stealing (use issue being tested) because of incidents that occurred in their early childhood, or perhaps later on in life, for which they now want to be punished. A psychologist would label a person like that a guilt complex reactor,

> which can play havoc with the test, so it's equally important that you be truthful to these two questions as I presume you have been to the others we have just reviewed.

Please note that this author used the word others, not three others, to avoid the inclusion of the Sacrifice/Preparatory relevant question 39 in that category. This is to have the two control questions compete against the two relevant questions 33 and 35, by the examinee's own selection.

The forensic psychophysiologist should tailor the above preamble to suit the issue being tested and his/her own style of question presentation. The idea is to make those two control questions important to the examinee, in that he or she wishes to be truthful but is reluctant to make admissions to crimes similar to the crime for which the test is being conducted for fear that it will reflect unfavorably on the claim of innocence to the target issue. This creates a conflict which should arouse a proportional response on the test. You would think that most examinees when confronted with the control question "Between the ages of ( ) and ( ) do you remember ever telling a serious lie?" would give an affirmative answer. However, when it is prefaced with the preamble, "Your credibility is at stake here, isn't it? (regarding the target issue) Are you a truthful person?" The examinee does not wish his or her credibility diminished by giving an affirmative answer to the control question. Over the years, forensic psychophysiologists have developed several successful and effective preambles for the introduction of control questions. The primary objective is to elicit a negative answer from the examinee to control questions that the examinee feels are important to the outcome of the PV examination.

During the review, this author holds a clipboard containing the worksheet with the test questions. This clipboard is held up in a manner which prevents the examinee from seeing what is being written. It has been this author's experience that examinees are generally not bothered when I am writing with the clipboard in that position. But when I drop the top of the clipboard down so that the examinee can readily see pen on paper, he or she becomes apprehensive, cautious and less talkative. The importance of this procedure will become obvious in a moment.

I now present and review control question #46 with the examinee. "Between the ages of 18 and 24, do you remember ever stealing anything?" If the examinee starts to make admissions, the forensic psychophysiologist should immediately express facial surprise, drop the top of his/her clipboard down while moving closer to the examinee and in a deliberate manner slowly and reluctantly start to write down the examinee's admission(s). This usually has the effect of stopping the examinee from making further admissions. The test question then is amended and reviewed with the examinee, as follows: "Between the ages of 18 and 24, besides what you have already told me, do you remember ever stealing anything?" The examinee should then provide a negative answer. The forensic psychophysiologist should then quickly proceed to the review of the next control question, number 47.

I now present and review control question #47 with the examinee. "During the first (l8) years of your life - Do you remember ever stealing anything from someone who trusted you?" Please note that this second control question deals with a different period of the examinee's life than control question 46 and the latter part of the question specifies "from someone who trusted you?" which is also different from control question 46. This difference in time-period and question syntax between control question 46 and 47 is essential for each control question to produce and maintain its independent, equally productive mental exercise and conflict. I have noted that some forensic psychophysiologists use the same age category and question for both control questions, which is therefore the same control question repeated in the same test. This in my view promotes habituation and significantly diminishes the mental effort and resultant conflict not only in the second control question but in subsequently administered charts.

Another example of different control questions within the same category, used for sex offenses, are set forth below:

46. Between the ages of (18) and (24) - Do you remember ever engaging in an unnatural sex act?

47. During the first (18) years of your life - Do you remember ever doing anything sexually that you're ashamed of?

The above control questions are within the same category (sex) but are different in time period and question type. They are also appropriate for their respective age categories.

A legitimate concern may arise when a forensic psychophysiologist is assigned the task of administering a PV examination to someone who is thoroughly familiar with the polygraph technique and its instrumentation, especially if the examinee is a forensic psychophysiologist. The forensic psychophysiologist conducting the PV examination might be apprehensive about his/her effectiveness in eliciting a negative answer to the control questions from such an examinee and of equal importance, will the control question(s) be effective as a competitor to the relevant question(s) on the same test. This author has personally conducted numerous PV examinations on examinees knowledgeable about the polygraph technique without experiencing any difficulty, and I have further conducted PV examinations on forensic psychophysiologists facing serious criminal charges resulting in conclusive results in each case. One case resulted in a truthful conclusion which was later verified by the conviction of another suspect.

The theme of the pre-test interview must be not only non-accusatory but also contain the presumption of innocence. This theme nourishes the examinee's desire to present his/her best and most innocent image to the forensic psychophysiologist, which in turn will inhibit the examinee from disclosing unfavorable information during the review of the control questions that would tarnish that image.

The primary concern of a forensic psychophysiologist facing the above situation is to develop control questions that are intimately connected to the relevant questions. For the examinee to make an admission to such a control question would appear to significantly increase the likelihood that the examinee committed the crime for which he/she is being polygraphed. In addition, the witnessing of the examination by the defense attorney or prosecutor or both as the case dictates (two-way mirror or closed circuit T.V.), with the full knowledge and consent of the examinee, should further inhibit the examinee from making admissions to control questions intimately connected to the crime. An example of control questions successfully used in such a case is set forth below:

Case: Male examinee accused of having sexual intercourse with his daughter who was under 16 years of age.

46. Between the ages of (18) and (28) - Do you remember ever thinking of having sex with anyone under the age of 16?

47. During the first (18) years of your life - Do you remember ever thinking of engaging in a sex act with anyone under the age of 16?*

[*Note: The word *anyone* includes both sexes increasing the probability. The word *child* could be used instead of *anyone* to further inhibit the examinee.]

Case: Male examinee accused of having his underage daughter ejaculate him.

46. Between the age of (18) and (35) - Do you remember ever being sexually aroused by anyone under 14 years of age?"*

[*Note: Initially 16 years of age was used but the examinee started to make an admission at which time it was quickly dropped to 14 to which he gave a negative answer.]

47. During the first (18) years of your life - Do you remember ever doing anything sexually that you're ashamed of?

An experienced and noted forensic psychophysiologist once told this author that he was reluctant to use sex control questions in sex offenses due to their strong arousal and false negative potential. However, I have had no such problem, especially with the Quadri-Track ZC technique, which assigns a minus one score when both the control and relevant questions elicit strong but equal responses in the pneumo and cardio tracings. We should remember that a sex offense, especially with children, carries an enormous social stigma, nearly indefensible, which can significantly increase the emotional content of the relevant question(s). Therefore, strong control questions must be used to compete with such emotionally charged relevant questions to protect the innocent.

The period of time of the aforesaid control questions can be increased by overlapping the time period of the two control questions with the use of control question #48 instead of control question #47. As an example: In a case of a 23 year old examinee whose cause of recent injury is suspicious.

46. Between the ages of 14 and 21 - Do you remember ever seriously considering taking your own life?

48. During the first 21 years of your life - Do you remember ever engaging in self-destructive behavior to gain attention?

<u>Review of the Error Questions</u>

We now proceed to the review of test questions #23 (fear of error) and #24 (hope of error). During the pre-test interview, the examinee was apprised of the accuracy of the polygraph instrument and the objectivity of the technique with its numerical scoring system of chart analysis by explanation of the various instrument recording components, and the results of research data supporting the numerical scoring system. It is hoped that the examinee now feels sufficiently confident about the accuracy of the test to furnish a negative reply to the following control question which is introduced as follows:

> I've explained to you about the accuracy of this test and that no errors will be made; the worst that can happen is that the results will be inconclusive which means that neither a finding of truthfulness or deception could be established from your polygraph charts, and that happens in only six percent of the cases. Now are you afraid an error will be made on this test regarding the target issue?

The term "target issue" is then explained to the examinee and feedback from the examinee is acquired for assurance that the term was clearly understood.

If the examinee answers "no" then the forensic psychophysiologist should ask the examinee why he or she is not afraid that an error will be made on this test. The usual explanation will be because they believe in the accuracy of the test and the expertise of the forensic psychophysiologist. But sometimes you may get explanations that do not correspond to the intent of the question, such as: "because I'm innocent, I didn't do it." or "I'm afraid you might make an error and not catch the person who did do it."

The latter explanation indicates that the person completely misinterpreted the intent of the question. In such case it is explained to the examinee that the question is directed at the examinee only. As to the statement, "because I'm innocent," it should be explained that the fact that they may be innocent has no bearing on the accuracy of the test; that it is the accuracy of the instrument and the expertise of the forensic psychophysiologist that affects the accuracy of the examination. That way, the examinee will not have a total lack of fear of error based on the erroneous assumption that an error can't be made because he or she is innocent. Thus the examinee will be left with some small potential for an error to be made, but not enough to resist giving a negative answer to that question. The Innocent examinee should therefore provide some physiological reaction to that control question (23), versus its neighboring relevant question #24.

Some examinees initially voice their poor opinion regarding the accuracy of the polygraph based on reports from the news media and from "friends" who "failed" their PV examination yet were truthful. All of these unfavorable opinions can be easily countered in an amiable fashion by producing abstracts from various research papers and other data supporting the high validity and reliability of the polygraph, which will add only a few minutes to the pre-test interview.

In rare cases, the examinee will insist on answering "yes" to the "fear of error" control question in spite of reassurances, in which case the forensic psychophysiologist should allow the examinee to answer in the affirmative to that question on the test. If the examinee is deceptive (as later verified) regarding the target issue, then he or she will be deceptive to both the "fear of error" question and the "Hope of Error" relevant question against which it is compared, which always elicits a negative reply from all examinees. The "Hope of Error" relevant question is more of a threat to the Guilty (as later verified) examinee than the "fear of error" control question, inasmuch he or she ***hopes*** but ***does not fear*** that an error will be made on his or her test, and the threat of discovery of his or her lie to the "Hope" relevant question is greater than his or her lie about his or her non-existent "fear of error." A "directed lie" to the "fear of error" control question is not recommended, nor necessary.

The innocent (as later verified) examinee who insists on giving an affirmative answer to the "Fear of Error" control question, while being truthful to that control question will still find that question more threatening than the "Hope of Error" relevant question to which that examinee is being completely truthful. Again, a *directed lie* to the "fear of error" control question is not recommended nor necessary.

We now proceed to the review of relevant question #24 as follows. The examinee is now told, 'The next question I expect everyone to answer "no" to, but the guilty person's "no" answer, of course, will be a lie.' Relevant question #24 is now read to the examinee, "Are you hoping an error will be made on this test regarding the target issue?" This will undoubtedly produce a negative answer. However, the forensic psychophysiologist should be on the alert for misinterpretation of that question. It is especially important that the examinee realize that this question is directed at the target issue (not the control question(s) he/she is probably lying to). I have heard examinees reply, "I hope there's no error made." Now they have made up their own question. They should be immediately corrected and the question repeated in its entirety with a thorough explanation of the question. Then get feedback from the examinee as assurance that the question was interpreted as intended and designed.

Review of the Neutral Question and Symptomatic Questions

We now review Neutral (Irrelevant) question #14J with the examinee. "Were you born in the United States?" Naturally, if the subject's birthplace is elsewhere, then use the actual birthplace. When there are several targets to be tested, the subject's last name (#13L) is used instead of the birthplace for the second target, and the subject's first name (#13F) is used for the third target. Rarely are there more than three targets in a PV examination, inasmuch as a minimum of two and as many as four charts have to be conducted for each target (issue), plus a Stimulation/Sensitivity test normally administered as the first test chart.

After Neutral (Irrelevant) question #14J is reviewed with the examinee, he/she is then advised, "These are the only questions you will be asked on this test. I'm giving you my word which is my bond that I will not ask you any questions except those that I have just reviewed with you, and in order for me to be assured that you are convinced of this, I'm going to ask you the following two questions on the test also." Now Symptomatic Question #25 is reviewed with the examinee, and if the answer is affirmative and the forensic psychophysiologist is confident through feedback that the examinee clearly understood that question, then he/she proceeds to review Symptomatic Question #26 which should elicit a negative answer, but may require some discussion with the examinee. Sometimes these symptomatic questions need to be reworded into a simpler form to accommodate examinees with limited command of the English language.

Conclusion

In conclusion, the principles enunciated in the above formulation, review, presentation and assurance of intended interpretation of test questions are applicable to all control question tests, but the administration of the tests is flexible. The above format is presented as a logical and successful method of preparing an examinee psychologically for the administration of a control question PV examination.

REFERENCES:

Capps, M. H. (1991). Predictive value of the sacrifice relevant question. *Polygraph*, 20(1), 1-6.

Horvath, F. (1991). The utility of control questions and the effects of two control question tests on field polygraph techniques. *Polygraph*, 20(1), 7-25.

Lee, C. D. (1953). *The Instrumental Detection of Deception*. Springfield, IL: Charles C. Thomas.

Matte, J. A. (1980). *The Art and Science of the Polygraph Technique*. Springfield, IL: Charles C. Thomas.

Matte, J. A. (1976). A polygraph control question validation procedure. *Polygraph*, 5(2), 170-177.

Matte, J. A. (1978). Quadri-Zone Comparison Technique. *Polygraph*, 7(4), 266-280.

Matte, J. A. (1993). Defense access to police polygraph tests. *New York State Bar Journal*, 65(5), 36-41.

Matte, J. A., Reuss, R. E. (1989). Validation study on the polygraph Quadri-Zone Comparison Technique. *Research Abstracts*, LAD 01452, 1502, University Microfilm International.

Raskin, D. C., Barland, G. H., Podlesny, J. A. (1978). *Validity and reliability of detection of deception*. Washington, D. C.: National Institute of Law Enforcement and Criminal Justice.

Reid, J. E., Inbau, F. E. (1977). *Truth and Deception*, 2nd ed. Baltimore, MD: The Williams & Wilkins Company.

Chapter 9

THE NUMERICAL APPROACH AND ZONE COMPARISON TESTS: METHODOLOGY CAPABLE OF ADDRESSING IDENTIFIED IMPEDING VARIABLES

Background

At the present, there are two basic methods used by forensic psychophysiologists (FP), the Clinical Approach and the Numerical Approach, in arriving at a determination of truth or deception. Initially, the Clinical method, also known as Global Evaluation, was predominant. The FP evaluated the case facts and examined the examinee's behavior and deportment during the pre-test interview which was used as an adjunct to the visual inspection and analysis of the physiological tracings recorded on the examinee's polygraph charts. In fact, some polygraph schools (Reid, Arther, Marcy) taught their polygraph students to use a behavior checklist which when completed would give the FP an assessment of the examinee's truthfulness or deceptiveness on the basis of his/her demeanor and behavior. This assessment would then be compared with the findings obtained from the examinee's polygraph charts. If the two evaluations did not match, inconclusive findings would be rendered. During the early years in the use of the polygraph instrument, from about the second decade through the end of the second world war, when the Relevant-Irrelevant polygraph technique was the primary technique used in criminal cases, the psychophysiological veracity (polygraph) test was used as an interrogative tool as much as a scientific means of determining truth or deception. (Reid & Inbau 1977). However, this attitude changed with the introduction of the Control Question Technique developed by John E. Reid in 1947. It should be noted that Father Walter G. Summers of Fordham University wrote of his use of controls, which he referred to as "emotional standards" some ten years earlier than Reid.(Summers 1939). Reid's test contained control questions designed to elicit a lie from the examinee, usually of the same type or category as the issue for which the examinee was being tested. These control questions are used to offer another threat on which the innocent examinee can focus, and more important, a means of comparison with the relevant or crime questions asked on the same test. In spite of the fact that Reid's test was more objective than its predecessor, the reliance on the examinee's behavioral cues as an adjunct to the polygraph charts persisted, to a lesser degree perhaps, but the FP's Approach was still clinical. (Reid & Inbau 1977). Reid's Approach was a significant improvement over the earlier ones, and is considered by most FP's as the fork in the road of forensic psychophysiology.

Footnote: The DoDPI has substituted Psychophysiological Detection of Deception Examination in lieu of Polygraph Examination. However, as explained in Chapter 1 of this book, the polygraph examination verifies the truth as well as detects deception, and consistent with the theme of our criminal justice system and the theme that should prevail during the conduct of the examination that examinees/suspects should be considered innocent until proven guilty, the proper title should be 'Psychophysiological Veracity Examination.'

Unlike earlier techniques which solely sought confessions, Reid's Control Question Test sought to verify the truthfulness of the examinee's statement(s), assisted by an evaluation of the examinee's behavioral cues. Clinical proponents assert that the clinical Approach minimizes inconclusive results because these FP's seem to rely on their analysis of the examinee's behavior when the polygraph charts are marginal. Indeed, Richard O. Arther, Director of the National Training Center of Lie-Detection stated in his article in the 1979 Journal of Polygraph Science "the correct observation and comparison of gestures will give me (FP) a pre-test opinion that has approximately the same validity and reliability as does the polygraph." "It is up to me - as a polygraphist - to blend my pre-test opinion and my chart analysis opinion into one final opinion as to the person's truthfulness." (Arther 1979). He offers no data to support this statement of validity and reliability. Other research discussed in this chapter refutes this statement.

The proponents of this Clinical Approach believe that the FP's decision regarding the truthfulness of an examinee has such important consequences for both the examinee and society that it is morally incumbent upon the conscientious FP to incorporate all relevant information including the examinee's demeanor and behavior in formulating a decision.

The second method was developed by Cleve Backster in 1959 which he named the Tri-Zone Comparison Technique. (Backster 1969, 1994, Bailey 1970). The major contribution this technique made to forensic psychophysiology was the introduction of a numerical scoring system using a seven-position scale in the analysis of the physiological data recorded on the polygraph charts. In addition, Backster also introduced two symptomatic questions into his test to determine if an outside issue was bothering the examinee and interfering with the examinee's "Psychological Set," a term adopted by Backster to explain that an examinee's focus of attention will be on the greatest threat to his/her well-being dampening out lesser threats also present on the same test which he labeled the anticlimax dampening concept. (Backster 1974).

Backster's Tri-Zone Comparison Test also differs from Reid's test in that Backster's Probable-Lie Control Questions have time bars which exclude the period of the crime or matter for which the examinee is being tested. Backster also limited his Zone Comparison Test to a single issue using only two relevant questions, differently worded, but covering that same issue, to optimize the intensity and distinctness of the examinee's psychological set thus avoiding competing variables, which further permits horizontal as well as vertical scoring thus establishing an internal reliability method inasmuch as the same questions worded differently are asked twice, doubling the number of spots scored for a determination. External reliability is established by the conduct of two or more polygraph charts on the same test. Backster further established a numerical threshold in the application of a numerical conclusion table to assure that conclusions are based on scores indicative of consistency hence reliability. Backster's Tri-Zone Comparison technique was structured and designed to eliminate those variables known to adversely affect the physiological data recorded on the polygraph charts, through a complex set of rules and quantification system including a Standardized Polygraph Notepack which attempted to numerically identify with a Target Selection Guide those issues most likely to produce conclusive results versus those issues most likely to produce inconclusive results. This system also attempted to identify any problems and variables appearing to interfere with the test through the use of Spot Analysis and a Scanning System of chart analysis (Fig. V-2) after the conduct of each chart and a numerical Examination Reliability Ratings (Fig. XI-1). Backster's method is often referred to as the Numerical Approach. Unlike the Clinical Approach, the Numerical Approach bases its conclusions as to truth or deception solely upon the numerical scores obtained from the analysis of the physiological data recorded on the examinee's polygraph charts, elicited through an objective, psychologically structured examination from which an inference can be made as to truth or deception. This scoring system is standardized so that other FP's trained in this Numerical Approach can independently score the physiological data recorded on the polygraph charts, offering an objective chart evaluation. (The issue of objectivity of scoring by FP's is examined in the Methodology section.)

Backster's Zone Comparison technique and quantification system was subsequently adopted in 1961 by the Federal Polygraph School managed by the U. S. Army C.I.D. School at Fort Gordon, Georgia, which immediately modified it as the U. S. Army Zone Comparison Technique. (DoD.1984 1.8.1.) The U. S. Army C.I.D. applied this new technique to their worldwide quality control and case review, permitting objective critique of psychophysiological veracity (PV) examinations conducted as far away as Asia and Europe. A report on "Polygraph Research in the Army" by Robert A. Brisentine, Jr., in March 1974, revealed that a validation study (Bersh 1969)* had been conducted consisting of an independent comparison of polygraph results with the investigative file, by comparing polygraph results in criminal cases against judgments of guilt or innocence made by a panel of lawyers having access to the complete investigative file from which all reference to the polygraph examination were removed. Cases were selected at random from the period 1963 to 1966, and of an initial 323 case files, a final number of 157 cases that were complete enough to permit a lawyer to judge guilt or innocence were selected. Cases were selected so that there were similar numbers of deception and no deception examiner

* The Bersh study contains a footnote #3 which states "The GQT type of examination begins with a control question but thereafter presents control and relevant questions in random order. In the ZOC type of examination, each relevant question is interpolated between a pair of control questions. The polygraph response to a relevant question is compared only with its surrounding control questions. In the case of the GQT type examination, the polygraph response to a relevant question is compared with the level of response to control questions in general." This statement by Bersh is in error and is misleading because the GQT (General Question Test) in that study began with a sacrifice relevant question, and thereafter only relevant and irrelevant questions were used, hence there were no control questions in the GQT because it was in fact a Relevant/Irrelevant test. (Brisentine 1995) The term control question in PV examinations is usually reserved for questions that are designed to elicit a lie from the examinee, whereas an irrelevant question is a neutral question, designed to lack any stimulating qualities for both the innocent and guilty examinee.

judgments and a mix of Zone Comparison tests and Relevant-Irrelevant tests referred to as General Question Tests. (Brisentine 1995). Seventy-two of the aforementioned cases had been interpreted by the forensic psychophysiologists (FPs) as deceptive and eighty-five as truthful. The attorneys had been instructed to disregard all legal technicalities and to judge each case solely on the evidence in the file. The results revealed that the polygraphists and the panel of lawyers agreed on 92 percent of all cases when the panel was unanimous in its findings. A breakdown of the statistics reflects deception indicated 90 percent agreement; no deception indicated 94 percent agreement. Of the 157 total cases, 89 were Zone Comparison tests divided into 37 deception indicated and 52 no deception indicated. These Zone Comparison tests had been administered by US Army CID and MI agents and US Air Force OSI agents. The General Question tests had been administered by US Navy ONI agents. All of the Zone Comparison tests were numerically scored and the decisions as to truth or deception were based solely on the test scores. Further, a group of 10 CID and MI Agent FPs and 10 OSI agent FPs independently scored the charts of all Zone Comparison tests without the benefit of the file. The percentages of agreement between FPs and the JAG panel were 92.6 % for (GQT) General Question cases, and 92.0% for (ZCT) Zone Comparison cases. A review of the data in Table 3 of Bersh's study necessitated a correction to the reported calculation of 91.0 agreement for Zone Comparison cases. Aforesaid table reflects that the FP correctly identified 34 of the 38 cases found Guilty by the JAG Panel, and the FP correctly identified 48 of the 51 cases found Not Guilty by the JAG Panel. Therefore the FP and JAG Panel agreed on 82 of the 89 cases for a 92.1% agreement. When Bersh released his report, Robert A. Brisentine, Jr., who carried out the data collection and was also a member of the Department of Defense Research Committee working group, objected to Bersh's statement that "the study did not permit isolation of the role played by the polygraph record itself, the examiner's judgment was considered the end product of his complete interrogation of a suspect" inasmuch as it did not correctly reflect the decision making process of the Zone Comparison tests (ZCT) which comprised half of the cases in the study. However Bersh, who at that time was convinced that global evaluation was the primary method of evaluating polygraph tests, declined to change his report for what he believed was a minor point.(Brisentine 1995). This is unfortunate because the data in this study shows that there was no statistical difference in the accuracy of tests decision (GQT) using global evaluation (Clinical Approach) versus the Numerical Approach (ZCT) where the decisions were based solely on the physiological data recorded on the polygraph charts, the latter providing better construct and internal validity hence superior reliability. Correlations between total numerical scores assigned by comparably trained numerical scorers usually exceed 93% (Raskin, 1982). Kircher and Raskin (1983) performed lens model analyses of the decision policies of five forensic psychophysiologists (FP) who performed numerical evaluations of polygraph charts and found only minor differences among them. Others have reported substantial differences among forensic psychophysiologists who used global methods (Clinical Approach) (Forman & McCauley, 1986). Those laboratory data are consistent with the results of a field study reported by Raskin (1976). Dr. Raskin found that field forensic psychophysiologists who used numerical methods of evaluation were significantly more accurate in their decisions than were global evaluators (98.9% vs 88.5%). (Kircher & Raskin 1988)

The second study consisted of statistics collected on U. S. Army C.I.D. examinations during the calendar year 1972. The quantity of polygraph examinations in 1972 was more than three times the number conducted during 1966. In all the examinations conducted by the U. S. Army C.I.D. worldwide, there were no examinations in which the FP reached a finding of truthful and the subject was later determined to be guilty of the crime. Furthermore, there was no instance in which a subject was found not guilty by a court after the FP reached a finding of deception. The U.S. Army's standardization of psychophysiological veracity examination procedures and quantification of physiological data in chart analysis, permitting one FP to read another FP's charts, resulted in a quality control that reduced the Army's yearly final inconclusive rate (after retest of initial inconclusives) from 5 percent to 1.8 percent. The U. S. Army's Quality Control unit made the ultimate and final decision regarding truth or deception. (Brisentine, 1974, 1986; Bersh 1969; Barland 1995)

Research conducted by Drs. Raskin, Barland and Podlesny (1978) pertaining to the reliability of chart interpretation revealed that "the 40 sets of polygraph charts obtained with the control question technique were scored numerically by the original examiner (Dr. Barland) and were independently scored by Dr. Raskin. Both examiners made a definite decision on 36 of the 40 subjects, and they were in agreement on 100 percent of them". "The outcome based on numerical scores by the original examiner (Dr. Barland) and those based on the blind evaluation of the charts by Dr. Raskin are shown in Table 6 (Raskin, et al. 1978). Both examiners obtained the same categorization in 86 of the 102 cases (84.3%) when inconclusives were included. On cases in which both examiners made a decision, they were in agreement 100 percent of the time. The correlation between the numerical scores assigned by the two examiners. was very high, r = .91." Research conducted by Drs. Matte and Reuss in 1989 pertaining to the reliability of chart interpretation also revealed a high correlation for the individual chart scores (.97 to .99) and for the total scores (.99).

This author (Matte), a graduate of the Backster School of Lie-Detection, developed the Quadri-Zone Comparison Technique in 1977 (renamed Quadri-Track Zone Comparison Technique in January 1995) which employs Backster's basic test structure and quantification system (Fig. XI-16 & XI-9) with some refinements and the addition of another Spot (Inside Track) or control/relevant question pair to deal with a variable not previously addressed. (Matte 1978).

During the five years preceding the development of the Quadri-Track Zone Comparison Technique (Quadri-Zone CT), this author (Matte) conducted experiments using fictitious crimes that the examinees believed to be real, to test the effectiveness of the probable-lie control questions before using those control questions in the actual crime test for which the examinee was being administered a psychophysiological veracity examination. These experiments were also used in the administration of Arther's Known Lie test which is similar to the Reid test. (Matte 1980). These experiments showed that when the control questions are weak or ineffective, the examinee will often show a mild reaction to the neighboring relevant questions, and in some cases will show a strong response to the relevant question(s). Experiments also showed that following the administration of a stimulation test, designed to convince the examinee that the test is able to detect deception, innocent examinees who previously showed a response to the relevant questions, now shifted their psychological set from the relevant questions to the probable-lie control questions. It became apparent to this author that a *fear that an error* might be made on the test was the major cause of responses to the relevant question by *truthful examinees* These experiments also showed that some *deceptive* examinees did not respond to the relevant questions to a degree that would produce the minimum scores necessary to reach a definite conclusion. Analysis of these cases by this author revealed that in the majority of cases, these *deceptive* examines had lost their fear of detection because they had in fact been detected, but the case against them had not been proven, and the psychophysiological veracity test was their major hope of escaping prosecution. Hence, they *hoped that an error* would be made on their test so that their *culpability* would not be *discovered.* It appeared that the guilty examinee's fear of detection was rechanneled into hope that an error would be made on the test regarding his/her involvement in the crime. This author (Matte) concluded that two additional areas needed to be probed during the conduct of a Single-Issue Zone Comparison Test; (1) Truthful examinee's fear of error and (2) Deceptive examinee's hope that an error would be made on the test. This apparent need resulted in the development of the Quadri-Zone Comparison Technique now known as the Quadri-Track Zone Comparison Technique, which was validated in a three-year field research study published in 1989.(Matte, Reuss 1989). It should be noted that in this study, 122 confirmed real-life cases representing 311 polygraph charts, obtained from two separate entities, correctly identified 91 percent of the Innocent as Truthful and 9 percent as Inconclusive, with no errors, and further correctly identified 97 percent of the Guilty as Deceptive and 3 percent as Inconclusive, with no errors. Inconclusive excluded, the Quadri-Track Zone Comparison Technique (Quadri-Zone CT) was 100 percent accurate in the identification of the Truthful and the Deceptive subjects. All of the decisions as to truth or deception were based solely upon the numerical scores obtained from the physiological data recorded on the polygraph charts. The emphasis in the Matte Quadri-Track Zone Comparison Technique (Quadri-Zone CT) as in the Backster Tri- Zone Comparison Technique is on the psychological preparation of the examinee and the proper administration of each polygraph chart without any effort at acquiring a confession unless and until all of the physiological data scores have been tallied and reveal deception. Backster now allows the use of the "Inside Track" for comparison of the Fear of Error against the Hope of Error questions as an additional "Spot" in his test structure. (Backster 1995).

Interestingly, this fear of error by the innocent examinee variable was later noted by Dr. Paul Ekman in his 1985 book "Telling Lies" devoted primarily to verbal and nonverbal behavior. In his chapter on the 'Polygraph as Lie Catcher' Dr. Ekman discusses the element of "fear" and states "The severity of the punishment will influence the truthful person's fear of being misjudged just as much as the lying person's fear of being spotted - both suffer the same consequence." Dr. Ekman feels that the psychophysiological veracity (polygraph) examination, like behavioral clues to deceit, is vulnerable to what he terms the "*Othello error*" because Othello failed to recognize that Desdemona's fear might not be a guilty adulterer's anguish about being caught but could be a faithful wife's fear of a husband who would not believe her.

The Matte Quadri-Track Zone Comparison Technique factors into the system the innocent examinee's fear of error and quantifies the results, hence addressing physiological responses produced by that emotion.

Under contact with the DoD, the Applied Physics Laboratory (APL) at Johns Hopkins University developed a new computer evaluation technology to score psychophysiological veracity tests automatically and with great accuracy. The APL software called PolyScore™ uses a highly sophisticated mathematical algorithm to analyze physiological signals recorded during a psychophysiological veracity examination. The program makes complex, statistical comparisons most of which would be difficult for forensic psychophysiologists to make. After the psychophysiological veracity test is completed, PolyScore™ displays a probability that indicates either Deception, No Deception, or in about 8 percent of the cases Inconclusive in the current version 3.0. The initial program was designed primarily to score Zone Comparison tests dealing with single issues. Dr. Dale E. Olsen, Program Manager and a Principal Staff member of APL's Strategic Systems Department stated that the program's scoring rules deliver consistent, objective results time after time. This allows the software to identify the physiological reactions of people who are telling the truth and of people attempting deception with an accuracy of over 98 percent (current version 3.0) in the confirmed sample of 218 cases. The analyzation program also helps to identify any chart abnormalities such as artifacts. (APA Newsletters, 26, (4); 26, (6). Olsen 1995; Harris 1995)

As supporting evidence, six hundred and twenty-four cases were used to develop the scoring algorithm. After subtracting an eight percent inconclusive finding, PolyScore ™ scored all but one of the remaining cases correctly. Two hundred and eighteen of these test cases were verified by confessions from either the subject or someone else. The remaining cases were judged by an independent team using traditional scoring methods and their results matched the programs' findings except for one case where the independent team disagreed with the PolyScore resulting in an unresolved finding.(Olsen 1995). The APL system had been under development for five years. The federal government has over two hundred computerized systems, and they are also being used by law enforcement agencies in most states and several foreign countries. (APA Newsletter 26, (4). Capps 1995, Olsen 1995).

Version 2.3 of the computerized system contains algorithms for scoring the Zone Comparison tests and another for rank ordering responses. Work to improve the algorithm of the Zone comparison continues. Work is also underway on other question sequences. Because the Zone Comparison test deals with a single issue, it is expected that the corresponding scoring algorithm will be more accurate than those for the other question sequences. (Olsen, Harris, Capps, Johnson, Ansley, 1994) The high validity and reliability obtained to date with this system supports the argument advanced by proponents of the Numerical Approach that the physiological data recorded on the polygraph charts can be relied upon as the sole determinant of truth or deception.

However, proponents of the Clinical Approach have challenged and openly criticized the Numerical Approach. Richard O. Arther stated "The polygraph expert who has been taught to depend 100% upon the charts and totally ignore gestures is a technician and not a polygraphist." (Arther 1980). Brian Jayne stated 'These examiners incorrectly believe that if opinions are based strictly on psychophysiological responses the error rate of the procedure is somehow reduced. However, it is precisely the utilization of auxiliary information that distinguishes between an examiner who merely reads charts and one who renders the most accurate opinion possible. This diagnostic procedure is termed "global evaluation."' (Jayne 1993).

The above statements (Arther & Jayne) ignore the fact that the Numerical Approach FP's tasks in implementing the following *Methodology* which precedes chart evaluation and quantification, comprise at least 90 percent of the overall psychophysiological veracity examination. Furthermore, the methodology and psychological test structure of the Numerical Approach, which is designed to address the known variables identified in *Methodology* below, are significantly different from the Clinical Approach, as demonstrated in the following *Methodology* and *Discussion* sections of this chapter.

METHODOLOGY

Most proponents of the Numerical Approach and the Clinical Approach to the verification of the truth and the detection of deception do agree that there is no *unique lie response* on polygraph charts. (Jayne 1993). The Forensic psychophysiologist (FP) therefore *infers* deception to the target issue by the elimination of all other possibilities that could have caused the significant and consistent physiological responses to the relevant questions, with a corresponding comparative absence of response to its neighboring control questions. Conversely, the forensic psychophysiologist *infers* truthfulness to the target issue by the presence of physiological responses to the control questions versus a comparative absence of physiological responses to the relevant questions. Where the two approaches depart is in the method by which those inferences are made.

Proponents of the Numerical Approach assert that valid and reliable results can be obtained through the use of a standardized examination procedure and chart analysis quantification system, without the need for supplemental information which they believe contaminates the objectivity of the psychophysiological veracity examination, and offer proof of its accuracy with field and analog studies. (Bersh 1969; Raskin, Barland, Podlesny 1978; Widacki 1982; Elaad , Schahar 1984; Patrick, Iacono 1987; Raskin, Kircher, Honts, Horowitz 1988; Matte, Reuss 1989; Arellano 1990) Proponents of the Clinical Approach deny the Numerical approach's assertion and ignore the results of aforementioned studies, while maintaining the need for auxiliary information including case information and the examinee's verbal and non-verbal behavior to augment their data base in arriving at a determination, explaining that the numerous variables which may affect the examination process cannot all be controlled or factored into the examination process.

Identification of Variables

The issue is not whether the Numerical Approach is valid and reliable; both analog and field studies demonstrate its accuracy and effectiveness. At issue is the demonstration of the Numerical Approach's methodology and capacity to cope with the numerous variables which may affect the examination process. Therefore we first seek to identify which variables have the capability to adversely affect the physiological responses to the critical questions recorded on the polygraph charts which are used to arrive at a determination of truth or deception. We then demonstrate how those relevant variables can be effectively controlled and/or factored into the examination process thereby providing the FP complete confidence in the physiological data recorded on the polygraph charts to reach a finding.

These variables can be categorized as follows:

A. Emotionally induced Sympathetic response.
B. Non-emotionally induced Sympathetic response.
C. Emotionally induced Parasympathetic response.
D. Factors affecting strength of emotional and non-emotional responses.

The sympathetic subdivision of the autonomic nervous system is the primary cause of the physiological response recorded as a reaction tracing segment indicative of deception (control or relevant) on polygraph charts. Therefore it is important that we identify emotional and non-emotional stimuli known as stressors which activate the sympathetic system, and the factors which determine or affect the strength of the emotional and non-emotional responses. A *stressor* is an event or stimulus that acts as a source of stress. (Rathus 1994). The emotionally induced parasympathetic response not associated with a preceding sympathetic response as indicated in category C is not selective of any particular test question, but has an effect on the overall emotional condition of the examinee.

A. **Emotionally Induced Sympathetic Responses**. Emotions which activate the sympathetic system causing a physiological reaction on the polygraph chart are known as *stressors* and are listed as follows:

1. **Fear of Detection by the deceptive (guilty) examinee**.(Rathus 1994)
   a. **Reticular Activating System - Arousal-Attention Filter**. (Rathus 1994)
   b. **Psychological set.- Selective Attention**. **Focus of attention on greatest immediate threat**.(Backster 1969,1974; Rathus 1994;Matte 1980;Abrams 1989)
      (1) **Fear of consequences if deception detected.** (Larson 1932; Keeler 1935; Marston 1938; Lee 1953; Reid & Inbau 1966; Matte 1980; Abrams 1989, Rathus 1994; Manners DoDPI 1994)
      (2) **Operant Conditioning - Guilt**. (Rathus 1994, Manners DoDPI 1994)

(3) **Cognitive Dissonance - Conflict**. (Rathus 1994,Manners DoDPI 1994)
  a. **Lie aversion vs. self-preservation**.(Matte 1995)
  b. **Attitude-Discrepant Behavior** (Rathus 1994, Manners DoDPI 1994)
(4) **Hope of error by Deceptive (guilty) examinee**. (Matte 1978, 1980)

2. **Fear of Error by the truthful (innocent) examinee**.(Matte 1978, 1980; Ekman 1985)
3. **Guilt by default (truthful -innocent examinee)**.(Matte 1995)
4. **Anger.** (Rathus 1994; Hunter 1974; Matte 1980; Abrams 1989)
5. **Surprise.** (Ekman, P.1980; Ekman, P., Davidson, R. J., Friesen, W.V. 1990; Rathus 1994)
   a. **Unreviewed question.** (Reid & Inbau 1977; Backster 1963, 1969; Matte 1980)
   b. **Inside/outside noise.** Lee 1953; Matte 1980)
6. **Shame**. (Relier 1985; Campbell 1989; Matte 1995)
7. **Embarrassment.** (Rathus 1994,)
8. **Classical Conditioning - Normally requires repetition of the act. However *Victim* may respond to a single traumatic event.** (Manners DoDPI 1994)
   a. **Words/thoughts of crime elicits response**. (Manners DoDPI 1994)
   b. **Environmental stimuli indirectly related to crime elicits response**. (Manners DoDPI 1994)

B. Non-Emotionally Induced Sympathetic Responses. Non-Emotional stimuli also known as *stressors* which can activate the sympathetic system causing a physiological reaction on the polygraph chart are listed as follows:

1. **Orienting response to external stimuli thru Reticular Activating System.** (Rathus 1994)
   a. **Change - question spacing, voice intonation.** (Lee 1953; Matte 1993)
   b. **First test instruction.** (Lee 1953; Backster 1969; Matte 1980)
   c. **First question on the test.** (Lee 1953; Backster 1969; Matte 1980)
   d. **First relevant (preparatory/sacrifice) question on the test.** (Backster 1969; Matte 1980, 1989, 1993; Capps 1991; Horvath 1994)
   e. **Physical sensation - increase/decrease pressure in blood pressure cuff.** (Manners DoDPI 1994)
   f. **Sudden, unexpected noise**.(Matte 1980)
   g. **Visual distraction.** (Golden 1966; Matte 1980)

2. **Cognitive appraisal/awareness**.(Rathus 1994)

   a. **Differentiation in signal value between relevant and control questions.** (Manners , DoDPI 1994).
   b. **Expectations**.(Bandura 1989,1991; Rotter 1972, 1990; Rathus 1994)

c. **Mental exercise.** (Lee 1953; Matte 1993)
   (1) **Complexity - length and structure of question**. (Lee 1953; Matte 1993)
   (2) **Ambiguity - unfamiliar terminology.** (Lee 1953; Matte 1993)

C. Emotionally Induced Parasympathetic Responses. Such a response lacks the *sympathetic response* component responsible for the physiological reaction tracing segment indicative of deception on the polygraph chart. The conditions listed below are adjustment disorders in response to stressors. (Carson & Butcher 1992).

1. **Depression**.(Carson & Butcher 1992; Rathus 1994)
2. **Grief.** (Carson & Butcher 1992; Rathus 1994)

D. Factors Affecting Strength of Emotional and Non-Emotional Responses.

1. **Drugs**.(Berman 1967,1975; Waid , Orne 1982; Matte 1980)
   a. **Stimulants.** (Berman 1967, 1975; Matte 1980)
   b. **Depressants.** (Berman 1967, 1975;Waid, et al 1982; Iacono, et al 1984; Iacono 1987; Gatchel, et al 1983; Matte 1980)
   c. **Beta Blockers** (Medical Drug Reference 1994; E. Elaad, et al. 1982; Gatchel, et al 1983)
2. **Degree of socialization - degree of response.** (Waid, Orne 1982)
3. **Respiratory Ailments.** (Lee 1953, Moss 1965, Matte 1980, Abrams 1989)
4. **Protection under Attorney-Client Privilege**. (Matte 1979)
5. **Biofeedback** (Corcoran, Lewis, Garver 1978; Corcoran, Wilson 1979; Barland 1995)
6. **Hypnosis** (Bitterman, Marcuse 1945; Cumley 1959; Provost Marshal General School 1959; Germann 1961; Weinstein, Abrams, Gibbons 1970.)

The Numerical Approach initially developed by Cleve Backster, was and still is a single-issue Zone Comparison test. Backster allows his students to use the "Inside Track" which deals with the truthful examinee's "fear of error" versus the deceptive examinee's "hope of error" developed by this author (Matte), as an additional "Spot" for quantification, therefore both the Backster Zone Comparison Technique and the Matte Quadri-Track Zone Comparison Technique are structured to cope with all of the variables and factors mentioned in paragraphs A, B, C, and D above. We consider the Multiple-Issue test a degradation of the Single-Issue test and have excluded it from the Numerical Approach as it does not possess the internal reliability present in the Single-Issue test which can be horizontally as well as vertically scored. (Raskin, Kircher, Honts, Horowitz, 1988)

Methodology Used to Address Identified Variables

The Matte Quadri-Track Zone Comparison Technique and test structure is employed here to show its method of addressing the variables and factors mentioned in paragraphs A, B, C, and D above. It is therefore important that the methodology and psychological test structure be fully explained. As in the Backster Zone Comparison Technique (Fig. XI-9), the Matte Quadri-Track Zone Comparison Technique (Fig. XI-3) employs the Black Zone to identify Symptomatic questions, the Red Zone to identify the strong Relevant questions used for comparison against the Control questions which are identified as the Green Zone.(Fig. XI-3). Backster defined *Zone* as follows: A twenty to thirty-five seconds block of polygraph chart time initiated by a question having a unique psychological focusing appeal to a predictable group of examinees.(Ansley 1990). **Each of the variables and factors mentioned in categories A, B, C, and D above will be noted and identified by their category and sub-category as they emerge and relate to the presentation and explanation of the methodology and test structure of the psychophysiological veracity examination depicted herein.**

We can look upon the psychophysiological veracity (PV) examination as a complex system encompassing the entire examination which includes all parts of the pre-test interview, to include test question formulation, their review and presentation and assurance of intended interpretation, to the conduct of the psychophysiological veracity test resulting in polygraph charts containing physiological data which are quantified for a determination. Therefore, the system includes all of the aforementioned interacting parts, any one of which if omitted or altered affects the results of the psychophysiological veracity examination. The whole is the sum of its parts and the interactions of its parts.

Case Preparation and Evaluation

Prior to the conduct of the PV examination, the forensic psychophysiologist (FP) reviews the case file and applies the Examination Reliability Rating Table (Fig. XI-1) using a five point system to determine which issue has the greatest likelihood of producing conclusive results, on the basis of its combined Adequacy of Information, Case Intensity, and Distinctness of Issue. (Backster 1969, Matte 1980). Compliance with this case evaluation system minimizes inconclusive results and assures that tests are conducted only in those cases where there is ample and accurate case information from which to formulate the test questions, and that the issue being covered is sufficiently distinct and intense to elicit the examinee's psychological set **(A.l.b.)** without offering an opportunity for rationalization.

During this discussion, the terms *Truthful* and *Deceptive* will be used to portray examinees who are either truthful or deceptive to the target issue. It is realized that an innocent examinee may be deceptive to the control questions but truthful regarding the (target) issue for which he or she is being examined. It is also acknowledged that an examinee may be found truthful to one target issue but deceptive to other target issue(s) during a psychophysiological veracity examination hence several different issues would each require a separate Single-Issue Zone Comparison test to meet the requirements imposed by the psychophysiological methodology described herein.

Examination Environment

Before we get involved with the examination procedure, we must first examine the environment in which the PV examination will be administered. The examination room should be near soundproof in that no outside noise will be cause for an *orienting response* to external stimuli. **(B.l.f.)** The examination chair should be of the type provided by polygraph manufacturers, either standard or portable, which have wide, elongated armrests which can be elevated in instances of obese examinees whose arms rest against their body resulting in pneumograph tracing distortion. This professional chair affords better posture hence better physiological tracings. The positioning of the examination chair across from the examination desk containing the polygraph instrument, facing the opposite direction in which the polygraph chart exits the polygraph instrument, provides the FP with a clear, direct view of the examinee's profile further inhibiting attempts at countermeasure by the guilty examinee. Furthermore, the examinee is instructed to close his/her eyes during the conduct of each test (chart), unless the examinee complains of claustrophobia, or wears contact lenses which irritate their eyes when closed for several minutes. This further reduces orienting response to external stimuli **(B.l.g.)** and increases correlation among the three physiological tracings. (Golden 1966). Therefore during the pretest interview, the examinee should be seated in a different, separate chair to the right and in close proximity to the FP who then has a vis-à-vis, tête-à-tête position to establish rapport with the examinee.

Presence of Non-Participant in Examination Environment

Some defense attorneys have insisted on being present inside the examination room during the pre-test interview and conduct of the PV examination, asserting their right to monitor the entire procedure in order to make note of any procedural violations which may affect the outcome of the physiological data recorded on the polygraph charts and insure that the defendant-examinee is afforded all of the safeguards guaranteed by the United States Constitution. Defense attorneys should be afforded the right to monitor the entire PV examination, but not from within the polygraph examination room. Such monitoring should be done through closed-circuit television or two-way mirror and speaker. The presence of an attorney or other representative of the defendant inside the examination room would add a critical variable in the examination process which could affect the psychological preparation of the examinee for the delicate introduction of the various types of test questions necessary to attain a valid and reliable test, which includes the sensitive and fragile development and presentation of the control questions which are an essential part of the psychological structure of the PV examination.**(A.l.b.(3); A.6: B.l.f. & g.)** An exception to the above is when the use of an interpreter-translator is required, but such instances do have the potential of adding a variable depending upon the professionalism and training of the interpreter functioning in this type of environment. **(B.2.c.(1) & (2)).**(Matte 1993).

Furthermore, the presence of a relative or close friend of the examinee, immediately outside of the examination room, should be avoided. The examinee should be requested to report for the examination alone or in the company of his attorney. The purpose of this rule is to avoid another potential variable which may arise as a result of the examinee's fear that the results if deceptive, will be voluntarily, involuntarily or unintentionally released to the relative sitting outside the examination room, in spite of promises by the FP to the contrary. This is especially true when the relative plays the dominant role.**(A7.)** The necessity for the FP to exit the examination room after each polygraph test has been administered, to conduct a spot analysis of the physiological data recorded on the polygraph chart before the conduct of the next chart, may arouse the examinee's suspicion that the data is being discussed with the relative whose presence may have been allowed under duress: a further cause for subdued anger or its arousal.**(A.4.).** Inasmuch as both the Truthful and the Deceptive examinee are withholding information from the control questions or the relevant questions respectively, they are both susceptible to the influence of aforementioned relative. Such a presence could also inhibit a deceptive examinee from rendering admissions or a confession during the post-test interview. **(A.l.b.(3)a).** While there is no evidence that such a presence would cause a false positive or negative result, it could raise an *outside issue* causing an inconclusive result. The attorney-client privileged communication that exists between the examinee and his attorney who requested the examination, is a tacit invitation and authorization for the attorney to receive the PV examination results, hence the presence of the attorney is not a threat to the examinee.**(D.4.)** The primary cognitive variable affecting behavior is *Expectations*. (Rathus 1994). The examinee who is administered a PV examination under Agreement and Stipulation *expects* the prosecution as well as the defense and the court to receive the results of his/her examination, hence no promise of confidentiality, therefore no threat to his/her *expectations*. However, the examinee tested under the umbrella of Privileged Communication *expects* total confidentiality, hence is vulnerable to any variable which might threaten that *expectation* of confidentiality.**(B.2.b)** Exceptions include the examination of children accompanied by a parent or guardian, and crime victims who need assistance. But every effort must be made to reassure the examinee of the confidentiality of the examination. The idea is to eliminate any potential variable which may arise during the conduct of the PV examination.

Pretest Interview

The pretest interview is designed to prepare the examinee psychologically for the administration of the PV test wherein the examinee's physiological responses to previously reviewed questions are recorded on a moving polygraph chart. The length of time required to conduct a proper pre-test interview depends on the number of issues to be tested, the complexity of the case, the mental aptitude of the examinee, and the examinee's cooperation. It is imperative that the FP maintain not only a non-accusatory approach, but convey to the examinee that all examinees including himself/herself are assumed to be truthful regarding the target issue(s) until and unless the physiological data on the polygraph charts indicate otherwise. This FP posture is objective because in this society, all persons are deemed innocent until proven guilty. The FP merely continues that assumption until all polygraph charts have been conducted and their physiological data have been quantified and indicate deception. This alleviates the potential arousal of *anger* from the unjustly accused truthful examinee. **(A.4.)** The FP does not convey to the examinee that he/she *believes* the examinee to be truthful, but that he *assumes* he/she is truthful regarding the target issue until all polygraph charts have been conducted and its results indicate otherwise. In fact, the sustained treatment of the examinee as possibly truthful during the entire pre-test interview, significantly increases cooperation from both the truthful and the deceptive as later verified examinee, and minimizes efforts at countermeasures by the deceptive as later verified examinees, because its potential discovery would be counter to the cooperation expected from the truthful. (Matte 1989, 1993). The unbiasness of this approach also reduces the *fear of error* by the truthful examinee. **(A.2.)** An explanation of the physiology recorded and the quantification system used in the analysis of the data from which a conclusion of truth of deception is acquired, is designed to further allay any *fear of error* by the truthful examinee, which may be further diminished by demonstration of the test's accuracy with data from validation studies. **(A.2.)**

Psychological Set - Selective Attention

When the mind registers only some of the information it is exposed to, it is engaging in *selective attention.* Selective attention is an indispensable adaptive function. We cannot process all the information that impinges on our faculties at any given moment, so we focus on what appears to us most important and filter out the rest. **(A.l.a.).** *Cognitive appraisal* is the link between stimulus and response. (Rathus 1994). The examinee, before reacting, evaluates the stimulus, and from the interpretation of the stimulus (or cognitive appraisal) will or will not respond to the stimulus. In other words, what determines the response is not the stimulus itself but the examinee's interpretation of the stimulus. **(B.2.)**

It is therefore imperative that following the scientific formulation of the test questions, a thorough review of all test questions with the examinee be conducted with examinee feedback for assurance that the test questions are clearly understood by the examinee in the manner intended. In concert with social-learning theorist/psychologist Albert Bandura's theory that the primary cognitive variable affecting behavior is *expectations* (Rathus 1994), it follows that the examinee's expectancies are influenced by the FP's apparent competency and impartiality. It is therefore imperative that an impartial, non-accusatory, non-interrogative pre-test interview and examination be conducted so that the examinee's *expectations* will not be prejudiced by the FP's behavior, demeanor, and deportment which might alter the examinee's *expectations*, hence his/her *psychological set*. (Backster 1974) **(A.l.b.)(B.2.b.)**

Fear and Anger

Recognizing that the underlying basis of the psychophysiological veracity examination is the emotion of *fear*, which is the most depressing of all emotions, we must also recognize that the emotion of *anger*, which is the most exciting emotion, also induces sympathetic excitation and adrenaline secretion. (Cannon 1929; Hunter 1974). Published data and neurological evidence suggest that *fear* and *anger* both cause a strong arousal of the sympathetic subdivisions of the autonomic nervous system.**(A.1;A.4)** Proponents of the Numerical Approach have a grave stake in the conduct of a pre-test interview that is non-accusatory, non-threatening, objective and impartial, with an assumption of examinee truthfulness, hence are motivated to eliminate any factors or variables which may adversely affect the examinee's psychological set normally self-directed onto either the relevant questions if deceptive or the control questions if truthful regarding the target issue, due to their complete reliance on the physiological data recorded on the ensuing polygraph charts which are quantified for a final determination. Dr. Stan Abrams (1989) states "The most important part of the entire test process is the pretest interview, for the validity of the procedure hinges on how effectively it is conducted. Numerous functions are served, and each one is significant. Rapport must be established, allaying the examinee's anger, suspicion and generalized anxiety. In part, this can be accomplished by the examiner's presenting himself or herself as being highly objective with an interest only in learning the truth. Trust can be developed with an assurance that there will be no surprise or trick questions and an explanation of the test procedure that reduces the fear of the unknown while enhancing the fear of a lie being detected."

Anger

Great pains must be taken to identify the presence of anger or resentment. The entire pre-test procedure is designed to be non-threatening and indeed reassuring to the truthful examinee. If there is any evidence of anger and the FP is unable to diffuse it, no examination should be conducted.**(A.4.)** Therefore whenever a psychophysiological veracity examination is conducted in the manner described herein to its completion and a definite decision is rendered, it can be readily assumed that the emotion of anger was not present or was satisfactorily dissipated and confirmed through examinee feedback, hence was not a variable affecting the examinee's physiological chart responses. Furthermore, an examination cannot be conducted without a signed Statement/Release form from the examinee attesting to the voluntary participation in the examination. The video recording of the entire examination is an additional measure of assurance to all parties that this emotion was not present when the test was administered. **(A.4)**

Symptomatic Questions

During the pretest interview, the examinee is assured that no *surprise* questions will be asked on the test; in fact, that all test questions will be reviewed word for word with the examinee by category, and that once all test questions have been finalized with the examinee, they will be read exactly as they have been written. It is explained to the examinee that the asking of a surprise question would invalidate the test, hence would be counterproductive. Furthermore, during the review of the test questions, two Symptomatic questions designed to determine whether the examinee is in fact convinced of the FP's promise not to ask an unreviewed question, and whether the examinee is afraid that a surprise question will be asked on the test, are reviewed with the examinee and inserted into the test structure (Black Zone) as *Outside Tracks*. (Fig. XI-3). **(A.5.a.)**

Research conducted by Capps, Knill, and Evans (1993) to determine the validity of the Symptomatic question revealed that "This research provides evidence to substantiate Backster's claim that the inclusion of symptomatic questions in the control question polygraph examination significantly reduces the inconclusive calls made by the examiner. The number of inconclusive calls were reduced by two-thirds, exactly as Backster predicted.

This study found, as Backster did, that the symptomatics do make a significant difference in terms of alleviating inconclusive results."

Sacrifice/Preparatory Relevant Question

The review of the test questions with the examinee begins with the Sacrifice/Preparatory Relevant question indicated as number 39 in Figures XI-3 & XI-9. This test question acts as a safeguard in that it allows for dissipation of excessive general nervous tension or undue anxiety prior to the asking of the primary relevant questions (33 & 35 in Fig. XI-3). **(B.1.d.)** It is structured as an orienting relevant question (Yellow/Red; not within Zone Comparison) under category B, but serves as both a Sacrifice Relevant Question which may elicit an emotionally induced sympathetic response under category A, and as a Preparatory Question under category B for the introduction of the two strong (Red Zone) relevant questions (33 and 35 in Fig XI-3.), hence a dual purpose question. It should not exceed the precise scope of its related relevant questions (33 and 35). The manner in which this orienting relevant question is introduced as a preparatory Question for the two strong relevant questions assures its function as a Sacrifice Relevant Question. (**Matte 1993). This question is used to fully identify the issue which is followed with a suffix "do you intend to answer truthfully each question about that?" The full identification of the target issue permits the first strong relevant question (33 in Fig. XI-3) to be short without fear of misinterpretation or rationalization.**(B.2.c.(l).** This also eliminates mental exercise as a possible cause for a physiological response to that first, strong relevant test question. **(B.2.c.(l).** The test questions must not be ambiguous and the use of unfamiliar terminology must be avoided. **(B.2.c.(2).** The second strong relevant question (35 in Fig. XI-3) identifies the same issue sufficiently to avoid the potential for examinee rationalization but not necessarily as long as the Preparatory question (39 in Fig. XI-3)

Formulation and Review of Quantifiable Relevant Questions

This author refined Backster's S/R question into a Preparatory/Sacrifice Relevant question to insure that it functioned as a Sacrifice Relevant Question, and further served to fully identify the issue to be tested so that the first strong relevant question (33 in Fig. XI-3) to be quantified for a determination could be short without the risk of rationalization. This was the result of experiments conducted and reported by Captain Clarence D. Lee in 1953, indicating that mental exercise during the test may cause a physiological arousal, therefore relevant test questions must be succinct, as short as possible, void of rationalization potential, and thoroughly reviewed with the examinee, and thus not elicit any mental exercise from the examinee. "All effort must be avoided except that involved in the deception syndrome." (Matte 1993) **(B.2.c)** Furthermore, research conducted by S. M. Patterson, D. S. Krantz, and S. Jochum (1995) to evaluate the effects of psychological stress on calculated plasma volume, the relationship of these changes to changes in hematologic and hemodynamic factors, and the time course of plasma volume changes in forty

**For a detailed presentation of test questions, see Chapter 8

healthy men and women during a mental arithmetic (math) or benign reading task and during postural change (standing), revealed that math and posture change produced a significant decrease in plasma volume (ps <.00l) and increases in blood pressure (ps <.00l), blood and plasma density (ps <.00l), and total plasma protein (p <.00l).Correlations were observed between plasma volume changes and changes in systolic (r =.55,p<.001), diastolic (r =.61,p <.0001), and mean (r = .65,p <.000l) arterial pressure during math. (Patterson, et al 1995). **(B.2.c.)**

The second quantifiable relevant question (35 in Fig. XI-3) is formulated to fully identify the same issue covered by the first quantifiable (short) relevant question but not as lengthily as the Sacrifice/Preparatory Relevant Question. This is to avoid potential rationalization. The positions of relevant questions 33 and 35 located in the Primary and Secondary Tracks (Fig. XI-3) are rotated with the administration of each polygraph chart so that each relevant question visits and is compared with each exclusive control question on the same test.

Victim Trauma Considerations

Care must be taken to avoid the use of embarrassing terms **(A.7.),** taking into consideration the examinee's educational level, socialization, and the use of alternative terms that meet the test's objective, especially when examining a victim. When testing a victim, where legally allowed, the FP should be cognizant of classical conditioning which normally requires repetition of the act, however a victim may respond to a single traumatic event. **(A.8.)** With victims, formulation of the relevant questions should avoid traumatic and personally embarrassing words which might elicit a physiological response by their very nature. **(A.7. & A.8.a)** Furthermore, the examination room should be void of any physical evidence of the crime, unless it is necessary in the conduct of the PV examination. **(A.8.b.)**

Shame

Shame has been defined as an emotional state produced by the awareness that one has acted dishonorably or ridiculously. The term is usually reserved for situations in which one's actions are publicly known or exposed to real or potential ridicule (Relier 1985). Shame has also been described as an affect that follows the revelation of one's previously hidden shortcomings. Shame is sometimes used as a defense against exhibitionism and voyeurism. Shame is given particular attention in self-psychology and developmental psychology, where it is regarded as a master emotion that influences all the others. (Campbell 1989). We must differentiate Shame **(A.6.)** from Guilt **(A.l.b.(2).** Guilt refers to feelings about an act, a real or imagined transgression. It does not usually bring with it self-loathing, as shame does.(Campbell 1989). Guilt may be described as an emotional state produced by the knowledge that one has violated moral standards. Most authorities recognize an emotional state as guilt only when the individual has internalized the moral standards of the society; thus it is distinguished from simple fear of punishment from external sources **(A.l.).** Guilt is, in a sense, a self-administered punishment, distinguished from shame, where knowledge of the transgression by others is part of the concept. (Relier 1985). Shame involves one's basic sense of self and is typically experienced as embarrassment **(A.7.)** or humiliation **(A.6.)** (Campbell 1989). It is therefore imperative that, when testing is appropriate and legally permitted, the FP recognize the potential for autonomic arousal to relevant questions by legitimate victims of transgressions which invoke shame (such as rape, though not limited to sex offenses), and formulate the relevant questions in a manner that does not debase the victim/examinee and arouse or cause shame. On the other hand, the control questions can encompass the element of shame as a competitor to the relevant questions which may be tainted by that emotion. (For example see Matte 1993).

Guilt by Default

A truthful examinee may suffer Guilt by Default **(A.3.)** due to feelings of responsibility for the occurrence of the crime or incident, e.g. , bank supervisor left safe unlocked resulting in a larceny within. Relevant questions should always be formulated to depict the perpetrator's active role in the commission of the crime or incident, e.g., "Did you steal that missing $5000.00?" not "Are you responsible for the theft of that missing $5000.00?" or "Did you shoot John Doe?" not "Did you cause John Doe's death?" Adequate case information assured through the *Examination Reliability Rating Table* or *Backster Pre-Examination Reliability Estimate* (Figs. XI-1 & XI-9b) and a proper, thorough pretest interview should reveal the potential for Guilt by Default and thus the formulation of test questions that will avoid misinterpretation, assuring the examinee that negligence or feelings of responsibility do not warrant guilt, unless he/she is actually guilty of committing the offense. Furthermore, while guilt may cause a response, it is not an essential nor the prevailing cause for a response to the relevant questions by the deceptive examinee; but fear of detection, fear of the consequences is the primary factor, as evidenced by the solid responses produced by psychopaths who lack guilt, as reported in research conducted by Drs. Raskin, Barland, and Podlesny (1978). The Inside Track's *Fear of Error* question also adjusts for this factor and adds confidence in the decision making process when this *fear* may be a factor, as evidenced by the Matte-Reuss (1989) study.

Exclusive Control Questions

The review of the two non-current exclusive control questions (Green Zone) follow the review of the relevant questions. This permits the structurally less intense control questions to have more impact on the Truthful as later verified examinee. The term *exclusive* indicates that the control questions exclude the period in which the crime or incident occurred, by using a time bar. Hence there is a clear division between the relevant questions and the control questions against which they are compared and quantified for a determination of truth or deception.**(A.l.a.).** The proper introduction of the two control questions (46 and 47 in Fig. XI-3) is critical to their effectiveness. The non-accusatory/presumption of innocence-truthfulness theme during the pre-test interview nourishes the examinee's desire to present his/her best and most innocent-truthful image to the FP, which in turn inhibits the examinee from disclosing unfavorable information during the review of the control questions that would tarnish that image. (Matte 1993) These earlier-in-life (non-current), exclusive control questions are formulated and introduced in a manner which presents them as a significantly greater stress/conflict producing threat to the innocent examinee who is truthful to the relevant questions, whereas the deceptive examinee's psychological set will be focused on the relevant questions which offer the greatest immediate threat **(A.l.b.)** due to fear of the consequences if deception is detected **(A.l.b.(1),** operant conditioning - guilt **(A.l.b.(2),** cognitive dissonance - conflict **(A.l.b.(3).** (Raskin, Barland, Podlesny 1978, Matte, Reuss 1989).

Unlike the *non-exclusive* control question used by proponents of the Clinical Approach, which includes the period in which the crime or incident occurred, the *non-current exclusive* control question with its time bar offers a clear distinction between the relevant and control questions which facilitates the reticular activating system's role as an arousal-attention filter, hence a more focused psychological set. **(A.l.a.)**

Fear of Error - Control Question

We now proceed to the review of test question 23 located in the Inside Track (Fig. XI-3) which is classified as a control question (Green Zone), which is designed to elicit a response from the truthful examinee who is fearful that an error will be made on his/her PV test regarding the target issue.**(A.2.)** During the pre-test interview, the examinee was apprised of the accuracy of the polygraph instrument and the objectivity of the technique with its numerical scoring system of chart analysis by explanation of the various instrument recording components, and the results of research data supporting the numerical scoring system. It is hoped that the examinee now feels sufficiently confident about the accuracy of the test to furnish a negative reply to the following control question: "Are you afraid an error will be made on this test regarding the target issue?" The field validation study on the Polygraph Quadri-Zone Comparison Technique (renamed Quadri-track Zone Comparison Technique) published in 1989 involving 122 confirmed cases from a metropolitan police department and a private polygraph firm reflected no instance wherein the FP was not successful in acquiring a negative answer to the "fear of error" question. That does not mean that none of those examinees were fearful of an error being made on their examination, but it does mean that the FP was able to dispel most if not all of their fear and obtain a negative answer from each examinee. If in fact an examinee has a "fear of error" then his/her answer will be deceptive which in turn should produce a response commensurate with the degree of their fear of error. This is not unlike the FP's attempt to acquire a negative answer to the exclusive control questions (46 & 47) which are structured as probable lies.

Hope of Error - Relevant Question

The aforementioned "fear of error" Control question 23 is located (Fig. XI-3) in the Inside Track at Spot #3 for comparison with the "hope of error" Relevant question 24 (Red Zone) which is worded as follows: "Are you hopeful an error will be made on this test regarding the target issue?" to which a negative reply is expected from both truthful and deceptive examinees. But only the deceptive examinee will hope that an error is made on the test regarding the target issue. **(A.1.b.(4).**

Fear of Error/Hope of Error Comparison

Both questions number 23 and 24 are compared and quantified to determine which of the two questions elicited the greatest autonomic arousal. If the scores are positive (plus scores), they will augment the scores produced by the exclusive Control questions, which may have been weakened by responses to the Relevant questions due to the truthful examinee's "fear of error." Conversely, if the scores are negative (minus scores), they will augment the scores produced by the Relevant questions, which may have been weakened by a deceptive examinee who has rechanneled his/her fear of detection into hope of passing or beating the test.**(A.1.b.(4)** This type of examinee has a defeatist attitude, whether because of overwhelming evidence against him/her, or some other factor, has lost the will to fight and has resigned himself/herself to whatever fate befalls him/her. This examinee has not confessed to his/her crime, but simply became passive. (Reid & Inbau 1977). The prospect of "passing" a PV examination which may be of assistance to his/her cause is of greater emotional importance than "fear of detection" to a crime he/she feels "detected" but not proved. In such an instance, crime questions may elicit only mild responses. (Matte, Reuss 1989)

Research Studies on Factors Affecting Strength of Responses

Interestingly, field research conducted by Stephen L. Kirby in 1981 compared the accuracy of the known solution and the unknown solution stimulation tests wherein a card is selected by the examinee to which he/she is requested to lie about its selection on the test. He found no statistical difference in the responsiveness of the examinees on their respective stimulation tests, which were administered as the second chart, after the conduct of the first relevant chart in accordance with the Reid Technique; hence both stimulation techniques were of equal value. It was further noted that the accuracy of the charts following the stimulation test for the truthful examinees increased an average of 4.3 percent, while deceptive subjects decreased 15.8 percent. Kirby opined that this data falls in line with the theory that some deceptive subjects who feel that the polygraph has detected their lie, give up, become less emotional, and therefore less responsive on each subsequent test (Reid & Inbau 1977).**(A.1.b.(4)** The Matte-Reuss Field Validation Study 1989, revealed that the Stimulation test administered as the second chart averages slightly greater countertrend scores for the truthful (as later verified), inconsistent with the general trend and ground truth, than when the Stimulation test is administered as the first chart or when no Stimulation test is administered. (See Chapter 10). In the Matte Quadri-Track Zone Comparison Technique, the Stimulation test is administered as the first chart so that it will have equal influence on all subsequent relevant charts. Furthermore, Relevant question 24, *Hope of Error*, has demonstrated its capacity to recoup negative scores lost as a result of aforementioned decrease in emotionality in the Matte-Reuss 1989 field study by increasing the negative scores of the Deceptive examinees by -5.4. A study on the "Effect of the Location of the Numbers Test on Examiner Decision Rates" by R. Widup and G. Barland in

1992, revealed that the location of the numbers test had no apparent practical effect on the distribution of examiners' decisions, but cautioned that the lack of ground truth and experimental control in real-life cases makes it difficult to draw firm conclusions. (See also Elaad & Kleiner 1986)

Remedial Function of Inside Track Questions

Equally important is the role that above Control question 23 and Relevant question 24 (Inside Track) play in the spot analysis conducted immediately after the administration of each polygraph chart to determine whether each test question within the zone comparison tracks is functioning as designed and remedial action may be warranted. While Control question 23 may recoup response scores lost as a result of an innocent examinee's fear of error, thereby possibly avoiding a false positive; negative scores from Relevant question 24 assure the FP that the negative scores from strong Relevant questions 33 and 35 are not due to an innocent examinee's "fear of error" thereby reinforcing the FP's conclusion of deception.**(A.1.2)** In a validation study (Matte, Reuss 1989) it was shown that the inclusion of the Inside Track containing questions 23 and 24 produced an increase in the plus scores for the Truthful from +5.89 to +13.1, and also produced an increase in the minus scores for the Deceptive from -19.7 to -25.1 thus avoiding a 5 percent false positive error rate and a 2 percent false negative error rate, with an inconclusive rate of only 6 percent. (Matte, Reuss 1989)**.(A.1.2 & A.1.b.(4)**

Neutral, Orienting Response Question

The neutral (irrelevant or norm) question which serves as the first test question asked on the test, identified as question 14J in Fig. XI-3, is next reviewed with the examinee. The examinee's place of birth, last name or first name is usually used for that purpose. This neutral question is designed to absorb an examinee's orienting response to the first question asked on the test. **(B.1.c.)**

Review of Symptomatic Questions

The examinee is now reassured that no unreviewed questions will be asked on the test, and in order for the FP to be assured that the examinee is in fact completely convinced of this, the two aforementioned symptomatic questions (25 & 26 in Fig. XI-3) are also reviewed with the examinee. **(A.5.a.)**

First Orienting Response Instruction

At the beginning of each test, prior to the asking of the first test question (Neutral, Irrelevant question 14J), the instruction "the test is about to begin" serves to absorb an orienting response to external stimuli. **(B.1.b.).**

Acquaintance Chart

Upon completion of the review of all test questions that will be asked on the first test (test A), the examinee is then seated in the examination chair and the polygraph instrument components are placed on his/her person. The examinee is then re-instructed about the importance of sitting perfectly still throughout the administration of each test (chart). The examinee is also informed that the pressure in the cardio cuff will be released twenty-five seconds after his/her answer to the last question on each chart, to reduce his/her anxieties regarding cuff pressure during the administration of the test. Usually when the cuff pressure is first applied, an orienting response is manifested on the polygraph chart. **(B.l.e.)** To acquaint the examinee to this cuff pressure, the examinee is requested to sit still for a couple of minutes while his physiology is monitored, at which time all physiological parameters are activated and recorded on the polygraph chart.

Sensitivity/Stimulation test

Following the aforementioned acquaintance chart, the examinee is informed that a sensitivity test will now be administered to determine the examinee's capability of response to a known lie. As described in detail in Chapters 8 and 10, a Sensitivity or Control/Stimulation test is administered which should result in the reassurance of the truthful examinee regarding the accuracy of the examination, thus allaying his/her potential fear of error regarding the target issue, thereby narrowing the truthful examinee's focus of attention to the control questions. **(A.l.b)** Conversely, the Stimulation test's demonstration of accuracy increases the deceptive examinee's fear of detection and/or hope of error regarding the target issue with a usual increase in autonomic response to the relevant questions(33, 35 and/or 24) as a result of a more focused psychological set affecting the reticular activating system which determines what is significant to the examinee. **(A.l.a.).** (Matte-Reuss 1989).

Interestingly, the Stimulation test has been cited by at least one psychologist (Reed 1992) as an example of physiological arousal caused by operant factors other than *fear of detection.* However the proper presentation of the Stimulation test with a preamble that makes the outcome of the Stimulation test important to the examinee, causes the deceptive examinee to *fear* the correct selection of his/her card number, because it indicates and reinforces the FP's ability to detect the examinee's lies to the crime questions. Some deceptive examinees may also *fear* the correct selection of their card number because of a preconceived false notion that the FP will then be able to compare his/her lie response on the Stimulation test to his/her response(s) on the actual crime test. Conversely, the innocent examinee will *fear* an incorrect selection of his/her card number because it would be indicative of the FP's inability to establish his/her innocence, hence a *fear of error.* (Matte 1978, 1980, 1989, 1993). Analog studies where students are employed in mock paradigms also experience the emotion of *fear* because of the effect that their failure would have on their pride. Admittedly, in mock paradigms, the absence of punishment or dire consequences, permits less prominent operant factors to produce physiological arousals such as mental exercise, conflict, lie aversion, but these operant factors are dominated or overridden when the powerful emotion of *fear* of detection or error is aroused as found in real-life cases. This would also explain the lack of response on Stimulation tests by innocent examinees who have been totally convinced by the FP of the accuracy of the examination, but nevertheless respond adequately to the control questions on the crime test.

Application of Reaction Combination Guide

After the administration of each test chart, the FP conducts a Spot Analysis referring to the Matte 23-Reaction Combination Guide to determine whether all *tracks* are functioning as designed and apply remedial action when necessary prior to the administration of the next test chart. This may necessitate an increase or decrease in the intensity or strength of one or both control questions, and perhaps a change in the type of control question. Remedial action could include the administration of a Silent Answer Test prior to the administration of the next relevant test chart. All of these remedies are included in aforementioned Reaction Combination Guide. Backster provides an 8-Reaction Combination Guide which he initially developed.

Effects of Drugs on PV Examination

The use of drugs, whether stimulants or depressants, by an examinee is always of concern to the FP, and the pretest interview probes that area. While some research has shown that certain drugs have had an effect on the outcome of PV examinations which lacked aforementioned control questions (Waid 1981)(OTA 1983), other research (Gatchel, et al. 1983) has shown that even with the use of propranolol, a beta-blocking drug **(D.l.c.)** the overall error rate was low but the inconclusive rate was high. However, a study by Iacono, et al. (OTA 1983) found that ingestion of neither 10 milligrams of diazepam (Valium®) nor 20 milligrams of methylophenidate (Ritalin®) affected the accuracy of detection.**(D.1.b.).** Results in both active drug conditions were more accurate than when subjects ingested a placebo containing lactose. (OTA 1983). A pilot study on the effects of beta blocking drugs on the polygraph detection rate conducted by E. Elaad, et al., using Trasicor, a beta blocking agent, revealed that while the GSR channel was the most efficient identification index for the placebo group in their analog study, it was also the most vulnerable to the effect of Trasisor.**(D.l.c.).** The results of Elaad, et al's study showed that both the GSR and the cardiovascular activity were significantly affected by Tracicor, however the beta blocking agent had no effect on the respiration recordings. Elaad, et al., concluded that "skin resistance responses are most vulnerable to BB (beta blocking) influences while respiration recordings are not affected by the drug. Following that conclusion it can be claimed that using beta adrenergic blocking drugs may be detrimental to polygraph techniques which emphasize the GSR responses (guilty knowledge technique) while the control question methods, which put more attention to changes in respiration, might be less affected."(Elaad, et al. 1982). It should be noted that in control question examinations, whatever effect the drug or medication may have on the relevant questions will also have the same effect on the control questions against which they are being compared. This variable may cause an inconclusive result but will not cause a false positive or negative outcome**.(D.l.a.b.c.).** It should also be noted that in the traditional scoring methods employed in the Backster, Matte, and DoDPI Zone Comparison techniques, all three parameters consisting of respiration, GSR, and cardiovascular activity are *treated equally* using a seven-position scale. However, the mathematical algorithm used in the Applied Physics Laboratory software called PolyScore employed in computerized polygraph systems devotes an average 54 percent of its criteria for deception to electrodermal activity, 24 percent to blood volume, 8 percent to pulse rate, and only 14 percent to respiration.(Johnson 1994; Olsen 1995). Our field study (Matte-Reuss 1992) on the relative effectiveness of physiological data in field polygraph examinations showed that the most productive of the physiological channels was the pneumo tracing at 43 percent, followed by the cardio at 32 percent and the electrodermal at 24 percent. Contrary to a report by Capps (1992) that we did not address *accuracy* of aforementioned parameters in above field study, we did in fact determine the *productivity/accuracy* of each tracing by "the tracing which accumulated the highest score *consistent with ground truth*." (Matte, Reuss 1992). While analog studies have generally found the electrodermal tracing to be the most effective parameter,(Raskin, et al 1978; Thackray & Orne 1968; Cutrow, et al 1972), several field studies have found opposite results with the pneumo tracing being the most effective parameter (Elaad & Eitan 1985; Elaad, Ginton, Jungman 1988; Ryan 1989; Elaad & Kleiner 1990; Jayne 1990; Matte, Reuss 1992; Suzuki 1975).We believe that the difference in psychodynamics between subjects in mock paradigms (laboratory studies) and field studies (real-life cases) explains the significant differences seen in the reported research for these different types of studies. The key factors for the psychodynamic differences are felt to be the *Fear of Detection* by the Guilty **(A.1)** and the *Fear of Error* by the Innocent. **(A.2).** The demonstrated effect of beta blockers on the GSR and cardio activity and the *lack* thereof on respiratory activity supports the continued usage of the traditional scoring system (Backster, Matte, DoDPI) wherein the respiratory channel alone can often provide the minimum scores required to arrive at a conclusive determination. The traditional scoring system can also be used as an adjunct to the computerized polygraph system's PolyScore which normally emphasizes the GSR (54%) and only applies its algorithm to the thoracic respiratory channel (in addition to cardio activity) for its results.(Johnson 1994; Olsen 1995). However, according to Dr. Olsen, while the two pneumograph channel tracings may appear to be quite different on the computer screen or polygraph chart, the PolyScore pre-processes the signals from both channels in such a manner that there is much less difference in the signals between the two channels. Furthermore, PolyScore compensates for channel(s) that produce inferior data by finding indicators of deception in those channels that are most productive. Therefore if an examinee is under the influence of a beta blocker, the PolyScore would shift its attention to the most productive channel, which existing research shows under that circumstance to be the pneumograph. Our field research (Matte, Reuss 1992) revealed a significant difference in the productivity of the thoracic and abdominal breathing tracings/channels of male versus female examinees, hence both channels are recorded on modern mechanical and electronic polygraph instruments. Furthermore, there were significant differences in the productivity of each channel (pneumo, GSR, cardio) for the truthful versus deceptive male and female examinees. The computerized polygraph system (APL) which enjoys an exceptionally high accuracy rate exceeding 98%, records and displays both respiratory channels which allows for traditional scoring, but in the final analysis applies the evaluating algorithm only to the thoracic channel which encompasses all of the traditional criteria for deception except for those baseline arousals which have no change in amplitude.(Olsen 1995). We cannot ignore the fact that beta blockers which are used to reduce heart strain for those who are at risk due to a heart problem are prescribed to a significant percentage of our population. Propranolol for instance is used in the treatment of angina (chest pain), hypertension, arrhythmias (Irregular heartbeats), migraine headaches, tremors, "thyroid storm" and pheochromocytoma. (Medical Drug Reference 1994). With the rapid growth of our aging population, more examinees suffering from a medical condition requiring the use of beta blockers will be seen by FP's who should become familiar with the various beta-blocking agents.

Effects of Socialization and Other Variables on PV Examination

Researchers Waid & Orne reported in 1982 that highly socialized examinees were more responsive electrodermally than examinees significantly less socialized, as measured by the socialization scale of the California Psychological Inventory (Gough 1964). However, only one physiological parameter was used in their study.**(D.2.)** The effect that socialization may have on the PV examination is not discriminatory, hence not problematic. Research conducted by Drs. Raskin, Barland, and Podlesny 1978, revealed that "With regard to a variety of personality, biographical, and circumstantial factors, the results failed to show any relationship between those variables and the polygraph outcomes. There were no differences attributable to aspects of personality as measured by the MMPI, age, sex, previous arrests or polygraph examinations, education attainment, or the type of crime involved. Thus, in the absence of very low intelligence or any incapacitating psychological or physical illness, it seems reasonable to conclude that polygraph examinations are effective with a wide variety of individuals with respect to the broad range of crimes typically investigated." **(D.2.)**

Respiratory Ailments

Symptoms of coughing, sneezing, or sniffing caused by respiratory ailments such as the common cold, influenza, pneumonia, bronchitis, tuberculosis can adversely affect the validity of the pneumograph recordings and indirectly the other physiological recordings (GSR and Cardio).**(D.3).** It has been this author's (Matte) policy and the practice of his colleagues that examinees suffering from any of the aforesaid symptoms be rescheduled for examination at a later date when they are symptom free. (Lee 1953, Moss 1965, Matte 1980, Abrams 1989).

Effects of Protection under Attorney-Client Privilege on Autonomic Arousal

PV Examinations conducted for defense attorneys have been criticized as having a high rate of false negatives due to a purported lack of *fear of detection* by the client examined. **(D.4)** It has been held that a defense FP may be unduly influenced to find the defendant examinee truthful to insure repeated business. (Orne 1975). The concept of the *Friendly Polygraphist* appears to have been accepted by many members of the psychological and legal community as reflected in United States v. Gipson, 24 M.J. 343 (C.M.A. 1987); People v. Adams, 53 Cal.App.3d l09 (1975); Cargill 1989). The common and consistent reasoning has been that "ex-parte examinations may be less reliable, because the ability to discard unfavorable test results eliminates or reduces an essential basis for the reliability of such results - the nervousness created by fear of detection." (Cargill 1989).**(D.4).** Whitman (1989) stated "The theory upon which the polygraph is based requires the examinee to be fearful when faced with the possibility of being caught in a lie. The military judge could determine that the accused had nothing to fear in the private examination, and therefore the reliability of the results would be questionable." (Matte & Reuss 1990)

However, a field study of the *Friendly Polygraphist* concept (Matte & Reuss 1989) involving confirmed cases from the files of a metropolitan police department and a private polygraph firm, revealed that from the total number of cases examined in aforementioned study, 39 PV examinations were conducted for defense attorneys under attorney-client privilege, and 34 of those were scored deceptive, and subsequently confirmed. Furthermore, defense attorney cases showed a mean chart score of -9.38 compared with police cases which showed a mean chart score of -9.10, which suggests similar states of autonomic arousal. Another group, commercial cases which were not tested under privilege, showed a mean chart score of -9.90. Because these guilty cases have similar scores, the idea that defense subjects lack the fear of arousal found in other populations is without merit, leaving the *Friendly Polygraphist* concept without support.**(D.4)** A study conducted by Drs. D. Raskin, G. Barland, and J. Podlesny in 1977 tested Dr. Martin T. Orne's hypothesis using three sets of data and found that the first sample showed that defense cases produced 78 % truthful, 20% deceptive, and 2% inconclusive outcomes. The law enforcement cases produced 76% truthful, 20% deceptive, and 5% inconclusive outcomes. Contrary to the *Friendly Polygraphist* hypothesis, there was no difference in the frequency of truthful outcomes for defense and law enforcement examinations. The second analysis produced mean numerical scores of -4.7 for defense cases and -2.0 for law enforcement and employer cases. Although the difference between those mean scores was not statistically significant, it was in the opposite direction from that predicted by the *Friendly Polygraphist* hypothesis. Another sample of numerical scores produced mean scores of -10.4 for defense cases and -0.7 for law enforcement cases. The difference between those mean scores was statistically significant and also in the opposite direction from that predicted by the *Friendly Polygraphist* hypothesis. Thus the three samples of data obtained in Raskin's study not only failed to produce any evidence to support Orne's hypothesis, but some of the results indicated effects which were totally contrary to Orne's speculation. Raskin et al. opined that the findings obtained with three different samples of criminal cases are contrary to the *Friendly Polygraphist* concept and there appears to be no increased risk of false negatives under such circumstances. **(D.4).** (Matte & Reuss 1990).

Use of Biofeedback Training as a Countermeasure

Biofeedback refers to the process where a person is given immediate information concerning his/her own biological functions, such as cardiovascular activity, temperature, galvanic skin response, or any other measurable physiological process. Biofeedback training aims at helping that person through the use of this biological information to voluntarily control a specific physiological process. Some analog studies using mock paradigms have shown varied success in the use of biofeedback training to control their responses during simulated polygraph examinations. (Corcoran, Lewis, Garver 1978). However no field study using all three polygraph parameters (pneumograph, GSR, cardiograph) employing a Zone Comparison Control Question test involving real-life criminal suspects to determine the effect of biofeedback training on PV examinations has yet been conducted. Corcoran and Wilson did report a case of a suspect in an actual larceny who had received treatment with biofeedback consisting of 21 one-hour sessions over a seventeen-month period to reduce the frequency and severity of her headaches. After two months of biofeedback training, this suspect underwent a psychophysiological veracity (PV) examination using the polygraph to determine whether or not she was criminally involved in the larceny of government property. Four MGQT (Mixed General Question Test) polygrams were administered which revealed that while she was able to volitionally suppress her responses to some of the questions on some of the parameters, she was not able to suppress her responses sufficiently to avoid detection, and the deceptive results were confirmed with her confession. (Corcoran & Wilson 1979). It is recognized that biofeedback training can successfully control long-term responses. However it is extremely doubtful that such training can be successful in controlling or suppressing short-term responses stimulated by the fear of detection and punishment from real-life consequences. The task becomes even more difficult when a Zone Comparison test is administered which requires that the examinee respond significantly and consistently to the control questions but not respond to the neighboring relevant questions contained in the same test. Furthermore, some test questions elicit an affirmative answer while others elicit a negative answer, and the positions of certain questions are rotated with each chart administered. Additionally, Stimulation, Sensitivity and when appropriate, Countermeasure tests, are normally included as part of the examination process. The psychodynamics between subjects in mock paradigms (laboratory studies) and field studies (real-life cases) are significantly different. Analog studies lack the elements of fear of detection by the guilty, fear of error by the innocent and the intense motivation found in subjects of field studies. As stated by Psychologists Carson and Butcher (1992), "By and large, such analogue studies have failed to make convincing connections." Dr. Stan Abrams in his studies and field testing of hypnotically induced subjects, concluded that the more motivated the subject, the more detectable that subject became. (Abrams 1995). In conclusion, there is no authoritative field research which indicates that biofeedback is an effective countermeasure in forensic psychophysiological veracity examinations using the polygraph. **(D.5)**

Use of Hypnosis as a Countermeasure

The question has often been raised regarding the possibility of an examinee defeating a psychophysiological veracity (polygraph) examination while under hypnotically induced amnesia. Hypnotically induced amnesia refers to a functional amnesia induced in the examinee by posthypnotic suggestion, and a posthypnotic suggestion refers to a suggestion concerning a phenomenon taking place subsequent to the "waking" of the examinee from the hypnotic trance. The question is answered in the review of literature on the subject, which revealed that, in 1945, E. M. Bitterman and F. L. Marcuse demonstrated by means of a Keeler polygraph that subjects showing complete symbolic posthypnotic amnesia for specific previously learned words retained the ability to recognize the words at the "unconscious" level. The subjects produced deceptive responses on their polygrams when they denied recognition of the previously learned words. In 1959, William E. Cumley and Robert L. Berry conducted an experiment involving a hypothetical burglary committed by two subjects in their normal state. The subjects were subsequently hypnotized and posthypnotic amnesia was induced by use of posthypnotic suggestion. After being hypnotized, the subjects while under polygraph instrumentation denied having committed the burglary, which produced deceptive responses to the relevant questions. In 1959, a research project was conducted by the Provost Marshal General's School at Fort Gordon, Georgia to study the effect of hypnotically induced amnesia upon the accuracy of the PV examination results. An analog study using twelve subjects revealed that only one subject produced a chart that was not disturbed or indicative of deception. Analysis of the results revealed that there is no specific depth in a hypnotic trance at which complete amnesia can be induced. It is extremely difficult to induce 100 percent amnesia in a subject. If only partial amnesia is induced and the subject retains a vague or hazy memory of the crime, or has an "uneasy feeling" concerning the crime, the subject will produce a deceptive response. (Berry 1960). In 1961, research was conducted by A. C. Germann to determine whether amnesia induced by hypnosis could surreptitiously defeat the PV examination. Fifteen PV examinations were administered, each repeated three times in accordance with field protocol. In eight examinations a significant response indicating deception was immediately detected by the Forensic Psychophysiologist (FP). In the other seven examinations, abnormal patterns were evaluated by the FP as indicative of excessive emotion, nevertheless were deemed somewhat inconclusive. This study concluded that the instrumental detection of deception technique relies upon subconscious as well as conscious reactions, and that amnesia hypnotically induced cannot surreptitiously defeat the PV examination. Experimental PV examinations administered to two volunteer subjects at Duquesne University in 1956 by Charles A. McInerney concluded that a wakeful subject cannot defeat the PV examination as the result of a post-hypnotic suggestion. Bryan (1962) studied this phenomenon by having a subject steal an object. Then he hypnotized her, suggested that she had stolen a second object, and had her forget the theft that she had committed. The PV examination showed a response to both objects, which suggests that the unconscious may produce anxiogenic responses which can be demonstrated psychophysiologically by the polygraph. An analog study conducted in 1970 by Edwin Weinstein, M.D., Stanley Abrams, Ph.D., and Donald Gibbons, Ph.D. used a group of six volunteer college students who were hypnotized to create amnesia regarding the theft of money. The conclusions of this study revealed that the FP was partially misled by the hypnotic approach since he could not state conclusively that the students were guilty. However, he was not completely deceived since he did not see them as innocent either. Interestingly, the aforementioned experiments were conducted under laboratory conditions totally lacking the *fear of detection* element found in field situations, which is a primary stimuli in the activation of the sympathetic subdivision of the autonomic nervous system causing a *reaction* on the polygraph chart. Furthermore, the techniques and instrumentation in use during that period lacked current knowledge and technology. Dr. Stan Abrams, a clinical and forensic psychologist informed this author that he personally administered PV examinations to several professional hypnotists in actual real-life cases who employed self-hypnosis as a countermeasure, but that none of them were able to defeat the PV examinations which produced very responsive physiological data, each confirmed by confessions. Dr. Abrams concluded that the more motivated, the more detectable the subjects become. Again, the psychodynamics of subjects in analog studies differ greatly from those in field studies where the consequences of detection are grave. Considering that post-hypnotic amnesia was not generally effective in aforementioned analog studies, it is expected to be even less effective in real-life cases, thus not an effective countermeasure to the PV examination. **(D.6)**

Effect of Emotionally Induced Parasympathetic Response on PV Examination

Reference category C, Emotionally Induced Parasympathetic Response. Depression **(C.l)** is an emotional condition, either normal or pathological, characterized by discouragement, feeling of inadequacy, helplessness, hopelessness, worthlessness which may be symptomized by inactivity, possible self-destructive tendencies, is a constant state throughout the examination and is not selective of either the control questions or the relevant questions, but could result in an unresponsive examinee producing inconclusive results. This condition lacks the sympathetic response component responsible for the physiological reaction tracing segment indicative of deception on the polygraph chart.**(C.l.)** The DSM-III-R diagnosis of major depression in interpersonal terms is described as a position of appeasement (hostile submission) toward another person's stance of accusation and blame (hostile dominance), which leads to internalized self-accusation and blame (hostile domination of self). (Carson & Butcher 1992). The DSM-III-R diagnosis provides another reason for the adoption of an impartial, non-accusatory Approach during the entire examination. Grief **(C.2)**can result in severe depression preceded by a period of numbness and shock punctuated by episodes of irritability and anger.(Janis, et al 1969). The FP should avoid the conduct of a PV examination on a grieving person until it has been determined that he/she has recovered.

Conclusion

The Matte-Reuss Field Validation Study (1989) on aforementioned methodology revealed a 100 percent accuracy with a 6 percent inconclusive rate from 122 confirmed cases provided by a Metropolitan Police Department and a Private Polygraph firm. This data supports the methodology of aforementioned Numerical Approach in addressing the variables listed in Categories A, B, C and D. In addition, Norman Ansley (1990) reported on the validity of polygraph in real cases conducted during the period from 1980 to 1990, which revealed that of the ten studies examined, six used the Numerical Approach with a combined accuracy of 97 percent. This indicates that in only 3 percent of those cases were they unable to correctly infer deception or truthfulness on the basis of the physiological data recorded on the polygraph charts.

DISCUSSION

Validity of Sacrifice Relevant Question

The validity and effectiveness of the Sacrifice Relevant question described in above methodology has been recently challenged by Dr. Horvath (1994) who invoked research conducted by Capps (1991) to show that "a sacrifice-relevant question does not reveal a response pattern that typifies that which occurs to actual relevant questions. More important, his findings suggested that while both truthful and deceptive examinees may indeed respond somewhat to the sacrifice relevant question, truthful examinees do not generally show misleading physiological indications of deception." (Horvath 1994).

However, Capps (1991) research regarding the Sacrifice Relevant question was designed to investigate "the value of the sacrifice relevant question in predicting the overall results of a polygraph examination in terms of 'deception indicated' versus 'no deception indicated.'" Capps' research was not designed to test the Sacrifice Relevant question's ability to absorb the orienting response of the truthful examinee on the first question dealing with the relevant issue, inasmuch as he did not make any comparison in the degree and magnitude of the Sacrifice Relevant's response to its related strong relevant questions on the same test. Furthermore, Capps did not structure nor present the Sacrifice Relevant question as a Preparatory question for the introduction of the two strong relevant questions, in accordance with the methodology of the Matte and Backster Zone Comparison Techniques.

Horvath's (1994) analogue study regarding the value and effectiveness of the Sacrifice Relevant Question fails to use a Zone Comparison format consistent with the Backster Zone Comparison Technique originated by Backster, nor the Matte Quadri-Track Zone Comparison Technique, both of which use only two relevant questions plus a Sacrifice/Preparatory question that is designed to function as an orienting relevant question which should not exceed the precise scope of its related two strong relevant questions. In his study, Horvath uses exclusive control questions that possess the same time frame within the test structure, versus Backster and Matte formats which use a different time frame for each control question within each test for each examinee. Furthermore, Horvath rotates the position of the control questions whereas Backster and Matte rotate the position of the relevant questions only. It should also be noted that in the Backster and Matte techniques, the Sacrifice Relevant question is presented to the examinee as a Preparatory question to enhance the focus of the deceptive as later verified examinee's psychological set onto the two strong relevant questions included in the same test, a procedure not used in the Horvath study. In order to effectively determine the validity and productivity of the Sacrifice Relevant question, it must be compared against the two relevant questions affected by it on the same test chart. However, Horvath's analog study did not make that comparison. Instead, Horvath compared the magnitude of the Sacrifice Relevant question in the Zone Comparison format to various relevant questions in the MGQT format (Mixed General Question Test), which is analogous to the comparison of apples and bananas. Even though the study design was faulty, there was no adverse impact showing on the results of the Zone Comparison test by the use of a Sacrifice Relevant question. The fact that Horvath's research is an analog study using mock paradigms which lack the essential emotions present in field cases leaves doubt as to the credibility of any conclusions based on his results. As stated by renowned psychologists Robert C. Carson and James N. Butcher, "Experiments of this kind are generally known as analogue studies - studies in which a researcher attempts to simulate the conditions under investigation...Apart from what many would regard as undiminished ethical problems in much research of this sort, the major scientific problem is of course to establish major commonality between the contrived behavior and the real thing as it occurs 'naturally.' By and large, such analogue studies have failed to make convincing connections." (Carson & Butcher 1992).

Major Differences in Test Structure of Numerical v. Clinical Approach

It is important to note that there are major differences in the test structure between the Numerical and the Clinical Approach which may account for the Clinicians' need for auxiliary information in their decision making process. Aside from the fact that the Clinical Approach test format does not include the *Inside* and *Outside Tracks* (Fig.XI-3) there are other major differences such as the *number* of relevant questions used and the *type* of control questions against which they are compared. Furthermore, Numerical Approach techniques such as the Backster and Matte Zone Comparison techniques segregate separate issues into single-issue tests which are then administered in order of their combined adequacy of case information, case intensity and distinctness of issue. This procedure limits undesirable variables to the manageable few described above. It should be noted that Guilty Knowledge questions, normally included in test formats employed by proponents of the Clinical Approach, are excluded from the Backster and Matte Zone Comparison tests; they are tested separately using Backster's S-K-Y test and Matte's S-K-G test. (Matte 1980). Dr. David T. Lykken, a proponent of the Guilty Knowledge Test but a severe critic of the "lie test", recognized the difference between the Clinical and Numerical Approach, stating "Polygraphers have not provided an agreed-upon name for the kind of examination taught by the Keeler, Reid, and Arther schools, in which the examiner himself serves as lie detector and the polygraphic information is combined with impressions of behavior and other data in arriving at a diagnosis. But we need to distinguish this approach from the Backster method, which attempts to let objective scoring of the charts alone determine the results. Both are psychological procedures aimed at arriving at a judgment about the subject's psychological state. The Backster technique is arguably a psychological test, but the Keeler-Reid-Arther procedure is clearly not a test at all, although it is commonly referred to in this way...these (Keeler-Reid-Arther) all can be described as clinical assessments rather than as tests." (Lykken 1981).

Exclusive Versus Non-Exclusive Control questions

As reflected in above Methodology, the Numerical Approach techniques such as Backster and Matte Zone Comparison Techniques, employ the Exclusive earlier-in-life control question, which uses a time bar to exclude the period in which the crime was committed from the period covered by the control question, in order to provide a distinct division between the two questions being intercompared, thus a clearer differentiation of physiological response data to control and relevant test questions, and a clear beacon to the examinee's psychological set. On the otherhand, the Clinical Approach techniques, which employ probable-lie control questions, use mostly Non-Exclusive control questions which are deliberately framed to include the relevant offense. (Horvath 1991). Clinicians reason that the inclusion of the crime period broadens the scope of the control question thereby increasing the likelihood of it being a lie by the truthful (innocent) examinee and further increases the examinee's concern about the accuracy of his/her answer to the control question.

The flaw in the reasoning offered by proponents of the Clinical Approach regarding the use of Non-Exclusive control questions is that since control questions are necessarily formulated to be in the same category of offense as the relevant questions, the guilty examinee may well choose the Non-Exclusive control question as a Relevant question because its scope does contain the crime for which he/she is being tested. Furthermore, the Non-Exclusive control question does not contain a time buffer between the time of the crime and the time covered by the control question(s) as found in the Exclusive control questions, therefore the Non-Exclusive control questions may not only contain the crime for which the deceptive (guilty) examinee is being tested, but also other similar crimes he may have recently committed, rendering the Non-Exclusive control question a significantly stronger threat to the deceptive (guilty) examinee than the relevant question against which it is being compared for a determination, thus a formula for false negatives.

Research Studies of Exclusive v. Non-Exclusive Control Questions

A review of the test structure employed by proponents of the Clinical Approach reveals that its two Non-Exclusive Control questions compete with four and five relevant questions, whereas proponents of the Numerical Approach such as the Backster and Matte Zone Comparison Techniques use only two relevant questions for comparison against their neighboring control questions. Yet this major distinction between the two test formats was overlooked by Horvath (1991) when he compared these two types of control questions to determine their effectiveness. Horvath, a dedicated researcher, used only the Non-Exclusive test format to test both types of control questions, and as expected, the two Exclusive control questions were overwhelmed by the five relevant questions on the same test. Another factor which reduced the strength and effectiveness of the two Exclusive control questions in Horvath's experiment was the use of the same age category for both Exclusive control questions, not a recommended practice (Matte 1993). But had Horvath also tested the Exclusive and Non-Exclusive control questions using the Exclusive control question format of two relevant questions compared against two controls or an equal number of each, he would have found a significant number of false negatives in that the Non-Exclusive control questions would have been too powerful for the two neighboring relevant questions. This view is supported by research conducted by Raskin, Barland, and Podlesny (1978) who reported the results of their comparison between the Backster (Exclusive) control questions, and the Reid (Nonexclusive) control questions, using the Exclusive control test format of three controls and three relevants, hence an equal number of comparative questions, stating "The tests using Backster control questions produced significant identification of innocent and guilty subjects. Quantitative analyses of physiological responses also produced some results which indicated a superiority for tests utilizing Backster control questions. As previously described, measures of skin conductance response recovery times and amplitude of negative skin potential responses showed stronger reactions to relevant questions by guilty subjects and to control questions by innocent subjects only with Backster control questions. The test which utilized Reid control questions showed no discrimination for either of those measures. Thus it appears that control questions which are separated from the relevant issue by age or time of occurrence have some advantages over control questions which do not have those exclusionary characteristics."

Defendability of Non-Exclusive Control Question

Furthermore, a case could be made against the defendability of the Non-Exclusive control question in a court of law where the truthfulness of a defendant is based on the defendant's consistently greater responses to the Non-Exclusive control questions than the relevant questions against which they were compared, by raising the point articulated above, that inasmuch as the Non-Exclusive control questions contain the crime as well as other offenses, the defendant could have identified the Non-Exclusive control question as a Relevant question imparting a greater threat to his/her well-being than the designated relevant question which dealt only with the current issue.

Objectivity of Quantification System

On the other hand, the Numerical Approach as used in aforementioned Zone Comparison techniques contains a numerical threshold which requires that the examinee produce reasonably consistent physiological responses to either the Exclusive control questions or the neighboring Relevant questions, but not to both questions, before a definite conclusion is rendered, thus avoiding errors. The numerical scores produced from the physiological data recorded on the polygraph charts represent the degree, strength, duration and consistency of physiological responses, to either the control questions indicative of truthfulness to the target issue, or the relevant questions indicative of deception. Hence, the stronger the score attained, the lesser the error rate expected and an increase in accuracy as the score increases. This scoring system provides the most objective and accurate analysis of the physiological data recorded on polygraph charts, and the required minimum score threshold provides an inconclusive safeguard against false positives and negatives. (Raskin, Barland, Podlesny 1978; Barland 1985; Matte, Reuss 1989, 1993).

Tasks Preceding Physiological Data Interpretation-Quantification

The reported high accuracy of the Numerical Approach does not imply that the FP has become nothing more than a "chart interpreter" as alleged by proponents of the Clinical Approach. (Jayne 1993). What it does mean is that all of the emotions and known variables affecting the physiological data recorded on polygraph charts have been factored into the examination process over a long evolutionary period of experimentation, which resulted in an objective, quantifiable procedure now known as the Numerical Approach. Approximately 90 percent of the examination process (some scientists place it at 99 percent (Reed 1992)) precedes the scoring of the polygraph charts, wherein the FP must review the case facts, apply an examination reliability rating estimate to determine numerically and objectively which issue being considered for testing contains the highest combined score for adequacy of case information, case intensity, and distinctness of issue, thereby eliminating those issues considered inadequate for testing, hence reducing the inconclusive rate. The FP must scientifically formulate relevant questions that avoid rationalization potential and undue mental exercise, and develop earlier-in-life exclusive control questions that are tailored to the relevant issue and the background of the examinee. The FP must conduct a complex pretest interview that identifies and/or eliminates undesirable variables, and establishes a proper psychological climate for the effective introduction of productive control questions. The FP must review each of the test questions with the examinee and insure proper interpretation through feedback before the administration of the actual test. Furthermore, the FP is responsible for conducting a spot analysis of the physiological data immediately after the conduct of each chart to determine whether each type of test question is functioning as designed, referring to his respective Reaction Combination Guide for remedial action as deemed necessary, and identify and counter any apparent examinee countermeasures, before administering the next polygraph chart in the same test. It can be readily seen from the above description of the FP's tasks that the duties prior to the final tally of the scores are enormous, requiring disciplined expertise. The manner in which the FP conducts those tasks determines the validity and reliability of the physiological data recorded on the charts. Therefore the FP who uses the Numerical Approach is not simply a chart interpreter, that's only a last function. The FP must have the required education, training and experience of a Forensic Psychophysiologist to administer the tasks which precede chart interpretation.

Research Into Verbal and Nonverbal Behaviors in the Decision Making Process

Proponents of the Clinical Approach (Arther 1980, Jayne 1993) advocate the use of verbal and nonverbal behaviors as an adjunct to the physiological data recorded on polygraph charts to arrive at a determination of truth or deception. However, research conducted by Drs. Raskin, Barland, and Podlesny revealed that "The predictions based upon the observation of behavior during the pretest phase of the polygraph examinations of criminal suspects were compared to the judgments of guilt or innocence made by a majority of the panel. The initial predictions agreed with the panel in 56 percent of the cases, and the later predictions agreed with the panel in 69 percent of the cases. Neither of those results was significantly above chance, indicating that systematic observation of behavior during the pretest phase of the polygraph examination was of no value in determining truth or deception." (Raskin, et al. 1978) Another study conducted under U. S. Department of Defense Grant #89-R-2323, 1990, by Dr. F. Horvath and B. Jayne, entitled "A Pilot Study of the Verbal and Nonverbal Behaviors of Criminal Suspects During Structured Interviews," Unpublished paper, revealed that the accuracy of nonverbal behaviors was dismal, about 52 percent, and overall accuracy was in the low seventieth percentile. (Capps 1994, Horvath 1994).

A recent study by Horvath, Jayne and Buckley (1994) to determine the effectiveness of trained evaluators in distinguishing truthful from deceptive suspects undergoing behavior Analysis Interviews, concluded that 78 percent of the judgments on actually truthful suspects were "truthful" decisions, 8 percent were erroneously found "deceptive" and 14 percent were "inconclusive." On deceptive suspects, the evaluators average 66 percent "deceptive" decisions, 17 percent were erroneously found "truthful" and 17 percent "inconclusive". Thus there were more false negatives than false positives. It should be noted that only larceny cases were included in this study, and even though they used well trained and highly experienced evaluators, they only obtained mediocre accuracy. Furthermore, research by Ekman and Sullivan (1991) indicates that there may be considerable variation in accuracy among those with a professional interest in the detection of deception from behavioral differences, hence another reason for our questioning its reliability. Horvath, et al's study established ground truth based on firm evidence (confession-verified) in only 41 percent of its cases. The remaining 59 percent of the cases used in their study were not confession-verified nor was there any other reasonably certain independent verification. In fact, "ground truth" in those cases (59%) was only established by systematic factual analysis. This author feels that the congruence between the outcome of the original Behavior Analysis Interview and the Evaluators' assessment of the suspects' truthfulness, revealed only a measure of the consistency between the original and subsequent evaluations, not the actual accuracy of the decisions. Inasmuch as the above study by Horvath, et al is based on the Behavior Analysis Interview which uses behavior-provoking questions, its relevance to the psychophysiological veracity examination is limited to its post-test interview, because such questions could arouse emotions known to cause undesirable variables affecting the examinee's psychological set and the inference process, hence should be avoided and not used during the pre-test interview nor during or between the administration of the psychophysiological veracity tests. This author believes that behavior-provoking questions are inconsistent with the presumption of innocence theme that should prevail throughout the administration of the psychophysiological veracity examination and comprise a subtle but unmistakable form of interrogation which even proponents of the Clinical Approach such as Reid and Arther have condemned. "At no time during the pretest interview should the examiner indulge in any interrogation aimed at determining the subject's deception or truthfulness, or at obtaining a confession of guilt"

(Reid 1977). "Especially important is that during the pretest interview I not only presume a person's truthfulness, but I believe that I know for sure he is truthful." (Arther 1982).

Use of Behavior-Provoking Questions

It was also suggested (Reed 1992) that behavior-provoking questions be used to arouse the guilty examinee's emotions such as guilt during the pretest interview. This author believes that this would be counterproductive for the reasons articulated above, and totally unnecessary. A thorough and proper non-accusatory pretest interview should convince the guilty examinee of the accuracy of the test, hence the imminent discovery of his/her guilt, thereby arousing his/her *fear* of detection. The success of this method is evidenced by the average score of minus 9 per chart for the deceptive-as-later-verified examinees (minimum -5 per chart required), and plus 6 per chart for truthful-as-later-verified examinees (minimum +3 per chart required), in the Matte-Reuss (1989) study involving one hundred and twenty-two confirmed cases (58 NDI, 64 DI).

Use of Auxiliary Information in Decision Process Usurps Function of the Court

A leading proponent of the Clinical Approach (Jayne 1993) suggests that an examinee's social history, opportunity, access, motivation, propensity, physical and circumstantial evidence, all be considered in forming an opinion as to truth or deception. However, to do so, would defeat the very purpose of the test, which is to furnish a separate, independent, objective evaluation which can be considered by the adjudicating authority who may weigh this evidence along with other evidence provided by investigators, expert and lay witnesses, etc. It is preposterous to presume that an FP can replace a judge and jury and make judgments as to guilt or innocence based on these criteria, without ever seeing the evidence or hearing the whole case. It is not the role of the FP to act as judge and jury. The expert FP prepares the examinee psychologically for the test, insuring that ideal conditions exist and variables known to affect the test have been eliminated or factored into the test, and that the test is administered objectively and its resulting charts quantified properly for an accurate, objective determination.

Effects of Merging Auxiliary Information with Physiological Data

From a scientific point of view, it seems absurd and illogical to augment the results of a technique that is for instance 95 percent accurate with another technique or method that is only 62.5 percent accurate (56% & 69% - Drs. Raskin, Barland, Podlesny 1978). By adding the two methods together you in effect realize a combined accuracy of only 78.7 percent, thus significantly reducing the accuracy by Global Evaluation.

Effects of Reliance on Auxiliary Information

This author (Matte) has observed that there is a tendency by many proponents of the Clinical Approach to underestimate the value of the physiological data recorded on the polygraph charts and rely rather heavily on auxiliary information including the examinee's verbal and non-verbal behavior during the pretest interview as well as between the administration of the polygraph charts. This should not be surprising in view of the statements quoted herein by its leading proponents but this appears to have a debilitating effect on the FP's ability at chart interpretation and confidence in its results. The effect of an accusatory or interrogative approach during any portion of the pretest interview or between the administration of the polygraph charts and tests can be disastrous to the innocent examinee's psychological set, and a sure-fire formula for false positive results.

Research Studies on the Effects of Other Variables in PV Examinations

Race

Critics argue that other variables such as an examinee's sex, education, number of previous arrests, age, race, physical condition, previous polygraph tests, etc., could affect the accuracy of PV examinations. A study conducted by Buckley and Senese (1991) on 1022 subjects who were administered specific issue polygraph examinations concluded that "After analyzing the frequency of truthful and deceptive opinions from specific issue examinations it was found that there were no statistical differences in polygraph results between Whites and Minorities."

Situational

The Department of Defense Polygraph Institute conducted research to assess situational variables and their effect on PV examination results. These variables included number of hours the subject had slept prior to the test; the subject's alertness during the test; the subject's general health; the subject's level of physical discomfort; the subject's use of alcohol, nicotine, and coffee prior to the test. In general the situational variables had little impact on test outcome. (U.S. Joint Security Commission Report 1994).

Gender, Age, Residence, Income, Education

The Department of Defense Polygraph Institute also conducted research to assess the effect the differences between recruits who are young, and in better shape than most people, but are often verging on exhaustion from their rigorous training, and the general civilian population recruited from communities near the Army base. The Institute compared polygraph outcomes from those populations on such variables as gender, age, urban or rural residence, income, and educational level. In general, these variables had little impact on PV examination outcome. (U.S. Joint Security Commission Report 1994).

Biographical and Personality

Furthermore, research conducted by Drs. Raskin, Barland and Podlesny (1978) revealed that "The subjects of the study of criminal suspects were also compared on a number of biographical and personality variables. Those comparisons were made for sex, education, number of previous arrests, religiousness, previous polygraph tests, age, and the MMPI scores for the lie scale, K-scale, hypochondriasis scale, and depression scale. There were no indications that any of those variables were related to the polygraph results."

Psychopathy

Raskin, et al., further investigated the problems associated with personality and psychopathy. 'The results were strongly contradictory to the common belief that psychopaths (sociopaths) can "beat the lie detector"' (Barland & Raskin, 1973. With convicted felons who were diagnosed psychopathic, not a single guilty subject was able to produce a truthful result. In fact, there were some indications that psychopaths may be somewhat easier to detect using polygraph examinations. The results with criminal suspects supported the position that deceptive psychopaths are as physiologically reactive and as readily detected as non-psychopaths. Thus, the fears that psychopathic criminals are able to be successful in deception during polygraph examinations can be dispelled. Perhaps the greatest danger is that a clever and convincing psychopath can talk a polygraph examiner into believing him, even though the polygraph charts indicate deception. Adequate training in chart interpretation and numerical scoring should prevent that from occurring."(Raskin, Barland, Podlesny 1978).

That last statement by Raskin, et al, was most prophetic when we consider the recent conviction of celebrated CIA spy Aldrich Ames who was administered a total of three periodic PV examinations by the CIA, using a multiple-issue test format employing the Clinical Approach (global evaluation). Ames' only advice by his Russian contact regarding his submission to a CIA PV examination was to be confident, remain calm, be friendly and make the FP think you like him. Ames' test charts contained physiological responses indicative of deception in all three PV examinations. When Ames failed the first test in 1986, the FP who interrogated him prepared a report for his superiors who simply shelved it. In 1991, he again failed a PV examination, was given a second one and failed again. But the FP for the CIA accepted Ames' explanation - that he was worried about his losing financial investments and that his concern had registered on the charts as deception. The FP concluded in his report that he didn't think Ames was a spy but did have money problems. (Kessler 1994, APA Newsletter 1994, Buffalo News 29 Apr 94). The FP for the CIA was deceived by Ames' verbal and non-verbal behavior. Interestingly, Ames showed no guilt or remorse when questioned in prison about his feelings for the ten intelligence agents who apparently lost their lives as a result of Ames' betrayal. Ames' psychological profile makes him a viable candidate as a sociopath. Ames' case provides proponents of the Numerical Approach with an excellent argument against the use of the Clinical Approach which relies on auxiliary information in their decision making process.

Empirical testimony

Albert D. Snyder, Senior Forensic Psychophysiologist for the Defense Investigative Service, Department of Defense, Past President of the American Polygraph Association, graduate of the Department of Defense Polygraph Institute, the Keeler Polygraph

Institute, and the FBI Academy, related to this author that as Chief of the Polygraph Division, Crime Records Center for the U. S. Army Criminal Investigations Command (C.I.D.) from 1976 to 1984 he supervised polygraph operations world-wide, including its Quality Control Unit which reviewed all polygraph examinations conducted by C.I.D. FP's world-wide. Quality Control FP's would first numerically score the polygraph charts for a determination as to truth or deception, without the influence of the case facts or test questions, then the test questions would be reviewed for assurance that they had been scientifically formulated, and if affirmative, the Quality Control Unit would form a conclusion based on the aforementioned polygraph chart interpretation and quantification. When the Quality Control Unit's conclusion differed with the original FP, a second chart quantification and test question review would be conducted by a member of the Quality Control Unit, and if both Quality Control Unit FP's conclusions were in agreement, the Quality Control Unit's final conclusion would prevail over the original FP who conducted the examination. The rate of return to the original FP for retest was about three percent, and in a significant number of these cases they were resolved through confession of the guilty and successful retesting of the innocent. Snyder opined that an FP who bases his conclusions on anything other than the numerical scores generated by the physiological data recorded on the polygraph charts is not a Forensic Psychophysiologist but merely an interrogator. The analysis of an examinee's verbal and non-verbal behavior may be useful in establishing rapport and proper controls during the pre-test interview, and may be of assistance in a post-test interview when the conduct of an interrogation is warranted, but should never be used in the formulation of a conclusion as to the truthfulness or deception of an examinee. Snyder's opinion should have special meaning to proponents of the Clinical Approach inasmuch as he is a member of Richard O. Arther's Academy of Certified Polygraphists, and is the author of a recent book (1994) entitled "Nonverbal Communication - An Investigator's Guide." Incidentally, the U. S. Army's Quality Control is now the model for all Federal agencies. (Snyder 1994).

This author recognizes that the aforementioned methodology is not employed in its pure form by all FP's who use the Numerical Approach, but it is hoped that the contents of this chapter will enlighten its critics and encourage FP's who seek an objective and independent means of verifying the truth and detect deception to employ its methodology and adopt its high standards.

REFERENCES

Abrams, S. (1989). *The Complete Polygraph Handbook.* Lexington, Massachusetts: Lexington Books.

Abrams. S. (1975). The Validity of the Polygraph Technique with Children. *Journal of Police Science and Administration,* 3(3), 310-311.

Abrams, S. (1995, Jun 8). Telephone Conversation with J. A. Matte.

Abrams, S. (1995, Jun 12). Audio tape review, comments and suggestion regarding instant thesis to J. A. Matte.

Ansley, N. (1990). The Validity and Reliability of Polygraph Decisions in Real Cases. *Polygraph*, 19(3), 169-181.

Ansley, N. (1992) Forensic Psychophysiology is in at DOD. *APA Newsletter*, 25(4), 11-12.

Ansley, N. (1993). Computerized 'Lie Detector' Scoring. *APA Newsletter*, 26(4), 3 July-August 1993.

Ansley, N. (1994). Polygraph Program, United States Department of Defense. *Polygraph*, 23(1), 61-84.

Ansley, N. (1994). Editorial "Aldrich Ames failed polygraph tests, results ignored." *APA Newsletter*, 27(2), Mar-Apr 94.

Ansley, N. (1995). Review notation on original manuscript '*Numerical versus Clinical Approach in Psychophysiological Veracity Examinations*' by J. A. Matte, 5 Oct 94.

Arellano, L.. R. (1990). The polygraph examination of Spanish speaking subjects. *Polygraph*, 19(2), 155-156. (abstract)

Arther, R. O. (1979). Observing Gestures, Part I. *The Journal of Polygraph Science*. Vol. XIV, Nr. 2, Sep-Oct 1979.

Arther, R. O. (1980). Observing Gestures, Part 4. *The Journal of Polygraph Science*. Vol. XIV, Nr. 5, Mar-Apr 1980.

Arther, R. O. (1982). Arther's Infamous Golden Rules. *The Journal of Polygraph Science*. Vol. XVI, Nr. 6. May-Jun 1982.

Backster, C. (1969). Technique Fundamentals of the Tri-Zone Polygraph Test. New York: *Backster Research Foundation.*

Backster, C. (1963/1979). Standardized Polygraph Notepack and Technique Guide: Backster Zone Comparison Technique. *Backster School of Lie Detection,* New York, N. Y.

Backster, C. (1974). Anticlimax Dampening concept. *Polygraph*, 3(1), 48-50.

Backster, C. (1994). 37th Annual Polygraph Examiner Work Conference Handout Notebook. San Diego, CA. 5-9 December 1994.

Bailey, F. L., Rothblatt, H. B. (1970). *Investigation and Preparation of Cases, Federal and State.* The Lawyers Cooperative Publishing Company, Rochester, N. Y.

Barland, G. H. (1985). A Method for Estimating the Accuracy of Individual Control Question Tests; Anti-Terrorism; Forensic Science; Psychology in Police Investigations. Proceedings of IDENTA-!85 *The International Congress on Techniques for Criminal Identification, Jerusalem, Israel: Heiliger and Company Limited* (1985): 142-147.

Barland, G. H. (1975). *Detection of Deception in Criminal Suspects: A Field Validation Study.* Unpublished dissertation. University of Utah.

Barland, G. H. (1995, Jun 5). Telephone conversation with J. A. Matte.

Berman, M. A. (1967). Drugs versus the polygraph. *The Journal of Polygraph Studies,* I (4): Jan-Feb 1967.

Berman, M. A. (1975). Prescription drugs and the polygraph. *Polygraph,* 4(4), 329-338.

Berry, R. L. (1960). *A Study of the Effect of Hypnotically Induced Amnesia Upon the Accuracy of the Lie Detector Test Results.* Lie Detector Committee, Department of Specialized Instruction. The Provost Marshal General's School, Fort Gordon, GA.

Bersh, P. J. (1969). A validation study of polygraph examiner judgments. *Journal of Applied Psychology.* 53, (5) 399-403.

Bitterman, E.M., Marcuse, F. L. (1945). Autonomic responses in post hypnotic amnesia. *Journal of Experimental Psychology.* 35:248-252.

Brisentine, R. A. (1974). Polygraph Research in the U. S. Army. *Polygraph,* 3(1), 66-80.

Brisentine, R. A. (1986). *Statement regarding inconclusive rate of polygraph examinations conducted by U. S. Army C.I.D.* Lecture at American Polygraph Association Seminar at Smuggler's North, Vermont. August 1986.

Brisentine, R. A. (1995, Oct 16). Telephone conversation with J. A. Matte.

Brisentine, R. A. (1995, Oct 19). Telephone conversation with J. A. Matte.

Brisentine, R. A. (1995, Nov 13). Telephone conversation with J. A. Matte.

Bryan, W. J., Jr. (1962). *Legal aspects of hypnosis.* Springfield, Illinois: Charles C. Thomas.

Buckley, J. P., Senese, L. C. (1991). The influence of race and gender on blind polygraph chart analysis. *Polygraph,* 20(4). 247-258.

Buffalo News Editorial. (1994, Apr 29). *Aldrich Ames Spy Case*.

Campbell, R. J. (1989). *Psychiatric Dictionary, Sixth Edition*. Oxford University Press, New York - Oxford.

Cannon, W. B. (1929). *Bodily Changes in Pain, Hunger, Fear, and Rage*. New York: Appleton.

Capps, M. H. (1991). Predictive value of the sacrifice relevant question. *Polygraph.* 20(l), 1-6.

Capps, M. H., Knill, B. L., Evans, R. K. (1993). Effectiveness of the Symptomatic Questions. *Polygraph,* 22(4), 285-298.

Capps, M. H. (1994, Sep 12, 16). Telephone conversation with J. A. Matte.

Cargill, R. V. (1989). United States v. Gipson: A leap forward or impetus for a step backward? *Polygraph*, 18(1), 33-42.

Carson, R. C., Butcher, J. N. (1992). *The World of Abnormal Psychology. A Special Edition of Abnormal Psychology and Modern Life*. Ninth Edition. Harper Collins Publishers, Inc. N.Y., N.Y.

Corcoran, J.F.T., Lewis, M.D., and Garver, R.B. (1978). Biofeedback Conditioned Galvanic Skin Response and Hypnotic Suppression of Arousal: A Pilot Study of their Reaction to Deception. *Journal of Forensic Science*. 23:155-162.

Corcoran, J.F.T., Wilson, D.H. (1979). Biofeedback Conditioned Responses and the Polygraph: A Case Report. *Polygraph,* 8(2). 120-126.

Cumley, W. E. (1959). Hypnosis and the Polygraph. *Police.*

Decker, R. E. (1995, Jun 13). Telephone Conversation with J. A. Matte.

Department of Defense (1984). *The Accuracy and Utility of Polygraph Testing.* Wash. D. C.

Ekman, P. (1985). *Telling Lies - A How-To-Guide for all Those Who Want to Detect Lies.* Berkley Books, New York. N. Y.

Ekman, P., O'Sullivan, M. (1991). Who Can Catch a Liar? *American Psychologist*. Sep. 1991, 913-919.

Ekman, P. (1980). The Face of Man. *Garland STPM Press.*

Ekman, P., Davidson, R. J., Friesen, W. V. (1990). The Duchene smile: Emotional expression and brain physiology II. *Journal of Personality and Social Psychology*, 58, 342-353.

Elaad, E., Schahar, E. (1985). Polygraph Field Validity. *Polygraph,* 14(3), 217-223.

Elaad. E., Bonwitt, G., Eisenberg, O., Meytes, I. (1982). Effects of Beta Blocking Drugs on the Polygraph Detection Rate: A Pilot Study. *Polygraph,* 11(3), 225-233.

Elaad E., Kleiner, M. (1986). The Stimulation Test in Polygraph Field Examinations: A Case Study. *Journal of Police Science and Administration.* 14(4), 328-333.

Gatchel, R. J., Smith, J. E., Kaplan, N. M., et al. (1983). *The Effect of Propanalol on Polygraphic Detection of Deception.* unpublished manuscript

Germann, A. C. (1961). Hypnosis as related to the scientific detection of deception by polygraph examination: A pilot study. *International Journal of Clinical and Experimental Hypnosis.* 9:309-311.

Golden, R. I. (1966). The Closed-Eyes Polygraph Technique. *Journal of Polygraph Studies.* I(2):1-4, Sep-Oct 1966.

Gouch, H. G. (1964). *Manual For the California Psychological Inventory.* Palo Alto; Consulting Psychologists Press

Harris, J. C. (1995, Jun 6). Telephone Conversation with J. A. Matte.

Honts, C. R. (1992). Bootstrap decision making for polygraph examinations. University of North Dakota, Grand Forks, ND, Grant #N000140-92-J-1794, Final Report, August 24, 1992. (Processed by PERSEREC and funded by DoDPI).

Horvath, F., Jayne, B. (1990). *A Pilot Study of the Verbal and Nonverbal Behaviors of Criminal Suspects During Structured Interviews.* Unpublished paper, U. S. Dept. of Defense Grant #89-R-2323.

Horvath, F., Jayne, B., Buckley, J. (1994). Differentiation of Truthful and Deceptive Criminal Suspects in Behavior Analysis Interviews. *Journal of Forensic Sciences.* 39(3), 793-807.

Horvath, F. (1991). The Utility of Control Questions and the Effects of Two Control Questions Tests on Field Polygraph Techniques. *Polygraph,* 20(1), 7-25.

Horvath, F. (1994). The Value and Effectiveness of the Sacrifice Relevant Question: An Empirical Assessment. *Polygraph*, 23(4), 261-279.

Horvath, F. (1994, Sep 12). Telephone Conversation with J. A. Matte.

Hunter, F. L. (1974). Anger and the Polygraph Technique. *Polygraph.* 8(4), 381-395.

Iacono, W. G., Boisvenu, G. A., Fleming, J. A. (1984). Effects of Diazepam and Methylphenidate on the Electrodermal Detection of Guilty Knowledge. *Journal of Psychology* 69: 189-299.

Iacono, W. G., Cerr, Am M., Patrick, C. J., Fleming, J. A. (1987). The Effect of Antianxiety Drugs on the Detection of Deception. *Psychophysiology* 24: 594 (abstract).

Janis, I. L., Mahl, G. F., Kagan, J., Holt, R. R. (1969). *From personality: Dynamics, development, and assessment*. New York: Harcourt Brace Jovanovich.

Jayne, B. C. (1989). *The Reid Control Question Technique*. Chapter 9 of the Complete Polygraph Handbook by Stan Abrams. Lexington Books, Lexington, Mass.

Jayne, B. C. (1993). The Use of Alternative Opinions in the Polygraph Technique. *Polygraph*. 22(4), 299-312.

Johnson, G. J. (1994). Information facsimile regarding APL Zone Scoring Results , Zone features, Algorithm Data, Scoring Weights and Response Intervals. U.S. Government Department of Defense, Office of Security Facsimile, 13 Oct 94 to Dr. James A. Matte.

Keeler, L. (1935). *Catching Criminals with the 'Lie Detector.'* Literary Digest.

Kessler, R. (1994, March 8). *Spies, Lies, Averted Eyes*. The New York Times. NY. NY

Kirby, S. L. (1981). The Comparison of Two Stimulation Tests and Their Effect on the Polygraph Technique. *Polygraph*. 10(2), 63-76.

Kircher, J. C., Raskin, D. C. (1988). Human vs computerized Evaluations of polygraph data in a laboratory setting. *Journal of Applied Psychology*, 73(2), 291-302.

Kircher, J. C., Raskin, D. C. (1989). *Computer-assisted polygraph systems, version 6.00 and 6.01 user's manual*, Scientific Assessments Technologies, Inc., 1865 Herbert Avenue, Salt Lake City, UT.

Kubis, J. F. (1962). *Studies in lie detection: Computer feasibility considerations*. Fordham University, New York, N. Y. RADC-TR-62205. Project No.5534,

AF30(602)-2270, prepared for Rome Air Development Center, Air Force Systems Command, USAF, Griffiss AFB, New York.

Larson, J. A. (1932). *Lying and its Detection.* Chicago: University of Chicago Press.

Lee, C. D. (1953). *The Instrumental Detection of Deception.* Springfield, Illinois: Charles C. Thomas.

Lykken, D. T. (1981). *A Tremor in the Blood: Uses and Abuses of the Lie Detector.* New York: McGraw-Hill Book Company.

Manners, R. M. (1994). Psychology for the Forensic Psychophysiologist. DoDPI presentation at the 29th Annual Seminar/Workshop of the American Polygraph Association, Nashville, TN.

Marcy, L. (1995, January). Telephone Conversation with J. A. Matte.

Matte, J. A. (1976). A Polygraph Control Question Validation Procedure. *Polygraph,* 5(2), 170-177.

Matte, J. A. (1977). A Case of Truth Serum Versus the Polygraph: Dissociative Neurosis - A Distinct Possibility. *Empire State Polygraph Society Newsletter.*

Matte, J. A. (1978). Polygraph Quadri-Zone Comparison Technique. *Polygraph,* 7(4), 266-280.

Matte, J. A. (1979). The Rights of the Examinee Polygraphed by a Law Enforcement Agency. *Polygraph,* 8(2). 150-154.

Matte, J. A. (1979). Privileged Communication between Attorney-Client-Polygraphist. *New York State Bar Journal.* 51(6), 466-469, 500-504.

Matte, J. A. (1980). A Technique for Polygraphing the Deaf. *Polygraph,* 9(3), 148-153).

Matte, J. A. (1980). *The Art and Science of the Polygraph Technique.* Charles C. Thomas - Publisher, Springfield, Illinois.

Matte, J. A. (1981). Polygraph Quadri-Zone Reaction Combination Guide. *Polygraph,* 10(3), 186-193.

Matte, J. A.. Reuss, R. M. (1989). A Field Validation Study of the Quadri-Zone Comparison Technique. *Polygraph,* 18(4), 187-202.

Matte, J. A., Reuss, R. M. (1989) Validation Study on the Quadri-Zone Comparison Technique. *Research Abstract,* LD 01452, Vol. 1502, 1989, University Microfilm International.

Matte, J. A., Reuss, R. M. (1990). A Field Study of the 'Friendly Polygraphist' Concept. *Polygraph,* 19(1), 1-9.

Matte, J. A., (1991). A Countermeasure That Failed, *APA Newsletter*, 24(4), 14-15.

Matte, J. A., Reuss, R. M. (1992). A Study of the Relative Effectiveness of Physiological Data in Field Polygraph Examinations. *Polygraph*, 21(1), 1-22.

Matte, J. A., Reuss, R. M. (1993). Predictive Tables for Estimating Accuracy and Error Rates in Single-Issue Control Question Tests. *The Truthseekers*, 5(3), 1-9.

Matte, J. A. (1993). Defense Access to Police Polygraph Tests. *New York State Bar Journal.* 65(5), 36-41.

Matte, J. A. (1993). The Review, Presentation and Assurance of Intended Interpretation of Test Questions is Critical to the Outcome of Polygraph Tests. *Polygraph,* 22(4), 299-312.

Medical Drug Reference (1994). Parsons Technology. CD-ROM Edition.

Moss Committee (1965). Committee on Government Operations, Tenth Report: *Use of Polygraphs as "Lie Detectors" by the Federal Government.* Union Ca. No. 88, House Report No. 198. Washington, U. S. Govt. Print Office, March 22, 1965.

Office of Technology Assessment (OTA). (1983). *Scientific Validity of Polygraph Testing - A Research Review and Evaluation.* Technical Memorandum for the Congressional Board of the 98th Congress of the United States, OTA-TM-H-15.

Olsen, D. E. (1995, Mar 8). Telephone Conversation with J. A. Matte.

Olsen, D. E. (1995, Apr 28). Telephone Conversation with J. A. Matte.

Orne, M. T. (1975). Implications of laboratory research for the detection of deception. In N. Ansley (ed.) *Legal Admissibility of the Polygraph.* Springfield, Illinois: Charles C. Thomas, 114-116.

Patrick, C.J., Iacono, W. G. (1987). Validity and Reliability of the Control Question Polygraph Test: A Scientific Invenstigation. *Psychophysiology*, 24, 604-605. (abstract)

Patterson, S. M., Krantz, D. S., Jochum, S. (1995). Time course and mechanisms of decreased plasma volume during acute psychological stress and postural change in humans. *Psychophysiology*, 32, 538-545.

Provost Marshal General's School. (1959). Lie Detector Committee: Preliminary Report on the Study of the Effect of Hypnotically Induced Amnesia upon the Accuracy of the Lie Detector Test Results. Fort Gordon. GA.

Raskin, D. C., Barland, G. H. Podlesny, J. A. (1978). Validity and Reliability of Detection of Deception. Washington, D. C.: *National Institute of Law Enforcement and Criminal Justice.*

Raskin, D. C., Kircher, J. C., Honts, C. R., Horowitz, S. W. (1988, May). A study of the validity of polygraph examinations in criminal investigation. *Final Report to The National Institute of Justice,* Grant No. 85-IJ-CX-0040. Department of Psychology, University of Utah, Salt Lake City, Utah.

Raskin, D. C., Kircher, J. C., Honts, C. R., Horowitz, S. W. (1988). Valitidy of Control Question Polygraph Tests in Criminal Investigation. *Psychophysiology*, 25(4), 474. (abstract)

Rathus, S. A. (1994). *Essentials of Psychology*. Fourth Edition. Harcout Brace College Publishers, Fort Worth, TX.

Reed, S. (1992, July). *Physiological Control.* Videotaped Lecture at the American Polygraph Association Seminar, Orlando, Florida.

Reed, S. (1992), July). So Why does this *?!* Work? Videotaped Lecture at the American Polygraph Association Seminar, Orlando, Florida.

Reed, S. (1992, July). *Who's right - Researchers or Examiners?* Videotaped Lecture at the American Polygraph Association Seminar, Orlando, Florida.

Reed, S. (1992, July) *What We Measure and How.* Videotaped Lecture at the American Polygraph Association Seminar, Orlando, Florida.

Reed, S. (1992, July) *Psychophysiological Principles.* Videotaped Lecture at the American Polygraph Association Seminar, Orlando, Florida.

Reed, S. (1992, July). *There's No Lie Response? So What?* Videotaped Lecture at the American Polygraph Association Seminar, Orlando, Florida.

Reed, S. (1992, July) *Are We Behind the times?* Videotaped Lecture at the American Polygraph Association Seminar, Orlando, Florida.

Reid, J. E., Inbau, F. E. (1977). *Truth and Deception*, 2nd Ed. Baltimore, MD: The Williams & Wilkins Company.

Relier, A. S. (1985). *The Penguin Dictionary of Psychology*. Penguin Books, N.Y. N. Y.

Schwartz, J. R. (1994, Oct 5). Telephone Conversation with J. A. Matte.

Snyder, A. (1994, Sep 12, Oct 5). Telephone Conversations with J. A. Matte.

Snyder, A. (1994). *Nonverbal Communication - An Investigator's Guide*. Severna Park, MD: JKP Publication Services.

Summers, W. G. (1939). Science can get that confession. *Fordham Law Review*. 8: 334-354.

U. S. Joint Security Commission Report. (1994). Redefining Security, A Report to the Secretary of Defense and the Director of Central Intelligence: Includes Polygraph Considerations. *Polygraph*, 23(1), 1-23.

Waid, W. M., Orne, E. C., Cook, M.R., Orne, M. T. (1981). Meprobamate Reduces Accuracy of Physiological Detection of Deception. *Science* 212:71-73.

Waid, W. M., Orne, M. T. (1982). The Physiological Detection of Deception. *American Scientist*. 70:402-409.

Weinstein, E., Abrams, S., and Gibbons, D. (1970). The validity of the polygraph with hypnotically induced repression and guilt. *American Journal of Psychiatry*. 126:1159-1162.

Widaki, J. (1982). *Analiza Przestanek Diagnozowania w. badanich poligraficznych*. (The analysis of diagnostic premises in polygraph examinations. Uniwersytetu Slaskiego, Katowice. (text in Polish)

Whitman, C. P. (1989). United States v. Gipson: Out of the Frye pan into the fire. *Polygraph*, 18(1), 24-32.

Chapter 10

THE CONTROL-STIMULATION TEST

During the pretest interview, every effort is made to allay any fears the innocent examinee may have regarding the accuracy of the outcome of the psychophysiological veracity (PV) examination, by explaining the scientific principles involved in the test, the sophistication of the instrument, and the complete objectivity of chart analysis through a numerical quantification system or computer algorithm. However, the best pretest interview by the most competent forensic psychophysiologist may sometimes fail to convince an examinee of the accuracy and reliability of the PV examination. In these cases, an innocent examinee may be concerned that the test may reflect that he/she lied to the relevant or crime questions, which in turn will cause the relevant questions to become a threat to his/her well-being. This threat will be competing with the control (probable-lie) questions rendering the charts more difficult to analyze and in some cases inconclusive findings may result.

The *Stimulation* test is designed to reassure the innocent examinee of the accuracy of the test and of the competency of the forensic psychophysiologist administering the PV examination. It also serves to stimulate the guilty examinee. But the Stimulation test further serves as a *Control* test to establish the examinee's capability and manner of response to a known lie under *controlled* conditions. (Hickman 1978, Lovvorn 1978). It can further serve to identify a *Spot Responder* or prove the falsity of such a claim by a deceptive examinee. (Decker 1996)

The theory of the Stimulation test postulates that once the innocent examinee is reassured that he/she will be found innocent of the crime for which he/she is being examined, his/her concern or psychological set will be focused strictly on the control questions to which he/she is lying. The forensic psychophysiologist (FP) then may expect clear charts showing consistency of response to the control questions and a comparative absence of response to the relevant questions. On the other hand, by convincing the guilty examinee through the use of the stimulation test of the accuracy of the test and competency of the FP, the guilty examinee will become more fearful of the discovery of his/her lie to the relevant questions and his/her psychological set will be focused directly on the crime questions, which are now definitely more threatening to his/her well-being, dampening out any concern over the control questions, due to anticlimax dampening as explained in Chapters 8 and 9. The stimulation test will in effect stimulate the guilty to more pronounced reactions on the relevant questions thereby producing clearer, more distinct charts due to anticlimax dampening of the control questions responses.

The lack of uniformity in the research construct and analog model of the various studies conducted on the Stimulation test have not surprisingly produced varied results. Ellson, Davis, Saltzman and Burke (1952) reported that examinees whose deception was detected, and who were informed of this, were actually more difficult to correctly evaluate on subsequent tests. Whereas Gustafson and Orne (1963) found a tendency, although not statistically significant, for motivated subjects to be more difficult to accurately diagnose in later tests. Those examinees who had not been given any feedback or who had been told that their deception had been discovered, demonstrated no change in detectability. In a follow-up study, Gustafson and Orne (1965) indicated that "successful detection maximizes subsequent detection." Another study conducted by Barland and Raskin (1972) reflected limited success in establishing the validity of the Stimulation test, stating "The manipulation of feedback on the card test failed to produce a reliable effect regarding detection of guilt or innocence." (Abrams 1978). A study on the "Effect of the Location of the Numbers Test on Examiner Decision Rates" by Widup and Barland (1992) revealed that the location of the numbers test had no apparent practical effect on the distribution of FP's decisions, but cautioned that the lack of ground truth and experimental control in real-life cases makes it difficult to draw firm conclusions. (see also Elaad & Kleiner 1986).

However, a field study by Louis Senese (1978) involving thirty (30) polygraph records from actual investigative cases which were equally divided with fifteen confirmed deceptive subjects and fifteen confirmed truthful subjects all of whom had been administered the Reid False Unknown Solution Stimulation test as the second chart following the first relevant test, were reviewed by seven staff FPs of John E. Reid and Associates who averaged 3.9 years of experience.

Senese's experiment was divided into two phases. In the first phase the seven FPs were given the first chart administered prior to the Stimulation test from the thirty verified cases used. The FPs were instructed individually to review each separate chart and state their opinion as to whether the subject was truthful or deceptive, or whether the test responses were inconclusive.

One month later the second and final phase of this experiment was completed. In this phase the same seven FPs were given the individual charts that immediately followed the Stimulation test. Each FP was instructed to interpret the records but was not informed as to the accuracy of his interpretation regarding the first one he had examined. As a final restriction, the project FPs were not allowed to see any of the Stimulation test charts. In fact, the FPs did not have any knowledge that a card test had been administered.

The results of aforementioned study revealed that the accuracy in correctly detecting deceptive subjects and identifying truthful subjects in the first chart was 55.7 percent. However, after the Stimulation test, the accuracy in the third chart rose to 71.4 percent, increasing the level of accuracy by 28.2 percent. Incorrect judgments of identifying truthful subjects as deceptive, or deceptive subjects as truthful was 13.3 percent in the first chart evaluation. Incorrect judgment of truthful subjects as deceptive and deceptive subjects as truthful in the third chart evaluation decreased to 9 percent, reducing errors by 32.3 percent. The inconclusive rate, which is the percentage of cases in which an FP could not evaluate a subject as being truthful or deceptive due to erratic or inconsistent responses, was 20.5 percent on the first chart evaluation. Results on the third chart evaluation after the card test showed a reduction to 14.3 percent for the inconclusive rate, reflecting a 30.2 percent decrease in inconclusive results. Senese also measured subject unresponsiveness, the lack of significant emotional disturbances on the relevant, irrelevant or control questions. On the first chart 10.5 percent of the FP's opinions were that the subjects were unresponsive. Results of unresponsiveness on the third chart evaluation decreased to 5.13 percent, yielding a 49.5 percent reduction in unresponsive results.(Senese (1978)

A field research (Matte, Reuss 1989) involving 122 confirmed actual criminal cases investigated the effect of the Stimulation test, traditionally administered as the second chart (after the first relevant chart), on the relevant chart following the Stimulation test compared to the first relevant chart, and further investigated the effect of the Stimulation test when administered as the first chart before the administration of any of the relevant test charts. In addition, the countertrend scores of subjects who were not administered a Stimulation test were also considered and reported. In the aforesaid study, the Quadri-Track Zone Comparison Technique was used by two separate polygraph agencies employing the Known-Solution Stimulation test and the True Unknown Solution Stimulation Test. In the Quadri-Track ZCT, each test or chart has nine separate spots that are scored; three in the pneumograph tracing, three in the galvanic skin resistance/conductance, and three in the cardiograph tracing. A minimum of two charts are required to reach a conclusion and as many as four charts are conducted. Therefore two charts offer 18 spots and three charts offer 27 spots for scoring. It is therefore not unusual for one or more spots to produce a score that does not follow the general trend consistent with ground truth, and these renegade scores are usually not strong enough to weaken the total tally of the general trend scores normally consistent with ground truth, into an Inconclusive or False Positive/Negative conclusion. It is imperative however that countertrend scores be kept to a minimum.

In examining the countertrend scores, scores that do not follow the true trend as later established by ground truth, it was found that in the Innocent cases, 20 subjects were administered the Stimulation Test after the conduct of the first relevant chart, experiencing a total countertrend score of -124 which averages -6.2 per subject, whereas the 6 subjects who were administered the Stimulation Test as the first chart before the conduct of the first relevant chart experienced a total countertrend score of -29 which averages -4.8 per subject. The 32 subjects which were not administered a Stimulation test nevertheless experienced a countertrend score of -142 averaging -4.4 per subject. For the Guilty (as later verified) subjects, 40 examinees were administered the Stimulation test after the first relevant chart for a total countertrend score of +110 averaging +3.0 versus 20 Guilty examinees who were administered the Stimulation test as the first chart with a total countertrend score of +39 averaging +2.0 countertrend per Guilty examinee, while 4 Guilty subjects who were not administered a Stimulation had a total countertrend score of +4 averaging +l per subject. (Matte, Reuss 1989, amended)

The above data suggests that the Innocent examinee is the most vulnerable to countertrend scores. There was no statistical difference in countertrend scores between those Innocent examinees who were not administered a Stimulation test and those Innocent examinees that were administered a Stimulation test as the first chart (-4.4 vs -4.8 respectively). However there was some statistical difference between Innocent examinees that were administered the Stimulation test after the first relevant chart (-6.2) and those Innocent examinees that were not administered a Stimulation test (-4.4). The Guilty cases show significantly lower overall countertrend scores but nevertheless showed the same trend of +l for Guilty examinees who were not administered a Stimulation test, +2 for those Guilty examinees who were administered a Stimulation test as the first chart, and +3 for those Guilty examinees who were administered a Stimulation test as the second chart. It would thus appear that the administration of the Stimulation test as the first chart causes no statistically significant increase in countertrend scores, while its administration as the second chart causes a moderate increase in countertrend scores. However, we must take into consideration the rather small number of Innocent cases (6) administered the Stimulation test as the first chart, versus 20 cases involving second chart Stimulation tests in evaluating the aforementioned data. Furthermore the statistical differences are mild. Further research in this area is certainly warranted. But the aforesaid Senese field study clearly shows a statistically significant increase in accuracy (28.2%), reduction in errors (32.3%), decrease in inconclusives (30.2%), and a reduction in unresponsive results of 49.5 percent, when the Stimulation test is administered.

Anecdotally, this author has personally observed over a period of two and a half decades of administering all types of PV examinations that when properly administered, the Stimulation test is a most useful tool in reassuring the innocent and stimulating the guilty examinee thus enhancing the selective attention process resulting in higher quality polygraph chart data.

The logic of administering the Stimulation test as the first test or chart (rather than as the second chart) does not escape the astute examinee, especially the innocent who may wonder why a test purportedly designed to determine the examinee's suitability for the test is being administered after the first relevant chart has already been conducted. The ensuing potential arousal of the examinee's fear of error regarding the first test or chart can only be felt by the Innocent subject, inasmuch as the Guilty examinee hopes that an error will be made on his/her test. Furthermore, the administration of the Stimulation test as the first test affects all relevant test charts equally, and provides the FP with a Control Test of the examinee's capability and manner of response with an opportunity of making necessary adjustments prior to the conduct of the relevant tests. Since completion and publication of the 1989 Matte-Reuss research on this topic, this author has been administering the Stimulation test as the first chart with continued success.

There are several different types of Stimulation tests, each with its own methodology of application. Those most widely used are described below. Some polygraph schools such as the Backster School of Lie Detection leave the use of the Stimulation test to the discretion of the forensic psychophysiologist, while others have a specific Stimulation test structure and method of application.

Since 1966, the U. S. Army Polygraph School has taught the use of a Stimulation test as a control procedure for use with the Zone Comparison Technique (ZCT), the Modified General Question Technique (MGQT), the General Question Technique (GQT), and Screening Tests (ST), but excludes the Peak of Tension Tests (POT). The US Army initially used the *Reid False Unknown-Solution Stimulation* test in the first position or as the first chart, although Reid recommended its use in the second position, but quickly changed to a Known-Solution Stimulation test format to avoid potential criticism from the use of marked cards and other trickery. In 1967, Ronald E. Decker, Director of the U.S. Army Polygraph School conducted experiments using the Stimulation test in the second position or as the second chart to observe the effects of the Stimulation test from the first relevant chart to the second relevant chart with the Stimulation test in between them. Decker found that the Stimulation test made no difference in PV examinations which had an effective pretest interview, but the Stimulation test had the effect of correcting the effects of poor pretest interviews. Henceforth, the U.S. Army Polygrah school adopted the *Known-Solution* Stimulation Test, administered as the second chart. That is, the examinee and the FP both know the number that is selected by the examinee and the examinee is fully aware that the FP also knows the number. (Decker 1996)

The aforementioned Stimulation test as taught by the U. S. Army Polygraph School and now by the Department of Defense Polygraph Institute is a Peak of Tension test in which the number is openly selected by the examinee. It is left to the discretion of the agencies who send their student FPs to the DoDPI as to whether the Stimulation test is administered as the first or second test (chart) (Weinstein 1996). However, if the examinee declares that he/she does not believe in the polygraph, the technique, or the forensic psychophysiologist, or the examinee brags that he has defeated another forensic psychophysiologist, then the Stimulation test is administered as the first chart. (Decker 1978).

The examinee is explained that this chart (Stimulation test) is to determine with certainty that the polygraph instrument is properly adjusted to the examinee. The examinee is then asked to select a number between 3 and 7, and write that number with a felt tip pen in a large figure on sheet of paper. The examinee is further instructed to write the number with his non-dominant hand, to assure memory of the selected number. This sheet of paper is then hung on the wall in front of the examinee at eye level. The examinee is then instructed to deny having selected the number appearing in front of him/her when it is mentioned in a series of numbers. If the selected number is 5, the list is 3, 4, 5, 6 and 7. If the examinee has picked 3, 4, 6 or 7, a buffer of two numbers is placed on each side of the selected number. Thus the total number of stimuli is five, to which the examinee gives four truthful answers and one lie. The forensic psychophysiologist may use a series of seven numbers instead of five if the examinee displays excessive nervousness or deliberate muscular movements during the first relevant chart.

The Stimulation test is given once, in sequence, with twenty-second intervals. The electrodermal component is employed in the manual mode so that the baseline trend is available. If a relevant chart has already been conducted, the cardio and pneumo channels remain at those settings that were satisfactory for the first relevant chart. The chart interpretation rules are those for the peak of tension in which the FP considers anticipatory, specific and relief responses. The Stimulation test begins with a preparatory question: "Regarding the number you wrote," followed by the series of questions regarding the numbers: "Did you write the number three?" "Did you write the number four?" "Did you write the number five?" "Did you write the number six?" "Did you write the number seven?" It should be noted that the preparatory question is asked only once, at the beginning of the test. The selected number is placed near the middle of the series.

The U.S. Army or DoDPI Stimulation test is a *Known-Solution* test which involves no trickery. The series is read only once, and when the physiological arousal is obvious, the chart is shown to the examinee. The purpose is to instill confidence in the polygraph technique which gives the truthful more confidence and creates more specific responses among the deceptive. It is a control procedure which has proven its value as an adjunct to all standardized government techniques. Additionally, the Known-Solution Stimulation test is useful in identifying a Spot Responder, or proving the falsity of such a claim by a deceptive examinee. (Decker 1978).

A *Fail-Proof Blind Numbers Stimulation* test reported by Dr. Gordon H. Barland who stated that he borrowed all the vital parts of this test from other forensic psychophysiologists, is described as follows. As in the U. S. Army's Known-Solution Stimulation test, the subject in this test also knows there can be no trickery, hence it is a *True Unknown Solution Stimulation test*. However, when the FP does not identify the correct number, the test nonetheless has the desired effect because the subject doesn't realize that the FP missed the correct number. (Barland 1978).

This Fail-Proof Blind Numbers Stimulation test (FPBNS) is usually administered as the second chart, after the first relevant chart. The examinee is informed that before a second relevant chart is conducted, he is going to be administered a short test completely unrelated to the target issue. The examinee is then asked to choose a number between 2 and 6 but not to divulge it to the FP. The examinee is then asked to write the selected number on a piece of paper provided by the FP who turns his/her back to the examinee while the examinee writes the number on the paper and is then instructed to fold the piece of paper in half and tuck it under his/her leg. Now facing the examinee, the FP instructs the examinee to answer all test questions in the negative, including the question number he wrote on the piece of paper, thus eliciting a lie from the examinee. The examinee is further instructed that the questions will be asked the first time in sequence, but the second time out of sequence, in a random order, then the examinee will be given some new instructions which he/she must follow, all while having his/her physiology recorded on the polygraph chart. (Barland 1978)

The test is then administered as follows:

Jim, regarding the number you just wrote down on that piece of paper tucked under your leg, did you write the number 1?

Did you write the number 2?
Did you write the number 3?
Did you write the number 4?
Did you write the number 5?
Did you write the number 6?

I'm going to repeat the numbers now, in a random order; continue to answer 'no' to all questions.

Did you write the number 6?
Did you write the number 4? (FP's first choice)
Did you write the number 2?
Did you write the number 3? (FP's second choice)
Did you write the number 5?

The examinee is now given the following instructions:

Jim, here are the new instructions I mentioned. I want you now to answer all questions truthfully, with either a yes or a no, depending upon what the actual truth is. Do you understand? (Upon acknowledgment of understanding, the FP continues)

Did you choose the number 4? (FP's first choice)

If the examinee answers above question in the affirmative, the FP immediately terminates the test. The examinee is then asked for the slip of paper containing the selected number, which the FP verifies, then studies the FPBNS test chart intently for a few seconds, then informs the examinee that he/she now knows exactly how the examinee's body reacts when he/she is telling the truth and also when they are lying (with emphasis on the truth). All of the aforementioned numbers tests are conducted on one chart at slightly lower cuff pressure than used during the relevant tests to minimize discomfort.

A misdiagnosis of the selected number is handled in the following manner:

When the examinee gives a negative answer to the first choice, the test continues but the FP places the Second choice at the end of the test sequence, in the following manner:

Did you choose the number 4? No.
Did you choose the number 5? No.
Did you choose the number 6? No.
Did you choose the number 1? No.
Did you choose the number 2? No.
(Pause).

"You have undoubtedly observed that I have repeated all of the numbers, except for one. I will now ask you that one number. Did you choose the number 3?" If the examinee gives an affirmative answer, the test is immediately terminated and the procedure as described for the correct selection of the first choice is applied. (Barland 1978)

When the examinee provides an affirmative answer to a question not anticipated by the FP, the sequence described above is continued, except that the comment about omitting one number is not mentioned. Should the examinee query the FP about his/her knowledge or lack thereof of the correct number, Barland recommends that the FP reply that he/she will be happy to go over the results of the tests as soon as all of the testing is completed. Following completion of the examination, the FP should bring up the numbers test, indicate that he/she had not known what number the examinee had selected, and debrief the examinee concerning the tests. Barland opined that occasionally such a result is due to countermeasures, and the resulting information increases the FP's competence in administering and interpreting such tests. (Barland 1978).

The Reid Stimulation test is a *False Unknown Solution Stimulation test,* inasmuch as the forensic psychophysiologist, unknown to the examinee, knows before the completion of the Stimulation test which card number the examinee has selected, by prior manipulation of the cards. The justification for this duplicity is that this test is a *control test* where ground truth must be known by the FP prior to the administration and completion of the test in order to discern and thwart invited attempts at countermeasures and identify and stimulate non-responsive examinees. In fact, one of the purposes of this test is to invite deceptive examinees to engage in acts of purposeful noncooperation by distorting their tracings during the test, thus providing additional, auxiliary information useful to clinicians who employ global evaluation. (Reid, Inbau 1966)

The Reid False Unknown Solution Stimulation test is routinely administered as the second chart, after the administration of the first relevant chart. Either five or seven card numbers may be used, such as 5, 3, 10, 8, and 12, or 5, 8, 12, 15, 8, 6, 3. Reid considers distortion attempts during a card test, a refusal to acknowledge the chosen card, an affirmative answer to the chosen card during the test, or his/her refusal to acknowledge his/her card when identified, as a reliable indication of deception. However Reid cautions that sole reliance should not be placed upon any one of these stratagems inasmuch as exceptions, although exceedingly rare, have been known to occur.(Reid, Inbau 1966).

This author has been using either the Known-Solution Stimulation (KSS) test or a True Unknown Solution Stimulation (TUSS) test with a False Unknown Solution Stimulation (FUSS) test backup for those rare instances when the TUSS test fails to identify the correct card number after two attempts. The KSS test used by this author is identical to that taught and utilized by DoDPI. In most instances this author uses the TUSS test with the FUSS test as backup. The procedure for its administration is as follows:

The TUSS test is always used as the first chart, preceding the first relevant test. Before the TUSS test is introduced to the examinee, all of the test questions of the first relevant test must first have been reviewed with the examinee and the examinee has moved from the interview chair to the polygraph examination chair where all of the polygraph instrument components have been placed on his/her person and a short acquaintance chart has already been conducted to accustom the examinee to the testing environment and to acquire a preliminary chart depicting the examinee's normal physiological tracing patterns. At this point the examinee expects the first relevant test chart to be administered, but instead he/she is informed that a *Sensitivity test* will first be administered to determine his/her capability and manner of response to a known lie. The examinee was explained during the pretest interview the function of the polygraph instrument in recording on the displayed polygraph chart physiological evidence of sympathetic and parasympathetic activity, and that 20 seconds will transpire between his answer to a test question and the beginning of the next question for all test questions on the test, to allow both of those systems to manifest themselves on the polygraph chart if they do activate. The examinee is now reminded that this test will provide physiological evidence of his/her sympathetic and parasympathetic systems to a known lie, as well as his/her truthful patterns. This preamble makes the TUSS test important to both the Guilty and Innocent as later verified subjects, inasmuch as it causes the Guilty examinee to *fear* the correct selection of his/her card number, because it indicates and reinforces the FP's ability to detect the Guilty examinee's lies to the crime questions. Some deceptive examinees may also *fear* the correct selection of their card number because of a preconceived notion that the FP will then be able to compare his/her lie response on the Stimulation test to his/her response(s) on the actual crime test. Conversely, the Innocent examinee will *fear* an incorrect selection of his/her card number because it would be indicative of the FP's inability to establish his/her innocence, hence a *fear of error*, which should be extinguished following the correct identification of the selected number.

An additional element may be introduced into the TUSS test preamble. The examinee may be told that the *Sensitivity test* will be administered to insure that the polygraph instrument is adjusted exactly to his/her sensitivity, not to the person tested before him/her. Further, that there is a chance, one in a hundred, that he/she may not be a testable subject that day or perhaps ever, due to some physiological impairment or other element not necessarily known to the examinee. A Guilty subject's self-preservation instinct will immediately focus his/her attention to this one in one hundred chance of not being discovered in his/her lie to the relevant question(s) by virtue of not being a testable subject. This then has the effect of making the stimulation test quite important to the Guilty examinee. In this fashion we have succeeded in introducing "fear of detection" into an otherwise innocuous test.

The examinee is then shown six cards, each containing a different number, usually numbers 3, 5, 8, 10, 12, 15, with the reverse side of the cards being blank. The numbers 7 and 13 should not be used because the overly superstitious examinee who accidentally selects one of these two numbers may believe that the FP selected the right number because he "knew" that the examinee would select that number or else the FP was able to see his overt, obvious reaction to the selection of such a meaningful number.

The cards are shuffled in the presence of the examinee, after which they are spread face down before the examinee who is then asked to select one card, memorize the number on the card selected, then place that card face down underneath one of his/her thighs (subject is seated).The remaining cards are then given to the examinee face down for him/her to examine as insurance that all of the cards bear a different number. The examinee is then requested to place these cards face down underneath his/her other thigh. Now the examinee has custody of all the cards. Since many FPs including this author use the closed-eyes technique, which requires that the examinee keep his/her eyes closed during the actual test when his/her autonomic nervous system is being monitored and recorded by the polygraph instrument, it is imperative that the examinee have custody of all the numbered cards during the stimulation test as assurance that the FP did not peek at the cards while the examinee's eyes are closed. It is further imperative that the card selected by the examinee be placed face down under one leg and the remaining cards be placed face down underneath the other leg, so that the examinee is not able to lie about the card he/she selected upon completion of the test. Prior to the adaptation of this procedure, some guilty (as later verified) examinees deliberately lied to the FP about the number they had selected in an attempt to sabotage the test, to create doubt in the FP's mind about the testability of the examinee. This required the administration of a second stimulation test, which resulted in the same countermeasure on the part of the examinee unless the FP was astute enough to segregate the card selected from the others.

The examinee, now in possession of all the numbered cards laying face down underneath his/her thighs, is ready to be administered the test. The examinee is of course in a sitting position in the polygraph chair with all sensors attached to the various areas of the body. The examinee is instructed to answer "no" to every question on the test, including the card he/she selected, which means that he/she will be lying to one numbered card on the test. After explaining this procedure to the examinee, he/she is then asked if he/she will be telling a little lie or a big lie. After his/her response, he/she will be advised that it is in fact just a little lie because he/she has nothing to lose by lying to a number. Nevertheless, his/her sympathetic and parasympathetic systems should activate even to that little lie, therefore, the FP will know the examinee's minimum capability of response.

The FP then proceeds with the test using the following format: Did you select card number 1? (Orienting number, not included in the choices); did you select card number 3?; did you select card number 5?; did you select card number 8?; did you select card number 10?; did you select card number 12?; did you select card number 15? No other questions except for the aforementioned card numbers should be inserted into this test. Upon identification of the number selected by the examinee, the FP should immediately mark that question on the chart by placing a half moon sign under the number in question.

The examinee should then be advised of the results of the test and asked for the card selected plus other cards. If the test is videotaped, the identified card should be received from the examinee and held in an unobtrusive manner for its number to be recorded on video.

If the test is successful, the FP will often witness elation, delight, a smile reflecting reassurance, from the innocent (as later verified) examinee. On the other hand, the FP will witness a worried look, anxiety, an attitude of defeat often depicted by the bowing of the head, the chin resting on the chest, staring at the floor, by the guilty (as later verified) examinee. The FP should never comment on these observations. The FP should however leave the examination room for a few minutes, leaving the examinee alone to reflect on the ramifications of the results of the Stimulation test. At this point a closed circuit television or one-way mirror is of value to the Clinical FP in observing the examinee's gestures and demeanor. Following the Stimulation test, no further comment should be made about the results to the examinee. The specific test should then proceed with the administration of the first relevant test chart.

An additional benefit of the Stimulation test provides an opportunity for the FP to make necessary instrument sensitivity adjustments in preparation for the first chart of the specific relevant test.

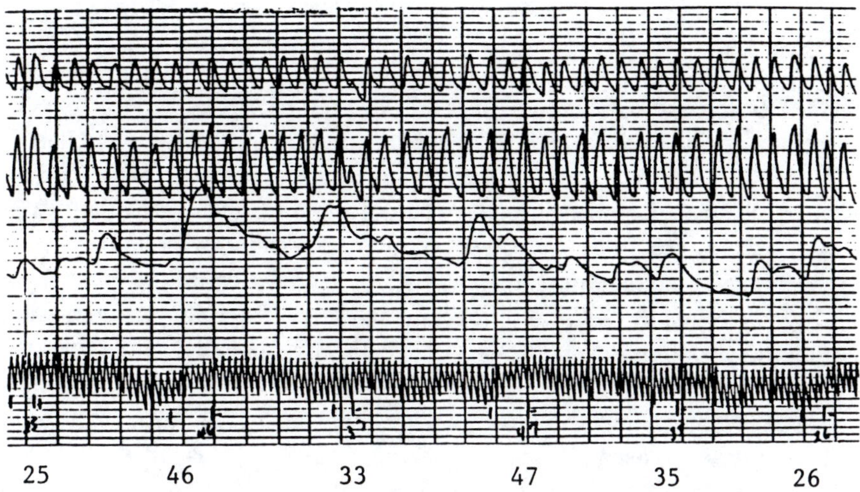

Backster Zone Comparison Test # 1 - Burglary Case

Figure X-1

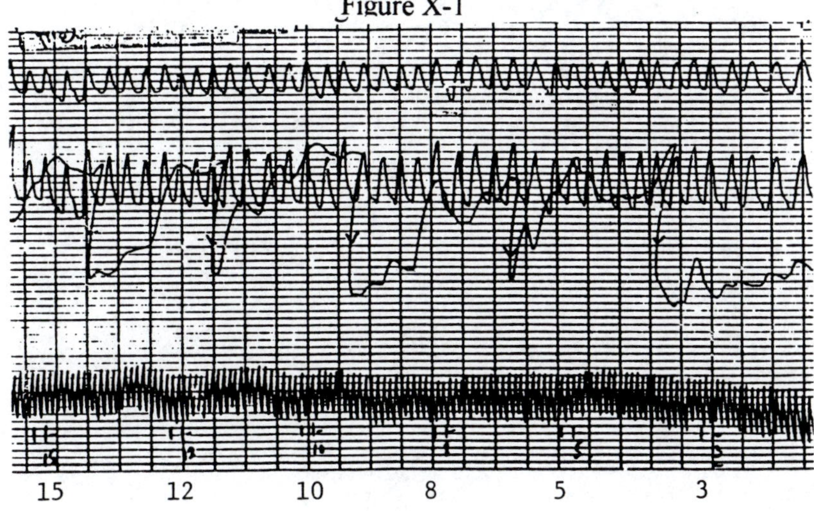

Figure X-2

Control-Stimulation Test Chart on Burglary Suspect

Backster Zone Comparison-Chart #3-burglary Case

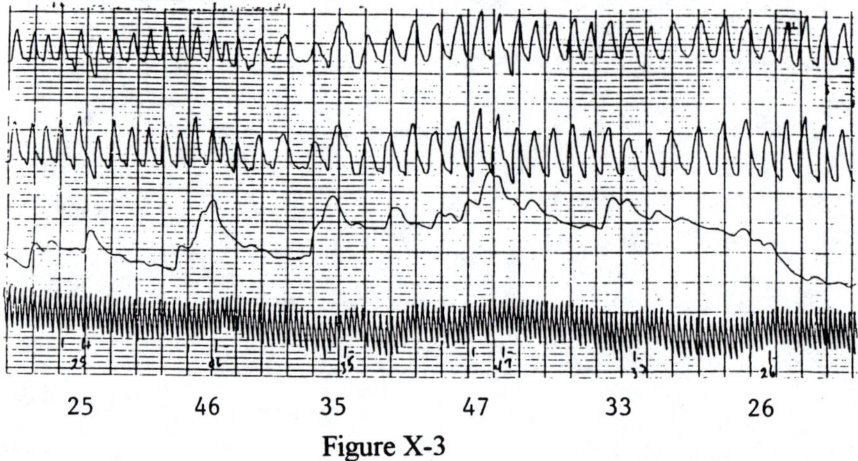

Figure X-3

Figures X-l through X-3 were obtained from a burglary suspect who manifested no fear of detection as evidenced by the lack of significant response on the first chart (Fig. X-1). However, after the administration of the Stimulation test (Fig. X-2, where card number 3 was selected), the examinee became convinced of the effectiveness of the test as demonstrated by the strong reactions to the relevant questions number 33 and 35. It must be noted that the strong reaction in the breathing tracing at control question number 46 is due to the fact that the examinee had stated he had committed a very serious crime during the period the control encompassed (at least two years preceding the crime for which the subject was being polygraphed) but refused to discuss it. Nevertheless, he still showed strong reactions at both relevant questions number 33 and 35. Normally, that control should have been changed because it was too strong; however, this author felt the subject would still react strongly to the relevant questions if guilty of the crime because of its intensity, which he did.

Control-Stimulation Test-Chart l - Arson-Murder

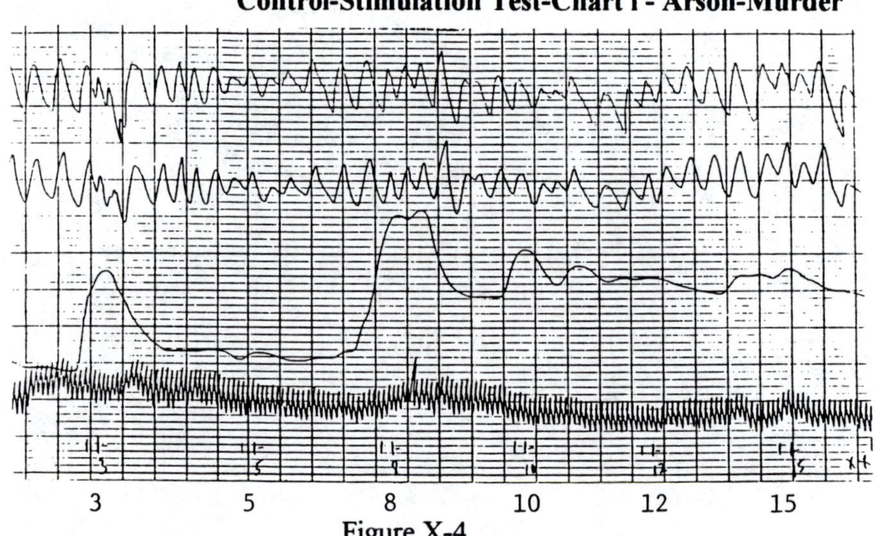

Figure X-4

In the examination depicted by Figures X-4 through X-6, the Stimulation test was administered first, followed by two charts dealing with an arson-murder case. Note the significant galvanic skin response arousal at number 8, which the subject selected and lied to in the True Unknown-Solution Stimulation test, and the blood pressure arousal.

Matte Quadri-Track Zone Comparison - Chart #2

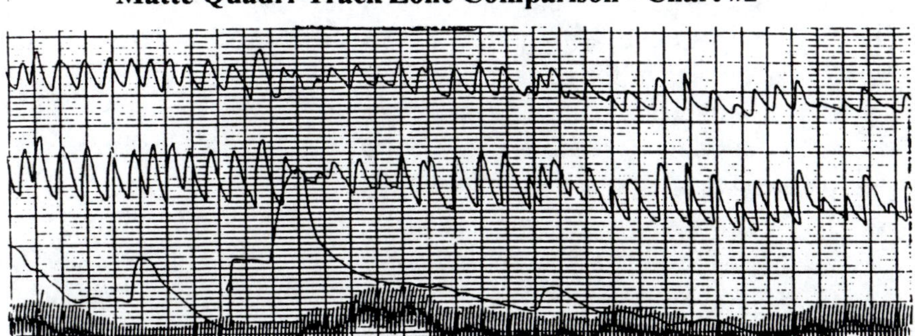

Figure X-5

Figure X-5, dealing with the arson, reflects very strong reactions in all three tracings at relevant question number 33 as opposed to a complete lack of reaction in the breathing and cardio tracing and mild reaction in the galvanic skin response tracing at neighboring control question number 46. Further note reactions in all three tracings at relevant question number 35 in contrast to an absence of reaction at neighboring control question number 47. When comparing "inside issue" factor question number 23 (fear of error) against question number 24 (hope of error) it can be seen that relevant question 24 surpasses control question 23 in strength of reactions.

Matte Quadri-Track Zone Comparison - Chart #3

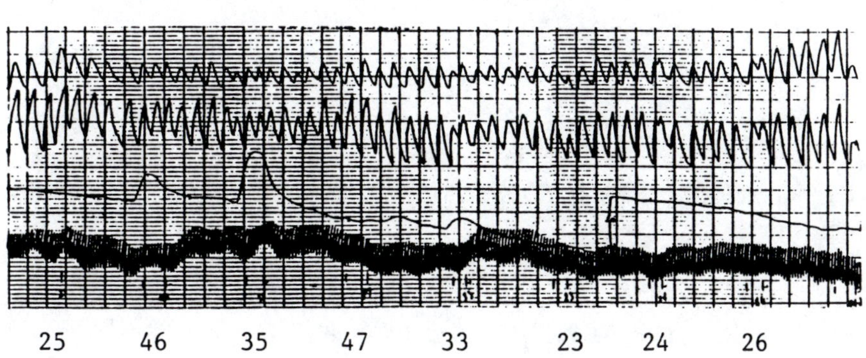

Figure X-6

Figure X-6 clearly support the findings of the first chart (Fig. X-4). Specifically note the galvanic skin response arousal nearly standing alone at relevant question number 35.

The pretest interview contains certain elements which are designed to inhibit the guilty (as later verified) examinee from using countermeasures.(see Chapter 8). Nevertheless, the FP may have the examinees remove their shoes after they are seated in the examination chair for the conduct of the actual tests. No reason should be given, but if asked the FP should reiterate that there should be no movement of the feet, toes or any other part of their body during the examination, implying that they will be under constant observation, while their eyes are closed (closed-eyes technique).

There are several other versions of the Stimulation Test such as the True Blue Control test (Scarce 1978); the Modified Controlled Stimulation Test Technique (Lovvorn 1978); A Control Test (Hickman 1978). Another type of stimulation test is known as the Silent Answer Test (SAT) which is fully described in Chapter 19.

REFERENCES:

Barland, G. H. (1978). A fail-proof blind numbers test. *Polygraph*, 7(3), 203-208.

Decker, R. E. (1978). The Army stimulation test - A control procedure. *Polygraph*, 7(3), 176-178.

Decker, R. E. (1996, January 16). Telephone conversation with J. A. Matte.

Hickman, R. C. (1978). Usefulness and Theory of the Stimulus Test. *Polygraph*, 7(3), 182-185.

Lovvorn, D. J. (1978). A Modified Controlled Stimulation test Technique. *Polygraph*, 7(3), 188-194.

Matte, J. A. (1980). *The Art and Science of the Polygraph Technique*. Springfield, IL: Charles C. Thomas.

Matte, J. A., Reuss, R. M. (1989). Validation Study on the Quadri-Zone Comparison Technique. *Research Abstract*, LD 01452, Vol. 1502, 1989, University Microfilm International.

Reid, J. E., Inbau, F. E. (1966). *Truth and Deception: The Polygraph ("Lie-Detector")* Technique. Baltimore, MD: The Williams & Wilkins Company.

Scarce, K. W. (1978). The True Blue Control Test. *Polygraph*, 7(3), 194-199.

Senese, L. (1978). Accuracy of the polygraph technique with and without card test stimulation. *Polygraph*, 7(3), 199-203.

Chapter 11

THE NUMERICAL APPROACH

TO

PSYCHOPHYSIOLOGICAL VERACITY EXAMINATIONS

The Numerical Approach developed by Cleve Backster in 1959 was initially designed for use in a *Single-Issue* test, namely the Backster Tri-Zone Comparison technique. The structure of the test optimizes the conditions for the function of the examinee's psychological set or selective attention process. Thus the test includes only two relevant questions dealing with a *same issue*, hence if the examinee is truthful to one of the relevant questions, he/she must also be truthful to the other relevant question on the same test. Conversely if the examinee is deceptive to one of the relevant questions, he/she must be deceptive to the other relevant question on the same test. It is important therefore to define the term Single-Issue, inasmuch as it may be argued that the perpetrator of a murder also broke into the house of the victim to commit the crime, thus a relevant question regarding the commission of the murder and a question regarding the break-in could be asked on the same test because the guilty examinee would be lying to both questions. However, those are considered two *separate actions*, thus two *separate issues* for the purpose of this type of test. The issue must be singular in scope, involving only one single action, which must be semantically distinct and specific. Hence the commission of the homicide would be treated as Single-Issue Test A, and the break-in would be treated as Single-Issue Test B. If a larceny had also been committed in the victim's house, it would be treated as Single-Issue Test C. Therefore, a Single-Issue test which addresses *primary involvement* should not contain a question involving *secondary involvement* such as a Knowledge question or an Evidence Connecting question. Those issues should be treated as separate tests.

The Single-Issue test is structurally designed to be numerically scored. A comparison is made between the control questions and their neighboring relevant questions which are identified as *Green Zone* and *Red Zone* questions respectively, using a seven-position scale in the analysis and quantification of the physiological data recorded on the polygraph charts. The type of control questions used vary with different polygraph techniques. The total scores acquired from the analysis and quantification of the physiological data on the polygraph charts constitute the sole determinant of truth or deception regarding the target issue. All non-polygraphic data is excluded from the decision-making process. Thus the pretest interview is designed to prepare the examinee psychologically for the proper processing of the essential information required for the unbiased administration of the psychologically structured test. Thus no accusatory or interrogative approach is permitted during any portion of the pretest interview or administration of the test(s).

Psychological Structure of the Zone Comparison Test: The psychophysiological veracity (PV) test is designed to pose a threat to the security of both the Innocent and Guilty examinee by offering them separate threats from which they must choose which one most endangers their well-being. Thus the relevant questions should pose the greatest threat to the deceptive examinee, and the control questions should pose the greatest threat to the examinee who is truthful to the relevant questions.

DEFINITION OF TERMS

Zone: Backster defined "Zone" as follows: A twenty to thirty-five seconds block of polygraph chart time initiated by a question having a unique psychological focusing appeal to a predictable group of examinees. (Ansley 1990). Backster color-coded each Zone as the *Green Zone* for the *Control* questions, the *Red Zone* for the *Relevant* questions, and the *Black Zone* for the *Symptomatic* questions. Their importance will become relevant when the test structures depicted below are examined.

Track: A *Track* identifies a pair of test questions related for evaluation as in the case of Symptomatic Questions, or a pair of test questions (Green and Red Zone) related for comparison which are located in a *Spot* for quantification.

Spot: Backster defines a Spot as one of four permanent locations on all zone comparison sequences which can only contain a relevant question. In the Matte Quadri-Track ZCT, a *Spot* also identifies a *Track* containing a pair of control/relevant questions which are *compared and quantified* for a determination of truth or deception to the target issue.

Psychological Set:. When the mind registers only some of the information it is exposed to, it is engaging in *selective attention*. Selective attention is an indispensable adaptive function. We cannot process all the information that impinges on our faculties at any given moment, so we focus on what appears to us most important and filter out the rest. Thus a person's (examinee) fears, anxieties, and apprehensions are channeled toward the situation (question) which holds the greatest immediate threat to his/her self-preservation or general well-being. The person's (examinee) focus is on that which indicates trouble or danger by having his/her sense organs and attention focused for a particular stimulus (question), and tune out that which is of a lesser threat (other question) to his/her legitimate security or general well-being. Thus the person (examinee) establishes his/her own psychological set.

Anticlimax Dampening Concept. In a PV examination, the examinee's psychological set will be drawn to the test question holding the *greatest threat* to his/her well-being thus engaging in *selective attention* which may *tune out* test questions of a lesser threat, hence causing an *anticlimax dampening effect* on all questions except that which has gained the examinee's selective attention. Therefore, when two distinctly separate crimes are included in the same test, the suspect who is guilty of both of them may respond only to that crime which he/she feels to be the greatest threat to his/her well-being. Furthermore, the relevant question offering the greatest threat to the guilty examinee will cause partial or complete dampening of control question reactions, thus an anticlimax.

Control Question. In a Zone Comparison Technique, the control question is designed to offer a threat to the well-being of the examinee who is expected to lie to that question, which is then used for comparison with the neighboring relevant question contained in the same test. It is expected that the *anticlimax dampening* effect of the question which elicited the examinee's psychological set will douse the potential arousal of its neighboring question, whether that be a control or relevant question. There are three types of control questions used for aforesaid purpose. (Directed Lie CQ is not included; see page 368).

a. *Non-Current Exclusive Control Question*. This control question, also known as the Backster control question, is formulated to be in the same category of offense or matter as the relevant question or issue. However, this control question is separated in time from the relevant issue with the use of a *time bar*, thus it is considered an *earlier-in-life* (non-current) control question. Thus this control question *excludes* the period in which the crime was committed, usually by at least two years or more, hence it is a Non-Current Exclusive Control Question.

Example (Subject is age 30): Between the ages of 18 and 25 - Do you remember ever stealing anything?

b. *Current Exclusive Control Question.* This control question is formulated to be in the same category of offense or matter as the relevant question or issue. However, this control question is not separated in time from the relevant issue with the use of a time bar, thus it is considered a current control question. However, this control question does excludes the specific crime or matter contained in the relevant questions. Thus it is called a Current Exclusive Control Question.

Example: Not connected with the larceny at ABC Market, did you ever steal anything?

c. *Non-Exclusive Control Question*. This control question, also known as the Reid control question, is formulated to be in the same category as the relevant question or issue. However this control question is not separated in time from the relevant issue nor does it exclude the crime or matter contained in the relevant question. Thus it is an inclusive control question but has been named by its employers as a Non-Exclusive Control question.

Example: Did you ever steal anything anywhere?

Symptomatic Question: This type of question developed by Backster is designed to determine whether the examinee is truly convinced that the FP will not ask an unreviewed question during the PV test, and whether there is something else the examinee is afraid the FP will ask him/her a question about, even though the FP promised the examinee he/she would not. A *super dampening* of both the relevant and control questions may occur when the examinee is more concerned about an *outside issue* being introduced in the form of an unreviewed question on his/her test in spite of reassurance to the contrary. This *Outside*

Issue factor may dampen out the response capability of the examinee to the question types that would ordinarily serve as a stimulus.

Preparatory/Sacrifice Relevant Question: This test question acts as a safeguard in that it allows for dissipation of excessive general nervous tension or undue anxiety prior to the asking of the primary relevant questions. It also serves to prepare the examinee for the introduction of the two primary relevant questions that follow it on the same test. It should not exceed the precise scope of its related relevant questions.

Inside-Issue Control Question: This type of question is designed to elicit a response from the Innocent (truthful as later verified) examinee who is *fearful that an error* will be made on his/her test.

Inside-Issue Relevant Question: This type of question is designed to elicit a response from the Guilty (deceptive as later verified) examinee who *hopes that an error* will be made on his/her test so that their deception to the target issue will not be detected.

Neutral (Irrelevant) Question: It is of a non-stimulating nature. In a Zone Comparison test format, this type of question is usually used as the first question on the test, to absorb an examinee's orienting response and reduce general nervous tension. The examinee's place of birth, last name or first name is usually used for that purpose. In other techniques it is also used to create a "norm" pattern at the beginning and end of each chart. It is also used between relevant questions where necessary to terminate lingering reactions to relevant or control questions and to nullify or terminate reactions due to extraneous stimuli or extended thought processes.

Spot Analysis: An analysis is made after each test (chart) is conducted on each Track and/or Spot, using the Matte or Backster Reaction Combination Guide as appropriate, to determine if each type of test question is functioning as designed and whether remedial action is needed prior to the conduct of the next test (chart).

There are five variations of the Single-Issue, Zone Comparison Technique: The Matte Quadri-Track Zone Comparison Technique, the Backster Tri-Zone Comparison Technique, the Department of Defense Polygraph Institute (DoDPI) Bi-Spot Zone Comparison Technique, the Integrated Zone Comparison Technique and the Utah Zone Comparison Technique. Each one of these techniques is described separately below:

SINGLE-ISSUE ZONE COMPARISON TESTS

The Matte Quadri-Track Zone Comparison Technique

The Matte Quadri-Track Zone Comparison Technique (MQTZCT) is a polygraph technique used exclusively for *Single-Issue* tests. It was developed in 1977 by this author after two years of research and experimentation with fictitious crime tests used in conjunction with actual crime tests in real-life situations (MCQV Test; Chap. 14) (Matte

1976, 1978). The MQT Zone Comparison Technique employs Backster's basic test structure and quantification system with some refinements and the addition of another *Spot* (Inside Track) consisting of a control/relevant question pair to deal with an Innocent examinee's "*fear of error*" and the Guilty examinee's "*hope of error*" discussed in chapters 8 and 9.

Case Preparation and Evaluation: Prior to the conduct of the PV examination, the forensic psychophygiologist (FP) reviews the case file and applies the *Examination Reliability Rating Table* (ERRT) (Fig. XI-1) using a five-point system to determine which issue has the greatest likelihood of producing conclusive results, on the basis of its combined *Adequacy of Information*, *Case Intensity*, and *Distinctness of Issue*. (Backster 1969, Matte 1980). Compliance with this case evaluation system minimizes inconclusive results and assures that tests are conducted only in those cases where there is ample and accurate case information from which to formulate the test questions, and that the issue being covered is sufficiently distinct and intense to elicit the examinee's psychological set without offering an opportunity for rationalization. Thus a PV examination should not be conducted unless the ERRT reflects a minimum rating of 3 for each of the three parameters on a scale of 1 to 5. Obviously, the higher the rating, the better expectancy of accurate, conclusive results.

EXAMINATION RELIABILITY RATING TABLE

Target Information "Adequacy" Rating

Inadequate	1	2	3	4	5	Adequate
Score	=7	=14	=21	=28	=35	:

Target "Intensity" Rating

Trivial	1	2	3	4	5	Serious
Score	=7	=14	=21	=28	=35	:

"Distinctness of Issue" Rating

Cloudy	1	2	3	4	5	Clear
Score	=6	=12	=18	=24	=30	:

EXAMINATION RELIABILITY RATING TOTAL: ______________

The highest reliability estimate would be a score of 100, lowest would be 20.

Figure XI-1

After the forensic psychophysiologist has determined from the ERRT the issues to be tested, the data regarding the first issue is studied and the relevant questions are formulated in accordance with the guidelines in Chapter 8. If more than one issue is to be addressed, the relevant questions are formulated for those issues also, on separate worksheets (see Fig. XI-6).

From the case information and subject background data, tentative control questions are selected from a pool of control questions that have shown success in that type of case with similar subjects. (see chapter 16). All of this information is entered on the FP's worksheet used for the administration of the PV examination. All administrative tasks are completed prior to the scheduled examination. Obviously, last minute changes are expected, mostly with the control questions; otherwise changes seldom occur, when the FP is adequately prepared.

PreTest Interview: The pretest interview is designed to prepare the examinee psychologically for the administration of the PV test(s) wherein the examinee's physiological responses to previously reviewed questions are recorded on a moving polygraph chart. The length of time required to conduct a proper pretest interview depends on the number of issues to be tested, the complexity of the case, the mental aptitude of the examinee, and the examinee's cooperation. It is imperative that the FP maintain not only a non-accusatory approach, but convey to the examinee that all examinees including himself/herself are assumed to be truthful regarding the target issue(s) until and unless the physiological data on the polygraph charts indicate otherwise. This FP posture is objective because in this society, all persons are deemed innocent until proven guilty. The FP merely continues that assumption until all polygraph charts have been conducted and their physiological data have been quantified and indicate deception. This alleviates the potential arousal of *anger* from the unjustly accused truthful examinee. The FP does not convey to the examinee that he/she *believes* the examinee to be truthful, but that he/she *assumes* he/she is truthful regarding the target issue until all polygraph charts have been conducted and their results indicate otherwise. In fact, the sustained treatment of the examinee as possibly truthful during the *entire* pretest interview, significantly increases cooperation from both the truthful and the deceptive (as later verified) examinees, because any uncooperativeness would be counter to the expected behavior of a truthful examinee. (Matte 1989, 1993). The unbiasness of this approach also reduces the *fear of error* by the truthful examinee. An explanation to the examinee of the physiology recorded and the quantification system used in the analysis of the data from which a conclusion of truth of deception is acquired, is designed to further allay any *fear of error* by the truthful examinee, which may be further diminished by demonstration of the test's accuracy with data from validation studies. During the pretest interview, background data is elicited from the examinee which is entered in the first page of a worksheet (Fig. XI-2).

The manner in which the test questions are reviewed and presented to the examinee is described in detail in chapter 8. Hence only the mechanics of their introduction is addressed in this chapter. (See Fig. XI-3 for Test Structure)

Order of Test Question Review: The test question review with the examinee starts with the Preparatory/Sacrifice Relevant question (#39), followed by Relevant Questions #33 and #35. Then a preamble is used to introduce the two Non-Current Exclusive Control Questions #46 and #47 which are also reviewed with the examinee.(See Chapter 8 for details). This is followed by the review of Inside-Issue Control Question #23 which like control questions 46 and 47 should elicit a reluctant negative answer. (See Chap. 8 for full

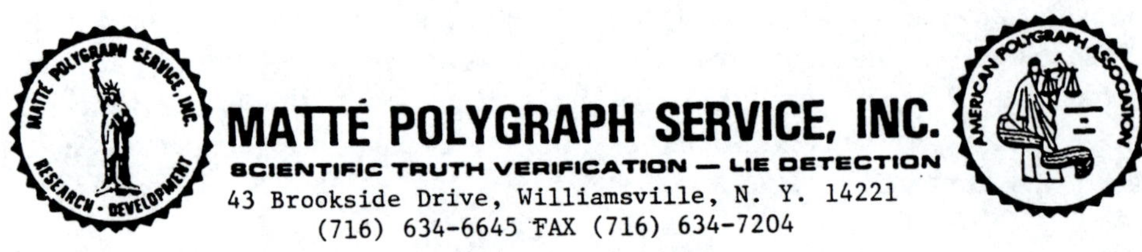

SPECIFIC POLYGRAPH EXAMINATION

WORKSHEET

CLIENT________________ DATE/TIME________
PLACE TESTED________________
SUBJECT________________ OCCUPATION________
PRESENT EMPLOYER________________
LENGTH OF EMPLOYMENT________ POSITION________
ADDRESS OF SUBJECT________________
SSAN________ DPOB________ AGE________
TELEPHONE________ DRIVER LICENSE NR.________
M F RACE____ HT____ WT____ HAIR____ EYES____ BUILD____ S M D SEP W CHILDREN________
SCHOOL GRADE FINISHED 1 2 3 4 5 6 7 8 9 10 11 12 GED COLLEGE 1 2 3 4 5 6 7 8 DEGREE____
MILITARY SERVICE A N M CG AF FROM________ TO________ DISCH________ RANK________
COURT-MARTIALS/ARRESTS________________
____
PRESENT PHYSICAL CONDITION: GOOD ○ FAIR ○ POOR ○ LAST PHYSICAL EXAM________
HOSPITALIZED PAST 2 YEARS________________
TROUBLE WITH NERVES REQUIRING MEDICATION________________
HEART DISEASE________________
TO SUBJECT'S KNOWLEDGE, BLOOD PRESSURE NORMAL ○ LOW ○ HIGH ○ ________
____
____
DIABETES (over 50 using 50 or more units of insulin by injection per day)________
____
EPILEPSY________ PREGNANCY________ PERMISSION FORM________
EVER UNDER CARE OF PSYCHIATRIST________ EVER PATIENT IN MENTAL HOSPITAL________
____
ANY MEDICATION OR DRUGS IN LAST 12 HOURS________________
NR OF HOURS SLEEP LAST NIGHT________ PERMISSION FORM SIGNED________
PREVIOUS POLYGRAPHS________________
INTERRUPTIONS________________
REMARKS________________
____
PREDICATION: Subject was administered a polygraph examination to determine________
____
____
____
____
CASE INFORMATION/SUBJECT'S VERSION: SEE ATTACHED SHEET
PRE-TEST/POST-TEST ADMISSIONS: SEE ATTACHED SHEET/CONFESSION.
TEST CONDUCTED: 1. QUADRI-ZONE 2. QUINQUE-ZONE 3. MCQVT 4. SAT 5. STIM 6. SKG
7. KS POT 8. P POT 9. BYP 10. MITT
CONCLUSIONS: TARGET A ( ) TRUTHFUL/DECEPTIVE TO RELEVANT QUESTIONS NR________
TARGET B ( ) TRUTHFUL/DECEPTIVE TO RELEVANT QUESTIONS NR________
TARGET C ( ) TRUTHFUL/DECEPTIVE TO RELEVANT QUESTIONS NR________
TARGET D ( ) TRUTHFUL/DECEPTIVE TO RELEVANT QUESTIONS NR________
TARGET E ( ) TRUTHFUL/DECEPTIVE TO RELEVANT QUESTIONS NR________

Figure XI-2

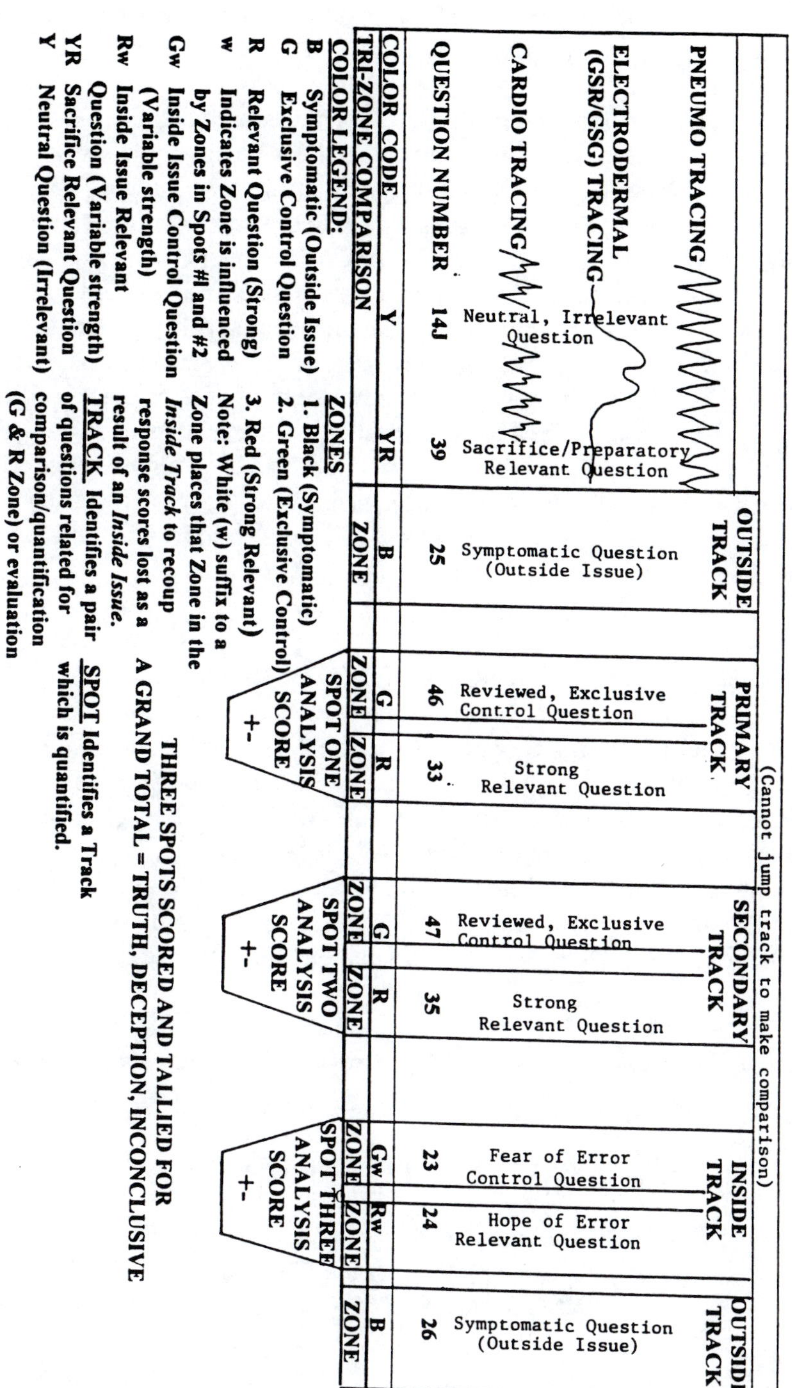
MATTE QUADRI-TRACK ZONE COMPARISON TEST STRUCTURE
(Cannot jump track to make comparison)
OUTSIDE TRACK
PRIMARY TRACK
SECONDARY TRACK
INSIDE TRACK
OUTSIDE TRACK
PNEUMO TRACING
ELECTRODERMAL (GSR/GSG) TRACING
CARDIO TRACING
Neutral, Irrelevant Question
Sacrifice/Preparatory Relevant Question
Symptomatic Question (Outside Issue)
Reviewed, Exclusive Control Question
Strong Relevant Question
Reviewed, Exclusive Control Question
Strong Relevant Question
Fear of Error Control Question
Hope of Error Relevant Question
Symptomatic Question (Outside Issue)
QUESTION NUMBER 14J 39 25 46 33 47 35 23 24 26
COLOR CODE Y YR B G R G R Gw Rw B
TRI-ZONE COMPARISON ZONE ZONE ZONE ZONE ZONE ZONE ZONE ZONE
SPOT ONE ANALYSIS SCORE +-
SPOT TWO ANALYSIS SCORE +-
SPOT THREE ANALYSIS SCORE +-
COLOR LEGEND:
B Symptomatic (Outside Issue)
G Exclusive Control Question
R Relevant Question (Strong)
w Indicates Zone is influenced by Zones in Spots #l and #2
Gw Inside Issue Control Question (Variable strength)
Rw Inside Issue Relevant Question (Variable strength)
YR Sacrifice Relevant Question
Y Neutral Question (Irrelevant)
ZONES
1. Black (Symptomatic)
2. Green (Exclusive Control)
3. Red (Strong Relevant)
Note: White (w) suffix to a Zone places that Zone in the Inside Track to recoup response scores lost as a result of an Inside Issue.
TRACK Identifies a pair of questions related for comparison/quantification (G & R Zone) or evaluation (B Zone).
THREE SPOTS SCORED AND TALLIED FOR A GRAND TOTAL = TRUTH, DECEPTION, INCONCLUSIVE
SPOT Identifies a Track which is quantified.

Figure XI-3

discussion). Then Inside-Issue Relevant Question #24 is reviewed which all examinees answer in the negative. The Symptomatic (Black Zone) Questions #25 and #26 are then reviewed which should elicit an affirmative and negative answer respectively. The last question reviewed is the Neutral, Irrelevant Question #14J.

Placement of Instrument Components: After all of the aforementioned test questions have been thoroughly reviewed with the examinee, he/she is then asked to be seated in the PV examination chair which faces away and in the opposite direction in which the chart exits the polygraph instrument, thus the examinee is seated with his/her right profile facing the FP when seated behind the polygraph instrument. (See Chapter 6) The pneumograph tube which records in the lower channel on the polygraph instrument is marked (red tape) so that the FP always places that tube over the abdominal area of the examinee, and the other pneumograph tube is placed over the chest area of the examinee which will be recorded in the upper channel on the polygraph instrument; thus the pneumograph tracings on the polygraph chart will correspond to their location on the examinee. The cardio cuff is then wrapped over the examinee's left arm with the bladder over the brachial artery area. Then the galvanic skin response/conductance electrodes are placed usually over the index and ring finger of the opposite (right) hand. These electrodes should be removed and wiped after the conduct of each polygraph test (chart).

First Test Administration: The examinee is first administered an Acquaintance Chart. The examinee is directed to remain quietly seated with eyes open but directed straight forward for a couple of minutes while the FP adjusts the instrument components to optimum tracing amplitude and sensitivity. The instrument is then turned off and the examinee is told that before the relevant test is administered, he/she is first going to be administered a Sensitivity Test to determine their capability and manner of response to a known lie. The Control-Stimulation Test is then administered . (See Chapter 10 for details). Approximately five minutes after the Control-Stimulation test has been conducted and the examinee has had time to physically recover from the pressure of the cardio cuff and psychologically processed the results of the Control-Stimulation, the examinee is administered the first Relevant test.

Administration of First Relevant Test: The first relevant test is administered in the order listed below:

Irrelevant (Neutral)	14J	Were you born in the United States?
Preparatory/Sacrifice	39	Regarding whether or not you shot Buffalo Police Officer John Doe on the morning of 20 January 1995: Do you intend to answer truthfully each question about that?
Symptomatic	25	Are you completely convinced that I will not ask you an unreviewed question during this chart?

Non-Current Exclusive Control	46	Between the ages of 19 and 28 - Do you remember being so mad at someone that you wished them dead?
Relevant question	33	Did you yourself shoot Officer John Doe?
Non-Current Exclusive Control	47	During the first 19 years of your life - Do you remember ever deliberately causing someone physical harm?
Relevant Question	35	On 20 January 1995, did you fire any of the shots that wounded Officer John Doe?
Inside-Issue Control	23	Are you afraid an error will be made on this test - regarding the target issue? (the shooting of Officer John Doe)
Inside-Issue Relevant	24	Are you hopeful an error will be made on this test - regarding the target issue? (the shooting of Officer John Doe)
Symptomatic	26	Is there something else you are afraid I will ask you a question about, even though I told you I would not?

The completed polygraph chart is removed from the examination room for Spot Analysis, using the Quadri-Track Reaction Combination Guide (Fig. XI-4). No comment is ever made to the examinee regarding the contents or results of the chart(s). The examinee was advised (see Chapter 8) that all tests have to be administered (for all issues), then scored for a determination. Thus no results are available to the examinee until all tests have been conducted and quantified. Figure XI-5 depicts the score tally for the Matte Control Question Validation (MCQV) Test for two charts with its Conclusion Table which when used precedes the administration of the Quadri-Track Zone Comparison Test. Figure XI-5 further depicts the score tally for four charts and a Conclusion Table for the number of charts conducted.

Please note that in Figure XI-3 there is a *notice* above the Primary, Secondary and Inside Tracks "Cannot Jump Track to Make Comparison." This means that each relevant question must be compared against the control question preceding it, or in the same Track. A minimum of two polygraph charts for each test must be administered before the FP can reach a conclusion regarding that test. If there is another (second) issue to be covered, then Test B is administered, without revealing the results of Test A. The same applies if there is a Test C to be administered. When all tests have been administered and quantified for a determination, then the examinee is advised of the results of each test. (See Chapter 8 for explanation of this procedure).

Figure XI-6 depicts the second page of the Quadri-Track Worksheet with a template for the formulation of test questions for the Matte Control Question Validation Procedure (when used) and the Quadri-Track Zone Comparison Technique.

Quadri-Track Reaction Combination Guide

COMBO	ZONE COMPARISON		COLOR CODE		PRESENCE OF REACTION		SCORE		INDICATION		REMEDY
	46	33	G	R		33	-1 to -9	A1	RESPONSE TO RED ZONE QUESTION (33) AND LACK OF RESPONSE TO GREEN ZONE (46) INDICATES DECEPTION TO RELEVANT QUESTION.	A1	NO REMEDY REQUIRED. RED ZONE QUESTION IDEALLY FORMULATED: FUNCTIONING AS DESIGNED.
	47	35	G	R		35	-1 to -9	A2	RESPONSE TO RED ZONE QUESTION (35) AND LACK OF RESPONSE TO GREEN ZONE (47) INDICATES DECEPTION TO RELEVANT QUESTION.	A2	NO REMEDY REQUIRED. RED ZONE QUESTION IDEALLY FORMULATED; FUNCTIONING AS DESIGNED.
A	23	24	G/W	R/W			0	A3	LACK OF RESPONSE TO GREEN/WHITE (23) AND RED/WHITE (24) ZONE INDICATES NO FEAR OF ERROR IS DAMPENING GREEN ZONE (46 & 47) AND FEAR OF DETECTION TO RED ZONE (33&35) NOT RECHANNELED INTO HOPE OF ERROR (24).	A3	NO REMEDY REQUIRED. NO EVIDENCE OF INSIDE ISSUE DAMPENING GREEN OR RED ZONES.
	25	26	B	B			NA	A4	LACK OF RESPONSE TO BOTH BLACK ZONE QUESTIONS (25 & 26) INDICATES NO OUTSIDE ISSUE BOTHERING SUBJECT DUE TO MISTRUST OF POLYGRAPHIST.	A4	NO REMEDY REQUIRED. SUBJECT APPEARS CONVINCED POLYGRAPHIST WILL NOT ASK UNREVIEWED QUESTION DURING EXAMINATION.
	46	33	G	R	46		+1 to +9	B1	RESPONSE TO GREEN ZONE QUESTION (46) AND LACK OF RESPONSE TO RED ZONE (33) INDICATES TRUTHFULNESS TO RELEVANT QUESTION.	B1	NO REMEDY REQUIRED. RED ZONE QUESTION IDEALLY FORMULATED; GREEN ZONE FUNCTIONING AS DESIGNED.
	47	35	G	R	47		+1 to +9	B2	RESPONSE TO GREEN ZONE QUESTION (46) AND LACK OF RESPONSE TO RED ZONE (33) INDICATES TRUTHFULNESS TO RELEVANT QUESTION.	B2	NO REMEDY REQUIRED. RED ZONE QUESTION IDEALLY FORMULATED; GREEN ZONE FUNCTIONING AS DESIGNED.
B	23	24	G/W	R/W			0	B3	LACK OF RESPONSE TO GREEN/WHITE (23) AND RED/WHITE (24) ZONE INDICATES NO FEAR OF ERROR IS DAMPENING GREEN ZONE (46 & 47) AND FEAR OF DETECTION TO RED ZONE (33&35) NOT RECHANNELED INTO HOPE OF ERROR (24).	B3	NO REMEDY REQUIRED. NO EVIDENCE OF INSIDE ISSUE DAMPENING GREEN OR RED ZONES.
	25	26	B	B			NA	B4	LACK OF RESPONSE TO BOTH BLACK ZONE QUESTIONS (25 & 26) INDICATES NO OUTSIDE ISSUE BOTHERING SUBJECT DUE TO MISTRUST OF POLYGRAPHIST.	B4	NO REMEDY REQUIRED. SUBJECT APPEARS CONVINCED POLYGRAPHIST WILL NOT ASK UNREVIEWED QUESTION DURING EXAMINATION.
	46	33	G	R	46	33	-1 to -3	C1	STRONG RESPONSE TO RED ZONE QUESTION (33) AND EQUAL STRONG RESPONSE TO GREEN ZONE (46) INDICATES SERIOUS GREEN ZONE DEFECT.	C1	ADMINISTER STIMULATION TEST TO REASSURE SUBJECT OF ACCURACY OF TEST. IF ALREADY GIVEN, REDUCE GREEN ZONE QUESTION INTENSITY BY ALTERING SUBJECT AGE CATEGORY OR CHANGING SCOPE OF GREEN ZONE.
	47	35	G	R	47	35	-1 to -3	C2	STRONG RESPONSE TO RED ZONE QUESTION (33) AND EQUAL STRONG RESPONSE TO GREEN ZONE (46) INDICATES SERIOUS GREEN ZONE DEFECT.	C2	REMEDY THE SAME AS C1 ABOVE.
C	23	24	G/W	R/W			0	C3	LACK OF RESPONSE TO GREEN/WHITE (23) AND RED/WHITE (24) ZONE INDICATES NO FEAR OF ERROR IS DAMPENING GREEN ZONE (46 & 47) AND FEAR OF DETECTION TO RED ZONE (33&35) NOT RECHANNELED INTO HOPE OF ERROR (24).	C3	NO REMEDY REQUIRED. NO EVIDENCE OF INSIDE ISSUE DAMPENING GREEN OR RED ZONES.
	25	26	B	B			NA	C4	LACK OF RESPONSE TO BOTH BLACK ZONE QUESTIONS (25 & 26) INDICATES NO OUTSIDE ISSUE BOTHERING SUBJECT DUE TO MISTRUST OF POLYGRAPHIST.	C4	NO REMEDY REQUIRED. SUBJECT APPEARS CONVINCED POLYGRAPHIST WILL NOT ASK UNREVIEWED QUESTION DURING EXAMINATION.
	46	33	G	R			0	D1	LACK OF RESPONSE TO RED ZONE QUESTION (33) AND GREEN ZONE QUESTION (46) USUALLY INDICATES INEFFECTIVE GREEN ZONE QUESTION: THIS RULE NULLIFIED BY BLACK ZONE RESPONSE.	D1	NO REMEDY REQUIRED. RED ZONE AND GREEN ZONE QUESTIONS WILL BE FUNCTIONING AS DESIGNED AFTER BLACK ZONE QUESTION RESPONSE SUBSIDES.
	47	35	G	R			0	D2	LACK OF RESPONSE TO RED ZONE QUESTION (33) AND GREEN ZONE QUESTION (46) USUALLY INDICATES INEFFECTIVE GREEN ZONE QUESTION: THIS RULE NULLIFIED BY BLACK ZONE RESPONSE.	D2	NO REMEDY REQUIRED. RED ZONE AND GREEN ZONE QUESTIONS WILL BE FUNCTIONING AS DESIGNED AFTER BLACK ZONE QUESTION RESPONSE SUBSIDES.
D	23	24	G/W	R/W			0	D3	LACK OF RESPONSE TO GREEN/WHITE (23) AND RED/WHITE (24) ZONE INDICATES NO FEAR OF ERROR IS DAMPENING GREEN ZONE (46 & 47) AND FEAR OF DETECTION TO RED ZONE (33&35) NOT RECHANNELED INTO HOPE OF ERROR (24).	D3	NO REMEDY REQUIRED. NO EVIDENCE OF INSIDE ISSUE DAMPENING GREEN OR RED ZONES.
	25	26	B	B	25	26	NA	D4	RESPONSE TO ONE OR BOTH BLACK ZONE QUESTIONS (25 & 26) INDICATES OUTSIDE ISSUE BOTHERING SUBJECT DUE TO MISTRUST OF POLYGRAPHIST.	D4	POLYGRAPHIST MUST GAIN SUBJECT'S CONFIDENCE REGARDING AVOIDANCE OF UNREVIEWED QUESTIONS EMBRACING OUTSIDE ISSUE.
	46	33	G	R		33	-1 to -9	E1	RESPONSE TO RED ZONE QUESTION (33) AND LACK OF RESPONSE TO GREEN ZONE (46) INDICATES DECEPTION TO RELEVANT QUESTION.	E1	NO REMEDY REQUIRED. RED ZONE QUESTION IDEALLY FORMULATED; FUNCTIONING AS DESIGNED.
	47	35	G	R		35	-1 to -9	E2	RESPONSE TO RED ZONE QUESTION (35) AND LACK OF RESPONSE TO GREEN ZONE (47) INDICATES DECEPTION TO RELEVANT QUESTION.	E2	NO REMEDY REQUIRED. RED ZONE QUESTION IDEALLY FORMULATED; FUNCTIONING AS DESIGNED.
E	23	24	G/W	R/W			0	E3	LACK OF RESPONSE TO GREEN/WHITE (23) AND RED/WHITE (24) ZONE INDICATES NO FEAR OF ERROR IS DAMPENING GREEN ZONE (46 & 47) AND FEAR OF DETECTION TO RED ZONE (33&35) NOT RECHANNELED INTO HOPE OF ERROR (24).	E3	NO REMEDY REQUIRED. NO EVIDENCE OF INSIDE ISSUE DAMPENING GREEN OR RED ZONES.
	25	26	B	B	25	26	NA	E4	RESPONSE TO ONE OR BOTH BLACK ZONE QUESTIONS (25 & 26) INDICATES OUTSIDE ISSUE BOTHERING SUBJECT DUE TO MISTRUST OF POLYGRAPHIST.	E4	POLYGRAPHIST MUST GAIN SUBJECT'S CONFIDENCE REGARDING AVOIDANCE OF UNREVIEWED QUESTIONS EMBRACING OUTSIDE ISSUE.

Figure XI-4a

Quadri-Track Reaction Combination Guide

COMBO	ZONE COMPARISON		COLOR CODE		PRESENCE OF REACTION		SCORE		INDICATION		REMEDY
	46	33	G	R	46		+1 to +9	F1	RESPONSE TO GREEN ZONE QUESTION (46) AND LACK OF RESPONSE TO RED ZONE (33) INDICATES TRUTHFULNESS TO RELEVANT QUESTION.	F1	NO REMEDY REQUIRED. RED ZONE QUESTION IDEALLY FORMULATED; GREEN ZONE FUNCTIONING AS DESIGNED.
	47	35	G	R	47		+1 to +9	F2	RESPONSE TO GREEN ZONE QUESTION (47) AND LACK OF RESPONSE TO RED ZONE (35) INDICATES TRUTHFULNESS TO RELEVANT QUESTION.	F2	NO REMEDY REQUIRED. RED ZONE QUESTION IDEALLY FORMULATED; GREEN ZONE FUNCTIONING AS DESIGNED.
F	23	24	G/W	R/W			0	F3	LACK OF RESPONSE TO GREEN/WHITE (23) AND RED/WHITE (24) ZONE INDICATES NO FEAR OF ERROR IS DAMPENING GREEN ZONE (46&47) AND FEAR OF DETECTION TO RED ZONE (33&35) NOT RECHANNELED INTO HOPE OF ERROR (24).	F3	NO REMEDY REQUIRED. NO EVIDENCE OF INSIDE ISSUE DAMPENING GREEN OR RED ZONES.
	25	26	B	B	25	26	NA	F4	RESPONSE TO ONE OR BOTH BLACK ZONE QUESTIONS (25 & 26) INDICATES OUTSIDE ISSUE BOTHERING SUBJECT DUE TO MISTRUST OF POLYGRAPHIST.	F4	POLYGRAPHIST MUST GAIN SUBJECT'S CONFIDENCE REGARDING AVOIDANCE OF UNREVIEWED QUESTIONS EMBRACING OUTSIDE ISSUE.
	46	33	G	R	46	33	-1 to -3	G1	STRONG RESPONSE TO RED ZONE QUESTION (33) AND EQUAL STRONG RESPONSE TO GREEN ZONE (46) INDICATES SERIOUS GREEN ZONE DEFECT.	G1	REDUCE GREEN ZONE QUESTION INTENSITY BY ALTERING SUBJECT AGE CATEGORY OR CHANGING SCOPE OF GREEN ZONE QUESTION.
	47	35	G	R	47	35	-1 to -3	G2	STRONG RESPONSE TO RED ZONE QUESTION (35) AND EQUAL STRONG RESPONSE TO GREEN ZONE (47) INDICATES SERIOUS GREEN ZONE DEFECT.	G2	REDUCE GREEN ZONE QUESTION INTENSITY BY ALTERING SUBJECT AGE CATEGORY OR CHANGING SCOPE OF GREEN ZONE QUESTION.
G	23	24	G/W	R/W			0	G3	LACK OF RESPONSE TO GREEN/WHITE (23) AND RED/WHITE (24) ZONE INDICATES NO FEAR OF ERROR IS DAMPENING GREEN ZONE (46 & 47) AND FEAR OF DETECTION TO RED ZONE (33&35) NOT RECHANNELED INTO HOPE OF ERROR (24).	G3	NO REMEDY REQUIRED. NO EVIDENCE OF INSIDE ISSUE DAMPENING GREEN OR RED ZONES.
	25	26	B	B	25	26	NA	G4	RESPONSE TO ONE OR BOTH BLACK ZONE QUESTIONS 25 & 26) INDICATES OUTSIDE ISSUE BOTHERING SUBJECT DUE TO MISTRUST OF POLYGRAPHIST.	G4	POLYGRAPHIST MUST GAIN SUBJECT'S CONFIDENCE REGARDING AVOIDANCE OF UNREVIEWED QUESTIONS EMBRACING OUTSIDE ISSUE.
	46	33	G	R	46	33	-1 to -3	H1	STRONG RESPONSE TO RED ZONE QUESTION (33) AND EQUAL STRONG RESPONSE TO GREEN ZONE (46) USUALLY INDICATES SERIOUS GREEN ZONE DEFECT. THIS RULE NULLIFIED BY GREEN/WHITE ZONE (23) RESPONSE.	H1	ADMINISTER STIMULATION TEST TO REASSURE SUBJECT OF ACCURACY OF TEST. IF ALREADY ADMINISTERED, THEN REVIEW BOTH INSIDE-ISSUE QUESTIONS (23 & 24) WITH SUBJECT TO INSURE UNDERSTANDING AND SUBJECT CONFIDENCE. FURTHER REVIEW GREEN ZONE QUESTIONS (46 & 47) ONLY WITH SUBJECT.
H	47	35	G	R	47	35	-1 to -3	H2	STRONG RESPONSE TO RED ZONE QUESTION (35) AND EQUAL STRONG RESPONSE TO GREEN ZONE (47) USUALLY INDICATES SERIOUS GREEN ZONE DEFECT. THIS RULE NULLIFIED BY GREEN/WHITE ZONE (23 RESPONSE.	H1	REMEDY THE SAME AS (H1) ABOVE.
	23	24	G/W	R/W	23		+1 to +9	H3	RESPONSE TO GREEN/WHITE ZONE (23) AND LACK OF RESPONSE TO RED/WHITE ZONE 24) INDICATES FEAR OF ERROR REGARDING RED ZONE QUESTIONS (33&35) MAKING RED ZONE QUESTIONS UNDULY THREATENING.	H3	REMEDY THE SAME AS (H1) ABOVE. BOTH GREEN ZONE AND RED ZONE QUESTIONS HAVE BEEN IDEALLY FORMULATED. IF (H1) REMEDY INEFFECTIVE, CHANGE GREEN ZONE QUESTIONS.
	25	26	B	B			NA	H4	LACK OF RESPONSE TO BOTH BLACK ZONE QUESTIONS (25 & 26) INDICATES NO OUTSIDE ISSUE BOTHERING SUBJECT DUE TO MISTRUST OF POLYGRAPHIST.	H4	NO REMEDY REQUIRED. SUBJECT APPEARS CONVINCED POLYGRAPHIST WILL NOT ASK UNREVIEWED QUESTION DURING EXAMINATION.
	46	33	G	R	46	33	-1 to -3	I1	STRONG RESPONSE TO RED ZONE QUESTION (33) AND EQUAL STRONG RESPONSE TO GREEN ZONE (46) USUALLY INDICATES SERIOUS GREEN ZONE DEFECT. THIS RULE NOT NULLIFIED BY RED/WHITE ZONE (24) RESPONSE.	I1	REDUCE GREEN ZONE QUESTION INTENSITY BY ALTERING SUBJECT AGE CATEGORY OR CHANGING SCOPE OF GREEN ZONE QUESTION.
	47	35	G	R	47	35	-1 to -3	I2	STRONG RESPONSE TO RED ZONE QUESTION (35) AND EQUAL STRONG RESPONSE TO GREEN ZONE (47) USUALLY INDICATES SERIOUS GREEN ZONE DEFECT. THIS RULE NOT NULLIFIED BY RED/WHITE ZONE (24) RESPONSE.	I2	REMEDY THE SAME AS (I1) ABOVE.
I	23	24	G/W	R/W		24	-1 to -9	I3	RESPONSE TO RED/WHITE ZONE (24) AND LACK OF RESPONSE TO GREEN/WHITE ZONE (23) INDICATES SUBJECT HOPES ERROR WILL BE MADE REGARDING RED ZONE QUESTIONS (33&35). INDICATING DECEPTION REGARDING TARGET ISSUE.	I3	GREEN/WHITE (23) AND RED/WHITE (24) ZONE QUESTIONS FUNCTIONING AS DESIGNED. REMEDY IN (I1) ABOVE SHOULD BE ADMINISTERED WITH THE REVIEW OF BOTH GREEN ZONE AND RED ZONE QUESTIONS.
	25	26	B	B			NA	I4	LACK OF RESPONSE TO BOTH BLACK ZONE QUESTIONS (25 & 26) INDICATES NO OUTSIDE ISSUE BOTHERING SUBJECT DUE TO MISTRUST OF POLYGRAPHIST.	I4	NO REMEDY REQUIRED. SUBJECT APPEARS CONVINCED POLYGRAPHIST WILL NOT ASK UNREVIEWED QUESTION DURING EXAMINATION.

Figure XI-4b

Quadri-Track Reaction Combination Guide

COMBO	ZONE COMPARISON		COLOR CODE		PRESENCE OF REACTION		SCORE		INDICATION		REMEDY
	46	33	G	R	46	33	-1 to -3	J1	STRONG RESPONSE TO RED ZONE QUESTION (33) AND EQUAL STRONG RESPONSE TO GREEN ZONE (46) USUALLY INDICATES SERIOUS GREEN ZONE DEFECT. THIS RULE <u>NOT</u> NULLIFIED BY RED/WHITE ZONE (24) RESPONSE.	J1	REDUCE GREEN ZONE QUESTION INTENSITY BY ALTERING SUBJECT AGE CATEGORY OR CHANGING SCOPE OF GREEN ZONE QUESTION.
	47	35	G	R	47	35	-1 to -3	J2	STRONG RESPONSE TO RED ZONE QUESTION (35) AND EQUAL STRONG RESPONSE TO GREEN ZONE (47) USUALLY INDICATES SERIOUS GREEN ZONE DEFECT. THIS RULE <u>NOT</u> NULLIFIED BY RED/WHITE ZONE (24) RESPONSE.	J2	REMEDY THE SAME AS (J1) ABOVE.
J	23	24	G/W	R/W		24	-1 to -9	J3	RESPONSE TO RED/WHITE ZONE (24) AND LACK OF RESPONSE TO GREEN/WHITE ZONE (23) INDICATES SUBJECT HOPES ERROR WILL BE MADE REGARDING RED ZONE QUESTIONS (33&35) INDICATING DECEPTION REGARDING TARGET ISSUE.	J3	GREEN/WHITE (23) AND RED/WHITE (24) ZONE QUESTIONS FUNCTIONING AS DESIGNED. REMEDY IN (J1) ABOVE SHOULD BE ADMINISTERED WITH THE REVIEW OF BOTH GREEN ZONE AND RED ZONE QUESTIONS.
	25	26	B	B	25	26	NA	J4	RESPONSE TO ONE OR BOTH BLACK ZONE QUESTIONS (25 & 26) INDICATES OUTSIDE ISSUE BOTHERING SUBJECT DUE TO MISTRUST OF POLYGRAPHIST.	J4	POLYGRAPHIST MUST GAIN SUBJECT'S CONFIDENCE REGARDING AVOIDANCE OF UNREVIEWED QUESTIONS EMBRACING OUTSIDE ISSUE.
	46	33	G	R	46	33	-1 to -3	K1	STRONG RESPONSE TO RED ZONE QUESTION (33) AND EQUAL STRONG RESPONSE TO GREEN ZONE (46) USUALLY INDICATES SERIOUS GREEN ZONE DEFECT. THIS RULE NULLIFIED BY GREEN/WHITE ZONE (23) RESPONSE.	K1	ADMINISTER STIMULATION TEST TO REASSURE SUBJECT OF ACCURACY OF TEST. IF ALREADY ADMINISTERED, THEN REVIEW BOTH INSIDE-ISSUE QUESTIONS (23 & 24) WITH SUBJECT TO INSURE UNDERSTANDING AND SUBJECT CONFIDENCE. FURTHER REVIEW GREEN ZONE QUESTIONS (46 & 47) ONLY WITH SUBJECT.
K	47	35	G	R	47	35	-1 to -3	K2	STRONG RESPONSE TO RED ZONE QUESTION (33) AND EQUAL STRONG RESPONSE TO GREEN ZONE (46) USUALLY INDICATES SERIOUS GREEN ZONE DEFECT. THIS RULE NULLIFIED BY GREEN/WHITE ZONE (23) RESPONSE.	K2	REMEDY THE SAME AS (K1) ABOVE.
	23	24	G/W	R/W	23		+1 to +9	K3	RESPONSE TO GREEN/WHITE ZONE (23) AND LACK OF RESPONSE TO RED/WHITE ZONE (24) INDICATES FEAR OF ERROR REGARDING RED ZONE QUESTIONS (33&35) MAKING RED ZONE QUESTIONS UNDULY THREATENING.	K3	REMEDY THE SAME AS (K1) ABOVE. BOTH GREEN ZONE AND RED ZONE QUESTIONS HAVE BEEN IDEALLY FORMULATED. IF (K1) REMEDY INEFFECTIVE, CHANGE GREEN ZONE QUESTIONS.
	25	26	B	B	25	26	NA	K4	RESPONSE TO ONE OR BOTH BLACK ZONE QUESTIONS (25 & 26) INDICATES OUTSIDE ISSUE BOTHERING SUBJECT DUE TO MISTRUST OF POLYGRAPHIST.	K4	POLYGRAPHIST MUST GAIN SUBJECT's CONFIDENCE REGARDING AVOIDANCE OF UNREVIEWED QUESTIONS EMBRACING OUTSIDE ISSUE.
	46	33	G	R	46	33	-1 to -3	L1	STRONG RESPONSE TO RED ZONE QUESTION (33) AND EQUAL STRONG RESPONSE TO GREEN ZONE (46) USUALLY INDICATES SERIOUS GREEN ZONE DEFECT. THIS RULE NULLIFIED BY GREEN/WHITE ZONE (23) AND RED/WHITE ZONE (24) RESPONSES.	L1	ADMINISTER STIMULATION TEST TO REASSURE SUBJECT OF ACCURACY OF TEST. IF ALREADY ADMINISTERED, THEN REVIEW BOTH INSIDE-ISSUE QUESTIONS (23 & 24) WITH SUBJECT TO INSURE UNDERSTANDING AND SUBJECT CONFIDENCE. FURTHER REVIEW GREEN ZONE QUESTIONS (46 & 47) ONLY WITH SUBJECT.
L	47	35	G	R	47	35	-1 to -3	L2	STRONG RESPONSE TO RED ZONE QUESTION (35) AND EQUAL STRONG RESPONSE TO GREEN ZONE (47) USUALLY INDICATES SERIOUS GREEN ZONE DEFECT. THIS RULE NULLIFIED BY GREEN/WHITE ZONE (23) AND RED/WHITE ZONE (24) RESPONSES.	L2	REMEDY THE SAME AS (L1) ABOVE.
	23	24	G/W	R/W	23	24	0	L3	EQUAL STRONG RESPONSE TO BOTH RED/WHITE (24) AND GREEN/WHITE (23) ZONE QUESTIONS INDICATES CONFUSION BY SUBJECT REGARDING ONE OR BOTH INSIDE-ISSUE QUESTIONS.	L3	REVIEW WITH SUBJECT BOTH RED/WHITE AND GREEN/WHITE ZONE QUESTIONS TO ASSURE COMPLETE UNDERSTANDING, AND SIMPLIFY WORDING OF QUESTION(S) IF NECESSARY.
	25	26	B	B			NA	L4	LACK OF RESPONSE TO BOTH BLACK ZONE QUESTIONS (25 & 26) INDICATES NO OUTSIDE ISSUE BOTHERING SUBJECT DUE TO MISTRUST OF POLYGRAPHIST.	L4	NO REMEDY REQUIRED. SUBJECT APPEARS CONVINCED POLYGRAPHIST WILL NOT ASK UNREVIEWED QUESTION DURING EXAMINATION.
	46	33	G	R	46	33	-1 to -3	M1	STRONG RESPONSE TO RED ZONE QUESTION (33) AND EQUAL STRONG RESPONSE TO GREEN ZONE (46) USUALLY INDICATES SERIOUS GREEN ZONE DEFECT. THIS RULE NULLIFIED BY GREEN/WHITE ZONE (23) AND RED/WHITE ZONE (24) RESPONSES.	M1	ADMINISTER STIMULATION TEST TO REASSURE SUBJECT OF ACCURACY OF TEST. IF ALREADY ADMINISTERED, THEN REVIEW BOTH INSIDE-ISSUE QUESTIONS (23 & 24) WITH SUBJECT TO INSURE UNDERSTANDING AND SUBJECT CONFIDENCE. FURTHER REVIEW GREEN ZONE QUESTIONS (46 & 47) ONLY WITH SUBJECT.
M	47	35	G	R	47	35	-1 to -3	M2	STRONG RESPONSE TO RED ZONE QUESTION (35) AND EQUAL STRONG RESPONSE TO GREEN ZONE (47) USUALLY INDICATES SERIOUS GREEN ZONE DEFECT. THIS RULE NULLIFIED BY GREEN/WHITE ZONE (23) AND RED/WHITE ZONE (24) RESPONSES.	M2	REMEDY THE SAME AS (M1) ABOVE.
	23	24	G/W	R/W	23	24	0	M3	EQUAL STRONG RESPONSE TO BOTH RED/WHITE (24) AND GREEN/WHITE (23) ZONE QUESTIONS INDICATES CONFUSION BY SUBJECT REGARDING ONE OR BOTH INSIDE-ISSUE QUESTIONS.	M3	REVIEW WITH SUBJECT BOTH RED/WHITE AND GREEN/WHITE ZONE QUESTIONS TO ASSURE COMPLETE UNDERSTANDING, AND SIMPLIFY WORDING OF QUESTION(S) IF NECESSARY.
	25	26	B	B	25	26	NA	M4	RESPONSE TO ONE OR BOTH BLACK ZONE QUESTIONS (25 & 26) INDICATES OUTSIDE ISSUE BOTHERING SUBJECT DUE TO MISTRUST OF POLYGRAPHIST.	M4	POLYGRAPHIST MUST GAIN SUBJECT'S CONFIDENCE REGARDING AVOIDANCE OF UNREVIEWED QUESTIONS EMBRACING OUTSIDE ISSUE.

Figure XI-4c

Quadri-Track Reaction Combination Guide

COMBO	ZONE COMPARISON		COLOR CODE		PRESENCE OF REACTION		SCORE		INDICATION		REMEDY
	46	33	G	R		33	-1 to -9	N1	RESPONSE TO RED ZONE QUESTION (33) AND LACK OF RESPONSE TO GREEN ZONE (46) INDICATES DECEPTION TO RELEVANT QUESTION.	N1	NO REMEDY REQUIRED. RED ZONE QUESTION IDEALLY FORMULATED; FUNCTIONING AS DESIGNED.
	47	35	G	R		35	-1 to -9	N2	RESPONSE TO RED ZONE QUESTION (35) AND LACK OF RESPONSE TO GREEN ZONE (47) INDICATES DECEPTION TO RELEVANT QUESTION.	N2	NO REMEDY REQUIRED. RED ZONE QUESTION IDEALLY FORMULATED; FUNCTIONING AS DESIGNED.
N	23	24	G/W	R/W	23	24	0	N3	EQUAL STRONG RESPONSE TO BOTH RED/WHITE (24) AND GREEN/WHITE (23) ZONE QUESTIONS INDICATES CONFUSION BY SUBJECT REGARDING ONE OR BOTH INSIDE-ISSUE QUESTIONS.	N3	REVIEW WITH SUBJECT BOTH RED/WHITE AND GREEN/WHITE ZONE QUESTIONS TO ASSURE COMPLETE UNDERSTANDING, AND SIMPLIFY WORDING OF QUESTION(S) IF NECESSARY.
	25	26	B	B			NA	N4	LACK OF RESPONSE TO BOTH BLACK ZONE QUESTIONS (25 & 26) INDICATES NO OUTSIDE ISSUE BOTHERING SUBJECT DUE TO MISTRUST OF POLYGRAPHIST.	N4	NO REMEDY REQUIRED. SUBJECT APPEARS CONVINCED POLYGRAPHIST WILL NOT ASK UNREVIEWED QUESTION DURING EXAMINATION.
	46	33	G	R		33	-1 to -9	O1	RESPONSE TO RED ZONE QUESTION (33) AND LACK OF RESPONSE TO GREEN ZONE (46) INDICATES DECEPTION TO RELEVANT QUESTION.	O1	NO REMEDY REQUIRED. RED ZONE QUESTION IDEALLY FORMULATED; FUNCTIONING AS DESIGNED.
	47	35	G	R		35	-1 to -9	O2	RESPONSE TO RED ZONE QUESTION (35) AND LACK OF RESPONSE TO GREEN ZONE (47) INDICATES DECEPTION TO RELEVANT QUESTION.	O2	NO REMEDY REQUIRED. RED ZONE QUESTION IDEALLY FORMULATED; FUNCTIONING AS DESIGNED.
O	23	24	G/W	R/W	23	24	0	O3	EQUAL STRONG RESPONSE TO BOTH RED/WHITE (24) AND GREEN/WHITE (23) ZONE QUESTIONS INDICATES CONFUSION BY SUBJECT REGARDING ONE OR BOTH INSIDE-ISSUE QUESTIONS.	O3	REVIEW WITH SUBJECT BOTH RED/WHITE AND GREEN/WHITE ZONE QUESTIONS TO ASSURE COMPLETE UNDERSTANDING, AND SIMPLIFY WORDING OF QUESTION(S) IF NECESSARY.
	25	26	B	B	25	26	NA	O4	RESPONSE TO ONE OR BOTH BLACK ZONE QUESTIONS (25 & 26) INDICATES OUTSIDE ISSUE BOTHERING SUBJECT DUE TO MISTRUST OF POLYGRAPHIST.	O4	POLYGRAPHIST MUST GAIN SUBJECT'S CONFIDENCE REGARDING AVOIDANCE OF UNREVIEWED QUESTIONS EMBRACING OUTSIDE ISSUE.
	46	33	G	R	46		+1 to +9	P1	RESPONSE TO GREEN ZONE QUESTION (46) AND LACK OF RESPONSE TO RED ZONE (33) INDICATES TRUTHFULNESS TO RELEVANT QUESTION.	P1	NO REMEDY REQUIRED. RED ZONE QUESTION IDEALLY FORMULATED; GREEN ZONE QUESTION FUNCTIONING AS DESIGNED.
	47	35	G	R	47		+1 to +9	P2	RESPONSE TO GREEN ZONE QUESTION (47) AND LACK OF RESPONSE TO RED ZONE (35) INDICATES TRUTHFULNESS TO RELEVANT QUESTION.	P2	NO REMEDY REQUIRED. RED ZONE QUESTION IDEALLY FORMULATED; GREEN ZONE QUESTION FUNCTIONING AS DESIGNED.
P	23	24	G/W	R/W	23	24	0	P3	EQUAL STRONG RESPONSE TO BOTH RED/WHITE (24) AND GREEN/WHITE (23) ZONE QUESTIONS INDICATES CONFUSION BY SUBJECT REGARDING ONE OR BOTH INSIDE-ISSUE QUESTIONS.	P3	REVIEW WITH SUBJECT BOTH RED/WHITE AND GREEN/WHITE ZONE QUESTIONS TO ASSURE COMPLETE UNDERSTANDING, AND SIMPLIFY WORDING OF QUESTION(S) IF NECESSARY.
	25	26	B	B			NA	P4	LACK OF RESPONSE TO BOTH BLACK ZONE QUESTIONS (25 & 26) INDICATES NO OUTSIDE ISSUE BOTHERING SUBJECT DUE TO MISTRUST OF POLYGRAPHIST.	P4	NO REMEDY REQUIRED. SUBJECT APPEARS CONVINCED POLYGRAPHIST WILL NOT ASK UNREVIEWED QUESTION DURING EXAMINATION.
	46	33	G	R	46		+1 to +9	Q1	RESPONSE TO GREEN ZONE QUESTION (46) AND LACK OF RESPONSE TO RED ZONE (33) INDICATES TRUTHFULNESS TO RELEVANT QUESTION.	Q1	NO REMEDY REQUIRED. RED ZONE QUESTION IDEALLY FORMULATED; GREEN ZONE QUESTION FUNCTIONING AS DESIGNED.
	47	35	G	R	47		+1 to +9	Q2	RESPONSE TO GREEN ZONE QUESTION (47) AND LACK OF RESPONSE TO RED ZONE (35) INDICATES TRUTHFULNESS TO RELEVANT QUESTION.	Q2	NO REMEDY REQUIRED. RED ZONE QUESTION IDEALLY FORMULATED; GREEN ZONE QUESTION FUNCTIONING AS DESIGNED.
Q	23	24	G/W	R/W	23	24	0	Q3	EQUAL STRONG RESPONSE TO BOTH RED/WHITE (24) AND GREEN/WHITE (23) ZONE QUESTIONS INDICATES CONFUSION BY SUBJECT REGARDING ONE OR BOTH INSIDE-ISSUE QUESTIONS.	Q3	REVIEW WITH SUBJECT BOTH RED/WHITE AND GREEN/WHITE ZONE QUESTIONS TO ASSURE COMPLETE UNDERSTANDING, AND SIMPLIFY WORDING OF QUESTION(S) IF NECESSARY.
	25	26	B	B	25	26	NA	Q4	RESPONSE TO ONE OR BOTH BLACK ZONE QUESTIONS (25 & 26) INDICATES OUTSIDE ISSUE BOTHERING SUBJECT DUE TO MISTRUST OF POLYGRAPHIST.	Q4	POLYGRAPHIST MUST GAIN SUBJECT'S CONFIDENCE REGARDING AVOIDANCE OF UNREVIEWED QUESTIONS EMBRACING OUTSIDE ISSUE.
	46	33	G	R	46 (mild)	33 (mild)	0	R1	MILD RESPONSE TO RED ZONE QUESTION (33) AND EQUAL MILD RESPONSE TO GREEN ZONE (46) USUALLY INDICATES SERIOUS GREEN ZONE DEFECT; UNLESS THERE IS STRONG RESPONSE TO RED/WHITE ZONE (24), THEN REFER TO REACTION COMBINATION (S).	R1	ADMINISTER STIMULATION TEST. IF ALREADY ADMINISTERED, INCREASE INTENSITY OF GREEN ZONE QUESTION (46) BY REVIEWING GREEN ZONE QUESTIONS ONLY BEFORE NEXT CHART; IF UNPRODUCTIVE, CHANGE GREEN ZONE QUESTION BY ALTERING AGE CATEGORY OR SCOPE OF GREEN ZONE QUESTION.
	47	35	G	R	47 (mild)	35 (mild)	0	R2	MILD RESPONSE TO RED ZONE QUESTION (35 AND EQUAL MILD RESPONSE TO GREEN ZONE (47) USUALLY INDICATES SERIOUS GREEN ZONE DEFECT; UNLESS THERE IS STRONG RESPONSE TO RED/WHITE ZONE (24), THEN REFER TO REACTION COMBINATION (S).	R2	REMEDY THE SAME AS (R1) ABOVE.
R	23	24	G/W	R/W			0	R3	LACK OF RESPONSE TO GREEN/WHITE (23) AND RED/WHITE (24) ZONE INDICATES NO FEAR OF ERROR IS DAMPENING GREEN ZONE (46 & 47) AND FEAR OF DETECTION TO RED ZONE (33&35) NOT RECHANNELED INTO HOPE OF ERROR (24).	R3	NO REMEDY REQUIRED. NO EVIDENCE OF INSIDE ISSUE DAMPENING GREEN OR RED ZONES.
	25	26	B	B			NA	R4	LACK OF RESPONSE TO BOTH BLACK ZONE QUESTIONS (25 & 26) INDICATES NO OUTSIDE ISSUE BOTHERING SUBJECT DUE TO MISTRUST OF POLYGRAPHIST.	R4	NO REMEDY REQUIRED. SUBJECT APPEARS CONVINCED POLYGRAPHIST WILL NOT ASK UNREVIEWED QUESTION DURING EXAMINATION.

Figure XI-4d

Quadri-Track Reaction Combination Guide

COMBO	ZONE COMPARISON		COLOR CODE		PRESENCE OF REACTION		SCORE	INDICATION	REMEDY
	46	33	G	R		33	-1 to -9	S1 RESPONSE TO RED ZONE QUESTION (33) AND LACK OF RESPONSE TO GREEN ZONE (46) INDICATES DECEPTION TO RELEVANT QUESTION.	S1 NO REMEDY REQUIRED. RED ZONE QUESTION IDEALLY FORMULATED; FUNCTIONING AS DESIGNED.
	47	35	G	R		35	-1 to -9	S2 RESPONSE TO RED ZONE QUESTION (35) AND LACK OF RESPONSE TO GREEN ZONE (47) INDICATES DECEPTION TO RELEVANT QUESTION.	S2 NO REMEDY REQUIRED. RED ZONE QUESTION IDEALLY FORMULATED; FUNCTIONING AS DESIGNED.
S	23	24	G/W	R/W		24	-1 to -9	S3 RESPONSE TO RED/WHITE ZONE (24) AND LACK OF RESPONSE TO GREEN/WHITE ZONE (23) INDICATES SUBJECT HOPES ERROR WILL BE MADE REGARDING RED ZONE QUESTIONS (33&35) INDICATING DECEPTION REGARDING TARGET ISSUE.	S3 NO REMEDY REQUIRED. RED/WHITE (24) AND GREEN/WHITE (23) QUESTIONS IDEALLY FORMULATED AND FUNCTIONING AS DESIGNED. RESPONSE TO RED/WHITE (24) QUESTION IN ADDITION TO RED ZONE QUESTIONS (33&35) PROVIDES FURTHER PSYCHOPHYSIOLOGICAL EVIDENCE OF DECEPTION REGARDING TARGET ISSUE.
	25	26	B	B			NA	S4 LACK OF RESPONSE TO BOTH BLACK ZONE QUESTIONS (25 & 26) INDICATES NO OUTSIDE ISSUE BOTHERING SUBJECT DUE TO MISTRUST OF POLYGRAPHIST.	S4 NO REMEDY REQUIRED. SUBJECT APPEARS CONVINCED POLYGRAPHIST WILL NOT ASK UNREVIEWED QUESTION DURING EXAMINATION.
	46	33	G	R		33	-1 to -9	T1 RESPONSE TO RED ZONE QUESTION (33) AND LACK OF RESPONSE TO GREEN ZONE (46) USUALLY INDICATES DECEPTION TO RELEVANT QUESTION. THIS RULE NULLIFIED BY GREEN/WHITE ZONE (23) RESPONSE INDICATING SUBJECT FEAR OF ERROR REGARDING TARGET ISSUE.	T1 ADMINISTER STIMULATION TEST TO REASSURE SUBJECT OF ACCURACY OF TEST. IF ALREADY ADMINISTERED, THEN REVIEW BOTH INSIDE-ISSUE QUESTIONS (23 & 24) WITH SUBJECT TO INSURE UNDERSTANDING AND SUBJECT CONFIDENCE. FURTHER REVIEW GREEN ZONE QUESTIONS (46 & 47) ONLY WITH SUBJECT.
T	47	35	G	R		35	-1 to -9	T2 RESPONSE TO RED ZONE QUESTION (35) AND LACK OF RESPONSE TO GREEN ZONE (47) USUALLY INDICATES DECEPTION TO RELEVANT QUESTION. THIS RULE NULLIFIED BY GREEN/WHITE ZONE (23) RESPONSE INDICATING SUBJECT FEAR OF ERROR REGARDING TARGET ISSUE.	T2 REMEDY THE SAME AS (T1) ABOVE.
	23	24	G/W	R/W	23		+1 to +9	T3 RESPONSE TO GREEN/WHITE ZONE (23) AND LACK OF RESPONSE TO RED/WHITE ZONE (24) INDICATES FEAR OF ERROR REGARDING RED ZONE QUESTIONS (33&35) MAKING RED ZONE QUESTIONS UNDULY THREATENING.	T3 REMEDY THE SAME AS (T1) ABOVE. IF (T1) REMEDY INEFFECTIVE, INCREASE INTENSITY OF GREEN ZONE QUESTIONS (46 & 47) BY ALTERING AGE CATEGORY OR CHANGING SCOPE OF GREEN ZONE QUESTIONS.
	25	26	B	B			NA	T4 LACK OF RESPONSE TO BOTH BLACK ZONE QUESTIONS (25 & 26) INDICATES NO OUTSIDE ISSUE BOTHERING SUBJECT DUE TO MISTRUST OF POLYGRAPHIST.	T4 NO REMEDY REQUIRED. SUBJECT APPEARS CONVINCED POLYGRAPHIST WILL NOT ASK UNREVIEWED QUESTION DURING EXAMINATION.
	46	33	G	R	46		+1 to +9	U1 RESPONSE TO GREEN ZONE QUESTION (46) AND LACK OF RESPONSE TO RED ZONE (33) INDICATES TRUTHFULNESS TO RELEVANT QUESTION.	U1 NO REMEDY REQUIRED. RED ZONE QUESTION IDEALLY FORMULATED; GREEN ZONE FUNCTIONING AS DESIGNED.
	47	35	G	R	47		+1 to +9	U2 RESPONSE TO GREEN ZONE QUESTION (47) AND LACK OF RESPONSE TO RED ZONE (35) INDICATES TRUTHFULNESS TO RELEVANT QUESTION.	U2 NO REMEDY REQUIRED. RED ZONE QUESTION IDEALLY FORMULATED; GREEN ZONE FUNCTIONING AS DESIGNED.
U	23	24	G/W	R/W		24	-1 to -9	U3 RESPONSE TO RED/WHITE ZONE (24) AND LACK OF RESPONSE TO GREEN/WHITE ZONE (23) USUALLY INDICATES SUBJECT HOPES ERROR WILL BE MADE REGARDING RED ZONE QUESTIONS. BUT PRESENCE OF RESPONSE TO GREEN ZONE QUESTIONS (46 & 47) AND LACK OF RESPONSE TO RED ZONE QUESTIONS (33 & 35) INDICATES SUBJECT MAY BE CONFUSED BY WORDING AND/OR PURPOSE OF RED/WHITE ZONE QUESTION (24).	U3 REVIEW WITH SUBJECT BOTH GREEN/WHITE AND RED/WHITE ZONE QUESTIONS (23 & 24) TO INSURE SUBJECT UNDERSTANDS WORDING AND PURPOSE OF QUESTIONS.
	25	26	B	B			NA	U4 LACK OF RESPONSE TO BOTH BLACK ZONE QUESTIONS (25 & 26) INDICATES NO OUTSIDE ISSUE BOTHERING SUBJECT DUE TO MISTRUST OF POLYGRAPHIST.	U4 NO REMEDY REQUIRED. SUBJECT APPEARS CONVINCED POLYGRAPHIST WILL NOT ASK UNREVIEWED QUESTION DURING EXAMINATION.
	46	33	G	R	46		+1 to +9	V1 RESPONSE TO GREEN ZONE QUESTION (46) AND LACK OF RESPONSE TO RED ZONE (33) INDICATES TRUTHFULNESS TO RELEVANT QUESTION.	V1 NO REMEDY REQUIRED. RED ZONE QUESTION IDEALLY FORMULATED; GREEN ZONE FUNCTIONING AS DESIGNED.
	47	35	G	R	47		+1 to +9	V2 RESPONSE TO GREEN ZONE QUESTION (47) AND LACK OF RESPONSE TO RED ZONE (35) INDICATES TRUTHFULNESS TO RELEVANT QUESTION.	V2 NO REMEDY REQUIRED. RED ZONE QUESTION IDEALLY FORMULATED; GREEN ZONE FUNCTIONING AS DESIGNED.
V	23	24	G/W	R/W	23		+1 to +9	V3 RESPONSE TO GREEN/WHITE ZONE (23) AND LACK OF RESPONSE TO RED/WHITE ZONE (24) INDICATES FEAR OF ERROR REGARDING TARGET ISSUE; BUT LACK OF RESPONSE TO RED ZONE QUESTIONS (33 & 35) INDICATES FEAR OR ERROR NOT MAKING RED ZONE QUESTIONS (33 & 35) UNDULY THREATENING TO SUBJECT.	V3 ADMINISTER STIMULATION TEST. IF ALREADY ADMINISTERED; NO FURTHER REMEDY REQUIRED. RESPONSE TO GREEN/WHITE ZONE (23) AND LACK OF RESPONSE TO RED/WHITE ZONE (24) IN ADDITION TO RESPONSE TO GREEN ZONE (46 & 47) AND LACK OF RESPONSE TO RED ZONE (33 & 35) QUESTIONS PROVIDES FURTHER PSYCHOPHYSIOLOGICAL EVIDENCE OF TRUTHFULNESS REGARDING TARGET ISSUE.
	25	26	B	B			NA	V4 LACK OF RESPONSE TO BOTH BLACK ZONE QUESTIONS (25 & 26) INDICATES NO OUTSIDE ISSUE BOTHERING SUBJECT DUE TO MISTRUST OF POLYGRAPHIST.	V4 NO REMEDY REQUIRED. SUBJECT APPEARS CONVINCED POLYGRAPHIST WILL NOT ASK UNREVIEWED QUESTION DURING EXAMINATION.

Figure XI-4e

Quadri-Track Reaction Combination Guide

COMBO	ZONE COMPARISON		COLOR CODE		PRESENCE REACTION		SCORE	INDICATION	REMEDY
	46	33	G	R			0	W1 LACK OF RESPONSE TO RED ZONE QUESTION (33) INDICATES TRUTHFULNESS REGARDING TARGET ISSUE BASED ON ASSUMPTION SUBJECT CAPABLE OF RESPONSE; BUT LACK OF RESPONSE TO GREEN ZONE QUESTION (46) AS WELL, INDICATES SERIOUS GREEN ZONE DEFECT, OR INCAPACITY OF SUBJECT TO RESPOND TO EITHER QUESTION ZONE FOR REASON(S) TO BE DETERMINED BY POLYGRAPHIST.	W1 FIRST, ADMINISTER STIMULATION TEST TO DETERMINE SUBJECT CAPABILITY OF RESPONSE. SECOND, INCREASE INTENSITY OF GREEN ZONE QUESTION (46) BY ALTERING AGE CATEGORY OR CHANGING SCOPE OF GREEN ZONE QUESTION. IF ABOVE REMEDY FAILS TO PRODUCE DESIRED RESPONSE, A URINE SPECIMEN MAY BE OBTAINED FROM SUBJECT TO DETERMINE THE PRESENCE OF ANY DRUG.
W	47	35	G	R			0	W2 LACK OF RESPONSE TO RED ZONE QUESTION (35) INDICATES TRUTHFULNESS REGARDING TARGET ISSUE BASED ON ASSUMPTION SUBJECT CAPABLE OF RESPONSE; BUT LACK OF RESPONSE TO GREEN ZONE QUESTION (46) AS WELL, INDICATES SERIOUS GREEN ZONE DEFECT, OR INCAPACITY OF SUBJECT TO RESPOND TO EITHER QUESTION ZONE FOR REASON(S) TO BE DETERMINED BY POLYGRAPHIST.	W2 REMEDY THE SAME AS (W1) ABOVE.
	23	24	G/W	R/W			0	W3 LACK OF RESPONSE TO GREEN/WHITE (23) AND RED/WHITE (24) ZONE INDICATES NO FEAR OF ERROR IS DAMPENING GREEN ZONE (46 & 47) AND FEAR OF DETECTION TO RED ZONE (33 & 35) NOT RECHANNELED INTO HOPE OF ERROR (24).	W3 NO REMEDY REQUIRED. NO EVIDENCE OF INSIDE ISSUE DAMPENING GREEN OR RED ZONE.
	25	26	B	B			NA	W4 LACK OF RESPONSE TO BOTH BLACK ZONE QUESTIONS (25 & 26) INDICATES NO OUTSIDE ISSUE BOTHERING SUBJECT DUE TO MISTRUST OF POLYGRAPHIST.	W4 NO REMEDY REQUIRED. SUBJECT APPEARS CONVINCED POLYGRAPHIST WILL NOT ASK UNREVIEWED QUESTION DURING EXAMINATION.

Figure XI-4f

Sometimes the FP encounters a deceptive (as later verified) examinee who employs countermeasures by attempting to control his/her breathing during the test. In such instances the employment of the Silent Answer Test (SAT) may be very useful as an anti-countermeasure test and a form of Control-Stimulation test. (See Chapter 19). This test is administered immediately after the chart suspected of deliberate distortion. As in the Control-Stimulation Test (Chapter 10) the SAT is not scored for a determination but its effect should be seen on the chart immediately following the SAT, and that chart is scored.

The total scores from each test are then compared to the Predictive Table of Accuracy and Error Rates for the Quadri-Track Zone Comparison Technique, for the Innocent or Guilty depending upon whether the scores are preceded by a plus or minus respectively. This Table (Fig. XI-7), based on the 1989 Matte-Reuss field study, will provide a *probability* that a Innocent or Guilty case will reach a mathematical score this high or higher (weaker); the *percentage* of the time an Innocent or Guilty case will score this value or lower than this value (stronger score); and the *potential for error* based on the probability that an opposite case will score this value or lower. Figure XI-8 depicts a graph of the predictive table data which shows the relation between the polygraph score and the distribution of scores for the Innocent and Guilty cases. (Matte, Reuss 1989)

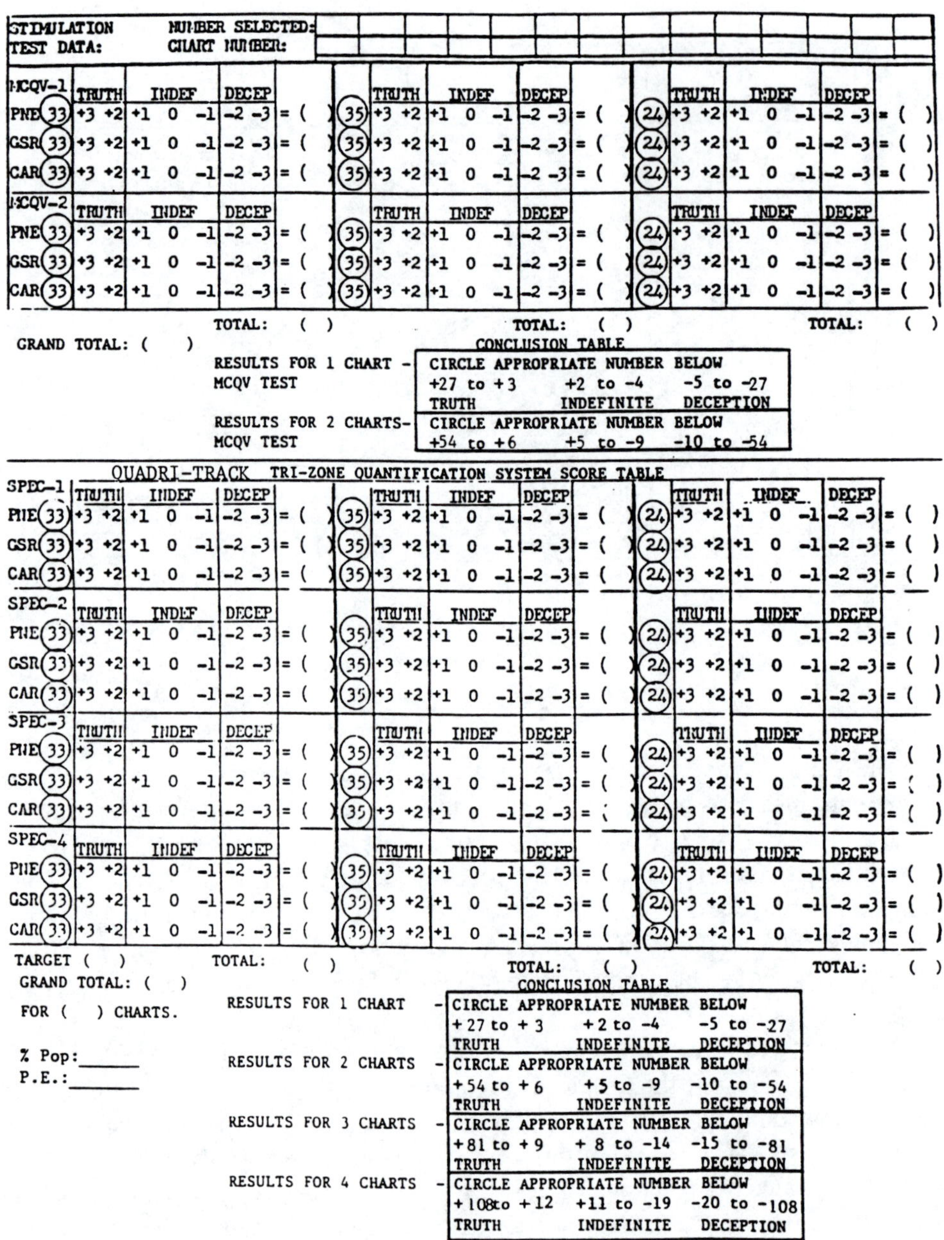

STIMULATION TEST DATA:	NUMBER SELECTED: / CHART NUMBER:

MCQV-1		TRUTH	INDEF	DECEP			TRUTH	INDEF	DECEP			TRUTH	INDEF	DECEP	
PNE	33	+3 +2	+1 0 -1	-2 -3	= ( )	35	+3 +2	+1 0 -1	-2 -3	= ( )	24	+3 +2	+1 0 -1	-2 -3	= ( )
GSR	33	+3 +2	+1 0 -1	-2 -3	= ( )	35	+3 +2	+1 0 -1	-2 -3	= ( )	24	+3 +2	+1 0 -1	-2 -3	= ( )
CAR	33	+3 +2	+1 0 -1	-2 -3	= ( )	35	+3 +2	+1 0 -1	-2 -3	= ( )	24	+3 +2	+1 0 -1	-2 -3	= ( )
MCQV-2		**TRUTH**	**INDEF**	**DECEP**			**TRUTH**	**INDEF**	**DECEP**			**TRUTH**	**INDEF**	**DECEP**	
PNE	33	+3 +2	+1 0 -1	-2 -3	= ( )	35	+3 +2	+1 0 -1	-2 -3	= ( )	24	+3 +2	+1 0 -1	-2 -3	= ( )
GSR	33	+3 +2	+1 0 -1	-2 -3	= ( )	35	+3 +2	+1 0 -1	-2 -3	= ( )	24	+3 +2	+1 0 -1	-2 -3	= ( )
CAR	33	+3 +2	+1 0 -1	-2 -3	= ( )	35	+3 +2	+1 0 -1	-2 -3	= ( )	24	+3 +2	+1 0 -1	-2 -3	= ( )
				TOTAL:	( )				TOTAL:	( )				TOTAL:	( )

GRAND TOTAL: ( )

CONCLUSION TABLE

	CIRCLE APPROPRIATE NUMBER BELOW		
RESULTS FOR 1 CHART - MCQV TEST	+27 to +3	+2 to -4	-5 to -27
	TRUTH	INDEFINITE	DECEPTION
RESULTS FOR 2 CHARTS- MCQV TEST	CIRCLE APPROPRIATE NUMBER BELOW		
	+54 to +6	+5 to -9	-10 to -54

QUADRI-TRACK TRI-ZONE QUANTIFICATION SYSTEM SCORE TABLE

SPEC-1		TRUTH	INDEF	DECEP			TRUTH	INDEF	DECEP			TRUTH	INDEF	DECEP	
PNE	33	+3 +2	+1 0 -1	-2 -3	= ( )	35	+3 +2	+1 0 -1	-2 -3	= ( )	24	+3 +2	+1 0 -1	-2 -3	= ( )
GSR	33	+3 +2	+1 0 -1	-2 -3	= ( )	35	+3 +2	+1 0 -1	-2 -3	= ( )	24	+3 +2	+1 0 -1	-2 -3	= ( )
CAR	33	+3 +2	+1 0 -1	-2 -3	= ( )	35	+3 +2	+1 0 -1	-2 -3	= ( )	24	+3 +2	+1 0 -1	-2 -3	= ( )
SPEC-2		**TRUTH**	**INDEF**	**DECEP**			**TRUTH**	**INDEF**	**DECEP**			**TRUTH**	**INDEF**	**DECEP**	
PNE	33	+3 +2	+1 0 -1	-2 -3	= ( )	35	+3 +2	+1 0 -1	-2 -3	= ( )	24	+3 +2	+1 0 -1	-2 -3	= ( )
GSR	33	+3 +2	+1 0 -1	-2 -3	= ( )	35	+3 +2	+1 0 -1	-2 -3	= ( )	24	+3 +2	+1 0 -1	-2 -3	= ( )
CAR	33	+3 +2	+1 0 -1	-2 -3	= ( )	35	+3 +2	+1 0 -1	-2 -3	= ( )	24	+3 +2	+1 0 -1	-2 -3	= ( )
SPEC-3		**TRUTH**	**INDEF**	**DECEP**			**TRUTH**	**INDEF**	**DECEP**			**TRUTH**	**INDEF**	**DECEP**	
PNE	33	+3 +2	+1 0 -1	-2 -3	= ( )	35	+3 +2	+1 0 -1	-2 -3	= ( )	24	+3 +2	+1 0 -1	-2 -3	= ( )
GSR	33	+3 +2	+1 0 -1	-2 -3	= ( )	35	+3 +2	+1 0 -1	-2 -3	= ( )	24	+3 +2	+1 0 -1	-2 -3	= ( )
CAR	33	+3 +2	+1 0 -1	-2 -3	= ( )	35	+3 +2	+1 0 -1	-2 -3	= ( )	24	+3 +2	+1 0 -1	-2 -3	= ( )
SPEC-4		**TRUTH**	**INDEF**	**DECEP**			**TRUTH**	**INDEF**	**DECEP**			**TRUTH**	**INDEF**	**DECEP**	
PNE	33	+3 +2	+1 0 -1	-2 -3	= ( )	35	+3 +2	+1 0 -1	-2 -3	= ( )	24	+3 +2	+1 0 -1	-2 -3	= ( )
GSR	33	+3 +2	+1 0 -1	-2 -3	= ( )	35	+3 +2	+1 0 -1	-2 -3	= ( )	24	+3 +2	+1 0 -1	-2 -3	= ( )
CAR	33	+3 +2	+1 0 -1	-2 -3	= ( )	35	+3 +2	+1 0 -1	-2 -3	= ( )	24	+3 +2	+1 0 -1	-2 -3	= ( )
TARGET ( )				TOTAL:	( )				TOTAL:	( )				TOTAL:	( )

GRAND TOTAL: ( )

FOR ( ) CHARTS.

% Pop:______

P.E.:______

CONCLUSION TABLE

	CIRCLE APPROPRIATE NUMBER BELOW		
RESULTS FOR 1 CHART -	+27 to +3	+2 to -4	-5 to -27
	TRUTH	INDEFINITE	DECEPTION
RESULTS FOR 2 CHARTS -	CIRCLE APPROPRIATE NUMBER BELOW		
	+54 to +6	+5 to -9	-10 to -54
	TRUTH	INDEFINITE	DECEPTION
RESULTS FOR 3 CHARTS -	CIRCLE APPROPRIATE NUMBER BELOW		
	+81 to +9	+ 8 to -14	-15 to -81
	TRUTH	INDEFINITE	DECEPTION
RESULTS FOR 4 CHARTS -	CIRCLE APPROPRIATE NUMBER BELOW		
	+108 to +12	+11 to -19	-20 to -108
	TRUTH	INDEFINITE	DECEPTION

Quadri-Track Numerical Score Sheet and Conclusion Table

Figure XI-5

MCQV TEST (Control Question Validation) USED ON CHART NR: [| | | | | | |]

14J	WERE YOU BORN IN THE U.S?	13L (Last Name)	13F (First Name)
39	RE: WHETHER (OR NOT) YOU	DO YOU INTEND TO ANSWER TRUTHFULLY EACH QUESTION ABOUT THAT?	
25	ARE YOU COMPLETELY CONVINCED THAT I WILL NOT ASK YOU AN UNREVIEWED QUESTION DURING THIS CHART?		
46	BETWEEN THE AGES OF ( ) AND ( ) - DO YOU REMEMBER:		
33			
47	DURING THE FIRST ( ) YEARS OF YOUR LIFE - DO YOU REMEMBER:		
35			
23	ARE YOU AFRAID AN ERROR WILL BE MADE ON THIS TEST?		
24	ARE YOU HOPEFUL AN ERROR WILL BE MADE ON THIS TEST?		
26	IS THERE SOMETHING ELSE YOU ARE AFRAID I WILL ASK YOU A QUESTION ABOUT, EVEN THOUGH I TOLD YOU I WOULD NOT?		
44J	REGARDING DRUGS - ARE YOU HOLDING BACK INFORMATION ABOUT ANY DRUGS OR MEDICATION YOU HAVE TAKEN DURING THE LAST 12 HOURS?		

CONTROL QUESTION CHANGES - USED ON CHART NR: [| | | | | | | | |]

46	BETWEEN THE AGES OF ( ) AND ( ) - DO YOU REMEMBER:
47	DURING THE FIRST ( ) YEARS OF YOUR LIFE - DO YOU REMEMBER:

QUADRI-TRACK ZONE COMPARISON TECHNIQUE

TARGET ( ) USED ON CHART NR: [| | | | | | |]

14J	WERE YOU BORN IN THE U. S?	13L (last Name)	13F (First Name)
39	RE: WHETHER (OR NOT) YOU	DO YOU INTEND TO ANSWER TRUTHFULLY EACH QUESTION ABOUT THAT?	
25	ARE YOU COMPLETELY CONVINCED THAT I WILL NOT ASK YOU AN UNREVIEWED QUESTION DURING THIS CHART?		
46	BETWEEN THE AGES OF ( ) AND ( ) - DO YOU REMEMBER:		
33			
47	DURING THE FIRST ( ) YEARS OF YOUR LIFE - DO YOU REMEMBER:		
35			
23	ARE YOU AFRAID AN ERROR WILL BE MADE ON THIS TEST : regarding		
24	ARE YOU HOPEFUL AN ERROR WILL BE MADE ON THIS TEST : regarding		
26	IS THERE SOMETHING ELSE YOU ARE AFRAID I WILL ASK YOU A QUESTION ABOUT, EVEN THOUGH I TOLD YOU I WOULD NOT?		
48	DURING THE FIRST ( ) YEARS OF YOUR LIFE - DO YOU REMEMBER:		
32			

Quadri-Track and MCQV Test Question Formulation Sheet

Figure XI-6

TABLE 10 Predictive Table For Estimating Error Rates

Table 10a-2. For Scores Obtained With the Quadri-Track Zone Comparison Technique for Innocent Cases

Z-score - based on the scores of the 58 innocent cases with the Quadri-zone adjustment

Probability - that an innocent case will reach a mathematical score that low or lower (weaker) is less than

Percent - of the time an innocent case will score this value or lower than this value (weaker score)

Potential Error (False Negative) - based on the probability that a guilty case will score this value or higher

SCORE FOR NUMBER OF CHARTS

AVERAGE SCORE	2	3	4	Z-SCORE	PROBABILITY	PERCENT	POTENTIAL ERROR
16.5	33	50	66	3.392	1.000	100%	0.0%
16.0	32	48	64	3.231	1.000	100	0.0
15.5	31	47	62	3.069	.999	99.9	0.0
15.0	30	45	60	2.908	.998	99.8	0.0
14.5	29	44	58	2.747	.997	99.7	0.0
14	28	42	56	2.585	.995	99.5	0.0
13.5	27	41	54	2.424	.992	99.2	0.0
13	26	39	52	2.263	.988	98.8	0.0
12.5	25	38	50	2.101	.982	98.2	0.0
12	24	36	48	1.940	.974	97.4	0.0
11.5	23	35	46	1.779	.962	96.2	0.0
11	22	33	44	1.617	.947	94.2	0.0
10.5	21	32	42	1.456	.927	92.7	0.0
10	20	30	40	1.295	.902	90.2	0.0
9.5	19	29	38	1.133	.871	87.1	0.0
9	18	27	36	.972	.835	83.5	0.0
8.5	17	26	34	.811	.791	79.1	0.0
8	16	24	32	.649	.742	74.2	0.0
7.5	15	23	30	.488	.687	68.7	0.0
7	14	21	28	.327	.628	62.8	0.0
6.5	13	20	26	.165	.566	56.6	0.0
6	12	18	24	.004	.502	50.2	0.0
5.5	11	17	22	-.157	.438	43.8	0.0
5	10	15	20	-.319	.375	37.5	0.0
4.5	9	14	18	-.480	.316	31.6	0.0
4	8	12	16	-.641	.261	26.1	0.0
3.5	7	11	14	-.803	.211	21.1	0.0
3	6	9	12	-.964	.167	16.7	0.0
2.5	5	8	10	-1.125	.130	13.0	0.0
2	4	6	8	-1.287	.090	9.0	0.0
1.5	3	5	6	-1.448	.074	7.4	0.0
1	2	3	4	-1.609	.054	5.4	0.0
0.5	1	2	2	-1.771	.038	3.8	0.0
0	0	0	0	-1.932	.027	2.7	0.0
-0.5	-1	-2	-2	-2.093	.018	1.8	0.1
-1	-2	-3	-4	-2.255	.012	1.2	0.2
-1.5	-3	-5	-6	-2.416	.008	1.0	0.4
-2	-4	-6	-8	-2.578	.005	1.0	0.6
-2.5	-5	-8	-10	-2.739	.003	0.3	1.0
-3	-6	-9	-12	-2.900	.002	0.2	1.5
-3.5	-7	-11	-14	-3.062	.001	0.1	2.3
-4	-8	-12	-16	-3.223	.001	0.1	3.5
-4.5	-9	-14	-18	-3.384	.001	0.1	5.1
-5	-10	-15	-20	-3.546	.000	0.0	7.1

Predictive Table of Error Rates for the Innocent

Figure XI-7a

TABLE 10 Predictive Table for Estimating Error Rates

Table 10b-2. For Scores Obtained With the Quadri-Track Zone Comparison Technique for Guilty Cases
Z-score - based on the scores of the 64 guilty cases with the Quadri-zone adjustment
Probability - that an guilty case will reach a mathematical score this high or higher (weaker) is less than
Percent - of the time a Guilty case will score this value or lower than this value (stronger score)
Potential Error (False Positive) - based on the probability that an innocent case will score this value or lower

SCORE FOR NUMBER OF CHARTS

AVERAGE SCORE	2	3	4	Z-SCORE	PROBABILITY	PERCENT	POTENTIAL ERROR
3	6	9	12	4.277	.000	100%	16.7%
2.5	5	8	10	4.101	.000	100	13.0
2	4	6	8	3.925	.000	100	9.0
1.5	3	5	6	3.750	.000	100	7.4
1	2	3	4	3.574	.000	100	5.4
0.5	1	2	2	3.398	.000	100	3.8
0	0	0	0	3.222	.001	100	2.7
-0.5	-1	-2	-2	3.046	.001	99.9	1.8
-1	-2	-3	-4	2.870	.002	99.8	1.2
-1.5	-3	-5	-6	2.694	.004	99.6	1.0
-2	-4	-6	-8	2.519	.006	99.4	1.0
-2.5	-5	-8	-10	2.343	.010	99.0	0.3
-3	-6	-9	-12	2.167	.015	98.5	0.2
-3.5	-7	-11	-14	1.991	.023	97.7	0.1
-4	-8	-12	-16	1.815	.035	96.5	0.1
-4.5	-9	-14	-18	1.639	.051	94.9	0.1
-5	-10	-15	-20	1.464	.071	92.9	0.0
-5.5	-11	-17	-22	1.288	.100	90.0	0.0
-6	-12	-18	-24	1.112	.133	86.7	0.0
-6.5	-13	-20	-26	.936	.175	82.5	0.0
-7	-14	-21	-28	.760	.224	77.6	0.0
-7.5	-15	-23	-30	.584	.280	72.0	0.0
-8	-16	-24	-32	.408	.342	65.8	0.0
-8.5	-17	-26	-34	.233	.408	59.2	0.0
-9	-18	-27	-36	.057	.477	52.3	0.0
-9.5	-19	-29	-38	-.119	.547	45.3	0.0
-10	-20	-30	-40	-.295	.616	38.4	0.0
-10.5	-21	-32	-42	-.471	.681	31.9	0.0
-11	-22	-33	-44	-.647	.741	25.9	0.0
-11.5	-23	-35	-46	-.823	.795	20.5	0.0
-12	-24	-36	-48	-.998	.841	15.9	0.0
-12.5	-25	-38	-50	-1.174	.880	12.0	0.0
-13	-26	-39	-52	-1.350	.912	8.8	0.0
-13.5	-27	-41	-54	-1.526	.937	6.3	0.0
-14	-28	-42	-56	-1.702	.956	4.4	0.0
-14.5	-29	-44	-58	-1.878	.970	3.0	0.0
-15	-30	-45	-60	-2.054	.980	2.0	0.0
-15.5	-31	-47	-62	-2.229	.987	1.3	0.0
-16	-32	-48	-64	-2.405	.992	0.8	0.0
-16.5	-33	-50	-66	-2.581	.995	0.5	0.0
-17	-34	-51	-68	-2.757	.997	0.3	0.0
-17.5	-35	-53	-70	-2.933	.998	0.2	0.0
-18	-36	-54	-72	-3.109	.999	0.1	0.0
-18.5	-37	-56	-74	-3.284	1.000	0.0	0.0
-19	-38	-57	-76	-3.460	1.000	0.0	0.0

Predictive Table of Error Rates for the Guilty

Figure XI-7b

TABLE 10-C GRAPH OF THE PREDICTIVE TABLE DATA WITH *INSIDE TRACK* (Formerly known as *Zone Four*).

This graph shows the relation between the Polygraph Score and the distribution of scores for the Innocent and Guilty cases. The graph is based on the average score per chart from Tables 10a-2 and 10b-2. The graph can be used for a given case by dividing the Total Score with the Inside Track by the number of charts scored to get the average score, or by referring to Tables 10a-2 or 10b-2, as appropriate, and then noting the location of the average score on the distribution.

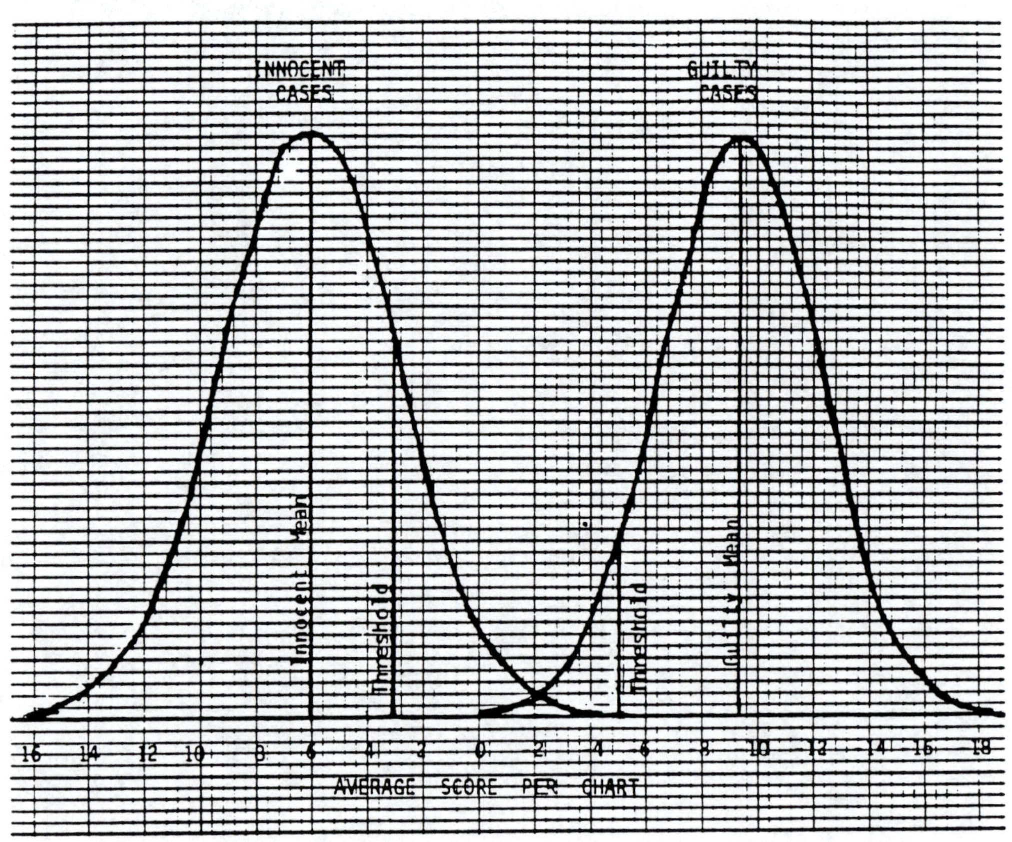

INNOCENT CASES Per Chart		GUILTY CASES Per Chart	
Threshold	+3	Threshold	-5
Mean	+6.0017	Mean	-9.1484
S. D.	3.099	S. D.	2.8433

Predictive Table Data Graph for Innocent & Guilty

Figure XI-8

If a computerized polygraph system was used to administer aforementioned examination, then both the scores from Quadri-Track Quantification System and the scores from the computer algorithm are reported.

The Backster Tri-Zone Comparison Technique

The Backster Zone Comparison Technique forms the basis of the above described Quadri-Track Zone Comparison Technique, therefore the definition of terms articulated above and the methodology used in the administration of the technique are hereto applicable. The current Backster Standardized Polygraph Notepack and Technique Guide (1979 Edition) which contains instructions in its application is partially set forth below. Backster permits his students/graduates to include the *Inside Track* "Fear of Error" Control Question #23, and the "Hope of Error" Relevant Question #24 in his "You" Phase (Single-Issue) Zone Comparison Test structure, in place of control question #48 and Optional/Not Recommended relevant question #37. When the Backster Zone Comparison Technique does incorporate the Fear/Hope of error questions, the only difference remaining in the *test structure* between the Matte Quadri-Track ZCT and the Backster Tri-Zone CT is in the position of Symptomatic Question #25 and Preparatory/Sacrifice Relevant Question #39 which are opposite.

The Backster scoring system uses a seven-position scale but its conversion table employs an increasing threshold that is slightly lower than the Quadri-Track ZCT, as can be seen in the Backster Notepack below. (Fig. XI-9a thru XI-9g).

Procedurally, Backster compares each relevant question against its neighboring control question as follows: To arrive at an interim spot analysis tracing determination of Truthful (+2) or Deception (-2) there must be a significant and timely tracing reaction in *either* the red zone (relevant) *or* green zone (control) being compared. If the red zone (relevant) indicates a lack of reaction, it should be compared with the neighboring green zone (control) containing the larger timely reaction. If the red zone (relevant) indicates a timely and significant reaction it should be compared with the neighboring green zone (control) containing no reaction or the least reaction. (Backster 1994) The aforesaid procedure differs from the Quadri-Track ZCT.

The diagram depicted below (Fig. XI-10) shows the test structure of Backster's You Phase, Single-Issue Zone Comparison Test; Backster's Exploratory (multiple-issue) test; and Backster's S-K-Y (Suspicion-Knowledge-You) test, which portray a consistency in the position of each Zone and Spot in all of the aforementioned test structures.

HA SUBJECT AND EXAMINATION DATA

HAA SUBJECT NAME DATA

Jr.
Sr.

Subject's Last Name | First Name | Middle Name or Initial

HAF EXAM. IDENT. DATA

File Number

HAB SUBJECT BIRTH DATA

U.S.A. | None

Birthplace (Town or County) | Birthplace (State and Country) | Nicknames – Aliases

File Number

Now ( )

Birthdate (Month, Day, Year) | Yrs. Old

1979 EDITION

STANDARDIZED POLYGRAPH NOTEPACK

and

TECHNIQUE GUIDE

PROFESSIONALIZATION
THROUGH
STANDARDIZATION

Backster

ZONE COMPARISON TECHNIQUE®

© 1979 By Cleve Backster | Printed in U.S.A.

Controlled Circulation

Date of This Examination

Own
Dept

For: Dept. Agency. Client

Polygraph Examiner

Offense-incident Category

HAC SUBJ. RESIDENCE DATA

Street Address

Town and State

Time at Present Address

None

Residence Telephone Number

HAE SUBJECT MISCELLANEOUS DATA

Race	Sex	Height	Weight	Hair	Eyes	Build
	M F	ft. in.	Lbs.			

Where Examined

HAD EXAMINATION TIME LOG

Appointment	Subject Arrived	Conference Start	Conference End	Pre-test Start	Exam Ended	Subject Left
am pm	am pm	am pm	am pm	am pm	am pm	am pm

Stop: am pm	Purpose: am pm	Start: am pm	Stop: am pm	Purpose: am pm	Start: am pm

Page 1

HWE

HA - SUBJECT AND EXAMINATION DATA

HAA Place Subject's last name, first name, and middle name or initial in space provided. This should be completed prior to subject's pre-test, if possible. Nicknames and aliases should be entered in the space provided. Circle "NONE" when applicable.

HAB Enter Subject's place of birth in space provided. Obtain date of birth (by asking "What does your birth certificate indicate as your month-day-and year of birth?") This date will later be compared with that on driving license, but do not ask for drivers license until you progress to page 7. Let Subject tell you his age - - which you enter in space to right of date of birth.

HAC During pre-test interview, obtain the actual address where Subject presently resides and length of time at that address. This will later be verified on page seven. Then obtain telephone number, by asking "What is the telephone number there?" - - do not ask "do you have a telephone".

HAD This space is provided for Subject's description. All entries except height and weight can usually be based upon observation.

HAE Examination time log: This space is provided for the logging of time from the moment the Subject arrives for his appointment until his departure from premises. Conference "start" and "stop" indicates the time you discussed the case information with investigators, etc. On lower spaces, log all significant interruptions such as Subject eating, going to the restroom etc.

HAF Examination Identification Information: The first two spaces are provided for file numbers. The date of the examination, name of your department, name of the client you are running the examination for, and the examiner's name follows. In the space provided for the "offense-incident category" goes the classification concerned.

HWE (1.3) | Page 1

Backster Standardized Polygraph Notepack and Technique Guide

Figure XI-9a

HC TARGET SELECTION GUIDE

Target | A | B | C

Pre-exam Target Information "Adequacy" Estimate

Inadequate	1	2	3	4	5	Adequate
	= 5	= 10	= 15	= 20	= 25	→

Pre-exam Target "Intensity" Estimate

Trivial	1	2	3	4	5	Serious
	= 8	= 16	= 24	= 32	= 40	→

Pre-exam "Distinctness of Issue" Estimate

Cloudy	1	2	3	4	5	Clear
	= 7	= 14	= 21	= 28	= 35	→

Pre-exam Overall Target Reliability Estimate Total →

Target | A | B | C

Pre-exam Target Information "Adequacy" Estimate

Inadequate	1	2	3	4	5	Adequate
	= 5	= 10	= 15	= 20	= 25	→

Pre-exam Target "Intensity" Estimate

Trivial	1	2	3	4	5	Serious
	= 8	= 16	= 24	= 32	= 40	→

Pre-exam "Distinctness of Issue" Estimate

Cloudy	1	2	3	4	5.	Clear
	= 7	= 14	= 21	= 28	= 35	→

Pre-exam Overall Target Reliability Estimate Total →

Target | A | B | C

Pre-exam Target Information "Adequacy" Estimate

Inadequate	1	2	3	4	5	Adequate
	= 5	= 10	= 15	= 20	= 25	→

Pre-exam Target "Intensity" Estimate

Trivial	1	2	3	4	5	Serious
	= 8	= 16	= 24	= 32	= 40	→

Pre-exam "Distinctness of Issue" Estimate

Cloudy	1	2	3	4	5	Clear
	= 7	= 14	= 21	= 28	= 35	→

Pre-exam Overall Target Reliability Estimate Total →

Page 4

HWE

HC - TARGET SELECTION GUIDE

HC The heading "PRE-EXAMINATION RELIABILITY ESTIMATE" should be entered at the top of the page 4 (omitted on final proof thru oversight). List up to three principle targets which compete for highest total score. Do not list more than one target if others are obviously unimportant by comparison to one already entered. Do not attempt to initially prearrange competing targets to reflect order of effectiveness. Select a position from 1 to 5 for each of the three estimates, namely "information adequacy", "target intensity" and "distinctness of issue". Then transfer the value assigned each position involved (red numbered) to the boxes provided at the right hand side of the page.

With "information adequacy" (1 to 5) #1 would indicate that a minimum of information was available, and #5 would indicate that all desired information was available and considered reliable. "Target intensity" refers to that which threatens the well being of the Subject or that which he can lose, such as loss of his job or loss of reputation (which would rate #1) to his very life itself (which would rate #5). "Distinctness of issue" is an anti-rationalization factor. If subject did it, does he know for sure that he did it, or is it possible for him to rationalize and feel that he did not.

Now add the three values which you entered at the right hand side of the page. The total score for each target considered is based on a 100 point possible total. The highest total should be indicated as target "A", the next highest target "B" and the lowest target "C". Target "A" should then be carried forward to page 10 and entered in space provided entitled "TARGET SELECTED".

HWE (4-3) Page 4

Backster Target Selection Guide

Figure XI-9b

Backster Relevant and Control Question Formulation Guide

HF- "YOU" PHASE TARGET "A" | Used on chart no: 1 | 2 | 3 | 4 | 5

HFA. TARGET SELECTION

…get …cted: | Overall Target Reliability Estimate:

Use below spaces as scratch sheet during formulation of questions 33, 35 and 39 insert.

(r) 33

Can subject be attempting deception to above question but not be guilty of offense? ( ) No: ( ) Yes – Eliminate question.

Can subject be answering above question truthfully but still be guilty of offense? ( ) No: ( ) Yes – Eliminate question.

(r) 35

Can subject be attempting deception to above question but not be guilty of offense? ( ) No: ( ) Yes – Eliminate question.

Can subject be answering above question truthfully but still be guilty of offense? ( ) No: ( ) Yes – Eliminate question.

If subject is attempting deception to one of above – must he be to both questions? ( ) Yes: ( ) No – Alter one question.

(y|r) 39 Re: Whether (or not) you (yourself): | Do you intend to answer truthfully each question about that?

Does above "Insert" avoid all "Guilty Aspects" except "Major Involvement"? ( ) Yes: ( ) No – narrow scope.

HFB- "PROBABLE LIE" QUESTION FORMULATION

Subject's Present Age: ____ | (g) 47 | During the first: [ ] years of your life do you remember?

Habitual Offender? + ? - | (g) 46 | Between the ages of: [ ] and [ ] do you remember?

(g) 48 | During the first: [ ] years of your life do you remember? (Combine span of questions 46 and 47.

…s target issue have earlier in life …ference danger? + ? - | How long has subject worked for current employer? ( ) Years ( ) Months

---

HWE

HF - "YOU" PHASE TARGET "A"

Page 10 is devoted to careful formulation of relevant questions #33, #35 and #39; also, Probable Lie Questions #46 and #47§48 Spaces provided should be used as "scratch sheets" to enable the examiner to properly refine the wording of each question before transferring its final version to the test question sheet, on page 11.

HFA From page 4, using the same wording, transfer that target which has the highest numerical "Reliability" total resulting from the "Pre-exam Target Reliability Estimate" procedure. Enter this target caption in the space provided. This is not referred to as "You" Phase Target "A". Questions #33 and #35 are then formulated to be as near perfect as possible, complying with the rules listed below each question formulation area. Question #39 is an "icebreaker" question confining itself to the same target issue covered by both Question #33, and Question #35. Care should be taken that the "scope" of Question #39 confines itself to the major involvement aspect only. When applying the rules to the question being formulated, be sure to check one of the boxes located to the right. Each of the 3 relevant questions must comply with the specific rules listed or your test may not be valid. The only rule violation exception is one where you realistically estimate your chances of getting into difficulty because of a rule violation--as one chance in ten or less.

HFB From page 1 of the Notepack enter "subjects present age" in the first block of the HFB section. Caution Areas, when formulating each of the Green Zone Questions Are:

1. Your "earlier in life" age splitting will be based on his actual present age.
2. End "habitual offender" #46 age scope at least 5 years prior to target.
3. Don't allow either of the Green Zone Questions to overlap subject's current place or period of employment, target involves incident where he works.
4. Be careful if your target issue has an earlier in life transference danger.

HWE (10-3) | Page 10

Figure XI-9c

HF-	"YOU" PHASE TARGET "A" *continued*			Used on chart no:	1 2 3 4 5
HFC-	"YOU" PHASE TEST				
—	(v)	13	(name) 14 (birth) 15 (residence)		
1	(b)	25	Do you believe me when I promise you I won't ask a question we haven't gone over — word-for-word?		
2	(v|r)	39	Re:	Do you intend to answer truthfully each question about that?	
3	(g)	46			
4	(r)	33			
5	(g)	47			
6	(r)	35			
7	(g)	48			
8	(r)	37	(Optional — not generally recommended..)		
	(b)	26	Even though I promised you I would not — are you afraid I'll ask a question we haven't gone over — word-for-word?.		

HWE

HF - "YOU" PHASE TARGET "A"

HFC Questions 14(J), 13 and represent a pool of "neutral" questions. Each is designed to help settle or calm the Subject. Only one of the three listed questions should be asked at the start of the "YOU" phase run. Either of the remaining two questions can be used later within the same chart if required to help terminate a lingering question reaction, or to keep question "pace" if something disrupts your planned question sequence. The remaining "neutral" question can also be used for one of the above reasons if necessary.

Questions 39, 46, 33, 47, &48 and 35 are transferred to this page (P.11) only after they have been "ideally" formulated on notepack page 10.

Black Zone Questions 25 and 26 are "symptomatic" questions and response to either or both of these questions indicates that an outside issue is bothering the subject due to a mis-trust of the examiner. It is very important that the examiner has the Subject's confidence regarding the avoidance of questions relating to outside issues and also avoidance of any question that has not been reviewed word for word with Subject prior to each particular chart. If the examiner does not have Subject's confidence in this regard, Subject's concern over the outside issue may dampen or completely eliminate response to either the red zone questions or the green zone questions.

HWE (11-3) Page 11

Backster "You" Phase Target "A"
Test Question Formulation

Figure XI-9d

HG SCANNING OF "YOU" PHASE "A" CHART – (FIRST RUN) – "TRI-ZONE" REACTION COMBINATIONS

HGA "TRI-ZONE" REACTION COMBINATIONS — CIRCLE ONE OF CAPITAL LETTERS (A) THRU (H) IMMEDIATELY AFTER CHART

Comb (A)=dd · Comb (B)=tt · Comb (C)=? · Comb (D)=?d (D-3, D-4) · Comb (E)=d (E-5, E-6) · Comb (F)=?d (F-3, F-4, F-5, F-6) · Comb (G)=t (G-5, G-6) · Comb (H)=t? (H-3, H-4) · also C-5, C-6 in Comb (C)

HGB SPOT ANALYSIS TALLY FOR QUESTIONS 33 "A" AND 35 "A" — FIRST "YOU" PHASE "A" CHART

1st Run

	Q	Truth		Indefinite			Deception			Q	Truth		Indefinite			Deception		
	33	tt	t	t?	?	?d	d	dd	(A-1)	35	tt	t	t?	?	?d	d	dd	(A-4)
Breathing Tracing	r	+3	+2	+1	0	-1	-2	-3	=	r	+3	+2	+1	0	-1	-2	-3	=
	33	tt	t	t?	?	?d	d	dd	(A-2)	35	tt	t	t?	?	?d	d	dd	(A-5)
G.S.R. Tracing	r	+3	+2	+1	0	-1	-2	-3	=	r	+3	+2	+1	0	-1	-2	-3	=
	33	tt	t	t?	?	?d	d	dd	(A-3)	35	tt	t	t?	?	?d	d	dd	(A-6)
Cardio Tracing	r	+3	+2	+1	0	-1	-2	-3	=	r	+3	+2	+1	0	-1	-2	-3	=

HGC SUBJECT DATA BETWEEN "YOU" PHASE "A" CHART — (FIRST RUN) AND STIMULATION TEST:

Next — run stimulation test (optional):

HH STIMULATION TEST — Used on chart no: 1 2 3 4 5

HHA TEST DATA:

HHB SUBJECT DATA BETWEEN "STIMULATION" TEST AND "YOU" PHASE "A" CHART (SECOND RUN):

HHC REPEAT "YOU" PHASE "A" — SWITCH QUESTION NO. 33 AND QUESTION NO. 35 POSITIONS:

HWE

HG - "YOU" PHASE TARGET "A" FIRST RUN AND FOLLOW-UP

HGA Tri-Zone Reaction Combination Scanning - Tri-Zone Reaction Scanning should be applied immediately after each "YOU" phase chart in order to determine the possible existence of one or more problem areas and apply the indicated remedy. To accomplish this, select the most clear cut tracing of the three. Within this tracing note the existance of reaction to one or both of the two questions in each of the three basic color zones, at the same time noting the lack of response to both questions in any of the color zones. As a result of this process, select the one appropriate box of the eight (A thru H) which denotes the combination involved. "Letter-number" codes (when appearing within the box selected), identify the existing problem areas and prescribe the remedies needed. Explanation of the "letter-number" codes are provided in the indication" and "remedy" sections of the "Tri-Zone Reaction Combinations" table.

HGB Spot Analysis Tally - It is desirable to assign "spot analysis" values immediately after each chart, using the "Seven Position Scale" (tt thru dd) to indicate a determination for each of the three tracings, as related to questions #33 and #35. Then convert each to a numerical value, which is entered in box (A-1) thru (A-6) by utilizing the (+3) to (-3) score indicated in red under each "seven position scale" selection. The values placed in box (A-1) thru (A-6) are then transferred to equivalent boxes (A-1) thru (A-6) on Notepack page 23. Although not desirable, it is permissable for the examiner who has a good indication of the "target trend" to postpone completion of this procedure until after the last of the "YOU" phase "A" charts.

HGC Additional information obtained from subject, following the "YOU" phase "A" chart (first run). Use of section HHA (stimulation test) and section HHB is optional.

HHC In the same order, repeat "You" phase "A" questions except for exchanging positions of questions #33 and #35, also positions of questions 44J and 44K.

HWE (12-3) Page 1:

Backster Scanning "You" Phase Chart I
Tri-Zone Reaction Combination

Figure XI-9e

HI. SCANNING OF "YOU" PHASE "A" CHART – (SECOND RUN) – "TRI-ZONE" REACTION COMBINATIONS

HIA "TRI-ZONE" REACTION COMBINATIONS – CIRCLE ONE OF CAPITAL LETTERS (A) THRU (H) IMMEDIATELY AFTER CHART

Comb (A)=dd	Comb (B)=tt	Comb (C)=?	Comb (D)=?d	Comb (E)=d	Comb (F)=?d	Comb (G)=t	Comb (H)=t?
r	–	–	r	r	r	–	–
–	g	–	g D-3 D-4	–	g F-3 F-4	g	– H-3 H-4
–	–	C-5 C-6	–	E-5 E-6	F-5 F-6	G-5 G-6	–

HIB SPOT.ANALYSIS TALLY FOR QUESTIONS 33 "A" AND 35 "A" – 2ND "YOU" PHASE "A" CHART

2nd Run

		Truth		Indefinite			Deception			
		tt	t	t ?	?	? d	d	dd		
Breathing Tracing	33 (r)	+ 3	+ 2	+ 1	0	- 1	- 2	- 3	=	(A-7)
G.S.R. Tracing	33 (r)	+ 3	+ 2	+ 1	0	- 1	- 2	- 3	=	(A-8)
Cardio Tracing	33 (r)	+ 3	+ 2	+ 1	0	- 1	- 2	- 3	=	(A-9)

	Truth		Indefinite			Deception			
	tt	t	t ?	?	? d	d	dd		
35 (r)	+ 3	+ 2	+ 1	0	- 1	- 2	- 3	=	(A-10)
35 (r)	+ 3	+ 2	+ 1	0	- 1	- 2	- 3	=	(A-11)
35 (r)	+ 3	+ 2	+ 1	0	- 1	- 2	- 3	=	(A-12)

HIC SUBJECT DATA AFTER "YOU" PHASE "A" CHART (SECOND RUN):

HID IF NO DETERMINATION REACHED – REPEAT "YOU" PHASE "A" TEST (THIRD RUN) (Again switch relevant question positions):

HWE

HI – "YOU" PHASE TARGET "A" SECOND RUN AND FOLLOW-UP

HIA TRI-Zone Reaction Combination Scanning – Apply Tri-Zone reaction scanning immediately after this "YOU" phase chart. Comply with section HGA instructions on page 12. Again, when appearing within the box selected, the "lette. number" codes will identify existing problem areas and prescribe needed remedies.

HIB Spot Analysis Tally – As recommended with the first run "YOU" phase "A" chart, it is desirable to assign "spot analysis" values immediately after completion of this second run.

If the examiner has a good indication of the "target trend" he may postpone completion of this procedure. Reference section HGB instructions. Be certain to allow for the exchange in position of questions #33 and #35, which should have been part of the "second run" procedure. Values in boxes (A-7) thru (A-12) are transferred to equivalent boxes (A-7) thru (A-12) on Notepack page 23.

HIC Indicate any additional information obtained from subject following this "YOU" phase "A" second run.

HID If no determination other than "indefinite" is indicated after this second "YOU" phase "A" chart you must re-evaluate each relevant question to be certain that none of the strict formulation rules on page 10 are being violated and that each relevant question is otherwise structurally sound. If this re-evaluation indicates no need to alter the structure or content of the relevant questions and if it is certain that all "Tri-Zone Reaction Combination" remedies have been applied, proceed with a third "YOU" phase "A" chart. In this chart return questions #33 and #35 to the original positions occupied in the first "YOU" phase "A" chart.

HWE (13-3) Page 13

Backster Scanning "You" Phase Chart 2
Tri-Zone Reaction Combination

Figure XI-9f

Backster ZCT Adjusted Distribution
Numerical Cutoffs

(December 15,1983 Revision)
BACKSTER ZONE COMPARISON TEST VARIATIONS
("ADJUSTED DISTRIBUTION NUMERICAL CUTOFFS")

"YOU" PHASE TEST WITH **TWO** RELEVANT QUESTIONS (Spot II & III used)						
ONE CHART (Projection)	(+ 18)	+ 12 TO + 3 TRUTH	+ 2 TO -4 INDEFINITE	-5 TO -12 DECEPTION	(-18)	(SPAN = 24)
TWO CHARTS	(+ 36)	+ 24 TO + 5 TRUTH	+ 4 TO -8 INDEFINITE	-9 TO -24 DECEPTION	(-36)	(SPAN = 48)
THREE CHARTS	(+ 54)	+ 36 TO + 7 TRUTH	+ 6 TO -12 INDEFINITE	-13 TO -36 DECEPTION	(-54)	(SPAN = 72)
FOUR CHARTS	(+ 72)	+ 48 TO + 9 TRUTH	+ 8 TO -16 INDEFINITE	-17 TO -48 DECEPTION	(-72)	(SPAN = 96)

"YOU" PHASE TEST WITH **THREE** RELEVANT QUESTIONS (Spot II, III & IV used)						
ONE CHART (Projection)	(+ 27)	+ 18 TO + 4 TRUTH	+ 3 TO -6 INDEFINITE	-7 TO -18 DECEPTION	(-27)	(SPAN = 36)
TWO CHARTS	(+ 54)	+ 36 TO + 7 TRUTH	+ 6 TO -12 INDEFINITE	-13 TO -36 DECEPTION	(-54)	(SPAN = 72)
THREE CHARTS	(+ 81)	+ 54 TO + 10 TRUTH	+ 9 TO -18 INDEFINITE	-19 TO -54 DECEPTION	(-81)	(SPAN = 108)
FOUR CHARTS	(+ 108)	+ 72 TO + 13 TRUTH	+ 12 TO -24 INDEFINITE	-25 TO -72 DECEPTION	(-108)	(SPAN = 144)

Figure XI-9g

Backster Spot Analysis for "You" Phase, Exploratory, and S-K-Y Tests

BACKSTER ZONE COMPARISON TECHNIQUE
NUMERICALLY SCORED "SPOT" ANALYSIS TESTS

				SPOT I		SPOT II		SPOT III		SPOT IV	
			BLACK ZONE	RED ZONE	GREEN ZONE	RED ZONE	GREEN ZONE	RED ZONE	GREEN ZONE	RED ZONE	BLACK ZONE
	(SEQUENCE DESIGNATION) →		1	2	3	4	5	6	7	8	9
YOU PHASE	ZONE COMPARISON "YOU" PHASE TEST (HORIZONTAL TOTAL) TWO "SPOTS"	(y) 13	(b) 25	(y|r) 39	(g) 46	(r) 33 SPOT II	(g) 47	(r) 35 SPOT III	(g) 48		(b) 26
YOU PHASE	ZONE COMPARISON "YOU" PHASE TEST (HORIZONTAL TOTAL) THREE "SPOTS"	(y) 13	(b) 25	(y|r) 39	(g) 46	(r) 33 SPOT II	(g) 47	(r) 35 SPOT III	(g) 48	(r) 37 SPOT IV	(b) 26
EXPLORATORY	ZONE COMPARISON EXPLORATORY TEST (VERTICAL TOTALS ONLY) THREE "SPOTS"	(y) 13	(b) 25	(y|r) 39	(g) 46	(r|y) 43 SPOT II	(g) 47	(r|y) 44 SPOT III	(g) 48	(r|y) 45 SPOT IV	(b) 26
EXPLORATORY	ZONE COMPARISON EXPLORATORY TEST (VERTICAL TOTALS ONLY) FOUR "SPOTS"	(y) 13	(b) 25	(r|y) 42 SPOT I	(g) 46	(r|y) 43 SPOT II	(g) 47	(r|y) 44 SPOT III	(g) 48	(r|y) 45 SPOT IV	(b) 26
SKY	ZONE COMPARISON "S-K-Y" TEST (VERTICAL TOTALS ONLY) THREE "SPOTS"	(y) 13	(b) 25	(y|r) 39	(g) 31 -S-	(r|y) 32 -K- II	(g) 47	(r) 33 -Y- III	(g) 48	(r|y) 34 SPOT IV	(b) 26
	(SEQUENCE DESIGNATION) →		1	2	3	4	5	6	7	8	9

Figure XI-10

The DoDPI Bi-Spot Zone Comparison Technique

The Zone Comparison technique taught at the Department of Defense Polygraph Institute (DoDPI) has changed very little from the original Backster Zone Comparison Technique of 1961 when adopted by DoDPI's predecessor, the U. S. Army Provost Marshal Polygraph School. However, Backster has since then made several changes to his tests formats, and the DoDPI has made some changes of its own to the Backster system. DoDPI has basically two Zone Comparison techniques; the first one contains relevant questions concerning Primary Involvement, Secondary Involvement, and S-K-Y (Suspicion-Knowledge-You) questions; thus is it a multiple-issue test which will be discussed and described under the heading of Multiple-Issue Tests. The second Zone Comparison technique is used when there is only one question (issue) that must be addressed in a PV examination; thus it is truly a Single-Issue Zone Comparison Test. It contains all of the elements of the Backster Zone Comparison Technique, as seen below. Unfortunately, DoDPI named it the Bi-Zone Comparison Technique, which is not in accordance with Backster's definition of the term "Zone". It is truly a Tri-Zone Comparison technique, but somehow, at some time, someone at the U. S. Army Provost Marshal General's Polygraph School mistook the term *Zone* to mean the area that covers a *control versus relevant question pair.* Since there are only two such pairs in this technique, it was labeled the Bi-Zone Comparison Technique. In fact, it is a Tri-Zone (Green, Red, Black) with two Spots for quantification. Thus, for comparison purposes and consistency in the explanation of the description of DoDPI's Single-Issue Test, this author has changed the title from Bi-Zone to DoDPI Bi-Spot Zone Comparison Technique. In the test structure it should be noted that DoDPI's Sacrifice Relevant Question is in the second position, similar to the Matte Quadri-Track ZCT but unlike the current Backster Tri-Zone CT which has its Preparatory/Sacrifice Relevant question in the third position. Unlike both the Backster ZCT and the Matte ZCT whose Sacrifice Relevant question is restricted to the precise scope of its related relevant questions (thus also acts as a Preparatory Question), the scope of the Sacrifice Relevant question in the DoDPI Bi-Spot ZCT is broad in nature; does not specifically identify the details of the issue; thus is formulated to function only as a Sacrifice Relevant question. (DoDPI 1994)

Inasmuch as DoDPI recommends the use of aforementioned Bi-Spot ZC test when only one question must be addressed in a PV examination, that is perhaps the reason for the lack of any mention of the use of the Target Selection Guidelines which are mentioned and set forth in DoDPI's multiple-issue Zone Comparison test. Interestingly, DoDPI's lesson plan states that some agencies require that the forensic psychophysiologist obtain approval from their Quality Control section before using this test. (DoDPI 1994)

<u>DoDPI Bi-Spot Zone Comparison Test Structure</u>.

1. Irrelevant — Is today Monday?
2. Sacrifice Relevant — Regarding the incident you reported, do you intend to answer truthfully each question about that?

3.	Symptomatic	Are you completely convinced that I will not ask you a question on this test that has not already been reviewed?
4.	Non-Current Exclusive Control	Prior to 1993, did you ever lie to anyone in a position of authority?
5.	Relevant	Did you lie about that man forcing you to have sexual intercourse with him?
6.	Non-Current Exclusive Control	Prior to this year, did you ever lie about something you are ashamed of?
7.	Relevant	Did you lie about that man forcing you to have sexual intercourse with him in his apartment?
8.	Non-Current Exclusive Control	Prior to 1990, did you ever lie to get out of trouble?
9.	Symptomatic	Is there something else you are afraid I will ask you a question about, even though I have told you I would not?

<u>Evaluation of Bi-Spot:</u>

1. To render a conclusion of deception (DI) there must be:
   a. A minus 3 or less in any spot. (question #5 or 7)
   b. <u>or</u> a grand total of minus 4 for both spots. (#5 & #7)

2. To render a conclusion of truthfulness (NDI), there must be:
   a. A plus in every spot.
   b. <u>and</u> a grand total of plus 4 or greater overall..

3. Any analysis between DI or NDI is inconclusive and requires additional testing.

SPOT 1	SPOT 2	Grand Total
+6	0	+6 Inconclusive
+4	-1	+3 Inconclusive
+2	+2	+4 NDI
-2	-2	-4 DI
+3	+1	+4 NDI
0	-3	-3 DI
+1	+2	+3 Inconclusive

A minimum of three polygraph charts containing the same test questions must be conducted before a determination of truth of deception can be rendered. However the minimum scores required to reach a conclusion or threshold is fixed to plus or minus 4.

<u>The Integrated Zone Comparison Technique</u>

The Integrated Zone Comparison Technique was developed in 1987 by Nathan J. Gordon, William M. Waid and Philip M. Cochetti. This technique has the most significant departure from the original Zone Comparison Technique developed by Cleve Backster.

The test structure and the order in which the test questions are delivered in the first relevant test chart is set forth below:

1. Irrelevant Question
2. Symptomatic Question
3. Sacrifice Relevant Question
4. Irrelevant Question (Optional)
5. Non-Current Exclusive Control Question
6. Relevant Question
7. Irrelevant Question (Optional)
8. Non-Exclusive Control Question.
9. Relevant Question
10. Irrelevant Question (Optional)
11. Non-Current Exclusive Control Question
12. Relevant Question.
13. Countermeasure Question (i.e. Did you deliberately do anything to try and beat this test?)

The first chart (above) administered to the subject is a Silent Answer Test (SAT) which is scored and included in the total tally for determination. The second chart conducted is a Known-Solution Stimulation test. In the second Relevant Chart, the position of the relevant questions are switched. The last relevant question (#12) is moved into position #6 and all other relevant questions are moved back one spot. In the third chart, the positions of the Control and Relevant questions are reversed: 6-5, 9-8, 12-11.

A minimum of three separate polygraph charts containing the same test questions must be conducted before a determination of truth or deception can be rendered. The Horizontal Scoring System developed by Gordon and Cochetti in 1984 is used to evaluate the physiological data. A minimum score of Plus or Minus 13 for 3 charts is required before a determination is made. The above test format can also be used to administer the Suspicion-Knowledge-You (S-K-Y) test depicted separately in Chapter 18.(Gordon 1996)

The Utah Zone Comparison Technique

The test structure of the Utah Zone Comparison Technique is basically the same for single issue tests as it is for multiple-issue tests. However, instead of using relevant questions that embrace several facets of a crime or matter under investigation, the single-issue test format uses relevant questions which address one single issue only. When there is a single issue, the total of all numerical scores is evaluated so that: (Honts 1996)

1. Total scores of -6 or less (greater score) are reported as deceptive.
2. Total scores of +6 or more are reported as truthful.
3. Total scores between -6 and +6 are considered inconclusive.

Richard S. Weaver (1980) described the Utah Zone Comparison technique, referencing Dr. Raskin's Fourth Annual workshop on the detection of deception conducted at the University of Utah, Salt Lake City, in September 1978. The test structure is depicted below:

Test Question Position:	1	2	3	4	5	6	7	8	9	10
Type of Question:	(I)	(S/R)	(SY)	(C)	(R)	(C)	(R)	(I)	(C)	(R)

At all times relevant test questions responses at each (R) position are compared only with the responses to the previous control question position (C). (Raskin 1979).

Further details regarding the Utah Zone Comparison Technique are described under Multiple-Issue Zone Comparison Tests below.

MULTIPLE-ISSUE ZONE COMPARISON TESTS

The multiple-issue test is a degradation of the single-issue test inasmuch as it contains varied relevant questions which may compete against each other rather than against the control questions for the guilty (as later verified) examinee's psychological set, thus permitting anticlimax dampening of one relevant question by another relevant question. Furthermore, because each relevant question is dealing with a different issue, the vertical scores of each Spot cannot be horizontally added or combined for a total score, thus the *internal reliability* present in Single-Issue tests is not present in Multiple-Issue tests. However the aforementioned weaknesses are reduced when the relevant questions all pertain to the same crime or matter wherein it is very likely that the guilty (as later verified) examinee will be deceptive to all of the relevant questions on the test. But since they do not deal with the same issue (single-issue as defined above), any one of the relevant questions may capture the guilty (as later verified) examinee's psychological set at the expense of the other relevant questions which may be dampened out by it. Some Multiple-Issue techniques are used to resolve multiple offenses within the same test, which increases potential anticlimax dampening of one or more relevant question by another relevant question on the same test. Such tests are known as *Exploratory* tests to "screen" a number of examinees regarding several issues. Obviously, the FP is not able to administer a separate test on each issue to each examinee, therefore he/she must resort to the use of aforementioned exploratory tests.

The Exploratory test is an excellent technique to use when the FP does have two or three separate issues of a general nature such as the theft of money, merchandise, and collusion with others from a particular store or firm to cover, and wishes to have control questions neighboring each relevant question in a test structure similar to the specific, single-issue test, such as the Matte Quadri-Track ZCT, the Backster ZCT, the DoDPI ZCT or the Integrated ZCT. The down side is that the safeguard against false positive/negative errors provided by the "Inside-Issue" Fear/Hope of Error questions pair identified as the *Inside Track* in the Matte Quadri-Track ZCT and also used in the Backster ZCT, cannot be used in multiple-issue tests because an examinee could be fearful of an error to one relevant question and hopeful of an error to one of the other relevant questions on the same test, thus obviating a comparison. The examinee's psychological set should be focused on either the "fear of error" control question or the "hope of error" relevant question, not both.

Each relevant question in the multiple-issue tests listed below is compared against its neighboring control question and scored vertically for a total score of each tracing (pneumo, GSR/GSG, cardio). However the tally from each Spot quantified cannot be added together because they deal with different issues. Hence in order to attain a near equivalent reliability, a greater number of charts should be conducted, keeping in mind that a Single-Issue test contains between two and three quantified spots per chart on the same issue, thus two of those charts would quantify a total of four to six spots. A multiple-issue test quantifies only one spot per chart dealing with that specific issue; thus it would take from four to six charts to equal the scoring reliability of the single-issue test: not a very practical solution. Hence the results of multiple-issue tests must be weighed by the number of charts conducted and the inherent weaknesses of the test structure of each type of test. Furthermore, there is sparse research to support their reliability and validity.

The Matte Quinque-Track Zone Comparison Technique

The Matte Quinque-Track Zone Comparison Technique worksheet, whose first page is similar to that used in the Matte Quadri-Track Zone Comparison Technique (Fig. XI-2) reflects the background information normally obtained from the examinee during the pretest interview, excluding information regarding prior arrests and courts martial. That information, if obtained, is gathered from sources other than the examinee to avoid raising outside issues with the examinee. This information is valuable to the forensic psychophysiologist (FP) in the formulation of control questions.

Figure XI-11 reflects the Matte Quinque-Track Comparison Test Structure showing each type of test question with color legend. Figure XI-12 reflects the format used for the Quinque-Track Zone Comparison Technique, with its quantification system and conclusion table. Figure XI-13 reflects a completed test question format. The format includes an optional knowledge (relevant) question, number 032, used only in the Exploratory test as needed. This Knowledge question is compared against Control question 031 which is a Suspicion question designed to offer the examinee who has strong suspicion but not knowledge, a related Spot on which to respond.

The only difference in numerical identification of the test questions between the Matte Quadri-Track Zone Comparison Technique and the Matte Quinque-Track Zone Comparison Technique is that in the Quinque-Track ZCT, the 45 series is used to identify relevant questions and 032 is used to identify a Knowledge (relevant) question. Non-Current Exclusive Control Question #48 is also added which includes the period of both

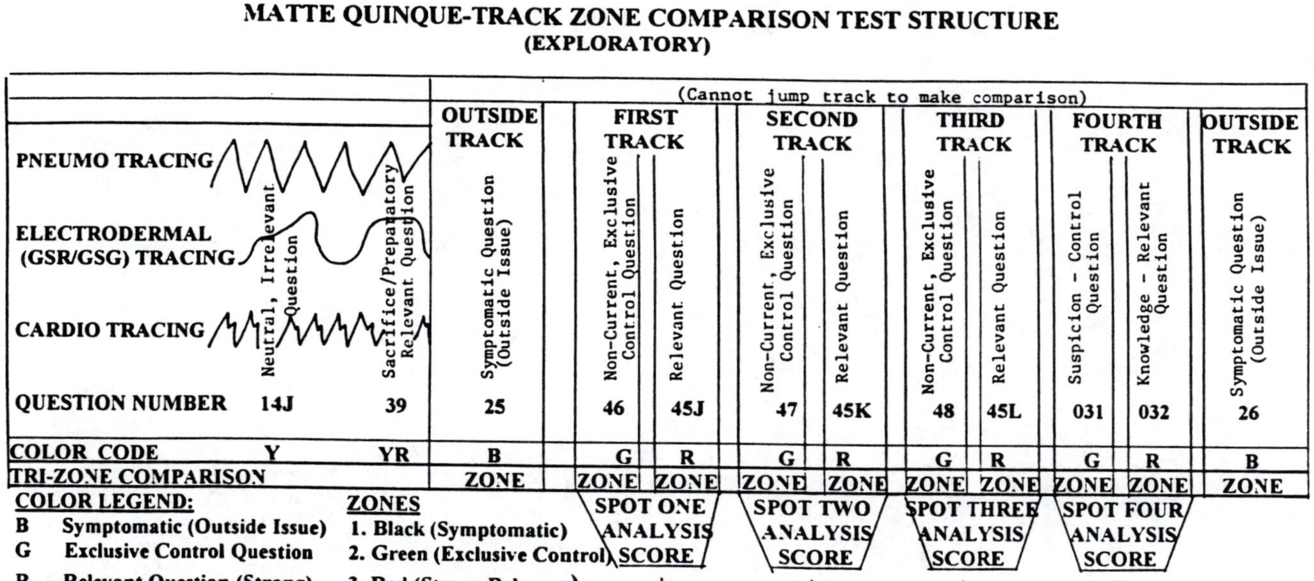

MATTE QUINQUE-TRACK ZONE COMPARISON TEST STRUCTURE
(EXPLORATORY)

(Cannot jump track to make comparison)

			OUTSIDE TRACK	FIRST TRACK		SECOND TRACK		THIRD TRACK		FOURTH TRACK		OUTSIDE TRACK
PNEUMO TRACING / ELECTRODERMAL (GSR/GSG) TRACING / CARDIO TRACING	Neutral, Irrelevant Question	Sacrifice/Preparatory Relevant Question	Symptomatic Question (Outside Issue)	Non-Current, Exclusive Control Question	Relevant Question	Non-Current, Exclusive Control Question	Relevant Question	Non-Current, Exclusive Control Question	Relevant Question	Suspicion - Control Question	Knowledge - Relevant Question	Symptomatic Question (Outside Issue)
QUESTION NUMBER	14J	39	25	46	45J	47	45K	48	45L	031	032	26
COLOR CODE	Y	YR	B	G	R	G	R	G	R	G	R	B
TRI-ZONE COMPARISON			ZONE	ZONE	ZONE	ZONE	ZONE	ZONE	ZONE	ZONE	ZONE	ZONE
				SPOT ONE ANALYSIS SCORE		SPOT TWO ANALYSIS SCORE		SPOT THREE ANALYSIS SCORE		SPOT FOUR ANALYSIS SCORE		
				+-		+-		+-		+-		

COLOR LEGEND:
- B Symptomatic (Outside Issue)
- G Exclusive Control Question
- R Relevant Question (Strong)
- YR Sacrifice Relevant Question
- Y Neutral Question (Irrelevant)
- O Prefix - Option Use.

ZONES
1. Black (Symptomatic)
2. Green (Exclusive Control)
3. Red (Strong Relevant)

TRACK Identifies a pair of questions related for comparison (G&R Zone) or evaluation (B Zone)

SPOT Identifies a Track which is quantified.

Note: Fourth Track includes Suspicion Question 031 Green Zone versus Knowledge Question 032 Red Zone.

ABOVE FOUR SPOTS ARE VERTICALLY AND INDEPENDENTLY SCORED BUT CANNOT BE HORIZONTALLY SCORED FOR A TOTAL TALLY BECAUSE EACH SPOT DEALS WITH A DIFFERENT ISSUE. A MINIMUM OF THREE CHARTS (IDEALLY FOUR) MUST BE CONDUCTED TO ATTAIN A MINIMUM NUMBER OF COMPARISONS FOR EACH SPOT.

Figure XI-11

MATTE QUINQUE-TRACK ZONE COMPARISON TECHNIQUE

TARGET ( )	USED ON CHART NR.		
14J	WERE YOU BORN IN THE U.S.?	13L (Last Name)	13F (First Name)
39.	RE: WHETHER OR NOT (YOURSELF)	DO YOU INTEND TO ANSWER TRUTH-TRUTHFULLY EACH QUESTION ABOUT THAT?	
25	ARE YOU COMPLETELY CONVINCED THAT I WILL NOT ASK YOU AN UNREVIEWED QUESTION DURING THIS CHART?		
46	BETWEEN THE AGES OF ( ) AND ( ) - DO YOU REMEMBER:		
45J			
47	DURING THE FIRST ( ) YEARS OF YOUR LIFE - DO YOU REMEMBER:		
45K			
48	DURING THE FIRST ( ) YEARS OF YOUR LIFE - DO YOU REMEMBER:		
45L			
031			
032			
26	IS THERE SOMETHING ELSE YOU ARE AFRAID I WILL ASK YOU A QUESTION ABOUT, EVEN THOUGH I TOLD YOU I WOULD NOT?		

QUANTIFICATION SYSTEM
QUINQUE-TRACK ZONE COMPARISON TECHNIQUE

CHART1	TI	INDEF	DI			TI	INDEF	DI			TI	INDEF	DI			TI	INDEF	DI	
PO 45J	+3+2	+1 0-1	-2-3	( )	45K	+3+2	+1 0-1	-2-3	( )	45L	+3+2	+1 0-1	-2-3	( )	32	+3+2	+1 0-1	-2-3	( )
GR 45J	+3+2	+1 0-1	-2-3	( )	45K	+3+2	+1 0-1	-2-3	( )	45L	+3+2	+1 0-1	-2-3	( )	32	+3+2	+1 0-1	-2-3	( )
CO 45J	+3+2	+1 0-1	-2-3	( )	45K	+3+2	+1 0-1	-2-3	( )	45L	+3+2	+1 0-1	-2-3	( )	32	+3+2	+1 0-1	-2-3	( )
CHART2	TI	INDEF	DI			TI	INDEF	DI			TI	INDEF	DI			TI	INDEF	DI	
PO 45J	+3+2	+1 0-1	-2-3	( )	45K	+3+2	+1 0-1	-2-3	( )	45L	+3+2	+1 0-1	-2-3	( )	32	+3+2	+1 0-1	-2-3	( )
GR 45J	+3+2	+1 0-1	-2-3	( )	45K	+3+2	+1 0-1	-2-3	( )	45L	+3+2	+1 0-1	-2-3	( )	32	+3+2	+1 0-1	-2-3	( )
CO 45J	+3+2	+1 0-1	-2-3	( )	45K	+3+2	+1 0-1	-2-3	( )	45L	+3+2	+1 0-1	-2-3	( )	32	+3+2	+1 0-1	-2-3	( )
CHART3	TI	INDEF	DI			TI	INDEF	DI			TI	INDEF	DI			TI	INDEF	DI	
PO 45J	+3+2	+1 0-1	-2-3	( )	45K	+3+2	+1 0-1	-2-3	( )	45L	+3+2	+1 0-1	-2-3	( )	32	+3+2	+1 0-1	-2-3	( )
GR 45J	+3+2	+1 0-1	-2-3	( )	45K	+3+2	+1 0-1	-2-3	( )	45L	+3+2	+1 0-1	-2-3	( )	32	+3+2	+1 0-1	-2-3	( )
CO 45J	+3+2	+1 0-1	-2-3	( )	45K	+3+2	+1 0-1	-2-3	( )	45L	+3+2	+1 0-1	-2-3	( )	32	+3+2	+1 0-1	-2-3	( )

TARGET ( ) TOTAL ( ) TOTAL ( ) TOTAL ( ) TOTAL ( )

CONCLUSION TABLE

	NDI	INCL	DI	45J	45K	45L	032
THREE CHARTS	+27 to +5	+4 to -7	-8 to -27	( )	( )	( )	( )
FOUR CHARTS	+36 to +7	+6 to -9	-10 to -36	( )	( )	( )	( )
FIVE CHARTS	+45 to +9	+8 to -11	-11 to -45	( )	( )	( )	( )

Each of the 4 SPOTS (45 series and 032) are scored, tallied and evaluated separately against the Conclusion Table according to the number of charts conducted.

STIMULATION TEST DATA - NUMBER SELECTED:_____CHART NR:_____________

Figure XI-12

MATTE QUINQUE-TRACK ZONE COMPARISON TECHNIQUE

TARGET (A)		USED ON CHART NR. 2, 3, 4	
14J	WERE YOU BORN IN THE U.S.?	13L Doe (Last Name)	13F John (First Name)
39	RE: WHETHER OR NOT (YOURSELF) stole any merchandise and/or money from ABC Market:	DO YOU INTEND TO ANSWER TRUTH- TRUTHFULLY EACH QUESTION ABOUT THAT?	
25	ARE YOU COMPLETELY CONVINCED THAT I WILL NOT ASK YOU AN UNREVIEWED QUESTION DURING THIS CHART?		
46	BETWEEN THE AGES OF (18) AND (22) - DO YOU REMEMBER: ever stealing anything?		
45J	Did you steal any money from ABC Market?		
47	DURING THE FIRST (18) YEARS OF YOUR LIFE - DO YOU REMEMBER: ever stealing anything from someone who trusted you?		
45K	Did you steal any merchandise from ABC Market?		
48	DURING THE FIRST (22) YEARS OF YOUR LIFE - DO YOU REMEMBER: ever stealing anything?		
45L	Did you ever enter into collusion with anyone to steal from ABC Market?		
031	Do you suspect anyone in particular of stealing from ABC Market?		
032	Do you know for sure of anyone who has stolen from ABC Market?		
26	IS THERE SOMETHING ELSE YOU ARE AFRAID I WILL ASK YOU A QUESTION ABOUT, EVEN THOUGH I TOLD YOU I WOULD NOT?		

NOTE: Bold Capital letters reflect the standardized template questions. The upper/lower case portion of question(s) reflects that portion of the question(s) acquired from case information.

Figure XI-13

Non-Current Exclusive Control Questions #46 and #47. As indicated in the previous paragraph, the Suspicion Question #031 is a control question which is compared exclusively with the Knowledge relevant question 032.

Figure XI-14 reflects an actual exploratory test, the results of which were confirmed by a written confession from the examinee. In this test, relevant question 45M was inserted in lieu of 032 (Knowledge Question). The results showed deception to relevant questions number 45J, 45K, 45L, and 45M. Question 45J, which dealt with the theft of money, reflects the most significant reaction to all parameters and, and as substantiated by the examinee's confession, reflected the most serious offense. Note the change in baseline of the breathing pattern at question number 45L, and the increase in blood pressure on the same question, indicating deception to that question as verified by the examinee's confession.

The Quinque-Track Zone Comparison Test

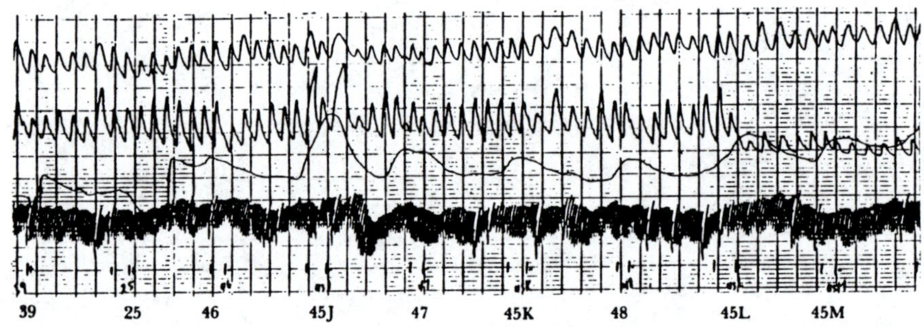

Actual Matte Quinque-Track ZCT
DI Chart in Larceny Case

Figure XI-14

Figure XI-15 reflects an actual exploratory test to determine whether the examinee had stolen any merchandise (45J), had made any improper discounts (45K), had entered into collusion with anyone to steal merchandise (45L), and had knowledge of anyone who had stolen merchandise from that company (32). In this test, the Suspicion Control question (03l) was not used (older test version). This examinee was found to be truthful regarding all relevant questions, as evidenced by clear reactions to the control questions 46, 47, and 48. Note the classic staircase pattern (suppression followed by hyperventilation) in the breathing at questions 46 and 47, and the superior GSR arousal at questions 46 and 48, plus the cardio blood pressure arousal at questions 47 and 48, as opposed to an absence of reaction in the breathing pattern at questions 45J, 45K, 45L, and 32 and comparatively mild reaction to the same questions in the GSR and cardio tracings. It should be noted that this examinee had ingested one Darvon tablet at 0930 hours and one tranquilizer at 1130 hours and was administered the PV examination at 1315 hours on the same day, yet was able to adequately respond on the test. The examinee was administered a stimulation test prior to the administration of the exploratory test.

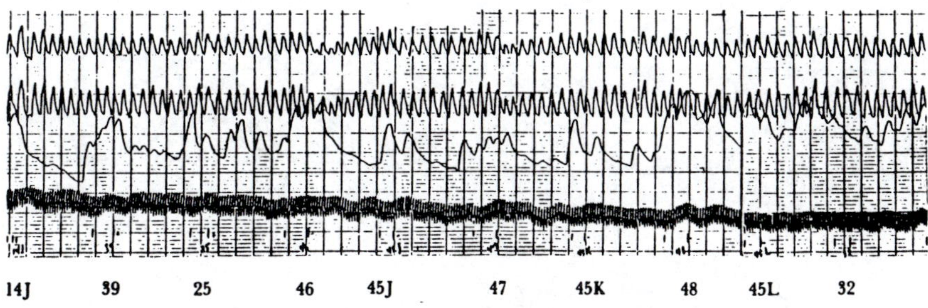

Actual Matte Quinque-Track ZCT
NDI Chart in Larceny Case

Figure XI-15

It should be noted that the Suspicion-Knowledge-Guilt (S-K-G) test described in Chapter 17 is more appropriate when a major involvement, some direct involvement, or guilty knowledge regarding the same case are to be addressed in the same test, usually to screen a number of suspects in a singular case to determine who warrants the administration of the Matte Quadri-Track Zone Comparison (Single-Issue) test. Sometimes the S-K-G test is administered after the Quadri-Track ZCT to address the Knowledge question.

Backster Zone Comparison Exploratory Test

The Backster Zone Comparison Exploratory Test structure as depicted in XI-16 below uses the same format as its "You" phase Zone Comparison Test in Figure XI-10 above which depicts both for comparison, but the numerical identification of its relevant questions has been changed from the 30 series to the 40 series, i.e. 42, 43, 44, and 45. It should be noted that the Sacrifice Relevant Question #39 can be replaced with a medium strength relevant question #42 which is formulated as follows: Regarding the (offense); before that (description of offense) occurred - did you definitely know it was about to happen? When Sacrifice-Relevant question #39 is replaced with Relevant Question #42, this creates a Fourth Spot for vertical scoring, as opposed to Three Spots when Sacrifice-Relevant Question #39 is used. (See Fig. XI-17 for numerical cut offs). Backster reminds his students that the lack of a minus score by any one of these question totals (vertical) cannot be trusted where deception is indicated by a vertical total on one or more of the other Relevant questions. Lack of reaction to all of the Relevant questions and presence of reaction to the Control questions still strongly infers truth.

Backster Zone Comparison Exploratory Test

EXPLORATORY											
ZONE COMPARISON EXPLORATORY TEST (VERTICAL TOTALS ONLY) THREE "SPOTS"	(y) 13	(b) 25	(y|r) 39	(g) 46	(r|y) 43 SPOT II	(g) 47	(r|y) 44 SPOT III	(g) 48	(r|y) 45 SPOT IV	(b) 26
ZONE COMPARISON EXPLORATORY TEST (VERTICAL TOTALS ONLY) FOUR "SPOTS"	(y) 13	(b) 25	(r|y) 42 SPOT I	(g) 46	(r|y) 43 SPOT II	(g) 47	(r|y) 44 SPOT III	(g) 48	(r|y) 45 SPOT IV	(b) 26

Figure XI-16

"EXPLORATORY" TEST AND "S-K-Y" TEST (SINGLE RELEVANT QUESTION TOTALS)						
ONE CHART (Projection)	(+9)	+6 TO +2 TRUTH	+1 TO -2 INDEFINITE	-3 TO -6 DECEPTION	(-9)	(SPAN = 12)
TWO CHARTS	(+18)	+12 TO +3 TRUTH	+2 TO -4 INDEFINITE	-5 TO -12 DECEPTION	(-18)	(SPAN = 24)
THREE CHARTS	(+27)	+18 TO +4 TRUTH	+3 TO -6 INDEFINITE	-7 TO -18 DECEPTION	(-27)	(SPAN = 36)
FOUR CHARTS	(+36)	+24 TO +5 TRUTH	+4 TO -8 INDEFINITE	-9 TO -24 DECEPTION	(-36)	(SPAN = 48)

Backster ZCT Conclusion Table for Exploratory and S-K-Y Tests

Figure XI-17

The DoDPI (Tri-Spot) Zone Comparison Technique

This particular format, which has changed very little from the original Backster technique of 1961, is the most frequently used by DoDPI in specific-issue tests. The relevant questions cover the Primary issue to test direct involvement, Secondary issue to test guilty or secondary knowledge, and in addition Backster's S-K-Y test is optionally included at the end of the other test questions. The relevant questions are compared against Non-Current Exclusive Control questions. A Sacrifice-Relevant question and two symptomatic questions are also used in this test. Three separate charts are conducted before a determination is made as to truth or deception. An example of the test format and question sequence is depicted below: (DoDPI 1994)

1. Irrelevant	Are the lights on in this room?
2. Sacrifice-Relevant	Regarding that stolen money, do you intend to answer truthfully each question about that?
3. Symptomatic	Are you completely convinced that I will not ask you a question on this test that has not already been reviewed?
4. Non-Current Exclusive Control	Prior to 1991, did you ever steal anything from someone who trusted you?
5. Strong Relevant	Did you steal any of that money?
6. Non-Current Exclusive Control	Prior to coming to Alabama, did you ever steal anything?
7. Relevant	Did you steal any of that money from that footlocker?
8. Symptomatic	Is there something else you are afraid I will ask you a question about, even though I have told you I would not?
9. Non-Current Exclusive Control	Prior to this year, did you ever steal anything from an employer?
10. Weak Relevant	Do you know where any of that stolen money is now?

S-K-Y (Optional)

11. Suspect (Control)	Do you suspect anyone in particular of stealing any of that money?
12. Knowledge (Relevant)	Do you know for sure who stole any of that money?
13. You (strong Relevant)	Did you steal any of that money?

NOTE: The S-K-Y is optional but some agencies require the S-K-Y and some do not. If the SKY is used, then test question #10 above should not include the wording of SKY test question #12. A Guilt Complex question which is a specialized control question based on a fictitious crime is used to identify a "guilt complex reactor." It may be used in lieu of the non-current exclusive control question #9, when it is believed that the examinee may be a guilt complex reactor.

Test Data Analysis:

a. Deceptive (DI). To make a determination that the examinee is deceptive on the above ZCT test, the score must be minus 3 or less in any spot or a grand total of minus 6 for all spots.

b. Non-Deceptive (NDI). To make a determination of non-deception, there must be a plus score in every spot with a grand total of plus 6 or greater overall.

c. Inconclusive (INC). If it is not DI or NDI, it is inconclusive.

SPOT 1	SPOT 2	SPOT 3	Grand Total
+6	0	+6	+12 = Inconclusive
+4	-1	-2	+1 = Inconclusive
-1	+6	+6	+11 = Inconclusive
+2	+2	+2	+6 = NDI
-2	-2	-2	-6 = DI
+3	+1	+2	+6 = NDI
+3	+2	-3	+2 = DI
0	0	-3	-3 = DI
+1	+1	+1	+3 = Inconclusive

It should be noted that in the above DoDPI (Tri-Spot) Zone Comparison Test, the relevant questions do not adhere to the Single-Issue rules defined by Backster and this author, yet DoDPI horizontally tallies the vertical scores from all of the Spots for a total tally from which a determination is made.

The DoDPI Modified General Question Test

The DoDPI Modified General Question Test (MGQT) is a modified version of the Reid technique developed by John E. Reid in 1953. The DoDPI MGQT also incorporated many of the principles utilized in Backster's Zone Comparison Test. The major difference between the Reid test and the DoDPI MGQT is that Reid did not use a numerical evaluation of the physiological data recorded on the polygraph charts, not were his control questions isolated by time or place from the relevant issue. (DoDPI FSC 502, 1 Nov. 1995)

The MGQT is thus a standardized control question test which allows for maximum number of relevant questions involving the selected target.

The psychology and concept of the MGQT is similar to the DoDPI Zone Comparison test in that it offers a threat to the security of the innocent examinee with the use of non-current exclusive control questions for comparison with the relevant test questions, and the test structure employs the concepts of Psychological Set, Anticlimax Dampening, Outside Super-Dampening, Spot Analysis, and Numerical Evaluation.

Both the Seven-Position Scale and the Three-Position Scale are used by the Federal Government in their numerical evaluation of the MGQT.

The MGQT uses four types of relevant questions.

(1) Primary Issue. This question tests direct involvement and is always the #5 question on the MGQT.

(2) Secondary Involvement. This question tests lesser actions of the crime than direct involvement. This test question is usually #3 question on the

MGQT, however it may also be placed at the #8 or #9 test question position if appropriate.

(3) Evidence-Connecting. This question is designed to determine if the examinee is aware of the nature or location of various items of evidence or fruits of the crime. The evidence-connecting question is most often used at the #8 position. Additional evidence-connecting questions may be used as the #3 or #9 question in certain circumstances.

(4) Guilty Knowledge. A question used to determine if the examinee has any knowledge of who committed the crime under investigation. This test question is usually the #9 question in the MGQT.

There are four Irrelevant test questions in the MGQT, which are positioned as #l, #2, #4, and #7. They are structured as:

(1) Neutral questions.
(2) Unrelated to the relevant issue.
(3) Designed to absorb initial (orienting) response to the first test question on the test.
(4) Worded so that the examinee answers "yes."
(5) Assist in overcoming artifacts, compensate for homeostatic changes and establish a tracing free of unwanted noise on the signal of interest.

The MGQT uses non-current exclusive control questions, as described earlier in this chapter, which are always placed in positions #6 and #10.

<u>MGQT Test Structure and Operations:</u>

A. Question Sequence.

(1) Irrelevant
(2) Irrelevant
(3) Relevant (Usually secondary involvement)
(4) Irrelevant
(5) Relevant (Always primary issue)
(6) Non-current exclusive control
(7) Irrelevant
(8) Relevant (Usually evidence connecting - can be secondary involvement)
(9) Relevant (Usually guilty knowledge)
(10) Non-current exclusive control.

There are normally three tests collected with the MGQT at DoDPI but some federal agencies allow two tests. The first two tests are conducted with the test questions asked in the order as shown above. The third test is always asked in the mixed order: I, I,

R, C, R, C, R, C, R, C. There are two options in sequencing the third test. One option is the order: 4, 1, 5, 6, 3, 10, 9, 6, 8, 10. The second option is to place the relevant question the examinee responded to the *least* in the previous tests as the first relevant question of the third test. A possible sequence for test three is: 7, 2, 8, 10, 3, 6, 5, 10, 9, 6. The control questions cannot be positioned back to back, thus they should alternate in the above sequence. Inasmuch as the control questions are repeated on the mixed test, the examinee should be advised during the pretest phase of the examination that at some time during the test, some questions may be repeated, and the examinee should be reminded of this again just prior to the administration of the mixed test. Furthermore, the examinee should be told that the order of the test questions will be changed; that some questions will be repeated and that some questions will not be asked; but that only the questions that were previously reviewed will be asked.

A Stimulation Test is used with the MGQT either before the MGQT is administered or between test number one and two. Hence in summary:

(1) Test One and Two: 1-2-3-4-5-6-7-8-9-10.
(2) Mixed Test: 4-1-5-6-3-10-9-6-8-10.

Irrelevant test questions may be inserted anywhere as needed. If additional irrelevant questions are needed, questions 1, 2, 4, and 7 can be repeated within a test.

<u>*MGQT Test Data Analysis:*</u>

(1) In the first two tests of the MGQT, relevant questions 3 and 5 are compared with non-current control question 6. Relevant question 8 can be compared with either non-current control question 6 or 10. Relevant question 9 can only be compared with control question 10.

(2) On the mixed order test (4-1-5-6-3-10-9-6-8-10), relevant question 5, or the least responding relevant in the first position, is only compared with the adjoining control question. All other relevant questions are compared with the control question most responsive (channel by channel) on either side of the relevant question.

(3) Test data analysis of the MGQT is done by *Spot Total only*. There is *no overall total* as in the Zone Comparison Test.

(a) For NDI: Each separate Spot total (questions 3, 5, 8, 9) must be a plus three (+3) or greater.

(b) For DI: At least one Spot total must be minus three (-3) or less.

(c) Anything else is *inconclusive*.

USAF Modified General Question Technique

The Air Force Modified General Question Technique (AFMGQT) is a modified version of the United States Army Military Police School's (USAMPS) own modification of the Reid Technique developed by John Reid in 1953. The major difference between the 1953 Reid Technique and the 1968 USAMPS MGQT was USAMPS adoption of the principles developed and used in Backster's Zone Comparison Test which included the use of a numerical evaluation (not used by Reid). USAMPS departed from Reid's non-exclusive control questions and adopted Backster's non-current exclusive control questions. In the mid 1970's the US Air Force modified the USAMPS MGQT by adding a Sacrifice Relevant question and restructured the basic Reid format. Thus the Air Force adopted Backster's Psychological set theory, AntiClimax dampening concept, Outside super-dampening concept and Spot analysis. The AFMGQT test format and question sequence is as follows:

1. Irrelevant Question
2. Sacrifice Relevant Question
3. Non-Current Exclusive Control Question
4. Relevant (usually secondary involvement)
5. Non-Current Exclusive Control Question
6. Relevant (always primary issue)
7. Non-Current Exclusive Control Question
8. Relevant (usually evidence connecting, can be secondary involvement)
9. Non-Current Exclusive Control Question
10. Relevant (usually guilty knowledge)

There are normally three charts (tests) collected with the AFMGQT; however some agencies allow two tests. The first test is conducted with the questions asked in the order shown above. The second is always asked as a mixed sequence I, S/R, C, R, C, R, C, R, C, R (1, 2, 5, 8, 3, 4, 9, 10, 7, 6). The Air Force conducts the Stimulation test as the first chart before the relevant charts are conducted, but recognizes its administration as the first or second test chart.

Test Data Analysis:

In the AFMGQT the relevant questions #4, 6, 8, and 10 are compared with their neighboring non-current exclusive control questions. Test data analysis of the AFMGQT is conducted by Spot total (vertical tally) only. The Spot totals are not horizontally tallied as in the Single-Issue Backster ZCT or Matte ZCT. Quantification for determination of truth (NDI) or deception (DI) or inconclusive (INC) is as follows: (Ahern. G. D. 1994)

a. NDI. Each separate Spot total (questions 4, 6, 8, and 10) must be plus three (+3) or greater.
b. DI. At least one Spot total must be minus three (-3) or less (-4, etc.).
c. INC. -2 thru +2.

The Utah Zone Comparison Technique

The Utah Zone Comparison Technique was initially developed by Drs. David C. Raskin and John Kircher in the course of their research studies using the control question test. Several versions have since been developed, two of which are described below (by Steve Bartlett and Charles R. Honts, both employers of the Utah Zone Comparison Technique). Some forensic psychophysiologists use some form of the original version of the Utah ZCT, such as Bartlett, while others such as Raskin and Honts have substituted exclusive non-directed-lie control questions with exclusive directed-lie control questions. The term "Directed-Lie" does not depict the structure of the control question, only the method in which the type of control question used is introduced to the examinee and the fact that the examinee is directed to lie to that control question on the test. Therefore, a "Directed-Lie" control question can incorporate any of the aforementioned control questions, i.e. Non-Current Exclusive Control Question, Current Exclusive Control Question, Non-Exclusive Control Question. However, many of the forensic psychophysiologists who have been using the original version of the Utah ZCT have resisted the use of the Directed-Lie control question and continue to use the original Utah ZCT format and methodology. Thus two formats are depicted below:

Bartlett Version of the Utah ZCT

(Y) 1. Irrelevant
(YR) 2. Sacrifice Relevant
(B) 3. Symptomatic
(G) 4. Non-Current Exclusive Control (NCEC)
(R) 5. Relevant
(G) 6. Non-Current Exclusive Control (NCEC)
(R) 7. Relevant
(Y) 8. Irrelevant
(G) 9. Non-Exclusive Control (NEC)
(R) 10. Relevant

Honts Version of the Utah ZCT

(Y) 1. Irrelevant
(YR) 2. Sacrifice Relevant
(Y) 3. Irrelevant
(G) 4. Directed Lie (NCEC)
(R) 5. Relevant
(Y) 6. Irrelevant
(G) 7. Directed Lie (NCEC)
(R) 8. Relevant
(Y) 9. Irrelevant
(G) 10. Directed Lie (NCEC)
(R) 11. Relevant

In both of the above technique formats the control questions are rotated in position with each chart conducted, but the ordinal position of the relevant questions does not change. In both technique formats the relevant questions are normally compared against the control question preceding the neighboring relevant question, unless the control zone was considered to be a distortion zone. If a control question is not scorable, the relevant question is compared to the control nearest in time that is acceptable for scoring. A minimum of three charts must be conducted for a determination. A Known Solution Stimulation test is normally used in the Bartlett version as the second chart, after the conduct of the first relevant chart. Backster's seven-position scale is used to score the control versus relevant question pairs or spots, and a fixed threshold of plus or minus 6 must be attained to reach a conclusion. Plus or minus 5 or lower are considered inconclusive. (Bartlett 1995; Honts 1996). Except in the Honts version when all of the relevant questions deal only with a true single-issue, neither technique format qualifies as a Single-Issue test inasmuch as the relevant questions cover direct involvement, secondary involvement or evidence connecting, and/or knowledge. Bartlett's formats tally all of the vertical scores of each spot for a total score from which a single determination is made regarding truth or deception. Honts reports each single relevant question as deceptive when the total vertical score is -3 or greater, and truthful when the total vertical score is +3 or greater. When the total vertical score is between -3 and +3 that relevant question is reported as inconclusive. (Bartlett 1995; Honts 1996; Abrams 1996). Research has indicated that in multiple-issue tests when the subject is truthful to some relevant questions, but is deceptive to others, the accuracy of all decisions decreases, and in particular, false positive errors increase. (Honts 1996).

REFERENCES

Abrams, S. (1996, January 25). Telephone conversation with J. A. Matte

Ahern, G. D. (1994) Air Force Modified General Question Technique (AFMGQT). Presentation at the American Polygraph Association's 29th Annual Seminar/Workshop, Nashville, TN 24-29 July 1994.

Department of Defense Polygraph Institute (1994). ZCT, Zone Comparison Test. Forensic Science 502. 15 pages.

Department of Defense Polygraph Institute (1995, November 1). Modified General Question Technique. Forensic Science 502.

Backster, G. C. (1994, December 5-9). 37th Annual Polygraph Examiner Work Conference. The *Backster School of Lie Detection*, San Diego, CA 92101.

Backster, G. C. (1979). Standardized Polygraph Notepack and Technique Guide: Backster Zone Comparison Technique. 24 pages.

Bartlett, S. K. (1995, December 20). Letter of reply to J. A. Matte.

Gordon, N. (1995, December 14). Telephone conversation with J. A. Matte.

Gordon, N. (1996, January 25). Telephone conversation with J. A. Matte.

Honts, C. R. (1996, February 9). Letter of reply to letter of inquiry by J. A. Matte dated 13 Jan 96.

Matte, J. A. (1976). A polygraph control question validation procedure. Polygraph, 5(2), 170-177.

Matte, J. A., Reuss, R. M. (1989). Validation study on the Quadri-Zone Comparison Technique. *Research Abstract*, LD 01452, Vol. 1502, University Microfilm International.

Matte, J. A., Reuss, R. M. (1993). Predictive tables for estimating accuracy and error rates in single-issue control question tests. *The Truthseekers*, 5(3), 1-9.

Raskin, D. C. (1978, September 13-16). Fourth annual workshop on the detection of deception. Conducted at the University of Utah, Salt Lake City, Utah.

Raskin, D. C. (1979). Nevada Supreme court rules that stipulated polygraph evidence is admissible: Background to the case. *Polygraph Law Reporter*, 2, 10.

Weinstein, D. A. (1996, January 25). Telephone conversation with J. A. Matte

Chapter 12

ANALYSIS, INTERPRETATION AND NUMERICAL QUANTIFICATION OF PHYSIOLOGICAL DATA RECORDED ON POLYGRAPH CHARTS

The second most critical part of any psychophysiological veracity (PV) examination is the analysis and interpretation of the physiological data recorded on the polygraph charts. The first is the scientific formulation of relevant and control questions in a valid psychological test that is properly administered, without which chart interpretation becomes useless.

The interpretation of polygraph charts requires the knowledge of physiology and psychology as they pertain to forensic psychophysiology. In this chapter we will interpret polygraph charts purely from a physiological standpoint.

While American Polygraph Association accredited polygraph schools such as the Department of Defense Polygraph Institute now have an excellent curriculum on physiology and its application to the interpretation of the physiological data recorded on polygraph charts, there are still many earlier graduates of polygraph schools whose curriculum on physiology was insufficient, who are currently practicing forensic psychophysiology. Many of those earlier graduates have attended continuing education seminars to augment their knowledge of physiology related to polygraphy through national and state association sponsored seminars/workshops. In addition to those who graduated from unaccredited polygraph schools whose curriculum may lack adequate physiology training, many earlier graduates of accredited polygraph schools have failed to supplement their initial limited knowledge of physiology in spite of continued advances in forensic psychophysiology. Thus many "polygraphists" are "technicians" who interpret chart tracings by memorizing known tracing patterns without knowing the physiological cause for the particular pattern analyzed. This can lead to errors in interpretation that otherwise could have been avoided. As an analogy, you would not want your x-rays to be analyzed by an x-ray technician; you want a medical doctor trained in radiology to interpret your x-rays.

While a knowledge of the various physiological patterns that may be recorded on polygraph charts is essential, an understanding of their etiology is also required in order to make an accurate evaluation.

A polygraph chart contains basically four separate physiological records, which are seen on the chart as four lateral tracings. Respiration patterns are recorded at the top portion of the chart by two separate pneumograph pens; one records thoracic breathing and the other records abdominal breathing. Older polygraph instruments used only one channel to record breathing patterns. The middle portion of the chart is reserved for the GSR (galvanic skin response) or GSG (galvanic skin conductance) tracing, which reflects relative changes in the subject's conductivity of minute induced electrical impulses. The cardio tracing, reflecting relative changes in blood pressure, pulse rate and pulse amplitude is recorded as the bottom tracing on the polygraph chart.

Test questions are spaced at 20 second intervals, from the answer to one question to the beginning of the next test question, to allow the sympathetic and parasympathetic systems to activate and manifest themselves on the chart. The subject is restricted to a simple *yes* or *no* answer on the test, since all test questions have been previously reviewed with the subject during the pretest interview. At the beginning of the test question, a short vertical line is placed at the bottom of the moving chart in line with the tip of the cardio pen, either manually with a felt tip pen or with the use of a stimulus marker. When the question is finished, another vertical line is marked on the moving chart. When the subject answers *yes* or *no*, a plus or minus marking is placed on the moving chart at the exact time the answer was given. Underneath the markings, the question number is inserted.

Uniform Chart Markings were developed by Cleve Backster (see Appendix A), to document on the polygraph chart at the exact time of occurrence any artifact caused by the examinee or the forensic psychophysiologist. This standardized procedure permits the reconstruction of the test conditions for subsequent evaluation by other forensic psychophysiologists.

A polygraph chart tracing can be dissected into four classifications or segments: an average tracing segment, a reaction tracing segment, a relief tracing segment, and distortion tracing segment. (Backster in Bailey 1970; Matte 1980; Weinstein 1995; DoDPI 1996)

The *average tracing segment* is a segment within a tracing that shows no physiological evidence of a change in the emotional level within the stress area on the polygraph chart (Backster 1970; Matte 1980). This condition is also as known as the *Tonic Level* (Weinstein 1995; DoDPI 1996).

The *reaction tracing segment* is a segment within a tracing that shows physiological evidence that the sympathetic subdivision of the autonomic nervous system has become more active, indicating a psychological change from the subject's average emotional level (Backster 1970; Matte 1980). This condition is also known as a *Phasic and/or Tonic Response* (Weinstein 1995; DoDPI 1996).

The *relief tracing segment* is a segment within a tracing that shows physiological evidence that the parasympathetic subdivision of the autonomic nervous system has become more active following the stress area on the polygraph chart, indicating a psychological return to the subject's exhibited average emotional level (Backster 1970; Matte 1980). This condition is also known as a *Homeostatic Change* (Weinstein 1995; DoDPI 1996).

The *distortion tracing segment* is a segment within a tracing that departs from the average emotional level but lacks physiological evidence of either sympathetic or parasympathetic activation within the stress area on the polygraph chart, indicating an absence of psychological origin (Backster 1970; Matte 1980). This condition is also known as *Artifact* (Weinstein 1995; DoDPI 1996).

Breathing Analysis

As discussed in Chapter 4, a person's inhalation causes the pneumo pen to climb proportionately clockwise on the chart. When a person exhales, the pen returns counter-clockwise to its normal baseline. Each inhalation/exhalation is considered one cycle. A series of consecutive cycles forms a tracing segment or pattern.

When a subject has no immediate fear of detection regarding a particular question on the test, the subject's breathing cycles should be of equal height and amplitude inasmuch as there is no psychological change that would inhibit the subject's diaphragm-intercostal muscular complex. Consequently, the subject has tidal air intake during inhalation and average residual air volume as a result of the relaxation of the diaphragm-intercostal complex not being inhibited.

Average tracing Segment

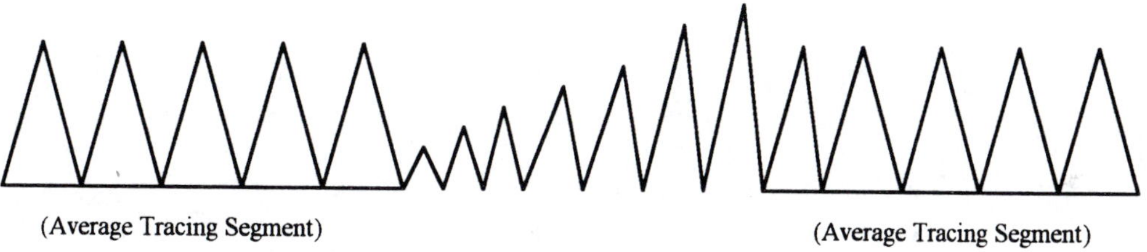

Figure XII-1

When a subject experiences a fear of detection regarding a particular question on the test that represents a threat to his/her well-being, a psychological change occurs that activates the subject's sympathetic system causing a related physiological change. During inhalation, the diaphragm-intercostal muscular complex is inhibited, causing a reduction in the tidal air intake. This results in either sustained, ascending, descending, or suppressed breathing cycles of less than average amplitude on a stable baseline. Sustained, ascending, descending, or suppressed cycles form reaction tracing segments (Fig. XII-2).

Reaction Tracing Segments

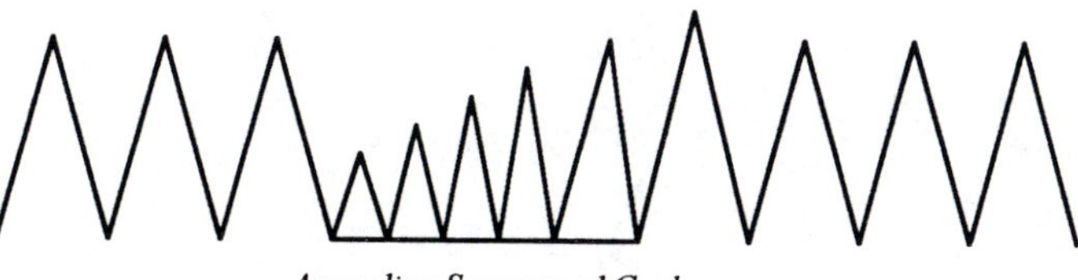

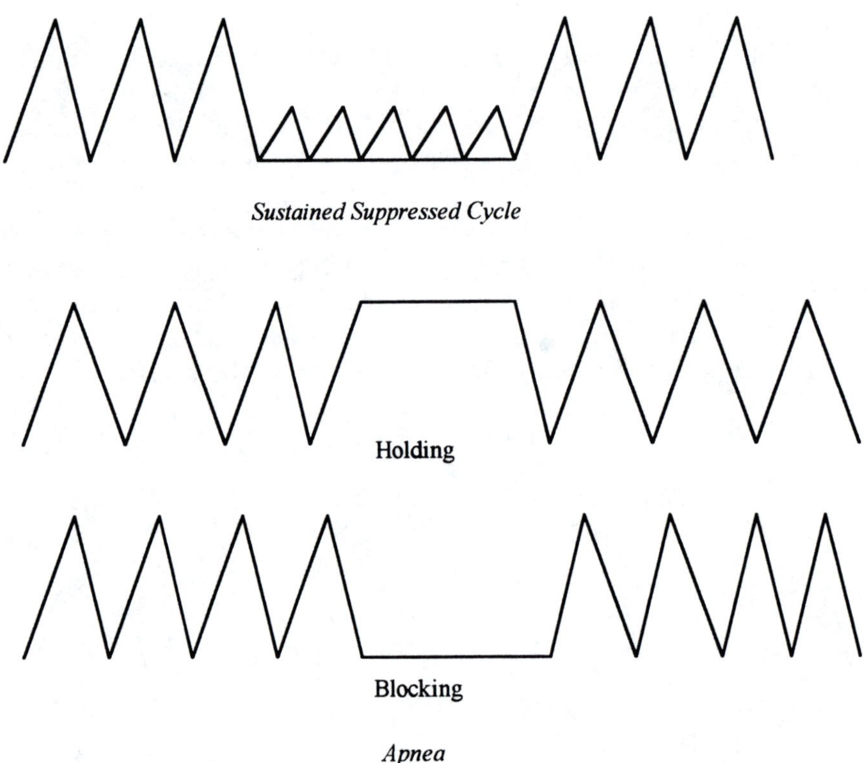

Sustained Suppressed Cycle

Apnea

An apnea is a momentary cessation of breathing by *Holding* at the end of the inspiration limb of the breathing cycle, or *Blocking* at the end of the expiration limb of the breathing cycle.

Caution: An *inspiration apnea* (holding) is usually a voluntary action which should be viewed as a suspected countermeasure if it occurs in the green zone or both in the green and red zone, whereas an *expiration apnea* (blocking) is usually an involuntary action of the pneumotaxic center of the Pons, constituting a legitimate reaction.

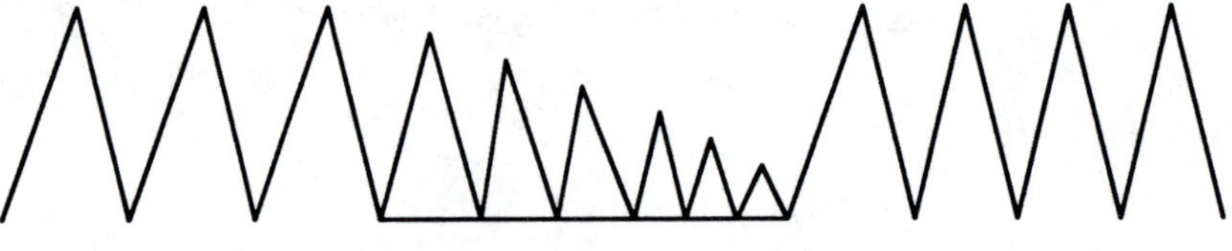

Descending Suppressed Cycle

Figure XII-2

If, during exhalation, relaxation of the diaphragm-intercostal muscular complex is being inhibited, impeding completion of the rib cage return causing less than average diminution of the chest cavity, the subject consequently has greater than average residual air volume resulting in a baseline arousal segment on an unstable baseline. (Figure XII-3)

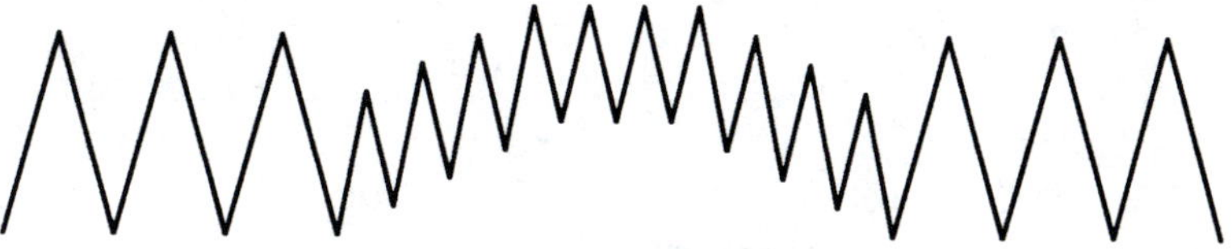

Baseline Arousal

Figure XII-3

If a baseline drops below the average baseline and stabilizes for the remainder of the test at the new baseline, this change was probably caused by either the pneumo tube slipping down from the chest or abdomen or the subject moved. In such cases the change has no interpretive significance. However in the absence of aforesaid artifact, a loss of baseline (up or down) is criteria for deception (DoDPI 1996). (Figure XII-4)

Loss of Baseline

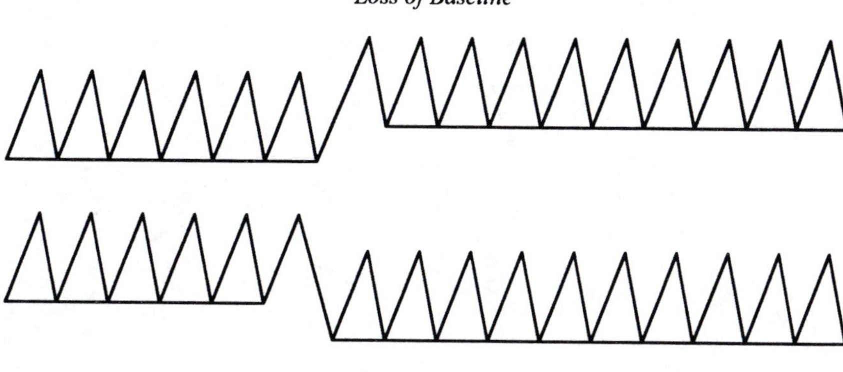

Figure XII-4

However, if the dropped baseline pattern returns to the original baseline and this was not caused by movement on the part of the subject, this is indicative of a reaction, probably the rarest of all deceptive breathing patterns. (Figure XII-5)

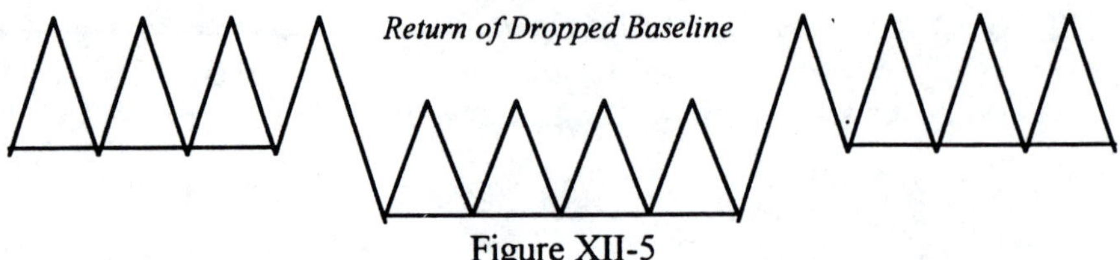

Figure XII-5

A decrease in breathing rate is also considered a reaction tracing segment for the same reason articulated above. It is usually followed by a marked increase in breathing rate which is considered a relief tracing segment. (Figure XII-6)

Decrease in Breathing Rate

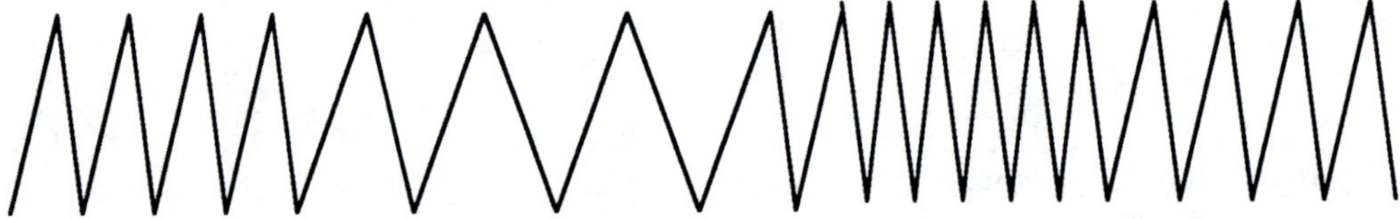

Figure XII-6

Change in Inhalation/Exhalation Ratio

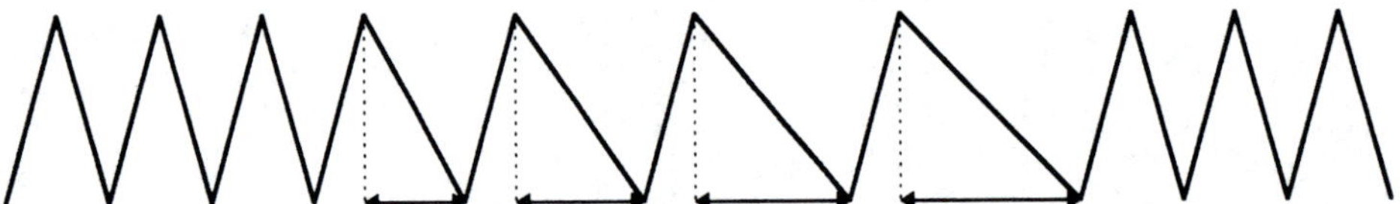

Figure XII-7

The subject's sympathetic system having already activated as a result of his/her fear of detection regarding a particular question on the test, the parasympathetic system now activates to reestablish the body's homeostasis. The subject's diaphragm-intercostal muscular complex must compensate for the preceding suppressed breathing by a greater than average enlargement of the chest cavity resulting in greater than average tidal air intake causing sustained, ascending, or descending hyperventilation cycles. Due to the relaxation of the diaphragm-intercostal muscular complex not being inhibited, the sustained, ascending, or descending hyperventilation cycles are on a stable baseline. Ascending, descending, or sustained hyperventilation cycles form relief tracing segments. (Figure XII-8)

Relief Tracing Segments

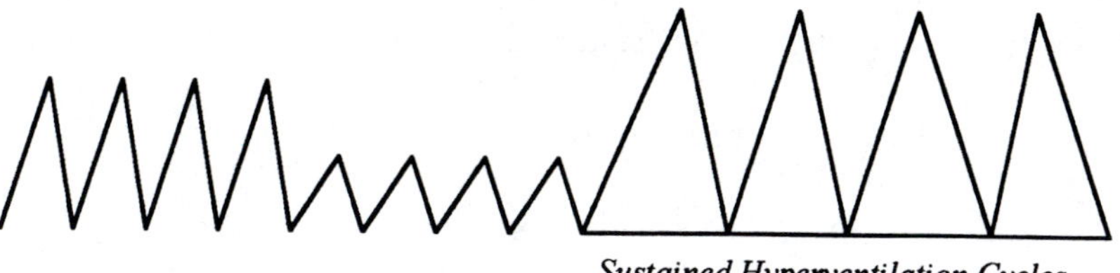

Sustained Hyperventilation Cycles

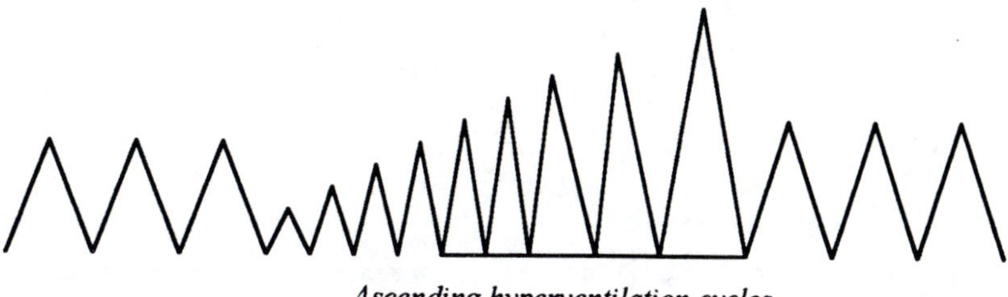

Ascending hyperventilation cycles

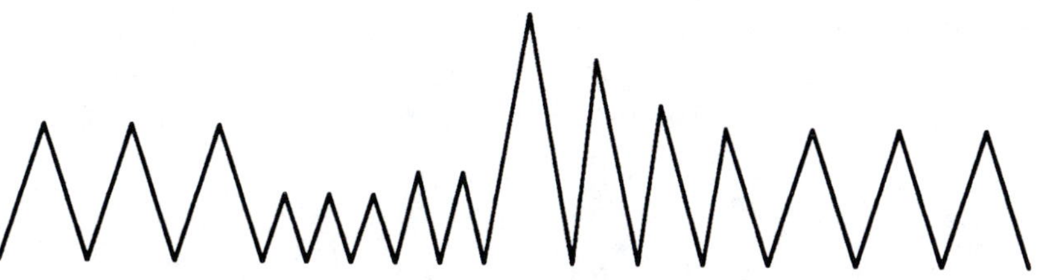

Descending Hyperventilation cycles

Figure XII-8

An increase in breathing rate is also considered a relief tracing segment which is usually a compensatory action to a previous decrease in breathing rate (reaction). (Figure XII-9)

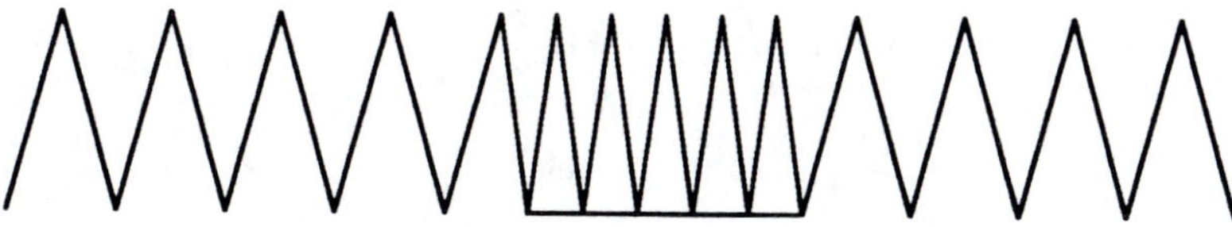

Increased Breathing Rate

Figure XII-9

A single breathing cycle not conforming to the average tracing segment among four other average tracing cycles is considered distortion and should be envisioned as possessing the same amplitude as its neighboring cycles. (Figure XII-10)

Distortion Tracing

Figure XII-10

The exception to this rule is when the nonconforming single cycle occurs during the listening of the question, preparation to answer, or when answering the question, but this phenomenon does not occur during the neighboring question against which it is being compared. (Figure XII-11). This would then constitute a reaction rather than a distortion. However, should the above phenomenon occur in both the relevant and neighboring control question, it would then constitute distortion rather than reaction. (Figure XII-12).

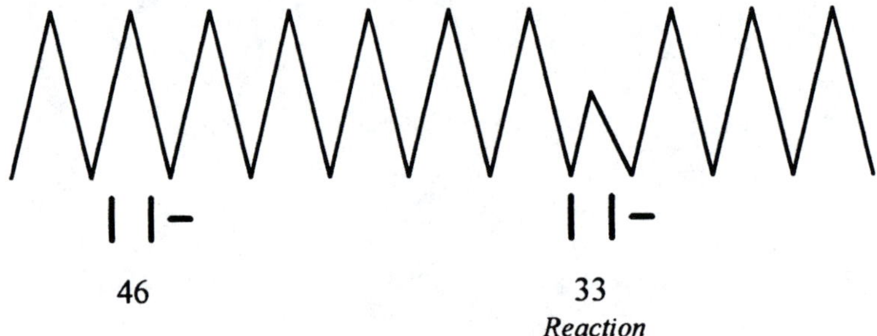

Figure XII-11

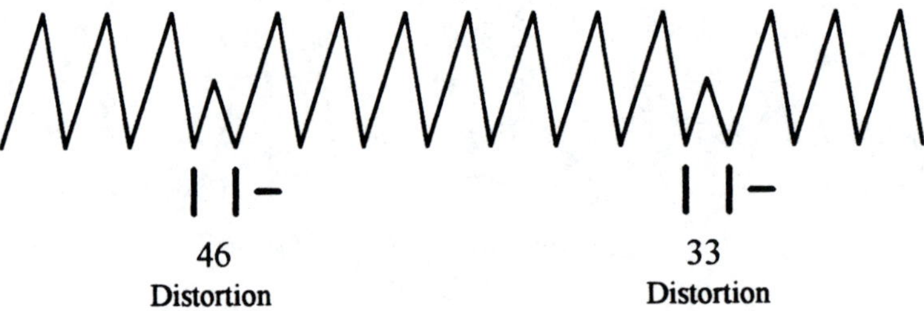

Figure XII-12

Distortion five seconds after the last answer or before the next question has no value. A series of equal but nonconforming breathing cycles interspersed within an average tracing segment is considered uniform distortion and should be envisioned as possessing the same amplitude as its neighboring average tracing cycles. (Figure XII-13).

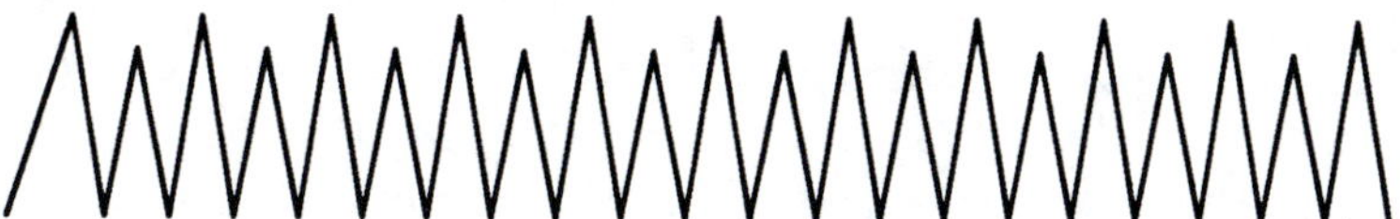

Figure XII-13

A subject may deliberately apply countermeasures to distort his/her breathing pattern in an attempt to prevent the forensic psychophysiologist (FP) from obtaining interpretable charts. The subject may breathe very deeply, very shallowly, very fast, or very slowly. The subject may deliberately cough, sniff, yawn, or any combination thereof.

Normal breathing rate ranges from ten to twenty-four cycles per minute. Breathing rate below ten cycles per minute usually indicates that the breathing is under conscious control. Once the FP has established that any of the above behavior is deliberate, the subject should be admonished. If the subject persists with the countermeasure, the test should be terminated and a post-test interview should be conducted to resolve the matter.

Galvanic Skin Response/Conductance Analysis

Galvanic skin response or conductance (GSR/GSG) is currently the best understood of the three parameters by scientists, but still the least understood by many practicing forensic psychophysiologists. While analog studies showed the GSR/GSG to be the most productive of the three parameters, field studies conducted and also reported by Matte, Reuss (1989, 1992) showed the GSR to be generally the least productive of the three parameters. However, a review of field studies by Capps (1991) revealed overall accuracy of the three parameters to be similar, with respiration at 81%, GSR at 81% and cardiovascular at 76%. (See Chapter 3 for full discussion). Since Backster's development of the numerical scoring system using the 7-position scale where each parameter/tracing is afforded equal value from zero to a maximum score of plus or minus three, no change has been made to this value system nor is it warranted at this time. Interestingly, the mathematical algorithm used in the computer software PolyScore developed by the Applied Physics Laboratory at Johns Hopkins University for use in computerized polygraph systems devotes an average 54% of its criteria for deception to GSR/GSG, 24% to blood volume, 8% to pulse rate, and 14% to respiration (Johnson 1994; Olsen 1995). However, it should be noted that development of an algorithm for the pneumo (respiration) was probably the most difficult, necessarily excluding some traditional criteria such as baseline arousal where the amplitude does not change, while the GSR/GSG was the least difficult to develop. Furthermore, the software system evaluates the GSR/GSG data using methods that are fundamentally different than traditional manual scoring by forensic psychophysiologists.

In order to properly interpret the GSR/GSG tracing, one must understand the causes and effect of the particular tracing to be analyzed. As we have seen in Chapter 4, the sweat glands are activated by sympathetic nerves that use acetylcholine as their chemical mediator, which is an exception to the usual situation where the sympathetic nerves use norepinephrine as the chemical mediator. Perspiration is an excellent conductor of electrical current because it is a saline fluid or chemical salt solution. By placing two electrodes on the last joint of the index and ring finger of the same hand for the purpose of measuring changes in the skin resistance to electricity, any increase in sweat glandular activity will cause a corresponding decrease in skin resistance to electrical current due to the increased saline fluid being emitted through the skin pores. Actually, the sweat need not reach the surface of the skin. As it rises into the epidermis, the moisture seeps out into the surrounding epidermis, hydrating it and lowering its resistance. Any minute flow of electrical current induced into the skin, moving from one point to another will increase its flow because of the resultant decrease in skin resistance.

At the outset, the forensic psychophysiologist obtains maximum GSR/GSG sensitivity, in the Manual Mode, while still able to maintain the GSR/GSG pen at mechanical center. The GSR/GSG pen will normally travel in a wavy motion within the center of the chart but will move rapidly in a clockwise motion when the flow of electrical current increases due to a decrease in the skin resistance to electrical current. The degree of the pen excursion is proportional to the amount of increase in electrical current. Inasmuch as the sympathetic system is responsible for this action, that portion of the pen excursion falls under the reaction tracing segment.

The GSR/GSG pen returns to its normal baseline (in a counterclockwise direction) when the excess sweat is reabsorbed by the surrounding skin pores, aided by evaporation. For this reason and also to prevent cut off of circulation, it is recommended that the GSR electrodes not be placed on the examinee's fingers too tightly. It must be remembered that when the sympathetic system activates, it causes a one-shot stimulation of the sweat glands. It is theorized that a secondary surge of the GSR/GSG pen often seen as a *saddle* pattern on the polygraph chart, also known as a *complex response* (Fig. XII-11), may be caused by the examinee's realization and fear that he/she may have reacted to that particular question thereby causing a second stimulation of the sweat glands. It was previously believed by some forensic psychophysiologists that the return of the GSR/GSG pen to normal baseline was caused by the release of a hormone called norepinephrine which is distributed throughout the body by arterial blood flow, chemically stimulating the constriction of the arterioles thereby affecting the tiny skin capillaries in the same manner which in turn purportedly reduced the volume of other body fluids from the skin surfaces in the outer extremities of the body, including the fingertips, resulting in an increase in the skin's resistance to electricity.* However this theory has no medical basis.

GSR/GSG Pen Excursion Indicative of a Reaction

Figure XII-14

In the illustration of the GSR/GSG pen excursion (Fig. XII-14), it must be remembered that the GSR/GSG pen is longer than the other pens and its tip rests half an inch further than the other pens on the chart, resulting in its recording five seconds earlier (Stoelting) or eight seconds earlier (Lafayette) than the other pens on the chart.

In the analysis of the GSR/GSG tracing pattern, an upward pen excursion of a magnitude of at least twice the neighboring control or relevant question (during the listening of the question, preparation to answer the question, or the answering of the question but not later than five seconds following the answer) constitutes a reaction tracing segment. The counterclockwise return of the GSR pen to established baseline constitutes the relief tracing segment.

In comparing GSR/GSG pen excursions between a relevant and a neighboring control question, the purity of the tracing must be considered, such as suddenness, rapidity of the pen movement, the clearness of the GSR tracing, and the free flowing nature of the GSR tracing.

A tracing that slowly eases up to a certain level cannot be considered to have had as strong a stimulus as the tracing that swiftly moves to the same level. However, in order to diagnose a tracing segment as a reaction, a two-to-one ratio must still exist.

According to research conducted by Abrams (1976), the duration of a response is as valid an indicator of deception as the height of a response. (Figure XII-15). Research conducted by Raskin, et al (1976) revealed that skin conductance responses that began after the onset of a question recovered more slowly following control questions for innocent subjects and following relevant questions for guilty subjects. These effects occurred only when Non-Current Exclusive (Backster) control questions were used and not with tests employing Non-Exclusive (Reid) control questions. Guilty-knowledge tests also reflected some indication of slower recovery responses following critical items for guilty

---

*Progressive Polygraph Studies, Vol. l, No. 4, Jul-Aug 75, Atlantic Security Agency, Baltimore, Md.

subjects. In light of the results of this research, secondary consideration should be given to the duration of the response; primary consideration is still the height of the response.

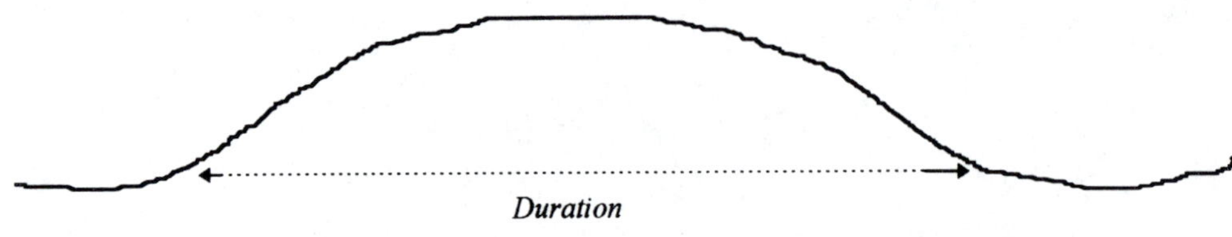

Figure XII-15

The Utah University research project (Raskin et al (1976) recommended that the automatic mode of the galvanic skin response (GSR) component be eliminated completely in view of aforementioned findings. While the manual or free-floating mode should be utilized whenever possible, there are times when the automatic mode is the only means of maintaining the galvanic skin response pen from falling and remaining at the bottom of the chart. In those cases, it is better to employ the automatic mode, which will furnish relative height of responses, than to have no recording of responses in the manual mode. For this reason, manufacturers should still make the automatic mode available to the forensic psychophysiologist.

On some occasions the GSR/GSG pen will travel up to the pen stop and remain there for several seconds before returning or being returned to baseline in preparation for the next test question. In the analysis of the pen excursion, the duration can be added to the height of the response by drawing imaginary lines from the ascending and descending limbs to its natural peak had there been no pen stop. An example is shown in Figure XII-16 below.

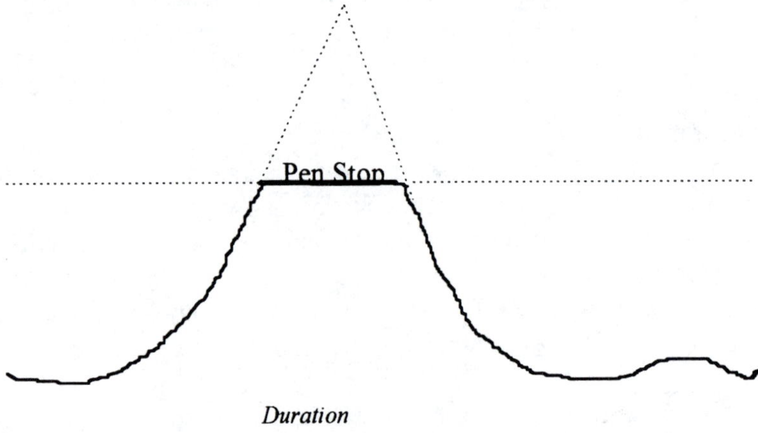

Figure XII-16

On rare occasions, a GSR/GSG pen that has been tracing a waving but steady horizontal line across the chart will suddenly plunge to the bottom of the chart during the reaction tracing segment of a threatening question. This phenomenon may be caused by the subject's endogenous electrical potential, which if in opposition to the voltages imposed by the polygraph instrument will cause the pen to plunge in a counterclockwise direction on the chart when stimulation occurs. Therefore, a plunging GSR/GSG tracing within the time frame of a question or within five seconds following the answer to a question within the zone comparison can be viewed as evidence of sympathetic activation. Care should be exercised to eliminate the possibility of subject hand movement or pressure on the GSG/GSG electrodes as the cause of the GSR/GSG pen plunge. A standard anti-countermeasure employed by this author is to routinely have the examinee wash his or her hands thoroughly with soap and water in the presence of the forensic psychophysiologist before commencement of the testing phase. Furthermore, the GSR/GSG electrodes should be removed after the conduct of each test (chart) and wiped clean and the corresponding fingers wiped dry.

Cardio Analysis

The basic purpose of the cardiograph component is to record from the brachial or radial artery at mean blood pressure relative changes in blood pressure and rate and strength of pulse beat. The cardio cuff is actually measuring changes in the volume of the arm; it is an occlusion plethysmograph. It measures the net volumetric changes in the arteries, arterioles, capillaries, venules, and veins, some of which may be dilating while others may be simultaneously contracting. It is also confounded by the fact that it is artificially preventing the return flows of blood until the pressures in the capillaries and veins reach a point higher than the air pressure in the cuff.

As explained in Chapter 4, the cardio pen moves upward on the chart in a clockwise motion when the heart pumps blood out into the aorta creating artery pressure. That upward movement of the pen is called a systolic or ascending limb. When the heart relaxes, the blood pressure drops and the pen on the chart commences its descent; if the cuff pressure is at mean blood pressure, when the pen descends to the halfway mark, it will suddenly stop and then resume its descent recording the dicrotic notch in the middle of the descending or diastolic limb as reflected in Figure XII-17. The dicrotic notch position within the diastole limb can be raised or lowered by decreasing or increasing the cuff pressure respectively.

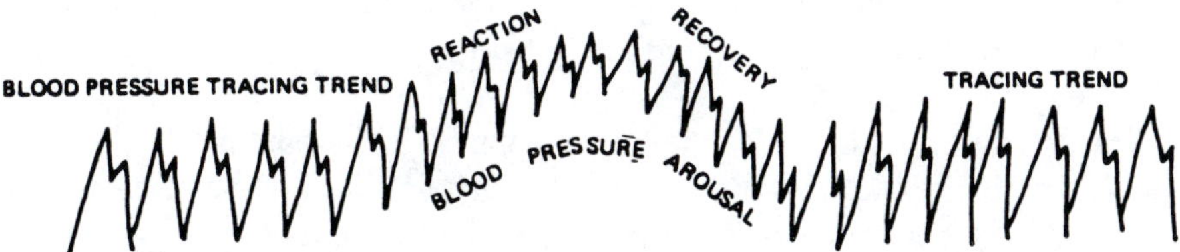

Figure XII-17

Activation of the sympathetic subdivision of the autonomic nervous system may cause an increase in mean blood pressure, a momentary increase or decrease in the pulse rate and an apparent decrease in pulse strength as a result of increased constriction of arterioles.

A relative change in blood pressure is a temporary deviation from blood pressure tracing trend and is therefore considered a reaction tracing (Fig. XII-18).

Polygraph Chart Interpretation

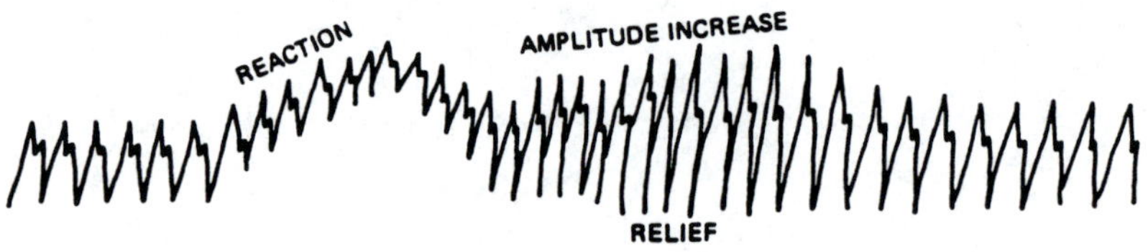

Figure XII-18

The strength of the pulse beat and the volume of blood ejected into the system's circulation creates a forceful pulse wave transmission. This force against the brachial artery wall increases air pressure within the arm cuff bladder, which causes corresponding air pressure in the polygraph's cardio tambour. This pressure in turn powers the cardio pen in an upward clockwise direction, which is called the ascending (systolic) limb of the cardio tracing.

The air pressure within the cardio cuff bladder decreases proportionately as the pulse wave passes beyond the cuff, thus causing the pen to descend in a counterclockwise direction to its baseline. This descending limb is known as the diastolic limb. The force of the pulse wave and the pulse pressure in the brachial artery do not alone determine the amplitude (height) of the cardio tracing. Vasoconstriction of the brachial artery through the release of norepinephrine* during activation of the sympathetic system greatly contributes to an increase in mean blood pressure, which accounts for a rise of the tracing on the chart during reaction time but also a decrease in amplitude (Fig. XII-14). Blood vessels, like the sweat glands, are (for all practical purposes) innervated by the sympathetic nervous system. Only a very few parasympathetic fibers go to a few blood vessels. Vasodilation occurs when the *number* of sympathetic nervous system impulses per second *decreases*. The partial contraction of blood vessels due to a moderate number of sympathetic nervous system impulses per second is called *tonus*.

The rate of the heart (pulse rate) is determined by its output of blood per minute. On a polygraph chart, each systolic tip denotes one heart beat. Manufacturers of kymograph paper have vertically lined the paper at one-half inch intervals, so a kymograph that drives chart paper at exactly six inches per minute will render each vertical line a five-second interval. By counting the number of systolic tips within a five second segment and then multiplying the figure by twelve, the forensic psychophysiologist (FP) obtains the subject's pulse rate per minute at that given moment of chart time. A change in the pulse rate is reflected by changes in the interval between beats or systolic tips (Fig. XII-19).

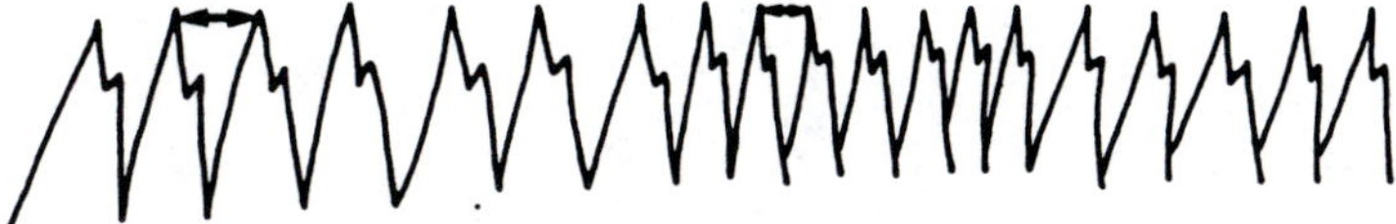

Change in Pulse Rate in the Cardio Tracing

Figure XII-19

As explained in Chapter 4, during activation of the sympathetic system, the heart rate may increase, decrease, or remain the same, depending on whether the beta adrenergic response dominated over the alpha adrenergic response, alpha dominated over beta, or both responses equalized each other.

TABLE 1** - ADRENERGIC RECEPTORS AND FUNCTION

Alpha Receptor	Beta Receptor
Vasoconstriction	Vasodilation (B2)
Iris dilatation	Cardioacceleration (B1)
Intestinal relaxation	Increased myocardial strength (B1)
Intestinal sphincter contraction	Intestinal relaxation (B2)
Pilomotor contraction	Uterus relaxation (B2)
Bladder sphincter contraction	Bronchodilation (B2)
	Calorigenesis (B2)
	Glycogenolysis (B2)
	Lipolysis (B1)
	Bladder wall relaxation (B2)

**From A. C. Guyton & J. E. Hall: Textbook of Medical Physiology, 9th Edition. Philadelphia, W. B. Saunders Company, 1996.

Therefore, a change in the heart rate within the reaction tracing segment of only one of two questions being intercompared can be considered a reaction tracing trend. A consistent, uniform lack of rate change to both questions being compared has no interpre-

*The sympathetic nervous system causes vasoconstriction primarily by nerve impulses to the smooth muscles in the walls of the arterioles and other vessels, the norepinephrine being secreted by the neurons; the norepinephrine circulating in the blood from the adrenal glands is a rarer, secondary method.

tive value inasmuch as both truthful and deceptive subjects may show no change in pulse rate during the reaction tracing segment if an equalization of influences by the alpha and beta adrenergic responses occurs. Figure XII-20 illustrates the types of blood pressure trends.

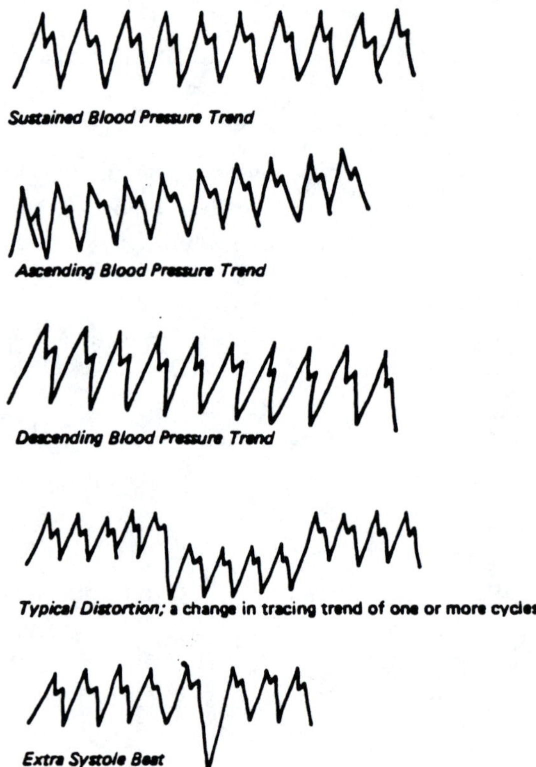

Illustration of Various Types of Blood Pressure Trends

Figure XII-20

The best indicator of sympathetic activation in the cardio tracing reflecting a reaction tracing is a change in the position of the diastolic tip. The second indicator is the systolic tip, and the last indicator is a change in the position of the dicrotic notch.

Figures XII-21a, XII-21b and XII-21c illustrate cardio reaction tracings. Figure XII-22 illustrates cardio relief tracings.

Illustration of Various Types of Cardio Reaction Tracings

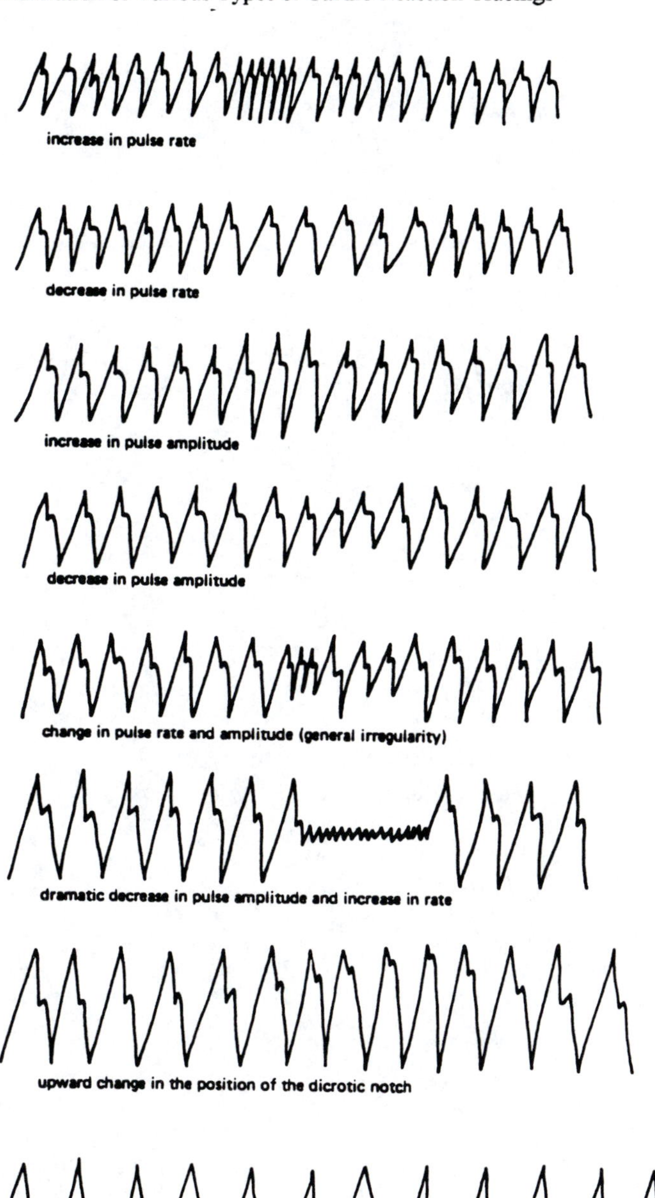

Figure XII-21a

Polygraph Chart Interpretation

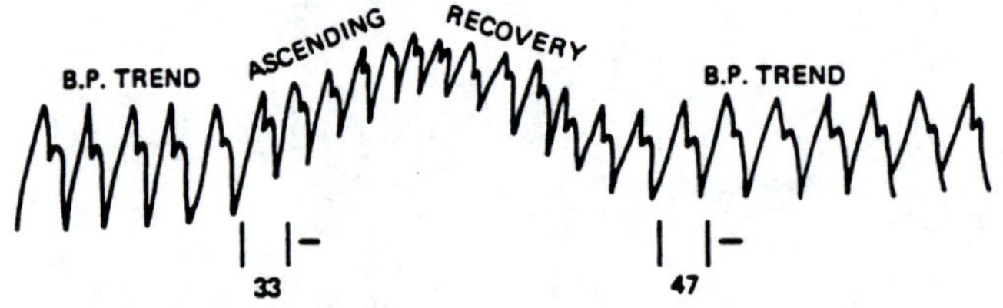

blood pressure arousal, there can be a primary and secondary recovery

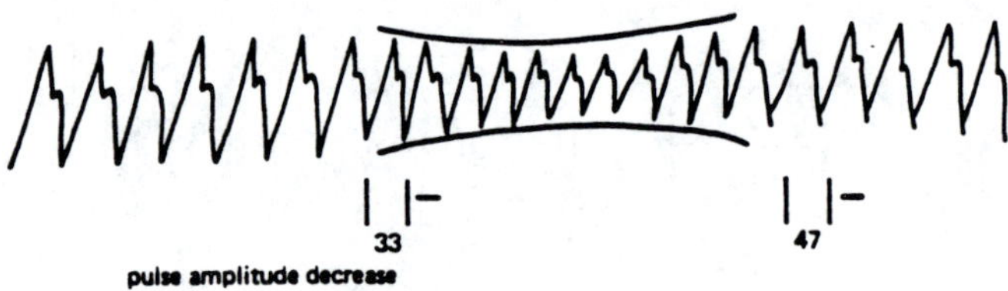

pulse amplitude decrease

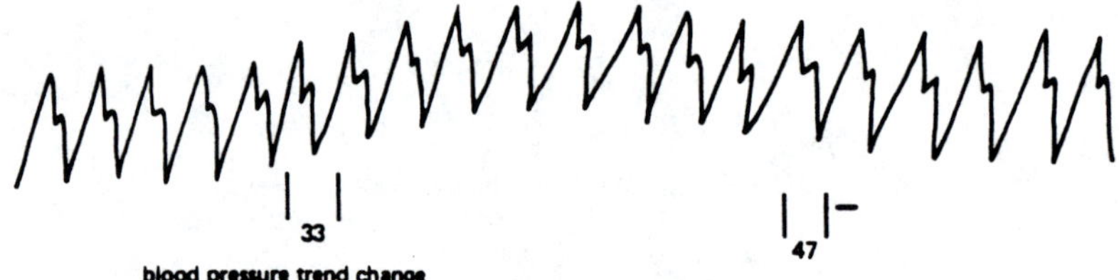

blood pressure trend change

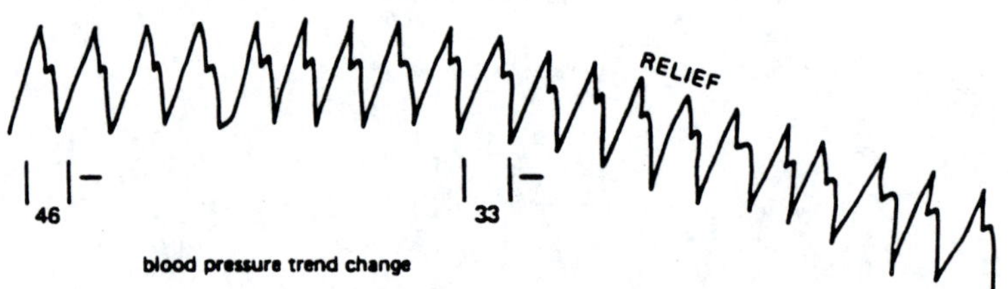

blood pressure trend change

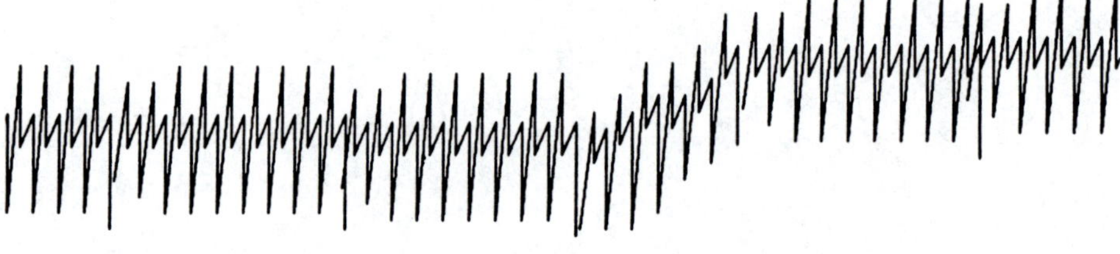

Increase only in baseline

Figure XII-21b

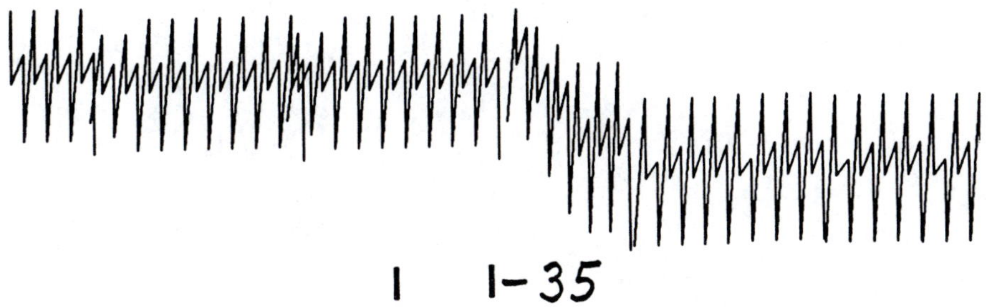

Decrease only in baseline

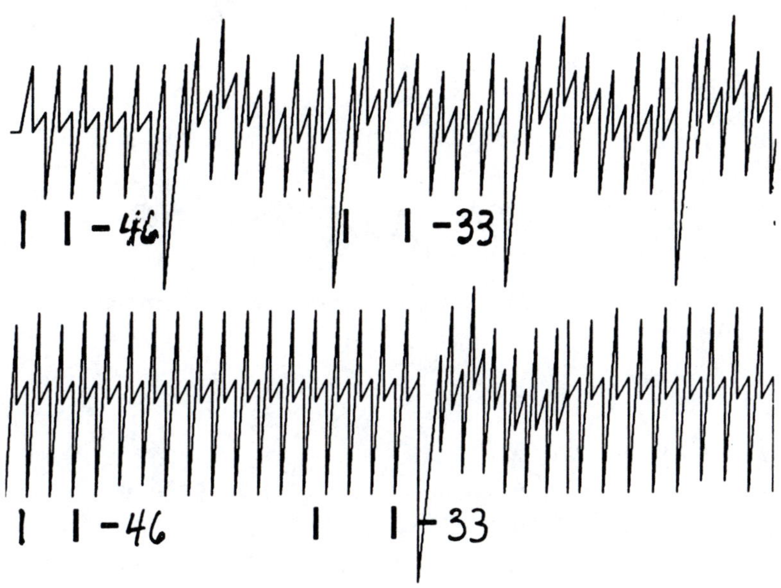

Premature ventricular contraction (PVC)

A PVC results in a sudden drop in blood pressure and blood volume. In the top tracing, the PVC occurs at almost regular intervals without specific stimulus thus is regarded as *uniform distortion*, whereas in the bottom tracing the PVC occurs only on a specific stimulus thus is regarded as a *reaction*.

Figure XII-21c

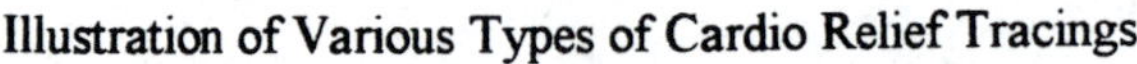
Illustration of Various Types of Cardio Relief Tracings

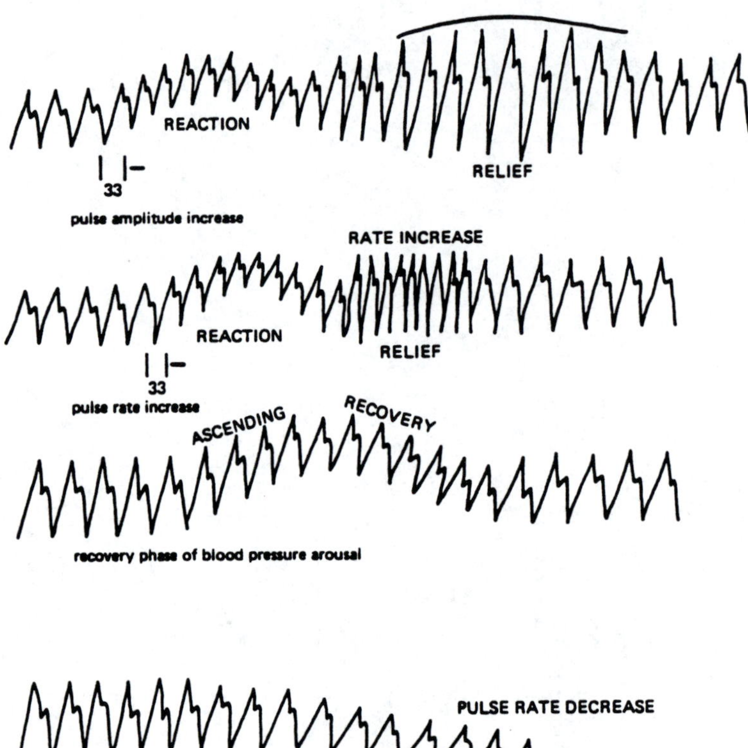

Figure XII-22

Distortions in the cardio tracing can be caused by the movement of subject's arm or tensing of the muscle(s) in the arm from which the recording is being obtained, general nervous tension, a vagus interaction, coughing, deep breath, etc. Distortion can occur when a subject is about to faint as demonstrated by a drop in blood pressure and a slowing down of pulse rate.

The forensic psychophysiologist who uses the cardio activity monitor (CAM) in lieu of the cardio arm cuff would normally expect to observe essentially the same reaction and relief tracing segments. However, this depends on the area of the body where the CAM is placed. As seen in Chapter 4, there are basically five areas to which the CAM is applied for best results. The first is over the radial artery at the wrist (See Fig. IV-10), and the four other areas consist of the thumbnail and three locations on the palmar side of the thumb(see Fig. IV-11).

The forensic psychophysiologist should understand that when the sympathetic subdivision of the autonomic nervous system activates, a major redistribution of the blood in the body occurs in which there is vasodilation of the main arteries in the larger skeletal muscles, and vasoconstriction of the arterioles at the extremities, causing a decrease in blood volume in the capillary bed.

Therefore, when the CAM is applied to the radial artery at the wrist, a similar reaction and relief tracing segment as found using the cardio cuff should be expected. However when the CAM is applied to the thumb nail or on the palmar side of the thumb, the forensic psychophysiologist is then recording capillary blood volume, which decreases when the sympathetic system activates. This results in a quick descent or plunge in the tracing as opposed to the rise in the tracing of the standard cardio pattern. Some forensic psychophysiologists (FP) refer to this latter CAM response as a "diving response."

Figure XII-23 is a section depicting the CAM tracing, recorded from the thumb nail area, containing a "diving response" at relevant question B7.

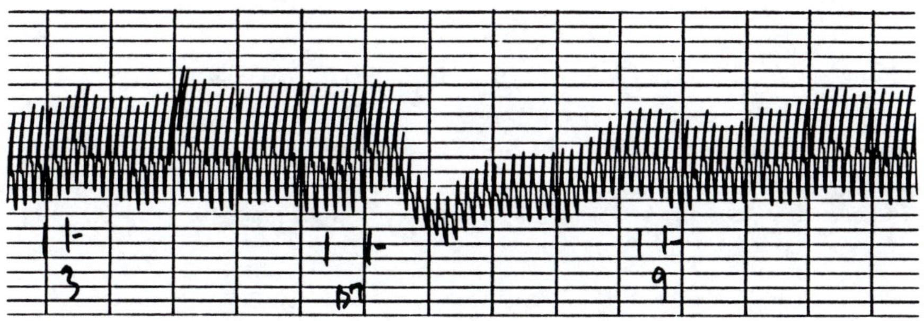

Cardio Activity Monitor (CAM) Reaction

Figure XII-23

In the interpretation of the cardio tracing, the FP must be aware of the possible effect that the breathing cycles may have on the cardio tracing. This phenomenon is called the *vagus* effect. The influence of the breathing upon the cardio pattern is caused by the change in the oxygen content of the blood, which in turn fluctuates with each inhalation of air bringing a fresh supply of oxygen to the bloodstream through the lungs. The vagus effect may also alter the galvanic skin response/conductance (GSG/GSG) pattern but it will be apparent only on the climbing limb, not on the descending limb of the GSR. The vagus effect, when apparent, is usually consistent in the cardio tracing throughout the chart, but not necessarily in the GSR/GSG because the GSR/GSG is not cyclic by nature. The vagus effect in the cardio tracing can be seen as a rise in the cardio pattern as the subject inhales and falls to normal baseline as the subject exhales. This same phenomenon can occur when the arm bearing the cardio cuff is resting against the subject's chest (usually obese). Care should be taken by the FP to use a chair whose arms will keep the examinee's arms in a comfortable position parallel to the ground at or above waist level, never below waist level, and away from the body.

Since the vagus effect is consistent, it produces uniform distortion that can be eliminated as a norm. Uniform distortion can also be produced by earaches, headaches, toothaches, etc., which may produce a cyclic pattern on the chart. Consistent cyclic patterns should be viewed by the FP as a norm and disregarded when seeking physiological evidence of sympathetic and parasympathetic activation.

The abdominal breathing can cause a milking action on the inferior vena cava and thus influence the amount of blood returning to the heart as the person breathes. This can also cause variations in the blood pressure and heart rate.

The polygraph charts depicted in Figures XII-24 thru XII-27 are from a verified examination where the subject was found to be truthful regarding the larceny of monies from a safe. This examination consisted of three charts. The Backster Zone Comparison technique was used in the first and third chart. The second chart consisted of a stimulation test to reassure the innocent examinee and stimulate the guilty examinee as the case may be.

Figure XII-24 shows the entire first chart. Note the sensitivity markings at the beginning of the chart in each tracing. The single X at the beginning of the test indicates that the examinee was advised that the test is about to begin. The XX (double X) at the end of the test denotes the end of the test and the exact time the test is ended is entered in international time. Each vertical line represents a five-second interval.

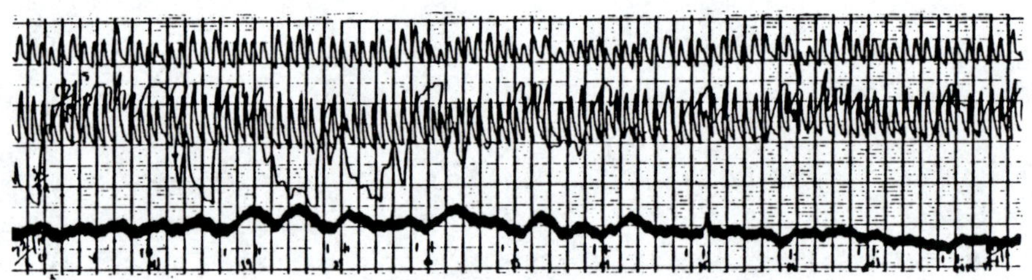

Actual Backster ZCT Chart l - NDI Suspect of Larceny

Figure XII-24

Figure XII-25 is a magnification of the zone comparison of the first polygraph chart. Question 46 and 47 are the control questions; question 33 and 35 are the relevant questions. Question 25 and 26 are the symptomatic questions. When comparing questions 46 and 33, there is clear evidence of suppression in the breathing pattern at question 46 (control). As a matter of fact, subject is actually hyperventilating (relief) on relevant question 33 as a result of reaction to control question 46. There is greater arousal of the galvanic skin reflex (GSR) on question 46 than 33. Control question 46 reflects a more sustained blood pressure arousal than question 33 where the arousal is delayed. When comparing question 47 and 35, average tracing is noted in the breathing pattern at question 35, but there is a baseline arousal at question 47 (control). The GSR pen excursion at question 47 is slightly higher and longer than at question 35 but not significant enough to score. In the cardio tracing, question 47 reflects a greater blood pressure arousal than at question 35. Questions 25 and 26 reflect mild reaction in all parameters indicating that the examinee is not completely convinced that he will not be asked an unreviewed question, but this factor is apparently not interfering with the examinee's psychological set on the control questions.

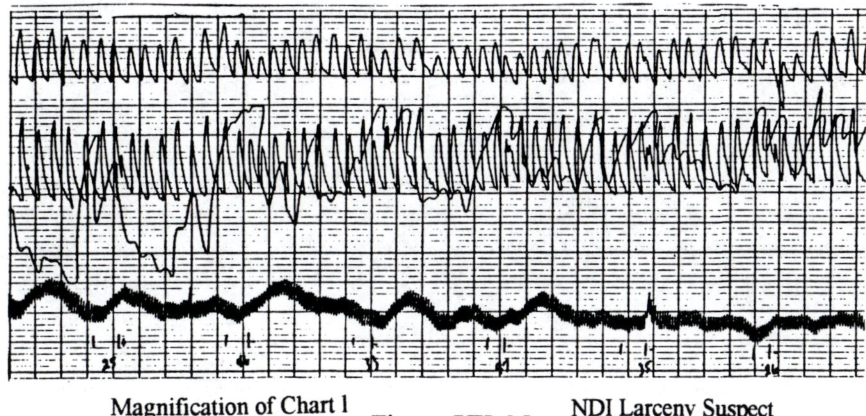

Magnification of Chart 1 NDI Larceny Suspect

Figure XII-25

The polygraph chart depicted in Figure XII-26 is the control-stimulation test. The examinee was requested to select one card from among a total of six cards, remember the number on the card selected, then place all cards face down under his legs. The examinee was then instructed to answer "no" to all questions on the test, including the card he had selected, so that he should be telling a lie on the test. The FP would determine which card the examinee had selected on the basis of physiological evidence of sympathetic and parasympathetic activation at the question to which the examinee lied. This served to determine the examinee's minimum capability of response, reassure the innocent examinee, and stimulate the guilty.

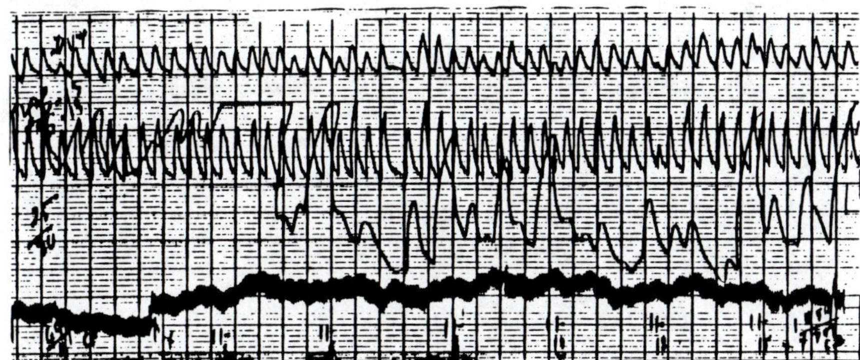

Actual Control-Stimulation Test conducted as Chart 2

Figure XII-26

The examinee selected number ten in the above stimulation test, as evidenced by the change in the baseline of the breathing pattern (stomach, lower pattern) and the staircase pattern especially evident in the upper tracing (chest). Note that the GSR is very active but becomes milder after question number 10 has been passed and resumes again at question 15. At question number 10 there is some evidence of relief in the cardio tracing after the question was asked. Question number 3 shows some reaction in the GSR and cardio tracing, which is expected from the first question asked in any test. Had there been no reaction to any question except question number 3, a second chart may have been run with question number 3 in a different position, to confirm the initial findings. Often, a guilty examinee will attempt distortion of the tracing by deliberate movement or focusing attention on a question other than the question selected in an attempt to convince the FP that he/she is not a testable subject.

Figure XII-27 is a magnification of the second test depicting the zone comparison only, which contains the same question as in the first test or chart, except that relevant questions number 33 and 35 have been switched in position. Note the clear suppression and hyperventilation in the breathing tracing at questions 46 and 47 and the absence of reaction at questions 33 and 35. The GSR tracing clearly shows a pen excursion at question 46 nearly three times greater than its neighboring relevant question 35, although questions 47 and 33 are of near equal amplitude. In the cardio tracing, question 46 shows greater blood pressure arousal than at question 35. Questions 47 and 33 appear to be of equal value except that the cardio tracing at question 33 is not graphically as high as question 47. The physiological evidence indicates that the examinee's psychological set is greatest on question 46 followed by question 47, indicating truthfulness to the relevant questions 33 and 35.

Actual Backster ZCT Magnification of Chart 3, NDI Suspect

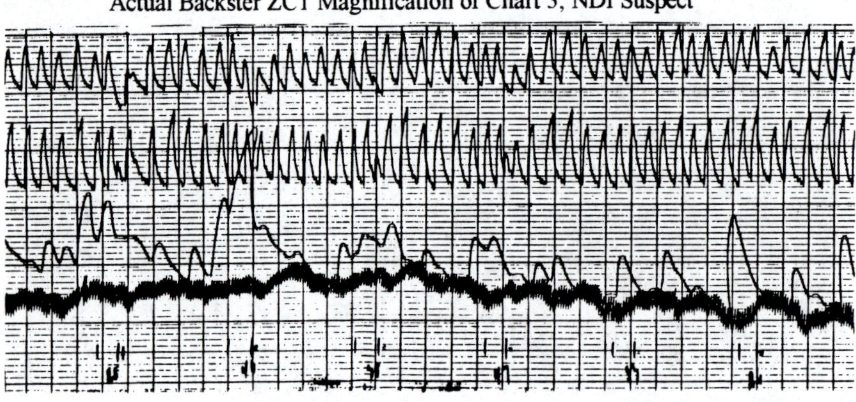

Figure XII-27

The polygraph charts depicted in Figures XII-28 through XII-30 are from an examination regarding the sale of narcotics. These charts indicated deception regarding the relevant questions, which was verified by a confession from the examinee in the post-test interview. This examination consisted of three charts. The Backster Zone Comparison

Technique was used in the first and third chart. The second chart consisted of a stimulation test to reassure the innocent examinee and stimulate the guilty examinee as the case may be.

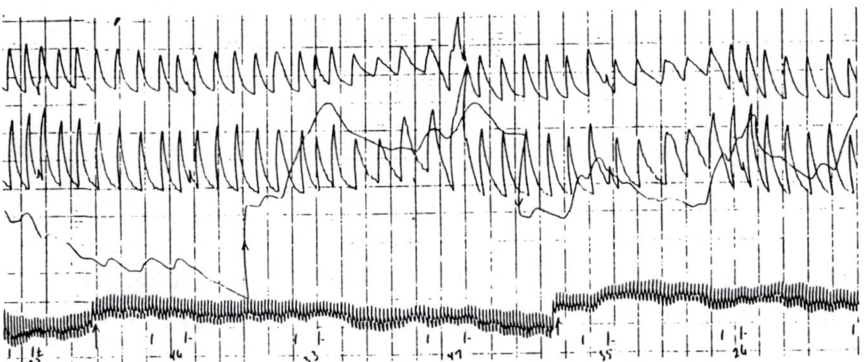

Actual Backster ZCT Chart 1 of DI Narcotic Suspect
Figure XII-28

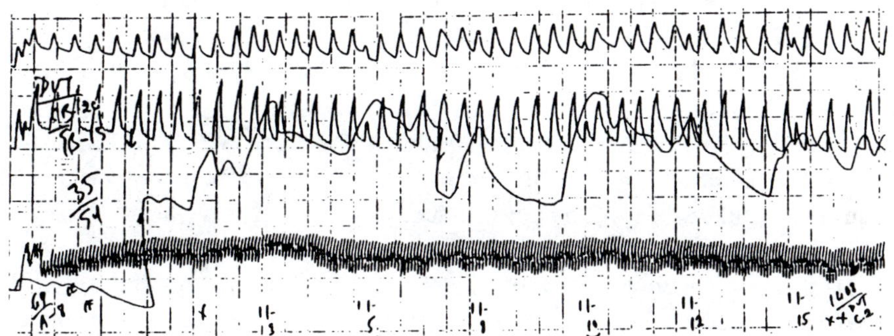

Actual Control-Stimulation Test Conducted as Chart 2

Figure XII-29

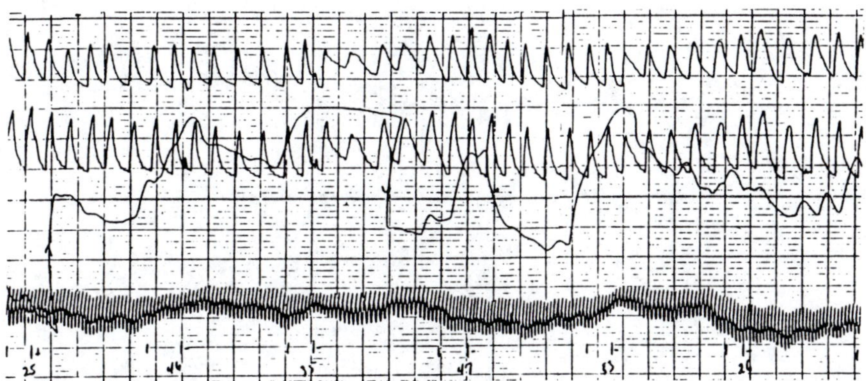

Actual Backster ZCT Chart 2 of DI Narcotic Suspect
Figure XII-30

Figure XII-28 is a magnification of the first chart depicting the zone comparison. Note the tremendous baseline arousal and hyperventilation in the breathing pattern in both upper and lower pneumograph at questions 33 and 35, the relevant questions, and the complete absence of reaction to the neighboring control questions 46 and 47. Also note the GSR arousal at 33 as compared to mild arousal at 46 and 47. Reaction is also indicated in questions 33 and 35 in the cardio tracing.

The polygraph chart depicted in Figure XII-29 is the control-stimulation test. This test was administered as the second chart. The examinee had selected number ten, as evidenced by the slight staircase pattern in the lower pneumograph tracing and the baseline arousal in the upper pneumograph tracing, plus the substantial rise in the GSR pen excursion.

Figure XII-30 is a magnification of the second test (third chart) following the stimulation test showing the zone comparison. The pneumograph tracing clearly demonstrates sympathetic and parasympathetic activation at relevant questions 33 and 35. Note the blood pressure arousal at question 33 as opposed to its neighboring control question 47, and the height of the GSR pen excursion at question 33 as compared to question 47.

Figure XII-31 is from a verified examination where the subject was found to be truthful regarding the murder of an exboyfriend. The Quadri-Track Zone Comparison Technique was used in this examination, which consisted of several issues each requiring at least two charts. The chart depicted below is the second chart of the first test following the stimulation test, regarding whether or not the examinee was present when the murder occurred. As can be seen below, there is ample physiological evidence that the examinee's psychological set was on the control questions 46 and 47, which dealt with her ever having hurt anyone during a period of her life at least two years preceding the date of the murder, thus non-current exclusive control questions.

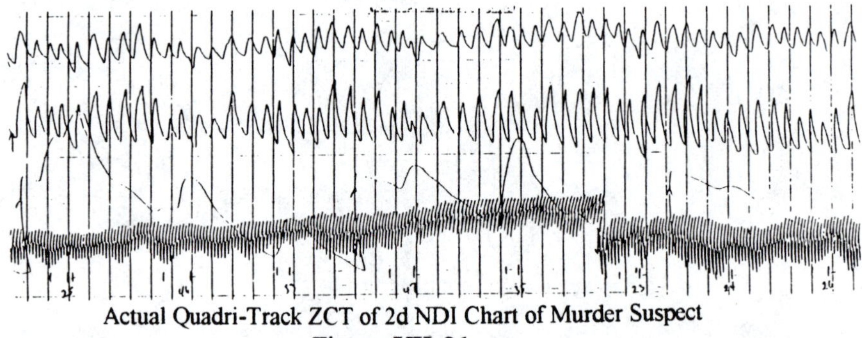

Actual Quadri-Track ZCT of 2d NDI Chart of Murder Suspect

Figure XII-31

Figures XII-32 and XII-33 were taken from a case of larceny involving the systematic theft of more than 5,000 dollars from cash receipts. The Quadri-Track Zone Comparison Technique was used in the examination of two office personnel. Figure XII-32 reflects that this examinee was truthful when she denied committing the larceny. The most significant response is found at control question 47 as evidenced by the staircase pattern in the pneumograph tracing and the significant GSR arousal and cardio relief. Also note the significant GSR arousal at the "inside issue" factor control question number 23 (Fear of Error), as compared to an absence of reaction to its neighboring "inside issue" factor relevant question number 24 (Hope of Error).

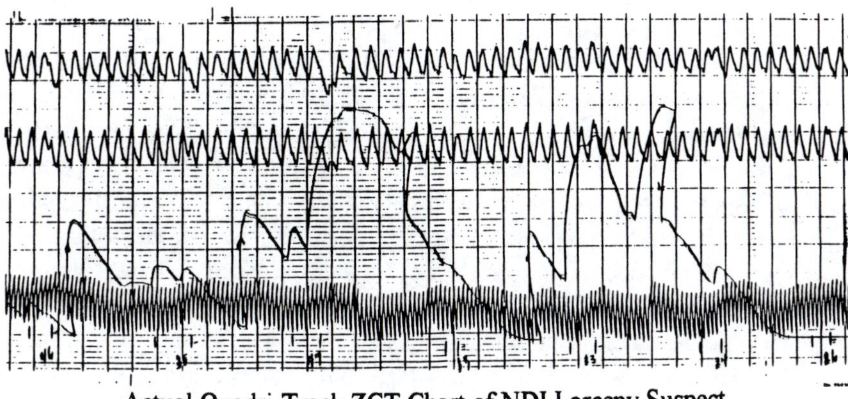

Actual Quadri-Track ZCT Chart of NDI Larceny Suspect

Figure XII-32

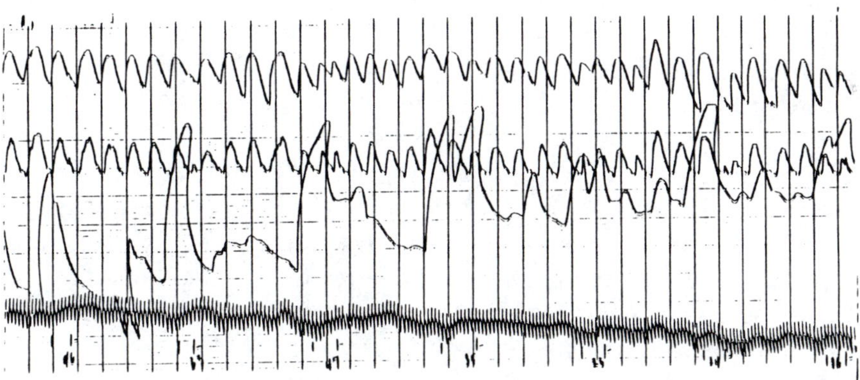

Actual Quadri-Track ZCT Chart of DI Larceny Suspect

Figure XII-33

Figure XII-33 is from the second examinee whose overweight condition necessitated the electronic amplification of the lower pneumograph tracing almost to maximum sensitivity (75 units). Interestingly, the greatest suppression is found in the lower breathing tracing at "Inside Issue" factor relevant question number 24 (Hope of Error), and duration of GSR response is also longest at that question, while GSR activity in the form of a double saddle is also significant at relevant question 35. After this examinee confessed to the aforementioned larceny, she stated that she had resigned herself to the fact that she was going to be discovered. Her demeanor during the entire examination was incredibly calm, cool, and void of gestures normally associated with a guilty person.

NUMERICAL QUANTIFICATION SYSTEM IN CHART ANALYSIS

The advantage of the comparison technique, where each relevant question is compared against its neighboring control (probable-lie) question for a presence or absence of sympathetic and parasympathetic activation, is that it lends itself to a numerical scoring system in the analysis of each chart tracing, i.e. breathing, galvanic skin resistance/conductance, and cardio. A score is assigned in each tracing to each set of relevant versus control questions on the basis of rules and standards established from logic, empirical data and analog/field research. As previously stated in this chapter, consistent presence of strong responses to the relevant question in two or more charts with a comparative absence of response to the control questions indicates an attempt at deception to the relevant questions. Consistent presence of strong responses to the control questions and a comparative absence or weak responses to the relevant questions in two or more charts indicates that no attempt at deception to the relevant questions was made. When all scores are tallied, a conclusion regarding truth or deception must be made from this tally by means of a conversion (conclusion) table based upon empirical data supported and refined through validation studies. (Raskin, et al 1976; Matte, Reuss 1989).

In chart interpretation, the forensic psychophysiologist (FP) must not allow a significant reaction in one tracing to influence his/her evaluation of that same relevant question in the other tracings. The FP must also not allow a strong reaction in any or all tracings to one relevant question to influence his/her evaluation of the other relevant questions on the same chart.

To attain an objective measure of the reactions or lack of reaction to each relevant question in each of the three tracings, a numerical scoring system was designed (Backster 1963) to provide the FP with a means of objectively evaluating each relevant question versus its neighboring control question, hereafter referred to as a *Spot* (control vs. relevant), in each tracing according to chart interpretation rules with penalties for violation of those rules, by the assignment or scoring of each *Spot* with a number from a seven-position scale:

VALUE

+3	MT	Maximum Truthful Score
+2	T	Truthful Score
+1	t	Minimum Truthful Score
0	?	
-1	d	Minimum Deception Score
-2	D	Deception Score
-3	MD	Maximum Deception Score

Numbers preceded by a minus sign fall into the deceptive area; numbers preceded by a plus sign fall into the truthful area. The following chart interpretation rules originally developed by Cleve Backster are depicted below, with some minor changes applicable to the Matte Quadri-Track Zone Comparison Technique and/or DoDPI Zone Comparison Technique where indicated.

Backster "Either-Or" Rule

To arrive at an interim spot analysis tracing determination of (+2) or (-2) there must be a significant and timely tracing reaction in either the red zone (relevant) or green zone (control) being compared.

Note: (Backster ZCT): If the red zone indicates a lack of reaction, it should be compared with the neighboring green zone containing the larger timely reaction. If the red zone indicates a timely and significant reaction it should be compared with the neighboring green zone containing no reaction or the least reaction.

Matte QTZCT: Red Zone is always compared with the green zone question preceding it. The red zone questions are switched in position with each chart conducted, thus are alternately compared against each green zone question.

Tracings Included: Breathing, GSR/GSG, and Cardio.

Backster "Non-Reinforcement" Rule

Each of the three tracings should be independently assigned spot analysis numerical values. Significant and even inconsistent reactions in one or both of the other two tracings will not be allowed to reinforce or detract from the appropriate numerical value due the single tracing being considered.

Note: It is permissible to note distortion indicators evident in either of the other two tracings.

Tracings Included: Breathing, GSR/GSG, Cardio.

Backster "Green Zone 'Yes' Answer Penalty" Rule

If a "yes" answer is given to a green zone question which is a reversal of the answer given during the pretest question review, that green zone cannot be used as a spot analysis "presence-of-reaction" zone.

A green zone involving such an answer reversal can be used as a spot analysis "lack-of-reaction" zone where no reaction, or a reaction significantly smaller than the red zone reaction, is indicated.

Note: (Backster ZCT) Such use should be avoided if another adjacent lack-of-reaction green zone, properly answered, is available.

Matte QTZCT: The forensic psychophysiologist (FP) cannot jump to another *Track* to make a comparison. See Figure XII-35 for Primary, Secondary and Inside Tracks.

Tracings Included: Breathing, GSR/GSG, Cardio.

Backster "Change in Amplifier Sensitivity" Rule

Spot analysis numerical tracing evaluations cannot be attempted when a change in amplifier sensitivity has been made within either of the two zones being inter-compared.

Note: Each change in amplifier sensitivity, no matter how small, must be indicated on the chart utilizing the appropriate chart marking symbols.

Tracings Included: Breathing (electronic/CPS), GSR/GSG, Cardio (electronic/CPS).

Backster "Timely Reaction" Rule

Any red zone or green zone reaction should be considered "timely" if it starts following the first word of the question being asked. Also, any reaction should be considered "timely" if it starts prior to five seconds past point-of-answer.

Note: Care should be taken, when evaluating the GSR/GSG tracing, to properly allow for the five (Stoelting) or eight (Lafayette) seconds apparent time displacement involved. It should also be noted that this time factor diminishes when the tracing arcs to the higher and lower portions of the chart.

Tracings Included: Breathing, GSR/GSG, Cardio.

Backster "Anticipatory Reaction" Rule

Regardless of its intensity, any red zone or green zone reaction which starts prior to the first word of the question that follows can be assigned a maximum numerical value of (+1) or (-1).

Note: This restriction applies even though the "either-or" rule is dramatically satisfied except for the prevailing reaction's timeliness.

Tracings Included: Breathing, GSR/GSG, Cardio

Backster "Lack of Reaction Via Deduction" Rule

If the red zone or the green zone tracing exhibits a presence of relief during the asking of a question, or starting prior to five seconds after subject's answer, that relief can be classified as a lack of reaction.

Note: The above is based upon the premise that a person cannot exhibit reaction and relief simultaneously.

Tracings Included: Breathing and Cardio.

Backster "Delayed Cardio Reaction Recovery" Rule

If a cardio reaction has not completed its recovery within the zone in which the question was asked, the continuation of that recovery into the zone that follows can be treated as a lack of reaction for that following zone.

Note: If zone that follows is utilized as part of the spot analysis evaluation, a maximum of (+2) or (-2) should be assigned.

Tracings Included: Cardio.

Backster "Minimum Lack of Reaction" Rule

During spot analysis when the GSR/GSG tracing displays no visible arousal magnitude, a minimum "unit count" value should be assigned.

Note: If one eighth inch is being utilized as the unit count, one unit (1) of linear arousal should be assigned that tracing location. If one tenth inch is being utilized as a unit count, two units (2) of linear arousal should be assigned that tracing location. If a metric ruler is being utilized, four millimeters of linear arousal should be assigned that tracing location.

Tracings Included: GSR/GSG.

Backster "Plunging GSR/GSG Baseline" Rule

During spot analysis a maximum numerical value of (+1) or (-1) should be assigned if the evaluation baseline created under the GSR/GSG tracing is rapidly plunging during either or both of the question zones being inter-compared.

Note: A downward baseline angle of 45 degrees or more should be considered as plunging.

Tracings Included: GSR/GSG.

Backster "Green Zone Abuse" Rule

If the intensity of a green zone reaction appears to be at least four times as dramatic as a minor reaction in the red zone, it is not proper to feature the minor red zone reaction and compare it with the other neighboring green zone which may show a lesser reaction or no reaction.

Note: Care should be taken to be reasonably certain that the larger green zone tracing change is not caused by accidental distortion or a deliberate countermeasure attempt.

Matte QTZCT: This Rule does not apply to the Quadri-Track ZCT inasmuch as the FP must compare each red zone question to the preceding green zone question, and cannot jump to another Track to make a comparison.

Tracings Included: Breathing, GSR/GSG, Cardio.

Backster "Tracing Average Trend Change" Rule

Where no significant tracing reactions are evidenced in the red zone or an adjacent green zone, a significant and meaningful change in the overall trend of the tracing average can be assigned a (+1) or a (-1) numerical value.

Note: In the cardio such a tracing average trend change can more often be noted by gradual blood pressure changes involving a combination of ascending, descending and sustained level trends.

Tracings Included: Principally Cardio; also Breathing and GSR/GSG.

Backster "Presence of Reaction Via Deduction" Rule

Where *relief* starts at a tracing location prior to five seconds past the point-of-answer to the question asked, and where the preceding question zone does not exhibit an apparent reaction, it can be inferred via deduction that some unrecognized reaction did occur *during that prior question.*

Where *relief* starts at a tracing location after five seconds past the point-of-answer to the question asked and where zone containing that question does not exhibit an apparent reaction, it can be inferred via deduction that some unrecognized reaction did occur *during that same zone*.

Note: Numerical values no higher than (+1) or (-1) can be assigned to deduced reactions.

Tracings Included: Breathing and Cardio.

Note from the Author: The forensic psychophysiologist must remember that a relief tracing segment represents a physiological compensation for a preceding physiological change in the subject's homeostasis. An increase in breathing rate or hyperventilation is normally due to a previous decrease in air intake below what is seen on the polygraph chart as an average tracing segment. This decrease in air intake can be in the form of an expiration apnea or decrease in breathing rate. Thus, a relief tracing pattern without an *apparent* preceding reaction tracing pattern may be due to a continuum of consecutive minute changes in the breathing cycles of equal amplitude (average tracing) lasting 15 or even 20 seconds after commencement of the test question which appear to be of the same frequency, but because of its many cycles, fail to reveal but to only the most discriminating eye or computer, the very slight decrease in breathing rate in each cycle.

A guilty subject may deliberately increase his or her breathing rate or hyperventilate during the reaction tracing segment to *mask* his or her expected physiological response to the relevant question. These could be seen by the forensic psychophysiologist as relief tracing patterns, without the usual reaction tracing patterns preceding them. Thus if Backster's Deduction Rule (1994) is applied and the control question preceding it exhibits no presence of reaction, it is nevertheless assigned a +1 score in the pneumo tracing due to the *Inferred Reaction via Deduction Rule*, and the *Lack of Reaction via Deduction Rule* which holds that "a presence of relief during the asking of a question, or starting prior to five seconds after subject's answer, that relief can be classified as a lack of reaction. This is based upon the premise that a person cannot exhibit reaction and relief simultaneously."

However, a guilty (as later verified) subject who attempts a countermeasure by masking his or her expected reaction to the relevant question by deliberately hyperventilating or increasing their breathing rate thus causing the appearance of a relief pattern during the reaction tracing segment of a relevant question, necessarily focuses his or her psychological set onto that relevant question, hence increasing the potential arousal in the GSR/GSG and Cardio tracings. Furthermore, the physiological change in the pneumo tracing caused by such a countermeasure will also affect a physiological change in the GSR/GSG and the cardio tracings, thus increasing the minus scores of those tracings. Inasmuch as the *Presence of Reaction Via Deduction Rule* limits the score of an *inferred reaction* to only a +l or -l, depending on which zone the *inferred reaction* is attributed to, the cited countermeasure in the breathing tracing could only produce an erroneous +l in that spot which would be more than neutralized by the expected increase in minus scores produced by the GSR/GSG and Cardio tracings of that same spot. It is doubtful that such a countermeasure could even produce an inconclusive result under that circumstance.

However, caution should be exercised in the identification of a relief tracing pattern so as not to mistake for relief a reaction tracing segment which starts with a sudden increase in breathing amplitude reminiscent of hyperventilation, but with decreasing amplitude cycles forming a descending staircase pattern. For a zone to be attributed an *inferred reaction*, it must have some physiological connection to the *relief tracing* pattern from which it acquires its deduction, such as a continuum change in the breathing cycle pattern.

DoDPI ZCT: It should be noted that the current teaching at the Department of Defense Polygraph Institute, given the above scenario, is that any *reaction* or *relief* pattern which occurs within the confines of a particular zone question would be attributable to that zone question, not to the previous zone question. (Weinstein 1996).

Backster "Single Cycle Trend Conformance" Rule

When a single non-distorted breathing cycle does not conform with that which would otherwise constitute a four-cycle horizontal trend, that non-conforming cycle can be envisioned as conforming.

Note: The horizontal pattern requirement disallows use of this rule when evaluating "baseline arousals." This rule will more often be utilized when the second or third cycle of a sustained suppressed cycle reaction trend does not conform.

Tracings Included: Breathing.

Backster "Question Pacing" Upgrading Rule

To upgrade a (+2) or (-2) interim spot analysis rating to a (+3) or (-3) final spot rating each of the two zones being intercompared must embrace a minimum of twenty seconds and a maximum of thirty-five seconds.

Note: Question pacing is measured from the first word of one question to the first word of the question that follows.

Matte QTZCT: Requires a minimum of twenty-seconds between the answer of a test question to the commencement of the next question that follows it, not to exceed thirty seconds.

Tracings Included: Breathing, GSR/GSG, Cardio.

Backster "Tracing Purity" Upgrading Rule

To upgrade a (+2) or (-2) interim spot analysis rating to a (+3) or (-3) final spot rating there must be an absence of tracing distortion in both of the zones being intercompared.

Note: Recording pen reorientation in either of the two zones will be considered a tracing distortion, for upgrading purposes only.

Tracings Included: Breathing, GSR/GSG, Cardio.

Backster "Reaction Intensity" Upgrading Rule

To upgrade a (+2) or (-2) interim spot analysis rating to a (+3) or (-3) final spot rating the intensity of the "presence-of-reaction" zone must be significantly more dramatic than that required by the "either-or" chart analysis rule.

Note: When attempting to upgrade the GSR/GSG inter-comparison a magnitude ratio close to or in excess of a four-to-one ratio is required.

Tracings Included: Breathing, GSR/GSG, Cardio.

Backster "Listening Reaction vs. Listening Distortion" Rule

When the red zone question or the green zone question was being asked and a subtle one-cycle or two-cycle suppression was evidenced on one, but not on both questions, this constitutes a mild listening reaction. If such a tracing variation occurred in each of the two zones being intercompared, both would be classified as mild listening distortions.

Note: If a listening reaction was not accompanied by additional tracing reaction variations even a (+1) or (-1) determination would not be warranted.

Listening distortions are more often encountered when a subject has difficulty in hearing the questions asked.

Tracings Included: Breathing.

Backster "Answer Reaction vs. Answer Distortion" Rule

When the red zone question or the green zone question was being answered and an additional vocal emphasis on one but not both questions caused the breathing tracing to exhaust more of the subject's residual air volume, this constitutes a mild answer reaction. If such a tracing variation occurred in each of the two zones being inter-compared, both would be classified as mild answer distortions.

Note: If an answer reaction was not accompanied by additional tracing reaction variations even a (+1) or (-1) determination would not be warranted.

Tracing Included: Breathing.

Backster "Stabilized Blood Pressure Trend" Rule

When a cyclic "general nervous tension" trend is evidenced throughout most of a chart, but stabilizes in one of the two zones being inter-compared, this may be an indication that the subject is focusing on selected questions as a form of "holding and hoping." If some numerical value seems appropriate in evaluating such an occurrence, it should not exceed a (+1) or (-1).

Note: With a subject exhibiting a "vagus pattern" which involves a cyclic rate reflecting the breathing activity, the apparent stabilization of the blood pressure cycles may be principally due to a series of suppressed breathing cycles.

Tracings Included: Cardio.

Backster "Extra Systole Cluster" Rule

It is felt that a series or cluster of extra systolic heartbeats, occurring primarily within the same "zone of influence" is more likely indicative of relief, rather than reaction.

Note: Caution must still be exercised when viewing a single extra systole, which may often be followed by an apparent blood pressure arousal, of short duration. It is advisable to treat such an event as distortion, rather than a reaction.

Tracings Included: Cardio.

Matte "Dual-Equal Strong Reaction" Rule

When the *red* and *green* zones being inter-compared both contain timely, specific and significant reactions of *maximum* and *equal* strength, a minus one (-1) score is assigned to that Spot.

Tracings Included: Pneumo and Cardio.

Note: When there is a presence of *mild* reaction in both the relevant question and its neighboring control question of *equal magnitude*, such as in Figure XII-34 where there is no presence of parasympathetic activation (46-33), a numerical value of zero (?) must be assigned to this spot in the breathing tracing. However when there is a presence of *strong* reaction manifested by distinct activation of both sympathetic and parasympathetic systems in both zones being inter-compared of *equal magnitude*, a minimum deception score (-1) must be given to this spot. This rule applies only to the *pneumo* and *cardio* tracings, not the GSR/GSG.

The aforesaid rule is based on the premise that both zone questions appear to be *equally* threatening to the examinee, the degree of threat being proportionate to the degree of the responses, which indicate that while the examinee may be attempting deception to the relevant question, its neighboring control question may be too intense due to faulty structure, embraces a more serious unknown crime, or a countermeasure attempt was made. A sophisticated guilty examinee may be able to cause a reaction on the control question but cannot control an oncoming reaction to the relevant question.

****

Now we will apply the seven-position scale in actual charts beginning with the top tracing on the chart, the breathing tracing.

The FP examines the first Spot containing the first control/relevant question pair located in the Primary Track on the polygraph chart. The control question #46 precedes the first relevant question #33, which is followed by the second and third Spots located in the Secondary Track and the Inside Track respectively as indicated in Figure XII-34. Figure XII-35 depicts the Tracks which contain Spots for quantification.

Figure XII-34 reflects a slight suppression of equal magnitude in both the relevant question #33 and the neighboring control question #46 indicating mild sympathetic activation to both questions, but no evidence of parasympathetic activation, inasmuch as there is no relief pattern in the form of hyperventilation because the suppression is mild. In the Quadri-Track Zone Comparison Technique, the FP must compare each relevant question with the neighboring control question *preceding* it, and *cannot jump the track* for comparison with another control question on the same chart. Inasmuch as each relevant question (33 & 35) is rotated in position with each chart conducted, each relevant question is eventually compared against each control question on the same test. (See Chapter 11 for each technique's rules of comparison).

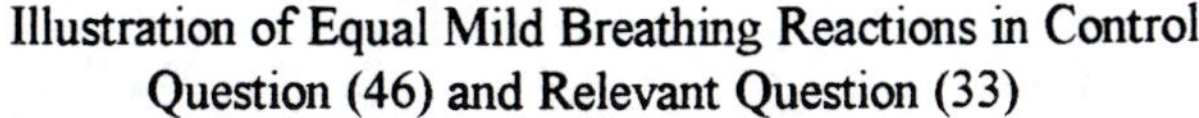
Illustration of Equal Mild Breathing Reactions in Control Question (46) and Relevant Question (33)

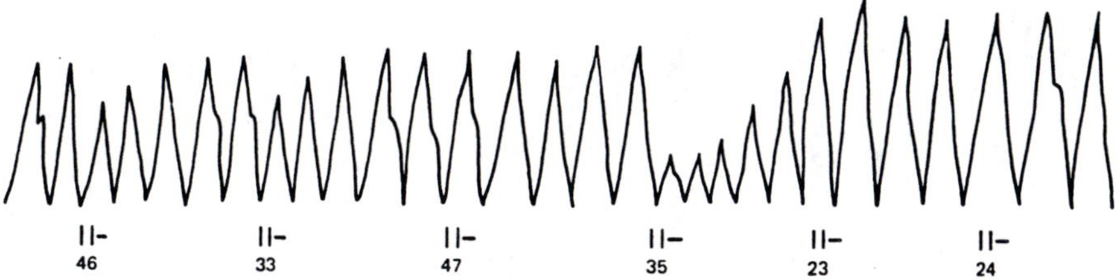

Figure XII-34

When there is a presence of *mild* reaction to both the relevant question and its neighboring control question of equal magnitude, such as in Figure XII-34 above where there is no presence of parasympathetic activation, a numerical value of zero (?) must be assigned to this Spot in the breathing tracing. However, when there is a presence of strong reaction manifested by distinct activation of both sympathetic and parasympathetic systems in both the relevant question and its neighboring control question of equal magnitude, a minimum deception score must be given to this Spot in the breathing tracing for a score of -1 (d), the rationale being that both questions appear to be equally threatening to the examinee, the degree of threat being proportional to the degree of the responses, which indicates that while the examinee may be attempting deception to the relevant question, its neighboring control question may be too intense due to faulty structure, embraces a more serious unknown crime, or a countermeasure attempt was made by deliberate intense concentration on the control question. The FP must keep in mind that an examinee may be able to cause a reaction on the control question but cannot control an oncoming reaction to the relevant question. However this rule applies only to the Pneumo and Cardio tracings inasmuch as the GSR/GSG tracing is more volatile and sensitive to extraneous stimuli.

Matte Quadri-Track Zone Comparison Test Structure

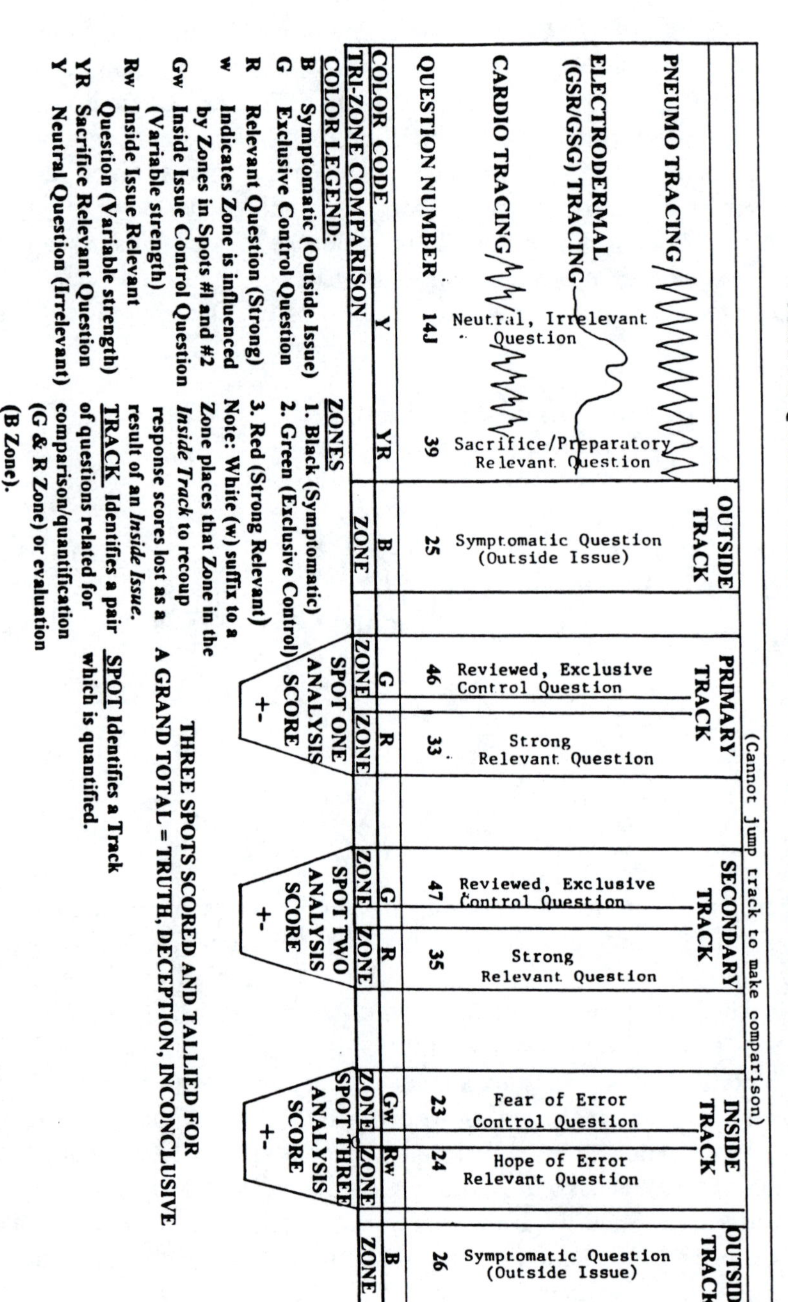

Figure XII-35

When the forensic psychophysiologist determines that a countermeasure such as an inspiration *apnea* has occurred in the reaction tracing segment of a *control* question, that deliberate action is deleted as a genuine reaction and is visualized as an average tracing segment when compared to its neighboring relevant question for quantification. Under such circumstances, a *significant response* to the *relevant* question would warrant a maximum score of minus 2. (See *Breathing Analysis* in this Chapter).

Due to the addition of the Inside Track containing questions #23 and #24, the FP is now able to determine whether a reaction on the relevant question, especially in the situation described above, is due to "fear of error" or genuine fear of detection. If there is equally mild reaction in control question #46 and relevant question #33 as illustrated in the diagram above, and there is also a presence of strong reaction in the "fear of error" question #23, the FP may safely assume that the mild reaction at relevant question #33 was caused by this "fear of error," therefore he/she should administer a stimulation test if one has not already been administered to reassure the innocent (as later verified) examinee. In the event a stimulation test has already been administered, empirical data has shown that the innocent (as later verified) examinee's anxiety towards the relevant questions will diminish with each additional chart conducted, but will conversely increase towards the control questions. One successful method of increasing the strength of the control questions for the innocent (as later verified) subject, without diminishing the strength of the relevant questions for the guilty (as later verified) subject, is to review only the two control questions with the examinee prior to the conduct of the next chart, but this procedure should only be used when recommended by the Quadri-Track Reaction Combination Guide with combinations B, K, L, M, R and T (see Fig. XI-4).

However, if there is a presence of strong reaction at the "resignation" relevant question #24 with an absence of reaction at question #23, the FP may assume that the presence of reaction at relevant question #33 is due to a genuine fear of detection, but that its neighboring control question is too intense for reasons that the FP should not attempt to uncover for fear of raising an "outside issue." Before the FP attempts to weaken that control question (usually by changing the age category), the FP should examine the other Spot to see which of the question pair (control vs relevant) predominates, for trend verification and assurance that the reaction to the "resignation" relevant question #24 was not due to misunderstanding/misinterpretation of the question by the examinee. If in doubt, the FP changes nothing and continues the examination with the administration of the next chart, where the control questions will be visited by a different relevant question, inasmuch as they are rotated in position with each chart conducted. When the relevant and control questions have been scientifically and ideally formulated, initial minor inconsistencies usually rectify themselves during the course of conducting several charts on the same issue.

The FP remains with this first question set and evaluates the next tracing (Fig. XII-36), which is the galvanic skin response (GSR) tracing.

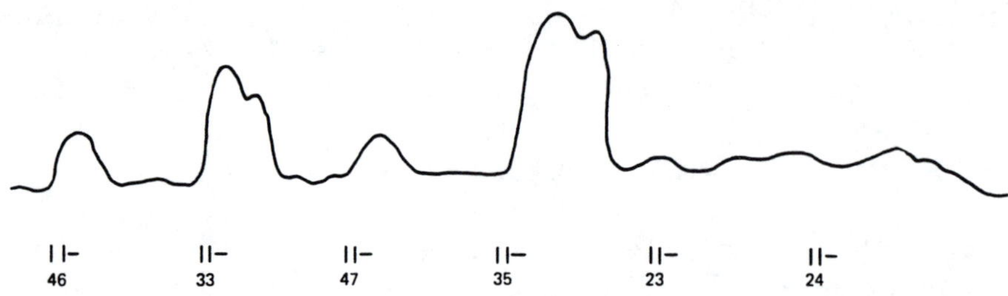

Figure XII-36

In the analysis of the GSR tracing a minimum ratio of two to one must be attained for a minimum truthful or minimum deception score (+l or -1). A ratio of three to one must be attained for a score of truthfulness or deception (+2 or -2). A ratio of four or higher to one must be attained for a score of maximum truthfulness or maximum deception (+3 or -3).

In Figure XII-36, the pen excursion in relevant question #33 reached a height double that of control question #46, affording a score of only -l (d).

The FP now drops his/her sight to the next tracing (Fig. XII-37), which is the cardio, and evaluates the first Spot in the Primary Track.

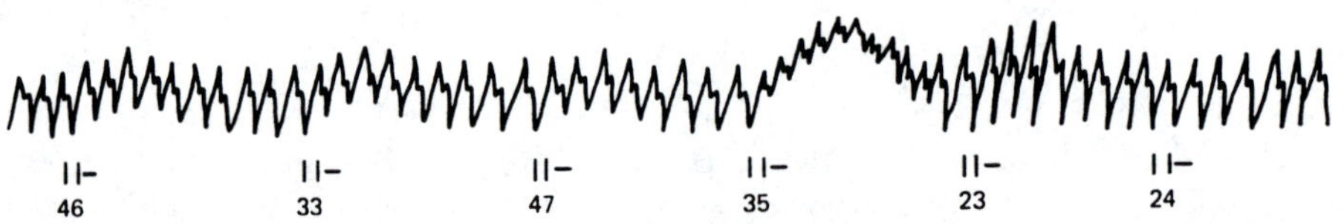

Figure XII-37

Inasmuch as there is equal mild blood pressure arousal in both questions #33 and #46 being intercompared, the same rule as outlined above in the breathing tracing applies. A score of zero (?) is assigned to this Spot.

We now turn to the secondary track containing Spot #2, and proceed from the top tracing downward in the same fashion as the first Spot (Fig. XII-38).

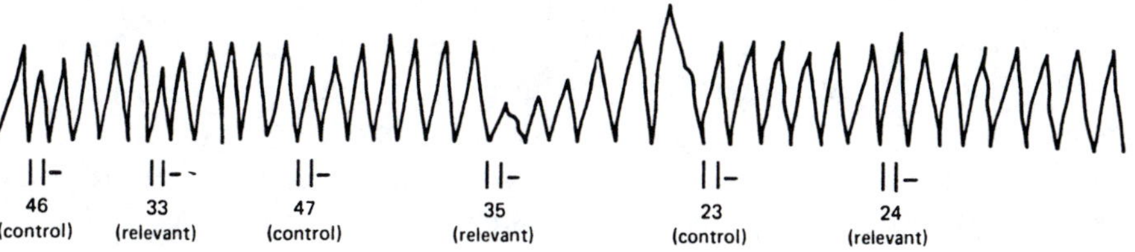

Figure XII-38

Question #35 above reflects significant suppression followed by hyperventilation signifying that both the sympathetic and parasympathetic systems activated on this relevant question. The neighboring control question #47 reflects mild suppression with no evidence of a relief pattern. Therefore, a score of -2 (D) or deception is given to this Spot in the breathing tracing.

The forensic psychophysiologist (FP) now examines the same Spot in the GSR tracing previously illustrated in Figure XII-36 and finds that the pen excursion of the relevant question #35 is three times as high as its neighboring control question #47. Inasmuch as the ratio is three to one in favor of the relevant question, a score of -2 (D) deception is given to that question set.

We now turn our attention to the bottom chart tracing (Fig. XII-37), namely the cardio and find that there is substantial blood pressure arousal at relevant question #35 and only mild arousal at control question #47, therefore we must arrive at a score of -2 (D) deception in the analysis of this tracing.

The FP now focuses his/her attention on the Inside Track containing control (fear or error) question #23 and relevant (hope of error) question #24, in Spot #3. It must be noted that this Spot is not expected to yield strong responses unless an "inside issue" factor is present. Should this occur, milder responses may be expected in the other Spots located in the Primary and Secondary Track. Spot #3 in the Inside Track enables the FP to determine whether a reaction on the relevant questions #33 and/or #35 located in Spots #l and #2, especially in the situation described above, is due to "fear of error" or genuine fear of detection. If there is equally mild reaction in control question #46 and relevant question #33 as illustrated in the diagram above, and there is also a presence of strong reaction in the "fear of error" question #23, the FP may safely assume that the mild reaction at relevant question #33 was caused by his/her "fear of error;" therefore the FP will not attempt to weaken the control question, and the plus scores acquired by the "fear of error" control question #23 should offset any minus scores produced by relevant question #33. However, if there is a presence of strong reaction at the Inside-Issue relevant question #24 with a comparative absence of reaction at question #23, the FP may assume that the presence of reaction at relevant question #33 is due to a genuine fear of detection, but that its neighboring control question is too intense, requiring remedial action as recommended in the Reaction Combination Guide (Fig. XI-4).

The analysis and scoring of any Spot, whether it is Spot #l, Spot #2, or Spot #3, should not be influenced by any of the other Spots. The score in each tracing in each Spot is based solely upon the physiological data at that location, and the strict application of aforementioned scoring rules. Thus the analysis and scoring of the Spot located in the Inside Track (questions 23 & 24) should never have any influence on the analysis and scoring of the previous two Spots located in the Primary and Secondary Tracks. All Spots, including Spot #3 (questions 23 and 24) are scored and those scores from Spots #l, #2, #3 are tallied for a total score from which a determination is made of truth or deception.

During the conduct of the PV examination, the FP conducts a Spot Analysis of each chart immediately after it is conducted to determine if each question is functioning as designed or whether remedial action needs to be taken before the administration of the next chart. It is at that time during the Spot analysis that the Inside Track questions #23 and #24 may alert the FP that a problem exists with the questions located in the Primary or Secondary Track which may require remedial action in accordance with the Quadri-track Reaction Combination Guide. While the Inside Track may alert the FP of the existence of a problem, this must never influence the scoring of any Spot. As indicated above, *the Inside Track not only alerts the FP to an existing problem, but rectifies it as well by contributing its compensatory scores to the total tally.*

Figure XII-39 depicts a chart with the strong presence of "fear of error" as evidenced by the clear presence of strong response in all three tracings at question #23 and the complete absence of response at relevant question #24. In the analysis of this Spot a score of +2 (T) is assigned to all three tracings. The scores obtained from this Spot serve to offset negative scores obtained from relevant question in Spot #l (46-33) and Spot #2 (47-35).

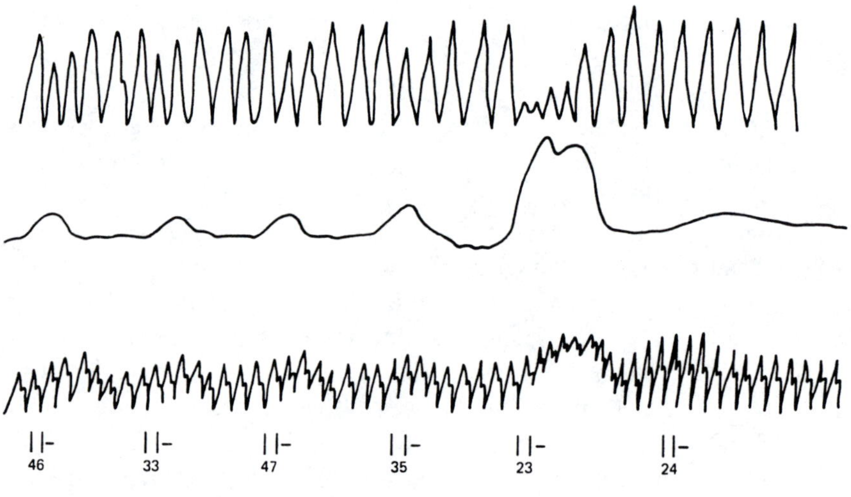

Figure XII-39

Spots can only be upgraded to +3 (MT) or -3 (MD) if there is a strong reaction and relief pattern with absolute purity of tracing in one question and a complete or near complete lack of reaction to its neighboring question being used for intercomparison. Purity means that the tracing contains typical characteristics that are distinct and clean with a lack of distortion or nontypical characteristics.

If either the relevant (Red) zone or the control (Green) zone being intercompared is less than twenty seconds of chart time from the examinee's answer to the beginning of the next question, or more than twenty-five seconds of chart time during that same zone, a score of truth (T) or deception (D) cannot be upgraded to maximum truth (MT) or maximum deception (MD). Furthermore, upgrading of truth or deception cannot be made if amplifier sensitivity has been increased or decreased during any portion of the two question zones being intercompared.

If a "yes" answer is given by the examinee to a control question (probable lie) during the actual examination in spite of instruction to the contrary during the review of the test question, that question zone cannot be used as an indication of reaction to that control question. However, a lack of reaction under the same circumstances can be used in comparing the control question to its neighboring relevant question; however, a maximum score of only -2 (D) can be given.

A minimum of two charts containing the same test questions must be conducted in each test in order to attain consistency of response, so that any stray emotion that may possibly cause a reaction will not have a serious effect on the overall trend. In order to arrive at a solid conclusion of either truthfulness or deception regarding the target issue we must have consistent responses to either the control questions or the relevant questions; thus consistency establishes reliability.

In tallying the scores obtained from each tracing in each Spot, there is no elimination of the weakest score or the score that does not follow the general trend as was the practice many years ago. As reflected in Figure XII-40, all scores are included in the Spot tally and the Total tally.

	QUESTION #33	QUESTION #35	QUESTION #24
Breathing	d= -1	D= -2	d= -1
GSR	t= +1	?= 0	d= -1
Cardio	D- -2	d= -1	?= 0
TOTAL:	-2	-3	-2

FIRST CHART GRAND TOTAL: -7

Figure XII-40

Matte Quadri-Track Zone Comparison Test

Tri-Spot Quantification System

	SPOT ONE					SPOT TWO					SPOT THREE			
SPEC-1	TRUTH	INDEF	DECEP			TRUTH	INDEF	DECEP			TRUTH	INDEF	DECEP	
PNE (33)	+3 +2	+1 0 -1	-2 -3	= ( )	(35)	+3 +2	+1 0 -1	-2 -3	= ( )	(24)	+3 +2	+1 0 -1	-2 -3	= ( )
GSR (33)	+3 +2	+1 0 -1	-2 -3	= ( )	(35)	+3 +2	+1 0 -1	-2 -3	= ( )	(24)	+3 +2	+1 0 -1	-2 -3	= ( )
CAR (33)	+3 +2	+1 0 -1	-2 -3	= ( )	(35)	+3 +2	+1 0 -1	-2 -3	= ( )	(24)	+3 +2	+1 0 -1	-2 -3	= ( )
SPEC-2	TRUTH	INDEF	DECEP			TRUTH	INDEF	DECEP			TRUTH	INDEF	DECEP	
PNE (33)	+3 +2	+1 0 -1	-2 -3	= ( )	(35)	+3 +2	+1 0 -1	-2 -3	= ( )	(24)	+3 ·2	+1 0 -1	-2 -3	= ( )
GSR (33)	+3 +2	+1 0 -1	-2 -3	= ( )	(35)	+3 +2	+1 0 -1	-2 -3	= ( )	(24)	+3 +2	+1 0 -1	-2 -3	= ( )
CAR (33)	+3 +2	+1 0 -1	-2 -3	= ( )	(35)	+3 +2	+1 0 -1	-2 -3	= ( )	(24)	+3 +2	+1 0 -1	-2 -3	= ( )
SPEC-3	TRUTH	INDEF	DECEP			TRUTH	INDEF	DECEP			TRUTH	INDEF	DECEP	
PNE (33)	+3 +2	+1 0 -1	-2 -3	= ( )	(35)	+3 +2	+1 0 -1	-2 -3	= ( )	(24)	+3 +2	+1 0 -1	-2 -3	= ( )
GSR (33)	+3 +2	+1 0 -1	-2 -3	= ( )	(35)	+3 +2	+1 0 -1	-2 -3	= ( )	(24)	+3 +2	+1 0 -1	-2 -3	= ( )
CAR (33)	+3 +2	+1 0 -1	-2 -3	= ( )	(35)	+3 +2	+1 0 -1	-2 -3	= ( )	(24)	+3 +2	+1 0 -1	-2 -3	= ( )
SPEC-4	TRUTH	INDEF	DECEP			TRUTH	INDEF	DECEP			TRUTH	INDEF	DECEP	
PNE (33)	+3 +2	+1 0 -1	-2 -3	= ( )	(35)	+3 +2	+1 0 -1	-2 -3	= ( )	(24)	+3 +2	+1 0 -1	-2 -3	= ( )
GSR (33)	+3 +2	+1 0 -1	-2 -3	= ( )	(35)	+3 +2	+1 0 -1	-2 -3	= ( )	(24)	+3 +2	+1 0 -1	-2 -3	= ( )
CAR (33)	+3 +2	+1 0 -1	-2 -3	= ( )	(35)	+3 +2	+1 0 -1	-2 -3	= ( )	(24)	+3 +2	+1 0 -1	-2 -3	= ( )
TARGET ( )	TOTAL:			( )				TOTAL:	( )				TOTAL:	( )

GRAND TOTAL: ( )

FOR ( ) CHARTS.

Figure XII-41

The score table in Figure XII-41 reflects three Spots, each containing a control-relevant question pair, which compose the nucleus of the Matte Quadri-Track Zone Comparison Technique. The Outside Track which contains two symptomatic questions (25-26), does not have a Spot for scores to be tallied because symptomatic questions are neither relevant nor probable-lie control questions; they are not designed to determine truth or deception, but are used to identify the presence of Outside Issues that might interfere with the test. Thus, of the four tracks in the Matte Quadri-Track Zone Comparison Technique, only three tracks have Spots which accumulate scores used to reach a conclusion of truth or deception, namely the Primary track, the Secondary track, and the Inside Track.

The grand total score for two or more charts obtained from the score table (Fig. XII-41) is applied to the conclusion table (Fig. XII-42), which reflects the numerical range that must be attained to reach a definite conclusion by the number of charts conducted. Although a range is given for a single chart, this by no means indicates a conclusion should be rendered in less than two charts. The single chart tally is furnished to show progression in the tally and further afford the FP a means of spot analyzing his/her charts after each test to identify and remedy any problem areas before continuing the examination.

CONCLUSION TABLE

	CIRCLE APPROPRIATE NUMBER BELOW		
RESULTS FOR 1 CHART -	+27 to +3	+2 to -4	-5 to -27
	TRUTH	INDEFINITE	DECEPTION
RESULTS FOR 2 CHARTS -	CIRCLE APPROPRIATE NUMBER BELOW		
	+54 to +6	+5 to -9	-10 to -54
	TRUTH	INDEFINITE	DECEPTION
RESULTS FOR 3 CHARTS -	CIRCLE APPROPRIATE NUMBER BELOW		
	+81 to +9	+8 to -14	-15 to -81
	TRUTH	INDEFINITE	DECEPTION
RESULTS FOR 4 CHARTS -	CIRCLE APPROPRIATE NUMBER BELOW		
	+108 to +12	+11 to -19	-20 to -108
	TRUTH	INDEFINITE	DECEPTION

Figure XII-42

The conclusion table (Fig. XII-42) reflects a lower score requirement to reach a conclusion of truthfulness than is required to reach a conclusion of deception. This is due to the fact that reactions to control questions, which are of lesser intensity than relevant questions, are not expected to be as pronounced.

It must be remembered that Spots #1 and #2 are designed to provide the decisive scores that determine truth or deception, and that Spot #3 is designed to recoup response energy lost by either of the other two Spots. However, as discussed in Chapters 8 and 9, there are times when Spot #3 draws the greatest scores for the reasons described earlier in this chapter and in aforementioned chapters 8 and 9.

Before the Matte-Reuss (1989) field validation study on the Matte Quadri-Track Zone Comparison Technique was conducted, the Conclusion Table was based on logic and empirical data. This author reasoned that the score requirement for a conclusion of deception should be based on the mandate that the four highest scores from the two decisive Spots (#l for questions 46-33 and #2 for questions 47-35) left for evaluation and tally after elimination of the two weakest scores in each chart must contain at least one -2 (D) score reflecting a strong response and the remaining three scores should produce a minimum total of -3. A finding of deception should not be based on charts that produce only four -l (d) scores, which are classified as minimum deception scores. Therefore, each chart used for evaluation should contain a minimum of one -2 (D) score plus a minimum total score of -3 from the other tracings in the same chart to reach a definite conclusion of deception.

The requirement for only one -2 (D) score on each chart is based upon the principle that the subject's psychological set may be focused upon only one of the relevant questions, that which offers the greatest threat to his/her well-being. That question may produce a -2 or even a -3 score; however, the other relevant question may produce only minimal response as a result of the examinee's strong focus on the question by which he/she feels most threatened.

The serious consequences deceptive polygraph results may have on an examinee, especially if the results are admitted into evidence, dictate that a convincing scientific argument be presented validating the results. An offer of four -l (d) scores, which are all minimum deception scores, although consistent throughout two or more charts, will not present a convincing argument to prove the guilt of an examinee.

If a person is guilty of a crime for which he/she is being administered a PV examination, at least one of the relevant questions should be of a sufficient threat to produce a -2 response in at least one of the three tracings on one of the relevant questions.

In order to establish reliability, two or more charts producing an absolute minimum in each chart of a -2 score plus a minimum total score of -3 from the other tracings in the same chart for a minimum grand total of -5 in each chart should be obtained before a definite conclusion of deception may be rendered. The only exception to this rule occurs when an inside issue factor dampens the responses to relevant question #33 and #35 but the lost response energy is recouped by relevant question #24; however, the total score for each chart must still meet the minimum score requirement set forth in the conclusion table. Obviously, evidence of a consistently greater score tally will correspondingly decrease the probability of error already reduced to an insignificant level.

The aforementioned required consistency and uniformity in the analysis and scoring of each chart are also applied in the truthful tally of the conclusion table. The lower score is justified on the basis that weaker responses are expected from control questions which are structurally less intense than the relevant questions. If each of the four remaining highest scores, after eliminating the two weakest scores, average a +l (t), each reflecting mild response to those control questions as opposed to comparatively no response to the neighboring relevant questions, it can be safely assumed that the results reflect truthfulness regarding the issue for which the examinee was tested. The +8 minimum score for two charts for a truthful conclusion is within the limits set forth in the Utah study (Raskin, et al 1976). (The weakest scores or countertrend scores are no longer eliminated from the score tally. The above merely explains the reasoning used to arrive at the *original* score threshold or cut off).

The above conclusion table formula is in compliance with the suggested minimum criteria furnished in the Utah study, based upon empirical data obtained from verified polygraph charts, and is further in compliance with the laws of logic and reliability. However, when this author with the assistance of Dr. Ronald M. Reuss completed the field validation study on the Quadri-Track Zone Comparison Technique involving 122 confirmed real-life cases from a Metropolitan Police Department and a private polygraph firm, the data from the 311 polygraph charts of those 122 verified cases revealed surprisingly that the cut off score or numerical threshold at which a zero error rate could be expected was -5 per chart for Deception and +3 per chart for a Truthful conclusion. Thus we were penalizing ourselves with a higher inconclusive rate by demanding a +4 per chart for a determination of truthfulness when a +3 could still have produced a zero error rate expectancy with fewer inconclusives. To our amazement, the -5 per chart for a determination of deception was apparently right on target, which is testimony to the logic initially used as the basis for the original conclusion table. (See Predictive Tables in Chapter 11)

The Zone Comparison Technique, which employs probable-lies as control questions, is ideally suited for a quantification system of chart analysis. Its standardized scoring based on scientifically objective rules and principles supported by validation studies (Raskin, et al 1976, Matte, Reuss 1989) provides a procedure that can be accurately reviewed. Polygraph techniques that do not lend themselves to a numerical quantification system of chart analysis will find it extremely difficult to survive in an age where complete objectivity is required for acceptance as a scientific procedure.

REFERENCES:

Abrams, S. (1976). The physiologic basis of polygraph transducers. *Polygraph*, 5(2).

Backster, G. C. (1963). *Backster Standardized Polygraph Notepack and Technique Guide*. New York: Backster School of Lie Detection.

Backster, G. C. (1994 December 5-9). 37th Annual Polygraph Examiner Work Conference. The *Backster School of Lie Detection*, San Diego, CA.

Backster, G. C. (1996, April 24). Telephone conversation with J. A. Matte.

Bailey, F. L., Rothblatt, H. B. (1970). *Investigations and Preparation of Criminal cases - Federal* and State. Chapter 14, Backster standardized polygraph notepack. Rochester, N.Y: The Lawyers Cooperative Publishing Co.

Capps, M. H. (1991). Accuracy of individual parameters in field polygraph studies. *Polygraph*, 20(2), 65-70.

Department of Defense Polygraph Institute. (Undated). *Test Data Analysis - DoDPI.* Transmitted to J. A. Matte on 13 May 1996 as the current DoDPI criteria for polygraph chart physiology analysis.

Guyton, A. C., Hall, J. E. (1996). *Textbook of Medical Physiology*. 9th Edition. Philadelphia, PA: W. B. Saunders Company.

Johnson, G. J. (1994). Information facsimile regarding APL Zone Scoring Results, Zone features, Algorithm Data, Scoring Weights and Response Intervals. U. S. Government Department of Defense, Office of Security Facsimile, 12 Oct 94 to Dr. James A. Matte.

Matte, J. A., Reuss, R. M. (1989) Validation Study on the Quadri-Zone Comparison Technique. *Research Abstract*, LD 01452, Vol. 1502, 1989, University Microfilm International.

Matte, J. A., Reuss, R. M. (1989). A field validation study of the Quadri-Zone Comparison Technique. *Polygraph*, 18(4), 187-202.

Matte, J. A., Reuss, R. M. (1992). A field study of the relative effectiveness of physiological data in field polygraph examinations. *Polygraph*, 21(1), 1-22.

Olsen, D. E., Harris, J. C., Capps, M. H., Ansley, N., Johnson, G. J. (1995, October 20). Computerized polygraph scoring system. Final draft, awaiting publication.

Olsen, D. E. (1995, Mar 8; Apr 28) Telephone conversations with J. A. Matte.

Olsen, D. E. (1996, April 25). Telephone conversation with J. A. Matte.

Raskin, D. C., Barland, G. H., Podlesny, J. A. (1976, August 30). *Validity and Reliability of Detection of Deception*. Final report. Contract 75-N1-99-0001. National Institute of Law Enforcement and Criminal Justice, Law Enforcement Assistance Administration, U. S. Department of Justice, Salt Lake City, University of Utah, Department of Psychology.

Suter, J. E. (1979). A field study of the usefulness of the cardio activity monitor. *Polygraph*, 8(2).

Weinstein, D. A. (1996, May 10). Facsimile reference Backster's Reaction via Deduction Rule, addressed to J. A. Matte.

Weinstein, D. A. (1995, August 13-18). *Anatomy and Physiology for the Forensic Psychophysiologist - Instrumentation and Physiological Recordings*. Presentation at the 30th Annual Seminar/Workshop of the American Polygraph Association, Las Vegas, Nevada.

Chapter 13

COMPUTERIZED POLYGRAPH SYSTEMS

Cleve Backster's development in 1961 of a standardized quantification system of the physiological data recorded on polygraph charts, which was introduced to the field of forensic psychophysiology in 1963 with the publication of Backster's Standardized Polygraph Notepack and Technique Guide, is the current standard for traditional scoring of polygraph charts. (see Chapter 11 for details). Variation in the threshold used in the conclusion table is the only significant modification to Backster's quantification system. In about 1985, the Horizontal Scoring System also known as the Rank Order Scoring System developed by Nathan J. Gordon and Philip M. Cochetti (Gordon, Cochetti 1987) introduced a hierarchy approach to numerical scoring. However, Backster's seven-position scale and standardized interpretation rules remain the preferred traditional method of numerical scoring of the physiological data recorded on polygraph charts. But implementation of aforementioned quantification systems requires formal training, adherence to the interpretation rules, and a good deal of experience in order to attain acceptable proficiency. In fact, in a study by Elaad and Kleiner (1990) it was reported that the *experienced* forensic psychophysiologists had significantly better detection rates with the respiration, but there was no significant difference between the groups in scoring electrodermal or cardio patterns. The greater difficulty in the interpretation of the breathing patterns did not escape subsequent computerization of the interpretation process.

The employment of computer technology in psychophysiological veracity (PV) examinations has been in the development stages since 1962 when Dr. Joseph F. Kubis, Fordham University, New York, N. Y., completed *Studies in Lie Detection, Computer Feasibility Considerations, for the Rome Air Development Center, Air Force Systems* Command, US Air Force. Dr. Kubis found that limitations in objectivity, uncontrolled invalidating influences and non-standardized instrumentation in the polygraph field at that time warranted further definitive research before the computer could be considered as an integral component of the lie detection decision. Dr. Kubis felt that there was a critical need for the objectification of the measurements of various aspects of the physiological patterns used in lie detection interpretation, and computer type programs could be of great service in the solution of this problem (Kubis 1962).

The second stage in the evolution process of polygraph computerization was the conversion of analog signals from electronic polygraph instruments to digital data (AD). The analog signals were taken off the pen drive motor from AC to a DC board digitizing the data into a series of numbers. A software program was developed to analyze the digitized data. However no algorithm was available to analyze the physiological data and determine the probability of truth or deception. (Barland 1996)

The third stage in the development of polygraph computerization occurred with the development of software to convert physiological waveforms to digital format, thus permitting the data to be recorded and stored on computer disks enabling the physiological data to be immediately or subsequently printed on traditional polygraph chart paper. This stage also included the development of software to analyze the physiological data and determine the probability of truth or deception regarding a subject's answers to relevant test questions. This third and current stage provides computerized polygraph systems with their own software to convert, record and examine the physiological data, and mathematical algorithms to evaluate and diagnose aforesaid data. Thus these new computerized polygraph systems are not interfaced with traditional polygraph instruments.

There are currently three stage III computerized polygraph systems manufactured in the United States. The first of these systems, in order of their appearance on the market, is produced and distributed by the Stoelting Company, Wood Dale, Illinois, as the Computerized Polygraph System (CPS) which is IBM compatible. The second systems, the Axciton which is IBM compatible, is produced and distributed by Axciton Systems, Inc., Houston, Texas. The third system, the Lafayette LX-2000-100 to 500 series which is either IBM or Macintosh compatible, is produced and distributed by Lafayette Instrument, Lafayette, Indiana.

The Stoelting CPS uses a proprietary algorithm (current version 2.13) developed by Scientific Assessment Technologies based on thirteen years of research conducted at the University of Utah by Dr. John C. Kircher and Dr. David C. Raskin. The models were field tested on a grant from the National Institute of Justice, U. S. Department of Justice, using data collected from examinations conducted during criminal investigations by an agency of the U. S. Department of the Treasury.

The Axciton and Lafayette computerized systems both use PolyScore 3.0 scoring algorithm developed by the Applied Physics Laboratory (APL) at the Johns Hopkins University with the assistance of the National Security Agency. In 1989, the APL team headed by Dr. Dale E. Olsen, Program manager, collected their first data from real-life law enforcement cases which used a common variant of the Control Question examination known as the Zone Comparison Technique. At that time the only computerized data collection systems available were the CODAS system (DATAQ Instruments, Inc.), the Computerized Polygraph System (CPS), and the Axciton System. However only the Axciton System met all of APL's computerized data collection requirements. Axciton contained a system for the rank order scoring of the responses, but the scoring system did not produce a probability of truth or deception. (Olsen, et al 1996)

By March 1994, APL had received data from 852 cases confirmed as deceptive (DI) or non-deceptive (NDI) by confession, guilty plea, or agreement between the original and two blind forensic psychophysiologists (FP) on the interpretation of the charts. Of the 852 cases, 228 were not used primarily due to (l) an inconclusive evaluation of the charts by two or more FPs, (2) a consensus could not be reached. However APL did use cases that one or more FP called inconclusive but that were eventually confirmed. The Polygraph Automated Scoring System (PASS) version 2.1 software was in service for a very brief period and was replaced by PolyScore® version 2.3 which was followed by the current version 3.0. This latest version was developed with 624 cases divided into 301 NDI and 323 DI cases. (Olsen, et al 1996)

During the development of APL's algorithm an attempt was made to determine the length of time that should elapse between questions. APL learned from their initial work that respiration reactions could last longer than eighteen seconds, therefore it was established that a twenty-five-second interval between test questions would be adopted although data with as few as eighteen seconds between questions were also used to develop the algorithm. (Olsen, et al 1996). Interestingly, three decades ago, Cleve Backster taught his students to space test questions a minimum of 20 seconds between the answer to a test question and the beginning of the next test question, effectively insuring that at least 25 seconds elapsed between the beginning of one question and the beginning of the next question.

Extreme control or relevant responses were classified as outliers if they accounted for more than 89% of the variability among the 18 responses, and were not used to develop the algorithm. An artifact-detection algorithm was constructed to detect distorted reactions not associated with legitimate, timely responses, which when identified were not used as a *reaction feature*. The algorithm was developed using seven basic steps. (1) Condition the data. (2) Standardize the data. (3) Develop data features. (4) Standardize features. (5) Evaluate features. (6) Develop the decision rule. (7) Evaluate the algorithm. (Olsen, et al 1996)

The features used in the algorithm were evaluated by testing them in a logistic regression-produced decision rule. This process ensured that the features were selected in a manner consistent with the properties of the decision rule which enabled the development of an effective algorithm based on a minimum number of features. Thus ten (10) features are used in version 3.0 of the PolyScore® model. It was found that many features not used by this algorithm, including those relating to traditional scoring criteria, are valuable for discrimination by themselves but do not improve the algorithm. The features used by the PolyScore® algorithm require a digitized signal and a computer to calculate due to their complexity. (Olsen, et al 1996)

The Decision Rule was developed using a logistic regression model which produced a "score" from various linear weight combinations of the features, which by "logit" conversion calculates a probability of deception. The logit conversion produces a number between 0 and 1 that reflects the probability that a given set of reactions are produced by a deceptive subject. Thus if a score is 0.95, the correct interpretation based on the data in the PolyScore® database is that 95% of the time when similar features are present, deception is indicated. Scores that are at or above 0.90 are interpreted as DI and scores at or below 0.10 are interpreted as NDI. Scores between 0.10 and 0.90 are identified as Inconclusive. (Olsen, et al 1996)

Of the 624 cases used to develop PolyScore® version 3.0, the algorithm scored 8% (50) of the cases as inconclusive and agreed with *known truth* or FP decisions in

99.8% (573) of the remaining cases. It disagreed with the FPs in only one case. Most of the cases were scored with probabilities less than 0.01 or greater than 0.99. The resulting computerized scoring system removed nearly all of the variation in chart interpretation. The computerized evaluation system differs fundamentally from traditional scoring systems in that the two methods use different scoring criteria and weight the channels differently. As an example, eight cases that were scored as Inconclusive by the original FP but were later confirmed as six deceptive and two truthful cases, were subsequently evaluated by PolyScore® which rendered a definite decision in seven of the eight cases and all seven decisions were correct. The one case was found Inconclusive. Thus it is apparent that the rules used by the algorithm are different than those used by FPs, which implies that the algorithm is evaluating the physiological data differently. (Olsen, et al 1996)

It should be noted that when using APL's PolyScore® the correct scoring algorithm should be selected depending upon whether the Zone Comparison Test (ZCT) format for a Single-Issue test is being used or the Modified General Question Test (MGQT) test format for a Multiple-Issue test is used, inasmuch as the scoring algorithm for the ZCT is different than the algorithm for the MGQT. Any mixed issue or exploratory test should be scored as a MGQT. The *Rank Field* should be used for Peak-of-Tension or Pre-Employment tests, or any other actual field test in which the relative strength of reactions among all the test questions is sought. (Wygant 1995). The rank scoring scales the *most* reactive question (spot) to a value of one. The relative rankings of the other questions are then provided. If the most reactive spot has a relatively small reaction, then other spots should have similar high values. If the most reactive spot is significantly greater than the other pots, then attention should be paid to that spot. (Olsen 1996).

It should be noted that in the traditional scoring methods employed in the Backster, Matte, and DoDPI Zone Comparison techniques, all three parameters consisting of respiration, GSR, and cardiovascular activity are treated equally using a seven-position scale. However, the mathematical algorithm used in APL's PolyScore® devotes an average 54 percent of its criteria for deception to electrodermal activity, 24 percent to blood volume, 8 percent to pulse rate, and only 14 percent to respiration (Johnson 1994; Olsen 1995). The algorithm used in CPS version 2.13 devotes 50 percent of its criteria for deception to electrodermal activity, 25 percent to the cardio and 25 percent to respiration.(Kircher 1996). A field study (Matte, Reuss 1992) on the relative effectiveness of physiological data in field polygraph examinations showed that the most productive of the physiological channels was the pneumo tracing at 43 percent, followed by the cardio at 32 percent and the electrodermal at 24 percent. (See Chapter 3 for full discussion). The demonstrated effect of Beta Blockers on the GSR and cardio activity and the *lack* thereof on respiratory activity (Elaad, et al. 1982) reflects the additional importance of the pneumograph channel, and supports the continued usage of the traditional scoring system (Backster, Matte, DoDPI) wherein the respiratory channel alone can often provide the minimum scores required to arrive at a conclusive determination. In fact, Dr. Charles R. Honts, a colleague of Dr. David R. Raskin and Dr. John C. Kircher who developed the Computerized Polygraph System (CPS) used in Stoelting computerized polygraph systems, uses the CPS as a quality control device. If there is a strong disagreement between the CPS and his traditional scoring of the physiological data and it cannot be resolved, which is rare, Honts goes with the traditional scoring inasmuch as their research indicates that the original FP's scoring is slightly more accurate than the CPS (Honts 1996). The traditional scoring system can thus be used as an adjunct to the computerized polygraph system's PolyScore® which normally emphasizes the GSR (54%) and only applies its algorithm to the thoracic respiratory channel (in addition to cardio activity) for its results. (Johnson 1994; Olsen 1995). It should be noted that the CPS 2.13 used by Stoelting evaluates both the thoracic and abdominal breathing patterns, standardizes and averages the scores for a probability decision. (Kircher 1996)

However, according to Dr. Olsen, while the two pneumograph channel tracings may appear to be quite different on the computer screen or polygraph chart, the PolyScore® pre-processes the signals from both channels in such a manner that there is much less difference in the signals between the two channels. Furthermore, PolyScore® compensates for channel(s) that produce inferior data by finding indicators of deception in those channels that are most productive; therefore if an examinee is under the influence of a Beta Blocker, the PolyScore® would shift its attention to the most productive channel which existing research shows under that circumstance to be the pneumograph. Field research by Matte, Reuss (1992) revealed a significant difference in the productivity of the thoracic and abdominal breathing tracings/channels of male versus female examinees, hence both channels are recorded on modern mechanical and electronic polygraph instruments. Furthermore, there were significant differences in the productivity of each channel (Pneumo, GSR, Cardio) for the truthful versus deceptive male and female examinees. The computerized polygraph system (APL) which enjoys an exceptionally high accuracy rate exceeding 98%, records and displays both respiratory channels which allow for traditional scoring, but in the final analysis applies the evaluating algorithm only to the thoracic channel which encompasses all of the traditional criteria for deception *except for those baseline arousals which have no change in amplitude*. (Olsen 1995). Apparently, the complexity of breathing pattern criteria of deception present the greatest difficulty in the development of computer *features.*

The Axciton Computerized Polygraph system which uses APL's algorithm also displays a Stress Analysis of both pneumograph channels whose signals are combined for a single numerical value. (White 1995, May 12). This is reminiscent of the old days when mechanical polygraph instruments contained only one pneumograph channel but the FP placed two pneumo sensors (corrugated rubber tubes) on the subject, one thoracic and one abdominal, and connected the two sensor hoses to a Y valve which combined the locked air of both pneumos into a single hose which fed into the single pneumograph bellows in the polygraph instrument. The mixing of the air or the signal, whether mechanical or electronic, deprives the FP of the separate and sometimes significantly different and/or more productive data that each channel can independently provide; thus the mixing of an unproductive channel with a productive one dilutes the productive data.

Interestingly, a Study of the Validity of Polygraph Examinations in Criminal Investigations by Dr. David C. Raskin, et al. in May 1988 found that "the overall accuracy of decisions made by the Secret Service examiners on individual relevant questions was 96% for confirmed truthful answers and 95% for confirmed deceptive answers." The study further found "the original examiners clearly outperformed all of the blind interpreters and the computer model." "The original examiners, one quality control, and one experienced blind interpreter outperformed the computer, but the computer outperformed the remaining five blind interpreters." "Comparisons of the computer-generated decisions and those produced by the human interpreters indicated that the computer was more accurate than the blind interpreters, but not as accurate as the original examiners."(Raskin, et al. 1988). It should be noted that the computer interpretation in aforesaid study used CAPS (Computer Assisted Polygraph System), which is the earliest version algorithm developed at the University of Utah. (Honts 1996; Kircher 1996). The later CPS version 2.13 is clearly superior to CAPS (Kircher 1996). Undocumented studies show that PolyScore does much better than blind examiners. (Olsen 1996).

Obviously, there are differences between the computer hardware and the software (algorithm) offered to forensic psychophysiologists by the three American manufacturers of computerized polygraph systems. All three systems provide chart evaluation and render an opinion regarding truth or deception. They also provide bar graphs that show relative strengths of responses to test questions. The Lafayette computerized system runs under Microsoft Windows. The Axciton and Stoelting systems run under DOS. The Axciton system runs under both DOS and Windows. The Axciton DOS system relies heavily upon function keys and requires exiting back to DOS from the chart recording program to evaluate the physiological data recorded on the polygraph charts with the separate PolyScore® software. The Stoelting CPS uses a series of menus, which can be slower to negotiate but easier to use. The evaluation portion of the Stoelting software is integrated into the main recording program. All three systems require an analog-to-digital converter box between the computer and the polygraph attachments (Pneumo, GSR, Cardio or Plethysmograph). The Lafayette box must be plugged into a SCSI adaptor on the computer. The Axciton and Stoelting units plugs into a common serial port, which can be a problem when using a PC (desktop) as opposed to a laptop computer, inasmuch as the serial port in a PC is often used for a modem, mouse or other device, which would require constant disconnecting and reconnecting. (Wygant 1995; Cross 1996). The Lafayette software can run without having the analog-to-digital converter box attached to the computer. This is an important feature because the PV examination can be conducted using a laptop equipped with the converter box and then displayed, reviewed and printed on another computer that has nothing special attached to it. On the other hand the Axciton system requires that the converter box be attached to the computer before the software will load, which presents a handicap for the FP who wishes to use a laptop to record PV examinations and a desktop to evaluate, review and/or print the data. (Wygant 1996). Some users of the Lafayette System have reported that printing a set of charts takes about 45 minutes, compared to claims for the Axciton System of about 7 minutes. Some of this will change rapidly as printers change. PolyScore can print charts in seconds on a laser printer, which does not produce a continuous, full-size chart. Most FPs using computerized instruments do their evaluation from the chart display on the computer screen. However printing becomes important if paper charts are required by a State Polygraph Licensing Law or review by another forensic psychophysiologist. (Wygant 1995). Whether using a traditional polygraph instrument or a computerized polygraph system, this author prefers to remove the polygraph chart from the examination room immediately after each test, in order to conduct a Spot Analysis of the chart data without observation from the subject which may otherwise generate questions from the subject about test results which should not be provided until all tests have been conducted. (See Chapter 8). Thus a *quiet, fast* printer should be acquired to produce paper charts from the computerized polygraph system preferably while the test is in progress, so as to avoid excessive delay in conducting Spot Analysis prior to the conduct of the next chart.

The table below depicts the various characteristics of the three computerized polygraph systems as of l October 1996.

Hardware/Software Characteristics of the Stoelting, Axciton, and Lafayette Systems

Characteristics	**Stoelting CPS**	**Axciton**	**Lafayette**
Algorithm	Proprietary CPS 2.13	PolyScore 3.3 and/or Axciton Chart Analysis	PolyScore 3.3
Algorithm included w/system	Yes	Yes	Yes
AD Converter Box needs to be attached to computer to run software.	No	Yes	No
Menu Driven	Yes	Yes	Yes
Mouse Driven	No	Yes	Yes
Program Pacing (question interval)	Yes/Adjustable	Yes/Adjustable	Yes/Adjustable
Tracing Enhancement After Test	No	Yes	Yes
Sensor Box - DC Current	AC/DC	Yes	Yes
Standard No. of Recording Channels	6	5	5
Optional Recording Channels	No	Motion/Auxiliary	No
IBM Compatibility	Yes	Yes	Yes
Mcintosh Compatibility	No	No	Yes
Type of Pneumo Attachment	Electronic Strain Gauge	Mechanical Conv. Tube	Mechanical Conv. Tube
Type Sphygmomanometer	Internal/Digital	Internal/Digital External/Analog	Internal/Digital External/Analog
Finger Electrode Attachment	GSG/SS Chloride	•GSG/Nickel Plated SS Chloride or Stainless Steel	•GSG/Nickel Plated •SS Chloride or •Stainless Steel
Internal Battery Power	Sensor Box requires AC Adapter	• Yes for CPU Box doesn't need it	•Yes, Optional External Supply
Independent of any AC Power	No	Yes	Yes
Prints Data During Test	No	Yes	Yes
Physiological Recordings Mirror Traditional Instrument	Most/GSG Pen Vertically Aligned	All/GSG Pen Vertically Aligned	All/GSG Pen Vertically Aligned

Characteristics	Stoelting CPS	Axciton	Lafayette
GSG Filtered (Auto)	No	Auto/Manual*	Man/Auto*
Color Display Chart on Screen	Yes	Yes	Yes
Chart Scrolls on Screen	Right-Left	Right-Left	Right-Left
Physiological Data collection Time Limit	10 minutes per chart	150 minutes per chart	15 minutes per chart
Noise Ratio	Not Available	<1 Part/8000 over Full Scale	Not Available
Print Centering Adjustment Indicators on Chart	No	Selectable	Selectable
Visual Reference of Edited Chart Segment	Yes	Yes	Yes
Sampling Rate	Not Available	•Samples per second to 120 Cardio 30 GSG & Pneumo Adjustable	•Samples per second 120 Data Collection 8 Cardio-Display 8 GSG/Pneumo-Disp
Display of Question List	Complete	Complete	Complete
Display of Test Question During Test	Maximum 240 Characters	Maximum 160 Characters	Maximum 110 Characters
WP Program Included	No	Yes	Yes
Synthetic Voice Questioning	No	Yes	Yes
Backster Computerized Notepack	No	No	Yes

* Axciton's GSG default is in Auto mode (White 1996). Lafayette's GSG default is in Manual mode (Fauset 1996) The APL algorithm basically can compute the detrended manual from the auto and the auto from the manual (Olsen 1996).

The above data was acquired from Yankee, Schwartz, Barland 1995; James Wygant 1995, 1996; Alfred J. Cross 1996; Lavern A. Miller; Bruce White 1996; Dale E. Olsen 1996; Douglas E. Spangler 1996; Chris L. Fausett 1996; John C. Kircher 1996.

NOTE: Lafayette's Synthetic Voice Questioning capability provides male and female voices with different pitches and tones for the delivery of the test questions. This capability addresses a potential variable caused by voice inflection during question delivery. (See Chapter 8). This capability could be further developed to deliver questions translated into the foreign language of choice. However, the *voice* of the forensic psychophysiologist who has established rapport and gained the trust of the innocent (as later verified) examinee may prove to be more effective in allaying his/her fear of the relevant questions thus eliciting the proper responses (to control questions). The FP's voice may have greater impact on the guilty (as later verified) examinee who has personally deceived the FP during the pretest interview and review of the test questions. Research in this area appears to be warranted. The Axciton Computerized Polygraph System permits the FP to record his/her voiced test questions for subsequent delivery by the computerized polygraph system during the conduct of PV tests.

The Display of Test Question During Test capability shown in above table reflects the number of characters that the forensic psychophysiologist is limited to in the formulation of the test questions he/she wishes to have appear on the screen during the administration of the PV test. The Zone Comparison Technique such as the Matte Quadri-Track ZCT and the Backster ZCT contain a *Preparatory/Sacrifice* relevant question that is necessarily lengthily in order to fully identify the issue to be tested. The related relevant questions that follow in the same test can then be formulated to be short and succinct, without fear of misinterpretation and/or rationalization. The importance of having short relevant questions is to avoid a potential reaction due to mental exercise which can be caused by a lengthly question, thus addressing a variable discussed in Chapter 9. The relevant questions themselves can sometimes be necessarily lengthly such as in fraud cases where rationalization was made an especially important issue in some court cases. Such involved cases may require from 160 to more than 200 characters to adequately identify the issue to the satisfaction of the forensic psychophysiologist and the court receiving the results. The use of acronyms and/or abbreviations to shorten sentences does not offer a desirable format for the FP busy with a multitude of tasks during the conduct of an examination. It is not up to the manufacturers of computerized polygraph systems to decide how long test questions should be; it should be left to the discretion of the forensic psychophysiologist. Normally 80 characters form one line on the computer screen. At the present time, only Stoelting's CPS provides adequate question space (240 characters or 3 lines).

A note of caution from James R. Wygant (July 1996) regarding the deletion of files in computerized polygraph systems with the command DEL*.*: "That command tells DOS to delete all files in whatever directory you are currently situated. If you are not attentive to your current location, you may accidentally erase the wrong files. The safest practice when using *.* to delete all files is to always use the full directory path. For instance, if you want to delete all files from C:\DEMO because you have copied them to floppy disks, the command should be DEL C:\DEMO*.* With Axciton systems, if you want to delete only test files in the directory C:\DEMO, the command should be DEL C:\DEMO\$$*.* since all Axciton test filenames begin with "$$"."

It should be noted that not all the aforementioned computerized polygraph systems use *stainless steel* electrodes which have been shown to be more effective than silver/silver chloride electrodes (Grimsley & Yankee 1986; Yankee & Grimsley 1987). Furthermore *stainless steel* electrodes are more resistant to corrosion and easier to maintain than nickel-plated brass electrodes and silver-silver chloride electrodes. (see Chapter 4 for full discussion).

REFERENCES:

Barland, G. H. (1996, February 27). Telephone conversation with J. A. Matte.

Cross, A. J. (1996, February 28). Telephone conversation with J. A. Matte.

Elaad, E., Bonwitt, G., Eisenberg, O., Meytes, I. (1982). Effects of Beta Blocking Drugs on the Polygraph Detection Rate: A Pilot Study. *Polygraph*, 11(3), 225-233.

Fausett, C. L. (1996, April). Telephone conversation with J. A. Matte.

Gordon, N. J., Cochetti, P. M. (1987). The horizontal scoring system. *Polygraph*, 16(2), 116-125.

Gordon, N. J. (1995, May 17). Letter of reply to J. A. Matte's letter of 26 Apr 95.

Grimsley, D. L., Yankee, W. J. (1986). The effect of multiple retests on examiner decisions in applicant screening polygraph examinations. NSA contract MDA 904-85-C-A962, 1986. A. Madley Corporation, Chalotte, N. C.

Honts, C. R. (1996, February 9). Letter to J. A. Matte

Kircher, J. C. (1996, February 28). Telephone conversation with J. A. Matte.

Kircher, J. C. (1996, March 15). Telephone conversation with J. A. Matte

Kircher, J. C., Raskin, D. C. (1988). Human versus computerized evaluations of polygraph data in a laboratory setting. *Journal of Applied Psychology*, 73(2), 291-302.

Kubis, J. F. (1962). *Studies in Lie Detection: Computer Feasibility Considerations*. Fordham University, New York, N. Y. RADC-TR-62-205. Project No. 5534, AF30(602)-2270, prepared for Rome Air Development Center, Air Force Systems Command, USAF, Griffiss AFB, New York.

Matte, J. A., Reuss, R. M. (1992). A study of the relative effectiveness of physiological data in field polygraph examinations. *Polygraph*, 21(1), 1-22.

Olsen, D. E. (1996, March 15). Letter of reply to J. A. Matte with critical review of chapter 12.

Olsen, D. E. (1996, June 14). Telephone conversation with J. A. Matte relating to Manual versus Auto mode of GSG in computerized polygraph systems using APL's algorithm.

Olsen, D. E. (1996, June 24). Telephone conversation with J. A. Matte relating to the APL algorithm's capacity to compute detrended manual data from the auto mode.

Olsen, D. E., Harris, J. C., Capps, M. H., Ansley, N. (1996). Computerized polygraph scoring system. Pending publication.

Raskin, D. C., Kircher, J. C., Honts, C. R., Horowitz, S. W. (1988 May). A study of the validity of polygraph examinations in criminal investigations. *Final Report to the National Institute of Justice*, Grant No. 85-IJ-CX-0040.

Spangler, Douglas E. (1996, February 28). Telephone conversation with J. A. Matte.

White, B. (1996, February 28). Telephone conversation with J. A. Matte.

White, B. (1996, June 14). Telephone conversation with J. A. Matte relating to the manual versus auto mode of GSG in computerized polygraph systems using APL's algorithm.

Yankee, W. J., Schwartz, J. R., Barland, G. H. (1995). Some things to consider before buying a computerized polygraph. Unpublished draft. Department of Defense Polygraph Institute.

Yankee, W. J. (1968, July 22-27). A report on the computerization of polygraphic recordings. Presented to Keeler Polygraph Institute Alumni Association, Fifth Annual Seminar, Chicago, Illinois.

Yankee, W. J., Grimsley, D. L. (1987). The effect of a prior polygraph test on a subsequent polygraph test. NSA contract MDA 904-84-C-4249. University of North Carolina at Charlotte, N. C.

Wygant, J. R. (1995, November). Computer polygraphs offer choices: three manufacturers compete for market. *News and Views*, 3(6), 1-2.

Wygant, J. R. (1996, January). Users report differences in computerized polygraphs. *News and Views*, 4(1), 1-2.

Wygant, J. R. (1996, July). Equipment Tips. *News and Views*, 4(4), 1-2.

Chapter 14

THE MATTE CONTROL QUESTION VALIDATION TEST

Prior to the development by this author of the Quadri-Track Zone Comparison Technique (Chapter 11), verification of the effectiveness of the control questions used in control question techniques became a special concern to this author when the polygraph charts of an examinee reflected consistent, strong physiological responses to the relevant questions with a complete absence of response to the neighboring control questions used for comparison. Theoretically, the aforesaid charts are considered ideal in that they indicate that the subject's psychological set was focused entirely on the relevant questions which dampened out the neighboring control questions which are structurally less intense. It is generally assumed that the control questions were ideally formulated, therefore the subject must be attempting deception to the relevant questions. However, what if the control questions were ineffective because the subject was not in his or her own mind lying to the control questions, or the lie was so trivial and the crime which he or she has been accused of committing so grave, that the control question(s) fail to capture the subject's psychological set? Under such circumstances, the possibility of a false positive cannot be ignored, thus the MCQV test offers a preventive and remedial procedure to address this infrequent but potential problem. Use of the MCQV is normally not required when the Matte Quadri-Track Zone Comparison Technique or the Backster Zone Comparison Technique which employ the Inside Track containing a "Fear of Error" control question versus a "Hope of Error" relevant question, are used. The Inside Track's function is described in detail in Chapters 11 and 8. However there will be times when the physiological data from the Inside Track will cause inconclusive findings thus avoiding a false positive or negative result. The ensuing retest could include the use of the MCQV test to verify the effectiveness of the usually new control questions.

The following case illustrates the need for effective control questions and the adverse psychological effect that an erroneously deceptive test result and interrogation can have on an innocent (as later verified) examinee's re-examination.

Late one night many years ago, a man returned home and to his surprise found the lights on, music blaring from the living room and the back door leading to the master bedroom slightly ajar. He sensed that something was wrong but never dreamed of the nightmare that was to follow. As he entered the lighted bedroom he was shocked to find his nude wife laying on her back on the floor in a pool of blood near the bed, her chest covered with a blood-soaked towel. He bent over his wife and as he removed the towel from her chest he became horrified at the sight of several stab wounds, one of which still held the knife blade broken at the handle. The savagery of the murder was well reflected by the blood-splattered wall nearest the body.

During the course of the investigation which followed, this man became a prime suspect, at which time he was requested to submit to a psychophysiological veracity (PV) examination using the polygraph by law enforcement authorities. His attorney decided to have his client polygraphed first by a private forensic psychophysiologist so as not to place his client in jeopardy should he in fact be guilty of the crime. The private forensic psychophysiologist, using a control-question technique, opined that the husband was truthful when he denied any involvement in the death of his wife. Reassured, the husband was advised by his attorney to submit to another PV examination, this time to be administered by the police. To the dismay of the husband and his attorney, the police forensic psychophysiologist, using an obsolete relevant-irrelevant technique, which did not employ either probable or known lies, or the situational control now used in the Modified Relevant-Irrelevant technique for comparison, opined that the husband was deceptive in his answers regarding the death of his wife. The attorney decided to obtain a third opinion by submitting his client to another PV examination by a private forensic psychophysiologist, which finally brought him to this author.

Using the Backster Zone Comparison Technique (Bailey 1970), three separate issues were covered in three tests, which were administered in order of their combined greatest adequacy of information, case intensity, and distinctness of issues. The first target sought to determine whether he had stabbed his wife. The second target sought to determine if he was at his house during the period of time the crime was committed. The third target sought to determine if he had hired or had knowledge of the person who perpetrated the homicide.

The first test dealing with the stabbing of his wife resulted in inconclusive findings due to inconsistent responses on the polygraph charts; neither a finding of truthfulness nor of deception could be established on the basis of the physiological data on the polygraph charts. However, the second and third tests dealing with his whereabouts and knowledge of the criminal resulted in truthful findings. It is important to note that a small percentage, less than 10 percent of all PV examinations conducted by scientifically cautious forensic psychophysiologists, result in inconclusive findings. Use of the quantification system in chart analysis has significantly reduced the number of inconclusives but nevertheless circumstances beyond the control of the forensic psychophysiologist will occasionally prevent the FP from arriving at a solid determination of truth or deception, in which case inconclusive results must be rendered. In such cases the subject is usually scheduled for a re-examination at a later date. In this particular case the results were deemed by the attorneys to be sufficiently supportive of the first PV examination to preclude a retest regarding the first issue, and charges were not preferred against the husband. However, it is doubtful under the circumstances whether a retest would have obtained conclusive results using the polygraph techniques available during that period. At that time the Quadri-Track Zone Comparison Technique had not yet been developed by this author.

The husband's failure to pass the police PV examination and the ensuring interrogation undoubtedly rendered the crime questions on any subsequent PV examination a definite threat to his well-being, inasmuch as he now knows that the police think he committed the murder and the strong possibility now exists that the next PV examination will also reflect deception regarding whether or not he himself stabbed his wife. The second factor for the inconclusive results may have been due to the trauma suffered as a result of the condition in which the husband found his wife, which would undoubtedly flash in his mind, when asked the relevant question "Did you yourself stab your wife?"

The question arises as to whether an effective control question sufficiently powerful to draw the examinee's psychological set away from such a threatening and emotionally packed relevant question can be formulated. In this particular type of offense, the problem is further compounded by the fact that inasmuch as the control question is designed to encompass behavior similar to that of the actual offense, control questions that can be developed will be narrower in scope and less probable as a lie than those more common, such as stealing. In homicides, the verbs "harm" or "hurt" normally form the basis of control questions, although when the motive is apparent, that category of control question can also be used. Therefore, can the forensic psychophysiologist be sure that the examinee is lying when he or she denies ever harming or hurting anyone? In larceny cases where the control question encompasses the verb "steal" the forensic psychophysiologist can be reasonably assured that the control question will be a *known lie*. However, in the case of a homicide the narrow scope and the nature of the control question provide the forensic psychophysiologist with a *probable lie*.

Ideally, the guilty examinee's psychological set will be focused onto the crime questions, which should completely dampen out the neighboring control questions, whereas the innocent examinee's psychological set will be focused onto the control questions, which should completely dampen out any concern he or she may have regarding the neighboring crime questions. This means that ideally there should be a presence of reaction in one type of question and a lack of reaction in the other type of question against which it is being compared. This is known as the "either-or-rule." However, as a practical matter, polygraph charts will more often reflect some reaction in one question and more in the other question being intercompared. Suppose we have ideal charts reflecting deception to the relevant questions. Inasmuch as there is a complete lack of reaction to the control questions due to anticlimax dampening by the relevant questions, how can the forensic psychophysiologist be certain that the examinee was in fact lying to the control questions. If he or she was not lying to the control questions, could the examinee possibly have released his or her anxieties onto the crime questions due to the lack of effective control questions upon which to relieve his or her anxieties?

Unless a forensic psychophysiologist uses a Zone Comparison Technique that employs the Inside Track (Chapter 11), which identifies the presence of inside issue factors that may affect the effectiveness of the control questions, the forensic psychophysiologist has no means of determining the effectiveness of the probable-lie control question; this is especially true in cases where reactions are found only on the relevant questions. The forensic psychophysiologist assumes that the subject is lying to the control questions and they are of sufficient concern to the innocent subject to dampen any concern he or she may have about the crime questions, even if they are somewhat threatening to him or her.

One method of verification that the examinee was lying to the control questions can be acquired during the post-test interview of the examinee. But when the examinee under such circumstances denies deception to both the relevant and control questions, the forensic psychophysiologist needs another form of verification. The Matte Control Question Validation (MCQV) test is designed to verify the effectiveness of the control questions prior to their use in the actual crime test. Albeit in aforesaid instance it would require a retest, but the MCQV test can be used before or after the actual crime test, with any type of control question test.

The MCQV test can also be useful in acquiring verified truthful charts in field PV examinations of actual criminal cases to be used in research studies, which are most difficult to obtain under the best of circumstances.

The Matte Control Question Validation (MCQV) Test:

Scope: The MCQV test is used in specific type psychophysiological veracity (PV) examinations which employ the Probable-Lie control question (Backster in Bailey & Rothblatt 1970) or the Known-Lie control question (Arther 1975).

Purpose: The MCQV test provides the forensic psychophysiologist (FP) with a means of determining the effectiveness of the control questions to be used in the actual crime test. It further provides the FP with a truthful chart from the examinee, dealing with issues of the same category and case intensity as the actual crime, for comparison and assistance in the analysis of the chart data acquired in the actual crime test.

Definition of Terms:

Control Question: A test question within a PV examination designed to produce a physiological reaction in the Innocent examinee, which is used for comparison with a relevant (crime) question.

Actual Crime Test: PV test regarding the specific issue(s) for which the examinee was scheduled to be administered.

MCQV Test: A PV test regarding a fictitious* crime of the same category and case intensity as the actual crime, designed to determine the control questions to be used in the actual crime test.

Stimulation Test: A test using numbers, numbered cards or money envelopes, with a known or unknown solution (Chapter 10), for the purpose of reassuring the Innocent examinee, stimulating the guilty examinee, and determining minimum capability of response.

PROCEDURE:

The pretest interview includes the gathering of personal data from the examinee, an explanation of the physiology recorded by the polygraph instrument, and then attentive listening to the examinee's version of the incident for which he or she is being examined. It is at this point in the pretest interview, when all information has been acquired from the examinee, and the forensic psychophysiologist (FP) is ready to finalize the formulation of the relevant and control questions, that the MCQV test is introduced. At this time, the FP informs the examinee that a crime similar to the actual crime occurred in the same area and is also under investigation; the subject is a prime suspect for both. It must be noted that when formulating a fictitious crime it is necessary that it be of the same case category and intensity as the actual crime. In the case of a nonrepeatable crime, such as the murder of one's wife, the FP's choice of fictitious crimes is more limited but nevertheless still feasible. For example, in such cases, the subject may be told that a few days prior to the death of his wife, a known "hit" man was killed in a car accident not far from where subject resides, and the police are attempting to determine the identity of the intended victim. At this time, a fictitious name of the "hit" man is furnished to the subject and he is asked if he has at any time contacted this man or contracted with anyone to murder his wife. The foundation has then been laid for the MCQV test.

The subject is then informed that he will be tested on this issue first. The FP then proceeds to formulate the relevant questions regarding the fictitious crime as well as the control questions. After all of the questions have been reviewed with the subject and he is ready for the examination, he is advised that a preliminary test must be conducted to insure that the instrument is adjusted to his sensitivity. At this point, the control-stimulation test is administered (Chapter 10), and of course the subject is informed immediately of the results, satisfying him that the instrument works on him and is in fact adjusted properly. The FP should then proceed with the MCQV test.

A minimum of two charts and preferably only two charts should be conducted on the MCQV test. This procedure is to establish consistency throughout each test. If only one chart is conducted on the MCQV test and two or more charts are run on the

---

*Reid & Inbau (1966) describe the use of a fictitious crime in a Guilt Complex Test for the overly responsive subject, usually after the third test, and only when the examinee gives pronounced, specific responses to both relevant and control questions in the actual crime test, or when behavior symptoms are inconsistent with recorded responses. It was not designed to verify the effectiveness of control questions and does not provide the FP with a means of modifying the control questions prior to their use in the actual crime test.

actual crime test, the innocent subject might become unduly upset or worried over the fact that it took only chart to resolve the first issue but two or more charts to resolve the second or actual issue. Hence, the subject should always be told at the outset that two or more charts will be conducted for purity of tracing and consistency of response, and that analysis of the physiological data on the polygraph charts will be conducted only upon completion of all tests (see Chapter 8 for details).

After completion of the first chart of the MCQV test, the FP should tear off the chart containing both the control-stimulation test and the first MCQV test and leave the polygraph suite to another room where he or she can analyze the physiological data on the collected charts.

A review of the control-stimulation test should ideally reflect some reaction to the number selected by the subject to which he or she deliberately lied during the test. In addition to determining the subject's minimum capability of response, this test can provide guidance to the FP in making necessary mechanical adjustments, such as the degree of increase or decrease required in the GSR/GSG response sensitivity. In the event no response is found in any of the tracings, the FP has two courses of action to follow; if he or she administered a known-solution stimulation test, he or she may proceed with the MCQV test on the assumption that the subject failed to respond on the stimulation test because the question posed no threat to him or her. On the other hand, the FP should postpone the examination if he or she suspects that subject's failure to respond on the stimulation test is due to fatigue, use of drugs, or other factors that will adversely affect the examination. It may be advisable for the FP to make arrangements with the attorney or agency requesting the PV examination, that the examinee be advised and consent prior to the scheduled PV examination, that in the event drug use by the examinee is suspected, the examinee will be administered a drug test at a nearby qualified laboratory. This author has standard arrangements with a drug testing laboratory located about five minutes driving distance from the polygraph laboratory. The examinee is driven by this author to the drug laboratory immediately after completion of the PV examination when circumstances warrant it. This author has found that this procedure of warning examinees prior to the PV examination of the possibility of a drug test, deters most guilty (as later verified) examinees from using drugs as a countermeasure.

A review of the first MCQV test chart should indicate reactions to the control questions if they were ideally formulated, which would then indicate that the control questions are functioning as designed. If the MCQV test shows no reaction to the control questions and no reaction to the relevant or fictitious crime questions, then obviously the control questions need to be changed. The FP should determine whether he or she simply needs to restrict or expand the age limitation prefacing control questions or to change the control questions completely by using alternate questions more fitting to the subject's background. It has been this author's experience that sometimes a mere reemphasis of the control questions by reviewing only the control questions with the subject prior to the conduct of the next chart, is sufficient to obtain the desired arousal on the control questions in the subsequent MCQV test. This author usually resorts to this remedy when the control questions are functioning at less than full capacity, that is, the subject's psychological set is not fully on the control questions in the first chart of the MCQV test. After remedial action has been taken, the second MCQV test chart should be conducted to measure the effectiveness of the reemphasized, ameliorated, or changed control questions.

Should the first chart of the MCQV test reflect no reaction to the control questions but reflect reaction to the relevant question(s), this may indicate that the control questions were not formulated properly. Therefore, the same remedial action as suggested above applies, excluding reemphasis of the control questions, which in this case are obviously ineffective. After remedial action has been taken, the second MCQV test chart should be run to measure the effectiveness of changed control questions.

In the event that subject continuously shows reaction only to the relevant questions in the MCQV test after all remedial action has been taken and at least two charts have been conducted, the subject should still be tested in the actual crime test. If the results show consistent reaction to the control questions, the most likely conclusion is that the subject is truthful regarding the actual crime questions. If, however, the results show consistent reaction to the relevant questions, the FP must call the results inconclusive, due to the lack of adequate control questions as demonstrated on the MCQV test.

After two charts have been collected using the MCQV test, the subject should not be apprised of the results. The FP should immediately review the previously formulated relevant questions dealing with the actual crime test. Relevant test questions should be formulated prior to the scheduled PV examination, subject to minor change(s) during the pretest interview. The reason for aforesaid procedure is threefold. First, there may be several issues to cover in the actual crime test, each requiring a minimum of two charts. These tests must be administered with the first test having the combined greatest adequacy of information, case intensity, and distinctness of issue. Since the subject is not apprised of the results until all test regarding the actual crime have been conducted, it would be inconsistent for the FP to apprise the examinee of the results of the MCQV test. Second, to apprise the examinee of the results of the MCQV test immediately after the last chart has been conducted would reduce the effectiveness of the control questions, inasmuch as the examinee may feel that he or she was found to be truthful regarding the fictitious crime in spite of the fact that he or she lied to the control questions. This author does not feel that advising the subject that he or she was truthful only to the relevant questions is sufficient to retain maximum effectiveness of the control questions. Third, this author does not fear the possible lingering effect of the fictitious crime on the actual crime test, by not apprising subject of the results of each test as they occur. This author feels that for the innocent subject, for whom the actual crime has been especially traumatic, the fictitious crime should serve to divide or diminish the subject's concern over the actual crime he or she did not commit, because of this new allegation, rendering the control questions more effective, whereas the guilty subject's concern would still be on the crime he or she did commit. An illustration of this was a case concerning an innocent subject accused of murder, who found his wife stabbed twelve times with part of the blade still in her chest. Obviously, when this subject was asked the relevant question "Did you yourself stab your wife?" he undoubtedly visualized the murder scene as he found it. Needless to say, control questions with enough threatening power to draw the subject's psychological set away from that traumatic "picture" are not easily developed. The fictitious crime would serve to draw subject's concern away from the actual crime, that is, to weaken it, by offering the subject's psychological set a third threat to his well-being, even though it is not included in the actual crime test, because it immediately precedes the actual crime test and he is not apprised of the results of the MCQV test. In short, the objective is to obtain good balance and consistency between the MCQV test and the actual crime test, so that credible comparisons can be made between the two.

This author has noted that when introducing the fictitious crime to guilty (as later verified) subjects, they generally welcome the test, sometimes too readily, suggesting to this author an attempt to delay the final outcome of the actual crime test. In not one instance has this author ever encountered a refusal or even a hesitation to answer fictitious crime questions, by either the guilty or innocent subjects.

After the relevant questions have been formulated and reviewed with the subject, the FP should then review the same control questions used in the MCQV test with subject, giving them the same emphasis as the relevant questions. Of course this review should be followed by a review of other questions as normally used in the technique employed. When all questions have been reviewed with the subject, he or she is then advised that a minimum of two charts will be conducted and the examination should proceed without delay.

After the first chart of the actual crime test has been conducted, the FP should leave the polygraph suite with all charts for the purpose of conducting a spot analysis to determine which questions show reaction and whether remedial action is necessary before continuing with a second chart. When using the Matte Quadri-Track Zone Comparison Technique (MQTZCT) or the Backster Tri-Zone Comparison Technique (BTZCT), the appropriate *Reaction Combination Guide* should be employed for that purpose. Obviously at this stage, the FP's concern is directed to the effectiveness of the relevant questions, which the FP should have formulated in accordance with the rules of the technique used. If this first chart reflects little or no reaction to the control questions and no reaction to the relevant questions, it may be assumed that the relevant questions have not been properly formulated; changes must be made before a second chart can be conducted. When the actual crime test employs the MQTZCT or BTZCT which would only be in cases where the initial test was inconclusive and this was a retest using the MCQV test to find the problem which caused the inconclusive result, then the FP has another guide, the *Inside Track* (fear/hope of error question pair), to assist the FP in determining which test questions need to be remedied.

When the spot analysis reveals that all questions are functioning as designed or when all remedial action has been made, the FP then may proceed with the administration of a second chart. When the FP has collected a sufficient number of charts showing consistency of response either to the control questions or the relevant questions, the FP has then achieved his or her objective.

As a practical matter, the addition of the MCQV test in a specific type PV examination requires basically two additional charts of approximately four minutes each; moreover, introduction of the MCQV test to the subject plus the analysis of the MCQV test charts requires about another 20 minutes. Therefore, excluding the required pretest preparation, only about one-half hour additional time is required to administer the MCQV test, a small price to pay for the results it provides.

Conclusion: The MCQV test provides for a determination of the effectiveness of control questions, allows the FP to obtain known truthful charts, and moreover, provides the FP with additional credibility when confronting a guilty subject with the results of both tests. More importantly, however, the FP who used the MCQV test can demonstrate the effectiveness of his or her control questions when requested to defend his or her PV examination in court.

Illustration of the MCQV test in a Verified Case

The following is an illustration of a verified psychophysiological veracity (PV) examination in which the MCQV test was used.

The subject, a twenty-one-year-old Caucasian, was arrested late one evening along with two Black males. All three persons were attempting to elude two police cars; pursuit was based upon an anonymous tip that three men, one armed with a sawed-off shotgun, were parked outside the Lilly White Tavern. The subject claimed that, while returning home, he was forced at gunpoint to admit these two Black males into his car and to drive them to the tavern in question. Further, he claimed that upon arrival of the police cars at said tavern, he was forced under threat of his life to elude the police. The subject admitted to his attorney that he was vaguely acquainted with one of the Blacks who had threatened him with the shotgun, due to the fact that the assailant's mother had rented a house from the subject's father. During the pretest interview, the subject mentioned that the police inferred that he was probably a dope pusher.

The following tests were administered (only the control and relevant questions are listed):

MCQV Test

Preparatory/Sacrifice Relevant Question:	Regarding whether or not you are the person named "Skip" who escaped a narcotic raid on 20 July 1973: Do you intend to answer truthfully each question about that?
Non-Current Exclusive Control Question:	Between the ages of 16 and 20 - Do you remember ever telling a serious lie?

Relevant Question: Are you the person known as "Skip" who escaped in a narcotic raid in Boston on 20 July 1973?

Non-Current Exclusive Control Question: During the first 16 years of your life - Do you remember ever lying to hurt someone?

Relevant Question: Regarding that narcotic raid on Samuel Street in Boston on 20 July 1973, were you on those premises at that time?

Results: Two charts were collected. Strong and consistent responses to the control questions were present; no strong or consistent responses to the relevant questions.

Actual Crime Test

Target A

Preparatory/Sacrifice Relevant Question: Regarding whether or not John Fiction and Joe Noname forced their way into your car on the evening of 1 November 1974: Do you intend to answer truthfully each question about that?

Non-Current Exclusive Control Question: Same as in MCQV test.

Relevant Question: Did John Fiction and Joe Noname force their way into your car?

Non-Current Exclusive Control Question: Same as in MCQV test.

Relevant Question: On the evening of 1 November 1974, under threat of your life, did John Fiction and Joe Noname force their way into your car?

Results: Two charts were collected. Strong and consistent responses were present on both relevant questions; no strong or consistent responses to the control questions.

Target B

Preparatory/Sacrifice Relevant Question: Regarding whether or not you were forced to speed away from the police on the evening of 1 November 1974: Do you intend to answer truthfully each question about that?

Non-Current Exclusive Control Question:	Same as in MCQV test.
Relevant Question:	Did John Fiction threaten you with a shotgun forcing you to speed away from the police?
Non-Current Exclusive Control Question:	Same as in MCQV test.
Relevant Question:	At the time the police car approached your car, did you speed away under threat of your life by Fiction?
Results:	Two charts were collected. Strong and consistent responses were present on both relevant questions. No strong or consistent responses to the control questions.
Final Results:	The subject was confronted with the results of the MCQV test, and the results of Actual Crime Tests A and B, where upon he confessed he had lied to the police and his own attorney.

The polygraph charts (Figs XIV-1 through XIV-10) taken from an actual sex offense case involving child molestation are illustrated in the order they were administered. Due to the sensitivity of the case, all references to the details of the incident, the date and place where it occurred, and the parties involved have been omitted.

The PV examination was predicated upon information that the examinee had picked up a young boy and molested him. Two distinct issues were covered in the examination, both relating to sexual acts allegedly perpetrated upon the victim. These issues were incorporated into two separate tests administered concurrently as test A and test B. The relevant questions, number 33 and 35 in each test, contained the actual alleged sex act as reported by the victim. Questions number 46 and 47 consist of non-current exclusive control questions encompassing earlier-in-life sexual activity the examinee denied committing. The results of this examination were confirmed by the examinee's subsequent confession to this author who conducted the examination.

A pretest interview was conducted during which time the control questions were developed and the relevant questions were refined to final wording and then reviewed word for word with the examinee.

In accordance with the previously outlined MCQV test procedure, the examine was first administered a control-stimulation test to reassure the innocent examinee, stimulate the guilty examinee, and determine his minimum capability of response. As illustrated in Figure XIV-1 by a half moon mark under the number chosen by the examinee to which he had been requested to lie, the examinee had selected card number ten, as evidenced by a baseline arousal and suppression in the pneumograph (breathing) tracing, and the significant upward excursion of the GSR pen in the electrodermal response tracing. The examinee was apprised of the card selected but showed no outward expression of either elation or depression over the results.

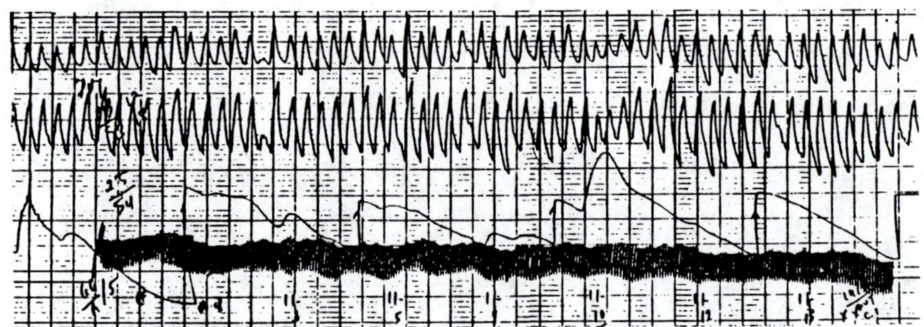

Actual Control-Stimulation Test, Chart 1 - Child Molestation Case

Figure XIV-1

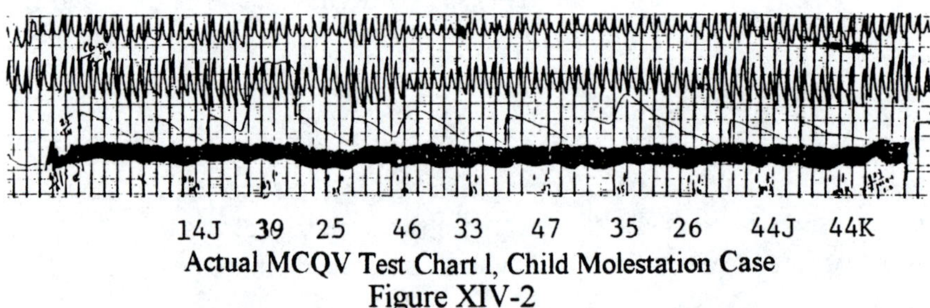

Actual MCQV Test Chart l, Child Molestation Case

Figure XIV-2

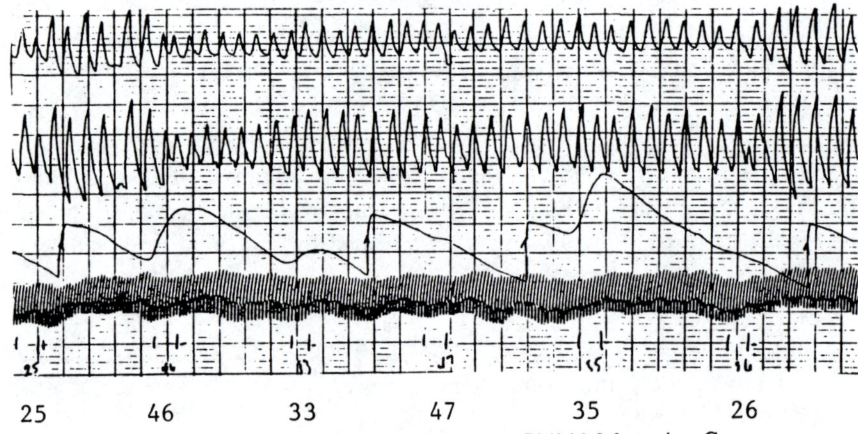

Actual MCQV Magnification of Chart l, Child Molestation Case

Figure XIV-3

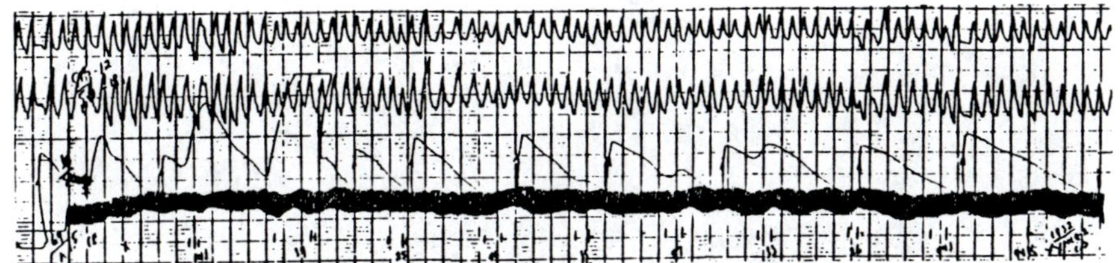

Actual MCQV Test Chart 2, Child Molestation Case

Figure XIV-4

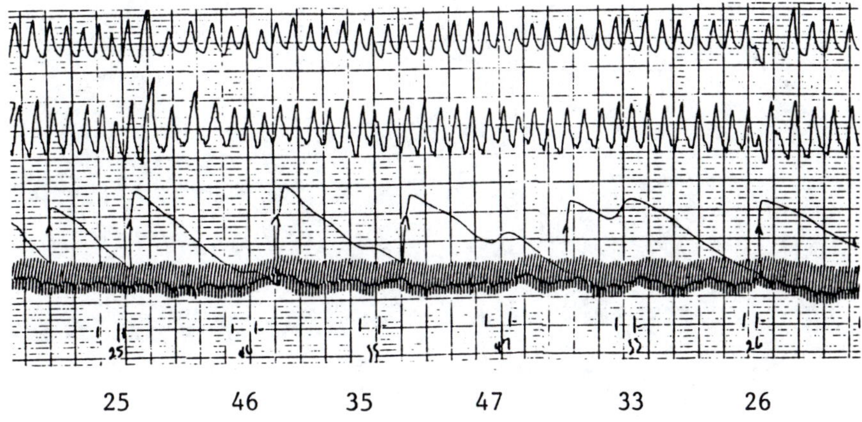

Actual MCQV Magnification of Chart 2, Child Molestation Case

Figure XIV-5

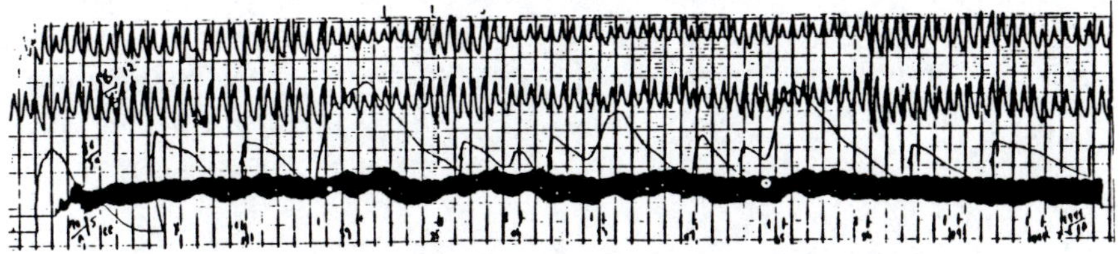

Actual Backster ZCT Chart lA, DI, Child Molestation

Figure XIV-6

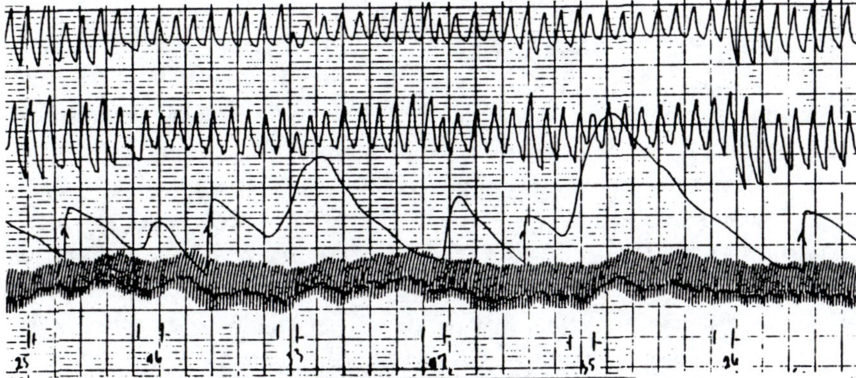

Actual Backster ZCT Magnification of Chart lA, Child Molest

Figure XIV-7

Actual Backster ZCT Magnification Chart 2A, Child Molest

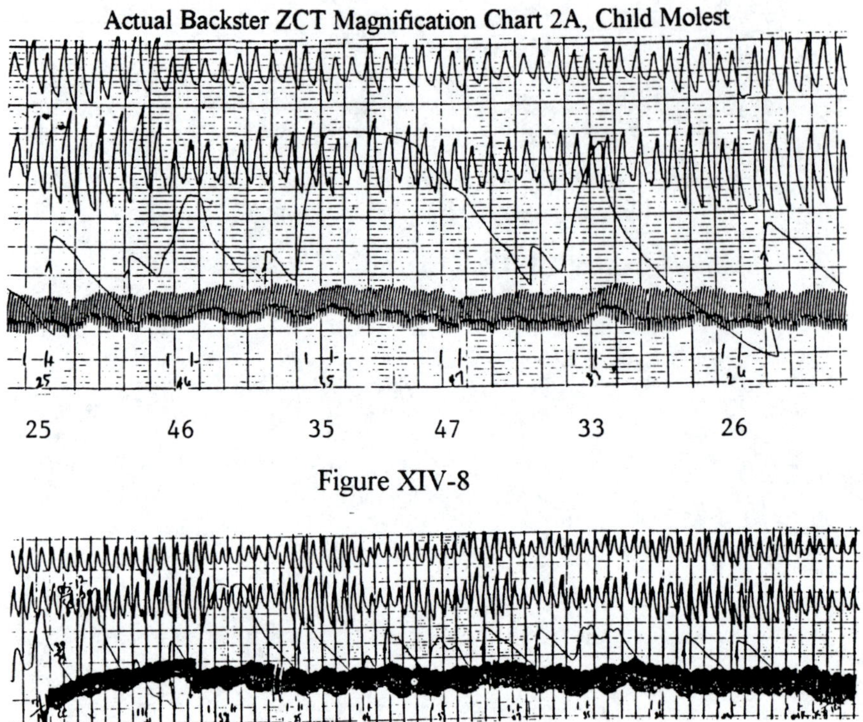

Figure XIV-8

Actual Backster ZCT Chart 1 B, DI, Child Molestation Case

Figure XIV-9

The examinee was then administered the first chart of the MCQV test to determine whether control questions number 46 and 47 were in fact effective. The relevant questions, number 33 and 35 in the MCQV test are formulated from a fictitious crime the examinee believes to be true. Figure XIV-2 depicts the entire first chart of the MCQV test. (The letters MCQ-1 at the end of the chart stand for Matte Control Question Test 1, the original title of this validation procedure.)

Figure XIV-3 is a magnification of Figure XIV-2 depicting the Primary and Secondary Tracks quantified for a conclusion. Note the tremendous baseline arousal and suppression in the pneumograph (breathing) tracing at the control question 46 and the lack of reaction at the neighboring relevant question 33 as evidenced by the constant average tracing cycles in the pneumograph tracing. Further, note the rise in the GSR pen of 3 to 1 ratio at question 46 compared to question 33. In the cardio tracing the mild blood pressure arousal is more sustained at question 46 than 33. In comparing control question 47 to relevant question 35 the suppression at question 47 in the pneumograph tracing, although mild, is still greater than at question 35. However, note the rise in the GSR pen at relevant question 35 (fictitious crime) is at least five to one compared with almost no rise in the GSR pen at control question 47. The cardio tracing reveals no substantial difference between the two questions. Clearly from this first chart, the examinee's psychological set is primarily focused on control question 46. The unexplained reaction in the GSR tracing at relevant question 35 involves only one parameter, but it indicated that perhaps control question number 47 was not functioning at full capacity, therefore question 47 was again reviewed with the examinee to increase the intensity of that probable lie control question.

Figure XIV-4 depicts the entire second chart of the MCQV test. Note the reaction in all parameters to question number 39, which is the sacrifice or first relevant question on the test. From the GSR tracing, it would appear that the examinee is getting tired as indicated by the falling GSR pen, which has to be manually brought back to mechanical center by the forensic psychophysiologist throughout this chart as indicated by the arrows on the tracing. The GSR becomes more active in subsequent charts.

Figure XIV-5 is a magnification of the second chart of the MCQV test, depicting the Primary, Secondary and Outside Tracks. In this chart, the position of relevant questions 33 and 35 have been switched. Note the baseline arousal in the pneumograph tracing at control question o46 as opposed to the very mild staircase pattern in the lower pneumograph tracing at question 35, and the larger blood pressure arousal at 46 compared to 35, but the lack of significant GSR arousal in either question. Further note the baseline arousal and suppression in the pneumograph tracing at question number 47 compared to the absence of any reaction in the pneumograph tracing at question number 33. The reactions found at questions 33 and 47 in the GSR and the cardio tracings equalize each other. Overall evaluation indicates that the examinee's psychological set is primarily focused on control question 46 and therefore question 46 is the most effective control question on the test. Control question 47 is sufficiently effective to neutralize any concern over its neighboring relevant question.

At this time the effectiveness of the control questions, number 46 and 47, have been verified and are therefore inserted in the actual crime test, which consists of two issues or targets labeled A and B administered in order of their combined greatest adequacy of information, case intensity, and distinctness of issue. Figure XIV-6 is the entire first chart of Test A. Note the substantial reaction in all tracings at the sacrifice relevant question number 39. The symptomatic questions, number 25 and 26, do not reveal any outside issue that is bothering the examinee.

Figure XIV-7 is a magnification of the first chart in test A, showing the test questions within the Primary and Secondary tracks quantified for a conclusion. In comparing relevant question number 33 with control question number 46, we find that while there is significant baseline arousal and suppression in the pneumograph (breathing) tracing at question number 46, there is equally significant baseline arousal and suppression at question number 33 plus greater relief pattern in the form of hyperventilation, indicating greater parasympathetic action was required at question number 33. In the GSR tracing the pen excursion is 2.5 times greater at question number 33 than at question number 46. The cardio tracing reflects a more sustained rise in blood pressure at question number 33 than at 46. In comparing relevant question 35 against control question 47 we find greater baseline arousal and hyperventilation in the pneumograph tracing at relevant question number 35, and the GSR tracing reflects a pen excursion of more than two to one ratio at relevant question number 35. Relevant question 35 also reflects a significant blood pressure arousal and a lack of reaction at control question 47. Clearly, the examinee's psychological set is focused onto the relevant questions number 33 and 35 in this first chart of Test A.

Figure XIV-8 is a magnification of the second chart of Test A reflecting the Primary, Secondary and Ooutside Tracks. The position of relevant questions number 33 and 35 have been switched. Although there is significant suppression in the pneumograph tracing at question number 46, there is also some suppression and hyperventilation at question number 35 but to a lesser degree. However, the GSR tracing reflects twice the rise in pen excursion at question number 35 than at question number 46. Furthermore, the cardio tracing reflects a greater blood pressure arousal at question number 35 than at question number 46. When comparing relevant question number 33 against control quest number 47, we find that although a baseline arousal occurred at question number 47, greater relief occurred at question number 33 as evidenced by the significant hyperventilation, which caused a return to the original pneumograph baseline last seen at symptomatic question number 25. The GSR tracing reflects a significant four to one rise in the pen excursion at relevant question number 33 as compared to control question 47. In the cardio tracing there is a presence of reaction in the form of a blood pressure arousal at question number 33 and a lack of reaction at control question number 47. Clearly, this chart shows that the examinee's psychological set was focused onto the relevant questions number 33 and 35.

Analysis of both charts in test A showed strong and consistent unresolved responses to the relevant questions number 33 and 35 indicating that the examinee was attempting deception when he answered them. However, the examinee was not apprised of this conclusion at this time because test B had yet to be administered.

Figure XIV-9 is the entire first chart of test B. Note the substantial reaction in all tracings at the sacrifice relevant question number 39, and the lack of reaction at the symptomatic questions number 25 and 26.

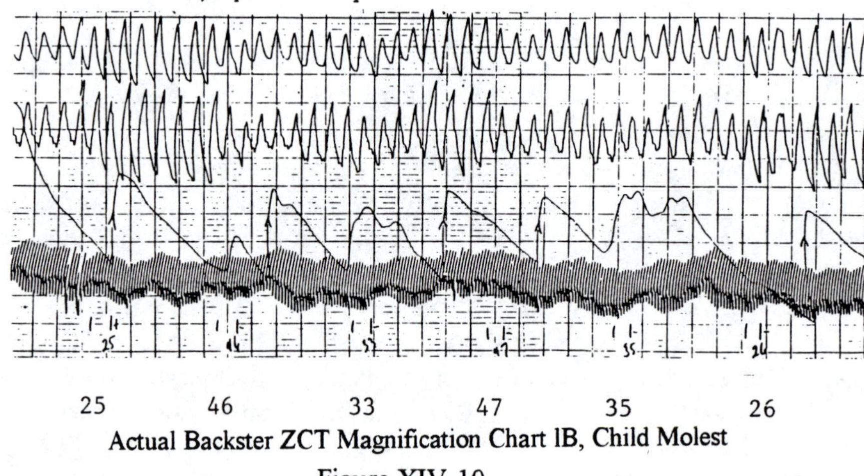

Actual Backster ZCT Magnification Chart lB, Child Molest

Figure XIV-10

Figure XIV-10 is a magnification of the first chart in test B reflecting the Primary and Secondary Tracks quantified for a conclusion. In comparing relevant question number 33 against control question number 46, we find a baseline arousal in the pneumograph tracing in both questions, but question number 33 reflects greater relief pattern (hyperventilation). The GSR tracing reflects greater pen excursion at question number 33 by a ratio of two to one over question number 46.

The cardio tracing reflects greater sustained blood pressure arousal at relevant question number 33 than at control question number 46. In comparing relevant question number 35 against control question number 47, there appears to be an equal amount of suppression and hyperventilation in both questions in the pneumograph tracing indicating a lean towards deception. However, the GSR tracing reflects a pen excursion at question number 35 of two to one over question number 47, and the cardio tracing reflects a blood pressure arousal at relevant question number 35 and an absence of any reaction at control question number 47.

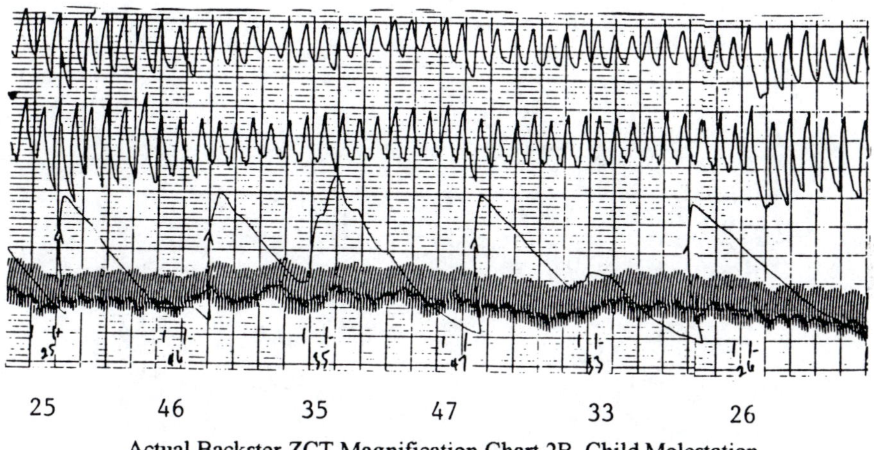

Actual Backster ZCT Magnification Chart 2B, Child Molestation

Figure XIV-11

Figure XIV-11 is a magnification of the second chart in test B reflecting the Primary, Secondary and Outside Tracks. The position of relevant questions number 33 and 35 have been switched. The upper pneumograph tracing reflects a greater baseline arousal at relevant question 35 when compared against control question number 46. The GSR tracing reflects a pen excursion at question number 35 of near four to one ratio when compared against question number 46. However, there is a greater blood pressure arousal at control question number 46 than its neighboring relevant question number 35. When comparing relevant question number 33 against control question number 47 we find that there is evidence of suppression and baseline arousal at question number 33 in the lower and upper pneumograph tracing respectively, and a lack of reaction at control question number 47. The GSR tracing reflects a mild pen excursion at relevant question number 33 but a complete absence of any reaction at control question number 47. The cardio trac-

EMPIRICAL DATA REGARDING EFFECTIVENESS OF MCQV TEST

				EFFECTIVENESS OF CONTROLS IN MCQ TEST REACTIONS FOUND IN					ACTUAL CRIME TEST REACTIONS FOUND IN					
OFFENSE	TECHNIQUES	VIOLATIONS IN QUESTION FORMULATION	VIOLATIONS IN EXAM PROCEDURES	CONTROL QUESTIONS CHART-1	RELEVANT QUESTIONS CHART-1	CONTROL QUESTIONS CHART-2	RELEVANT QUESTIONS CHART-2	REMEDIAL ACTION TAKEN	CONTROL QUESTIONS CHART-1	RELEVANT QUESTIONS CHART-1	CONTROL QUESTIONS CHART-2	RELEVANT QUESTIONS CHART-2	FINAL TEST RESULTS	RESULTS CONFIRMED
Larceny	Arther	None	None	Yes	No	Yes	No	None	Yes	No	Yes	No	Truthful	No
Larceny	Arther	None	None	No	No	Yes	No	Re-emphasis of controls	Yes	No	Yes	No	Truthful	No
Larceny	Arther	None	None	Yes	No	Yes	No	None	Yes	No	Yes	No	Truthful	No
Larceny	Arther	None	None	No	No	Yes (mild)	No	Changed controls after Chart-2	No	Yes	No	Yes	Deceptive	Yes Confession.
Breaking & Entering	Arther	None	None	No	Yes (mild)	Yes	No	Changed controls After Chart-1	No	Yes	No	Yes	Deceptive	No
Assault-Kidnap	Backster	None	None	Yes	No	Yes	No	None	No	Yes	No	Yes	Deceptive	Yes Confession
Larceny	Backster	None	None	No	No	No	No	Re-emphasis of controls Chart-1. Changed Controls after Chart-2	Yes	No	Yes	No	Truthful	No
Assault Robbery	Backster	None	None	Yes	Yes (mild)	Yes	No	Re-emphasis of controls Chart-1.	No	Yes	No	Yes	Deceptive	Yes Confession
Narcotics Smuggling	Backster	None	None	Yes (mild)	No	Yes	No	Re-emphasis Controls Chart-1	No	Yes	No	Yes	Deceptive	Partial Confidential Source.
Larceny	Backster	None	None	Yes	Yes (mild)	Yes	No	Re-emphasis Controls Chart-1	Yes	No	Yes	No	Truthful	Yes No Inventory shortage

NOTE: The Arther Technique employed non-exclusive control questions. The Backster technique employed non-current exclusive control questions.

Figure XIV-12

ing reflects a significant blood pressure arousal at relevant question number 33 and a lack of reaction at its neighboring control question number 47.

Analysis of both charts in test B reflects strong and consistent unresolved responses to all relevant questions (33 and 35), indicating that the examinee was attempting deception when he answered them.

The examinee was confronted with the results of the MCQV test indicating truthfulness to its relevant questions, and the results of tests A and B indicating deception to its relevant questions. The examinee at first denied any attempt at deception but when shown and explained the lack of any reaction to the relevant questions in the MCQV test and the consistent presence of strong responses to the relevant questions in Tests A and B, the examinee realized the futility of his denial against such obvious scientific evidence and confessed to his crime.

Figure XIV-12 depicts empirical data regarding the effectiveness of the MCQV test utilizing the Backster Zone Comparison technique (Chap. 11) and the Arther Specific Accusation Test (Chap. 15).

REFERENCES

Arther, R. O. (1975, Nov-Dec). The eight known-lie question principles. *Journal of Polygraph Science*, X(3)

Bailey, F. L., Rothblatt, H. B. (1970). *The Use of the Polygraph. Investigation and Preparation of Criminal Cases - Federal and State*. Rochester, NY: The Lawyers Cooperative Publishing Company.

Reid, J. E., Inbau, F. E. (1966). *Truth and Deception: The Polygraph ("Lie Detector") Technique*. Baltimore, MD: Williams and Wilkins.

Chapter 15

THE CLINICAL APPROACH TO PSYCHOPHYSIOLOGICAL VERACITY EXAMINATIONS

The *Clinical Approach* differs from the *Numerical Approach* in arriving at a determination of truth or deception in that it does not depend entirely upon the physiological data recorded on the polygraph charts in the decision making process. The forensic psychophysiologist (FP) employing the *Clinical Approach* evaluates the case facts (factual analysis) and the examinee's verbal and non-verbal behavior (behavior assessment) during the pretest interview which the FP uses as an adjunct to the visual inspection, analysis and in some cases quantification of the physiological data recorded on the polygraph charts for a *Global* evaluation. The examinee's behavior may be assessed with the use of a behavior checklist which when completed is compared with the findings obtained from the examinee's polygraph charts. Generally, when the two findings do not match, inconclusive findings are rendered. In fact, Richard O. Arther (1979), Director of the National Training Center of Lie Detection, stated "the correct observation and comparison of gestures will give me a pretest opinion that has approximately the same validity and reliability as does the polygraph." "It is up to me - as a polygraphist - to blend my pretest opinion and my chart analysis opinion into one final opinion as to the person's truthfulness." Hence the method is referred to as *Global* evaluation. The global evaluation is a psychological procedure which has been described by Dr. David L. Lykken (1981) as a *clinical assessment* rather than a *test*, hence named the Clinical Approach. However for ease of reporting and consistency in the description of the techniques by their authors, they will be referred to as tests. The inclusion of factual analysis and behavior assessment introduces a strong subjective element to the decision making process. While the Clinical Approach is subjective in its methodology, it nevertheless has enjoyed a high level of accuracy, at times exceeding ninety percent (Bersh 1969; Elaad & Schahar 1985; Murray 1989; Ryan 1989) in determining truth and deception when administered by properly trained, competent, and experienced forensic psychophysiologists.

As in the Numerical Approach, the Clinical Approach prohibits the use of accusatory or interrogative methods during the pretest interview or during the administration of the PV examination. (Arther 1982; Reid & Inbau 1977). However the use of behavior-provoking questions during the pretest interview is permitted and used in the Clinical Approach (Jayne in Abrams 1989). (See Chapter 9). Inasmuch as clinicians (Arther 1979) place equal importance on the examinee's verbal and non-verbal behavior as they do on the physiological data on the polygraph charts and use behavior-provoking questions during the pretest interview, the temptation to interrogate before the actual administration of the test charts may prove irresistible. This emphasizes the importance of having all PV examinations videotaped in their entirety to assure all parties that there were no procedural violations during the conduct of the examination which could have had an adverse psychophysiological effect on the polygraph chart data, which clinicians also must produce to support their findings. (See Chapter 9 and 23).

Within the Clinical Approach there are five techniques which are widely used and will be discussed herein. They are the Reid Technique, the Arther Technique, the Marcy Technique, the Modified Relevant-Irrelevant (MRI) technique, and the DoDPI General Question Test (GQT). Of the aforesaid techniques, only the Marcy technique and the MRI technique employ a quantification system that contains a *conversion table with cut-off scores to reach a conclusion*. However the *conversation table* is *Vertical* in that it tallies the scores vertically for each parameter or tracing, but does not add up the scores *horizontally* for a total of all the vertical scores inasmuch as each vertical score represents a different issue. The Clinical FP inspects and analyzes the physiological data using standardized chart interpretation rules (Reid & Inbau 1977). The Reid Technique uses a three-position numerical scale (+l 0 -1) as a means of visualizing response discrimination within each question, each parameter and each test, but no conversion table or established cut-off score is used in determining truth or deception (Jayne in Abrams 1989). The Arther technique uses a chart analysis form wherein each tracing is assigned a large check mark for the largest reaction, a medium size check mark for the next largest reaction, and a small check mark for the third largest reaction in that same tracing. Each tracing is marked in that manner to compel the FP to individually analyze the four polygraph tracings to each and every question and further determine the magnitude of every emotional change to each question and then compare it to the magnitude of all the other emotional changes in that test. The DoDPI General Question Test (GQT) permits the FP to analyze and evaluate the responses by visual observation only, without any assigned numerical value to any attribute, *or* to use a seven-position numerical scale as a means of visualizing response discrimination within each question, each parameter and each test. The Marcy Technique and the Modified Relevant-Irrelevant (MRI) Technique both use a seven-position numerical scale in a vertical scoring system containing a threshold (cut-off score) of plus or minus 3 for two/three charts for each relevant question which are compared against the control question exhibiting the greatest reaction. However, in the numerical evaluation of the pneumograph tracings, the Marcy technique scores both the thoracic and abdominal breathing patterns and thus affords the pneumograph tracings a 50% weight, the GSR 25% and the Cardio 25% in the numerical evaluation of the physiological chart data. (Decker 1996; Minor 1996)

Each of the aforesaid techniques have their own complex set of rules, methodology and unique test structure. Various types of control questions are used in aforesaid techniques for comparison with the relevant questions, such as the *Non-Exclusive* control question in the Reid and Arther techniques, the *Current Exclusive* control question used in the Marcy technique, the *Situational* control question in the Modified Relevant-Irrelevant (MRI) technique, and the *Disguised* control question in the DoDPI General Question Test (GQT). The definitions of those control questions, some of which were previously discussed during the description of the Numerical Approach, are set forth below in the description of the techniques which employ them. The *Psychological Set* theory and the *Anticlimax Dampening* concept previously described in the Numerical Approach apply equally to the Clinical Approach. The description of each technique set forth below is limited to the test structure and basic application.

The Reid Technique

In the Reid Control Question Technique a test is defined as a single reading of the test questions to the examinee during which time the examinee's physiology is being recorded. In the Reid technique there are six types of test: The Straight-Through Test (ST), the Stimulation Card Test (CT), the Mixed Question Test (MQT), the Silent Answer Test (SAT), the Yes Test (YT), the Guilt-Complex Test (GCT). Thus a psychophysiological veracity (PV) examination can encompass any or all of the aforementioned tests. Hence a Reid PV examination includes the pretest interview, the administration of all of the tests, the evaluation of the chart data and auxiliary data such as verbal and non-verbal examinee behavior and other appropriate data for a global evaluation resulting in an opinion of truth or deception. A post-test interview/interrogation is not part of the examination procedure. In the Reid Technique, all test questions are reviewed with the examinee prior to the administration of test.

Non-Exclusive Control Question: This control question, also known as the Reid control question, is formulated to be in the same category as the relevant question or issue. However this control question is not separated in time from the relevant issue nor does it exclude the crime or matter contained in the relevant question. Thus it is an inclusive control question but has been named by its employers as a Non-Exclusive control question.

Straight-Through Test (ST): This test consists of Irrelevant questions, Relevant questions, Non-Exclusive Control questions, asked in a sequential order but the examinee does not know the order of the test questions during the first test. Usually, the ST is administered as the first and third test of the series of tests used in the PV examination. The second test is the Stimulation Card Test (CT). Below is the sequence of the Straight-Through Test (ST):

1. (Irrelevant) 2. (Irrelevant) 3. (Relevant) 4. (Irrelevant) 5. (Relevant) 6. (Non-Exclusive Control) 7. (Irrelevant) 8. (Relevant) 9. (Relevant) 10. (Not Used) 11. (Non-Exclusive Control). All of the aforesaid test questions are presented to the examinee during the testing phase in the order depicted above. (Reid & Inbau 1977; APA Seminar 1981; Jayne in Abrams 1989)

Stimulation Card Test (CT): Usually administered as the second test, after the administration of the first Straight-Through Test (ST), the Stimulation Card Test is designed to increase the examinee's responsitivity thus increase question discrimination. The CT further assures both the Innocent and the Guilty examinee of the accuracy of the test, thus allaying the Innocent's fear of error regarding the target issue while increasing the Guilty's fear of detection regarding the target issue. The CT also invites the Guilty examinee to engage in acts of purposeful noncooperation and/or countermeasures. (Reid & Inbau 1977; Jayne in Abrams 1989)

The above Stimulation Card Test is classified as a *False Unknown-Solution Stimulation (FUSS) Test* inasmuch as the forensic psychophysiologist, unknown to the examinee, knows before the completion of the Stimulation Test which card number the examinee has selected, by prior manipulation of the cards. Brian Jayne (in Abrams 1989) explains "The reasons the examiner should know which card the subject selected before running the test is to take precautions against a subject who engages in acts of purposeful noncooperation that will render the charts uninterpretable or who lies about which card he or she selected from the deck."

However there are occasions when a *Known-Solution Stimulation (KSS) Test* involving no trickery wherein the card number is known to both the examinee and the FP with each other's knowledge, is preferred over the *False Unknown-Solution Stimulation (FUSS) Test*. The KSS should be administered for examinees of lower intelligence who may not comprehend the procedure and instructions of the FUSS, and examinees who have expressed suspicion towards the FP or the test. The procedure calls for the FP to present some numbers during the conduct of the CT that were not contained in the deck from which the examinee selected his/her card number. These additional numbers serve as a buffer at the beginning and in between the relevant numbers and further act as a counter-countermeasure device against the guilty examinee who may deliberately lie about which card he/she had selected. (Reid & Inbau 1977; Jayne in Abrams 1989).

Following the Stimulation Card Test, the second Straight-Through Test is administered as the third test in the series.

Mixed Question Test (MQT): Usually administered as the fourth test, after the second Straight-Through Test, the MQT employs the same test questions as the ST but they are presented on the test in a different order, and some of the questions are repeated with the prior knowledge of the examinee, as a means of increasing the threatening quality of the control questions for the Innocent examinee and the relevant questions for the Guilty examinee. The mixing of the test questions also allows for a variety of comparisons between the relevant and control questions, and purportedly aids in identifying a *spot responder*. The arrangement of the questions should be based on the type and location of responses which occurred during the prior tests. If there were reactions, for instance, to question number 3 and it was located in the first position, the reaction may have been caused by the fact that it was the first test question, thus it should be moved to another position and substituted with a question which elicited little or no response on the previous test. The typical sequence of the test questions for the MQT when three relevant questions are included is as follows: 7(I)-8(R)-2(I)-3(R)-6(C)-l(I)-5(R)-11(C)-8(R)-6(C). When four relevant questions are included, the following sequences are applicable: 7(I)- 9(R)-1(I)-3(R)-6(C)-5(R)-11(C)-2(I)-3(R)-6(C)-(8R-11C) and/or 7(I)-8(R)-4(I)-9(R)-6(C)-5(R)-11(C)-2(I)-3(R)-6(C)-(8R-11C). (Reid & Inbau 1977; Jayne in Abrams 1989).

Silent Answer Test (SAT): This test has the same test sequence as the Straight-Through Test (ST) and the examinee is informed that he/she will be asked the same questions as on his/her previous test and in exactly the order they were asked before. Furthermore the examinee is informed that he/she is not to answer orally any test questions, but must answer all test questions silently in his/her mind with only truthful answers. (Reid & Inbau 1977). The SAT has a stimulation effect on the examinee's response potential and eliminates answer distortions from obese examinees and those suffering from pulmonary disease. (Jayne in Abrams 1989). (See Chapter 19 for details).

<u>The Yes Test (YT):</u> This test is administered when the FP suspects or has evidence that the examinee has engaged in purposeful acts of noncooperation to distort his/her physiological chart recordings. By instructing the examinee to answer 'Yes' to all of the test questions, except for the two Non-Exclusive Control questions which are purposely omitted, any continued distortions on the Yes test will in most cases confirm the FP's suspicion that the examinee was engaged in purposeful acts of noncooperation or countermeasures. The control questions are omitted from the Yes test to assure the FP that if the examinee attempts to distort the test, he/she is doing so because of efforts to conceal his/her deception regarding the target issue. (Reid & Inbau 1977; Jayne in Abrams 1989).

<u>Guilt Complex Test (GCT):</u> This test, not to be confused with the Matte Control Question Validation (MCQV) test described in Chapter 14, is used primarily for overly responsive examinees, or when the examinee's behavior or factual analysis indicates truthfulness but the physiological data on the polygraph charts indicate deception; when the examinee exhibits equal responses to the relevant and control questions; or when the examinee exhibits pronounced emotions about the target issue during the pretest interview and the physiological chart data shows deception. The GCT is usually administered to overly sensitive examinees after their Mixed Question Test (MQT). Prior to the conduct of the GCT the examinee is advised that he will now be tested regarding another incident which he/she is led to believe is real, but in fact is a fictitious crime in the same category as the actual crime for which he/she is being examined. The GCT is then conducted with relevant questions dealing only with the fictitious crime. Following the GCT the examinee is then instructed that on the next test he/she will be asked questions about both incidents, which means that this test will include relevant questions regarding the fictitious crime juxtaposed with relevant questions regarding the actual crime. When an examinee shows equal response to both the guilt complex questions and the actual crime questions, it is recommended that a Mixed Question Guilt Complex (MQGC) test containing both the fictitious and actual crime relevant questions be administered, with one major change. The examinee is now advised that the guilt complex test questions are fictitious and they were used to further evaluate his/her responses on the test. If the examinee continues to show equal responses to the fictitious relevant questions as he/she does to the actual crime questions, then the results are reported as Inconclusive. (Reid & Inbau 1977; Jayne in Abrams 1989).

The Reid technique relies heavily on the judgment and interaction of the forensic psychophysiologist (FP) with the examinee during the examination. The role of the FP should be objective in the administration of the examination, and each assessment to include *factual analysis*, *behavioral analysis*, and *chart analysis*, must be mutually exclusive and independent from the others. (Jayne in Abrams 1989). In this global evaluation process, Reid & Inbau (1977) caution that while an examinee's behavior symptoms should be taken into consideration in arriving at a diagnosis of deception, if the recorded physiological data on the polygraph charts *very clearly* indicate deception, the physiological data should be given precedence over contrary behavior symptoms.

The Arther Technique

The Arther technique also known as the Arther Specific-Accusation Test, employs behavior analysis and chart analysis similar to the Reid technique in its decision-making process. When there is a conflict between the behavior analysis and the chart analysis, the subject is re-examined. Its chart analysis system uses various size check marks in a Chart Analysis Form depicted at the end of this discussion, to discriminate responses. The Arther test is composed of a series of normally ten test questions in a format depicted below: (Arther 1996)

Question Number	*Question Type*	*Question Example*
1	Irrelevant	Do you live in the United States?
3T	Known Truth	
3K/B	Knowledge	Do you know for sure who...
5	Relevant	
6	Non-Exclusive Control	During your entire life, even once did you ever...
8	Relevant	
8T	Known Truth	
9	Relevant	
10	Non-Exclusive Control	During your entire life, even once did you ever...
11	Irrelevant	Do you live in Canada?

The two non-exclusive control questions, number 6 and 10 contain sub-categories 6a, 6b and 10a, 10b each of which represent a different non-exclusive control question. The issue to be tested determines which control questions are used.

In the formulation of the control and relevant test questions, the Arther technique has criteria of Eight Known-Lie Question Principles, Four Golden Rules, and Ten Commandments (Arther 1983, 1984, 1996). They are listed and quoted as follows:

The Eight Known-Lie Question Principles:

1. The KLQ MUST be a question to which we can automatically presume a person lying.
2. A KLQ must NOT be a crime question.

3. The KLQ MUST be of lesser emotional impact than are the crime questions.
4. The KLQ MUST be generally worded.
5. The KLQ MUST be a question whose motive basically matches the motive of the crime question it follows.
6. The reason (justification) given to the person for using the KLQs MUST be thoroughly and properly explained during EVERY pretest interview.
7. During the pretest interview, the KLQs MUST be read verbatim to the person and he answers them exactly as he is going to answer them on the first test.
8. The KLQs MUST be as carefully chosen as are the crime questions.

The Four Golden Rules:

"I must always ask myself two questions regarding each and every crime question."

1. Should This Issue Even be Asked?
   Presuming the answer is "Yes" to the above question, then the Second Golden Rule takes effect:
2. Is The Proposed Crime Question Properly Worded?
   (In addition to the above two Golden Rules of Crime-Question Wording, there are two others:)
3. Every Crime Question Must be Emotionally Charged.
   An emotionally charged crime question is obtained in two ways:
   First: Using an "Explosive" Verb.
   Second: Keeping the Question Short.
   The main way to keep a question short is to eliminate prepositional phrases. Each prepositional phrase makes a question longer, can confuse the listener, and introduces a new case fact. If a prepositional phrase is truly needed, if possible limit it to just one and if possible have it at the beginning of the question.
4. Never Count Upon My Fantastic Pretest Interview to Make up for a Poorly Worded Crime Question.

The Ten Commandments:

1. Each crime question must deal with only *one issue*. Never use the words **and** or **or**.
2. Regardless of how the person answers, never ask a question that implies guilt. That is, never use as a crime question a "Are you still beating your wife?" type of question.
3. Never *unintentionally* ask a crime question that gives away the key to a good Known-Solution Peak-of-Tension test.

4. Remember that very likely at least some of the case facts may be wrong.
5. Is it possible that the liar can answer this crime question truthfully? If that issue is crucial and must be asked, try to limit the crime questions to just one question of this type.
6. Is it possible that a truthful person will lie to one of the proposed crime questions? If so, NEVER ask it! The reason is that some truthful have tried to "beat the lie detector" when such a question is asked, thus misleading the expert into thinking the person was lying.
7. Ask only four crime questions during any one session.
8. Word the questions so that they flow smoothly.
9. Make sure that even if the person had a minor part in the crime, he will be lying to at least one of the crime questions.
10. Each word used in every question must be completely understood by the person. The best way to assure that he understands is to use the very terms and verbs he used.

In the Arther technique, four crime questions is the number in any one polygraph test. Thus the four crime questions are asked in one series of questions; there is no second set of test questions with different crime questions. Typically, these four crime questions are asked on three separate tests. A Polygraph Sensitivity Test using colored cards (red, yellow, and yellow with a red dot), is administered shortly after the pretest interview begins and a different type of stimulus test, namely the Double Verification Test (DVT) which is a numbered card test, is administered between the first specific-accusation test and the second specific-accusation test.

In the formulation of the relevant (crime) questions, number 5 is the most important in that it deals with *primary* participation or *direct* involvement. 3K is the *knowledge* question and must deal exactly with the same specific issue as question number 5. The second most important relevant question is number 9 which deals with secondary participation. Relevant question number 8 deals with this particular person and his/her possible involvement in the crime. This question (8) can relate to the person's knowledge regarding the location of the stolen property or conspiracy to commit the crime. There are times when the knowledge question (3K) is not appropriate for the occasion, in which case it can be replaced with a fourth relevant (crime) question numbered 3B. After formulation of the relevant questions has been completed, the polygraphist should determine whether any of the crime questions reveal the *Key* which could be used in a Known-Solution Peak-of-Tension test. If affirmative then the polygraphist must ascertain whether that is the only *Key* available and whether or not it is critical. When in doubt, the crime questions take precedence over peak-of-tension tests. When formulating the aforesaid crime questions, the polygraphist should first make a list of six crime questions from which to choose from, in order to avoid missing an important issue. From these crime questions, the polygraphist narrows the list to those that meet the aforementioned criteria. (Arther 1984; 1996).

ARTHER'S KNOWN-LIE TEST
CHART ANALYSIS FORM

Using three different size check marks for all four tests and starting with each test's second question, check ONLY the two largest reactions in each recording of each test.

Do the DVT checks indicate that the examinee might be a spot responder? Y/N. (Circle Yes/No)
Is the breathing pattern the same in the PST as in the SATs? Y/N.
Is the breathing pattern the same in the DVT as in the SATs? Y/N.
During warm-up periods, when BP cuff is being inflated, and after cuff is deflated, is the breathing the same as in PST? Y/N. DVT? Y/N. SATs? Y/N.

		3T	3K/B	5	6	8	8T	9	10	11
	Chest-Breath	B	B	B	B	B	B	B	B	B
	Stomach-Breath	B	B	B	B	B	B	B	B	B
T-1	GSR	G	G	G	G	G	G	G	G	G
	Cardio	C	C	C	C	C	C	C	C	C
	Chest-Breath	B	B	B	B	B	B			
	Stomach-Breath	B	B	B	B	B	B			
DVT	GSR	G	G	G	G	G	G			
	Cardio	C	C	C	C	C	C			
	(3)	(5)	(7)	(8)	(10)	(13)	(15)			
	Chest-Breath	B	B	B	B	B	B	B	B	B
	Stomach-Breath	B	B	B	B	B	B	B	B	B
T-3	GSR	G	G	G	G	G	G	G	G	G
	Cardio	C	C	C	C	C	C	C	C	C
	Chest-Breath	B	B	B	B	B	B	B	B	B
	Stomach-Breath	B	B	B	B	B	B	B	B	B
T-4	GSR	G	G	G	G	G	G	G	G	G
	Cardio	C	C	C	C	C	C	C	C	C
FINAL OPINION (T, or L, or I)										

The Marcy Technique

The Marcy technique employs Current Exclusive Control questions (described below) in its test format. The first test is a Silent Answer Test (SAT) (See Chap. 19) in that the test concerning the relevant issue(s) is conducted with instructions for the examinee to think about the test questions but not to answer them out loud. The SAT is followed by a Stimulation test, usually a Known-Solution Stimulation (KSS) test (See Chap.10), then the third and fourth tests require the examinee to give a verbal answer (Verbal Answer Test - VAT) to the same test questions asked in the SAT. The physiological data in the

SAT is evaluated and included in the decision-making process along with the VAT. The Marcy technique also utilizes the 'Yes Test' (described in Reid Technique) and the 'True/Lie Sample Stimulation Test' when there is evidence that the examinee may be employing countermeasures during the VAT. The 'Yes Test' requires the examinee to answer all test questions with a 'Yes' answer. The 'True/Lie Sample Stimulation Test' requires the examinee to answer out loud truthfully first, and lie when the question is repeated. (See Chap. 2 and Chap. 5 for details). The Marcy test structure is depicted below:

<u>Current Exclusive Control Question:</u> This control question is formulated to be in the same category of offense or matter as the relevant question or issue. However, this control question is not separated in time from the relevant issue with the use of a time bar, thus it is considered a current control question. However, this control question does exclude the specific crime or matter contained in the relevant questions. Thus it is called a Current Exclusive Control Question. The Marcy technique employs the Clinical Approach which includes factual analysis, behavior assessment and chart analysis for a Global evaluation. Its chart analysis includes a seven-position numerical scale and a *vertical* conversion table with a cut-off score of plus or minus 3 for a minimum of 2 polygraph test charts.

Color Code	Question Number	Question Type	Question Description
Yellow	1	Irrelevant	Are you now in________? ("No" answer design)
Green	2T	Sacrifice/ Control	Have you now told me the absolute and complete truth about every single thing we talked about here today?
Red/Yellow	3	Relevant	Do you know who (Aimed at knowledge of ultimate issue perpetrator, including fact detail, dates, names, etc. Except, a detailed "withholding information" question where knowledge is not at issue.)
Yellow	4	Irrelevant	Are you now in_______? ("Yes" answer design)
Red	5	Relevant	Did you (Aimed at one element of the ultimate issue if bifaceted; or sequentially preliminary to the ultimate issue, as in "plan" or "try" to do the issue, for POT affect; or directly addressing the ultimate issue.)
Green	6	Current Exclusive Control	(Not connected with______) did you ever______?
Red	7	Relevant	Did you (Aimed at the other element of the ultimate issue if bifaceted; or addressing the ultimate issue directly.)
Yellow	8	Irrelevant	Are you now in_________? ("Yes" answer design)
Red/Yellow	9	Relevant	Do you know (Aimed at knowledge of identity, location, or disposition of evidence or persons to subsequent Exploratory POT testing; secondary

			evidence connection or secondary involvement as in "Present When")
Green	10	Current Exclusive Control	(Not connected with______) did you ever_______?
Red/Yellow	11	Relevant	Are you deliberately lying (to the investigator; the judge; to your attorney; to me) about any true facts in this case?
Black	12	Symptomatic	(If used, a Symptomatic Question of "Yes" answer design).
Yellow	13	Irrelevant	Are you now in ______? ("No" answer design).

Note: Question sequence modified in Verbal Answer Test (No. 3) by control question reversal; in Verbal Answer Test (No. 4) by question reversal of #13 and #7, and by restoration of the position of the Control questions as in SAT (No. l).(Marcy 1994 & 1995)

The Modified Relevant/Irrelevant (MRI) Technique

The original *Relevant-Irrelevant* technique known as the *Keeler* technique comprised a simple format of relevant questions interspersed with irrelevant questions. In its early evolution, emotionally charged questions such as a *personally embarrassing question* or a *surprise question* were introduced into the test structure to verify the examinee's capability of response, and as a form of control question, but were later abandoned due to their counterproductivity. However in 1980, Paul K. Minor modified the *Relevant/Irrelevant* (R/I) technique to include control questions of measured relevance to the target issue but not designed to cause an arousal. Instead, they serve as a vehicle to introduce the examinee to the issue in a logical interrogatory form and allow possible guilt feelings, anger, frustration, and so forth to be vented in areas other than at the direct relevant questions. These *relevant connected* questions referred to as *Situational Controls* provide a means for the truthful examinee to respond to the reasons he/she is tied to or associated to the target issue. These *Situational Control* questions provide a baseline of comparison that includes the excitement level of the target issue itself. This later modification of the R/I technique is thus known as the *Modified Relevant/Irrelevant (MRI) technique*. (Minor 1995, 1996).

The MRI technique employs the Clinical Approach which includes factual analysis, behavior assessment and chart analysis for a global evaluation. In its chart analysis, the MRI technique uses the seven-position numerical scale with a *vertical* conversion table with cutoff scores of plus or minus 3 for a minimum of two polygraph test charts. In the MRI technique, only the Irrelevant test questions are normally specifically reviewed with the examinee. The Relevant questions are asked during the course of the pretest interview but are not normally specifically reviewed word for word prior to the administration of the test. But there are no surprise test questions, that is a question regarding a topic that has not been discussed during the pretest interview. The test question progression should:

1. Identify the relevant issue (target).
2. Determine the examinee's relationship to the offense or event.
3. Explore examinee's suspicions.
4. Explore examinee's knowledge regarding the event.
5. Explore examinee's indirect involvement.
6. Explore examinee's direct involvement.

Because the laws in several states require the review of all test questions verbatim with the examinee prior to the administration of the test, the review of all questions is optional and has been deemed by authorities in the MRI technique not to have any adverse effect on the test. (Minor 1995, 1996)

MRI Test Structure:

Color Legend	Question Number	Question Type	Description/Example	Answer
Yellow	A	Irrelevant	Is your first name John?	Yes
Yellow	B	Irrelevant	Are you employed at the First National Bank of Buffalo?	Yes
Yellow/Red	1	Sacrifice/ Relevant	Do you intend to try to mislead me about anything during this examination?	No
Yellow/Green	2	Situational Control	Were you working at the First National Bank on 2 January 1996?	Yes
Yellow	3	Irrelevant	Are you now in the State of New York?	Yes
Green/Red	4	Situational Control	Did you report $5,000.00 missing from your bank on 2 January 1996?	Yes
Red/Green (Optional)	5	Situational Control	Do you suspect anyone in particular of stealing that money?	No
Yellow	6	Irrelevant	Do you live in the county of Erie?	Yes
Red	7	Relevant	Do you know for sure what happened to that missing money?	No
Red	8	Relevant	Did you steal any of that money?	No
Yellow	9	Irrelevant	Are you now in the State of New York?	Yes
Red (Optional)	10	Relevant	Do you know where the money is now?	No
Green/Yellow	11	Situational Control	Did you prepare in any way for this test?	No

The DoDPI General Question Test (GQT)

The Department of Defense Polygraph Institute's General Question Test (DoDPI GQT) is a modification of Keeler's Relevant/Irrelevant technique. It is useful when multiple issues need to be explored with a large number of suspects. It is also a useful technique when the forensic psychophysiologist is restricted to a non-control question technique, the examinee has been trained in forensic psychophysiology, or the examinee has been routinely polygraphed in the past. In DoDPI's GQT, formalized control questions in the form of Disguised Controls are used as the first and last test question. The DoDPI GQT uses Irrelevant questions (Yellow), Disguised control questions (Green), and Relevant questions (Red). No more than 13 questions per test with no more than three relevant questions in succession are used. The forensic psychophysiologist (FP) has the option of using global analysis wherein the attributes are observed by the FP utilizing only visual observation of the physiological data without any assigned numerical value to any attribute, but an outcome is declared, or the FP may use a numerical test data analysis employing a seven-position scale with a *vertical* conversion table containing a cutoff score of plus or minus 3 with a minimum of three test charts. The DoDPI GQT methodology is as follows: (DoDPI 1995)

Pretest Interview Phase:

1. The pre-test interview is adapted for an expanded discussion of general control material.
2. Relate disguised controls to background when collecting biographical data. (Integrity, honesty, parental upbringing, etc. - but be brief)
3. Introduction of relevant areas is accomplished by asking questions like "Why are you here?" and/or "Why have you been asked to take this PV examination?

Pretest Interview Phase Sequence:

1. Introduction. (Identification, Examination Suite & Overview).
2. Rights Form/Consent Form.
3. Biographical/Medical Information. (Lay foundation for disguised controls)
4. Explain PV examination procedure and what the instrument records.
5. Case facts review/discuss incident.
6. Review/discuss test questions.

Discussing Incident with Examinee: Review the crime with the examinee as if you were walking him/her through the *crime scene one step at a time.*

Test Question Review Sequence:

1. First disguised control: "Do you intend to lie to any of the questions on this test?"
2. All relevant questions.
3. All irrelevant questions.
4. Second disguised control: "Have you lied to me in any way since we have been talking today?" (Last Question Reviewed).

DoDPI GQT - Question Sequence Example:

Color Legend	Question Number	Question Type	Question Example
Irrelevant	A	Irrelevant	Is today Monday?
Irrelevant	B	Irrelevant	Is this the month of November?
Green	1	Disguised Control	Do you intend to lie to any of the questions on this test?
Red	2	Relevant (Plan)	Did you plan with anyone to steal any of that money?
Red	3	Relevant (Knowledge)	Do you know for sure who stole any of that money?
Yellow	C	Irrelevant	Is your first name Jim?
Red	4	Relevant (Primary)	Did you steal any of that money?
Red	5	Relevant (Secondary)	Do you know where any of that stolen money is now?
Green	6	Disguised Control	Have you lied to me in any way since we have been talking today?
Yellow (Optional)	D	Irrelevant	Is your last name Jones?

NOTE: An irrelevant question may be inserted in test as needed. The "Have you lied..." disguised control is *always* last or next to last question in format.

DoDPI GQT Data Collection Phase Rules:

1. No more than 13 questions per test, with no more than three relevant questions in succession.
2. Numerical analysis, if utilized, is the most significant reaction of each disguised control against all relevants. (Component-by-component tracing).
3. Length of the pretest is flexible.
4. Examinee is not told the order of the questions, *but all are reviewed.*
5. Three tests are collected at DoDPI.
6. Minimum of three but no more than five relevant questions per examination.
7. Relevant questions should "walk" examinee through the crime.
8. Different offenses may be asked in examination, however, they must be continuation of same crime (e.g., burglary & rape).
9. No sensitivity/pressure changes allowed after first disguised control is asked.
10. Relevants may be resequenced after first test; however, disguised control questions remain in same position for all three tests.
11. Stimulation (acquaintance) test is optional. *If conducted, it is the first test.*
12. All other DoDPI test question construction and operations rules apply.

Test Data Analysis:

Global Evaluation:

1. Reactions must be consistent, specific and significant.
2. Two out of three component tracings per test.
3. Two out of three askings of the relevant questions per examination.

Numerical Evaluation:

1. Most significant reaction of each disguised control question is compared against all relevants - component-by-component tracing, using a 7-position numerical scale.
2. A vertical conversion table containing a cutoff score of plus or minus 3 is used separately for each relevant question.
3. A minimum of three test charts will be conducted before an evaluation is made.

REFERENCES:

Abrams, S. (1989). *The Complete Polygraph Handbook.* Chapter 9, The Reid Control Question Technique, Brian C. Jayne. Massachusetts: Lexington Books.

Arther, R. O. (1984, November-December). How to correctly word crime questions. *The Journal of Polygraph Science*, XIX(3), 1-4.

Arther, R. O. (1983, March-April). How to word the known-lie questions. *The Journal of Polygraph Science*, XVII(5), 1-4.

Decker, R. E. (1981, August). Comparative technique flowchart and test structures. Handout material at Seminar/Workshop of the American Polygraph Association.

Decker, R. E. (1996, Mar 10). Telephone conversation with J. A. Matte

Department of Defense Polygraph Institute. (1995). DoDPI General Question Test (GQT).

Jayne, B. C. (1993). The use of alternative opinions in the polygraph technique. *Polygraph*, 22(4), 313-322.

Marcy, L. P. (1994, September 15). School Handouts of Marcy Technique. The American Institute of Polygraph Technology and Forensic Psychophysiology. 5 pages.

Marcy, L. P. (1995, January 30). Letter with 5 enclosures of polygraph school handouts to J. A. Matte.

Marcy, L. P. (1995, January 28). Telephone conversation with J. A. Matte.

Minor, P. K. (1995, January 10). Telephone conversation with J. A. Matte.

Minor, P. K. (1996, March 13). Telephone conversation with J. A. Matte regarding same date facsimile from J. A. Matte to P. K. Minor pertaining to MRI technique.

Reid, J. E., Inbau, F. E. (1977). *Truth and Deception: The Polygraph ("Lie-Detector") Technique*. 2d Ed. Baltimore: The Williams & Wilkins Company.

Chapter 16

A COMPENDIUM OF CONTROL QUESTIONS

In psychophysiological veracity (PV) examinations, control questions are generally used to absorb the anxieties of the truthful (as later verified) examinee and elicit or draw that examinee's psychological set away from the relevant questions contained in the same test. In control question tests, this is accomplished by formulating control questions that are designed to elicit a probable lie from the examinee to questions broadly similar to the crime or matter for which the examinee is being tested. Ideally, the control question should be structurally weaker than the relevant question against which it will be compared. A control question of equal strength as the relevant question could cause an inconclusive finding from a deceptive (as later verified) examinee who would find both test questions equally threatening. There are various types of control questions currently in use, depending on the technique employed in the PV examination. Also listed in this compendium are *disguised* control questions, *relevant connected* control questions, and *screening* control questions. The merits and usage of the control questions listed below are explained in Chapters 8, 9, 11 and 15. They are set forth below:

Non-Current Exclusive Control Question: This control question, also known as the Backster control question, is formulated to be in the same category of offense or matter as the relevant question or issue. However, this control question is *separated in time* from the relevant issue with the use of a *time bar*, thus it is considered an *earlier-in-life* (non-current) control question. Thus this control question *excludes* the period in which the crime was committed, usually by at least two years or more, hence it is a Non-Current Exclusive Control question.

Current Exclusive Control Question: This control question is formulated to be in the same category of offense or matter as the relevant question or issue. However, this control question is *not separated* in time from the relevant issue with the use of a time bar, thus it is considered a *current* control question. However, this control question does *exclude* the specific crime or matter contained in the relevant questions by using a prefix such as "Not connected with this (crime). Thus it is called a Current Exclusive Control Question.

Non-Exclusive Control Question: This control question, also known as the Reid control question, is formulated to be in the same category as the relevant question or issue. However this control question is *not separated* in time from the relevant issue *nor does it exclude* the crime or matter contained in the relevant question. Thus it is an *inclusive* control question but has been named by its employers as a Non-Exclusive Control Question.

Disguised Control Question: This type of test question is usually *general in nature* and relates to the examinee's truthfulness to the relevant test questions. As in DoDPI's General Question Technique (GQT), this type of question which inquires whether the examinee intends and/or has lied to any of the questions on the tests, is usually positioned as the first and/or last test question. While these test questions appear to be relevant questions, empirical data shows that due to their location on the test and the general nature of these questions, they elicit physiological responses from the Innocent as well as the Guilty (as later verified) examinee. (See Chapter 15 for details).

Screening Control Question: As in the Disguised Control Question, this type of test question is structured for use in General Question Tests, but they can be located almost anywhere within the test. They are designed to pose a dilemma and provoke mental exercise from the innocent (as later verified) examinee; e.g. "In the future, if you had a chance, would you steal from this company?" or "Would you lie to even one of these questions if you thought you could get away with it?"

Relevant Connected Control Question: This type of control question is formulated to appear as a relevant question by its connection to the relevant issue and the victim of the crime. However its usage is restricted to cases in which the examinee is acquainted with the victim. The relevant connected control question never overlaps the occurrence of the relevant issue. This type of control question asks the examinee whether he or she ever considered the same or similar behavior to that specified in the relevant questions, except that the examinee is not asked about having actually committed similar acts with the current victim. When specific names and/or dates are used in the relevant questions, these should be incorporated into the relevant connected control questions to equalize their impact whenever possible, but with an exclusionary phrase that removes the control question from the relevant incident or crime, such as "before that .... incident" or "without regard to that ....incident." (Wygant 1979)

NOTE: Except for the Disguised Control Question which is normally used in General Question Tests such as DoDPI's GQT, the above described control questions are generally used in Control Question Techniques such as the various Zone Comparison Techniques listed in Chapter 11, and the Reid, Arther, Marcy, and DoDPI Control Question techniques listed in Chapter 15. However there is one type of control question which is not listed in this compendium because its scope is limited and it is adequately described in Chapter 15. That is the *Situational Control Question* used in the Modified Relevant/Irrelevant (MRI) technique.

Except for the aforementioned Disguised and Screening Control Questions which are listed in this Compendium by their title (D & S respectively), the control questions listed in this compendium are categorized by the type of crime or incident in which they would be most effective and appropriate. Some control questions can be used in a number of different crimes or incidents, such as stealing, cheating and lying, thus will be repeatedly seen in several categories of crimes. The formulation of control questions is fully discussed in Chapter 8. However some helpful notes have been included in the various categories of control questions listed herein. Although the Non-Current Exclusive Control Question format is used in this compendium to described the control questions, they can be reformatted for use in the Current Exclusive Control Question format and the Non-Exclusive Control Question Format.

The abbreviated prefix **DYR** before each control question represents the words "Do You Remember" normally used in Non-Current Exclusive Control Questions.

The following control questions are formulated to be used as Non-Current Exclusive Control Questions. Non-current exclusive control questions use a *time bar* (not reflected below) followed by the words: Do you remember (**DYR**) ever: These non-current exclusive control questions can be reformulated to be used as non-exclusive control questions by omitting the *time bar*. Current Exclusive Control Questions substitute the *time bar* with the prefix "Not connected with this (crime)."

ALCOHOL

DYR ever drinking any alcoholic beverage? (includes whiskey, wine or beer)
DYR ever tasting an alcoholic drink?
DYR ever thinking of drinking an alcoholic beverage?
DYR ever driving a car after you had been drinking alcohol?
DYR ever driving a car while under the influence of alcohol?
DYR ever driving a car while you were drunk?
DYR ever getting sick from drinking any alcoholic beverage?
DYR ever drinking any alcoholic beverage before you were 21 years of age?
DYR ever drinking more than______since______? (Time and/or date)
DYR ever lying to anyone about your drinking?
DYR ever coming close to having an accident because you were drinking?
DYR ever having any alcoholic drinks since____? (date and/or time of last drink admitted)
DYR ever drinking any alcoholic beverages while working?

ARSON

DYR ever deliberately damaging any property?
DYR ever deliberately destroying any property?
DYR ever thinking about destroying any property and not go through with it?
DYR ever cheating on an insurance claim?
DYR ever thinking of starting a fire to cover a theft or loss?
DYR ever starting a fire for excitement?
DYR ever having the urge to start a fire?
DYR ever threatening to damage any property?
DYR ever destroying any property that did not belong to you?
DYR ever being fascinated by fire?
DYR ever doing anything destructive?
DYR ever committing any spiteful act?
DYR ever doing any vandalism of any kind?
DYR ever doing anything because you felt you couldn't resist doing it?
DYR ever masturbating while watching a fire?
DYR ever ejaculating while watching a fire?
DYR ever enjoying seeing a fire?

DYR ever lying to anyone in authority?
DYR ever making a false report?
DYR ever cheating on your income tax?
DYR ever cheating anyone out of anything?
DYR ever cheating by buying/selling goods you knew were stolen?
DYR ever cheating an employer out of anything?
DYR ever cheating an employer by maliciously destroying his property[9]

NOTE: Stealing (from someone who trusted you); intentionally defraud anyone in a deal; make good controls in arson cases

ASSAULT

DYR ever hurting someone?
DYR ever hurting someone who trusted you?
DYR ever hurting someone when you could have avoided it?
DYR ever hurting someone without (serious) provocation?
DYR ever hurting someone except for genuine self-protection?
DYR ever doing anything excessive or unreasonable in any dispute?
DYR ever endangering someone else by your own recklessness?
DYR ever creating any risk or injury to someone else by your own actions?
DYR ever provoking any dispute?
DYR ever taking up anything as a weapon in a dispute? (only if weapon involved in present case)
DYR ever wanting to hurt someone?
DYR ever deliberately hurting anyone?
DYR ever physically hurting anyone?
DYR ever threatening anyone with physical harm?
DYR ever doing something that would hurt someone?
DYR ever wanting to see someone get hurt?
DYR ever causing physical damage to anyone?
DYR ever doing anything to get aback at someone[9]
DYR ever hurting anyone by word or deed?
DYR ever wishing someone you knew would die?
DYR ever endangering someone else by your own recklessness?
DYR ever creating a risk of injury to someone else by your own actions?

HOMICIDE

Use of any of the above Assault controls plus the following:

DYR ever wishing someone were dead?
DYR ever thinking about what it would be like to kill someone?
DYR ever being so mad at someone that you wanted that person dead?
DYR ever being so mad at someone that you wanted to hurt him/her?

DYR ever thinking that you were capable of killing someone?
DYR ever being so angry that you momentarily lost control?

BRIBERY

Bribery control questions for persons in authority who overlook their sworn duty for some reward or compensation (government agents, policemen, judges, inspectors, licensing personnel, politicians and citizens who offer bribes or gratuities or who as employees take kickbacks or gratuities) Includes accepting a bribe, soliciting, blackmailing, offering, receiving, confidence game or kickbacks. Also gratuities of any description or amount. Control questions relating to fraud, cheating and stealing can also be used in this category.

DYR ever receiving a gratuity?
DYR ever giving a gratuity to anyone?
DYR ever receiving anything for doing a favor?
DYR ever giving anyone anything for doing a favor?
DYR ever being offered anything for doing a favor?
DYR ever asking for anything for doing a favor?
DYR ever giving anything to have a violation overlooked?
DYR ever receiving anything to overlook a violation?
DYR ever asking for anything to overlook a violation?
DYR ever offering anything to have a violation overlooked?
DYR ever receiving any money from any other source than your (job title) policeman's salary?
DYR ever tricking anyone out of anything?
DYR ever making a false official report?
DYR ever breaking any rules or regulations?
DYR ever doing anything that would jeopardize you position as a (job title) policeman?

BURGLARY

Controls used in Larceny and theft can also be used in burglaries, plus the following:

DYR ever going anyplace you weren't supposed to be?
DYR ever considering going in anyone's residence without permission? (residential burglaries only).

CHILDREN

DYR ever stealing anything?
DYR ever doing anything dishonest?
DYR ever doing anything bad in your life?
DYR ever doing anything wrong?
DYR ever doing anything mean?
DYR ever telling a lie? (parents, teacher, etc.)
DYR ever disobeying your parents? (teacher, etc.)

DYR ever taking anything not yours?
DYR ever lying to your parents or teacher about anything?
DYR ever doing anything you should have been punished for?
DYR ever doing anything to get even with somebody?
DYR ever blaming someone else for something you did yourself?
DYR ever cheating anyone? (games, tests, friends, or baby sitter, etc.)
DYR ever cheating anyone out of anything?
DYR ever doing anything without permission?
DYR ever hurting anyone/anything? (animal, insect, etc.)
DYR ever borrowing pencils or books without asking?
DYR ever doing anything that you wouldn't want your parents to find out?
DYR ever damaging property/things of others deliberately (on purpose)?
DYR ever writing or drawing pictures on walls or woodwork?
DYR ever committing a sin?
DYR ever copying the school work of others?
DYR ever breaking a rule? (boy scout, girl scout, school, club, etc.)
DYR ever breaking a law? (crossing street against the light, etc.)
DYR ever having a wet dream?
DYR ever being punished by your parents? An affirmative answer may establish the basis for a control question).
DYR ever lying about your age on the bus or movies?
DYR ever damaging property? (school, neighbors, etc.)
DYR ever skipping school?
DYR ever faking illness to skip school?
DYR ever forging your parent's name on your own report card?
DYR ever withholding a teacher's note from your parents?

CHILD SEX ABUSE CASES

DYR ever being sexually aroused by a child under 16 years of age?
DYR ever thinking of having sex with a child under the age of 16?
DYR ever taking sexual liberties with a child under the age of 16?
DYR ever thinking of having sex with anyone under the age of 16?
DYR ever thinking of engaging in a sex act with anyone under the age of 16?
DYR ever engaging in an unnatural sex act?
DYR ever feeling any improper sexual attraction for someone who was too young?
DYR ever taking sexual liberties with a child under the age of 16?
DYR ever doing anything sexually that you're ashamed of?

CONSPIRACY

DYR ever encouraging someone else to do something illegal?
DYR ever engaging in (any/serious) prohibited conduct with anyone else?
DYR ever being willingly involved in someone else's illegal act?
DYR ever putting personal loyalty above truthfulness?

DYR ever lying to cover for someone?
DYR ever figuring that any lie that helped you was excusable?
DYR ever lying about something when you thought it couldn't be proved?
DYR ever considering that lying was OK under certain circumstances?
DYR ever trying to blame some one else for your own mistake?
DYR ever trying to discredit someone in authority? (best use when there are claims of police misconduct).
DYR ever participating in any way in someone else's illegal act?
DYR ever lying to get yourself out of trouble?

CRIMINALS

Control questions for known criminals; persons who have been convicted of previous or current crime(s) which includes criminals on parole or probation. These control questions are predicated upon the belief that ex-convicts have committed previous undetected crimes. Furthermore, criminals on parole or probation are expected to have committed a minor violation of the parole or probation which if discovered could jeopardize their freedom, thus control questions encompassing such probable violations create effective controls. Career criminals seldom admit to any past crimes and often deny the commission of the crime for which they were most recently convicted.

DYR ever committing a crime?
DYR ever taking part in a crime?
DYR ever committing a crime you were not arrested for?
DYR ever committing a crime the police don't know about?
DYR ever committing a crime that was not found out by the police?
DYR ever lying in court?
DYR ever lying to the police?
DYR ever lying to anyone in authority? (Police, Judge, Warden, Parole/Probation Officer).
DYR ever selling any stolen goods?
DYR ever selling any goods that you knew were stolen?
DYR ever committing any crime since you got out of jail? (prison)
DYR ever violating parole?
DYR ever violating your probation?
DYR ever entering a building without permission?
DYR ever stealing a large amount of money?
DYR ever stealing a large amount of merchandise?
DYR ever thinking of robbing a bank?
DYR ever stealing by threatening someone?
DYR ever committing more than_____burglaries?
DYR ever committing more than_____robberies?
DYR ever buying any stolen goods?
DYR ever breaking any law?
DYR ever committing a crime you were not arrested for?

DYR ever committing any undetected crime?

EMPLOYMENT

Control questions relating to employment (malicious & negligent acts)

DYR ever thinking of getting even with your boss?
DYR ever breaking any company rules or regulations?
DYR ever taking credit (pay) for work you did not do?
DYR ever purposely destroying any company property or equipment?
DYR ever going into a work area you were not supposed to go?
DYR ever thinking of breaking or losing equipment so you didn't have to work?
DYR ever horseplaying on the job?
DYR ever doing anything on your job you cold be fired for?
DYR ever trying to get even with another employee?
DYR ever being jealous of another employee?
DYR ever wasting any good materials at the company[9]
DYR ever thinking of selling any company property?
DYR ever purposely goofing off on the job?
DYR ever purposely throwing away any good company material?
DYR ever thinking of breaking a security rule?
DYR ever revealing any business secrets to anyone?
DYR ever stealing anything from a place where you worked?
DYR ever cheating your employer out of anything?
DYR ever doing anything you could be fired for?
DYR ever lying about anything in your job application?
DYR ever receiving a kickback from anyone?
DYR ever giving a kickback to anyone?
DYR ever asking for a kickback from anyone?
DYR ever receiving a gratuity from a company supplier?
DYR ever padding an expense account?
DYR ever cheating a customer out of anything?
DYR ever cheating your employer (company) on any deal (sale or purchase)?
DYR ever arranging (conspiring) with anyone to cheat your company?
DYR ever suggesting to anyone how to cheat your company (employer)?
DYR ever making a false report to your company (employer)?
DYR ever misrepresenting the facts in any deal?

FIDELITY

DYR ever engaging in an unnatural sex act?
DYR ever engaging in illicit sexual activity?
DYR ever being unfaithful to someone who trusted you?
DYR ever violating the trust of someone who loved you?

DYR ever doing anything sexually that you are ashamed of?

FRAUD

Fraud includes cheating, arson for financial gain, bribery, conspiracy, confidence game, counterfeiting, entrapment, embezzlement, extortion, homicide for financial gain, libel and slander, selling alcohol to minors, narcotics seller or buyer.

Definitions:

Malicious mischief - Deliberate destruction of personal property due to resentment or ill will toward owner or occupant.

Misfeasance - The doing of a lawful act in an unlawful manner.

Malfeasance - Wrongdoing or misconduct, especially in handling public affairs..

Non-feasance - Failure to do what duty requires to be done.

DYR ever cheating anyone out of anything?
DYR ever making a false report?
DYR ever lying about anyone?
DYR ever tricking anyone out of anything?
DYR ever lying to anyone in authority? (Judge, police, member of clergy, teacher, parent, warden, parole or probation officer, etc.)
DYR ever cheating on your income tax returns?
DYR ever misrepresenting the facts in any deal?
DYR ever cheating by lying to someone?
DYR ever being unfaithful to your wife? (husband, girl/boy friend, parent, employer, friend, country, etc.)
DYR ever buying any goods you knew were stolen?
DYR ever knowingly selling any liquor to a minor? (bartenders)
DYR ever writing a check knowing there was not enough funds in the bank?
DYR ever making a false bookkeeping entry?
DYR ever cheating anyone out of anything while gambling?
DYR ever cheating your wife and/or children by using necessary money for gambling?
DYR ever cheating a person out of his reputation by spreading false rumors?
DYR ever trying to fix a traffic ticket?
DYR ever offering a policeman money to be freed on a traffic violation?
DYR ever cheating on an insurance claim?
DYR ever attempting to cheat an insurance company?
DYR ever cheating by paying a bribe?
DYR ever cheating by keeping a kitty? (bank tellers)
DYR ever cheating by borrowing money or goods without authorization?
DYR ever cheating by buying goods you knew were stolen?
DYR ever cheating by selling goods you knew were stolen?

DYR ever cheating by using someone else's credit card?
DYR ever cheating by violating your probation? (Parole?)
DYR ever dealing in illegal goods?
DYR ever buying any goods you thought were stolen?
DYR ever being asked as a cab driver to arrange for a prostitute? (prior employer)
DYR ever cheating a passenger out of any money? (prior employer)
DYR ever cheating the cab company out of any money? (prior employer)
DYR ever thinking of cheating an insurance company out of anything?
DYR ever thinking of starting a fire to cover a theft or loss?
DYR ever lying to get out of a social obligation?
DYR ever listening in on someone else's conversation?
DYR ever cheating an employer out of anything?
DYR ever cheating a customer out of his change?
DYR ever making any false entries on the company records?
DYR ever taking credit (money) for work you did not do?
DYR ever cheating a boss by using a false excuse for tardiness or absence?
DYR ever cheating an employer by taking gratuities or kickbacks from suppliers?
DYR ever cheating an employer by lying on a job application?
DYR ever cheating an employer by padding expense accounts?
DYR ever cheating an employer out of time?
DYR ever cheating an employer out of his property?
DYR ever giving an unauthorized discount?.
DYR ever cheating the government by unauthorized moonlighting?
DYR ever using any government property illegally?
DYR ever accepting a bribe? (as a civil servant)
DYR ever cheating an employer by the malicious destruction of company property?
DYR ever cheating an employer out of time by falsification of a time card?
DYR ever having another employee falsify our time card?
DYR ever cheating a customer out of any money? (bartender, waiter/waitress, cashier)
DYR ever cheating the company by sleeping on the job?
DYR ever breaking any rules or regulations? (any act of non-feasance, misfeasance or malfeasance).
DYR ever allowing a customer to steal from the company?
DYR ever purposely destroying any company records?
DYR ever doing anything that would cause you to lose your job?
DYR ever cheating anyone by having sex with their spouse?
DYR ever cheating on your wife? (husband)
DYR ever cheating by watering down drinks?
DYR ever stealing anything?
DYR ever stealing anything from a place where you worked?
DYR ever borrowing money from any of your accounts?
DYR ever thinking of stealing a large amount of money from your employer?
DYR ever falsifying any company records?

GENERAL - UNIVERSAL

DYR ever stealing anything?
DYR ever cheating anyone?
DYR ever deliberately hurting anyone by word or deed?
DYR ever taking advantage of someone who trusted you?
DYR ever lying to someone who trusted you?
DYR ever blaming someone for something you did?
DYR ever breaking the law?
DYR ever telling a lie of importance?
DYR ever telling a serious lie?
DYR ever lying to get yourself out of trouble?
DYR ever lying to anyone in authority?
DYR ever lying to stay out of trouble?
DYR ever going anything that made you feel guilty?
DYR ever stealing anything from a placed where you worked?
DYR ever cheating anyone out of anything?
DYR ever lying to a person in authority? (Judge, policeman, school teacher, preacher, parent)
DYR ever breaking any rules or regulations?
DYR ever intentionally breaking the law?
DYR ever doing any illegal act?
DYR ever doing anything dishonest?
DYR ever committing a sin?
DYR ever withholding any information from your spouse? (parents, police, priest, judge)
DYR ever being ashamed of any of your acts?
DYR ever being jealous of anyone?
DYR ever committing a crime?
DYR ever lying about anyone?
DYR ever lying to your spouse?
DYR ever doing anything you could be arrested for?
DYR ever hurting anyone?
DYR ever damaging any property?
DYR ever starting an argument?
DYR ever thinking of trying to get even with anyone?
DYR ever doing anything you could be fired for?
DYR ever doing anything that would cause you to lose your job?

HOMICIDE (Murder)

DYR ever wishing someone were dead?
DYR ever thinking about what it would be like to kill someone?
DYR ever being so mad that you momentarily lost control?
DYR ever deliberately hurting anyone?
DYR ever deliberately hurting anyone physically?
DYR ever thinking of killing someone and not do it?

DYR ever wishing any person you knew would die?
DYR ever threatening any person with physical harm?
DYR ever wanting to see someone get hurt?
DYR ever doing anything that would hurt someone?
DYR ever thinking of destroying anybody?
DYR ever causing physical damage to anyone?

LARCENY

Control questions used in crimes involving dishonesty may include many control questions listed under the categories of Fraud, Criminals and General-Universal. Generally, the "steal" control question is most appropriate in larceny cases.

DYR ever stealing anything?
DYR ever thinking of stealing anything from a store?
DYR ever keeping a cash overage?
DYR ever failing to charge a customer for anything?
DYR ever giving someone an authorized discount?
DYR ever padding your expense account?
DYR ever thinking of stealing a large amount of money from your employer?
DYR ever falsifying any company records?
DYR ever setting any merchandise aside with the intention of stealing it?
DYR ever stealing anything from someone who trusted you?
DYR ever stealing anything from someone who loved you?
DYR ever stealing anything from someone you loved?

MALICE

Malicious, revengeful, negligent or mischievous acts, usually for personal satisfaction rather than personal gain, includes: assault, battery, brutality not sex related to sadism, negligent conduct, sabotage, libel or slander, malicious mischief and vandalism, also malfeasance and non-feasance.

Cheating and stealing control questions may also be used in addition to the control questions listed below:

DYR ever destroying any property?
DYR ever thinking of damaging (destroying) any property (anything)?
DYR ever doing anything to get back at someone?
DYR ever threatening anyone with physical harm?
DYR ever lying to a public official? (Judge, policeman)
DYR ever lying to anyone in authority? (Judge, police, teacher, parent, priest)
DYR ever threatening to damage any property?
DYR ever hurting anyone?
DYR ever wanting to see someone get hurt?

DYR ever hitting anyone?
DYR ever starting an argument?
DYR ever starting a fight?
DYR ever doing anything that could hurt someone?
DYR ever hitting anyone with a hard object during a fight?
DYR ever lying about facts in any deal?
DYR ever thinking of causing physical damage to anyone (property)?
DYR ever destroying any property that did not belong to you?
DYR ever trying to ruin someone to better your own position?
DYR ever saying anything about anyone that was not true?
DYR ever lying about anyone?
DYR ever thinking of getting even with anyone?

NARCOTIC

This type of control question includes primarily "users" and "sellers" also known as "Peddlers or pushers." If the examinee scheduled for a PV examination is a narcotic addict, it is advisable to use control questions related to drugs or narcotics. Otherwise control questions from the "cheat or steal" category or the standard control questions listed below can be used:

DYR ever doing anything against the law?
DYR ever doing anything you could be arrested for?
DYR ever lying to anyone about using drugs?
DYR ever using any drugs illegally?
DYR ever thinking of using any illegal drugs?
DYR ever using any narcotics since you got out of jail?
DYR ever smoking marihuana more than___times? (use the number of time admitted)
DYR ever using any narcotics since____? (date of last use admitted by subject)
DYR ever getting sick from using drugs?
DYR ever getting "high" from using drugs?
DYR ever missing work because of using drugs?
DYR ever taking any medication without a doctor's authorization? (medical prescription)
DYR ever smoking anything containing a drug?
DYR ever inhaling anything containing a drug?
DYR ever smoking (using) marihuana?
DYR ever using any narcotics? (illegally)
DYR ever using any drugs since you've been on parole? (probation)
DYR ever selling any drugs illegally? (Pharmacist or assistant)
DYR ever doing anything which would cause you to lose your license? (for pharmacists, bar/night club owners, bartenders, theater owners).
DYR ever being more involved with drugs than what you told me?
DYR ever dealing (selling) drugs for a profit?
DYR ever considering yourself a drug dealer?
DYR ever selling any drugs when it was more than just a favor to a friend?
DYR ever considering selling any addicting drugs?

DYR ever doing anything illegal to make money?
DYR ever selling anything illegal for a profit?
DYR ever deliberately hurting anyone?
DYR ever thinking of selling narcotics?
DYR ever buying any drugs illegally?
DYR ever trying to get someone to smoke marihuana?
DYR ever trying to get someone to use illegal drugs?
DYR ever lying to anyone about smoking marihuana (or using illegal drugs)?
DYR ever falsifying an official report? (pharmacist)

PATERNITY

Paternity suit: Involves bastard children; children born out of wedlock.

It is unnecessary to confine the control questions in this category to sex questions for either the complainant (mother) or the defendant (the suspected father).

Control questions relating to lying, cheating or stealing are proper, but general sex type control questions can also be used.

For the defendant: The control questions should not be related with sexual intercourse with the *complainant* at any other time, since this can be a relevant issue. The above suggested types of control questions (lying, cheating, stealing, etc.) are more appropriate.

For the complainant (mother):

DYR ever having sexual intercourse more than___times during that period?
DYR ever having sexual intercourse with more than___men during that period?(Use the number the subject admitted as the basic question).
DYR ever having sexual intercourse with any man other than the (defendant) during (period of conception)?

POLICE - INTERNAL

DYR ever making any kind of false report about any incident?
DYR ever violating any department rules or policies?
DYR ever doing anything while on duty that you knew you shouldn't have done?
DYR ever lying about your own conduct while on duty?
DYR ever trying to cover up improper conduct by any other officer?
DYR ever abusing your authority as a police officer?
DYR ever doing anything while on duty for which you could have been disciplined?
DYR ever using excessive force in effecting an arrest? (when brutality is the issue).
DYR ever violating a suspect's rights in effecting an arrest?
DYR ever using improper methods in effecting an arrest?
DYR ever tampering with evidence?
DYR ever fabricating evidence?

DYR ever destroying evidence?
DYR ever using a police vehicle for unauthorized purposes?
DYR ever leaving your police weapon in an unsecured place?
Also:
DYR ever telling a serious lie?
DYR ever lying to get yourself out of trouble
DYR ever making a false or inaccurate statement?
DYR ever lying to anyone in authority?

PROPERTY

DYR ever damaging anyone's property to get even?
DYR ever damaging anyone's property?
DYR ever encouraging someone else to do anything illegal?
DYR ever enticing someone else to commit an illegal act?
DYR ever being involved in someone else's illegal act?
DYR ever engaging in an illegal act with someone else?

RAPE

For additional control questions see SEX offenses.

Review the following possible controls in the order of the most severe first, to the last severe, and use the control that elicits a negative answer.

DYR ever forcing anyone to have sex with you?
DYR ever trying to have sex with a woman against her will?
DYR ever continuing beyond genuine objections to your sexual advances?
DYR ever thinking of forcing someone to have sex with you?
DYR ever considering forcing a woman to have sex with you?

Also may use the following:

DYR ever engaging in an unnatural sex act?
DYR ever doing anything sexually that you're ashamed of?

RELEVANT CONNECTED CONTROLS

General:
If you committed this crime, should you get the maximum sentence?
Should the person who stole that $________ receive the maximum sentence?
Do you feel that the person who committed this crime is mentally ill?
If this test shows you to be guilty of this________________,should you be severely punished?

Larceny:
Before you worked for Acme, **DYR** ever stealing anything from an employer?
Before last week's theft, **DYR** ever considering stealing anything from Acme?

Assault:
Excluding Joe's complaint, **DYR** ever doing anything excessive or unreasonable in a dispute?

Murder:
Without regard to Martha, **DYR** ever being so mad at someone you wanted them dead?
Before Martha's (victim) death, **DYR** ever being seriously angry with her?

Rape:
Without regard to Robert (alleged rapist), **DYR** ever teasing a man sexually?

ROBBERY

DYR ever stealing anything?
DYR ever deliberately hurting anyone?
DYR ever thinking of robbing someone?
DYR ever doing something that would hurt someone?
DYR ever causing physical harm to anyone?
DYR ever threatening anyone with physical harm?
DYR ever deliberately hurting someone physically?
DYR ever threatening anyone with a weapon?
DYR ever forcing anyone to do anything they didn't want to do?
DYR ever considering using force to get what you wanted?
DYR ever taking anything from anyone by force?
DYR ever figuring it was all right to use force to get what you wanted?
DYR ever threatening anyone to get them to do something?
DYR ever using a threat to get what you wanted?
DYR ever taking up anything as a weapon against another person?

SCREENING CONTROLS

Were you born in the United States?

Would you lie to even one of these questions if you thought your job depended on it?

Did you ever use any name besides what you told me?

Excluding this application, **DYR** ever making any misrepresentation in an attempt to get any job?

Excluding this application, **DYR** ever falsifying information on a job application?

Excluding this application, **DYR** concealing information about:
your gambling? your drinking? your use of illegal drugs? your traffic violations record? your education and training? your honesty with previous employers? your military service record? any dishonest acts you may have committed? any theft from any employer? any shoplifting you may have committed?

DYR ever justifying to yourself an actual theft you had committed?
DYR ever figuring that stealing was all right?
DYR ever considering doing anything illegal to get goods or money?
DYR ever buying or selling anything you suspected was stolen?
DYR ever taking or receiving anything you weren't entitled to?
DYR ever doing something for which you could lose your job?

SEX CONTROLS

Sex control questions are used only instances where the *relevant issue* involves the commission of a sex act (i.e. rape, child molestation, sexual assault) or the incident or crime is sexually motivated (e.g. some cases of arson, homicide).

DYR ever maturbating?
DYR ever having sexual contact with anyone?
DYR ever taking part in an unnatural sex act?
DYR ever thinking of having anything to do sexually with anyone?
DYR ever thinking of touching a girl's private parts?
DYR ever playing with your private parts?
DYR ever sexually touching your own naked body?
DYR ever having a wet dream?
DYR ever sexually touching your private parts while looking in a mirror?

When the *sex offense* is committed by someone of the same sex, the following control questions are quite appropriate.

DYR ever taking part in an act of sexual perversion?
DYR ever masturbating?
DYR ever taking part in an unnatural sex act?
DYR ever thinking of yourself taking part in a homosexual act?
DYR ever being approached by a man for sexual relations?
DYR ever taking part in a homosexual act?
DYR ever taking part in a 69 act with any other man?
DYR ever desiring a sex act with another man?
DYR ever approaching a male for sexual relations?
DYR ever taking an active part in a homosexual act?
DYR ever taking the passive part in a homosexual act?
DYR ever sexually kissing another man on the lips?
DYR ever fondling another man's penis?
DYR ever masturbating another man?

DYR ever taking part in a mutual masturbation?
DYR ever sexually contacting another man?
DYR ever putting your penis between another man's legs?
DYR ever touching another man's penis?
DYR ever putting your penis against another man's buttocks?
DYR ever putting on any female clothing?
DYR ever putting your penis in a man's rectum?
DYR ever putting another man's penis in your rectum?
DYR ever allowing another man to put his penis in your rectum?
DYR ever allowing another man to kiss your penis?
DYR ever taking a man's penis in your mouth?
DYR ever thinking of having sex with a young boy?
DYR ever having sexual contact with anyone?
DYR ever trying to force another person (male or female) to have sex with you?
DYR ever thinking of having sex with anyone other than your wife?
DYR ever trying to have anything to do sexually with a girl against her will?
DYR ever touching a girl sexually against her will? (kissing, etc.)
DYR ever being tempted to touch a strange girl?
DYR ever exposing your penis to anyone?
DYR ever taking part in an unnatural sex act? (cunninlingus, fallatio, sodomy, bestiality, etc.)
DYR ever having anything to do sexually with any girl under the age of 16? (use the highest age possible that the subject denies having sexual contact.)
DYR ever looking into someone else's window for sex purposes?
DYR ever thinking of having sex with a prostitute?
DYR ever peeping in a bedroom window?
DYR ever thinking of having sex with a young girl?
DYR ever wanting to have sex with any other woman besides your wife?
DYR ever taking indecent liberties with anyone?
DYR ever committing adultery?
DYR ever taking part in an act of fornication?
DYR ever taking part in a 69 act with anyone?
DYR ever feeling a girl's breast?

In *sex offense* cases, *engaging in an unnatural sex act* is often used as a control question, and can be described as a sex act contrary to regular sexual intercourse between a male and female. Includes: cunninlingus, fallatio, sodomy, bestiality, exhibitionism, transvestism, masochism, flagellation, sadism.

DYR ever masturbating? (Jack oft)
DYR ever taking part in an unnatural sex act?
DYR ever having anyone masturbate you?
DYR ever putting your finger in a girl's vagina?
DYR ever putting your tongue in a girl's privates?
DYR ever having anyone take your penis into their mouth?
DYR ever putting your penis in a person's rectum?

DYR ever taking part in a 69 act with anyone?
DYR ever having anything to do sexually with an animal?
DYR ever rubbing your penis against another person in a crowd?
DYR ever having a deep passion to rub someone's hair?
DYR ever rubbing your penis against the buttocks of a woman (man) in a crowd?
DYR ever exposing your privates to a female (male) who was a stranger to you?
DYR ever witnessing a sex act between other persons?
DYR ever inserting anything into your anus for sexual purposes?
DYR ever playing with your penis secretly in someone else's presence?
DYR ever having anything to do sexually with a child under 14?
DYR ever putting on female clothing for sexual purposes?
DYR ever stealing anything? (theft of female items for sex purposes).

Female subjects do not ordinarily offend sexually, but often are the victims. Therefore, generally, cheat and steal controls can be used. See cheat and steal.

DYR ever inviting any sexual advancements from any man?
DYR ever flirting with a man?
DYR ever gossiping about anyone?
DYR ever reading someone else's mail? (diary)
DYR ever thinking of having sex with any man? (besides your husband? if married).
DYR ever thinking of dating any other man besides your husband?
DYR ever teasing a man for sexual purpose?
DYR ever teasing a man to have sex with you?
DYR ever being sexually jealous of another woman?
DYR ever sexually kissing another woman?
DYR ever thinking about cheating on your husband?
DYR ever masturbating?
DYR ever being unfaithful to your husband?
DYR ever thinking of divorcing your husband?
DYR ever thinking of killing your husband?
DYR ever committing adultery?
DYR ever having sexual intercourse? (unmarried)
DYR ever having sexual contact with anyone? (unmarried)\
DYR ever trying to "make" any man?
DYR ever taking part in an unnatural sex act?
DYR ever considering forcing any girl/woman/female to (submit to sex/do something sexual)?
DYR ever fantasizing about forcing sex on a stranger? (if victim was a stranger)
DYR ever figuring it was all right to force sex on a certain kind of girl/woman?
DYR ever ignoring a girl's/woman's resistance to (sex/sexual contact)?
DYR ever doing something sexual because you couldn't resist it?
DYR ever feeling any improper sexual attraction for someone too young? (child victim only)
DYR ever having sexual interests that were anything other than normal (for that age)?

DYR ever doing anything sexual that most other men/women the same age would not do?
DYR ever doing something sexual that (was/others would consider) improper for that age?
DYR ever doing something sexual that others would consider excessive?
DYR ever doing something sexual (alone or with another) that you didn't want your wife/husband to know about?
DYR ever handling your own body or another's in an improper sexual way?
DYR ever wanting to have sex with a man (woman) whose name you didn't know?
DYR ever attempting to encourage the interests of a man other than your husband?
DYR ever (dressing/appearing in public) in a way intended to arouse sexual interest?
DYR ever teasing a man sexually?
DYR ever considering forcing a girl/woman to (submit to sex/do something sexual?)
DYR ever forcing any kind of sexual contact/attention on anyone?
DYR ever fantasizing about forcing sex on a stranger? (if victim was a stranger)
DYR ever figuring it was all right to force sex on a girl/woman?
DYR ever ignoring a girl's/woman's resistance to sex?
DYR ever doing something sexual because you couldn't resist it?
DYR ever feeling any improper sexual attraction for some one too young? (See Children Victim).
DYR ever having sexual interests that were anything other than normal for that age?
DYR ever committing any sex act that most other men/women (that age) would not do?
DYR ever doing something sexual that (was/others would consider) improper for that age?
DYR ever masturbating?
DYR ever engaging in any unusual sex activity?
DYR ever having sexual intercourse with anyone other than your husband/wife since your marriage?
DYR ever doing something sexual that others would consider excessive?
DYR ever doing something sexual (alone or with another) that you didn't want your wife/husband to know about?
DYR ever having a desire to have someone watch you in a sex act? (exposure cases)
DYR ever wanting to have sex with a man whose name you didn't know?
DYR ever attempting to encourage the interests of a man other than your husband/boyfriend? **DYR** ever (dressing/appearing in public) in a way intended to arouse sexual interest?
DYR ever teasing any man sexually?

VICTIMS

DYR ever lying about anything important?
DYR ever lying to protect yourself?
DYR ever lying to protect someone else?
DYR ever lying to save yourself embarrassment?
DYR ever lying to cover a mistake?
DYR ever making an erroneous statement and afraid to admit you made a mistake?

DYR ever making an inaccurate statement and afraid to admit it because it would make you look like a fool?
DYR ever blaming someone for something you did?
DYR ever lying to anyone in authority?
DYR ever hurting anyone by word or deed?
DYR ever cheating anyone out of anything?
DYR ever lying about anyone?
DYR ever cheating on an insurance claim?
DYR ever thinking of cheating an insurance company out of anything?
DYR ever making a false claim to an insurance company?

REFERENCES

Abrams, S. (1989). The Complete Polygraph Handbook. Lexington, MA: Lexington Books, D. C. Heath and Company.

Decker, R. E. (1995). Training materials; USAMPS Polygraph Training School.

Department of Defense Polygraph Institute (1995). DoDPI General Question Test (GQT).

Marcy, L. P. (1994, September 15). School Handouts of Marcy Technique. The American Institute of Polygraph Technology and Forensic Psychophysiology. 5 pages.

Matte, J. A. (1982). Training Materials; Matte Institute of Polygraph Science.

Minor, P. K. (1995, January 10). Telephone conversation with J. A. Matte.

Reid, J. E., Inbau, F. E. (1977). *Truth and Deception: The Polygraph ("Lie-Detector")* 2d Ed. Baltimore, MD: The Williams & Wilkins Company.

Wygant, J. (1979). The relevant-connected control. *Polygraph*, 8(1), 309-324.

Chapter 17

THE MATTE S-K-G TEST AND THE BACKSTER S-K-Y TEST

The Matte Suspicion-Knowledge-Guilt Test, hereafter referred to as the S-K-G test, and the Backster Suspicion-Knowledge-You Test hereafter referred to as the S-K-Y test were designed to provide the forensic psychophysiologist with a single test capable of identifying the examinee(s) who has major involvement, some direct involvement, or guilty knowledge, yet containing similar controls to that found in the Matte Quadri-Track Zone Comparison Technique and the Backster Tri-Zone Comparison Technique respectively. (See Chapter 2 for the history of S-K-Y and S-K-G Tests). The S-K-G will be described first, followed by the S-K-Y test.

The Matte S-K-G Test

The S-K-G test is usually administered in instances where a group of people are scheduled for examination to determine guilty knowledge as well as the identity of the perpetrator(s) of an offense. This test serves to eliminate those persons with no direct or indirect involvement and identify those persons who do by category. The forensic psychophysiologist can then use the results of the S-K-G test to determine whether the Matte Quadri-Track Zone Comparison Technique with its numerical scoring system of chart analysis should be administered to support findings of major or direct involvement, conduct a Known-Solution Peak of Tension Test (see Chapter 18) or simply interrogate if S-K-G test results indicate guilty knowledge only. Interrogation should not be conducted on the basis of S-K-G test results alone where major or direct involvement is indicated because, although the test deals with only one offense, several targets are covered with only one control (probable-lie) question available for comparison. It must be remembered that a psychophysiological veracity (PV) examination is limited in duration due to the medical cuff pressure, which is constant against the examinee's upper arm, therefore a PV examination is limited in duration to a maximum of twelve questions whenever a medical cardio cuff is used. Use of electrically enhanced cardiographs does not alleviate this limitation because a minimum of 60 mm of pressure is still required in most cases to obtain an efficient tracing and valid, reliable results. Use of the cardio activity monitor (CAM) over the radial artery at the wrist or the thumb, while more comfortable and a definite advance in technology, does not produce the strong, dramatic responses of the cardiograph because it obtains its recordings significantly further from the heart. The S-K-G test is a valid and reliable technique in the elimination of suspects by virtue of the fact that consistent responses to the control (probable-lie) question and the absence of response to any of the relevant questions is most certainly an indication of truth regarding the offense upon which the relevant questions are based. Furthermore, an absence of response to the relevant questions, but the presence of response to the question regarding suspicion of someone, in addition to a response to the control question, must remove that examinee from direct or indirect involvement in the crime in question.

Once an examinee has been identified by the S-K-G test as having major or direct involvement in a crime, he/she is then administered the Matte Quadri-Track Zone Comparison Technique requiring a minimum of two charts numerically scored before any type of interrogation can be initiated. The interrogation of a major suspect immediately after the administration of the S-K-G test will undoubtedly cause the suspect's psychological set to be riveted to any relevant question asked during subsequent tests, rendering the control questions too weak to compete against relevant questions that now have become a real threat to the well-being of the examinee: he or she now realizes that the S- K-G test reflects that he or she is guilty of the offense, although he or she may still be innocent of the crime. The examinee will now fear that the outcome of the Matte Quadri-Track Zone Comparison test will be the same as the S-K-G test.

While the S-K-G test and the Matte Quadri-Track Zone Comparison (MQTZC) test both contain the "inside issue" factor questions designed to identify and measure the degree of the examinee's "fear of error," premature interrogation will cause abnormal anxiety and fear of the relevant questions to a degree greater than control question #23 is able to negate, resulting in inconclusive findings. Interrogation when appropriate must always follow, never precede, a polygraph examination.

In the administration of the S-K-G test, each question is reviewed word for word with the examinee. The relevant questions (39, 42, 34, 33, 32) followed by control question 31 are first reviewed with the examinee. Then control question 48 is reviewed with the examinee followed by review of control question 23 and relevant question 24. Finally symptomatic questions 25 and 26 followed by irrelevant question 13L (examinee's last name) are reviewed with the examinee.

As in the MQTZC test, the examinee is not apprised of the exact order that the questions will be asked during the examination. However, unlike the MQTZC test, during the second and subsequent charts of the S-K-G test, there is no exchanging of the positions of any of the questions; they are always asked in the same order as on the first chart. Figure XVII-1 depicts the format for the S-K-G test.

Control question #48 should not encompass the period of the crime for which the subject is being examined. If the subject is twenty-seven years of age and the crime occurred while at that age, the control question should not go beyond the examinee's twenty-fifth birthday. Control question #48 is located at the peak tension area immediately prior to the major involvement question, to allow the innocent examinee an opportunity to relieve his or her anxieties prior to the major involvement question and further allow a strong response to the control question to dampen out any concern the (innocent as later verified) examinee may have regarding the major involvement (relevant) question that follows it. By the same token, the examinee guilty of major involvement will have his or her psychological set focused on the relevant question because it will be the most threatening question on the test thereby dampening out subject's concern for the preceding control question, which as a result will show little or not response in comparison to the response elicited by the (relevant) major involvement question.

Consistent responses in two or more charts to questions 34 and 42 indicate some direct involvement. Consistent response to question 33 indicates major involvement.

Consistent response to question 32 indicates guilty knowledge. Consistent response to questions 25 and 26 indicate that an outside issue is bothering the examinee.

S-K-G Test Structure and Quantification System

S-K-G Test	13L	Used on Chart Nr.____
25	Are you completely convinced that I will not ask you an unreviewed question during this chart?____	
39	Regarding the:	Do you intend to answer truthfully each question about that?
42	Same as above	Before that ____ occurred - Did you definitely know it was about to happen?____
34	Same as above	At the very time that ____ occurred - were you ____ (on the scene)____
48	During the first ( ) years of your life - Do you remember:	
33	Same as above	Did you (yourself)
32	Same as above	Do you know for sure (who)
31	Same as above	Do you suspect anyone in particular of
23	Are you afraid an error will be made on this test regarding: (whether or not you were involved in this crime)____	
24	Are you hopeful an error will be made on this test regarding: (whether or not you were involved in this crime)____	
26	Is there something else you are afraid I will ask you a question about, even though I told you I would not?____	

S-K-G QUANTIFICATION SYSTEM SCORE TABLE

SKG-1				
PNE 42 Score ( )	34 Score ( )	33 Score ( )	32 Score ( )	24 Score ( )
GSR 42 Score ( )	34 Score ( )	33 Score ( )	32 Score ( )	24 Score ( )
CAR 42 Score ( )	34 Score ( )	33 Score ( )	32 Score ( )	24 Score ( )
SKG-2				
PNE 42 Score ( )	34 Score ( )	33 Score ( )	32 Score ( )	24 Score ( )
GSR 42 Score ( )	34 Score ( )	33 Score ( )	32 Score ( )	24 Score ( )
CAR 42 Score ( )	34 Score ( )	33 Score ( )	32 Score ( )	24 Score ( )
42 Total ( )	34 Total ( )	33 Total ( )	32 Total ( )	24 Total ( )

S-K-G CONCLUSION TABLE

	TRUTH	INCONCLUSIVE	DECEPTION
RESULTS FOR 1 CHART:	+2 or more	+1 to -2	-3 or more
RESULTS FOR 2 CHARTS:	+4 or more	+3 to -5	-6 or more

S-K-G CONCLUSIONS: TRUTHFUL to relevant question(s) ____________

DECEPTIVE to relevant question(s)____________

TARGET ( ) INCONCLUSIVE to relevant question(s)__________

Figure XVII-1

Consistent response to question 31 indicates unfounded suspicion; consistent response to question 31 and a lack of response to the other questions is an indication of truthfulness regarding any major or direct involvement or guilty knowledge of the crime in question. Consistent response to questions 48 and 23 indicate truthfulness regarding all (crime) relevant questions on the test.

When the examinee has a legitimate reason for being on the scene of the crime, question number 34 may be substituted or changed as indicated in the example. Normally question number 34 attempts to place the examinee at the scene of the crime.

In order to quantify this test, each relevant question must be compared separately against a control question for the purpose of determining whether the control or the relevant question offers the greatest threat to the examinee's well-being. The insertion of four control questions into the test is impractical, because it would make the test too long, and not desirable (inasmuch as one control may be less effective than another, because the subject's psychological set may be focused onto that control question that offers the greatest threat, dampening out the other controls). The insertion of control question #48, which encompass both control question 46 and 47 as found in the MQTZC technique, makes it the most powerful and effective control inserted at the center of the test immediately preceding the strongest and most direct relevant question. Each relevant question is compared separately, tracing by tracing, against control question 48 for a numerical score in the plus or minus area according to rules set forth in Chapter 12. After two (or more) charts, a total score is accrued either in the plus or minus area for a conclusion regarding truthfulness or deception regarding each relevant question on the part of the examinee.

Question 31, which regards unfounded suspicion on the part of the examinee, is not a relevant question but rather a control, inasmuch as it can be readily assumed that an examinee who shows no reaction to any of the relevant questions but shows a reaction to suspicion can be excluded as a participant or witness in the crime. Therefore, the forensic psychophysiologist (FP) can choose between control question 48 and control question 31 for the greatest physiological evidence of sympathetic and parasympathetic action, which the FP then uses as the control question to compare against relevant questions 42, 34, 33, and 32 individually (see Fig. XVII-2)

COMPARISON SCORE TABLE

Relevants	42	34	33	32	24
Controls	48or31	48or31	48or31	48or31	23
TALLY	(+/-)	(+/-)	(+/-)	(+/-)	(+/-)

Figure XVII-2

The control-relevant question set 23-24 serves the same purpose as in the Matte Quadri-Track Zone Comparison Technique (MQTZCT): to correct countertrue scores by recouping response energy lost from either the control or relevant questions as a result of inside issue factors present in the test.

Empirical data reflects few occasions when question 31 (control) will exceed control question 48 in overall sympathetic/parasympathetic activity. However, its inclusion is necessary to offset the chance that an examinee's suspicion of someone may be so strong that, without the suspicion question on the test, he or she may show reaction on the knowledge question because there is no other question in that general category to relieve the energy.

In order to obtain test reliability, we must have consistency of response; therefore two or more charts must be conducted, after which the scores are tallied. A conclusion must be rendered on the basis of the score obtained from each relevant question versus the control questions.

Since here we are using only one control versus one relevant question (rather than two controls versus two relevant questions regarding the same issue as in the Matte Quadri-Track Zone Comparison Technique), it could be argued that only half the score is required to render a conclusion. Using the Utah study (Raskin, et al 1976) scoring system of +6 or -6 we could halve that to a +3 or -3 for a determination of truthfulness or deception respectively in the S-K-G test. However, using the same logical basis for conclusion score requirements of the MQTZC technique, the expected +3 or -3 cutoff for two charts is augmented to satisfy the laws of logic, as explained in the next paragraph.

When comparing a relevant question against the control question, in the case of results reflecting deception, we must expect at least one of the tracings in the relevant question area to yield at least a -2 score, and one of the other tracings a -l score. We cannot expect all three tracings to yield a score, but in order to render a conclusion of deception, a score must be obtained in at least two of the three tracings and one of them must be a minimum of -2 (D). This means that each chart must yield a total minus score of at least -3 for a grand total of -6 in two charts to render a conclusion of deception. Examination of the conclusion table in the MQTZC technique reveals that a score of -5 or more per chart is required to render a conclusion of deception, which is supported by a field study (Matte, Reuss 1989). It would appear that a -3 score for the S-K-G test is inconsistent with the score requirement in the MQTZC technique, but in fact is not inconsistent because in the MQTZC technique we only expect the examinee to show a strong reaction in one of the two relevant questions, that which offers the greatest threat to the examinee's well-being or that which his or psychological set is focused upon. Therefore, only one -2 (D) score is required on one of the tracings in one or the other relevant question, hence the score of -5 per chart instead of -6 per chart in the MQTZC technique. With the S-K-G test we have only one relevant and one control and one score for the three tracings.

As for results reflecting truthfulness, strong scores cannot be expected from a control question, which is structurally less intense than the relevant question because of its earlier-in-life threat as opposed to the immediate threat offered by the relevant question. Therefore, using the rule above, a minimum score of +1 for two of the three tracings for a total of +2 per chart for a grand total of +4 for two charts should be the cutoff point.

S-K-G CONCLUSION TABLE

RESULTS FOR 1 CHART: CIRCLE APPROPRIATE NUMBER BELOW

+2 or more	+1 to -2	-3 or more
TRUTH	INCONCLUSIVE	DECEPTION

RESULTS FOR 2 CHARTS: CIRCLE APPROPRIATE NUMBER BELOW

+4 or more	+3 to -5	-6 or more
TRUTH	INCONCLUSIVE	DECEPTION

Figure XVII-3

In the past this author has often administered the S-K-G test after other targets have been conducted using the Quadri-Track Zone Comparison technique to satisfy questions regarding nondirect involvement or knowledge. Using the S-K-G test in that manner offers a nice change of pace. The subject finds that the two control questions previously used in the Quadri-Track test are now being combined into one question. The examinee has perhaps become habituated to the other control questions (46 and 47) and is used to being asked the relevant questions. However, this new control question, which we now know to be effective by the performance of 46 and 47 in the prior tests, is inserted immediately prior to the prime relevant question the examinee has been accustomed to being asked. As in a beam of light, the narrower the beam, the more intense the light. We have new relevant questions (42 and 34) inserted prior to the control question (48) that should elicit a response from the person attempting deception to them, but the truthful examinee's psychological set will ride over those weaker relevant questions and hit upon that single, strong control question, which will in turn dampen out any concern for the following strong relevant (33) question. The knowledge question (32) and the suspicion question (31) are placed at the end of the test so that if an examinee does respond to either of these questions, he or she will have had a chance to respond to stronger questions first.

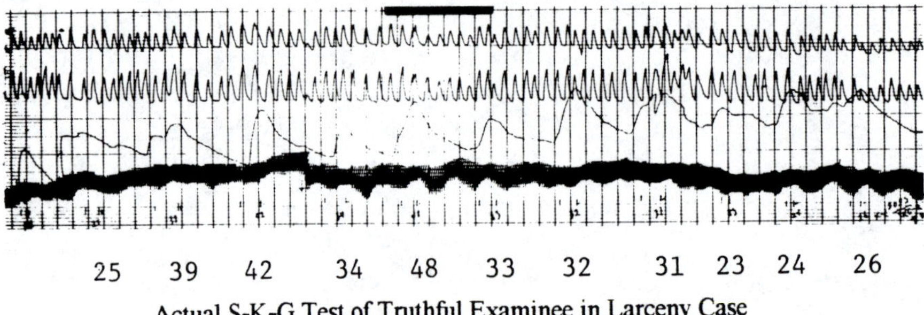

Actual S-K-G Test of Truthful Examinee in Larceny Case

Figure XVII-4

Figure XVII-4 reflects that the examinee was truthful in his denial of involvement in the larceny of merchandise from his employer as evidenced by the reaction at control question 48 regarding thefts committed by the examinee during a period preceding his current employment; the reaction at question 31 indicates that he does suspect someone else of perpetrating the larceny, which therefore absolves him of any involvement since he showed no reaction to relevant question 33 (direct involvement) and 32 (actual knowledge regarding identity of perpetrator).

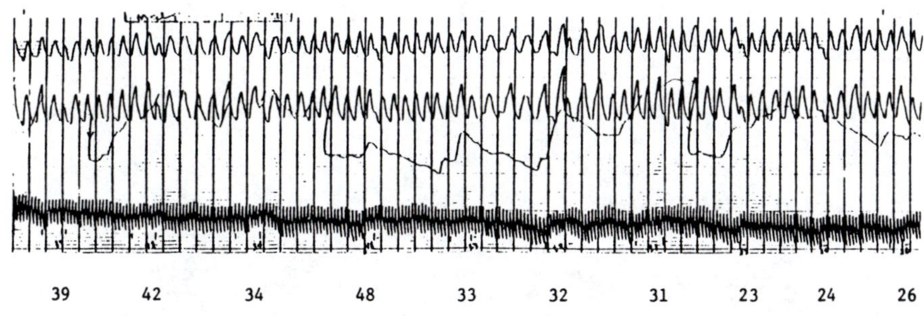

Actual S-K-G Test of Deceptive Examinee in Larceny Case

Figure XVII-5

Figure XVII-5 reflects that the examinee was directly involved in the burglary for which he was polygraphed. Note significant change in breathing rate, suppression followed by hyperventilation in both upper and lower pneumograph tracings. This test followed the Quadri-Track Zone Comparison test, also reflecting deception regarding the commission of the burglary.

The Backster S-K-Y Test

Target selection for the S-K-Y phase series should utilize the most successful of those targets pursued where two or more different "YOU" phase series (See Chapter 11), were utilized. If only one "YOU" phase series was utilized prior to S-K-Y testing, the same target is brought forward from notepack pages 10 and 11 along with the "Did You" question 33 or 35, one of which is then used with a minimum of variation as a basis for the entire examination chart where the target does not embrace "direct involvement." On such occasions, return to the notepack and utilize the pre-examination target selection guide. Using the same wording, transfer that target which has the highest numerical "Reliability" total resulting from the "Pre-exam Target Reliability Estimate" procedure. Enter this target caption in the space provided.

Formulate question 33, the first half of which then becomes the nucleus for all of the remaining questions in this series (other than question #25 and 26). While formulating question #33 be certain that you apply the rules provided. Now complete the last half of each remaining question utilizing the available guide material.

In reference to question #34, where subject had a legitimate reason to be "on the scene" at the time of the incident, another question may be substituted.

Question #42, which involves "prior knowledge" can be used in most situations, except those that lack any significant degree of planning.

Figure XVII-6 below depicts the horizontal structure of Backster's SKY test.

Zone Comparison	Y	B	Y/R	G	R/Y	G	R	G	R/Y	B
S-K-Y Test	13	25	39	31	32	47	33	48	34	26
(Vertical Totals Only)				-S-	-K-		-Y-			
Three "SPOTS"				II	III		IV			

Figure XVII-6

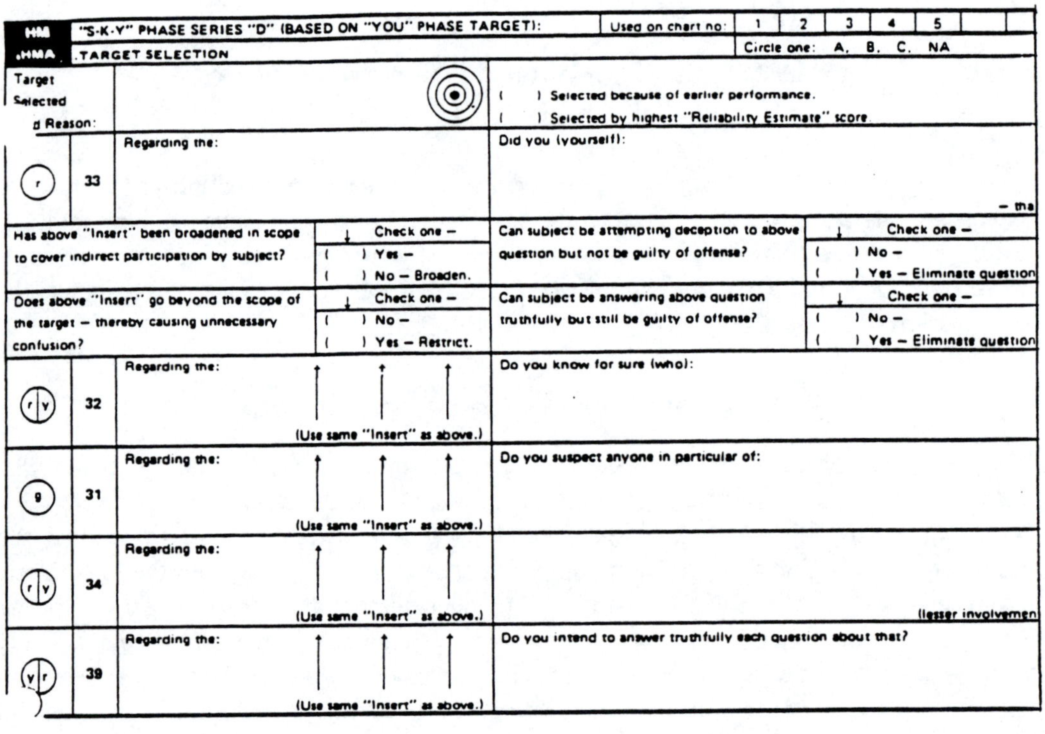

HM "S-K-Y" PHASE SERIES "D" (BASED ON "YOU" PHASE TARGET): Used on chart no: 1 2 3 4 5

.HMA .TARGET SELECTION Circle one: A. B. C. NA

Target Selected d Reason:

( ) Selected because of earlier performance.

( ) Selected by highest "Reliability Estimate" score.

(r) 33 Regarding the: Did you (yourself): — tha

Has above "Insert" been broadened in scope to cover indirect participation by subject? Check one — ( ) Yes — ( ) No — Broaden.

Can subject be attempting deception to above question but not be guilty of offense? Check one — ( ) No — ( ) Yes — Eliminate question

Does above "Insert" go beyond the scope of the target — thereby causing unnecessary confusion? Check one — ( ) No — ( ) Yes — Restrict.

Can subject be answering above question truthfully but still be guilty of offense? Check one — ( ) No — ( ) Yes — Eliminate question

(r|y) 32 Regarding the: (Use same "Insert" as above.) Do you know for sure (who):

(g) 31 Regarding the: (Use same "Insert" as above.) Do you suspect anyone in particular of:

(r|y) 34 Regarding the: (Use same "Insert" as above.) (lesser involvemen

(y|r) 39 Regarding the: (Use same "Insert" as above.) Do you intend to answer truthfully each question about that?

Backster S-K-Y Target Selection & Question Formulation Format

Figure XVII-7

Figure XVII-7 depicts the SKY test Target Selection and Question Formulation format.

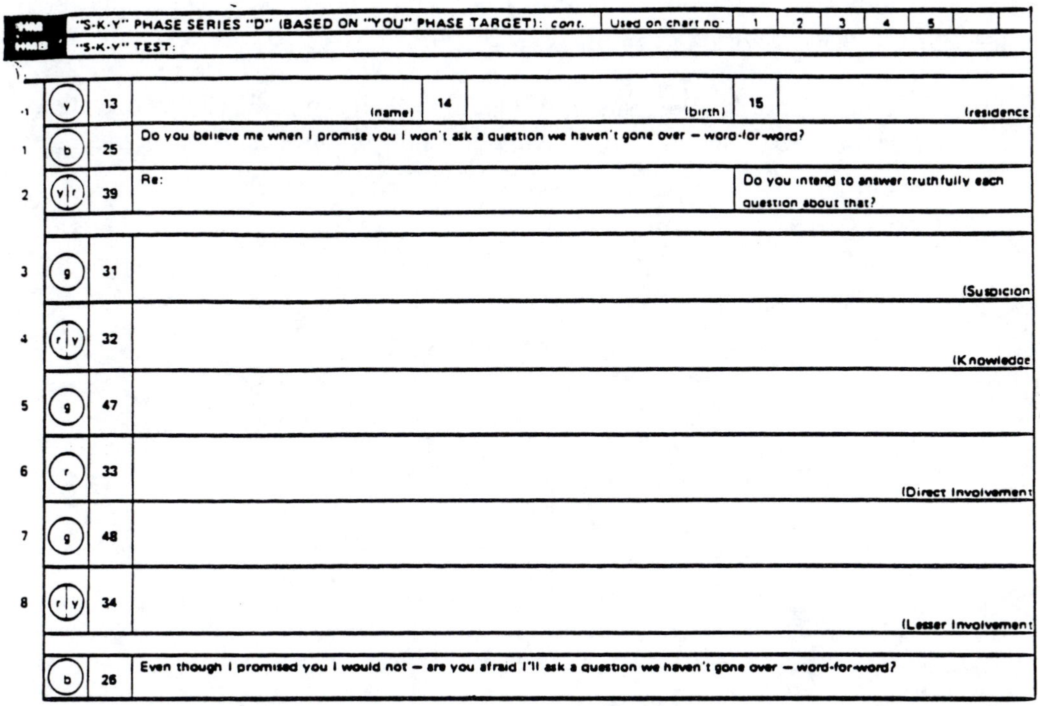

"S-K-Y" PHASE SERIES "D" (BASED ON "YOU" PHASE TARGET): *cont.* | Used on chart no: 1 2 3 4 5

"S-K-Y" TEST:

-1	v	13	(name) 14 (birth) 15 (residence
1	b	25	Do you believe me when I promise you I won't ask a question we haven't gone over – word-for-word?
2	v | r	39	Re: Do you intend to answer truthfully each question about that?
3	g	31	(Suspicion
4	r | y	32	(Knowledge
5	g	47	
6	r	33	(Direct Involvement
7	g	48	
8	r | y	34	(Lesser Involvement
	b	26	Even though I promised you I would not – are you afraid I'll ask a question we haven't gone over – word-for-word?

Backster SKY Test Format in Order of Question Presentation

Figure XVII-8

Figure XVII-8 depicts the SKY test format in the order that the test question are presented during the test.

REFERENCES

Backster, C. (1994, December 5-9). 37th Polygraph Examiner Work Conference. *The Backster School of Lie Detection*, San Diego, CA.

Matte, J. A. (1980). *The Art and Science of the Polygraph Technique*. Springfield, IL: Charles C. Thomas - Publisher

Matte, J. A., Reuss, R. M. (1989). Validation study on the Quadri-Zone Comparison Technique, *Research Abstract*, LD 01452, Vol. 1502, 1989, University Microfilm International.

Matte, J. A., Reuss, R. M. (1989). A field validation study of the Quadri-Zone Comparison Technique. *Polygraph*, 18(4), 187-202.

Raskin, D. C., Barland, G. H., Podlesny, J. A. (1978). Validity and reliability of detection of deception. Washington, D. C.: *National Institute of Law Enforcement and Criminal Justice*.

Chapter 18

GUILTY KNOWLEDGE TESTS

Dr. David T. Lykken who conducted extensive research and popularized the Guilty Knowledge test (GKT) among scientists, described the GKT as follows: "I consider a GKT to be any procedure that uses some involuntary physiological response to indicate whether the subject identifies the 'correct' or crime-related alternative as distinctive or different from a set of control alternatives that are not in fact crime-related but chosen to seem equally plausible to an innocent suspect. And the crucial thing about the procedure is that, in contrast with the CQT (Control Question Test), the incorrect alternatives provide genuine controls in the scientific sense of that term. That is, the subject's mean response to the incorrect alternatives provides an estimate of how this person ought to react to the correct alternative if he is innocent and does not recognize the correct alternative as being crime-related." (Lykken 1992).

Dr. Gershon Ben-Shakhar refers to Known-Solution Peak-of-Tension and Probing Peak-of-Tension Tests as special cases of the Guilty Knowledge test. Ben-Shakhar holds the broad view that the GKT "refers to a set of procedures which are constructed like a multiple choice test such that the one alternative (the relevant alternative) is related to a specific event (assumed to be known to any individual who participated in that event, or has knowledge of the event), whereas all other alternatives (the control alternatives) are unrelated to the event, but are equivalent to the relevant one in the sense that an individual who has no knowledge of the event cannot discriminate between the relevant and the control alternatives (i.e., cannot guess at a better than chance rate which alternative is the relevant one)." (Ben-Shakhar, 1992)

Hence, the above descriptions of the Guilty Knowledge Test suggests that the GKT is broad in definition and thus includes the Known-Solution Peak-of-Tension and the Probing (Searching) Peak-of-Tension Tests which have been widely used by field forensic psychophysiologists since the 1930s. The field forensic psychophysiologist will use a Guilty Knowledge Test to either discover the examinee who has knowledge of a particular case fact of a crime which is only known to the *perpetrator* of the offense and the *police* *(FP)* in which case the FP could administer a Known-Solution Peak-of-Tension Test; or to discover a case fact known *only* to the *perpetrator* of the offense in which case the FP could administer a Probing Peak-of-Tension Test. The FP could in fact employ several variations of the Guilty Knowledge Test (Harrelson 1964, Lykken 1981; Arther 1970; Backster 1969, Reid & Inbau 1977, Widacki 1986, Furedy & Ben-Shakhar 1991, Suzuki 1978, Bradley & Rettinger 1992, Fukomoto 1982, Nakayama & Yamamura 1990, Matte 1980, DoDPI 1991). The major distinction between Lykken's GKT and the traditional Peak-of-Tension Tests is that in Lykken's GKT format, the critical or key item is placed anywhere in the list, by chance, except in the first position because of the need for a buffer, and the sequence of the items is unknown to the subject of the test. If the list is used more than once, or there is more than one list, the sequence for each list is varied by chance selection, excluding the buffer. Whereas in POT tests, the critical or key question in Known Solution POT tests is usually placed near the middle of the list of test questions, and in Probing POT tests, the position of the most likely item is usually central in the list of test questions. Stimulation tests and laboratory simulations where the subject is not seriously involved or concerned about the outcome should be more appropriately named *Concealed Knowledge* tests. (Ansley 1992).

In this chapter, two Guilty Knowledge test formats which have been successfully used in the field for many years by this author and colleagues are described in detail with actual cases, followed by three tables developed by Norman Ansley (1992) reflecting field validity studies and laboratory studies conducted during the period from 1930 through 1991, and a cumulative table of the studies' results.

Early one Monday morning, the manager of a store reviewed the previous Saturday's daily receipt balance sheet left on his desk by one of his assistants. Sales had been very good that particular Saturday. The sheet reflected $4020.00 in checks and $6215.18 in cash. As customary, the manager opened the office combination safe to recount the receipts and deposit the money in the bank that morning. However, to his chagrin he discovered that the envelope containing both the checks and the cash was missing from the safe. There was no evidence of tempering or forced entry into the safe. Only three persons had the combination to the safe: the manager and his two assistants. No other person including former employees had the current safe combination. The manager was therefore convinced that one of his two assistants had stolen the money or had forgotten to place the envelope in the safe, thereby allowing someone else to steal it while unprotected.

The manager and both assistants agreed to submit to a psychophysiological veracity (PV) examination using the polygraph to remove the cloud of suspicion, and to the manager's surprise, the results showed that neither the manager nor his assistants were in any way involved in the theft or disappearance of the missing money. This author suggested that an employee might have obtained the safe combination one number at a time over a period of several weeks or months by being in the office when the safe was opened, on busy days when security precautions were lax. It was, therefore, feasible that an unauthorized employee might have the combination to the office safe. As a precautionary measure, the combination was immediately changed and the decision was made that all employees would be administered a PV examination to determine guilty knowledge regarding the safe combination.

A Known-Solution Peak-of-Tension (KSPOT) test was administered, which consisted of the actual combination plus six other combinations derived from the actual combination, hereafter referred to as the "key" question, as outlined in Figure XVIII-1.

As indicated below, the question containing the actual combination is called the "key" question, also known as the "true key" question. Question number 2 is a control question in the form of a fictitious key question. This question does not necessarily have to be in position number 2, but it should never be in position number 1 or immediately before or after the "true key" question. The "true key" question should be placed in position number 5 or 6.

During the pretest interview, the basic principles of the peak-of-tension test, with emphasis on the blood pressure tracing, were explained to the examinee. The examinee was advised that a truthful person's blood pressure would remain the same throughout the test but the deceptive person's blood pressure would slowly rise and continue to rise until the question to which he was lying has been asked, at which time his blood pressure would commence its descent to normal. While explaining this phenomenon to the examinee, the forensic psychophysiologist (FP) moved his hand across horizontally, raising it slowly up and down when describing the lying subject, for effect. As an additional power of suggestion tool, the examinee was further told that he might even start hearing his heart pound louder and louder until he reached the question to which he was lying.

Actual Known-Solution POT Test Format in Larceny Case

"KNOWN SOLUTION" PEAK-OF-TENSION TEST	USED ON CHART NR.
PREPARATORY QUESTION If you know the combination to the safe at Moran's Market -	
PREFIX QUESTION Do you know the combination to be:	
BUFFER QUESTIONS (Must contain fictitious key only)	
1	5 - 44 - 09
2	6 - 45 - 10 (Fictitious Key Question)
3	7 - 46 - 11
BUFFER QUESTIONS (Plus True Key Only)	
4	8 - 47 - 12
5	9 - 48 - 13 (Key Question)
6	10 - 49 - 14
7	11 - 50 - 15
BUFFER QUESTIONS (Cannot contain either Key)	
8	12 - 51 - 16
9	

Figure XVIII-1

Each test question was then reviewed with the examinee but not in the order asked on the test. When discussing the fictitious key question during the review, the FP deliberately looked the examinee in the eye and accentuated that particular question, whereas all other questions were asked in a monotone and routine manner. The examinee was advised that a minimum of two charts would be conducted, however, he was not told the actual order of the questions. The "true" key question in the second chart was moved to another position but not next to the "fictitious" key.

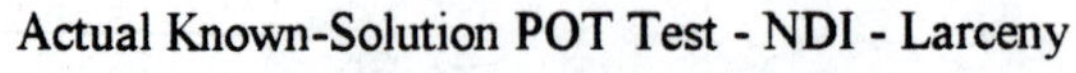
Actual Known-Solution POT Test - NDI - Larceny

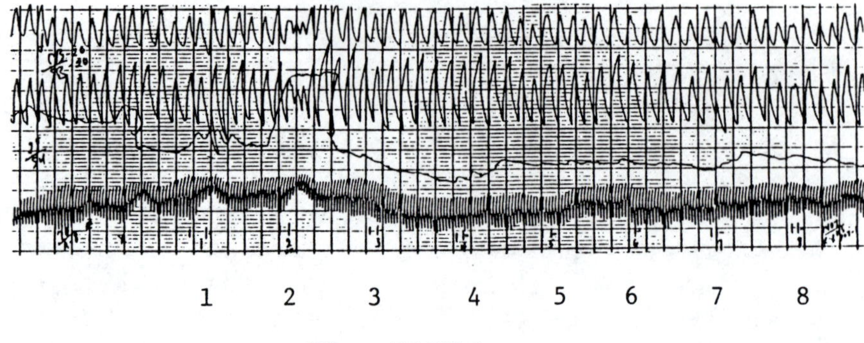

Figure XVIII-2

The first four examinees all showed from mild to strong responses to the "fictitious" key question but no response to the "true" key question. However, the fifth examinee showed consistent strong responses to the "true" key question and a lack of response to the fictitious key. The deceptive subject was shown his charts, asked to follow with his finger the cardio tracing to its highest peak then read aloud the question number. He was asked to repeat this with the second chart. He was then shown the question sheet and asked to read aloud the question corresponding to the number he had peaked on his charts. Holding back tears, he admitted stealing the money so he could go to Florida with a girl friend. The checks of which he had not yet disposed, and most of the money were returned. As suspected, he had obtained the combination one number at a time by glancing over the shoulder of the person opening the safe in unguarded moments.

Chart of innocent examinee (Fig. XVIII-2) shows reaction at fictitious key question (#2) as evidenced by suppression and hyperventilation in the breathing patterns, the significant galvanic skin response, and the diminishing blood pressure pattern following the false key question.

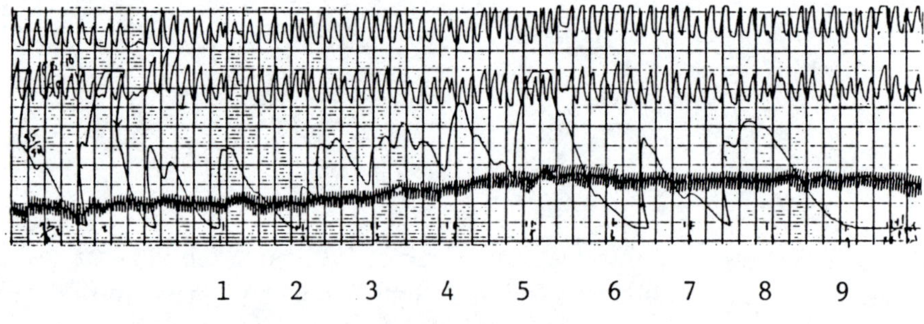

Actual Known-Solution POT Test - DI - Larceny

Figure XVIII-3

The chart of the guilty examinee (Fig. XVIII-3) above, reflects reaction at question #5, the "true" key question, indicating guilty knowledge regarding the safe combination, as evidenced by the baseline arousal and "blocking": in the breathing pattern, the superior height and duration of the galvanic skin response, and the slow rising cardio pattern, which ends its ascent with a sudden blood pressure increase at the true key question before commencing its slow descent.

The Known-Solution Peak-of-Tension Test is normally used after a specific type test has been administered, to support the results of the specific test. In cases where the specific test reflects deception to the crime questions, interrogation should immediately follow the specific test; when unproductive, the Known-Solution Peak-of-Tension Test is then administered. However, when a Known-Solution Peak-of-Tension Test is administered after a specific test reflects deception, the preparatory question in the Known-Solution Peak-of-Tension Test should commence with the words "Regarding the...."rather than "If you..." in order not to convey any uncertainty about the results of the specific test to the examinee.

The Known-Solution Peak-of-Tension Test is feasible only when an item of information regarding an incident or an offense is known to the investigator, the perpetrator of the offense, and the forensic psychophysiologist (FP) but, for practical purposes, is not known to the general public or among the scheduled examinees except the person guilty of the offense. Sometimes more than one item of information may be useful as key questions. Care must be exercised by those in possession of that information not to unintentionally or intentionally divulge this valuable information to any person who later may become the subject of a PV examination regarding that same issue. Care must also be exercised by the FP not to divulge key information during the conduct of the specific test, which normally precedes the known-solution POT test.

Sometimes a forensic psychophysiologist will inadvertently divulge a secondary key in the administration of the primary Known-Solution POT test. As an example, in a house burglary a white leather purse containing 176 dollars was stolen in addition to other things. The primary or first Known-Solution POT test should not reveal that the money was in a white leather purse. The test should simply determine if he or she has guilty knowledge regarding the amount of money stolen. The second Known-Solution POT test will then determine guilty knowledge regarding the description of the purse, or the fact that the money was contained inside a purse.

Ideally, Known-Solution POT tests should be prepared prior to the scheduled examination so that the forensic psychophysiologist (FP) will have the necessary time to "think out" his questions carefully and select the best, most likely "true" key question from known case facts. In this manner, only minor adjustments or refinements will be required at a time when the FP is under pressure with limited spare time. With the Known-Solution POT test prepared before the scheduled PV examination, the FP is less likely to give away the "key" during the pretest interview. It further reduces the amount of time the examinee is left alone to marshal his or her psychological forces.

Another type of Peak-of-Tension test available to the forensic psychophysiologist is known as the Probing Peak-of-Tension Test. This test is used to identify key information not known to the investigator or the FP. It may be used to locate accomplices, determine extent of involvement, locate weapons, loot, evidence, determine amounts of money stolen, and methods of entry. A "fictitious" key is not used in the Probing POT test. The choices are listed in order of least likely, most likely, least likely, finally followed by an all inclusive question such as "any other place I haven't mentioned?" Probing POT tests should be prepared prior to the scheduled examination with a view towards determining those facts deemed most important to the investigators in solving their case.

In one particular case where a Probing POT test was used successfully, a cashier employed at a department store was observed by a team of professional shoppers not ringing up a six dollar sale. In a subsequent interview by store security personnel, the cashier admitted that she had intentionally failed to ring up that particular sale for the purpose of stealing the six dollars but denied committing similar thefts during her two years of employment there and agreed to verify her statement by submitting to a psychophysiological veracity (PV) examination using the polygraph.

A specific PV examination was first administered to determine if she had stolen more than six dollars from that department store. The results indicated deception. In the ensuing interrogation the cashier weakly admitted to more thefts of money from the store but was evasive regarding the approximate amount stolen. In an attempt to determine the approximate amount of money she had stolen from the department store and further convince the cashier of the futility of further resistance, a Probing POT test was administered as shown in Figure XVIII-4.

"PROBING" PEAK-OF-TENSION TEST	USED ON CHART NR.
PREPARATORY QUESTION Regarding the total amount of money you have stolen from ABC Dept Store in the past 2 years	
PREFIX QUESTION Did you steal at least:	
LEAST LIKELY CHOICES	
A	$50
B	$100
MOST LIKELY CHOICES	
C	$250
D	$500
E	$700
F	$1000
LEAST LIKELY CHOICES	
G	$2000
H	$5000
ALL INCLUSIVE CHOICE	
I	More than $5000

Actual Probing POT Test with List of Test Questions

Figure XVIII-4

The questions were reviewed with the cashier in the same order they were asked on the test and a total of two charts were conducted (Fig. XVIII-5). Strong and consistent unresolved responses were reflected at question F, indicating that she believed she had stolen a total of at least 1,000 dollars from the company. During the post-test interview, the cashier was confronted with the charts, after which she admitted that shortly after being hired she started stealing money by not ringing up sales and continued her thefts, averaging at least ten dollars per week until her discovery by security. While the aforementioned case was successful in determining the approximate amount of money stolen, the forensic psychophysiologist should exercise extreme caution in rendering a decision based upon the results of a Probing POT test *involving amounts of money stolen over a long period of time*, without other confirmatory evidence, inasmuch as this type of test is vulnerable to psychological variables beyond the control of the FP or the examinee. As Dr. David T. Lykken once stated "The Searching Peak of Tension test is its own justification when it leads to the discovery of useful physical evidence or elicits a valid confession. The mere occurrence of consistent responding to some item in the series, by itself, is hopelessly ambiguous and provides no legitimate basis for any conclusions about the veracity of the subject." (Lykken 1981).

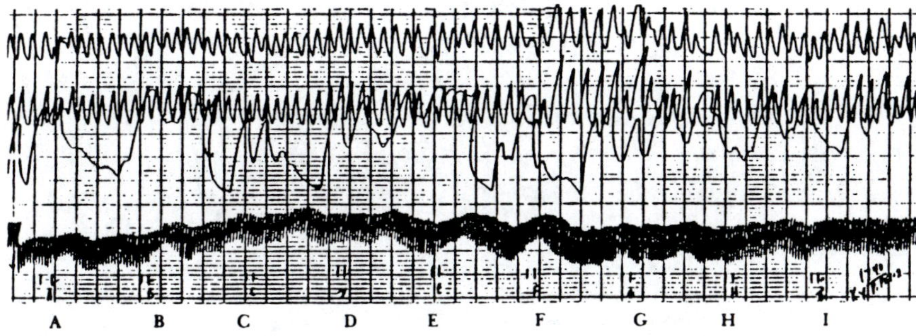

Actual Probing POT Test - DI - Larceny Case

Figure XVIII-5

In another case, a murder suspect was administered a PV examination and the results indicated deception. Post-test interrogation failed to elicit a confession. However, the subject still provided valuable information which produced evidence of his crime by use of a Probing POT test. In this instance the murder weapon had not been found, therefore the Probing POT test was formulated as shown in Figure XVIII-6.

During the review of the test questions, the subject apparently realized the futility of further resistance and confessed to his crime. However, had he not confessed and had showed strong and consistent unresolved responses in two charts to one of the above questions, the subject would have been interrogated, and if the FP again failed to acquire a confession, he would have pursued the matter further by administering another Probing

"PROBING" PEAK-OF-TENSION TEST	USED ON CHART NR.
PREPARATORY QUESTION Regarding the present location of the gun you used to shoot John Doe on 7 March 1976:	
PREFIX QUESTION Is that gun right now:	
LEAST LIKELY CHOICES	
A	buried in the ground?
B	under water?
MOST LIKELY CHOICES	
C	out in the open?
D	in a residence?
E	in a vehicle?
F	in a commercial building?
LEAST LIKELY CHOICES	
G	in a cellar?
H	in an attic?
ALL INCLUSIVE CHOICE	
I	somewhere I have not mentioned?

Probing POT Test Format - Homicide Case
Figure XVIII-6

POT test, this time narrowing down the location of the weapon with the use of the results from the previous Probing POT test. For example, if the subject reacted to question D, his Probing POT test would be formulated as shown in Figure XVIII-7.

"PROBING" PEAK-OF-TENSION TEST	USED ON CHART NR.
PREPARATORY QUESTION Regarding the present location of the gun you used to shoot John Doe on 7 March 1976:	
PREFIX QUESTION is the gun right now at:	
LEAST LIKELY CHOICES	
A	your in-law's residence?
B	a relative's residence?
MOST LIKELY CHOICES	
C	your parents residence?
D	your own residence?
E	a female friend's residence?
F	a male friend's residence?
LEAST LIKELY CHOICES	
G	an unoccupied residence?
H	an incompleted residence?
ALL INCLUSIVE CHOICE	
I	a residence I haven't yet mentioned?

Probing POT Test Format - Homicide Case
Figure XVIII-7

In the location of evidence or accomplices, the forensic psychophysiologist (FP) is limited only by his imagination. For instance, in locating evidence, a map encompassing the most distant point where the subject could have hidden the evidence should be obtained and a gridiron drawn on the map dividing it into areas numbered l, 2, 3, etc. The examinee is then thoroughly familiarized with the map and its respective areas and allowed to study it so that he/she can readily recognize the area number where he/she knows the evidence is hidden. A Probing POT test is then administered to determine to which area he/she consistently shows a response. A map of this area is now obtained and gridiron is drawn over it following the same procedure as in the first Probing POT test. In this manner the FP can conceivably narrow it down to a street or even a house.

In cases involving unknown accomplices, a Probing POT test can be formulated to encompass the names of former accomplices or friends, using an all-inclusive question as the last question.

Whether a forensic psychophysiologist is using a Known-Solution or Probing Peak-of-Tension test, special care should be taken not to inflate the cardio cuff beyond 85 mm of pressure, since excessive cuff pressure will cause pain or discomfort to the examinee, who will then become more concerned about his or her arm than the questions on the test.

Question formulation is equally important in Peak-of-Tension tests as it is in specific tests. Each question must be clear, concise, encompass only one issue, and serve the purpose for which it is intended. In the first example described in Figure XVIII-1 above, the prefix question used the words "Do you know the combination to be?:" In this particular case, the use of the prefix "Do you know.?" was necessary because the purpose of the test was to determine whether or not he had '*knowledge*' of the combination. However in most cases, use of the prefix "Do you know...?" should be avoided inasmuch as the guilty (as later verified) subject *does know* and is *lying* when he or she answers "no" to each choice on the list of test questions. The Keeler Polygraph Institute of Training Guide (Harrelson 1964) specifically warned against the use of the prefix "Do you know...?" and in September 1991, the Department of Defense Polygraph Institute made a technical correction in its construction of Peak-of-Tension tests, with the use of more direct prefix such as "Is it....?" or "Was it...?" For instance: "Regarding the location of that bomb, Is it located in: Atlanta? Is it located in Birmingham?" etc. (Ansley 1992). Care must be taken during the pretest to establish the question format so that "no" answers can logically be given. No format should allow an "I don't know" answer. (Yankee 1991)

Validity and Reliability of Guilty Knowledge and Peak of Tension Test Formats.

The following three tables reflecting field and laboratory studies on Guilty Knowledge and Peak of Tension tests (GKT & POT) and a Cumulative table for all GKT and POT tests, were compiled by Norman Ansley (1992). Ansley summarizes the results as follows: "Only two studies exist that describe the field accuracy of POT and GKT tests. They are quite different. The Japanese study by Yamamura and Miyake (1978) involved known solution peak of tension tests, and for those who were deceptive, searching peak of tension tests on the specific acts suspects committed during a riot that included arson and murder. Their accuracy is based on those cases for which there were eventual verification. The results are well above chance (see Table 1). The other study (Elaad 1990) is a reliability study in which the researcher in Israel drew confirmed deceptive and truthful sets of charts from police files in which one or more GKT tests followed control question tests. Analyzing those GKT charts globally, blind to the status of the cases, the independent reviewer was quite accurate with the truthful but only right on half of the deceptive cases (See Table 1). There isn't enough information on these disparate research projects to arrive at a generalization. Table 2 represents the accuracy of peak of tension tests and guilty knowledge tests conducted in a laboratory setting. While they are all placed on one table, they are so different that the totals are of little value. Whether they were POT or GKT was based on what the author called them, or if not called, what they appeared to be. If the reader is interested in totals, despite the varied nature of the projects, see Table 3." (Ansley 1992).

TABLE 1

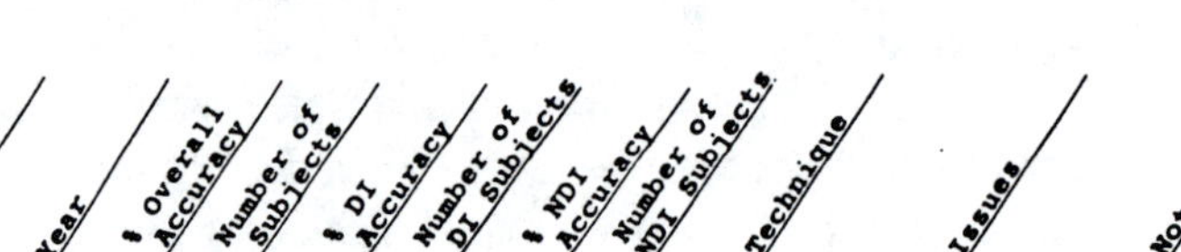
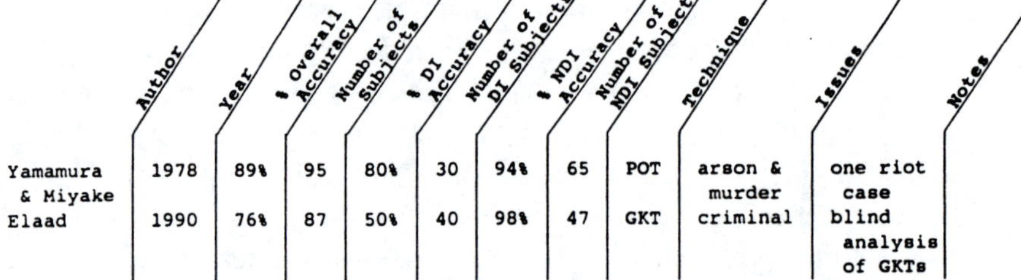

Field Validity of POT and GKT Testing
Where Results Were Confirmed

Author	Year	% Overall Accuracy	Number of Subjects	% DI Accuracy	Number of DI Subjects	% NDI Accuracy	Number of NDI Subjects	Technique	Issues	Notes
Yamamura & Miyake	1978	89%	95	80%	30	94%	65	POT	arson & murder	one riot case
Elaad	1990	76%	87	50%	40	98%	47	GKT	criminal	blind analysis of GKTs

Notes: No inconclusives in Yamamura & Miyake
Inconclusives excluded from Elaad

TABLE 2-1

Peak of Tension (POT) and Guilty Knowledge Tests (GKT)

Author	Year	% Overall Accuracy	Number of Subjects	% DI Accuracy	Number of DI Subjects	% NDI Accuracy	Number of NDI Subjects	Subject Type	Incentive	Technique	Chance	Notes
Balloun & Holmes #1	79	73%	34	61%	18	87%	16	S	who cheated	GKT	17%	GSR, HR, FPV
Balloun & Holmes #2	79	53%	34	17%	18	94%	16	S	who cheated	GKT	17%	no answer
Barber	64	26%	60	26%	60	--	--	S	--	POT A	17%	field instruments
Barland	84	75%	20	75%	20	--	--	P	$15	POT	20%	SRR
Barland	84	95%	20	95%	20	--	--	P	$15	GKT	20%	SRR
Beijk	80	80%	228	80%	228	--	--	S	--	POT	10%	SCR
Ben-Shakhar, et.al.	70	77%	27	77%	27	--	--	S	--	GKT	20%	SRR
Davidson	68	87%	48	50%	12	100%	36	S	--	GKT	25%	SRR
Day & Rouke	74	44%	80	44%	80	--	--	S	--	POT	20%	SRR; 'no' answer
Diaz	85	64%	120	64%	120	--	--	P/S	$3	POT	20%	SRR
Dufek #1	69	83%	30	83%	30	--	--	P	--	POT	11%	GSR + odd
Dufek #2	69	90%	20	90%	20	--	--	P	--	POT	17%	GSR + odd
Dufek #3	69	100%	10	100%	10	--	--	P	--	POT	10%	GSR + odd
Dufek #4	69	85%	20	85%	20	--	--	P	--	POT	17%	GSR + odd
Dufek, et.al.	75	73%	30	73%	30	--	--	S	keep wine	POT	10%	field
Forman & McCauley	89	72%	40	45%	20	100%	20	S	$2 - $10	GKT		
Frese	78	51%	75	51%	30	--	--	S	--	POT	20%	field
Furedy & Ben-Shakhar	91	86%	21	86%	21	--	--	S	$ .75 + ego	GKT	20%	SCR; 'no' answer; low motivation
Furedy & Ben-Shakhar	91	48%	21	48%	21	--	--	S	$ .75 + ego	GKT	20%	SCR; 'yes' answer; low motivation

TABLE 2-2

Furedy & Ben-Shakhar	91	55%	20	55%	20	--	--	S	$ .75 + ego	GKT	20%	SCR; mute answer; low motivation
Furedy & Ben-Shakhar	91	62%	21	62%	21	--	--	S	$ .75 + ego	GKT	20%	SCR; 'no' answer; high motivation
Furedy & Ben-Shakhar	91	45%	20	45%	20	--	--	S	$ .75 + ego	GKT	20%	SCR; 'yes' answer; high motivation
Furedy & Ben-Shakhar	91	55%	20	55%	20	--	--	S	$ .75 + ego	GKT	20%	SCR; mute answer; high motivation
Geldreich	41	74%	50	74%	50	--	--	S	--	POT	20%	GSR meter
Geldreich (fatigued)	41	100%	50	100%	50	--	--	S	--	POT	20%	GSR meter
Geldreich	42	86%	50	86%	50	--	--	S	electric shock	POT	20%	GSR meter
Giesen & Rollison	80	97%	40	95%	20	100%	20	S	--	GKT	20%	SRR
Gudjonsson	77	85%	123	85%	123	--	--	P	--	POT	14%	GSR meter
Gustafson & Orne	63	64%	18	64%	18	--	--	S	$1 + ego	POT	20%	SRR
Gustafson & Orne	63	28%	18	28%	18	--	--	S	--	POT	20%	SRR
Gustafson & Orne	64	48%	47	48%	47	--	--	S	--	POT	20%	SRR; no answer
Gustafson & Orne	64	69%	49	69%	49	--	--	S	--	POT	20%	SRR
Gustafsor & Orne	64	79%	24	79%	24	--	--	S	--	POT	20%	SRR; guilty person
Gustafson & Orne	64	33%	24	33%	24	--	--	S	--	POT	20%	SRR; guilty information
Gustafson & Orne	64	75%	24	75%	24	--	--	S	--	"RI" GKT	20%	SRR; guilty person
Gustafson & Orne	64	62%	24	62%	24	--	--	S	--	"RI" GKT	20%	SRR; guilty information
Gustafson & Orne	65	54%	50	54%	50	--	--	S	--	POT & GKT	20%	SRR; no answer
Gustafson & Orne	65	69%	42	69%	42	--	--	S	--	POT & GKT	20%	SRR
Horneman & O'Gorman	85	54%	121	29%	78	100%	43	S	--	POT	20%	SCR; no answer
Horneman & O'Gorman	85	64%	121	44%	78	100%	43	S	--	POT	20%	SCR
Horneman & O'Gorman	85	50%	121	22%	78	100%	43	S	--	POT	20%	SCR; answer "yes"
Horvath	78	69%	20	69%	20	--	--	S	--	POT	20%	SRR; with cuff pressure
Horvath	78	42%	20	42%	20	--	--	S	--	POT	20%	SRR; no cuff pressure
Horvath	79	52%	64	52%	64	--	--	S	—	POT	50%	SRR & PSE
Iacono, et.al.	84	91%	60	88%	45	100%	15	S	$5	GKT	20%	SCR & HR; drug no effect included
Jones & Salter	89	100%	8	100%	3	100%	3	P	--	GKT		

TABLE 2-3

Keeler #1	30	95%	75	95%	75	--	--	P	--	POT	10%	BP & Pneumo; no GSR
Keeler #2	30	93%	30	93%	30	--	--	S	--	POT	33%	BP & Pneumo; no GSR
Kizaki, et.al.	76	53%	40	53%	40	--	--	S	--	POT	20%	SRR; "no" to the word
Kizaki, et.al.	76	65%	40	65%	40	--	--	S	--	POT	20%	SRR; "no" to an associated word
Konieczny, et.al.	84	80%	30	80%	30	--	--	S	--	POT	20%	normal test; autopsy details
Konieczny, et.al.	84	93%	30	93%	30	--	--	S	--	POT +	20%	personality & bio-feedback by GSR
Konieczny, et.al.	84	87%	30	87%	30	--	--	S	--	POT	20%	no answer
Krapohl	84	60%	60	60%	60	--	--	P	$5	GKT	20%	field instrument
Krapohl	84	20%	60	20%	60	--	--	P	--	GKT	20%	field instrument
Krenbergerova & Dufek	69	97%	10	97%	10	--	--	P	--	POT	6%	SRR; random "yes"s with "no"s
Kugelmas, et.al.	67	59%	27	59%	27	--	--	P/S	--	POT	17%	SRR; answer "no"
Kugelmas, et.al.	67	70%	27	70%	27	--	--	P/S	--	POT	17%	SRR; answer "yes"
Lahri & Ganguly	78	90%	40	90%	40	--	--	P	--	POT	12%	criminal suspects; field instrument
Lahri & Ganguly	78	70%	40	70%	40	--	--	P	--	POT	12%	office workers; field instrument
Lieblich, et.al.	76	62%	39	62%	39	--	--	Pr	$5 + cigarettes	POT	20%	SRR; prison inmates
Lieblich, et.al.	70	70%	44	70%	44	--	--	S	--	POT	50%	SRR; two cards
Lieblich, et.al.	70	61%	44	61%	44	--	--	S	--	POT	25%	SRR; four cards
Lieblich, et.al.	70	52%	44	52%	44	--	--	S	--	POT	12%	SRR; eight cards
Lieblich, et.al.	74	50%	8	50%	8	--	--	S	Pride	POT	20%	SCR; high motivation; intelligent can
Lieblich, et.al.	74	48%	28	48%	28	--	--	S	--	POT	20%	SCR; low motivation; ten series
Lieblich, et.al.	74	42%	20	42%	20	--	--	S	Pride	POT	20%	SCR; high motivation; + countermeasures
Lykken	59	96%	49	100%	35	86%	14	S	shock	GKT	20%	SRR
Lykken	60	100%	20	100%	20	--	--	S/P	$10	GKT	17%	SRR; medical students, psychologists; CMs ineffective
Miyake	78	63%	20	63%	20	--	--	S	--	POT	20%	SRR; eye movement, 43%; vasomotor, 47%
Moroney	72	25%	26	25%	26	--	--	S	pride	POT	10%	SRR
Ohkawa #1	63	87%	40	87%	40	--	--	?	--	POT	12%	SRR; answered "no" to theft item
Ohkawa #2	63	87%	40	87%	40	--	--	?	--	POT	12%	silent

TABLE 2-4

Ohkawa #3	63	75%	40	75%	40	--	--	?	--	POT	12%	"no" answer; "yes" to correct item
Pennebaker & Chew #1	85	65%	10	65%	10	--	--	S	--	POT	20%	SRR; normal test
Pennebaker & Chew #2	85	72%	30	72%	30	--	--	S	--	POT	20%	SRR; closely watche to inhibit
Podlesny, et.al.	76	90%	60	90%	30	90%	30	P	$10	GKT	20%	research instrument
Ralloff & Johnson	88	71%	28	71%	28	--	--	?	--	GKT	10%	SCR; motor response push a button
Ralloff & Johnson	88	86%	28	86%	28	--	--	?	--	GKT	10%	SCR; no motor respc
Richardson, et.al.	90	82%	70	82%	70	--	--	M	--	POT	17%	SCR
Ruckmick	38	78%	89	78%	89	--	--	S	--	POT	10%	SRR; meter
Steller, et.al.	87	92%	87	85%	47	100%	40	Po	--	GKT	17%	SCR
Stern, et.al. #1	81	50%	48	50%	48	--	--	S	--	GKT	20%	SRR; with feedback GSR, geometric fig
Stern, et.al. #2	81	67%	48	67%	48	--	--	S	--	GKT	20%	SRR
Stern, et.al. #3	81	88%	52	88%	52	--	--	S	--	GKT	25%	SRR; hostage/murder plot; no feedback
Stern, et.al. #4	81	96%	52	96%	52	--	--	S	--	GKT	25%	SRR; hostage/murder plot; GSR-tone fee
Suzuki	80	49%	24	49%	24	--	--	S	--	GKT	20%	SRR (?)
Suzuki, et.al. #1	69	60%	10	60%	10	--	--	S	--	POT	20%	SPR; no feedback
Suzuki, et.al. #2	69	70%	10	70%	10	--	--	S	--	POT	20%	SPR; feedback
Suzuki, et.al. #3	69	80%	10	80%	10	--	--	S	--	POT	20%	SPR; feedback + fak to first item
Timm	82	82%	270	82%	270	--	--	S	--	GKT	20%	SRR + respiration
Timm	89	87%	61	100%	5	86%	56	S	course credit	GKT	20%	SRR + respiration
VanBuskirk & Marcuse	54	72%	50	72%	50	--	--	S	--	POT	12%	cardio & pneumo onl
Voronin, et.al. #1	72	26%	22	26%	22	--	--	Ch	--	POT	20%	8/9-yr-old children first test
Voronin, et.al. #2	72	44%	22	24%	22	--	--	Ch	--	POT	20%	second test; HR & G
Voronin, et.al. #3	72	86%	22	86%	22	--	--	Ch	threat of pain	POT	20%	third test; 30 days later; + threat
Waid, et.al.	78	77%	34	79%	23	72%	11	?	--	GKT	17%	SRR
Waid, et.al.	78	71%	28	61%	18	90%	10	?	shock	GKT	25%	SRR
Waid, et.al.	78	76%	30	73%	15	80%	15	?	--	GKT	17%	SRR
Waid, et.al.	81	86%	44	82%	33	100%	11	?	pride	POT	25%	w/o meprobamate and placebo groups

TABLE 2-5

Waid, et.al.	81	65%	74	55%	40	76%	30	?	pride	GKT	25%	SCR
Wakamatsu	76	60%	20	60%	20	--	--	P	1000 yen or shock	POT	20%	field instrument; w/o CM & "carefree" groups
Wakamatsu	76	55%	20	55%	20	--	--	P	pride	POT	20%	3 tests with field instrument
Wakamatsu	76	35%	20	35%	20	--	--	P	pride	POT	20%	3 tests with field instrument
Yamaoka & Suzuki	73	77%	13	77%	13	--	--	?	--	POT	20%	SPR; skin blood flow, 33%; SRR, 15%
Yamaoka & Suzuki	73	55%	31	55%	31	--	--	?	--	POT	20%	skin potential - numbers
Yamaoka & Suzuki	73	48%	31	48%	31	--	--	?	--	POT	20%	skin resistance - numbers
Yamaoka & Suzuki	73	45%	31	45%	31	--	--	?	--	POT	20%	pulse rate - numbers
Yamaoka & Suzuki	73	35%	31	35%	31	--	--	?	--	POT	20%	breathing amplitude - numbers
Yamaoka & Suzuki	73	29%	31	29%	31	--	--	?	--	POT	20%	breathing cycle time - numbers
Yamaoka & Suzuki	73	77%	31	77%	31	--	--	?	--	POT	17%	skin potential - name
Yamaoka & Suzuki	73	81%	31	81%	31	--	--	?	--	POT	17%	skin resistance - name
Yamaoka & Suzuki	73	62%	31	62%	31	--	--	?	--	POT	17%	pulse rate - name
Yamaoka & Suzuki	73	32%	31	32%	31	--	--	?	--	POT	17%	breathing amplitude - name
Yamaoka & Suzuki	73	29%	31	29%	31	--	--	?	--	POT	17%	breathing cycle time name

Abbreviations on Table 2

-- = no data

Population:
- S = student
- P = general population
- M = military
- Pr = prisoners
- Po = police
- Ch = children
- ? = unstated

Notes:
- GSR = galvanic skin response
- HR = heart rate
- FPV = finger pulse volume
- SRR = skin resistance response
- SCR = skin conductance response
- SPR = skin potential response
- meter = no strip chart recording
- field instrument = cardio, respiratory and electrodermal recordings
- PSE = psychological stress evaluator
- BP = blood pressure
- pneumo = respiration
- CM = countermeasure group deleted

TABLE 3

Cumulative Table

	Overall Accuracy	No. of Subjects	DI Accuracy	No. of Subjects	NDI Accuracy	No. of Subjects
All Tests	68%	4,874	65%	4,396	93%	478
Labeled GKT	76%	1,519	72%	1,181	91%	338
Other POTs	66%	3,355	65%	3,215	100%	140

Note: The only generalization one might be tempted to make from this is that POT/GKT formats may be better at detecting or supporting truthfulness than they are at detecting deception.

REFERENCES

Ansley, N. (1992). The history and accuracy of Guilty Knowledge and Peak of Tension tests. *Polygraph*, 21(3), 174-247.

Arther, R. O. (1970). Peak of tension: Question formulation. *Journal of Polygraph Studies*, 4(5), 1-4.

Backster, C. (1969). Standardized Polygraph note pack and technique guide: Backster Zone Comparison Technique. New York: Backster Institute of Lie Detection.

Ben-Shakhar, G. (1992, February 2). Letter to Norman Ansley. Excerpt reported in *Polygraph*, 21(3), 174-247.

Bradley, M. T., Rettinger, J. (1992). Awareness of crime-relevant information and the guilty knowledge test. *Journal of Applied Psychology*, 77(1), 55-59.

Decker, R. E. (1978). The Army stimulation test; A controlled procedure. *Polygraph*, 7(3), 176-178.

Elaad, E. (1990). Detection of guilty knowledge in real-life criminal investigations. *Journal of* Applied Psychology, 75(5), 521-529.

Federal Bureau of Investigation (1985). *Peak of tension (POT) test construction*. Paper distributed at the annual seminar of the American Polygraph Association, Reno, NV.

Fukumoto, J. (1980). A case in which the polygraph was the sole evidence for conviction. *Polygraph*, 9(1), 42-44.

Fukomoto, J. (1982). Psychophysiological detection of deception in Japan: The past and present. *Polygraph*, 11(3), 234-238.

Furedy, J. J., Ben-Shakhar, G. (1991). The roles of deception, intention to deceive, and motivation to avoid detection in the psychophysiological detection of guilty knowledge. *Psychophysiology*, 28(2) 163-171.

Harrelson, L. H. (1964). *Keeler Polygraph Institute Training Guide*. Chicago, IL: Keeler Polygraph Institute.

Lykken, D. T. (1959). The GSR in the detection of guilt. *Journal of Applied Psychology*, 43(6), 383-388. Reprinted in *Polygraph*, 7(2), 123-128.

Lykken, D. T. (1960). The validity of the guilty knowledge technique: The effect of faking. *Journal of Applied Psychology*, 44(4), 258-262. Reprinted in *Polygraph*, 7(1), 42-48.

Lykken, D. T. (1981). *A Tremor in the Blood: Use and Abuses of the Lie Detector*. New York: McGraw-Hill Book Company.

Matte, J. A. (1980). *The Art and Science of the Polygraph Technique*. Springfield, IL: Charles C. Thomas - Publisher.

Nakayama, M., Yamamura, T. (1990). Changes of respiration pattern to the critical question on guilty knowledge technique. *Polygraph*, 19(3), 188-198. Abstract in *Psychophysiology*, 26(4A), 45.

Reid, J. E. (1952, March 6). Psychological advantages of the card control test in lie detector examinations. In *Proceedings of The American Academy of Forensic Sciences*, Atlanta, GA.

Reid, J. E., Inbau, F. E. (1977). *Truth and Deception: The Polygraph ("Lie-Detector") Technique* (2d ed.) Baltimore, MD: Williams & Wilkins.

Suzuki, A. (1978). A survey of polygraph examinations in Japan. *Polygraph*, 7(4), 295-308.

Widacki, J. (1986). Polygraph testing in Japan. *Archiwum Medycyny Sadowej I Kriminologii*, 36-(4), 229-233.

Yankee, W. J. (1991, September 24). Memorandum: Technical correction of curriculum. Department of Defense Polygraph Institute.

Chapter 19

THE SILENT ANSWER TEST

Several years ago, while conducting a psychophysiological veracity (PV) examination using the polygraph for a defense attorney on a suspected arsonist, this author observed that in both the first and second polygraph charts, the examinee consistently took a deep breath while listening to the relevant questions, which caused a substantial rise in the electrodermal response (GSR) pen. The excessive amount of air taken in by the examinee as a result of the deep breath naturally caused a need for less air intake in subsequent breathing cycles, causing a suppression pattern commonly found in a reaction tracing segment. However, the cause for the rise in the GSR pen and the breathing suppression could not be attributed to the activation of the sympathetic system while a logical scientific explanation for this physiological occurrence could also be attributed to another factor, the deep breath.

The fact that this examinee only took deep breaths while listening to the relevant questions and not while listening to the control questions would tend to indicate that the examinee's greatest concern or psychological set was focused onto the relevant questions. The possibility that the deep breaths may be a form of attempted countermeasure must also be considered.

In order to eliminate the distortion caused by the deep breath, this author decided to administer a Silent Answer Test (SAT) as the third chart. The examinee was advised that a third chart would be conducted using the same identical questions, but that this time, instead of answering the questions aloud, he was to listen carefully and then answer each question to himself truthfully but silently, in other words, he remains silent throughout this third chart.

A review and interpretation of the third chart containing the silent answer test revealed strong and consistent responses to the relevant questions and a lack of any deep breath or other distortion in the entire chart. A fourth chart was then administered similar to charts one and two requiring a verbal response from the examinee, which subsequently revealed a deep breath on the last relevant question only, but which clearly indicated strong responses in all tracings on the relevant questions. The conclusion of attempted deception to the relevant questions was verified by a confession from the examinee who admitted taking the deep breaths in an attempt to distort the chart tracings.

Research conducted by Frank S. Horvath and John E. Reid (1972) revealed that the Silent Answer Test produces better respiratory patterns by eliminating causes of distortions from the examinee who prepares himself or herself to answer each question aloud by inhaling a great amount of air; from the examinee who loudly bellows his or her answer to emphasize his or her denial; from the examinee who feels compelled to give an elaborate answer instead of a simple "yes" or "no" as instructed; and from the examinee whose throat is dry or irritated necessitating the clearing of his or her throat or coughing at intervals during the test.

Their research further indicated an enhancement of the utility of the electrodermal (GSR) recording. The SAT not only produced a chart with greater purity of tracing but also acted as an effective stimulation test for the subsequent polygraph tests/charts requiring a verbal answer.

The stimulating effect of the silent answer test on the guilty examinee may be due to the dilemma encountered when told he or she is not to answer the questions aloud but truthfully and silently to himself or herself. Previously the examinee has geared his or her defenses so that his or verbal answer to the relevant questions would not betray him or her. Now the examinee wonders whether he or she should answer those questions truthfully to himself or herself and presumably not show a reaction, which may reflect a different pattern than the previous charts, or silently answer them the same way as before and perhaps show a strong reaction as he or she may have on previous charts. This causes an inner conflict, a feeling of helplessness, which carries over into the subsequent test requiring a verbal response. The guilty examinee must now readjust his or her defenses again in preparation for his or her verbal responses to the relevant questions, which causes his or mind to race inasmuch as the two tests are administered back-to-back. The examinee's concern is on the relevant questions, which are now an even greater threat to his or her well-being which increases the strength of his or her psychological set onto the relevant questions and creates greater and clearer responses. The Silent Answer Test has the effect of enhancing the threatening power of the relevant questions to the guilty examinee, and conversely also enhances the innocent examinee's concern over the probable-lie control questions inasmuch as the relevant questions should be of no concern to him or her.

While most polygraph techniques employ the Silent Answer Test as a stimulation test and/or countercountermeasure, usually after the second chart, some polygraph techniques use the SAT as the very first test prior to the administration of the relevant issue test and include the SAT data in their decision-making process.

There is no literature on the use of a silent answer method or a no-answer method with field applications of the Guilty Knowledge Test including Peak of Tension formats. There are, however, research reports on this topic. Most of them have produced detection rates above chance (Ben-Shakhar 1977; Ben-Shakhar, Lieblich & Kugelmass 1975; Day & Rouke 1974; Dufek, Widacki & Valkova 1875; Elaad & Ben-Shakhar 1989; Gudjonsson 1977; Gustafson & Orne 1963, 1964, 1965; Horneman & O'Gorman 1985; Janisse & Bradley 1980), Minouchi & Kimura 1965; and Stern, Breen, Watanabe & Perry 1981). (Ansley 1992)

Konieczy, Fras and Widacki (1984) gave peak of tension tests to two groups of Polish students, one group that had watched an autopsy and one group that were told all the details, including the details that would be used in the test. Three Peak-of-Tension tests were administered to each person: routine, no answer, and with biofeedback. The detection rates for both groups were the same for each type of test: routine detection was 12 of 15 for each group (80%), no answer 13 of 15 (87%), and biofeedback 14 of 15 (93%). Stern, Breen, Watanabe and Perry (1981) had a higher detection rate for a no-answer group than the routine group, but the experiments were so dissimilar that the difference in answering may not be significant. (Ansley 1992)

Ellson (1952) used a galvanometer and eight students in which he attempted to detect the month of their birth. He broke the year into three groups of four months and asked, "Were you born in _____?" twice for each month in the group in a semi-random order for each; semi-random in that no month was repeated until the four were asked once. In this experiment the subject lied during one of the three phases of four-month groups. Each of the eight subjects were given three such tests in offsetting order for sequence, with one series answered "no," one answered "yes," and one mute. Ellson's detection rate for the eight students was four of the "no" answers, two of the "yes" answers, and one from the mute tests. (Ansley 1992)

While some polygraph techniques include their evaluation and quantification of the physiological data acquired in the Silent Answer Test into their final decision making process as to truth or deception, this author *does not* for the reasons set forth below.

(a) The guilty (as later verified) examinee may answer silently to himself/herself all test questions truthfully, thus the potential for no distinctive response to any of the test questions.

(b) The guilty (as later verified) examinee may answer silently to himself/herself truthfully to the relevant questions, thus the potential for significant reduction or elimination of response to the relevant questions.

(c) Inasmuch as the examinee is to remain mute during the SAT, the examinee may elect to disassociate himself/herself from the test entirely by not listening to the presentation of the test questions.

(d) The innocent (as later verified) examinee's expected concern about the control questions, may prompt him or her to give a silent truthful answer to the control questions, thus potentially negating their role and safeguard against false positives.

(e) At the present time, there is insufficient research data supporting the use of the physiological data provided by the Silent Answer Test in the decision-making process regarding truth or deception.

In analog studies conducted by Eitan Elaad and Gershon Ben-Shakhar (1989, 1991) it was found that when no motivational instructions were given and *no verbal answers* to the GKT questions were required, significantly lower levels of psychophysiological detection were attained, compared to the group required to give a *verbal answer* and *employ countermeasures* to the critical item. (See Chapter 21).

The above cited reasons for not including the Silent Answer Test results into the decision-making process, do not diminish the SAT's usefulness as an effective Stimulation Test and/or Counter-Countermeasure Test.

Figures XIX-1 through XIX-3, obtained from an actual case, present an unusual development resulting from the administration of the silent answer test, which proved the subject truthful regarding the larceny of a sapphire ring.

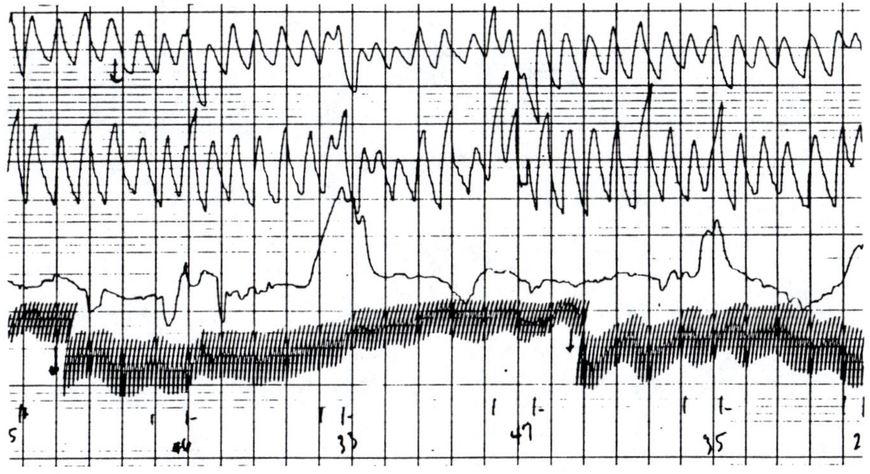

Actual Non-Silent Answer Test - Chart 1 -Larceny Case

Figure XIX-1

The first chart depicted above is a magnification of the Tracks (Spots) which are quantified for a determination. There is significant presence of reaction in all four tracings (two pneumos) at relevant question number 33 and an apparent lack of reaction to the neighboring control questions (46 and 47). Other than a mild electrodermal (GSR) response at relevant question 35, there is no significant presence of reaction to that relevant question. If the forensic psychophysiologist (FP) were to have made a decision on the basis of that one chart, he would have found the subject deceptive. However a Silent Answer Test was administered after this chart.

In the Silent Answer Test depicted in Figure XIX-2, the breathing tracing reflects significant suppression and hyperventilation in both control questions 46 and 47, but especially at question 46, compared to their neighboring relevant questions 33 and 35. In the electrodermal (GSR) response tracing the responses are of about equal magnitude except for question 35, which is double that of its neighboring control question. In the cardio tracing there is significant blood pressure arousal at question 46 as opposed to question 33. At question 47 there is some blood pressure arousal but there is an apparent

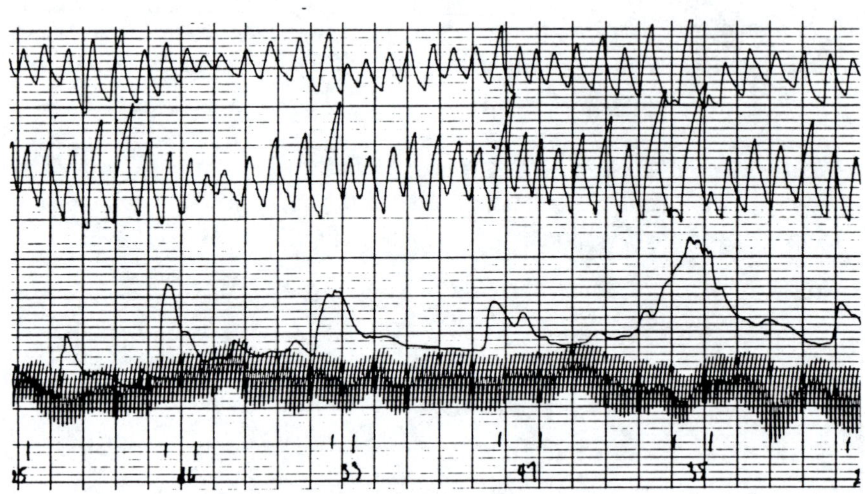

Actual Silent Answer Test - Chart 2 - Larceny Case

Figure XIX-2

greater blood pressure arousal at question 35. However, it must be noted that the subject was hyperventilating at question number 35 while relieving from question number 47 (control), which can cause a GSR and blood pressure arousal.

The chart depicted in Figure XIX-3 was administered immediately after the above depicted Silent Answer Test. In the breathing tracing there is a slight baseline arousal and suppression at control question 46, but average tracing cycles at question 35. There is a significant suppression and hyperventilation at control question 47 but average tracing cycles at relevant question 33. In the electrodermal (GSR) tracing, questions 35 and 46 are of apparent equal magnitude, but at question 47 there is a clear, significant arousal and a complete lack of response to its neighboring relevant question 33. In the cardio tracing there is evidence of a blood pressure arousal at control question 46 and an apparent lack of arousal at its neighboring relevant question 35. There is a significant blood pressure arousal at control question 47 and an apparent lack of arousal at its neighboring relevant question 33. It was subsequently confirmed that this subject had not stolen the sapphire ring.

While many forensic psychophysiologists claim that their Silent Answer Tests track consistently with the relevant test charts; in the absence of rigorous and definitive research data and answers regarding aforementioned psychological variables (a through e), it is premature at this time to consider and include the quantified and/or evaluated physiological data of the Silent Answer Test in the final determination of the examinee's truthfulness or deceptiveness regarding the target issue. However the SAT has empirically demonstrated its usefulness as an effective stimulation test and counter-countermeasure test.

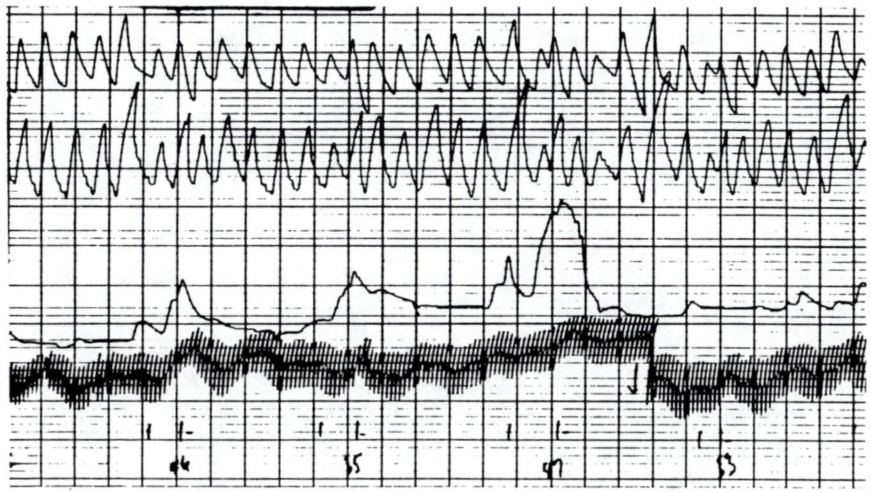

Actual Non-Silent Answer Test - Chart 3 - Larceny Case

Figure XIX-3

REFERENCES

Ansley, N. (1992). The history and accuracy of guilty knowledge and peak of tension tests. *Polygraph*, 21(3), 174-247.

Day, D. A., Rouke, B. P. (1974). The role of attention in lie detection. *Canadian Journal of Behavior Science*, 6(3), 270-276.

Dufek, M., Widacki, J., Valkova, V. (1975). Experimental studies of the use of the polygraph for a house search. *Archiv Med. Sad. I Krym.*, 25(2), 163-166.

Elaad, E., Ben-Shakhar, G. (1989). Effects of motivation and verbal response type on psychophysiological detection of deception. *Psychophysiology*, 26(4), 422-451

Ellson, D. G. (1952, Sep 15). A report on research on detection of deception; Office of Naval Research Contract No. N6-ONR -18011. Lafayette, IN: Indiana University.

Gudjonsson, G. H. (1977). *The efficacy of the galvanic skin response in experimental lie detection: Some personality variables*. Unpublished Master of Science Thesis, University of Surrey.

Gustafson, L. A., Orne, M. T. (1963). Effects of heightened motivation on the detection of deception. *Journal of Applied Psychology*, 47(6), 408-411.

Gustafson, L. A., Orne, M. T. (1964). *The effect of 'lying' on 'lie detection' studies*. Paper presented at the 35th annual meeting of the Eastern Psychological Association, Philadelphia, PA.

Gustafson, L. A., Orne, M. T. (1965). Effects of perceived role and role success on detection of deception. *Journal of Applied Psychology*, 49(6), 412-417.

Horneman, C., O'Gorman, J. G. (1985). Detectability in the card test as a function of the subject's verbal response. *Psychophysiology*, 22(3), 330-333. Reprinted in *Polygraph*, 15(4), 261-270.

Horvath, F. S., Reid, J. E. (1972). The polygraph silent answer test. *Journal of Criminal Law, Criminology and Police Science*, 63(2).

Konieczny, Jerzy, Fras, Miroslav, Widacki, J. (1984). The specificity of so-called emotional traces and certain features of personality in the polygraph examination. *Journal of Forensic Medicine and Criminology*, 34(1), 25-30.

Janisse, M. P., Bradley, M. T. (1980). Deception information and the pupillary response. *Perceptual and Motor Skills*, 50, 748-750.

Matte, J. A. (1980). *The Art and Science of the Polygraph Technique*. Springfield, IL: Charles C. Thomas - Publisher.

Minouchi, M., Kimura, T. (1965). Response of silence and forced to answer during peak of tension tests. Research materials No. 35, *Polygraph Reports*, National Institute of Police Science, pp. 25-29.

Reid, J. E., Inbau, F. E. (1977). *Truth and Deception: The Polygraph ("Lie-Detector") Technique* (2d ed) Baltimore, MD: Williams & Wilkins.

Stern, R. M., Breen, J. P., Watanabe, T., Perry, B. S. (1981). Effect of feedback on physiological information on response to innocent associations and guilty knowledge. *Journal of Applied Psychology*, 66(6), 677-681.

Suzuki, A., Yatsuda, J. (1965). Case study of silent answer of murder suspect in polygraph test. Research Materials No. 35, *Polygraph Reports*, pp. 17-29, National Institute of Police Science.

Chapter 20

THE EFFECTS OF DRUGS IN PSYCHOPHYSIOLOGICAL VERACITY EXAMINATIONS

Polygraph tracings can be described as physiologically recorded products of autonomic activity influenced by adrenergic stimulation which can possibly be modified by the intake of drugs. Because some drugs have the ability to alter polygraph tracings, the subject of drugs and psychophysiological veracity (PV) examinations becomes a very important one to forensic psychophysiologists. While it is generally true that the use of drugs by an examinee will not prevent valid and reliable PV examination results when a control question technique is used, unless the dosage is so great that the examinee is unable to participate in the pretest interview, a good comprehension of the effects of certain drugs on the physiological systems is necessary for the forensic psychophysiologist to accurately evaluate and assess test results.

Even though an impaired condition due to drug use would be readily apparent to any competent forensic psychophysiologist, there are times when the forensic psychophysiologist will test an examinee who is under the influence of prescribed medication or is under the influence of a drug by his or her own admission. This condition should not normally impair the examination and an examinee should never be advised to disregard his or her doctor's orders and/or refrain from prescribed medication prior to the PV examination because it could cause serious medical consequences, and from a scientific point of view could suddenly cause an imbalance in the examinee's metabolism, thereby upsetting his or her *normal state*. However, the examinee's medical history and use of drugs, especially in the twenty-four hours prior to the PV examination, should be obtained by the forensic psychophysiologist who should be familiar with the various drugs generally in use today and the expected effects on the physiological systems of the examinee and the charts that will be produced.

Drugs used in the treatment of disease today have become markedly more specific in their effects as more research has revealed more and more of the characteristics of receptor sites in the human body. Still, it is very possible that while ameliorating conditions for which they are prescribed, many drugs have undesirable effects which not only are unpleasant for the individual but pose possible challenges for the forensic psychophysiologist. Several categories of drugs will be discussed in this chapter and their primary and secondary effects will be given.

Beta-adrenergic receptor antagonists, or beta blockers, are medications used primarily for hypertension. Beta-blocking drugs block the uptake of norepinephrine by the beta-adrenergic receptors in cardiac tissue. Some beta blocking drugs are cardio specific, while others block beta-1 as well as beta-2 receptors. It is not necessary for the forensic psychophysiologist to be able to distinguish between the two types of beta-blocking drugs, but the beta blockers will include:

Generic Name	Trade Name	Generic Name	Trade Name
acebutolol	Sectral®	emmolol	Brevibloc®
atenolol	Tenormin®	penbutolol	Levatol®
bisoprolol	Zebeta®	betaxolol	Kerlone®
metoprolol	Lopressor®	carteolol	Cartrol®
nadolol	Corgard®	timolol	Blocarden®
pindolol	Visken®	sotalol	Betapace®
propanolol	Inderal®		

A drug which possesses alpha and beta blocking qualities is:
Labetalol Normodyne®, Trandate®

The primary effects a forensic psychophysiologist should expect from beta-blocking drugs are:

a. GSR/GSG reduced responsiveness due to the decreased sympathetic tone. Some experienced forensic psychophysiologists believe that the GSR/GSG is the channel in which the most effect is exhibited by the beta-blocking drug.

b. Cardio-responsive but reduced amplitude and rate. Other effects that can be expected from beta-blocking drugs are dizziness, vertigo, visual disturbances, sleep disturbances, and sedation.

Depressant drugs, a category which includes alcohol, tranquilizers, antihistamines, and anti-psychotics have a general effect of depressing the central nervous system (CNS). The varying degrees of depression range from mild sedation or relaxation to coma. Depressant drugs can cause physiological changes that may affect each tracing of the polygraph chart by decreasing the breathing rate and/or increasing the tracing amplitude; by creating slower and/or smaller electrodermal responses; and by decreasing the heart rate and/or creating slower/smaller reactions. The effects of the drug are constant throughout the chart, and do not selectively exert an influence on any one group of questions.

The primary effects that will be witnessed with depressant drugs will be a decreased responsiveness of the GSR/GSG and decreased amplitude and reactivity of the cardio. Some change may be seen in the pneumograph tracing in the form of a slower breathing rate, although experiments have shown that subjects on tranquilizers generally give excellent charts which still exhibit characteristic reaction criteria. Often the effects of a depressant such as a tranquilizer are observed in the GSR/GSG in that the pen will continuously fall to the bottom of the chart regardless of the sensitivity setting, and when the unit is placed in the automatic or self-centering mode, there is no movement of the pen regardless of the sensitivity setting. Before making that assumption though, the forensic psychophysiologist should have the examinee wash his or her hands in the presence of the forensic psychophysiologist who should wipe the GSR/GSG electrodes, preferably before each and every test/chart. When aforesaid remedial action proves unsuccessful, the forensic psychophysiologist should then check out the GSR/GSG unit by placing the electrodes on his or her own fingers and/or recalibrating that unit. It is expected that the GSR/GSG unit and other components are always calibrated on a regular basis.

The most common tranquilizers on the market today are:

Generic	**Trade Name**	**Generic Name**	**Trade Name**
diazepam	Valium®	chlordiazepozide	Librium®
oxazepam	Serax®	lorazepam	Ativan®
alprazolam	Zanax®	chlorazepate	Tranxene®
butalbital	Butisol®	mephobarbital	Mebaral®
phenobarbital	Luminal®	hydroxyzine	Atarax®

Some common antihistamines that may cause drowsiness and/or a decreased responsiveness are:

Generic Name	**Trade Name**	**Generic Name**	**Trade Name**
diphenhydramine	Benadryl®	clemastine Fumarate	Tavist®
tripelennamine	PBZ®	pyrilamine	No trade name
dexchlorpheniramine	Polaramine®	chlorpheniramine Maleate	Chlor-Trimeton®
brompheniramine	Dimetane®	trimeprazine	Temaril®
methdilazine	Tacaryl®	cyproheptadine	Periactin®

Antidepressants, except for fluoxetine (Prozac®), paroxetine (Paxil®), and sertraline (Zoloft®) which are the more recent introductions to the United States market, produce varying levels of sedation, particularly during the first few weeks of treatment. When a patient/examinee is being treated with an antidepressant, as much or more concern should be given to the underlying condition as to the drug. In most cases, the effect of the drug itself is predictable. However, combining the antidepressant drug with the residual effect of the underlying condition may give unexpected and surprising results, particularly if accompanied by other drugs. The anticholinergic (atropine-like) effect of most of the antidepressant drugs on today's market will normally cause a faster than normal heart rate. The pneumograph pattern should not be affected and normal reactions should be detected in the pneumograph, GSR/GSG and cardiograph tracings. The degree of change in the GSR/GSG depends on the condition of the examinee, the dosage level of the antidepressant and the length of time the antidepressant has been a part of the dosage regimen of the examinee. Therefore, the GSR/GSG is the channel in which more difficulty is encountered in predicting a given response. However, even with all of that, just the mere fact that an examinee reports having taken an antidepressant is no cause within itself to expect a chart that displays other than normal reactions sufficiently adequate for a forensic psychophysiologist to render an opinion.

Generic	Trade Name	Generic Name	Trade Name
amitriptyline	Elavil®	clomipramine	Anafranil®
doxepin	Sinequan®, Adapin®	imipramine	Tofranil®
trimipramine	Surmontil®	amoxapine	Asendin®
desipramine	Noroparamin®	nortriptyline	Aventil®,Pamelor®
protriptyline	Vivactil®	maprotiline	Ludiomil®
trazodone	Desyrel®	bupropion	Wellbrutrin®
fluoxetine	Prozac®	paroxetine	Paxil®
sertraline	Zoloft®	venlafaxine	Effexor®

Anti-psychotic drugs commonly cause a sedative effect in individuals as well as a faster than normal heart rate, due to the anti-cholinergic influence of many of the drugs in the anti-psychotic class. Here again, as much or more concern should be given to the underlying condition as to the effect of the drug. If an examinee appears responsive in the pre-test interview and is alert, there is no reason not to test the person solely on the basis of their disclosure of having taken an anti-psychotic drug. Some anti-psychotic drugs frequently seen are:

Generic Name	Trade Name	Generic Name	Trade Name
chlorpromazine	Thorazine®	promazine	Sparine®
triflupromazine	Vesprin®	thioridazine	Mellaril®
mesoridazine	Serentil®	trifluoperazine	Stelazine®
perphenazine	Trilazon®	acetophenazine	Tindal®
prochlorperazine	Compazine®	fluphenazine	Prolixin®
thiothixene	Navane®	haloperidol	Haldol®
molindone	Moban®	loxapine	Loxitane®
clozapine	Clozaril®	risperidone	Risperdal®
pimozide	Orap®	lithium	Lithionate®
			Eskalith®

Narcotic analgesics or *pain killers* should be of interest to the forensic psychophysiologist, not only because they may influence the physiological data on the chart of the examinee but because of their chemical relation to some of the illegal street drugs. Narcotic analgesics are classified as agonists, mixed agonist-antagonist, or partial agonist by their activity at *opioid* receptors. These drugs may result in euphoria, drowsiness, apathy, mental confusion, and respiratory depression while providing direct pain relief and antitussive activity. The two pharmacological properties of interest to the forensic psychophysiologist relate to respiratory depression and sedation. These effects are dose related and may vary with different individuals. Drugs in this category which the forensic psychophysiologist will sometimes see are:

Generic Name	Trade Name	Generic	Trade Name
codeine	No trade name	hydrocodone	Lorcet, Lortab®
hydromorphone	Dilaudid®	levorphanol	Levo-Dromoran®

Generic Name	Trade Name	Generic Name	Trade Name
oxycodone	Roxicodone®	oxymorphone	Numorphan®
alfentanil	Alfenta®	fentanyl	Sublimaze®, Duragesic®
meperidine	Demerol®	sufentanil	Sufenta®
methadone	Dolophine®	propoxyphene	Darvon®, Dolene®
dezocine	Dalgan®	butorphanol	Stadol®
nalbuphine	Nubain®	buprenorphine	Buprenex®
methotrimeprazine	Levoprome®	tramadol	Ultram®
morphine	Duramorph® & MSIR®, MS Contin®	pentazocine	Talwin® & Talwin NX®

Heroin is chemically similar enough to morphine to exhibit some of the physiological effects of the drugs of this class. Heroin is rapidly hydrolyzed to monoacetyl morphine (MAM), which in turn, is hydrolyzed to morphine in the body. Morphine and "MAM" are responsible for the pharmacological actions of heroin. Despite obvious respiratory depression from doses that cause toxicity, the blood pressure is usually maintained until relatively late in the course of intoxication and then falls largely as a result of hypoxia. The main effects seen with heroin use are pain relief and intense euphoria followed by a period of somnolence and lassitude, referred to as "on the nod." The examinee who is a heroin addict will have pinpoint pupils, constipation, a desire for sweets, and varying degrees of respiratory depression. Initial signs of withdrawal appear about 12 hours after the last drug administration. During this time, the addict will be anxious and crave another dose. Symptoms which develop include watery eyes, yawning, runny nose, and perspiration. As the withdrawal progresses, irritability, restlessness, diarrhea, vomiting, gooseflesh, and muscle aches occur. Finally, symptoms will include chills, alternating flushing and sweating, pain in muscles of the back and extremities, as well as muscle spasms and kicking movement.

Stimulant drugs, both in the prescription only category and some which are available over the counter cause a number of actions in the body. Of interest to the forensic psychophysiologist is the central nervous system excitatory action such as respiratory stimulation and the cardiac excitatory action which is responsible for an increase in heart rate and force of contraction. Under the influence of stimulant drugs, both systolic and diastolic blood pressure are raised and pulse pressure is usually increased, although with large doses, the heart rate may be reflexively slowed. Cardiac arrhythmias may occur as well as headaches, palpitation, dizziness, vasomotor disturbances, agitation, confusion, dysphoria, apprehension, delirium or fatigue. The respiratory center will be stimulated and the rate and depth of respiration will be increased, though not appreciably. The changes seen by the forensic psychophysiologist will be changes in breathing rate, decreased pneumo amplitude, faster and/or greater electrodermal responses, and an increased heart rate and/or greater cardiac reactions. Some of the drugs in this category are:

Generic Name	Trade Name	Generic Name	Trade Name
dextroamphetamine	Dexedrine®	mazindol	Sanorex®
methamphetamine	Desoxyn®	diethylpropion	Tepanil®
benzphetamine	Didrex®	phendimetrazine	Bontril PDM®
phentermine	Fastin®, Adipex® & Ionamin®		

Cocaine is a powerful CNS stimulant and sympathomimetic agent, which produces its sense of well-being through potentiation of neurotransmitters. The euphoric effect of cocaine has a relatively short duration of action and is dependent on the route of administration. Cocaine hydrochloride may be insufflated as well as used intravenously (IV). It may be free-based into a dried paste which is known as crack or rock which may be smoked. Initial doses of cocaine result in euphoria, hyperactivity, and restlessness which progressively leads to tremors, hyperreflexia, and convulsions, leading to tachycardia and hypertension. It can produce nausea and vomiting as well as diarrhea and abdominal cramps. All channels of the polygraph will be exaggerated as long as the drug is producing a physiological effect, followed by a "crash" or flat charts which is characteristic of the use of other stimulants.

Commonly available over the counter are preparations containing caffeine, phenylpropanolamine, and ephedrine.

Any discussion of street drugs should be prefaced by the fact that there is no standardization of dosage, leading to a wide array of individualized effects. Combine that with the fact that individuals whose lifestyle includes common illicit drugs may use combinations of different drugs, and the issue of predicting physiological responses becomes immensely clouded. The consoling factor is that if the examinee is deemed capable of being tested, most likely any unusual tracing will present a "*norm*" throughout the test and will not adversely affect his or her physiological ability to react to the questions on the test.

Marijuana (marihuana) also referred to as pot, maryjane, grass, hooch, hemp or reefer, is a composite of dried leaves and flowering buds of the plant *Cannabis sativa* L. The compounds that produce the hallucinogenic and euphoric effects of marihuana are called cannabinoids. The cannabinoid, delta-9-tetrahydrocannabinol (THC), is the principal psychoactive ingredient in marijuana and hashish. The compound THC is almost completely metabolized after it is quickly absorbed through smoking or ingestion. Elimination of urinary metabolites begin within hours after exposure to cannabinoids. Concentrations depend on the total amount of THC absorbed, frequency of abuse, rate of release from fatty tissue, and time of sample collection with respect to use. The prevalent theory is that THC is distributed in and absorbed by various fatty tissues and then is very slowly released to the blood stream; it is then metabolized in the liver and eventually excreted in the urine and feces. In chronic users, THC may accumulate in fatty tissues faster than it can be eliminated. This accumulation leads to longer detection times in urinalysis for chronic users than for occasional users. Detection of THC could be up to three months in the every-day user (Booth 1996). For most of the recreational users, one or two marijuana cigarettes (joints) a week, the drug is recovered in urine specimens 14 to 28 days later (Booth 1996). Marijuana continues to be one of the most commonly used recreational drugs in the United States. A user's response to the drug is dependent on a number of factors, including personality and expectations, prior experience, and the amount of the active ingredient (THC) absorbed. The setting in which the drug is used also influences the effect it will have on the individual. In an isolated environment, users experience euphoria, relaxation and sleepiness. Smoking in a group setting, however, results in social interaction, friendliness, and laughter. Time seems to pass more slowly, and sensory perceptions become more vivid. Higher doses elicit more intense reactions, including image distortion, altered self-identity, and hallucinations. Vigilance, coordination and reaction time may be impaired for 12 to 14 hours after the "high" from the drug is gone. The most consistent effects on the cardiovascular system are an increase in heart rate, an increase in systolic blood pressure, and a marked reddening of the conjunctivae. Increases of 20 to 50 beats per minute are usual, but a tachycardia of 140 beats per minute is not uncommon. There is no consistent change in respiratory rate but the GSR is characteristically very flat and unresponsive.

It cannot be overemphasized that examinees should *never* be advised to refrain from taking or using their prescribed medication either before or on the day of their scheduled PV examination. All medications should continue to be taken as prescribed with no deviations. This includes all insulin or diabetic medications, anticonvulsants, blood pressure medications, etc. Not only can serious medical consequences result from omission of the medicine, but its effect on the PV examination itself can be serious.

Drug effects on the physiological systems should be constant throughout the collection of the physiological data and all examinees must still produce reactions either to the control questions if truthful to the target issue, or to the relevant questions if deceptive to the target issue, of sufficient magnitude, purity of tracing, and consistency of response of a combined value that will attain a numerical score scientifically sufficient to render a valid and reliable conclusion. No drug effect exists which will change a truthful diagnosis to a deceptive diagnosis or vice versa. The worst outcome is that the physiological tracings may be affected to the extent that an inconclusive outcome would result.

The subject of drug effects on PV examination results is long overdue for more controlled studies. While the effects of most drugs may be predicted, reliable studies are woefully lacking. With the present state of knowledge, the forensic psychophysiologist who is well versed on drugs will often have logical explanations for abnormal physiological tracings on the polygraph charts.

In the final analysis, the forensic psychophysiologist has the responsibility and final decision regarding the feasibility of a psychophysiological veracity (PV) examination but should never disregard medical authority that warns against the administration of a PV examination.

Thus far we have seen the effects of drugs on the examinee of a PV examination. We shall now discuss the effectiveness of the PV examination in narcotics investigations.

Investigations into the use and primarily the sale of illegal drugs and narcotics rely heavily upon information from informants who for the most part are "users" and/or "pushers" of narcotics themselves, generally on a small scale. They often become informants to eliminate their competition, to learn investigative procedures and operations, and to learn the identity of narcotics investigators so as to avoid detection of their own current or future criminal activities. The informant who consistently provides law enforcement with reliable information believes himself or herself indispensable, therefore relatively immune from arrest and exposure regarding minor narcotics or other criminal activities. The narcotic underworld is composed of criminals who will lie, cheat, and steal to support their drug habit. Since narcotics informants generally come from that environment, narcotics agents or investigators must be especially cautious in their dealing with them. Each year a number of narcotic investigators are compromised or betrayed by their informants, sometimes costing the investigator's life. For this reason, a number of law enforcement agencies have started using the services of a forensic psychophysiologist to verify the truthfulness of evidentiary information supplied by a narcotics informant and his or her motive.

Favorable PV examination results regarding information supplied by a narcotics informant serve to buttress the notoriously poor credibility of informants whose testimony or affidavit forms the basis of search warrants in narcotics investigations.

The polygraph technique can be used on persons charged with the unlawful possession of narcotics to develop information regarding the identity of his or her source. Once the identity of the source has been verified by the polygraph, the investigator should attempt to elicit the cooperation of this person to effect an introduction of an undercover investigator to the developed source (the "pusher"). The pretest interview will usually develop background information (this person's occupation, employment, and financial status). The narcotics user will be hard pressed to explain the source of the additional income required to support his or her drug habit. In addition to developing information regarding unsolved burglaries, the investigator will also develop information concerning larcenies from suspects' employers, since it is easier to steal from a place of employment than to commit burglaries.

The PV examination can be administered to convicted narcotics violators prior to sentencing to determine whether the extenuating and mitigating circumstances offered by the defendant are true, and further verify the accuracy of information provided by the defendant as a gesture of cooperation with law enforcement officials. PV examination results would be invaluable to the court in sentence determination.

Since narcotics users and addicts are preoccupied with drugs, their knowledge of drugs is usually extensive. It therefore behooves the forensic psychophysiologist to acquire as much knowledge as possible regarding drugs and the terminology used by the drug culture. An excellent source of information on prescription drugs is the Physician's Desk Reference (PDR) and/or the Medical Drug Reference by Parsons Technology on computer CD ROM. A list of drug terms employed by the drug culture can be obtained by law enforcement agencies from the Drug Enforcement Agency (DEA) or from any Law Enforcement Drug Investigation School.

REFERENCES

Arther, R. O. (1973, Mar-Apr). Drugs, medicines, alcohol - and chart analysis. *The Journal of Polygraph Studies.* 7(5).

Bazil, M. K., Gabriel, G. (1996, February). Review of therapy for hypertension. *U. S. Pharmacist.*

Berman, M. A. (1967, Jan-Feb). Drugs versus the polygraph. *The Journal of Polygraph Studies.* 1(4).

Booth, P. (1996, April). Marijuana. *Lablink*, Corning Clinical Laboratories, Vol. 2, Nr. 1.

Cantrell, J. A. (1995, August 16). Drugs and the effect of drugs on polygraph examinations. Presentation at the 30th Annual Seminar/Workshop of the American Polygraph Association, Las Vegas, NV.

Elaad, E., Bonwitt, G., Eisenberg, O. Meytes, I. (1982). Effects of beta blocking drugs on the polygraph detection rate: A pilot study. *Polygraph*, 11(3), 225-231.

Gatchel, R. J., Smith, J. E., Kaplan, N. M. (1983). The effect of propranolol on polygraphic detection of deception. Unpublished manuscript, University of Texas Health Sciences Center.

Gilman, A. G., Goodman, L. S., Gilman A. (1980). *The Pharmacological Basis of Therapeutics.* Sixth Edition. New York: MacMillan Publishing Co., Inc.

Iacono, W. G., Boisvenu, G. A. (1984). Effects of diazepam and methylphenidate on the electrodermal detection of guilty knowledge. *Journal of Applied Psychology*, 69(2), 289-299.

Iacono, W. G., Cerri, A. M., Patrick, C. J., Fleming, J. A. (1992). Use of antianxiety drugs as countermeasures in the detection of guilty knowledge. *Journal of Applied Psychology*, 77(1), 60-64.

Matte, J. A. (1980). *The Art and Science of the Polygraph Technique*. Springfield, IL: Charles C. Thomas.

Olin, B. R. (Ed.) (1996). Drug facts and comparisons. *Facts and Comparisons*. St. Louis: A Wolters Kluwer Company.

Parsons Technology. (1994). Medical Drug Reference: For windows. CD-ROM. Hiawatha, Iowa

Physicians' Desk Reference (1994). PDR 48 edition. Montvale, NJ: Medical Economics Data Production Company.

Rothschild, A. J.,(1995). Optimizing care of the depressed patient: Choosing appropriate antidepressant therapy. Proceedings of a symposium presented in conjunction with the 52d annual meeting of the American Society of Hospital Pharmacists in Miami Beach, Florida. Published through the facilities of U. S. Pharmacist. Pfizer Labs, NHO, Pratt, Roerig, U.S. Pharmaceuticals Group.

Scaros, L. P., Westra, S., Barone, J. A. (1990, May). Illegal use of drugs: A current review. *U. S. Pharmacist*. Pgs 17-39.

Waid, W. M., Orne, E. C., Cook, M. R., Orne, M. T. (1981). Meprobamate reduces accuracy of physiological detection of deception. *Science* 212:71-73.

Chapter 21

COUNTERMEASURES

A psychophysiological veracity (PV) examination comprises a pretest interview to psychologically prepare the examinee for the conduct of the PV tests (Phase I), and the conduct of PV tests for the collection of physiological data (Phase II). Analysis and quantification of the physiological data for a conclusion (Numerical Approach) or global evaluation of factual analysis, behavior assessment and analysis of the chart data for a conclusion (Clinical Approach) comprise Phase III. A post-test interview following Phase III is not considered part of the PV examination inasmuch as it does not play any role in the acquisition of the physiological data from which a determination of truth or deception is made. Indeed some courts have dismissed post-test confessions because the forensic psychophysiologist associated the post-test interview to the PV examination process. (Johnson v. State, 208 Ga.App. 87, 429 S.E.2d690 (Ga.App.1993); State v. Craig, 50 St.Repo. 1533,___P.2d___(Montana 1993); Amyot v. Her Majesty the Queen, Province of :Quebec, District of Montreal, Nos. 500-10-000015-837, 500-10-000141-877, and (705-01-000137-8353). Countermeasures when employed are used during one or both of the first two phases of the PV examination.

Proponents of the Numerical Approach normally focus their attention to countermeasure attempts during Phase II of the PV examination. In 1984, Dr. Gordon H. Barland defined polygraph countermeasures as "Those deliberate techniques which a deceptive subject uses in an attempt to appear nondeceptive when his physiological responses are being monitored during a polygraph examination." Dr. Barland excluded from this definition "all false positive errors" "all false negative errors occurring naturally" and "attempts to explain away reactions after they have occurred."

Proponents of the Clinical Approach normally focus their attention to countermeasure attempts during the first two phases and some include all phases including the post-test interview, inasmuch as the Clinical Approach includes a *behavior assessment* in their decision making process known as global evaluation. Thus a broader definition offered by the Gormac polygraph training school* emerged as follows: "Any intentional attempt, method or action taken by an examinee to influence the outcome of the polygraph examination" (Marcy 1995).

However, Lynn P. Marcy, a proponent of the Clinical Approach offered this working definition: "Any behavior(s) employed by an examinee deliberately during the testing protocol and intended to assist continued concealment of verbal deception directed at some aspect of the perceived issue under examination." (Marcy 1995).

---

*See Appendix P for list of polygraph schools accredited by the American Polygraph Association.

Regardless of which approach is used, the forensic psychophysiologist (FP) should be on the alert for the application of countermeasures during the first two phases of the PV
examination until all physiological data charts have been collected for analysis. While proponents of the Numerical Approach do not factor into the decision making process any behavior assessment which would include deliberate countermeasure attempts, such behavior when noticed is combated with countercountermeasures, and when warranted, is factored into the analysis of the physiological data.

Countercountermeasures were defined by Marcy as "those *reactive* question sequence strategies; verbal stimuli; and special testing methodologies introduced into the examination protocol when countermeasures become suspected at some point in the pretest or testing process. Then it becomes an added part of the examiner's mission to utilize some reactive countercountermeasure technique(s) to investigate whether some countermeasure is probably being attempted." (Marcy 1995)

Anticountermeasures were defined by Marcy as "those *proactive* question sequence strategies; verbal stimuli; and special testing methodologies to be introduced into the examination protocol routinely through the deliberate advance design of the examiner independently of any suspected countermeasure." (Marcy 1995).

Both the Numerical Approach and the Clinical Approach to PV examinations include anticountermeasures in Phase I, the pretest interview, which includes the psychological preparation of the examinee for Phase II. These anticountermeasures vary with each technique as modified by the knowledge and experience of each forensic psychophysiologist and available equipment designed for that purpose. An example of such anticountermeasures incorporated into a pretest interview is described in Chapters 6, 8 and 9.

In addition to a structured pre-test interview designed to deter the guilty (as later verified) examinee from employing countermeasures, the forensic psychophysiologist can also employ other anticountermeasures such as the routine use of drug testing immediately after completion of a PV examination. Notification of this practice to all examinees prior to their scheduled PV examination is a useful deterrent. Another anticountermeasure is the use of a motion or activity sensor attached to the examination chair which records on the polygraph chart at the exact moment, the most minute examinee movement. In at least one book on the use of countermeasures, the reader is advised to avoid all physical countermeasures when the PV examination chair contains a motion or activity sensor.

It has been this author's experience, that when adequate anticountermeasures are included in the psychophysiological methodology used, and the forensic psychophysiologist implements them, the need for countercountermeasures is minimal if not rare. In a field validation study conducted by this author and Dr. Ronald M. Reuss (1990), 39 defense attorney cases were tested by this author under attorney-client privilege and their conclusions were confirmed. Of these 39 confirmed cases, 34 of them were scored deceptive, 3 truthful, and 2 inconclusive. While it may be easier to acquire a confession which under those circumstances cannot be used against the examinee, the guilty (as later verified) examinee's motivation to defeat the PV examination is still very strong judging by the mean chart score of -9.38 versus the police cases used in the same study which employed the same polygraph technique, who realized a mean chart score of -9.10. A mean chart score of -5 is required to render a decision of deception. In none of the aforementioned attorney cases were countercountermeasures required, indicating that either the anticountermeasures were effective or the countermeasures used were ineffective.

Countercountermeasures available to the forensic psychophysiologist include specialized psychological tests and techniques, described in chapters 8, 9, 19 and 22, plus the video taping of the PV examination for subsequent review and analysis.

This chapter is devoted primarily to *research* conducted on the effectiveness of mental, physical and pharmaceutical countercountermeasures in psychophysiological veracity examinations.

MENTAL

Mental countermeasures require employment of the mind only, thus are not readily apparent to the forensic psychophysiologist (FP). This includes rationalization, and mental exercise covered in Chapters 8 and 9, and hypnosis which will be addressed in this chapter. Biofeedback which is covered in chapter 9, is not in itself a countermeasure, but refers to the process where a person is given immediate information concerning his or her own biological functions. Such biofeedback training aims at helping that person through the use of this biological information to voluntarily control a specific physiological process.

Hypnosis

The question has often been raised regarding the possibility of an examinee defeating a psychophysiological veracity (PV) examination while under hypnotically induced amnesia. Hypnotically induced amnesia refers to a functional amnesia induced in the examinee by posthypnotic suggestion, and a posthypnotic suggestion refers to a suggestion concerning a phenomenon taking place subsequent to the "waking" of the examinee from the hypnotic trance. The question is answered in the review of the literature on the subject, which revealed that, in 1945, E. M. Bitterman and F. L. Marcuse demonstrated by means of a Keeler polygraph that subjects showing complete symbolic posthypnotic amnesia for specific previously learned words retained the ability to recognize the words at the "unconscious" level. The subjects produced deceptive responses on their polygrams when they denied recognition of the previously learned words.(Bitterman & Marcuse 1945)

In 1959, William E. Cumley and Robert L. Berry conducted an experiment involving a hypothetical burglary committed by two subjects in their normal state. The subjects were subsequently hypnotized and posthypnotic amnesia was induced by use of posthypnotic suggestion. After being hypnotized, the subjects, while under polygraph instrumentation, denied having committed the burglary, which produced deceptive responses to the relevant questions. (Cumley 1959)

In 1959, a research project was conducted by the Provost Marshal General's School at Fort Gordon, Georgia to study the effect of hypnotically induced amnesia upon the accuracy of the PV examination results. (Lie Detector Committee 1959).

The project was limited to tests concerning hypothetical crimes perpetrated by the subject prior to hypnosis using a total of twelve examinees. The general relevant-irrelevant question test and the peak-of-tension test were used.

The experiments were conducted in two phases. The subject was first tested after the commission of a hypothetical crime in his conscious state without the influence of hypnosis. In the second phase the subject was placed in a hypnotic trance and an attempt was made to induce amnesia concerning the hypothetical crime by use of a posthypnotic suggestion. The subject was then administered a PV examination concerning the offense.

The researchers encountered difficulty in developing a technique that would induce a sufficiently deep hypnotic trance to insure complete amnesia. To insure valid results it was necessary to place the subject in as deep a trance as possible. It was found that very few individuals will go into a deep trance the first time they are hypnotized; even after several encounters only a limited number will go into such a trance.

The experiment revealed that of the twelve subjects examined, only one failed to indicate deception when examined on the polygraph. Prior to hypnosis, this subject gave deception responses during the PV examination when he denied the commission of the hypothetical crime. After amnesia was induced through hypnosis, the subject was reexamined, and he failed to give deceptive responses. During the pretest interview and the posttest interrogation he emphatically denied the commission of the hypothetical crime.

After hypnosis, the other eleven subjects retained a partial or hazy memory of the hypothetical crime. During a reexamination, their denial regarding the commission of the crime produced deceptive responses similar to the responses produced prior to hypnosis.

Analysis of the results obtained by the research project conducted by the Provost Marshal General's School indicates the following:

a. The degree of amnesia the hypnotist can induce is dependent upon the subject and upon the depth of the hypnotic trance.
b. There is no specific depth in a hypnotic trance at which complete amnesia can be induced.
c. It is extremely difficult to induce 100 percent amnesia in a subject.
d. If only partial amnesia is induced and the subject retains a vague or hazy memory of the crime, or has an "uneasy feeling" concerning the crime, the subject will produce a deceptive response.

e. In one instance, a subject who had previously indicated deception concerning a hypothetical crime failed to do so after amnesia was hypnotically induced.

NOTE: The aforesaid study by the Provost Marshal General's Polygraph School was an *analog* study which used a mock paradigm. It would appear even more difficult to induce amnesia to an actual crime importing dire consequences of discovery.

In 1961, research (analog) was conducted by A. C. German to determine whether amnesia induced by hypnosis could surreptitiously defeat the polygraph. Of a total of twenty volunteers, five were selected for the study on the basis of their suggestibility and deep trance capability - based on eye and limb catalepsy; tactile, olfactory, auditory, gustatory, and visual illusions and hallucinations, positive and negative; anesthesia; response to posthypnotic suggestion, normal and bizarre; age regression; and perceptual transcendence. Fifteen PV examinations were administered, each repeated three times. The suggestions for amnesia consisted of writing on sand, after which waves would erase the writing; the examinee would write on a blackboard and would then erase with gasoline-soaked rags; and the examinee would write on paper and then burn the paper to ashes.

In eight of the PV examinations, a significant response indicating deception was immediately detected by the forensic psychophysiologist (FP). In the other seven examinations, abnormal patterns were evaluated by the FP as indicative of excessive emotion, nevertheless were deemed somewhat inconclusive as indicative of either truthfulness or deception. This study concluded that the instrumental detection of deception technique relies upon subconscious as well as conscious reactions, and that amnesia hypnotically induced cannot surreptitiously defeat the psychophysiological veracity (PV) examination.

Interestingly, the aforementioned experiments were conducted under laboratory conditions totally lacking the "fear of detection" element found in field situation, which is the primary stimulus that activates the sympathetic subdivision of the autonomic nervous system causing a "reaction" on the polygraph chart. The fact that the forensic psychophysiologists in the aforementioned studies were able to detect deception while employing techniques in use from 1945 to 1961, should not escape the reader's attention.

A later study conducted in 1970 by Edwin Weinstein, M.D., Stanley Abrams, Ph.D., and Donald Gibbons, Ph.D., relates different conclusions. Using a group of six volunteer college students divided into two subgroups of three students each, one group was instructed to take a one-dollar bill, a five-dollar bill, or a twenty-dollar bill from an empty office. Each of these three students was then hypnotized to create amnesia for the act of taking the money and the suggestion was made that no guilt would be associated with the act. The second group was hypnotized and it was suggested that they had stolen the money, after which they were awakened and instructed to deny their guilt when tested on the polygraph. The results of this experiment revealed that the forensic psychophysiologist (FP) determined that the latter group, which had not in fact stolen the money, had according to the polygraph charts stolen the money in the denominations suggested while under hypnosis. Regarding the three students who had actually taken the money, the FP was unable to conclusively determine whether or not they were guilty of the theft. Under pressure for a definite conclusion, however, the FP indicated that this group had probably taken the money but was not definite enough to present this evidence in a court of law. Furthermore, when asked which of the three bills each student might have taken, the FP was correct in only one instance. (Weinstein, Abrams, Gibbons, 1970).

The conclusions of the aforesaid study revealed that the FP was "partially misled by the hypnotic approach since he could not state conclusively that the students were guilty. However, he was obviously not completely deceived since he did not see them as innocent either." (Weinstein, Abrams, Gibbons, 1970).

Experimental psychophysiological veracity (PV) examinations administered to two volunteer subjects at Duquesne University in 1956 by Charles A. McInerney concluded that a wakeful subject cannot defeat the PV examination as the result of a posthypnotic suggestion.

W. J. Bryan, Jr. (1962) studied this phenomenon by having a subject steal an object. Then he hypnotized her, suggested that she had stolen a second object, and had her forget the theft that she had committed. The PV examination showed a response to both objects, which suggests that the unconscious may produce anxiogenic responses which can be demonstrated psychophysiologically by the polygraph.

Dr. Stanley Abrams, a clinical and forensic psychologist informed this author that he personally administered PV examinations to several professional hypnotists in actual real-life cases who employed self-hypnosis as a countermeasure, but that none of them were able to defeat the PV examinations which produced very responsive physiological data, each confirmed by confessions. Dr. Abrams concluded that the more motivated, the more detectable the subjects become. Again, the psychodynamics of subjects in analog studies differ greatly from those in field studies where the consequences of detection are grave. Considering that posthypnotic amnesia was not generally effective in aforementioned analog studies, it is expected to be even less effective in real-life cases, thus not an effective countermeasure to the PV examination. (Abrams 1995).

Dissociation

Eitan Elaad and Gershon Ben-Shakhar (1991) conducted an analog study on the effects of specific dissociation from the relevant stimulus and continuous dissociation throughout the entire Guilty Knowledge test in mock crime paradigms. A control no-countermeasure condition was also used in this study. Two experiments were conducted:

---

*Cardiovascular recordings at pressures below 70 mmHg produce decreasingly less dramatic amplitude changes during a reaction because the percent change in the mismatch (MABP and MCAP) during a response at low cuff pressure is relatively small. (see Chapter 4 for full explanation.)

one in a field setup using a Lafayette Pentograph field model polygraph instrument (which recorded thoracic and abdominal breathing patterns, electrodermal response (GSR), and cardiovascular activity recorded by a pneumatic blood-pressure cuff inflated to a pressure between 40 and 50 mmHg*); the other experiment employed only a constant voltage system to measure skin conductance.

However in experiment one the authors reported their results based only on the GSR inasmuch as it proved to be the most effective parameter. Both experiments revealed that the item-specific countermeasures tended to *increase* psychophysiological detection, whereas the continuous dissociations tended to decrease detection efficiencies. The authors stated that "the results support the notion that manipulations designed to enhance the attention to the relevant information and which make the relevant stimuli more difficult to ignore are associated with greater differential autonomic responsivity and with better psychophysiological differentiation. The practical implication of this finding is that validity studies of the GKT based on experimental setups and on simulated conditions probably provide underestimated validity levels. The motivation level in real-life settings is much greater than in simulated conditions and therefore the attention paid to the relevant items is likely to be greater in the real-life context." (Elaad, Ben-Shakhar 1991). The expected increase in responsivity of subjects in real-life cases is supported by research conducted by Matte and Reuss (1989) comparing mean scores of control question tests in selected analog studies (Barland 1985) with mean scores in selected field studies (Matte, Reuss 1989). (See Chapter 3 for details).

PHYSICAL

Physical countermeasures require the deliberate manipulation or treatment of some part of the body for the purpose of affecting the physiological data recorded on the polygraph chart. The most common of these is the subject's attempted control of his or her breathing rate. Both anticountermeasures and countercountermeasures for respiration control identification are discussed in Chapters 8, 9, and 12.

Other physical countermeasures include movements, which may cause distortion of the physiological tracing, or pain, which can cause a physiological reaction and/or distortion. Again, anticountermeasures can be most effective in the prevention and identification of such attempts to defeat the PV examination. One such anticountermeasure is the motion or movement detection chair discussed and depicted in Chapter 2.

Polygraph manufacturing companies such as Stoelting, Lafayette and Axciton have responded to claims made by polygraph critics (Lykken 1978) that countermeasures in the form of physical movement during the PV examination can successfully defeat the polygraph, by manufacturing and marketing a "movement sensing chair." But the first movement chair was designed by John Reid, noted forensic psychophysiologist in 1946. It consisted of metal bellows in the arms and seat bottom of the chair which pneumatically activated recording pens on the polygraph chart. This instrument was so effective in identifying physical movements that it prompted attorney F. Lee Bailey to offer a reward of $10,000.00 to anyone who could beat the polygraph. Dr. Lykken admits in his book (Lykken 1981) that Mr. Bailey's money is quite safe if the test is administered by a competent forensic psychophysiologist utilizing a movement sensing chair. Dr. Lykken explains however that a forensic psychophysiologist of Reid's experience would be looking for the slightest movement which would be interpreted as a deliberate countermeasure, which is consistent with the anticountermeasure theme and procedure described in Chapters 8 and 9. Dr. Lykken raises the question of tongue biting as one covert self-stimulation which Reid's special chair cannot detect. Dr. Lykken admits that "there is no doubt that it would be hard to beat a lie test when the examiner expects you to try and knows how you mean to do it." (Lykken 1981).

Over the years, the motion chair has been refined from a bulky, mechanical pneumatic device to the current electrically enhanced strain-gauge transducer type of device. Research conducted by Mike Stephenson and Glenn Barry at the Canadian Police College Polygraph School (Stephenson 1988) involving twelve subjects who used thirty-six physical countermeasures such as pushing left/right foot onto the floor, contraction of anal sphincter, curling toes, right/left thigh contraction, left/right forearm push, pressing on GSR plates, right/left heel press, right/left palm press, left/right elbow pushed down, resulted in a percentage detection rate for the forensic psychophysiologist using the movement chair of 85 percent. Without the benefit of the movement chair the forensic psychophysiologist obtained a detection rate of only 9 percent. An observer placed directly in front of the subject obtained a detection rate of 36 percent. It must be noted that the subjects of Stephenson-Barry's research were forensic psychophysiologist trainees who had completed ten weeks of a twelve-week polygraph examiners course, well versed on physical countermeasures in a non-test situation. The results indicate that the motion chair is a very useful piece of equipment for the forensic psychophysiologist in a time when various ways to defeat the psychophysiological veracity (PV) examination are broadly published. However Stephenson and Barry specifically directed subjects to move parts of their bodies and observed whether these movements could be detected, and whether or not they could be evaluated on the charts as countermeasures, with and without the Lafayette Activity sensor. Dr. Stanley Abrams and Lt. Michael Davidson (Abrams 1988) conducted a study to evaluate the impact of movement as a countermeasure upon PV examinations and to ascertain further if the activity sensor is an effective counter to these attempts to distort the findings. In this study additional movements were incorporated in the form of tongue biting, stepping on a tack, tensing of the jaw, and tightening of the buttocks. The results of this study revealed that in every movement made by the subjects, a change resulted in the tracings in at least one of the three measures being employed. In 36 percent of the cases, the tracings demonstrated distortion caused by the movements which were readily interpreted as movements. This was particularly the case when the movement was on the upper portion of the body and on the same side as the blood pressure cuff. Despite concentrating on that part of the body to be moved, only 12 percent of the movements were actually observed. In 5 percent of the movements that were seen, no changes in the tracings occurred that would indicate that a movement had been made. Combining both the behavioral reactions nor seen in the tracings and those indications of movement present in the tracings, a total of 44 percent of the countermeasures were detected. The activity sensor, however, was able to detect 92 percent of these movements. This included both the tongue biting and stepping down on a tack. As Dr. Abrams points out in his discussion of the study, it would take a sophisticated subject to create responses to the right questions (control questions) and he or she would still face the problem of suppressing an arousal at the relevant questions. Inasmuch as this study involved a mock paradigm where the "Fear of Detection" is not present, the question arises regarding a real-life situation where the relevant questions offer a real threat to the subject, as to whether that real threat would still elicit a greater arousal from the Guilty subject than the control questions to which the subject is applying a physical countermeasure. It appears from the higher rates of accuracy reported in the research for deceptive subjects, that the majority of individuals are not employing countermeasures of this nature (Patrick and Iacono, 1987; OTA study, 1983). An unofficial survey by this author of several forensic psychophysiologists, one of whom was in charge of the polygraph unit at a public defender's office, revealed that nine out of ten defendants tested produced deceptive results. It may be that the reactions to the relevant questions in real-life testing exceed the reactions of the controls even though purposeful movements are made. (See Chapter 3 for research on difference in magnitude of response between analog and field studies, Matte, Reuss 1989).

The aforesaid question is partially answered by the following event which occurred at this author's polygraph office in 1991. An adult male was administered a PV examination employing the clinical approach by a law enforcement agency regarding the commission of a crime, but the results were inconclusive. Before submitting to a retest by the police, his new attorney decided to have him tested privately and brought him to this author. I administered the Quadri-Track Zone Comparison Technique consisting of a Control-Stimulation Test followed by four separate charts dealing with the same issue. Each chart was scored as follows: Chart 1 was -10, Chart 2 was -2, Chart 3 was -13, Chart 4 was -8 for a total score of -33. For the Quadri-Track Zone Comparison Technique, a minimum score of -20 for 4 charts is required before a definite conclusion of Deception can be rendered. A minimum score of +12 for 4 charts is required before a definite Truthful conclusion can be rendered. The suspect was confronted with the results of his PV examination and after some interrogation, the suspect confessed to the crime. During his explanation of the details surrounding the commission of the crime, the suspect, still sitting in the polygraph chair (which did not have an activity sensor), reached down and unlaced his right boot, took off the boot and removed the insole, From the tip of the insole the suspect calmly removed a thumbtack from the toe area and placed it on the polygraph desk. The tack would most likely have escaped detection because it was in the insole which required pressure for the tip to surface. The suspect stated that he had read a booklet that told how to beat the polygraph, primarily by controlling his breathing and placing a tack in his shoe. I asked the suspect which questions did he press his toe on the tack and the suspect replied. "to all of the test questions except the two relevant questions." However, he did not use that countermeasure on the stimulation test. The high scores from this suspect's polygraph charts clearly show that the subject's *fear of detection* regarding the target issue created significantly greater physiological responses to the relevant questions than the physiological responses caused by the self-inflicted pain.

There is no doubt however from aforementioned research that when either pain, muscular tension or movements are used, the activity sensor is highly effective in detecting these countermeasures. It should be noted that no movement activity sensor was employed in the administration of 122 confirmed real-life cases conducted by the Buffalo Police Department and at this author's private polygraph firm, which were used in a field validation study that revealed the correct identification of 91 percent of the Innocent as Truthful with 9 percent Inconclusive, and the correct identification of 97 percent of the Guilty as Deceptive with 3 percent Inconclusive, and no errors. All three forensic psychophysiologists involved in the aforesaid study were trained in and employed the Quadri-Track Zone Comparison technique, whose methodology includes anticountermeasures.

An analog study using a *concealed knowledge test* (CKT) (Honts, Devitt, Winbush, Kircher, 1996) revealed that when the polygraph charts were evaluated and scored by Human Evaluation, the Innocent were correctly identified in 100% of the cases, the Guilty 70%, but when physical countermeasures were applied, correct decisions dropped to 10% and mental countermeasures dropped them to 50%. But when the Kircher and Raskin (1988) Discriminant Analysis Algorithm was used, it correctly classified 80% of the Innocent, 80% of the Guilty control, 40% of the physical countermeasure, and 80% of the mental countermeasure subjects. Some knowledgeable subjects were informed about the nature of the CKT and were trained in the use of a countermeasure. It should be noted that in this experiment, Honts, Devitt, Winbush and Kircher used a Lafayette Model 761-65GA field polygraph instrument but only recorded thoracic and abdominal breathing patterns, plus galvanic skin response. <u>No cardiovascular recording was used</u>. Many experts including this author believe that the cardio cuff pressure has a psychophysiological effect on the breathing patterns, and the cardiograph channel provides an excellent means of detecting some countermeasures. Furthermore, Honts, et al., relied solely on the physiological data on the polygraph charts to detect countermeasures in their evaluations whereas in a field situation, the forensic psychophysiologist would be observing the examinee seated with profile directly in front of him or her, with many forensic psychophysiologists using the Closed-Eyes technique. Honts, et al, make no mention of the availability of motion detection devices attached to polygraph examination chairs (Stoelting, Lafayette, Axciton) which research has shown were able to identify 92% and 85% of countermeasure movements by Abrams & Davidson 1988, and Stephenson & Barry 1988, respectively. The *concealed knowledge test* as used in this study is the weakest of test structures in the battery of tests available to the forensic psychophysiologist (See Chapter 18). Thus this analog study did not replicate the psychophysiological dynamics and instrumentation as found in a field situation.

Dr. David T. Lykken conducted an analog study (1960) using a guilty knowledge test which in this instance could more appropriately be called a concealed knowledge test inasmuch as it is an analog study employing a mock paradigm. The twenty subjects used in this study included a number of medical students, several staff psychologists and psychiatrists, and a number of female members of the secretarial staff, all of whom were given training in the theory of the GSR and the guilty (concealed) knowledge method, were allowed to practice inhibiting or producing false GSRs, and instructed concerning the interrogation procedure and scoring system to be used. The aforesaid subjects were then offered $10.00 if they could defeat the test. Correct classification was obtained in 100% of these cases without ambiguity, using objective scoring of the GSR protocol alone. (Lykken 1960)

However, Honts, Devitt, Winbush and Kircher (1996) fault the aforesaid study by Lykken (1960) in that it contained no innocent subjects, and there is no guidance in Lykken's study on how to evaluate a subject who does not have a key pattern. Furthermore, the Lykken study and analysis used 25 CKT series, which is virtually impossible in a field situation. Finally, Lykken used items of personal history for the key items in the CKT, rather than items from the episodic memory of a witnessed/perpetrated event. Honts, et al., opined that the psychophysiological processes associated with the recognition of overlearned items of personal history may be quite different from the recognition of items from an episodic memory of a single event. (Honts, Devitt, Winbush, Kircher, 1996). However, it must be remembered that in a field situation, the key item to a guilty subject would represent a significantly greater threat than an item from the episodic memory of a mock crime such as in Lykken's analog study; thus Lykken appears to be justified in using items of personal history as key items, which, it could be argued, still fail to compare to the intensity of the threat offered by keys to actual crimes which if discovered could cost the examinee his or her freedom.

PHARMACEUTICAL

The use of drugs, whether stimulants or depressants, by an examinee is always of concern to the forensic psychophysiologist, and the pretest interview should probe that area. Anticountermeasures should be built into the examination process as described in chapters 6, 8, 9, and 20. While some research has shown that certain drugs have had an effect on the outcome of psychophysiological veracity (PV) examinations which lacked control questions as defined in chapters 11 and 16 (Waid 1981; OTA 1983), other research (Gatchel, et al. 1983) has shown that even with the use of propranolol, a beta-blocking drug, the overall error rate was low but the inconclusive rate was high. However, a study by Iacono, et al (OTA 1983) found that ingestion of neither 10 milligrams of diazepam (Valium®) nor 20 milligrams of methylophenidate (Ritalin®) affected the accuracy of detection. Results in both active drug conditions were more accurate than when subjects ingested a placebo containing lactose (OTA 1983).

A pilot study on the effects of beta-blocking drugs on the polygraph detection rate conducted by E. Elaad, et al, using Trasicor, a beta blocking agent, revealed that while the GSR channel was the most efficient identification index for the placebo group in their analog study, it was also the most vulnerable to the effect of Trasicor. The results of Elaad, et al's study showed that both the GSR and the cardiovascular activity were significantly affected by Trasicor, however the beta-blocking agent had no effect on the respiration recordings. Elaad, et al., concluded that "skin resistance responses are most vulnerable to BB (beta-blocking) influences while respiration recordings are not affected by the drug. Following that conclusion it can be claimed that using beta adrenergic blocking drugs may be detrimental to polygraph techniques which emphasizes the GSR responses (guilty knowledge technique) while the control question methods, which put more attention to changes in respiration, might be less affected." (Elaad, et al. 1982). It should be noted that in control question examinations, whatever the effect the drug or medication may have on the relevant questions, it will also have the same effect on the control questions against which they are being compared. This variable may cause an inconclusive result but will not cause a false positive or negative outcome. It should also be noted that in the traditional scoring methods employed in the Backster, Matte, and DoDPI zone comparison techniques, all three parameters consisting of respiration, GSR, and cardiovascular activity are *treated equally* using a seven-position scale quantification system.

It should be noted that the term "Control Question" as used in the Guilty Knowledge Test is different in construction and purpose than the "Control Question" used in Control Question Tests. For instance Bradley and Ainsworth (1984) in describing the research conducted by Waid, et al. (1981) on the effects of a tranquilizer, Meprobamate, on guilty subjects attempting to conceal information, state "That is, skin resistance responses in a Guilty Knowledge Test examination were reduced to critical questions but not to control questions." A person not familiar with the Guilty Knowledge Test might not realize that the *control questions* in a GKT are not designed to elicit a response from either the guilty or innocent examinee; they merely act as buffer questions, whereas the Control Question Test contains *control questions* which are specifically designed to elicit a response from the innocent (as later verified) examinee. Thus the tranquilizer Meprobamate cannot discriminate between the relevant and the control questions in a Control Question Test. (See Chapters 11 and 16)

The mathematical algorithm used in the Applied Physics Laboratory software called PolyScore employed in computerized polygraph systems devotes an average 54 percent of its criteria for deception to Electrodermal activity, 24 percent to Blood Volume, 8 percent to Pulse Rate, and only 14 percent to Respiration. (Johnson 1994; Olsen 1995). A field study by this author and Dr. Ronald M. Reuss (1992) on the relative effectiveness of physiological data in field psychophysiological veracity examinations showed that the most productive of the physiological channels was the pneumo tracing at 43 percent, followed by the cardio at 32 percent and the electrodermal at 24 percent. In that study we determined the productivity/accuracy of each tracing by the tracing which accumulated the highest score consistent with ground truth. (Matte, Reuss 1992). While *analog* studies have generally found the electrodermal tracing to be the most effective parameter (Raskin, et al., 1978; Thackray & Orne 1968; Cutrow, et al., 1972), several *field* studies have found opposite results with the pneumo tracing being the most effective parameter (Elaad & Eitan 1985; Elaad, Ginton, Jungman, 1988; Ryan 1989; Elaad & Kleiner 1990; Jayne 1990; Matte, Reuss 1992; Suzuki 1975). This author believes that the difference in psychodynamics between subjects in mock paradigms (laboratory studies) and field studies (real-life cases) explain the significant differences seen in the reported research for these different types of studies. The key factors for the psychodynamic differences are felt to be the *Fear of Detection* by the Guilty, and the *Fear of Error* by the Innocent. The demonstrated effect of beta blockers on the GSR and cardio activity and the *lack* thereof on respiratory activity supports the continued usage of the traditional scoring system (Backster, Matte, DoDPI) wherein the respiratory channel alone can often provide the minimum scores required to arrive at a conclusive determination. The traditional scoring system can also be used as an adjunct to the computerized polygraph systems's PolyScore which normally emphases the GSR (54%) and only applies its algorithm to the thoracic respiratory channel (in addition to the cardio activity) for its results. (Johnson 1994; Olsen 1995).

However, while the two pneumograph channel tracings may appear to be quite different on the computer screen or polygraph chart, the PolyScore pre-processes the signals from both channels in such a manner that there is much less difference in the signals between the two channels. Furthermore, PolyScore compensates for channel(s) that produce inferior data by finding indicators of deception in those channels that are most productive, therefore if an examinee is under the influence of a beta blocker, the PolyScore would shift its attention to the most productive channel which existing research shows under that circumstance to be the pneumograph. (Olsen 1995).

We cannot ignore the fact that beta blockers which are used to reduce heart strain for those who are at risk due to a heart problem are prescribed to a significant percentage of our population. Propranolol for instance is used in the treatment of angina (chest pain), hypertension, arrhythmias (irregular heartbeats), migraine headaches, tremors, "thyroid storm" and pheochromocytoma. (Medical Drug Reference 1994). With the rapid growth of our aging population, more examinees suffering from a medical condition requiring the use of beta blockers will be seen by forensic psychophysiologists who should become familiar with the various beta blocking agents. The methodology used by the forensic psychophysiologist should include a methodical medical history acquisition system, plus a contractual arrangement with a local drug testing laboratory for impromptu as well as routine drug tests which should include the presence of ataractics such as chlordiazepozide hydrochloride, diazepam, meprobamate, propanolol and atenolol.

Alcohol

Bradley and Ainsworth (1984) attempted to determine the effect that alcohol would have on the detection rate of subjects who had committed a mock crime while under the influence of alcohol, and subjects who had committed a mock crime while sober but were administered a psychophysiological veracity (PV) examination while under the influence of alcohol. These two guilty groups were further subdivided in such a manner that half of each group were administered a PV examination while intoxicated and the other half while sober. Forty male university students were used in this study and two polygraph techniques were used; the Control Question Test (Backster, 1969) and the Guilty Knowledge Test (Lykken, 1959). The mock crime paradigm involved a fictitious murder, the theft of money ($1.00), and information (safe combination). The instrument used was Grass polygraph which recorded heart rate with a Grass photoelectric transducer embedded in an elasticized foam finger attachment. The pulse wave was recorded on one channel and pulse rate, in bpm, was recorded from a Grass cardiotachograph on a second channel. Respiration was measured by chest bellows positioned in the thoracic area immediately above the diaphragm. Skin resistance was measured using Grass cup-shaped silver-silver chloride electrodes attached to the medial phalanges of the first and second fingers. The pretest interview was short (5 to 10 minutes).

The results of aforesaid study reflect that alcohol intoxication during the enactment of a mock crime affects detection rates on both the Control Question Test and the Guilty Knowledge Test. It further revealed that alcohol intoxication during the PV examination does not significantly affect the test results, which argues against its use as an effective countermeasure.

It should be noted that the authors (Bradley and Ainsworth) of aforesaid study employed a polygraph instrument significantly inferior than that used by field forensic psychophysiologists. In aforesaid study they used only one pneumograph component and placed said component in the thoracic area of the all-male subjects. Research (Matte, Reuss 1992) shows that the abdominal area is the most productive pneumograph recording area for male subjects and the thoracic area was the least productive for male subjects. Furthermore, field FPs mostly use the blood pressure cuff which has significant psychophysiological effects on the pneumograph. Bradley and Ainsworth refer to Backster (1969) for the Control Question Test used in their study, but their test question formulation is in violation of Backster's question formulation rules in that the relevant test question #5 actually contains three questions, to wit: "Did you shoot the man and steal the money and information?" A three-position rather than Backster's seven-position scale of quantification was used in this study. The 5-10 minute pretest interview is inadequate by any standard, as this is precisely when the forensic psychophysiologist establishes rapport and evaluates the examinee for the administration of the PV tests.

This author believes that the aforementioned study by Bradley and Ainsworth fail on several counts as mentioned above to replicate field instrumentation, polygraph technique, and the emotional psychodynamics found in a real-life situation. Yet in spite of all the aforesaid weaknesses in the aforementioned study, *the use of alcohol as a countermeasure failed*. But the study also showed that alcohol intoxication during the crime reduced detectability with detection scores derived from the measurement of skin responses on the Control Question Test and the Guilty Knowledge Test. Intoxication during the enactment of a crime is dealt with in chapter 8.

Subsequent research on the effects of alcohol and the physiological detection of deception was conducted by Dennis O'Toole, John C. Youille, Christopher J. Patrick and William G. Iacono (1994) wherein eighty male volunteers participated in an analog study of the *effects of alcohol intoxication at the time of a mock crime* on the physiological detection of deception using a Control Question Technique and a Guilty Knowledge Technique. As in the Bradley and Ainsworth study (1984), O'Toole, et al., used a single chest bellows positioned above the diaphragm to record and measure respiration. The systolic blood pressure was monitored with a low-weight sphygmomanometer with pressure cuff, but the systolic blood pressure was not recorded during the polygraph test; rather, it was measured at various times during the experiment and served as a measure of physiological arousal. The authors admittedly recognized that this was not the typical instrument used in field polygraph examinations, stating that this type of recording was not available for the Sensor Medics polygraph used in this experiment. Unlike Bradley and Ainsworth, the O'Toole et al study used a single-issue control question test, but they mixed *non-current exclusive* control questions with *non-exclusive* control questions. Furthermore their sacrifice relevant question embraced both the control and the relevant questions. (see Chap. 8). Again, this study failed to replicate field instrumentation, polygraph technique, and the emotional psychodynamics found in a real-life situation. Nevertheless, O'Toole, et al's study found that intoxication at the time of the crime *had no significant effect* on polygraph test outcomes nor resulted in any false negatives on either the Control Question Test or the Guilty Knowledge Test, in spite of the fact that the dose of alcohol administered to subjects in the present study exceeded that used by Bradley and Ainsworth (1984).

Scientists in academia appear to be influenced by prior analog research which indicates that the electrodermal response is the best discriminator of truth and deception, which may be the reason for so many analog studies conducted with inferior cardio and respiratory equipment. However field research (Matte, Reuss 1992; Ryan 1989; Slowik, Buckley 1975; Jayne 1990) show the pneumograph as the best discriminator of truth and deception. But the hierarchy of parameter effectiveness can vary according to each subject's physiology, thus Backster's concept of equal treatment for each parameter which has been validated in analog and field studies (Raskin, et al 1977, 1978; Matte, Reuss 1989) is the approach that should be taken by research scientists. Scientists should adhere to the polygraph instrumentation and techniques used in the field in order to replicate as closely as possible the conditions under which field psychophysiological veracity examinations are conducted. Furthermore, research models (hybrid and field studies) recommended in Chapter 3 would be more appropriate and accurate in approximating the accuracy of the various PV examination techniques and their vulnerability to countermeasures.

In the past, many forensic psychophysiologists feared that publication of the essential elements of the polygraph techniques currently in use would aid the guilty (as later verified) subject to defeat the psychophysiological veracity (PV) examination. After several years of publication of the various techniques' composition in professional and public literature the aforesaid fear of disclosure was discovered to be unfounded by field forensic psychophysiologists and in studies designed to test that hypothesis (Rovner 1986; Lykken 1960). A similar fear has emerged regarding the open discussion of countermeasures used in the field, disregarding their publication in the professional and public media including the Internet. This author believes that this fear is also unfounded when proper safeguards incorporated into the techniques' methodology and instrumentation are implemented by qualified expert forensic psychophysiologists. But forensic psychophysiologists must maintain a constant vigil for new countermeasures. Computer algorithms and polygraph techniques must be periodically revised and/or adjusted to cope with the forever changing technology available in our open society.

REFERENCES

Abrams, S., Davidson, M. (1988). Countermeasures in polygraph testing. *Polygraph,* 17(1), 16-20.

Abrams, S. (1995, June 8). Telephone conversation with J. A. Matte.

Backster, C. (1969). Technique fundamentals of the Tri-Zone Polygraph Test. New York: *Backster Research Foundation.*

Barland, G. H. (1985). A method for estimating the accuracy of individual control question tests; Anti-Terrorism, Forensic Science, Psychology in Police Investigations. Proceedings of IDENTA-!85. *The International Congress on Techniques for Criminal Identification,* Jerusalem, Israel: Heiliger and Company Limited. 142-147.

Barland, G. H. (1994, July 27). *Countermeasures and how to detect them.* Paper presented at the 29th Annual Seminar/Workshop of the American Polygraph Association at Nashville, TN.

Bitterman, E. M., Marcuse, F. L. (1945). Autonomic responses in post hypnotic amnesia. *Journal of Experimental Psychology.* 35:248-252.

Bradley, M. T., Ainsworth, D. (1984). Alcohol and the psychophysiological detection of deception. *Polygraph* 13(2), 177-192.

Bryan, W. J., Jr. (1962). *Legal aspects of hypnosis.* Springfield, Illinois: Charles C. Thomas.

Cumley, W. E. (1959). Hypnosis and the Polygraph. *Police.*

Elaad, E., Bonwitt, G., Eisenberg, O., Meytes, I. (1982). Effects of beta blocking drugs on the polygraph detection rate. A pilot study. *Polygraph,* 11(3), 225-233.

Elaad, E., Ben-Shakhar, G. (1991). Effects of mental countermeasures on psychophysiological detection in the guilty knowledge test. *International Journal of Psychophysiology,* 11(2), 99-108.

Gatchel, R. J. Smith, J. E., Kaplan, N. M, et al. (1983). *The effects of Propanalol on Polygraphic Detection of Deception.* Unpublished manuscript.

German, A. C. (1961). Hypnosis as related to the scientific detection of deception by polygraph examination: A pilot study. *International Journal of Clinical and Experimental Hypnosis.* 9:309-311.

Honts, C. R., Devitt, M. K., Winbush, M., Kircher, J. C. (1996). Mental and physical countermeasures reduce the accuracy of the concealed knowledge test. *Psychophysiology*, 33(1), 84-92.

Jayne, B. (1990). Contributions of physiological recordings in the polygraph technique. *Polygraph*, 19, 105-117.

Johnson, G. J. (1994). Information facsimile regarding APL zone scoring results, zone features, algorithm data, scoring weights and response intervals. U. S. government Department of Defense, Office of Security Facsimile, 13 Oct 94 to Dr. James A. Matte.

Kircher, J. C., Raskin D. C. (1988). Human vs computerized evaluations of polygraph data in a laboratory setting. *Journal of Applied Psychology*. 73(2), 291-302.

Lie Detector Committee. (1959, September). *Preliminary report on the study of the effect of hypnotically induced amnesia upon the accuracy of the lie detector test results.* Fort Gordon, GA: The Provost Marshal General's School.

Lykken, D. T. (1959). The GSR in the detection of guilt. *Journal of Applied Psychology*, 43(6), 385-388.

Lykken, D. T. (1960). The validity of the guilty knowledge technique: The effects of faking. *Journal of Applied Psychology*, 44(4), 258-262.

Lykken, D. T. (1978). Testimony. Hearings before the Subcommittee on the Constitution, U. S. Senate on S1845. Polygraph Control and Civil Liberties Protection Act. U. S. Government Printing Office. 8-33.

Lykken, D. T. (1981). *A Tremor in the Blood, Uses and Abuses of the Lie Detector*. New York: McGraw-Hill.

Marcy, L. P. (1995, August 14). *Countermeasures*. Paper presented at the 30th Annual Seminar/Workshop of the American Polygraph Association at Las Vegas, NV.

Matte, J. A., Reuss, R. M. (1989). Validation Study on the Quadri-Zone Comparison Technique. *Research Abstract*, LD 01452. Vol. 1502, 1989, University Microfilm International.

Matte, J. A., Reuss, R. M. (1990). A field study of the 'Friendly Polygraphist' concept. *Polygraph*, 19(1), 1-8.

Matte, J. A., Reuss, R. M. (1992). A study of the relative effectiveness of physiological data in field polygraph examinations. *Polygraph*, 21(1), 1-22.

Medical Drug Reference (1994). Parsons Technology. CD-ROM Edition.

Office of Technology Assessment (OTA). (1983). *Scientific Validity of Polygraph Testing - A Research Review and Evaluation.* Technical Memorandum for the Con gressional Board of the 98th Congress of the United States, OTA-TM-H-15.

Olsen, D. E. (1995, March 8). Telephone conversation with J. A. Matte.

O'Toole, D., Yuille, J. C., Patrick, C. J., Iacono, W. G. (1994). Alcohol and the physiological detection of deception: Arousal and memory influences. *Psychophysiology*, 31(3), 253-263.

Patrick, C. J., Iacono, W. G. (1987). Validity and reliability of the control question polygraph test: A scientific investigation. *Psychophysiology*, 24, 604-605. (abstract).

Raskin, D. C., Barland, G. H., Podlesney, J. A. (1977). Validity and reliability of detection of deception. Polygraph, 6(1), 1-39.

Raskin, D. C., Barland, G. H., Podlesny, J. A. (1978). Validity and reliability of detection of deception. Washington, D. C.: National Institute of Law Enforcement and Criminal Justice.

Ryan, R. (1989). Relative validity and utility of examiner diagnosis of truth and deception utilizing respiration, cardiovascular, and galvanic skin response parameters. Unpublished Master's thesis, Reid College of Detection of Deception.

Rovner, L. I. (1986). The accuracy of physiological detection of deception for subjects with prior knowledge. *Polygraph*, 15(1), 1-39.

Slowik, S., Buckley, J. (1975). Relative accuracy of polygraph examiner diagnosis of respiration, blood pressure, and GSR recordings. *Journal of Police Science and administration*, 3(3), 305-310.

Stevenson, M., Barry, G. (1988). Use of a motion chair in the detection of physical counter-measures. *Polygraph* 17(1). 21-27.

Waid, W. M., Orne, E. C., Cook, M. R., Orne, M. T. (1981). Meprobamate reduces accuracy of physiological detection of deception. *Science*, 212: 71-73.

Weinstein, E., Abrams, S., Gibbons, D. (1970). The validity of the polygraph with hypnotically induced repression and guilt. *American Journal of Psychiatry*, 126: 1159-1162.

Chapter 22

THE DEAF OR HEARING IMPAIRED

AND

THE USE OF INTERPRETERS

In 1978 this author attended a seminar on forensic psychophysiology in New York City and the topic of using interpreters in the administration of psychophysiological veracity (PV) examinations arose. From the group's comments, it appeared that deaf persons offered the greatest problem to the forensic psychophysiologist (FP). Inasmuch as one of this author's clients had a department manned by deaf persons, it became necessary for this author to develop a technique to facilitate the conduct of their PV examinations and insure the integrity of the examinations. This technique is useful not only in the conduct of PV examinations on hearing impaired persons, but also in any PV examination requiring the use of an interpreter where the loyalty and/or qualifications of the interpreter may be in question by the attending forensic psychophysiologist or the judicial body that may receive the PV examinations results.

Most deaf persons can utter sounds; some never develop intelligible sounds, while others do, which is largely dependent upon the age of onset of deafness and their ensuing education. Some deaf persons will not orally express themselves with non-deaf persons because of embarrassment over their poor speech. A good percentage of deaf persons can read lips if the words are spoken slowly. Communication between deaf persons or between a deaf person and an interpreter for deaf persons is conducted through the "Sign Language in Straight English" or "American Sign Language (AMESLAN)"[1] each requiring the use of the hands in communicating. When the individual communicating with a deaf person does not know the sign language, use of the written word becomes necessary.

When confronted with the task of conducting a PV examination on a deaf person, one might believe the task impossible without the use of an interpreter for deaf persons. Usually the company or agency requesting the PV examinations(s) has a person on their staff knowledgeable in the deaf person sign language, especially if there are several deaf persons employed there, to provide essential communication between deaf employees and non-deaf employees. The temptation of the forensic psychophysiologist to use such a person as an interpreter in the conduct of PV examinations must certainly be hard to resist, yet great caution must be exercised, for the following reasons:

---

1. Sign language in Straight English requires that every word be visually represented in sign or fingerspelling, whereas in American Sign Language just the concept is visually represented.

a. The loyalty of the interpreter may be with the subject, not the company and forensic psychophysiologist.
b. The interpreter who is also a co-worker of the subject may be an accomplice.
c. The interpreter may yield to an offer of a bribe by the subject with whom he or she is acquainted.
d. The interpreter may yield to blackmail by the subject (co-worker) knowledge able about the interpreter's own illegal activities at the company.
e. The interpreter may inadvertently make an error in communicating the test question(s) as a result of ineptitude or own misinterpretation.

The interpreter so inclined may sabotage the PV examination by:

a. Not actually conveying the relevant question.
b. Rewording the relevant question(s) (in sign language) so that the examinee's answer(s) will not be a lie to the examinee.
c. Substituting an irrelevant or neutral question for the relevant question(s).

The forensic psychophysiologist not knowledgeable in the sign language for deaf persons would be unable to detect any of the above means of sabotage. However the following technique which this author developed in about 1974 and has since used on many occasions has proved effective in eliminating countermeasure attempts by the subject, and the need for an interpreter for deaf persons during the actual administration of the PV examination, and if necessary, the entire examination. Ideally the forensic psychophysiologist should be assisted by an interpreter to facilitate the conduct of the pretest interview. The interpreter would also assist in the presentation of the cards containing the test questions during the actual examination, although this could be done by any third party selected by the forensic psychophysiologist.

Administration of this technique requires that one of the examinee's hands and arms, preferably the right, be free of any instrument attachments. For best results, an electronic polygraph instrument equipped with a Cardio Activity Monitor (CAM) or a computerized polygraph system equipped with a plethysmograph (CAM not yet available) is recommended. The CAM is placed over the radial artery of the left wrist with palm facing upward, or over the thumb nail with palm facing downward, while the left arm and hand is in a limp, relaxed position. When using the plethysmograph, the palm usually faces downward. Other positions for the CAM and plethysmograph may be used as recommended by the manufacturer at the discretion of the forensic psychophysiologist. The electrodermal (GSR/GSG) electrodes are then placed on the index and ring fingers (or other alternate fingers) of the same hand (left hand). This author has noted no adverse effects on the GSR tracing as a result of the fingers bearing the GSR electrodes being in an upward position or palmar side up. This procedure leaves the right hand completely free.

A 3 x 5 card as depicted below is taped near the end of the right arm rest of the polygraph examination chair, so that the examinee's right index finger may reach the card without moving his right arm or hand. This author has noted that movement of right hand during the polygraph examination did not cause tracing distortion as long as the arm itself was not moved.

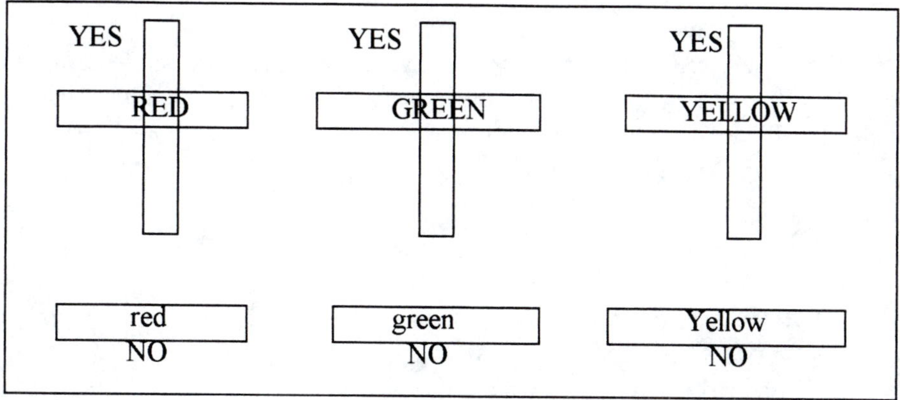

Figure XXII-1

The card depicted in Figure XXII-1 above offers three choices for an affirmative answer and three choices for a negative answer; in red, green, and yellow.

All of the test questions are typed in large capital letters, double spaced, each on a separate 3 x 5 card numbered consecutively. Within the text of each question is inserted the word RED, or GREEN, or YELLOW. Example: "WERE YOU BORN IN THE GREEN UNITED STATES?" or "DID YOU STEAL THAT MISSING $100? RED" or "DURING THE FIRST 18 YEARS OF YOUR LIFE - DO YOU REMEMBER GREEN EVER STEALING ANYTHING?"

The subject is instructed to point his or her finger at the plus or minus sign of the color reflected somewhere in the question. This necessitates that the subject read the question in order to answer it properly; that is with a "yes" or "no" answer in the appropriate color.

The cards containing the test questions are presented to the subject by a third person sitting directly in front of the subject as depicted in the photograph below. This assistant is given a signal by the forensic psychophysiologist (FP) with his free hand while the FP marks the beginning of the question on the polygraph chart with his or her writing hand. However the forensic psychophysiologist does not attempt to mark the end of the question since his only reliable clue is when the examinee places his finger on the appropriate sign at which time the FP marks the subject's answer on the polygraph chart at the exact time given.

The assistant is cautioned not to make any sound nor make any unnecessary movement that may distract the subject. The forensic psychophysiologist must follow the sequence of each question with his own question formulation worksheet, containing the same color code he assigned to each question on the 3 x 5 cards. The forensic psychophysiologist should be very attentive to the examinee's answers and be on the alert for answer(s) given in the wrong color code as this is an indication that the examinee has not read the question.

The normal procedure of not reviewing the test questions in the same order they are asked on the test, some eliciting an affirmative and some a negative answer, further provides the FP with a means of determining whether the subject read the question by verifying a correct answer was given.

Figure XXII-2

Above figure depicts a deaf person posed by Dr. Ronald M. Reuss, being shown a 3 x 5 card containing a test question by Thomas E. Armitage, Forensic Psychophysiologist, Buffalo Police Department, and the author administering the mock PV examination.

Two sets of 3 x 5 cards containing the test questions should be made; one set with the color code inserted into each question, and one set without the color code. The subject should be given an opportunity to read each card (without the color code) to assure the FP that he or she fully understands each and every word on those cards.[2]

---

2. A deaf person's ability to read may be below normal because of his or her deafness and lack of natural development of language and vocabulary.

Use of the color coded answer signs assures the forensic psychophysiologist that the examinee understands each and every question, that he or she has read each test question before giving his or her answer, and that his or her answer is clear and emphatic, free from chart tracing distortion caused by speech impediment and undesired stimulus resulting from the emotion of embarrassment it may cause the examinee.

Figure XXII-3

The above figure offers another view of the technique used to polygraph the deaf.

The aforementioned technique removes the possibility of subject countermeasure, or interpreter sabotage, and identifies the presence of communication problems at the most critical stage of the psychophysiological veracity examination.

REFERENCES

Matte, J. A. (1980). A technique for polygraphing the deaf. *Polygraph*, 9(3), 148-152.

Chapter 23

LEGAL ASPECTS
OF THE
PSYCHOPHYSIOLOGICAL VERACITY EXAMINATION

In this chapter, we will discuss the legal status of psychophysiological veracity (PV) examinations (Part I), the selection of a forensic psychophysiologist (FP) (Part II), defense access to police PV examinations (Part III), and defense conditions for police PV examinations of defendants (Part IV).

Part I - Legal Status of PV Examinations

Since 1923 when a Federal court in *Frye v. United States*, 54 App. D. C. 46, 47, 293 F. 1013, 1014 (1923), stated that expert opinion based on a scientific technique is inadmissible unless the technique is "generally accepted" as reliable in the relevant scientific community, the results of psychophysiological veracity (PV) examinations using the polygraph have been generally held inadmissible as evidence in Federal and State courts in the United States. The aforesaid *Frye* decision became the *Frye* Standard for the admissibility of scientific evidence in Federal courts which was emulated by most State courts.

There have been a few exceptions to the aforesaid standard as some states permitted the introduction of the results of PV examinations when agreed and stipulated by both the prosecution and the defense. The first such stipulation was *State v. Loniello* in the Circuit Court of Columbia County, Wisconsin in 1935. Stipulations have been useful in avoiding trials when the suspect accepts a previously worked out plea bargain wherein the prosecutor agrees to drop the charges if the test results reveal no deception to the target

---

*Occasionally the judge wants to be involved in the wording of the relevant questions. The lawyers involved in the agreement and stipulation will have agreed upon the wording of the relevant questions and have them inserted into the agreement and stipulation. Unfortunately this prevents the forensic psychophysiologist from formulating and/or revising the test questions with the examinee to achieve the necessary clarity and dichotomy, essential to produce effective polygraph test questions which conform to the requirements of the technique's psychological format. Legal language does not lend itself to good communication between the examinee and the forensic psychophysiologist. The topic(s) or issue(s) should be agreed upon and inserted into the stipulation, but the formulation of the test questions and their exact wording should be left to the expertise of the forensic psychophysiologist named to conduct the PV examination. The stipulation should not be worded to exclude other essential questions not related to the relevant issue but necessary to the integrity and scientificity of the test format, such as various types of control questions, symptomatic questions, sacrifice relevant questions, irrelevant questions, et al. that insure and preserve the construct validity of that particular technique.

issue, but a plea of guilty to a lesser offense if found deceptive. In some jurisdictions and in some circumstances the judges are involved in the agreement,* and the judge may even be one of the signatories to the agreement and stipulation. Stipulations often state who is to conduct the PV examination, either by name or by office or agency. The stipulation may merely state a forensic psychophysiologist agreeable to all parties of the agreement and stipulation, and may include minimum qualifications.

The state of California passed Proposition 8, a constitutional amendment that barred exclusion of any relevant evidence, which caused the California courts to be flooded with defense cases from non-stipulated PV examinations. At the urging of district attorneys, the California legislature enacted an urgency statute Section 351.1 to be added to the Evidence Code on 12 July 1983, which requires stipulation prior to the admission of PV examination results as evidence. This author believes that the aforesaid *flood* could have been avoided, had the district attorneys and the courts enacted the basic *acceptance criteria* set forth later in this chapter, which would have allowed the rejection of any PV examination which failed to meet the basic criteria. Rule 702 of the Federal Rules of Evidence confides to the judge some gatekeeping responsibility in that the judge must ensure that any and all scientific testimony or evidence admitted is not only relevant, but reliable, and evidentiary reliability must be based upon scientific validity.

Some states such as Pennsylvania, have consistently refused to admit PV examination results into evidence, but in isolated instances have admitted PV test results into evidence such as in *Commonwealth v. Smith*, 227 A.2d 653 (Pa. 1967). Several states have admitted the results of PV examinations into evidence over objection, but those are also isolated cases, such as *Patterson, v. State*, 633 S. W. 2d 549 (Tex.Cr.App. 1982); *People v. Daniels*, 422 NYS2d 832, 102 Misc2d 540 (1979); *People v. Glenn Battle*, reported in NY Law Journal 18 Apr 89, Page 26, Col. 3, Justice Lewis Douglass, NYS Supreme Court, Brooklyn, NY; *People v. Kenny*, 3 N.Y.S.2d 348, 167 Misc. 51 (Queens County Ct. 1938). *People v. Vernon*, 391 N.Y.S. 2d 959 (1977). *In the matter of Jennifer Meyer and Jessica Meyer*, 132 Misc2d 415, 504 N.Y.X.2d 358. and many others from several states. (See Polygraph and the Law, Volumes I, II, III, by Norman Ansley, 1990).

In each instance of objection, the *Frye standard* was called upon for the court to reject the results of PV examinations as having failed to meet the "general acceptance" requisite. As indicated above, some court judges decided that the Frye standard had been met and allowed its use as evidence at trial, but the majority of such efforts failed, until 1989 when the U. S. Court of Appeals for the 11th Circuit in *U. S. v. Piccinonna* declared in a precedent setting decision that "there is no question that in recent years polygraph testing has gained increasingly widespread acceptance as a useful and reliable scientific tool" "The Science of polygraphy has progressed to a level of acceptance sufficient to allow the use of polygraph evidence in limited circumstances when the danger of unfair prejudice is minimized." 885 F.2d 1529 (11th Cir. 1989). The 11th Circuit also cited the Third, Sixth, Seventh, Ninth and Tenth Circuits and the Court of Military Appeals that permit admission of polygraph evidence even in the absence of a stipulation when special circumstances exist. *U. S. v. Johnson* 816 F2d 918, 923 (3rd Cir. 1987; *Wolfell v. Holbrook*, 823 F2d 970 (6th Cir. 1987); *U.S. v. Kampiles*, 609 F2d 1233, 1245 (7th Cir. 1979); *U. S. v. Miller*, 874, F2d 1255, 1262 (9th Cir. 1989) and *U. S. v. Bowen*, 847 F2d 1337, 1341 (9th Cir. 1988); *U. S. v. Hall*, 805 F2d 1410 (10th Cir. 1986); *U.S. v. Gipson*, 24 M.J. 343 (C.M.A. 1987).

Interestingly, in 1978 an "Experimental Investigation of the Relative Validity and Utility of the Polygraph Technique and three Other Common Methods of Criminal Identification" namely Fingerprint Identification, Handwriting Analysis, and Eyewitness Identification, were conducted by Drs. J. Widacki and F. Horvath. This analog study, although conducted in a laboratory context, generally believed to decrease the effectiveness of the polygraph technique (Abrams 1973; Horvath 1976), insured that "ground truth" was known and that the circumstances in which the data was collected were similar in nature. The need for such a comparison was made explicit by J. Reid and F. Inbau (1966) who claimed that the polygraph technique (PV examination) "possesses a degree of accuracy commensurate with, and even superior to, most of the presently approved forms of evidence, scientific as well as non-scientific, that feature in criminal and civil trials."

The aforesaid study comprised forty-two males and thirty-eight females between the ages of 19 and 24. All subjects provided handwriting specimens, full face photographs and fingerprints. The subjects were then assigned various roles in the commission of a crime and were subsequently administered a PV examination to determine their guilt or innocence. The PV examinations were conducted "blind"; the forensic psychophysiologist was not aware of who had been assigned the role of perpetrator or of innocent suspect. Independent of the PV examinations, a fingerprint expert and a handwriting expert analyzed and processed the mock crime evidence. Two eyewitnesses who had talked and observed the perpetrators for about two minutes were subsequently shown a photographic lineup of suspects. The results shown in Tables 1 and 2 reveal that the forensic psychophysiologist (polygraph) correctly resolved 95% of the cases, the handwriting expert 94% of the cases, the eyewitnesses 64% and the fingerprint expert 100% of the cases. However, when Inconclusives are included, the percentage of correctly resolved cases changes dramatically to 90% polygraph; 85% handwriting; 35% eyewitnesses; and 20% fingerprint. It should be noted that the greatest number of inconclusives (16) was from

Table 1 - Distribution of case decisions made in each identification method.

	Decision		
Identification Method	Correct	Incorrect	Inconclusive
Polygraph	18	1	1
Handwriting	17	1	2
Eyewitness	7	4	9
Fingerprint	4	0	16

fingerprint identification, and the number of false positives (innocent erroneously found deceptive) was greatest for eyewitness identification (9.1%), followed by handwriting analysis (1.4%), PV examinations (1.3%), and fingerprint identification (0.0%), (Table 2). (Widacki and Horvath 1978)

It should also be noted that unlike real-life situations, the eyewitnesses in this analog study had advance knowledge of their role, made identification based on contemporary photographs, were relatively uninfluenced by emotional involvement in a criminal offense, and made identification within a reasonable time following the offense. Yet the eyewitnesses' performance was the least impressive. Inasmuch as the psychodynamics of the mock paradigm lack the emotion of "fear of detection" prevalent as a causative factor of autonomic arousal in field (real-life) psychophysiological veracity examinations, the polygraph technique in this analog study was the most disadvantaged by the laboratory context. On the other hand, the physical evidence on which the handwriting and fingerprint experts and the eyewitnesses based their decisions was collected and analyzed in rather auspicious circumstances which would appear to work in favor of those methods. Thus, the aforesaid study supports Reid and Inbau's statement that the accuracy of the psychophysiological veracity (PV) examination is commensurate with and even superior to most of the presently approved forms of evidence. (Widacki & Horvath 1978).

Table 2 - Distribution of false positive errors made in each identification method.

Identification Method	Definite Decisions Made Number	False Positive Errors Percentage
Polygraph	78	1.3
Fingerprint	16	0.0
Handwriting	72	1.4
Eyewitness	44	9.1

NOTE: See Addendum (P. 593) for 1993 forensic disciplines study by Light & Schwartz.

In 1987, the United States Court of Military Appeals declared in *U. S. v. Gipson* that the accused should have been allowed to attempt to lay a foundation for polygraph evidence. In its decision the Court of Military Appeals concluded that the U. S. v. Frye test should be abandoned in favor of a test using the Military Rules of Evidence and expressed the opinion that the state of polygraph evidence is such that it should be admitted in courts-martial. Although following this decision the Military Rules of Evidence were amended by executive order to preclude polygraph evidence at courts-martial, the judicial finding that advances in polygraph techniques have enhanced reliability remains uncontroverted. 24 M.J. 343 (C.M.A. 1987).

In February 1992, the Appellate Division of the New York State Supreme Court, 3rd Judicial Department overturned a judgment of the Supreme Court and the New York state Division of Parole and ordered that the petitioner be discharged from custody and returned to parole status. The Appellate Division noted that "Expert polygraph evidence was also received which demonstrated that petitioner was not lying when he stated that he did not attack J.S." *People of the State of New York ex. rel. Kenneth Johnson, Appellant v. New York State Board of Parole et al, Respondents* (App. Div. 3; Op) 2/20/92).

The following year, on 28 June 1993, the Supreme Court of the United States, No. 92-102, in *William Daubert, et ux., etc, et al., Petitioners v. Merrell Dow Pharmaceuticals, Inc.* 113 S.Ct 2786, 125 L.E.2d 469, 509 U.S. on a Writ of Certiorari to the United States Court of Appeals for the Ninth Circuit, *rescinded* the *Frye standard* of "general acceptance" test, and adopted in its stead the *Federal Rules of Evidence* as the standard for admitting expert scientific testimony in a federal trial. The court in its ruling stated that "nothing in the Rule as a whole or in the text and drafting history of Rule 702, which specifically governs expert testimony, gives any indication that 'general acceptance' is a necessary precondition to the admissibility of scientific evidence. Moreover, such a rigid standard would be at odds with the Rules' liberal thrust and their general approach of relaxing the traditional barriers to 'opinion' testimony." The court further stated that "the trial judge, pursuant to Rule 104(a), must make a preliminary assessment of whether the testimony's underlying reasoning or methodology is scientifically valid and properly can be applied to the facts at issue. Many considerations will bear on the inquiry, including whether the theory or technique in question can be (and has been) tested, whether it has been subjected to peer review and publication, its known or potential error rate, and the existence and maintenance of standards controlling its operation, and whether it has attracted widespread acceptance within a relevant scientific community." The court also stated that "Cross-examination, presentation of contrary evidence, and careful instruction on the burden of proof, rather than wholesale exclusion under an uncompromising 'general acceptance' standard, is the appropriate means by which evidence based on valid principles may be challenged."

Rule 702, governing expert testimony, provides:

> If scientific, technical, or other specialized knowledge will assist the trier of fact to understand the evidence or to determine a fact in issue, a witness qualified as an expert by knowledge, skill, experience, training, or education, may testify thereto in the form of an opinion or otherwise.

The displacement of the *Frye* standard by the *Federal Rules of Evidence* did not remove all limits on the admissibility of purportedly scientific evidence, nor is the trial judge disabled from screening such evidence. Rule 702 confides to the judge some gatekeeping responsibility in that the judge must ensure that any and all scientific testimony or evidence admitted is not only relevant, but reliable.

Rule 702 holds that the subject of an expert's testimony must be "scientific knowledge" and in order to qualify as "scientific knowledge" an *inference* or *assertion* must be derived by the scientific method. Proposed testimony must be supported by appropriate validation, i.e. "good grounds," based on what is known. The Court recognized that "it would be unreasonable to conclude that the subject of scientific testimony must be 'known' to a certainty; arguably, there are no certainties in science." While the Court acknowledged that scientists typically distinguish between "validity" and "reliability," its reference is to *evidentiary* reliability or trustworthiness, and "in a case involving scientific evidence, *evidentiary reliability* will be based upon *scientific validity*."

Rule 702 further requires that the evidence or testimony "assist the trier of fact to understand the evidence or to determine a fact in issue." This condition goes primarily to relevance. "Expert testimony which does not relate to any issue in the case is not relevant and, ergo, non-helpful." 3 Weinstein & Berger Para. 702(02). p. 701-18. *United States v. Downing*, 753 F.2d 1224, 1242 (CA 3 1985). "Another aspect of relevancy is whether expert testimony proffered in the case is sufficiently tied to the facts of the case that it will aid the jury in resolving a factual dispute."

Considering the number of polygraph techniques currently in use (See chapters 11 and 15) the Supreme Court's discussion of the evaluation of the *theory* or *technique* upon which the scientific testimony is based is pertinent. "Another pertinent consideration is whether the theory or technique has been subject to peer review and publication. Publication (which is but one element of peer review) is not a sine qua non of admissibility; it does not necessarily correlate with reliability, see S. Jasanoff, The Fifth Branch: Science Advisors as Policymakers 61-76 (1990), and in some instances well-grounded but innovative theories will not have been published, see Horrobin, The Philosophical Basis of Peer Review and the Suppression of Innovation, 263 J. Am. Med. Assn. 1438 (1990). Some propositions, moreover, are too particular, too new, or of too limited interest to be published. But submission to the scrutiny of the scientific community is a component of '*good science*,' in part because it increases the likelihood that substantive flaws in methodology will be detected. See J. Ziman, Reliable Knowledge: An exploration of the Grounds for Belief in Science 130-133 (1978); Relman and Angell, How Good Is Peer Review?, 321 New Eng. J. Med. 827 (1989). The fact of publication (or lack thereof) in a peer-reviewed journal thus will be a relevant, *though not dispositive*, consideration in assessing the scientific validity of a particular technique or methodology on which an opinion is premised."

The Supreme Court in *Daubert v. Merrell Dow Pharmaceuticals* summarized that "'general acceptance' is not a necessary precondition to the admissibility of scientific evidence under the Federal Rules of Evidence, but the rules of Evidence --especially Rule 702--do assign to the trial judge the task of ensuring that an expert's testimony both rests on a reliable foundation and is relevant to the task at hand. Pertinent evidence based on scientifically valid principles will satisfy those demands."

Nonetheless, in *United Sates v. Black*, 831 F.Supp. 120 (E.D.N.Y. 1993) the Second Circuit Court stated that nothing in *Daubert v. Merrell Dow Phamaceuticals, Inc.*, would disturb the settled precedent that polygraph evidence is neither reliable nor admissible (in the Second Circuit). *United States v. Rea*, 938 F.2d 1206 (2nd Cir. 1992).

However in a bribery case before federal trial judge Sonia Stotmayer, the defendant Wlodek Jan Lech, attempted to enter into evidence the results of a PV examination in which he answered such questions as, "Did you try to bribe any Board of Education official to obtain asbestos removal contract?" and "Did you take part in trying to bribe Board of Education officials to obtain asbestos removal contract?" While conceding that the U. S. Court of Appeals for the Second Circuit has intimated that polygraph results are generally inadmissible, Mr. Lech questioned that bar in light of the U. S. Supreme Court 1993 ruling on scientific evidence in *Daubert v. Merrell Dow Pharmaceuticals, Inc.* 113 S.Ct. 2786.

Judge Stotmayer did not solve the question whether polygraph evidence would be admissible as reliable under *Daubert* and *Rule* 702. Instead, she assumed it would be for the purposes of the motions. Then she found, after applying rule 403 of the *Federal Rules of Evidence*, that the polygraph evidence is precluded because "its probative value is substantially outweighed by the danger of unfair prejudice, confusion, or misleading of the jury." She explained that, "Each of the questions Lech seeks to introduce calls for his belief about the legal implications of his actions, without setting forth the factual circumstances underlying such conclusion." In other words, she wrote, "the jury would receive evidence showing Lech's personal belief that he did not violate any federal criminal statute, but would not receive any information that would assist its inquiry to find facts." In a footnote, the Judge indicated the outcome may be different if a defendant sought to introduce answers "to an exam where he or she completely denied any connection or involvement" with the alleged crime. (New York Law Journal, 28 Jul 95) (Question...1995)

On 20 September 1991, Marty Gadson was convicted of first-degree murder and felony firearms violation and was sentenced to life without parole. Subsequently new evidence in the form of witnesses previously afraid to testify, exculpated Gadson and inculpated two other individuals as the murderers of the victim. Also admitted in evidence in Gadson's request for a new trial was the result of a psychophysiological veracity (PV) examination of Gadson which reflected Gadson as non-deceptive to the relevant questions relating to the shooting of the victim, whether he was at the scene of the crime when the victim was shot and whether he had conspired with anyone to shoot the victim. On 13 April 1994, the Michigan Court of Appeals remanded a request by Gadson to file a motion for a new trial to the Recorder's Court for the City of Detroit. Upon hearing the evidence from new witnesses and the results of the PV examination, Gadson's motion for a new trial was granted. The polygraph (PV exam) evidence was admissible in this situation under a state precedent, *People v. Mechura*, 205 MA 474 (1994) which affirmed the first ruling on the use of PV examination results in a motion for a new trial, *People v. Barbara*, 400 Mich. 352, 255 N.W.2d 171 (Mich. 1977) (Michigan...1995).

The U. S. District Court in Arizona accepted polygraph evidence in the case of *Dock Gray v. Safeway, Inc., John Does I-X, Jane Does I-X, White Entities I-X.* The PV examination was conducted in this civil case for the plaintiff on 7 January 1995 and entered by affidavit. The forensic psychophysiologist's evidence included his credentials as an expert, the exact questions asked during the PV examination, his opinion that Dock

Gray was truthful regarding the target issue, and a copy of his PV examination report. CIV 93-2165 PHX RCB. (U.S. District Court in Arizona accepts...1995)

Interestingly, in United States v. Williams, 39 M.J. 555, 1994 W.L. 23841 (ACMR 9202646, U.S. Army Court of Military Review, 28 Jan. 1994) the United States Army Court of Military Review, Morgan, J. held that military rule of evidence which foreclosed discretion and compelled exclusion of polygraph evidence was unconstitutional as applied to facts of the case. Returned for remand. The Accused's Fifth Amendment right to fair trial by court-martial, combined with his Sixth Amendment right to produce favorable witnesses on his behalf, afforded him the opportunity to be heard on foundational matters regarding admissibility or arguably exculpatory polygraph examination results, and allowed for possibility of admitted polygraph evidence, notwithstanding explicit prohibition of Military Rules of Evidence 707, precluding admission of polygraph evidence. U.S.C.A. Const.Amends 5, 6; Military Rules of Evid., Rules 403, 707.

The aforesaid Army Appellate Court quoted the Court of Military Appeals in United States v. Gipson, 24 M.J. 246, 253 (C.M.A., 1987) which assessed the state of the polygraph technique in the following language: "Depending on the competence of the examiner, the suitability of the examinee, the nature of the particular testing process employed, and such other factors as may arise, the results of a particular examination may be as good as or better than a good deal of expert and lay evidence that is routinely and uncritically received in criminal trials. Further, it is not clear that such evidence invariably will be so collateral, confusing, time-consuming, prejudicial, etc., as to require exclusion. The court clearly felt that polygraph evidence has evolved to the point where it can no longer be 'rejected out of hand,' and concluded that the admissibility determination could and should be made by the trial judge, with this caveat: We do not suggest that all polygraph evidence is admissible or that this particular evidence should have been admitted. Appellant still bears the burden of establishing the foundational predicates outlined above. Our holding here is only that appellant was entitled to attempt to lay that foundation. Judge Cox, speaking for the court, outlined the comprehensive scheme for processing expert testimony envisioned under Mil.R.Evid. 401, 402, 403, and 702, and observed that 'the judge has considerable room to exercise judgment.'" This comprehensive scheme closely parallels the analytical approach to scientific evidence outlined by the Supreme Court six years later in Daubert v. Merrell Dow Pharmaceuticals, Inc. (1993).

The aforesaid Court noted that the Supreme Court has not been reluctant to strike down evidentiary rules that restrict an accused's ability to present favorable evidence at trial, citing Washington v. Texas, 388, U.S. 14, 87 S.Ct. 1920, 18 L.Ed2d 1019 (1967) which held that the Compulsory Process Clause of the Sixth Amendment provides an accused the right to obtain witnesses in his or her favor and have them testify, notwithstanding the effect of state statutes regarding competence of codefendants to the contrary. In Chambers v. Mississippi, 410 U.S. 384, 93 S.Ct. 1038, 35L.Ed.2d 297 (1973), the court recognized that the right to call witnesses in one's own behalf is also an essential component of constitutional due process, and held that a state hearsay rule which compromised this right must yield. And in Rock v. Arkansas, 483 U.S. 44 at 61, 107 S.Ct. 2704 at

2714, 97L.Ed.2d 37 (1987, the court explained that "a state's legitimate interest in barring unreliable evidence (the defendant's hypnotically refreshed testimony) does not extend to per se exclusions that may be reliable in an individual case."

A footnote in United States v. Rodriguez, 37 M.J. 448 (C.M.A. 1993) of the majority opinion suggested that Mil.R.Evid. 707 may ironically survive constitutional scrutiny only to the extent that it excludes polygraph evidence offered by the prosecution, but not for the defense. Our military justice system is replete with examples of safeguards for the rights of military accused which are not available to their civilian counterparts. Recognizing yet another of these advantages not only enhances the perception of fairness that is so vital to the integrity of our system, it also reinforces the basic tenet of Anglo-American jurisprudence that we are better served by protecting the innocent than by convicting the guilty. (Ansley 1994)

In *United States v. Posado*, 1995 WL 368417 (5th Cir. (TX)), the defendants were convicted of one count of conspiracy to possess and one count of possession with intent to distribute in excess of five kilograms of cocaine. Their convictions in the U.S. District Court for the Southern District of Texas was appealed. The issue was admissibility of polygraph evidence in a pretrial hearing to suppress forty-four kilograms of cocaine recovered after an airport interdiction and search of the defendants' luggage. The District Court refused to consider the polygraph evidence offered by defendants to corroborate their version of events preceding the arrest. Fifth Circuit rulings, with few variations, have held an absolute ban on polygraph test results as evidence (*Barrel of Fun v. State Farm Fire & Gas Co.*, 732, F.2d 1028, 5th Cir. 1984). However, the Fifth Circuit now states that prior rulings did not survive *Daubert v. Merrell Dow Pharmaceuticals, Inc.*, 113 S. Ct. 2786, 125 L.Ed.2d 469 (1993). The Court therefore reversed and remanded the *Posado* case for a district court determination of the admissibility of the proffered polygraph evidence in light of the principles embodied in the federal rules of evidence and the Supreme Court decision in Daubert. (Fifth...1995)

Massachusetts has had for many years an evidentiary decision allowing admissibility of PV examination results as evidence. But in a 1989 decision, the state high court barred such evidence. Early in 1996, the state's highest court reconsidered the matter in a case called *Lanigan II*. The court questioned the *Frye* rule as too stringent, possibly considering the Supreme Court's rejection of Frye in *Daubert v. Merrell Dow Pharmaceutical, Inc*. The Massachusetts court concluded that although general acceptability in the field was a significant factor in determining validity, it was not the only factor. In an article by attorney Richard W. Murphy in the Patriot Ledger of 8 July 1995, the author states that "Lawyers have since interpreted the decision to mean that polygraph evidence may be admissible to the extent in which lawyers can prove that the polygraph test produces reliable results." (Massachusetts... 1995)

In *United States v. Crumby*, CR-94r-122-RGS, Crumby moved for an evidentiary ruling to introduce polygraph test results, to demonstrate his innocence. The District Court noted that the Ninth U.S. Circuit Court of Appeals has traditionally been inhospitable toward polygraph evidence, with two exceptions: Stipulated polygraph evidence and polygraph evidence used for the purpose of demonstrating an operative fact. The District Court found a significant increase in polygraph reliability in recent years, and said it is now sufficiently reliable to be admitted as scientific evidence under Rule 702, in accordance with the Supreme Court decision in Daubert v. Merrell Dow Pharmaceuticals, Inc. The Court was also influenced by the Piccinonna decision in the 11th Circuit. (BDE, WCL 3 Nov. 95 *U.S. v. Crumby*, 2 Oct 95 National Law Journal.) (U.S. District Court in Arizona sets odd...1995).

In Louisiana, U.S. District Court Judge F. A. Little, Jr. has ruled the results of polygraph tests are admissible, in a case involving two defendants (Ulmer and Savoie) who sued State Farm Insurance Company for refusing to pay a claim after their home in Montgomery was destroyed by fire, in spite of the fact that both defendants had passed a PV examination administered by a Louisiana State Police examiner for the State Fire Marshal's Office. In his decision, Judge Little said that lie detector tests, while not infallible, have a good record of accuracy when administered by licensed testers and are now widely used in industry and government. The ruling is in keeping with a recent decision of the Fifth Circuit Court of Appeals (*U.S. v. Posado*, 57F.3d 428 (5th Cir. 1995)), which in turn depended on the decision of the U.S. Supreme Court in *Daubert v. Merrell Dow Pharmaceuticals*. (Alexandria Daily Town Talk 10 Oct 95) (U.S. District Court admits... 1995).

While the demise of the *Frye* standard in favor of the Federal Rules of Evidence has opened the door for the admissibility of the results of psychophysiological veracity (PV) examinations using the polygraph, it is evident from the language of the courts which have addressed this issue before and after *Daubert* that PV examinations are regarded as an instrumental testing device rather than a group of diverse psychological techniques which employ the same physiological recordings with a polygraph instrument. Thus it is not surprising to hear some judges quoting decades-old precedents rejecting the admissibility of the results of a PV examination, inasmuch as the current polygraph instruments record basically the same physiological parameters. That current electronic and computerized polygraph systems have vastly improved the quality of the recordings has apparently not had much impact on the courts. But the courts need to understand that the role of the polygraph instrument is minor compared to the methodology and application of the selected psychological test (also known as the PV examination *technique*) which precedes the collection of the physiological data by polygraph. And as described in chapters 11, 15, 17 and 18, there are numerous *accepted* techniques currently in use, each with their own method of addressing those variables capable of affecting the examination process, as identified in chapter 9.

It is therefore imprudent to summarily reject the results of a PV examination without knowing the type of PV examination *technique* used to acquire the proffered results, which might contain significant validated improvements compared to the *technique* previously used in the court precedent rejecting its admissibility. In addition, the administering forensic psychophysiologist has far more research studies supporting his or her technique than his or her predecessors. It behooves judges and lawyers to become acquainted with the contents of at least chapters 3, 6, 7, 8, 9, 11, 15 and 18 in addition to this chapter, in order to understand the complexity and differences of the various techniques whose results may come before them for evaluation. The sixteen techniques described in chapters 11 and 15 which employ the Numerical Approach or the Clinical Approach have distinct philosophical and methodological differences which may be relevant under Rule 702 of the federal rules of evidence.

A proposed set of criteria for court acceptance of psychophysiological veracity (PV) examination techniques is set forth below with a definition of the term *technique* as used in forensic psychophysiology.*

A technique is defined as: A psychological method of implementing a scientifically structured test which includes the following:

a. Analysis of case information.
b. Issue selection and question formulation.
c. Completion of test format.
d. Psychological preparation of examinee for test.
e. Collection of physiological data.
f. Interpretation of data.
   (1) Quantification of physiological data and application of conversion table.
   (2) Factual analysis (optional - clinical approach only)
   (3) Behavior assessment (optional - clinical approach only)
g. Technique control
   (1) Consistency of process.
   (2) Evaluation of examinee's physical and mental state.
   (3) Countermeasure identification.

Criteria for General Acceptance and Published Validation:

The Court could consider any PV examination technique which has received *General Acceptance* within the field of forensic psychophysiology or *Published Validation*.

1. <u>General Acceptance</u>.

A technique which has been in wide use for at least ten years and taught at an APA accredited polygraph school, has been published in a professional journal (not house organs) related to forensic psychophysiology such as *Polygraph* or in a textbook on forensic psychophysiology used in an American Polygraph Association (APA) accredited polygraph school, warrants *general acceptance*.

---

*A committee has been formed under the auspices of the American Society for Testing and Materials (ASTM) to promulgate standards in the discipline of Forensic Psychophysiology Using The Polygraph. Sub-committees are developing standards in research, instrumentation, quality control, examiner education/training, standardization and ethics.

2. <u>Published Validation:</u>

   a. Extensive use (1000 or more field tests); plus a *field validation study* comprising 100 or more real-life cases supervised at the doctorate level, which demonstrates construct and criterion validity and reliability that is subsequently published in *Polygraph* journal of the APA or other national/international journal involved in publishing research related to forensic psychophysiology, warrants *published validation* acceptance.

   or

   b. No extensive use of technique, but:
      (1) *Analog* (laboratory) *study* involving at least 50 cases demonstrating construct and criterion validity and reliability, the results of which are published in *Polygraph,* journal of the APA or other national/international journal involved in publishing research related to forensic psychophysiology, which is replicated by:

      (2) *Field validation study* comprising 100 or more real-life cases supervised at the doctorate level, which demonstrates construct and criterion validity and reliability, the results of which are published in Polygraph, journal of the APA or other national/international journal involved in publishing research related to forensic psychophysiology. Fulfillment of b.(1) and (2) warrants *published validation* acceptance.

In addition to the aforesaid acceptance criteria, the proffered PV examination must have been videotaped in its entirety to provide the court, the prosecution and the defense counsel an opportunity to critique and/or have their expert forensic psychophysiologist review the entire examination process. An audio tape recording may be substituted when the examination is conducted in a prison or similar institution or at a distant location where video equipment is not available and/or feasible.

In addition to the aforesaid criteria for acceptance of a PV examination technique, the judicial system could also require that the forensic psychophysiologist who conducted the proffered PV examination meet specific educational, training and experience standards as set forth below in Part II of this chapter.

Part II - Selection of a Forensic Psychophysiologist.

Before a prosecution or defense attorney embarks on the selection process for the employment of a forensic psychophysiologist, it is highly recommended that he or she thoroughly read chapters 6, 9, 11 and 15 of this textbook. In the final analysis, the attorney must decide whether the Numerical Approach or the Clinical Approach to forensic psychophysiology best suits his or her legal objectives. Once that has been decided, then the attorney's selection process is narrowed to those forensic psychophysiologists who have received formal training and extensive experience in the selected approach/technique.

In the selection process, it should be remembered that the psychophysiological veracity (PV) examination consists of three phases: (1) the pretest interview, (2) the collection of physiological data, and (3) the analysis and interpretation of the data for a conclusion. The focus of the forensic psychophysiologist is to determine whether the examinee is truthful or deceptive to the target issue(s). This three-phase process should be objective and unbiased. There should be no attempt to acquire a confession until all three phases have been completed and the results of the PV examination conclusively indicate deception to the target issue(s). Thus when the interrogation of an examinee is warranted, it must be conducted after the PV examination is completed, which can be performed by the forensic psychophysiologist who conducted the PV examination, or the investigator of the case, or a chosen interrogator. In view of recent court decisions denying admissibility of a confession because of its direct connection to the PV examination process, the aforementioned division between the two procedures is highly desirable. (Johnson v. State, 208 Ga.App. 87, 429 S.E.2d.690 (GA.App.1993); State v. Craig, 50 St.Repo. 1533,___P.2d__(Montana 1993); Amyot v. Her Majesty the Queen, Province of Quebec, District of Montreal, Nos. 500-10-000015-837, 500-10-000141-877, and (705-01-000137-8353)).

Many forensic psychophysiologists (FP) have graduated from polygraph schools which teach a methodology which is confession oriented. Many forensic psychophysiologists were recruited from their police departments to attend polygraph school because of their aptitude at interrogation. The temptation to form an opinion of guilt and interrogate prior to the completion of Phase III would appear to be greater from forensic psychophysiologists who use the Clinical Approach and include factual analysis and behavior assessment in their decision-making process. There are also former interrogators who have attended polygraph schools that teach either the Numerical or Clinical Approach, who ignore proper objective procedures in favor of their perceived superior ability to detect deception through interrogation methods which use the polygraph instrument primarily as a psychological lever to obtain confessions. Many such '*polygraph interrogators*' have developed impressive credentials based on their enviable confession rate. But both prosecution and defense attorneys should be wary of confession-oriented forensic psychophysiologists, especially those who refuse to allow their PV examination and ensuing polygraph charts to be viewed and reviewed by opposing attorneys and/or forensic psychophysiologists. Both prosecution and defense attorneys should desire the service of an objective forensic psychophysiologist who has had formal training and much experience in implementing the psychological procedures (depicted in chapters 8 and 9) necessary to attain a valid and reliable test result. The acid test may well be the courtroom where procedural violations cannot be hidden from the Court which requires a videotape of the entire PV examination as part of its criteria for admissibility. Furthermore, procedural violations impact on the validity and reliability of the proffered test which must be proven to the satisfaction of the court.

In the selection of a forensic psychophysiologist, the attorney should not be swayed by the type of polygraph instrument used, inasmuch as it comprises less than ten percent of the overall PV examination procedure. Both the electronic and the computerized polygraph systems record the same physiological parameters (See Chapter 13). The computerized polygraph systems have an algorithm which analyzes the physiological data and produces a statistical probability that the examinee was truthful or deceptive. But the computer algorithms identify few countermeasures, whereas the forensic psychophysiologist who manually analyzes and quantifies the physiological data is capable of identifying most known countermeasures and factoring them into his or her analysis and quantification of the data. However, the computerized systems do produce charts and display the data on screen for the forensic psychophysiologist to manually score the physiological data which most forensic psychophysiologists use as the primary source for their conclusions, with the algorithm's statistical probability as a secondary source or backup. Thus, at this time, whether the forensic psychophysiologist uses an electronic or computerized polygraph instrument should not be a factor in the attorney's selection process.

The most important factors to consider in the selection process of a forensic psychophysiologist are the type and quality of formal training, successful completion of an internship immediately following the formal training, number of continuing education seminars/workshops related to forensic psychophysiology, extent of experience, and membership in the American Polygraph Association which has stringent standards for its members. Other factors can also contribute to the credentials of the forensic psychophysiologist, such as authorship and publication of research articles and books related to forensic psychophysiology, non-political appointments to positions involving research, development and supervision of projects pertaining to forensic psychophysiology, and qualifying as an expert forensic psychophysiologist in a judicial proceeding. The attorney may request a curriculum vitae from the forensic psychophysiologist detailing his or her credentials.

If the selection process appears to be tedious, the results are well worth the effort to both the prosecution and the defense attorney.

There is an old saying that "he who is his own counsel usually has a fool for a client." An analogous phrase would be that "he who is his own lie-detector is usually fooled by his client."

Approximately 87 percent of the examinees referred to this author by defense attorneys were guilty of the offense for which they were polygraphed, as evidenced by the PV examination results that were in most cases substantiated by their own post-test admissions or confessions (reported in a field validation study conducted by Matte & Reuss) (1989, 1990). A great number of those attorneys were thoroughly convinced of their client's innocence and were merely seeking scientific corroboration to present to the district attorney in an attempt to have the charges against their client dismissed. One attorney even had his client examined by a psychiatrist who administered a truth serum test (sodium pentothal) opining that the defendant was innocent of the charges against him. A PV examination was subsequently administered to buttress the findings of the truth serum test. To the astonishment of both the defense attorney and the psychiatrist, the PV examination results indicated deception and the defendant confessed his crime to this author.

It is apparent that a competent forensic psychophysiologist can save the defense attorney a lot of time and effort by providing the defense attorney with scientific reassurance of his or her client's innocence or his or her client's true version of the incident. The attorney can then formulate his or her defense strategy on the basis of what he or she now knows to be a full and accurate account of the relevant facts. A competent forensic psychophysiologist can provide the prosecution attorney with accurate and objective information which can be most useful in prosecutorial decisions which may rely on the veracity of defendants, witnesses, victims and informants.

The forensic psychophysiologist hired by a defense attorney is acting as an agent of that attorney. Therefore the umbrella of privileged communication between attorney and client extends to the polygraphist acting on behalf of the attorney (People v. George 1980; Matte 1979). Any and all information obtained by the forensic psychophysiologist during such an examination is therefore privileged and cannot be released by the forensic psychophysiologist to anyone other than the defense attorney who requested the PV examination unless explicit permission is given by the attorney and his or her client. This usually occurs when a client is found truthful, in which case a written report of the expert opinion is submitted to the requesting attorney, who normally furnishes a copy of it to the district attorney in an effort to have the charges dismissed or to plead to a lesser charge.

Often a suspect, after being arrested, will be asked to submit to a PV examination, to be administered by a police forensic psychophysiologist. It is wise for a defense attorney to delay his or her client's response to such a request until he or she has had his or her client discreetly polygraphed by a competent private forensic psychophysiologist. In this manner, if the client is in fact guilty of the offense, the results of the private examination will be protected from disclosure to the police, and subsequent refusal by the client to submit to a police examination cannot be held against him or her, nor can his or her refusal even be mentioned in a court of law. To allow a client to submit to a police PV examination without the above precaution will place the client in serious jeopardy especially if he or she is guilty of the offense, since police forensic psychophysiologists are recruited from the detective force for their ability as interrogators. Once the examination reveals that the client attempted deception to the crime questions, interrogation is certain to follow and the chances are excellent for a confession from the client. The fact that the client is innocent does not remove him or her from jeopardy. Although a great percentage of law enforcement forensic psychophysiologists are well trained, experienced, and dedicated officers, there are still many who have received inferior formal training and use obsolete techniques.

In addition to those police forensic psychophysiologists who have received inferior formal training and use obsolete techniques, others have had no formal training but simply had on-the-job training from their predecessor, whose own training may have been no more than such an apprenticeship. Such forensic psychophysiologists are no more than '*polygraph interrogators*' who use the polygraph instrument as a lever or psychological rubber hose to elicit a confession. A mimeograph machine would undoubtedly accomplish the same results if the examinee did not know the difference between the two instruments.

In view of the above situations, there is a distinct possibility that an innocent client may be found deceptive in a PV examination conducted by a forensic psychophysiologist lacking proper training and experience. However, when a police forensic psychophysiologist knows that the client was previously examined regarding the same issue by a competent, reputable private forensic psychophysiologist, who found the client to be truthful, his or her own expertise and competence are then challenged if his or her findings are different from the private forensic psychophysiologist. Due to this additional scrutiny and pressure, the police forensic psychophysiologist will exercise greater caution in the administration of the PV examination.

A knowledgeable attorney will only allow a police forensic psychophysiologist that employs a polygraph technique that meets the *General Acceptance and Published Validation Criteria* previously articulated in this chapter and listed in chapters 11 and 15, to administer a PV examination to his or her client. In addition, the defense attorney should enter into an agreement with the prosecuting and/or law enforcement agency which will assure the defense counsel that all of the *Conditions For Polygraph Tests Conducted By The Police On Defense Attorney Clients* (which are listed at the end of this chapter) will be met and complied with. As discussed later in this chapter, there is no legal or scientific justification for the rejection of these conditions, thus the defense attorney should view such a rejection with suspicion, and rather than merely refusing to submit his client to an unmonitored examination, the defense attorney should obtain a court order compelling the law enforcement agency to administer the PV examination in compliance with the aforesaid *Conditions*.

In the selection of a forensic psychophysiologist, the defense attorney should whenever possible consult the directory of the American Polygraph Association (APA). Historically, it has been the unifying force in the field of forensic psychophysiology, establishing and enforcing standards of practice and a code of ethics as well as minimum educational and training requirements for membership. It must be noted that there are nine classes of membership in the American Polygraph Association: Full member, Intern member, Associate member, Life member, Science & Technology member, Honorary member, Retired member, Divisional member, International member. For practical purposes, active forensic psychophysiologists fall into one of the first four classes. The defense attorney should be aware of the difference in educational and training requirements between the four classes of membership in the APA.

To qualify as an APA *Full Member*, the individual must have:

1. Graduated from an APA accredited school.
2. Completed not less than two hundred (200) actual PV examinations using a standardized polygraph technique as taught at an APA accredited school and hold a current and valid license to practice forensic psychophysiology issued

by any state or federal agency requiring such license.

3. Received a Baccalaureate degree from a college or university accredited by a regional accreditation board.
4. Those individuals applying for membership who have not graduated from an APA accredited school must apply as Associate Members prior to upgrade to Full Membership.

To qualify as an *Intern Member*, the individual must:

1. Be in attendance at an APA accredited polygraph training school or who is completing requirements of such training school shall be eligible for member ship as an *Intern* provided that he or she meets all requirements for membership as a *Full Member* except for the experience requirements as set forth in A 2 and 3 of the Full membership requirements.
2. Persons admitted under this provision shall, upon completion of the polygraph experience requirement for *Full Member*, be upgraded to *Full Member*, without examination, upon petition to the Board certifying satisfactory fulfillment of the experience requirement within 36 months following the date of completion of the polygraph training school. *Intern members* who fail to complete the experience requirement within 36 months, shall be required to complete satisfactorily an APA approved examination, to be administered by the APA Membership Committee, before upgrading to *Full Member* status. *Intern members* who do not become *Full Members* within 48 months of completion of the polygraph training school requirements shall be required to petition the Board for an extension of their *Intern member* status. The Board, at its discretion, may prescribe further experience, examination and time period requirements or may take other actions as it deems necessary.

To qualify as an *Associate Member*, the individual must:

1. A person who is a practicing forensic psychophysiologist and who can document to the satisfaction of the Board of Directors of the APA successful completion of a formal polygraph training program, but who does not meet the requirements of membership as a *Full* or *Intern Member* shall be eligible for membership in the APA as an *Associate Member*.

2. An Associate Member shall be eligible to be upgraded to Full Member status provided that the following conditions have been satisfied:

    a. Has satisfactorily completed a qualifying examination attesting to his or her knowledge of and competence in the administration of PV examination procedures. This examination shall consist of an oral and written assessment of both academic and practical knowledge of PV examination procedures and shall be administered by the APA Membership Committee.

b. Has been an *Associate Member* for not less than 36 months and,
c. Within the 36 months preceding upgrading he or she has successfully completed either:

 (1) At least 108 hours of continuing education in topics directly related to PV examination testing, including at least one APA annual seminar, during their *Associate* membership; or,

 (2) An APA approved refresher course administered by a polygraph training school accredited by the APA; and,

  (a) Is in attendance at an APA annual seminar at the time of consideration of his or her request for upgrading to Full Member; and,
  (b) Submits proof of having completed not less than 200 satisfactory PV examinations; and,
  (c) Holds a current and valid license as a forensic psychophysiologist in the state or other similar governmental jurisdiction of his or her practice if at the time of application such license is required by law.

To qualify as a *Life Member*, the individual must:

1. Be a *Member* of the APA:
   a. Who has been nominated by another *Member* for *Life Membership*, and,
   b. Whose nomination has been approved by a two-thirds (2/3) majority vote of the Board, and,
   c. Whose nomination has been confirmed by a majority vote of all *Voting Members* present at a meeting of the General Membership.

Attorneys should note that several polygraph schools do not consider the mere completion of the 300 or more hours of classroom instruction as sufficient training to issue a graduation certificate. Schools such as the Backster School of Lie Detection require that students satisfactorily complete a minimum of thirty psychophysiological veracity examinations in the field within a year following completion of the academic portion of the course before they are issued a certificate of graduation. In the years past, a surprising number of students have failed to complete the aforesaid internship which has been called by at least one polygraph school a *Certification* program, thus some students who have successfully completed their internship are *Certified* while others who have also successfully completed their internship have *Graduated* because their school does not use the term *certified*. Hence the attorney making inquiries in that area should focus on the successful completion of the work project required in the internship.

Basically, the defense attorney should select a forensic psychophysiologist who is well educated (ideally a college graduate), has *graduated* from a polygraph school accredited by the American Polygraph Association, is experienced, and is a person of integrity and mature judgment.

The forensic psychophysiologist should be agreeable to having his or her charts and related data reviewed by another competent forensic psychophysiologist *trained in the same technique* for double verification of the findings if the attorney so desires, in order to strengthen the PV examination results and his or her case. A forensic psychophysiologist who claims that he or she is the only one who can interpret his or her charts indicates that his or her technique lacks standardization or is not a validated technique, or he or she lacks confidence in his or her chart interpretation and/or procedure and, therefore, should be avoided by the attorney.

The forensic psychophysiologist should be a good witness in court. Since PV examination results have only occasionally been admitted as evidence in courts throughout the country, very few forensic psychophysiologists have therefore had occasion to testify in a court of law regarding PV examination results. However, a forensic psychophysiologist possessing federal, state, or local law enforcement investigative experience is normally no stranger to courtroom procedures; therefore, he or she should not find it difficult to offer credible testimony regarding his or her PV examination results if he or she is in fact a competent, expert forensic psychophysiologist. Courtroom experience will further enable the forensic psychophysiologist to maintain a professional posture during cross-examination.

The defense attorney must remember that the strength and credibility of the PV examination results are based upon the qualifications and expertise of the forensic psychophysiologist who administered the examination. A careful selection will protect the results from attack by the prosecution and lessen the chance of the prosecution obtaining contradictory results from their own forensic psychophysiologist.

The forensic psychophysiologist will require certain essential information from the defense attorney in order to develop effective control questions and scientifically formulate relevant questions that will be accurate in content and penetrate to the heart of the matter. Therefore, the defense attorney should furnish the forensic psychophysiologist with all available discovery reports and information concerning the charges. This includes all information relating to the matter including all statements, accusatory instruments, and available transcripts. The defense attorney should also furnish the forensic psychophysiologist with as much background data regarding the defendant as possible. This information will be used by the forensic psychophysiologist to develop control questions, whose effectiveness may be diminished if the attorney discusses the reason and purpose of the background data with his or her client. The defense attorney must remember that effective control questions are essential to prove the truthfulness of an innocent client, therefore release of information that would sabotage the effectiveness of control questions would be counterproductive in that it could produce inconclusive polygraph results.

The defense attorney should also furnish the forensic psychophysiologist with all known psychological and medical data including the use of drugs and current prescribed medication by his or her client so that appropriate medical precautions are taken. The attorney should never advise his client to abstain from prescribed medication, but he or she should always advise the forensic psychophysiologist prior to the PV examination of the medication or drug used by his or her client. If the client is an habitual user of illegal drugs, he or she should be scheduled for a PV examination at a time when he or she is not suffering from withdrawals, and of course the forensic psychophysiologist should be apprised of this prior to the PV examination. Full disclosure of the usage of all drugs will undoubtedly assist the competent forensic psychophysiologist, although in all probability he or she will conduct an independent urinalysis for the presence of any drugs in the examinee's system immediately upon completion of the PV examination.

It can be anticipated that a properly conducted PV examination will last anywhere from two to four hours, and sometimes longer, depending on the number of issues to be tested, therefore the attorney should advise his client to acquire a good night's rest and further attempt to schedule the examination at a particular time of the day that will not cause the client to miss a meal.

The defense attorney should make clear to the forensic psychophysiologist at the outset whether he or she wants the forensic psychophysiologist to interrogate his or her client should the PV examination results reflect that his or her client was attempting deception to the relevant questions. Normally it is to the attorney's advantage to allow the forensic psychophysiologist wide latitude in the post-test interview of his or her client, since all information obtained from the interview is privileged (Matte 1979), yet provides the attorney with the truthful version of the incident. However, it is doubtful whether a written statement incorporating admissions or a confession from the client is recommended under these circumstances. Most defense attorneys instruct the forensic psychophysiologist to obtain only a verbal confession from the client, which the forensic psychophysiologist may reduce to writing only for purposes of subsequent accurate recall when furnishing verbal results to the attorney.

There are times, however, when the defense attorney desires a written report plus a written confession from a deceptive client in order to protect him or her from any claim of ineffective representation.

The defense attorney should expect a sensitivity test to be conducted on his client, plus a minimum of two polygraph charts on each issue to be covered during the PV examination. Each polygraph chart must contain identifying data, uniform chart markings depicting instrument adjustment and sensitivity settings, plus the client's signature in the top middle of each chart to avoid any question of chart switching.

The psychophysiological veracity (PV) examination should whenever possible be video tape recorded in its entirety for possible use in court. This will provide the court with evidence that proper procedures were followed and prevent the opposition from raising questions regarding the manner in which the examination was conducted.

When a written report of the PV examination results is rendered, it should include a predication, laboratory results regarding the presence or absence of drugs if performed, the examinee's version of the event as related to the forensic psychophysiologist, if substantially different from his previous version to the attorney, the type of examination PV examination technique and instrumentation used, the expert opinion of the forensic psychophysiologist and the basis for the FP's conclusion.

The procedure for introducing the PV examination results into evidence requires that the forensic psychophysiologist who conducted the PV examination be examined in the court for the purpose of determining his or her qualifications as an expert witness. When the attorney examines the forensic psychophysiologist on the witness stand, he or she must first qualify him or her as an expert, by eliciting from the FP information regarding his or her formal education, polygraph training and certification or graduation from the polygraph school, experience, research conducted and published if any, and active membership in organizations related to forensic psychophysiology.

In cases where the attorney is attempting to have the PV examination results admitted into evidence and is therefore laying a foundation regarding its acceptance within the scientific community, the attorney may find it desirable to precede the testimony of his or her forensic psychophysiologist with the testimony of a psychologist or physiologist knowledgeable about forensic psychophysiology, establishing the validity and reliability of the PV examination technique as used by the testifying forensic psychophysiologist. It may be advisable to have a second forensic psychophysiologist of authoritative stature or possessing impressive credentials testify as to his or her opinion regarding his or her analysis of the technique used by the examining forensic psychophysiologist and his or her interpretation of the resulting charts, to buttress the expert opinion of the examining forensic psychophysiologist.

This testimony may be supplemented by the introduction of various validity studies supportive of the PV examination technique used, and the validity and reliability of PV examinations in general.

In the majority of cases, PV examination results admitted as evidence in a court of law were submitted under agreement and stipulation. Both the defense counsel and the prosecutor executed a written agreement stipulating that they would allow the results of a PV examination conducted by a specific forensic psychophysiologist agreeable to both parties to be admitted into evidence at trial regardless of the outcome of the examination. Obviously, the prosecutor must have great faith in the competency and neutrality of the forensic psychophysiologist selected and the defense attorney must have similar confidence to enter into such an agreement. This agreement, however, does not prevent either party from cross-examining the forensic psychophysiologist, especially when the results are other than expected by either party.

One of the most serious and enduring problems encountered by many forensic psychophysiologists who have testified in court, is the lack of adequate pretrial court testimony preparation by the attorney with the forensic psychophysiologist. The attorney should review with his forensic psychophysiologist all of the data that the FP intends to present at trial, and discuss the strengths and weaknesses of his or her testimony. A determination should be made regarding the use of visual aids to show the judge and jury the structure of the examination and related test questions, and perhaps a display of the polygraph charts pinned to a classroom board to graphically display the examinee's physiological tracings and their meaning. The attorney should learn from his expert witness what questions to ask that will increase the credibility of his or her testimony, and conversely what questions may be expected in cross-examination and the expert witness' planned testimony in reply. In short, the attorney must prepare his expert witness at least a day before trial and be prepared for lengthly testimony.

Whenever an attorney anticipates cross-examining a forensic psychophysiologist, he or she should first consult with a reputable expert forensic psychophysiologist for the purpose of learning about the *technique* used by the forensic psychophysiologist to be cross-examined. The attorney should attempt to obtain a copy of the polygraph report and related documents, including all the questions used in each test, controls as well as relevant questions, and the respective polygraph charts for the consulting expert forensic psychophysiologist to review. In this manner, the consulting expert can advise the attorney of any procedural violations and/or chart misinterpretation found in his or her review, and further advise the attorney of necessary steps that must be taken to expose the errors. The attorney may elect to call the consulting expert forensic psychophysiologist as a witness and/or he or she may elect to call an expert witness who has done specific research in that area of forensic psychophysiology that the consulting forensic psychophysiologist feels has been violated.

Inasmuch as the attorney cannot have his or her own consulting forensic psychophysiologist cross-examine the opposing forensic psychophysiologist, it behooves the attorney to become thoroughly familiar with the PV examination *technique* by reading available books regarding the subject. In addition, the attorney should have his consulting forensic psychophysiologist with him or her in the courtroom for instant advice. The forensic psychophysiologist can recognize faulty polygraph testimony that would otherwise go undetected by the most astute attorney.

In the cross-examination of a forensic psychophysiologist, the first area to be scrutinized should be his or her testimony regarding his or her qualifications since this forms the basis of his or her credibility as an expert and yet is his or her most vulnerable area.

After establishing that the forensic psychophysiologist did in fact satisfactorily complete the academic portion of the polygraph school, the attorney should determine whether or not following the academic portion of the school, the forensic psychophysiologist completed the number of specific type of cases that he or she was required to submit to the school for review (normally thirty cases), then determine whether or not he or she was certified or graduated from that polygraph school. In the years past, only a small percentage of forensic psychophysiologists actually satisfactorily completed the required field project and obtained their graduation certificate (certification). During the examination of the forensic psychophysiologist in court, the number of years of polygraph experience and the total number of tests are elicited from the forensic psychophysiologist to impress the court as to his or her expertise. In cross-examination, the forensic psychophysiologist should be made to repeat the number of PV examinations he or she claims to have personally conducted. Then the attorney should ascertain the beginning period and ending period in which these examinations were conducted. The attorney should then determine from the forensic psychophysiologist what percentage of this total number of examinations represent specific type PV examinations, what percentage represents pre-employment type examinations, and what percentage represents routine periodic or screening examinations. Police forensic psychophysiologists will normally reflect a high percentage of specific type tests; however, private forensic psychophysiologists will normally reflect a low percentage inasmuch as commercial polygraph work entailed (until enactment of EPPA in 1988) a large number of pre-employment and screening examinations, which normally employ a Relevant-Irrelevant or General Question technique. In this manner, the attorney has succeeded in segregating the number of specific type tests from all other types, thereby offering the court a more accurate picture of the testifying forensic psychophysiologist's experience in the type of PV examination being submitted to the court as evidence, which in many cases will be dramatically reduced by the above procedure.

The attorney should understand human nature, in that an inexperienced forensic psychophysiologist may be tempted to inflate the total number of PV examinations he or she has conducted. He or she may fear that a low number of tests will disqualify him or her as an expert, which will cause him or her to lose face and business from other attorneys. A sharp attorney will determine from the forensic psychophysiologist the number of hours per day, the number of days per week, and the number of years he or she has conducted PV examinations. The attorney will then divide the actual number of full workdays into the total number of all tests, including pre-employments and periodics, to determine the average number of tests the forensic psychophysiologist conducted in any one day. By previously cross-examining the forensic psychophysiologist regarding the average amount of time he or she spends on each type of examination, it becomes quite evident when a forensic psychophysiologist has inflated the total number of tests conducted. As an example, a forensic psychophysiologist initially claims a total of 6,000 tests yet has had only one year of experience. This would require that he or she conduct an average of twenty-four PV examinations per day. If he or she claimed an eight-hour average, it can be easily seen that the tests lasted an average of twenty minutes, a totally unacceptable figure, especially when specific type tests are included in that time frame. The simplest test requires a minimum of one hour if proper procedures and safeguards are followed. A reasonable average of total tests conducted should not exceed six General Question tests or two Specific-Issue cases per day which may involve several single-issue tests in each case. This takes into account that on some days this number may be exceeded due to longer hours expended but this should be offset by those days when fewer tests were conducted.

If voluntariness of the examinee is an issue, then the next step is to determine the voluntariness of the examination by examining the release or permission form signed by the examinee at the beginning of the test.

Most permission forms or waiver of constitutional rights provide a space at the beginning of the form for the examinee's printed name, and a line at the bottom of the form for the examinee's signature.

The attorney should determine whether the printed name was executed by the forensic psychophysiologist or the examinee. This author, for example, has the examinee print his or her name at the beginning of the first paragraph, initial any typographical errors or changes in the text, and sign the form with the time and date. Furthermore, the examinee will insert the time and sign an exit paragraph reiterating the voluntariness of his or her submission to the test and the time that it concluded.

If a statement or a confession was obtained by the forensic psychophysiologist from the examinee, the same cross-examination procedures as utilized to determine the voluntariness of the instrument in criminal cases is employed.

Many forensic psychophysiologists including this author enter the time and date at the end of each polygraph chart. If the time is also entered in the statement, the defense attorney can determine the amount of time the interrogation that resulted in the confession lasted.

The forensic psychophysiologist is now cross-examined regarding the pretest interview of the examinee, which is perhaps the most crucial segment of the entire psychophysiological veracity examination, inasmuch as the validity of the physiological data upon which is based the decision of truth or deception, depends not only on the scientific formulation of the test questions, but also on the proper psychological preparation of the examinee for the collection of the physiological data. *Any procedural violations uncovered during this cross-examination could result in the invalidation of the test results.*

The forensic psychophysiologist's worksheet containing background data and other information elicited from the examinee should be available to the attorney conducting the cross-examination. The attorney should determine whether the forensic psychophysiologist made necessary inquiries into the examinee's state of health, present use of drugs that would have an effect on the test, and the amount of rest or sleep the examinee had the night before the test. The attorney should then go over the pretest interview with the forensic psychophysiologist for any evidence that an accusatory approach or interrogation was used prior to the collection of the physiological data with the polygraph instrument, which would invalidate the test (See chapter 9).

A determination should be made as to when the polygraph instrument used to produce the charts submitted into evidence was last calibrated prior to the PV examination of the defendant. Calibration is usually performed by the forensic psychophysiologist on a monthly basis and sometimes more frequently. It is a relatively simple procedure. When a polygraph instrument malfunctions, it becomes apparent to the competent forensic psychophysiologist the same as a television set to the viewer. One either gets a good picture, a poor picture, or no picture. However, the competent forensic psychophysiologist (unlike the television viewer) usually knows the nature of the malfunction. Most polygraph instruments are composed of modules that can be quickly removed and shipped to the manufacturer with a replacement within forty-eight hours. Computerized polygraph systems are calibrated at the factory only.

The next step is to cross-examine the forensic psychophysiologist regarding any apparent deficiencies in the polygraph charts, which should have been brought to the attorney's attention prior to trial by his consulting forensic psychophysiologist. For this purpose, the charts or copies thereof should be displayed on a board for the court and the jury to see as the charts are being scrutinized by the attorney. A blackboard should also be available for the forensic psychophysiologists on both sides to provide the court and jury with visual demonstrations of any physiological explanations they may have regarding their interpretation of the charts submitted into evidence.

Effective cross-examination of an expert forensic psychophysiologist requires much preparation by the attorney, who may expect a seasoned courtroom veteran. The attorney should have a definite plan of action, know the specific areas of the procedure he or she will attack, and be armed with credible scientific data to support the testimony of his or her expert witnesses.

There are numerous areas where the defense attorney can use PV examination results. Whenever there is a factual dispute regarding a distinctive issue, the PV examination may be used to prove or disprove essential elements of his/her client's version of the incident or matter. The following are some of the areas where the PV examination is frequently used.

Plea Bargaining: Even inadmissible PV examination results can be used to bargain with the prosecution for a lesser charge or outright dismissal. Verification of the essential elements of information in the subject's version of the incident will prevent unnecessarily lengthy investigations into sometimes incredible versions, when the other evidence against the subject is overwhelming and a very appealing offer by the prosecution is available if the case is resolved by a negotiated plea.

Motions To Suppress Evidence: Conflicting testimony between the defense attorney's client and the arresting officer concerning the legality of a search and/or advisement of his or her rights can be resolved by the administration of a PV examination.

Settlements: Acceptance of PV examination results prior to trial often results in settlements, thereby saving the time, expense, agony, and embarrassment of a trial.

Sentencing: PV examination results may be used to disprove unfavorable information found in presentencing reports that was not used to arrive at a guilty verdict, or to determine the veracity of a convicted subject's assertion of assets which may be an issue at sentencing.

Supporting Evidence: Quite often, a criminal defense depends upon psychiatric opinion testimony as to the defendant's ability to understand the charges and assist in his or her defense or his or her legal culpability for actions he or she may have committed. The opinions of the expert witness in this area often depend heavily upon statements made to the expert by the defendants. Prosecutors often attack the expert's opinions by challenging the truthfulness of the defendant's statements. The PV examination used in conjunction with a psychiatric examination can provide the expert with verified information upon which to base his or her opinion.

Parole and Probation: The PV examination can be an invaluable aid in verifying the accuracy of information to be used as a basis for granting or revoking parole or probation. In fact, several states have adopted a program of monitoring sex offenders with the use of PV examinations as a condition of their parole or probation. (See Chapter 24).

Arbitration: Forensic psychophysiology has been successfully used in federal and state arbitrations to resolve conflicting testimony.

Civil Actions: PV examination results can be used to resolve paternity suits, effect marital reconciliation, settle child custody and visitation right disputes, and determine the veracity of accusations often made in domestic relation cases. Disputes in automobile accidents or transactions between businessmen can also be resolved by the use of PV examinations.

The defense attorney who intends to introduce PV examination results as evidence in a court of law on behalf of his or her client must realize that the supersedence of the Frye standard in favor of the Federal Rules of Evidence by Daubert v. Dow Pharmaceuticals, Inc., is merely an invitation for forensic psychophysiology to show that it is worthy of acceptance by the court. It therefore behooves the attorney who has such an aspiration to present to the court a most competent and well-prepared forensic psychophysiologist.

The benefits that the attorney will derive from the use of the psychophysiological veracity examination are by no means exhausted. The bulk of his or her practice involves a constant effort to verify those facts that will further his or her cause. Awareness of the utility of forensic psychophysiology will open new vistas for the attorney in his or her daily practice.

Part III - Defense Access to Police Psychophysiological Veracity Examinations.

Some law enforcement agencies have been allowing defense attorneys and their expert forensic psychophysiologist to witness a defendant's psychophysiological veracity

(PV) examination, but a great number do not, i.e., the New York State Police, the Federal Bureau of Investigation, to name a few. Interestingly, some of the supervising forensic psychophysiologists employed by those agencies which prohibit access to defense attorneys have privately informed this author that they are not personally opposed to a policy of affording defense attorneys and their expert to witness audiovisually the entire PV examination and provide the defense access to the polygraph data. Thus, this author submitted a proposal to the American Polygraph Association in August 1995 to adopt a policy which supports and encourages all law enforcement agencies and district attorneys to afford defense attorneys such access, which is quoted verbatim below:

> The lofty mission of the American Polygraph Association (APA) necessitates that it hold itself to the highest standard of justice, above the adversary criminal justice system, in order to provide all of society equal protection from mendacity. To fulfill that mission, the APA hereby declares that all examinees must be afforded the ability to protect themselves from potential human error or incompetence by permitting a representative of the examinee to monitor and/or inspect the audiovisual and documentary records of the entire psychophysiological veracity (PV) examination. The APA holds that the PV examination is a validated scientific procedure not unlike other scientific techniques that are routinely subjected to the closest scrutiny. The APA postulates that this complete access policy will galvanize its membership to adhere to superlative standards of practice which will earn the respect of the scientific community and the confidence of the criminal justice system, its courts, and the public it serves.

This author believes that the adoption of aforesaid complete access policy would foster a better understanding, greater respect and a unity of support from the legal community for psychophysiological veracity examinations, which would most assuredly impact on their acceptance and admissibility as evidence in Court. This view was supported by Stephen K. Bartlett, President (1995-1996) of the American Polygraph Association who stated that "I personally believe that this should be allowed and, of course, that all law enforcement examinations should be open to review by all defense attorneys who wish to review their client's examinations even if they do not witness them during the exam." (Bartlett 1995)

The Board of Directors of the APA voted against the adoption of aforesaid policy in 1996, not because they disagreed with its contents and merits, but because such a policy could be construed as a directive to APA members employed at law enforcement agencies whose own policies and directives would be in conflict with the APA policy. However it is encouraging to note that several regional law enforcement agencies have adopted a complete access policy which hopefully will be emulated by the national law enforcement agencies that administer psychophysiological veracity examinations.

Historically, prosecutors' offices and law enforcement agencies have been extremely reluctant to provide the defense with any information that may be useful to the defendant's case; thus the pretrial discovery rule was enacted to correct that inequity. However, this rule is not effective until the defendant is actually charged with a crime. Most psychophysiological veracity (PV) examinations are offered to a defendant by the police or prosecutor prior to charges being preferred, and it is at this stage of the proceedings that the innocent (as later verified) defendant has the best opportunity to "prove" his or her innocence and avoid the agony and expense of a trial. Generally, when such an offer is made by the prosecutor or the police to a defendant, it is a "take it or leave it" proposition. Take and pass the test and the charge(s) will be dropped. Failure to pass the test usually results in a plea bargain or trial. A test refusal is often interpreted in the same light as a test failure thus significantly increasing the potential for trial. This scenario can present a serious problem for the defense attorney, especially if his or her client is innocent.

A psychophysiological veracity (PV) examination, when properly conducted in accordance with the standards of the American Polygraph Association by a competent, expert forensic psychophysiologist, is no longer merely an interrogation tool, but a validated scientific procedure which has demonstrated a high degree of reliability in identifying truthful and deceptive examinees. As indicated in Part I of this chapter and Chapter 3 relating to the scientific status of PV examinations, the results of continuing research and development in forensic psychophysiology have significantly improved the potential for admissibility of PV examination results in court, especially under the current *Federal Rules of Evidence* which superseded the *Frye* standard for the admissibility of scientific evidence in a court of law. Thus a defendant has an inherent right to ensure that any scientific test performed on him or her be conducted by a competent expert, using a scientifically accepted procedure which can be reviewed and critiqued by his or her own expert.

It has already been established by the Daubert Court and the scientific community that the competency of the expert, the validity and reliability of the technique, and the scientificity of the methodology used to administer the test are critical in the evaluation of the test results. Thus it seems reasonable that a defendant who is requested to submit to a psychophysiological veracity (PV) examination which has been scientifically validated be afforded the same safeguards against error and/or incompetency that other scientific tests and/or procedures currently enjoy, which include access to all of the data that was used to conduct the test for critical review by a defense or independent expert.

However, in psychophysiological veracity (PV) examinations, the critical review and analysis of the physiological data collected from a defendant without a videotape of the pretest procedure and methodology used to collect the data, rely entirely on the *enormous assumption* that the attending forensic psychophysiologist was totally competent and his or her procedure/methodology was flawless. As indicated in chapters 8 and 9, the validity and reliability of the physiological data recorded on polygraph charts depend entirely on the competency of the forensic psychophysiologist in administering a validated technique sans procedural violations. The alternative to the videotape is a live viewing through a two-way mirror and speaker. Thus the production by the prosecution of the defendant's polygraph charts containing the physiological data from which a decision was made as to truth or deception, to the defense counsel without a videotape demonstrating the conduct of the pretest interview and the collection of the physiological data, is totally inadequate because procedural violations which can affect the validity of the collected physiological data, are most often committed during the pretest interview and during the collection of the data.

Research has shown that when an error is made in a psychophysiological veracity (PV) examination, it is more likely to be a false positive where an innocent examinee is found deceptive, rather than a false negative where a guilty examinee is erroneously found truthful regarding the target issue. The Office of Technology Assessment's 1983 report evaluated both analog and field studies conducted on polygraph tests pertaining to specific incident criminal investigations and found that in field studies examined, false positives average 19.1 percent and false negatives average 10.2 percent. It should be noted however that the OTA included Inconclusives as errors. (See Chapter 3). A report by Norman Ansley, Department of Defense on "The Validity and Reliability of Polygraph Decisions in Real Cases" for the past 10 years revealed that of the 7 studies involving 7 different PV examination techniques (Backster Tri-Zone Comparison, Matte Quadri-Track Zone Comparison, Reid CQT, Arther CQT, Utah CQT, Canadian CQT, MGQT), the combined false positive rate (Innocent found Deceptive) was 5 percent, and the combined false negative rate (Guilty found Truthful) was 1 percent. (Ansley 1990; OTA 1983).

Judging from the findings of the above studies, there appears to be a greater potential for making errors against the Innocent than against the Guilty examinee. However it should be remembered that the aforementioned studies embrace several different polygraph techniques employing either the clinical approach or the numerical approach and involving many forensic psychophysiologists with varied training and experience. Modern PV examination techniques, most of which employ a numerical scoring system of chart analysis, are not structurally biased against the Innocent examinee. The problem occurs during the pretest interview when the control questions and the relevant questions are improperly formulated and/or introduced/presented to the examinee. Furthermore, several procedural violations can occur during the pretest interview and during the collection of the physiological data with the use of a polygraph instrument and between the conduct of each polygraph chart that may significantly increase the potential for or cause a false positive result.

The two major factors that forensic psychophysiologists must recognize (many do not) which can produce a physiological reaction/arousal on the relevant (crime) questions from an Innocent examinee are "fear of error" and "anger." Field research has shown that if an Innocent examinee's fear of error is strong enough, it will display itself onto the relevant test questions. The physiological reaction on the polygraph chart caused by the "fear of error" cannot be distinguished from the physiological reaction caused by "fear of detection." Dr. Paul Ekman in his book *"Telling Lies"* devoted primarily to verbal and nonverbal behavior, discusses the element of "fear" in his chapter on the "Polygraph as Lie

Catcher" and states "The severity of the punishment will influence the truthful person's fear of being misjudged just as much as the lying person's fear of being spotted - both suffer the same consequence." Dr. Ekman feels that the PV examination, like behavioral clues to deceit, is vulnerable to what he terms the "*Othello error*" because Othello failed to recognize that Desdemona's fear might not be a guilty adulterer's anguish about being caught but could be a faithful wife's fear of a husband who would not believe her. Both cause an autonomic nervous response. (Ekman 1985; Hunter 1974).

Published field research by this author (Matte 1976, 1980; Matte, Reuss 1989) has clearly demonstrated that when an Innocent examinee is fearful that the examination will err against him or her, that fear will often transfer onto the relevant questions with a corresponding physiological reaction which when strong enough could be interpreted as deception. But when this same Innocent examinee is reassured and convinced of the accuracy of the test and the unbiasedness of the forensic psychophysiologist, the physiological reaction formerly displayed on the relevant questions will shift on subsequent charts from the relevant questions to the control questions indicating truthfulness to the target issue. This research resulted in the development of the Matte Quadri-Track Zone Comparison Technique to help correct this problem.

The second factor often overlooked by forensic psychophysiologists is the emotion of anger. Recognizing that the underlying basis of the PV examination technique is the emotion of fear, which is the most depressing of all emotions, we must also recognize that the emotion of anger, which is the most exciting emotion, also induces sympathetic excitation and adrenaline secretion. Published data and neurological evidence suggest that fear and anger both cause a strong arousal of the sympathetic subdivision of the autonomic nervous system. (Hunter 1974).

Thus it is quite apparent that the pretest interview is critical in identifying the presence of either of the aforesaid emotional states and adopt remedial action before proceeding with the actual administration of the PV examination. The adroit expert forensic psychophysiologist who looks for the presence of those negative emotions and finds them, will attempt and usually succeed in subsiding them. Since he or she is aware of their presence, he or she will also be aware of their dissipation. If the examinee's "fear of error" persists, the Matte Quadri-Track Zone Comparison Technique or the Backster Zone Comparison Technique with the Fear/Hope of Error Spot, can be used to address that emotion. However, if the anger still persists, then the examination should be postponed. Forensic psychophysiologists seldom encounter examinee anger unless the examinee has been coerced into taking the PV examination, in which case the examination should not be administered. The emotion of anger is usually aroused by the deportment of the forensic psychophysiologist who may use an accusatory or interrogative approach during the pretest interview. If those negative emotions are no longer apparent to the forensic psychophysiologist and the test is administered, any lingering negative emotions may cause countertrend scores sufficient to render the total charts scores in the Inconclusive range but not great enough to cause a false positive result, especially in those polygraph techniques that have an increasing threshold that requires a higher score with each chart conducted to reach a conclusion. (Matte, Reuss 1989).

It therefore behooves the forensic psychophysiologist to adopt safeguards that will preclude the elements of "anger" and "fear of error" from entering and interfering with PV examination. The best safeguard against these two elements is to search for their existence prior to and during the PV examination. Pretest information should be obtained to determine the subject's attitude towards the examination whenever possible. The best source of information about a subject's behavior is usually the subject himself/herself.

It is quite obvious that any accusatory or interrogative approach by the forensic psychophysiologist during any portion of the pretest interview and/or during any portion of the administration of the psychophysiological veracity test will arouse one or both emotional states described above which are largely responsible for false positives. Leading proponents of both the Numerical Approach and the Clinical Approach to forensic psychophysiology have condemned the use of accusatory or interrogative methods during the pre-test interview and/or the collection of the physiological data (Reid & Inbau 1977; Arther 1982; Matte 1980, 1989, 1993, 1994; Abrams 1989). While some polygraph schools have recognized those factors as problematic, many forensic psychophysiologists are not aware of their existence, which is evident in the conduct of their pretest interview and polygraph test procedure. Many forensic psychophysiologists are prosecution-oriented and have a "get the confession" mentality. Some even brag that they seldom have to turn on the polygraph instrument. Obviously they use the polygraph instrument as nothing more than a psychological lever to obtain confessions. These procedural violations do not adversely affect the Guilty examinee but most assuredly will invalidate the polygraph charts of an Innocent person. Fortunately they do not represent the polygraph profession. Unfortunately, lawyers don't know who they are. Graduation from an accredited polygraph school and/or member of a reputed law enforcement agency or national/state polygraph association is no guarantee that such procedural violations will not occur. Furthermore, most lawyers are not equipped to critique the many facets of a psychophysiological veracity examination which would best be left to the expertise of a forensic psychophysiologist hired by the Defense Attorney to view and critique the examination of his or her client. To quote Dr. William J. Yankee, Director of the Department of Defense Polygraph Institute in his welcoming remarks at the 1990 Federal Interagency Polygraph Seminar, FBI Academy, "We must recognize that an examiner is more than a skilled operator, more than a cop. We must realize that a polygraph examination is one of the most complex psychophysiological examinations ever developed." (Yankee 1990). In fact, the United States Department of Defense has dropped the title "*polygraph examiner*" and substituted "*forensic psychophysiologist*" in its place, and A.P.A. accredited polygraph schools have formed a new organization entitled "*International Association of Forensic Psychophysiological Institutes.*" (Appendix P)

The lawyer who finds himself or herself in the difficult position of critiquing a police psychophysiological veracity (PV) examination of his or her client without the benefit of an expert forensic psychophysiologist should find the following brief explanation and overview of the PV examination procedure of value.

It has been well established that no accusatory or interrogative approach by the forensic psychophysiologist should be used during any portion of the pretest interview of the PV examination or between the conduct of the tests to collect the physiological data recorded on the polygraph charts. Furthermore, the actual examination should be conducted without emphasis on a particular question. No accusatory or interrogative approach should be used until all polygraph charts have been conducted and a determination of deception has been concluded from the physiological data recorded on the polygraph charts. In the final analysis, truth or deception is determined by the examinee's consistent physiological responses on the polygraph charts either to the control questions if he/she is Innocent, or to the relevant (crime) questions if he/she is Guilty. The examinee's psychological set must be self-directed onto those test questions that he/she finds most threatening, either the control questions or the relevant questions. *The forensic psychophysiologist must not introduce any factors that will increase the threat of the relevant questions and/or the Innocent examinee's fear of them.* This is especially important because the earlier-in-life exclusive control questions are structurally less intense than the relevant questions. The pretest interview is used to gather background data and the examinee's version of the event, refinement of the formulation of the test questions, and preparation of the examinee psychologically for the administration of the psychophysiological veracity (PV) examination, including the dissolution of any anger and the promotion of confidence in its impartiality and reliability. (Matte 1980, 1993; Matte, Reuss 1995).

Most of the errors in PV examinations stem from an improper pretest interview. Therefore the conduct of the forensic psychophysiologist during the pretest interview and the administration of the polygraph test must be impartial and non-accusatory. Violation of this procedure may result in invalid polygraph charts. The attorney should instruct his or her client/examinee to sign all of his or her polygraph charts above the tracings in the middle of each chart prior to exiting the polygraph examination room, for their subsequent identification. This will prevent an unscrupulous forensic psychophysiologist from successfully switching charts at a later date to support his or her position or findings.

It becomes obvious even to the layman that without a recording or live viewing of the pretest interview and examination by a knowledgeable representative of the examinee, the right of the examinee to a scientifically prepared, impartial and objectively administered PV examination cannot be assured him or her. The examinee is not capable of evaluating the examination, and his or her protests when erroneously found deceptive appear to be self-serving. Furthermore, he or she has no record to document or support his or her criticism of the test.

The PV examination room and its forensic psychophysiologist must not smack of a police setting, but rather of a truth verification laboratory where all examinees, regardless of the case information, are deemed and treated as innocent unless and only until all of their polygraph charts containing their physiological data have been collected and reveal deception.

There has been a persistent myth among members of the psychological and legal community (judges and prosecutors) that PV examinations conducted for defense attorneys lack the essential "fear of detection" because unfavorable results are protected from disclosure under the privileged communication umbrella. In *United States v. Gipson* the Court of Military Appeals in admitting polygraph evidence articulated their concern for "maximizing" the "fear of detection" by having only one PV examination conducted under agreement and stipulation where the results are available to all parties. This was an uncritical adoption of Dr. Martin Orne's unsupported theory of the "*Friendly Polygraphist*" (Orne 1975). Some police forensic psychophysiologist have *maximized* the examinee's "fear of detection" by using an accusatory or interrogative approach during the pretest interview of the PV examination. In 1989, this theory was challenged by this author and Dr. Ronald M. Reuss (Matte, Reuss 1990) with solid data from a large field study of the "*Friendly Polygraphist*" concept using confirmed real-life cases from a Metropolitan Police Department and cases from a Private Polygraph firm where all of the polygraph decisions were quantified and fed into a computer. The data showed that defense attorney cases had a mean chart score of -9.38 compared with police cases which showed a mean chart score of -9.10, which suggests similar states of autonomic arousal. Another group, commercial cases which were not tested under privilege, showed a mean chart score of -9.90. In addition, of the 39 defense attorney cases in this study, 34 of those were scored deceptive and subsequently confirmed. Because these guilty cases have similar scores, the idea that defense subjects lack the fear of arousal found in other populations is without merit, leaving the "*friendly polygraphist*" concept without support. The scientific study of confirmed cases should carry more judicial weight than judgments based on an unsupported opinion, even when offered by a scientist. Police forensic psychophysiologists should not be afraid to adopt the same non-threatening posture that private forensic psychophysiologists have used with success for decades. (Matte, Reuss 1990).

Police interrogators from the various squads, such as homicide, robbery, fraud, etc., should work closely with the polygraph unit to insure that their methods of interrogation do not impede the proper administration of PV examinations. Defense attorneys should ensure that their client is not administered a PV examination soon after a police interrogation. Both parties should understand that the administration of a PV examination immediately following an interrogation by one of the police units increases the potential for false positive or inconclusive PV examination results. Understandably, police investigators/interrogators are reluctant to allow much time to elapse between their interrogation and the scheduled PV examination for fear that the suspect may change his or her mind and/or seek the advice of an attorney. However, it is surprising how many suspects willingly submit to a police PV examination when their attorney is permitted to view the test, either through closed-circuit television or two-way mirror. An example is the Buffalo Police Department Polygraph Unit headed by Detective Thomas E. Armitage. All PV examinations are videotaped and both the District Attorney and the Defense Counsel are permitted to view the PV examination. This practice has been going on for the past fifteen years, with great success. Detective Armitage's scoring of the polygraph charts in plain view of both counsels lends credibility to his findings and instills a trust in his impartiality which encourages defense counsels who believe their clients' innocence to submit their client to a police PV examination.

Since an Innocent (as later verified) examinee's fear that an error will be made on his or her PV examination can increase the threat of the relevant (crime) questions, creating a potential for false positive results, the presence of the examinee's attorney and/or representative expert during the examination via closed circuit television or two-way mirror with the examinee's knowledge and consent should have a calming, reassuring effect on the Innocent examinee that should significantly reduce the potential for false positive results.

The expert forensic psychophysiologist, public or private, who uses a scientifically accepted PV examination technique and conducts a proper pre-test interview and examination, should welcome an opportunity to show those who question the results of his or her PV examination the objectivity of his or her pre-test procedure and chart analysis. This author videotapes the entire PV examination which is made available with the charts to anyone having a need to know, approved by the examinee and his or her attorney.

Police forensic psychophysiologists who fear that a defense attorney viewing the examination live might interrupt the examination when the client starts to confess can enter into a prior agreement with the attorney promising no interference (Annot. 1) or use closed-circuit television in a room removed from the examination room, or videotape the entire examination for subsequent showing to the attorney which will allow the attorney and his or her expert forensic psychophysiologist an opportunity to critique the examination and the charts, safeguarding the examinee's right to a fair, impartial and scientifically accurate PV examination. Objections to the review of the PV examination, the questions used and the polygraph charts by the defense attorney or his expert forensic psychophysiologist are weak and without scientific substance

The recent introduction of computerized polygraph systems does not diminish in any way the need for recording and viewing of the entire PV examination by the defense attorney. The computerized polygraph systems' criteria for deception have a narrower scope than the physiological criteria used by the experienced forensic psychophysiologist, but even when they are fully developed, estimates of their value to the entire psychophysiological veracity examination is still less than ten percent. The value of the compu-

---

Annot. 1. If a confession is obtained by means considered illegal, the viewing attorney can make note of it for later submission to the court to have the confession excluded. Some attorneys believe that permitting or entering into an agreement with the police to allow the conduct of a post-test interview involving an interrogation of a defense attorney's client is tantamount to malpractice, thus the agreement should only permit the conduct of the PV examination with no post-test interview, unless the attorney is present in the examination room with his client during the post-test interview.

terized polygraph system is in its objective and reliable analysis and quantification of the physiological data recorded on the polygraph charts which afford the forensic psychophysiologist with a built-in chart interpretation quality control. Research conducted at the University of Utah's Psychology Department (Raskin, et al. 1988) revealed that the original experienced forensic psychophysiologist clearly outperformed the Computerized Polygraph System, but since then the computer software (CPS and APL) and hardware (Stoelting, Axciton, Lafayette) (See chapter 13) have significantly improved, and it is expected that the computerized polygraph systems will equal and surpass the expert forensic psychophysiologist in chart interpretation and quantification. At the moment, there are still some restrictive features in the computerized polygraph systems (see Chapters 12 & 13) that have delayed many forensic psychophysiologists from making the transition. Nevertheless, the defense attorney should remember the computer axiom "garbage in, garbage out" which aptly describes the value of the polygraph charts when procedural violations occur during the pretest interview or during the administration of the PV test, whether the charts are produced by a mechanical polygraph instrument, a fully electronic polygraph instrument, or a computerized polygraph system.

The necessity to preserve an adequate record to review the fairness and accuracy of the testing procedure, and the individual's right to counsel during the investigatory process should be balanced against whatever legitimate fears may exist by police forensic psychophysiologists that interruptions and disruptions might render adequate testing procedures impossible. An analogy may be made with line-up procedures where such a balancing test has been applied. There the courts have determined that a limited right to counsel exists enabling the defendant's attorney to view the line-up and preserve objections to and evidence of the procedures used for subsequent judicial review without enabling the defendant or his attorney to disrupt the line-up itself (Annot. 2, citations). Similar procedures could easily be adopted in PV examinations. In fact they must be adopted if an individual is to be protected from inadequate or improper PV examinations.

Some police agencies feel that since their offer to conduct a PV examination on a suspect is solely at their discretion, the conditions under which the examination is conducted and its monitoring permitted are also at their sole discretion. The reasoning advanced is that its use is only for that agency in the furtherance of their investigation and the test results are not for court use since they are generally not admissible. However, an innocent suspect who refuses to submit to such a test because of lack of representation by his or her defense attorney is denied an opportunity of clearing himself/herself which often results in dismissal of charges, hence avoiding the agony and expense of a trial not to mention the potential for an erroneous conviction.

Annot. 2. *United States v. Wade* (1967) 388 U.S. 218, 87 S.Ct. 1926, 18 L.Ed.2d 1149. *Gilbert v. State of California* (1967) 388 U.S. 263, 87S.Ct. 1951, 18 L.Ed.2d 1178. *Stovall v. Denno* (1967) 388 U.S. 293, 87 S.Ct. 1967, 18 L.Ed.2d 1199. *Kirby v. State of Illinois* (1972) 406 U.S. 682, S.Ct. 1877, 32 L.Ed.2d 411

Honoring the defense's request for representation during the administration of a PV examination on a defendant is now even more warranted with the recent supersedence of the *Frye* standard by the *Federal Rules of Evidence* and the advent of precedent-setting Federal and State Court decisions set forth in Part I, admitting PV examination results into evidence. With the recognition of forensic psychophysiology as a valid, scientific procedure goes the responsibility of assuring its fair and just application.

Without regard to whether or not an accused person has a right to demand the opportunity to take a PV examination, and regardless whether the offer to take a PV examination is made before or after the examinee is charged, unreasonably restrictive procedures violate an individual's right to due process of law and equal protection under the law. Once a governmental body extends to individuals a right or privilege, it must administer that right or privilege fairly and even-handedly and cannot arbitrarily hamstring the exercise of that right or privilege with unreasonable limitations and conditions. Furthermore, the privilege against self-incrimination and right to counsel assure an individual of at least minimal safeguards once he or she becomes the subject of a criminal investigation.

The cases cited in Annotation 2 hold that a defendant is entitled to counsel in a line-up once adversary proceedings have been initiated. In the case of a PV examination, the privilege against self-incrimination and other considerations would make the right to counsel apply at an earlier stage in the investigatory process.

For too many years the psychophysiological veracity examination has been cloaked in secrecy for fear that knowledge of its substance would defeat it. Yet all PV examination techniques accepted by the scientific community and recognized by the American Polygraph Association have been written about in detail in books and scientific journals.

Objections to full disclosure will no doubt be heard from "polygraph interrogators" who use the polygraph as an extension of their interrogation technique rendering the polygraph as nothing more than a psychological lever to obtain confessions; from those forensic psychophysiologists who rely on factors other than the physiological data recorded on the polygraph charts, to reach a conclusion; from those forensic psychophysiologists who have neglected to change their procedure to conform to the latest advances and developments in forensic psychophysiology; and from some of the forensic psychophysiologists who have been enjoying complete autonomy and immunity from critique because of their status as the sole forensic psychophysiologist in their department.

This author fails to see any reason, scientific or otherwise, for denying an examinee the right to have a representative such as his or her attorney or a forensic psychophysiologist of his or her choice witness the PV examination either through a two-way mirror or closed circuit television. Nor is there any valid reason for denying his or her representative an opportunity to review the PV examination charts, or furnish him or her a copy for evaluation by another expert.

It seems logical that if cardiology charts obtained from a patient can be reviewed by other cardiologists, developed latent fingerprints examined by opposing fingerprint experts, photographs of ballistic comparison and identification examined by opposing experts, then PV examination charts should also become available for examination by the opposition.

The right of the examinee to protect himself/herself against error that might cause him/her the loss of liberty or life supersedes the right that any law enforcement agency may have that would deny him or her that right. If forensic psychophysiologists expect the courts to ever afford forensic psychophysiology judicial notice of acceptance as a scientific means of truth-verification and lie-detection, they must forever remove this unnecessary cloak of secrecy and afford it recognition as a fair, impartial, scientifically structured examination, recorded by a scientifically accurate and reliable instrument, resulting in polygraph charts that are objectively analyzed through the use of a quantification system that permits its objective and accurate review by any other expert forensic psychophygiologist trained in the same technique.

Forensic psychophysiology provides the criminal justice system with a tool that significantly enhances its ability to identify the Guilty and exonerate the Innocent. The modern psychophysiological veracity examination with proper safeguards should have its rightful place within the criminal justice system. This will happen only when those who administer the test willingly submit it to the scrutiny of all parties involved. But defense attorneys should not expect those law enforcement and prosecuting agencies entrenched in a *non-access* policy to voluntarily provide the defense access to their PV examinations without some legal prodding. Thus defense attorneys have a responsibility to those clients who may benefit from a police PV examination to seek *court orders* compelling those police agencies to afford their client adequate and fair representation.

Part IV - Defense Conditions For Police PV Examinations of Defendants.

The following conditions are recommended for submission by defense attorneys to prosecuting and/or law enforcement agencies desiring to administer a psychophysiological veracity examination using the polygraph, to the attorney's client,

1. The forensic psychophysiologist must be a member or be eligible for membership in the American Polygraph Association. (Attorney may specify *Full* or *Associate* member).

2.
   a. The defense attorney and/or his forensic psychophysiologist (polygraph expert) shall be afforded an ability to witness audiovisually the entire psychophysiological veracity examination including the pretest interview phase, the actual testing phase, and the post-test interview phase through a two-way mirror and speaker or closed-circuit television system.

or

b. The entire psychophysiological veracity (PV) examination will be videotape recorded for subsequent release to and review by the defense attorney and/or his forensic psychophysiologist.

3. All contact between the examinee/client and the police agency to include the entire psychophysiological veracity examination consisting of the pretest interview phase, the actual testing phase, and the post-interview phase must be audiovisually recorded with a video recording system.

4. Only those relevant issues set forth in the enclosed letter will be covered in aforesaid psychophysiological veracity examination, and all of the relevant test questions will address those issues only. Only those additional test questions such as control, symptomatic, preparatory/sacrifice relevant, irrelevant and other non-relevant questions which are an integral part of the psychological structure of the validated technique will be used in the PV examination. Administration of a Control-Stimulation Test and/or Silent Answer Test is permitted at the discretion of the forensic psychophysiologist. .

NOTE: Unless specifically stated, the forensic psychophysiologist may use a PV technique that employs either the Numerical Approach (Chap. 11) or the Clinical Approach (Chap. 15). Therefore the attorney may wish to specify which *category* of techniques may be used on his client by adding a sentence to paragraph 4 above. As an example if the attorney elects the Numerical Approach, then the following sentence would be appropriate.

Each issue will be examined using a single-issue, numerically scored, validated Zone Comparison Test that employs non-current exclusive control questions, and a decision-making process based exclusively on the numerical scores acquired from the physiological data collected from the examinee's polygraph charts.

5. The polygraph instrument used will record continuously, permanently and simultaneously on a moving chart or computer media, changes in cardiovascular, electrodermal, abdominal and thoracic breathing patterns. Each test will be administered at least two times, that is, a minimum of two polygraph charts will be used on each issue tested to reach a determination of truth, deception or inconclusive. Whether a mechanical, electronic or computerized polygraph instrument is used, polygraph charts will be produced for the examinee's signature, which will be maintained for a period or three years and made available to proper authorities upon request.

6. The psychophysiological veracity examination will be conducted in a quiet room at a comfortable temperature, and during the testing phase the examinee will be seated in a standard or portable specifically designed polygraph chair with the wide, elongated armrests to afford the best posture, hence optimum physiological chart tracings.

7. The examinee will be afforded an opportunity and will be requested to sign all polygraph charts in the middle of each chart above the top tracing for subsequent identification before exiting the polygraph examination room and before any of the polygraph charts are

removed from the polygraph examination room. Such signature will be accomplished while recorded by the audiovisual recording system being employed.

8. There will be no interrogative or accusatory approach by the forensic psychophysiologist or other police personnel during any portion of the pretest interview phase or the testing phase, nor between the administration of the polygraph charts nor the psychophysiological veracity tests on each of the aforementioned issues.

9. (Optional) There will be no post-test interview nor interrogation of the examinee other than the announcement of the results of the polygraph test(s) without the express consent and presence in the examination room of the attorney representing the examinee.

10. The defense attorney will be advised at least five business days prior to the commencement of the psychophysiological veracity examination of any additional psychological test such as SCAN (Scientific Content Analysis) and/or MITT (Morgan Interview Theme Technique) which may be used during any portion of the psychophysiological veracity (polygraph) examination, and the defense attorney will have the option to have such additional psychological tests omitted from the standard psychophysiological veracity (polygraph) examination format. The defense attorney will also be advised of any additional psychophysiological veracity (polygraph) tests planned for administration on the defense attorney's client such as the Guilty Knowledge or Known Solution Peak-of-Tension Test and/or the Probing Peak-of-Tension Test, at least five business days prior to the commencement of the psychophysiological veracity examination, and the defense attorney shall have the option to have such additional psychophysiological veracity (polygraph) test(s) omitted from the agreed psychophysiological veracity (polygraph) examination format articulated in paragraph four.

11. The defense attorney shall be afforded the following no later than seven business days after such request:

a. At no cost, a complete copy of the audiovisual tape(s) of the entire psychophysiological veracity examination, plus an actual full-size continuous copy (such as produced by fax machine) of each and all polygraph charts signed by the examinee containing all instrument sensitivity and other chart markings made by the forensic psychophysiologist including any completed polygraph charts on the examinee not used for a determination, and any Acquaintance Test, Control-Stimulation Test, Sensitivity Test, Silent Answer Test(s), Control Question Validation Test, Guilt Complex Test administered to the examinee. The defense attorney shall also be provided with a copy of the forensic psychophysiologist's entire worksheet to include the background data, all test questions including control and other types of test questions used, plus the detailed scoring sheet for each physiological tracing on each question pair evaluated and/or used for a determination. The defense attorney will furnish the law enforcement agency provider of aforementioned material with an affidavit assuring all concerned that no copies of any audio-visual tape recording of the PV examination will be made and said audio-visual tape recording will be shown and used only by the attorney representing the client/examinee and his expert forensic psychophysiologist. Aforesaid material will be returned intact by certified mail or its equivalent to the providing law enforcement agency not later than ten working days after its receipt.

or

b. Or, the defense attorney and his independent forensic psychophysiologist (Name:________________________________) at defense expense, shall be given access to all of the police forensic psychophysiologist's original polygraph charts, including all Stimulation, Acquaintance, Sensitivity, Guilt Complex, Control Question Validation, and/or Silent Answer tests and the worksheet containing background data, all test questions and the detailed scoring sheet for each physiological tracing on each question pair evaluated and/or used for a determination, plus a viewing of the video tape for the purpose of independent review. Such review, may at the desire of the police agency that administered the psychophysiological veracity examination, be conducted in the presence of one or more police agents and at a location within (County:____________________) to be selected by the police agency.

c. The defense attorney shall be given a written report of the results and conclusions, including detailed scores of each separate test conducted during the psychophysiological veracity examination administered by the police on said examinee within fourteen (14) business days after that examination was conducted. Said reports shall be either personally delivered to the attorney or mailed to him at his law office.

The aforesaid *Conditions* could include a clause that the client/examinee will be removed as a suspect or subject of the police investigation and/or any pending charges will be dismissed if the results of the psychophysiological veracity (PV) examination reveal the client to be truthful regarding the target issue(s). Additionally, should the police PV examination results be unfavorable to the client, and the defense attorney has objections to the methodology and/or conduct of instant examination, he/she may elect to have the police records concerning the PV examination plus the defense's noted observations and objections submitted to the polygraph school or authoritative expert qualified to conduct a critical review of the particular polygraph technique used in aforesaid examination, as agreed by both parties, and both parties would abide by its determination.

ADDENDUM

The following summary of a study conducted by Gary D. Light and John R. Schwartz, Department of Defense Polygraph Institute, entitled "The Relative Utility of the Forensic Disciplines" published in March 1993, represents the first comprehensive research effort in which actual field data has been utilized to compare the effectiveness and utility of the findings routinely provided by a major crime laboratory in support of felony investigations. The reports of investigations and the findings of 1,069 forensic examinations involving 920 felony investigations conducted between 1 Jul 90 and 30 Dec 90 by the United States Army Criminal Investigations Command (USACIDC) are presented in Tables 1 through 5. Eight primary forensic disciplines that were used in support of the USACIDC criminal investigative mission were used in this study which are identified as follows: Firearms, Latent Prints, Questioned Documents, Trace Evidence, Illicit Drugs, Psychophysiological Detection of Deception (PDD), Serology, and Photographic. (Light and Schwartz, 1993). Term PDD used by DoDPI is synonymous with PV Examination.

The traditional laboratory disciplines combined conducted 584 (55%), and the Psychophysiological Detection of Deception (PDD) discipline conducted 485 (45%) of the examinations. The PDD discipline provided the investigator with 432 (89%) opinions that contained positive results and the laboratory disciplines provided positive results in 431 (74%) examinations. In all categories assessed, regardless of the type of crime, a higher solve rate was achieved for USACIDC when multiple forensic disciplines were used. The PDD discipline was the most utilized and effective of the individual disciplines, but all forensic disciplines demonstrated a high degree of utility in specific criminal offense categories. Of the 1,069 examinations reviewed, there were no instances in which the findings of one discipline contradicted the results of any other discipline. (Light and Schwartz, 1993)

The findings of greater utility with certain disciplines based upon the examination and analysis of various physical evidence types is consistent with the findings of Widacki and Horvath (1978) described earlier in this chapter. When using an analog study, Widacki and Horvath found a 100% accuracy rate with fingerprint examinations but found that fingerprints could only render a positive opinion with subjects in 20% of examinations. Wickaki and Horvath also found PDD and handwriting examinations resulted in a high accuracy (90% and 85%, respectively) while rendering a positive result with subjects in 95% and 94% of the examinations. The fingerprint, handwiting and PDD results were consistent with the results in this study. (Light and Schwartz, 1993)

Table 1

UTILITY OF THE FORENSIC DISCIPLINES

Discipline	Positive Results	Positive Results With Subject	Positive Results Without Subject	Negative Results	Total #s Percent-age
PDD	432 (89%)	289 (60%)	143 (29%)	53 (11%)	485 (100%)
Latent Finger-Prints	90 (59%)	31 (20%)	59 (38%)	64 (42%)	154 (100%)
Questioned Documents	105 (72%)	66 (45%)	39 (27%)	40 (28%)	145 (100%)
Illicit Drugs	125 (93%)	106 (80%)	19 (14%)	8 (6%)	133 (100%)
Firearms	39 (76%)	14 (27%)	25 (49%)	12 (24%)	51 (100%)
Trace Evidence	33 (65%)	14 (28%)	19 (37%)	18 (35%)	51 (100%)
Serology	34 (85%)	20 (50%)	14 (35%)	6 (15%)	40 (100%)
Photo-graphic	5 (50%)	1 (10%)	4 (40%)	5 (50%)	10 (100%)

TABLE 2

IMPACT OF THE FORENSIC DISCIPLINES							
Total Exams	Laboratory Exams	PDD Exams	USACIDC Solve Rate	Interdis-cipline Solve Rate	Non-Dis-cipline Solve Rate	PDD Solve Rate	Laboratory Solve Rate
914	421	493	81%	86%	78%	82%	81%

TABLE 3

CRIMES AGAINST PROPERTY SOLVE RATE											
Crimes Against Property		Laboratory Exams		PDD Exams		Latent Finger Prints		Questioned Documents		All Other Laboratory Disciplines	
# of Exams/ Solve Rate		# of Exams Con-ducted	Solve Rate	# of Exams Con-ducted	Solve Rate	# of Exams Con-ducted	Solve Rate	# of Exams Con-ducted	Solve Rate	# of Exams Con-ducted	Solve Rate
473	71%	234	75%	239	67%	95	69%	102	77%	37	80%

TABLE 4

CRIMES AGAINST PERSONS SOLVE RATE											
Crimes Against Persons		Laboratory Exams		PDD Exams		Latent Finger Prints		Trace Evidence		Serology	
# of Exams/ Solve Rate		# of Exams Con-ducted	Solve Rate	# of Exams Con-ducted	Solve Rate	# of Exams Con-ducted	Solve Rate	# of Exams Con-ducted	Solve Rate	# of Exams Con-ducted	Solve Rate
309	93%	124	91%	185	94%	30	90%	30	97%	26	90%

TABLE 5

ILLICIT DRUGS SOLVE RATE				
Total Exams: Illicit Drugs	Laboratory Exams		PDD Exams	
	# of Exams Con-ducted	Solve Rate	# of Exams Con-ducted	Solve Rate
132	63*	100%	69	97%

REFERENCES

Abrams, S. (1989). *The Complete Polygraph Handbook.* Lexington, MA: Lexington Books.

Ansley, N. (1990). *Polygraph and the Law.* Volumes I, II and III. JKP Publication Services.

Ansley, N.(Ed.) (1993). Supreme Court of the United States No. 92-102: William Daubert, et. ux., etc. et al., Petitioners v. Merrell Dow Pharmaceuticals, Inc., 113 S.Ct.2786, 125 L.E.2d 469, 509 U.S.___. *Polygraph*, 22(3), 270-283.

Ansley, N. (Ed.) (1994). Army Appellate Court reconsiders polygraph ban. *Polygraph*, 23(4), 324- 328.

Arther, R. O. (1982, May-June). Arther's infamous golden rules. *The Journal of Polygraph Science*. Vol. XVI, Nr. 6.

Cargill, R. V. (1989). United States v. Gipson: A leap forward or impetus for a step backward? *Polygraph*, 18(1), 33-42.

Fifth U.S. Circuit remands case for hearing on polygraph admissibility. (1995, Jul-Aug). *American Polygraph Association Newsletter*, 28(4), 1.

Ishida, J., Sevilla, C. M. (1981). The friendly polygrapher concept and admissibility. *Polygraph*, 10(3), 175-178.

Light, G. D., Schwartz, J. R. (1993, March). The Relative Utility of the Forensic Disciplines. Department of Defense Polygraph Institute, Ft McClellan, AL.

Massachusetts reconsidering polygraph admissibility. (1995, Jul-Aug). *American Polygraph Association Newsletter*, 28(4), 3.

Matte, J. A. (1979, October) Privileged communication between attorney-client-polygraphist. *New York State Bar Journal*, 51(6), 466-469, 500-504.

Matte, J. A. (1980). *The Art and Science of the Polygraph Technique*. Springfield, IL: Charles C. Thomas.

Matte, J. A., Reuss, R. M. (1989). Validation Study on the Polygraph Quadri-Zone Comparison Technique. *Research Abstract*, LD 01452, Vol. 1502, 1989, University Microfilm International.

Matte, J. A., Reuss R. M. (1989). A field validation study on the Quadri-Zone Comparison Technique. *Polygraph*, 18(4), 187-202.

Matte, J. A., Reuss, R. M. (1990). A field study of the 'Friendly Polygraphist' concept. *Polygraph*, 19(1), 1-8.

Matte, J. A. (1993). The review, presentation and assurance of intended interpretation of test questions is critical to the outcome of polygraph tests. *Polygraph*, 22(4), 299-312.

Matte, J. A., Reuss, R. M. (1995, August 16). *Methodology in Numerically Evaluated Psychophysiological Veracity Examinations*. Presented at the 30th Annual

Seminar/Workshop of the American Polygraph Association at Las Vegas, Nevada.

Matte, J. A. (1994, November 5). *Numerical versus Clinical Approach in Psychophysiological Veracity Examinations.* Thesis presented before the School of Continuing Studies of the Florida Polygraph Association.

Michigan allows polygraph evidence in motion for a new trial. (1995, Mar-Apr). *American Polygraph Association Newsletter*, 28(2), 41.

Orne, M. T. (1975). Implications of laboratory research for the detection of deception. In N. Ansley (ed.) *Legal Admissibility of the Polygraph.* Springfield, Illinois: Charles C. Thomas, 114-116.

People v. George (1980, June 2). Supreme Court, Bronx county, 428 N.Y.S.2d 825.

Question formulation factor in Federal admissibility ruling. (1995, Sep-Oct). *American Polygraph Association Newsletter,* 28(5), 21.

Raskin, D. C., Barland, G. H., Podlesny, J. A. Validity and reliability of detection of deception. *Polygraph*, 6(1), 1-39.

Reid, J. E., Inbau, F. E. (1966). *Truth and Deception - The Polygraph ("Lie-Detector") Technique.* Baltimore, MD: The Williams & Wilkins company.

U. S. District Court in Arizona accepts polygraph evidence. (1995, Mar-Apr). *American Polygraph Association Newsletter*, 28(2), 41.

U.S. District Court in Arizona sets odd admissibility rules.(1995, Nov-Dec). *American Polygraph Association Newsletter*, 28(6), 4.

U.S. District Court admits polygraph results in Louisiana. (1995, Nov-Dec). *American Polygraph Association Newsletter*, 28(6), 4.

Whitman, C. P. United States v. Gipson: Out of the Frye pan into the fire. *Polygraph*, 18(1), 24-32.

Widacki, J., Horvath, F. (1978). An experimental investigation of the relative validity and utility of the polygraph technique and three other common methods of criminal investigation. *Polygraph*, 7(3), 215-222.

Yankee, W. J. (1990). Welcoming remarks of Dr. William J. Yankee at the 1990 Federal Interagency Polygraph Seminar FBI Academy, Quantico, Virginia. *Polygraph*, 19(3), 182-187.

Chapter 24

Psychophysiological Veracity Examinations Using The Polygraph In Sex Offenses

In Part I of this chapter, the use of psychophysiological veracity (PV) examinations using the polygraph in the treatment and monitoring of convicted sex offenders on parole or probation is presented in its current state of operation, with some caveats and recommendations for improved methodology. Part II discusses the role of PV examinations in the investigation of sex offenses and the positive and negative aspects of its application to sex offense victims.

Part I - Probationary Psychophysiological Veracity Examinations

In the United States, a new application for psychophysiological veracity (PV) examinations using the polygraph has emerged. Initially, in the late nineteen sixties, two judges from Chicago, Illinois, and Walla Walla, Washington, frustrated by the high rate of recidivism, conceived the idea of administering PV examinations on those individuals whom they had placed on probation. They discovered that the use of PV examinations was successful not only in apprehending those who reoffended but in deterring others from committing additional acts. Although this approach was found to be most effective, its utilization was completely discontinued in Chicago and was continued in Washington at a minimal level.

In 1973, Dr. Stan Abrams, a clinical psychologist and forensic psychophysiologist initiated the use of the PV examination in the state of Oregon on a group of convicted child molesters, who, because of their past record, never would have been placed on probation. These individuals were given the option of being sentenced to prison or probation with periodic PV testing. In 1986, Dr. Stan Abrams and Dr. Ernest Ogard reported that 68 percent of individuals on probation for burglary, substance abuse and sex offenses who had PV examination supervision did not reoffend and successfully completed their probation, whereas only 28 percent of those individuals on probation supervision without the use of PV testing abstained from reoffending and successfully completed their probation. The Abrams-Ogard research demonstrated that the use of PV examinations was a very effective deterrent for the general criminal population on probation, and the PV examination results had a high degree of validity. Included in their research was a small number of sexual abusers, which revealed that 71 percent of those on PV examination supervision were successful versus only 43 percent for the control population. (Abrams, Ogard 1986).

A recidivism study of 173 sex offenders conducted in 1991 by Charles F. Edson, Parole and Probation Officer and Sex Offender Specialist for the Medford Department of Correction, Oregon, during the period from 1982 to 1991 revealed that 95 percent of individuals in the PV examination program were free of new sex crime conviction, 96 percent were free of new felony conviction, 89 percent were crime free in terms of any new criminal conviction, and 65 percent experienced no parole/probation revocations. Due to the epidemic nature of child sexual abuse and the compulsive nature of the disorder, Dr. Abrams strongly recommended that disclosure and periodic PV testing should be used with child abusers rather than the criminal population in general. Furthermore, the heinous nature of the acts committed by these sex offenders made their testing by PV examination more acceptable to the community. As a result, a very high number of pedophiles on probation in the states of Oregon and Washington are currently under PV examination surveillance. The success of this program has been so great that other states such as California, Texas, Tennessee, Florida, Massachusetts, Indiana, and Colorado, have adopted the use of PV examinations in the supervision, treatment and monitoring of individuals on parole/probation. The impact of these programs can be seen in the reduction of the prison population and the cost of housing these individuals, and the saving of supervisory time by busy probation officers which can be applied to other probationers whose reoffending was discovered by the PV examination, plus the deterrent effect on the majority of the others on probation, which amount to additional protection for society. In addition, therapists involved in these programs believe that the use of PV examinations has helped the treatment process because if a pedophile was reoffending, he or she would be reinforcing the very behavior they were attempting to eliminate. (Abrams 1992, Morris 1994).

Probationary PV examination programs currently involve the conduct of three types of PV examinations. The first type is known as the Disclosure Examination: Convicted Offense. The second type is known as the Disclosure Examination: Sexual History. The third type is known as the Maintenance/Monitoring Examination.

In order to avoid confusion between the two aforementioned disclosure examinations, this author has renamed the first examination *Conviction Verification,* the second *Complete Disclosure Examination*, and the third *Maintenance Examination*.

While the emphasis in the use of Probationary PV examinations has been on sex offenders, its broader use in other types of offenses amenable to such a program should also be contemplated. But inasmuch as the current Probationary PV examination programs deal exclusively with sex offenders, this chapter will focus its attention to the methods currently employed in that offense category and where appropriate, recommendations for improved methodologies.

The Conviction Verification Examination is deemed essential to the therapist in the treatment of a sex offender who is in denial regarding the commission of the offense for which he or she was convicted. Thus a convicted sex offender who agrees to the conditions of his or her probation requiring his or her submission to aforesaid Probationary PV examinations must first be administered a Conviction Verification Examination, to overcome his/her denial of the offense, unless he/she already has made a full confession to the court and/or attending therapist. This type of examination is usually quite lengthly, normally involving one to three single-issue zone comparison tests. As indicated in chapters 3 and 11, the Single-Issue Zone Comparison Test has been validated as the most objective and accurate test procedure in the arsenal of the forensic psychophysiologist. In fact, the Texas Polygraph Examiners Board (1995) in their recommended Guidelines in the use of Probationary PV examinations require the use of Single-Issue Control question examinations. The number of offenses that result in a conviction of a sex offender are normally limited for the forensic psychophysiologist to conduct a reasonable number of Single-Issue Zone Comparison tests.

The Complete Disclosure examination is used to explore and extract from the convicted sex offender his/her sexual history, in the belief that such full disclosure will improve the effectiveness of the treatment by breaking the offender's denial system, with the additional benefit of identifying new victims who can be contacted for treatment. However ethical and legal questions have been raised (Wygant 1992) regarding Complete Disclosure examinations inasmuch as the subject is compelled under the threat of revocation of parole or probation to reveal his or her *entire sexual history* and disclose sex offenses for which he or she was not charged and/or convicted. Abrams (1992) a proponent of the Complete Disclosure Examination cites a precedent by the Oregon Court of Appeals in State v. Wilson (1974) which found that the test was voluntary since probationers had the choice of prison for their crime or probation with polygraph supervision. The appellant claimed that this was no choice at all, but the Appellate court disagreed indicating that the appellant had made that decision and thus had to live with it. Proponents of the Complete Disclosure examination will cite statistics of great numbers of undiscovered offenses resulting from such examinations, but no statistical evidence of its *singular* impact on the offender's recidivism is available.

Convicted persons eligible for parole or probation may elect to serve the entire term of their sentence rather than subject themselves to a Complete Disclosure examination that would compel them to reveal undetected crimes which could result in additional prison sentence(s). On the other hand, if the parolee or probationer is guaranteed immunity from prosecution for any offenses he/she reveals as a result of the Complete Disclosure examination, this would encourage them to be truthful during the Complete Disclosure examination, resulting in the potential identification of new victims for treatment. In many jurisdictions, an agreement is entered into by the Probation Department with the District Attorney's office wherein sex offenders on probation who reveal formerly undisclosed victims during their therapy session or PV examination will not be prosecuted for those offenses. In other jurisdictions an informal understanding exists between the Probation Department and the District Attorney's office.

Some forensic psychophysiologists involved in Probationary PV examinations have limited their Complete Disclosure examinations to undisclosed victims rather than the examinee's entire sexual history with much success (Wygant 1996; Lundell 1996). This makes the PV examination procedure more manageable inasmuch as the issues are specific in nature.

Oftentimes the parolee/probationer has been convicted of a minor sex offense; thus the conditions for parole/probation which form the basis for the Maintenance PV examination are tailored to those conditions. However, the administration of a Complete Disclosure Examination which reveals new, undisclosed victims of *more serious offenses*, permits the forensic psychophysiologist to increase the scope and depth of the Maintenance PV examination for more effective treatment/monitoring.

However, research should be conducted to determine the therapeutic value and necessity of the Complete Disclosure examination to the overall effectiveness of the Probationary Program. Furthermore, ethical and legal considerations should be applied to either limit the scope of inquiry to those areas deemed essential to the treatment and rehabilitation of the offender or delete the Complete Disclosure examination from the Probationary Program.

The Maintenance Examination is used to monitor the sex offender's activities, behavior, and sexual interests after conviction and while on parole or probation. This type of PV examination is generally administered every three to six months to determine if the offender has been complying with his or her conditions of parole or probation. It is also used to determine if the offender has complied with his or her treatment conditions commensurate with their convicted offense such as refraining to associate with school children or contact with prior victims or exposure to pornographic material or the performance of certain deviate sex acts. The success of the Probationary PV examination program depends largely on the effectiveness of the Maintenance Examination in monitoring the activities of the offender.

Historically, the Probationary PV examination has been part of a team effort involving the probation officer, the treatment provider and the forensic psychophysiologist in the treatment and rehabilitation of the offender. Information is shared by law enforcement agencies, probation officers, therapists and other treatment specialists with the forensic psychophysiologist in order to provide all of the essential information required in the conduct of the aforementioned Probationary PV examinations. During the offender's initial treatment by the therapist, the offender is constantly reminded of the importance in being completely truthful and this reminder is continued by the forensic psychophysiologist during the course of his or her Probationary PV examinations.

The Jackson County Sex Offender Treatment Program (JCSOTP) developed by the Oregon Department of Corrections Community Programs Division offers insight into the roles played by the various members of the team involved in such a program (Grindstaff 1993). Jackson County combines specialized supervision, qualified treatment, and probationary psychophysiological veracity (PV) examinations using the polygraph to monitor and manage sex offenders on community supervision. This team approach results in a low rate of new sex offenses, new crimes, and parole/probation revocations to prison. The model is recognized internationally as an effective approach to the management of sex offenders in the community.

The purposes of the Jackson County Sex Offender Treatment Program are to protect the community, advocate for victims, reduce the reoffense rate, and block the sex offender's efforts to manipulate the treatment provider and the parole/probation officer. The key components of the program are court-ordered treatment, long term intensive supervision, psychological evaluation, behavioral treatment with a strong confrontational approach, immediate sanctions for failure/non-compliance, and monitoring of behavior and treatment using Probationary PV examinations (polygraph). The parole/probation officer, the treatment provider, and the forensic psychophysiologist (polygraphist) work cooperatively, sharing information and providing a consistent response to sex offender behaviors.

Sex offenders are often characterized by a strong need for power and control. They frequently deny or minimize their wrongdoing, both about the offense of conviction and past behaviors. The use of polygraph examinations is key in breaking through this denial. The information obtained in these exams, as well as in treatment and through supervision, is shared between team members and is instrumental in neutralizing the sex offender's ability to manipulate one side against the other to his/her advantage. The JCSOTP model requires offender accountability; the sex offender must accept responsibility for his/her crime of conviction and past sexual abuses. It promotes community safety by identifying behavior cycles, thinking errors, and/or inappropriate contacts that may lead to further offenses.

Supervision

Most sex offenders are classified as high or medium risk. Parole/probation officers working under the JCSOTP model carry a caseload of about 50 sex offenders. Due to the complexity of treatment issues impacting this population, and the demands of communication and networking, the parole/probation officers specialize in sex offender supervision. A caseload of 50 allows for frequent contacts, including home visits. In addition, sex offenders are seen weekly by their therapists. The conditions of supervision usually include the successful completion of a sex offender treatment program, no contact with minors, payment of their own and victim treatment costs, and payment for PV examinations. Supervision under the JCSOTP model usually continues for the entire length of parole or probation.

Treatment

At the beginning of supervision, the offender must choose a treatment provider from a list of providers approved by the court. Approved providers meet certain professional standards, are members of the Association for the Behavioral Treatment of Sex Abusers, hold at least a Masters Degree, and offer educational and treatment components that are consistent with the JCSOTP model. Once an offender has selected a therapist, he/she must stay with that therapist until he/she graduates. It takes an average of twenty-four months for a sex offender to complete treatment, although many stay in treatment for the duration of supervision, around five years. Subsidies may be available to assist indigent offenders with treatment costs.

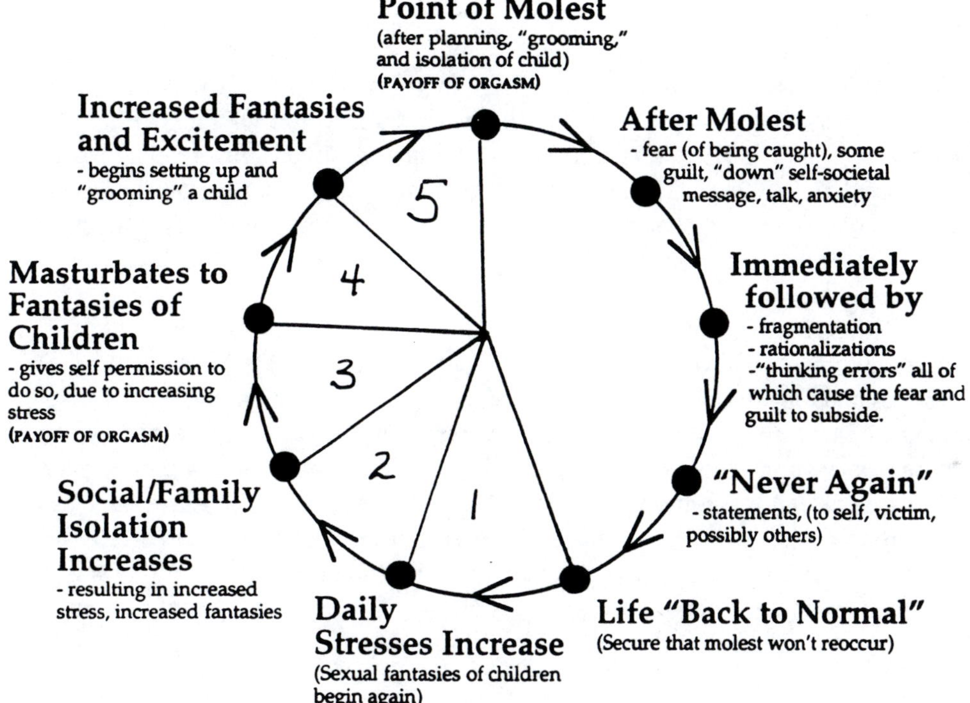

Specific details will vary from person to person, but the general pattern applies in virtually all cases. It must be assumed that the offender does not act without planning (i.e., "on impulse"), as he would otherwise be caught sooner.

Figure XXIV-1: Reproduced with permission from "Why Did I Do It Again?" by Bays and Freeman-Longo (1989) Safer Society Press; Box 340, Brandon, VT 05733-0340 (802) 247-3132.

The treatment approach is multi-modality, with an emphasis on behavioral techniques. Treatment components include cycle behaviors, thinking errors, victim impact, intervention techniques, offender victimization, family dysfunction, self concept, communication and self-concept skills. Treatment is usually provided in groups. There are five specialty groups: low functioning, aged, new to treatment, regular, and post treatment monitoring. If the offender fails treatment, the therapist and the parole/probation officer decide jointly on a course of action. Failure to continue in treatment will likely result in arrest for a supervision violation. Usually a recommendation is made for revocation and incarceration.

PV Examination

Jackson County has two forensic psychophysiologists with particular expertise in sex offender issues. The JCSOTP model hinges on the information verified by the forensic psychophysiologists. The PV examinations are vital in confirming offender reports of behavior. Information gathered in the PV examination process is shared with both the parole/probation officer and the therapist. PV examination information assists in responding quickly to offender behaviors which may lead to reoffense.

The JCSOTP uses two types of Probationary PV examinations: Complete Disclosure and Maintenance. In group treatment, the offender is required to admit to the current offense and past sexual abuses. The Complete Disclosure examination verifies the comprehensiveness of these disclosures. Maintenance examinations occur every six months or less. These examinations explore compliance with conditions and requirements of supervision and treatment. Information obtained in the full disclosure and maintenance PV examinations are reported to the parole/probation officer and the treatment provider. Both the parole/probation officer and the treatment group confront deceptions. PV examination failures are not reported to the releasing authority. However, information about new crimes, supervision violations and treatment failures are reported.

Team Approach

The team approach and the support of the wider criminal justice community are key to the success of the JCSOTP model. Cooperation and coordination enable the consistent response to sex offender behaviors which is essential to effectiveness with this particular population. Considerable communication occurs between the parole/probation officer, the treatment provider, and the forensic psychophysiologist on a routine, practical level. In addition, a spectrum of agencies working with sex offenders and sex offender issues meets monthly to discuss issues, maintain consistency of practice, and solidify the coalition. These meetings include the specialized sex offender parole/probation officers, assistant District Attorneys focusing on sex crimes, treatment providers, forensic psychophysiologists, Children's Services Division, victim's advocates, juvenile sex offender therapists, and corrections personnel from adjoining jurisdictions.

Evaluation

A study was conducted of one hundred and seventy-three JSCOTP cases supervised between 1982 and 1990. The study covered all open cases and a random sample of closed cases. For over 60% of the cases, the offender had been on community supervision for more than three years. The study showed the following: (Grindstaff 1993)

No subsequent sex crime convictions	95%
No other new criminal convictions	89%
No other new felony convictions	96%
No parole/probation violations	65%
No parole/probation revocations to prison	87%

The following application of the Probationary PV examination program was presented by Robert G. Lundell and Susan A. Holmes, Polygraph Associates of Oregon, at the American Polygraph Association's 29th Annual Seminar/Workshop in July 1994.

Preparing Offenders For Full Sexual History Disclosure Examinations

The primary purpose of full sexual history disclosure examinations is two-fold. Number one, to verify that the offender has fully disclosed the kinds and frequency of sexual abuse involving himself and the victim of conviction. Number two, to verify the offender has disclosed all *other* victims of abuse. This includes victims of child molest, rape, public indecency, etc. (all sexually motivated crimes - not just similar to his crime of conviction).

If the offender is in denial regarding the crime of conviction, generally no progress in treatment can occur. Our experience has shown that until the offender is willing to take full responsibility for his crime of conviction no meaningful disclosure process can begin. When the offender first enters treatment from either a probation status or returning on parole from the institution, he must be made fully aware that he is going to be required to accept the responsibility for his crime of conviction. While some minimization and rationalization of behavior can be expected, if the offender completely denies the crime of conviction efforts now must focus on that issue alone. It is our recommendation that the offender be given a timetable during which he will be closely monitored and evaluated regarding his progress in treatment as it relates to the victim of conviction. It serves no legitimate purpose to prolong this process if the offender is in absolute denial. Although this may vary among treatment programs, a standard timetable where some breakthrough must occur would generally be about four group sessions. If after four group sessions the offender is still entrenched in his absolute denial, we recommend that a single-issue specific polygraph examination be conducted to resolve the issue. The offender also must realize the consequences for not disclosing the truth about the victim. There needs to be some sanction if the offender clearly is deceptive on this examination regarding the victim. Again, our recommendation would be to return the offender to treatment to deal again with the therapist and other offenders with the failed polygraph results and attempt in a final effort to have the offender disclose the truth. Ultimate consequences for continued denial should be dismissal from the group treatment process. If dismissal does not occur, then every other group member now has received the message that lying about something as important as the victim of conviction carries with it no consequence. Therefore, the entire group process will begin to deteriorate with no offenders wanting to tell the truth since the consequences are non-existent.

When the offender takes the responsibility for the crime of conviction either from the beginning of probation or parole or after failing the specific issue examination, the process of accounting for full sexual history can begin. Methods may vary from program to program as to how the offender accounts for his past behavior. Some treatment programs require the offender to write out a sexual autobiography dealing with their first sexual experiences all the way up to the present day. Some programs require the autobiography along with attached sheets to identify all paraphilias. Additionally, for those offenders who have committed hands-on crimes with victims, additional disclosure sheets should be prepared on all identifiable victims. Victims should not be given a number but should be identified truly, by name. On the disclosure forms the issue regarding maximum numbers of specific forms of sexual behavior is an issue quite often in question. Most offenders do not know exactly how many times a specific sexual act occurred, particularly if it was a frequent occurrence over a period of months or years. The important thing to remember is that we are trying to hold the offender accountable by making him list specifically what happened as well as the most number of times the particular behavior may have occurred. For this reason, the numbers column should represent the *most* possible times that behavior occurred. While offenders' sexual histories vary, it is a general recommendation that at least 90 days of intensive group treatment should occur before the offender undergoes the sexual history PV examination. The offender should review all of the information in a group setting and should also do a review of that information, perhaps in a more condensed form, with his probation officer. The therapist should be in possession of either the presentence investigation or the actual police report in which the victim has detailed the specific abuse. Both therapist and probation officer should compare the allegations of the victim with that disclosure now made by the offender. Again, any major differences should be supplied to the forensic psychophysiologist. Our experience has shown that most offenders will often disclose more kinds and frequency of abuse than that which was originally alleged by the victim. Quite often this new information provided by the offender is extremely helpful in the treatment of the victim.

Once the offender has prepared in full all disclosure forms and all sexual history information required by treatment, he is now as ready as he will ever be to undergo the sexual history disclosure examination. It is not unusual for offenders to "remember" more details about their history as the date for the PV examination approaches. It is also normal for more information to surface during the actual pretest interview of the PV examination. If during this pretest interview information surfaces that is extremely significant and has been concealed from probation and treatment, there is a good likelihood that the actual examination will not take place. In other words, if the offender has been concealing the truth about a multitude of other victims and decides at the last minute just prior to testing to disclose, he will be returned to treatment to resolve these issues before the actual examination can occur.

The pass or fail probability with sexual history testing is largely dependent upon the intervention and persistence of the treatment provider and the probation officer.

All offenders when reporting for their sexual history testing should bring with them all written information from treatment. This should include their individual disclosure forms on victims, their sexual history autobiography in whatever form it has been prepared, and any current fantasy logs, anger logs, or treatment reports that have been prepared during the week the test is to occur and that have not yet been submitted to the therapist. Offenders will be expected to review in detail all of the information they bring with them to the examination. The actual questions which make up the examination will be developed by the forensic psychophysiologist and the offender on the day the PV examination takes place.

If the examination results clearly indicate the offender is withholding additional information regarding other victims or ongoing behavior or other information related to his sexual history, it will most likely be necessary to conduct a follow-up examination at a later date.

Instructions For Preparing Your Sexual History Disclosure

PART 1

Instructions:

The first step in treatment is to be open and honest with the therapist and with other group members. You need to prepare a description of the crime you have committed and you need to also write down any other crimes or inappropriate behavior. You need to list all of the other victims that you have sexually offended. You must list each victim separately and describe, in detail, everything that has happened with that victim. We should have a clear picture of what occurred with each victim. Remember, you have nothing to lose by giving us all of the information. You have everything to gain by being totally honest and clear.

Directions:

1. You are to take each victim separately and answer only questions about one victim at a time. You will follow these instructions completely through for one victim and then start over for another victim.

2. The first thing you should do is write Sexual History Disclosure on the top of a lined piece of paper, and then place your full name, your therapist's name, and your probation/parole officer's name in the top right hand corner.

3. The next thing you must do is put a number "1" on the page and the victim's name or some identifying characteristic like, "the victim I exposed to at the shopping center," in the top left hand corner of the first page. **Remember:** When filling out a **Victim Form**, only use this form for those victims with whom you've had physical sexual contact (see example of **Victim Form** attached).

4. You should then put a number "2" and write down how the person is related to you, such as "sister, friend, neighbor, etc." An example of this answer would be "number 2 - Sharon S. is my neighbor's little girl." If on item #1, you did not know the victim's name, then put "Unknown" and simply describe how you came into contact with this person.

5. You should then put a number "3" on your paper and list your age and the age of the victim, child, or adult at the time you began doing something that was inappropriate. An example of this answer would be, "I was ten years old and Sharon S. was approximately five years old," or "The woman was about 30 years old and I was 24."

6. List a number "4" and then describe what happened the very first time you did anything sexually improper with this victim. It is on this number that you should list sexual things that you did and that you tried to do. Pretend as though the person reading this is from a foreign country and does not understand anything unless it is carefully explained. **Remember**: Describe all actions/behaviors in detail.

7. List a number "5" on your paper and write down the number of times you did something that was sexually inappropriate with this person. Example: "I molested Sharon Approximately once a week for two years," or "I exposed to a 30-year-old woman with blond hair on one occasion."

8. List a number "6" on your paper and describe where the abuse occurred. If the abuse happened in several different places, describe the kinds of places where the abuse happened. Example: "This would usually take place in her bedroom at her house on 12th Street" or "sometimes I would get her to go into the backyard where I could touch her there too."

9. List a number "7" on your paper and describe what you said to the victim in order for the victim to feel the need to cooperate. It is important for us to know how you were able to get the victim to do what you wanted. If you did not say anything, but you used some kind of force, bribe or trick, be sure to tell us what you used. It should be very clear exactly how you were able to sexually assault the victim.

10. List a number "8" on your paper and describe how you kept the victim from telling. It is important that we know exactly how you were able to keep the sexual assault a secret. Examples are: "I would pretend as though I was playing with my brother, so he kept the secret because he didn't know that what I was doing was wrong," or "I told her if she told, she would get in trouble," or "I would wear a ski mask when I exposed to women, so they could not identify me."

11. List a number "9" on your paper and tell us how someone found out if you were caught. You must tell us about how the offense was discovered, and how you got caught.

12. Make sure you start over on a new sheet of paper with each new victim, and that you list the victim's name in the top right hand corner of the page (same as instruction #l).

13. When you are finished, put the entire package of information together in one report. Number all pages of your sexual history in the middle of the bottom of each page beginning with a Title Page. Identify the Title Page with the words **"Sexual History Disclosure."** Then, print your full name, your therapist's name, your probation/parole officer's name, the offense you were convicted of, and the date you began treatment.

14. Last, you must make a "TABLE OF CONTENTS" and list each victim and the number of the page where the information about that victim begins. This is the page number you placed at the bottom of the relevant page (see #13 of directions). For example, you would be listing such things as: Sharon S., Page 1, Johnny Jones, Page 3, etc. You will list these down in a row with the page number beside the name of the child you abused.

Example: **"TABLE OF CONTENTS"**

Sharon Smith - Page 1
Johnny Jones - Page 3

15. These papers should be handled in an organized form. They should be easy to read and, you must include a completed **"Victim Form"** for only those victims with whom you've had **physical sexual contact**. When you have completed this sexual history disclosure, you will begin the process of explaining to the group and your therapist about your history.

Instructions For Preparing Sexual History Disclosure

Part II

Instructions:

Part II of your Sexual History requires you to complete a sheet on each of the categories listed below. Prepare a sheet for the category even if you were never involved with that type of sexual activity. Remember, these are suggestions and may not have occurred in your history. You may have had other sexual activities not included on this list. If affirmative, make a sheet for those also.

Directions:

Write the title of each activity listed below. One activity only per page. Then develop each section starting from the age you were when the activity began. Include who else participated, if any, how old they were, and as much of your thinking that was involved in each activity. This is very important. Even though it is important to organize your history according to age, if you remember additional items, do not hesitate to include them. The purpose of this exercise, as with Sexual History Part I, is to help you to be honest with us and yourself.

1. Sexual play with other children (playing doctor or "show me" games).

2. Masturbation (when did it start? what was the approximate frequency ? what types of fantasies did/do you have? and any/all use of pornography).

3. Involvement with pornography without masturbation.

4. Stealing of or masturbating with underwear or any form of under clothing.

5. Public masturbation (include all public places, e.g., outdoors, restrooms, etc.).

6. Bestiality (sexual involvement with animals).

7. Voyeurism (peeking for sexual purposes).

8. Exhibitionism (exposing your sexual anatomy to others).

9. Necking, Petting and Consensual Sexual Activities with same-age peers. Give approximate number of consensual peer-age sexual partners.

10. Homosexual behavior (any sexual activity with the same sex).

11. Obscene phone calls or 1-900 numbers (sex lines).

12. Frottage (Rubbing up against or grabbing the sexual area(s) of nonconsensual others).

13. Abusing or torturing animals. Was this behavior sexually motivated?

14. Setting fires for fun or sexual arousal.

15. Prostitution (either paying for sex or being paid for sex).

16. Rape (penetration of a male or female adult without consent).

17. Sodomy - anal penetration or attempted penetration with an adult.

18. Oral copulation - mouth to penis, mouth to vagina, or mouth to anus contact with an adult.

19. "French kissing" a minor when you were an adult.

20. Transsexuallism - (thoughts or interest in wanting to be the opposite sex).

21. Transvestitism - (activities involving dressing in the opposite sex's clothing).

22. Fetishism - (sexual arousal to inanimate objects, e.g., underwear, feet, shoes, tampons, kotex, vibrators, or putting objects in your anus for sexual arousal.

23. Sadism - (deriving sexual pleasure from another's pain or humiliation).

24. Masochism - (deriving sexual pleasure from being hurt or humiliated).

25. Urolagnia - (Use of urine for sexual excitement)

26. Coprophilia - (use of feces or filth for sexual excitement).

27. Arousal to odors (any odor associated with sexual arousal).

28. Sexual arousal to memories (fantasies) of your own sexual victimization experience(s).

29. Necrophilia - (sexual contact with dead animals or people).

30. Taking photographs of or video taping minors for sexual purposes.

31. Taking photographs of or video taping adults for sexual purposes.

32. Sexual Victimization (description of your own victimization if you have ever been sexually abused).

- **Also do an individual sheet on each of the following:**

1. Criminal History (any crime, reported or unreported - shoplifting - taking things from an employer because "he owes me," etc.).

2. Drug History (include alcohol - it is a drug). Identify specific drug(s) used and approximate frequency of use.

After your sexual history disclosure has been **thoroughly** reviewed by your therapist, you will be asked to again review it with your probation/parole officer. Your treatment provider and your probation/parole officer will be working together to see that you have been completely honest throughout your sexual history report.

The final requirement for completing your sexual history disclosure involves submitting to a Comprehensive Psychophysiological Veracity (PV) Examination using the Polygraph in order to verify that you have told the **complete truth** about your sexual history. The forensic psychophysiologist (polygraphist) will review with you your **Sexual**

History Disclosure report and all of your **Victim Forms**. Keep in mind that you should have your sexual history disclosure report and victim forms completed and reviewed by all parties previously identified and be ready to schedule your first PV examination 90 days (3 months) after your entry date into the sexual offender treatment program.

See your treatment provider or probation/parole officer before scheduling a PV examination date. They will give you the required instruction.

VICTIM FORM

VICTIM'S NAME____________________________**SEX: M-F**_____**AGE:**________
MY AGE AT TIME OF CONTACT______

TYPE OF CONTACT	Yes/No	Most Possible Times
1. Rubbed/touched breast through clothing		
2. Rubbed/touched bare breasts.		
3. Rubbed/touched vagina/penis area through clothing.		
4. Rubbed/touched bare vagina/penis.		
5. Put finger inside vagina (even a little bit).		
6. Placed mouth on crotch-vagina/penis area through clothing		
7. Placed mouth/tongue on bare vagina/penis.		
8. Victim rubbed my penis through clothing.		
9. Victim placed mouth on my bare penis.		
10. Victim touched/rubbed my bare penis.		
11. Rubbed penis against bare vagina/penis		
12. Put penis inside vagina (even a little bit).		
13. Put penis against (or in) anus.		
14. Put finger in anus (even a little bit).		
15. Put mouth on anus (even a little bit).		
16. Victim placed penis against (or in) my anus.		
17. Victim put finger in my anus (even a little bit).		
18. Put foreign object in vagina/anus (vibrator, sticks, utensils, etc. Also include ointments).		
19. Masturbate using victim's clothing - pictures.		
20. Masturbate in front of victim.		
21. Ejaculate in or on victim (anus, vagina or body).		
22. Taking of or possessing nude photographs or videos of victim.		

List other contact with victim not included above that you know is important to disclose.

____

____

The first sexual contact of any kind happened when? ______________(month/year)
The last sexual contact of any kind happened when?_______________(month/year)
Can you now answer this question with a "No": Did you have more sexual contact with this victim than what is on this form? Answer:__________**(yes** or **no)**

Print your full name:____

Signature:____

* *

POLYGRAPH ASSOCIATES of Oregon
123 West 10th St., Suite 205
Medford, Oregon 97501
(503) 776-2941

Robert G. Lundell
Susan A. Holmes
Licensed Examiners

EXAMINEE:__________________________DATE:__________TIME:_____

Parole & Probation Issues: Since your last examination on______________have you:
Explain fully all "yes" answered questions.

1. Lied on any part of your monthly report to the probation office?

2. Drunk any alcoholic beverage? (If so, how much?)

3. Seen anyone using any illegal drug, <u>or</u> in possession of any?

4. Been with anyone when they sold or bought illegal drugs?

5. Set up or arranged for anyone to buy or sell illegal drugs?

6. Used any illegal drug yourself? (Include when, where, what, how many times.)

7. Been with anyone when they stole something?

8. Stolen anything yourself? (Stores, work, etc.)

9. Been with anyone when they committed any other kind of a crime?

10. Used anyone else's prescription medication?

11. Been contacted by the police for any official reasons?

12. Driven a vehicle on the highway without a valid driver's license?

13. Committed any law violations you could be cited or arrested for? (Damage to property, assaults or disorderly conduct, weapons or firearms violations, fish and wildlife offenses, etc.)

14. Violated any special or general conditions of parole or probation we haven't discussed?

15. Done anything else that could affect your parole or probation you haven't told me?

I have answered all questions truthfully and completely:

SIGNED:__________________________________

* * * * * * * * * * * * * * * * * * * *

POLYGRAPH ASSOCIATES of Oregon
123 West 10th Street, Suite 205
Medford, Oregon 97501
(503) 776-2941

Robert G. Lundell
Susan A. Holmes
Licensed Examiners

TREATMENT ISSUES: (Sexual Behavior) Since:______________________________

1. List everyone with whom you've had ANY sexual contact or relationship.

2. List all locations where these sexual acts have occurred (house, car, outdoors, etc.)

3. Have you viewed any sexually explicit movies or looked at any pornography? (Explain)

4. Describe any contact with past victims (phone, letters, direct, etc.)

5. Describe your masturbation habits (all locations, how often per day, week or month).

6. While masturbating have you had sexual fantasies about children or past victims?

7. Have you been truthfully reporting in treatment your conduct related to masturbation? (Explain how you report: verbally or written)

8. Have you been left alone anywhere with children? (Explain)

9. Have you had any physical contact with a minor child (touching, hugging, kissing, wrestling, etc.)? (Explain).

10. Have you felt sexually aroused by looking at, or having any contact with a person under 18? (Explain).

11. Have you been in contact with anyone under 18 that might violate probation or treatment?

12. Have you told group treatment and/or your probation officer about all sexual contact

or partners?

13. Have you engaged in ANY sexual activity by yourself or with a partner that might be considered improper, unnatural or illegal? (Explain).

14. Have you been doing anything of a sexual nature that has not already been listed on this form? (Explain).

I Have told the complete truth to each question on this form:________________________
(Signature)

POLYGRAPH ASSOCIATES of Oregon
123 West 10th Street, Suite 205
Medford, Oregon 97501
(503) 776-2941
Fax (503) 779-4011

Robert G. Lundell
Susan A. Holmes
Licensed Examiners

RELEVANT QUESTIONS - SEXUAL HISTORY

1. In the last 10 years, have you fondled the sex organs of any child under 12 besides the ones we've talked about?

2. Since the age of 18, have you had penis-to-vagina (or mouth-to-vagina) contact with any of the children you molested?

3. In the last 20 years, have you fondled the bare sex organs of any child besides the two you've reported?

4. Since you've been a teenager, have you fondled the sex organs of any other child under 10 besides Amber?

5. Since the age of 21, have you fondled the sex organs of any young child besides your two daughters?

6. Did you fondle Amber's bare sex organs more times than you put on the form?

7. Have you now told the truth on the victim form about all sexual acts between you and Amber?

8. Was there ever any mouth-to-sex organ contact between you and Jamie?

9. Did you ever show X-rated movies (magazines) to Sara?

10. Was there ever any criminal sexual acts between you and Joshua?

RELEVANT QUESTIONS - PERIODIC MAINTENANCE

1. Since your last test, have you touched the sex organs of any minor child?

2. In the last 6 months, have you had sexual relations with anyone under 18?

3. Besides your wife, have you touched anyone else's sex organs since your last test?

4. Is Jennifer the only person you've had sexual relations with since your last test?

5. Have you fondled anyone else's sex organs since your last test?

6. In the last 6 months (since your last test), have you been in a home or vehicle with any minor child?

7. Since your last test, have you been all alone in a home or vehicle with any minor child? (or specific sex: male...female)

8. Besides that one time you've reported, were you in a home with a child any other time since your last test?

9. Have you been having secret contact with any children since your last test?

10. Have you had any face-to-face contact with your daughter in the last 6 months?

11. Have you been inside your wife's home even one time since your last test?

12. Have you been secretly masturbating and not reporting it since your last test?

13. Have you exposed your bare penis to anyone in a public place since your last test?

14. In the last 6 months, have you purposely shown your penis to any female in a public place?

15. Have you made any sexually obscene phone calls since your last test?

16. Have you viewed any X-rated movies since your last test?

17. Since your last test, have you stolen anything from a store? (house) (or anything else besides...)

18. Since your last test, have you personally consumed any alcoholic beverage? (or any 'other' alcohol besides...)

19. Have you personally used any illegal street drug since...or last test? (or...any other

drug besides marihuana)

20. Have you personally exchanged any illegal drugs for money since...(starting probation, the last test, etc.)?

RELEVANT SECONDARY OR SUPPLEMENTAL QUESTIONS

1. In the last 6 months, have you done anything that could violate probation you haven't told me?

2. Since your last test, have you committed any kinds of probation violations you haven't told me?

3. Are you purposely concealing any other probation violations since your last test?

4. Have you left any important information off the probation form today?

5. Have you purposely falsified any of the probation information you told me about today?

6. Since starting probation, have you done anything that you could be violated for we haven't talked about?

7. Before starting probation, did you commit any kinds of crimes <u>more serious</u> than what you've disclosed in treatment?

8. Have you told the complete truth to each question on the probation form?

9. Is there even one question on the probation form you haven't answered truthfully?

* * * * * * * * * *

10. In the last 6 months, have you done anything considered sexually improper you haven't told me?

11. Since your last test, have you engaged in any kind of improper sexual behavior you haven't reported?

12. Are you purposely concealing any kind of sexual behavior since your last test?

13. Have you left any important information off the treatment form today?

14. Have you done anything sexual since your last test you're too embarrassed to tell me?

15. Have you lied to any of the questions on the treatment form today?

16. Have you falsified any information on your weekly treatment reports?

17. Have you been 'under-reporting' your deviant fantasies?

CONTROL QUESTIONS

(non-adjudicated cases and sexual history testing)

1. Before you entered high school, did you do anything sexually improper you haven't told me?

2. While in high school, did you do anything sexually unnatural while all alone?

3. Before you joined the Army, did you participate in any sexual acts you know your friends would never do?

4. When you were in the Army, did you do anything sexually improper?

5. Did you ever try to physically force someone your own age to perform a sex act against their will?

6. Besides what you've reported, did you do anything else of a sexual nature with animals?

7. When you lived in California, were you involved in any sexual acts with an adult you were later ashamed of?

8. Before you were married, did you lie to a close friend about a personal sexual issue?

9. Have you ever engaged (or tried to engage) in any improper sexual acts while using the telephone?

10. Do you currently have any ongoing sexual fantasies concerning young children?

11. Did you ever tell someone you might use a weapon if they didn't agree to a sexual act?

12. Is there anything about your sexual history as a young child you're too embarrassed to tell me?

13. Did you ever continue a sexual act with someone your own age after they asked you to stop?

14. Did you ever engage in a sexual act with a complete stranger as a way of getting even with someone?

15. Have you ever engaged in any unnatural sex act when you knew someone was watching you?

Any of the sample Secondary or Supplemental questions could be used on sexual history disclosure examinations. (Lundell & Holmes 1994).

Note from this Author: The above described control questions are a mix of Non-Current Exclusive control questions, Current Exclusive control questions, Non-Exclusive control questions, and Relevant Connected or Disguised control questions. See Chapter 16 for explanation in the use of the various types of control questions.

Obviously, the above described test formats may require a multiple-issue test structure to accommodate the numerous relevant test questions/issues. But as mentioned earlier in this chapter, several probationary programs emphasize the use of the single-issue control question test format in the administration of the three types of Probationary PV examinations. It appears that the demonstrated success of the single-issue control question test has blinded some forensic psychophysiologists to the effectiveness of other test formats which in some instances are more appropriate and effective in resolving a particular task. In order to comply with the single-issue control test mandate, some forensic psychophysiologists have consolidated the several issues normally covered during the Complete Disclosure Examination and/or the Maintenance Examination into a single statement form which is then treated as a single issue by asking the offender on the test whether he or she was completely truthful regarding the contents of his or her statement.

This manipulation of the single-issue concept creates the potential for a false positive result because any question regarding the accuracy of a statement containing the articulation of multiple issues and associated events is apt to generate mental exercise from a factually uncertain but truthful offender/examinee. As mentioned in chapter 8, relevant test questions must be succinct, as short as possible, void of rationalization potential, and thoroughly reviewed with the examinee and thus not elicit any mental exercise from the examinee: "all effort must be avoided except that involved in the deception syndrome."

Another problem envisioned by this author is the submission of an offender/examinee to the repeated administration of the Control Question Test in the conduct of the Complete Disclosure examination and especially the Maintenance Examination which may be conducted as often as every three months. Habituation from repeated exposure to the exclusive and non-exclusive control questions normally used in control question tests can significantly reduce their effectiveness, hence also the accuracy of the examination. Use of the directed-lie control question does not alleviate the effects of habituation and raises the potential for false negatives (see Chapter 5). The Single-Issue Control question test may more appropriately be used in the initial Conviction Verification Examination, and thereafter only in the final resolution of unresolved responses found in the Complete Disclosure and/or Maintenance Examinations which would employ a General Question Test (GQT) with *disguised* controls (not exclusive/non-exclusive) described in chapters 15 and 16.

An example of a Maintenance Examination employing a General Question Test format is set forth below:

Irrelevant	1. Is today Monday?
Irrelevant	2. Is your last name Smith?
Control	3. Do you intend to lie to any of the questions on this test?
Relevant	4. Since you have been on probation (or Since your last Probationary Examination or Since (date)): have you violated your probation by having any undisclosed contacts with a person under the age of 18?
Control	5. Do you sometimes behave in a manner designed to sexually attract underage persons?
Relevant	6. Since you have been on probation have you made any attempts to engage in sexual activity with anyone under the age of 18?
Irrelevant	7. Is today (day of the week)?
Relevant	8. Since you have been on probation have you engaged in sexual activity with anyone under the age of 18?
Irrelevant	9. Were you born in (place of birth)?
Relevant	10 Since you have been on probation have you visited any adult book store?
Control	11. Would you lie to even one of these questions if you thought you could get away with it?
Relevant	12. Since you have been on probation have you viewed any pornographic material?
Control	13. Have you lied to me in any way since we have been talking today?
Irrelevant	14. Is your first name John?

Any or all of the above disguised control questions are designed to elicit a potential response from the truthful (to the target issues) offender/examinee. If the examinee fails to respond to any of the relevant test questions but responds significantly to one or more of the control questions on two or more charts, this indicates that the examinee was capable of response to the relevant questions but felt more threatened by the structurally less intense control question(s) which elicited the examinee's psychological set, thus indicating truthfulness regarding the target issues (relevant questions). On the other hand, if the examinee does show significant and consistent unresolved responses to one of the relevant test questions, but not to the other relevant questions, it should not be assumed that the examinee was truthful to those relevant questions which did not elicit a response due to the anti-climax dampening concept explained in Chapters 9 and 11.

When the test results indicate consistent unresolved responses on two or more polygraph charts to a particular relevant test question, the forensic psychophysiologist does not interrogate the examinee, but immediately queries the examinee employing the *broad approach* as to whether any of the test questions bothered him or her on the test. It is surprising how often an examinee will provide some additional information regarding the very question to which he or she showed a response not revealed by the forensic psychophysiologist. Sometimes the information merely clarifies the issue of the question and at other times it is an admission against self-interest. When the *broad approach* yields no information from the examinee, then the *specific* approach is used by asking the examinee what he or she was thinking about when he or she was asked that specific relevant question, with no mention that he or she showed a physiological response to that test question. By directing the examinee to the exact test question to which the examinee showed a response, the deceptive examinee will realize without being told that he or she responded to that test question, thus raising the examinee's apprehension level without using any accusatory approach. At this point there is a strong likelihood that a deceptive examinee will reveal the information which caused the response on the test. However, when this approach fails to resolve the response to the relevant question, the examinee should then be advised in a non-accusatory, non-threatening manner that there is an unresolved response to that test question and a dialogue with the examinee should be initiated to resolve the response. When the examinee does furnish information which appears to satisfy and resolve the response, another General Question Test with the critical relevant question amended to exclude the admission, must be administered to determine the veracity of the examinee's answers to all of the relevant test questions.

When the General Question Test (GQT) fails to resolve a significant and consistent reaction to a relevant test question, the examinee is then rescheduled for a Single-Issue Control Question Test such as the Zone Comparison Test to resolve the matter. Thus the most powerful and objective test format is reserved and its critical exclusive or non-exclusive control questions preserved for those cases when an examinee's truthfulness is in serious question and his or her probation is in jeopardy of revocation. Hence the GQT should only be used to verify the examinee's truthfulness, but deception should only be determined with the use of the Single-Issue Control Question Test. In this manner, we have a very effective and utilitarian Maintenance Examination which is supported by the Single-Issue Control Question Test, which demonstrated its effectiveness to the examinee in his or her initial Conviction Verification examination.

The impact of the Probationary Psychophysiological Veracity Examination Program can be seen in the reduction of the prison population and the cost of housing these individuals, and the saving of supervisory time by busy probation officers which can be applied to other probationers whose reoffending was discovered by the Probationary PV examination, plus the deterrent effect on the majority of the others on probation, which amount to additional protection for society. In addition, therapists involved in these programs believe that the use of Probationary PV examinations has helped the treatment process because if a pedophile was reoffending, he or she would be reinforcing the very behavior they were attempting to eliminate. (Abrams 1992; Morris 1994).

However, we must guard against the abuses discovered during congressional hearings which led to the enactment of the Employee Polygraph Protection Act (EPPA) of 1988. Many State agencies offer a polygraph contract to administer Probationary PV examinations on convicted sex offenders on parole or probation to the lowest bidder. This is reminiscent of the pre-EPPA era when employers would award polygraph contracts to the polygraph firm or forensic psychophysiologist who charged the lowest fee, with little or no regard for the forensic psychophysiologist's qualifications. Many employers used the polygraph as a psychological threat to acquire admissions and a deterrent to future dishonesty rather than as a scientific procedure to determine an examinee's truthfulness, therefore did not want to pay for the additional time required for a properly conducted PV examination. In order to secure a contract, a polygraph firm would offer a very low bid, then make up the loss by spending less time on each examination, thus more examinations conducted, which translated into more money but reduced accuracy and increased error rate. Some polygraph firms expected their forensic psychophysiologists to conduct as many as 25 or more examinations per day. This led to the restrictions now found in the EPPA. A more appropriate method of contracting for Probationary PV examination services is to appoint a knowledgeable administrator to represent the governmental agency, who would be empowered to visit, inspect and enforce the standards of practice included in the contract. A reasonable flat fee for each type of test or an hourly rate that would attract the best qualified forensic psychophysiologists would be set by the governmental agency, and a list of qualified forensic psychophysiologists willing to work for that fee would be employed on a rotation basis as needed. The enforcement of the following standards would preclude the type of abuses mentioned in the EPPA hearings.

1. The forensic psychophysiologist must be a graduate of a polygraph school accredited by the American Polygraph Association who has completed the required post-academic field project study and internship to the satisfaction of the accredited polygraph school which issued the certificate of graduation.

2. The forensic psychophysiologist must possess a polygraph license when required by the county or state in which he or she practices forensic psychophysiology (polygraphy).

3. The forensic psychophysiologist must have conducted at least 700 PV examinations, of which no less than 250 must be specific single-issue PV examinations with at least three years of experience in the conduct of PV examinations, or be a ***full member*** of the American Polygraph Association in good standing for at the past three years.

4. The Probationary PV examinations will be conducted with the use of a polygraph instrument which records simultaneously on a moving chart, both thoracic and abdominal breathing patterns, electrodermal response, and cardiovascular activity.

5. The Probationary PV examination report shall be a factual, impartial, and an objective account of the pertinent information developed during the examination and the examiner's professional conclusion shall be based on analysis of the collected physiological data.

6. A forensic psychophysiologist will not conduct more than three (3) Single-Issue Control Question Tests in any one Conviction Verification Examination, Complete Disclosure Examination, or Maintenance Examination, in any one day. Each Single-Issue Control Question Test will encompass two or more polygraph charts. Thus three Conviction Verifi-

cation Examinations each with only one Single-Issue Control Question Test would meet the three Single-Issue Control Question Test limit in any one day. Probationary PV examinations using the General Question Test (GQT) format in Complete Disclosure and/or Maintenance Examinations will not exceed five tests in any one day. Each General Question Test may encompass two or more polygraph charts.

7. A forensic psychophysiologist's decision or conclusion of truth or deception must be based on a minimum of two polygraph charts containing the same test questions to establish consistency hence reliability.

8. A forensic psychophysiologist will not conduct a Probationary PV examination without the examinee's knowledge and consent.

9. All Probationary PV examinations will be videotape recorded and held in the files of the forensic psychophysiologist and/or polygraph agency for a period of three (3) years.

10. A forensic psychophysiologist will not conduct a Probationary PV examination on an individual whom he or she believes to be physically or emotionally unsuitable for testing.

11. A forensic psychophysiologist will use only those polygraph techniques which have been received *General Acceptance* within the field of forensic psychophysiology or *Published Validation*. (See Chapter 23).

12. All polygraph charts containing the physiological data will be signed in ink by the examinee who provided the physiological data, in the middle but at the top of each polygraph chart before he or she is released from the examination room at the conclusion of the Probationary PV Examination.

13. All polygraph charts will contain and reflect the sensitivity settings of each parameter recorded, any and all artifact which occurred during the conduct of the PV test, and the chart number, time and date that the test ended, to be written at the chart location when the test was concluded.

14. No one will be permitted to be present in the examination room during the conduct of any portion of the Probationary PV Examination other than the examinee and the forensic psychophysiologist except for an interpreter/translator when required. This requirement is based on the premise that the presence of a third person in the examination room would add a critical variable in the examination process which could affect the psychological preparation of the examinee for the delicate introduction of the various types of test questions necessary to attain a valid and reliable test, which includes the sensitive and fragile development and presentation of the control questions which are an essential part of the psychological structure of the PV examination.

The success of the Probationary Psychophysiological Veracity Examination program depends to a large extent on the enforcement of the conditions of parole or probation. The offender must know with certainty that violation of any of the conditions of his or her parole or probation will result in some form of discipline with the possibility of parole/probation revocation. The enforcement of parole/probation conditions provides the reoffender with the "fear of detection" deterrent which is useful in the treatment process, and the underlying basis of the psychophysiological veracity examination. (Chapter 9).

The alternative to the use of Probationary PV examinations offers a bleak scenario wherein the parole/probation officer must periodically interview the offender, using basically the same questions that would be used by a forensic psychophysiologist with one exception. The officer must make a judgment regarding the truthfulness of the offender's answers by evaluating the offender's verbal and non-verbal behavior which is known as behavior assessment or demeanorology, without the benefit of any instrument that would record the offender's physiology for evaluation by an expert forensic psychophysiologist. The absence of the PV examination from the probationary program removes an effective psychological deterrent for the potential reoffender and motivational aid in the treatment of the offender.

Part II - Use of PV Examinations on Victims of Sex Offenses.

Since about 1990, the United States has experienced a near epidemic increase in reported sex offenses, from victims of rape to allegations of child abuse/molestation by parents in child custody disputes, and most notably from adults who recalled being sexually abused as children by one of their parents. In fact, the latter caused such turmoil that in March 1992, a group of distinguished psychologists and psychiatrists formed the False Memory Syndrome (FMS) Foundation headquartered in Philadelphia, Pennsylvania to combat what they felt were dubious therapeutic practices which included the use of hypnosis, dream analysis, visual imagery, soporific agents and so-called truth serums such as sodium amytal or pentothal on adult females in attempts to effect recall of childhood sexual traumas, presumably obliterated for decades. This phenomenon is called Decades Delayed Disclosure or DDD. The FMS does not deny that childhood sexual assaults occur, but in almost every case the event is never forgotten. Indeed, it festers as a lifelong source of shame and anger. (Gardner 1993). However, many clinicians believe that complete repression can occur in some children who have been sexually molested and they maintain that amnesia can persist well into adulthood when recall may be stimulated by a dream, a similar experience, or as a result of therapy. S. Abrams and J. Abrams (1995) in their article on FMS vs. Total Repression, cite Briere and Conte's (1995) evaluation of the responses of many adults who had been sexually abused as children. They reported that 59% responded that they had no memory of their abuse. Briere and Conte (1993) also reported that there were soldiers who had no memory of their participation in particular battles. Williams (1992) reported that of one hundred women admitted to emergency rooms as children because of sexual abuse, 38% had no recall of it when subsequently questioned as adults.

Proponents of DDD and FMS do not claim that every case of complete repression or false memory respectively is genuine, but both sides offer data to support their theory; Fredrickson (1992) states that millions of people have repressed childhood traumas, and Loftus (1993) cites numerous examples supporting the false memory syndrome. Interestingly, Dr. Stan Abrams, a clinical psychologist and forensic psychophysiologist, stated in aforesaid article (1995) that he has tested hundreds of alleged sexual abusers and obtained deceptive findings in about 85% of the cases. In contrast he has seen very few cases associated with repression. Only three women assumed to be victims were examined, and all three of them failed the PV examination. Because they seemed so believable and because they were still involved in reliving their experiences in therapy, it was felt that they were not fit subjects for testing. However, much later, five men who were allegedly perpetrators of abuse that occurred years before were each administered a PV examination and every one of them was found to be truthful. Dr. Abrams admits that other forensic psychophysiologists have not found the same degree of truthfulness in cases of this nature. Dr. Abrams suggests that it is virtually impossible to document whether sexual abuse did or did not occur years before, thus the psychological associations can only evaluate this issue indirectly, whereas the forensic psychophysiologist can administer a PV examination using the polygraph on the alleged *perpetrators* and determine the degree of truth or deception that exists. Data of this nature is not only useful to the medical and legal system, but is also highly valuable to the American Psychological and Psychiatric Associations.

These and other allegations of sex offenses are easily made and almost impossible to defend inasmuch as they are usually committed in privacy and in the aforesaid two categories (Custody disputes and DDD) there is no physical evidence to corroborate the allegation. Yet juries are increasingly more often judging a parent guilty without any confirming evidence other than the alleged victim's testimony which may be true, knowingly false or unknowingly untrue.

The temptation by some law enforcement personnel is to offer the adult victim an opportunity to confirm her or his allegation by submitting to a psychophysiological veracity (PV) examination using the polygraph. However allegations of sexual abuse based on DDD could well be real to the alleged victim who underwent lengthly and suggestive therapy, thus producing truthful PV examination results to an event that did not actually occur. Thus, in such cases, it is the alleged *perpetrator* who should be requested to submit to a PV examination inasmuch as he or she *would know* whether he/she did or did not commit the alleged offense. This author is in complete agreement with Dr. Abrams's statement (1995) that because of difficulties associated with confirmatory testing, the subjects of PV examinations in DDD cases should be the alleged perpetrators rather than the victims. As indicated in Chapter 9, when testing a victim, when legally allowed, especially in a sex offense of someone of a tender age, the forensic psychophysiologist should be ultra sensitive to the victim's emotional state regarding the traumatic event, and thus in the formulation of the relevant test questions the forensic psychophysiologist should avoid traumatic and personally embarrassing words which might elicit a physiological response by their very nature. This may be accomplished by having the victim write a *very short* statement regarding the single-issue offense, which then can be the used on the PV examination to determine the truthfulness of the victim's statement with the further precaution of eliciting affirmative answers to the relevant test questions. This is in contrast to the lengthly *multiple-issue* statement used in some of the Probationary examinations to comply with the mandate of the single-issue test, discussed in Part I of this chapter, which is not recommended. Furthermore, the examination room should be devoid of any physical evidence of the crime, unless it is necessary in the conduct of the PV examination. The conduct of PV examinations on victims of sex offenses should also take into consideration the effects of *shame* and *anger* which are fully discussed in Chapter 9.

In child custody disputes where one parent accuses the other of sexually molesting or abusing one or more of their children, it is almost always preferable to have the alleged perpetrator of the offense submit to a PV examination, especially when the victim is a child. Children below the age of eleven usually do not make good subjects of PV examinations (Abrams 1975, 1989) and should not be compelled to relive the event.

In a study conducted by Steven A. Adang on The Use of the Polygraph with Children, Adang reports that research done by Ceci, Toglia & Ross (1987), and Haugaard et al. (1991) found that as a general rule, children between ages four and six could determine that saying something that was not true to a policeman was a lie, even if the parents of the children prompted the child to make the statement. In a summary of findings on children's testimony, Adang reports that Dr. Gibson of the Wisconsin Polygraph Association, stated:

> ...Younger children's memories are not as detailed as older persons with the same learning opportunity, and therefore, contain less inaccuracies. However, because of poorer memory and lack of supporting information, their memory is more precarious to the manner of questioning (suggestibility;...etc.). ...Children can sometimes be more accurate when question(ed), because they don't fill in 'what must have happened' owing to their naiveness. Allowing children to give free recall and account for the incident in their own words, without questions provided for the fewest incidents inaccuracies. However, such accounts lack completeness. (Gibson 1991).

Rape cases present a different problem in that usually the perpetrator and the victim are both adults and the rate of unfounded allegations of rape is statistically significant. In a research study conducted by Saxton, Kanin and Brocki in 1988, the results showed that the distribution of unfounded rape complaints averaged 14 percent when no PV examination was offered to the victim. When a few victims were offered PV examinations, the rate was 16 percent. When some PV examinations were offered to victims the rate rose to 22 percent. When most or all of the victims were offered PV examinations the unfounded rape rate was 30 percent. This research also showed that the gender composition of the investigating officers had no effect on the percentage of unfounded rapes, citing all male officers 23% unfounded rape, all female officers 26% unfounded rape. Thus the issue of gender composition as an affect on the rate of unfounded rape cases appears to be without merit. However this does not imply that female officers are not more effective than male officers in other areas of rape investigations requiring rapport, empathy and preservation of victim dignity. The point is that in approximately 30 percent of allegations of rape, an innocent person is wrongfully accused of a crime which requires minimum corroboration.

Several states such as New York have enacted laws that prohibit law enforcement agencies and district attorneys from requiring any victim of a sexual assault to take a polygraph examination as a prerequisite to initiating a criminal investigation (NY Bill S-2789, Sen. Kehoe, and A-3743, Assym. Saland, eff. 3 Sep 87), and in some states the prohibition is absolute, as evidenced by the subsequent passage in New York State of Senate bill #3769 in 1996 which amends its earlier statute limiting the use of polygraph tests with alleged victims of sexual assault. Section l, subdivision l of section l60.45, l990 as amended , reads as follows: "No district attorney, police officer or employee of any law enforcement agency shall request or require any victim of a sexual assault crime to submit to any polygraph test or psychological stress evaluator examination."(Ansley, ed. 1996). Understandably, the legitimate victim of a rape should not be subjected to any procedure that questions her or his veracity, however the high percentage of false allegations of rape cannot be ignored. The Buffalo News reported in their 7 June 1996 edition that the Erie County District Attorney's office dropped its monthlong investigation into the allegations that a Buffalo music teacher had sex with a 13-year old student, because the 13-year old girl failed a PV examination and subsequently admitted that she had lied. The girl even planted a condom wrapper behind the bookcase in the teacher's classroom. The News quoted the president of the Buffalo Teachers Federation as saying "What we have here is a case of a complete fabrication by a disturbed child who has tainted the career of a teacher who did absolutely nothing wrong." The exonerated teacher stated "In the blink of an eye, I almost lost everything." (Warner 1996)

The US Army C.I.D.'s protocol for making PV examinations available to rape victims involves a number of safeguards that protect the victim. First, the accused must have refused to submit to a PV examination. Secondly, if the accused maintains that there was consent, and the victim maintains that there was no consent, and there is no other evidence in the case, a point of conflict arises and a PV examination may be conducted at the request of the victim to resolve the issue. (Hardy, 1994; Williams, 1995).

Psychophysiological veracity (PV) examinations of sex offense victims should not be conducted without the permission of the attending psychiatrist or psychologist who is treating the victim/patient. The longer the delay in administering a PV examination to a sex offense victim, the less potential there will be for a false positive result due to the emotional trauma suffered by the victim. On the other hand, the alleged perpetrator of a sex offense should be administered a PV examination, with his/her consent, as soon as possible, provided he/she was not interrogated immediately prior to the scheduled examination.

REFERENCES:

Abrams, S. (1975). The validity of the polygraph technique with children. *Journal of Police Science and Administration*, 3(3), 310-311.

Abrams, S. (1989). *The Complete Polygraph Handbook*. Lexington, MA: Lexington Books.

Abrams, S. (1992). A response to Wygant's critique of the discovery test. *Polygraph*, 21(3), 248-253.

Abrams, S. (1996, July 1). Telephone conversation with J. A. Matte regarding Probationary PV examinations.

Abrams, S., Abrams, J. (1995). False memory syndrome vs. total repression: Only polygraphy can know. *Polygraph*, 24(4), 297-301.

Abrams, S., Ogard, E. (1986). Polygraph Surveillance of Probationers. *Polygraph*, 15(3), 174-182.

Abrams, S., Weinstein, E. (1974). The validity of polygraph with retardates. *Journal of Police Science and Administration*, 2(1), 11-14.

Ansley, N. (ed) (1996, July-August). Polygraph in the news. New York Law banning tests of victims of sexual assault. Newsletter, American Polygraph Association, 29(4), 11.

Bays & Freeman-Longo, R. E. (1989). Why Did I Do It Again?. Brandon, VT: Safer Society Press.

Briere, J. (1993). Repressed memory controversy and sex abuse. Debate at the 101st Annual Convention of the American Psychological Association, Toronto, Canada.

Briere, J., Conte, J. (in press). Self-reported amnesia for abuse in adults molested as children. Journal of Traumatic Stress.

Ceci, S.J., Taglia, M. P. Ross, D. F. (1987). *Children's Eyewitness Memory*. New York: Springer-Verlag. at pp. 89-90.

Fredrickson, R. (1992). *Repressed Memories: A Journey to Recovering from Sexual Abuse*. N. Y.: Simon & Schuster.

Gardner, M. (1993). Notes of a fringe-watcher: The false memory syndrome. *Skeptical Inquirer*, 17, 370-375.

Gibson, K. (1991, June). *Children's competency as eyewitnesses*. Paper presented at the Spring Meeting of the Wisconsin Polygraph Association.

Grindstaff, R. (1996, July 1). Telephone conversation with J. A. Matte regarding sex offender management.

Hardy, L. H. (1994, July). *Polygraph testing of victims: Focus on sex crime victims.* Paper presented at the 29th Annual Seminar/Workshop of the American Polygraph Association, Nashville, TN.

Haugaard, J. J., Repucci, N. D., Laird, J., Nauful, T. (1991). Children's definition of the truth and their competency as witnesses in legal proceedings. *Law and Human Behavior*, 15(3), 253-271.

Jaroff, L. (November 27, 1993). Lies of the Mind, *Time*, 52-59.

Keifer, R. W. (1996, June 12). Telephone conversation with J. A. Matte regarding the testing of the victims of sex offenses and kidnapping by the Federal Bureau of Investigation.

Loftus, E. F. (1993). The reality of repressed memories. *American Psychologist*, 48, 518-537.

Lundell, R. G. (1996, July 1). Telephone conversation with J. A. Matte regarding Probationary PV Examinations.

Lundell, R. G., Holmes, S. A. (1994, July 24-29). Polygraph testing of the sexual offender-specific, sexual history and periodic. Presentation at the American Polygraph Association's 29th Annual Seminar/Workshop, Nashville, TN.

Morris, J. R. (1994, July 24-29). *How to set-up and manage a court-ordered polygraph testing program for sexual offenders on probation and parole.* Paper presented at the 29th Annual Seminar/Workshop of the American Polygraph Association, Nashville, TN.

Saxton, G. N., Kanin, E. J., Brocki, S. J. (1988). Unfounded rape complaints and the polygraph. *Polygraph*, 17(3), 97-105.

Warner, G. (1996, June 7). False allegations take toll on teacher. *The Buffalo News*, Buffalo, N. Y.

Williams, L. M. (1992). Adult memories of childhood abuse: Preliminary findings from a longitudinal study. *The Advisor*, 5, 19-20.

Williams, V. L. (1995). Response to Cross & Saxe's 'A critique of the validity of polygraph testing in child sexual abuse cases.' *Journal of Child Sexual Abuse*, 4(3), 55-71.

Wygant, J. R. (1996, July 1). Telephone conversation with J. A. Matte regarding Probationary PV Examinations.

Chapter 25

Application of the Employee Polygraph Protection Act

On 27 June 1988, President Ronald Reagan signed Public Law 100-347, the Employee Polygraph Protection Act of 1988 (EPPA), to prevent the denial of employment opportunities by prohibiting the use of lie detectors by employers involved in or affecting interstate commerce. The EPPA prohibits private employers from suggesting, requesting or requiring a job applicant or employee to submit to a lie detector test except under limited circumstances. The term "commerce" has the meaning provided by section 3(b) of the Fair Labor Standards act of 1938 (29 U.S.C. 203(b)). The term "employer" includes any person acting directly or indirectly in the interest of an employer in relation to an employee or prospective employee. The term "lie detector" includes a polygraph, deceptograph, voice stress analyzer, psychological stress evaluator, or any other similar device (whether mechanical or electrical) that is used, or the results of which are used, for the purpose of rendering a diagnostic opinion regarding the honesty or dishonesty of an individual. The term "polygraph" is defined by EPPA as an instrument that records continuously, visually, permanently, and simultaneously changes in cardiovascular, respiratory, and electrodermal patterns as minimum instrumentation standards; and is used, or the results of which are used, for the purpose of rendering a diagnostic opinion regarding the honesty or dishonesty of an individual.

The employer who is contemplating the use of the polygraph for any purpose should first contact the nearest office of the Wage and Hour Division of the Federal Labor Department and request that the following items be sent to him or her. (1) a *Notice* (W.H. Publication 1482) which summarizes the pertinent provisions of EPPA, which must be posted in a conspicuous place where notices to employees are customarily posted. (2) A copy of Public Law 100-347, June 27, 1988, Employee Polygraph Protection Act of 1988. (3) The Federal Register, Part IV, Department of Labor, Employment Standards Administration, Wage and Hour Division, 29 CFR Part 801, Application of the Employee Polygraph Protection Act of 1988; Final Rule. The employer should thoroughly familiarize himself/herself with the above three items and when possible, furnish a copy of the EPPA and its related Federal Register Application to the employer's attorney for review and familiarization, inasmuch as the employer at some point will undoubtedly want to consult with his/her attorney for insurance that the employer's actions comply with EPPA. This chapter is intended only as a guide based on seminars pertaining to EPPA and the author's experience in implementing the EPPA and interactions with the W & H Division of the Federal Labor Department.*

---

* This chapter is only intended as a guide and should not be relied upon for legal advice. The reader should consult with his or her attorney for any legal questions.

The EPPA contains several limited exemptions which authorize polygraph tests under certain conditions, including the testing of: (1) Employees who are reasonably suspected of involvement in a workplace incident that results in economic loss or injury to the employer's business; (2) certain prospective employees of private armored car, security alarm, and security guard firms; and (3) certain current and prospective employees in firms authorized to manufacture, distribute, or dispense controlled substances. Federal, State and local government employers are exempted from the Act, with respect to polygraph testing of their employees. In addition , an exemption permits testing by the Federal Government of experts, consultants, or employees of Federal contractors engaged in national security intelligence or counterintelligence functions. Employers who violate any of the Act's provisions may be assessed civil money penalties up to $10,000.00 per infraction. (See EPPA Civil Money Penalty Report in Appendix M). Thus six exemptions are included in the Employee Polygraph Protection Act of 1988. They affect the government, national defense, national security, ongoing investigations, security services, and drug security. However, these exemptions do not diminish a private employer's obligation to comply with applicable state and local law as well as any negotiated collective bargaining agreements that may limit or prohibit the use of lie detector tests. The last three named have limited exemptions which are discussed below:

Ongoing Investigations.

This limited exemption permits any employer, regardless of the industry in which it does business, to request an employee to submit to a polygraph test, provided that the employer complies with the following four prerequisites:

1. The test must be administered in connection with an *ongoing investigation* involving economic loss or injury to the employer's business.

2. The employee must have had *access* to the property or money that is the subject of the investigation.

3. The employer must have a *reasonable suspicion* that the employee was involved in the incident or matter under investigation.

4. The employer must execute a written letter addressed to the employee to be polygraphed, wherein the employer articulates in detail the specific loss or injury sustained by the employer, and describe the employee's access. Furthermore the employer must also articulate his/her basis of the employer's *reasonable suspicion* that the employee was involved in the incident. *Access* cannot be used as the basis for the *reasonable suspicion* (with one exception discussed below), and this *basis* must be directly related to the incident. This letter must also include a notice to the employee/addressee that he or she has 48 hours, excluding weekend days and holidays, in which to consult with an attorney or employee representative before the scheduled examination. That the employee also has the right to consult with legal counsel or an employee representative before each phase of the polygraph examination. However, the employee's attorney or employee representative may be excluded

from the room where the examination is administered during the actual testing phase. This letter must be signed by a person other than the forensic psychophysiologist who is legally authorized to bind the employer. (See Appendix N for Model Letter from Employer to Employee).

Failure by the employer to fully describe in detail the *loss* or *injury* to the employer, the *access* by the employee, and the basis for the employer's *reasonable suspicion* in aforesaid letter to the employee to the subsequent satisfaction of a compliance officer of the Federal Labor Department can invalidate the polygraph test and subject the employer to severe penalties and civil litigation.

The aforesaid exemption does not allow for the polygraph examination of prospective employees, nor does it allow for examinations with any equipment other than the polygraph instrument previously described herein.

Once the employer has satisfied the above requirements, and the suspected employee has had 48 hours, excluding weekend days and holidays, in which to consult with an attorney or employee representative, the employee can either agree or refuse to submit to the polygraph examination. If the employee refuses to submit to a polygraph examination after all of the conditions have been satisfactorily met, the employer can discharge or terminate the employee's employment based on the employee's refusal supported by proof of access and the basis for the employer's reasonable suspicion. The EPPA states in 801.20 of the Federal Register's Rules and Regulations, that Section 8(a) (1) of the Act provides that the limited exemption in section 7(d) of the Act and 801.12 of this part for ongoing investigations shall not apply if an employer discharges, disciplines, denies employment or promotion or otherwise discriminates in any manner against a current employee based upon the analysis of a polygraph test chart or the refusal to take a polygraph test, without additional supporting evidence. The additional supporting evidence for purposes of section 8(a) of the Act, includes, but is not limited to the following:

1. Evidence indicating that the employee had *access* to the missing or damaged property that is the subject of an *ongoing investigation*; and

2. Evidence leading to the employer's *reasonable suspicion* that the employee was involved in the incident or activity under investigation.

or

3. Admissions or statements made by an employee before, during or following a polygraph examination.

In order for the employer to legally request and submit an employee to a polygraph examination, he/she had to first acquire the aforementioned supporting evidence (1 & 2) for inclusion in his/her letter of request to the employee. Thus the employer can legally terminate an employee who refuses to submit to a polygraph test inasmuch as the employer has already acquired the supporting evidence (1 & 2) as reflected in his letter to the employee.

It is therefore of paramount importance that the employer be absolutely certain that all of the elements of the required letter to the employee meet and even exceed EPPA requirements.

The employer may also terminate an employee on the basis of the results of a polygraph examination supported by the aforementioned supporting evidence reflected in the required letter to the employee or admissions/statements made by the employee before, during or following a polygraph examination.

Many reporters of the EPPA have stated that the exemption does not apply if the employee can show that he or she has been discharged or disciplined solely on the outcome of a polygraph test or on his or her refusal to submit to the test, but these same reporters have failed to mention that if the test was legally administered, the employer would have necessarily had to acquire the supporting evidence (para. 1 & 2 above) for inclusion in the letter he/she is required to furnish the employee prior to the administration of the polygraph test, thus the employer needs only the results (deceptive) of the polygraph test or a refusal to submit to the test to take adverse employment action. However, in the employer's dismissal action he or she must reiterate and articulate the supporting evidence in addition to the unfavorable results of the polygraph examination or its refusal, as appropriate.

Reasonable Suspicion Based on Access: Normally *access* cannot be used as the basis for *reasonable suspicion.* However Page 9068 of the Federal Register states "in an investigation of a theft of an expensive piece of jewelry, an employee authorized to open the establishment's safe no earlier than 9 a.m., in order to place the jewelry in a window display case, is observed opening the safe at 7:30 a.m. In such a situation, the opening of the safe by the employee one and one-half hours prior to the specified time may serve as the basis for *reasonable suspicion*. On the other hand, in the example given, if the employer asked the employee to bring the piece of jewelry to his or her office at 7:30 a.m., and the employee then opened the safe and reported the jewelry missing, such *access*, standing alone, would not constitute a basis for *reasonable suspicion* that the employee was involved in the incident unless *access* to the safe was limited solely to the employee. If no one other than the employee possessed the combination to the safe, and all other possible explanations for the loss are ruled out, such as a break-in, the employer may formulate a basis for *reasonable suspicion* based on *sole access* by one employee."

Reasonable Suspicion Based on Behavior/Demeanor: Section 801.12(f)(1), EPPA Final Rule, states: "As used in section 7(d)(3), the term *'reasonable suspicion'* refers to an observable, articulable basis in fact which indicates that a particular employee was involved in, or responsible for, an economic loss." "Information from a co-worker, or an employee's behavior, demeanor, or conduct may be factors in the basis for reasonable suspicion. Likewise, inconsistencies between facts, claims, or statements that surface during an investigation can serve as a sufficient basis for reasonable suspicion. While access or opportunity, standing alone, does not constitute a basis for reasonable suspicion, the totality of circumstances surrounding the access or opportunity (such as its unauthorized or unusual nature or the fact that access was limited to a single individual) may constitute a factor in determining whether there is a reasonable suspicion."

Courts have used the term *reasonable suspicion* primarily in the law enforcement context. A law enforcement officer is not allowed to *stop and frisk* or *pat down* a criminal suspect unless he/she has a *reasonable suspicion* that criminal activity is in progress. Thus the *reasonable suspicion* required for a *stop and frisk* or *pat down* is significantly less than the *probable cause* required for an *arrest*. Hence, the term *reasonable suspicion* simply means that the officer must have specific reasons that he can describe for his/her suspicion that justifies the *frisk*. As an example, an individual dressed in dark clothes, who is observed walking around a jewelry store for an unusual amount of time, late at night long after it is closed, may be subject to a *stop and frisk*. While such behavior, standing alone, would not be sufficient for an arrest, it does give rise to a *reasonable, describable suspicion*. However, if an individual is simply observed in front of the same jewelry store during the daytime, an officer who *stops and frisks* that individual would probably violate his/her constitutional rights. (Nagle 1989)

While in the latter example, there is no reasonable or objective factor which would give rise to a suspicion, in the former example, the officer can describe two or three factors which arouse a *reasonable suspicion*, or which cause an objective and experienced officer to be suspicious. In the law enforcement context, the term *reasonable suspicion* simply requires something more than a mere *gut instinct*, or *hunch*. The suspicion may not be based on a whim, or racial or ethnic prejudice, or be arbitrary or capricious. On the other hand, an individual's *demeanor* is a sound basis to give rise to a *reasonable suspicion*, so long as the officer can articulate the basis for his/her suspicion. As an example, "I didn't like the way he looked" is insufficient, while the statement "His eyes were bloodshot, he appeared nervous and avoided eye contact when I questioned him" is the kind of articulation of a basis for suspicion which would meet the test. Thus, while a *hunch* is not good enough, if the officer can articulate the factors which gave rise to his *hunch*, and those factors are recognized by experienced police officers as indicia that something is awry or that suspicious behavior is present, the officer's suspicion will be deemed reasonable. Hence the reasonable requirement does not appear to present a severe or stringent obstacle, and so long as the suspicions are not based on whimsical or unreasonable factors, the EPPA requirement would be met. Although the Department of Labor's Regulations under EPPA borrow terminology from the criminal context, the Senate has made clear that the EPPA's reasonable suspicion requirement is even less stringent than that required in the criminal law enforcement context, as articulated in Section 801.12(f)(1) above. While the factors that constitute reasonable suspicion obviously will be unique to each case, they may include unusual displays of nervousness, suspicious statement during questioning, peculiar demeanor during questioning, information from co-workers or others, or other observations about the individual's behavior or habits which arouse suspicion. (Nagle 1989)

On the basis of the above description of factors which constitute *reasonable suspicion*, it would appear that the results of the following psychologically structured Bio-Kinetic™ interview would satisfy EPPA's *reasonable suspicion* requirement. The Bio-

Kinetic interview comprises the administration of Scientific Content Analysis (SCAN) which consists of an analysis of the contents of an individual's statement relating his/her activities during the period in question, by an investigator certified in the process, and further includes the administration of the Morgan Interview Theme Technique (MITT) which is a derivative of the Thematic Apperception Test (TAT) often administered by psychologists. The Bio-Kinetic™ interview also includes the listening by the subject of an audio motivational tape prior to the MITT, and an evaluation of the individual's verbal and non-verbal behaviors is monitored and evaluated against the Matte Checklist of one hundred and seventy-six documented behaviors associated with truthtelling and non-truthtelling styles developed by this author. In this instance, the Bio-Kinetic™ interview was administered by this author with three decades of experience in interviewing and interrogating suspects. Under these circumstances, one would have to believe that a Bio-Kinetic™ Interview report articulating with specificity, a subject's *behavior and demeanor* which give rise to *reasonable suspicion*, would carry at least as much if not more weight than an evaluation offered by a police officer as described above with no interrogative training. Yet when such a Bio-Kinetic™ interview was submitted as the basis for *reasonable suspicion* to the Wage and Hour Division, it was judged *inadequate* in satisfying the basis for the *reasonable suspicion* requirement. This reflects the *extreme restrictiveness* of the W&H Division's interpretation of the *reasonable suspicion* requirement under EPPA.

The employer should be most careful about accepting the opinion of a forensic psychophysiologist regarding the adequacy of the three requirements described above, especially the basis for the employer's *reasonable suspicion*, unless his/her integrity and knowledge of EPPA is well known to the employer, and even so, the employer should double check the information with his/her attorney for insurance. The employer should also exercise caution in accepting the verbal advice of an official of the Wage and Hour Division of the Federal Labor Department regarding the adequacy of the three requirements described above without written confirmation. It is the *employer*, not the forensic psychophysiologist, who is held liable for any of the violations of the EPPA. Thus an unscrupulous forensic psychophysiologist seeking business may agree to conduct polygraph examinations knowing that the employer is in violation of EPPA because it is the employer who will have to pay the fines and be subjected to lawsuits. However, in at least one instance, a Federal Judge ruled that the forensic psychophysiologist could be sued along with the employer by the employee in Rubin, et al. v. Tourneau, Inc., and Jeffrey L. Gwynne and Associates, Inc. No. 92 Civ. 0078 (MBM) July 9, 1992 in U. S. District Court, Southern District of New York. However, that is little comfort to the employer who is the subject of litigation as a result of inaccurate information provided by the forensic psychophysiologist.

The Wage and Hour Division of the Federal Labor Department has shown little interest in assisting employers and/or forensic psychophysiologists in their efforts to comply with EPPA, and has adopted an extremely restrictive interpretation of the EPPA. In one instance, this author contacted an official of the Wage and Hour Division of the Labor Department at Buffalo, New York to determine whether a larceny of money from the rectory of a church whose janitor was the only suspect, fell under EPPA jurisdiction. This author was advised that in this case the EPPA did not apply. This author subsequently contacted the pastor and advised him to contact the same Labor Department official for confirmation and request the exemption *in writing*. Shortly thereafter, the pastor notified this author that the Labor official informed him that his church and this case were not exempt from the conditions of EPPA. We thus proceeded with the usual caution in implementing all of the requirements of EPPA and the matter was legally resolved. The lesson learned from this incident is that *verbal* advice from the Wage & Hour Division of the Labor Department is not always dependable, and as will be seen in the next case, *written* advice is unattainable.

This author was visited by a compliance officer of the Wage and Hour Division of the Labor Department, Rochester, New York as a result of an employer who had terminated an employee on the basis of his refusal to submit to a polygraph test, supported by aforesaid supporting evidence. After several hours of reviewing my files without finding fault, the officer while exiting my office stated that he had not seen any notice of the *Nature and Characteristics of the Polygraph Test* on the release form submitted to the employee/examinee. This author pointed out to the officer that the first paragraph of the release form articulated almost verbatim the nature and characteristics of the polygraph test from the American Polygraph Association's manual on EPPA written by the law firm of F. Lee Bailey. The officer read that first paragraph, and then left without comment. Some time later the employer was notified that he was in violation of EPPA and cited the failure to notify the employee of the *Nature and Characteristics of the Polygraph Test*. Only after this author discussed the matter with the regional director and produced a lengthly audio tape containing a thorough explanation of the physiological and psychological aspect of the test and the instrumentation used, was this violation removed. But the story doesn't end there. In order to assure that this matter would not be raised again, this author formulated a new release form (Appendix H) and in a separate paragraph, under the heading of Nature and Characteristics of the Polygraph Test, described in minute detail the nature and characteristics of the polygraph test, which was then submitted to the regional director of the Wage and Hour Division of the Labor Department who informed this author that he would forward my release form to their legal department in New York City for comment. In addition this author's letter requested an opinion from the W&H Division regarding the use of an audio tape recording and headphones to read the Notice to Examinee which is required by EPPA in addition to its presentation in writing to the examinee. This author explained that the use of an audio recording assures both the examinee and the W&H Division that the Notice is consistently read in a slow, distinct and precise manner without mistakes or editing, time after time, and an audio record of the tape with a written version is always available for review by the W&H Division. In contrast, a live reading of the Notice to the Examinee is subject to a hurried, edited and/or inaccurate rendition without the knowledge of the examinee, and with no record for review; thus the reading of the Notice by audio recording should meet EPPA conditions. Several months later this author received a telephone call from an official of the W&H Division of the Labor Department in New York City advising me that they had reviewed my new release form and could not comment on the adequacy of the paragraph under the heading of Nature and Characteristics of the Polygraph Test because they were not forensic psychophysiologists therefore were not qualified to render an opinion as to its adequacy but would accept it as meeting EPPA requirements. It thus appears that by simply adding a *descriptive title* in consonance with EPPA requirements to a paragraph, one will hopefully meet the requirement. The official further stated that he could not render an opinion regarding whether the aforesaid audio tape recording for the reading of the Notice to Examinee met EPPA requirements. The EPPA official refused to send this author a letter confirming the adequacy of my new release form (Appendix H), even though we both knew that it met all of the requirements of EPPA. This author was left with the impression that the W&H Division does not wish to provide employers and their agents with solid guidelines that will ease their burden and risk of fines and litigation.

The frustration felt by many employers who have come in contact with the EPPA can be summarized by this recent incident. This author was contacted by an employer who had placed one of her male employees on a paid leave of absence as a result of a female employee filing a complaint against the aforesaid employee alleging that she had been sexually assaulted while at work on the company premises. The employee/victim reported the incident to the police department having jurisdiction and inasmuch as their forensic psychophysiologist had recently retired from the police department, they suggested that the employer contact a private forensic psychophysiologist to determine who was telling the truth inasmuch as there were no witnesses to the alleged sexual assault and the alleged perpetrator/employee denied the allegation.

The first requirement by EPPA is that the employer must have suffered an *economic loss or injury*. In this instance, it was felt that the employer had indeed suffered an economic loss in that the employer felt obliged to protect the employee/victim from the alleged employee/perpetrator by placing the latter on a paid leave of absence, thus depriving the company of that employee's work and the employee/victim's full performance as a result of the suffered trauma. There was no question in this instance of the employer meeting the requirements of *access* and *reasonable suspicion* on the part of the suspected employee due to the written statement containing a direct accusation from the victim/employee. However, in order to play it safe, this author contacted an official of the local Federal Wage & Hour Division to verify whether the instant employer met the *economic loss or injury* requirement of the EPPA. After much discussion of the case, the Wage & Hour EPPA investigator opined that the instant employer *did not suffer an economic loss or injury* thus was not legally permitted to request either employee to submit to a polygraph examination, even though each of the employees had volunteered to take the test. The W&H investigator admitted that this was a nebulous area of the EPPA and suggested that this author contact an official of their Washington bureau who was an expert on EPPA matters. This author immediately contacted the mentioned EPPA expert in Washington and we were joined by a second EPPA expert in a telephone conference call. The Washington experts opined that the instant employer did not have to place the alleged perpetrator/employee on paid leave of absence; that this was a voluntary action by the employer who under current state statutes could have terminated his employment inasmuch as the employee does not have a *right to work* there. Thus the employer did not meet the EPPA economic loss/injury requirement because the employer's economic loss was due to a voluntary decision on the part of the employer. This author raised the question about the employer's vulnerability to legal action by the victim if the employer failed to protect the victim from contact at the work place by the alleged employee/perpetrator, but the EPPA officials raised the point of the employee's *right to work* suggesting that the employer had the option of terminating the suspected employee's employment. The EPPA officials recognized that the employer's action was an ethical one, but under EPPA rules, the instant employer did not meet the Economic Loss or Injury requirement, thus could not legally submit either employee to a polygraph examination. To further compound the problem, had the police department agreed to conduct polygraph examinations on one or both employees, the results of the examinations could not be legally released to the employer, nor could the employer use the results of any police polygraph test.

In the aforesaid incident, the EPPA fails to address and protect employees victimized by other employees and the employer who is responsible for their protection at the work place. It appears that the EPPA would rather see a wrongfully accused employee dismissed from employment with the ensuing destruction of his family, rather than allow the use of a psychophysiological veracity examination which has been scientifically validated and is currently being admitted on a more frequent basis in the courts of the United States.

There is little doubt that the Employee Polygraph Protection Act (EPPA) needs to be amended to correct many of its inequities which Labor Department officials are compelled to enforce.

However, the Labor Department as well as other governmental agencies who are supported by our taxes have an obligation to assist *all* citizens who are genuinely attempting to comply with the law. Instead we find a governmental agency whose actions or lack thereof appear to beg the employer and the forensic psychophysiologist to violate the EPPA so that the ensuing fines will discourage other employers from using the polygraph. Hopefully, this book, and especially chapter 3 pertaining to the scientific status of psychophysiological veracity examinations using the polygraph, will be read by Labor Department officials with the effect of removing their apparent bias against forensic psychophysiology. The Federal Labor Department's Wage and Hour Division should show equal treatment and respect for the rights of the employer as well as the employee and adopt an attitude and policy that promotes compliance with EPPA rather than punishment for non-compliance.

Exemptions for Employers Providing Security Services. (801.14)

Section 7(e) of the Act provides an exemption from the general prohibition against polygraph tests for certain armored car, security alarm, and security guard employers. Subject to the conditions set forth in sections 8 and 10 of the act and 801.21, 801.22, 801.23, 801.24, 801.25, 801.26 and 801.35 of this part, section 7(e) permits the use of polygraph tests on certain prospective employees provided that such employers have as their primary business purpose the providing of armored car personnel, personnel engaged in the design, installation, and maintenance of security alarm systems, or other uniformed or plainclothes security personnel; and provided the employer's function includes protection of:

(1) Facilities, materials, or operations having a significant impact on the health or safety of any State or political subdivision thereof, or the national security of the United States, such as:

a. Facilities engaged in the production, transmission, or distribution of electric or nuclear power.
b. Public water supply facilities.
c. Shipments or storage of radioactive or other toxic waste materials, and
d. Public transportation; or

(2) Currency, negotiable securities, precious commodities or instruments, or proprietary information.

Section 7(e) permits the administration of polygraph tests only to prospective employees. However, security service employers may administer polygraph tests to current employees in connection with an ongoing investigation, subject to the conditions of section 7(d) of the Act and 801.12. EPPA rules governing Security Services are exhaustively set forth in the Rules and Regulations of the Federal Register.

Security Services employers who elect to have prospective employees polygraphed must submit a letter to each applicant advising the prospective employee of the time, date, place and purpose of the polygraph examination, plus the same 48 hour consultation with an attorney or employee representative warning contained in aforesaid ongoing investigation letter, signed by an official of the company legally authorized to bind the employer. The employer should familiarize himself/herself with pages 9070-9073, paragraph 801.14, Rules and Regulations of the Federal Register, Vol. 56, No. 42, 4 March 1991, EPPA Final Rule.

Exemption of Employers Authorized to Manufacture, distribute, or dispense controlled substances.

Section 7(f) provides an exemption from the Act's general prohibition regarding the use of polygraph tests for employers authorized to manufacture, distribute, or dispense a controlled substance listed in schedule I, II, II, or IV of section 202 of the Controlled Substances Act (21 U.S.C. 812). This exemption permits the administration of polygraph tests, subject to the conditions set forth in sections 8 and 10 of the Act and 801.21, 801.23, 801.24, 801.25, 801.26 and 801.35.

1. A prospective employee who would have direct access to the manufacture, storage, distribution, or sale of any such controlled substance; or

2. A current employee if the following conditions are met:

   a. The test is administered in connection with an ongoing investigation of criminal or other misconduct involving, or potentially involving, loss or injury to the manufacture, distribution, or dispensing of any such controlled substance by such employer; and

b. The employee had access to the person or property that is the subject of the investigation.

In each of aforementioned cases, whether for a prospective employee or an employee, the usual letter containing the previously discussed warnings and notices must be issued by the employer to the applicant or employee to be scheduled for a polygraph examination (See Appendix O). The employer should familiarize himself/herself with pages 9069-9070, paragraph 801.13 Rules and Regulations of the Federal Register, Vol. 56, No. 42, 4 March 1991, EPPA Final Rule.

Conduct of Polygraph Test Within EPPA Guidelines.

The exemptions provided under sections 7 and 8 of the EPPA for private employers do not apply unless the procedures set forth in the *Notice to Examinee* (See Appendix H) and the requirements of the forensic psychophysiologist are adhered to throughout the examination. This includes six paragraphs with nineteen sub-paragraphs. This *Notice* is inserted by this author on the reverse side of the release/permission form (Appendix H) which is presented to the applicant/employee/examinee at the commencement of the PV examination for the applicant/employee/examinee to read and sign. In addition, the *Notice to Examinee* is read to the applicant/employee/examinee in compliance with EPPA. All of the test questions are reduced to writing and presented by the forensic psychophysiologist to the applicant/employee/examinee for his/her review prior to the conduct of the testing phase of the PV examination. Page 9060 Federal Register - Final Rule states "Section 801.22(c)(1)(ii) has been modified accordingly to make clear that the questions to be asked during a test can be presented in writing and reviewed with the examinee *any time prior to the actual testing phase*." The forensic psychophysiologist is prohibited from asking test questions not presented in writing for review by the forensic psychophysiologist prior to the test. The PV examination must be at least ninety minutes long, from the greeting of the examinee by the forensic psychophysiologist to the examinee's departure from the examination room. The forensic psychophysiologist cannot conduct more than five complete PV examinations in one day and must maintain a daily log of PV examinations conducted. Some of the examinee's rights include:

(a) The examinee shall be permitted to terminate the test at any time.
(b) The examinee is not asked questions in a manner designed to degrade, or needlessly intrude on, such examinee.
(c) The examinee is not asked any questions concerning:
  (1) religious beliefs, or affiliations.
  (2) beliefs or opinions regarding racial matters.
  (3) political beliefs or affiliations.
  (4) any matter relating to sexual behavior; and
  (5) beliefs, affiliations, opinions, or lawful activities regarding unions or labor organizations; and
(d) The examiner does not conduct the test if there is sufficient written evidence by a physician that the examinee is suffering from a medical or psychological

condition or undergoing treatment that might cause abnormal responses during the actual testing phase.

Prior to the conduct of a PV examination, the employer must provide the prospective examinee with *notice* of the test and of the examinee's right to consult with an attorney or employee representative before each phase of the test. The employee must be informed in writing of the *nature and characteristics of the test and the instrument* involved, including whether the testing location contains a two-way mirror or any other device through which the test may be observed and whether any recording devices will be used in addition to the polygraph instrument. The employee must be provided with a written statement (included in the *Notice to Examinee* - Appendix H) reiterating that the examinee cannot be required to take the test as a condition of employment and that any statement made during the test may be used as evidence against the examinee. The statement also must list the legal rights and remedies available to the examinee if the test is not conducted in a manner prescribed by law. Before any adverse employment action, the employer shall:

(a) further interview the examinee on the basis of the results of the test; and
(b) provide the examinee with:
  (1) a written copy of any opinion or conclusion rendered as a result of the test, and
  (2) a copy of the test questions asked during the test along with the corresponding charted responses (polygraph charts).

Qualifications of the Forensic Psychophysiologist:

(a) Has a valid and current license granted by licensing and regulatory authorities in the State in which the test is to be conducted, if so required by the State; and
(b) Maintains a minimum of a $50,000.00 bond or an equivalent amount of professional liability coverage.

NOTE: The above EPPA qualifications fail to recognize that more than half the states in the United States have no polygraph licensing statutes and many of those that do have minimum standards. This author recommends that the employer hire a forensic psychophysiologist whose credentials can withstand the scrutiny of the judicial system's adversary proceedings in the event that the employer has to defend any adverse employment action based on the PV examination report. (See Chapter 23, Selection of a Forensic Psychophysiologist).

Requirements of the Forensic Psychophysiologist:

(a) Renders any opinion or conclusion regarding the test:
  (1) In writing and solely on the basis of an analysis of polygraph charts,
  (2) that does not contain information other than admissions, information, case facts, and interpretation of the charts relevant to the purpose and stated objectives of the test, and

(3) that does not include any recommendation concerning the employment of the examinee; and

(b) Maintains all opinions, reports, charts, written questions, lists, and other records relating to the test for a minimum period of 3 years after administration of the test.

Disclosure of Information.

Under Section 9, a person, other than the examinee, may not disclose information obtained during a PV examination (polygraph test), except as provided in this section.

Permitted Disclosures: A forensic psychophysiologist (polygraph examiner) may disclose information acquired from a PV examination (polygraph test) only to:

(a) the examinee or any other person specifically designated in writing by the examinee;
(b) the employer that requested the test; or
(c) any court, governmental agency, arbitrator, or mediator, in accordance with due process of law, pursuant to an order from a court of competent jurisdiction.

Disclosure by Employer: An employer (other than an employer described in subsection (a), (b), or (c) of section 7) for whom a polygraph test is conducted may disclose information from the test only to:
(a) a person in accordance with Permitted Disclosures; or
(b) a governmental agency, but only insofar as the disclosed information is an admission of criminal conduct.

EPPA Rules Regarding Employer's Use of Police Polygraph Test Results.

Page 9047 and 9048 of the Federal Register's Final Rule reflect that a new paragraph (b) has been added to 801.4 to make clear that employers are not responsible under EPPA for any test police authorities might decide to administer during the course of their investigation of any theft or other incident involving economic loss which the employer reported to such authorities. This new paragraph also clarifies the type of cooperation or assistance which may be given by an employer at the request of police authorities without incurring any liability under the Act. For example, allowing a test on the employer's premises during working time and similar types of cooperation would not be construed as being within the Act's prohibited conduct. The question also arose concerning practices in some local communities where employers reimburse police examiners for tests conducted on employees suspected by the employer of wrongdoing, and practices in some communities where police authorities request employer testing of employees before an investigation is initiated on a reported theft. Activities within the Act's prohibitions would include all tests in which employer participation is direct, i.e., employer administers the test at the request/direction of police authorities, or indirect, i.e., employer reimburses police authorities for the costs of tests they administer. These limitations are necessary to prevent evasion of the Act's prohibitions through such actions. Additionally, a new subsection (c) makes clear that a fairly common practice of police authorities to disclose test results to employers, particularly when the test indicates deception on the part of an employee, causes the employer to violate section 3(2) of the Act, which prohibits employers from "using, accepting, or inquiring" about the results of a lie detector test.

24 hours Waiver Reduction.

Reference legally administered *Pre-Employment Polygraph tests*, the Federal Register Page 9057 states that "Section 801.23(a)(1) formerly 801.22(c)(1)(i)(A) is accordingly modified to allow prospective employees the option of voluntarily waiving the 48-hour time period and to proceed to a test 24 hours after receipt of the required written notice. Employers would be well advised to include this 24 hours waiver in the letter of notice to the prospective employee (See Appendix O). When a prospective employee chooses that waiver option, his/her signature is affixed to the employer's copy of the letter as well as the original, thus the employer has recorded proof of the waiver agreement.

Employee's Rights Cannot Be Waived.

It should be noted that the employee's rights under the Act may not be waived, either *voluntarily* or *involuntarily* (Federal Register page 9075, 801.23 (E)(xv)), which means that although an employee may volunteer to take a polygraph test to satisfy his/her employer, the employee cannot be requested to submit or be administered a polygraph test without the employer meeting all of the EPPA requirements.

Criminal Conduct May be Disclosed by Employer.

An employer may disclose information from the polygraph test at any time to an appropriate governmental agency without the need of a court order where, and only insofar as, the information disclosed is an admission of *criminal conduct*. (Federal Register - Page 9076, 801.35 (b).

Methods of Compliance with EPPA.

The most difficult task for employers who wish to use the polygraph under EPPA rules is the establishment of an *articulable*, *observable basis* for their *reasonable suspicion* that the employee they wish to have tested meets EPPA standards. One successful method developed by this author to acquire the aforesaid *legal basis* for the *reasonable suspicion* is in the use of the Bio-Kinetic™ Interview Technique which is *not* under the jurisdiction of the EPPA.

When an employer is unable to meet the *basis* for the *reasonable suspicion* requirement but has several employees who meet the *access* requirement, the employer may then submit all of the employees who had *access* to a Bio-Kinetic™ interview, preferably in the order of the least likely suspect first and the most likely suspect last to be interviewed.

While the results may prove the order wrong, employers have historically shown good instincts in this selection process due to their knowledge and experience with their employees. This author has been employing the Bio-Kinetic™ Interview Technique since its development in 1987 with much success in developing relevant new information, previously unknown to the employer. Some of the relevant information was provided by employees not involved in the crime who were reluctant witnesses. As the information accumulates during the interviews, the identity of the perpetrator becomes more distinct, thus effecting any needed correction to the interview order. Oftentimes, the testimonial evidence becomes so compelling that it results in a confession from the developed suspect. But in the absence of a confession, the *testimonial* evidence may be sufficiently strong to serve as the *basis* for the *reasonable suspicion* to request the developed suspect to submit to a psychophysiological veracity (PV) examination using the polygraph.

The Bio-Kinetic™ Interview Technique commences with the interviewee executing a handwritten statement of his or her activities during the period that the offense presumably occurred, which is immediately followed by the interviewee listening to an audio motivational tape (Matte, 1987), while the contents of the statement (SCAN) is analyzed by the interviewer. The interviewee is then administered an Interview Theme technique (MITT) based on the psychological principles of projection (TAT), using a series of sketches within a structured psychological interview which is monitored by closed-circuit television. During the course of the Bio-Kinetic interview, the suspect's verbal and non-verbal behaviors are assessed against one hundred and seventy-six categorized behaviors denoting truthtelling and non-truthtelling styles (Matte, 1987). The Bio-Kinetic™ Interview Technique does not purport to be a method of truth verification or lie-detection, thus does not render a decision or conclusion of truth or deception, but merely uses the SCAN, MITT, and Matte Behavior Assessment to *acquire information* from reluctant interviewees. This interview technique ensemble enables the Bio-Kinetic™ interviewer to narrow a field of suspects in any type of crime to the party or parties most likely involved with a reasonable degree of success.

Polygraph and Other Techniques No Basis For Reasonable Suspicion.

Interestingly, the Federal Register (pages 9051-9052) reflects that there is no basis in the legislative history or in the case law for reaching a conclusion that reasonable inferences of involvement in incidents under investigation can be drawn from the results of PV examination (polygraph) or "pen and pencil" tests. Hence, if only two employees had access to a missing item and a basis for reasonable suspicion can only be acquired for one of the two employees and that employee subsequently produces truthful PV examination results, these PV examination results cannot be used as a basis for reasonable suspicion to administer a PV examination to the other employee. Likewise, the results of paper and pencil honesty tests or security interviews which produce no testimonial evidence cannot be used as the basis for reasonable suspicion to request that an employee submit to a PV examination. It was apparently assumed when the EPPA was written that no technological advances would be made in forensic psychophysiology, yet substantial research reported in Chapter 3 of this book reflects a general accuracy of psychophysiological veracity examinations in the upper ninety percentile and research conducted by the Applied Physics Laboratory at Johns

Hopkins University with the Department of Defense using the computerized polygraph system with APL's algorithm revealed an accuracy exceeding 98%. Clearly, the results of such PV examinations exceed the validity and reliability of any behavior analysis, especially an evaluation by a police officer articulated in the above example used to describe the criteria for reasonable suspicion.

There is a legislative effort at this time by the American Polygraph Association to effect some changes to the EPPA that would make it easier for employers to use psychophysiological veracity (PV) examinations using the polygraph. However these changes will not be forthcoming without the assistance of the business community. While the PV examination can only be used by employers in very limited circumstances, employee theft has continued to rise to an intolerable level, placing some employers in the unenviable position of having to choose between the burdensome requirements of the EPPA with its high risk of litigation and fines, or the distasteful and unfair discharge of *all* suspects without raising the issue of PV examinations, under the "termination at will" right of most employer-employee relationships, thus solving the employer's problem at the expense of innocent employees. The current EPPA rules need to be ameliorated to include educational and training requirements that will assure that only qualified forensic psychophysiologists practice under EPPA rules, and those rules be amended to permit more flexibility by the employer in the use of psychophysiological veracity examinations using the polygraph.

REFERENCES

Federal Register (1988, October 21). *Application of the Employee Polygraph Protection Act of 1988; Final Rule*. Part IV, 29 CFR Part 801. Department of Labor, Employment Standards Administration, Wage and Hour Division.

Kerschner, A. (1996, July 10). Telephone conversation with J. A. Matte.

Nagle, D. E. (1989). Questions and answers regarding the Employee Polygraph Protection Act of 1988. Seminar/Workshop, Pennsylvania Polygraph Association, Philadelphia, PA.

Matte, J. A. (1988). The Bio-Kinetic Pre-Employment Interview; The Bio-Kinetic Employee Evaluation, The Bio-Kinetic Interrogation Technique. Brochure - Bio-Kinetic™ Interview Center, Williamsville, N.Y.

Morgan, R. C. (1988, August 13-19). The Morgan Interview Theme Technique (MITT). 23rd Annual Seminar/Workshop, American Polygraph Association, Miami, Florida.

Public Law 100-347 (1988, June 27). *Employee Polygraph Protection Act of 1988*. 102 Stat. 646-653, 29 USC 2001-2009. 100th Congress. U.S. Government Printing Office.

Rubin, et al. v. Tourneau, Inc., and Jeffrey L. Gwynne and Associates, Inc., No. 92 Civ. 0078 (MBM),(1992, July 9). U. S. District Court, Southern District of New York. Federal Statute - Independent examiner's status as 'employer' - Private enforcement action >215.07 >110.07 >505.03. 7 IER Cases 993-997.

Sapir, A. (1988, August 13-19). Scientific Content Analysis (SCAN). 23rd Annual Seminar/Workshop, American Polygraph Association, Miami, Florida.

U.S. Dept. of Labor (1991, October). *Civil Money Penalty Report - Employee Polygraph Protection Act*. Form WH-525, Employment Standards Administration, Wage and Hour Division.

APPENDIX A

BACKSTER SERIES ON POLYGRAPH TECHNIQUES

UNIFORM CHART MARKINGS

by Cleve Backster

NECESSITY OF UNIFORM CHART MARKING

In order that a polygraph examiner might more accurately interpret charts after an examination is completed, or when called upon to review the charts at some subsequent date, it is extremely important that he be able to reconstruct the test conditions as exactly as possible. Certain test conditions may have been relevant in causing fluctuations or distortions in the polygraph tracing. Without adequate knowledge of these conditions some of these fluctuations might unjustly be considered as natural deception reactions. To attempt to re-establish the test conditions is difficult enough without being burdened with a lack of adequate information. A uniform chart marking system will also be of great help when an examiner with limited experience seeks additional instruction, or advice concerning his techniques, from a more experienced polygraph examiner who uses the same uniform chart marking procedure.

PERMANENCY OF CHART MARKINGS

All chart markings should be made with a free-flowing fountain pen and, where necessary to make them following a test, all changes should be initialed by the examiner. Possible criticism may be averted by avoiding the use of a pencil in marking your charts.

NEATNESS OF CHARTS

Wherever possible all questions should be first written on the question sheet and only the question number recorded on the chart. Excessive writing on moving chart paper is difficult, clutters the charts unnecessarily, and tempts the examiner to use hastily constructed questions.

SYMBOLS AND ABBREVIATIONS

In order that writing be kept to a minimum it is suggested that uniform symbols and abbreviations be used. The listings below are primarily classified by sector locations on standard 6 inch chart paper. Most of the suggested locations are based on placement nearest the recording which is most often affected by the phenomena involved (See Figure 1): (a) Sector One primarily involves a record of what is said by the examiner and marks indicating the exact time that it was said; (b) Sector Two primarily involves a record of the restricted standard answers the subject is limited to giving; (c) Sector Three primarily involves a record of adjustments of the cardio tracing, and movement or discomfort of subject that might affect the cardio tracing; (d) Sector Four primarily involves a record of adjustments of the G.S.R. tracing and noises which might have an effect on this tracing; and (e) Sector Five primarily involves a record of adjustments of the breathing tracing and unexpected phenomena distorting the breathing tracing.

The symbols and abbreviations below are also classified by purpose or function as follows: (a) question identification, (b) examiner comments, (c) behavior of subject, (d) special instructions, and (e) extraneous factors.

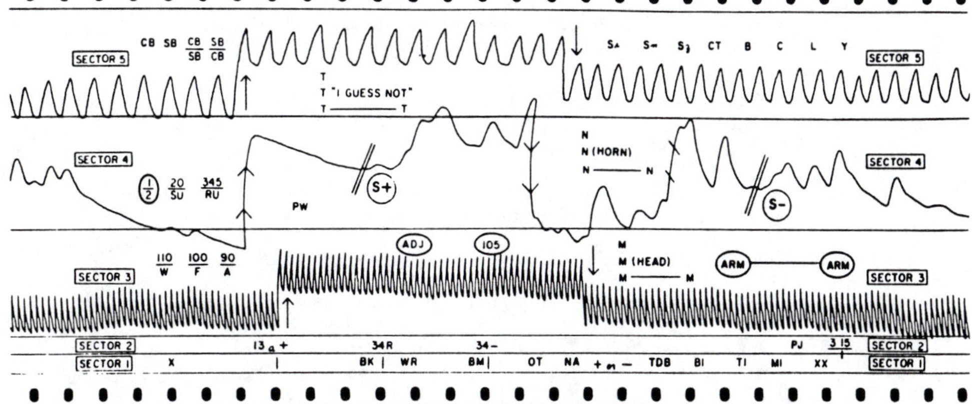

POLYGRAPH CHART

Published by C.H. STOELTING CO. 424 N. Homan Ave., Chicago 24, Illinois

APPENDIX A

SECTOR ONE

Area extends from ½ inch above bottom chart edge to ¾ inch above bottom chart edge.

QUESTION IDENTIFICATION to indicate exact location of question on chart:

I Stimulus mark placed on chart, directly below cardio recording pen, as the last word of question is spoken.

EXAMINER COMMENTS or deviations from prepared questions:

X Subject notified that questions are about to begin. This symbol also used in computing "total chart minutes".

XX Subject notified that questions are completed on that chart and told to sit quietly until instrument is turned off. This symbol also used in computing "total chart minutes".

OT "Other than you have already told me________________________________?"

BK "To the best of your knowledge________________________________?"

BM "To the best of your memory________________________________?"

WR "Will repeat" used to acknowledge subject's request for examiner to repeat a question. Also used to notify subject that examiner is about to repeat some or all of the questions in the series.

NA Subject told that question examiner alerted him for will "not be asked".

SPECIAL INSTRUCTIONS given while chart is actually in progress:

+ or − Subject reminded to answer "yes or no" only.

TDB Subject instructed to take a deep breath to check "vagus" effect.

BI Subject tactfully instructed regarding deep breaths (Breathing Instruction).

TI Subject tactfully instructed regarding talking (Talk Instruction).

MI Subject tactfully instructed regarding movement (Movement Instruction).

SECTOR TWO

Area extends from ¾ inch above bottom chart edge to 1 inch above bottom chart edge.

QUESTION IDENTIFICATION to designate by number or letter the corresponding question written on the question sheet:

34 Number or letter placed above and slightly to the left of stimulus mark.

BEHAVIOR OF SUBJECT relating to his standard verbal responses to questions asked:

+ Subject answered "yes", location of symbol identifies time of answer.

− Subject answered "no", location of symbol identifies time of answer.

R Subject asked for "repeat" of question.

EXTRANEOUS FACTORS accounting for inaccuracy or association of chart time constant with time of day:

PJ Chart drive "paper jam".

$\frac{3:15}{1}$ "Time of day" mark at specific point during chart or toward end of chart, just after air is released from cardio cuff.

APPENDIX A

SECTOR THREE

Area extends from 1 inch above bottom chart edge to 2½ inches above bottom chart edge.

INSTRUMENT ADJUSTMENT relating to cardio tracing:

110/W Indicates pressure (MM of mercury) to which wrist cuff was initially inflated.

100/F Indicates pressure (MM of mercury) to which arm cuff, placed on forearm, was initially inflated.

90/A Indicates pressure (MM of mercury) to which arm cuff was initially inflated.

(105) All subsequent references to cuff pressure during same chart.

↑ Indicates an upward adjustment of baseline of cardio tracing.

↓ Indicates a downward adjustment of baseline of cardio tracing.

(ADJ) Any adjustment of a more complex nature, such as a cuff pressure change by examiner as compared to pressure change due to movement.

BEHAVIOR OF SUBJECT involving body movement by him during examination:

M Subject moved, portion of body unspecified.

M( ) Subject moved, portion of body specified.

M —— M Prolonged movement indicated by placing first "M" when movement is noticed and second "M" when movement stopped.

EXTRANEOUS FACTORS due to blood pressure cuff discomfort:

(ARM) When it seems apparent that subject is concerned with discomfort or skin color change due to cuff pressure.

SECTOR FOUR

Area extends from 2½ inches above bottom chart edge to 4 inches above bottom chart edge.

INSTRUMENT ADJUSTMENT relating to G.S.R. unit:

∧ Indicates an upward adjustment of baseline of G.S.R. tracing.

∨ Indicates a downward adjustment of baseline of G.S.R. tracing.

(½) G.S.R. "amplifier sensitivity" estimated at ½ of total range, where control is not calibrated.

20/SU G.S.R. "amplifier sensitivity" set at 20 sensitivity units (SU) on scale, where control is calibrated.

345/RU G.S.R. "position on chart" control set at 345 resistance units (RU), where control is calibrated.

(S+) G.S.R. amplifier sensitivity increased.

(S-) G.S.R. amplifier sensitivity decreased.

/ / Long double slash lines drawn across G.S.R. tracing, with tops of marks leaning to right, to emphasize location of G.S.R. sensitivity change.

APPENDIX A

EXTRANEOUS FACTORS affecting G.S.R. activity:

N Noise during chart, source or nature unspecified.

N(   ) Noise during chart, source or nature specified.

N——N Prolonged noise indicated by placing first "N" when noise was perceived and second "N" when noise stopped.

PW Poorly worded or awkwardly executed question.

∮ Short widely separated marks drawn across G.S.R. tracing, with tops of marks leaning to left, to indicate that G.S.R. activity started prior to question or arrival of pertinent portion of question.

SECTOR FIVE

Area extends from 4 inches above bottom chart edge to ½ inch below top chart edge.

INSTRUMENT ADJUSTMENT to indicate initial and subsequent adjustments of breathing unit tracing and location of breathing tube or tubes:

↑ Indicates an upward adjustment of baseline of breathing tracing.

↓ Indicates a downward adjustment of baseline of breathing tracing.

CB "Chest breathing" from single breathing tube fastened around chest.

SB "Stomach breathing" from single breathing tube fastened around stomach.

CB/SB Top tracing is "chest breathing" and bottom tracing is "stomach breathing", where two tubes are used simultaneously.

SB/CB Top tracing is "stomach breathing" and bottom tracing is "chest breathing", where two tubes are used simultaneously.

BEHAVIOR OF SUBJECT involving identifiable breathing distortions:

T Subject talked, short in duration.

T"   " Subject's comment.

T——T Prolonged talk by subject.

Si Subject sighed audible sigh.

Sn Subject sniffed.

Sz Subject sneezed.

CT Subject cleared throat.

B Subject burped.

C Subject coughed.

L Subject laughed or chuckled.

Y Subject yawned.

INTERIM CHART IDENTIFICATION

In order that charts will be properly identified it is suggested that the items of information below, at a minimum, be placed in the upper left hand corner of the chart immediately after its completion.

Subject's full name or code designation.

Chart number.

ADDITIONAL CHART IDENTIFICATION

Use of many of the items below is necessary to fulfill organizational requirements. This additional data is also recorded in extreme upper left hand corner of the over-all chart.

File number.

Place "L" after the sequence number of the last chart.

Date of Examination.

Examiner's name or code designation.

Instrument type or serial number, or short designation.

Interrogation room number, if more than one is in use.

Case name or client's name.

Subject's signature in ink or right thumb print on each chart, especially if case is controversial.

MATTÉ POLYGRAPH SERVICE, INC.

SCIENTIFIC TRUTH VERIFICATION - LIE DETECTION

43 Brookside Drive • Williamsville, New York 14221-6915
(716) 634-6645 • FAX (716) 634-7204

FULL MEMBER:
American Polygraph Assoc.
Empire State Polygraph Society
Florida Polygraph Assoc.
Assoc. Former OSI Special Agents
C.I.D. Agents Assoc.
HONORARY LIFE MEMBER:
Pennsylvania Polygraph Assoc.

FULL MEMBER:
Society For Psychophysiological Research
American Psychological Society
REGIONAL DIRECTOR:
Research-Instrumentation Committee
American Polygraph Association

MODEL PV EXAMINATION REPORT FOR SPECIFIC TEST

APPENDIX B

PRIVILEGED AND CONFIDENTIAL

John H. Doe, Attorney at Law   Date
111 Mason Blvd.., Suite 222
Buffalo, N. Y. 14202

Dear Mr. Doe:

At your request, SSAN: was administered a psychophysiological veracity (PV) examination using the polygraph to determine whether or not ....

Before being administered a PV examination ________________________________read and signed a statement assuring all concerned that the examination was being taken voluntarily.

A urine specimen was obtained from ____________________________immediately (prior to) (after) the psychophysiological veracity examination. This specimen was transmitted to the____________________ for forensic drug assay - urine, which revealed .... (no presence of any drug).

Upon completion of Test(s) A, B, and C above, ____________________________ was transported to CPF MetPath Laboratories, Williamsville, New York, where a urine specimen was obtained from _____________________________________for forensic drug assay - urine, which revealed .... (no presence of any drug).

The Polygraph Quadri-Track Zone Comparison Technique employing exclusive earlier-in-life control questions and a numerical scoring system of chart analysis as recommended in the Validation Study on the Polygraph Quadri-Track Zone Comparison Technique[1] was utilized throughout the examination, using equipment which indicated and recorded on a moving chart relative changes in blood pressure, rate and strength of pulse beat, electrodermal response, thoracic and abdominal breathing patterns.

During the pre-test interview, ...(relate any information provided by the examinee deemed relevant to the issue(s) being examined).

Three principal targets were covered in this examination which were administered as Test A, Test B, and Test C, in order of their combined information adequacy, target intensity, and distinctness of issue. A minimum of two polygraph charts were conducted in each test in accordance with American Polygraph Association standards.

TEST A. The following relevant questions were among those asked during Test A:

Preparatory/Sacrifice Relevant Question:

39.

Relevant Questions Quantified and Used for Determination:

33.

35.

answered in the affirmative to Preparatory Question 39 and in the (negative/affirmative) to Relevant Questions 33 and 35 in above test A.

TEST B. The following relevant questions were among those asked during Test B:

Preparatory/Sacrifice Relevant Question:

39.

Relevant Questions Quantified and Used for Determination:

33.

35.

answered in the affirmative to Preparatory Question 39 and in the (negative/affirmative) to Relevant Questions 33 and 35 in above Test B.

TEST C. The following relevant questions were among those asked during Test C:

Preparatory/Sacrifice Relevant Question:

39.

Relevant Questions Quantified and Used for Determination:

33.

35.

answered in the affirmative to Preparatory Question 39 and in the (negative/affirmative) to Relevant Questions 33 and 35 in above Test C.

Conclusions:

(Model Opinion for the Truthful)

In the opinion of the undersigned, ______________________________'s polygrams in Test A above showed no strong or consistent unresolved responses to aforementioned relevant questions. Careful analysis and quantification of ____________________________'s polygrams revealed a total score of plus 27 for 3 charts. A minimum score of plus 9 for 3 charts is required before a definite truthful conclusion can be rendered. It is therefore the opinion of the undersigned that ________________________________was Truthful when he gave the above indicated answers to aforementioned relevant questions 33 and 35 in Test A above.

According to the Predictive Table for Estimating Error Rates,[1] in 83.5 percent of the time, a Truthful subject will score this value (+27 for 3 charts) or lower than this value (weaker score). Based on the Statistical Table of Probability that a Deceptive subject will score this value (+27) or higher, the Potential for Error is 0.0 percent.

(Model Opinion for Deception)

In the opinion of the undersigned, ______________________________ 's polygrams in Test A above showed strong and consistent unresolved responses to aforementioned relevant questions. Careful analysis and quantification of ____________________________'s polygrams revealed a total score of minus 18 for 3 charts. A minimum score of minus 15 for 3 charts is required before a definite conclusion of Deception can be rendered. It is therefore the opinion of the undersigned that ____________________________ was Deceptive when he gave the above indicated answers to aforementioned relevant questions 33 and 35 in Test A above.

According to the Predictive Table for Estimating Error Rates,[1] in 86.7 percent of the time, a Deceptive subject will score this value (-l8 for 3 charts) or lower than this value (stronger score). Based on the Statistical Table of Probability that a Truthful subject will score this value (-l8) or lower, the Potential for Error is 0.0 percent.

(Model for Inconclusives)

In the opinion of the undersigned, ______________________________'s polygrams in above test ( ) showed inconsistent unresolved responses to the above-listed relevant questions. Careful analysis and quantification of ___________________________'s polygrams revealed a total score of minus 3 for 4 charts. A minimum score of plus l2 for 4 charts is required before a definite truthful conclusion can be rendered. A minimum score of minus 20 for 4 charts is required before a definite conclusion of deception can be rendered. The results of______________________'s psychophysiological veracity (polygraph) examination are therefore Inconclusive, which translated means that neither a finding of truthfulness or deception could be established from ______________________________'s polygrams in above test ( ).

Please be advised that Indefinite conclusions are not uncommon in the polygraph community. A numerical scoring system in chart analysis as recommended in the Validation Study on the Quadri-Track Zone Comparison Technique[1] was employed which contains a conclusion table requiring a high truthful or deceptive score be attained before a definite conclusion can be rendered. This Inconclusive area is designed to prevent false positive or negative conclusions, so that conclusive results will enjoy exceptionally high validity and reliability.

Sincerely,

James Allan Matte, Ph.D.
Forensic Psychophysiologist
President

Enclosures:

1. Graph of Predictive Table
2. Copy of Release Form signed by

1. Validation Study on the Polygraph Quadri-Track Zone Comparison Technique, James Allan Matte, Ph.D., and Ronald M. Reuss, Ed.D., June 1989, published in *Research Abstract*, LD 01452, Vol. 1502, 1989, University Microfilm International, and *Polygraph*, Vol. 18, Nr. 4, 1989, Journal of the American Polygraph Association.

MATTÉ POLYGRAPH SERVICE, INC.

SCIENTIFIC TRUTH VERIFICATION - LIE DETECTION

43 Brookside Drive • Williamsville, New York 14221
(716) 634-6645 • FAX (716) 634-7204

APPENDIX C

PRE-EMPLOYMENT POLYGRAPH REPORT

Date ____________________

Company ______________________________ Location ____________________

Name of Examinee ____

Position Sought ______________________________ SSAN ____________________

Present Address ____

Driver's License (when applicable) State: __________ Class: __________ Nr. ____________________

REMARKS:

____

____

____

____

EDUCATION:

School Grade Finished: 1 2 3 4 5 6 7 8 9 10 11 12 GED College 1 2 3 4 5 6 7 8

Degree ____________________ Other Schooling or Training ____________________

____

Now Attending ____

MILITARY SERVICE:

Status ______________ Active Duty A AF N MC CG NG From ________ To________ Rank ______________

Active Reserves A AF N MC CG NG From ________ To________ Rank ______________

Discharge ____________________ Court-Martials Y N ______________________________

REMARKS:

____

____

____

(A Dishonorable, Undesirable or General Discharge is not an absolute bar to employment and that other factors will affect a final decision to hire or not to hire).

CONFIDENTIAL

EMPLOYMENT HISTORY

Company	City	State	Position	Salary	From	To	Reason for Leaving
1.							
2.							
3.							

1. Quit 2. Fired 3. Lay Off 4. Better Job 5. More Money 6. Argument with Company 7. Transferred 8. Moved Residence 9. Join Military Service 10. School 11. Marriage 12. Pregnancy 13. Poor Working Conditions 14. Personality Conflict with Supervisor 15. Business Closed 16. Harassment by Boss 17. No Chance for Advancement 18. Just Didn't Like Job 19. Wanted to Travel 20. Spend More Time with Family 21. Didn't Want to Work Anymore 22. Retired 23. Other, See Remarks

DELINQUENT DEBTS (Debts which are behind more than 60 days): **YES** _________ **NO** _________

COMPANY OWED	TOTAL AMOUNT OF DEBT	MONTHLY PAYMENTS	NUMBER OF MONTHS PAST DUE

POLYGRAPH EXAMINATION

Relevant Questions:

1. Did you tell the complete truth on your job application?
2. Have you deliberately withheld information from your job application?
3. Have you ever been fired from a job?
4. Are you seeking a permanent position with this company?
5. Have you ever committed an undetected crime?
6. Have you ever been convicted of a crime?
7. Are you currently using marihuana?

7a. Are you currently using any other narcotics illegally?
7b. Have you ever sold marihuana or other narcotics illegally?

8. Did you ever steal merchandise from any of your employers?
9. Did you ever steal monies from any of your employers?
10. Have you ever used a system to cheat any of your employers?
11. Have you told me the truth regarding your financial status?

0 12. Have you ever had your driver's license suspended or revoked?
0 13. Have you ever had any traffic citations in the past five (5) years?
0 14. Are you withholding any information regarding vehicle accidents in the past five (5) years?
0 15. Are you seeking a job with this company for any reason other than legitimate employment?

16. ____________________

17. ____________________

100. Have you deliberately lied to any of these questions?

ADMISSIONS - COMMENTS: ____________________

REACTIONS: ____________________

Verbal to ____________________ **Date** ____________

LEGEND: The letter "B" in front of any question indicates that the question was preceded by the words: "Besides what you have already told me. . ."
The letter "O" in front of any questions indicates that it is optional and used only when appropriate.

CONFIDENTIAL

MATTÉ POLYGRAPH SERVICE, INC.

SCIENTIFIC TRUTH VERIFICATION - LIE DETECTION

43 Brookside Drive • Williamsville, New York 14221
(716) 634-6645 • FAX (716) 634-7204

APPENDIX D

PERIODIC POLYGRAPH EXAMINATION REPORT

Date ______________________

Company ______________________ Location ______________________

Name of Examinee ______________________

Address ______________________

SSAN ______________________ Present Position ______________________

Length of Employment with Company ______________ Date last Polygraphed with this Company ______________

Present Physical Condition: ☐ Good ☐ Fair ☐ Poor Date of Last Physical Examination ______________

REMARKS:

____

____

POLYGRAPH EXAMINATION

☐ Amnesty Program – Prefix Question: ______________________

Relevant Questions:

22. Do you know of anyone who has been stealing merchandise from this company?
23. Did you steal any merchandise from this company?
24. Do you know of anyone who has been stealing money from this company?
25. Did you steal any money from this company?
26. Have you ever helped anyone to steal from this company?
27. Have you ever used any method to cheat or steal from this company?

O28. Have you ever falsified company records for your own personal gain?
O29. Have you ever made an improper discount for yourself or anyone else?
O30. Have you ever intentionally damaged or defaced company property?
31. Did you ever use marijuana or other narcotics illegally while employed by this company?
31a. Did you ever use marijuana or other narcotics illegally on company premises?
31b. Did you ever sell narcotics illegally on company premises?
32. Have you ever taken monies from a register for your own personal gain?
33. Have you ever intentionally failed to record all or part of a sale?
34. Has the drinking of alcoholic beverages interferred with your work?
35. Have you ever given away any merchandise?
O36. Have you ever received money from the sale of stolen merchandise?
O37. Have you ever made a time clock violation?
38. Have you failed to report any thefts or shortages known to you?
O39. Have you been involved in the issuance of a false refund?
O40. Have you been involved in any phony voids?
O41. Have you ever falsified expenses for your own personal gain?
42. Have you ever entered into collusion with anyone to steal from this company?

43. ______________________

44. ______________________

45. ______________________

46. ______________________

47. ______________________

O97. Is your written statement the complete truth?
O98. Did you intentionally falsify any portion of your statement?
O99. Have you deliberately withheld any information from your statement?
100. Have you deliberately lied to any of these questions?

CONFIDENTIAL

Additional Relevant Questions for Super Markets:

48. **Have you ever gone through a register and not been charged the proper amounts?**
49. **Have you cashed in coupons and kept the money?**

O 50. **Have you asked anyone to record on the wrong department key?**
O 51. **Has anyone asked you to record on the wrong department key?**
O 52. **Have you ever falsified any credit invoices?**

Additional Relevant Questions for Truck Drivers:

53. **Have you received any traffic citations while driving a company vehicle?**
54. **Have you been involved in any company vehicle accidents not known to this company?**
55. **Have you ever driven a company vehicle while intoxicated?**
56. **Have you ever driven a company vehicle while under the influence of drugs or narcotics?**
57. **Have you ever unloaded merchandise anywhere other than its legitimate destination?**

☐ QUINQUE-TRACK EXPLORATORY TEST:

Relevant Questions:

E45J ____________________

E45K ____________________

E45L ____________________

E45M ____________________

032 ____________________

PRE-TEST/POST-TEST ADMISSIONS: Statement Obtained Y N

____

____

____

____

____

____

____

REACTIONS: ____________________

____

COMMENTS: ____________________

____

Verbal to ____________________ **Date** ____________________

LEGEND: **The letter "B" in front of any question indicates that the question was preceded by the words: "Besides what you have already told me . . ."**
The letter "O" in front of any question indicates that it is optional and used only when appropriate.
Quinque-Zone Exploratory Test Questions are preceded by the letter "E" as indicated above.

CONFIDENTIAL

APPENDIX E

Place ______________________________ Date ____________________

I, ______________________________ do hereby voluntarily agree, without duress, coercion, threats, promises of reward or immunity, to submit to an interview and verification procedure utilizing the Polygraph (Lie Detector). I have had the nature of this interview and verification procedure explained to my complete satisfaction, and do hereby consent to the placing of the necessary apparatus upon my person. I further consent to the use of electronic audio and visual recording devices, and I voluntarily request and authorize MATTE POLYGRAPH SERVICE, INC., to now proceed with the actual examination. I do hereby authorize that MATTE POLYGRAPH SERVICE, INC., its officers, employees, and/or agents to disclose both orally and in writing the examination results and opinions to officers, employees, and/or agents

of ____

I understand that this is being used as an interview procedure for my attorney and to be made use of by my attorney and with my consent. I understand that this is in a nature of privilege communication with my attorney and this may not be used against me without my voluntary and knowledgeable waiver of the attorney-client privilege. I am fully aware that the expert opinion may be that I have not been truthful. Notwithstanding such, in consideration of and as an inducement for MATTE POLYGRAPH SERVICE, INC., to give me this polygraph examination, I for myself and my successors, assigns, heirs, executors, and administrators, hereby release, absolve, remise, covenant, promise agree to save harmless, forever discharge, and hold free from all harm, liability, or damage to me, MATTE POLYGRAPH SERVICE, INC., and its officers, employees, and agents individually, collectively, and personally. In addition, I knowingly remise, release, waive, and forever discharge each and all the above-named from any and all suits, actions, or causes of actions at law, claims, demands, or liabilities either in law or in equity including but not limited to false arrest, false imprisonment, libel, slander, or invasion of all my rights which I, my successors, assigns, heirs, executors, or administrators have now or may ever have resulting directly, indirectly, or remotely from my taking said examination, possible liabilities or damages flowing from the operation of all electronic audio, visual and polygraph recording devices, the rendered oral and written opinions and statements, and/or all future actions taken by any and/or all of the above based upon the examination. As a further consideration and inducement to have MATTE POLYGRAPH SERVICE, INC., conduct the examination, I represent that not only am I in good mental and physical condition but that I know of no mental or physical ailment which might be impaired by the examination.

______________________ ______________________________ __________

(Witness) (Signature of Examinee) TIME

This examination was concluded at ______________ on the above date. I completely re-affirm in its entirety my above agreement. I also certify that during the entire time I was well-treated, submitted myself freely to the examination knowing that I could stop any time I so desired by merely saying I wished to stop or that I wished to consult an attorney or any other person. I remained of my own free will knowing that I could leave this room at any time I so desired, and that there were no threats, promises, or any harm whatsoever done to me during the entire period I have been here, either in connection with the examination or my again signing of this agreement and release form.

______________________________ ______________________________

(Witness) (Signature of Examinee)

APPENDIX F

AGREEMENT AND STIPULATION

(INSERT LEGAL CAPTION)

It is hereby agreed and stipulated between the undersigned parties and attorneys in this action as follows:

1. That the said defendant/plaintiff voluntarily agrees to submit to a psychophysiological veracity (PV) examination using the polygraph (truth verification - lie detector) to be administered by James Allan Matte, Ph.D., a forensic psychophysiologist employed by Matte Polygraph Service, Inc.

2. This PV examination will be administered on ____________199__ at Matte Polygraph Service, Inc., 43 Brookside Drive, Williamsville, New York 14221.

3. The purpose of this PV examination is to: ___________________________________

____

____

4. The forensic psychophysiologist (FP) will be provided complete access to all parties' reports, records, transcripts, work sheets, audio and/or video tapes, and statements (written or verbal reduced to writing) which are related to the investigation or matter which is the subject of this PV examination. The attorneys for all parties in this matter agree to fully cooperate and provide any and all information requested by the forensic psychophysiologist regarding this matter.

5. Selection of the PV examination technique(s) and polygraph instrument that will be used, including the scope and actual wording of the relevant test questions, the place and conditions under which the PV examination will be administered, as well as all other aspects of the examination will be at the sole discretion of the forensic psychophysiologist.

6. The examinee (defendant/plaintiff) agrees to fully cooperate and answer truthfully all questions posed by the forensic psychophysiologist concerning the matter for which he is submitting to a PV examination. Should the forensic psychophysiologist believe that the examinee (defendant/plaintiff) is not fully cooperating, the PV examination can be terminated at the forensic psychophysiologist's discretion, and testimony by the forensic psychophysiologist can be given in court regarding the reason for such termination.

7. The examinee (defendant/plaintiff) agrees to sign the forensic psychophysiologist's standard permission/release form immediately prior to commencement of the PV examination. The examinee and his/her attorney understand that his/her refusal to sign aforesaid permission/release form will be cause for cessation or abortion of the PV examination.

8. The examinee (defendant/plaintiff) agrees to return for additional testing at a subsequent time(s) and date(s) if requested by the forensic psychophysiologist, who may testify to any refusal for such additional testing.

9. Should the examinee (defendant/plaintiff) confess his/her guilt or make any admissions against self-interest, or changes any previously given statements or testimony, all such statements, whether oral and/or written, will be admissible at any trial or hearing without objection by the defense or any of the attorneys representing any of the parties.

10. The results and/or opinions resulting from the PV examination which may encompass several tests will be incorporated into a written report which will be furnished to all of the attorneys representing the parties in this matter within five working days after completion of the final PV examination. Such written report will be introduced into evidence without objection by any of the attorneys representing any of the parties, at the time the forensic psychophysiologist gives testimony regarding his findings at any trial or hearing involving this matter. The polygraph chart recordings containing the examinee's physiological data acquired during the conduct of the PV examination(s) plus related worksheets containing all of the test questions and the numerical scores derived from the analysis and evaluation of the aforesaid polygraph chart recordings may be introduced and admitted into evidence.

11. Should the forensic psychophysiologist be unavailable to testify by reason of death, disability, illness, or any other just reason, none of the attorneys representing any of the parties will object to the introduction of the forensic psychophysiologist's PV examination report and statement or curriculum vitae containing the forensic psychophysiologist's qualifications/expertise.

12. The forensic psychophysiologist is acknowledged by all parties and attorneys in this matter to be an expert in forensic psychophysiology which includes the psychological structure of the PV examination, the methodology used in the administration of the PV examination, and in the analysis, evaluation and numerical scoring of the physiological data recorded on the polygraph charts. The attorney offering the forensic psychophysiologist as a witness will be permitted to fully develop his expertise and offer into evidence his expert opinion regarding the truthfulness or deceptiveness of the examinee's answers to the relevant test questions reflected in the forensic psychophysiologist's written report introduced at trial or hearing. The attorneys for all parties in this matter expressly waive any and all objections of such testimony as to the competency, weight, relevancy, remoteness, or admissibility of such testimony based upon public, legal, judicial, social policy, or due process of law.

13. Opposing attorney(s) shall have the right to cross-examine (except at Grand Jury proceedings) the forensic psychophysiologist as to his qualifications, the methodology used in the conduct of the PV examination, the wording and sequence in which the test questions were asked the examinee (defendant/plaintiff), the physiological data analysis and evaluation method used to reach a conclusion as to the examinee's veracity to the relevant test questions, the accuracy of the results and the possibility of error.

14. Upon reasonable belief that the examinee (defendant/plaintiff) may have taken some drug, alcohol, or medicine other than prescribed previous to the execution of this Agreement and Stipulation, the forensic psychophysiologist may request that blood, urine, and/or saliva samples be given by the examinee as soon as possible at the CPF MetPath Laboratories, Williamsville, New York or other laboratory or hospital selected by the forensic psychophysiologist, for analysis. Should the results of the laboratory analysis reveal positive results regarding the presence of drug(s), alcohol, and/or a medicine other than prescribed previous to the signing of this Agreement and Stipulation, both the laboratory technician or doctor and the forensic psychophysiologist will be allowed to testify. If the examinee refuses to provide aforesaid samples, the forensic psychophysiologist will be allowed to testify and corroborate such refusal.

15. The examinee (defendant/plaintiff) and his/her attorney(s) do completely exonerate and forever release the forensic psychophysiologist, his employer, and its directors, officers, and employees together with the attorneys representing all parties in this matter, from any and all liability in regard to the PV examination, the forensic psychophysiologist's opinions, the dissemination of the examination results and/or opinions, and the testimony of the forensic psychophysiologist.

16. It is understood by all parties that upon signing this Agreement and Stipulation, it is not only binding upon them individually but upon all further parties and their successors in interest, and such other counsel as the State of New York or the examinee (defendant/plaintiff) may retain or employ for any trial or hearing regarding this matter.

The parties hereby acknowledge that they have read and understood all of the above terms and conditions and by signing below they knowingly and voluntarily stipulate and agree that such terms and conditions shall become final, irrevocable and binding upon them.

Dated:______________________________ ______________________________
(Defendant/Plaintiff)

Dated______________________________ ______________________________
(Attorney for Defendant)

State of New York }
ss
County of Erie }

On this _____day of_____________, 19___ before me personally appeared ______________________________, the Defendant/Plaintiff in the above captioned action, and ________________________________, his/her attorney, to me personally known and known to me to be the same persons described in and who executed the within instrument, and they duly acknowledged to me that they executed the same.

____
(notary public)

APPENDIX G

Place ______________________________ Date ______________

I, ______________________, voluntarily — without threats, duress, coercion, force, promises of immunity or reward, agree and stipulate to take a polygraph (truth-verification) examination for the mutual benefit of myself, MATTE POLYGRAPH SERVICE, INC., and

____

I fully realize that: I am not required to take this examination, I may remain silent the entire time I am here, anything I say can be used against me in any court of law, I may first consult with an attorney or anyone I wish to before either signing this form or taking the examination, I may have an attorney present, if I cannot afford an attorney and desire one an attorney will be appointed for me prior to any questioning, and I have the opportunity to exercise all these rights at any time I wish to during the entire time I am here. Nevertheless, I consent to the use of electronic audio and visual recording devices at the discretion of MATTE POLYGRAPH SERVICE, INC. and I voluntarily request and authorize MATTE POLYGRAPH SERVICE, INC., to now proceed with the actual examination.

I do hereby authorize MATTE POLYGRAPH SERVICE, INC., its officers, employees, and/or agents to disclose both orally and in writing the examination results and opinions to officers, employees and/or agents of ______________

____

I am fully aware that the expert opinion may be that I have not been truthful. Notwithstanding such, in consideration of and as an inducement for MATTE POLYGRAPH SERVICE, INC., to give me this polygraph examination, I — for myself and my successors, assigns, heirs, executors, and administrators, hereby release, absolve, remise, covenant, promise, agree to save harmless, forever discharge, and hold free from all harm, liability, or damage to me MATTE POLYGRAPH SERVICE, INC., and its officers, employees, and agents individually, collectively, and personally. In addition, I knowingly remise, release waive, and forever discharge each and all the above-named from any and all suits, actions, or causes of actions at law, claims, demands or liabilities either in law or in equity including but not limited to false arrest, false imprisonment, libel, slander, or invasion of all my rights which I, my successors, assigns, heirs, executors, or administrators have not or may ever have resulting directly, indirectly, or remotely from my taking said examination, possible liabilities or damages flowing from the operation of all electronic audio, visual and polygraph recording devices, the rendered oral and written opinions and statements, and/or all future actions taken by and/or all of the above based upon the examination.

As a further consideration and inducement to have MATTE POLYGRAPH SERVICE, INC., conduct the examination, I represent that not only am I in good mental and physical condition, but that I know of no mental or physical ailment which might be impaired by the examination.

I have been advised that pursuant to section 6, paragraph a.4. of Erie County Local Law number 4, 1984, I have the right to request that an audio record of this interview and examination be made and held for a period of 45 days during which period the recording will be kept confidential and not exposed to public display and available only to the proper authorities upon request. I (DO) (DO NOT) request that such audio record be made.

Important notice: This agreement and release form is a legally binding contract. If not completely understood do not sign but seek competent advice, such as that rendered by an attorney.

______________________ ______________________ ________

WITNESSED SEAL (Signature of person to be examined) TIME

This examination was concluded at ______________ on the above date. I completely re-affirm in its entirety my above agreement. In addition, I knowingly and intelligently continued to waive all my rights, including those listed in the second paragraph above, and I willingly made all the statements that I did make.

I also certify that during the entire time I was well-treated, submitted myself freely to the examination knowing that I could stop any time I so desired by merely saying I wished to stop or that I wished to consult an attorney or any other person. I remained of my own free will knowing that I could leave this room at any time I so desired, and that there were no threats, promises, or any harm whatsoever done to me during the entire period I have been here, either in connection with the examination or my again signing of this agreement and release form.

______________________ ______________________

WITNESSED SEAL ((Signature of person examined)

APPENDIX H

The author has viewed with great interest the progress of the New York State Legislature regarding licensing of polygraphists. The following model polygraph licensing act embodies the author's suggestions for legislation in the State of New York.

MODEL POLYGRAPH LICENSING ACT

Section 1-A INTRODUCTION.

This article applies to the polygraph profession.

Section 1-B DEFINITIONS.

As used in this article:

1. "Polygraphy" is defined as the art and science of truth verification and lie detection through the use of polygraph technique and instrumentation.
2. "Polygraph Instrument" signifies any instrument or any device of any type used or allegedly used to test or question individuals for the purpose of determining truthfulness, regardless of the name or design of the instrument or device used, provided the instrument or device meets the minimum standards set by Section 4 of this article.
3. "Secretary" shall mean the Secretary of State of New York.
4. "Department" shall mean the Department of State.

Section 1-C USE OF TITLE "POLYGRAPHIST."

1. Only a person licensed under this article shall be authorized to use the title "polygraphist."
2. It is unlawful for any person to administer polygraph examinations or any other detection of deception examinations, or attempt to hold himself out as a polygraphist or detection of deception examiner, without a license issued by the Department under this article.

Section 1-D STATE BOARD OF POLYGRAPHY.

1. The Secretary of State shall appoint not less than five polygraphists to compose a Board created for the purpose of assisting the Department. The Board shall consist of a committee on licensing and one or more committees on professional practice and conduct, as may be appointed by the Board chairman.
2. The Board, or its committee on licensing, shall investigate all applicants for licensing to assure they meet all requirements set forth in this bill.
3. The Board, or its committee or committees on professional conduct, shall conduct disciplinary proceedings pursuant to the provisions of Section 8 and Section 11 of this article and shall assist in other professional conduct matters as prescribed by the Department.
4. Members of the Board shall be appointed by the Secretary for three year terms, except that the terms of those first appointed shall be arranged so that as nearly as possible an equal number shall terminate annually. A vacancy occurring during a term shall be filled by an appointment by the Secretary for the unexpired term.
5. Each member of the Board shall receive a certificate of appointment, shall before beginning his term of office file a constitutional oath of

office with the Secretary of State and shall be reimbursed for his necessary expenses. No member shall serve beyond the age of seventy. Any member may be removed from a Board by the Secretary for misconduct, incapacity, or neglect of duty.

6. The Board shall elect from its members a chairman and vice-chairman annually, shall meet upon call of the chairman or the Secretary, and may adopt by-laws consistent with this article and approved by the Secretary. A quorum for the transaction of business by the Board shall be not less than three members.
7. An executive secretary to the Board shall be appointed by the Secretary. Such executive secretary shall not be a member of the Board, shall hold office at the pleasure of and shall have the powers, duties, and annual salary prescribed by the Secretary.

Section 2 REQUIREMENTS FOR A PROFESSIONAL LICENSE.

A. To qualify for a license as a polygraphist, an applicant shall fulfill the following requirements:

1. *Application:* File with the Department of State a written application on the form provided by such department containing such information and documentation, including fingerprints, as the Secretary may require.
2. Education
   (a) Has graduated from a polygraph school accredited by the American Polygraph Association consisting of a minimum of two hundred hours, and has an academic degree at least at the baccalaureate level from a college or university accredited by the Regional Accreditation Board or has an academic degree at the associate level in criminology or psychology from a college or university accredited by the Regional Accreditation Board.
   (b) or may be issued a one-year temporary license if the following conditions are met:
      (1) Applicant has successfully completed the academic portion of an accredited polygraph school within the past eighteen months but has not yet graduated from the polygraph school due to non-completion of the post-academic field project study necessary for school certification and graduation.
      (2) Applicant must submit letter from polygraph school indicating applicant is actively pursuing school certification and the applicant's polygraph examinations are monitored by the school or a polygraphist fully licensed by this state.
      (3) Meets all other requirements as set forth in subdivision A of Section 2 of this article.
3. *Age*: be at least twenty-one years of age.
4. *Citizenship*: be a citizen of the United States.
5. *Character*: be of good moral character as determined by the Department. Applicant should further show that he has not been convicted of any crime that is a felony in the State of New York or convicted anywhere of any misdemeanor involving moral turpitude or of a felony, or has not been released or discharged under other than honorable conditions from any of the Armed Services of the United States.

6. *Fees*: a filing fee of twenty-five dollars shall be required along with an initial licensing fee of one hundred dollars.

B. On recommendation of the Board, the Secretary may waive the requirements of paragraph two of subdivision A of Section 2 of this article in the cases of applicants who have practiced in the polygraph profession since January 1, 1975, using a polygraph instrument as defined in Section 4 of this article; have completed at least three hundred polygraph examinations; and have successfully passed a written examination administered by a representative of the Board.

C. *Reciprocity*: An applicant who is a polygraphist licensed under the laws of another State or Territory of the United States may be issued a license without examination by the Department, in its discretion, upon payment of a fee of $150.00 and the production of satisfactory proof that:
1. The applicant is at least twenty-one years of age.
2. The applicant is a citizen of the United States.
3. The applicant is of good moral character.
4. The requirements for the licensing of polygraphists in such particular State or Territory of the United States were, at the date of licensing, substantially equivalent to the requirements of this licensing act.
5. The applicant had lawfully engaged in the administration of polygraph examinations under the laws of such State or Territory for at least two (2) years prior to his application for license hereunder.
6. The other State or Territory under which the applicant is licensed grants similar reciprocity to license holders of this State.

Section 3 ISSUANCE OF LICENSE.

When the application shall have been received and such further inquiry and investigation made as the Secretary of State shall deem proper, and when the Secretary of State shall be satisfied therefrom of the good character, competency and integrity of such applicant, he shall cause to be issued and delivered to such applicant a certificate of license to practice as a polygraphist.

The license as a polygraphist granted pursuant to this article shall be valid for a period of two years but shall be revocable at all times by the Department of State for cause shown.

The license certificate shall be in a form to be prescribed by the Secretary of State.

Section 4 INSTRUMENT.

No polygraph instrument shall be used by a polygraphist unless it is approved by the Department and it is capable of measuring and permanently recording simultaneously at least the following three physiological phenomena: cardiovascular reactions, breathing, and galvanic skin response.

Section 5 GUARANTEEING RIGHTS.

The conduct of polygraph examinations and the use of its results will be in compliance with the provisions of this section.

A. The examinee will be advised that he has the right to terminate the polygraph examination at any time, and this advice will be incorporated into the consent form for his signature.

B. The examinee will be advised that he has the right to refuse to answer any question in the polygraph examination, and this advice will be incorporated into the consent form for his signature.

C. The results of a preemployment polygraph examination will not be divulged by either the polygraphist or polygraph firm nor by the client for whom the polygraph examination was conducted to any person or firm other than that person or firm indicated on the permission form signed by the examinee.

D. The results of a polygraph examination conducted at the request of a defense attorney on behalf of his client will fall under the protection of privilege communication between attorney-client-polygraphist, and as such will not be released by the polygraphist or polygraph firm to any person or entity other than the examinee and/or his defense attorney without the express written authorization of the examinee.

Section 6 STANDARDS OF PRACTICE.

A. Each polygraph examination will be conducted privately, in a room that provides for confidentiality in a professional setting that does not offend or injure the dignity of the examinee. No third person will be present either during the pretest interview or during the actual examination unless that person is assisting the polygraphist in that interview, with the understanding that the examinee may terminate the interview at any time.

B. The polygraphist will review with the examinee each test question prior to the actual polygraph examination, and the examinee will be afforded an opportunity to qualify any of his answers prior to the polygraph test.

C. A polygraphist shall not initiate an accusatory interview or interrogation for the purpose of eliciting an admission or confession against interest from the examinee until after he has conducted at least two polygraph charts regarding the issue(s) submitted for determination. No polygraphist shall render a conclusive verbal or written decision or report based on chart analysis without having administered two or more polygraph charts.

D. All polygraph charts will be signed at the termination of the examination by the examinee above the top tracing in the middle of the chart.

E. The time will be entered at the end of each polygraph chart. The beginning of each polygraph chart will reflect the breathing area recorded, and the sensitivity setting of the galvanic skin response and cardiograph components. All artifacts will be noted on each chart at the exact location it occurred on the polygraph chart.

F. No polygraphist will administer more than twelve (12) polygraph examinations in any one day.

G. All polygraph charts and related polygraph examination papers/documents will be retained for a period of three years and will be subject for review by the Licensing Board upon request.

H. Each polygraph instrument in use shall be calibrated at least once each month and a record reflecting the date of calibration, notation of any malfunction, and signature of calibrator will be maintained for at least three years.

Section 7 **APPLICATION**

The provisions of this article shall not apply to officers and employees of the federal government who operate a polygraph as part of their regular employment.

Section 8 **ENFORCEMENT OF ARTICLE: INVESTIGATIONS.**

1. The Secretary of State shall have the power to enforce the provisions of this article and, upon complaint of any person or on his own initiative, to investigate any violation thereof or to investigate the business, business practices, and business methods of any person applying for or holding a license as a polygraphist, if in the opinion of the Secretary of State such investigation is warranted. Each such applicant of licensee shall be obliged, on request of the Secretary of State, to supply such information deemed necessary or required concerning his business practices or business methods. Failure to comply with a lawful request of the Secretary shall be grounds for denying an application for a license, or for revoking, suspending, or failing to renew a license issued under this article.
2. For the purpose of enforcing the provisions of this article, and in making investigations relating to any violation thereof, and for the purpose of investigating the character, competence and integrity of the applicants or licensees hereunder, and for the purpose of investigating the business, business practices, and business methods of any applicant or licensee, the Department shall have the power to subpoena and bring before the Board any person in this State and require the production of any books, records, or papers he deems relevant to the inquiry and to administer an oath to and take testimony of any person or cause his deposition to be taken, except that any applicant or licensee shall not be entitled to fees and/or mileage. A subpoena issued under this section shall be regulated by the civil practice law and rules. Any person, duly subpoenaed, who fails to obey such subpoena without reasonable cause or without such cause refuses to be examined or to answer any legal or pertinent question as to the character or qualification of such applicant or licensee or such applicant's licensee's business, business practices, and business methods, or such violations, shall be guilty of a misdemeanor. The testimony of witnesses in any investigative proceeding shall be under oath, which the Secretary of State or one of his deputies, or a subordinate of the Department of State designated by the Secretary of State, may administer, and willful false swearing in any such proceeding shall be perjury.

Section 9 **RENEWAL OF LICENSE.**

A license granted under the provisions of this article will be renewed by the Department of State upon application therefor by the holder thereof, in such form as the Department may prescribe and payment of a fee of one hundred dollars. The application shall be filed six weeks before the expiration date of the license unless the application is accompanied by a late filing fee of fifteen dollars. In no event will renewal be granted more than six months after the date of expiration of a license. No person shall carry on any business subject to this article during any period which may exist between the date of expiration of a license and the renewal thereof.

Section 10 **REVOCATION OF LICENSE.**

Every license certificate shall be surrendered to the Department of State within seventy-two hours after notice in writing to the holder that such license has been revoked. Failure to comply with this provision is a misdemeanor.

Section 11 **HEARINGS, NOTICE, DETERMINATIONS, REVIEW.**

1. The Department of State shall have the power to revoke or suspend any license, or in lieu thereof to impose a fine not exceeding one thousand dollars payable to the Department of State, or reprimand any licensee or deny an application for a license or renewal thereof upon proof:
   (a) that the applicant or licensee has violated any of the provisions of this article or the rules and regulations promulgated hereunder;
   (b) that the applicant or licensee has practiced fraud, deceit, or misrepresentation;
   (c) that the applicant or licensee has made a material misstatement in the application for a renewal of his license;
   (d) that the applicant or licensee has demonstrated incompetence or untrustworthiness in his actions.
2. The Department of State shall, before denying an application for a license or before revoking or suspending any license, excepting a temporary suspension as provided in subdivision five hereof, or imposing any fine or reprimand, at least fifteen days prior to the date set for the hearing and upon due notice to the complainant or objector, notify in writing the applicant for or holder of such license of any change made and shall afford said applicant or licensee an opportunity to be heard in person by counsel in reference thereto. Such written notice may be served by delivery of same personally to the applicant or licensee, or by mailing same by registered mail to the last known business address of such applicant or licensee.
3. The hearing on such charges shall be at such time and place as the Department of State shall prescribe and shall be conducted by the State Board at the Secretary of State's request, who shall have the power to subpoena and bring before the Board any person in this state, and administer an oath to and take testimony of any person or cause his deposition to be taken. A subpoena issued under this section shall be regulated by the civil practice law and rules. Such officer or person in the Department of State designated to take such testimony shall not be bound

by common law or statutory rules of evidence or by technical or formal rules of procedure.

4. In the event that the Department shall deny the application for, or revoke or suspend any such license, or impose any fine or reprimand, its determination shall be in writing and officially signed. The original or such determination, when so signed, shall be filed in the office of the Department and copies thereof shall be mailed to the applicant or licensee and to the complainant within two days after the filing thereof as herein prescribed.
5. The Department, acting by the State Board to conduct the hearing pursuant to subdivision 3 above or by such other officer or person in the Department as the Secretary of State may designate, shall have the power to suspend the license of any licensee who has been convicted in this state or any other state or territory of a felony or of any misdemeanor for a period not exceeding thirty days pending a hearing and a determination of charges made against him. If such hearing is adjourned at the request of the licensee, or by reason of any act or omission by him or on his behalf, such suspension may be continued for the additional period of such adjournment.
6. The action of the Department of State — in granting or refusing to grant or to renew a license under this article or in revoking or suspending or refusing to revoke or suspend such a license or imposing any fine or reprimand — shall be subject to review by a proceeding instituted under Article 78 of the civil practice law and rules at the instance of the applicant for such license, the holder of a license that is revoked, suspended, fined, or reprimanded, or the person aggrieved.

Section 12 VIOLATIONS

1. Any person who willfully violates any of the provisions of this article shall be guilty of a misdemeanor punishable by a fine of not more than one thousand dollars, or imprisonment for more than one year or both.
2. Attorney General to prosecute. Criminal actions for violations of this article shall be prosecuted by the Attorney General, or his deputy, in the name of the people of the state, and in any such prosecution the Attorney General, or his deputy, shall exercise all the powers and perform all the duties the district attorney would otherwise be authorized to exercise or to perform therein. The Attorney General shall, upon a conviction for a violation of any provisions of this article, and within ten days thereafter, make and file with the Department of State a detailed report showing the date of such conviction, the name of the person convicted, and the exact nature of the charge.
3. Penalty recoverable by person aggrieved. In case the offender shall have received any sum of money as commission, compensation, or profit by or in consequence of his violation of any provision of this article, he shall also be liable to a penalty of not less than the amount of the sum of money received by him as such commission, compensation, or profit and not more than four times the sum so received by him, as may be determined by the court, which penalty may be used for and recovered by any person aggrieved and for his use and benefit, in any court of competent jurisdiction.

Section 13 **DISPOSITION OF FEES AND OTHER REVENUE.**

All fees and other monies derived from the operation of this article shall on the fifth day of each month be paid by the Department of State into the state treasury.

This act shall take effect on the first day of September next succeeding the date on which it shall have become a law.

Place____Date______________________________

I,___________________________________do hereby voluntarily agree, without duress, coercion, threats, promises of reward or immunity, to submit to a psychophysiological veracity examination using the polygraph (Lie Detector). I have had the nature of this interview and verification procedure explained to my complete satisfaction, and do hereby consent to the placing of the necessary apparatus upon my person., I further consent to the use of electronic audio and visual recording devices, and I voluntarily authorize Matte Polygraph Service, Inc., its officers, employees, and/or agents to disclose both orally and in writing the examination results and opinions to officers, employees, and/or agents of _____________________________________

____

I am fully aware that the expert opinion may be that I have not been truthful. Notwithstanding such, in consideration of and as an inducement for Matte Polygraph Service, Inc., to give me this psychophysiological veracity (polygraph) examination, I, for myself and my successors, assigns, heirs, executors, and administrators, hereby release, absolve, remise, covenant, promise, agree to save harmless, forever discharge, and hold free from all harm, liability, or damage to me, Matte Polygraph Service, Inc,, and its officers, employees, and agents individually, collectively, and personally. In addition, I knowingly remise, release, waive and forever discharge each and all the above-named from any and all suits, actions, or causes of actions at law, claims, demands, or liabilities either in law or in equity including but not limited to false arrest, false imprisonment, libel, slander, or invasion of all my rights which I, my successors, assigns, heirs, executors, or administrators have now or may ever have resulting directly, indirectly, or remotely from my taking said examination, possible liabilities or damages flowing from the operation of all electronic audio and visual recording devices, the rendered oral and written opinions and statements, and/or all future actions taken by any and/or all of the above based upon the examination. As a further consideration and inducement to have Matte Polygraph Service, Inc., conduct the examination, I represent that not only am I in good mental and physical condition but that I know of no mental of physical ailment which might be impaired by the examination.

________________________________ ____
(Witness) (Signature of Examinee (Time)

This examination was concluded at___________on the above date. I completely re-affirm in its entirety my above agreement. I also certify that during the entire time I was well-treated, submitted myself freely to the examination knowing that I could stop any time I so desired by merely saying I wished to stop or that I wished to consult an attorney or any other person. I remained of my own free will knowing that I could leave this room at any time I so desired, and that there were no threats, promises, or any harm whatsoever done to me during the entire period I have been here, either in connection with the examination or my again signing of this agreement and release form.

________________________________ ____
(Witness) (Signature of Examinee (Time)

APPENDIX J

AGREEMENT

It is hereby agreed on this _____th day of ______________19____, that the ______________ ______________________________will pay Matte Polygraph Service, Inc., $__________for case preparation which precedes the psychophysiological veracity (PV) examination(s) using the polygraph and $__________for each specific single-issue PV examination conducted during the period from ____ __________to______________at the offices of Matte Polygraph Service, Inc., Williamsville, New York. Additional issues are $____________each. This fee includes a written report but does not include copies of related polygraph charts, which when required will cost an additional fee of $__________per chart. It is further agreed that ________ ________________________________will pay Matte Polygraph Service, Inc., the sum of $___________for any No Shows, Cancellations made after 1:00PM on the day preceding the day of the examination, or Postponements due to the examinee's medical/health condition or other reasons deemed by the Forensic Psychophysiologist (FP) to be adverse to a proper PV examination which are made after 4:30PM on the day preceding the date of scheduled examination. ______________________________________agrees to abide and comply with all of the requirements of the Employee Polygraph Protection Act of 1988 (EPPA), that it is solely responsible for its implementation, and will not hold Matte Polygraph Service, Inc., and/or its Forensic Psychophysiologist James Allan Matte responsible and/or liable for any fines, suits or other judgments levied against ________________________________ and further agrees to hold harmless and indemnify Matte Polygraph Service, Inc., against any of aforementioned legal actions resulting from the conduct or scheduling of PV examination(s) on behalf of ____. It is understood and agreed that if Matte Polygraph Service, Inc., and/or its FP James Allan Matte are required to appear at any hearing or court in conjunction with any PV examination conducted for the __________ ____________________and/or as a result of any action taken against any employee examined or scheduled for a PV examination by Matte Polygraph Service, Inc., the Matte Polygraph Service, Inc., will then be compensated by the _________________________ at the rate of $___________for each half day or part thereof spent by Matte Polygraph Service, Inc., James Allan Matte, or its representative at such hearing and/or court, or time spent addressing any official complaint generated by the ___________________________'s use of the results of any PV examination(s) conducted by Matte Polygraph Service, Inc., on behalf of _________________________________. It is further understood that PV examination(s) conducted by Matte Polygraph Service, Inc., at a location other than its office in Williamsville, New York will cost an additional fee of $________if within Erie or Niagara County, and $__________plus expenses if outside of aforementioned counties. It is further understood and agreed that all of the above fees are subject to an __% New York State Sales Tax which will be added to above fees to be paid to Matte Polygraph Service, Inc. It is agreed that Matte Polygraph Service Inc., will charge a service charge of 1.5 percent per month on all balances remaining unpaid 60 days from the date of invoice. It is further agreed that in the event payment is not made when due and any action is brought by Matte Polygraph Service, Inc., to effect collection thereof, the ______________________________agrees to pay Matte Polygraph Service, Inc., all reasonable attorney's fees and costs incurred in such action, and any other costs incurred by virtue of such non-payment including but not limited to fees of any collection agencies. It is understood that this is the complete agreement and that there are no promises, verbal understandings or agreements of any kind other than specified herein.

______________________________	______________________________
Matte Polygraph Service, Inc.	(Name of Company or Corporation)
______________________________	______________________________
(Signature)	(Signature)

APPENDIX K

Place____Date______________________

I, ______________________________do hereby voluntarily agree, without duress, coercion, threats, promises of reward or immunity, to submit to an interview and verification procedure utilizing the Polygraph (Lie Detector). I have had the nature of this interview and verification procedure explained to my complete satisfaction, and do hereby consent to the placing of the necessary apparatus upon my person. I further consent to the use of electronic audio and visual recording devices, and I voluntarily request and authorize MATTE POLYGRAPH SERVICE, INC., to now proceed with the actual examination. I do hereby authorize that MATTE POLYGRAPH SERVICE, INC, its officers, employees, and/or agents to disclose both orally and in writing the examination results and opinions to officers, employees, and/or agents of__________

____

I am fully aware that the expert opinion may be that I have not been truthful. Notwithstanding such, in consideration of and as an inducement for MATTE POLYGRAPH SERVICE, INC., to give me this polygraph examination, I, for myself and my successors, assigns, heirs, executors, and administrators, hereby release, absolve, remise, covenant, promise, agree to save harmless, forever discharge, and hold free from all harm, liability, or damage to me MATTE POLYGRAPH SERVICE, INC., and its officers, employees, and agents individually, collectively, and personally. In addition, I knowingly remise, release, waive and forever discharge each and all the above-named from any and all suits, actions, or causes of actions at law, claims, demands, or liabilities either in law or in equity including but not limited to false arrest, false imprisonment, libel, slander, or invasion of all my rights which I, my successors, assigns, heirs, executirs, or administrators have now or may ever have resulting directly, indirectly, or remotely from my taking said examination, possible liabilities or damages flowing from the operation of all electronic audio and visual recording devices, the rendered oral and written opinions and statements, and/or all future actions taken by any and/or all of the above based upon the examination. As a further consideration and inducement to have MATTE POLYGRAPH SERVICE, INC., conduct the examination, I represent that not only am I in good mental and physical condition but that I know of no mental or physical ailment which might be impaired by the examination.

____________________ ______________________________

(Witness) (Signature of Examinee) TIME

This examination was concluded at__________on the above date. I completely re-affirm in its entirety my above agreement. I also certify that during the entire time I was well-treated, submitted myself freely to the examination knowing that I could stop any time I so desired by merely saying I wished to stop or that I wished to consult an attorney or any other person. I remained of my own free will knowing that I could leave this room at any time I so desired, and that there were no threats, promises, or any harm whatsoever done to me during the entire period I have been here, either in connection with the examination or my again signing of this agreement and release form.

____________________ ______________________________

(Witness) (Signature of Examinee)

I hereby authorize MATTE POLYGRAPH SERVICE, INC., and its polygraphist________________

________________________who reviewed the results of this polygraph examination with me to disclose and discuss the results of this polygraph examination to________________

____

____________________ ______________________________

(Witness) (Signature of Examinee)

APPENDIX L

Place____Date____________________

I,___________________________________voluntarily, without threats, duress, coercion, force, promises of immunity or reward, agree and stipulate to take a polygraph (truth-verification) examination utilizing an instrument which records continuously, permanently and simultaneously changes in cardiovascular, respiratory and electrodermal patterns, for the mutual benefit of myself, MATTE POLYGRAPH SERVICE, INC., and-

____.

I fully realize that: I am not required to take this examination. I may remain silent the entire time I am here. Anything I say may be used against me in any court of law. I may first consult with an attorney or anyone I wish to before either signing this form or taking the examination, and I may have an attorney present.

I do hereby authorize MATTE POLYGRAPH SERVICE, INC., its officers, employees and/or agents to disclose both orally and in writing any information that I volunteer, the examination results and opinions to officers, employees and/or agents of____

I am fully aware that the expert opinion may be that I have not been truthful. Notwithstanding such, ion consideration of and as an inducement for MATTE POLYGRAPH SERVICE, INC., to give me this polygraph examination, I, for myself and my successors, assigns, heirs, executors, and administrators, hereby release, absolve, remise, covenant, promise, agree to save harmless, forever discharge, and hold free from all harm, liability, or damage to me MATTE POLYGRAPH SERVICE, INC., and its officers, employees, and agents individually, collectively, and personally. In addition, I knowingly remise, release, waive, and forever discharge each and all the above-named from any and all suits, actions, or causes of actions at law, claims demands or liabilities either in law or in equity including but not limited to false arrest, false imprisonment, libel, slander, or invasion of all my rights which I, my successors, assigns, heirs, executors, or administrators have not or may ever have resulting directly, indirectly, or remotely from my taking said examination, possible liabilities or damages flowing from the operation of all electronic audio, visual and polygraph recording devices, the rendered oral and written opinions and statements, and/or all future actions taken by and/or all of the above based upon the examination.

As a further consideration and inducement for MATTE POLYGRAPH SERVICE, INC., to give me this polygraph examination, I agree that in the event I do commence any suits, actions or make claims of any sort against MATTE POLYGRAH SERVICE INC., and its officers, employees, and agents individually, collectively and personally, and such suits, actions or claims are found to be without merit, I agree that I shall indemnify MATTE POLYGRAPH SERVICE, INC., and its officers, employees, and agents for any loss, damage, and/or inconvenience suffered as a consequence, including but not limited to lost income, attorneys fees and legal costs of defending any such suits, actions or claims.

Pursuant to Section 8(b) 2(e) of the Employee Polygraph Protection Act to conduct the examination, I represent that not only am I in good mental and physical condition, but that I know of no mental or physical ailment which might be impaired by the examination.

I have been advised that pursuant to section 6, paragraph a.4 of Erie County Local Law Number 4, 1984, I have the right to request that an audio record of this interview and examination be made and held for a period of 45 days during which period the recording will be kept confidential and not exposed to public display and available only to the proper authorities upon request. I (DO) (DO NOT) request that such audio record be made.

I have carefully read and understand the above material and I am fully aware of my legal rights and remedies available to me in accordance with Public Law 100-347, Employee Polygraph Protection Act of 1988. I realize that nothing in this release is meant to supersede these rights as explained in the following Notice promulgated by the Department of Labor as Appendix A to Regulations 29 CFR 801.22:

____________________________________ __________________

(Signature of Examinee) (Date)

NATURE AND CHARACTERISTICS OF THE POLYGRAPH TEST

The polygraph examination you will be administered today will include the use of a fully electronic polygraph instrument which will record continuously, permanently and simultaneously on a moving chart changes n cardiovascular, respiratory and electrodermal patterns. Prior to the use of aforementioned instrument, a pre-test interview will be conducted with you wherein you will first listen to a recording made by Dr. Matte who will explain to you in more detail the physiology involved, the procedure used, and how the results are obtained. You will also be re-advised of your rights under the Employee Polygraph Protection Act of 1988. You will also be explained that all of the test questions will be reviewed with you and presented to you in writing before the actual administration of the polygraph test, and that no other questions will be asked on the test except those questions that will have been reviewed with you; in other words there are no surprise questions on the test. On the test itself you will be restricted out of necessity to just a yes or no answer, but during the review of these same questions prior to the test, you have every opportunity to qualify our answers and explain anything you wish. A minimum of two separate polygraph charts, each containing the same questions, will be conducted on each test, to establish consistency hence reliability which is required by the National standards and Erie County Law. The results of each test will be determined solely by the physiological tracings on your polygraph charts. Thank you for your cooperation.

____________________ (Date)   ____________________________________ (Signature of Examinee Acknowledgment)

NOTICE TO EXAMINEE

Section 8(b) of the Employee Polygraph Protection Act, and Department of Labor regulation (29 CFR 801.22) require that you be given the following information before taking a polygraph examination.

1. (a) The polygraph examination area (does) (does not) contain a two-way mirror, a camera, or other devices through which you may be observed.

(b) Another device, such as those used in conversation or recording, (will) (will not) be used during the examination.

(c) Both you and the employer have the right, with the other's knowledge, to record electronically the entire examination.

2. (a) You have the right to terminate the test at any time.

(b) You have the right, and will be given the opportunity, to review all questions to be asked during the test.

(c) You may not be asked questions in a manner which degrades, or needlessly intrudes.

(d) You may not be asked any questions concerning: Religious beliefs or opinions; beliefs regarding racial matters; political beliefs or affiliations; matters relating to sexual behavior; beliefs, affiliations, opinions, or lawful activities regarding unions or labor organizations.

(e) The test may not be conducted if there is sufficient written evidence by a physician that you are suffering from a medical or psychological condition or undergoing treatment that might cause abnormal responses during the examination.

3. (a) The test is not and cannot be required as a condition of employment.

(b) The employer may not discharged, dismiss, discipline, deny employment or promotion, or otherwise discriminate against you based on the analysis of a polygraph test, or based on your refusal to take such a test without additional evidence which would support such action.

(c) (1) In connection with an ongoing investigation, the additional evidence required for an employer to take adverse action against you, including termination, may be (A) evidence that you have access to the property that is the subject of the investigation, together with (B) the evidence supporting the employer's reasonable suspicion that you were involved in the incident or activity under investigation.

(2) Any statement made by you before or during the test may serve as additional supporting evidence for an adverse employment action, as described in 3(b) above, and any admission of criminal conduct by you may be transmitted to an appropriate government law enforcement agency.

4. (a) Information acquired from a polygraph test may be disclosed by the examiner or by the employer only:

(1) To you or any other person specifically designated in writing by you to receive such information;

(2) To the employer that requested the test;

(3) To a court, governmental agency, arbitrator, or mediator that obtains a court order;

(4) To a U. S. Department of Labor official when specifically designated in writing by you to receive such information.

(b) Information acquired from a polygraph test may be disclosed by the employer to an appropriate governmental agency without a court order where, and only insofar as, the information disclosed is an admission of criminal conduct.

5. If any of your rights or protections under the law are violated, you have the right to file a complaint with the Wage and Hour Division of the U.S. Department of Labor, or to take action in court against the employer. Employers who violate this law are liable to the affected examinee, who may recover such legal or equitable relief as may be appropriate, including employment, reinstatement, and promotion, payment of lost wages and benefits and reasonable costs, including attorney's fees. The Secretary of Labor may also bring action to restrain violations of the Act, or may assess civil money penalties against the employer

6. Your rights under the act may not be waived, either voluntarily or involuntarily, by contract or otherwise, except as part of a written settlement to a pending action or complaint under the Act, and agreed to and signed by the parties.

I acknowledge that I have received a copy of the above notice, and that it has been read to me.

________________ (Witnessed)   ______________________________ (Signature of Examinee)   ________________ (Time) (Date).

APPENDIX M

Employee Polygraph Protection Act
Civil Money Penalty Report

U.S. Department of Labor
Employment Standards Administration
Wage and Hour Division

Name of Employer

Location

Region	SIC Code	Total Employees	Case No.	DO NOT GIVE THIS FORM TO EMPLOYERS

Violations:

The following amounts are to be computed per employee/per violation under Sections I and II:

First Investigation	2,000
Second Investigation	5,000
Subsequent Investigations (or in any investigation where future compliance is not assured)	10,000

Assessments

		Number of Employees	Total CMPs
I. Improper Lie Detector Test			
II. Improper Polygraph Test			
A. No exemption	☐		
B. Exemption conditions not satisfied			
1) Ongoing investigation	☐		
a) No specific incident	☐		
b) No access	☐		
c) No reasonable suspicion	☐		
d) No written statement	☐		
i Was not properly signed	☐		
ii Was not complete	☐		
iii Was not timely	☐		
2) Controlled substances			
a) Prospective employee without direct access	☐		
b) Current employee without access or no ongoing investigation	☐		
3) Security services			
a) Primary business test not met	☐		
b) Not hired to protect covered facilities or assets	☐		
c) Not a prospective employee	☐		
III. Adverse Employment Action (Amounts to be computed per violation/per employee)			
A. Discharge or denial of employment	10,000		
B. Other discriminatory action with loss of pay or benefits	5,000		
C. Other discriminatory action without loss of pay or benefits	1,500		
D. Threaten adverse action	1,500		
E. Discriminated against employee for exercising his /her rights (Sec. 3(4))	10,000		
		SUBTOTAL	

Form WH-525
Rev. Oct. 1991

APPENDIX M

EPPA - Civil Money Penalty Report (continued)

IV. Failure to meet one or more of the exemption restrictions listed in Section 8 of EPPA results in the computation of the following CMP amounts per employee.

First investigation	1,000		
Second investigation	3,000		
Subsequent investigations	5,000		

V. Recordkeeping (charged per investigation)

First investigation	1,000		
Second investigation	2,000		
Subsequent investigations	3,000		

VI. Other Violations

A. Recurring failure to post*	100/500		
B. Interfering with an investigation*	5,000		
C. Suggesting, requiring, requesting....(801.4(a))	1,000		
D. Inquiring into and/or using test results....(801.4(b))	1,000		
E. Improper disclosure of polygraph test information	5,000		

* Not Per Employee

GRAND TOTALS: No. of EE's ________
Total Amount ________

INVESTIGATOR (signature) Date (mo., day, yr.)

APPENDIX N

USE EMPLOYER'S LETTERHEAD
MODEL LETTER
from
EMPLOYER TO EMPLOYEE
To be Polygraphed

TO: Name and Address
of EMPLOYEE

Date:______________

You are hereby requested to submit to a psychophysiological veracity (PV) examination using the polygraph on (DATE) at (TIME) with Dr. James A. Matte, Matte Polygraph Service, Inc., 43 Brookside Drive, Williamsville, N. Y. 14221, (716) 634-6645. Please be advised that you have forty-eight hours, excluding weekend days and holidays, in which to consult with an attorney or employee representative before the scheduled examination. You also have the right to consult with legal counsel or an employee representative before each phase of the PV (polygraph) examination. However, your attorney or employee representative may be excluded from the room where the examination is administered during the actual testing phase.

This test is administered in connection with an ongoing investigation involving *(Describe with detail the economic loss or injury to Employer's business).*

You had access to the (Property, Money, Merchandise, in detail) that is the subject of this investigation because *(Describe with detail the Employee's access).*

We have reasonable suspicion of your involvement in the above-described incident, based on the following: *(Describe with detail the basis for reasonable suspicion).*

Signed:_______________________________
(Must be signed by any person, other than Polygraphist, who is legally authorized to bind Employer).

____
(Signed by Employee at Time he/she receives this letter)

____
(Time & Date of Receipt of this Letter by Employee).
(FAX executed copy to Polygraphist (716) 634-7204

NOTICE: Matte Polygraph Service, Inc., and James Allan Matte are not responsible for adequacy of the information contained in this letter. The completed letter should be reviewed and approved by the lawyer representing the employer and/or an official of the Wage & Hour Division, U.S. Dept. of Labor prior to the issuance of letter to the employee. (The above NOTICE is only to the Employer. It is not to be included in the letter to the employee by the employer).

APPENDIX O

USE EMPLOYER'S LETTERHEAD

MODEL LETTER
from
EMPLOYER TO APPLICANT
To be Polygraphed

TO: Name and Address
of APPLICANT

Date:________________

You are herewith being offered a job at this company contingent upon your satisfactorily meeting all of the job requisites and standards based on your verified completed job application and employer interview. You are hereby requested to submit to a pre-employment polygraph examination on___________199_ at ______hours with Dr. James Allan Matte, Matte Polygraph Service, Inc., 43 Brookside Drive, Williamsville, N.Y. 14221, (716) 634-6645. Please be advised that you have forty-eight hours, excluding weekend days and holidays, in which to consult with an attorney or an employee representative before the scheduled examination. You also have the right to consult with legal counsel or an employee representative before each phase of the polygraph examination. However, your attorney or employee representative may be excluded from the room where the examination is administered during the actual testing phase. You may at your sole option give written consent to the administration of the polygraph test within 48 hours but no earlier than 24 hours after receipt of this notice.

(I DO) (DO NOT) WAIVE THE 48 HOURS REQUIREMENT___________________
(Circle & Initial) (Signature of Applicant)

____
(Signed by Job Applicant)

____
(Must be signed by any person other than polygraphist who is legally authorized to bind employer)

____
(Time and Date of Receipt of this Letter by Applicant)

(FAX executed copy to polygraphist)
at (716) 634-7204

APPENDIX P

AMERICAN POLYGRAPH ASSOCIATION (APA) ACCREDITED POLYGRAPH SCHOOLS
As of January 16, 1996

ACADEMY FOR SCIENTIFIC INVESTIGATIVE TRAINING
1704 Locust Street, 2nd Floor
Philadelphia, PA 19103
Director: Nathan J. Gordon
(215) 732-3349

AMERICAN INSTITUTE OF POLYGRAPH
25000 Ford Road, Suite 1-A
Dearborn Heights, MI 48127-3106
Director: Lynn P. Marcy
(313) 274-3810

ARGENBRIGHT INTERNATIONAL INSTITUTE OF POLYGRAPH
4854 Old National Highway, Suite 210
Atlanta, GA 30337-6222
Director: Von Jennings
(404) 663-3552 or (800) 305-9559

ARIZONA SCHOOL OF POLYGRAPH SCIENCE
3118 W. Thomas Road, Suite 716
Phoenix, AZ 85017-5308

Director: Thomas R. Ezell
(602) 272-8123

BACKSTER SCHOOL OF LIE DETECTION
861 Sixth Avenue, Suite 403
San Diego, CA 92101-6379
Director: Cleve Backster
(619) 233-6669

CANADIAN POLICE COLLEGE POLYGRAPH TRAINING SCHOOL
P. O. Box (CP) 8900
Ottawa, ON, Canada K1G 3J2
Director: John W. Kaster
(613) 998-0889

DoD POLYGRAPH INSTITUTE
(ATZN-DPI-030)
Building 3195
Fort McClellan, AL 36205-5114
Director: Michael H. Capps
(205) 848-3803

INTERNATIONAL ACADEMY OF POLYGRAPH
1885 W. Commercial Blvd., Suite 125
Fort Lauderdale, FL 33309-3066
Director: Charles G. Michaels
(305) 771-6900

MARYLAND INSTITUTE OF CRIMINAL JUSTICE
8424 Veterans Highway, Suite 3
Millersville, MD 21108-0458
Director: Billy H. Thompson
(410) 987-6665

TEXAS DEPARTMENT OF PUBLIC SAFETY
LAW ENFORCEMENT POLYGRAPH SCHOOL
P. O. Box 4087
Austin, TX 78773-0001
Director: Lt. Gordon W. Moore
(512) 483-5912

VIRGINIA SCHOOL OF POLYGRAPH
7909 Brookfield Road
Norfolk, VA 23518-3279
Director: Billy A. Franklin
(804) 583-1578

WESTERN OREGON STATE COLLEGE SCHOOL OF POLYGRAPH
Division of Continuing Education
Monmouth, OR 97361
Director: Stan Abrams, Ph.D.
(503) 838-8483

APPENDIX Q

PV EXAMINATION DOCUMENTS REQUIRED FOR INDEPENDENT REVIEW

1. Written report from forensic psychophysiologist (FP) who conducted the psychophysiological veracity (PV) examination, which should describe the type/name of polygraph technique used in instant PV examination.

2. Continuous, actual size, polygraph charts containing the physiological data collected during the instant PV examination, including all sensitivity and other chart markings, to include all polygraph charts on all tests conducted, any Acquaintance chart, Stimulation Test chart, Silent Answer Test chart, and also any chart or test conducted but not used for the forensic psychophysiologist's conclusions. (Charts should contain examinee's signature).

3. A copy of the forensic psychophysiologist's worksheet which reflects the individual scores of each Spot quantified for each tracing (Pneumo, GSR/GSG/Cardio, other channels) and the final tally of the scores, plus the scores threshold or cut-off used to reach conclusion and determination made from aforesaid scores.

4. A copy of the forensic psychophysiologist's worksheet reflecting the background and other information provided by the examinee during the pre-test interview.

5. Type and model of polygraph instrument used in instant PV examination.

6. Type and model of any motion/movement detection sensor used in instant PV examination.

7. A complete list of all test questions used in each test, including all types of control questions.

8. The order in which the test questions were reviewed with the examinee and the order in which the test questions were asked during each test.

9. Any instructions, review and/or introduction of a question to the examinee between the conduct of any of the PV tests (charts).

10. A copy of any video and/or audio recording of the PV examination.

11. (Optional) Any written statement executed by the examinee during any portion of the PV examination including Pre-test, Actual test, Post-test.

GLOSSARY OF TERMS

Acetylcholine (ACh): A chemical neurotransmitter substance released by some nerve endings.

Active Reabsorption: A biologically adaptive mechanism which keeps the skin from becoming overly moist and returns the sweat gland duct to its normal, empty state.

Activity Monitor: Also known as a Movement or Activity *Sensor,* an electronic device which fastens to the rear leg or the front legs of a polygraph chair, depending on the manufacturer of the device.

Adrenal Glands: Hormone producing glands located superior to the kidneys, each consisting of the medulla and cortex areas

Adrenalin: Trademark name for epinephrine. A hormone produced by the adrenal medulla that stimulates the sympathetic division of the autonomic nervous system (ANS).

Adrenal Medulla: The inner part of the adrenal gland which produces adrenaline.

Adrenergic Fibers: Nerve fibers whose terminals release norepinephrine and epinephrine upon stimulation.

Affect: In psychology, the emotional reactions associated with an experience.

Afferent: Carrying impulses toward a center, i.e. a sensory nerve carries a message toward the brain. Opposite of efferent.

Afferent Neuron: Also known as sensory neuron. A neuron that transmits messages from sensory receptors to the spinal cord and brain.

Affidavit: A written or printed declaration or statement of facts, made voluntarily that is confirmed by the person's oath or affirmation.

Agonist: A muscle whose contraction opposes the action of another muscle, its antagonist, which at the same time relaxes.

Agoraphobia: Fear of open, crowded places.

Alarm Reaction: The first stage of the general adaptation syndrome, which is triggered by the impact of a stressor and characterized by heightened sympathetic activity.

Alternating current (AC): Electrons that flow alternately in both directions.

Alveolus: (Pulmonary) One of the terminal saccules of an aveolar duct where gases are exchanged in respiration.

Amplitude: Height of response from baseline. The extreme range of a variable quantity.

Amygdala: A small oval-shaped structure located at the end of the hippocampus and imbedded in the underside of the cerebral hemispheres, the amygdala is the emotional seat of the human body.

Anabolism: The constructive phase of metabolism by which a cell takes from the blood the substance required for repair and growth, building it into a cytoplasm, thus converting a non-living material into the living cytoplasm of the cell.

Analog Studies: Laboratory studies that use mock crimes that attempt to simulate field conditions involving actual crimes.

Anatomy: The science of the structure of organisms, i.e. organs of the human body.

Anticlimax Dampening Concept: Cleve Backster's theory that a person's fears, anxieties, and apprehensions are channeled toward the situation which holds the greatest immediate threat to his/her self-preservation or general well-being. In PV examinations this can occur to an extent where concern over the more intense relevant question may completely dampen response to the lesser relevant question and/or cause partial or complete dampening of control question reactions with the guilty subject which is an anticlimax to the guilty person.

Antisocial Personality Disorder: Formerly called *psychopath* or *sociopath*. Individual with a personality disorder involving a marked lack of ethical and moral development who is in frequent conflict with society and experiences little or no guilt and anxiety and is undeterred by the threat of punishment.

Aorta: The main trunk of the arterial system of the body which arises from the left ventricle of the heart.

Apnea: A temporary cessation of breathing.

Arousal: A state or level of preparedness of an organism to act.

Arterioles: Minute and microscopic continuations of arteries, composed of three layers with progressively thinner walls and less elastic tissue.

Artery: An elastic, three-layer, tubular vessel that carries blood from the heart to the tissues.

Arther Technique: A psychophysiological veracity examination using the polygraph which uses non-exclusive control questions and employs the clinical approach in its decision making process. (See Chapter 15).

Applied Psychology: The investigation and solution of human problems through the application of fundamental psychological knowledge and methods.

Autonomic Balance: The extent to which the sympathetic nervous system or the parasympathetic nervous system is dominant in an individual.

Autonomic Nervous System (ANS): The division of the peripheral nervous system that functions involuntarily and is responsible for the innervation of cardiac muscle, smooth muscle, and glands.

Axon: An efferent process of a neuron by which impulses are carried away from the cell to other neurons.

Backster Zone Comparison Technique: A single-issue psychophysiological veracity examination using the polygraph comprising relevant questions, non-current exclusive control questions, symptomatic questions, preparatory/sacrifice relevant question, irrelevant question and optional inside-issue fear/hope of error questions. This technique uses a seven-position numerical scoring system and conversion table in its decision making process known as the numerical approach. (See Chapter 11).

Backster Zone Comparison Exploratory Test: A multiple-issue test which employs non-current exclusive control question. The numerical approach is used in its decision making process by means of vertical scoring for each spot. . (See Chapter 11)

Band Pass Filter: Particular range of frequencies - blocks others.

Baseline: Tonic level.

Beta Blocker: A chemical which blocks the receptors for adrenalin like substances.

Bias Potential: Same as *polarization*.

Bio-Electrical Recordings: Endosomatic (inside).

Bipolar-Disorder: Formerly called manic-depression, it is a disorder in which the mood of the patient inappropriately alternates between extremes of elation and depression. (See Chapter 7)

Black Zone: A twenty to thirty-five seconds block of polygraph chart time initiated by a *symptomatic* question having a unique psychological focusing appeal to the examinee who is fearful that a question dealing with an *outside issue* may be introduced in the form of an unreviewed question.

Brachial Artery: The artery located in the inner upper arm to which the blood pressure cuff is affixed.

Bradycardia: A slow heartbeat characterized by a pulse rate that is under sixty beats per minute.

Brain Stem: The stemlike part of the brain comprising the medulla oblongata, the pons, and the midbrain that connects the cerebral hemispheres with the spinal cord.

Bronchi: The two main branches of the trachea leading to the lungs.

Capillary: A minute blood vessel connecting arterioles with venules.

Cardiac Cycle: The period from the commencement of one beat of the heart to the commencement of the next heartbeat, which includes the systole and diastole.

Cardiac Reflex: A change in cardiac rate by stimulation of sensory nerve endings in the wall of the carotid sinus by increased arterial blood pressure which decreases heart rate, or stimulation of vagus fibers in the right side of the heart by increased venous return which reflexly increases heart rate.

Cardiac Output: Blood volume ejected per minute by the left or right ventricle.

Cardio Activity Monitor (CAM): A dry type transducer with silicon strain gages which monitors volumetric blood pressure variations and heart rate with the placement of the transducer on the finger, thumb, or wrist using its artery feeler.

Cardiograph: The sensor component in polygraph instruments that measures blood pressure, blood volume, and heart rate.

Cardio Notch Knob: Reverberation circuit.

Cardio Response Knob: High pass filter.

Catabolism: The opposite of anabolism. The destructive phase of metabolism in which living cells break down and convert complex substances into simpler substances with the release of energy.

Cell: The basic biological unit of structure of living organism comprising a mass of protoplasm containing a nucleus.

Central Nervous System (CNS): The brain and spinal cord with their nerves and end organs that control voluntary and involuntary reflexes.

Cerebellum: Located in the posterior region of the cranium, it is the largest part of the hindbrain and controls muscle coordination and balance.

Cerebral Cortex: The convoluted surface area of the cerebrum often referred to as *gray matter* because of its appearance, it is comprised of two hemispheres which are bridged by the corpus coloseum permitting impulses to travel between the two hemispheres.

Cheyne Stokes Respiration: Characterized as an irregular breathing pattern where there is a series of shallow breaths that increase in depth and rate, followed by breaths that decrease in depth and rate, usually interspersed with an apnea between cycles. This pattern is generally attributed to an individual who has suffered a brain injury or an abuser of narcotics which have a dramatic affect on the central nervous system.

Classical Conditioning: Also referred to as *respondent* or *Pavlovian* conditioning, it is a basic form of learning in which one stimulus begins to elicit a response usually elicited by a second stimulus by repeatedly associating the first stimulus with the second stimulus. However *cognitive theorists* explain classical conditioning by the manner in which stimuli provide information that allows an organism to reorganize mental impressions of its environment.

Cognitive Awareness: Based on signal value - significance of stimulus to examinee. It requires the examinee to differentiate between control and relevant test questions.

Cognitive Dissonance: The theory that humans are motivated to have *consistency* in our cognitions or beliefs. The commission of an act which is *inconsistent* with an individual's inherent beliefs and attitudes can generate discomfort, tension, conflict with ensuing emotional and physiological arousal.

Complete Disclosure Examination: Also known as Full Disclosure Examination. A psychophysiological veracity examination using the polygraph usually administered at the beginning of a sex offender's probationary treatment program in which the convicted sex offender's is required to reveal his/her entire sexual history for verification by PV testing, which is subsequently used by a therapist in the treatment of the sex offender.

Computerized Voice Stress Analyzer (CVSA): A device that detects stress related changes in the voice (laryngeal) microtremor for the purpose of detecting deception. (See Chapter 2)

Conductance: Ease of current passage.

Conductivity: It is the specific electric conducting ability of a substance and the reciprocal of unit resistance.

Construct Validity: Refers to whether a test adequately measures the underlying trait it is designed to assess. To measure construct validity, it is necessary to both describe the construct and show its relation to a conceptual framework. (See Chapter 3).

Contractility: In cardiac physiology, the force with which left ventricular ejection occurs.

Contraction: In muscle physiology, a shortening or tightening of the muscle.

Control-Stimulation Test: See *Stimulation Test*.

Control Question: A non-relevant test question used for comparison against a relevant test question. In Guilty Knowledge tests the non-critical questions are used as *controls* against the critical item question. In Control Question tests, the relevant question is compared to either *non-current exclusive* control questions, *current exclusive* control questions, *non-exclusive* control questions, which are designed to elicit the innocent examinee's psychological set and autonomic arousal. The Modified Relevant-Irrelevant test employs *situational* control questions. The General Question Test uses *disguised* control questions. (See chapters 11, 15, 16).

Control Question Technique: A procedure employed in psychophysiological veracity examinations which use control questions for comparison with neighboring relevant questions to reach a decision of truth or deception. (See Chapters 11 and 15).

Conversion Disorder: Anxiety or unconscious conflicts are converted into physical symptoms that sometimes have the effect of helping the person cope with the anxiety or conflicts.

Corneal Hydration: The passive reabsorption of sweat diffused through the duct wall into the corneum.

Corneum: The outermost layer of the epidermis, made up of dead, dry skin cells.

Craniosacral: Involving the skull and sacrum.

Criterion Validity: Theoretically, construct validity is most important, but practically, criterion validity is the central component of a validity study. In PV examinations, this aspect of validity refers to the relationship between test outcomes and a criterion of ground truth. (See Chapter 3)

Current Exclusive Control Question: This control question is formulated to be in the same category of offense or matter as the relevant question or issue. However, this control question is not separated in time from the relevant issue with the use of a time bar, thus it is considered a current control question. However, this control question does exclude the specific crime or matter contained in the relevant questions. (See Chapter 11)

Dampening Effect: Cleve Backster's concept that the potential deceptive response to a test question can be completely dampened or reduced by test question(s) or outside issue offering a greater threat.

Data Analysis: A component of Construct Validity, it is the method by which the physiological data produced from the administration of the psychological structure test is analyzed and evaluated for a conclusion of truth or deception, i.e., traditional numerical scoring system (Backster) or mathematical algorithm (APL, CPS).

DDD: *Decades Delayed Disclosure* refers to repressed childhood sexual traumas and memories which emerge as an adult under therapeutic treatment.

Dendrite: A branched protoplasmic process of a neuron that conducts impulses to the cell body which form synaptic connections with other neurons.

Dermis: Also referred to as *corium,* it is the deep layer of dense, irregular connective tissue just beneath the epidermis.

Diastole: A period of relaxation and dilation of the heart between contractions during which it fills with blood.

Dicrotic Notch: The upward movement of the cardio pen during diastole as a result of a pressure wave in the aortic blood after it rebounds off the aortic valve.

Differential Attenuation: Uneven reduction in signal due to the filtering of low frequency signals, i.e., GSR automatic mode.

Direct Current (DC): Electrons flow in only one direction..

Directional Fractionation: A term used to describe the phenomena of two different systems of the same organism responding in opposite directions than what might be expected, to the same stimuli.

DoDPI Bi-Spot Zone Comparison Technique: A single-issue psychophysiological veracity examination using the polygraph based on the Backster Zone Comparison test format which employs two relevant questions dealing with the same issue which are compared against non-current exclusive control questions. Decisions are based on the numerical approach which uses the seven-position numerical scoring system with a conclusion table which employs a fixed threshold of plus/minus four. (See Chapter 11).

DoDPI General Question Test (GQT): This test format is a modification of Keeler's Relevant-Irrelevant technique which is used when multiple issues need to be explored with a large number of suspects or the forensic psychophysiologist is restricted to a non-control question technique. Disguised controls are used in this test format. Either the clinical or numerical approach with vertical conversion table may be used. (See Chapter 15).

DoDPI Tri-Spot Zone Comparison Technique: Considered a multiple-issue test due to its inclusion of primary and secondary relevant issues, it employs non-current exclusive control questions, and as an option may also include Backster SKY questions. The numerical approach is used in its decision making process employing the seven-position scale with a conclusion table that uses a fixed threshold of plus/minus six. (See Chapter 11)

Duration: Entire length of time response occurs - from response onset.

DSM: *Diagnostic and Statistical Manual* of the American Psychiatric Association.

Eccrine Sweat Gland: Glands distributed over the entire body which secrete sweat in the form of H^2O and NaCl, or sodium chloride and certain other bodily waste products such as urea and uric acid. Their primary function is thermoregulation but they also respond to psychological and emotional stimuli.

Efferent: The carrying away or away from, especially a nerve fiber that carries away impulses away from the central nervous system.

Polarization: In psychophysiological veracity examinations, it is the gathering or build-up of electrical properties on the electrodes used for recording electrodermal activity, causing its own electrical charge.

Electrodermal Response (EDR): A measure of physiological arousal determined by the skin's resistance (GSR) or conductivity (GSG) to electricity.

Endocrine gland: A ductless gland that empties its internal secretion directly into the blood stream.

Endosomatic: (Inside - body) (EKG, EEG).

Epidermis: The outer layer of cells of the skin.

Epinephrine: Also called adrenalin, is the primary hormone produced by the adrenal medulla that stimulates the sympathetic division of the autonomic nervous system

EPPA: Employee Polygraph Protection Act of 1988. An act which severely limits the use of psychophysiological veracity examinations using the polygraph in the private sector by business and industry.

Examination Reliability Rating Table: A procedure that uses a five-point system to determine which issue has the greatest likelihood of producing conclusive results, on the basis of its combined *Adequacy of Information*, *Case Intensity*, and *Distinctness of Issue*.

Exclusive Control Question: A type of control question which is formulated to be in the same category of offense as the crime in question but employs a time bar to exclude the period in which the crime was committed.

Exosomatic: (Outside - body) (GSR, GSG).

Exploratory Test: A non-specific control question test that contains relevant questions which deal with multiple issues.

External Reliability: In PV examinations, external reliability is established by repetition of the test itself, hence two or more polygraph test (charts) are required to be administered before a conclusion of truth or deception can be rendered. (See Chapter 3)

External Validity: Refers to the nature of the subjects and settings tested. The broader the population examined and the type of setting investigated, the wider that study's results can be generalized. (See Chapter 3)

Extra Systole: An extra beat of the ventricle caused by a number of possible sources such as AV nodal, Perkinje fiber, or scar in ventricle muscle.

Face Validity: The evaluation of a test by its author based on his/her own logical analysis without subjecting his/her device to comparison with external standards. (See Chapter 3).

False Memory Syndrome (FMS): A condition in which an individual's memory of an earlier-in-life traumatic experience is distorted or confabulated and objectively false but which the individual strongly believes to be true.

False Negative: The erroneous diagnosis of a deceptive subject as truthful.

False Positive: The erroneous diagnosis of a truthful subject as deceptive.

Federal Rules of Evidence: On 28 June 1993, the Supreme Court of the United States in William Daubert v. Merrell Dow Pharmaceuticals, Inc., declared that the Frye standard established in 1923 for the admissibility of scientific evidence in court was superseded by the Federal Rules of Evidence which assigns to the trial judge the task of ensuring that an expert's testimony both rests on a reliable foundation and is relevant to the task at hand. Thus pertinent evidence based on *scientifically valid principles* rather than *general acceptance* will satisfy those demands. (See Chapter 23).

Field Research: Studies conducted on real-life suspected criminals involving actual crimes as opposed to analog studies which employ mock paradigms such as in laboratory experiments.

Forebrain: Located above the midbrain, the forebrain consists of the telencephalon and the diencephalon.

Frequency: A number of cycles over a period of time (High or Low = Fast or Slow).

Frye Standard: The standard established by the Federal Court in 1923 in Frye v. United States and adopted by most State courts which rejected the admissibility of polygraph due to its lack of acceptance by the scientific community, but which became the standard for admissibility of all scientific evidence. (See Chapter 23)

Full Disclosure Examination: Same as *Complete Disclosure Examination.*

Functional Psychosis: A psychotic disorder in which there is no apparent pathology of the central nervous system.

Galvanic Skin Response: A measure of physiological arousal determined by the amount of decrease in the skin's resistance to electricity purportedly due to an increase in sweat gland activity. (See Electrodermal Response).

GSR/GSG Auto/Manual Mode: Duration of response is recorded only in the Manual Mode when the output signal is essentially unfiltered. Auto Mode is a high pass filter which filters out low frequency signals, thus returns the recording pen to baseline almost immediately after reaching height of response.

Generalization: The process of going from the specific to the general.

Gland: An organ specialized for secretion or excretion of substances for use in the body or elimination..

Global Evaluation: The decision making process known as the Clinical Approach in psychophysiological veracity examinations which includes the *interpretation of the physiological data* recorded on the polygraph charts together with an evaluation of the case facts known as *factual analysis*, and an assessment of the examinee's verbal and non-verbal behavior known as *behavior assessment*. (See Chapters 9 and 15)

Green Zone: A twenty to thirty-five seconds block of polygraph chart time initiated by a non-current exclusive control question having a unique psychological focusing appeal to the innocent (truthful) examinee.

Ground Truth: An objective, factual basis such as a confession or recovered physical evidence which supports the results of a psychophysiological veracity examination.

Guilt: A feeling of responsibility from behavior or desires in conflict with our moral and/or ethical code. It usually involves both self-devaluation and detection apprehension which includes fear of punishment. Although detection apprehension and fear of punishment can be experienced without the emotion of guilt such as a person with an *antisocial personality disorder* formerly known as psychopath or sociopath.

Guilt Complex Test: a psychophysiological veracity examination which includes a fictitious crime in the test structure to determine whether the examinee is reactive to any accusatory test question.

Guilty Knowledge Test (GKT): A procedure that uses some involuntary physiological response to indicate whether the examinee identifies the correct or crime-related alternative as distinctive or different from a set of control alternatives that are not in fact crime-related but chosen to seem equally plausible to an innocent suspect. The GKT is broad in definition and includes the Known-Solution Peak-of-Tension and the Probing (Searching) Peak-of-Tension tests. (See Chapter 18)

Habituation: The process by which a person's responses to the same external stimulus lessens with repeated presentations. In PV examinations, the more significant the stimulus (question) is to the examinee, the longer it takes to habituate to that stimulus.

Heart: A muscular pump divided into four hollow chambers constructed of two *syncytia* known as the *atria* and the *ventricles*, comprised of specialized muscle called *cardiac* muscle. The entire heart structure is covered by a serous membrane called the *pericardium*.

Hering-Bruer Reflex: A reflex mechanism which stops inspiration if the lungs are stretching too much, and causes expiration to begin.

High Pass Filter: Allows passage of higher frequencies - blocks lower frequencies.

Hindbrain: Also referred to as the *old brain* because it is the first part of the brain that develops in the embryo, it governs autonomic functions including heart rate and respiration and is responsible for human survival.

Homeostasis: The body's internal equilibrium maintained by dynamic processes of feedback and regulation.

Hormone: The secretion of endocrine glands that promote development of body structures or regulate bodily functions.

Hyppocampus: A horn-like structure primarily concerned with cognition and memory, the hyppocampus extends from the end of a group of nerve fibers called the *fornix*.

Hypothalamus: A bundle of nuclei located in the region of the diencephalon below the thalamus involved in the regulation of body temperature, motivation and emotion. It is responsible for the control of the sympathetic and parasympathetic systems.

Hysterical disorder: Former term for Conversion Disorder.

Inconclusive: Psychophysiological veracity examination results which failed to produce sufficient data to render a decision of truth or deception.

IC1 and IC2: Preamplifier and Power amplifier.

Inside-Issue Control Question: A test question used in a single-issue zone comparison test which is designed to elicit a response from the Innocent (truthful as later verified) examinee who is *fearful that an error* will be made on his/her test. (See chapter 11).

Inside-Issue Relevant Question: A test question used in single-issue zone comparison test which is designed to elicit a response from the Guilty (deceptive as later verified) examinee who *hopes that an error* will be made on his/her test so that their deception to the target issue will not be detected.

Integrated Zone Comparison Technique: This technique may be employed as a single or multiple-issue test. The test format includes non-current exclusive control questions and a non-exclusive control question interspersed with relevant and irrelevant test questions. The Horizontal Scoring System is used to evaluate the physiological data. (See Chapter 11)

Intent Questions: A relevant test question which lacks the element of *certainty* regarding the commission of an offense, thus determines only an *intent* to commit an offense.

Internal Reliability: In PV examinations, internal reliability is established by repetition of a test segment within the same test. (See Chapter 3)

Internal Validity: Refers to the degree to which a study has control over extraneous variables which may be related to the study outcome. (See Chapter 3).

Ions: Electrically charged (positive and negative) particles.

Irrelevant Question: An irrelevant question is a *neutral* question, designed to lack any stimulating qualities for both the innocent and guilty examinee.

Known Solution Peak-of-Tension Test: A guilty knowledge test wherein the guilty examinee and the investigator(s) and/or forensic psychophysiologist know the critical test question also known as the Key question. (See Chapter 18)

Kymograph: The motor in a polygraph instrument that drives and controls the flow of chart paper at six inches per minute. (See Chapter 4)

Latency: Time from stimulus onset to response onset.

Level: Pre-stimulus activity.

Limbic System: A group of brain structures that form a fringe along the inner edge of the cerebrum, which are involved in memory and motivation.

Lobes: The brain is geographically divided into four lobes. *Frontal* which involve personality, judgment. reasoning and motor area, *parietal* which involve sensory functions, the *occipital* which involves visual functions and *temporal* which involves auditory functions.

Low-Pass Filter: Allows lower (slower) frequencies to pass.

Maintenance Examination: A psychophysiological veracity examination using the polygraph which is employed in Probationary PV examinations to monitor the offender on a periodic basis to insure and deter the parolee/probationer from reoffending.

Manic Depression: Former term for bipolar disorder. (See Chapter 7)

Marcy Technique: This test format includes current exclusive control questions and uses a seven-position numerical scoring system with a vertical conversion table but employs the clinical approach in its decision making process.(See Chapter 15)

Matte Control Question Validation Test (MCQV): This test is designed to verify the effectiveness of the control questions planned for use in an actual crime control question test. The control questions are inserted in a fictitious crime control question test similar in nature to the actual offense, which is administered immediately prior to the actual crime test to determine the efficacy of the control questions prior to their use in the actual crime test. (See Chapter 14)

Matte Quadri-Track Zone Comparison Technique. A single-issue psychophysiological veracity examination using the polygraph comprising relevant questions, non-current exclusive control questions, preparatory-sacrifice relevant question, inside-issue fear/hope of error questions, symptomatic questions and irrelevant question. This technique uses a seven-position numerical scoring system and conclusion table in its decision making process known as the numerical approach. (See Chapter 11).

Matte Quinque-Track Zone Comparison Technique. This is an exploratory, multiple-issue test which includes a guilty knowledge question in addition to direct and indirect involvement relevant questions. The numerical approach is used in its decision making process employing a vertical scoring/tally system with a conclusion table that uses an increasing threshold. (See Chapter 11)

Medulla: An oval-shaped area of the hindbrain also referred to as the medulla oblongata, which regulates reflex mechanisms such as oxygen level, heart rate and respiration in the maintenance of homeostasis.

Metabolism: The sum total of all physical and chemical changes that occur in the body.

Metarterioles: Smaller branches of arterioles.

Methodology: A component of Construct Validity, it refers to the methodology used to administer the psychologically structured test (PST) which must consider and address all of the known variables (Chap. 9) that may affect the physiological data produced from the administration of the PST. (See Chapter 3)

Midbrain: Located just below the center of the cerebrum, the midbrain assumes the responsibility for coordination between body movements and auditory and visual stimuli.

Minnesota Multiphasic Personality Inventory (MMPI): An objective, widely used and empirically validated personality test.

Multiple Personality: A dissociative disorder in which a person has two or more distinct and relatively independent personalities.

Myelin: A lipid and protein substance which wraps around the axon, insulating it, which permits faster transmission of the action potentials along the length of the axon.

Nerve Impulse: The electrochemical discharge of a neuron or nerve cell.

Neuron: A nerve cell - the structural and functional unit of the nervous system.

Neurosis: Some leading psychologists have abandoned the term *neurosis* and *psychoneurosis* and replaced them with *anxiety disorders* such as panic states, phobias and obsessive-compulsive behavior, and *somatoform disorders* such as hysteria, conversion symptoms and hypochondriasis (see Chapter 7). *Neurosis* is characterized chiefly by anxiety, feelings of dread and foreboding, and avoidance behavior, theorized to stem from unconscious conflict.

Neutral Question: A question of a non-stimulating nature. (See Irrelevant Question).

Non-Current Exclusive Control Question: Also known as the Backster Control Question, it is formulated to be in the same category of offense or matter as the relevant question or issue. However, this control question is separated in time from the relevant issue with the use of a *time bar*, thus it is considered an *earlier-in-life* (non-current) control question. Thus this control question excludes the period in which the crime was committed.

Non-Exclusive Control Question: Known as the Reid control question, it is formulated to be in the same category as the relevant question or issue. However it is not separated in time from the relevant issue not does it exclude the crime or matter contained in the relevant questions. Thus it is an inclusive control question but has been named by its employers as a Non-Exclusive control question.

Notch Filter: Blocks passage of a specified frequency - allows others to pass.

Numerical Analysis: A numerical system by which a consistent set of values are used to describe the observable physiological responses recorded on the test. The two systems most often used are the Seven-Position Scale and the Three-Position Scale.

Numerical Approach: A procedure developed by Cleve Backster which employs a standardized scoring system in the evaluation of the physiological data recorded on polygraph charts from which a determination is made regarding the examinee's truthfulness or deception to the target issue.

Onset: This term is used in forensic psychophysiology to describe either the initial application of a stimulus, as in *stimulus onset*, or the very first indication of a physiological change from the pre-stimulus level, or *response onset*.

Operant Conditioning: A simple form of learning in which an organism learns to engage in behavior because it is reinforced. Thus guilt is a learned emotion associated with morals and values, subject to internalized consequences such as a sense of right and wrong. Hence guilt translates into emotion resulting in a physiological arousal.

Organ: A part of the body that serves a specific function.

Orienting Response: An unlearned, reflex response to external stimulus.

Oxygen Debt: The oxygen required in the recovery period after strenuous physical activity.

Parasympathetic Nervous System (PNS): The craniosacral division of the autonomic nervous system that controls most of the basic metabolic functions essential to life. In

PV examinations, the PNS is responsible for the examinee's recovery from sympathetic activity.

PDD: Psychophysiological Detection of Deception. The term *polygraph examination* was replaced by DoDPI with the term *PDD*.

Peak-of-Tension Test (POT): There are two types of Peak-of-Tension Tests; the Known-Solution POT and the Probing (Searching) POT. Both are classified as Guilty Knowledge tests. The Known-Solution POT is used to determine whether the examinee knows the critical item known as the Key question which is known to the forensic psychophysiologist. The key question is interspersed with similar questions used as controls. The Probing POT is used to develop information known only to the examinee who perpetrated the crime. (See Chapter 18).

Pedophile: An adult who engages in or desires sexual relations with a child.

Penile Plethysmograph: A sensor that measures blood flow to the penis.

Peripheral Nervous System: The part of the nervous system which is comprised of the *somatic nervous system* which regulates contractions of the skeletal (striated) muscle, and the *autonomic nervous system* which regulates the contraction of smooth muscle, cardiac muscle and the secretion of the glands.

Phasic Change/Response: Change in Tonic Level or average tracing as a result of specific stimulus.

Physiological Psychology: Also known as Biological Psychology - The study of the relationship between biological processes and behavior.

Physiology: The study of the functions of the body and its components and the chemical and physical processes involved.

Plethysmograph: A device for finding variations in size of a segment of the body due to variations in the amount of blood passing through or contained in that segment. In forensic psychophysiology there are two types of plethysmographs. The *Cardio Activity Monitor* which measures volumetric blood *pressure* by a means of a transducer which performs similarly to a blood pressure cuff. When applied to the radial artery of the wrist, the CAM records arterial blood flow which increases during autonomic arousal, however when placed on the thumb nail the CAM records the effects of vascular activity at the limb extremity which reflects a decrease in blood volume during autonomic arousal. The second type of plethysmograph is the *Photoelectric Plethysmograph.* There are two types of Photoelectric plethysmographs; one type operates via light transmission, the other employs light reflection. Basically a change in the volume of blood in the transmission or reflecting path will alter the amount of light presented to the photoelectric detector. Both photoelectric plethysmographs record capillary blood volume from the examinee's fingertip. (See Chapter 4).

Pneumograph: A mechanical or electronic device that measures thoracic and/or abdominal breathing patterns. (See Chapter 4)

Pons: A bulbous structure lying between the midbrain region and the medulla, the pons connect the cerebellum with the brain stem providing linkage between upper and lower levels of the central nervous system. It hosts some of the respiratory regulatory centers and is a sensory relay between the cerebellum and the remainder of the nervous system.

Post-Ganglionic: Refers to a neuron of the autonomic nervous system having its cell body in a ganglion with the axon extending to an organ or tissue.

Post-Test Interview: The interview which follows the conclusion of the psychophysiological veracity examination.

Predictive Table of Accuracy and Error Rates: Based on a 1989 field study of the Matte Quadri-Track Zone Comparison Technique, this table provides a *probability* that an Innocent or Guilty case will reach a mathematical score this high or higher (weaker); the *percentage* of the time an Innocent or Guilty case will score this value or lower than this value (stronger score); and the *potential for error* based on the probability that an opposite case will score this value or lower. (See Chapter 11)

Pre-ganglionic: Refers to a neuron of the autonomic nervous system having its cell body in the spinal cord or the brain and its axon in terminating in a ganglion.

Preparatory/Sacrifice Relevant Question: Presented during the test as the first relevant question, it is formulated as a preparatory relevant question to the introduction of the two or three relevant questions which follow it. Due to its position as the first relevant question, it is anticipated that it may elicit a response from both the innocent and the guilty examinee, thus it is treated as a sacrifice relevant question which is not evaluated or used in the decision making process.

Pre-Test Interview: The first phase of the psychophysiological veracity examination which precedes the collection of the physiological data recorded on the polygraph charts, comprising the acquisition of examinee background data, refinement and finalization of test question formulation, and explanation of the examination procedure.

Probationary PV Examination: Refers to psychophysiological veracity examinations using the polygraph on convicted felons placed on parole or probation for the purpose of treatment and monitoring. Probationary PV Examinations are most used on convicted sex offenders which include a Conviction Verification PV examination, a Complete Disclosure PV examination, and periodic Maintenance/Monitoring PV examinations. (See Chapter 24)

Protoplasm: The substance that constitutes the physical basis all living activities exhibiting the properties of assimilation, growth, mobility, secretion and reproduction.

Psychiatry: The branch of medicine concerned with the diagnosis, treatment and prevention of mental disorders.

Psychological Set: Also known as Selective Attention, it is an adaptive psychophysiological response to fears, anxieties, and apprehensions with a selective focus on the particular issue or situation which presents the greatest threat to the legitimate security of the examinee while filtering out lesser threats.

Psychological Stress Evaluator (PSE): A device that detects inaudible and involuntary frequency modulations (FM) whose strength and pattern are inversely related to the degree of stress in a speaker which are believed to be a result of physiological tremor or microtremor that accompanies voluntary contraction of the striated muscles involved in vocalization.

Psychological Structure: A component of Construct Validity, Psychological Structure refers to the psychological components that make-up the test structure which must initially be in conformance with acceptable scientific principles, have face validity, and be in harmony with the theory's objectives. (See Chapter 3)

Psychologist: A person who is schooled and trained in methods of psychological analysis, therapy and research.

Psychology: The scientific study of behavior and mental processes.

Psychopath: Also known as Sociopath - See *Antisocial Personality Disorder*.

Psychophysiological Veracity Examination (PVE): Abbreviated as *PV examination* or PVE, and formerly known as a polygraph examination, it is a psychologically structured test designed to determine the veracity of an examinee's answers to the relevant or critical test questions incorporated into the test structure which is evaluated with the use of a polygraph instrument capable of recording on a moving chart as a minimum an examinee's heartbeat, pulse rate and strength, electrodermal response, and thoracic and abdominal breathing patterns. A PV examination includes the pre-test interview phase and the administration of all PV tests necessary for the collection of the physiological data used to make a determination of truth or deception. (See Chapters 8, 9 and 11).

Psychosis: A major psychological disorder wherein a person suffers personality disintegration and loss of contact with reality.

Pulmonary Circuit: The particular route that the blood follows when traveling to the lungs to be oxygenated and then back to the heart for distribution throughout the body.

Radial Artery: One of the two arteries located in the forearm and wrist, which descend from the *brachial* artery in the upper arm. The other is called the *ulnar* artery.

Rationalization: Ego-defense mechanism in which a person engages in self-deception, finding justifications for unreasonable or illogical ideas or behaviors.

Recovery Time: From peak to baseline.

Red Zone: A twenty to thirty-five seconds block of polygraph chart time initiated by a relevant question having a unique psychological focusing appeal to the guilty (deceptive) examinee.

Reid Technique: This psychophysiological veracity examination test format includes non-exclusive control questions and employs the clinical approach in its decision making process. (See Chapter 15)

Relevant-Irrelevant Technique (R-I): The basic R-I technique compares the relevant questions to irrelevant (neutral) questions. However the Modified Relevant-Irrelevant Technique compares the relevant questions to situational control questions. (See Chapter 15).

Relevant Question: This test question is related to the crime at issue which generated the test. It is designed to pose a threat to the security of the deceptive or guilty examinee and elicit his/her psychological set.

Reliability: The assessment of the validity of any psychophysiological veracity test is based on the assumption that the test consistently measures the same properties. This consistency, known as *reliability*, is usually the degree to which a test yields repeatable results, .i.e the extent to which the same examinee retested is scored similarly. Reliability also refers to consistency across forensic psychophysiologists/scorers. (See Chapter 3).

Resistance: Galvanic Skin Response (GSR).

Response Onset: Observable beginning of physiological change from tonic level.

Reticular Activating System (RAS): Fibers going from the reticular formation to higher brain centers. The RAS functions as a general arousal system.

Rise Time: Response onset to the peak of a given response.

Schizophrenia: A psychotic disorder of at least six months duration characterized by a breakdown of integrated personality functions and thought processes, and impaired reality and emotions.

Searching Peak-of-Tension Test: A guilty knowledge test wherein only the examinee but not the investigator and/or forensic psychophysiologist, has guilty knowledge of the sought information, such as the location of physical evidence.

Semilunar Valve: A valve that prevents blood return to the ventricle after contraction.

Serial Criminal: An individual who commits a series of *similar* crimes such as a serial murderer or a serial rapist.

Signal: *Electrical impulses* received by the polygraph instrument to a transducer, coupler, preamplifier and power amplifier enabling the pen motor.

Silent Answer Test: Utilized as a counter-countermeasure test for examinees who appear to be attempting countermeasures. The examinee is directed to *not verbalize* his/her answer on the SAT but *silently* answer each test question truthfully. The SAT is currently also being used as an anti-countermeasure test. (See Chapter 19).

Somatic Nervous System: The division of the peripheral nervous system also known as the *voluntary nervous system* which connects the central nervous system (spinal cord and brain) with sensory receptors, muscles and the surface of the body.

Sphincter: A ringlike muscle surrounding and enclosing a body orifice.

Sphygmomonometer: An instrument that measures arterial blood pressure.

Spinal Cord: An oval-shaped column of nervous tissue within the spine that transmits messages from the sensory receptors to the brain and from the brain to muscles and glands throughout the body.

Spot: A term originated and defined by Backster as one of four permanent locations on all zone comparison sequences which can only contain a relevant question. In the Matte Quadri-Track ZCT, a *Spot* also identifies a *Track* containing a pair of control/relevant questions which are *compared and quantified* for a determination of truth or deception to the target issue. (See Chapter 11)

Spot Analysis: The numerical evaluation of a relevant question by comparing it to a control question no further than one position to the left or right of that spot location. (See Chapter 11)

Stimulation Test: Also known as the *Control-Stimulation Test*, it is designed to reassure the innocent (as later verified) examinee, and stimulate the guilty (as later verified) examinee by showing the accuracy of the test using a Peak-of-Tension Test format. (See chapter 10).

Stimulus Onset: Initial application of stimulus.

Sub-Dermis: Also referred to as the *subcutaneous*, it is that layer beneath the dermis where the sweat glands originate.

Super Dampening Effect: Backster's concept that the presence of an outside issue which is of greater concern to an examinee than either the relevant or control questions, may have a dampening effect on the examinee's capability of response to all of the test questions. Backster's remedy was the development of the Symptomatic question.

Suspicion-Knowledge-Guilt Test (SKG): A single test capable of identifying the examinee's major involvement, some direct involvement or guilty knowledge yet containing similar controls to that found in the single-issue Matte Quadri-Track Zone Comparison Technique.

Suspicion-Knowledge-You Test (SKY): A single test capable of identifying the examinee's major involvement, some direct involvement or guilty knowledge to a single issue yet containing similar controls to that found in the single-issue Backster Zone Comparison You-Phase Technique.

Sympathetic Nervous System (SNS): The division of the autonomic nervous system (ANS) that is most active when the body's reserve energy is summoned in emergency conditions of extreme cold, strong emotions and violent effort.

Symptomatic Question: Developed by Cleve Backster, this type of question is designed to identify subject's mistrust of the forensic psychophysiologist regarding the asking of an unreviewed question embrassing an outside issue that may be bothering the subject which may have the effect of dampening out the response capability of the examinee to the question types that would ordinarily serve as a stimulus. (See chapter 11).

Synapse: Non-contact, chemical transmissions between the terminal knob of the axon of a neuron and the dendrite of another neuron.

Systemic Circuit: The route that the blood takes as it is supplying the body, including the aorta, the largest of the arteries and all of its branches that lead to the body tissues.

Systole: The ventricular contraction phase of a cardiac cycle which is reflected on polygraph charts as the first and upward limb.

Technique: A psychological method of implementing a scientifically structured test. (See P. 564, Chapter 23).

Thalamus: The mass of gray matter at the base of the brain which is involved in the relay of sensory information ascending from other parts of the nervous system to the cerebral cortex and in the functions of sleep and attention.

Tissue: A group of similar cells and fibers that act together in the performance of a particular function.

Tone: Refers to the periodic firing of a particular nerve at a particular rate when not being *specifically* used which is a function of *homeostasis*. Inasmuch as the sympathetic and parasympathetic division of the autonomic nervous system are continually active, the base rates of this activity are referred to as sympathetic and parasympathetic tone, respectively.

Tonic Change/Level: Change in baseline or average tracing amplitude.

Total Test Minutes Concept: Refers to that period of time when examinee reactivity is at maximum relative effectiveness. This time period includes only that period of time when the physiological data is being collected from the examinee with the polygraph instrument.

Track: A term used in the Quadri-Track Zone Comparison Technique to identify a pair of test questions related for *evaluation* as in the case of Symptomatic questions (Black Zone), or a pair of test questions (Green and Red Zone) related for *comparison* which are located in a *Spot* for quantification. (See Chapter 11)

Traditional Polygraph Instrument: Non-computerized polygraph instrument that is powered by Alternating Current (AC) which is comprised of frequencies that fluctuate. This Alternating Current is subsequently *rectified* or changed from Alternating Current to Direct Current (DC), which is current that is relatively constant. The recording components (pneumo, cardio and GSR) that are supplied on the traditional polygraph instruments are powered by this Direct Current. These components are designed to use only Direct Current to produce an output signal.

Transduced Recording: A recording from signals that were changed from mechanical to electrical to mechanical energy.

Tri-Zone Indication-Remedy Table: A "First Aid" technique to immediately detect and remedy any Zone Comparison technique defect.

Ulnar Artery: One of the two arteries located in the forearm and wrist, which descend from the *brachial* artery in the upper arm. The other is called the *radial* artery.

USAF Modified General Question Technique: A multiple-issue test which employs non-current exclusive control questions interspersed with relevant questions of primary and secondary involvement, evidence connecting and guilty knowledge. Test data analysis is conducted by Spot total with vertical tally only, employing a fixed threshold. (See Chapter 11)

Utah Zone Comparison Technique: This technique has developed into three separate formats (Raskin, Honts, Bartlett), all of which employ the numerical approach using a seven-position scale and a fixed threshold, but only one of the formats is designed for a single-issue. The Bartlett version employs non-current exclusive control questions and one non-exclusive control question. The Honts and Raskin versions employs directed-lie non-current exclusive control questions. (See Chapter 11)

Vagus Nerve: A pneumogastric cranial nerve having motor and sensory functions with a greater distribution than any of the other cranial nerves.

Validity: The state, quality or fact of being valid. An index of validity shows the degree to which a test measures what it purports to measure, when compared with accepted criteria, hence the validity of a PV examination using the polygraph depends on whether it can accurately determine truth and deception. (See Chapter 3)

Vasoconstriction: The narrowing or reduction in diameter of blood vessels due to smooth muscle contraction in the walls of the blood vessels stimulated by innervation from the sympathetic division of the autonomic nervous system.

Vasodilation: The relaxation of the smooth muscles of the vascular system resulting in dilated blood vessels due to the blood volume and pressure pushing outward on the wall..

Vein: A tubular vessel which carries unaerated blood to the heart (except pulmonary vein which carries oxygenated blood). Veins contain inner, middle and outer coats as in arteries but differ from arteries in their thinner walls and larger more frequent anastomoses and presence of valves that allow one-way flow of blood toward the heart, preventing backward circulation

Vein Valves: Flap-like structures that close when blood begins to back up in a vein, particularly in the arms and legs.

Viscera: Internal organs of the body.

Zone: A twenty to thirty-five seconds block of polygraph chart time initiated by a question having a unique psychological focusing appeal to a predictable group of examinees. Backster color-coded each Zone as the Green Zone for the Control questions, the Red Zone for the Relevant questions, and the Black Zone for the Symptomatic questions. (See Chapter 11)

Zone Comparison Test (ZCT): A technique developed by Cleve Backster that encompasses three Zones (Black, Red, Green), two of which (Red & Green) are compared and quantified for a determination of truth or deception. It is designed to pose a threat to the security of the examinee, regardless of their innocence or guilt, and compel them to focus their attention on a specific zone question(s). (See Chapter 11)

TABLE OF FIGURES

Index

B